Law, Business, and Society

Law, Business, and Society

Eighth Edition

Tony McAdams
University of Northern Iowa

Nancy Neslund
Widener University

Kristofer Neslund
Golden Gate University

Boston Burr Ridge, IL Dubuque, IA Madison, WI New York San Francisco St. Louis
Bangkok Bogotá Caracas Kuala Lumpur Lisbon London Madrid Mexico City
Milan Montreal New Delhi Santiago Seoul Singapore Sydney Taipei Toronto

McGraw-Hill
Irwin

LAW, BUSINESS, AND SOCIETY

Published by McGraw-Hill/Irwin, a business unit of The McGraw-Hill Companies, Inc., 1221 Avenue of the Americas, New York, NY, 10020. Copyright © 2007 by The McGraw-Hill Companies, Inc. All rights reserved. No part of this publication may be reproduced or distributed in any form or by any means, or stored in a database or retrieval system, without the prior written consent of The McGraw-Hill Companies, Inc., including, but not limited to, in any network or other electronic storage or transmission, or broadcast for distance learning.

Some ancillaries, including electronic and print components, may not be available to customers outside the United States.

This book is printed on acid-free paper.

1 2 3 4 5 6 7 8 9 0 DOC/DOC 0 9 8 7 6

ISBN-13: 978-0-07-304810-9
ISBN-10: 0-07-304810-0

Editorial director: *John E. Biernat*
Senior sponsoring editor: *Kelly H. Lowery*
Editorial assistant: *Kirsten Guidero*
Senior marketing manager: *Lisa Nicks*
Producer, Media technology: *Damian Moshak*
Lead project manager: *Christine A. Vaughan*
Senior production supervisor: *Sesha Bolisetty*
Senior designer: *Mary E. Kazak*
Media project manager: *Joyce J. Chappetto*
Cover image: © *Larry Brownstein/Getty Images*
Cover design: *Jillian Lindner*
Typeface: *10/12 Times Roman*
Compositor: *GTS—New Delhi, India Campus*
Printer: *R. R. Donnelley*

Library of Congress Cataloging-in-Publication Data

McAdams, Tony.
    Law, business, and society / Tony McAdams, Nancy Neslund, Kristofer Neslund.—8th ed.
      p. cm.
    Includes bibliographical references and index.
    ISBN-13: 978-0-07-304810-9 (alk. paper)
    ISBN-10: 0-07-304810-0 (alk. paper)
      1. Business enterprises—Law and legislation—United States.   2. Trade regulation—United States.   3. Business ethics—United States.   4. Industries—Social aspects—United States. I. Neslund, Nancy. II. Neslund, Kristofer. III. Title.
KF1355.M28 2007
346.73'065—dc22

                                        2005040188

About the Authors

Tony McAdams

Tony McAdams is a professor of management at the University of Northern Iowa. He earned a B.A. in History from the University of Northern Iowa, a J.D. from the University of Iowa and an MBA from Columbia University. Professor McAdams' primary teaching interests include government regulation of business, business and society, and employment law. Professor McAdams' research interests include managerial accountability, business ethics, and employment law. His scholarly articles have appeared in such journals as *The Harvard Business Review, The Academy of Management Review, The Journal of Business Ethics,* and *The American Business Law Journal.* Professor McAdams has received the Iowa Board of Regents Award for Faculty Excellence, the Distinguished Teacher of the Year Award from the student government at the University of Kentucky, and the University of Northern Iowa College of Business Administration Excellence in Teaching Award.

Nancy Neslund, author of Chapters 16, 17, and 18

Nancy Neslund is currently a visiting associate professor at Widener Law School in Harrisburg, Pennsylvania. She earned a B.A. in Economics from Willamette University, a J.D. from Columbia University, and an LL.M. from New York University. Prior to entering academia, she was a lawyer in private practice for 14 years. During the academic year 2004–2005, she was a visiting professor on the law faculty of Europa Universität Viadrina, in Germany on its border with Poland. She teaches business organizations, business law, and tax law. Her research interests include the World Trade Organization, international and domestic taxation of e-commerce, and international professional regulation.

Kristofer Neslund, author of Chapter 9

Kris Neslund is an associate professor of taxation and the associate dean of the school of taxation at Golden Gate University. He holds a D.B.A. from Kent State University, a J.D. from Lewis & Clark College, and an LL.M. in taxation from New York University. He is a CPA and a member of the Oregon bar. Prior to entering academia, he was a tax partner in two law firms, as well as the CFO of a telecommunications company operating in three western states. During academic year 2004–2005 he was a visiting professor in the master of professional accountancy program at UNITEC in New Zealand, and a visiting professor of law at both the Europa Universität Viadrina in Germany and La Trobe University in Australia. He taught courses in corporate governance, the regulation of the accounting profession, and U.S. taxation. Professor Neslund helped lead the United Way's low-income tax return preparation effort in Rochester, New York, which was named one of the best programs in the U.S. for working-class families by the U.S. Council of Mayors in 2003.

Preface

NEW DIRECTIONS

For various reasons, including the recent changes in the CPA Examination, the 8th edition of *Law, Business and Society* departs a bit from our format of previous years. The primary changes:

- Chapter 6 (Contracts) is new to this text and Chapter 7 (Business Torts and Product Liability) includes substantially expanded attention to business torts themes.
- In order to increase ethics coverage and to demonstrate the role of ethics throughout law and business, each chapter now features at least one designated "Practicing Ethics" vignette or discussion.
- We have expanded and updated our discussions of corporate governance, Sarbanes-Oxley, and the corporate scandals of recent years.

OVERVIEW

This text is directed to courses at both the upper-division undergraduate and masters levels in the legal environment of business, government and business, and business and society. Authors of textbooks in these areas often rely on a single discipline (for example, law, economics, or management) as the foundation for their efforts. In this text we take an interdisciplinary approach, using elements of law, political economy, international business, ethics, social responsibility, and management. This large task necessarily requires certain trade-offs, but we hope the product will more accurately capture the fullness of the business environment.

We want to emphasize that our primary goal is to produce an interesting, provocative reading experience. Naturally, accuracy and reasonable comprehensiveness cannot be sacrificed. Our feeling, however, is that a law text can be both intellectually and emotionally engaging without sacrificing substantive ends. To meet our objective we have given extensive attention to readings, provocative quotes, and factual details (surveys, data, and anecdotes) that add flesh to legal theory and practice.

The book is divided into five units as follows:

Unit I—Business and Society. We do not begin with the law. Rather, in Chapter 1 (Capitalism and the Role of Government), Chapter 2 (Business Ethics), and Chapter 3 (The Corporation and Public Policy: Expanding Responsibilities), we describe some of the economic and social forces that shape our legal system.

The goals of Unit I are to (*a*) enhance student awareness of the many societal influences on business, (*b*) establish the business context from which government regulation arose, and (*c*) explore the roles of the free market, government intervention, and individual and corporate ethics in controlling business behavior.

The student must understand not merely the law but the law in context. What forces have provoked government intervention in business? What alternatives to our current "mixed economy" might prove healthy? These considerations help the students respond to one of the critical questions of the day: To what extent, if any, *should* we regulate business?

Unit II—Introduction to Law. Chapter 4 (The American Legal System) and Chapter 5 (Constitutional Law and the Bill of Rights) survey the foundations of our legal system. Here we set out the "nuts and bolts" of law, combining cases, readings, and narrative. Then with Chapters 6 (Contracts) and 7 (Business Torts and Product Liability), we examine the foundations of business law.

Unit III—Trade Regulation and Antitrust. Chapter 8 (Government Regulation of Business) examines federal administrative law but also directs significant attention to state and local regulations. Chapter 9 (Business Organizations and Securities Regulation), Chapter 10 (Antitrust Law—Restraints of Trade), and Chapter 11 (Antitrust Law—Monopolies and Mergers) survey the core of government oversight of business.

Unit IV—Employer–Employee Relations. Chapter 12 (Employment Law I: Employee Rights), Chapter 13 (Employment Law II: Discrimination), and Chapter 14 (Employment Law III: Labor–Management Relations) are intended not only to survey the law in those areas, but also to introduce some of the sensitive and provocative social issues that have led to today's extensive government intervention in the employment relationship.

Unit V—Selected Topics in Government–Business Relations. Two of the closing chapters of this book—Chapter 15 (Consumer Protection) and Chapter 17 (Environmental Protection)—emphasize the dramatic expansion of the public's demands for socially responsible conduct in business. Chapter 16 (International Ethics and Law) provides an overview of the legal and ethical issues emerging from global business practice, while Chapter 18 (Internet Law and Ethics) surveys some cyberlaw and ethics problems.

ACCREDITATION

Our text conforms to AACSB accreditation standards.

Two chapters are devoted exclusively to ethics, and ethics themes emerge throughout the book. The chapter on employment discrimination should be quite helpful in aiding students' understanding of diversity issues.

Furthermore, as required by the rapidly changing nature of commerce and as recommended by the AACSB, the text devotes extensive attention to legal and ethical issues arising from international business. Various topics throughout the text (for example, comparative economic systems, the Foreign Corrupt Practices Act, and global pollution) afford the student a sense of the worldwide implications of American business practice, and Chapter 16 is entirely devoted to international themes.

At the same time, the text's central theme remains the role of law, if any, in regulating the business and society relationship.

PHILOSOPHY

As noted, our primary goal is to provoke student thought. To that end, we place heavy emphasis on analysis. We consider the questions we ask more important than the answers to those questions. The student is acquainted with existing policy in the various areas, not merely for the purposes of understanding and retention, but also to provoke inquiry as to the desirability of those policies.

Our book takes a strong public policy orientation. Unit I of the text is a necessary foundation on which the student can build a logical understanding of the regulatory process, but the business and society themes don't stop there. In virtually every chapter, we look beyond the law itself to other environmental forces. For example, in the antitrust chapters economic philosophy is of great importance. Antitrust is explored as a matter of national social policy. We argue that antitrust has a good deal to do with the direction of American life generally. Law is at the heart of the fair employment practices section, but we also present material from management, sociology, history, and popular culture to treat fair employment as an issue of social policy rather than as a series of narrower technical legal disputes. These kinds of approaches characterize most chapters as we attempt to examine the various problems as a whole and in context. But with all this, the law remains the core of the book.

KEY FEATURES/DEPARTURES

Journalistic and scholarly readings seek to give the book a stimulating, real-world quality.

Ethics and social responsibility are at the heart of the text rather than an afterthought to meet accreditation standards.

International issues receive extensive attention.

Law cases are long enough to clearly express the essence of the decision while challenging the reader's intellect.

The law is studied in the economic, social, and political context from which it springs.

Critics of business values and the American legal system receive attention.

Approximately 200 selected Web sites appear in the eighth edition, and each chapter includes at least one Internet Exercise.

Perhaps the key pedagogical tactic in the book is the emphasis on questions rather than on answers.

INSTRUCTOR'S MANUAL

A package of supplementary materials is included in the instructor's manual. Those materials include (1) chapter outlines, (2) general advice regarding the goals and purposes of the chapters, (3) summaries of the law cases, (4) answers for the questions raised in the text, and (5) a test bank.

COMPUTERIZED TEST BANK

This version of the Test Bank includes all of the material in the printed version with added flexibility. Instructors can add, remove, modify, and shuffle questions according to their preference and teaching style.

BOOK WEB SITE

This site, located at **www.mhhhe.com/mcadams8e,** enriches the text. In addition to offering instructors a downloadable version of the Instructor's Manual and Test Bank, it also contains additional cases, readings, and student quizzes for the benefit of both instructors and students.

ACKNOWLEDGMENTS

Completion of the eighth edition of this book depended, in significant part, on the hard work of others.

The authors are pleased to acknowledge the contributions of these good people: John Biernat, editorial director; Andy Winston, publisher; Kelly Lowery, senior sponsoring editor; Christine Vaughan, lead project manager; and Kirsten Guidero, editorial assistant.

The authors also thank the 35 reviewers from past editions, and the following professors who reviewed portions of the text and otherwise provided valuable guidance for this edition: Martha Broderick, University of Maine; Debra Burke, Western Carolina University; Frank Cavico, Nova Southeastern University; Suzanne Cummins, University of Arizona; Heidi Noonan-Day, University of Northern Iowa; Jeffrey Pittman, Arkansas State University; Craig Stilwell, Michigan State University; and Keith D. Swim Jr., Texas A&M University.

SUGGESTIONS

The authors welcome comments and criticism from all readers.

Tony McAdams

Brief Contents

Contents

Chapter 3
The Corporation and Public Policy:
Expanding Responsibilities   77

UNIT TWO
INTRODUCTION TO LAW   121

Chapter 4
The American Legal System   122

UNIT THREE
TRADE REGULATION AND ANTITRUST   293

Chapter 8
Government Regulation of Business   294

Chapter 10
Antitrust Law—Restraints of Trade   386

Chapter 11
Antitrust Law—Monopolies and
Mergers   415

UNIT FIVE
SELECTED TOPICS IN GOVERNMENT–BUSINESS RELATIONS   583

Chapter 15
Consumer Protection   584

Chapter 16
International Ethics and Law   617

Chapter 17
Environmental Protection   658

Business and Society

Capitalism and the Role of Government

Part One—Introduction

Are you a capitalist?

Are you a capitalist? If so, what role, if any, should the law play in your business life? How much government does America need? These themes, examining the relationship between government and business in America, are the core of this text. Since the fall of the Soviet Union and the general decline of communist influence, free market reasoning has dominated worldwide economic discourse. Indeed, former U.S. State Department policy planner Francis Fukuyama has argued that capitalism and Western democracy have so thoroughly proven their worth that the capitalism/collectivism debate is over.[1] Democracy and markets, Fukuyama claims, are so clearly triumphant that no new forms of civilization are likely to emerge. Thus, he says, we are at the end of history.

On the other hand, distinguished management scholar Henry Mintzberg says we have misunderstood the lesson of the ascendance of capitalism:

> "Capitalism has triumphed." That was the pat conclusion reached in the West as, one by one, the communist regimes of Eastern Europe began to fall. It has become such an article of faith that we have become blind to its effects. Those effects are highly negative—indeed, dangerous—because the conclusion itself is wrong.

> * * * * *

> Capitalism did not triumph at all; balance did. We in the West have been living in balanced societies with strong private sectors, strong public sectors, and great strength in the sectors in between. The countries under communism were totally out of balance. In those countries, the state controlled an enormous proportion of all organized activity. There was little or no countervailing force.

> The belief that capitalism has triumphed is now throwing the societies of the West out of balance, especially the United Kingdom and the United States. That the imbalance will favor private rather than state ownership will not help society.[2]

> * * * * *

Challenging Capitalism/Globalization   Whether a victory for capitalism (Fukuyama) or for balance (Mintzberg) or for something else altogether, the new global, technologically based economy is leading us in directions we can only dimly foresee. Does that uncertain future call for strengthened government controls, or are we wisest to let the market sort out our lives on a case-by-case basis? As scholar Robert Heilbroner notes, we are in an era of "warp-speed capitalism,"[3] fired by unprecedented faith in market-based decision making. That faith in the market is being severely tested, however. For example, the World Alliance of Reformed Churches [http://www.warc.ch/], representing 75 million Christians in 100 countries, recently expanded the ideological attack on capitalism and corporations by arguing that United States–style capitalism is the biggest threat to world welfare.

> ## Capitalism, as currently practiced, is "unfaithful to God"

Capitalism, as currently practiced, should be blamed, the clergy claim, "for job loss and grinding poverty, an unprecedented rise in crime and violence, ecological degradation, and the spread of HIV/AIDS."[4] The alliance, in its 2004 meeting, went on to claim that capitalism, as currently practiced, is "unfaithful to God":

> We live in a scandalous world that denies God's call to life for all. The annual income of the richest 1 percent is equal to that of the poorest 57 percent, and 24,000 people die each day from poverty and malnutrition.

> *   *   *   *   *

> The policies of unlimited growth among the most industrialized countries and the lust for profits of the multinational corporations have so badly damaged the planet that by the year 2000 one species was disappearing every hour.
> This is a global system that defends and protects the interests of the powerful. . . . [I]n Biblical terms such a system of wealth accumulation at the expense of the poor is seen as unfaithful to God.[5]

Political theorists Michael Hardt and Antonio Negri likewise condemn American capitalism and globalization. They argue that we are in an era of a new American "empire" where multinational businesses and political units are allied to influence and control all corners of American and world interests.[6] Edward Rothstein, writing in *The New York Times,* explains Hardt and Negri's view:

> Nothing escapes what the authors call the capitalist system of "global apartheid." And war is perpetual, pursued for profit and power. Even the purpose of the "war on terrorism," in their view, is "to organize global violence," to ensure that the power to use violence remains in hands of those who already have it.[7]

But we cannot deny the obvious productive power and idealized pursuit of individual freedom that characterizes capitalism—at least as most Americans see it. Robert Bartley, former editor of *The Wall Street Journal* and one of the most influential journalists in American history, was convinced of the merits of the market:

> For all our momentary problems, at the turn of the century the Soviet empire had collapsed, democracy was spreading to unlikely places, and the American free-enterprise model was established as the route to development. Even with today's problems, the United States has no serious rival. . . . What I think I have learned over 30 years is that in this society, rationality wins out, progress happens, and problems have solutions. This, I like to think, is what happens when a society incorporates the editorial credo of my newspaper, free markets and free people.[8]

September 11, 2001 The terrorist attacks on the World Trade Center and the Pentagon necessitate a reevaluation of our previous understanding of global politics, economics, and social values. How can we now so confidently conclude that capitalism is the only meaningful economic voice for the globe? How can we conclude, as Fukuyama claims, that we are at the end of history when the terrorists have told us so brutally and tragically that they are not satisfied with the current Western-dominated global culture? Is Fukuyama wrong about the long-term and indestructible triumph of capitalism/democracy and Samuel Huntington more nearly correct when he claims that the world is mired in a clash of six or seven major cultures that will not converge and that cannot happily coexist?[9]

Fukuyama has referred to September 11 as an attack on the "centre of global capitalism."[10] Certainly the Twin Towers were an emphatically visible symbol of American and global business; but can the terrorist attack legitimately be seen as a repudiation of capitalist, American, Western values? We don't precisely know the motivations of the terrorists, but experts have pointed to such explanations as America's allegedly pro-Israeli tilt in the conflict with Palestine, a general resentment of American global power, and anger over alleged American protection of autocratic Middle Eastern governments. Each of these explanations may have played a role in causing the terrorists to fly planes to their deaths and the deaths of 3,000 others. However, part of the answer probably resides in capitalism itself and in the onrushing process of *globalization.* Experts differ about the nature and impact of globalization; but we certainly see compelling evidence that international trade is breaching national boundaries, technology is shrinking the globe, and multinationals are increasingly viewing the globe as one giant market. As we discuss later (see Chapters 3 and 16), globalization suggests the promise of dramatic advances in worldwide prosperity. Perhaps greater social and political understanding will also emerge from our "shrinking" globe. But as the following editorial suggests, the September 11 terrorists and doubtless millions of others around the globe see the advance of capitalist, American, Western values on all fronts as a direct assault on their way of life.

READING ▶ **"Cultural Imperialism"? No**

Omaha World-Herald, November 24, 2001

American troops don't have to take over the world. American culture—which, more accurately, is an amazingly multicultural phenomenon—is achieving conquests of its own.

"Cultural imperialism" is one of Osama bin Laden's more frequent indictments of the United States. He and others who want to beat up on this country make it sound like it is promoting an insidious plot. But what's happening is really more cultural osmosis, in many cases happily embraced. "Imperialism" implies the imposition of one nation's will upon another. The conquer-and-spread cultural imperialism practiced by

Greece, for instance, was evident when its armies took over parts of the ancient Middle East and its civilizing influence and public baths "took over," in a sense, the people living there.

But cultural infiltration as it is seen these days is more subtle, traveling not via arrows or bullets but in knowledge, information, understanding. It is people listening to the music, eating the food, reading the books, watching the television shows of a foreign country—and liking them. It is attitude, atmosphere, expectations. It is the potential for change where no change is wanted, at least by the people in authority.

This kind of "imperialism" is what the United States stands accused of by bin Laden and others around the world, some less violent than he but no less contemptuous of American society.

American culture, of course, is itself an amalgam. It is portions of the cultures of all of the ethnic groups that have come here, stayed, and melted into the melting pot, adding their uniqueness. Some of the most "American" of our cultural icons—the Statue of Liberty, the ubiquitous taco, even the traditions of the Christmas season—are imports.

Americans count by using Arabic numerals (learned by Europeans from Arabs, though the numerals' origin apparently was in India). Even the tune to the national anthem is an old English drinking song.

American culture? It's a patchwork.

Unfortunately, defending some of the tackier patches exported to the world is not easy.

Baywatch is said (let us hope facetiously) to be the most popular television show on the planet. The McD-ing of the world, the homogenization of fast-food tastes, means that the people of Tokyo and Buenos Aires, Seoul and Bahrain, Canberra and Reykjavik all have the opportunity to chow down on some version of the quintessentially American burger, fries, and a shake.

The idea that so many people have enthusiastically embraced some of the worst aspects of American culture may be dismaying, but it comes with the territory. MTV, low-slung jeans, slang, and vomit-and-flatulence movies aren't necessarily what Americans might want to be known for by the people of other nations.

But that's the way it goes. When you offer up your culture for other people to see and accept, they take what they need. More significantly, they take what they like. No one forces Iranians to turn on their illicit televisions when *Baywatch* is illicitly scheduled via illicit satellite broadcast. But some—reportedly a lot of them—do.

That's free will; that's freedom. It is inherently destabilizing for the dictators of the far left and the far right and the fundamentalist mullahs of the world. It's just what the bin Laden types can't stand. In a closed, tightly controlled society, all actions are dictated by the interpretations and biases of the leaders. There is no choice, no dissent. Therefore, freedom—and the American culture that springs from it—is subversive.

It is far more comfortable for the enemies of freedom to define Americans by possessions rather than by core beliefs and ideals. How much easier it is to hate the self-indulgence of bottled water and *Ally McBeal* and movies that swagger with exaggerated American pride than it is to deal with the depth and breadth of the American spirit. And with the virtues of tolerance, freedom and justice that have few equals in any other time or place.

Source: *Omaha World-Herald,* November 24, 2001, p. 6b. Reprinted by permission.

Questions

1. *a.* Is America deliberately seeking to convert the balance of the globe to American, free market, democratic values?

   b. Would all nations be well served if they adopt American, free market, democratic values? Explain.

2. In what ways might American culture be viewed as offensive and threatening to Muslims and others around the globe?

3. What role did oil play in the September 11 attack?

4. Intellectuals Michael Hardt and Antonio Negri claim that a new global economic system is emerging, which they refer to as an "empire" bound together by a network of agreements arranged and monitored by global organizations such as the World Trade Organization, the International Monetary Fund, the World Bank, and the United Nations. A reviewer explained their central ideas:

   > It is not a nation–state. It is not an aligned superpower bloc. It has no seat like the Roman Empire. It is a distributed network, like the Internet, created by international agreements binding nations big and small into relationships that none of them fully control.[11]

   What role do giant American multinational corporations, such as McDonald's, allegedly play in the emerging "empire?"

[For arguments in support of globalization, see **http://www.iccwbo.org/home/menu_case_for_the_global_economy.asp**]
[For a critique of "capitalist globalization," see **http://flag.blackened.net/revolt/wsm/global.htm**]

Our Purpose Thus the ongoing globalization movement, the struggle between government intervention and free markets, and the battle between corporations and their critics provide the unstable context in which American business operates. Within that context, then, the purpose of this book is to ask two questions:

1. What is the proper role of business in American and global society?
2. How much, if any, government regulation of business is necessary to secure that role?

Markets and Governments In the United States, we certainly cannot understand our system of laws without a firm appreciation for the principles of capitalism from which those laws spring. We chose a capitalist, democratic approach to life. Other cultures have placed less faith in the market and more in government planning. The legal systems in those countries reflect a preference for greater central authority.

In this chapter we will explore the full range of the economic spectrum, moving from a laissez-faire, free market approach on the extreme right to a brief reminder of command economy principles on the far left. But the bulk of our attention will rest where the world is at this moment; that is, we will examine the notion of the *mixed economy,* a combination of markets and rules.

The pure free market approach assumes that we can operate our business structure and our society at large free of all but foundational legal mechanisms such as contract and criminal law. The wisdom of the market—our individual judgments, in combination with our individual consciences—would "regulate" American life. Most forms of government including regulatory agencies, consumer protection, environmental rules, occupational licensure, zoning restrictions, antitrust law, and all but the most basic government services (perhaps limited to the police, the courts, and the army) would be eliminated.

As noted, today's debate is no longer about capitalism versus communism but about the mixed economy—that is, about what combination of capitalism and government best serves the world's needs. Substantially open markets have shown themselves to be the stronger vehicle for productivity, efficiency, and personal freedom. But are they also the stronger vehicle for improving living conditions for all citizens, for maximizing democracy, for discouraging crime and corruption, and for building strong communities? In this era of rapid globalization, are America and the world best served by the speed and efficiency of largely unrestrained markets, or do we still need the "civilizing" influence of government rules?

Law Finally, this chapter should be read as a foundation for the study of law that follows. Once a society settles on some broad political and economic principles, it pours a thin veneer or many heavy coats (depending on the system chosen) of social control on that foundation. The law serves as a primary method of social control. So to understand the law, we need to understand its roots in the economic, political, and social preferences of the world's people.

Questions—Part One

1. Former Secretary of Labor Robert Reich speculated about five possible scenarios for the political economy of the current century. Which do you think is the more likely direction? Explain.
    a. History is ending in bureaucratic corporatism. . . . Key decisions are shifting away from elected politicians and legislative bodies toward multinational bureaucracies (such as the G-8) and global corporations unaccountable to any single population.
    b. History alternates between periods of central control and chaos, and we are again entering the latter. The 40-year interval of superpower stability is giving way to tribal fragmentation and warfare with ethnic tensions flaring over Eastern Europe and the former Soviet Union, the Asian subcontinent, and even within advanced industrial nations.

    c. History is ending in cultural authoritarianism. Societies like Japan and Germany, which reward group loyalty and investment, are gaining economic power over societies organized around individual liberty and personal consumption. Meanwhile, much of the Third World is succumbing to Islamic fundamentalism.

    d. History is ending in liberal democracy and individual liberty. Modern economies depend on educated workforces, which in turn are demanding rights and freedoms that only liberal democracies can provide (look at Latin America).

    e. All of the above. See Robert Reich, "Is Liberal Democracy the Hallmark of Our Era?" *The Wall Street Journal,* February 6, 1992, p. A12.

2. In 1999 *The Wall Street Journal* asked leading economists, executives, and others whether capitalism's triumph over socialism is, in fact, complete, or whether challenges remain. What challenges threaten capitalism in this millennium? See Paul Hofheinz, "What Now?" *The Wall Street Journal,* September 27, 1999, p. R25.

Part Two—Capitalism

Capitalism in Theory—Ayn Rand

Capitalism in America was built on a strong theoretical foundation and was stimulated by the promise of unprecedented general welfare. These forces, in combination with America's natural resources and an ambitious population, led to the development of a powerful economic machine. But that machine, in the view of many Americans, ran out of control for a time. Business abuses brought widespread popular sentiment for governmental restraints on capitalism. Thus, as is discussed in subsequent chapters, America's substantially free market economy was gradually placed under government regulation. And despite the striking rhetoric and significant deregulation strides of the current free market era, America remains a nation of big government.

Our purpose now is to reconsider the merits of a purer form of capitalism. Did we turn too hastily from the market? Should we further shed our governmental role in economic affairs and restore our faith in the "invisible hand"? Can we, in large measure, do without regulation by law? Will a genuinely unfettered market better serve our needs than our current amalgam of business restrained by government? To answer these questions, we need a firm understanding of capitalism in a pure form, which has almost entirely slipped from view. The controversial philosopher and novelist Ayn Rand was an uncompromising advocate of free market principles. She believed the necessary categories of government were only three in number: the police, the armed services, and the law courts. Via her philosophy of objectivism, Rand argued that the practice of free market principles is necessary to the pursuit of a rational, moral life. Rand's viewpoint has been the subject of vigorous criticism. Its merits are for the reader to assess, but it is fair to say that she was among America's most ardent and articulate apostles of a genuine free market. [See The Center for the Moral Defense of Capitalism at **http://www.moraldefense.com/**]

Ayn Rand

If one wishes to advocate a free society—that is, capitalism—one must realize that its indispensable foundation is the principle of individual rights. If one wishes to uphold individual rights, one must realize that capitalism is the only system that can uphold and protect them.

"Rights" are a moral concept—the concept that provides a logical transition from the principles guiding an individual's actions to the principles guiding his relationship with others—the concept that preserves and protects individual morality in a social context—the link between the moral code of a man and the legal code of a society, between ethics and politics. *Individual rights are the means of subordinating society to moral law.*

Every political system is based on some code of ethics. The dominant ethics of mankind's history were variants of the altruist-collectivist doctrine which subordinated the individual to some higher authority. Consequently, most political systems were variants of the same statist tyranny.

* * * * *

Under all such systems, morality was a code applicable to the individual, but not to society. Society was placed *outside* the moral law, and the inculcation of self-sacrificial devotion to social duty was regarded as the main purpose of ethics in man's earthly existence.

Since there is no such entity as "society," since society is only a number of individual men, this meant, in practice, that the rulers of society were exempt from moral law; subject only to traditional rituals, they held total power and exacted blind obedience—on the implicit principle of "The good is that which is good for society, and the ruler's edicts are its voice on earth."

This was true of all statist systems, under all variants of the altruist-collectivist ethics, mystical or social. As witness: the theocracy of Egypt, with the Pharaoh as an embodied god—the unlimited majority rule or *democracy* of Athens—the welfare state run by the Emperors of Rome—the Inquisition of the late Middle Ages—the absolute monarchy of France—the welfare state of Bismarck's Prussia—the gas chambers of Nazi Germany—the slaughterhouse of the Soviet Union.

All these political systems were expressions of the altruist-collectivist ethics—and their common characteristic is the fact that society stood above the moral law. . . . Thus, politically, all these systems were variants of an *amoral* society.

The most profoundly revolutionary achievement of the United States of America was *the subordination of society to moral law.*

The principle of man's individual rights represented the extension of morality into the social system—as a limitation on the power of the state. . . . The United States was the first *moral* society in history.

All previous systems had regarded man as a sacrificial means to the ends of others, and society as an end in itself. The United States regarded man as an end in himself, and society as a means to the peaceful, orderly, *voluntary* coexistence of individuals. All previous systems had held that man's life belongs to society, that society can dispose of him in any way it pleases, and that any freedom he enjoys is his only by favor, by the *permission* of society, which may be revoked at any time. The United States held that man's life is his by *right,* that a right is the property of an individual, that society as such has no rights, and that the only moral purpose of a government is the protection of individual rights.

A "right" is a moral principle defining and sanctioning a man's freedom of action in a social context. There is only *one* fundamental right (all the others are its consequences or corollaries): a man's right to his own life. . . .

America's inner contradiction was the altruist-collectivist ethics. Altruism is incompatible with freedom, with capitalism, and with individual rights. . . .

It was the concept of individual rights that had given birth to a free society. It was with the destruction of individual rights that the destruction of freedom had to begin.

A collectivist tyranny dare not enslave a country by an outright confiscation of its values, material or moral. It has to be done by a process of internal corruption. . . . The process entails such a growth of newly promulgated "rights" that people do not notice the fact that the meaning of the concept is being reversed. . . .

The Democratic Party platform of 1960 summarizes the switch boldly and explicitly. It declares that a democratic administration "will reaffirm the economic bill of rights which Franklin Roosevelt wrote into our national conscience 16 years ago."

Bear clearly in mind the meaning of the concept of *rights* when you read the list which that platform offers:

1. The right to a useful and remunerative job in the industries or shops or farms or mines of the nation.

2. The right to earn enough to provide adequate food and clothing and recreation.

3. The right of every farmer to raise and sell his products at a return which will give him and his family a decent living.

4. The right of every businessman, large and small, to trade in an atmosphere of freedom from unfair competition and domination by monopolies at home and abroad.

5. The right of every family to a decent home.

6. The right to adequate medical care and the opportunity to achieve and enjoy good health.

7. The right to adequate protection from the economic fears of old age, sickness, accidents, and unemployment.

8. The right to a good education.

A single question added to each of the above eight clauses would make the issue clear: *At whose expense?*

Jobs, food, clothing, recreation (!), homes, medical care, education, etc. do not grow in nature. These are man-made values—goods and services produced by men. *Who* is to provide them?

If some men are entitled *by right* to the products of the work of others, it means that those others are deprived of rights and condemned to slave labor.

*   *   *   *   *

Observe, in this context, the intellectual precision of the Founding Fathers: they spoke of the right to *the pursuit* of happiness—*not* of the right to happiness. It means that a man has the right to take the actions he deems necessary to achieve his happiness; it does *not* mean that others must make him happy. . . .

Property rights and the right of free trade are man's only "economic rights" (they are, in fact, *political* rights)—and there can be no such thing as "an *economic* bill of rights." . . .

And while people are clamoring about "economic rights," the concept of political rights is vanishing. . . .

Such is the state of one of today's most crucial issues: *political* rights versus "*economic* rights." It's either-or. One destroys the other. But there are, in fact, no "economic rights," no "collective rights," no "public-interest rights." The term *individual rights* is a redundancy: there is no other kind of rights and no one else to possess them.

Those who advocate laissez-faire capitalism are the only advocates of man's rights.

Source: From *The Virtue of Selfishness* by Ayn Rand. Copyright © 1961, 1964 by Ayn Rand. Copyright, © 1962, 1963, 1964 by the Objectivist Newsletter, Inc. Reprinted by arrangement with New American Library, New York, New York, and with permission of the Estate of Ayn Rand. [For more information about Ayn Rand and objectivism, see **http://www.aynrand.org**]

Questions

1. *a.* As measured by the level of taxation and regulation, protection for property rights, the liberality of trade policy, and the like, would you say the world is increasingly free or increasingly subject to government oversight?

    b. Of all the nations of the world, does the United States enjoy the greatest level of economic freedom? Explain. [See **www.heritage.org**]

2. In 1999 an ad was placed in Ivy League college newspapers offering $50,000 for ovarian eggs from women with minimum credentials of a combined SAT score of 1400 and a height of 5 feet, 10 inches. Similarly, an Internet site auctioned eggs from models and actresses.

    a. Does capitalism encourage us to treat people as products?

    b. Are people, in fact, products? Explain.

3. Gwyneth Paltrow reportedly was to earn $3.6 million to sing one three-minute song, "This Thing Called Love," in a cameo appearance playing singer Peggy Lee in the movie *Every Word Is True,* a biographical treatment of the author/celebrity Truman Capote.[12] Has the market failed, or has it worked as it should when an individual is paid $3.6 million for a work product that will total three minutes? Explain.

4. The navy wants to keep its skilled workers happy so that they will reenlist. At the same time, those skilled workers are needed in locales abroad where many do not want to go. Historically, the navy simply ordered those sailors to serve wherever they were needed. Now the navy has turned to a free market strategy to find sailors willing to accept undesirable assignments abroad. Using free market reasoning, explain how the navy can achieve its goals. See Greg Jaffe, "Navy Turns . . . ," *The Wall Street Journal*, August 11, 2003, p. B3.

Capitalism in Practice—"Privatization" in America and Abroad

Around the globe, from Russia to Eastern Europe and from the United Kingdom to Southeast Asia, expanded faith in the free market was the singular economic message of the 1980s and 1990s. Nations increasingly embraced the free market argument that virtually all services performed by government may be more efficiently and more equitably "managed" by the private sector forces of the market.

Most commonly, privatization follows two patterns: (1) contracting out where government, in effect, turns over a portion of its duties, such as garbage collection, to a private firm; and (2) the sale of public assets, such as an airport, to a private purchaser. Contracting with private firms to provide public services has become widespread in the United States and includes activities such as tree trimming, building maintenance, computer services and providing welfare services for the indigent.

Toll Roads   Should users pay direct fees for access to highways? About a dozen states are taking that direction as fuel taxes fail to keep up with road building and repair costs.[13] Some drivers are delighted:

> Mike Cunningham is so tired of fighting traffic on the way to work in his Ford Explorer that he can't wait for 66 miles of new roads to open north of (fast-growing Austin, Texas)—even though he'll be charged a toll of at least $1 every time he uses them. . . . His 13-mile drive to the office usually takes 45 minutes, up from 25 minutes five years ago.[14]

Missouri officials hope to impose a toll on Interstate 70 from Illinois to Kansas. Virginia plans a toll for its I-81, and toll roads have been in place in the Houston, Texas, area for four years. The result in Houston is an average speed of 60 miles per hour on the toll roads as compared with 40 on nearby major roads without tolls.[15] But not everyone is happy with the fees. Double taxation is one of the primary complaints because drivers pay gasoline taxes to build and improve roads, and truckers feel especially pinched by the tolls.

Critics worry about creating fast-moving "Lexus lanes" for rich people.

Some states are now experimenting with privately funded highways and so-called congestion pricing. In crowded Orange County, California, drivers pay to take a privately funded and operated, 10-mile stretch of highway rather than suffer the frustrations of the public road.[16] The idea is that traffic jams are caused by not requiring drivers to pay for the costs (delays) they impose on others. The market-based solution, then, is to charge for driving where congestion is a problem. Experts, note, however, that the Orange County toll road is one of the few successes in privately financed transportation,[17] and critics worry about creating fast-moving "Lexus lanes" for rich people. [For a large database supportive of privatization, see **http://www.privatization.org/**]

Should nongolfing taxpayers subsidize those who choose to play?

Golf Courses   Golf is a great game, beloved by many; but should nongolfing taxpayers subsidize those who choose to play? Studies show that payrolls for city-operated golf courses are about 13 percent higher than for privately operated courses.[18] According to the Reason Foundation, five of six privatized courses in Los Angeles County increased revenues "between 24 percent to 400 percent in the first year of private operation."[19] Detroit's $500,000 deficit became a $200,000 profit under private management. Similar results were reported in New York City and Chicago.[20] Reason explained,

> [Private contractors] deliver better services at lower costs than the public sector and make a profit all at the same time . . . by increasing the number of rounds played, cutting overhead costs, purchasing materials and supplies in volume, improving golf course management techniques, and reinvesting revenues in capital improvements.[21]

Questions

1. Author Joan Didion referred to our highways as America's only communion. Would it be a social/ethical wrong to adopt widespread "congestion fees" and privately operated toll roads that would permit those with money to avoid the democracy of the highways? Explain.

2. *Governing Magazine* labeled golf courses "perhaps the most nonessential of the nonessential public services." Why do we subsidize golf, and should we continue doing so? Explain.

Prisons   Private prisons have become important economic development/job creation projects for many communities across America. But earning a profit in housing prisoners amounts to "a commerce in souls," according to one critic.[22] Corrections Corporation of America, the largest private prison firm in the nation, manages 66,000 beds in 65 facilities in 20 states.[23] In Colorado, for example, 20 percent of the prison population is in private hands,[24] but for the nation as a whole only about 6.5 percent of the population is in for-profit facilities.[25] Private prisons have clear short-term cost advantages in that they ordinarily are built more quickly at a smaller cost, and their generally lower wages allow operating costs that fall significantly beneath state-run facilities. Of course, the long-term costs are unknown; and legislators are increasingly worried that safety is a bigger issue in private prisons than in those run by government. Sacrifices in programs, basic care, and security may accompany the less expensive private-sector prisons. [For labor union opposition to privatization, see **http://www.afscme.org/private/**]

Schools   Is capitalism the answer to poor school performance? Can the competitive power of the market reform America's struggling public school systems? The idea was unthinkable a few decades ago, but some increasingly frustrated parents and school boards have adopted a free market "fix." Schools are experimenting with free market approaches such as open enrollment (students attend the school of their choice regardless of their place of residence), charter schools (funded by taxes but freed of much government oversight), and vouchers (students "spend" their taxpayer-provided dollars on the school of their choice). Some 23 states have taken the dramatic step of contracting with private education providers, most notably Edison Schools Inc., to manage some of their more troubled schools. The basic idea of these experiments is to introduce competition into the education "market." Edison hopes to make money running schools and improving student performance. After two years of managing 20 of Philadelphia's most troubled inner-city schools, Edison appears to have achieved some significant performance improvements with reported double-digit reading and math gains along with a tripling of the number of schools meeting the federal government's No Child Left Behind standards.[26] On the other hand, Edison's pre-Philadelphia test in the impoverished suburb of Chester, Pennsylvania, appears, after three years, to have had little success in improving student performance.[27]

Privatization Abroad   Much of the globe has adopted the American- and British-led policy of government downsizing via privatization. Nations as economically diverse as Italy, Japan, Guyana, Hungary, and Australia have all aggressively pursued privatization initiatives. Predictably, results have been mixed, although experts continue to believe that privatization offers enormous advantages in efficiency, productivity, and output over state-controlled enterprises. Russia has particularly struggled with privatizing its oil industry, and talks of "de-privatization" of one of its largest hydroelectric power plants raise concerns about the future course of privatization in Russia. China has likewise taken halting steps toward privatization of its vast state-owned assets. A recently created bureaucratic structure, the State-Owned Assets Supervision and Administration Commission (SASAC), is designed to "preserve the value of state assets" and may prove to be a "powerful obstacle to privatization at all levels."[28] Nonetheless, hundreds of privatizations by local government units are in the offing, as China carefully balances its movement toward open markets against its continuing commitment to government control.[29] [For information on privatization abroad, see **http://www.adamsmith.org.uk/ policy/publications/world-privatization.htm**]

Privatization in Sum   Studies indicate that contracting out services reduces costs by 10 to 20 percent.[30] Privatization supporters also point to improved managerial skills and increased expertise when turning government services over to private-sector specialists. Critics, however, argue that those savings result simply from paying substandard wages and cutting corners on quality. Professor Jonathan Goodrich lists these primary concerns regarding privatization:

- Unemployment of government workers.
- Lower quality of services.
- Government loss of control and accountability.
- Excessive government payments for private-sector work.
- Corruption and scandal.[31]

On balance, privatization has proven efficient and useful in many instances; and the larger relationship between the market and government, around the globe, has been dramatically altered. But the efficiency virtues of privatization do not mean that Americans want to turn their backs on government. Daniel Yergin and Joseph Stanislaw remind us of our insecurities:

> Americans are willing to tolerate more insecurity than people in other industrial nations, but there are still limits to how much insecurity they will accept. Elections and opinion polls demonstrate that while the public does not want government to extend its reach, neither does it want this rich country to abandon its American-style safety net.[32]

Questions—Part Two

1. *a.* Should we turn the U.S. Postal Service over to the private sector? Explain.
   b. Which segments of society would be harmed most by that move? Explain.

2. From the capitalist viewpoint, why is the private ownership of property necessary to the preservation of freedom?

3. Ayn Rand argued, "Altruism is incompatible with freedom, with capitalism, and with individual rights."

    a. Define *altruism.*

    b. Explain why Rand rejected altruism.

4. In describing life in aggressively commercialized Hong Kong, Alvin Rabushka praised the "single-minded pursuit of making money" and the "emphasis on the material things in life." Rabushka admitted to finding "Hong Kong's economic hustle and bustle more interesting, entertaining, and liberating than its lack of high opera, music, and drama."

    a. Although it is often criticized in America, is materialism the most certain and most interesting path to personal happiness? Explain.

    b. Would "sophisticated" culture (such as opera and drama) substantially disappear in America without government support? Explain.

    c. If so, how may we justify that support? If not, how may we justify that support?

5. Assume the federal government removed itself from the purchase and maintenance of its parks.

    a. Left to the private sector, what sorts of parks would develop under the profit incentive?

    b. Would Yellowstone, for example, survive in substantially its present state? Explain.

    c. How can it be argued that the federal parks are an unethical, undemocratic expropriation of private resources?

6. Assume the abolition of the federal Food and Drug Administration. How would the free market protect the citizenry from dangerous food and drug products?

7. Should education be returned to the free market? Explain. How would poor Americans finance a private sector education?

8. Scholar Amitai Etzioni argues that America must choose between rededication to economic growth and emphasis on a quality-of-life society (slower growth, emphasis on ecology, concern for safety, harmony with oneself and others). He argues that the monetary costs and the social–psychic strains of pursuing these two divergent courses exceed America's resources, both physical and emotional.

    a. Do you agree with Etzioni? Explain.

    b. Which path would you choose? Explain.

    c. Will the market support the quality-of-life approach? Explain.

9. Puritan leaders felt concern over the morality of merchants selling goods for "more than their worth." That concern was particularly grave when the goods were scarce or in great demand.

    a. Should our society develop an ethic wherein goods are to be sold only "for what they are worth"? Explain.

    b. Can a seller make an accurate determination of worth? Explain.

    c. Does a product's worth differ from the price that product will bring in the marketplace? Explain.

    d. Personalize the inquiry: Assume you seek to sell your Ford car for $5,000. Assume you know of several identical Fords in a similar state of repair that can be purchased for $4,500. Assume you find a buyer at $5,000. Will you unilaterally lower your price or direct the purchaser to the other cars? Explain.

e. If not, have you acted justly? Explain.

10. Critics of our capitalist system contend that ability and effort often are less responsible for one's success than "unearned" factors such as family background, social class, luck, and willingness to cheat. Do you agree? Explain.

11. Commentator Irving Kristol asked whether it was "just" for Ray Kroc (now deceased, formerly of McDonald's) to have made so much money by merely figuring out a new way to sell hamburgers. He concluded that capitalism says it is just because he sold a good product; people want it; it is fair.

a. Do you agree with Kristol? Explain.

b. Does contemporary American capitalism offer excessive rewards to those clever enough to build near-term paper profits (lawyers, accountants, financial analysts) through mergers, tax write-offs, and the like while diverting scarce resources from long-term productive ventures (such as new product development or more efficient production processes)? Explain.

c. If so, is capitalism fatally flawed? Explain.

12. Professor Robert E. Lane argued that the person who is motivated by needs for affiliation, rather than by needs for achievement, does less well in the market. Such a person is not rewarded so well as autonomous, achievement-oriented people.

a. Is Lane correct? Explain.

b. Is capitalism, in the long run, destructive of societal welfare in that achievement is better rewarded than affiliation? Explain.

13. Make the argument that the federal highway program, although well-intentioned, was merely one in a series of federal interventions that distorted the market, leading, in this instance, to the long-term decline of inner cities.

14. How would poor people be cared for in a free market society?

15. Kevin Mattson, a researcher at Rutgers University, fears the gated community, where people shut themselves off from public life. "The privatization of everything including garbage service," he said, "disassociates people from contributing to the public good and from their responsibility to other people."

Do you agree? Explain. See Lisa Rathke, "School Choice Experts Discuss Impact of Choice," *Associated Press State & Local Wire,* February 8, 1999.

Part Three—Collectivism

The term *collectivism* embraces various economic philosophies on the left of the political–economic spectrum: principally communism and socialism. Capitalism is characterized by economic individualism. Communism and the various styles of socialism feature economic cooperation and varying degrees of centralized control.

Communism

While China, Cuba, North Korea, Vietnam, and a few other nations continue to practice communism, the balance of the world has clearly rejected *Marxist–Leninist* totalitarianism, and China, as noted above, is gradually but aggressively embracing important elements of free market thought. Even the closed and aggressively hostile communist state of North Korea is feeling the gradual pressure of free market forces, ranging from a private market near the nation's capital to buy consumer goods that are scarce in the state stores to the private, "illegal" sale of mobile phones along the Chinese–North Korean border.[33] Despite the decline of communism, we need to briefly remind ourselves of some fundamental Marxist principles because, as *The Wall Street Journal* noted a few years ago, "His Shadow Persists: Marx Can't Be Ignored. In His Critique of Capitalism the Great Analyst Helped to Shape Today's Agenda."[34] Lenin, not Marx, created the communist dictatorship in Russia. Lenin and the other communist totalitarians, most notably Stalin and Mao, cannot be defended. However, Marx, along with Freud and Einstein, are among the thinkers who most profoundly shaped the 20th century. For our purposes, Marx's central message concerns the severe abuses that can accompany unrestrained capitalism. Marx was particularly concerned about the growing imbalance between rich and poor. Moreover, he felt that the pursuit of wealth and self-interest would erode society's moral core. More broadly, Marx built an economic interpretation of history, arguing that "the mode of production in material life determines the general character of the social, political, and spiritual processes of life."[35] [For an introduction to communist thought, see **http://www.maths.tcd.ie/~belle/comm.html**]

Poland and the Free Market

Ambivalence about capitalism is apparent in many former communist nations. According to a 2004 survey, over 58 percent of Poles, for example, support the free market, but the more the market develops the more problems emerge: fierce competition, the wealth gap, unemployment, and bankruptcies. Only 29 percent of Poles believe that privatization has been good for the nation. Forty-four percent expressed a willingness to pay high taxes to enjoy free education, health care, and other public services, but 43 percent support lower taxes and a copayment system. In short, after 15 years of transformation the Poles continue to look for a "better" capitalism, whatever that may prove to be.

Source: "Fifteen Years after Communism's Fall, Poles Remain Deeply Distrustful of the Free Market," *Polish News Bulletin,* August 26, 2004 [**http://web.lexis-nexis.com/universe/document?_m=fc1577b058fa59 . . .**].

Socialism

Communism appears to have run its course philosophically. However, the problems that generated its appeal—poverty, oppression, political inequality, and so on—remain. Hence the world continues to look to government intervention. The question is, How much? We will briefly remind ourselves of the socialist response to that question. Socialists reject communist totalitarianism and embrace democracy while calling for aggressive government intervention to correct economic and social ills. Historically, socialism has been associated with democratic governments and peaceful change, whereas communism has been characterized by totalitarianism and violent revolution.

Socialists aim to retain the benefits of industrialism while abolishing the social costs often accompanying the free market. The government is likely to be directly involved in regulating growth, inflation, and unemployment. In the contemporary Western world, Austria, Norway, Denmark, Sweden, South Africa, and France are among the nations where socialist principles have retained a significant presence. Now those nations have embraced free markets, although socialist concerns and principles remain influential.

Socialist Goals

A critical distinction between socialists and capitalists is that the former believe a society's broad directions should be carefully planned rather than left to what some take to be the whimsy of the market. Furthermore, socialists are convinced that problems of market failure (inadequate information, monopoly, externalities, public goods, and so on—see Chapter 8) mean that the free market is simply incapable of meeting the needs of all segments of society. The socialist agenda includes these elements:[36]

1. **Liberty.** To the capitalist, socialism appears to harshly restrain individual freedom. To the socialist, the freedoms of capitalism are largely an illusion, accessible only to the prosperous and powerful.

2. **Social welfare.** Socialists reserve much of their concern for the condition of the lower class—poverty, exploitation, cultural deprivation, and so on. Socialists feel that the economy must be directed toward the general interest rather than left free to multiply the welfare of successful capitalists. Hence socialists advocate income supports, free education, free health care, generous sick pay, family planning, and so on to correct the wrongs of capitalism.

3. **Fulfilling work.** Socialists object to the harshness of working life where a large segment of society is chained to degrading labor.

> Socialists seek a communitarian approach to life

4. **Community.** Socialists seek a communitarian approach to life where the excessive individualism of capitalism is muted by a concern for the welfare of all.

5. **Equality.** Class distinctions are anathema to the socialist. All humans are equally meritorious, and distinctions among them are inherently unjust.

6. **Rationality.** Socialists fear the "irrationality" of a society based on competition and unrestrained pursuit of industrial growth.

The following account of a visit by some Santa Clara University professors to a coffee plantation in Guatemala reminds us why collectivists fear unrestrained capitalism while finding great strength in community.

Finca la Victoria

James Reites and Don Dodson

We stand in a circle, our attention focused on Julio César Archilla as he tells us the heartbreaking story of his community—the campesinos of Finca Los Cerros, a large coffee plantation in the southwestern highlands of Guatemala. As two of his young children look on, he explains how 88 families stood up to the finca owner's decision to throw them off the land where they had lived and worked for generations.

The trouble at Finca Los Cerros began in 1995, when the workers started organizing. Before they created the union, they had earned 12.50 quetzales ($2.10) a day; afterward, their pay was increased to 15.50 quetzales a day. The workers thought they had won a major concession when they were told they could take a vacation—a right they had never had before. But in April 1995 when 10 men returned from their vacations, they no longer had jobs.

When the people complained to the local magistrate, the situation escalated. The *finca* owner tried to evict the workers, cutting off electricity and sending his servants to pull up banana and papaya trees. Thirteen people starved to death, 11 of them children. At one point, the women of the community surrounded the owner's men and held them for two weeks.

The impasse was broken when the bishop of San Marcos, Alvaro Ramazzini (himself under death threats for supporting the campesinos), successfully negotiated a settlement that allowed the 88 families to move to new land—land that, for the first time in their lives, they would own.

That the parcel is not large enough to sustain them and that access to drinking water is extremely difficult do not diminish their pride. "We are very happy because we have succeeded with this struggle," the leader of the women tells us. "We are joyful because we have someplace to go—*our* place."

While we talk, we watch men and boys dismantle the simple sheds where they had lived at Finca Los Cerros and carry them, piece by piece, to their new land. There they will make a clearing for a dirt floor and reconstruct their dwellings, albeit without roofs because they are not allowed to take the corrugated tin that had covered their former homes.

Julio is full of plans for the new *finca.* He wants to raise money for a pump to get water from a nearby stream, and he even hopes some organization will donate enough for the families to purchase another piece of land for cash crops. He also speaks proudly of plans to build a school, a church, and a community center on the new land, pointing out the location of each.

"The *campesinos* are down underneath your shoe," says Julio, stamping his foot. "We care for ourselves because, if we don't, there are people out there who are bigger who will eat us up. We, as *campesinos,* have to group together to contradict that."

Source: Markkula Center for Applied Ethics, Santa Clara University © 1996 Markkula Center for Applied Ethics. Reprinted by permission [http://www.scu.edu/Ethics/]

Coping with Capitalism—China and Russia

China—Economics Business is booming in China. The nation of 1.3 billion people is aggressively competing around the globe. Western nations have rushed to China to get a foothold in the world's largest market. After 25 years of increasing capitalism, the signs of material progress are obvious: skyscrapers, cars rapidly replacing bicycles, and McDonalds, KFC, and the like on many urban corners. The 1,100 private cars in 1985 Beijing have been supplemented by more than 2 million today. China is moving toward its goal of a "moderately well off" society with an economy quadrupled by 2020 allowing the Chinese at that time to enjoy a standard of living roughly comparable to the average Westerner's life in 1990.[37] Several tens of millions of Chinese live in poverty (depending on how poverty is defined), but that number is down dramatically from more than 250 million when reforms began in 1978.[38] So economic progress in China is indisputable, and China's power in the global economy is certain to grow rapidly. At the same time, enormous problems remain. In general, China is beset with a dual economy of advancing and sometimes spectacular prosperity, particularly in the urban coastal areas, and wretched poverty in the rural provinces and among the urban underclass. Unemployment is common as the economy gradually shifts from state ownership to the free market. China's so-called "Number 1 Document" for 2004 commits the Communist Party and the nation to increasing income for the rural poor. And the Chinese government is aggressively developing a social security net to help the millions of workers who were laid off in the 1990s as state-owned companies tried to take a free market orientation. The program will provide subsistence income for the persistently unemployed, but the problem is enormous with 47 million urban workers laid off from money-losing, state- or community-owned companies between 1996 and 2000. Meanwhile, emerging private-sector businesses have added about 15 million new jobs.[39] So China's free market initiatives have had a profound impact, but enormous changes remain to be implemented before China can accurately be considered a free market economy. Indeed, the European Union and the United States in 2004 affirmed their view that the state is still much too involved in the Chinese economy and that China's legal system, bankruptcy regime, banking sector, and corporate governance systems are still too underdeveloped and too tied to the state to treat China as a free market economy.

> The Communist Party employs 30,000 "Internet security agents" to monitor online communications.

China—Politics   Of course, China remains a dictatorship governed by the Communist Party. Human rights appear to have improved, but repression remains common. The Communist Party controls all media and employs 30,000 "Internet security agents" to monitor online communications. Hundreds of thousands of Chinese are confined to labor camps, and state executions are estimated to total about 4,000 annually—more than the balance of other nations combined.[40] But political progress is also evident. For the first time since 1949, party leaders were able to achieve a peaceful transfer of power in 2004 when former leader Jiang Zemin gave full control of the military to President Hu Jintao. [For the latest Chinese news, see **http://thebeijingnews.net/**]

Russia   Communist totalitarianism is gone from Russia, and life there has improved in some important ways. Russia quickly and aggressively converted itself to a market-based economy after the fall of the Soviet Union. The economic results in recent years have been encouraging. The bulk of the economy is now privately owned, total economic growth has been steady with a 7.2 percent increase in 2003, the number of mobile phones doubled in 2003 to 36 million, and the percentage of Russians who consider themselves middle class rose from 28 in 1999 to 48 in 2003.[41] On the other hand, those economic gains remain unrealized for many Russians. Russian sociologist Boris Kagarlitsky explains:

• Many Russians believe that although they may have had less freedom under communism, they had more rights when all of their basic material needs were met and relative equality was achieved.

- Under the communist state, medical care was administered reliably and was free to all. Today even a pair of boots may shake the family budget.
- Under communism most people were provided apartments, whereas today homelessness is common and poverty is epidemic. At the same time, a capitalist elite lives in luxury.[42]

Perhaps most disturbingly, the democracy that was expected to accompany economic liberalization has not materialized, and Russian faith in the idea of democracy seems to be eroding quickly. The pressure of change, corruption in the private sector and in government, and ongoing terrorism, among other forces, cause many Russians to doubt the merits of democracy. In late 2004 after three major terrorists attacks killed over 400, Russian President Vladimir Putin announced new plans that would restore more power to the Kremlin and reduce citizens' opportunities to elect legislators and governors.

Questions

1. What Americans would think of as organized crime—the Mob, the Mafia—plays a powerful and destructive role in capitalist Russia. Does a rise in crime inevitably accompany the movement from collectivism to capitalism? Explain.
2. Believing tourism and its economic benefits can best be realized via the profit incentive, China is turning over some of its state-controlled parks, nature reserves, and monuments to the private sector. Critics worry that this shift will destroy those Chinese treasures. Explain the critics' fears.

Part Four—Middle Ground? A Mixed Economy (The Third Way)

Communism has failed. Socialist principles, to the extent that they call for central planning, bloated bureaucracies, and restraints on personal freedom, are discredited. An era has passed, but the shape of the future is unclear. Some middle ground in free market and welfare state principles may be the next step, but the appropriate mixture is proving elusive. For years, the Nordic states of Sweden, Norway, Denmark and Finland practiced their market socialism or social democracy with such success that it was labeled a "third way" between the harsher extremes of capitalism and communism. Their welfare states provided healthy economic growth with cradle-to-grave social care for all in a system emphasizing the collective welfare over individual preferences.

Sweden   Life expectancy in Sweden is 80.4 years, among the highest in Europe. Education, health care, child care, maternity and paternity leave, unemployment protection, and more are provided by the government. To pay for its comprehensive welfare benefits, Sweden has among the world's highest tax rates with state spending equal to 53 percent of the total gross domestic product.[43] (In the United States, the comparable figure is 30 percent.[44]) The state employs nearly one-third of workers, and state-owned companies produce 20 percent of corporate revenues.[45] So Sweden retains a strong welfare state, but changes are emerging. To remain competitive in the global economy, Sweden (along with Denmark and Norway) has aggressively streamlined its business regulations and now ranks, according to the World Bank, among the top 10 nations in the world in easing the time and cost involved in doing business (getting credit, hiring/firing workers, enforcing contracts, and so on).[46] In recent years Sweden has forced tens of thousands of long-term unemployed welfare recipients back into the labor pool. Certainly Sweden is not abandoning its welfare preferences; rather the nation has recognized the new realities of the global market. To continue to provide generous cradle-to-grave care and to expand that care (such as a proposed personal assistant for each elderly person), Sweden has acknowledged the power of the market while striving for a balanced economy.

Speeding Ticket

Nokia vice president Anssi Vanjoki of Helsinki, Finland, was fined $103,600 for driving 47 miles per hour in a 30 mph zone. Consistent with its collectivist principles, Finland assesses fines based on the offender's income.

Source: Steven Landsburg, "Highway Robbery," *The Wall Street Journal,* February 11, 2002, p. A22.

Germany   Labor–management cooperation and joint decision making (labeled *codetermination*) have been the distinguishing features of Germany's specialized form of post–World War II capitalism. German law requires employee representation on the boards of Germany's larger companies. For decades, the codetermination system and Germany's highly capable business/technical community provided both a powerful economic engine and welfare for all. The resulting prosperity has meant that the unemployed in Germany often live better than low-wage Americans.[47] Germany's protection of workers and of a particular vision of a "good life" are evidenced by laws forbidding stores from being open on Sundays and holidays and requiring early closing hours.[48] Now, however, the German cooperative version of capitalism is changing. Welfare benefits have been reduced, employers' power to fire workers has increased, and more dramatic changes are being considered. Indeed, the powerful system of codetermination itself may be reformed under the pressure of the new globalization realities.

> The unemployed in Germany often live better than low-wage Americans.

American Capitalism in Europe?   Globalization and the universally acknowledged power of the market have put great pressure on Sweden, Germany, France, and other European states to trim their welfare policies. Broadly, they want the benefits of aggressive capitalism, especially its proven power in wealth creation, without the problems that they observe in America: slums, poverty, the wage and wealth gaps, the uncertainties of the market, the lack of public services such as trains, and what they view as our extravagant and tasteless commercialism.

However noble the European welfare goals, the American approach seems to be carrying the day. Over the past 25 years, the American economy has grown 55 percent faster than Germany's.[49] A 2004 study, "The EU vs. USA" by Swedish economists Fredrik Bergstrom and Robert Gidehag, found a big and growing gap in economic performance between America and Europe. Gross domestic product per capita in the United States was 32 percent higher than the European Union average in 2000.[50] That higher GDP means the average American can spend about $9,700 more annually on consumption than the average European.[51] The average living space of "poor" American households is about 1,200 square feet, whereas *all* European households average about 1,000 square feet.[52] Even poverty and low-income concerns come down somewhat on the side of the United States, according to the study. For example, about 25 percent of American households were considered low income according to a 1999 study. By that study's standard, 40 percent of Swedish households would be considered low income.[53] The authors speculated as to why the EU has fallen behind the United States:

> The expansion of the public sector into overripe welfare states in large parts of Europe is and remains the best guess as to why our continent cannot measure up to our neighbor in the west.[54]

But the news is certainly not all bad for the European welfare states. Despite their very high tax rates, the four Nordic, Third Way nations (Finland, Sweden, Norway, and Denmark) rank in the top six countries worldwide in economic competitiveness.[55] Indeed, Finland ranked first in a World Economic Forum study, just ahead of the United States. Taiwan was number four with China at 46, India at 55, and Russia at 70.[56] According to the study, high taxes remain the biggest drawback to global competitiveness in the Nordic nations; but those taxes buy education, training, and infrastructure that produces a more sustainable competitiveness than what is found in low-tax nations.[57] The Nordic nations were also particularly notable for their low level of corruption, whereas the biggest strength of the United States was its decisive global lead in technological innovation.[58] So while the European Union as a whole seems to be lagging the United States, the Nordic Third Way states, notwithstanding their heavy taxes, remain quite competitive economically while providing an extraordinary degree of social welfare.

Of course, economic performance measures alone do not capture all of the important ingredients in a good life: a clean environment, an equitable distribution of wealth, opportunity for leisure, and so on. For example, workers in the United States are the most productive in the world, according to a 2003 United Nations study; but that rank was achieved, in part, by working more hours.[59] American workers in 2002 put in an average of 1,825 hours annually on the job (the equivalent of 46 40-hour weeks) as compared with about 1,380 hours in Norway.[60] American output was fourth in the world at $32 per hour, while the Norwegians led at $38 per hour followed by the French ($35) and the Belgians ($34).[61]

So America enjoys unparalleled wealth, but we have to work harder to achieve it.

So America enjoys unparalleled wealth, but we have to work harder to achieve it. Does our brand of aggressive, hardworking capitalism translate into the best life for all? The European states do not think so; however, the weight of globalization has swept them into a demanding market that has forced them to rethink their systems and to move reluctantly toward the American approach. But is the American approach best for America? We examine that question in the next section. [For an overview of "Europe vs. America," see **http://www.nybooks.com/articles/17726**]

Questions—Parts Three and Four

1. Billionaire investor George Soros, in his book *Open Society,* sees "market funda-mentalism as a greater threat to open society today than communism."[62] Soros fears contemporary capitalism's extreme commitment to self-interest, which results, he says, in our greatest challenge today: "to establish a set of fundamental values."[63]
   a. What does Soros mean?
   b. Do you agree with him? Explain.

2. Americans feel a great deal of faith in the free market. Explain some of the weak-nesses in the market. That is, where is the free market likely to fail?

3. Writing in *Dissent,* Joanne Barkan says, "[A]lmost all Swedes view poverty, extreme inequalities of wealth, and the degradation that comes with unemployment as unacceptable."[64]
   a. Do you agree with the Swedes? Explain.
   b. Why are Americans more tolerant of those conditions than are the Swedes?

4. In the late 1970s, correspondent R. W. Apple of *The New York Times* reported that Sweden had willfully pursued a policy of economic leveling:

   > As a result almost every family living near the sea has a boat, but almost all are small boats. A large percentage of families have summer houses, but none of them rivals the villas of the Riviera or the stately manor houses of Britain. Virtually no one has servants.
   >
   > Even among the handful of people who might be able to afford it, conspicuous consumption is frowned upon. There are fewer than 25 Rolls Royces in Sweden.[65]

   a. Is that Swedish approach preferable to the extreme conspicuous consumption permitted—and even encouraged—in this country? Explain.
   b. Is the opportunity to garner luxuries necessary to the successful operation of the American system? Explain.
   c. Does our system generate guilt among those who enjoy its fruits in quantities well beyond the norm? Explain.

5. *a.* Should an American citizen's primary duty be to herself or himself or to all other members of society? Explain.
   b. Should all humans be regarded as of equal value and thus equally worthy of our individual support? Explain.
   c. Can social harmony be achieved in a nation whose citizens fail to regard the state as a "superfamily"? Explain.

6. *a.* In your view, is an individual's possession of extravagant wealth a moral wrong?
   b. Would economic justice require that we treat "being rich" as a social wrong? Explain.
   See George Scialabba, "Asking the Right Questions," *Dissent,* Spring 1988, p. 114.
   c. Where do you stand on that favorite American question, "Does money buy hap-piness?" Put another way, if the market works rationally, as we believe it does, wouldn't we find greater happiness in those who earn more money? Explain. See Sharon Begley, "Wealth and Happiness . . ." *The Wall Street Journal,* August 13, 2004, p. B1.

7. In questioning Oakland Athletics general manager Billy Beane, *The Wall Street Jour-nal* described professional football as "socialist" and baseball as "capitalist":

The NFL (National Football League) has been successful as a socialist league, equally divvying up the league's revenue among all the teams. Major league baseball, on the other hand, is a capitalist league, with a clear divide between big-market and small-market teams. Do you think some of baseball's financial rules have to be changed to better balance the playing field?

Do you think "socialism" or "capitalism" is the better system for professional sports? Explain. See Jim Chairusmi, "Winning with Smaller Pockets," *The Wall Street Journal,* October 18, 2004, p. R2.

8. In Sweden, spanking children is a violation of the law.
   a. What reasoning supports that legislation?
   b. Would such legislation help reduce violence in America? Explain.

9. Eskimos, among other cultures, regarded all natural resources as free or common goods to be used but never possessed by any individual or group. What arguments may be raised to justify our notion of private ownership of natural resources?

Part Five—America's Economic Future: Where Are We Going?

Greed Is Good

Michael Douglas, as Gordon Gekko in the movie *Wall Street:* "Greed is good! Greed is right! Greed works! Greed will save the USA!"

According to a United Nations report, in 1998 the world's 200 richest people had combined incomes equal to the poorest 40 percent of the world's population, a total of 2.4 billion people.

Source: Alan Guebert, "Less Competition, More Poverty," Waterloo/Cedar Falls Courier, November 25, 2001, p. C3.

We have inspected the entire economic continuum. We know that communism has been discredited. Hence the far left has little to offer. America has led the revival of open markets both domestically and around the globe. Should we expand our faith in capitalism, or do we need to move our present mixed economy a bit closer to the welfare state model, which itself is under great pressure? Or must a new model emerge? In sum, how much government do we need?

Uncertainty

America is strong but struggling. The September 11 attacks scratched our confidence and undermined our economy. We have been through a period in the middle and late 1990s when crime fell sharply, employment reached new records, gender and racial equality appeared to be improving, children were healthier than ever, and we were making at least some progress with our considerable environmental problems. But serious concerns remain. Economic uncertainty abounds, as the skyrocketing layoffs in 2001 and 2002 and corporate bankruptcies of giants like WorldCom, Enron, and Kmart indicate. In a broad sense, should we have doubts about the top-to-bottom fairness of our American system? Certainly we approve of America in the abstract, and we are generally comfortable with our overall prosperity and our expansive freedoms; but we also recognize that tens of millions are not achieving the American Dream. Let's examine a series of concerns that continue to cast a shadow on America's many free market victories.

Overall Quality of Life   At the turn of the century, Americans have enjoyed a remarkable economic boom that has produced one of the most prosperous eras in our history. Not surprisingly, that boom was accompanied by a general decline in many social ills, such as crime and unemployment. Thus, to most Americans we appear to be enjoying the best the world can currently offer; and according to the United Nations' 2004 report on the overall quality of life in 177 nations (based on 2002 data),

> In overall quality of life, the United States ranked eighth in the world

we are doing well, but some others are doing a little better. In overall quality of life, the United States ranked eighth in the world behind Norway, Sweden, Australia, Canada, the Netherlands, Belgium, and Iceland[66] and ahead of Japan and Ireland.[67] Niger and Sierra Leone ranked at the bottom of the list.[68] The United States ranked fourth in gross domestic product per capita ($35,750) behind Luxembourg ($61,190), Norway ($36,600) and Ireland ($36,360), with Germany ($27,100) and Japan ($26,940) lagging quite significantly.[69] On the other hand, we rank first among industrial nations (excluding China and Russia) in percentage of the population living below the poverty line; more than double the rates in Sweden and Norway with their aggressive welfare policies.[70] Similarly, our infant mortality rate (the probability of dying between birth and age one per 1,000 live births) of seven is the highest among industrial nations (excluding China and Russia).[71] Sweden, for example, is at three and Norway at four.[72] Life expectancy in the United States is 77.1 years, which is lowest among industrial nations except for Ireland (77) and Denmark (76.6).[73] Japan leads at 81.6 and Sweden is second at 80.1.[74] Thus the United States is clearly the most economically productive nation, but in some important respects we have not been successful in securing a high quality of life for all. [For other international quality of life data, see **http://hdr.undp.org/reports/global/2004/** or change the year for updates.]

Poverty   After significant improvement in the 1990s, the number of Americans living below the poverty line ($19,307 for a family of four) has since been rising and reached 12.7 percent of the population in 2004.[75] A disturbing total of 17.8 percent of children (under 18) fell below the poverty line.[76] In a similar vein, nearly 46 million people (15.7 percent of the population) lacked health insurance.[77] A particularly striking example of poverty extremes in the United States is the city of Cleveland, Ohio—once a thriving industrial center and now America's poorest big city (population 500,000)

> Only Mexico among 29 industrial nations has a higher rate of children's poverty than the United States.

with nearly one-third of that number living in poverty.[78] According to the United Nations Children's Fund, only Mexico among 29 industrial nations has a higher rate of children's poverty than the United States.[79] Our poor poverty standing relative to other wealthy nations is attributable to much greater wage inequality in America than in those nations and to the fact that we allocate only about 4 percent of our gross domestic product to "social spending" whereas the other wealthy nations spend about twice that.[80] Perhaps the greater frustration is that many of those who work are nevertheless poor, at least for a time. The Working Poor Families Project reported in 2004 that nearly 39 million Americans, including 20 million children, are members of low-income working families whose income barely meets their most basic needs.[81] *BusinessWeek* recently summarized the perilous life on the edge for those who are trying but barely managing:

> [M]ost (of the working poor) labor in a netherworld of maximum insecurity, where one missed bus, one stalled engine, one sick kid means the difference between keeping a job and getting fired, between subsistence and setting off the financial tremors of turned-off telephones and $1,000 emergency-room bills. . . .
>
> At any moment, a boss pressured to pump profits can slash hours, shortchanging a family's grocery budget—or conversely, force employees to work off the clock, wreaking havoc on child care plans. Often, as they get close to putting in enough time to qualify for benefits, many see their schedules cut back. The time it takes to don uniforms, go to the bathroom, or take breaks routinely goes unpaid. Complain, and there is always someone younger, cheaper, and newer to the United States willing to do the work for less.[82]

Historically we have accepted difficulties for a significant share of the population in the belief that they would move up, in time, if they worked hard; but as *BusinessWeek* reports, upward mobility is slower and less likely today than in the past:

> Five of the 10 fastest-growing occupations over the next decade will be of the menial, dead-end variety, including retail clerks, janitors and cashiers.[83]

At the same time, the cost of college has "exploded" such that fewer than 5 percent of students from low-income families can now earn degrees.[84] The result is an often harsh life in this astonishingly wealthy nation. For example, the World Health Organization (WHO) ranked the United States 37th in quality of health care among 190 nations surveyed.[85] France and Italy ranked first and second.[86] Our system ranked so low, according to the WHO, because it is so expensive and yet fails to provide adequate health care for the poor:

> The United States is really three Americas. The top 10 percent here are the healthiest in the world. The middle bulk does mediocre. But it's the bottom 5 or 10 percent—made up of Native Americans living on reservations, the inner city poor, rural blacks, and Appalachia—that is a third America.[87]

In fact, we are the only major industrialized nation that does not assure health care for all of its citizens. [For more data on U.S. poverty, see **www.census.gov/hhes/www/poverty.html**]

Are Americans Stingy?

Americans think of themselves as the most generous people on earth. A *Los Angeles Times* look at global giving challenges that conclusion:

> By total money, the United States by far donates more than any other country in the world. . . . But when aid is calculated per U.S. citizen or as a percentage of the economy, the United States ranks among the least generous in the industrial world.

One study found that U.S. foreign aid in 2002 amounted to 13 cents per American each day, and private donations came to 5 cents per day per citizen. Sixteen governments gave more than the United States, and in Switzerland, Ireland, and Norway private citizens gave more. Indeed, the Norwegian government provided $1.02 per citizen per day, while private giving totaled 24 cents per day per citizen.

Of course, the United States "gives" a great deal by providing worldwide peacekeeping.

Source: Sonni Efron, *Los Angeles Times,* "Are Americans Generous or Stingy? Depends on How You Measure," *Cedar Falls/Waterloo Courier,* December 31, 2004, p. A4.

Good News   Life in the United States is quite wonderful in many respects, and the good news should not be ignored. For example, children in recent years have become less likely to commit a crime and less likely to become victims of a crime.[88] The teen birthrate hit a record low in 2002.[89] Furthermore, as compared with the suffering of large parts of the world, life in the United States is generally magnificent:

- One in six of the world's adults is illiterate.
- 30,000 children die each day of preventable illnesses.
- Once enrolled, the odds of an African child completing primary school are one in three.
- The World Health Organization estimates that $35–40 per capita in public health spending is necessary for basic health services; but in the least developed nations that figure, in the late 1990s, averaged about $6 per capita—as compared with $1,356 per capita in high-income countries.
- Some 54 nations are poorer in 2004 than they were in 1990.
- One in every five humans (1.2 billion people) survives on less than one dollar per day.[90]

The Gap   As *The Sacramento Bee* characterized it, the United States is the richest industrial nation, but it is also the poorest;[91] that is, the United States has the highest levels of both wealth and poverty among the industrial nations. Extravagant wealth, side by side with punishing poverty, is perhaps the greatest disappointment and injustice, from the critics' point of view, in the great, global victory of the free market. Harvard economist Richard B. Freeman wonders whether the United States is headed toward an "apartheid economy"—"one in which the wealthy and powerful prosper while the less well-off struggle."[92] Considerable data support his concern.

> Harvard economist Richard B. Freeman wonders whether the United States is headed toward an "apartheid economy"

- Wage inequality—the gap between America's highest- and lowest-paid workers—has been growing steadily since the 1970s except for a break in the late 1990s. For example, the wealthiest 20 percent of households in 1973 earned 44 percent of total U.S. income, whereas that share jumped to 50 percent in 2002. For the bottom fifth, the share fell from 4.2 percent to 3.5 percent.[93] The share going to the bottom fifth was the lowest on record.[94] America's income gap is the biggest among advanced industrial nations.

- The 400 richest Americans hold nearly as much wealth as the 100 million Americans in the bottom half of the U.S. wealth pyramid.[95]

- Corporate CEOs continue to stretch the gap in pay between themselves and those who work for them. U.S. CEOs made 44 times as much as workers in 1980 and 254 times as much in 2003.[96] U.S. CEOs make five times as much as those in Japan and three times as much as those in the United Kingdom, France, and Italy.[97]

PRACTICING ETHICS) Are the Gaps Too Big?

Should we care about these vast and growing gaps in income and wealth? Commentator Dan Seligman says we should not be troubled because the number of poor is really all that matters, not the gap between the poor and the rich.[98] Furthermore, the Heritage Foundation/*Wall Street Journal* Index of Economic Freedom suggests that the greater the degree of freedom in an economy, the better off the people are at *all* income levels, and that the income gap is smallest in countries with the "freest" economies.[99] According to the 2005 Index, the United States is 12th among the world's free economies (with, Hong Kong first, the United Kingdom seventh, Australia 10th, and Sweden 14th).[100] Nonetheless, ethicist William Sundstrom argues, among other things, that fairness does matter, that the income we receive should bear some reasonable relationship to what we "deserve," and that democracy may not be able to tolerate too much social stratification.[101] [For more on the Index of Economic Freedom, see **http://heritage.org/research/features/index/**]

Questions

1. *a.* Should income bear some reasonable relationship to what we "deserve"?
   b. How would we identify what we deserve?
   c. Based on your personal sense of fairness, is a large and growing gap in income and wealth between the rich and poor an ethical wrong? Explain.

2. Bhutan, the isolated Buddhist kingdom located in the Himalayas, now measures national progress by a model labeled "gross national happiness." Bhutan is seeking to build a measure of societal well-being that extends beyond gross domestic product (GDP) to include considerations such as environmental quality, protecting natural resources, and providing democratic governance. Bhutan has consciously rejected the notion that a rising GDP will inevitably bring other benefits and with them happiness.

   a. Must a socially responsible society actively pursue life satisfaction for its citizens rather than being content to build wealth? Explain.
   b. Does the market, with its focus on wealth accumulation, fail to accurately capture all of the features of a fulfilling, meaningful, ethical life? Explain.

3. Microsoft Corporation cofounder Paul Allen contracted for a new yacht, the 414-foot *Octopus*, complete with a 59-foot speedboat, personal submarine, swimming pool, music studio, and helicopter pad. The boat was expected to cost $250 million to build and $10 million annually to operate. Responding to the challenge, Oracle boss Larry Ellison expanded plans for his own new yacht from 393 to 452 feet. The $200 million *Rising Sun* is, at this writing in 2005, the world's longest yacht, but a Saudi family's new boat, *Platinum*, is expected to reach 525 feet.

   Even if we have the money and we earned it legitimately, do we commit an ethical wrong when we spend our money on extravagances like colossal yachts? Explain. See Robert Frank, "New Luxury Goods Set Super-Wealthy Apart from Pack," *The Wall Street Journal*, December 14, 2004, p. A1.

Crime/Women in Prison   Americans are fascinated with records, but an interesting new standard in criminal incarcerations presumably is not a matter of national pride.

women in Prisons reached an all-time high in 2004

The number of women in state and federal prisons reached an all-time high in 2004 at 103,310.[102] Female prison growth has averaged about 5 percent annually in recent years as compared with about 3.3 percent for males. The total number of inmates in prisons and jails on June 30, 2004, was 2,131,180. Thus about 1 in every 138 U.S. residents was in jail or prison. An estimated 12.6 percent of all black males in their late twenties were in prison while the comparable figure for Hispanics was 3.6 and 1.7 for whites.[103] The seemingly relentless rise in incarceration, despite a declining crime rate, is attributed to longer sentences, fewer probations and paroles, and the "war on drugs" that commenced in the 1980s. [For "research on the prison industrial complex," see [**http://www.prisonsucks.com**]

Community   So crime, poverty, inequality, and unfairness are among the criticisms of American capitalism despite its extraordinary successes. But perhaps the bigger and more interesting concern, for all Americans, rich and poor alike, is rising evidence that our lives are increasingly solitary, distant, alone, and unshared. The market is driven by and rewards individual achievement; could that struggle for success be depriving us of the full satisfaction of our humanity? In his now famous book *Bowling Alone,* Robert Putnam meticulously documents the decline of what he labels *social capital,* the community and commitment bonds that seem to emerge in a culture where people regularly interact with each other by volunteering, socializing, participating in clubs, engaging in group recreation, and the like.[104] Thus, Putnam explains, in the early 1970s, 1 person in 16 worked for a political party, but that figure had fallen to 1 in 30 for the mid-1990s.[105] The following review of *Bowling Alone* summarizes Putnam's point.

"Bowling Alone" the New National Pastime; Author Decries Disengaged Society

R E A D I N G

Jack Cox, *Denver Post,* August 27, 2000

Thanks to cell phones, Americans appear to be doing more talking to one another than they've done in years. But ironically, they're probably less connected than ever.

That's the message that Harvard social scientist Robert Putnam rolls out in *Bowling Alone,* an influential new book that documents a steady decline in social and civic involvement over the past generation.

"It's not just that we've stopped voting. It's also that we've stopped playing cards and going to picnics," Putnam told a Denver audience recently. "Virtually every measure of social interaction is down, big time, over the last 25 years."

The most vivid illustration of the trend, Putnam suggests, may be the decrease in league bowling, which has plummeted more than 40 percent since 1980, even though the total number of bowlers in the United States has risen 10 percent—hence the notion of "bowling alone."

But regular surveys of consumer behavior, he says, chronicle similar declines in numerous other indicators of social engagement, from church attendance to charitable giving to membership in what he jokingly calls "the animal clubs" (Lions, Elks, Moose, Eagles, and so on). Even the tradition of having people over for dinner has fallen by 40 percent, he reports.

Putnam points to several factors as possible explanations for this apparent disengagement, including the migration of women from home to workplace and the increase in suburban sprawl.

"Every 10 minutes of additional commuting time," he asserts, "cuts all forms of social interaction by 10 percent, and 20 minutes more cuts it by 20 percent."

But the chief culprit, he suspects, is television. And we're not talking about public affairs shows like *Face the Nation,* he remarks. "Watching *Cheers* or *Survival* is what's really lethal in terms of social interaction."

In short, we're devoting more time to watching *Friends* than making them.

To those who see little harm in unwinding in front of the tube, Putnam points out that communities tend to work better when their inhabitants devote a fair amount of time to talking face-to-face—as he demonstrated in a 1993 book showing that local governments in Italy functioned best, oddly enough, in places where choral societies were strong.

"If you live in a community where people are connected with each other in a positive way, where there's plenty of trust and reciprocity, you are more productive," he says. "Social

networks have value, and this is true whether people are organized into groups or just hanging out together."

* * * * *

Source: *Denver Post,* August 27, 2000, p. H01. Reprinted by permission.

Questions

1. Is Putnam correct? Explain.
2. Putnam points to women in the workplace, commuting, and television as primary culprits in the decline of social capital. A 2001 study by professors from the Massachusetts Institute of Technology and Tufts University found that rising income inequality was a primary force in weakening community ties. Explain that finding. See Gene Koretz, "Why Americans Grow Apart," *BusinessWeek,* July 23, 2001, p. 30.
3. President George Bush and Congress are considering laws to mandate community service:

   Heralding "the responsibilities of active citizenship," Senators John McCain and Evan Bayh recently introduced the Call to Service Act. This bill would force universities to increase student participation in community service programs.[106]

   a. How do you feel about mandatory community service?
   b. From a capitalist perspective, how would you argue that mandatory community service is a philosophical wrong?

PRACTICING ETHICS) Technology and Loneliness

In his book *Interpersonal Divide: The Search for Community in a Technological Age* (Oxford University Press, 2005), Iowa State University professor Michael Bugeja argues that excessive dependence on media technologies such as e-mail, cell phones, television, radio, and video games is destroying face-to-face relationships, causing each of us to become increasingly isolated.

Questions

1. In your view, is Bugeja correct? Explain.
2. How might our ethical standards and performances be affected by excessive reliance on media technology?

Source: Steve Weinberg, "Prof Bemoans Loss of Direct Contact," *Des Moines Register,* February 20, 2005, p. 5OP.

Too Much Capitalism? or Too Little?

Has America placed too much faith in the market and too little in government? Is the alleged decline in community in some sense a product of capitalism itself? Are poverty, inequality, crime, and corporate scandals such as the Enron case inevitable by-products of a "selfish, greedy" market? Even some conservatives are concerned:

> "What I'm concerned about is the idolatry of the market," says conservative intellectual William Bennett, a former education secretary and author of the *The Book of Virtues*. He worries particularly that the market for popular music and movies with sexual or violent content has a corrosive effect. "Unbridled capitalism . . . may not be a problem for production and for expansion of the economic pie, but it's a problem for human beings. It's a problem for . . . the realm of values and human relationships."[107]

> "Capitalism is more efficient . . . But it is not more fair."

The dilemma, in brief, was expressed by a 20-year-old Cuban student and communist organizer: "Capitalism is more efficient . . . But it is not more fair."[108]

The EU Dream   Fair or not, America's aggressively capitalist approach to life is the dominant model for the globe at the moment. Dramatic changes, however, seem inevitable. The rise of China and India, among others, certainly will profoundly adjust the world economic and political order. And the new European Union of 25 nations and 457 million people (compared with 296 million in the United States) suggests that our status as the world's only superpower will be challenged in the future. If so, European economic and social values will confront those of America. Author Jeremy Rifkind, in his 2004 book *The European Dream: How Europe's Vision of the Future Is Quietly Eclipsing the American Dream,* raises the possibility that America's methods for achieving well-being and prosperity may someday be surpassed by the "European Dream." Rifkind explains that European companies currently dominate major segments of the world economy. Fourteen of the 20 largest commercial banks are European.[109] Sixty-one of the 140 biggest companies on the global *Fortune* 500 are European, while 50 are American.[110] As we have noted, many European nations lead the United States in quality of life measures such as distribution of wealth, poverty rates, and crime rates. Europeans accept heavy gasoline taxes and small cars as part of the price for the energy-efficient, sustainable life they contrast with our profligate consumption practices. Rifkind explains the very dissimilar values that are leading America and Europe to differing conceptions of the good life:

> The old dream, the American Dream that made the individual the master of his fate and emphasized the personal accumulation of wealth, is faltering. . . . In today's world, the European Dream, with its emphasis on inclusivity, diversity, sustainable development, and interconnectedness, is the world's first attempt at creating a global consciousness. And it deserves our close attention.

*   *   *   *   *

Americans have always associated freedom with autonomy, and autonomy with property. The wealthier you are, the more independent you are, and the more secure you are. Europeans find freedom not in autonomy, but in embeddedness. For most Europeans, the community's quality of life is more important than individual financial success. . . . Belonging—not belongings—is what brings security.

* * * * *

Europe has articulated a vision of the future that differs from ours in fundamental ways. Romano Prodi, the president of the European Commission, has admitted that the EU's goal is to establish "a superpower on the European continent that stands equal to the United States." When I asked him to explain what he meant, he spoke of the European vision as one of a new type of power, based not on military strength but on economic cooperation and the construction of communities of conscience, a new kind of superpower based on waging peace.[111]

Questions—Part Five

1. *a.* Explain the American and European Union dreams for the good life of the future.
   b. Do Americans remain committed to the American Dream?
   c. Which of those dreams is most consistent with your personal values?
   d. Which of those dreams is most likely to prevail in the future? Explain.

2. *a.* What does William Bennett mean by "the idolatry of the market?"
   b. In what sense do we have a market in "values and human relationships"?
   c. What does Bennett mean about the corrosive effect of popular culture?
   d. Can we have a free market in economic affairs without harming our social values and relationships? Explain.

3. Journalist Lauren Soth says, "Let's challenge the sacred goals of economic growth, greater output of goods and services, greater productivity."[112] How could we have a better life if we were to diminish our attention to those seemingly central requirements?

Internet Exercise

The Global Policy Forum is generally critical of the globalization movement. Sample those views at [http://www.globalpolicy.org] and explain whether the criticisms have merit, in your judgment. Then turn to this Global Policy Forum page: "Goodbye Uncle Sam, Hello Team Europe" [http://www.globalpolicy.org/empire/analysis/2005/0414byeunclesam.htm]. Explain author John Feffer's argument that the European Union should be more influential in world affairs than the United States. Do you agree? Explain.

Chapter Questions

1. The gravestone of the late baseball great Jackie Robinson is inscribed with this advice: "A life is not important except in the impact it has on other lives." Will your life be meaningful only if you contribute to the well-being of others? Explain.

2. Commenting in *Newsweek,* economist Robert Samuelson said, "The . . . pervasive problem of capitalist economies is that almost no one fully trusts capitalists."[113] Do you agree? Why?

3. Dartmouth English professor Noel Perrin laments the explosive growth of the world population, which amounts to about 2 million additional persons per week. In 1987 the

world population was 5 billion, and at the turn of the century the total is about 6 billion. Perrin says, "Why not stem the population explosion by paying women not to have babies?"[114] He proposes government payments to each fertile woman each year commencing with $500 at puberty and rising by $100 for each year thereafter so long as the woman does not give birth. That total would reach nearly $100,000 by age 53, but he compares that with, for example, the nearly $200,000 cost of bringing up one abandoned child in New York City. In sum, he argues that the plan would be less expensive than our current welfare program.

a. Would you support Professor Perrin's market-based approach to birth control? Explain.

b. Do you consider such a program immoral? Explain.

4. "America's real problem," said former Council of Economic Advisers Chairman Herbert Stein, a conservative Republican, is that it has "serious deficiencies that one would not expect in so rich a country . . . the public is saying that even though we are very rich, we have too much crime, too much homelessness, too much illiteracy and ignorance."[115]

a. Do you agree? Explain.

b. How do you account for our problems?

c. Do we need a greater measure of government intervention to correct these problems? Explain.

5. a. Noted economist Lester Thurow argues that the economic demands of the market are destroying the traditional two-parent, nuclear family. Explain his argument.

b. Child development authority Benjamin Spock likewise blamed capitalism for the "destruction of the American family," but his reasoning differed from Thurow's:

> The overriding problem is excessive competition and our glorification of it. It may contribute to our rapid technological advancement, but it has done so at a great price. We are taught to be rugged individualists, and we are obsessed with getting ahead. The family gets lost in this intense struggle. In a healthy society, family should come first, community second, and our outside jobs third. In this country, it is the other way around.[116]

Comment.

c. If Spock was correct, how did we reach this condition?

6. Barbara Ehrenreich, author of *Nickel and Dimed,* recently criticized Wal-Mart in a *New York Times* column. Ardent capitalist Sally Pipes summarized Ehrenreich's position:

> This could be the central battle of the 21st century: Earth People vs. the Wal-Martians," Ehrenreich wrote. "No one knows exactly when the pod landed on our planet," but when it did Wal-Mart began to experience "recklessly metastatic growth." Wal-Mart, contends Ehrenreich, is "a creature afflicted with the appetite of a starved hyena."[117]

a. Ehrenreich certainly is not alone in complaining about Wal-Mart. List some of those criticisms.

b. Explain how a capitalist like Pipes would respond to the Wal-Mart critique.

7. We often read that many college professors actively criticize capitalism and support welfare state principles.

   a. Has that been your experience? Explain.

   b. If that assessment is accurate, how do you account for the leftist inclinations among intellectuals?

8. As noted in the readings, privatization is enjoying immense popularity.

   a. Make the arguments for and against turning our prisons and jails over to private enterprise.

   b. Would you favor a penal system operated for profit? Explain.

9. If we are fundamentally selfish, must we embrace capitalism as the most accurate and, therefore, most efficient expression of human nature? Explain.

10. Economist and jurist Richard Posner has suggested a free market in babies. Given that "production costs" are relatively low and the value of babies to childless people is high, Posner observed the possibilities for mutually beneficial transactions.

    a. Explain some of the advantages and disadvantages of a market in babies.

    b. Would you favor the legalization of the sale of babies? Explain.

11. Is capitalism a necessary condition for successful democracy? Or, put another way, in a democracy will increasing state control necessarily result in the destruction of that democracy? Explain.

12. Commentator Thomas Friedman reflects on the Islamic terrorists' hatred for America:

    > Their constant refrain is that America is a country with wealth and power but "no values." The Islamic terrorists think our wealth and power is unrelated to anything in the soul of this country. . . . Of course, what this view of America completely misses is that American power and wealth flow directly from a deep spiritual source—a spirit of respect for the individual, a spirit of tolerance for differences of faith or politics, a respect for freedom of thought as the necessary foundation for all creativity, and a spirit of unity that encompasses all kinds of differences. Only a society with a deep spiritual energy, that welcomes immigrants and worships freedom, could constantly renew itself and its sources of power and wealth.[118]

    * * * * *

    a. Do you agree that the "spiritual source" Friedman cites is the foundation for American success? Explain.

    b. Is America without a meaningful "soul"? Explain.

13. Socialist Michael Harrington argued for life "freed of the curse of money":

    > [A]s long as access to goods and pleasures is rationed according to the possession of money, there is a pervasive venality, an invitation to miserliness and hostility to one's neighbor.[119]

    Should we strive to make more goods and services "free"? Raise the competing arguments.

14. The intellectual Adolph Berle once said, "A day may come when national glory and prestige, perhaps even national safety, are best established by a country's being the

most beautiful, the best socially organized, or culturally the most advanced in the world."[120]

a. Is government intervention necessary to achieving Berle's goal? Explain.

b. If faced with a choice, would most Americans opt for Berle's model or for a nation preeminent in consumer goods, sports, and general comfort? Explain.

15. Edward Luttwak, in his book, *Turbo Capitalism,* says it is dangerous for the United States to export its mostly unregulated capitalism around the world because many other nations do not have firmly in place two central forces that balance capitalist power in the United States.

a. What are those two forces?

b. Do you agree with Luttwak that many other nations are not ready to fully embrace our free market system? Explain.

16. Benjamin Barber, writing in *The Atlantic,* sees two possible political futures, which he labels the "forces of Jihad" and the "forces of McWorld":

> The first is a retribalization of large swaths of humankind by war and bloodshed . . . culture is pitted against culture, people against people, tribe against tribe—a Jihad in the name of a hundred narrowly conceived faiths against every kind of interdependence. . . . The second is being borne in on us by the onrush of economic and ecological forces that demand integration and uniformity and that mesmerize the world with fast music, fast computers, and fast food—with MTV, Macintosh, and McDonald's pressing nations into one comercially homogeneous global network: One McWorld tied together by technology, ecology, communications, and commerce.[121]

a. Do either of these scenarios make sense to you? Explain.

b. Which would you prefer? Explain.

17. Critics argue that socialism requires a uniformity, a "sameness" that would destroy the individuality Americans prize.

a. Are Americans notably independent and individualistic? Explain.

b. Explore the argument that socialism would actually enhance meaningful individualism.

18. Hilda Scott wrote a book to which she affixed the provocative title *Does Socialism Liberate Women?*

a. Answer her question. Explain.

b. Are minority oppression and oppression of women inevitable by-products of capitalism? Explain.

19. In Wisconsin, members of the Old Order Amish religion declined to formally educate their children beyond the eighth grade. The U.S. Supreme Court held that their First Amendment right to freedom of religion was violated by the Wisconsin compulsory education statute, which required school attendance until the age of 16. Chief Justice Burger explained:

> They object to the high school, and higher education generally, because the values they teach are in marked variance with Amish values and the Amish way of life; they view secondary school education as an impermissible exposure of their children to a "worldly" influence in conflict with their beliefs. The high school tends to emphasize

intellectual and scientific accomplishments, self-distinction, competitiveness, worldly success, and social life with other students. Amish society emphasizes informal learning-through-doing; a life of "goodness," rather than a life of intellect; wisdom, rather than technical knowledge; community welfare, rather than competition; and separation from, rather than integration with, contemporary worldly society.[122]

    a. Have the Amish taken the course we should all follow? Explain.

    b. Could we do so? Explain.

20. Distinguished economist Gary Becker argues for a free market approach to America's immigration difficulties:

> In a market economy, the way to deal with excess demand for a product or service is to raise the price. This reduces the demand and stimulates the supply. I suggest that the United States adopt a similar approach to help solve its immigration problems. Under my proposal, anyone willing to pay a specified price could enter the United States immediately.[123]

Comment on this view.

21. Management scholars Rabindra Kanungo and Jay Conger remark that "'Altruism' is a word rarely associated with the world of business," but they ask, "Does altruism have a place in our business lives? And does it make good economic sense?"[124] Answer their questions.

Notes

1. Francis Fukuyama, "Are We at the End of History?" *Fortune,* January 15, 1990, p. 75.
2. Henry Mintzberg, "Managing Government—Governing Management," *Harvard Business Review* 74, no. 3 (May–June 1996), p. 75.
3. Robert Heilbroner, "Warp-Speed Capitalism," *Los Angeles Times Book Review,* February 8, 1998, p. 5.
4. Editorial, "The Manchurian Multinational," *The Wall Street Journal,* August 20, 2004, p. A12.
5. "Covenanting on a Matter of Life and Death," October 7, 2004 [**http://warc.jalb.de/warcajsp/side.jsp?news_id=159navi=1**].
6. Gary Rosen, "They Say They Want a Revolution," *The Wall Street Journal,* August 3, 2004, p. D8.
7. Edward Rothstein, "For Radical Visionaries, the Evil Empire Is Us," *The New York Times,* August 7, 2004, p. A21.
8. Karen House, "A Report to *The Wall Street Journal's* Worldwide Readers," *The Wall Street Journal,* January 8, 2004, p. A23.
9. Francis Fukuyama, "The West Has Won: Radical Islam Can't Beat Democracy and Capitalism. We're Still at the End of History," *The Guardian (London),* October 11, 2001, p. 21.
10. Ibid.
11. Dean Kuipers, "The Rise of the New Global 'Empire,'" *Los Angeles Times,* October 1, 2001, Part 5, p. 1.
12. "It'll Be a Good Day for Gwyneth," *Des Moines Register,* September 29, 2004, p. 2A.
13. Daniel Machalaba, "Highway Nirvana, at a Price," *The Wall Street Journal,* July 6, 2004, p. A15.
14. Ibid.

15. Ibid.

16. Kim Clark, "How to Make Traffic Jams a Thing of the Past," *Fortune,* March 31, 1997, p. 34.

17. David Wessel and John Harwood, "Capitalism Is Giddy with Triumph; Is It Possible to Overdo It?" *The Wall Street Journal,* May 14, 1998, p. A1.

18. Editorial, "City-Owned Golf Courses Cannot Be Sacred Cows," *Waterloo/Cedar Falls Courier,* July 13, 2003, p. C7.

19. Ibid.

20. Ibid.

21. Ibid.

22. Michael Chandler, "Looking to Privately Run Lockups," *Salt Lake Tribune,* August 22, 2004, p. E1.

23. Sean Kelly, "Riot Reignites Debate over Private Prisons," *Denver Post,* July 22, 2004, p. A06.

24. Ibid.

25. Chandler, "Looking to Privately Run Lockups," p. E1.

26. Editorial, "Edison's Discovery," *The Wall Street Journal,* August 25, 2004, p. A10.

27. Helen Gym, "Edison Schools' Failure in an Impoverished Town," *The Wall Street Journal,* September 3, 2004, p. A11.

28. "Say Goodbye to Financial Reform," *South China Morning Post,* September 20, 2004, p. 17.

29. "Trouble Brewing: China Should Sell State Assets to the Highest Bidder," *Financial Times (London),* May 7, 2004, p. 18.

30. David Wessel, "The American Way?" *The Wall Street Journal,* October 2, 1995, p. R8.

31. Jonathan N. Goodrich, "Privatization in America," *Business Horizons* 31, no. 1 (January–February 1988), pp. 11–16.

32. Wessel and Harwood, "Capitalism Is Giddy," p. A1.

33. Martin Himel, "Flirting with Capitalism," *The Vancouver Sun,* July 10, 2004, p. A17.

34. Henry Myers, "His Statues Topple, His Shadow Persists: Marx Can't Be Ignored," *The Wall Street Journal,* November 25, 1991, p. A1.

35. Ibid.

36. Elements of this list are drawn from Agnes Heller and Ferenc Feher, "Does Socialism Have a Future?" *Dissent,* Summer 1989, p. 371.

37. David J. Lynch, "China Finds Western Ways Bring New Woes," *USA TODAY,* May 19, 2004, p. 13A.

38. "Chinese Policy to Concentrate on Helping Rural Workers, Urban Poor," *BBC Monitoring Asia Pacific—Political,* October 6, 2004 [**http://web.lexis-nexis.com/universe/document?_m=fca014051fff3 . . .**].

39. Paul Wiseman, "Deep Financial Problems Threaten to Bury China," *USA TODAY,* October 18, 2001, p. 1B.

40. David Wallechinsky, "The World's 10 Worst Dictators," *Parade,* February 22, 2004, p. 5.

41. Andrew Higgins, "Reform in Russia: Free Market, Yes; Free Politics, Maybe," *The Wall Street Journal,* May 24, 2004, p. A1.

42. Boris Kagarlitsky, "10 Years after Soviet Rule," *Milwaukee Journal Sentinel,* December 22, 2001, p. 15A.

43. Editorial, "Size Matters," *The Wall Street Journal,* November 4, 2003, p. A18.

44. Ibid.
45. Almar Latour, "Sweden Seeks Utopia from Tech Boom," *The Wall Street Journal,* July 17, 2000, p. A1.
46. Michael Schroeder and Terence Roth, "World Bank Faults Tight Regulation," *The Wall Street Journal,* October 7, 2003, p. A2.
47. David Wessel, "American Economy Offers a Model Others Both Envy and Fear," *The Wall Street Journal,* January 18, 2001, p. A1.
48. Ibid.
49. Editorial, "Das Cowboy Kapital," *The Wall Street Journal,* September 28, 2004, p. A22.
50. Editorial, "Europe vs. America," *The Wall Street Journal,* June 18, 2004, p. A10.
51. Ibid.
52. Ibid.
53. Ibid.
54. Ibid.
55. Marcus Walker, "Most Competitive? Nordic Nations Trump China," *The Wall Street Journal,* October 14, 2004, p. A17.
56. Ibid.
57. Ibid.
58. Ibid.
59. "Study: Americans Most Productive Workers," *China Daily,* September 1, 2003 [**www.chinadaily.comcn/en/doc/2003-09/01content_260175.htm**].
60. Ibid.
61. Ibid.
62. Adrian Karatnycky quoting Soros in "The Merits of the Market, the Perils of 'Market Fundamentalism,'" *The Wall Street Journal,* January 9, 2001, p. A20.
63. Ibid.
64. Joanne Barkan, "Not Yet in Paradise, But . . . ," *Dissent,* Spring 1989, pp. 147, 150.
65. R. W. Apple, Jr., "Swedes Feel They're Lumped Together in 'National Blandness,'" *Lexington Leader,* July 26, 1978, p. A15.
66. "Human Development Report 2004," United Nations Development Program [**http://undp.org/reports/global/2004/**].
67. Ibid.
68. Ibid.
69. Ibid.
70. Ibid.
71. Ibid.
72. Ibid.
73. Ibid.
74. Ibid.
75. "Income Stable, Poverty Rate Increases, Percentage of Americans without Health Insurance Unchanged," *U.S. Census Bureau News* [**http://www.census.gov/Press-Release/www/releases/archives/income_wealth/005647.html**].
76. Ibid.
77. Ibid.

78. M. R. Kropko, Associated Press, "Cleveland Ranked Nation's Poorest City," *Seattle Post-Intelligencer* [**http://seattlepi.nwsource.com/national/apus_story.asp?category=11 . . .**].

79. Rob Morse, "Who Are We Kidding When We Say We Love Children?" *Des Moines Register,* September 7, 2000, p. 11A.

80. Gene Koretz, " . . . And the Home of the Poor," *BusinessWeek,* March 12, 2001, p. 32.

81. Associated Press, "Study: 39 Million Americans Live in Working Poor Families," *Waterloo/Cedar Falls Courier,* October 12, 2004, p. D6.

82. Michelle Conlin and Aaron Bernstein, "Working . . . and Poor," *BusinessWeek/online,* May 31, 2004 [**http://www.businessweek.com/print/magazine/content/04_22/b3885 . . .**].

83. Ibid.

84. Ibid.

85. Rita Mishra, "Survey: U.S. Health Care Lags, Is Called Inferior," *Des Moines Register,* June 21, 2000, p. 10A.

86. Ibid.

87. Ibid.

88. Siobhan McDonough, "Children Gain: Health, School and Weight," *Des Moines Register,* July 17, 2004, p. 2A.

89. Ibid.

90. "Millennium Development Goals: A Compact Among Nations to End Human Poverty" [**http://hdr.undp.org/reports/global/2003/**].

91. Leo Rennert, "U.S. Ranked Richest—and Poorest—Industrial Nation," *Sacramento Bee,* September 9, 1998, p. A9.

92. Richard Freeman, "Toward an Apartheid Economy?" *Harvard Business Review* 74, no. 5 (September–October 1996), p. 114.

93. Associated Press, "Income Gap Up over Two Decades, Data Show," August 16, 2004 [**http://www.forbes.com/associatedpress/feeds/ap/2004/08/16/ap1506713.html**].

94. Holly Sklar, "Boom Time for Privileged Billionaires," *Des Moines Register,* October 16, 2004, p. 11A.

95. Ibid.

96. Holly Sklar, "Outsource CEOs, Not Workers," *Des Moines Register,* May 7, 2004, p. 9A.

97. Ibid.

98. Dan Seligman, "Gap-osis," *Forbes,* August 25, 1997, p. 74.

99. Bryan T. Johnson, Kim R. Holmes, and Melanie Kirkpatrick, "Freedom Is the Surest Path to Prosperity," *The Wall Street Journal,* December 1, 1998, p. A22.

100. Heritage Foundation, "Index of Economic Freedom" [**http://www.heritage.org/research/features/index/indexoffreedom.cfm**].

101. William A. Sundstrom, "The Income Gap," *Issues in Ethics,* Fall 1998, p. 13.

102. United States Department of Justice, "Nation's Prison and Jail Population Grew by 932 Inmates Per Week" [**http://www.ojp.usdoj.gov/bjs/pub/press/pjim04pr.htm**].

103. Siobhan McDonough, "Inmate Intake Outpaces Releases," *Des Moines Register,* April 25, 2005, p. 3A.

104. Robert Putnam, *Bowling Alone* (New York: Simon & Schuster, 2000).

105. Peter Schrag, "'Bowling Alone'; As Americans Quit Being Joiners, Our Social Fabric Begins to Unravel," *San Diego Union-Tribune,* August 20, 2000, p. G6.

106. Alex Epstein, *Tribune* Media Service, "Federal Act Would Force College Students to Do Community Service," *Northern Iowan,* January 25, 2002, p. 8.

107. Wessel and Harwood, "Capitalism Is Giddy with Triumph," p. A1.

108. Associated Press, "A Threat to Castro," *Des Moines Register,* August 30, 1994, p. 8A.

109. Jeremy Rifkin, "Whose Vision Will Prevail?" *Des Moines Register,* December 4, 2004, p. 9A.

110. Ibid.

111. Ibid.

112. Lauren Soth, "Seek Better Care of People and Earth," *Des Moines Register,* April 24, 1993, p. 5A.

113. Robert Samuelson, "Economics Made Easy," *Newsweek,* November 27, 1989, p. 64.

114. Noel Perrin, "A Nonbearing Account," *Newsweek,* April 2, 1990, pp. 10–11.

115. Karen Pennar, "The Free Market Has Triumphed, But What about the Losers?" *BusinessWeek,* September 25, 1989, p. 178.

116. Carla McClain, "Dr. Spock: Restore the Family," *Des Moines Register,* November 7, 1993, p. 3E.

117. Sally Pipes, "Wal-Mart's Success Makes It Unfair Target," *Des Moines Register,* August 7, 2004, p. 17A.

118. Thomas L. Friedman, "Eastern Middle School," *New York Times on the Web,* October 2, 2001.

119. Michael Harrington, "Why We Need Socialism in America," *Dissent,* May–June 1970, pp. 240, 286.

120. Adolph Berle, *Power* (New York: Harcourt Brace Jovanovich, 1969), pp. 258–59.

121. Benjamin Barber, "Jihad v. McWorld," *The Atlantic* 269, no. 3 (March 1992), p. 53.

122. *Wisconsin v. Yoder,* 406 U.S. 205, 210–11 (1972).

123. Gary Becker, "Why Not Let Immigrants Pay for Speedy Entry?" *BusinessWeek,* March 2, 1987, p. 20.

124. Rabindra Kanungo and Jay Conger, "Promoting Altruism as a Corporate Goal," *The Academy of Management Executive* 8, no. 3 (August 1993), p. 37.

Business Ethics

Corporate misconduct of historic proportions has recently called into question the integrity of the American business community while bringing financial and moral hardship to millions. Most of America's great corporate names remain untouched by the tidal wave of crimes, but neither can we credibly argue that only "a few bad apples" are to blame. We seem to be witnessing the exposure of some fundamental and systemic flaws in big patches of American business practice. Some great names have been besmirched with allegations and/or convictions: Adelphia (misuse of corporate funds), Arthur Andersen (auditing irregularities), Enron (off-books partnerships to hide debts and losses), Global Crossing (deceptive accounting), Merrill Lynch (stock fraud), Tyco (corporate looting), WorldCom (hiding billions in expenses), and Xerox (misstating revenues). Even Martha Stewart, that paragon of propriety in the home, spent five months in federal prison for lying to the government regarding some insider trading allegations.

> Even Martha Stewart spent five months in federal prison for lying

What went wrong? The facts are not yet clear, but we know that accounting irregularities were commonplace. Many corporate bosses (and many of us) were caught up in the glittering financial promises of the "New Economy," where technology seemed to guarantee success without some of the dreary demands of the old smokestack economy. The government, with its well-meant and often quite sound deregulation policies, seemed to signal that the road was clear for fast, efficient growth without a lot of bothersome oversight. Old-fashioned greed and arrogance may, however, have been the most powerful motors in this great scandal. The article that follows gives us the government's version of some of the factors motivating former Qwest CEO Joe Nacchio, who, at this writing, faces Securities and Exchange Commission civil charges of fraud involving allegedly false and misleading statements about Qwest's financial condition. The alleged $3 billion fraud resulted in Qwest stock prices plunging from a high of $60 to under $4.00 and led to Qwest agreeing to pay a $250 million fine to settle accounting fraud allegations.

SEC Says "Culture of Fear" Led to Qwest's Acts

Associated Press

Denver, Colo.—Joe Nacchio gathered his employees on a January day five years ago and laid it on the line: The key to the success of Qwest Communications wasn't the customers, products, or even the workers—it was the numbers, the money.

"It's more important than any individual product, it's more important than any individual philosophy, it's more important than any individual cultural change we're making," Qwest's then–chief executive said, according to federal regulators. "We stop everything else when we don't make the numbers."

According to a Securities and Exchange Commission lawsuit, Nacchio and his executives exerted so much pressure to meet those targets that they created a "culture of fear" where harried employees did whatever they could, even resorting to illegal actions, to paint a false and rosy financial picture for investors.

Business goals are commonplace, but setting targets can create a boiler-room atmosphere in which employees step outside the law to comply or become afraid to report wrongdoing, legal experts say. The accounting problems at Denver-based Qwest forced the telecommunications company for 14 states to erase some $3 billion in revenue.

The commission's lawsuit against Nacchio and six other executives cited a time when Nacchio referred to revenue targets and told one person, "You do this or I'll find someone who will."

During a criminal trial last summer for four former Qwest midlevel managers, former chief financial officer Robin Szeliga said there was significant pressure from Nacchio to meet targets, enough to create a "pressure-cooker" atmosphere.

Source: *Des Moines Register*, March 22, 2005, p. 10C. Reprinted by permission of the copyright holder, The Associated Press.

Question

1. Is obsessive attention to "the numbers, the money" a practical necessity in today's highly competitive, global economy? Explain.

Part One—Introduction to Ethics

Can we count on self-regulation (ethics) as a useful means of controlling managerial/corporate behavior? Put another way, can we count on the free market as discussed in Chapter 1 along with managerial and corporate ethics to guide business conduct such that government regulation can be significantly reduced? Obviously, the Qwest story does not provide an encouraging answer to those questions. Indeed, we appear to be in the midst of a collapse in corporate decency. Nonetheless, we know that good behavior remains the norm and the goal in America and presumably in the corporate community. Thus this chapter will examine the ethical climate of business and the role of ethics in business decision making. Our goal here is not to *teach morality* but to sensitize the reader to the vital role honor plays in building a sound career and a sound corporate community. We will return from time to time to the ongoing corporate scandals; but for now we will consider a pair of personal, practical ethical dilemmas of the kind that affect all managers' lives; the first a tragic loss for a working mother, the second a choice between money and ideals.

PRACTICING ETHICS Career and Family

5:45 PM, June 26, 2001. Upon leaving work, Kari Engholm, a mother and chief administrator of the Dallas County Hospital in Perry, Iowa, found her seven-month-old daughter, Clare, dead in her car seat in the rear of the Engholm family van. Clare died of elevated body temperature (hyperthermia). The official death certificate declared the death an accident.

Ms. Engholm's husband, Dennis, ordinarily took Clare to the babysitter's house; but because of Dennis's work schedule at Iowa State University, Kari intended to take the Engholm's $3\frac{1}{2}$-year-old son, Eric, to day care as usual and then leave Clare at her babysitter's home. She dropped Eric off at his day care on the morning of June 26, 2001, then apparently forgot that Clare was in her car seat in the back of the family minivan. After dropping Eric off, Ms. Engholm headed directly to "a tense board meeting during which members decided to sell an Adel medical practice to a doctor for $55,000 because of criticism that the hospital was not renewing the doctor's contract." Ms. Engholm completed her workday in the normal manner, and then when entering her minivan after work, discovered her daughter who had expired during the day.

Ms. Engholm was charged with criminal violations of neglect of a dependent person and involuntary manslaughter, but she was acquitted of both charges because, in the judgment of the court, the facts did not establish that Ms. Engholm's behavior met the statutory criminal standards of willfully or recklessly causing harm to her daughter. (A *Des Moines Register* review of 39 similar cases nationwide found 11 instances of parents facing criminal charges after such episodes.)

Prior to the Engholm trial, a letter to the *Des Moines Register* criticized parents and American society for giving too much attention to career advancement and wealth at the expense of children:

> Baby Clare might be considered an extreme example of the defenseless victims of a culture of selfishness and materialism. Far too many American couples are opting for two incomes and two careers at the expense of their children. Sending children off to be raised by $6 per hour "child care specialists" in order to have a bigger house, more vacations, an SUV, ad infinitum, is a form of child abuse in itself.

Sources: Dan Frommelt, "Children Are Victims of Parents' Careers," (Letter to the Editor) *Des Moines Register*, July 4, 2000, p. 8A, and various other *Des Moines Register* news accounts.

Questions

a. Do you agree with the letter writer? Explain.

b. Are your career and family goals ethically compatible? Explain.

AFTERWORD

Through the first eight months of 2003, at least 36 children died in the United States in overheated cars. Those deaths have generally been increasing from 25 in 1998, to 31 in 1999, to 28 in 2000, to 34 in 2001. According to the advocacy group Kids and Cars [**www.kidsandcars.org**], at least nine states make it illegal to leave a child alone in a vehicle.[1]

One Parent at Home?

Forty-one percent of Americans surveyed in a 2001 Gallup Poll believe that one parent should stay at home solely to raise children, while 24 percent felt the ideal arrangement would involve both parents working outside the home: one full-time, the other part-time.

Source: Chris McComb, "Few Say It's Ideal for Both Parents to Work Full-Time Outside of Home," *The Gallup Poll Monthly,* May 2001, p. 24.

PRACTICING ETHICS   Pat Tillman's Ideals

The Associated Press

Pat Tillman walked away from millions in the NFL to fight for his country in Afghanistan.

He paid with his life.

The former Arizona Cardinals safety was killed in a firefight while on combat patrol. A sergeant with the elite Army Rangers, he was 27.

"He is a hero," Cardinals vice president Michael Bidwill said. "He was a brave man. There are very few people who have the courage to do what he did, the courage to walk away from a professional sports career and make the ultimate sacrifice."

Lt. Col. Matt Beevers, a spokesman for the U.S. military in Kabul, said a soldier was killed by anticoalition militia forces about 25 miles from a U.S. military base at Khost, the site of frequent attacks.

A military official at the Pentagon confirmed it was Tillman, and the White House praised him as "an inspiration both on and off the football field."

The 5-foot-11, 200-pound Tillman was an overachiever as an athlete. Too slow to be a great safety, too small for an NFL linebacker, he got by on toughness and effort.

Those attributes undoubtedly served him well in the Army Rangers, whom he joined in May 2002 after abandoning his career with the Cardinals. He moved from a violent game to the reality of war.

"Pat Tillman personified all the best values of his country and the NFL," commissioner Paul Tagliabue said. "He was an achiever and leader on many levels who always put his team, his community, and his country ahead of his personal interests."

Six months after the September 11 terrorist attacks, Tillman walked into the office of then-coach Dave McGinnis, pulled up a chair and said, "Mac, we have to talk."

Tillman and his brother Kevin—a minor league baseball player in the Cleveland organization—were going to join the Army Rangers, soldiers sent where the fighting is toughest.

"It was his wish that this not be something that would draw a lot of attention," McGinnis said. "He truly felt committed and felt a sense of honor and duty at this point in his life that this is what he wanted to do."

Tillman never said a word publicly about his decision.

Tillman turned down a more lucrative offer from the St. Louis Rams in 2001 to stay with the Cardinals. A year later, he walked away from a three-year, $3.6 million offer from Arizona to join the army.

"What other person do you know who would give up a life in the NFL to defend what he believes in with his own life?" said former teammate David Barrett, now with the New York Jets. "That is a humble guy."

Source: Associated Press, "Former Arizona Cardinal Pat Tillman Is Killed in Afghanistan after Walking Away from an NFL Contract to Join the Army," *Waterloo/Cedar Falls Courier*, April 24, 2004, p. C1. Reprinted by permission of the copyright holder, the Associated Press.

Questions

1. Is Corporal Tillman a hero because he walked away from money and fame or because he joined the military to do what he believed to be his duty? Explain.

2. Is forgoing money in itself an heroic act? Explain.

3. *a.* Can you envision yourself doing as Corporal Tillman did, were you similarly situated?

   b. Would you do so given your current circumstances in life? Explain.

AFTERWORD

In late 2003, after Corporal Tillman had completed a tour of duty in Iraq, his agent had received a number of calls from National Football League teams who were interested in signing Tillman for the 2004 season. NFL executives thought Tillman could secure an early discharge because he had already served one tour of duty overseas. Tillman, however, said that he owed the service three years, and that he would do another tour. He then proceeded, as ordered, to Afghanistan where he was killed. Subsequent inquiries by the army and journalists concluded that Tillman was killed by "friendly fire," a finding the army apparently hid for some time.

Ethics Survey

The Ethics Officer Association and the Ethical Leadership Group sampled a cross-section of workers at large companies nationwide. How would you respond?

1. "Is it wrong to use company e-mail for personal reasons?"
2. "Is it wrong to play computer games on office equipment during the workday?"
3. "Is it OK to take a $100 holiday food basket?"
4. "Due to on-the-job pressure, have you ever abused or lied about sick days?"

Source: "The Wall Street Journal Workplace-Ethics Quiz," *The Wall Street Journal,* October 21, 1999, p. B1.

Ethics Theories

Volumes of literature are devoted in general terms to the question of defining *ethics.* We cannot hope to advance that discussion here. Ethics, of course, involves judgments as to good and bad, right and wrong, and what ought to be. *Business ethics* refers to the measurement of business behavior based on standards of right and wrong, rather than relying entirely on principles of accounting and management. (In this discussion, the word *morals* will be used interchangeably with the word *ethics.* Distinctions certainly are drawn between the two, but those distinctions are not vital for our purposes.)

Finding and following the moral course is not easy for any of us, but the difficulty may be particularly acute for the businessperson. The bottom line is necessarily unforgiving. Hence the pressure to produce is intense, and the temptation to cheat may be great. Although the law provides useful guideposts for minimum comportment, no clear moral guidelines have emerged. Therefore, when the businessperson faces a difficult decision, a common tactic is simply to do what he or she takes to be correct at any given moment. Indeed, in one survey of ethical views in business, 50 percent of the respondents indicated that the word *ethical* meant "what my feelings tell me is right."[2]

Philosophers have provided powerful intellectual support for that approach. Existentialists, led by the famed Jean-Paul Sartre, believe standards of conduct cannot be rationally justified and no actions are inherently right or wrong. Thus each person may reach his or her own choice about ethical principles. That view finds its roots in the notion that humans are only what we will ourselves to be. If God does not exist, there can be no human nature, because there is no one to conceive that nature.

Existence precedes essence
In Sartre's famous interpretation, existence precedes essence. First humans exist; then we individually define what we are—our essence. Therefore, each of us is free, with no rules to turn to for guidance. Just as we all choose our own natures, so must we choose our own ethical precepts. Moral responsibility belongs to each of us individually.

Universal Truths?

Have we then no rules or universal standards by which to distinguish right from wrong? Have we no absolutes? Philosophers seek to provide guidance beyond the uncertainties of ethical relativism. We will survey two ethical perspectives, teleology and deontology, which form the core of ethical analysis. Before proceeding to those theories, we will note the important role of religion in ethics and take a brief look at two additional formulations—libertarianism and virtue ethics—that have been increasingly influential in contemporary moral analysis.

1. **Religion.** Judeo–Christian beliefs, Islam, Confucianism, Buddhism, and other faiths are powerful ethical voices in contemporary life. They often feature efforts such as the Golden Rule to build absolute and universal standards. Scholarly studies indicate that most American managers believe in the Golden Rule and take it to be their most meaningful moral guidepost. From a religious point of view, the deity's laws are absolutes that must shape the whole of one's life, including work. Faith, rather than reason, intuition, or secular knowledge, provides the foundation for a moral life built on religion. [For worldwide coverage of ethics issues, see "Religion & Ethics" at **http://www.bbc.co.uk/religion/ethics/**]

Religion at Work

A 2004 Gallup Poll reported that 84 percent of American adults believe religion is either "very" or "fairly" important in their lives. Business scholars and reporters note a renewed interest in religion and spirituality in the workplace. In one survey, 40 percent of those responding to a *Fortune* 1,000 survey felt that "religious principles and values were an integral part of

---

their organization's culture." Scholars Ian Mitroff and Elizabeth Denton undertook a "spiritual audit of corporate America" and concluded that managers desire a way to express their spiritual selves at work and that managers often are unable to bring their "complete selves" to work. They argue that business must acknowledge the soul to maximize performance.

Do you think corporate America must now make room for spirituality and the soul in the workplace to maximize success? Explain.

Sources: The Gallup Poll, May 2–4, 2004 [**www.pollingreport.com/religion.htm.**] Karen C. Cash and George R. Gray, "A Framework for Accommodating Religion and Spirituality in the Workplace," *Academy of Management Executive* 14, no. 3 (2000), p. 124. Ian I. Mitroff and Elizabeth A. Denton, *A Spiritual Audit of Corporate America: A Hard Look at Spirituality, Religion, and Values in the Workplace* (San Francisco: Jossey-Bass, 1999).

2. **Libertarianism.** Contemporary philosopher Robert Nozick built an ethical theory rooted in personal liberty. For him, morality coincided with the maximization of personal freedom. Justice and fairness, right and wrong are measured not by equality of results (such as wealth) for all, but from ensuring equal opportunity for all to engage in informed choices about their own welfare. Hence Nozick took essentially a free market stance toward ethics.

3. **Virtue ethics.** In recent years, an increasing number of philosophers have argued that the key to good ethics lies not in rules, rights, and responsibilities but in the classic notion of character. As Plato and Aristotle argued, our attention should be given to strategies for encouraging desirable character traits such as honesty, fairness, compassion, and generosity. Aristotle believed that virtue could be taught much as any other skill. Virtue ethics applauds the person who is motivated to do the right thing and who cultivates that motivation in daily conduct. A part of the argument is that such persons are more morally reliable than those who simply follow the rules but fail to inspect, strengthen, and preserve their own personal virtues. The article that follows describes a bar owner in a Des Moines, Iowa, suburb, who decided to do what he apparently thought was the "right thing," the virtuous act. [For an overview of virtue ethics, see **http://plato.stanford.edu/entries/ethics-virtue/**]

READING

Concerned Owner Closes Bar's Doors

April Goodwin, *Register* Staff Writer

Vieux Carre, the spacious West Des Moines nightclub that pioneered all-you-can-drink specials in the metro area, has closed after the owner had an attack of conscience.

Dick Davis said he had moral concerns with how the bar was being run and had fought with his managers.

"Morally, I just wanted out," he said. "I closed it up."

Davis said he thought some of the promotions, which he did not approve in advance, tarnished his reputation. "That just irritated the hell out of me," he said of the all-you-can-drink special.

Vieux Carre opened last May in a former movie theater that Davis owned.

Davis, 75, said he worried about his customers getting hurt or driving drunk.

"I'm going to sleep so good this weekend," he said Friday. . . .

Donna Mahers of Des Moines was stunned Thursday night—her 21st birthday—to discover that the club was closed. "We pulled in and there were no stinking cars," she said.

Mahers said she had trouble finding anywhere fun to go. "I didn't even puke on my 21st birthday. I wanted to go dancing. I took the whole day off today, thinking I'd have a hangover. It was kind of a waste."

Davis said he plans to reopen the bar, which he said reaped an average of $85,000 in profits monthly, under new management.

Downtown Des Moines bar owner Larry Smithson said Vieux Carre's image was hurt by a radio ad featuring a character who says he got so drunk he didn't remember the night before.

Source: *Des Moines Register,* March 16, 2002, p. 1B. Reprinted by permission.

Questions

1. *a.* Would all "virtuous" persons do as Davis did? Explain.
    b. Would you? Explain.
    c. From a libertarian perspective, would all bar owners be morally required to act as Davis did? Explain.
    d. Does religion provide any guidance for a bar owner in Davis's position? Explain.

2. Are bar owners generally, and Davis particularly, in any way responsible for the values Donna Mahers expressed in discussing her 21st birthday plans and disappointments? Explain.

Teleology or Deontology—An Overview

Teleological ethical systems (often referred to as *consequentialist ethical systems*) are concerned with the consequences of an act rather than the act itself. A teleological view of life concerns itself with ends, goals, and the ultimate good. Duty and obligation are subordinated to the production of what is good or desirable. For the teleologist/consequentialist, the end is primary and that end or result is the measure of the ethical quality of a decision or act.

To the *deontologist,* on the other hand, principle is primary and consequence is secondary or even irrelevant. Maximizing right rather than good is the deontological standard. The deontologist might well refuse to lie even if doing so would maximize good. *Deontology,* derived from the Greek word meaning *duty,* is directed toward what ought to be, toward what is right. Relationships among people are important because they give rise to duties. A father may be morally committed to saving his son from a burning building, rather than saving another person who might well do more total good for society. Similarly, deontology considers motives. For example, why a crime was committed may be more important than the actual consequences of the crime.

The distinction here is critical. Are we to guide our behavior in terms of rational evaluations of the consequences of our acts, or are we to shape our conduct in terms of duty and principle—that which ought to be? Let's take a closer look at *utilitarianism,* the principal teleological ethical theory, and *formalism,* the principal deontological ethical theory.

Teleology

Utilitarianism   In reaching an ethical decision, good is to be weighed against evil. A decision that maximizes the ratio of good over evil for all those concerned is the ethical course. Jeremy Bentham (1748–1832) and John Stuart Mill (1806–1873) were the chief intellectual forces in the development of utilitarianism. Their views and those of other utilitarian philosophers were not entirely consistent. As a result, at least two branches of utilitarianism have developed. According to *act-utilitarianism,* one's goal is to identify the consequences of a particular act to determine whether it is right or wrong. *Rule-utilitarianism* requires one to adhere to all the rules of conduct by which society reaps the greatest value. Thus the rule-utilitarian may be forced to shun a particular act that would result in greater immediate good (punishing a guilty person whose constitutional rights have been violated) in favor of upholding a broader rule that results in the greater total good over time (maintaining constitutional principles by freeing the guilty person). In sum, the principle to be followed for the utilitarian is the greatest good for the greatest number. [For an extensive database exploring utilitarianism, see **http://www .hedweb.com/philsoph/utillink.htm**]

Deontology

Formalism   The German philosopher Immanuel Kant (1724–1804) developed perhaps the most persuasive and fully articulated vision of ethics as measured not by consequences (teleology) but by the rightness of rules. In this formalistic view of ethics, the rightness of an act depends little (or, in Kant's view, not at all) on the results of the act. Kant believed in the key moral concept of "the good will." The moral person is a person of goodwill, and that person renders ethical decisions based on what is right, regardless of the consequences of the decision. Moral worth springs from one's decision to discharge one's duty. Thus the student who refuses to cheat on exams is morally worthy if his or her decision springs from duty, but morally unworthy if the decision is merely one born of self-interest, such as fear of being caught.

How does the person of goodwill know what is right? Here Kant propounded the *categorical imperative,* the notion that every person should act on only those principles that he or she, as a rational person, would prescribe as universal laws to be applied to the whole of humankind. A moral rule is "categorical" rather than "hypothetical" in that its prescriptive force is independent of its consequences. The rule guides us independent of the ends we seek. Kant believed that every rational creature can act according to his or her categorical imperative because all such persons have "autonomous, self-legislating wills" that permit them to formulate and act on their own systems of rules. To Kant, what is right for one is right for all, and each of us can discover that "right" by exercising our rational faculties.

Using Utilitarianism and Formalism: Layoffs, Part I

Obviously, ethical theory does not provide magical answers to life's most difficult questions. However, those theories are useful in identifying and sorting the issues that lead to better decision making. Apply those theories to the reading that follows, and think about when layoffs are ethical.

Richard Lorant, Associated Press

As he watched Malden Mills burn, Michael Lavallee was sure the factory where he had worked for 25 years was being reduced, building by building, to a memory. "We just kept staring at the place, saying, 'It's over. It's done. It's gone,'" said Lavallee, an engineer.

* * * * *

The next morning, [mill owner Aaron] Feuerstein vowed to rebuild Malden Mills Industries without layoffs, embarking on a road that would lift him to national prominence as a symbol of corporate compassion in a seemingly heartless era.

At Malden Mills, Feuerstein appears to be succeeding in his effort to rebuild after the December 11, 1995, fire that threatened 3,100 high-paying manufacturing jobs in this economically depressed region north of Boston. The blaze injured 33 people, 8 of them severely. Six have not yet returned to work, and at least one will never work again.

Feuerstein has said everything about his Jewish upbringing and his 50-year history in the local business told him to rebuild. "It was the right thing to do and there's a moral imperative to do it, irrespective of the consequences," Feuerstein said.

The new plant is scheduled to open in February. Filled with shining machinery, it was designed to boost production of the mill's patented Polartec fabric, which has become the fleece of choice for manufacturers of name-brand winter clothes. All Malden Mills' employees received full pay and benefits for three months after the fire. Since then, 85 percent have returned to work on makeshift production lines located in once and future warehouses. About 400 workers remain idle—a shortcoming Feuerstein regards as a failure—but he pledges to restore those jobs "come hell or high water" within two years.

Feuerstein has spent more than $300 million to build the new plant, replace lost machinery, and cover business losses. Insurers have paid half that amount so far. The rest has come from bank loans and from his family's savings.

After falling off because of the fire, production of Polartec and Polarfleece is back to previous levels. "Unquestionably, in the long run, it will pay dividends," he said.

But while Feuerstein defends his decision to rebuild as a good business move, it originated in the old-fashioned way his family has run the mill since it was founded by his grandfather in 1906. Despite its technical innovations, Malden Mills is in some ways a throwback to the days when a mill was like an extended family, with the owner at its head. Almost all of the many mills in the area have closed, following cheap labor to the South and then overseas.

Whole families in the immigrant-filled neighborhoods of Methuen and nearby Lawrence see the mills as their tickets into the middle class. If their $11-an-hour jobs were to disappear, many would end up with lower-paying service jobs.

If the fire provided Feuerstein with a challenge of the magnitude few business owners face, he also had two key advantages that helped him take the high road and stand by his workers. First, Malden Mills was a profitable company offering a patented product, Polartec, that had carved out a $3 billion market and a loyal customer base. Second, as a privately held company, Malden Mills Industries was free of the pressure to produce short-term profits and satisfy Wall Street analysts faced by publicly traded businesses.

"He's still pretty lonely, but the idea has appeal," said Michael Useem, a professor at the University of Pennsylvania's Wharton School. "The thinking is: employees can be seen as an ultimate competitive advantage. If you treat them well, they'll pay you back in really hard work later on."

Source: Richard Lorant, Associated Press. Reprinted in *The Chicago Tribune,* December 10, 1996, p. 8. Reprinted by permission.

Questions

1. Aaron Feuerstein became something of an overnight national hero by protecting his workers. Feuerstein said, "It was the right thing to do and there's a moral imperative to do it, irrespective of the consequences."

   a. Was Feuerstein employing utilitarian or formalist reasoning? Explain.

   b. In your view, was he correct to say that the consequences, in this instance, did not matter? Explain.

2. Commenting on Feuerstein's approach to his employees' needs, Wharton School professor Michael Useem said, "The thinking is: employees can be seen as an ultimate competitive advantage. If you treat them well, they'll pay you back in really hard work later on."

   a. Was Useem expressing formalist or utilitarian reasoning?

   b. In a 1986 pastoral letter, the U.S. Catholic bishops argued that "every economic decision and institution must be judged in light of whether it protects or undermines the dignity of the human person."[3] Does the thinking summarized by Useem undermine that dignity and as such require rejection under either utilitarian or formalist reasoning? Explain.

3. *a.* Are we in the midst of a "heartless" era as the author suggests? Explain.

b. Are you "heartless"? Explain.

4. If you were a successful entrepreneur with the flexibility of Aaron Feuerstein, would you operate your business like "an extended family"? Explain.

Layoffs, Part II

In November 2001, Malden Mills was forced to enter Chapter 11 bankruptcy proceedings (see Chapter 15) for the purpose of reorganizing its finances under court protection. At the time, Malden Mills was bearing a $140 million debt load. Lenders demanded the bankruptcy action as a condition for extending an additional $20 million to keep the company afloat. In late 2003 Malden Mills emerged from bankruptcy. Creditors control the board of directors with Aaron Feuerstein occupying the family's one seat. Malden's precarious financial position was the product of a variety of forces: customers were lost during the rebuilding after the fire, cheaper fleece substitutes entered the market, the company took on substantial debt in rebuilding and in keeping on its employees following the fire, and the company probably overbuilt following the fire. As a result, the Malden Mills workforce shrunk to 1,200 employees. The article that follows contrasts Feuerstein's ethical reasoning with the apparent values of those who built Enron and then led it to bankruptcy in 2001. (Remember that Malden Mills is privately held, whereas Enron is a publicly traded company.)

READING Tale of Two Bankruptcies

Mary McGrory

In this anxious hour of pink-slip dread, it is restoring to think of Aaron Feuerstein, a Massachusetts manufacturer who prizes his employees and risks profits on their behalf.

The CEO of Malden Mills, located in Lawrence, the 23rd poorest community in the country, stepped clear of the greedy stereotype of his kind in 1995 when, just before Christmas, his factory burned down. Rather than taking the insurance money and retiring or moving the plant to some Third World country, he promptly announced that he would rebuild. He gave bonuses to the help and paid them while they waited for the factory reopening. Last Monday, this paragon of corporate virtue held a rally at the plant he inherited from his father. The idea was to kick off a campaign for Malden Mills' special product, Polartec, a light, warm fabric that is keeping U.S. Marines cozy in the grinding cold of Afghanistan. Sen. John Kerry hailed Malden Mills as a mill with soul and a mill with heart.

Feuerstein has not had all the good fortune he may deserve. Sales dipped, and he recently filed for bankruptcy under Chapter 11 and negotiated a $20 million loan. Feuerstein would have liked the money without the Chapter 11—"I hate to put any stain on our beautiful name"—but he told cheering workers that together they would win.

Columnist Mark Shields was the first to make the striking contrast between Feuerstein and today's most celebrated bankruptcy case, that of Enron, the monstrous Texas energy outfit. Most of its 21,000 workers lost jobs. For 11,000, it was a lump of coal, the loss of life savings invested in Enron stock. Enron employees were urged to buy the stock with their retirement funds, their 401(k)s. When Enron started going south in October, however, the employees were forbidden to sell. Enron

CEO Kenneth Lay and his fellow executives were exempt from the lockdown and sold, often at tremendous profits.

Stricken ex-Enron workers told the Senate Commerce Committee of being seduced, betrayed, and abandoned by their bosses. Enron lied about earnings, cooked its books, and left its employees in the lurch, while its top brass made out like bandits.

Janice Farmer, a Florida widow, had her daughter with her to help her through her testimony. A year ago, she retired with $700,000 in Enron stock. Today it is worth $4,000. When she saw that Enron was ailing, she tried to sell. She was locked out.

If Lay is sorry about all this, he hasn't said so. Acting committee chairman Byron Dorgan, D-N.D., said Lay had been invited to testify but declined and promised to come later. Lay is a good friend to the president and is his biggest contributor. White House strategist Karl Rove owned a big bloc of Enron stock, and when Vice President Cheney was devising his strange energy plan, Lay was consulted. There are other Texas ties: Wendy Gramm, wife of Sen. Phil Gramm, is a member of the Enron board and chairman of the auditing committee.

Where Feuerstein and Lay differed most sharply was on devotion to the bottom line. To Lay, we are almost forced to conclude, it was paramount; Feuerstein put the excellence of his product above the entries in his ledgers. To Lay, employees were as disposable as Kleenex; Feuerstein thinks they are partners.

Where did Feuerstein get his extraordinary ideas about worker–management relations? "At my father's table. We all had to be there. No pizza in the kitchen. I was 7 years old when I heard my father tell a story I never forgot."

Aaron's father had watched his father, who founded the factory, go around at the end of the day and give money to every one of his workers. Aaron's father explained to his father, a Hungarian immigrant, that this was not the American way. Aaron's grandfather screamed at Aaron's father that it was against the Torah to do it any other way.

Young Aaron consulted his rabbi, who happened to be his maternal grandfather. His other grandfather, he was told, was right. In Leviticus, it is written, "You are not permitted to oppress the working man because he is poor and needy." Aaron memorized the passage in Hebrew—and lives by it.

Such a rabbi Kenneth Lay should have had.

Source: *Pittsburgh Post-Gazette,* December 22, 2001, p. A15, Reprinted by permission of the copyright holder, The Universal Press Syndicate.

Questions

1. *The Wall Street Journal* raised the question, "Are layoffs moral?"[4]

    a. Should we establish a universal, formalist rule forbidding layoffs of all hard-working, competent employees, or should we rely on utilitarian reasoning, libertarian thought, virtue theory, or religious beliefs to answer that question? Explain.

    b. Is morality irrelevant to the question of when layoffs are necessary? Explain.

2. Do you think it would be accurate and fair to say that Feuerstein's ethical choice to protect his employees led to the decline of his business? Explain.

3. Did Feuerstein make an error in judgment in relying on an absolute principle—that is, the protection of his workers at all costs? Explain.

4. How might Feuerstein's workers have benefited by being laid off after the fire?

5. John MacKenzie, in a letter to *The New York Times,* says he has a duty to help Aaron Feuerstein and Malden Mills: "Of course I have an ethical obligation to buy from Malden Mills if I have a choice and if my purchase can make a difference. It would reward Mr. Feuerstein for what he has done and what he is trying to do, and the system needs more of that."[5]

    Do you have a duty to buy Malden Mills products? Explain.

Loyalty Pays Off?

Sometimes employer generosity works out more favorably than has been the case at Malden Mills. The *Des Moines Register* recently applauded an Ames, Iowa, company whose boss, Roger Underwood, said, "It's the employees who made us successful, and we decided to reward them." The *Register* explained:

> Every once in a while, an employer comes along that renews one's faith in business. Becker Underwood, a 22-year-old Ames company that makes landscaping and agricultural products, last week spent $1.4 million giving bonuses to 238 employees at eight locations around the world. Each worker received $2,000 for each year worked for the company.

Finally loyalty pays off.

* * * * *

That's a rare attitude in corporate America—a winning attitude, apparently, considering how well the company is doing. Is there a lesson there?

Source: "A Rare Recognition," *Des Moines Register,* September 6, 2004, p. 10A.

Questions—Part One

1. Think about ethical dilemmas in your own life.
   a. Do you find yourself turning primarily to teleological or deontological reasoning to resolve those problems? Or neither? Explain.
   b. Have you developed any systematic means of addressing ethical issues? Explain.
2. Do you think that philosophers' analyses of ethics, as we have briefly explored them in this text, can be of value in your future professional life? Explain.
3. On January 31, 2001, United Airlines' Web site erroneously listed international flights for remarkably low prices, including $24.98 round-trip from San Francisco to Paris, and similar amazing bargains to Hong Kong and other destinations. United blamed a computer error. One hundred forty-three tickets were sold at the bargain rates during a 55-minute period.
   a. Was UAL ethically obliged to honor the low fares? Explain.
   b. Can purchasers honorably take advantage of the UAL error? Explain.
4. Sociologist/philosopher Zygmunt Bauman says the Holocaust (the mass extermination of Europeans Jews by the Nazis) was not an historical aberration or a moral anomaly; rather, he says, it was a somewhat predictable product of modern bureaucratic life. Explain how a bureaucratic society might be expected to produce immoral, even horrific, decisions and policies. See Zygmunt Bauman, *Modernity and the Holocaust* (Ithaca, NY: Cornell University Press, 2001).

Part Two—Managerial Ethics: Evidence and Analysis

America's Moral Climate

Perhaps more than ever Americans are questioning the nation's moral health. Certainly we must wonder why we are so deeply hated that terrorists would attack on 9/11 and kill 3,000 of us along with themselves. But the list of concerns is much longer: highly publicized corporate corruption, mistreatment of war prisoners in Iraq, steroid use by professional athletes, journalists making up phony stories, government officials apparently exaggerating intelligence evidence, and so on, including our personal lives.

Sociologist David Callahan's 2004 book *The Cheating Culture: Why More Americans Are Doing Wrong to Get Ahead*[6] argues that we are a society in moral decline. Reviewer Jackson Lears summarized Callahan's position:

> As economic inequalities have deepened during the last several decades, the renewed worship of money has bred temptation at all levels. Executives at Enron, World Com, and other corporations, intoxicated by the heady atmosphere of deregulation, defraud shareholders of billions and get away with little or no punishment. The little guy naturally says, If the big shots can get away with it, why not me? So he cheats on his taxes, steals from his company, and downloads music without paying for it.
>
> These may be trivial matters, but Callahan believes they are symptomatic of a deeper disease in the body politic. The infection takes hold as early as high school or college (cheating is rampant on campus), feeding (and feeding on) the conviction that success in life requires cutting moral corners, that success is ultimately defined in monetary terms.[7]

The result of this winner-take-all ethos, Callahan thinks, is a nation increasingly falling into two groups: a "winning class" who cheated their way to the top and an "anxious class" who fear falling behind if they too do not cheat.[8]

Do you think Callahan is correct? Is America in moral decline? When the Gallup organization polled Americans about their primary concerns, moral decline was cited by about 10 percent of those whom we might label "conservatives" but only 1 percent of "liberals."[9] If we look just at the facts of individual behavior, we can actually find some reasons for optimism. For example, violent crime has been in steady decline, falling by one-third from 1994 to 2003.[10] Likewise, teen sexual activity, cocaine and marijuana use, and welfare case loads have been on the decline for sometime.[11] Not surprisingly, then, the record is mixed; but certainly we can all point to ample room for improvement. [For the Josephson Institute of Ethics, see **http://www.jiethics.org/**]

Sex or Cell Phone?

Fourteen percent of cell phone users admit to having interrupted sex to answer their cell phones. A 2005 survey of more than 3,000 people, 15 to 35 years of age in 15 nations, found Germans and Spaniards (22 percent) most likely to answer the phone, with Italians least likely at 7 percent and Americans in the middle at 15 percent. Almost half of those responding worldwide thought their cell phones said as much about them as a car, while one-third of the Americans surveyed felt the same way.

Advertising giant BBDO commissioned the survey. Christine Hannis, BBDO head of communications explained, "People can't bear to miss a call. Getting so many calls . . . fulfills a fundamental insecurity."

Sources. Bill Hoffman, "Cell Users Put Sex on Hold," *New York Post Online Edition*, "BBDO Releases Cell Phones and Sex Acts Reports," [**http://adage.com/news.cms?newsId=44753** or **http://www.furl.net/item.jsp?id=2605994**].

College Students

Ninety-five percent of 3,000 undergraduate business students polled in 31 universities admit they cheated in high school or college, although only 1 to 2 percent admit having done so "frequently."[12] Professor Joseph Petrick, coauthor of the study, attributes the cheating to "the academic welfare mentality. Business school students feel morally entitled to get what they need to do well in business."[13] Academic ethics expert Donald McCabe's surveys find about 75 percent of college students cheating on either a test or paper at some point, with business majors, fraternity and sorority members, and male students being among those most likely to cheat.[14] Technology now facilitates cheating with papers available on demand and cell phones as handy storage devices. McCabe finds that about 35 percent of American college students admit to Internet-based cut and paste plagiarism, with 10 percent admitting to buying papers online.[15] [For the Center for Academic Integrity, see **www.academicintegrity.org**]

These contemporary cheating behaviors are an interesting contrast to the views of a 1928 Princeton University freshman writing home:

> Father, you suggest that the greatest benefit from college is to be found in . . . habits of intellectual diligence and application. I am nonetheless putting my chief emphasis on the study of right and wrong.[16]

UCLA's annual survey of college first-year students provides further evidence of dramatically changing values. Responding to the 2003 survey, 73.8 percent of new freshmen identified financial success as a very important objective, whereas a record-low 39.3 percent considered developing a "meaningful philosophy of life" important.[17] Those results represent essentially a reversal of freshmen objectives from 30–40 years ago.

Questions

1. *a.* Are you more committed to making money or finding a philosophy of life?
   b. Does it matter? Explain.
2. The 1928 Princeton freshman ranked learning about right and wrong ahead of his father's advice to pursue intellectual growth.
   a. What do you think your parents most hope you will achieve from your college years?
   b. What do you value most? Explain.

Business Practice

The corporate scandals at Enron, Arthur Andersen, WorldCom, Adelphia, and others brought front-page attention to long-felt doubts about the integrity of the business community. As the following Gallup Poll results depict, Americans for decades have had little faith in the ethics of businesspeople. Respondents were asked to rate the honesty and integrity of people in various fields on a scale of very high, high, average, low, or very low.

Honesty and Ethics in Various Professions

	Percentage Saying Very High or High					
	1977	1985	1995	2000	2002	2004
Nurses				79	79	79
Druggists/pharmacists		65	66	67	67	72
Medical doctors	51	58	54	63	63	67
Police	37	47	41	55	59	60
Clergy	61	67	56	60	52	56
Bankers	39	38	27	37	36	36
Congressional representatives	16	20	10	21	17	20
Business executives	19	23	19	23	17	20
Lawyers	26	27	16	19	18	18
Stockbrokers		20	16	19	12	
Advertising practitioners	10	12	10	10	9	10
Car salespeople	8	5	5	7	6	9

Source: David Moore, "Nurses Top List in Honesty and Ethics Poll," December 7, 2004, [http://www.gallup.com/poll/content/login.aspx?ci=14236]. Reprinted by permission.

Are the recent scandals mere aberrations? Is the public mistaken in its assessment of business ethics? We don't have a definitive answer, but polling data provide some insights. A 2000 KPMG survey of 2,390 employees nationwide found that 76 percent of the respondents had observed what they believed to be illegal and/or unethical conduct on the job.[18] A similar 2000 survey, however, found only about one-third of employees reporting "misconduct" at work, and that number fell to 22 percent in 2003.[19] A 2003 Wirthlin Worldwide survey of the general public as well as 150 executives examined trust in corporations after the scandals involving Enron, WorldCom, and others:

- Just over a third of adults surveyed believed that top U.S. businesses operate ethically.
- 79 percent of the executives believed most major firms operate ethically.
- 61 percent of the public agreed that mistrust of major U.S. employers is justified by the corporate scandals.
- 71 percent of the executives said the scandalous behavior of a few had unfairly tarnished the image of many corporations.[20]

So the evidence suggests that we have reason to be concerned about the ethics of business practice. At the same time, we can be greatly encouraged by the intense current interest of businesses, scholars, think tanks, and others in ethical concerns.

Why Do Some Managers Cheat?

Moral Development

Scholars argue that some individuals are better "educated" to make ethical judgments than others. Psychologist Lawrence Kohlberg built and empirically tested a comprehensive theory of moral development in which he claimed that moral judgment evolves and improves primarily as a function of age and education.

Kohlberg, via interviews with children as they aged, was able to identify moral development as movement through distinct stages, with the later stages being improvements on the earlier ones. Kohlberg identified six universal stages grouped into three levels:

1. **Preconventional level:**
   Stage 1: Obey rules to avoid punishment.
   Stage 2: Follow rules only if it is in own interest, but let others do the same. Conform to secure rewards.

2. **Conventional level:**
   Stage 3: Conform to meet the expectations of others. Please others. Adhere to stereotypical images.
   Stage 4: Doing right is one's duty. Obey the law. Uphold the social order.

3. **Postconventional or principled level:**
   Stage 5: Current laws and values are relative. Laws and duty are obeyed on rational calculations to serve the greatest number.
   Stage 6: Follow self-chosen universal ethical principles. In the event of conflicts, principles override laws.[21]

At Level 3 the individual is able to reach independent moral judgments that may or may not conform with conventional societal wisdom. Thus the Level 2 manager might refrain from sexual harassment because it constitutes a violation of company policy and the law. A manager at Level 3 might reach the same conclusion, but his or her decision would be based on independently defined universal principles of justice.

Kohlberg found that many adults never pass beyond Level 2. Consequently, if Kohlberg was correct, many managers may behave unethically simply because they have not reached the upper stages of moral maturity.

Kohlberg's model is based on extensive longitudinal and cross-cultural studies over more than three decades. For example, one set of Chicago-area boys was interviewed at 3-year intervals for 20 years. Thus the stages of moral growth exhibit "definite empirical characteristics" such that Kohlberg was able to claim that his model had been scientifically validated.[22] Although many critics remain, the evidence, in sum, supports Kohlberg's general proposition. [For more information about Kohlberg's theory of moral development, see **http://snycorva.cortland.edu/~ANDERSMD/KOHL/content.HTML**]

Feminine Voice   One of those lines of criticism requires a brief inspection. Carol Gilligan, a colleague of Kohlberg, contends that our conceptions of morality are, in substantial part, gender-based.[23] She claims that men typically approach morality as a function of justice, impartiality, and rights (the ethic of justice), whereas women are more likely to build a morality based on care, support, and responsiveness (the ethic of care). Men, she says, tend to take an impersonal, universal view of morality as contrasted with the feminine "voice" that rises more commonly from relationships and concern for the specific needs of others. Gilligan criticizes Kohlberg because his highest stages, 5 and 6, are structured in terms of the male approach to morality while the feminine voice falls at stage 3. Further, Kohlberg's initial experimental subjects were limited to young males. The result, in Gilligan's view, is that women are underscored. Of course, a danger in the ethic of care is that it might be interpreted to restore and legitimize the stereotype of women as care-giving subordinates not deserving of moral autonomy.[24] Furthermore, other scholarly studies have failed to find a meaningful difference in moral reasoning by gender.[25] [For an organization of young business leaders committed to "responsible management practice," see **http://www.net-impact.org/**]

Testing Honesty around the World

Reader's Digest intentionally "lost" more than 1,100 wallets in 117 cities to see how many would be returned. The wallets contained up to $50 along with a name and phone number. Some of the results:

- 44 percent were not returned.
- All wallets in Norway and Denmark were returned.
- Nearly 70 percent were returned in the United States.

Source: Lori Joseph and Marcy E. Mullins, "Testing Honesty around the World," *USA TODAY,* May 1, 2001, p. 1A.

Organizational Forces

The businessperson's individual moral stance obviously plays a role in workplace wrongs, but a considerable body of evidence suggests that forces external to the individual are also quite influential. A 2004 survey found corporate CEOs clearly affirming that business ethics has achieved new prominence in corporate practice because of the scandals of recent years:

> 81 percent of the CEOs believe that standards for corporate ethics have risen since the scandals.

- 81 percent of the CEOs believe that standards for corporate ethics have risen since the scandals.
- 74 percent of the CEOs indicated that their companies had changed their ethics policies in recent years.[26]

More important, perhaps, employees affirm that changes have been made. A 2003 nationwide survey shows that employees clearly have better feelings about their companies' ethical posture than they did in 2000:

- 82 percent of employees in 2003 felt that top management kept promises as compared with 77 percent in 2000.
- Both actual observed misconduct and pressure to compromise ethics declined from 2000 to 2003. Observed misconduct fell from 31 percent to 22 percent and pressure fell from 13 to 10 percent.
- Of special importance to students, the survey notes that managers under 30 years of age and with less than three years in the organization were twice as likely to feel pressure to cheat (21 percent to 10 percent).
- The types of misconduct most frequently observed included intimidating behavior (21 percent), misreporting of hours worked (20 percent), and lying (19 percent).
- 44 percent of nonmanagement employees do not report the misconduct they observe, and only 58 percent of all employees reporting misconduct are satisfied with the

organizational response.[27] [For the Business Roundtable Institute for Corporate Ethics, see **www.corporate-ethics.org**]

The pressure to produce is, of course, very great for those at the bottom of the power structure; but it often does not go away with advancement. Thirty graduates of the Harvard MBA program agreed to in-depth interviews about their on-the-job ethics experiences. One interesting conclusion from the interviews was the degree to which these younger subordinates understood and empathized with the pressure felt by their primarily middle-manager bosses:

> I really feel for people who are middle management, with a wife and four kids, under financial strain. . . .You see it happen all the time, that people are indicted for fraud or larceny. You can empathize with their situation. The world is changing fast. And a lot of people have been blindsided by it—so they've done things that they don't like. I can't say that will never happen to me. It's easy for me as a single person . . . but when you're desperate, you're desperate. [My boss] was not willfully unethical. It was the pressure of the time. . . . I have no idea what pressures were on him to drive the project. It probably wasn't [his] initiative to fudge the numbers. There may have been a good intention at some point in the organization. But as it got filtered through the organization, it changed. Some executive may have said, "This is an interesting project." Unfortunately this got translated as, "The vice president really wants this project." This sort of thing can happen a lot. Things start on high. As they go down they are filtered, modified. What was a positive comment several levels above becomes "do this or die" several levels down.[28] [For a variety of business ethics links, see **http://www.ethics.ubc.ca/resources/business/**]

> [My boss] was not willfully unethical. It was the pressure of the time

The Boss

Scholarly evidence and common sense suggest that bosses are crucial in setting the ethical climate in an organization. *The Wall Street Journal* reviewed Dial Corporation (the soap company) CEO Herb Baum's new leadership book:

> In *The Transparent Leader,* Herb Baum argues that a climate of integrity is crucial to the success of a public company and that it begins at the top.
> Mr. Baum . . . is at the top himself, but he drives a VW Beetle to work, he tells us, and doesn't have a reserved parking space. Not that he minds: He arrives at 5 AM, ahead of the crowd. He espouses straight talk, solid values, and hiring literally good people—as opposed to people who are merely good at their jobs. His catchall term for this ethos is "transparency."
> How to create it? Mr. Baum rightly insists that it has to come from the chief executive's office. He emphasizes valuing people by keeping an open door, communicating honestly, listening carefully, and making sure that integrity permeates every aspect of the company. Hypocrisy is anathema: "A lot of CEOs, including me, are overpaid," he says bluntly—and at one point he distributed his annual bonus to Dial's lowest-paid employees.[29]

> Managers are the ethics teachers of their organizations.

Ethics Teachers? Harvard business ethics professor Joseph Badaracco has said "managers are the ethics teachers of their organizations."[30] If so, we would be forced to conclude that many corporate leaders have been teaching the wrong ethics lessons. As Business for Social Responsibility observed,

> The Enron debacle has made it crystal clear that a failure of ethical leadership at the rarefied heights of a corporation—in the executive suite boardroom—can destroy a company.[31]

At this writing, Andrew Fastow, former Enron chief financial officer, has pleaded guilty to committing federal crimes that helped destroy the now bankrupt energy giant, formerly the seventh largest American corporation. Fastow is cooperating in the government's case against former Enron bosses Kenneth Lay (chairman), Jeffrey Skilling (chief executive), and Richard Causey (chief accounting officer). In the first criminal case emerging from the scandal, one midlevel Enron boss and four former Merrill Lynch bankers were found guilty in 2004 of conspiracy and fraud. A crucial part of Lay's early defense strategy seems to be a classic for many corporate bosses: He claims he did not know what was happening beneath him. *The Wall Street Journal* reports that several scandal-tied CEOs are making a similar claim:

> Call it the reverse Nuremberg strategy. Chief executives of scandal-ridden companies such as WorldCom, Sotheby's Holdings Inc., Cendant Corp., and now Enron Corp. all have claimed that they didn't know about the alleged fraud at their businesses and blamed it largely on underlings.
>
> It is the opposite of the defense used at the Nuremberg trials, when Hitler's minions claimed they were only carrying out orders from above. In the corporate fraud cases, the argument is that the top dog was so above the fray that he didn't know what directives were being issued or carried out by those below him. . . .
>
> The Sarbanes-Oxley Act, which requires CEOs and their chief financial officers to sign all financial statements attesting to their veracity, was designed in part to short-circuit such defenses.[32]

[For the Business Roundtable Institute for Corporate Ethics, see **http://www.darden .virginia.edu/corporate-ethics/**]

Keep On Cheating?   Some corporate officers not only cheat stockholders, employees, and the public while in office, but they continue to loot the corporate treasury after they have left. Many of these executives have "just cause" clauses in their contracts that make firing them difficult. If they are forced out, they often have "golden parachute" arrangements that let them collect millions as severance pay. Former PeopleSoft CEO Craig Conway reportedly managed a nice deal for himself despite his dubious conduct:

> They often have "golden parachute" arrangements that let them collect millions as severance pay.

> The former chief executive of PeopleSoft Inc. lied to Wall Street analysts about the company's business. So what happened to him? He got to keep his job for a year, and when he was finally fired, he walked away with a huge severance package. . . .
>
> Conway was ousted about a month ago, in part because of his clashes with other senior managers. But there was also the big lie that got him in trouble. Conway played down the effect on PeopleSoft's business when he was asked at a September 2003 meeting with Wall Street analysts whether customers were holding back purchases because of a potential sale (of PeopleSoft) to Oracle. "The last remaining customers whose business decisions were being delayed have actually completed their sales and completed their orders. So I don't see it as a disruptive factor," Conway said.[33]

Conway later admitted he knew that statement to be untrue, but he said it anyway because he was "promoting, promoting, promoting."[34] So what happened to Conway? According to newspaper accounts, his severance package may total as much as $50 million.[35] In response to these situations, 40 percent of the biggest American corporations now do not have written contracts with their CEOs, in part so that firing is easier and less expensive.[36] [For extensive data on more than 1,500 corporations, see Hoover's Online at **http://www.hoovers.com**]

Bank Robber to Boardroom

Some bosses go wrong but correct their lives—none more dramatically than James Joseph Minder, 74-year-old former chairman of Smith & Wesson Holding Corp. In his twenties, Minder was the notorious "Shotgun Bandit" of Michigan. He committed dozens of armed holdups, some while a student at the University of Michigan. On one occasion he terrorized employees before stealing $53,000 from a branch of Manufacturers National Bank. He served time in prison and was free of trouble, he says, after 1965. After release from prison in 1969, he spent 20 years successfully setting up group homes and programs for troubled children and young adults. After retiring in the 1990s Minder got involved in the gun industry and eventually became chair of Smith & Wesson. Then in 2004 a reporter came to his home asking about his past, a life he had not hidden but one he had not advertised either. At first he denied he was the "Bandit," but he reconsidered and decided, "I had better tell the truth." He later told the other members of the Smith & Wesson board and resigned as chairman.

Source: Vanessa O'Connell, "How Troubled Past Finally Caught Up with James Minder," *The Wall Street Journal,* March 8, 2004, p. A1.

Questions—Part Two

1. *a.* Do you think it is important for our character development to have heroes in our lives? Explain.
   b. Do you think we have fewer heroes today than in the past? Explain.
   c. Do you have a hero? Explain.

2. Rank the following by the standard, "the most important problem facing the country today is . . .":
   a. Poverty.
   b. Education.
   c. Morality/ethics/family values.
   d. Social Security.
   e. Teen violence in school.
   f. Drugs/alcohol.
   g. Too many guns/gun control.
   h. Health care cost/availability.

3. What forces would you say are chiefly responsible for misconduct in the workplace?

4. Does a corporation have a conscience? Explain. See Kenneth Goodpaster and John B. Matthews, Jr., "Can a Corporation Have a Conscience?" *Harvard Business Review,* January–February 1982, p. 136.

5. As explained earlier, psychologist Lawrence Kohlberg developed a theory of moral development holding that humans proceed through six stages before reaching moral maturity. Kohlberg built his theory from interviewees' responses to a series of moral dilemmas.

For example (stated briefly), should you steal drugs if doing so is the only way to save your spouse's life?

a. Is Kohlberg's theory consistent with your own view of moral development? Explain.

b. Rank your moral development using Kohlberg's scale.

c. Carol Gilligan has argued that men and women have differing moral languages. Gilligan suggests women make moral decisions based on responsibility and caring, whereas moral decision making for males is founded in rules and justice. Comment.

d. Many men continue to have negative attitudes toward women as managers/executives. Would you expect to find lower levels of moral development in these men? Explain.

Part Three—Business Ethics in Practice

Introduction: Ethics Codes

Having established a general ethics foundation, we turn now to ethics in practice. A long-favored device for institutionalizing ethical standards is the ethics code. Most big companies have voluntarily developed ethics codes; but with the passage and continuing implementation of the federal Sarbanes-Oxley Act (SOX), all publicly traded companies now must develop and use ethics codes. Sarbanes was passed after Enron and other recent corporate scandals as a way to reduce financial and accounting fraud, thus maintaining confidence in America's financial markets. Section 406 of Sarbanes specifically requires publicly traded companies to adopt a code of ethics for senior financial officers or to explain why they have not done so. Section 406 defines *code of ethics* as written standards that are reasonably designed to deter wrongdoing and to promote such behaviors as honest conduct, full disclosure in reports, compliance with all applicable laws and rules, prompt reporting of violations, and methods for conforming to the code's expectations. Section 406 also requires public disclosure (as in a company's annual report) of the code. Furthermore, the New York Stock Exchange and the NASDAQ National Market listing standards require listed companies to adopt and publicly disclose ethics codes for *all* directors, officers, and employees. Topics to be addressed include conflicts of interest, insider trading, fair dealing, and so on.

So at least for publicly traded companies, the once voluntary and often underutilized code of ethics now has become a matter of law with potentially serious consequences if ignored. Therefore, companies are rewriting their codes to make them more detailed and specific. German software giant SAP, for example, has a 14-page code with sections describing acceptable conduct with customers, vendors, and competitors.[37] Codes are being more prominently displayed, and frequently all employees are being required to read and sign the codes. Companies are also creating training sessions to be sure that their codes are well understood and to push the codes more firmly into the total decision-making process. [For the Ethics Officers Association, see **http://www.eoa.org/**]

Whether the new attention to codes will prove beneficial remains to be seen. At worst the codes are a starting point for building a more ethically alert and concerned company culture. And importantly, the company that can show clear compliance with code expectations may be more generously treated by the justice system if criminal problems do emerge. (Additional Sarbanes-Oxley discussion follows in this chapter and in Chapter 9.) [For the Ethics Resource Center, see **http://www. ethics.org/index.html;** for information on global corporate governance and citizenship, see **http://www.conference-board.org/**]

Bribery Abroad

As just explained, strategies for curbing corrupt business practices around the world have become a matter of urgency in this era of closely entwined stock markets and financial institutions. What was once merely a Western standard of ethical business practice has now become, the American business community believes, a necessity for the entire global economy; but that new expectation raises complex ethical dilemmas for America's multinational businesses. In many cultures, the payment of bribes—*baksheesh* (Middle East), *huilu* (China), *vzyatku* (Russia), *mordida* (South America), or *dash* (Africa)—is accepted as necessary and, in some cases, a lawful way of doing business. American firms and officers wishing to succeed abroad have faced great pressure to engage in practices that are illegal and unethical in the American culture. For example, Lucent Technologies, the telecommunications equipment maker, announced in 2004 that it had fired four executives based in China for possible violations of the Foreign Corrupt Practices Act (FCPA), the chief federal weapon against bribery abroad. The possible violations were not detailed, but the problems in China were discovered as part of a series of FCPA compliance audits by Lucent that were implemented after the company allegedly paid $15 million in bribes to a Saudi Arabian minister in exchange for favorable treatment.[38]

The FCPA was enacted in 1977 in response to disclosure of widespread bribery by American firms. In brief, the FCPA, provides that U.S. nationals and businesses acting anywhere in the world, as well as foreign nationals and companies acting in the United States, are engaging in criminal conduct if they offer or provide bribes to foreign government officials to obtain "any improper advantage." In addition, the FCPA requires rigorous internal accounting controls and careful record keeping to ensure that bribes cannot be concealed via "slush funds" and other devices. The act does not forbid "grease" payments to foreign officials or political parties where the purpose of the payments is "to expedite or to secure the performance of a routine governmental action,"[39] such as processing papers (like visas), providing police protection, and securing phone service. And those accused may offer the affirmative defense that the alleged payoff was lawful in the host country or was a normal, reasonable business expenditure directed to specific marketing and contract performance activities. Criminal penalties include fines of up to $2 million for companies, while individuals may be fined $100,000 and imprisoned for as long as five years if they either participate in a violation, know of a violation, or are "aware of the high probability of the existence" of a bribery situation "unless the person actually believes that such circumstance does not exist."[40] That is, corporations and individuals cannot use "head-in-sand" tactics to avoid knowledge of wrongdoing. [For a summary of the FCPA, see **http://www.fcpaenforcement.com/ explained/explained.asp**]

Controversy

The FCPA has been controversial from the outset. Some businesspeople see it as a blessing both because it is an honorable attempt at a firm moral stance and because it is often useful for an American businessperson abroad to say, "No, our laws forbid me from doing that." On the other hand, some have seen the act as damaging to our competitiveness. Now other nations are recognizing that corruption is a great risk to the global economy. Once believing that bribery aided the poor, most industrial countries are now moving toward the zero tolerance view held by the United States, recognizing that the money mainly goes to the well connected and that bribery is inefficient, harmful to democratic institutions, and a threat to world financial stability. In addition to the FCPA, the United States also participates in several other anticorruption initiatives including the United Nations Convention against Corruption, the OECD Anti-Bribery Convention, and the Inter-American Convention. The United States has an immense interest in a level playing field and sound international financial practices. A recent State Department study found over $24 billion in lost international contracts for U.S. firms over a five-year period where bribes allegedly influenced the outcome.[41] German firms have legally spent an estimated $3 billion per year in bribes,[42] although the Anti-Bribery Convention is expected to change that practice. [For details on the OECD Anti-Bribery Convention, see **www.oecd.org**]

United States Corruption   Although the United States has been the clear world leader in pursuing anticorruption efforts, we should not be unduly prideful. Indeed, the United States is tied for 17th in the world on Transparency International's 2004 Corruption Perceptions Index, which ranks countries based on the degree of *perceived* corruption among public officials and politicians.[43] Finland is regarded as least corrupt in government, and most of northern Europe as well as the United Kingdom and Canada are viewed as less corrupt than the United States. Our chief economic rivals, Germany (15) and Japan (24), rank just above and somewhat below the United States.[44] Not surprisingly, corruption was perceived to be highest in poorer nations, with Haiti and Bangladesh tied for last in the Transparency ranking.[45]

Corruption in Practice   A 2002 Gallup Poll of private-sector leaders in 15 emerging market nations, including India, the Philippines, and South Korea, asked the leaders' sense of how frequently corporations bribe senior public officials in their nations. Corporations from Australia, Sweden, and Switzerland were perceived to be first, second, and third in employing the *least* amount of bribery, whereas Russian and Chinese companies were considered to employ the *greatest* amount. U.S. corporations ranked 13th and showed "a high propensity" to pay bribes to foreign government officials.[46]

A Transparency International survey found about 10 percent of people worldwide saying they or a member of their household had actually paid a bribe in the previous year.[47] Remarkably, every third student in Lithuania reports having given a bribe to a teacher to improve grades, avoid being expelled, or to solve some other problem.[48] Forty percent of firms pay bribes according to a World Bank survey of 3,600 companies in 69 countries,[49] but the World Bank found some good news in a 2004 report showing a likely decline in corruption in many Eastern European and Central Asian nations.[50] Likewise, survey data in Mexico indicate that bribes to achieve a public service such as garbage pickup have fallen significantly in recent years.[51]

"Massive" Bribes

"The scale of bribe-paying by international corporations in the developing countries of the world is massive. Actions by the majority of governments of the leading industrial countries to curb international corruption are modest. The results include growing poverty in poor countries, persistent undermining of the institutions of democracy, and mounting distortions in fair international commerce."

Source: Peter Eigen, Chair, Transparency International, January 20, 2000 [**http://www.transparency.org/cpi/ 1999/bps.html**].

Questions

1. To some, the FCPA and the Anti-Bribery Convention are merely further evidence of American paternalism or imperialism. What do they mean?

2. America ranked 17th in the 1998 Corruption Perception Index, about the same ranking as in infant mortality. Journalist Martin Dyckman says that every nation ahead of us in the Corruption Index is also ahead of us in preventing infant deaths.[52] Everyone, Dyckman explains, also has a national health care system. Do you see any relationship between our comparatively poor showing in the Corruption Index and our comparatively poor showing in infant mortality? Explain.

3. Carl Kaufmann of Du Pont raised the following bribery issue. As the head of a multinational corporation, you learn that one of your plant managers has been arrested in a distant republic. His alleged crime is that goods found in your warehouse lack the proper customs stamp and papers. But the truth is more complicated. For years, *grease* has been a way of life in this country's bureaucracy, and your plant manager has been paying gratuities to the customs officers. But he knows it is against home office policy, and so he stops. Their inspection follows. The price for dropping all charges: $18,000.

   a. Would you pay up? Or let your manager be put in jail? Explain.

   b. Which alternative is more ethical?[53] Explain.

4. Your employer, as you see it, is taking advantage of poor, powerless production workers in an overseas subsidiary located in a country where jobs are in short supply. You are a midlevel manager in the home office.

   a. Do you have any responsibility in the situation abroad?

   b. What should you do? Explain.

Corporate/White Collar Crime

Martha Stewart has served
her time in prison

At this writing, Martha Stewart has served her time in prison for lying and obstruction of justice, Enron's top executives are facing prosecution and others are in jail, accounting giant Arthur Andersen has been destroyed by its part in the Enron scandal, and on and on and on. Are we in the midst of a corporate crime wave? We cannot be sure, but the evidence suggests that corporations and their bosses may be at greater risk of prosecution than ever before in American history. *The Wall Street Journal* summed up that risk:

> There may never have been a worse time to be a corporate criminal. . . . The reason: After a wave of corporate-fraud cases, prosecutors want to send a signal that executives aren't above the law. What's more, tough federal sentencing guidelines that take into account the number of investor victims and how much money they lost have resulted in extremely long recommended sentences.[54]

Fraud is so commonplace that 10 percent of all publicly traded companies have been forced to restate their earnings from 1999 to 2004.[55] Since the formation of a special federal task force in mid-2002, more than 500 of 900 individuals indicted in 400 corporate fraud cases have been convicted with many prosecutions not yet complete.[56] Perhaps to an unprecedented degree, those indictments and convictions have reached to the top of the American wealth and power pyramid. In addition to Martha Stewart, former Tyco CEO Dennis Koslowski, former WorldCom chief, Bernard Ebbers, Adelphia founder John Rigas, and his son Timothy are among those who have been convicted of fraud, conspiracy, or other crimes. Furthermore, the sentences emerging from these convictions have not been mere hand slaps. For example, Ebbers, who oversaw the largest corporate fraud in American history, was sentenced to 25 years in prison. In addition, Ebbers settled the civil claims against him by forfeiting some $45 million, leaving his wife with a modest Mississippi home and about $50,000. At this writing, the only exception to the striking setbacks for corporate chiefs is Richard Scrushy, Health South founder, who was accused of playing a leading role in a $2.7 billion accounting scheme. Scrushy was acquitted of all charges, but he faces civil claims from the Securities and Exchange Commission. [For the National White Collar Crime Center, see **http://www.nw3c.org/**]

Shoplifting—Not a Sin?

In 1997 a British priest, the Reverend John Papworth, reportedly suggested that shoplifting is not a sin—as long as the victim is a big supermarket. In a radio interview Reverend Papworth then explained, "With these institutions, all you are confronted with are these boardroom barons . . . plotting how to take the maximum amount of money out of people's pockets for the minimum in return." Papworth said he did not mean to encourage shoplifting, although "if people wander in and wander out without paying for the stuff I think it is a perfectly comprehensible action."

Do you feel any sympathy for Papworth's position?

Source: Associated Press, "Thou Shalt Not Steal, Except . . . ," *Des Moines Register,* March 16, 1997, p. 8A.

Punishment   Responding to public outrage as Enron and the other corporate scandals surfaced, Congress felt great pressure to strengthen federal criminal laws dealing with corporate fraud. The result was the aforementioned 2002 Sarbanes-Oxley Act (SOX), which significantly increased penalties and provided other aggressive measures for attacking corporate crime by publicly traded companies. Among its major provisions, the bill

- Establishes an independent board to oversee the accounting profession.
- Requires corporate executives to personally certify the accuracy of their financial reports.
- Creates new crimes and raises penalties to as much as 25 years imprisonment along with heavy fines.
- Requires publicly traded companies to establish internal control systems designed to assure the accuracy of financial information (Section 404, perhaps the key provision).
- Requires publicly traded companies to disclose whether they have adopted an ethics code for senior financial management, and if not, why they have not done so (see p. 61 for greater detail).

Along with Sarbanes, rules from the Justice Department, the SEC, the stock exchanges, and the Federal Sentencing Guidelines have all been toughened to attack corporate crime.

To achieve greater predictability and consistency in punishment for both white-collar and street crime, the sentencing guidelines provide ranges (such as 10–12 months imprisonment) within which judges are advised to impose sentences. Basically, the guidelines employ a chart that considers the crime's "offense level" and the defendant's "criminal history" to establish the appropriate punishment range. The sentencing guidelines for organizations now specifically expect companies to vigorously promote an organizational culture of ethical behavior and compliance with the law. Companies are to establish standards and procedures to prevent and detect crime, and the burden for achieving compliance is placed squarely on the board of directors and top-level executives. Compliance and ethics training are to be provided for all employees, and compliance programs are to be audited, monitored, and evaluated for effectiveness.[57]

> Across America, corporations have created ethics and anticrime programs

Those companies, officers, and directors who comply with the guidelines may receive leniency if punishment is imposed. Aggravating factors such as a leadership role in an offense can increase the punishment. Thus, across America, corporations have created ethics and anticrime programs, along with sophisticated financial monitoring systems to ensure compliance. Corporations are operating in a new criminal law environment where white-collar crime, once treated more gently than street crime, is now a law enforcement target:

> The current climate for white-collar wrongdoers is similar to the climate that arose for street criminals in the 1980s and 1990s when "three strikes" laws and mandatory penalties became fashionable. Now an office worker holding a bag of shredded documents may as well be holding a bag of cocaine. Authorities are anxious to prosecute; they have the resources to identify and pursue the wrongdoers; and the penalties are severe, equaling or exceeding those being given to convicted drug dealers.[58]

The new intensity in pursuing corporate crime comes, of course, at a heavy price both for the government and for the corporations that must comply:

Tom Martin, audit operations manager for Boise Cascade Corp. in Boise, Idaho, estimates that his company will spend about $7 million a year on Sarbanes-Oxley compliance, including 20,000 auditor hours this year, after recording 17,000 auditor hours on Sarbanes-Oxley compliance last year.[59]

Guidelines Now Uncertain

The Federal Sentencing Guidelines, once mandatory for judges, are, at this writing in 2005, to be treated as recommendations as a consequence of a recent Supreme Court decision. Judges are now expected to consult the guidelines for advice in sentencing, but they are no longer required to strictly adhere to them. The practical consequences of the decision are uncertain, but many experts think that judges will continue to be significantly influenced by the guidelines in sentencing both individuals and corporations. Congress may choose to respond to the Supreme Court decision with new legislation.

Source: United States v. Booker, 125 S. Ct. 738 (2005).

Too Much?   Critics of this regulatory activism see the open market as the best protection against corporate misconduct. To the critics, the existing laws were adequate, and the new measures are a politicized overreaction to scandals affecting a relatively small part of the economy. From a free market perspective, the greatest concern is that SOX, the revised sentencing guidelines, and the other new rules are another government-inflicted drag on the economy—both in the cost of compliance and in reducing the willingness to take the risks that are a crucial motivator for a growing economy. [For the United States Sentencing Commission, see **http://www.ussc.gov/**]

The following article details an effort by the University of Maryland to educate and frighten its MBA students into compliance with the law once on the job.

READING

Inmates Teach MBA Students Ethics from behind Bars

James Cox, Cumberland, Maryland

Before getting diplomas Wednesday night, the University of Maryland's MBA graduates got a lesson in life from distinguished alumnus Gerard Evans.

A lawyer renowned as the state's highest-paid lobbyist, he boasts deep ties to the university. He earned a master's degree at Maryland, taught there, and served on the school's board of visitors. Currently he is a doctoral candidate in the American Studies program.

Evans does his doctoral work at a distance, though, because he also happens to be prisoner No. 33950-037 at the Cumberland, Maryland, Federal Correctional Institution here.

A trip to prison is mandatory for second-year Maryland MBA students, part of an ethics class intended to puncture their sometimes sizable egos just weeks before they graduate and leap to the corporate world. Maryland officials describe the one-day prison field trip as a kind of "scared-straight" program for MBAs. The purpose is to show them how smart, successful, business-savvy overachievers—people like them—can land in the slammer.

Murders, rapes, assaults, and other violent crimes have been declining across the United States over the past two decades. But rates of embezzlement, fraud, and other white-collar crimes have proved stubbornly resistant, remaining steady despite beefed-up law enforcement efforts.

Experts say computers and cross-border commerce have made white-collar crimes easier to commit and easier to conceal. At the same time, the growing ranks of women in top jobs have led to a surge in the number of women convicted of embezzlement and other financial crimes, says the National White-Collar Crime Center.

Few graduates will confront more on-the-job pressure, responsibility, and temptation than the latest U.S. crop of 100,000 MBA graduates. In an annual rite of spring, Wall Street investment banks, consulting firms, and consumer products marketers are scooping them up and launching them on high-flying careers.

Many of Maryland's 188 MBA graduates are leaving school with dream jobs in hand—at Marriott, Deloitte & Touche, Accenture, Booz Allen & Hamilton, Johnson & Johnson, Intel, Citibank, and other companies. Their starting salaries, with bonuses, are likely to top last year's average of $85,959.

It's important that hubris doesn't bring these newly minted MBAs crashing to earth, says Larry Penley, dean of the college of business at Arizona State University.

"A single person with an MBA makes decisions that have a huge impact on a business," he says. "If you look at some of the recent scandals, you (typically) see a person with a lot of autonomy in a global corporation that has a centralized information system. The damage you can do under those circumstances is considerable."

SKILLS GONE AWRY

Hubris was central to the downfall of Evans and two other white-collar offenders telling their tales to the Maryland MBA students.

"I felt that I could do no wrong," says inmate Monte Greenbaum, former CEO of a property management firm now serving 18 months at the prison camp for fraud.

Greenbaum, who holds an accounting degree from Maryland, describes the networking skills that brought him wealth and got him elected president of the state board of public accounting. "I had everything.... I could have retired five years ago. We were looking at retirement properties in Arizona."

Retirement was off when he was nabbed shifting funds between buildings he owned and those he managed for the Department of Housing and Urban Development.

Greenbaum, 52, says he informed HUD of his moves and had every intention of eventually squaring accounts. "But if you rob a bank and put all the money back, you still robbed a bank," he says.

Ego also may have gotten the better of Evans, once a $1 million-a-year lobbyist in Annapolis. The 45-year-old was sentenced to 30 months for fraud after he was accused of conspiring to get a lawmaker to sponsor a bogus bill intended to bring panicky clients to his lobbying firm.

*   *   *   *   *

Evans, Greenbaum, and convicted embezzler Greg Gamble, 49, sound other common themes. They say it's the little gray-area decisions that ultimately lead to more serious ethical and legal breaches.

"That got to me," student Patricia Martinez says later. "It made me think we're all just one decision away from the big decision that leads to trouble."

Source: *USA TODAY,* May 25, 2001, p. 2B. Copyright 2001, USA TODAY. Reprinted with permission.

Questions

1. In your judgment is cheating in school likely to lead to cheating on the job? Explain.
2. Does the market punish corporate criminals? Explain.

Whistle-Blowing

Erin Brockovich, with a boost from Julia Roberts, may be the most famous whistle-blower, but Sherron Watkins of Enron must be among the most courageous. She decided to speak out against her employer, Enron, one of the most financially and politically powerful organizations in America:

Enron executive Sherron Watkins never intended to become a whistle-blower by helping expose the practices that triggered her company's financial collapse.

When Jeffrey Skilling, president of the Houston energy concern, abruptly quit in August [2001], Enron officials set up a special letter-collection box so employees could anonymously vent their worries. Ms. Watkins, vice president for corporate development, wrote an unsigned, one-page note to then-Chairman Kenneth Lay. "Has Enron become a risky place to work?" her letter asked, after questioning its irregular accounting methods.

"I am incredibly nervous that we will implode in a wave of accounting scandals," she continued. "My eight years of Enron will be worth nothing on my résumé."[60]

Today employees seem increasingly inclined to follow the dictates of conscience in speaking out—publicly, if necessary—against wrongdoing by their employers. Historically, complaints were taken to management and resolved there. "Going public" was considered an act of disloyalty. Americans continue to maintain a strong tradition against "squealing." Indeed, management has good reason to discourage irresponsible, precipitous whistle-blowing that might disclose legitimate trade secrets, cause unnecessary conflict among employees, unfairly tarnish the company image, and so on.

> Americans continue to maintain a strong tradition against "squealing"

However, Enron and other recent scandals have caused Congress to include new whistle-blower protections in Sarbanes-Oxley. SOX specifically requires auditors to set up what amounts to a whistle-blowing hotline for employees who want to report accounting and auditing complaints. SOX also forbids employer retaliation against an employee who reports information about corporate fraud, and it makes a crime of interfering with "the lawful employment or livelihood of a person" in retaliation for reporting potential federal offenses to law enforcement authorities. The Whistleblower Protection Act of 1989 and a number of other federal laws help federal employees, and some of those laws also protect private-sector whistle-blowers. [For an overview of whistle-blower activity and protections, see **http://www.whistleblowers.org/**]

Many states now offer whistle-blower protection for public- and/or private-sector employees. And some court decisions have protected whistle-blowers by denying employers the right to fire *at-will* employees (those not working under contract; see Chapter 12) because of their decision to report misconduct. [For a law firm dedicated to representing whistle-blowers as well as the stories of some of those whistle-blowers, see **http://www.phillipsandcohen.com/**]

Retribution   Despite expanded legal protection, whistle-blowers often pay a high price for exercising their consciences. Jack Liles wrote a letter to *The Wall Street Journal* cautioning readers about the risks.

> Folks such as Sherron Watkins at Enron are rarely given a special status or legal protection merely for uncovering an ugly practice or incident, legal or not.
>
> After only four months in a management position at a large *Fortune* 500 firm, I discovered within my department an unethical practice and culture of soliciting for and accepting lavish gifts from vendors and suppliers in exchange for favorable consideration and favoritism in purchasing decisions and contract negotiations.
>
> When I confronted management on the issue and its clear violation of company rules and basic business ethics standards, I was quickly escorted to the parking lot where the

parking decal was scraped from my car and my company I.D. confiscated. I was history.[61]

Questions

1. Why is the role of "squealer" or whistle-blower so repugnant to many Americans?

2. *a.* How would you feel about a classmate who blew the whistle on you for cheating on an examination?

   b. Would you report cheating by a classmate if it came to your attention? Explain.

Internet Exercise

Can ethics be taught? Many people say no. Experts at the Markkula Center for Applied Ethics at Santa Clara University explored that question. Look for their answer at [**http://www.scu.edu/ethics/practicing/decision/canethicsbetaught.html**].

   a. Explain their conclusion.
   b. Do you agree? Explain.

Chapter Questions

1. Can the realistic businessperson expect to be both ethical and successful? Explain.

2. Resolve this ethical dilemma posed by Carl Kaufmann of Du Pont:[62]

   > Assume that federal health investigators are pursuing a report that one of your manu-facturing plants has a higher-than-average incidence of cancer among its employees. The plant happens to keep excellent medical records on all its employees, stretching back for decades, which might help identify the source of the problem. The govern-ment demands the files. But if the company turns them over, it might be accused of violating the privacy of all those workers who had submitted to private medical exams. The company offers an abstract of the records, but the government insists on the complete files, with employee names. Then the company tries to obtain releases from all the workers, but some of them refuse. If you give the records to the feds, the company has broken its commitment of confidentiality. What would you do?

3. Among your classmates, would you expect to find a difference between males and females in the incidence of cheating? Explain.

4. a. In her book *Lying,* Sissela Bok argues that lying by professionals is common-place. For example, she takes the position that prescribing placebos for experi-mental purposes is a lie and immoral. Do you agree with her position? Explain.
   b. Is the use of an unmarked police car an immoral deception? Explain.
   c. One study estimates that Americans average 200 lies per day if one includes "white lies" and inaccurate excuses. On balance, do you believe Americans approve of lying? Explain.

5. *Tonight Show* host Jay Leno performed in commercials encouraging his audience to "eat your body weight in Doritos."[63] He says that he turned down alcohol ads at twice the money. "I don't drink . . . And I don't like to sell it. You don't see dead teenagers on the highway with bags of Doritos scattered around them."[64]

    a. Are you in agreement with the moral distinction that Leno draws between encouraging the consumption of alcohol and encouraging the consumption of Doritos? Explain.

    b. Given the influence of television and of "stars," is all television advertising by celebrities inherently unethical? Explain.

6. The following quote and questions are drawn from Leonard Lewin's "Ethical Aptitude Test."

> As with other goods and services, the medical care available to the rich is superior to that available to the poor. The difference is most conspicuous in the application of new and expensive lifesaving techniques.[65]

    a. Is ability to pay an acceptable way to allocate such services? Explain.

    b. If not, how should such services be apportioned?

    c. Many lifesaving drugs can be tested effectively only on human beings. But often subjects are exposed to such dangers that only those who feel they have nothing to lose willingly participate. Are there any circumstances in which it would be right to conduct such tests without ensuring that the persons tested clearly understood the risks they were taking? Explain.

    d. How much in dollars is the average human life worth?

7. Aaron Burr said, "All things are moral to great men." Regardless of your personal point of view, defend Burr's position.

8. A pharmacist in Lexington, Kentucky, refused to stock over-the-counter weight reducers. His reasons were (1) the active ingredient is the same as that in nasal decongestants; (2) he feared their side effects, such as high blood pressure; and (3) he felt weight reduction should be achieved via self-discipline.[66] Assume the pharmacist manages the store for a group of owners who have given him complete authority about the products stocked. Was his decision ethical? Explain.

9. When *Business and Society Review* surveyed the presidents of 500 large U.S. companies, 51 responded with their reactions to hypothetical moral dilemmas. One question was this:

> Assume that you are president of a firm that provides a substantial portion of the market of one of your suppliers. You find out that this supplier discriminates illegally against minorities, although no legal action has been taken. Assume further that this supplier gives you the best price for the material you require, but that the field is competitive. Do you feel that it is proper to use your economic power over this supplier to make them stop discriminating?[67]

Respond to this question.

10. a. Do you think taking office supplies home from work for personal use is unethical? Explain.

    b. Are employers committing a serious ethics breach when they monitor their employees' e-mail? Explain.

11. Commentator Robert Scheer asks, "What does it mean that a whopping 70 percent of Americans, according to a recent *New York Times*–CBS News poll, believe that mass culture is responsible for debasing our moral values?"[68]

    a. Answer Scheer's question.

    b. Scheer went on to say;

> Worse, these national moralists—dominated these days by evangelical Christians—politicize the issue by blaming "liberal Hollywood" for what deregulation and the free market have wrought. Never mind that Arnold Schwarzenegger made all those violent movies, it is the Democrats and their ilk who are corrupting youth by promulgating our "relativistic" morality. But that's just bunk.[69]

    Do you agree with Scheer's "that's just bunk" position? If not, why? If so, who is to blame for our arguable moral decay?

12. In general, does the American value system favor "cheaters" who win in life's various competitions over virtuous individuals who "lose" with regularity? Explain.

13. If you were an executive about to hire a new manager, which of the following qualities would you consider most important/least important: verbal skills, honesty/integrity, enthusiasm, appearance, sense of humor? Explain.

14. In general, do smaller firms have higher ethical standards than larger firms? Explain.

15. a. Rank the following occupations as to your perception of their ethical quality: businesspeople, lawyers, doctors, teachers, farmers, engineers, carpenters, librarians, scientists, professional athletes, letter carriers, secretaries, journalists.

    b. In general, do you find educated professionals to be more ethical than skilled but generally less-educated laborers? Explain.

    c. Can you justify accepting an occupation that is not at or near the top of your ethical ranking? Explain how your ranking affects your career choices.

16. Can businesspeople successfully guide their conduct by the Golden Rule?

17. Comment on the following quotes from Albert Z. Carr:

> [M]ost bluffing in business might be regarded simply as game strategy—much like bluffing in poker, which does not reflect on the morality of the bluffer.
>
>   I quoted Henry Taylor, the British statesman who pointed out that "falsehood ceases to be falsehood when it is understood on all sides that the truth is not expected to be spoken"—an exact description of bluffing in poker, diplomacy, and business.

*　*　*　*　*

> [T]he ethics of business are game ethics, different from the ethics of religion.

*　*　*　*　*

>   An executive's family life can easily be dislocated if he fails to make a sharp distinction between the ethical systems of the home and the office—or if his wife does not grasp that distinction.[70]

18. Anthropology professor Lionel Tiger has argued for the creation of "moral quality circles" to help improve business conduct. Tiger notes,

> [O]ur species evolved in small groups of perhaps 25 to 200 hunters and gatherers, groups in which there was no place to hide. Over 200,000 generations or so we

evolved great face-to-face sensitivity and a lively skill for "whites-of-their-eyes" assessments of others.

*   *   *   *   *

These ancient but still lively emotions can be tied into the nature of organizational life to help overcome the all-too-evident capacity of large groups to yield to "if you want to get along, go along." My hunch is that moral laxity emerges when members of such groups receive little or no dignified opportunity to define their moral views on practical matters without the risk of endangering their occupational health.[71]

Tiger says that our moral systems sprang from that small-group context; but today, with complex industry replacing hunter–gatherers, those moral systems no longer correspond to contemporary needs. Tiger goes on to argue that we have a kind of "gene for morality" and that most of us have a rather clear sense of right and wrong. Given these conditions, he proposes the moral quality circle, in which workers would discuss the ethical implications of their duties and of the company's conduct in much the same manner that quality circles are now used to improve productivity and reliability. Do you see any value in Tiger's proposal? Explain.

19. Assume that you are working as manager of women's clothing in a large department store. You observe that the manager of equivalent rank to you in men's clothing is performing poorly in that she arrives late for work, she keeps her records ineptly, and she is rude to customers. However, her work has no direct impact on your department.
    a. Do you have any responsibility either to help her or to report her poor performance? Explain.
    b. If the store as a whole performs poorly, but you have performed well, do you bear any degree of personal responsibility for the store's failure when you confined your efforts exclusively to your own department even though you witnessed mismanagement in other departments? Explain.

20. We are often confronted with questions about the boundaries of our personal responsibilities.
    a. How much money, if any, must you give to satisfy your moral responsibility in the event of a famine in a foreign country? Explain.
    b. Would your responsibility be greater if the famine were in America? Explain.

Notes

1. Matt Slagle, "36 Kids Perish in Hot Vehicles So Far in 2003," *Des Moines Register,* August 26, 2003, p. 1A.
2. Raymond Baumhart, *Ethics in Business* (New York: Holt, Rinehart & Winston, 1968), p. 10.
3. Timothy Schelhardt, "Are Layoffs Moral? One Firm's Answer: You Ask, We'll Sue," *The Wall Street Journal,* August 1, 1996, p. A1.
4. Ibid.
5. John P. MacKenzie, "Lending a Hand if a Company Asks," *The New York Times,* February 3, 2002, Sec. 3, p. 11.
6. New York: Harcourt, 2004.
7. Jackson Lears, "Cheater, Cheater," *In These Times,* June 21, 2004, p. 28.
8. Eriq Gardner, "Cheat Sheet," *Corporate Counsel,* June 2004, p. 131.

9. David Moore, "Country's Problems Seen through Partisan Lens," *Gallup Poll News Service,* June 18, 2004.

10. Bureau of Justice Statistics, "Crime and Victims Statistics" [**http://www.ojp.usdoj.gov/ bjs/cvict.htm**].

11. "Immoral Americans?" *Des Moines Register,* February 23, 1999, p. B9.

12. Lee Berton, "Business Students Hope to Cheat and Prosper, New Study Shows," *The Wall Street Journal,* April 25, 1995, p. B1.

13. Ibid.

14. Susan C. Thomson, "Internet Helps Swell E-Cheating on Campuses," *The Washington Post,* March 14, 2004, p. A08.

15. Pauline Tam, "Students Like to Brag about Cheating Exploits," *The Ottawa Citizen,* August 27, 2003, p. C1.

16. Mary Rourke, "What Happened to America's Moral Climate?" *Los Angeles Times,* April 26, 2001, p. E1.

17. Shaena Engle, "Political Interest on the Rebound among the Nation's Freshmen, UCLA Survey Reveals" [**www.gseis.ucla.edu/heri/03_press_release.pdf**].

18. KPMG, "2000 Organizational Integrity Survey." A summary may be accessed at [**http:// ecampus.bentley.edu/dept/cbe/research/surveys.html**].

19. Joshua Joseph, "2003 National Business Ethics Survey 2000" [**http://www.ethics.org/ nbes2003/index.html**].

20. "Corporate Trust a Matter of Opinion" [**http://bostonworks.boston.com/globe/out_field/ archive/112303.shtml**].

21. For an elaboration of Kohlberg's stages, see, for example, W. D. Boyce and L. C. Jensen, *Moral Reasoning* (Lincoln, NE: University of Nebraska Press, 1978), pp. 98–109.

22. Lawrence Kohlberg, "The Cognitive–Development Approach to Moral Education," *Phi Delta Kappan* 56 (June 1975), p. 670.

23. Carol Gilligan, "In A Different Voice: Women's Conceptions of Self and Morality," *Harvard Educational Review* 47, no. 4 (November 1977), p. 481.

24. For an overview of the justice versus care debate, see Grace Clement, *Care, Autonomy, and Justice* (Boulder, CO: Westview Press, 1996).

25. James Weber and David Wasieleski, "Investigating Influences on Managers' Moral Reasoning," *Business & Society* 40, no. 1 (March 2001), pp. 79, 83.

26. "Business Roundtable Institute for Corporate Ethics Announces Key Findings from 'Mapping the Terrain' Survey of CEOs," *Business Wire,* June 8, 2004 [**http://web.lexis-nexis.com/ universe/document?_m=85aa4f7ae2f804…**].

27. Ethics Resource Center Research Department, "2003 National Business Ethics Survey," (Executive Summary) [**http://www.ethics.org/nbes2003/2003nbes_summary.html**].

28. Joseph L. Badaracco, Jr., and Allen P. Webb, "Business Ethics: A View from the Trenches," *California Management Review* 37, no. 2 (Winter 1995), pp. 8, 12.

29. Daniel Akst, "Room at the Top, for Improvement," *The Wall Street Journal,* October 26, 2004, p. D8.

30. Joseph L. Badaracco, Jr., *Defining Moments: When Managers Must Choose between Right and Wrong* (Boston: Harvard Business School Press, 1997), p. 65.

31. "Do Your Employees See You as an Ethical Leader?" *Business for Social Responsibility* [**http://www.bsr.org/BSRMagazine?InDepth/analysis.cfm**].

32. Susan Pulliam, "The 'It Wasn't Me' Defense," *The Wall Street Journal,* July 9, 2004, p. B1.

33. Rachel Beck, Associated Press, "Bucks Still Flow to Troubled CEOs," *Des Moines Register,* November 7, 2004, p. 1D.

34. Ibid.

35. Ibid.

36. Ibid.

37. Amey Stone, "Putting Teeth in Corporate Ethics Codes," *BusinessWeek Online,* February 19, 2004 [**http://web.lexis-nexis.com/universe/document?_m=d73al58fa54c7e…**].

38. Stephen Taub, "Lucent First Four on Bribery Suspicions," *CFO.com,* April 7, 2004 [**http://www.cfo.com/printable/article.cfm/3013085?=options**].

39. 15 U.S.C. 78dd-1(b)-2(b) (1982), as amended by 1988 Trade Act 5003(a), (c).

40. Foreign Corrupt Practices Act Amendments of 1988, 15 U.S.C. 78dd-1 A (f) (2) (A) (B).

41. "Bribes Cost U.S. Firms $24B in Contracts," *Ottawa Citizen,* April 8, 1999, p. D4.

42. Richard Bray, "Stiff Penalties for Doing 'Business as Usual,' " *Ottawa Citizen,* April 8, 1999, p. D14.

43. "Transparency International Corruption Perceptions Index 2004" [**http://www.transparency.org/pressreleases_archive/2004/2004.10.20…**].

44. Ibid.

45. Ibid.

46. "Transparency International's Bribe Payers Survey" [**http://www.transparency.org/pressreleases_archive/2002/2002.05.14.bpi.en.html#bpi**].

47. U.S. Department of State, "International Organizations and Africa," *Africa News,* December 9, 2004 [**http://web.lexis-nexis.com/universe/document?_m=4c913b507a35a…**].

48. "Every Third Lithuanian Student Has Given Bribe—Study," *Baltic News Service,* February 23, 2004 [**http://web.lexis-nexis.com/universe/document?_m=4c913b507a35a…**].

49. Thomas Omestad, "Bye-Bye to Bribes," *U.S. News & World Report,* December 22, 1997, pp. 39, 42.

50. "Eastern Europe/Central Asia: World Bank Report Encouraging on Business-Related Corruption," *Euro-East,* April 22, 2004 [**http://web.lexis-nexis.com/universe/document?_m=4c913b507a35a…**].

51. Laurence Iliff, "Poll Shows Bribery in Mexico May Be on the Decline," *Dallas Morning News,* December 28, 2003 [**http://web.lexis-nexis.com/universe/document?_m=4c913b507a35a…**].

52. Martin Dyckman, "Taking a Reading on Corruption around the World," *St. Petersburg Times,* October 11, 1998, p. 3D.

53. Carl Kaufmann, "A Five-Part Quiz on Corporate Ethics," *Washington Post,* July 1, 1979, pp. C-1, C-4.

54. Shawn Young and Peter Grant, "More Pinstripes to Get Prison Stripes," *The Wall Street Journal,* June 20, 2005, p. C1.

55. Craig Rose, "Only a Few Bad Apples?" *San Diego Union-Tribune,* May 4, 2003, p. H1.

56. Deborah Solomon and Anne Marie Squeo, "Crackdown Puts Corporations, Executives in New Legal Peril," *The Wall Street Journal,* June 20, 2005, p. A1.

57. Portions of this paragraph relied on Robert G. Morvillo and Robert J. Anello, "White-Collar Crime, Corporate Compliance Programs: No Longer Voluntary," *New York Law Journal,* December 7, 2004, p. 3.

58. Anton R. Valukas, Robert R. Stauffer, and Seth A. Travis, "Enforcement Actions in the Post-Enron World: Zero Tolerance in the White-Collar Arena," *S&P's The Review of Securities & Commodities Regulation,* July 1, 2004, p. 133.

59. Dennis Callaghan, "Ready, Set, Comply; Sarbanes-Oxley: Road to Compliance," *eWeek,* February 16, 2004, p. 1.

60. Joann S. Lublin, "Saving Your Career after Earning a Name as a Whistle-Blower," *The Wall Street Journal,* February 5, 2002, p. B1.

61. Jack Liles, "Blow the Whistle . . . Then Watch Out," *The Wall Street Journal,* February 21, 2002, p. A19.

62. Kaufmann, "Five-Part Quiz," p. C4.

63. "Short Takes," *Des Moines Register,* February 5, 1990, p. 2T.

64. Ibid.

65. Leonard C. Lewin, "Ethical Aptitude Test," *Harper's,* October 1976, p. 21.

66. Reported on WKYT TV, Channel 27, *Evening News,* Lexington, Kentucky, May 12, 1980.

67. "Business Executives and Moral Dilemmas," *Business and Society Review,* no. 13 (Spring 1975), p. 51.

68. Robert Scheer, "The Invisible Hand Holds the Remote," *Los Angeles Times,* November 30, 2004, p. B13.

69. Ibid.

70. Albert Z. Carr, "Is Business Bluffing Ethical?" *Harvard Business Review* 46, no. 1 (January–February 1968), pp. 143–52.

71. Lionel Tiger, "Stone Age Provides Model for Instilling Business Ethics," *The Wall Street Journal,* January 11, 1988, p. 22.

The Corporation and Public Policy: Expanding Responsibilities

Introduction

The bulk of this book is devoted to the law regulating business conduct, but before turning in that direction we need to remind the reader of the context—the environment—in which the law developed. Therefore, a major purpose of this chapter is to raise some critical issues regarding the business community's relationship to the larger society. Should we "free" business from government intervention to achieve greater productivity and profit? Should business play a larger role in politics, education, and other public-sector activities? Should business assume greater responsibilities in correcting societal ills? The reader is expected to use this chapter to make a tentative assessment of the very large question, What is the proper role of business in society? Only after acquiring some preliminary grasp of that issue can one logically and fruitfully turn to various "control devices" (such as law) as a means of enforcing that proper role.

The second major goal of this chapter is to alert the reader to some of the primary criticisms raised against the corporate community. The successful businessperson and the good citizen must understand and intelligently evaluate the objections of those who criticize the role of the corporation in contemporary life. Of course, government regulation is, in part, a response to those criticisms. (A detailed investigation of the forces generating government intervention is offered in Chapter 8.)

Finally, this chapter is designed to introduce what might be labeled *corporate public policy*. Tomorrow's leaders must understand the interdependent relationship between business and the larger society. They must understand the public policy issues that have emerged from that relationship, and they must build the skills necessary to successfully manage that relationship. In the 1960s the public began to demand more of business than simply producing products and services. We began to expect the business community to make a broad contribution to general societal welfare—to become a corporate citizen with all of the responsibilities that corporate wealth and power suggest. Those new demands led to the evolutionary development of public policy. We will examine that evolution in four parts: (1) criticism of corporate America, (2) the emergence of the expectation of *corporate social responsibility*, (3) the management of social responsibility, and (4) the examination of some specific business and society issues.

Part One—Corporate Power and Corporate Critics

Corporate critics have long argued that the public interest has not been well served by America's big corporations. We recognize that colossal size and the economies of scale that accompany it have been critical to American competitiveness in today's unforgiving global market. At the same time, that very size, the critics say, permits continuing abuse of the American public. Of course, we recognize that big companies are a fixture of the American landscape. However, a reminder of the specifics may be useful.

Wal-Mart is now the largest company in America (see Table 3.1) and in the world and is the first service company to hold the top spot. Wal-Mart sales have exploded from $1 billion in all of 1979 to $1 billion on some single good days in 2001.[1] Wal-Mart is, by a wide margin, America's number one employer with some 1.6 million workers.[2] Second-place McDonald's employs 438,000.[3]

TABLE 3.1 **America's Largest Corporations**

Corporation	Location	Sales Revenue (in billions)
Wal-Mart Stores	Bentonville, AK	$288.2
Exxon Mobil	Irving, TX	270.8
General Motors	Detroit, MI	193.5
Ford Motor	Dearborn, MI	172.2
General Electric	Fairfield, CT	152.4

Source: "*Fortune* 500 Largest U.S. Corporations," *Fortune*, April 18, 2005, p. F-1.

The extraordinary wealth of America's corporate institutions is such that they tower over most countries of the world in economic might. If we compare corporate sales with gross national products, Wal-Mart, General Motors, Exxon Mobil, Ford Motor, and DaimlerChrysler annually rank around the 25th to 30th largest economic entities in the world.[4] The annual sales of each of those companies exceed the GNPs of, for example, Norway, South Africa, Saudi Arabia, or Greece.[5] Of the globe's 100 largest economic entities, 51 are corporations and 49 are countries.[6]

The 300 largest global corporations hold one-quarter of the entire globe's productive assets.[7] Corporate wealth and power are similarly concentrated in the United States, where the revenues of the top 500 corporations equal about 60 percent of America's total economic output.[8] (Do you see any risk in corporations holding greater economic muscle than many of the nations of the world? Certainly the danger in these numbers is transparent to the critics—too much power in too few hands. For further detail on global corporate power, see **[http://www.uaw.org/solidarity/9610/11_2.html]**.)

> Only 24 percent of Americans expressed "a great deal" or "quite a lot" of confidence in big business.

The critics' concerns seem to be shared by many Americans. In a 2004 Gallup Poll only 24 percent of Americans expressed "a great deal" or "quite a lot" of confidence in big business. Indeed, among the 15 major institutions listed, only health maintenance organizations ranked lower (18 percent) than big business. The military (75 percent), the police (64 percent), organized religion (53 percent), and banks (53 percent) topped the list.[9]

The Corporate State

Historically, the foundation of the critics' argument has been that giant companies hold monopoly power, permitting them to secure "excess profits" at the expense of the consumer. Considerable evidence supported that view,[10] but it has been rendered somewhat passé in this era of fierce international economic competition. Further, many of America's old-line titans (GM, IBM, Sears, and so on) are struggling to retain their strength, suggesting that bigness does not guarantee success in the contemporary market.

At the same time, the extraordinary authority of the corporate community in contemporary American and global life is simply undeniable. An interesting example of that influence is the evolution of American tax policy in recent years. A General Accounting Office study showed that 61 percent of U.S. corporations paid no federal income taxes from 1996 through 2000.[11] During the same period, IRS audits of corporate tax returns declined while those of individuals increased.[12] As billionaire investor Warren Buffett put it, "If class warfare is being waged in America, my class is clearly winning."[13]

Of course, the stunning corporate scandals of recent years (Enron, Martha Stewart, Tyco, Adelphia, and so on) have deepened doubts about corporate honor. *The Wall Street Journal* reports,

> Big corporations are stuck in the doghouse. More than two years after a wave of accounting scandals shook the public's trust, the reputation of many of the best-known companies continues to decline. In their latest corporate-reputation study, Harris Interactive and the Reputation Institute found that the public is still mad at many of the 60 companies in this year's ranking: Three-quarters of the survey respondents graded the image of big corporations as either "not good" or "terrible."
>
> But the public's scorn runs deeper than the scandals. Americans also feel less positively about customer service, the treatment of employees, and the environmental policies at many companies measured in the survey.[14]

So complaints about the corporate role in pollution, discrimination, white-collar crime, misleading advertising, and so on remain commonplace. But in a democratic, free market society like America's, presumably we all must share some of the blame for our problems. If we are not happy with, for example, Wal-Mart's treatment of its employees, we are free to shop elsewhere. Arguably, then, the role of business in American life merely reflects the values of the American people. Thus the critics' broader concern is that America has committed its very *soul* to business values in a way that is progressively undermining our national well-being. We will briefly examine that argument prior to turning to our more detailed study of corporate social responsibility and government regulation of business.

Corporations as Psychopaths?

The 2004 movie documentary *The Corporation* argues that the corporation has become the dominant institution in American life, exceeding the influence of both religion and government. One result is that corporations often demonstrate the "traits of the prototypical psychopath." The contemporary corporation is depicted as an "exploitative monster" driven not by the greater good but by its first responsibility to stockholders.

Source: Jim Keough, "Film Sees Evil in Corporations," *Worchester Telegram & Gazette,* September 29, 2004, p. C5.

America's Soul?

Generally, critics contend that the power of the business community has become so encompassing that virtually all dimensions of American life have absorbed elements of the business ethic. Values commonly associated with businesspeople (competition, profit seeking, reliance on technology, faith in growth) have overwhelmed traditional humanist values (cooperation, individual dignity, human rights, meaningful service to society). In the name of efficiency and productivity, the warmth, decency, and value of life have been debased.

> **Objects dominate our existence**

We engage in meaningless work in an artificial culture. Objects dominate our existence. We operate as replaceable cogs in a vast, bureaucratic machine. Our natural environment is shredded in the pursuit of progress. Indeed, we lose ourselves, the critics argue.

Charles Reich, former Yale University law professor, addressed the loss of self in his influential book of the Vietnam War era, *The Greening of America:*

> Of all of the forms of impoverishment that can be seen or felt in America, loss of self, or death in life, is surely the most devastating. . . . Beginning with school, if not before, an individual is systematically stripped of his imagination, his creativity, his heritage, his dreams, and his personal uniqueness, in order to style him into a productive unit for a mass, technological society. Instinct, feeling, and spontaneity are repressed by overwhelming forces. As the individual is drawn into the meritocracy, his working life is split from his home life, and both suffer from a lack of wholeness. Eventually, people virtually become their professions, roles, or occupations, and are henceforth strangers to themselves.[15]

Some interesting empirical evidence supports Reich's view that we have become hollow men and women dominated by the demands of big institutions. The Harris Alienation Index shows a generally steady rise in Americans' feelings of powerlessness from 1966 when the index stood at 29 to the 1999 poll in which the index stood at 62.[16] *Alienation,* as defined in the survey, includes feelings of economic inequity (the rich get richer, the poor get poorer), feelings of disdain about the people in power, and feelings of powerlessness (being left out and not counting for much.) The results since 1999, however, have improved. The index fell to 50 in 2004, probably as a result of the presidential race in that year.[17]

Questions

1. According to some polls, nearly three-quarters of Americans think corporations have too much power.

   a. Do you agree that corporations are too powerful? Explain.

   b. How did American corporations expand their power in the 1980s and 1990s?

2. Management theorist John Nirenberg writes,

   > In a world where democracy is breaking out in some of the unlikeliest places and in a world now committed to the idea of liberty, it is sadly ironic that Americans have so thoroughly surrendered themselves to corporate tyranny.
   >
   > How have we come to accept so thoroughly the sacrifice of over half of our waking consciousness to the god of earning a living without the slightest thought to the propriety of the relationships in the workplace and the fact that we must surrender ourselves to an impersonal bureaucracy that defies our influence? How have we so completely surrendered ourselves to the rule of the dollar and the powers of an unelected, often unaccountable boss?[18]

   a. Do you agree with Nirenberg? Explain.

   b. Answer Nirenberg's questions.

Politics

We can detail the case of the corporate critics by directing our attention to some areas of special concern. We will begin with politics, where critics charge that superior resources enable the business community to unfairly slant the electoral and law-making processes in favor of corporate interests.

In recent decades, the corporate community took an increasingly direct and vigorous role in the political process. As a result, corporate critics have been concerned that the financial weight of big business will prove so influential that our pluralist, democratic approach to governance may be significantly distorted. Today money is central to winning elective office, and dollars to finance lobbying on Capitol Hill can be critical in shaping congressional opinion.

Corporate funds cannot lawfully be expended for federal campaign contributions. However, corporations (as well as labor unions, special interest groups, and others) can lawfully establish *political action committees* (*PACs*) to solicit and disburse voluntary campaign contributions. That is, corporations can solicit contributions from employees, shareholders, and others. That money is then put in a fund, carefully segregated from general corporate accounts, and disbursed by the PAC in support of a federal election campaign.

Although PAC contributions are voluntary, corporate employees often feel pressured to participate. *The New York Times* explained the PAC expectations that the Enron scandal revealed:

> On June 15, 2000, Enron's political action committee sent a memo to employees suggesting "voluntary" contributions for Enron employees, from $500 for a low-level manager to $5,000 for a top executive. The memo said the money would assist the company as it faced numerous legal and regulatory challenges and a variety of environmental and tax issues.[19]

PAC contributions are limited to $5,000 per candidate in each election cycle, while individuals are limited to $2,000 per candidate in each election.

Nonetheless, the public has no doubt that big money continues to buy votes. Responding to a 2000 *BusinessWeek* poll, 74 percent of Americans agreed that "big companies have too much political influence."[20] Certainly business has poured substantial money into the process: "In 2002, businesses pumped $215 million into the political process, or about 42 percent of the $507 million given to party committees in unregulated donations"[21] (so-called *soft money* donations that go directly to the political parties rather than to candidates). Those remarkable sums and the fear that elections were in danger of being purchased led Congress to act.

Reform

After years of bickering, Congress and President Bush agreed to campaign finance reforms in 2002. Basically, the new McCain-Feingold legislation curbs soft money and relaxes rules on regulated hard money. In 1999–2000, of the $495 million the national parties raised in soft money, nearly two-thirds came from just 800 contributors who provided at least $120,000 each.[22] The most powerful voice for campaign finance reform, Senator John McCain of Arizona, explained the general concern about soft money:

> Campaign contributions from a single source that run to hundreds of thousands or millions of dollars are not healthy to a democracy.[23]

The bill imposes limits on raising soft money by labor unions, companies, and individuals and requires greater disclosure of sources of financing for campaign advertising. It also bars corporations and unions from funding radio or TV ads for federal candidates within 60 days of a general election. [For an overview of concerns about campaign financing and reform concepts, see **http://lwv.org/~lwvus/cfrcon.html**]

Corporate Response

The new soft money legislation, having passed several challenges in the courts, has effectively blocked that route to corporate political contributions. The soft money approach has been replaced by independent but partisan groups called *527s* (referring to the section of the tax code that governs them) that take contributions that cannot go directly to parties. Those 527s then spend money for their favored candidates. Many corporations have declined to make contributions through the loosely controlled 527s, favoring more direct political roles. One such tactic is the reenergized PAC route, where some 201 corporate PACs contributed $111 million in 2003.[24] Total corporate contributions are significantly smaller than in the pre-McCain-Feingold days of soft money, but many corporations still look for ways to be heard. For example, corporate money played a big role in funding the 2004 presidential nominating conventions. ABC News reported some of the details:

> [Corporations are] throwing hundreds of parties to entertain and influence the powerful GOP politicians in town [New York City] for the Republican National Convention. "This is the place where the elite get to mingle with the people who write the laws overseeing them," said Micah Sifry, an analyst for Public Campaign, a nonprofit, nonpartisan organization.

*   *   *   *   *

General Motors invited former House Majority Leader Dick Armey to New York as one of its lobbyists. When asked if attending these parties was key for lobbyists like himself, Armey told ABC News, "Well, I guess so. I'm here because of my relationship with the speaker" (Republican Speaker of the House of Representatives, Dennis Hastert, Illinois).[25]

Lobbying

As Dick Armey's words suggest, influencing legislators is an important business strategy. Sophisticated and expensive lobbying is a staple of the business community's efforts to implement its legislative agenda. Lobbying is defended as an efficient method of better acquainting busy politicians with the subtleties of the diverse issues they must address. Of course, lobbying is not confined to the "big spenders" of the business community— witness the many influential consumer and environmental interest groups. Washington lobbying has become an enormous industry. Congress has passed rules requiring registration of lobbyists, greater disclosure of their activities, and limiting or banishing gifts from lobbyists to politicians, but the impact of those rules seems negligible.

The clubby, personal nature of Washington power building was apparent with a glance at the Enron Field (now Minute Maid Park) "Diamond Club" seating for the Houston Astros' April 2000 opener:

> In the state-of-the-art baseball stadium's most exclusive section, behind home plate, there were the Bushes—a former president and a president to be—along with the younger Mr. Bush's running mate, Dick Cheney, and his successor as governor, Rick Perry. Nearby was Senator Kay Bailey Hutchison, whose husband, Ray, is a lawyer with Enron's chief law firm, Vinson & Elkins. And then came the executives of Houston's biggest companies, who had vied to become the younger Bush's most prominent fund-raisers, just as they had jockeyed to buy the prized luxury seats. And at the center of it all, down on the pitcher's mound, was Kenneth L. Lay, the man responsible for building Enron into an American powerhouse, throwing out the first ball.[26]

Buy Votes?

In the end, does all of the money buy votes? In most cases probably not, but it certainly buys access and returned phone calls; and we have considerable evidence that money influences voting patterns. For example, an analysis by the Campaign for Tobacco-Free Kids found that members of Congress who took money from tobacco companies were three times more likely to vote against a bill to fight cigarette sales to minors.[27] Of course, contributions are most likely to go to those who are predisposed to favor the tobacco industry position. A recent academic study found that "PAC contributions are negatively related to new firm entry in manufacturing industries."[28] Basically the research argues that existing firms use contributions to create political barriers to entry (laws, rules, and enforcement practices) by new competitors. Though the research does not establish a causal relationship between PAC contributions and difficulty of entry, "the results suggest that corporate PACs may play a role in inhibiting new entry to an industry.[29] And at a practical level, the effects of lobbying are readily observable. For example, Diageo PLC, controlling 27 percent of the U.S. liquor market, has recently led the liquor industry in aggressive lobbying of states to build a rules climate more favorable to liquor sales. With a presence in every state capital, Diageo has recently played a big role in convincing nine states to allow some form of Sunday liquor sales, raising the nationwide total to 30 states.

Similarly, the liquor industry's lobbying group, the Distilled Spirits Council of the United States, has helped defeat liquor tax increases in 26 of the 30 states that have considered such increases.[30] For the Center for Responsive Politics and its extensive database on money in politics, see [**http://www.opensecrets.org/home/index.asp.**]. The article that follows details UPS's political campaign to secure federal approval of a highly lucrative cargo air route to China.

READING | **Congress Helps UPS Win Route**

Larry Margasak, Associated Press

United Parcel Service landed its first cargo planes in China last week, the culmination of a 19-month, multimillion-dollar lobbying campaign.

Known for its brown, box-shaped delivery trucks, UPS won its new China air route from the Transportation Department after persuading a remarkable two-thirds of the House and Senate to serve as company pitchmen, according to documents and interviews by The Associated Press.

UPS provided draft letters for lawmakers to sign and send to the transportation agency. And the company handed out $1.2 million in political donations to congressmen who signed the letters. Twenty-seven House and Senate members got UPS checks within a week before or after the dates on the letters they signed, and 120 had received checks within two months, an AP analysis found.

Company officials also appeared at congressional offices with Teamster Union members—reminding both pro-corporate Republicans and pro-labor Democrats that the company provides nearly 350,000 jobs in virtually every city in the nation.

The package carrier also lent its town house to lawmakers for fund-raising events.

In all, 368 of the 535 members of Congress wrote to the Transportation Department in favor of granting the Beijing and Shanghai air route to UPS.

* * * * *

The company estimates the route will be worth $300 million in new revenue annually after the first year. It will allow UPS to compete with Federal Express, which has been flying to China since 1995.

The status of Federal Express, a nonunion company, as the only U.S. cargo carrier with direct access to China helped persuade the Teamsters to put aside any bitterness from a 1997 strike against UPS and join the company in its lobbying campaign.

"It was a pretty easy decision to put on a full court press on this," said Fred McLuckie, the Teamsters' legislative director.

The lobbying campaign overwhelmed Delta, American, and Polar Air Cargo, the three rivals competing for the same route.

UPS spokesman Tad Segal said the company won "because of the strength of our arguments."

Source: *Rocky Mountain News,* April 11, 2001, p. 30A. Reprinted by permission of the copyright holder, the Associated Press.

Questions

1. How would you defend UPS's powerful influence in Congress?

2. Then-Defense Secretary William Perry repeatedly told Congress that the Pentagon did not want more B-2 Stealth bombers than the 20 planes already delivered or on order. Nonetheless, in 1995 Congress agreed to spend nearly one-half billion dollars more on the bombers. Explain why Congress would approve weapons not wanted by the Pentagon.

3. Richard Goodwin, aide to former President John F. Kennedy, speaks out on PACs:

    Morally the system is bribery. It is not criminal only because those who make the laws are themselves accomplices. Government is for sale. But the bids are sealed, and the prices are very high.

    There is an easy way out: Eliminate PACs. We should place a rigorous ceiling on all congressional campaigns, allocate public funds to finance campaigns, and require television stations—the most costly component of modern political campaigns—to give a specified amount of air time to candidates.[31]

    a. Should we forbid PACs? Explain.

    b. Would such action be constitutionally permissible? Explain.

Too Much Business?

Clearly, the business community's influence in America's political life is enormous, but the critics' concerns only begin there. The corporation is arguably the central institution in contemporary America. In every dimension of American life, business values are increasingly pervasive. To those who criticize the corporation, that near-blanket adoption of the business ethic signals a dangerous distortion of the nation's priorities. In an editorial, the *Des Moines Register* commented that commercials have become so interwoven with our total existence that they cannot effectively be "separated out." Commentator Jane Eisner laments the increasing immersion of very young children in America's commercial culture:

> The typical first grader can name 200 brands and acquires an average of 70 new toys a year. American children view an estimated 40,000 commercials annually. Teen purchasing power has risen so rapidly that teenagers spend on average $100 a week.

*   *   *   *   *

> Despite having only 4.5 percent of the world's population, the United States consumes 45 percent of global toy production—but all those toys are not buying happiness, as rates of childhood depression, anxiety, and suicide are increasing.[32]

*   *   *   *   *

Business products and business values saturate and dominate all corners of American life, the critics claim. Judge for yourself as we take a quick look at several areas of concern.

Schools

In the face of nationwide alarm about elementary and secondary education, the corporate community has played an increasingly aggressive role in supporting and reforming our schools. And considerable good may come from that corporate pressure and assistance, as evidenced by a RAND study that concluded that a day-to-day business commitment was the primary reason for faster reform progress in Texas and North Carolina than in other states.[33] In 2001 more than 200 Pennsylvania corporations pledged some $8.5 million primarily for private school scholarships, in return for which the corporations will receive tax credits.[34] In a striking development, the struggling Philadelphia schools turned to the profit-making Edison Schools, Inc., to help manage the public school system and to take direct control of some of the worst schools. Philadelphia is the biggest of some 40 school districts that have been privatized although several cities, including Baltimore and Minneapolis, have hired Edison to run individual schools.[35] Critics, however, are concerned that cash-short schools become vulnerable to corporate marketing strategies, and perhaps unwittingly, encourage the indoctrination of students in business values and practices. The National School Boards Association summarized commercial activities being directed to some elementary and high school students:

- Advertising is placed on school buses by Old Navy (San Francisco) and Burger King (Colorado Springs).
- Nike, Gatorade, and Calvin Klein are among the companies providing free book covers with ads.
- Campbell Soup provided science kits measuring whether Prego is thicker than Ragu.

- Dr. Pepper paid the Grapevine–Colleyville School District in Texas $3.45 million over 10 years to put its logo on the school roof, which happens to be in a flight path for the Dallas–Fort Worth airport.[36]

Since 1989, Channel One has supplied educational programming and television sets to schools. The 12-minute programs include two minutes of advertising often featuring junk food and violent movies.[37] [For the Channel One news, see **http://www .channelonenews.com**]

Anxious to keep the valuable assistance, some school officials appear to have become promoters of the corporate sponsors:

> [I]n Colorado Springs, Colo., a school district official sent a memo to principals, exhorting them to crank up sales of Coke products to meet a quota or risk losing revenue. Signing the letter "The Coke Dude," he urged schools to consider allowing students to drink Coca-Cola's juices and teas—if not soft drinks—in classrooms.[38]

> The San Francisco school board declared their children "not for sale"

The San Francisco school board, on the other hand, declared their children "not for sale," and approved a policy limiting ads and paid endorsements in the schools and forbidding districtwide, exclusive contracts for soft drinks and snack foods.[39] Faced with these commercialism complaints, in 2001 Coca-Cola urged its bottlers and competitors to end exclusive sales arrangements with schools.[40] The schools, however, want the money (as one example, $1.77 million for a five-year deal with the 35 schools in Sarasota, Florida's county school district), and the deals often continue.[41]

From kindergarten through graduate school, the "business mentality" is ever-present. Students and their parents call for a "quick fix" of skills (such as accounting, management, and marketing) as a replacement for occupationally uncertain disciplines such as history, literature, and philosophy. Education is consumed much like pizza, and the student hopes to proceed into the Corporate State. But did that student buy a good life or an empty existence? Charles Reich offers his opinion:

> The process by which man is deprived of his self begins with his institutionalized training in public school for a place in the machinery of the State. The object of the training is not merely to teach him how to perform some specific function; it is to make him become that function, to see and judge himself and others in terms of functions, and to abandon any aspect of self, thinking, questioning, feeling, loving, that has no utility for either production or consumption in the Corporate State. The training for the role of consumer is just as important as the training for a job, and at least equally significant for loss of self.[42]

Religion

Mel Gibson's movie *The Passion* emphatically affirmed the spectacular commercial potential of religion as one of America's most marketable products. Religion as the subject of books, music, and movies is hardly a new phenomenon; but the aggressive marketing of the religious message and the explicit adoption of business principles in the name of religion is, for the most part, a development of recent decades. Craig Karpel, cocreator of Jewcy, an online boutique featuring clothing linked to the Jewish faith, explains the new commerce of religion:

People that are more conservative think it is commercializing or lessening the value of religion, but that's not what we are doing. This is a very different world than it was even 30 years ago. When it comes to spreading religion, the methods have gotten a lot savvier and smarter than they ever were.[43]

To many Christians, Jesus is a pop-culture icon[44] and thus is the inspiration for a vast array of commercial expressions from T-shirts to license plates and bobblehead dolls. Clever marketers and designers are now combining religious messages with familiar secular symbols such as the shirt that displays what looks like a Jack Daniels whiskey label but says, "Living Water: Never Thirst Again."[45]

One of the most visible Christian leaders, the Reverend Robert Schuller, builder of the Crystal Cathedral church complex in Garden Grove, California, and popularizer of drive-in churches, announced in 1998 that he intended to add a food court to his church along with an exhibition hall honoring the great "Christian capitalists." Benjamin J. Hubbard, chair of comparative religion at California State University–Fullerton, criticized Schuller's blending of faith and convenience: "It smacks of the mall mentality gone crazy. You shop for religion and then swing by the food court."[46] [For a review of *Christianity Incorporated: How Big Business Is Buying the Church*, see **http://www.usask.ca/relst/jrpc/br4-VanDyke.html**]

Questions

1. Do you see any risks to religion in treating it as a product to be marketed and sold? Explain.
2. *a.* Why has religion increasingly become a product in the commercial world?
   b. Is everything a product in some sense?

Culture

Does America possess a cultural life? For decades, the concern was that so-called "high" culture—classical music, opera, ballet, and the like—would give way to rock and roll, television, and video games. Now that battle is over; Americans (and the world) have clearly voted for *South Park* and the like. Corporate America deserves our respect for its generous financial and organizational support to the traditional intellectual culture. At the same time, corporate bottom-line concerns appear to the critics to be steadily degrading America's cultural life. For example, the esteemed Metropolitan Museum of Art in New York City has been criticized for allowing corporate money to shape some of its shows. Reportedly, Tommy Hilfiger's $1 million donation to the museum allowed the designer "considerable influence" on one exhibit—a fashion show—and its accompanying fund-raiser.[47] Even popular culture (rock, movies, television, hip hop, and so on), already considered a wasteland, has been further debased, not merely by a mindless market (that's us), but by limitless corporate greed and indifference to quality.

The evolution of pop music on the radio demonstrates the fear of suffocating corporate control. Corporate ownership of radio stations has dramatically consolidated since the 1996 Telecommunications Act deregulated the industry and allowed widespread

Americans (and the world) have clearly voted for *South Park* mergers. The result is standardized, national play lists that leave little room for music that strays even slightly from the massive middle of the market. Although some 30,000 new CDs are issued annually, *Rolling Stone* reports that "in one recent week," the biggest 45 Top 40 stations in the nation added only 20 new songs to their play lists.[48]

> "Most of the country is based on lowest-common-denominator programming: Play the fewest songs that appeal to the most people," says Alexandra Inzer, program director for WMPS, a Memphis adult alternative station that is one of the few independent commercial broadcasters left in a major metropolitan market.[49]

The resulting repetition and predictability in programming confirms the critics' complaints, but the market may be demanding change. Radio listening time dropped some 13 percent from the early 1990s through the turn of the century.[50] Teen listening dropped 10 percent from 1998 to 2001.[51]

Sports

> The fight against crass commercialism was lost a long time ago.
> If there's an extra buck out there, everyone wants a share.[52]

As the current steroid scandals suggest, the pursuit of money by virtually any means has consumed the sports landscape. Consider some examples:

> **Ralph Nader called it a "greedy new low"**

- Ralph Nader called it a "greedy new low" when the Yankees and the Devil Rays wore Ricoh logos on their uniforms and helmets during the 2004 season opening major league baseball series in Tokyo.[53]

- The University of Missouri gave naming rights to its new sports center to billionaires Bill and Nancy Laurie in return for their $25 million donation toward the construction of the $75 million building. Mr. and Mrs. Laurie (she is an heir to the Wal-Mart fortune) chose to name the building Paige Sports Arena after their daughter, Elizabeth Paige Laurie. That decision was criticized for its glorification of a young woman whose parents' money put her name on the world's "biggest dollhouse," as one unhappy alum expressed it. As it turned out, the name was changed after a few weeks to Mizzou Arena when Paige Laurie's freshman roommate at the University of Southern California accused Laurie of paying her about $20,000 over three and one-half years to write papers and complete various assignments for Laurie.[54]

- Sports shoemaker New Balance decided in 2005 to speak directly to the influence of money in sports with its advertising theme: "There are two motivations in sports. Which is yours? For love or money?" The New Balance ad campaign tried to associate its brand with those who value sports for their emotional satisfactions and to celebrate "the spirit and authenticity of the true athlete."[55]

The conversion of athletics, both professional and collegiate, from sport to business is essentially an accomplished fact, but its significance remains unclear. What have we lost when the innocence and idealism of sports are forfeited in favor of profit? Or are innocence and idealism simply a myth? Perhaps we are better off when corporate and personal profit—the free market—drives sports. Or is the pursuit of profit the route to the slow but sure death of meaningful sports, as one fan recently lamented?

> We would be a healthier society if professional sports did not exist. The love of money, or greed, takes all the fun out of sports, demeans the integrity of the games, corrupts the athletes and belittles the fans. . . . The love of money is slowly, subtly destroying sports and America.[56]

Of course, as the University of Missouri example suggests, the influence of money in sports certainly is not limited to professional sports. As Reverend Theodore Hesburgh, former president of Notre Dame, put it, "These sleazebags have come in over the last 30 years and taken the tradition of learning at our universities and colleges and just gutted it by making it an adjunct to the pro leagues or simply entertainment."[57]

What does the future hold? One critic imagines the following:

> One day, perhaps the New York Yankees may morph into the IBM Yankees, ballplayers will decorate their uniforms with soft drink brands, and the Exxon Cowboys might win the General Motors Super Bowl.[58]

We have already received glimpses of that direct merger of sports and business. The article that follows explains how Nike not only sponsored individual participants in the 1998 Winter Olympics, but in effect created its own team.

READING   Kenyan Skiers Nike Products?

Associated Press

One of the feel-good stories of the Nagano Olympics began two years ago with a brainstorm at Nike's marketing department: What if we transform a couple of Kenyan runners into cross-country skiers?

Now Nike's backing of the two athletes may have backfired, with some accusing the company of going too far to put its swoosh on a good story.

"These are not athletes clearing hurdles to reach their Olympic dream," wrote *Detroit News* columnist Bob Wojnowski. "These are marketing pawns financed by well-heeled publicity seekers."

Details of Nike's involvement began to emerge even before one of the great photo moments of the game—Kenyan cross-country skier Philip Boit crossing the finish line dead last in the 10-kilometer race and being embraced by the gold medal winner from Norway.

Nike, which had its signature swoosh on Boit's hat, collar, and sweater, hatched the idea two years ago to send Kenyan distance runners Boit and Henry Bitok to Finland to learn cross-country skiing.

They would be like the celebrated Jamaican bobsled team at the Calgary Games in 1988.

Nike paid for their move and spent a reported $200,000 for their lodging and a Finnish coach. The athletes even got custom ski uniforms, courtesy of the company.

Nike spokeswoman Martha Benson said Nike has financially backed Kenyan runners since 1991, and the move into cross-country skiing came out of a series of meetings between Nike and Kenyan running officials.

Steve Miller, a senior Nike executive in Japan, conceded that less idealistic goals also figured into the company's support.

"People forget, we are a business, and part of our objective as a business is to get attention," he said.

Source: *Des Moines Register,* February 14, 1998, p. 4S. Reprinted by permission of the Associated Press.

Question

1. In the future, will "amateur" athletes compete for corporations—for example, Team Nike—rather than universities or nations?

Home or Corporate Office?

The New York City Museum of Modern Art, in 1999, previewed the "architecture of the next century" with images of 26 homes of the future. Architecture writer Peter Whoriskey reviewed the exhibit:

> What's scary is what has happened to the idea of home. In the exhibit's designs, the forces of business have invaded the domestic refuge. Home and office have become one, a union enabled by the electronic "freedom" to work at home. In some instances, it's hard to tell, for example, whether a home is in fact a home, or just a corporate office where people happen to sleep over.

Questions

a. Do you think the house of the future will be as much a place of work as a home?

b. If so, should we be concerned about that development? Explain. See Peter Whoriskey, "Brave New House," *Miami Herald*, August 1, 1999, p. 5M.

Globalization

All of the critics' concerns about the domination of American life by big corporations and business values are now being applied to the entire globe. With the fall of the Soviet Union and the triumph of capitalism, the world has come to understand that free markets are simply more efficient than government rules. As a result, national boundaries are receding in importance, technology is shrinking the world, multinational companies are treating the world as one big market, less developed countries are trying to improve living standards by connecting to that market, financial assets flow freely and almost instantaneously from one side of the globe to the other, and the world becomes one highly greased, interconnected mass market. A lot of good news emerges from globalization: less developed countries have the opportunity to raise their standard of living, the benefits of competition and efficiency (better products at lower prices) reach more people, and as one Canadian journalist expresses it, the world is now at our door:

> I can buy Paris- or New York–designed garments at Philippines or Indonesian prices at what amounts to my local corner store. Where strong coffee was unobtainable a dozen years ago, I now have four espresso-equipped cafes within three blocks. In my small town, I can have delivered to my door *Le Monde, The Asian Wall Street Journal,* and *Izvestia.* After coming home in my Swedish car, I can watch on my Japanese TV set the BBC news at 1800 hours, news from Paris at 1900, and news from Brussels at 2200 hours.[59.]

Fears

America has enjoyed unprecedented prosperity; from our view, globalization simply looks like the welcome spread of capitalist values to the entire world. Not surprisingly, however, many people are alarmed. They see a world rapidly coming under the thumb of America, and more particularly, America's giant, multinational corporations. Capital, technology, goods, and services can be moved rapidly throughout the world aided by the new free trade arrangements such as the North American Free

> They see a world rapidly coming under the thumb of America

Trade Agreement, the World Trade Organization, the European Union, and so on. These free trade mechanisms, in the critics' view, have essentially nullified the regulatory power of national governments and left corporations free to do largely as they wish. They see a world ruled by corporate interests with the following results:

- The rich get richer and the poor fall further behind.
- Whole ecosystems, such as the Amazon Basin, are despoiled for profit-seeking purposes.
- Rural cultures are displaced and an urban migration follows.
- Financial instability, like the Asian financial crisis of the late 1990s, is inevitable.
- Labor is exploited to satisfy market demands.
- Consumerism swells and traditional values are submerged.

[For the World Trade Association, see **http://www.wto.org**]

An Assessment

Are the critics correct that America's multinational corporations and our thorough commitment to business values are a threat to the well-being of the world? Certainly markets are imperfect. Many economists concede that financial instability, in the short term at least, is likely to accompany globalization.[60] And we don't yet have any meaningful global mechanism for dealing with the monopoly concerns that American antitrust laws address. (See Chapters 10 and 11.) Furthermore, the developed nations, led by the United States, clearly are complicit in some degree of labor exploitation, and we clearly do consume more than our "fair" share of the world's dwindling supply of fish, forests, clean air, and other resources. In general, then, while markets are clearly more efficient than rules, we still must doubt whether largely unrestrained markets produce increased fairness.

Rich/Poor   Scholar James Mittelman raises perhaps the fundamental globalization question:

> Is it ethically sustainable? Morally and politically, is it possible to maintain a global system in which the world's 225 richest people have a combined wealth equal to the annual income of 2.5 billion people, the poorest 47 percent of the world's population? In which the three richest people have assets that exceed the combined GDP of the forty-eight least developed countries?[61]

Of course, some of that rich–poor gap must be attributed to corruption and mismanagement, but moral sensitivity and our own interests require that we reflect a bit on the world's sharp division between haves and have-nots.

Consider Haiti, an example very close to home, but one that clearly has not profited from that proximity. Haiti is the poorest country in the Western Hemisphere and the fourth poorest in the world, with a life expectancy of 52 years for women and 48 for men and unemployment near 70 percent.[62] Haitian sweatshop wages are often under 50 cents per hour. American corporations control much of the Haitian economy, and about 60 percent of the small country's imports and exports involve the United States. As the

U.S. Network for Economic Justice reports, those close ties between America and Haiti have meant little to the Haitian people:

> Whereas corporations receive vast incentives to set up plants in Haiti . . . returns to the Haitian economy are minimal. . . . Decades of public investments and policy manipulation by the World Bank, the IMF, and the U.S. government have deliberately created an environment where the exploitation of workers is hailed as an incentive to invest in Haiti.[63]

Outsourcing   As in the Haitian example, globalization critics accuse the industrial world and particularly the United States of exploitation under the banner of free trade. To many in the West, however, that so-called exploitation really represents the wholesale export of good jobs to the low-wage, underdeveloped nations. Millions of American jobs have moved or will move to India, China, Mexico, and other low-wage nations. So what looks like low-wage exploitation to some represents enormous job losses, especially for blue-collar workers in the United States. The outsourcing furor in America has increased in recent years because the job losses have shifted to the influential middle classes now that white-collar jobs such as accounting and programming are also sailing out of the United States in large numbers. Some predictions expect 3.3 million American white-collar jobs to move to low-cost countries by 2015.[64] To corporate managers these dramatic labor shifts reflect a healthy market that will pay off for industrial nations by providing savings that will lead to new investments and new products while putting money in the hands of new customers in the low-wage nations. But to those losing their jobs, outsourcing doesn't work as the market theorizes:

> "The consulting firm I work for is sending jobs to India," said Steve Ward, a computer programmer in Philadelphia. . . . Ward, holding a sign—"Will Code for Food"—dismissed the notion that everyone benefits from the corporate savings generated by offshore outsourcing. "Companies are predatory institutions, and they have to be controlled," he said.[65]

Terrorism   Globalization, some critics say, is at least partly responsible for the terrorist violence that defaces contemporary life. Obviously, the 9/11 terrorists hated America or at least parts of American life. Certainly no rational, ethical person can find any credible justification for their horrific harm to innocents. But perhaps we can understand that others are threatened by an American culture that encourages women to assume commanding leadership roles; that allows everyone an open voice; that tolerates what must appear to be an unrestrained sexuality; and that, via its corporate community, exports those values to the Islamic world, much of which deplores these Western, capitalist preferences. A big share of the terrorists' anger certainly has to do with the Arab–Israeli conflict and America's role in it; but to some extent the terrorists and many Islamic people generally see America and its culture as a direct threat to what they value in life.

But to French political philosopher Jean-Francois Revel, all of this anger toward America and American corporate success can be summarized in one word: envy.[66] Critics, Revel thinks, try to convert the United States into a scapegoat in an effort to discredit capitalist, free market thinking. "Thus," Revel comments, "a practically uninterrupted economic growth over 17 years (1983–2000), a technological revolution without precedent since the 19th century, the creation of tens of millions of new jobs, an unemployment level fallen to a little over 4 percent, a tremendous population increase (going from 248 to 281 million between 1990 and 2000), all this was but a 'dream.' If only France had dreamt that way!"[67]

Corporate Duty?   Whether the criticisms are fair or not, as the market increasingly "Americanizes" or "Westernizes" the globe, do American corporations bear some responsibility for addressing the resulting conflict? Certainly these problems, to the extent they are addressed at all, have traditionally been the province of government; but as globalization has magnified corporate power, we must wonder whether corporations won't increasingly be expected to fulfill expanded and, doubtless, uncomfortable new roles. Harvard Business School professor Christopher Bartlett explains:

> In our collective post–September 11 struggle to build a safer, more harmonious world, those leading today's multinational corporations must become much more attuned to the ways in which their actions can and do impact the fragile social, political, and economic environments in which they operate worldwide. Yet far too often these powerful companies have been so focused on their core economic role that they have ignored the huge social and political impact they have.[68]

Of course, as corporations do give more attention to global social and political concerns, they are also criticized for exercising too much power, as examined in the article that follows.

READING ▸ ## Rise of the Corporate Nation–State

Laurent Belsie, *Christian Science Monitor*

Around the globe, more and more corporations are beginning to act like governments.

They negotiate with guerrilla leaders, build roads, and set up schools. Increasingly, they're setting labor standards in places where nations can't or won't.

There's only one problem.

By accepting more social responsibility, they're taking on more power just as a small but growing backlash against rising corporate power is taking hold in the United States. The movement burst on the scene . . . during demonstrations against the World Trade Organization (WTO) in Seattle last year. . . .

At the heart of this debate lies a simple question: Who should set society's agenda—big business or big government? . . .

"The real question out there is the conflict between mobile international capital on the one hand versus nationalism on the other," says John Ellwood, professor of public policy at the University of California at Berkeley. . . .

By most accounts, corporations are getting stronger while governments are getting weaker. "Business has taken a much more central role in our society," says Michael Maccoby, an anthropologist and management consultant in Washington.

Reasons given for this shift vary. Some observers say the trend is irreversible because globalization will make the corporation, not the nation–state, the primary entity on the world stage in the 21st century. Others see only a temporary pendulum swing.

Either way, signs of the new business activism lie everywhere:

- In Colombia last month, two American entrepreneurs met with a guerrilla leader to negotiate for peace—over the objections of the U.S. State Department.

- Reebok International built a school three years ago in Pakistan as part of its effort to move children from factories into schools. The company, based in Stoughton, Massachusetts, guarantees that its soccer balls are not made with child labor—one of the very few corporations to make such an explicit commitment.

- Recognizing the growing importance of business, the United Nations has created a global compact that urges businesses to uphold certain environment, labor, and human rights principles.

The trend draws sharp criticism from some activists. "Do we want a social responsibility movement, where we have the corporations throw us some crumbs while they accumulate more power?" asks Russell Mokhiber, editor *of Corporate Crime Reporter,* a legal weekly in Washington. "Or do we want to challenge the notion of the corporation? They shouldn't have the power that they have."

For example, Mokhiber likens current campaign finance laws to legalized bribery of government officials by corporations. "There's no comparison in terms of straight raw power," he says. "[Corporations] dominate the political process."

Other would-be reformers take the opposite tack. If they can't get governments to act, they turn to a corporation—even if such a move increases its power.

"In some ways, it's government default, it seems to me, that puts companies in this position," says Sam Brown, executive director of the Fair Labor Association, a coalition of corporations and nonprofit groups aiming to protect the rights of apparel and footwear workers worldwide. "And if the only economic authority around to make this happen is corporations, then OK."

Leading companies in the social responsibility movement defend their actions. "It's not about power," says Holly Carver, acting director of government affairs for Levi Strauss & Co. in San Francisco. "It's about making sure that people are treated well."

These companies say they're eager to have governments take the power back. "It isn't because we're in the business of operating schools," says Doug Cahn, Reebok's vice president of human rights programs. "We want to use it as an example of how government can do better. It's to drive change."

*   *   *   *   *

Source: *Christian Science Monitor,* April 10, 2000, p. 1. Reprinted by permission.

Questions
1. *a.* Should corporations take on bigger social duties around the globe, or will that direction lead to a dangerous concentration of power in corporate hands? Explain.
   b. Are corporations likely to be the "savior" of less developed nations around the world, or are they being expected to take on roles for which they are ill-suited? Explain.
2. Why might corporations decide to involve themselves in closing the global rich–poor gap?
3. Why should nations worry about the loss of their traditional cultures?
4. Does cultural diversity matter to the welfare of the world? Explain.

[See the Corporate Watch Web site for an extensive database of concerns about globalization: **http://www.corpwatch.org**]

Questions—Part One

1. Journalist Eric Liu complained, in early 1999, about the conversion of public spaces (parks, streets, schools, stadiums) to advertising "vessels":

   > Rollerblade now hawks its wares in Central Park under the banner "The Official Skate of New York City Parks." Buses in Boston and other cities don't just carry ad placards anymore; some of them have been turned into rolling billboards. . . . [W]e haven't yet draped Mount Rushmore with a Nike "swoosh." But things are heading in that general direction.
   >
   >   You might say at this point, "What's the big deal? America is commercialized—get over it!" And I admit my views may sound a bit old-fashioned. But this isn't a matter of priggishness or nostalgia. Public spaces matter.[69]

   Why should we be concerned about the "commercialization" of public spaces?

2. According to *The Wall Street Journal,* "[S]hopping can be all things to all people. It can alleviate loneliness and dispel boredom; it can be a sport and can be imbued with the thrill of the hunt; it can provide escape, fulfill fantasies, relieve depression."[70]

  a. Is shopping an American addiction that requires treatment in the manner of alcoholism, for example? Explain.

  b. Does shopping fill a void of some sort in our lives? If so, how was that void created? Or was it always there? Explain.

  c. If you reduced shopping in your life to that which is required to meet only the necessities, how would you use the time that would then be available to you?

  d. Are shopping malls replacing the family in American life? Explain.

  e. Even if shopping has assumed excessive importance in our lives, is the business community in any way to blame for that condition? Explain.

3. Tom Bratz, in a *Newsweek* commentary, spoofed America's willingness to make a buck in any way possible. He argued that we need to be more aggressive in our efforts to balance the federal budget. His suggestion: advertising.

> The first step would be to name the official products of various government agencies. The Ford Probe is an obvious choice as the official automobile of the Department of Justice. . . . Next would come the subtle placement of various products at televised events—when the president addresses the nation from the Oval Office, what could possibly look more natural than a Big Mac and some french fries sitting on his desk? . . . Then we'd start to have corporate sponsors for all government functions. We'd no longer have a State of the Union Address; it would be the Miller Lite State of the Union Address.[71]

  Comment.

4. Bob Ortega, reporter for *The Wall Street Journal:*

> To denizens of the counterculture, Wal-Mart stands for everything they dislike about American society—mindless consumerism, paved landscapes, and homogenization of community identity.
>   "We've lost a sense of taste, of refinement—we're destroying our culture and replacing it with . . .Wal-Mart," says Allan B. Wolf [an Ohio high school teacher].[72]

  Is Wal-Mart a threat to America's long-term well-being? Explain.

5. *a.* Has your education been designed primarily to prepare you for a utilitarian role as a producer and/or consumer in the Corporate State? Explain.

  b. Is business America's dominant art form? Explain.

6. *The Wall Street Journal* recently observed that outsourcing will not destroy the American jobs of the future, but that the real problem may be whether outsourcing (and technology) could widen the gap between good "brainpower" jobs and poorly paid physical jobs. Explain how outsourcing may exacerbate the rich–poor income gap. (See David Wessel, "The Future of Jobs," *The Wall Street Journal,* March 2, 2004, p. A1.)

7. How do you explain the terrorists' September 11, 2001, attack on America?

8. Nicholas Lemann reminds us that various "elite" groups have dominated American life over the years. More than a century ago, capitalist titans such as J. P. Morgan, John D. Rockefeller, and Andrew Carnegie were in charge. They were followed in the forepart of the 20th century by white (male), Anglo-Saxon Protestants (WASPS) who were then displaced by an "SAT meritocracy" of very bright people who attended America's most distinguished colleges and universities. Lehman says the SAT giants

have now been replaced by a new elite. Who are they? (See Nicholas Lemann, "Who Will Be the Next Elite?" *Time,* February 21, 2000.)

9. In your judgment, does the following quote accurately express the current American attitude toward the accumulation of money? Explain. Michael Novak of the American Enterprise Institute writes,

> The vast majority of Americans choose what they want to do, and they don't choose merely to seek wealth. Most of the people I know seek the work that satisfies them most completely. Of course a sliver of people want money, money, money, but I think they're only a small number.[73]

10. *a.* Do Americans trust the business community? Explain.
    b. Does it matter? Explain.

11. In 1980 Ted Peters, an associate professor of systematic theology at the Pacific Lutheran Seminary and the Graduate Theological Union, asked,

> How will the advancing postindustrial culture influence the course of religion? It is my forecast that religion will become increasingly treated as a consumer item.
>
> Because our economy produces so much wealth, we are free to consume and consume beyond the point of satisfaction. There is a limit to what we can consume in the way of material goods—new homes, new cars, new electronic gadgets, new brands of beer, new restaurants, and so on. So we go beyond material wants to consume new personal experiences—such as broader travel, exotic vacations, continuing education, exciting conventions, psychotherapy, and sky diving.
>
> What will come next and is already on the horizon is the consumption of spiritual experiences—personal growth cults, drug-induced ecstasy, world-traveling gurus, training in mystical meditation to make you feel better, etc. Once aware of this trend, religious entrepreneurs and mainline denominations alike will take to pandering their wares, advertising how much spiritual realities "can do to you." It will be subtle, and it will be cloaked in the noble language of personal growth, but nevertheless the pressure will be on between now and the year 2000 to treat religious experience as a commodity for consumption.[74]

    a. Is Peters's forecast coming true? Explain.
    b. Is marketing necessary to the survival and growth of religion? Explain.
    c. Is marketing a threat to the legitimacy and value of religion? Explain.

12. In your opinion, which of the following will be the biggest threat to America in the future: big government, big labor, or big business?

13. In 1993 a scholarly book, *The Concept of Honest Poverty,* attacking Japan's money-centered society, became a huge best-seller (600,000 copies sold in eight months). The author, Koki Nakano, explained his thesis:

> However rich Japan becomes, it will never get the respect of the world. To earn respect, we need dignity, chivalry, and the philosophy of honest poverty. Our image is that of a country that's good at making things but has no culture. Foreigners say Japanese lack character and dignity, and think of us just as people with money.[75]

    a. What does he mean by *honest poverty?*
    b. Do we honor honest poverty in America? Explain.
    c. Do you admire the Japanese? Explain.

      d. Aren't rich people highly respected in America? Explain.

      e. Why is American culture so widely admired?

      f. In the end, is culture more important to the fate of a nation than wealth? Explain.

14. Do you think allegiance to the company will become more important than allegiance to the state? Is that a desirable direction? Raise the arguments on both sides of the latter question.

15. As expressed in *BusinessWeek,* "Increasingly, the corporation will take over the role of the mother, supplying day care facilities where children can be tended around the clock."[76] How do you feel about the corporation as mother? Explain.

Part Two—Corporate Social Responsibility

Introduction

As illustrated in Chapter 2 and in Part 1 of this chapter, the business community has been the subject of intense criticism. Journalist Daniel Seligman put it this way:

> A standard view of the American corporation . . . is that it is an efficient deliverer of goods and services, yet also a wellspring of social injustice. Driven by a narrow calculus of profits, it is oblivious to the common good. And so, the litany goes, it degrades the environment, promotes unsafe products, skimps on workplace safety and (current indictment No. 1), lays off workers who have given it years of service.[77]

That broadly shared perception of business misdeeds or indifference, in conjunction with the growing influence of business values throughout American life, has led in recent decades to the development of the notion of *corporate social responsibility* (sometimes also referred to as *corporate citizenship*). The issue is as follows: Must business decision making include consideration not merely of the welfare of the firm but of society as a whole? For most contemporary readers, the answer is self-evident—of course business bears a social responsibility. Business has enjoyed a central and favored role in American life. As such, it must assume a measure of the burden for the welfare of the total society. Indeed, businesspeople themselves now generally endorse businesses' responsibility to help solve society's problems. Companies continue to put profits first; but responding to a *Wall Street Journal*–Harris poll, 77 percent of corporate recruiters said it is important to hire students with an awareness of social and environmental responsibility.[78] And students themselves are increasingly interested in the social responsibility/corporate citizenship approach to business practice. Similar philosophies such as the *triple bottom line* (giving close accounting attention to social and environmental performance as well as financial performance) and the *sustainable* corporation (operating the business with a focus on environmentally sensitive practices that will husband scarce resources and maintain a healthy community now and in the future) have powerful appeal to many students and managers. Those approaches are of interest to the corporate community; and as the following article suggests, MBA programs have begun to aggressively reflect these newer goals. [For the "Global Reporting Initiative" on sustainability practices around the world, see **http://www.globalreporting.org/**]

Schools Turning Out Kinder, Gentler MBAs

Associated Press

At business schools across the country, future business leaders are learning to be kinder, gentler managers. In fact, if you're thinking about getting an MBA, be prepared to learn how to use your financial analysis, accounting, and marketing skills to help the environment and the community.

While that may come as a surprise to those who think of business school as a breeding ground for hard-charging executives obsessed with bottom-line results, it also reflects the realities that businesses are dealing with today. As companies go global, their shareholders are demanding more responsible business practices.

Jen Boulden, 30, is a big believer that businesses can be powerful agents of change in the environment. After working in technology marketing for eight years, she decided to get her MBA at George Washington University, in part because the school's curriculum would allow her to combine her passion for the environment with her business skills. "I wouldn't have gone back to school if I didn't find an environmentally oriented program within an MBA structure," said Boulden.

Once relegated to the fringes of a business school's curriculum, schools are slowly integrating ethics and social and environmental management into their classes. At Stanford University, for example, classes on social and environmental issues are woven into 12 of the 14 courses that business school students are required to take. At some schools, students can choose a concentration in environmental management or sustainability, the idea that a company can meet its financial goals without hurting the environment. And outside of the classroom, schools are holding more seminars and conferences on corporate social responsibility.

The Aspen Institute's Business & Society Program and the World Resources Institute's Sustainable Enterprise Program recently issued a report on the trend titled "Beyond Gray Pinstripes 2003." The study found about 45 percent of the schools that participated require students to take one or more courses on such subjects as ethics and corporate social responsibility.

That's up from 34 percent in 2001, the last time the survey was conducted.

* * * * *

"The idea of just focusing on shareholder value isn't enough for companies," said Meghan Chapple, manager of business education at WRI. Now companies have to work with broader constituencies, such as the community, the environment, and employees, she noted.

Student interest also is rising. At UNC's Kenan-Flagler Business School, about 20 percent of students attend the school because of its concentration in sustainable enterprise.

At Michigan Business School, when Timothy Fort started teaching business ethics 10 years ago his biggest hurdle was trying to convince students it was an important issue. Today, with the number of students in his class having more than quadrupled to over 400, his biggest challenge is trying to convince them that they won't be able to solve all the world's problems immediately.

Meanwhile, participation in Net Impact, a network of MBAs with an interest in social and environmental business issues, has grown to 8,000 members today from 1,350 in 1998, while the number of chapters jumped to 85 from 45 over the same period. "It's not just the tree-huggers anymore; it's more mainstream," said Benjamin Klasky, executive director of Net Impact.

Source: *Waterloo/Cedar Falls Courier,* October 20, 2003, p. B6. Reprinted by permission of the Associated Press.

Questions

1. *a.* Would America be better off with "kinder, gentler" managers in charge of the corporate community? Explain.

   b. If you were in charge of a corporation, would you be looking for "kinder, gentler" managers? Explain.

2. Have your business school courses given sufficient attention to social responsibility issues? Explain.

3. Do consumers care whether companies are socially responsible? Explain.

A New Ideology

The ascendance of the social responsibility concept represents one of the most striking ideological shifts in American history. From the colonial period until roughly 1950, business was expected to concentrate on one goal—the production and distribution of the best products at the lowest possible prices. Of course, social responsibility arguments were raised, but business was largely exempt from any affirmative duty for the resolution of social problems. Business scholars and critics began in the 1950s to consider a larger role for corporate America. Now in the 21st century, the role of business in society has been radically altered. Profit seeking remains central and essential, but for most businesspeople, the rather unwieldy ingredient of social responsibility must be added to the equation.

What Is Social Responsibility?

The sweeping notion of corporate social responsibility is not readily reduced to a brief definition, but Davis and Blomstrom some years ago captured the core ingredients: "The idea of social responsibility is that decision makers are obligated to take actions which protect and improve the welfare of society as a whole along with their own interests."[79] More systematically, the social role of business can be thought of as an ideological continuum, corresponding roughly to the familiar American political spectrum of conservative/Republican views on the right, moderates in the middle, and liberal/Democrats on the left. Figure 3.1 depicts that continuum and is best understood by reading "backward" from right to left. On the right side of the spectrum lies the free market view where *profit maximization* is considered the best measure of social responsibility. Across the middle lies a viewpoint that is commonly thought of as the *long-term company interest* where profits are the first consideration, but where satisfied workers, customers, and community members are also of importance, within some reasonable limits, in order to secure the firm's long-term survival. On the left side of the spectrum lies the *triple bottom line/sustainability* movement that calls for a revolutionary re-visioning of corporate goals and practices such that profit maximization is only one of three key measures of success. Triple bottom line advocates specifically call for accounting practices that measure and respect the firm's *social* and *environmental* performance just as the firm's *financial* performance is measured and respected. The goal is to ensure the long-term viability (sustainability) of the organization and the total society.

Now let's examine the continuum in a bit more detail. [For the Corporate Social Responsibility home page, see **http://www.elca.org/dcs/Corp.html**]

FIGURE 3.1
A Social Responsibility Continuum

| Triple bottom line/ sustainability (social + environmental + financial) | Long-term company interest (profit + good deeds) | Profit maximization (profit) |

Profit Maximization   Here the dominant concern lies in maximizing shareholders' interests. Those shareholders, after all, are the owners of the firm. They are taking the financial risk. Hence, from a profit maximization point of view, the only responsible and moral course of behavior is to reap the highest return possible, within the law. Nobel prize–winning economist Milton Friedman is the most prominent advocate of the profit maximization view:

> The only responsible and moral course of behavior is to reap the highest return possible, within the law.

> [In a free economy] there is one and only one social responsibility of business—to use its resources and engage in activities designed to increase its profits, so long as it stays within the rules of the game, which is to say, engages in open and free competition, without deception or fraud.[80]

Friedman, employing free market reasoning, believes the firm that maximizes its profits is necessarily maximizing its contribution to society. He asks how managers can know what the public interest is. He also argues that any dilution of the profit-maximizing mode—such as charitable contributions—is a misuse of the stockholders' resources. The individual stockholder, he contends, should dispose of assets according to her or his own wishes.

Herbert Stein, former chair of the President's Council of Economic Advisers, shares Friedman's doubts about the idea of social responsibility, but Stein's concerns are of a more pragmatic nature. He argues that business is simply ill suited for solving social problems:

> Efficiency in maximizing the nation's product . . . is not the only objective of life. But it is the one that private corporations are best qualified to serve. I don't want to be a purist about this. I don't object to corporations contributing to the United Givers Fund. . . . But to rely on corporations' responsibility to solve major social problems—other than the problem of how to put our people and other resources to work most efficiently—would be a wasteful diversion from their most important function. Our other objectives can be better served in other ways, by individuals and other institutions.[81]

Long-Term Company Interest   Across the broad middle ground of our social responsibility continuum lie those firms, doubtless the great majority, who believe that a strong bottom line, in many cases, requires considerations beyond the immediate, short-run, profit-maximizing interests of the firm. In a sense, these managers are merely taking a longerterm view of profit maximization. They recognize the imperative of a strong return on the shareholder's investment, but they also believe that achieving that return may require heightened sensitivity to the welfare of employees, consumers, and the community. Furthermore, they often embrace the view that socially responsible behavior, within reasonable bounds, is simply the "right thing" to do.

Triple Bottom Line/Sustainability   Managers, whether traditional profit maximizers or those embracing the longer-term, more socially conscious attitude, are being pushed by scholars, activists, government, and often the larger community to adopt a bigger, broader conception of social responsibility—one that significantly redefines the corporate role and calls for values and tactics that will produce a sustainable, healthy global community. This redefinition is explained by Steve Rochlin:

> The new corporate citizenship challenges executives to find alternatives to zero-sum solutions that often emphasize shareholder value at the cost of social and environmental welfare. Instead, the new corporate citizenship challenges companies to deliver not just financial returns but also environmental and social value—together marking the pillars of what is called a "triple bottom line." . . .
>
> The new corporate citizenship requires business transparency and accountability regarding the ways in which business practices generate benefits and costs for issues ranging from employee diversity, community development, working conditions, clean air and water, human rights, poverty, and corruption.[82]

The triple bottom line/sustainability approach recognizes the necessity for financial success but also argues that social and environmental responsibilities are of equal importance and that corporations giving close attention to those social and economic duties have a powerful competitive advantage that will contribute to both organizational and societal sustainability. As Rochlin notes, the firm committed to triple bottom line principles and sustainability will be concerned about social equity issues such as community philanthropy, employee satisfaction, lawful corporate governance, transparency in business practices, fair treatment of customers, and so on. In the environmental domain, sustainability will require attention to energy efficiency, waste minimization, recycling, and the total ecological agenda. All of this will be achieved via market principles, but the market is expected to work more effectively through a new spirit of cooperation between business, government, nongovernmental organizations (NGOs), and the citizenry. In sum, the idea is that the survival (sustainability) of the corporation and of the global community requires new values and new decision-making tactics that will take a balanced view of the triple bottom line while implementing accounting procedures that measure success not just in profits but in social and environmental goals as well. Figure 3.2 depicts the change in values that presumably would need to accompany a shift to the sustainability approach. [For a critique of triple bottom line thinking, see **www.businessethics.ca/3bl**]

FIGURE 3.2

Values

Who Will Satisfy the Demand for Caring Capitalism?		
Old Paradigm	$\rightarrow$	**New Paradigm**
Careless	$\rightarrow$	Careful, caring
Control	$\rightarrow$	Stewardship
Me	$\rightarrow$	We
Monocultures	$\rightarrow$	Diversity
Growth	$\rightarrow$	Sustainability[83]

Social Responsibility Pyramid

Another way of visualizing socially responsible business practice is depicted in Figure 3.3. Social responsibility, or corporate citizenship as Carroll sometimes labels it, necessarily begins with making a profit in a lawful fashion; but simultaneously the socially responsible firm moves beyond the minimal demands of economics and law to find the ethical course of action—the behavior best suited to the demands of virtue and moral principle. In striving for profitable, lawful, ethical conduct, that company may also choose to engage in discretionary philanthropic (charitable) efforts (money, time, facilities, programs) to build a better community.[84] [For a "comprehensive, worldwide information resource on corporate social responsibility," see **http://www.bsr.org/BSRResources/index.cfm**]

FIGURE 3.3
The Social Responsibility Pyramid

Source: Archie B. Carroll, "The Pyramid of Corporate Social Responsibility: Toward the Moral Management of Organizational Stakeholders." Reprinted from *Business Horizons* 34, no. 4 (July–August 1991), pp. 39, 42. Copyright 1991 by the Foundation for the School of Business at Indiana University. Used with permission.

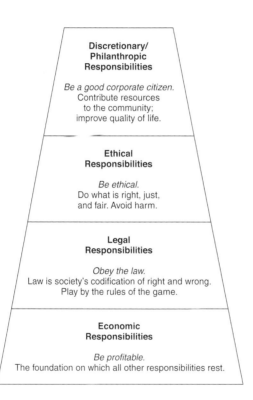

Discretionary/ Philanthropic Responsibilities

Be a good corporate citizen.
Contribute resources
to the community;
improve quality of life.

Ethical Responsibilities

Be ethical.
Do what is right, just,
and fair. Avoid harm.

Legal Responsibilities

Obey the law.
Law is society's codification of right and wrong.
Play by the rules of the game.

Economic Responsibilities

Be profitable.
The foundation on which all other responsibilities rest.

Corporations Practicing Social Responsibility

Obviously we have no shortage of social problems both domestically and globally. In recent years the corporate community has become convinced that it needs, for various reasons, to take a more active role in addressing those problems.

PRACTICING ETHICS Big Business—A Social Issues Leader?

Journalist Marc Gunther argues that big business is becoming a leader in addressing social problems:[85]

> Despite the understandable cynicism about the corporate world that has been fed by Enron and other scandals, many of America's big companies are becoming more socially responsible, more green, more diverse, more transparent, and more committed to the common good—as well as the bottom line.[86]

Gunther points to Hewlett-Packard, Dell, and IBM, which have agreed on a code of conduct to audit and ensure the health, safety, and human rights of the people in developing countries who work for the computer giants' electronics suppliers around the globe.[87] Likewise, Gunther notes that 227 *Fortune* 500 companies provide domestic partner benefits and that corporate America is a strong supporter of affirmative action.[88] The environmental movement clearly is influencing business practice as, for example, giant lumber retailers Home Depot and Lowe's have pledged to stop buying wood from endangered forests, and DuPont has cut its greenhouse gas emissions by 65 percent since 1990.[89] Finally, Gunther argues that leading companies have decided that they must become more open—more *transparent*—in describing their business practices. Gap recently followed that path in acknowledging that some overseas workers who make its clothes have been mistreated.

Questions

1. *a.* Do you think Gunther is correct in arguing that big business is responding in meaningful ways to the corporate social responsibility movement? Explain.

   b. Should corporations do so? Explain.

2. What forces would move corporations to give increased attention to social issues?

Ben & Jerry's Probably the most highly publicized example of intentionally conducting business according to social responsibility principles is the famous Ben & Jerry's ice cream chain. "Hippie" capitalists Ben Cohen and Jerry Greenfield built ice cream flavors like Cherry Garcia into consumer favorites, and they did so in a socially conscious way that brought them admiration and fame. Their Vermont-based company paid above-market prices for local milk. Each employee received three free pints of ice cream per day. Seven and one-half percent of pretax profits went to charity. Then in 2000, under pressure from shareholders to accept a generous offer, Cohen and Greenfield sold Ben & Jerry's to Unilever, the multinational conglomerate. Doubtless the deal looked like a sellout to some, but Unilever contractually committed itself to carry on Ben & Jerry's charitable efforts. And Ben Cohen has since formed an investment fund to buy companies in low-income neighborhoods where he intends to raise wages. Cohen's plan is a prominent example of the recent movement toward *venture philanthropy,* where entrepreneurs start or buy companies expressly for the purpose of generating profits for charitable and socially responsible projects.

Invest Responsibly

Students at some of America's top universities have developed an advocacy group, Responsible Endowments Coalition, to push universities to invest their many billions of endowment dollars in companies that follow ethical business practices. [Learn about this student initiative at **www.SRIendowment.org**]

But Is Corporate Responsibility Good Business?

The evidence is mixed, but generally supportive of the idea that the market rewards good conduct and punishes bad conduct. A 1999 review of the sound, scholarly work to date found 33 studies showing a positive relationship between socially responsible behavior and favorable financial performance, while 5 studies found a negative relationship and 14 found no effect or were inconclusive.[90] Another review of 27 studies found convincing statistical evidence that the stock market punishes firms caught in illegal or socially irresponsible behavior by reducing shareholder wealth, at least in the short term.[91] On the other hand, a 2004 study could not establish that philanthropical giving had an effect on corporate financial performance, although "firm owners do not lose when firms contribute to charitable causes."[92]

Question

1. Build a list of the arguments for and against social responsibility for business.

Part Three—Managing Social Responsibility

Stakeholder Approach

As the principle of social responsibility has become increasingly acceptable to the corporate community, the nature of the debate has shifted to identifying the new duties and assessing whether the corporation is meeting those duties. Many corporations, particularly those of great size, are confronting the practical notion of how best to manage the firm's response to social issues. Corporations are increasingly considering what scholars have labeled the *stakeholder model* of social responsibility. Under that model, the corporation identifies all of the groups (stockholders, customers, employees, communities, governments, unions, schools, and the like) that may affect the firm's performance or be affected by it. These are groups with a "stake" in the activities of the corporation. Of course, we have wide divisions of opinion about how expansive the list of stakeholders should be; and once identified, we have wide divisions of opinion about the extent of the corporation's duties toward those stakeholders. Certainly, scholarly advocates of the stakeholder approach see it as a redefinition of the nature of the corporation. Simply maximizing the interests of the primary stakeholders, the shareholders, would not, from the advocates' point of view, satisfy the corporation's social duties.

Building Stakeholder Relationships   Should stakeholder theory and social performance concerns significantly influence actual business practice? Business consultant Ann Svendsen points to Microsoft's enormously publicized difficulties as an example of a company harmed by poor stakeholder relations.[93] Antitrust losses in court, insensitive treatment of suppliers, efforts to manipulate the political process, and arm-twisting of corporate customers have brought storms of unfavorable publicity. And what about the firm that tries to do the socially responsible thing and offends its customers? What managerial response should we expect from American giant Procter & Gamble with its much-loved consumer products (Tide, Crest, Pampers) that were subjected to a 2004 boycott by conservative groups objecting to P & G's support of gay rights?

Svendsen argues that most business leaders have accepted the claim that companies have multiple stakeholders, but the difficult question lies in the attention given to each stakeholder relationship.[94] Historically, of course, shareholders towered over all other stakeholders in their perceived importance. Now that other stakeholders are asserting claims, how much attention must the firm pay to them? What sort of relationship should be developed with them? Can stakeholder relationships be regarded as opportunities for corporate growth and advantage rather than as burdensome claims on scarce resources? Recently scholars have theorized that the importance of a particular stakeholder to the corporation is determined by three factors:

- **Legitimacy.** Does the stakeholder have some kind of legal, ethical, or moral claim on the corporation?
- **Power.** Does the stakeholder have sufficient power to meaningfully affect the corporation?
- **Urgency.** Is the stakeholder demanding immediate attention?[95]

Manage or Collaborate? One plausible and common approach to stakeholders is to "manage" them—that is, to influence and perhaps control the behavior of those stakeholders. Thus the marketing department deals with consumers, human resources deals with employees, public affairs deals with the media, and so on.[96] Each department is expected to anticipate and mediate the stakeholder relationship in ways that are most advantageous to the firm. An alternative and arguably more "progressive" approach to stakeholders involves a collaborative strategy in which stakeholder relationships are regarded as being mutually defined, cooperative, reciprocal, and thus not subject to "management" by the firm.[97] The firm endeavors to understand and balance the interests and needs of all stakeholders with the view that this collaborative effort results in enhanced firm performance over the long term while building a healthier society. The collaborative view presumes that firms and stakeholders are significantly interdependent.[98]

Some recent theorizing refines stakeholder practice by suggesting that the attention given to a particular stakeholder depends on the firm's life-cycle stage.[99] Thus in a new firm's first stage (start-up), shareholders, customers, and creditors are likely to be dominant stakeholders because of their importance in generating and maintaining necessary revenue; but as the firm moves through stage two (emerging growth) to stage three (maturity), attention to the various stakeholders shifts according to firm needs. Then in stage four (decline/transition) the firm will again shift its stakeholder strategy, giving maximum time and resources to those who are most critical to its survival.[100] Of course, respect for stakeholders and social responsibility concerns generally will also vary depending on the industry the firm is part of. For example, environmental, governmental, and community groups are likely to receive much closer attention from a waste disposal firm than one involved in financial services.[101] [For an overview of stakeholder research, see **http://www.mgmt.utoronto.ca/~stake/**]

All of this new complexity requires the contemporary manager to learn about a much broader range of issues than was the norm historically. Profit now rests not merely in providing the best product or service at the lowest price, but in understanding and dealing with the complex interplay between the corporation, government, and society. Thus today's manager is likely to be increasingly involved in identifying and addressing social issues and stakeholder concerns. A measure of the emerging importance of corporate social performance is the fact that firms increasingly are linking executive pay to success in addressing social issues. Nearly two-thirds of the 106 big manufacturing firms responding to a 2000 survey said that environmental performance was a factor in setting senior executive pay, and a growing number of companies consider workforce diversity, customer satisfaction, and employee satisfaction in making compensation decisions.[102]

Stakeholder Results   Measuring the success of social responsibility activism is very difficult. Recently, however, a public interest group, the Council on Economic Priorities, has developed the first global standard, SA8000 (social accountability 8000), that measures companies' social and environmental records.[103] SGS-ICS, an independent Swiss certification agency, will accredit companies that meet the SA8000 standards in the areas of child labor, forced labor, health and safety, freedom of association, discrimination, disciplinary practices, working hours, compensation, and management systems.[104] [See **www.sa8000.org**]

The Global Reporting Initiative, supported by the United Nations and various foundations, was established to develop consistent global guidelines for reporting the economic, environmental, and social performance of corporations (and, eventually, other organizations). GRI's specific task is to devise a generally accepted reporting system, equivalent to financial reporting, to measure and display corporations' success in achieving "sustainable" development.[105] [For more, see **www.globalreporting.org**]

Another way of looking at the results of stakeholder activism is to observe how the business community responds when wrongs occur. The devastating 1984 chemical spill at Bhopal, India, was one of the great tragedies in world industrial history. A chemical leak at a Union Carbide plant resulted in more than 3,000 deaths and tens of thousands of injuries. Legal and market pressures were intense, of course, but as *The Wall Street Journal* reported, the entire chemical industry was compelled to respond to the "public outcry and concern" that followed the disaster:[106]

> The chemical leak . . . spurred a revolution in approaches to safety, pollution, and community relations that have made chemical plants in the United States more accessible and more accountable to their neighbors. New laws forced plants to disclose safety and pollution data. And an army of community activists won new powers.[107]

Shareholder Approach

Stakeholder theory and corporate social performance have gained great credibility with academics and many managers. Others, however, argue that profits and shareholders must remain the consuming concern of management, and that a skilled focus on the bottom line will, incidentally but inevitably, result in the greatest good for society. That is, the company that maximizes its profits necessarily does not only what is best for its shareholders but also what is best for society generally. The shareholder/stakeholder debate is well illustrated by the heated competition between massive retailers Wal-Mart and Costco. Each week Wal-Mart serves some 140 million shoppers worldwide and saves those customers billions annually by its relentless focus on the bottom line and hence on the interests of its shareholders. Costco, on the other hand, has drawn great praise from management scholars for its close attention to worker welfare. Costco workers average about $16 per hour versus $11.50 at Wal-Mart. Costco annually pays $5,375 per employee for health care and contributes $1,400 to each employee's retirement plan, while the comparable figures for Wal-Mart are $3,500 and $745.[108] As a result, Costco's employee turnover is about one-third that of Wal-Mart. At the bottom line, both companies are highly profitable; but Wal-Mart's net profit margin of 3.4 percent doubles Costco's 1.7 percent—which means, for every dollar of revenue, Wal-Mart makes 3.4 cents versus 1.7 cents for Costco.[109] Journalist/financial adviser Malcolm Berko explains why, in his view, the tough, bottom-line, shareholder-focused approach of Wal-Mart will, in the end, whip the kinder, gentler stakeholder approach of Costco:

> **In this business of investing, it's the bottom line that counts while kindness and goodness aren't worth a pickled herring.**

COST (Costco) may be a good neighbor, but WMT (Wal-Mart) is certainly a better-managed company. In this business of investing, it's the bottom line that counts while kindness and goodness aren't worth a pickled herring. While COST may have a kind, empathetic, and sensitive social conscience, hard-driving, hard-hearted, and hard-headed WMT is doing precisely what its shareholders want it to do. WMT is making money, lots of money, and paying a dividend that has increased fivefold in the last eight years.

If you and your broker want to be socially conscious people, donate money to a charity or various charities of your choice. Investing is for making money, not for appeasing your soul by making feel-good choices.[110]

Of course, Wal-Mart, however profitable its operations, is the target of relentless criticism for its allegedly irresponsible business practices. Wal-Mart is facing a class-action lawsuit involving 1.6 million women who claim they are victims of sex discrimination in pay, promotion, and job assignments.

> **Entire communities have banished Wal-Mart's big boxes.**

Other lawsuits accuse Wal-Mart of failing to pay overtime. Entire communities have banished Wal-Mart's big boxes. By a large margin in 2004, the citizens of Inglewood, California, voted to block a proposed 60-acre development. Wal-Mart's low wages, vast parking lots, and gigantic, ugly stores are despised by many Americans. *BusinessWeek* commented recently on the Wal-Mart versus Costco debate:

> The larger question here is which model of competition will predominate in the United States. Costco isn't alone; some companies, even ones like New Balance Athletic Shoe Inc. that face cheap imports from China, have been able to compete by finding ways to lift productivity instead of cutting pay. But most executives find it easier to go the Wal-Mart route, even if shareholders fare just as well either way over the long run.
>
> Yet the cheap-labor model turns out to be costly in many ways. It can fuel poverty and related social ills and dump costs on other companies and taxpayers, who indirectly

pick up the health care tab for all the workers not insured by their parsimonious employers. What's more, the low-wage approach cuts into consumer spending and, potentially, economic growth. . . . Says Costco CEO James D. Sinegal, "Paying your employees well is not only the right thing to do but it makes for good business."[111]

Questions

1. Costco CEO Sinegal says high employee pay makes for good business. How can that be so?

2. William Beaver writes, "And what of the stakeholder model? Beyond generating some academic interest, perhaps the best that can be said is that although corporations will not be unmindful of their other stakeholders, the latter's concerns will remain a distant second to those holding the share."[112] Will shareholders or other stakeholders dominate corporate thought in the coming years? Explain.

3. In 1999 Bob Thompson sold his road-building firm for $422 million. Then he divided $128 million among his 550 workers, more than 80 of whom became millionaires. Thompson explained his generosity by saying, "I wanted to go out a winner, and I wanted to go out doing the right thing."[113]

   a. Which management strategy, Wal-Mart's low wages or Thompson's bonuses, is the more socially responsible? Explain.

   b. Can Wal-Mart, a publicly traded company owned by its shareholders, practice the same kind of generosity to employees that Thompson followed in distributing money that was literally his own? Explain.

   c. Stanford professor Jeffrey Pfeffer reflecting on the bonus strategy: "It's how you look at your workforce. . . . When I look at you, do I see a cost or do I see you as the only thing that separates me from my competition?"[114] Comment.

   d. Do you agree with Thompson that he did the "right thing"? Explain.

4. Layoffs can destroy worker trust. Is worker trust a critical ingredient in socially responsible management? Explain.

Part Four—Social Responsibility Cases: Case One: Workplace Diversity

Corporate leaders must produce a profit, but they also must conform to society's expectations for responsible conduct. Will the business community successfully shape its own behavior, or must the government intervene? Workplace discrimination continues to require extensive government oversight (see Chapter 13.). But now many corporations have moved beyond mere legal compliance to recognize the power of a diverse workforce combining the strengths of America's various demographic groups. In recent years, that attention to diversity has broadened to embrace gay, lesbian, bisexual, and transsexual Americans, as employers strive to "do the right thing" and to compete in a global market that requires all of our available resources.

Coming Out in Corporate America

CLIFF EDWARDS

One chilly fall day last year, Gary Osifchin trooped into a mandatory training session at S.C. Johnson & Son Inc. The privately held company, located in Racine, Wisconsin, which was voted 2003's "all-American city" by the National Civic League, manufactures Raid insecticide and Glade air fresheners. It's the kind of place where factory workers ride to the assembly line on Harley-Davidsons, dine on local bratwurst, and chase it down with Milwaukee beer.

About 20 plant managers were seated in a circle in a drab conference room. Osifchin, an S.C. Johnson marketing exec, walked into the center and started telling stories—about his boyfriend, his romantic life, and his experiences as a homosexual. He told coworkers, for instance, that one constant source of stress was having to come out anew every time he sat down with a new supervisor or switched units. "Somebody might see a picture of a guy on my desk, and that just sparks conversation," he said.

The frank talk was the kickoff of Gay 201, the upper-level course in gay sensitivity training offered at S.C. Johnson. It's available only to graduates of Gay 101, an introductory seminar that debunks stereotypes. The classes at Johnson are hardly anomalous. Eastman Kodak Co. offers similar sessions. Lucent Technologies, Microsoft, Southern California Edison, and dozens of others, meanwhile, send executives to weeklong training courses for gay managers at the University of California–Los Angeles Anderson School of Management.

The programs are just one small piece of a growing gay, lesbian, bisexual, and transgender (GLBT) rights movement in corporate America. Following in the footsteps of African Americans, women, and other traditionally marginalized groups, corporate gays are increasingly standing up for their rights. Defense contractors such as Raytheon Co. and Lockheed Martin Corp. now sponsor gay support groups. American Express Co. and Lehman Brothers Inc. promote their gay financial advisers in GLBT publications. Even culturally conservative Wal-Mart Stores Inc., which bans racy magazines and compact disks with offensive lyrics, this year adopted a nondiscrimination policy toward gays.

GALLOPING CHANGE

Of the nation's top 500 companies, 95 percent now offer policies that preclude discrimination based on sexual orientation, and 70 percent offer domestic partner benefits for same-sex couples. In 2000 the numbers stood at 51 percent and 25 percent, respectively. "To be competitive, we need to be able to get the best from people when they're at work, and to do that they need to bring their whole selves to the table," says Marge Connelly, director of operations at credit card issuer Capital One Financial Corp. She should know—she's a lesbian. "Being out is imperative for me to be a good leader," Connelly says. "You've got to let people know you. People have to trust you."

TOUGHER AT THE TOP

Still, it comes as no surprise that, as is the case with society at large, gays still face plenty of discrimination in their jobs. In a study by researcher Harris Interactive Inc. and marketer Witeck Combs Communications Inc., 41 percent of gay employees said they had been harassed, pressured to quit, or denied a promotion because of sexual orientation. Homosexuality is still legitimate legal grounds for firing an employee in 36 states.

So while gays may have won more acceptance at work, that does not mean they have gained legal, financial, and occupational equality. Intolerance that has built up over centuries does not disappear because of the sudden emergence of harassment-training videos and rainbow flags in cubicles. Many members of the GLBT community believe that discrimination increases as they rise up the corporate hierarchy into the executive suites, boardrooms, and country clubs where true power is wielded.

Need proof? Just look at a list of openly gay corporate leaders. While there are some big names—including DreamWorks SKG cofounder David Geffen, former Quark CEO Tim Gill, and Ford vice chairman Allan D. Gilmour—it is a pretty paltry roster for a highly educated minority that comprises, by some estimates, 6 percent of the population. In fact, many corporate CEOs who are widely believed to be gay are not comfortable discussing their sexuality on the record. The price of success may be having to stay in the closet.

Ironically, many of the companies that are most progressive about GLBT rights are reluctant to stand up for them in public for fear of being identified too closely with the issue—an apprehension that is likely only to mount if gay marriage touches off a national culture battle. Several companies that were more than willing to discuss their benefits and programs were unwilling to allow gay employees to pose for photographs that might wind up prominently displayed in the pages of *BusinessWeek*. Coors Brewing Co., whose products were boycotted by the gay community in the 1970s for giving money to anti-gay groups, adopted its sexual nondiscrimination policy in 1978. Since 1988 it has offered financial support to gay community causes. But the Golden (Colorado) company would not allow Scott Coors, the gay vice president and marketing director who is the son of vice chairman William Coors, or any other spokespeople, to talk to *BusinessWeek* about its programs.

ORDINARY PEOPLE

The people driving the gay rights revolution in corporate America by and large are not working in the executive suite. They're ordinary employees like Daniel Kline. The United Parcel Service Inc. supervisor last year applied for the company's Management Initiated Transfer, which allows employees to follow spouses to other cities and keep their jobs and seniority. An employee for more than two decades, Kline wanted to move with his longtime partner, who was reassigned by United Airlines Inc. from San Francisco to Chicago. After receiving approval at district and regional levels to take an open position in Chicago, Kline was rejected at the corporate level.

UPS backed down this August after the couple enlisted Lambda Legal Defense & Education Fund, a gay advocacy organization, to sue on their behalf, contending the company violated California antidiscrimination laws. A spokesman says UPS's policy on so-called trailing partners now includes same-sex couples. "I' am not looking to change the world. I simply want to live with the person with whom I've shared the last 27 years," says Kline.

While the gay experience in corporate America is far from monolithic, most gay managers interviewed by *Business-Week* say it has become easier in recent years to be themselves in the workplace. Displaying a picture of a same-sex lover on a desk or bringing a partner to a corporate gathering is no longer quite as intimidating as it used to be. Many now attend events such as the Out & Equal Workplace Summit, held this year in Minneapolis in October. "I used to keep my worklife and my private life separate, never talking about what I did on the weekend," says IBM microelectronics vice president Scottie Ginn. "Once you come out, you feel a much more whole person."

Broadly speaking, there is a generational divide among gay workers. Younger employees, typically those below 35, saw Roseanne Barr kiss another woman on TV and comedian Ellen DeGeneres declare publicly that she was a lesbian. They tend to come into the workplace as unashamedly gay and to demand equal rights more aggressively. Older workers, raised in times of greater stigma, tend to be quieter about their sexual identity to both coworkers and customers. Says James Law, a gay adviser at American Express Financial Advisers Inc., "With my older clients, I'm less prone to bring it up. With my younger clients, it's a nonissue."

CONTROVERSY AWAITS

[The legal controversy over gay marriage] will surely make life more complicated for CEOs trying to navigate this contentious issue. While they may not want to alienate cultural conservatives, they will also be loath to drive away the gay community. After all, the GLBT universe in the United States includes some 15 million consumers. Many have high disposable incomes. Research from online company MarketResearch.com pegs GLBT buying power this year at $485 billion.

Of course, the path of gay rights in corporate America is not a line angling boldly upward. When Exxon bought Mobil Oil in 1999, it rescinded the target company's policy of offering medical benefits to gay partners and disowned Mobil's written policy against discrimination based on sexual orientation (arguing that gay partners are not legal spouses and that gays are covered under its broader nondiscrimination policies). But despite such setbacks, far more companies are expanding gay rights than contracting them. There's no doubt that full legal equality for gays is many years away. But for the first time, it seems reasonable for gays in corporate America to dream of a day when Gay 101 will no longer be necessary.

Source: *BusinessWeek*, December 15, 2003, p. 64, Reprinted by permission.

Questions

1. What managerial risks and problems accompany gay and lesbian diversity policies in the workplace?

2. In your view, do the gay and lesbian diversity policies described in the article constitute socially responsible corporate behavior? Explain.

3. List the issues that you would consider if you were a CEO deciding whether to extend health insurance to the same-sex partners of your employees.

4. Christopher Mossey wrote in a letter to *The Wall Street Journal,*

   > Your Oct. 11 "In Marketing to Gays, Lesbians Are Often Left Out," raises a provocative question about the direction of the gay advocacy movement: Must gay men and lesbians be "recognized" by the marketing departments of large corporations? The comments in the article by Kate Kendell, executive director of the National Center for Lesbian Rights, suggest that it is a social responsibility of corporations to pitch products to gay people.

   In your judgment, do corporations have a social responsibility to "recognize" and practice targeted marketing towards gays and lesbians? Explain. See Christopher Mossey, "Marketing to Gays: Why Is It Needed?" *The Wall Street Journal,* October 29, 1999, p. A19.

Social Responsibility Case Two: Kobe Bryant and Nike

Los Angeles Lakers basketball star Kobe Bryant has been one of the world's most prominent and well-paid product endorsers. Then in June 2003 Bryant, a married man with a child, was accused of raping a 19-year-old woman in a Colorado hotel room. Bryant faced criminal sexual assault charges, but the case was dismissed in September 2004 because the alleged victim did not want to proceed. Bryant issued a written apology. Thereafter, in March 2005, a civil lawsuit filed by the woman was settled. The terms of the settlement were not disclosed.

Bryant had signed a $40 million endorsement deal with Nike shortly before his arrest. Following the sexual assault allegations, McDonald's and Nutella dropped Bryant from their endorsement rosters, but Nike did not do so.[115] Then in early 2005 Bryant's name, but not his image, appeared in a Nike ad and was followed in the summer of 2005 with a Nike footwear ad; this time including Bryant's picture. The substance of the ad contrasted insults sometimes directed at Bryant such as "Selfish" and "Overrated" with elements of Bryant's workout routine such as "1,000 made jumpers" and "Curls 15 x 3". Below Bryant's picture was the Nike swoosh and the company slogan, "Just Do It."

> Below Bryant's picture was the Nike swoosh and the company slogan, "Just Do It."

Questions

1. *a.* As an ethical matter, was it wrong for Nike to renew its use of Bryant as an endorser of its products? Explain.
   b. From a business point of view, was the renewed use of Bryant a good move by Nike? Explain.
2. Sales of Bryant's No. 8 basketball jersey reportedly fell dramatically in 2004.
   a. Do you think the market was punishing Bryant for his alleged sexual misconduct?[116]
   b. In your view, are moral issues like those associated with Bryant automatically incorporated in the market's information processing in much the same manner as price, quality, etc.? Explain.

American Consumers and Sweatshops Abroad

Margaret Mills, then an undergraduate at Washington University of St. Louis, described her 2001 junior-year visit to a carpet factory in Nepal:

> Today I toured carpet factories. The factories are not factories. They are sweatshops. They are nonventilated brick rooms with huge hand looms that look like something out of a period movie. It is the worst, most traumatic, heart-wrenching thing I have ever seen. The women have giant bandages on their hands because the fabric is so tough it cuts them. Those hand-made, expensive rugs you buy have human blood in them. You can't breathe because the air is filled with dust and fabric. There are giant makeshift cradles hanging from the ceilings that have babies in them. Women nurse and weave at the same time. They work 16 hours a day, and most of them never see their wages because they are supposedly paid in provided

housing. The "provided houses" are cement blocks with no lighting or toilets. There is raw sewage in the corners of the hallways, and I saw a rat today that I first mistook for a dog.

They treated me like a celebrity. It was horrible. They think I am some sort of real person with real capabilities. I'm just trying to get credit for my junior year abroad.

Source: Reprinted by permission of Margaret Mills.

Internet Exercise

1. Many critics, activists, international scholars, and others are concerned that corporate/governmental interests threaten global human rights and the global natural environment. Using the Corporate Watch Web site [**http://www.corpwatch.org/**], explain those concerns in more detail.

2. Using the Web site Opensecrets.org., find the latest campaign finance data for your congressperson or one of your senators. While there, perhaps you will want to take a look at the personal financial condition of those same politicians. See [**http://www.opensecrets.org/home/index.asp**].

Chapter Questions

1. a. In general, do you think employers are more concerned with profits or with delivering quality goods and services? Explain.
   b. Which *should* they be more concerned about? Explain.
   c. Are you most concerned about receiving a quality education or earning a degree? Explain.

2. Scholar Denis Goulet argued that we will find no facile resolution to the conflict between the values of a just society and the sharply opposing values of successful corporations.[117]
   a. Do you agree that the values of a just society oppose those of successful corporations? Explain.
   b. Can a solution be found? Explain.

3. Recently some major American corporations have begun establishing or expanding child care and elder care programs. Ford Motor Company, in a partnership with the United Auto Workers, expects to open on-site, 24-hour-a-day child care centers in 14 states over the next several years.[118] Likewise, Ford in 2001 began offering free house calls by geriatric care specialists who assess the health of elderly relatives and develop plans for their health maintenance.[119] Are child care and elder care necessary additions to companies' benefits menus? Explain.

4. "Sex seems to be on everyone's mind in the beer business these days," says George Hacker, director of the Alcohol Policies Project at the Center for Science in the Public Interest. "It's the particular portrayal of essentially drunken, riotous behavior by young people that is so problematic." One-quarter of alcohol advertising on television in 2001 was more likely to be seen by youths than adults. See Brian Sternberg and Suzanne Vranica, "Brewers Are Urged to Tone Down Ads," *The Wall Street Journal,* June 23, 2003, p. B4.

a. Lawsuits were filed in 2004 claiming that some prominent alcohol companies have negligently targeted underage drinkers. What evidence can you cite in support of the plaintiffs' and defendants' claims?

b. Does advertising influence your drinking habits?

c. Does alcohol advertising endanger underage Americans? Explain.

5. a. Under what conditions would you consider a layoff/termination to be ethically justified?

b. Do layoffs as dictated by business circumstances make good long-term sense for stockholders? Explain.

6. Worried about Junior misbehaving? Here's an answer: Call a board meeting. As crazy as it sounds, some Americans are trying to keep tabs on the kids by bringing business strategies into the traditional family meeting. They're hashing out everything from vacations to disputes over toys with techniques that seem right out of a management textbook: mission statements, rotating chairmanships, motivational seminars, even suggestion boxes. The most corporate of clans hire professional meeting facilitators, just to smooth over family squabbles.[120]

a. List some of the strengths and weaknesses of the business approach to raising children.

b. Do you regard the business approach in the home as a promising development or another encroachment of business values into life outside of work? Explain.

7. Sam Wong, speaking during his sophomore year at Iowa State University:

Materialism, like patience, is a virtue. Ever since my parents bought me my first Transformer, almost everyone has tried to convince me that owning a lot of toys wouldn't make me happy. Oh, how wrong they were. Toys make me very, very happy. That's why today I have more of them than ever. I own every Nintendo. I own two CD-R burners. My drum set cost as much as a semester of school. I drive a Miata. What's more, I'm not ashamed to be a consumer. I consider it part of my American heritage, and I'm proud of it.[121]

Do you share Wong's values? Explain. Is materialism in America's best interests? Explain.

8. a. Do you, as a student, have a responsibility to protest if your college logo appears on sportswear made in low-wage sweatshops? Explain.

b. Have you ever inquired about the manufacturing source of a product your were considering, or have you declined, as a matter of principle, to buy certain garments or other items because you believe the manufacturer engages in unfair labor practices? Explain.

9. Should American companies refuse to do business in countries

a. That do not practice democracy?

b. That routinely practice discrimination?

c. That tolerate or even encourage the abuse of children? Explain.

10. In criticizing General Motors, Ralph Nader is reported to have said,

Someday we'll have a legal system that will criminally indict the president of General Motors for these outrageous crimes. But not as long as this country is populated by people who fritter away their citizenship by watching TV, playing bridge and Mah-Jongg, and just generally being slobs.[122]

a. Is the citizenry generally unconcerned about unethical corporate conduct? Explain.

b. To the extent that corporations engage in misdeeds, does the fault really lie with the corporate community or with society at large?

11. Journalist Michael Kinsley expresses some serious reservations about corporate social responsibility:

> In particular, I am not impressed by corporate charity and cultural benefaction, which amount to executives playing Medici with other people's money. You wouldn't know, from the lavish parties corporate officers throw for themselves whenever they fund an art exhibit or a PBS series, that it's not costing them a penny. The shareholders, who aren't invited, pick up the tab.[123]

Comment on Kinsley's statement.

12. The Pennsylvania garment maker AND1 developed a line of T-shirts directed to young males and adorned with sayings such as "Your game is as ugly as your girl" and "You like that move? So does your girl." A feminist group complained that the shirts "put down" girls and implied that "girls are the property of boys." JC Penney, which was selling the shirts, withdrew them after the complaints.[124] Was JC Penney's decision the socially responsible course of action, or did JC Penney cave in to "politically correct" pressure? Or did JC Penney simply make a wise business move? Explain.

13. *USA TODAY:*

> The friendly folks at Ford have outfitted their 18.9-foot Excursion, which debuted Friday, with a "blocker beam," a kind of under-the-bumper bumper designed for collisions. That's nice of them. If the biggest sports utility vehicle of all time, chugging along at 10 miles per gallon of gas, rams a Toyota compact with a Sierra Club bumper sticker, the latter won't get decapitated.
>
> The Excursion, big enough to hold nine finger-wagging environmentalists and 44 gallons of their gas, is earning piles of scorn half a year before going on sale. Among other no-nos, it is so big that federal fuel economy standards for cars and small trucks don't apply.[125]

a. Are giant cars a social wrong?

b. If so, who is to blame—the manufacturers or us?

c. If not, how do we justify those vehicles in the face of the economic struggles of most of the world's citizens? Explain.

14. In 1992 the rapper Ice-T released a song titled "Cop Killer" as part of his album *Body Count.* Then-President Bush labeled the rap a "sick" glorification of killing law enforcement officers. Some music retail chains removed *Body Count* from their shelves. However, Time Warner continued to distribute the album. Ice-T eventually decided to remove "Cop Killer" from the album.

a. Was Time Warner socially irresponsible in its decision to market the album while it included the "Cop Killer" tune?

b. Defend Time Warner.

c. Assume the rap had said "fag killer" or "black killer" or "Jew killer" or "woman killer." Explain what you would have done if you had been in charge of Time Warner and Ice-T included one of those raps on his album.

d. Rap and heavy metal music often degrade women and glorify sexual violence. Do you decline to purchase music of that character? Explain.

15. You are the sole owner of a neighborhood drugstore that stocks various brands of toothpaste. Assume that scientific testing has established that one brand is clearly superior to all others in preventing tooth decay.

    a. Would you remove from the shelves all brands except the one judged best in decay prevention? Explain.

    b. What alternative measures could you take?

    c. Should the toothpaste manufacturers be required to reveal all available data regarding the effectiveness of their products? Explain.

16. *The Wall Street Journal:*

    TAMPA, Fla.—A lip-licking lizard leers from an ad in the liquor section adjacent to the Albertson's supermarket here. "Ask Me About My Tooters!" the ad says.

    Tooters Lingo Liqueurs are potent, single-serve cocktails made from vodka, tequila, and other liquors. With such frat-boy names as Yellin Melon Balls, Bamama Hama, and Blu-Dacious Kamikaze, they come in a "Party Pack" that looks like something from chemistry class. Thirty foil-sealed test tubes sit on a cardboard rack, and each contains a single shot of fruit-colored liquid with a hefty alcohol content of 15%. Albertson's sells the 750-milliliter Party Pack for $12.99.[126]

    Activists against underage drinking are outraged by products they believe to be targeted to young people. They point to products like Flugel, the label of which features a bug-eyed pink duck and the expression, "It's dynamite." As one critic said, "There aren't a lot of adults that relate to frogs or lizards in advertising, and I don't think mature adults are the ones choosing to use Jell-O shots."[127] Do you consider these marketing practices socially irresponsible? Explain.

17. Approximately $10 million is expended annually for alcohol ads in college newspapers. Many millions more are expended in other youth-oriented publications such as *National Lampoon* and *Rolling Stone.* The beer industry sponsors many campus athletic contests. And brewers have established promotional relationships with rock bands. Is beer and liquor advertising directed to the youth market unethical? Explain.

18. Increasingly, U.S. corporations are farming out programming, customer support, data entry, and various back-office jobs to lower-paid workers in countries as diverse as India, Romania, and Ghana. The average programmer commands $60 an hour in the United States, six times the rate in India.

* * * * *

"In a research report in mid-2003, Gartner Inc. predicted that at least 1 out of 10 technology jobs in the United States would move overseas by the end of 2004. Forrester Research predicts at least 3.3 million white-collar jobs and $136 billion in wages will shift from the United States to low-cost countries by 2015.

    a. Is outsourcing good for America? Explain.

    b. Are you confident that you will be competitive in the American market of the future where outsourcing seems destined to strip away big pieces of the job market? Explain. See Associated Press, "Corporations Explore New Ways to Ship Jobs Overseas," *Waterloo/Cedar Falls Courier,* January 22, 2004, p. D6.

19. In 1999, when President Clinton advocated a plan to "save Social Security" that would have involved the government buying up about 4 percent of the stock market, the Reverend Jesse Jackson remarked, "I think he should not invest in gun manufacturers, and shouldn't invest in liquor companies, and shouldn't invest in tobacco companies."[128] When you invest in the stock market will you avoid the product lines Jackson singles out? Explain.

20. Former General Motors vice president John Z. DeLorean wrote in his book, *On a Clear Day You Can See General Motors,*

> It seemed to me then, and still does now, that the system of American business often produces wrong, immoral, and irresponsible decisions, even though the personal morality of the people running the business is often above reproach. The system has a different morality as a group than the people do as individuals, which permits it willfully to produce ineffective or dangerous products, deal dictatorially and often unfairly with suppliers, pay bribes for business, abrogate the rights of employment, or tamper with the democratic process of government through illegal political contributions.[129]

a. How can the corporate "group" possess values at odds with those of the individual managers?

b. Is DeLorean merely offering a convenient rationalization for corporate misdeeds? Explain.

c. Realistically, can one expect to preserve individual values when employed in a corporate group? Explain.

21. Do you agree or disagree with the following statements? Explain.

a. "Social responsibility is good business only if it is also good public relations and/or preempts government interference."

b. "The social responsibility debate is the result of the attempt of liberal intellectuals to make a moral issue of business behavior."

c. "'Profit' is really a somewhat ineffective measure of business's social effectiveness."

d. "The social responsibility of business is to 'stick to business.'"[130]

Notes

1. Matt Moore, "Wal-Mart Inc. Claims Top Spot on *Fortune* 500," *Des Moines Register,* April 1, 2002, p. 10A.

2. "*Fortune* 500, How the Companies Stack Up," *Fortune,* April 18, 2005, p. F-33.

3. Ibid.

4. Sarah Anderson and John Cavanagh, "Of the World's 100 Largest Economic Entities, 51 Are Now Corporations and 49 Are Countries" [**http://www.corporations.org/system/top100.html**].

5. Ibid.

6. Ibid.

7. "Facts from the Corporate Planet: Ecology and Politics in the Age of Globalization," Corporate Watch Web site [**http://www.corpwatch.org/trac/feature/planet/fact_1.html**], citing Joshua Karliner, *The Corporate Planet* (San Francisco: Sierra Club Books, 1997).

8. Ibid.

9. "Major Institutions," *Polling Report.com* [**http://www.pollingreport.com/institut.htm**].

10. Peter Asch, *Industrial Organization and Antitrust Policy* (New York: John Wiley & Sons, 1983), p. 16.

11. *Los Angeles Times,* "60% of Corporations Avoid Income Taxes," *Waterloo Courier,* April 7, 2004, p. B6.

12. Associated Press, "Business Tax Audits Decline," *Waterloo Courier,* April 12, 2004, p. A2.

13. Associated Press, "Buffett in Berkshire's Annual Report: Tax Cuts Favor Corporations, Wealthy," *Waterloo Courier,* March 7, 2004, p. A2.

14. Ronald Alsop, "Corporate Scandals Hit Home," *The Wall Street Journal,* February 19, 2004, p. B1.

15. Charles Reich, *The Greening of America* (New York: Bantam Books, 1970), pp. 7–8.

16. "Nation's Alienation Index Decreases as Fewer People Feel Powerless," *Harris Poll,* no. 96, December 1, 2004 [**http://www.harrisinteractive.com/harris_poll/index.asp?PID=525**].

17. Ibid.

18. John Nirenberg, *The Living Organization* (Homewood, IL: Business One Irwin, 1993), p. 65.

19. Don Van Natta, Jr., John Schwartz, and Jim Yardley, "Enron's Collapse: Backdrop," *The New York Times,* January 20, 2002, Sec. 1, p. 25.

20. Aaron Bernstein, "Too Much Corporate Power?" *BusinessWeek,* September 11, 2000, pp. 144, 149.

21. Jeanne Cummings, "In New Law's Wake, Companies Slash Their Political Donations," *The Wall Street Journal,* September 3, 2004, p. A1.

22. David Rogers, "Senate Approves Measure to Curb Big Donations," *The Wall Street Journal,* March 21, 2002, p. A24.

23. Ibid.

24. Jeanne Cummings, "In New Law's Wake, Companies Slash Their Political Donations," *The Wall Street Journal,* September 3, 2004, p. A1.

25. Brian Ross and Rhonda Schwartz, "Money and Influence," ABCNEWS.com, August 30, 2004.

26. Van Natta, Jr., et al., "Enron's Collapse," Sec. 1, p. 25.

27. Associated Press, "Study Shows Influence of Tobacco Contributions," *Waterloo/Cedar Falls Courier,* September 2, 1997, p. C6.

28. Thomas J. Dean, Maria Vryza, and Gerald E. Fryxell, "Do Corporate PACs Restrict Competition?" *Business & Society* 37, no. 2 (June 1998), pp. 135, 149.

29. Ibid.

30. Deborah Ball and Christopher Lawton, "In Its Long War with Brewers, Liquor Industry Gets Aggressive," *The Wall Street Journal,* May 24, 2004, p. A1.

31. Richard N. Goodwin, "PACs Gobbling Up Congress," *Waterloo Courier,* December 17, 1985, p. A4.

32. Jane Eisner, "Peer Pressure, Ads Aimed at Youth Lead to Culture of Overconsumption," *Waterloo/Cedar Falls Courier,* September 19, 2004, p. C9.

33. Editorial, "Business Leaders' New Tack Poses Challenge to Public Schools," *USA TODAY,* February 25, 1999, p. 14A.

34. Knight Ridder Newspapers, "Corporate America Becoming More Important to School Improvement," *Waterloo/Cedar Falls Courier,* August 19, 2001, p. A8.

35. Associated Press, "Philadelphia Schools Become Experiment in Privatization under State, City Control," *The Wall Street Journal,* December 24, 2001, p. B5.

36. Jane Eisner, "Soft Sell: Check the Advertisements Plastered in Schools," *Des Moines Register,* November 24, 2000, p. 9A.

37. Andrea Sachs and Juliet Schor, "Author Juliet Schor Explores how Marketing Has Invaded Childhood," *Time Online* [**http://www.time.com/time/connections/article/0,9171,1101041004-702127,00.html**]

38. *Los Angeles Times,* "San Francisco Takes Stand against Campus Commerce," *Waterloo/Cedar Falls Courier,* July 16, 1999, p. A9.

39. Ibid.

40. Betsy McKay, "Coke Finds Its Exclusive School Contracts Aren't So Easily Given Up," *The Wall Street Journal,* June 26, 2001, p. B1.

41. Ibid.

42. Reich, *Greening of America,* pp. 141–42.

43. Stacey Palevsky, "Fashion & Faith," *Waterloo/Cedar Falls Courier,* September 20, 2004, p. B4.

44. Ibid.

45. Ibid.

46. *Los Angeles Times,* "Schuller Adding Food Court to Complex," *Waterloo/Cedar Falls Courier,* September 8, 1998, p. A4.

47. Ken Bensinger, "Metropolitan Museum of Art Cancels Commercially Charged Chanel Show," *The Wall Street Journal,* June 20, 2000, p. B8.

48. Greg Kot, "What's Wrong with Radio?" *Rolling Stone,* August 16, 2001, p. 25.

49. Ibid.

50. Ibid.

51. Ibid.

52. Steve Wilstein, "Let Commercialism Reign," *Waterloo/Cedar Falls Courier,* April 29, 2004, p. C2.

53. Darren Rovell, "The Tangled Web of Sports and Advertising," *ESPN.com,* May 5, 2004.

54. Josh Flory, "Curators Pick Mizzou Arena as New Name," *Columbia Daily Tribune,* November 27, 2004 [**http://www.showmenews.com/2004/Nov/20041127News002.asp**].

55. "New Balance Debuts 'For Love or Money' Advertising Campaign for 2005," *PRNewswireUS,* February 28, 2005 [**http://www.prnewswire.com**].

56. Paul Whiteley, Sr., "Fan Fears Greed Is Ruining Sports," *Des Moines Register,* August 27, 1995, p. 9D.

57. Welch Suggs, "College Presidents Urged to Take Control of College Sports," *The Chronicle of Higher Education,* July 6, 2001, p. 35.

58. Wilstein, "Let Commercialism Reign," p. C2.

59. Kristian Palda, "How to Enjoy Globalization in One Easy Lesson," *Ottawa Citizen,* May 7, 1998, p. A15.

60. Robert J. Samuelson, "Globalization's Downside," *Washington Post,* December 17, 1997, p. A25.

61. James H. Mittelman, *The Globalization Syndrome* (Princeton, NJ: Princeton University Press, 2000), p. 246.

62. Yifat Susskind, "Haiti—Insurrection in the Making," February 25, 2004 [**www.zmag.org**].

63. "50 Years Is Enough: Corporate Welfare in Haiti" [**http://www.50years.org**].

64. Associated Press, "Corporations Explore New Ways to Ship Jobs Overseas," *Waterloo/Cedar Falls Courier,* January 22, 2004, p. D6.

65. Ibid.

66. Carlin Romano, "Why Does the World Dislike America? One Word: Envy," *Des Moines Register,* December 28, 2003, Opinion, p. 5. Reviewing Jean-Francois Revel, *Anti-Americanism* (Encounter Books, 2003).

67. Ibid.

68. Christopher A. Bartlett, "Losing in the Court of Public Opinion," *Across the Board,* Jan.–Feb. 2002, p. 27.

69. Eric Liu, "Remember When Public Space Didn't Carry Brand Names?" *USA TODAY,* March 25, 1999, p. 15A.

70. Betsy Morris, "As a Favored Pastime, Shopping Ranks High with Most Americans," *The Wall Street Journal,* July 30, 1987, pp. 1, 13.

71. Tom Bratz, "Your Ad Here," *Newsweek,* February 5, 1996, p. 12.

72. Bob Ortega, "Aging Activists Turn, Turn, Turn Attention to Wal-Mart Protests," *The Wall Street Journal,* October 11, 1994, p. A1.

73. Forum, "Is There Virtue in Profit?" *Harper's,* December 1986, pp. 37, 42.

74. Ted Peters, "The Future of Religion in a Post-Industrial Society," *The Futurist,* October 1980, pp. 20,22.

75. Richard Holman, "Book Captures Japan's New Mood," *The Wall Street Journal,* May 6, 1993, p. A11.

76. "More Leisure in an Increasingly Electronic Society," *BusinessWeek,* September 3, 1979, pp. 208, 212.

77. Daniel Seligman, "Helping the Shareholder Helps the Society," *The Wall Street Journal,* June 21, 1996, p. A12.

78. Ronald Alsop, "Corporations Still Put Profits First, But Social Concerns Gain Ground," *The Wall Street Journal,* October 30, 2001, p. B12.

79. Keith Davis and Robert L. Blomstrom, *Business and Society: Environment and Responsibility,* 3rd ed. (New York: McGraw-Hill, 1975), p. 6.

80. Milton Friedman, *Capitalism and Freedom* (Chicago: University of Chicago Press, 1962), p. 133.

81. Herbert Stein, "Corporate America, Mind Your Own Business," *The Wall Street Journal,* July 15, 1996, p. A10.

82. Steven A. Rochlin, "The New Corporate Citizenship," *BusinessWeek,* December 13, 2003, p. 66.

83. John Elkington, *Cannibals with Forks* (Gabriola Island, British Columbia: New Society Publishers, 1998), p. 327.

84. Archie Carroll and others have pointed to some descriptive and theoretical limitations associated with his social responsibility pyramid; and Carroll has proposed a new three-domain approach of economic, legal, and ethical responsibilities arrayed in a Venn framework. The newer model appears to satisfy some of the concerns of Carroll and others about Carroll's pyramid, but for both teaching and research purposes, the pyramid remains a useful construct. For Carroll's new construct, see Mark S. Schwartz and Archie B. Carroll, "Corporate Social Responsibility: A Three Domain Approach," *Business Ethics Quarterly* 13, no. 4 (October 2003), p. 503. For an example of recent research employing the Carroll pyramid and a discussion of some of the strengths and weaknesses of the pyramid, see Dane K. Peterson, "The Relationship between Perceptions of Corporate Citizenship and Organizational Commitment," *Business & Society* 43, no. 3 (September 2004), p. 296.

85. Marc Gunther, "Corporations Go for the Green," *Des Moines Register,* November 22, 2004, p. 9A.

86. Ibid.

87. Ibid.

88. Ibid.

89. Ibid.

90. Ronald Roman, Sefa Hayibor, and Bradley Agle, "The Relationship between Social and Financial Performance," *Business & Society* 38, no. 1 (March 1999), pp. 109, 121.

91. Jeff Frooman, "Socially Irresponsible and Illegal Behavior and Shareholder Wealth," *Business & Society* 36, no. 3 (September 1997), p. 221.

92. Bruce Seifert, Sara A. Morris, and Barbara R. Bartkus, "Having, Giving, and Getting: Slack Resources, Corporate Philanthropy, and Firm Financial Performance," *Business & Society* 43, no. 2 (June 2004), pp. 135, 154.

93. Ann Svendsen, *The Stakeholder Strategy* (San Francisco: Berrett-Koehler, 1998), p. 7.

94. Ibid., p. 49.

95. Ibid.

96. Ibid., p. 3.

97. Ibid.

98. Ibid., p. 4.

99. I. M. Jawahar and Gary L. McLaughlin, "Toward a Descriptive Stakeholder Theory: An Organizational Life Cycle Approach," *The Academy of Management Review* 26, no. 3 (July 2001), p. 397.

100. Ibid.

101. Ibid.

102. "Linking Executive Pay to Social Performance" [**http://www.bsr.org/resourcecenter/custom** . . . **659=281&659=282&659=283&659=3025&659=285**].

103. Simon Buckby, "Global Standard for Business Ethics Launched," *Financial Times,* June 11, 1998, p. 10.

104. Ibid.

105. "A Common Framework for Sustainability Reporting" [**www.globalreporting.org/AboutGRI/Overview.htm**].

106. Susan Warren, "Chemical Companies Keep Lessons of Bhopal Spill Fresh," *The Wall Street Journal,* February 13, 2001, p. B4.

107. Ibid.

108. "S.P." letter to Malcolm Berko, "Bottom Line Speaks Louder Than Employees," *Waterloo/Cedar Falls Courier,* May 25, 2004, p. C5.

109. Malcolm Berko, "Bottom Line Speaks Louder Than Employees," *Waterloo/Cedar Falls Courier,* May 25, 2004, p. C5.

110. Ibid.

111. Stanley Holmes and Wendy Zellner, "Commentary: The Costco Way," *BusinessWeek/Online*, April 12, 2004 [**http://www.businessweek.com/print/magazine/content/04_15/b3878 . . .**].

112. William Beaver, "Is the Stakeholder Model Dead?" *Business Horizons* 42, no. 2 (March–April 1999), p. 8.

113. Associated Press, "Boss Rewards Workers' Loyalty—Shares $128 Million," *Waterloo/Cedar Falls Courier,* September 12, 1999, p. B1.

114. Greg Miller, "Extreme Generosity Shocks Firm's Employees, Analysts," *Des Moines Register,* December 18, 1996, p. 1A.

115. Associated Press, "Kobe Bryant Resumes Endorsement Career," July 9, 2005 [**http:// start.earthlink .net**].

116. For an assessment of Bryant's marketing fortunes, see "Fans Shunning Kobe Bryant's Jersey," January 7, 2005 [**http://www2.chinadaily.com.cn/english/doc**].

117. For an overview of Denis Goulet and his work, see [**http://www.nd.edu/~krocinst/faculty_staff/fellows/goulet.html**]

118. Associated Press, "Ford Motor Co. to Offer Child Care Services," *Waterloo/Cedar Falls Courier,* November 21, 2000, p. C6.

119. Kelly Greene, "A Renewed Push to Help Workers with Elder Care," *The Wall Street Journal,* March 29, 2001, p. B1.

120. Nancy Jeffrey, "Kids, Come to Order," *The Wall Street Journal,* August 10, 2001, p. W1.

121. SamWong, "Materialism Makes Me Feel Happy, Not Guilty," *Des Moines Register,* September 10, 2000, p. 11A.

122. Charles McCarry, *Citizen Nader* (New York: Saturday Review Press, 1972), p. 301.

123. Michael Kinsley, "Companies as Citizens: Should They Have a Conscience?" *The Wall Street Journal,* February 19, 1987, p. 29.

124. "Penney Hears Protests, Agrees to Trash T-Shirts," *Des Moines Register,* July 6, 1999, p. 2A.

125. Editorial, "King of the Road," *USA TODAY,* March 1, 1999, p. 14A.

126. Alejandro Bodipo-Memba, "'Shooter' and Other Alcoholic Novelties Face Scrutiny," *The Wall Street Journal,* April 14, 1999, p. B1.

127. Ibid.

128. Editorial, "The Rubin-Jackson Raid," *The Wall Street Journal,* February 1, 1999, p. A20.

129. John Z. DeLorean with J. Patrick Wright, "Bottom-Line Fever at General Motors" (excerpted from *On a Clear Day You Can See General Motors*), *The Washington Monthly,* January 1980, pp. 26–27.

130. Steven N. Brenner and Earl A. Molander, "Is the Ethics of Business Changing?" *Harvard Business Review* 55, no. 1 (January–February 1977), p. 68.

Introduction to Law

The American Legal System

Introduction

Presumably, we can agree that some business practices have unfavorable consequences for society. Thus the issue becomes this: What should be done, if anything, to change those consequences? The fundamental options in the United States have been fourfold: let the market "regulate" the behavior; leave the problem to the individual decision maker's own ethical dictates; pass a law; or rely on some combination of the market, ethics, and law. Market regulation was discussed in Chapter 1. Self-regulation through ethics was explored in Chapters 2 and 3. This chapter, then, begins the discussion of the legal regulation of business with a brief outline of the American legal system and how it functions.

This chapter also introduces an additional alternative for addressing business–society conflicts. This alternative looks at conflict resolution processes such as negotiation, mediation, and arbitration that do not resort to the legal system. Although these alternatives are not new, they have been receiving much more attention in recent years.

Before turning to our detailed examination of the technical dimensions of the law, we should remind ourselves of the central purpose of our legal system—the pursuit of justice. As you read this chapter, ask yourself repeatedly, "Does this rule (this procedure, this case) contribute to the search for justice?"

Justice

Most Americans believe we have the best justice system in the world, but concerns are widespread:

- A Columbia Law School survey found that two-thirds of Americans do not think of lawyers as even "somewhat honest."[1] About the same percentage of Americans think that lawyers are more interested in making money than in serving their clients.[2]

- Americans seem particularly skeptical of the criminal portion of the nation's justice system. Seventy-two percent of those responding to a 2000 survey say police distort the truth on the witness stand often (20 percent) or sometimes (52 percent) to get a conviction.[3] Eighty percent say race is a factor in criminal trials always (12 percent) or sometimes (68 percent).[4] Ninety percent think defense attorneys will hide facts often (56 percent) or sometimes (34 percent) to protect their client.[5] [For a daily update of legal news, see **http://www.law.com/**]

Law and the Market   So Americans recognize some weaknesses in our justice system; but whatever the doubts may be, the crucial role of a reliable legal system in fostering and maintaining capitalism is indisputable. The following law review excerpt explains.

READING

The Importance of Law to the Private Enterprise System

Deb Ballam

Nobel economist Frederich von Hayek describes the theoretical importance of law to private enterprise. According to Hayek, law that secures property rights in modern society is a prerequisite to private enterprise. Without the order of law enforcing private property ownership and facilitating the transfer of property rights, business enterprise in a complex, heterogeneous culture is simply infeasible.

The importance of law to the conduct of private enterprise is evident in economic developments in the former Soviet Union and the Republic of China. In moving from state-controlled to private enterprise, these countries have faced substantial difficulties arising from the lack of a legal system that would secure property ownership and the contractual transfer of property rights. Reports from Russia indicate continuing economic turmoil due largely to the absence of adequate legal institutions and the absence of social experience in observing legal rules securing the marketplace. Not law, but extortion, intimidation, and violence today control much private enterprise in Russia. . . .

In contrast to the economy of the former Soviet Union, China's economy has grown steadily in recent years. Minxin Pei, a political scientist at Princeton University, explains law's contribution to that growth: "Legal reform has become one of the most important institutional changes in China since the late 1970s. . . . Within China, the changing legal institutions have begun to play an increasingly important role in governing economic activities, resolving civil disputes, enforcing law and order, and setting the boundaries between the power of the state and the autonomy of society." Pei reports that the number of lawyers

in China grew threefold between 1986 and 1996 and that the number of commercial disputes adjudicated by the courts grew from about 15,000 annually in the early 1980s to some 1.5 million annually in the mid-1990s. . . .

Of course, the importance of law to private enterprise goes far beyond its initial support as an institutional framework guaranteeing ownership rights. As the market system grows more complex both nationally and internationally, the legal recognition of promise keeping becomes increasingly significant in facilitating business. A condition for emerging economies entering international trade is learning how to keep promises to strangers, and whether enforced through litigation or arbitration, promise keeping in business requires the ordering presence of contract law.

In a democracy, law is important to business for another reason quite separate from its function in establishing ownership rights and facilitating promise keeping necessary to their transfer: It provides the formal expression of democratic social will. That expression implicates private enterprise in a plethora of ways, including regulation of the environment, employment laws, securities regulation, consumer protection statutes, and product liability. As contemporary society becomes increasingly diverse, law grows, not diminishes, in its importance to private enterprise; and in spite of valid concerns about the impact of law on efficiency, future business managers will need to know more, not less, about how law affects business operations. No evidence suggests any other conclusion.

Source: Deb Ballam, quoting from "The Importance of Law to the Private Enterprise System," The American Legal Studies in Business Task Force Report by O. Lee Reed. *American Business Law Journal* 36, no. 1 (Fall 1998), p. ix. Reprinted by permission.

Questions

1. *a.* Do you expect to see greater reliance on law as our society becomes increasingly complex?

   b. Can you think of any meaningful substitutes for law as we now practice it? Explain.

2. A recent study concludes that girls are punished more harshly than boys for minor criminal conduct. Girls arrested for more serious crimes receive fewer services and placement opportunities than boys. Girls are less likely than boys to engage in violence, and girls are less likely to be repeat offenders.[6] Why does our criminal justice system apparently treat girls more harshly than boys?

3. The police found three marijuana plants in an Iowa man's home. The man admitted smoking marijuana with his six-year-old son and was sentenced to 27 years in prison on various drug and child endangerment charges. He was to be eligible for parole in five years.[7]

   a. Does the sentence seem fair and just? Explain.

   b. Would you legalize marijuana? Explain.

4. Sociologist Franz Schurmann says,

   > No issue so suggests the existence of a dual justice system in America as the composition of its prison population. Those being fed into the prison system are overwhelmingly young, poor, or dark-skinned. They are the people without rights, who are, in effect, its modern, legal slaves.[8]

   a. In your opinion, is ours a dual justice system? Explain.

   b. Are the young, poor, and dark-skinned of our prisons the equivalent of slaves? Explain.

5. Bernard McCummings was shot in the back and paralyzed from the waist down while he was robbing and beating a 72-year-old man in a subway station. McCummings was shot by a plainclothes police officer. McCummings pleaded guilty to robbery and served 32 months in prison. McCummings brought a civil action for his injuries. At trial, the officer testified that he shot when McCummings lunged at him. McCummings testified that he was running away when he was shot. Some corroborating evidence supported McCummings's testimony, and McCummings won a $4.3 million negligence judgment. New York's highest court upheld the jury's judgment for McCummings, saying the officer "did not exercise that degree of care which would reasonably be required of a police officer under similar circumstances."

   On the other hand, dissenting high court justice Bellacosa said the decision was an "inversion of justice." He went on to say, "The instant case approaches the surreal zone. It involves split-second decisions by public safety employees made in the most dangerous and volatile circumstances."

   In your judgment, was justice achieved in this case? Explain. See *McCummings v. New York City Transit Authority,* 613 N.E. 2d 559 (NY 1993); cert. den. *New York City Transit Authority v. McCummings,* 114 S. Ct. 548 (1993).

Part One—Legal Foundations

Objectives of the Law

Americans differ wildly in their personal conceptions of the role the law should play in our lives. For some, the courts and the police primarily act as obstructions to personal freedom and to a fully efficient marketplace. Others seek much more law to ensure that everyone is cared for who is in need and everyone is sheltered from wrongdoers. We are in constant conflict about the law's precise path in our lives, but most of us can agree on some foundational expectations that a fair, efficient legal system should achieve. Certainly we expect the law to *maintain order* in our diverse, rapidly changing society. Of course, we rely on law to peacefully, fairly, and intelligently *resolve conflict.* Perhaps less obvious, but no less important, the law serves to *preserve dominant values.* Americans differ dramatically about core values, but we have reached a workable accord about our most fundamental beliefs. Some of those, such as freedom of speech, press, and religion, are guaranteed by our Bill of Rights, thus serving to set a steady foundation for an enduring nation. Thus we can see that the law is a vital force in *guaranteeing free-dom.* (But freedom can be confusing: Are you free to smoke wherever you wish, or do I have a right to smoke-free air?) Broadly, we count on the law to *achieve and preserve justice.* All legal studies, in the end, must involve the search for justice. The *Graff* case that follows does just that. Where does justice lie when someone is hurt but the one being blamed did not directly cause the harm? [For help with legal research on the Internet, see **http://www.virtualchase.com**]

Too Many Rules in Britain?

All societies struggle with the question of how important law should be in directing the course of affairs. In 1999 Great Britain introduced its antisocial behavior orders (ASBO) to discourage "loutish" conduct. Then in 2004 the government began its Antisocial Behavior Action Plan, which is designed to address everyday headaches from "nuisance neighbors" to begging to graffiti. Nearly 2,500 ASBOs have been issued nationwide, and the courts have upheld all but 42 as of this writing. But many Brits wonder if the law hasn't gone a bit too far:

> A teenager is forbidden to say "grass" (slang for informer). A great-grandfather is banned from being sarcastic. Two record companies are told not to put up advertising posters. All have run afoul of the British government's latest weapon against petty crime, vandalism, and hooliganism: the antisocial behavior order, or ASBO. The orders have been used to ban thousands of people, some as young as 10, from associating with certain people or engaging in activities as varied as shouting, swearing, spray-painting, playing loud music, and walking down certain streets. Breaching an order is a crime, punishable by up to five years in prison.

Source: Jill Lawless, Associated Press, "Britain Tries to Rein in Louts with Bans on Misbehavior," *Des Moines Register,* September 1, 2004, p. 5A.

The Case Law: Locating and Analyzing

To prepare for *Graff,* the first law case in this text, a bit of practical guidance may be useful. The study of law is funded largely on the analysis of judicial opinion. Except for the federal level and a few states, trial court decisions are filed locally for public inspection rather than being published. Appellate opinions, on the other hand, are generally published in volumes called *reports.* State court opinions are found in the reports of that state, as well as a regional reporter published by West Publishing Company that divides the United States into units, such as South Eastern (S.E.) and Pacific (P.).

Within the appropriate reporter, the cases are *cited* by case name, volume, reporter name, and page number. For example, *Royce Graff, Debra Graff, Bobby Hausmon, and Betty Hausmon v. Brett Beard and Dorothy Beard,* 858 S.W.2d 918 (Texas S.Ct. 1993) means that the opinion will be found in volume 858 of the South Western Reporter, 2nd series, at page 918 and that the decision was reached in 1993 by the Texas Supreme Court. Federal court decisions are found in several reporters, including the *Federal Reporter* and the *United States Supreme Court Reports.* In practice, of course, those cases can most readily be found via online databases such as LexisNexis and Westlaw. [For a broad database of law topics, see **http://www.findlaw.com** or **http://www.yahoo.com/law**]

Briefing the Case

Most law students find the preparation of *case briefs* (outlines or digests) to be helpful in mastering the complexities of the law. A brief should evolve into the form that best suits the individual student's needs. The following approach should be a useful starting point:

1. Parties   Identify the plaintiff and the defendant.
2. Facts   Summarize only those facts critical to the outcome of the case.
3. Procedure   Who brought the appeal? What was the outcome in the lower court(s)?
4. Issue   Note the central question or questions on which the case turns.
5. Holding   How did the court resolve the issue(s)? Who won?
6. Reasoning   Explain the logic that supported the court's decision.

Royce Graff, Debra Graff, Bobby Hausmon, and Betty Hausmon v. Brett Beard and Dorothy Beard

LEGAL BRIEFCASE   858 S.W.2d 918 (Texas S.Ct. 1993)

Justice John Cornyn

We are asked in this case to impose a common-law duty on a social host who makes alcohol available to an intoxicated adult guest who the host knows will be driving. . . .

Houston Moos consumed alcohol at a party hosted by the Graffs and Hausmons, and allegedly left in his vehicle in an intoxicated condition. En route from the party, Moos collided with a motorcycle, injuring Brett Beard. Beard sued both Moos and his hosts for his injuries. The trial court ultimately dismissed Beard's claims against the hosts for failure to state a cause of action. An en banc divided court of appeals reversed the trial court's judgment and remanded the case, holding for the first time in Texas jurisprudence that social hosts may be liable to third parties for the acts of their intoxicated adult guests.

Under the court of appeals' standard, a social host violates a legal duty to third parties when the host makes an alcoholic beverage available to an adult guest whom the host knows is intoxicated and who will be driving. In practical effect, this duty is twofold. The first aspect of the host's duty is to prevent guests who will be driving from becoming intoxicated. If the host fails to do so, however, a second aspect of the duty comes into play—the host must prevent the intoxicated guest from driving.

The legislatures in most states, including Texas, have enacted dram shop laws that impose a statutory duty to third parties on commercial providers under specified circumstances. We have recently held that when the legislature enacted the Texas dram shop statute it also imposed a duty on the provider that extends to the patron himself. Because the dram shop statute applies only to commercial providers, however, it does not govern the duty asserted in this case.

We think it significant in appraising Beard's request to recognize common-law social host liability that the legislature has considered and declined to create such a duty. A version of the bill that eventually became our dram shop statute provided for social host liability. Although that version passed the Senate, the House rejected it. The Senate–House conference committee deleted social host liability from the bill the legislature eventually enacted.

The highest courts in only four states have done what we are asked to do today: judicially impose a duty to third parties on social hosts who make alcohol available to adult guests. In two of these states, California and Iowa, the legislatures subsequently abrogated the judicially created duty. Neither of the two remaining jurisdictions, Massachusetts and New Jersey, had dram shop statutes when their courts acted. Rather, their courts first imposed a common-law duty to third parties on commercial establishments and then extended the duty to social hosts.

* * * * *

Deciding whether to impose a new common-law duty involves complex considerations of public policy. We have said that these considerations include "'social, economic, and political questions,' and their application to the particular facts at hand." Among other factors, we consider the extent of the risk involved, "the foreseeability and likelihood of injury weighed against the social utility of the actor's conduct, the magnitude of the burden of guarding against the injury, and the consequences of placing the burden on the defendant." We have also emphasized other factors. For example, questions of duty have turned on whether one party has superior knowledge of the risk, and whether a right to control the actor whose conduct precipitated the harm exists.

Following our decisions in *Seagrams* and *Otis Engineering Corp.,* we deem it appropriate to focus on two tacit assumptions underlying the holding of the court of appeals: that the social host can reasonably know of the guest's alcohol consumption and possible intoxication, and possesses the right to control the conduct of the guest. Under Texas law, in the absence of a relationship between the parties giving rise to the right of control, one person is under no legal duty to control the conduct of another, even if there exists the practical ability to do so.

* * * * *

Instead of focusing on the host's right of control over the guest, the court of appeals conditioned a social host's duty on the host's "exclusive control" of the alcohol supply. The court defined "exclusive control," however, as nothing more than a degree of control "greater than that of the guest user." Under the court's definition, at a barbecue, a wedding reception, a backyard picnic, a pachanga, a Bar Mitzvah—or a variety of other common social settings—the host would always have exclusive control over the alcohol supply because the host chooses whether alcohol will be provided and the manner in which it will be provided. The duty imposed by the court of appeals would apparently attach in any social setting in which alcohol is available regardless of the host's right to control the guest. Thus, as a practical matter, the host has but one choice—whether to make alcohol available to guests at all.

But should the host venture to make alcohol available to adult guests, the court of appeals' standard would allow the host to avoid liability by cutting off the guest's access to alcohol at some point before the guest becomes intoxicated. Implicit in that standard is the assumption that the reasonably careful host can accurately determine how much alcohol guests have consumed and when they have approached their limit. We believe, though, that it is far from clear that a social host can reliably recognize a guest's level of intoxication. First, it is unlikely that a host can be expected to know how much alcohol, if any, a guest has consumed before the guest arrives on the host's premises. Second, in many social settings, the total number of guests present may practically inhibit the host from discovering a guest's approaching intoxication. Third, the condition may be apparent in some people but certainly not in all. . . .

* * * * *

This brings us to the second aspect of the duty implicit in the court of appeals' standard: that should the guest become intoxicated, the host must prevent the guest from driving. Unlike the court of appeals, however, we cannot assume that guests will respond to a host's attempts, verbal or physical, to prevent the guests from driving. Nor is it clear to us precisely what affirmative actions would discharge the host's duty under the court of appeals' standard. Would a simple request not to drive suffice? Or is more required? Is the host required to physically restrain the guests, take their car keys, or disable their vehicles? The problems inherent in this aspect of the court of appeals' holding are obvious.

* * * * *

Ideally, guests will drink responsibly, and hosts will monitor their social functions to reduce the likelihood of intoxication. Once a guest becomes impaired by alcohol to the point at which he becomes a threat to himself and others, we would hope that the host can persuade the guest to take public transportation, stay on the premises, or be transported home by an unimpaired driver. But we know that too often reality conflicts with ideal behavior. And, given the ultimate power of guests to control their own alcohol consumption and the absence of any legal right of the host to control the guest, we find the arguments for shifting legal responsibility from the guest to the host, who merely makes alcohol available at social gatherings, unconvincing. As the common law has long recognized, the imbiber maintains the ultimate power and thus the obligation to control his own behavior: to decide to drink or not to drink, to drive or not to drive. We therefore conclude that the common law's focus should remain on the drinker as the person primarily responsible for his own behavior and best able to avoid the foreseeable risks of that behavior.

We accordingly reverse the judgment of the court of appeals and render judgment that Beard take nothing.

DISSENTING OPINION—JUSTICE GAMMAGE JOINED BY JUSTICE DOGGETT

I respectfully dissent. The majority errs in holding that the legislature must "create" the duty for social hosts not to send intoxicated guests driving in our streets to maim and kill. Logic, legal experience, and this court's own earlier decisions dictate a contrary result. The legislature may enact a statute that creates a duty. But the legislature's failure to act does not "un-create" an existing duty. A duty created by the common law continues to exist unless and until the legislature changes it, and such an existing common law duty applies to the defendants here.

The majority confuses issues of proof with issues of whether to recognize the tort duty. The majority is concerned that the social host might not be able to persuade or control his intoxicated guest to keep him or her from driving. The host, however, clearly does control whether alcohol is being served, and in what quantities and form. The answer to the "duty" question is that the host should not let the driving guest have the alcohol in intoxicating quantities. If the guest becomes inebriated, however, just as with any other dangerous situation one helps create, the host has the duty to make every reasonable effort to keep the dangerously intoxicated guest from driving. If the guest resists those efforts, then there is a question for the factfinder to resolve whether the host's efforts were all that reasonably could be done under the circumstances.

The majority expresses concern that "the reasonably careful host" may not be able to detect when some guests are intoxicated. If that is so, then the factfinder should have no difficulty determining that the host did not serve them while they were "obviously intoxicated." The majority further asserts, without citation to authority, that the "guest . . . is in a far better position to know the amount of alcohol he has consumed" than the host.

This assertion defies common sense, because from personal observation we know that most persons, as they become intoxicated, along with losing their dexterity and responsive mental faculties, gradually become less and less cognizant of how much they've had and how badly intoxicated they are. Even if the host is also intoxicated, as a third party viewing the guest, the host is probably in a better position to evaluate the guest's intoxication. Intoxicated guests need someone to tell them not to drive. . . .

If circumstances do not permit the social host to adequately monitor and control the quantity of alcoholic beverages a guest consumes, the host still retains absolute control over whether alcoholic beverages should be served at all. . . .

* * * * *

. . . All culpable parties should be liable—the social host who knowingly intoxicated the guest and the guest who drunkenly caused the accident. I am persuaded that both should be liable to the extent of their responsibility for the accident. The television commercial says, "Friends don't let friends drive drunk." That is sound public policy. But today the majority says, "Intoxicate your friends and send them out upon the public streets and highways to drive drunk. Don't worry; you won't be liable." That is, in the kindest term I can muster, unsound policy.

Questions

1. Who won this case and why?
2. What do the dissenting justices mean by saying "the majority confuses issues of proof with issues of whether to recognize the tort duty"?
3. In your judgment, does the Texas Supreme Court decision represent a just result? Explain.
4. Nichols, age 26, and Dobler, a minor, were guests at Maldonado's party. Dobler was served alcohol and, while intoxicated, repeatedly hit Nichols with a hammer. Nichols sued Maldonado for negligence in serving alcohol to a minor. The jury found for Nichols. Maldonado appealed. How would you rule on that appeal? Explain. See *Nichols v. Dobler*, 655 N.W. 2d 787 (Mich. Ct. App. 2002).

[For the National Center for State Courts, see **http://www.ncsconline.org/**]

Classifications of Law

Some elementary distinctions will make the role of law clearer.

Substantive and Procedural Law

Substantive laws create, define, and regulate legal rights and obligations. Thus, for example, the federal Civil Rights Act of 1964 forbids discrimination in employment and other matters (see Chapter 13).

Procedural law embraces the systems and methods available to enforce the rights specified in the substantive law. So procedural law includes the judicial system and the rules by which it operates. Questions of where to hear a case, what evidence to admit, and which decisions can be appealed fall within the procedural domain.

Law by Judicial Decision and Law by Enactment

In general, American rules of law are promulgated by court decisions (*case law*) or via enactments, which include constitutions, statutes, treaties, administrative rules, executive orders, and local ordinances.

Case Law (Judicial Decisions)   Our case law has its roots in the early English king's courts, where rules of law gradually developed out of a series of individual dispute resolutions. That body of law was imported to America and is known as the *common law.* (This term may be confusing because it is frequently used to designate not just the law imported from England of old but also all judge-made or case law.)

The development of English common law rules and American judicial decisions into a just, ordered package is attributable in large measure to reliance on the doctrine of *stare decisis* (let the decision stand). That is, judges endeavor to follow the precedents established by previous decisions. Following precedent, however, is not mandatory.

As societal beliefs change, so does the law. For example, a United States Supreme Court decision approving racially separate but equal education was eventually overruled by a Supreme Court decision mandating integrated schools. However, the principle of stare decisis is generally adhered to because of its beneficial effect. It offers the wisdom of the past and enhances efficiency by eliminating the need for resolving every case as though it were the first of its kind. Stare decisis affords stability and predictability to the law. It promotes justice by, for example, reducing "judge-shopping" and neutralizing judges' personal prejudices.

Statutes (Enactments)   Here our primary concern is with the laws that have been adopted by the many legislative bodies—Congress, the state legislatures, city councils, and the like. These enactments are labeled *statutory law.* Some areas of law, such as torts, continue to be governed primarily by common law rules, but the direction of American law lies largely in the hands of legislators. Of course, legislators are not free of constraints. Federal legislation cannot conflict with the U.S. Constitution, and state legislation cannot violate either federal law or the constitutions of that state and the nation.

Law and Equity

Following the Norman conquest of England in 1066, a system of king's courts was established in which the king's representatives settled disputes. Those representatives were empowered to provide remedies of land, money, or personal property. The king's courts became known as *courts of law,* and the remedies were labeled *remedies of law.* Some litigants, however, sought compensation other than the three provided. They took their pleas to the king.

Typically the *chancellor,* an aide to the king, would hear these petitions and, guided by the standard of fairness, could grant a remedy (such as an injunction or specific performance—see the glossary of legal terms in the back of the book) specifically appropriate to the case. The chancellors' decisions accumulated over time such that a new body of remedies—and with it a new court system, known as *courts of equity*—evolved. Both court systems were adopted in the United States following the American Revolution, but today actions at law and equity are typically heard in the same court.

Public Law and Private Law

Public law deals with the relationship between government and the citizens. Constitutional, criminal, and administrative law (relating to such bodies as the Federal Trade Commission) fall in the public law category. *Private law* regulates the legal relationship between individuals. Contracts, agency, and commercial paper are traditional business law topics in the private category.

Civil Law and Criminal Law

The legislature or other lawmaking body normally specifies that new legislation is either *civil* or *criminal* or both. Broadly, all legislation not specifically labeled criminal law falls in the civil law category. *Civil law* addresses the legal rights and duties arising among individuals, organizations such as corporations, and governments. Thus, for example, a person might sue a company raising a civil law claim of breach of contract. *Criminal law,* on the other hand, involves wrongs against the general welfare as formulated in specific criminal statutes. Murder and theft are, of course, criminal wrongs because society has forbidden those acts in specific legislative enactments. Hence, wearing one's hat backward would be a crime if such a statute were enacted and if that statute met constitutional requirements. [For a brief discussion of business and white-collar crime and the federal sentencing guide lines, see Chapter 2.]

Crimes   Crimes are of three kinds. In general, *felonies* are more serious crimes, such as murder, rape, and robbery. They are typically punishable by death or by imprisonment in a federal or state penitentiary for more than one year. In general, *misdemeanors* are less serious crimes, such as petty theft, disorderly conduct, and traffic offenses. They are typically punishable by fine or by imprisonment for no more than one year. *Treason* is the special situation in which one levies war against the United States or gives aid and comfort to its enemies.

Elements of a Crime   In a broad sense, crimes consist of two elements: (1) a wrongful act or omission (*actus reus*) and (2) evil intent (*mens rea*). Thus an individual who pockets a ball-point pen and leaves the store without paying for it may be charged with petty theft. The accused may defend, however, by arguing that he or she merely absentmindedly and unintentionally slipped the pen in a pocket after picking it off the shelf to consider its merits. Intent is a state of mind, so the jury or judge must reach a determination from the objective facts as to what the accused's state of mind must have been.

Criminal Procedure   In general, criminal procedure is structured as follows: For more complex, arguably more serious, crimes the process begins with the prosecuting officials bringing their charges before a grand jury or magistrate to determine whether the charges have sufficient merit to justify a trial. If so, an *indictment* or *information* is issued, charging the accused with specific crimes. (Grand juries issue indictments; magistrates issue informations.) In instances where action by a grand jury or magistrate is not required, cases are initiated by the issuance of a warrant by a judge, based on a showing of probable cause that the individual has committed or will commit a crime. Where necessity demands, arrests may be made without a warrant, but the legality of the arrest will be tested by probable cause standards.

After indictment or arrest, the individual is brought before the court for *arraignment*, where the charges are read and a plea is entered. If the individual pleads not guilty, he or she will go to trial, where guilt must be established *beyond a reasonable doubt.* (In a civil trial, the plaintiff must meet the lesser standard of *a preponderance of the evidence.*) In a criminal trial, the burden of proof is on the state. The defendant is, of course, presumed innocent. He or she is entitled to a jury trial, but many choose to have the case decided by the judge alone. If found guilty, the defendant can, among other possibilities, seek a new trial or appeal errors in the prosecution. If found innocent, the defendant may, if necessary, invoke the doctrine of *double jeopardy* under which a person cannot be prosecuted twice in the same tribunal for the same criminal offense. [For an extensive criminal justice database, see **http://www.ncjrs.org**]

PRACTICING ETHICS) Punishment

How do we decide what penalties are appropriate to the wrongs we suffer? Some wrongs are intentional or inexcusably negligent, and we may treat those as crimes. Some wrongs are the product of ordinary carelessness and mistakes (such as auto accidents or defective products) and usually are treated as civil wrongs to be remedied by money. Some wrongs give rise to both criminal and civil complaints. In the lives of college students, those wrongs, both criminal and civil, often spring from excessive drinking. The story that follows depicts a tragedy that government attempts to address with the law but that ultimately requires a wrenching personal assessment of right and wrong and responsibility that each of us must face on our own terms.

Scott Krueger of Orchard Park, New York, was about five weeks into his first semester at the Massachusetts Institute of Technology (MIT) when he attended a September 26, 1997, "Animal House Night" initiation party for pledges at the MIT chapter of Phi Gamma Delta fraternity. Krueger, 18 years old, died that night. The pledges had been instructed to drink a specified amount of beer and whiskey. No one knows how much drinking Krueger did, but apparently he drank a bottle of Bacardi Spiced Rum reportedly given to him by his fraternity "big brother." As the evening went on, Krueger became ill and began to lose consciousness. Two "big brothers" carried him to his room and left him lying on his stomach. About 10 minutes later, he was discovered unconscious. Emergency personnel were called, but by the time they arrived Krueger's face had turned blue, and he was choking on his own vomit. Police indicated that Krueger had sustained severe alcohol poisoning with a blood-alcohol level of

.401—more than five times the legal driving limit. Krueger, in a coma for about 40 hours, died at a Boston hospital after life-support mechanisms were removed.

Officers charged the Phi Gamma Delta local chapter with serving alcohol to a minor; the second such citation for the fraternity in a 19-month period. The local chapter was later indicted for misdemeanor hazing and criminal manslaughter. Prosecutors saw the wrongdoing as a collective behavior and decided against indicting any individual fraternity members. The Phi Gamma Delta local chapter disbanded the day after the indictment was issued, thus derailing the criminal claims unless the fraternity were to reorganize at MIT. The national headquarters of Phi Gamma Delta announced that it would ban alcohol from all of its chapter houses.

Krueger's parents took their son's body home in the back of their 1988 Buick station wagon. The local funeral home had closed when they returned. Rather than leave her son alone, Mrs. Krueger spent the night in the car with him. The Kruegers, while conceding that their son bore significant responsibility for his own death, later negotiated with MIT until reaching a $6 million settlement that included an apology from MIT's president, Charles A. Vest, delivered personally in the Kruegers' home. Scott Krueger had joined Phi Gamma Delta, in part, in order to secure freshman-year housing. MIT agreed to require all freshmen to live in university housing, to strictly enforce antidrinking rules, and to forbid fraternity recruiting during freshmen orientation. The Kruegers also settled with the Phi Gamma Delta national fraternity and some of its officers, who agreed to produce and distribute a video on the dangers of drinking and to pay a total of $1.75 million.[9]

Questions

1. A letter to the *Buffalo News* questioned MIT's responsibility for Scott Krueger's death:

   > . . . Unless Krueger was held down against his will and forced to drink alcohol, how can the blame be put on the school? Ultimately, Krueger was responsible for his own death. We all have to make choices, and he made the choice to drink in excess. Colleges should not be expected to babysit their students. Young adults must start taking responsibility for their own actions.[10]

   a. Do you agree with the letter writer? Explain.

   b. How would you apportion blame for Scott Krueger's death?

   c. In your opinion, did the Phi Gamma Delta chapter commit a criminal act? Explain.

AFTERWORD

Mrs. Krueger spoke of what a "big difference" it made that President Vest would hear the parents' anger, "look us in the eye," and say we were right and they were wrong.[11] As one commentator later said, an apology can be a miraculously healing act:

> [S]uch a real apology clearly works, even here, with a lawsuit pending; in politics, almost anywhere. It's what the wronged party wants and needs. It enlarges the heart of the one who's done wrong.[12]

Questions—Part One

1. Julie Rabideau, a Racine, Wisconsin, woman, watched as her dog was shot by an off-duty city police officer. The parties' accounts of the facts differ as to whether the dog was a threat to the officer and others at the scene. Rabideau sued seeking $5,000 in damages for emotional distress, and the case reached the Wisconsin Supreme Court.

   a. Explain the central issue facing the court.

   b. How would you rule on Rabideau's claim? Explain.

   c. What monetary value, if any, would you assign to the dog? Explain. See *Rabideau v. City of Racine*, 627 N.W. 2d 795 (Wis. S. Ct. 2001).

2. Jonathan Rauch argues that America is making a mistake in allowing what he calls Hidden Law to be replaced by what he calls Bureaucratic Legalism. Hidden Law refers to unwritten social codes, whereas Bureaucratic Legalism refers to state-provided due process for every problem. Thus universities formerly expected insults and epithets among students to be resolved via informal modes such as apologies, while today many universities have written codes forbidding offensive or discriminatory verbal conduct. Similarly, four kindergarten students in New Jersey were suspended from school for three days because they were observed "shooting" each other with their fingers serving as guns.

   a. Would we be better off leaving campus insults and school-yard finger "shootings" to the Hidden Law? Explain.

   b. Can you think of other examples where we have gradually replaced Hidden Law with Bureaucratic Legalism?

   c. Rauch argues that the breakdown of one Hidden Law, the rule that a man must marry a woman whom he has impregnated, may be "the most far-reaching social change of our era." Do you agree? Explain. See George Will, "Penalizing These Kids Is Zero Tolerance at a Ridiculous Extreme," *Des Moines Register*, December 27, 2000, p. 11A.

3. Iowa, a state particularly troubled by methamphetamine abuse, imposed a new criminal penalty in 1999 providing that sales of meth to minors or producing the drug with that intent would lead to a 99-year prison term, and a second offense would bring life without parole. What concerns would you raise about that stern law?

4. In 1999 Denmark legalized prostitution.

    a. Should the United States do the same?

    b. Should we remove criminal penalties from all of the so-called victimless crimes including vagrancy, pornography, and gambling? Should we regulate those practices in any way? Explain.

5. *The Wall Street Journal* commented on the criminal justice system in Japan:

    > [D]espite its image of dealing tough justice, Japan's legal system is surprisingly lenient, geared toward reinstating most suspects into the cultural mainstream. Many who are arrested for minor crimes are let off the hook before indictment if they show remorse, legal experts say. And those who are indicted tend to get much lighter sentences if they confess, show remorse, compensate victims, and demonstrate that they have a strong family to return to.
    >
    > That gives a big incentive for an indicted suspect to cooperate with prosecutors and use the trial as a stage for shows of contrition. That may explain why 60 percent of those convicted and sentenced to prison terms last year had their sentences suspended.[13]

    Should American judges and prosecutors adopt the lenient Japanese response to crime? Explain.

6. A Rhode Island man pleaded guilty to child molestation. As an alternative to imprisonment and as a condition of his probation, the judge ordered him to purchase a newspaper ad displaying his picture, identifying himself as a sex offender, and encouraging others to seek assistance. A number of courts across the country have required apologies or other forms of humiliation in criminal cases.

    a. What objections would a defendant's lawyer raise to that method of punishment?

    b. Would you impose a "humiliation sentence" if you were the judge in a case like that in Rhode Island? Explain.

Part Two—The Judicial Process

Most disputes are settled without resort to litigation, but when agreement cannot be reached, we can turn to the courts—a highly technical and sophisticated dispute resolution mechanism.

State Court Systems

While state court systems vary substantially, a general pattern can be summarized. As shown in Figure 4.1, at the base of the court pyramid in most states is a *trial court of general jurisdiction,* commonly labeled a *district court* or a *superior court.* Most trials—both civil and criminal—arising out of state law are heard here, but certain classes of cases are reserved

FIGURE 4.1 **State and Federal Court Systems**

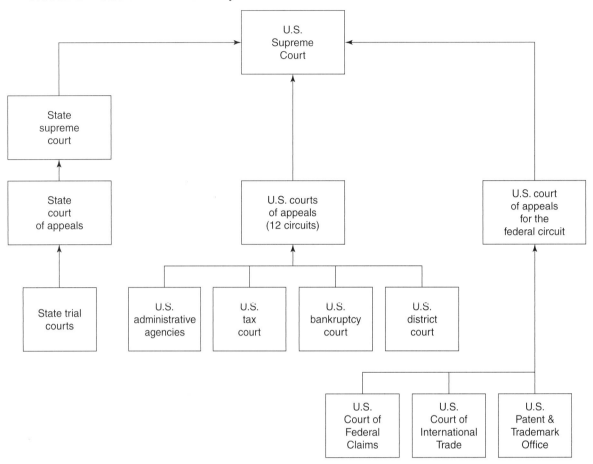

to courts of limited subject-matter jurisdiction or to various state administrative agencies (such as the state public utilities commission and the workers' compensation board). Family, small claims, juvenile, and traffic courts are examples of trial courts with limited jurisdiction. At the top of the judicial pyramid in all states is a court of appeals, ordinarily labeled the *supreme court.* A number of states also provide for an intermediate court of appeals located in the hierarchy between the trial courts and the highest appeals court.

Federal Court System

District Courts

The district courts provide the foundation of the federal judicial system. The Constitution provides for a Supreme Court and such inferior courts as Congress shall authorize.

Pursuant to that authority, Congress has established at least one district court for each state and territory. These are trial courts where witnesses are heard and questions of law and fact are resolved. Most federal cases begin in the district courts or in a federal administrative agency (such as the Federal Communications Commission). Congress has also provided for several courts of limited jurisdiction, including a tax court and the U.S. Court of International Trade.

[For access to all federal court Web sites, see the Federal Judicial Center at **http:// www.fjc.gov/**]

Courts of Appeals

Congress has divided the United States geographically into 11 judicial circuits and the District of Columbia and has established a court of appeals for each. Those courts hear appeals from the district courts within their circuit and review decisions and enforce orders of the various federal administrative agencies.

In 1982 Congress created the U.S. Court of Appeals for the Federal Circuit. That court hears, among others, all patent appeals and all appeals from the U.S. Court of Federal Claims (monetary claims against the United States).

Supreme Court

The Supreme Court consists of nine justices appointed for life by the president and confirmed by the Senate. Almost all of the Supreme Court's work consists of reviewing lower court decisions, principally from the courts of appeal with a small number from state high courts. Virtually all parties seeking Supreme Court review must petition the Court for a *writ of certiorari,* which commands the lower court to forward the trial records to the Court.

Decisions regarding those petitions are entirely discretionary with the Court. Typically it will hear those cases that will assist in resolving conflicting courts of appeal decisions, as well as those that raise questions of special significance about the Constitution or the national welfare. The Supreme Court caseload has grown steadily over the years and now totals approximately 7,000 cases per term. Formal, written opinions, however, are issued in only about 80 to 90 cases, a decline from, for example, 170 in 1981. Thus, in terms of numbers alone, the Court has backed away from its more activist approach of the 1960s, 1970s, and 1980s. [For a Web site tracking Supreme Court arguments and opinions see **http://docket.medill.northwestern.edu**]

Jurisdiction

A plaintiff may not simply proceed to trial at the court of his or her preference. The plaintiff must go to a court with *jurisdiction*—that is, a court with the necessary power and authority to hear the dispute. The court must have jurisdiction over both the subject matter and the persons (or, in some instances, the property) involved in the case.

Subject-Matter Jurisdiction

Subject-matter jurisdiction imposes bounds on the classes of cases a court may hear. The legislation or constitution creating the court will normally specify that court's jurisdictional authority. For example, state courts of general jurisdiction may hear most types of cases, but a criminal court or probate court is limited in the subject matter it may hear.

The outer bounds of federal jurisdiction are specified in the Constitution, while Congress has further particularized that issue by statute. Essentially, the federal district courts may hear two types of cases: (1) those involving a federal question and (2) those involving diversity of citizenship and more than $75,000.

Federal question jurisdiction exists in any suit where the plaintiff's claim is based on the U.S. Constitution, a U.S. treaty, or a federal statute. Thus litigants can bring to the federal courts cases involving, for example, the federal antitrust statutes, federal criminal laws, constitutional issues such as freedom of the press, and federal tax questions. Federal question jurisdiction does not require an amount in controversy exceeding $75,000. Further, federal and state courts have *concurrent jurisdiction* for some federal questions. Thus some federal question cases are decided in state courts applying federal law. Federal courts can also hear cases involving state laws. Congress has accorded the federal courts exclusive jurisdiction over certain subjects, including federal criminal laws, bankruptcy, and copyrights. Under *diversity jurisdiction,* federal district courts may hear cases involving more than $75,000 where the plaintiff(s) and the defendant(s) are citizens of different states. (Corporations are treated as citizens both of their state of incorporation and the state in which their principal place of business is located.) Diversity cases may also be heard in state courts, but plaintiffs frequently prefer to bring their actions in federal courts. The quality of the federal judiciary is generally believed to be superior to that of the states, and the federal courts are considered less likely to be influenced by local bias. Federal court action may also have procedural advantages, such as greater capacity to secure witnesses' testimony.

Personal Jurisdiction

Judicial authority over the person is known as *in personam jurisdiction.* In general, a state court's powers are limited to the bounds of the state. While the matter is fraught with complexities, it is fair to say that state court jurisdiction can be established in three ways: (1) When the defendant is a resident of the state, a summons may be served at that residence. (2) When the defendant is not a resident, a summons may be personally served should he or she be physically present in the state. (3) Most states have legislated "long-arm" statutes that allow a state or federal court to secure jurisdiction against an out-of-state party where the defendant has committed a tort in the state or where the defendant is conducting business in the state. Hence, in an auto accident in Ohio involving both an Ohio resident and a Kentucky resident, the Ohio resident may sue in Ohio and achieve service of process over the Kentucky defendant as a consequence of the jurisdictional authority afforded by the long-arm statute.

A state court may also acquire jurisdiction via an *in rem action.* In that instance the defendant may be a nonresident, but his or her property, which must be the subject of the suit, must be located within the state.

The following case involves a dispute about the commercial use of the name of an early rock star, "The Big Bopper." Both subject matter and personal jurisdiction questions regarding a *federal district court's* authority to resolve the dispute are at issue as an Iowa corporation sues an estate composed of Texas residents.

Judge Bennett

I. INTRODUCTION
A. Procedural Background
On June 2, 1999, plaintiff Wells' Dairy, Inc., ("Wells") filed its complaint in the Northern District of Iowa seeking declaratory judgment that use of its federally registered trademark, Reg. No. 2,031,929, did not violate or misappropriate any property interest owned by the defendant, The Estate of J.P. Richardson, Jr., a/k/a Richardson Family Trust, p/k/a "The Big Bopper" ("the Richardson Estate"). In short, Wells seeks declaratory relief to determine the rights to the use of the "Big Bopper" name. Thereafter, on June 18, 1999, the Richardson Estate filed a complaint in Texas state court against Wells based on a Texas state property statute, which is likewise pending. On August 2, 1999, the Richardson Estate filed a motion to dismiss the action in the Northern District of Iowa for lack of subject matter jurisdiction [and] lack of personal jurisdiction. . . .

B. Factual Background
Plaintiff Wells' Dairy, Inc., is an Iowa corporation with its principal place of business in LeMars, Iowa. The defendant, which the court collectively refers to as the Richardson Estate, consists of the heirs of J.P. Richardson, Jr., namely, his son, Jay Perry Richardson, his wife Adrianne Richardson Wenner, and his daughter, Debra Richardson Bridges, all of whom reside in the state of Texas. J.P. Richardson, Jr., otherwise known as "The Big Bopper," a famous musician best known for his hit "Chantilly Lace," died in a plane crash near Clear Lake, Iowa, on February 3, 1959. Perishing with "The Big Bopper" were rock sensations Buddy Holly and Ritchie Valens. At the time of their death, all three musicians, while not of equal prominence, left an indelible mark in the music and entertainment industry. Consequently, February 3, 1959, became known as "the day the music died." [http://www.officialbigbopper.com/story.htm[n1]]

On or about April 22, 1996, Wells began to commercially use the name "Big Bopper" to identify ice cream novelties, namely its large size chocolate chip cookie ice cream sandwich. On or about January 1, 1997, Wells received Registration No. 2,031,929 from the United States Trademark Office for

[n1]Musician Don McLean wrote and sang the song titled "American Pie," which coins the phrase "the day the music died." The entire song is a tribute to Buddy Holly, The Big Bopper, and Richie Valens, and a commentary on how rock and roll changed in the years since their deaths.
[http://www-ccs.ucsd.edu/svc/music/american_pie.html]

a registration on the Principle Register of "Big Bopper" for such ice cream novelties and frozen confections. Thereafter, on or about April 30, 1999, Wells received a cease and desist letter from attorney David Showalter, who represents the heirs of the Richardson Estate, requesting that Wells cease using its trademark and pay restitution to the Richardson Estate for the unauthorized use of the name "Big Bopper" on its ice cream products. Receipt of this letter precipitated Wells to file suit.

II. LEGAL ANALYSIS
A. Subject Matter Jurisdiction
1. The Jurisdictional Amount in Controversy
The court must first look to the face of the complaint to determine the sum or value in controversy. . . .

* * * * *

In this case, the Richardson Estate claims that the matter in controversy does not exceed the [diversity of citizenship] jurisdictional amount of $75,000.00. The court does not agree. In support of its claim that the jurisdictional amount is satisfied, the president and CEO of Wells submitted an affidavit in which he stated that "Wells began to use the commerce name 'Big Bopper' to describe an ice cream confection in 1996," and that "this trademark to Wells alone exceeds $75,000.00." Additionally, Fred Wells stated that "if Wells is required to stop using the trademark, the cost to develop and promote a new trademark would exceed $75,000.00." Therefore, based on Fred Wells's affidavit, and the defendants' lack of proof otherwise, the court concludes that Wells, in good faith, satisfies the requisite jurisdictional sum.

2. Federal Question Jurisdiction
In the alternative, Wells asserts that federal question jurisdiction exists by reason of the Federal Lanham Act, Title 15. Jurisdiction premised upon a federal question is set forth in § 28 U.S.C. 1331, which provides:

> The district courts shall have original jurisdiction of all civil actions arising under the Constitution, laws, or treaties of the United States.

The Lanham Act is codified at 15 U.S.C. §§ 1051–72, 1091–96, 1111–21, and 1123–27 (1976). Significantly, 15 U.S.C. § 1121 provides the following:

> The district and territorial courts of the United States shall have original jurisdiction and the courts of appeal of the United States shall have appellate jurisdiction, of all actions arising under this chapter, without regard to the amount in

controversy or to diversity or lack of diversity of the citizenship of the parties.

Based on the foregoing, the court concludes that it has jurisdiction over Wells's Lanham Act claim.

B. Personal Jurisdiction

* * * * *

The determination of whether or not a federal court has personal jurisdiction over a nonresident defendant involves a two-step analysis. First, the court must decide whether the facts satisfy the forum state's long-arm statute. If the statute has been satisfied, then the court must address whether the facts show that the nonresident has minimum contacts with the forum state such that the court's exercise of jurisdiction would be fair and in accordance with the due process clause of the Fourteenth Amendment.

1. Long-Arm Authority
In this case, the long-arm authority for defendant's service was Iowa Rule of Civil Procedure 56.2, which gives Iowa courts jurisdiction to the fullest constitutional extent. Because the rule has been interpreted to confer jurisdiction to the fullest extent permitted by the due process clause, the personal jurisdiction inquiry here collapses into the single question of whether exercise of personal jurisdiction comports with due process.

2. Minimum Contacts
Under the due process clause, the constitutional touchstone is whether defendant Richardson Estate has established sufficient minimum contacts with Iowa such that the exercise of jurisdiction here does not offend traditional notions of fair play and substantial justice.

* * * * *

The Five Factor Test. The test for evaluating the propriety of personal jurisdiction under the due process clause requires the court to consider the following five factors: (1) the nature and quality of the contacts with the forum state; (2) the quantity of the contacts with the forum state; (3) the relation of the cause of action to the contacts; (4) the interest of the forum state in providing a forum for its residents; and (5) the convenience of the parties. Of these factors, the first three are the most important. The record in this case shows that the Richardson Estate does have some of these traditional contacts with the State of Iowa.

In order to demonstrate that personal jurisdiction exists, Wells contends that the Richardson Estate has transacted business in the state of Iowa. To support this contention, Wells

points to three separate licensing agreements that the Richardson Estate granted to the Easter Seal Society of Iowa, Inc. ("Easter Seals"). This agreement gave the Easter Seals permission to use the name "The Big Bopper" in connection with a weekend event held at the Col Ballroom in Davenport, Iowa.

* * * * *

In addition, Wells contends that the Richardson Estate directly solicited business within the State of Iowa through personal visits. Wells maintains that on at least four occasions, Jay Perry visited the State of Iowa on behalf of the Richardson Estate to actively promote the music, memory, and good name of his father, "The Big Bopper." Three of these visits occurred at the Surf Ballroom in Clear Lake, Iowa, where "The Winter Dance Party" is held. This event commemorates and celebrates "The Big Bopper," and in the summer of 1989 a memorial was dedicated to "The Big Bopper." Wells claims that during the party in 1989, Jay Perry and his representatives sold compact discs of "The Big Bopper's" music, pictures of himself with the caption "Big Bopper, Jr.," and buttons that showed the likeness of J.P. Richardson, Jr.

Wells also claims that the Richardson Estate solicited business in Iowa through the official Big Bopper Web site.

In contrast, the Richardson Estate claims that personal jurisdiction does not exist, and states that it neither entered into a license agreement with the Easter Seals, nor received any consideration from the Easter Seals. The Richardson Estate maintains that it merely allowed the Easter Seals to use "The Big Bopper" name for the event. In so doing, it claims that it did not transact business within the state of Iowa.

The Richardson Estate likewise claims that it did not directly solicit business within Iowa. Specifically, the estate claims that plaintiff Wells's reference to Jay Perry's involvement with the Winter Dance Party is greatly embellished, when in fact his involvement was extremely limited. The Richardson Estate claims that its contacts with Iowa are sporadic and primarily indirect. Also, the Richardson Estate claims that the Web site is likewise not sufficient to establish jurisdiction in Iowa, because the level of activity involved with the Web site is minimal. . . .

The court must look at facts in the light most favorable to Wells as the nonmoving party. . . . [T]he court concludes that there has been a consistent series of business contacts and visits by the Richardson Estate, through Jay Perry, in the State of Iowa for the purpose of transacting and soliciting business to sustain personal jurisdiction as to the Richardson Estate. The contacts of the Texas-based Richardson Estate with this forum have been more than "random," "fortuitous," or "attenuated." For example, the Richardson Estate has transacted business for a period of several years in the State of Iowa as is evidenced by the licensing agreement with the Easter Seals of Iowa. In so doing, and taking the facts in the light most favorable to Wells's *prima facie* showing of jurisdiction, the Richardson Estate availed itself of the laws of Iowa by entering into a licensing agreement executed in this state.

[N]ot only has the Richardson Estate transacted business in the State of Iowa, but the Richardson Estate solicited business in Iowa. The Richardson Estate maintains a Web site, which is used to promote the name of "The Big Bopper" and to sell products. The Richardson Estate also participates in entertainment events with the similar purpose of promoting the name of "The Big Bopper" and selling products of "The Big Bopper." The sale of these products involves the trademark at issue in the present case, and, accordingly, such acts are related to the subject matter of Wells's Lanham Act claim. Moreover, advertisements with the name, "The Big Bopper," appeared, and continue to appear, in Iowa's newspapers to promote entertainment events. All these contacts with the State of Iowa prove that the Richardson Estate "purposefully availed" itself of transacting and soliciting business in Iowa and that the heirs of the Estate could have reasonably expected to be sued here. . . .

III. CONCLUSION

In considering defendant Richardson Estate's request that the complaint be dismissed on the grounds of lack of the required jurisdictional amount and lack of federal question jurisdiction, the court concludes that plaintiff Wells has made a good faith claim that satisfies the requisite jurisdictional sum, and that a federal question is present. Therefore, defendant Richardson Estate's motion to dismiss for lack of subject matter jurisdiction is **denied.** Also, the court concludes that the plaintiff has established a *prima facie* case that this court may exercise personal jurisdiction over defendant Richardson Estate. Therefore, because the due process clause does not prohibit the exercise of personal jurisdiction over defendant Richardson Estate, defendant Richardson Estate's motion to dismiss for lack of personal jurisdiction is **denied.**

Questions

1. *a.* Explain the reasoning that allowed the court to rule that it had subject matter jurisdiction in the case.

   b. Explain the reasoning that allowed the court to rule that it had personal jurisdiction over the Richardson estate.

2. What damages did Wells secure for its victory in this case? Explain.

3. In your view, is this decision fair to the Richardson Estate? Explain.

4. The Robinsons filed a product liability suit in an Oklahoma state court to recover for injuries sustained in an automobile accident in Oklahoma. The auto had been purchased in New York from the defendant, World-Wide Volkswagen Corp. Oklahoma's long-arm statute was used in an attempt to secure jurisdiction over the defendant. World-Wide conducted no business in Oklahoma. Nor did it solicit business there.

   a. Build an argument to support the claim of jurisdiction for the Oklahoma court.

   b. Decide. See *World-Wide Volkswagen Corp. v. Woodson*, 100 S. Ct. 559 (1980).

5. Burger King conducts a franchise, fast-food operation from its Miami, Florida, headquarters. John Rudzewicz and a partner, both residents of Michigan, secured a Burger King franchise in Michigan. Subsequently, the franchisees allegedly fell behind in payments, and after negotiations failed, Burger King ordered the franchisees to vacate the premises. They declined to do so, and continued to operate the franchise. Burger King brought suit in a federal district court in Florida. The defendant franchisees argued that the Florida court did not have personal jurisdiction over them because they were Michigan residents and because the claim did not arise in Florida. However, the district court found the defendants to be subject to the Florida long-arm statute, which extends jurisdiction to "[a]ny person, whether or not a citizen or resident of this state" who, "[b]reach[es] a contract in this state by failing to perform acts required by the contract to be performed in this state." The franchise contract provided for governance of the relationship by Florida law. Policy was set in Miami, although day-to-day supervision was managed through various district offices. The case ultimately reached the U.S. Supreme Court.

   a. What constitutional argument would you raise on behalf of the defendant franchisees?

   b. Decide. See *Burger King Corp. v. Rudzewicz*, 471 U.S. 462 (1985).

Venue

Once jurisdictional authority—that is, the power to hear the case—is established, the proper *venue* (geographic location within the court system) for the case comes into question. Ordinarily, a case will be heard by the court geographically closest to the incident or property in question or to where the parties reside. Thus a lawsuit springing from a crime ordinarily would be filed in the county where the crime took place. Sometimes pretrial publicity or other factors may cause one of the parties to seek a *change of venue* on the grounds that a fair trial is impossible in the original location. At this writing, former Enron Chairman Kenneth Lay and Chief Executive Jeffrey Skilling have asked to have their conspiracy and fraud trial moved out of Houston, Texas, where the collapse of their giant energy company cost thousands of jobs while damaging local real estate and charitable interests. The executives claim the hatred for them in Houston is so personal and emotional that they cannot receive a fair trial:

> The former Enron executives have been compared to Satan, al Quaida, Adolf Hitler, and O.J. Simpson in reports in the local media. . . . In a survey, nearly one in three Houston residents used negative statements to describe Skilling.[14]

Sometimes the choice of venue is a strategic decision reflecting the attorneys' knowledge of the tendencies of judges and juries in various locales around the nation. At this writing, the pharmaceutical giant Merck & Co. is beginning its defense against billions of dollars in claims linking the Merck painkilling drug Vioxx (now withdrawn from the market) to heart attacks and strokes. *The Wall Street Journal* explains that "both sides seek friendly venues":

> Whether Merck & Co. ends up winning or losing in the courts over Vioxx is going to depend in large part on the location of the playing field and the leanings of the referee. . . . [B]oth sides are battling for the courtroom advantage—seeking to have many of the cases . . . assigned to the courthouse and judge each thinks will be most open to its arguments.

> *   *   *   *   *

> Merck . . . asked a judicial panel to move the nearly 80 federal Vioxx cases filed around the country into one court, the U.S. District court in Maryland. The court is in the Fourth District, considered to have among the most conservative judges on the federal bench. In a court filing, the company described the Maryland court as ideal since it has tried consolidated product liability cases in the past, it already has three Vioxx cases filed there, and it is near major airports and in an area that has many hotels.

> By contrast, a faction of attorneys representing a few hundred plaintiffs want all the federal cases transferred to the U.S. District Court in Houston. "South Texas is considered a very, very attractive place for plaintiffs," Prof. [David] Logan says. "The juries in southern Texas are among the most generous in the United States."[15]

Sometimes trials, such as the one described next, are moved to avoid hardship or inconvenience (the doctrine of *forum non conveniens*).

PER CURIAM

Kia Motors America, Inc., headquartered in California; Kia Motors Corporation, headquartered in Korea (Kia Motors America, Inc., and Kia Motors Corporation are hereinafter collectively referred to as "Kia"); and Emerald Auto Sales, Inc. ("Emerald"), located in Houston County, Alabama, petition this Court to grant their motions to dismiss these cases based on the doctrine of forum non conveniens.

Facts and Procedural History

On October 16, 1999, Marilyn Elise Jeffreys, her daughter Danielle Jeffreys, Justin Valieres, and Christopher Allen Durden were in a 1998 Kia Sephia automobile when they were involved in a high-speed crash with another vehicle in Jackson County, Florida. The force of the crash caused the Sephia to leave the roadway; it came to rest in a pasture, where it caught fire and burned. The only occupant to survive the accident was Danielle Jeffreys.

On September 7, 2001, Howard Jeffreys, as the administrator of the estate of Marilyn Elise Jeffreys; Patricia Foxworth, as the administratrix of the estate of Christopher Allen Durden; and Debra Woodward, as the administratrix of the estate of Justin Valieres (Howard Jeffreys, Foxworth, and Woodward are hereinafter collectively referred to as "the respondents"), sued Kia and Emerald in the Houston Circuit Court on theories of product liability, breach of warranty, and negligence and wantonness as to Kia, and product liability and breach of warranty as to Emerald.

On October 11, 2001, Kia filed a motion to dismiss the Alabama actions on the ground of forum non conveniens. . . . [I]t requested the trial court to dismiss the actions and allow them to be filed in Jackson County, Florida. Subsequently, Kia filed an evidentiary submission in support of its motion to dismiss, presenting the affidavits of 25 witnesses who are residents of Florida and who stated that it would be more convenient if the actions were brought in Jackson County, Florida, where the crash occurred. From the facts before us, it appears that the accident site, the decedents, the plaintiffs, nonparty witnesses, rescue personnel and medical examiners who might testify, and documents related to this accident are located in Florida. The wrecked vehicle is currently being stored in Birmingham [Alabama].

* * * * *

Analysis

Kia and Emerald allege that in denying their motions to dismiss on the basis of forum non conveniens the trial court exceeded its discretion. Specifically, they argue that because the decedents were, and the plaintiffs are, residents of Florida and because the accident occurred in Florida and the majority of witnesses and accident-related documents are located in Florida, in the interests of justice the trial court should dismiss these actions so that they may be brought in Jackson County, Florida.

* * * * *

The doctrine of forum non conveniens requires a court to determine whether to accept or to decline jurisdiction of claims arising outside the state. . . . "Initially, the party seeking dismissal must show that the claims arose outside Alabama. Next, that party must show that an alternative forum exists."

* * * * *

Thus, the trial court is compelled to dismiss an action . . . if, upon a defendant's motion, it is shown that there exists a more appropriate forum outside the state, taking into account the location where the acts giving rise to the action occurred, the convenience of the parties and witnesses, and the interest of justice. . . . In addition, in determining whether a dismissal of the action on the ground of forum non conveniens should be granted, the trial court should consider "the relative ease of access to sources of proof, the location of the evidence, the availability of compulsory process for the attendance of unwilling witnesses, the cost of obtaining the attendance of willing witnesses, the possibility of a view of the premises, if a view would be appropriate to the action, and any other matter in order to assess the degree of actual difficulty and hardship that would result to the defendant in litigating the case in the forum chosen by the plaintiff." Ex parte Ben-Acadia, Ltd., 566 So. 2d 486, 488 (Ala. 1990).

* * * * *

In the instant case, for the doctrine of forum non conveniens to be applicable, the claims must have arisen outside Alabama. The respondents' complaints allege product liability and breach-of-warranty claims against both Kia and Emerald. Additionally, the respondents allege that Kia was negligent or wanton in its design and manufacture of the Sephia. It is undisputed that the product liability and negligence claims against Kia arose in Florida. However, the parties disagree as to where the breach-of-warranty claim against Emerald arose. The respondents, in their brief, state,

In this case, Florida's substantive law will apply to the product liability, negligence, and wantonness claims brought against the Defendants Kia Motors America, Inc., and Kia Motors Corporation. However, the Plaintiffs' breach of warranty claims against Emerald Auto Sales, Inc., arise under Alabama law since the subject car was purchased in Alabama.

In contrast, Kia and Emerald allege that all of the respondents' claims, including the breach-of-warranty claim against Emerald, arose in Florida.

* * * * *

In the present case, Jackson County, Florida, is clearly a more appropriate forum for these actions than is Houston County, Alabama. Applying Alabama law, we are satisfied that all of the causes of action occurred in Florida. Furthermore, 25 nonparty witnesses that Kia and Emerald plan to call on the issue of liability reside in Florida and cannot be subpoenaed and made to personally appear in the Houston Circuit Court. The inability to have live testimony in Alabama from these nonparty witnesses in the liability phase of this action, we believe, clearly favors dismissal.

* * * * *

Conclusion

We hold that the trial court exceeded its discretion in failing to dismiss the actions. Therefore, we grant the petition and order the trial court to dismiss these actions so that they can be refiled in Jackson County, Florida.

DISSENT: SEE, JUSTICE (DISSENTING)

I respectfully dissent from the majority opinion holding that the trial court exceeded its discretion in failing to dismiss this case pursuant to Alabama's forum non conveniens statute.

* * * * *

I agree with the majority that, for the forum non conveniens statute to apply, all of the claims in the present case must have arisen outside Alabama. However, I submit that Kia and Emerald have not met their burden of showing that the respondents' breach-of-warranty claim against Emerald arose outside this State.

* * * * *

In the present case, Emerald warranted the car as fit for its intended purpose when the purchaser accepted delivery of the car in Houston County. The respondents allege that the car was not fit for its intended purpose. The act giving rise to the breach-of-warranty claim against Emerald was Emerald's delivery of an allegedly defective car at its dealership in Houston County, not the accident in Florida. Therefore, the breach-of-warranty claim against Emerald arose in Houston County. . . .

* * * * *

Questions

1. *a.* Why did the court consider Florida to be the more "convenient" location for the case?

   b. Explain the dissenting opinion.

2. Why do you think the plaintiffs/respondents wanted the case heard in Alabama rather than in Florida?

Standing to Sue

All who wish to bring a claim before a court may not be permitted to do so. To receive the court's attention, the litigant must demonstrate that she or he has *standing to sue*. That is, the person must show that her or his interest in the outcome of the controversy is sufficiently direct and substantial as to justify the court's consideration. The litigant must show that she or he personally is suffering, or will be suffering, injury. Mere interest in the problem at hand is insufficient to grant standing to sue.

The Civil Trial Process

Civil procedure varies by jurisdiction. The following generalizations merely typify the process. (See Figure 4.2.) [For a vast "catalog" of law on the Internet, see **http://www. catalaw.com/**]

FIGURE 4.2 **Stages of a Lawsuit**

Pleading stage	Discovery stage		Trial stage	Appellate stage
Complaint	Deposition	Written interrogatories	Jury selection	Filing the appeal
Answer	Request for admissions	Production of documents	Opening statements	Submission of briefs
Reply			Cases in chief	Arguing the case
	Request for physical examination		Arguments	Decision of the court
	Request for mental examination		Instruction to jury	
			Verdict	
			Judgment	

Pleadings

Pleadings are the documents by which each party sets his or her initial case before the court. A civil action begins when the plaintiff files his or her first pleading, which is labeled a *complaint.* The complaint specifies (1) the parties to the suit, (2) evidence as to the court's jurisdiction in the case, (3) a statement of the facts, and (4) a prayer for relief (a remedy).

The complaint is filed with the clerk of court and a *summons* is issued, directing the defendant to appear in court to answer the claims alleged against him or her. A sheriff or some other official attempts to personally deliver the summons to the defendant. If personal delivery cannot be achieved, the summons may be left with a responsible party at the defendant's residence. Failing that, other modes of delivery are permissible, including a mailing. Publication of a notice in a newspaper will, in some instances, constitute good service of process. Ordinarily, a copy of the complaint accompanies the summons, so the defendant is apprised of the nature of the claim.

The defendant has several options. He or she may do nothing, but failure to respond may result in a default judgment in favor of the plaintiff. The defendant may choose to respond by filing *a demurrer* or *a motion to dismiss,* the essence of which is to argue that even if the plaintiff's recitation of the facts is accurate, a claim on which relief can be granted has not been stated. For example, a student may file suit objecting to a teacher's "bizarre" manner of dress; but, barring unusual circumstances, the student could not, as a matter of law, successfully challenge the teacher's costume.

Alternatively, the defendant may file with the court an initial pleading, called an *answer,* wherein the defendant enters a denial by setting out his or her version of the facts and law, or in which the defendant simply concedes the validity of the plaintiff's position. The answer may also contain an *affirmative defense* that would bar the plaintiff's claim. For example, the defendant might assert the statute of limitations or the statute of frauds. The defendant's answer might include a counterclaim or cross-claim. A *counterclaim* is the defendant's assertion of a claim of action against the plaintiff.

A *cross-claim* is the defendant's assertion of a claim of action against a codefendant. In some states, these would be labeled *cross-complaints.* In the event of a counterclaim or the assertion of new facts in the answer, the plaintiff will respond with a *reply.* The complaint, answer, reply, and their components are the pleadings that serve to give notice, clarify the issues, and limit the dimensions of the litigation. [For a summary of "Famous Trials" in history, see **http://www.law.umkc.edu/faculty/projects/ftrials/ftrials.htm**]

Motions

As necessary during and after the filing of the pleadings, either party may file motions with the court. For example, a party may move to clarify a pleading or to strike a portion deemed unnecessary. Of special importance is a motion for a judgment on the pleadings or a motion for summary judgment. In a *motion for a judgment on the pleadings,* either party simply asks the judge to reach a decision based on the information in the pleadings. However, the judge will do so only if the defendant's answer constitutes an admission of the accuracy of the plaintiff's claim, or if the plaintiff's claim clearly has no foundation in law.

In a *motion for a summary judgment,* the party filing the motion is claiming that no facts are in dispute. Therefore, the judge may make a ruling about the law without taking the case to trial. In a summary judgment hearing, the court can look beyond the pleadings to hear evidence from affidavits, depositions, and so on. These motions avoid the time and expense of trial.

Discovery

Discovery is the primary information-gathering stage in the pretrial process. That information clarifies the trial issues, promotes pretrial settlements, and helps prevent surprises at the trial, among other things. Discovery may consist of *depositions* (recorded, sworn testimony in preparation for trial), physical and mental examinations, answers to written questions (*interrogatories*), requests for access to documents and property to inspect them prior to trial, and *admissions* (agreement by the parties to stipulated issues of fact or law prior to trial).

Pretrial Conference

Either party may request, and many courts require, a pretrial meeting involving the attorneys, the judge, and occasionally the parties. Usually following discovery, the conference is designed to plan the course of the trial in the interests of efficiency and justice. The participants seek to define the issues and settle the dispute in advance of trial. If no settlement is reached, a trial date is set.

The Judge and Jury

The federal Constitution and most state constitutions provide for the right to a jury trial in a civil case (excepting equity actions). Some states place dollar minimums on that guaranty. At the federal level and in most states, unless one of the parties requests a jury, the judge alone will hear the case and decide all questions of law and fact. If the case is tried before a jury, that body will resolve questions of fact; but all questions of law will be resolved by the judge, who will also instruct the jury as to the law governing the case.

Jurors are selected from a jury pool composed of a cross section of the community. A panel is drawn from that pool. The individuals in that panel are questioned by the judge, by the attorneys, or by all to determine if any individual is prejudiced about the case such that he or she could not reach an objective decision on the merits. The questioning process is called *voir dire.*

From an attorney's point of view, jury selection is often not so much a matter of finding jurors without bias as it is a matter of identifying those jurors who are most likely to reach a decision favorable to one's client. To that end, elaborate mechanisms and strategies have been employed—particularly in criminal trials—to identify desirable jurors. For example, sophisticated, computer-assisted surveys of the trial community have been conducted to develop objective evidence by which to identify jurors who would not admit to racial prejudice but whose "profile" suggests the likelihood of such prejudice.

After questioning, the attorneys may *challenge for cause,* arguing to the judge that the individual cannot exercise the necessary objectivity of judgment. Attorneys are also afforded a limited number of *peremptory challenges,* by which the attorney can have a potential juror dismissed without the judge's concurrence and without offering a reason. However, peremptory challenges may not be used to reject jurors on the basis of race or gender.

Jury selection and the jury system are the subject of considerable debate in the legal community. Are juries necessary to a just system? How small can a jury be and still fulfill its duty? Is the jury process too slow and expensive? Should very long and complex cases, such as those in the antitrust area, be heard only by judges?

Misleading the Jury?

The case that follows examines allegations of trial misconduct by the plaintiff's attorney in an apparent effort to prejudice the jury.

LEGAL BRIEFCASE

Minichiello v. Supper Club

296 A.D.2d 350 (S.Ct. N.Y., App. Div., 1st Dept. 2002)

Judges Buckley, Rosenberger, Lerner, Rubin, Marlow

[P]laintiff alleges that he was verbally and physically abused by defendants because of his sexual orientation and then wrongfully discharged when he refused to voluntarily relinquish his position at the Supper Club.

The Supper Club is a dining and dancing establishment operated by defendant, Edison Associates, L.P. (hereinafter Edison), a limited partnership. Defendant Martin Theising is a partner in Edison and defendant Andre Cortez is the general manager of The Supper Club and is responsible for its day-to-

day operations. Defendant Oliver Hoffman was an independent consultant to The Supper Club.

In November 1992, plaintiff was hired as The Supper Club's late night manager initially responsible for its disco and later for its cabaret until he was discharged in July 1995. Plaintiff alleges in his complaint, that during the course of his employment, he was repeatedly subjected to humiliation and to discriminatory epithets regarding his sexual orientation and that, two weeks before he was discharged, he was physically held down by Hoffman and another individual while Cortez threatened to cut off his ponytail with a pair of scissors.

After a lengthy trial, the jury found that plaintiff had been subjected to a hostile work environment and had been discharged because of his sexual orientation and that Cortez had committed assault and battery. The jury awarded $160,000 in lost wages, finding that plaintiff could not have mitigated his damages. It further awarded $8,000,000 for past pain, suffering, and emotional distress and $2,000,000 for such future damages. The jury also awarded punitive damages of $1,000,000 against The Supper Club, $54,000 against Cortez and $2,200,000 against Theising with respect to the discrimination claims.

Defendants contend that the damages awarded were so grossly excessive as to be the result of passion and prejudice born of plaintiff's counsel's misconduct and judicial error, that a mere reduction of the awards would not be an adequate remedy.

"When misconduct of counsel in interrogation or summation so violates the rights of the other party to the litigation that extraneous matters beyond the proper scope of the trial may have substantially influenced or been determinative of the outcome, such breaches of the rules will not be condoned." (*Kohlmann v. City of New York*, 8 AD2d 598, 598.) Although evidence of hostility and harassment to other minorities may be relevant to a claim of a hostile work environment based on sexual orientation, the cumulative effect of the many irrelevant and highly prejudicial comments made by plaintiff's counsel in the course of this trial only served to incite the jury's passion and sympathy and effectively prevented a fair and dispassionate consideration of the evidence. Plaintiff's counsel referred to Theising, a German national with an apparent accent, as someone who exhibited an "attitude of hatred" and made forced analogies to Nazi Germany and the Holocaust. While the issue of this case was sexual orientation discrimination, plaintiff's counsel presented to the jury inappropriate matters involving African Americans, Latinos, and Jews that went far beyond any permissible boundaries and served no other purpose than to incite the jury's passions. Similarly, plaintiff's counsel elicited testimony about an alleged physical attack by an assistant to Cortez on an employee dying of AIDS and extensive testimony from several witnesses regarding the consumption of alcoholic beverages by Cortez, Hoffman, and Theising which was highly prejudicial with little or no probative value.

We find that the aggregate effect of such comments and conduct of plaintiff's counsel, which cannot be characterized as inadvertent or harmless, inflamed the jury's passion and sympathy to such an extent as to render the resulting judgment meaningless. . . .

The trial court erred in refusing to allow defendants to introduce evidence that no other employees were treated abusively . . . and in denying defendants' requested jury charge on mitigation. Likewise, it was error to deny defendants a missing witness charge upon plaintiff's failure to produce his therapist, Susan Corcoran, and a treating physician, Dr. Keston, since both had provided extensive treatment to plaintiff and their testimony would not have been cumulative. Further, the trial court made a number of demeaning comments in the presence of the jury demonstrating a marked antipathy toward defense counsel which, in light of the totality of circumstances at trial, warrant a new trial.

Were this Court not to reverse and remand for a new trial for the reasons stated above, we would have nevertheless reversed on the issue of damages. The jury's grossly excessive compensatory and punitive damages awards totaling approximately $20,000,000 have no rational basis. . . . [Reversed. Remanded to "a different justice."]

Questions

1. *a.* Why did the appeals court reverse the decision of the lower court?

   b. Why was the case remanded to "a different justice"?

2. Did this decision conclude that the plaintiff had not been a victim of sexual harassment, wrongful dismissal, or the like? Explain.

3. According to the appeals court, what errors were made by the judge at trial?

Eminem

A Michigan trial judge dismissed a 2003 defamation claim by DeAngelo Bailey against rapper Eminem. Bailey claimed that Eminem falsely depicted him as a bully in a song called "Brain Damage." The song's lyrics recount a childhood attack when Bailey allegedly beat up Marshall Mathers (Eminem). Perhaps inspired by the famous rapper, the judge added a rap footnote to her 13-page opinion. A portion follows:

Mr. Bailey complains that his rep is trash/so he's seeking compensation in the form of cash/Bailey thinks he's entitled to some monetary gain/Because Eminem used his name in vain."

The lyrics are stories no one would take as fact/they're an exaggeration of a childish act." It is therefore this Court's ultimate position/that Eminem is entitled to summary disposition.

The Michigan Court of Appeals affirmed the trial court decision.

Sources: "Eminem Delivered Favorable Verdict by Rap-Lovin' Judge" [**http://www.chartattack.com/damn/2003/ 10/2106.cfm**]; *Bailey v. Mathers,* No. 252123, 2005 WL 857242 (Michigan Ct. App., April 14, 2005).

The Trial

The trial begins with the opening statement by the attorney having the burden of proof. Then the opposing attorney offers his or her statement. Each is expected to outline what he or she intends to prove. The plaintiff then presents evidence, which may include both testimony and physical evidence, such as documents and photos, called *exhibits.*

The attorney secures testimony from his or her own witness via questioning labeled *direct examination.* After the plaintiff's attorney completes direct examination of the plaintiff's own witness, the defense attorney may question that witness in a process labeled *cross-examination. Redirect* and *re-cross* may then follow. After all of the plaintiff's witnesses have been questioned, the plaintiff rests his or her case.

At this stage, the defense may make a motion for a *directed verdict,* arguing, in essence, that the plaintiff has offered insufficient evidence to justify relief, so time and expense may be saved by terminating the trial. Understandably, the judge considers the motion in the light most favorable to the plaintiff. Such motions ordinarily fail, and the trial goes forward with the defendant's presentation of evidence.

At the completion of the defendant's case, both parties may be permitted to offer *rebuttal* evidence, and either party may move for a directed verdict. Barring a directed verdict, the case goes forward, with each party making a *closing argument.* When the trial is by jury, the judge must instruct the jurors as to the law to be applied to the case. The attorneys often submit to the judge their views of the proper instructions. Because the law lacks the clarity that laypersons often attribute to it, framing the instructions is a difficult task, frequently resulting in an appeal to a higher court. Finally, the verdict of the jury is rendered and a judgment is entered by the court. [For companies providing mock or practice trials, see **www.e-jury.net** or **www.virtualjury.com**]

Experts

In this highly technological and scientific era, one of the biggest dilemmas facing judges and juries is the weight to give to expert testimony. Very often, in cases such as medical malpractice and product liability (see Chapter 7), the testimony of experts is decisive to the outcome; but that testimony varies wildly in its reliability and credibility. The golfing case that follows investigates the theme of experience as a qualification for expert testimony.

Justice Gilbertson

Larry Nickles, the guardian of Mark Nickles, appeals the trial court's admission of expert testimony.

FACTS

On May 5, 1996, Jay Schild (Schild), Mark Nickles and Schild's younger brother drove to the Human Services Golf Course in Yankton, South Dakota, to play golf. All three boys were minors. Both Nickles and Schild had previously received golf instructions and had been taught some golfing rules.

After playing five holes, Schild and Nickles proceeded to the next tee box. Schild's younger brother was still on the fifth hole green retrieving his ball, which Nickles had knocked a short distance from the green. Schild proceeded to tee up his ball at the front center of the tee box and was preparing to hit his next drive. In the meantime, Nickles moved off the tee box approximately 10 feet and was facing the previous green watching Schild's brother. Schild, who had seen Nickles walk off the tee box, stepped back from his ball and took three practice swings. On the third practice swing, Schild hit Nickles in the head, fracturing his skull and permanently injuring his left eye.

Guardian commenced a personal injury action against Schild for damages sustained as a result of Schild's negligence and failure to exercise reasonable care in swinging his golf club. Schild denied he was negligent and claimed that Nickles was contributory negligent and assumed the risk of his injuries. During trial, Schild called Robert Boldus as an expert witness. Boldus was a former member of the Professional Golfer's Association and golf professional at Fox Run Golf Course in Yankton, South Dakota. Boldus had often given golfing lessons to junior golfers while at Fox Run.

Schild asked Boldus whether "as a golf professional," he had "formed any opinions as to what had happened in this case?" Nickles immediately requested permission to briefly interrogate Boldus for purposes of objecting to his opinion. During this interrogation, the following discussion occurred:

Q: (Nickles's attorney): Mr. Boldus, as a professional golfer, a member of PGA or based upon your experience, have you had any training in evaluating liability or standards of care required in golf liability cases?

A: (Boldus): No, I haven't.

Nickles then objected to the opinion by Boldus regarding standards of care or the ultimate issue. The trial judge overruled Nickles's objection and allowed Boldus to give his opinion:

Q: (Schild's attorney): And could you tell the jury what opinions you have come to?

A: (Boldus): In my opinion it was an accident. But one of the players moved, and when you're in your preshot routine if you move, you back away from the ball six inches to a foot or one step, and then you take your practice swings. My opinion, somehow Mark Nickles had moved in the way of the swing and got hit.

Q: (Schild's attorney): In your opinion did [Schild] violate any standards of care?

A: (Boldus): No.

The jury returned a verdict in favor of Schild. Nickles appealed, raising the following issue:

> Whether the trial court abused its discretion by permitting expert testimony from Boldus.

STANDARD OF REVIEW

Our standard of review in reviewing admissibility of expert testimony is well settled. We have often stated that

> we review questions of admissibility of an expert witness's testimony under an abuse of discretion standard. We have long acknowledged that the trial court has broad discretion concerning the admission of expert testimony. The trial court's decision on such matters will not be reversed absent a clear showing of an abuse of discretion.

DECISION

*   *   *   *   *

[A]n expert is not limited to testifying only upon those areas in which he or she has received formal training. Rather, when giving an opinion, an expert is allowed to draw upon all the knowledge, skill, or experience that he or she has accumulated.

[W]hile Boldus may not have had any formal classroom "training" in the applicable liability standards, it is clear Boldus was no novice at the game of golf. He was a former member of the PGA and a golf professional at Fox Run Golf Course in Yankton. While at Fox Run, he had often given golf lessons to junior golfers, which included golf etiquette and safety. He had even previously given golf lessons to Nickles. By any of these methods of acquiring the appropriate expertise or combination thereof, he could have qualified himself as an expert to testify as to "what happened."

It is quite clear from the testimony of Boldus and his vitae that he did have an opinion on the standards of care required in golf and the expertise to give such an opinion. The following testimony regarding the standard of care applicable to the game of golf was elicited from Boldus during direct testimony:

Q: When someone has addressed the ball and stepped back and they're doing their practice swings, what is the person's duty when they're doing those practice swings?

A: Well, basically there's nothing stated that says that you have to look around. You should be, when you begin your preshot routine, prior to taking your practice swings you should look and kind of [get] an idea where people are at so they are out of your way so you can take a swing. Once you begin your practice swings I think it's a duty of the other person to stay out of the way.

Q: So once, right before you start your preshot routine is when you have the duty to check what's going around?

A: Yes.

Q: And then as you start your preshot routine then it's the duty of those around you to become aware that that's what you're going to do, to watch?

A: Yes.

* * * * *

Boldus merely described, in his opinion, "what happened in this case" and that Schild's actions did not violate any standard of care concerning the game of golf. He did not invade the province of the jury as Nickles suggests. Boldus did not testify as to the ultimate issue of negligence. In fact, Boldus did not discuss the issue of liability at all until he was asked upon cross-examination, "but one party is liable, aren't they?" Boldus responded, "I wouldn't—yah—I don't know about liable, but somebody [is responsible for that]."

Nickles', objection as to the qualifications of Boldus goes in part to formal training concerning the issue of ultimate liability. The ultimate liability of one of the parties is not the same as standard of care. One can violate a standard of care and still not be held liable. There could be further potential questions of

contributory negligence, assumption of the risk, financial responsibility of a minor and/or his parents, questions of duty to supervise a minor and the like, all of which can have a decisive effect on liability and which clearly are outside the expertise of a golf pro and his knowledge of golf standards of care. Boldus did not testify as to any of these issues; his testimony was limited to describing the standard of care for the game of golf.

Affirmed.

DISSENT

Justice Sabers
I dissent.

I write specially to point out that the majority opinion misses the point—not once, but several times.

Whether Boldus was qualified as an expert witness is immaterial. The point is that under the pretense of being an expert witness, Boldus cannot testify as a fact witness. He was not present at the scene. He does not know what happened. Only fact witnesses can testify "as to what happened?" Therefore, under these circumstances it was totally improper for Boldus to testify to his opinion "as to what happened in this case."

Questions
1. What were Nickles's objections to the expert, Boldus's, testimony?
2. What objection was raised by the dissenting Justice Sabers?
3. Do you agree with the expert, Boldus, that once a golfer has properly started the preshot routine the duty of care shifts to those around the golfer to be aware of what is happening and to keep themselves out of harm's way? Explain.
4. Dodge slipped leaving work and claimed that she suffered knee, ankle, and back injuries. Dodge sued the cleaning service, but she provided no expert testimony to establish that the fall caused the injuries. Rather Dodge provided her own explanation of the fall and resulting injuries. Did the trial court err in admitting Dodge's lay person testimony? Explain, See *Dodge-Farrar v. American Cleaning Services Co.,* 54 P. 3d 954 (Ida. App. 2002).

Posttrial Motions

The losing party may seek a *judgment notwithstanding the verdict (judgment n.o.v)* on the grounds that in light of the controlling law, insufficient evidence was offered to permit the jury to decide as it did. Such motions are rarely granted. The judge is also empowered to enter a judgment n.o.v on his or her own initiative.

Either party may also move for a new trial. The winning party might do so on the grounds that the remedy provided was inferior to that warranted by the evidence. The losing party commonly claims an error of law to support a motion for a new trial. Other possible grounds for a new trial include jury misconduct or new evidence.

Appeals

After the judgment is rendered, either party may appeal the decision to a higher court. The winner may do so if he or she feels the remedy is inadequate. Ordinarily, of course, the losing party brings the appeal. The appealing party is the *appellant* or the *petitioner,* while the other party is the *appellee* or *respondent.* The appeals court does not try the case again. In theory, at least, its consideration is limited to mistakes of law at the trial level. For example, the appellant will argue that a jury instruction was erroneous or that the judge erred in failing to grant a motion to strike testimony alleged to have been prejudicial. The appeals court does not hear new evidence. It bases its decision on the trial record, materials filed by the opposing attorneys, and oral arguments.

The appellate court announces its judgment and ordinarily explains that decision in an accompanying document labeled an *opinion.* (Most of the cases in this text are appellate court opinions.) If no error is found, the lower court decision is *affirmed.* In finding prejudicial error, the appellate court may simply *reverse* (overrule) the lower court. Or the judgment may be to *reverse and remand,* wherein the lower court is overruled and the trial court must try the case again in accordance with the law as articulated in the appeals court opinion. After the decision of the intermediate appellate court, a further appeal may be sought at the highest court of the jurisdiction. Most of those petitions are denied.

Questions—Part Two

1. What are the purposes and uses of the concept of jurisdiction? Why do we limit the courts to which a claim can be taken?

2. Law cases often read like soap operas even as they reveal important truths. A woman and man, each married to others, had engaged in a long-term love affair. The woman's husband died, and she pleaded with her paramour to leave his New York home to visit her in Florida. She affirmed her love for the man. They made arrangements to meet in Miami, but on his arrival at the airport he was served a summons informing him that he was being sued. His Florida "lover" sought $500,000 for money allegedly loaned to him and for seduction inspired by a promise of marriage.

   a. Does the Florida court have proper jurisdiction over him?

   b. What if he had voluntarily come to Florida on vacation? See *Wyman v. Newhouse,* 93 F.2d 313 (2d Cir. 1937).

3. Sea Pines, a privately owned suburban community on Hilton Head Island, South Carolina, was designated a wildlife sanctuary by the state legislature. After study, the state Department of Natural Resources decided to issue permits to allow limited deer hunting on the land to reduce overpopulation. Various environmental groups challenged the issuance of the permits. What defense would you expect the state to offer in court? Explain. See *Sea Pines Ass'n for Protection of Wildlife v. South Carolina Dept. of Natural Resources,* 550 S.E. 2d 287 (S. C. S. Ct. 2001).

4. In dealing with crime, which of the following would you advocate: (*a*) job training, family counseling, and youth activities or (*b*) stricter sentencing, capital punishment for more crimes, and fewer paroles for convicted felons? Explain.

5. *a.* Would a prosecutor who is seeking a conviction against a black male for armed robbery prefer to try the case before an all-white jury? That is, do the demographics of the jury significantly influence the outcome of a case? Explain.

   b. Could that prosecutor legally exclude blacks and women from the jury by use of peremptory challenges? Explain.

Part Three—Criticism and Alternatives

Criticism

To many Americans, our system of justice is neither systematic nor just. A big portion of that concern is the view that we are awash in lawyers and lawsuits.

Too Many Lawyers and Lawsuits?

In 1991, then–Vice President Dan Quayle asked whether "America really needs 70 percent of the world's lawyers."[16] In fact, most countries do not collect reliable data regarding lawyer numbers, and definitions of what actually constitutes a lawyer vary widely. Nonetheless, the theme generated enormous, generally favorable, publicity. So in 1999, then–presidential candidate Quayle again attacked what he called the "legal aristocracy."[17]

Many lawyers, of course, means many lawsuits: too many, according to the critics. For example, Wal-Mart alone faces, at any given moment, about 8,000 lawsuits. In 2003–4, 33 potential *class actions* (similarly situated plaintiffs joined together in a single action rather than each filing individual claims) faced Wal-Mart with one of those (a sex discrimination suit) potentially involving some 1.6 million claimants.[18] Increasingly, the lawyers themselves are criticized for manufacturing many of these lawsuits, effectively making a business of the search for justice. *BusinessWeek* recently explained the power of the class action and activist lawyers in building lawsuits more as profit-making devices than as justice-seeking vehicles:

> How is it possible to profit from . . . flimsy lawsuits? Because of the power of the class action—a legal procedure that allows plaintiffs' attorneys to represent tens of thousands of individuals at once. With numbers that large, corporate defendants face the prospect of multibillion-dollar verdicts. Thus many companies will surrender the moment a judge officially "certifies" a class action. . . .
>
> What frustrates corporate lawyers the most is that some plaintiffs' lawyers have managed to turn the legal system upside down. Rather than waiting for clients to call, they come up with ideas for lawsuits and hunt down clients. These aggressive attorneys treat class actions as investment ventures rather than vehicles for helping consumers, argues Lewis H. Goldfarb, vice president and associate general counsel at DaimlerChrysler. "The plaintiffs' lawyers are capitalists," says Goldfarb. "For many of them, it's just a business."[19]

The result, as one expert explains, is that dealing with legal problems has become a central ingredient in management practice:

> Only a few decades ago, the law was peripheral to the core activities of doing business. When I became a business lawyer in the late 1950s, for example, our involvement was generally limited to forming a corporation or partnership for a client, providing for the investment capital, doing a lease for an office or factory, and maybe handling a key contract with a CEO or a major supplier. . . . Today the law can affect almost every action a manager takes. It has moved closer to the core activities of conducting business and succeeding in a red-hot, competitive environment. More people now have "rights" they can assert against your company, so you face claims from employees, consumers, competitors, and the government. Consequently, today's manager needs to know something about employment law, discrimination claims, sexual harassment rules, product safety issues, the rules of advertising and competition, antitrust rules, environmental law, the value of intellectual property, and more.[20]

Reform   In an effort to reduce litigation, Congress and President Bush in 2005 approved new legislation to curb "abusive" class actions. The Class Action Fairness Act shifts most interstate class actions seeking more than $5 million to the federal courts, where plaintiffs will face stern challenges. One effect of the new legislation is that plaintiffs, in most cases, will be unable to "shop" for a state court favorable to their claims. (For more on class action reforms, see Chapter 7. For a database of lawyer jokes, see [**http://dir. yahoo.com/Entertainment/Humor/Jokes/Lawyer_Jokes/**].

***Penthouse:* More of Paula**

David Joyner, Texas prisoner and self-proclaimed Minister of Law of the Mandingo Warriors prison gang, sued *Penthouse* magazine for $500,000 because the December 2000 centerfold of Paula Jones (who sued President Clinton for sexual harassment) was insufficiently revealing. U.S. District Judge Sam Sparks dismissed the claim and explained his reasoning in a take-off of "Twas the Night Before Christmas," a portion of which read,

> The minute his *Penthouse* issue arrived,
> the Minister ripped it open to see what was inside.
> But what to his wandering eyes should appear—
> not Paula Jones's promised privates, but only her rear.

Source: "Frustrated Felon," *ABA Journal,* March 2001, p. 16.

Law as a Global Business

The powerful role of litigation in the American market has, in recent years, begun to be mimicked by other economic powers around the globe. Globalization has brought American-style capitalism to all corners of the world, and American-style litigation is following. One of the perhaps unexpected consequences of globalization is the remarkable growth in lawyers and litigation in nations that once prided themselves on avoiding what they derided as the irrational practices of a litigation-crazy America.

Europe As European nations deregulate their economies and reduce their protective social welfare programs, the law seems to be taking on increasing importance:

> Some lawyers suggest the trend is the outcome of a broad political shift in Europe away from the generous welfare state of the late 20th century. "People are beginning to resort to self-help remedies," Mr. Bowden [London-based lawyer Paul Bowden] says. He points to Spain's decision two years ago to allow a version of class actions as an example of a "strong liberalizing trend in Europe" prompted by governments shifting responsibility for costly entitlements such as pensions off the state's balance sheet.[21]

European labor unions, long accustomed to relying on demonstrations and strikes to achieve change, are increasingly turning to coordinated legal claims.[22] Insurers are particularly concerned about the new litigiousness:

> "The biggest emerging risk for insurance groups worldwide is the proliferation of the U.S. tort system or elements of it," says Allianz A.G.'s chief risk officer, Raj Singh. Although a number of crucial elements of the U.S. system—such as class actions—aren't available in many places, it is only a matter of time before lawyers or consumer activists find ways around the problem, insurance executives say.[23]

Despite these shifts in European litigation practice, damages remain tiny compared to those in America. As noted, class actions are not allowed in much of Europe, and contingency fee arrangements (lawyers paid a percentage of the damages) are also unavailable. Indeed, in the United Kingdom and Ireland, plaintiffs who lose their cases may be required to pay the defendant's legal fees—a practice designed to discourage frivolous, speculative lawsuits.[24] But European lawyers are beginning to find ways to pursue litigation in the more wide-open American manner, and in another surprise, the Japanese are adopting similar moves.

Japan Globalization and its resultant deregulation are changing Japan's historically cooperative corporate culture. Until recently the Japanese government maintained enormous influence over a cartel-bound, clubby private sector; but the pressure of global competition is provoking more friction, and lawsuits are soaring in a culture that once favored working things out quietly. That litigation explosion would have been cause for alarm in the past, but the Japanese recently opened 68 new law schools:

> The schools—the first U.S.-style law schools in Japan—started classes this month with 5,600 students enrolled. They are part of the Japanese government's ambitious plan to boost the number of lawyers to 50,000 by 2018, from 23,000 now. That pales in comparison with the United States, which has an estimated 1 million lawyers. Part of that discrepancy with the United States, however, is because many tasks that lawyers handle in the United States are performed by nonlawyers in Japan.[25]

China As in Japan, aggressive capitalism and globalization have brought a booming legal industry to China:

> Starting from scratch in the late 1970s, the country now has more than 200,000 judges, 100,000 lawyers, 10,000 law firms, and 400 law schools. Even so, the system remains

deeply flawed. Many Chinese judges come from military backgrounds and have little legal training. Government prosecutors often lack basic skills in evidence discovery and collection.[26]

The article that follows describes the ups and downs of developing a more robust Chinese legal system. [For "Chinese law resources on the Internet," see **http://www.law.wustl.edu/chinalaw/intersou.html**]

Developing a Capitalist Taste for Litigation

James Harding

Just as Qian Yuan was leaving Watson's, a pharmacy on one of Shanghai's busiest shopping streets, the store alarm went off.

The 19-year-old university student was taken down to the basement and searched for shoplifting. She was scanned with a portable electronic detector. Then, much to her embarrassment, she says, the female security guard asked her to unzip her trousers, twice. On both occasions, nothing was found.

The incident might have remained nothing more than a personal humiliation, but Qian decided to take Watson's to court.

Last September, she sued the store, which is owned by the Hong Kong–based company Hutchison Whampoa in which the magnate Li Ka-shing has a substantial stake, demanding compensation for her mental anguish. She said she was "picking up the legal weapon to demand justice and safeguard her human dignity."

The district court found resoundingly in Qian's favor—Watson's was ordered to place an apology in Shanghai's most popular daily newspaper and pay damages of Rmb 250,000 ($30,000), equivalent to roughly 20 years' pay for an average Shanghai worker.

Qian is one of a growing breed of litigants in China. Where once disputes were handled by an official, adjudicated by a neighborhood Party committee, or simply and frequently left unresolved, these days more and more Chinese people are turning to the courts.

And handsome payouts for personal injury, emotional distress, and mental anguish are turning the business of accidents into something of a legal industry. When misfortune strikes, many Chinese people now call a lawyer.

Zhang Yuqi, a former Shanghai policeman-turned-attorney, says he was inundated with requests for representation after he secured a Rmb 130,000 compensation last year for a client who walked into a glass wall at a department store in which foreigners had invested.

"Ordinary people have tended to solve their problems between themselves. Average consumers do not know how they can protect their legal rights through the courts. But things are changing. They are beginning to realize how the law can help them," he says.

The signs that Chinese people are starting to show a litigious streak may suggest that a Communist-run country is moving toward a rule-based society. But the cases themselves illustrate how very far China has to go—they have exposed a patchy set of legal statutes and an often arbitrary court system.

* * * * *

The scale of the award for Qian created something of a stir in Shanghai, simply because the size of the compensation payment seemed astronomical to ordinary people. But the government seemed to consider the level of damages a mark of progress.

"Greater contact with other countries since the reforms and opening up began, has made the Chinese understand the importance of reparations," an official report explained.

More modest damages underestimated the extent of the victim's suffering and "did not teach others a lesson." Lawyers, too, have naturally been in favor of higher compensation payments, as they tend to be paid on a percentage of the final award.

* * * * *

Last month, the [Qian] case took a puzzling turn. Watson's appealed. The store has maintained that Qian was never body-searched. The Shanghai No. 2 Intermediate People's Court still judged that Watson's had violated the human dignity of Ms. Qian, but decided the award was too high. Instead of damages of Rmb 250,000, the sum was reduced to Rmb 10,000.

* * * * *

The speculation has been that pressure—either from other foreign retailers or domestic political interests eager not to displease Watson's chief owner, the powerful Li Ka-shing—was brought to bear on the Shanghai courts.

Indeed, a spokeswoman for Hutchison Whampoa, which owns the shop, acknowledges that there was "a lot of pressure from retail people. It was not just a Watson's issue. It became a supermarket operator issue." But, she says, Hutchison left the Shanghai division of Watson's to handle the case. Certainly, she says, Li was not involved.

Whatever the background to the revised verdict, it has left many people perplexed. Like many other areas of the law in China, the rules governing personal injury and emotional distress awards are a collage of statutes, regulations, and directives that sometimes overlap, sometimes contradict, and often leave large areas blank. "There is not a very clear basis in China's civil law for emotional compensation for personal injuries," says Zhang.

Indeed, the experiences of the eager new band of Chinese litigants suggests that recourse to the rule of law in China by no means guarantees a transparent, level, and fair hearing.

Source: Courtesy of *Financial Times* (London), February 26, 1999, p. 18.

Questions

1. List some of the services performed by lawyers and the legal system that are necessary to an efficient free market.
2. Do you see it as a sign of progress that China is encouraging the growth of its legal infrastructure? Explain.
3. *a.* In your opinion, why do lawyers in America have such an unfavorable image?
   b. Is that image deserved? Explain.

On the Other Hand—Litigation as a Last Resort

Almost everyone seems to be unhappy about lawyers and lawsuits, but we see considerable evidence that Americans increasingly expect the courts to correct problems that legislatures and regulators decline to address. Faced with giant problems involving dangerous drugs, handguns, environmental decline, and so on, angry jurors are increasingly anxious to send a message to big business and big government:

> "We are witnessing the emergence of an activist jury pool," says University of Georgia law professor Ron Carlson. "People are frustrated by the inaction of other branches of government and realize that as jurors they hold incredible powers of change."[27]

A recent study found 700 cases since 1990 in which jurors publicly declared that they intended their verdicts to have an impact beyond the immediate case, whereas the study found fewer than 100 such declarations in the prior two decades.[28] Of course, almost all policy makers agree that juries are inefficient, messy vehicles for solving problems, and jurors often are not the best informed, best qualified parties to address those problems. The point, however, is that American society seems to be demanding action, and the courts are often the only available weapon. So whatever frustration we may be feeling about exploding litigation may be attributable to us as much as to greedy lawyers.

Furthermore, those greedy lawyers turn out to be indispensable in maintaining freedom, fairness, and democracy for all. As columnist Anthony Lewis observed, "[L]aw . . . meets the fundamental human desire for both freedom and order."[29]

Even the broadly criticized class action, as *BusinessWeek* explains, often plays a vital role in achieving justice in some kinds of cases:

> There are plenty [of class actions] that do exactly what class actions are designed to do: efficiently offer relief to a large group of people who have suffered real injuries. Even opponents of the plaintiff's bar admit that some class actions are justifiable and speak favorably of cases such as the race discrimination suits against Texaco and Denny's and the antitrust claims against . . . vitamin manufacturers.[30]

Likewise, laws and lawyers are central to economic efficiency. Lawyers devise the rules, processes, and structures that permit capitalism to operate effectively. As we have read, the balance of the world is coming to recognize that law and lawyers are prerequisites to economic stability and progress.

Reform: Judicial Efficiency

Governments, businesses, lawyers, judges—all are frustrated with the expense and inefficiency of our overburdened judicial system. Some small businesses are now buying legal services insurance or prepaid legal services for a flat monthly fee.

Some cities have taken novel approaches to adjudication such as business courts that hear only commercial claims, thus allowing jurists to become very efficient handling contract problems, shareholder claims, and the like. Those systems are variations on the small claims courts that have long proven effective in settling minor disputes.

Small Claims Courts

Suppose you move out of your apartment and your landlord refuses to return your $500 damage deposit even though the rooms are spotless. Hiring a lawyer doesn't make good financial sense and is beyond your means anyway, but a small claims court may provide an effective solution. Small businesses have been particularly satisfied with the small claims courts as an efficient device for collecting unpaid bills without the expense of bill collectors and lawyers. The article that follows outlines the primary features of the small claims process.

READING ▶ **Small Claims Court FAQ**

Nolo

CAN ANY KIND OF CASE BE RESOLVED IN SMALL CLAIMS COURT?

No. Small claims courts primarily resolve small monetary disputes. In a few states, however, small claims courts may also rule on a limited range of other types of legal disputes, such as evictions or requests for the return of an item of property (restitution). You cannot use small claims court to file a divorce, guardianship, name change, or bankruptcy, or to ask for emergency relief (such as an injunction to stop someone from doing an illegal act).

* * * * *

ARE THERE TIME LIMITS IN WHICH A SMALL CLAIMS COURT CASE MUST BE FILED?

Yes. States establish rules called "statutes of limitations" that dictate how long you may wait to initiate a lawsuit after the key event giving rise to the lawsuit occurs or, in some instances, is discovered. Statutes of limitations rules apply to all courts, including small claims.

You'll almost always have at least one year to sue (measured from the event or, sometimes, from its discovery). Often, you'll have much longer. . . .

HOW MUCH CAN I SUE FOR IN SMALL CLAIMS COURT?

The limit is normally between $3,000 and $7,500, depending on your state. For instance, the maximum is $3,000 in New York, $5,000 in California, $7,500 in Minnesota, and $3,500 in Vermont. Recently there has been a trend toward increasing small claims court limits. . . .

WHERE SHOULD I FILE MY SMALL CLAIMS LAWSUIT?

Assuming the other party lives or does business in your state, rules normally require that you sue in the small claims court district closest to that person's residence or headquarters. In some instances, you also may be able to sue in the location (court district) where a contract was signed or a personal injury occurred (such as an auto accident). Check with your small claims clerk for detailed rules.

If a defendant has no contact with your state, you'll generally have to sue in the state where the defendant lives or does business. . . .

WILL I GET PAID IF I WIN THE LAWSUIT?

Not necessarily. The court may decide in your favor, but it won't handle collection for you. So before you sue, always ask, "Can I collect if I win?" If not, think twice before suing.

Worrying about whether or not you can get paid is reasonable, because some people and businesses are "judgment proof"—that is, they have little money or assets and aren't likely to acquire much in the foreseeable future. If they don't pay voluntarily, you may be out of luck. Ask yourself whether the person you're suing has a steady job, valuable real property, or investments. If so, it should be reasonably easy to collect by garnishing his wages if you win. If not, try to identify another collection source, such as a bank account, before going forward. . . .

WHAT SHOULD I DO TO PREPARE MY SMALL CLAIMS CASE?

Whether you are a plaintiff (the person suing) or the defendant (person being sued), the key is to realize that it's usually what you bring with you to court to back up your story—not what you say—that determines whether you'll win or lose. This makes sense if you understand that the judge has no idea who you are and whether your oral (spoken) testimony is reliable.

After all, your opponent is likely to claim that the "true story" is exactly the reverse of your version.

In short, your chances of winning will greatly increase if you carefully collect and prepare your evidence. Depending on the facts of your case, a few of the evidentiary tools you can use to convince the judge you are right include eyewitnesses, photographs, letters from experts, advertisements falsely hyping a product or service, and written contracts.

CAN I BRING A LAWYER TO SMALL CLAIMS COURT?

In a handful of states, including California, Michigan, and Nebraska, you must appear in small claims court on your own. In most states, however, you can be represented by a lawyer if you like. But even where it's allowed, hiring a lawyer is rarely cost-efficient. Most lawyers charge too much given the relatively modest amounts of money involved in small claims disputes. Happily, several studies show that people who represent themselves in small claims cases usually do just as well as those who have a lawyer.

WILL MY WITNESSES NEED TO TESTIFY IN PERSON IN SMALL CLAIMS COURT?

If possible, it's best to have key witnesses present in court. But if this isn't convenient, a clearly written memo or letter will be allowed under the rules of most small claims courts. (Be sure to check your state's rules.) Have the witness start the statement by establishing who he or she is. ("My name is John Lomox. I've owned and managed Reo's Toyota Repair Service for the last 17 years.") In clear, unemotional language, the witness should explain what he or she observed or heard. ("I carefully checked Mary Wilson's engine and found that it has been rebuilt improperly, using worn-out parts.") Finally, the witness should try to anticipate any questions a reasonable person might ask and provide the answers. ("Although it can take a few days to get new parts for older engines, such as the one Mary Wilson owned, it is easy and common practice to do so.")

IF I LOSE MY CASE IN SMALL CLAIMS COURT, CAN I APPEAL?

The answer depends on the state in which you live. Many states allow either party to appeal within a certain period of time, usually between 10 and 30 days, and obtain a new trial. In many states, appeals must be based solely on the contention that the judge made a legal mistake, and not on the facts of the case. Other states have their own unique rules. . . .

Source: Reprinted with permission from the publisher, NOLO. Copyright 2002, **http://www.nolo.com.**

Alternative Dispute Resolution (ADR)

Businesses, in particular, are increasingly looking outside the judicial system for dispute resolution strategies. Dot-com entrepreneurs are developing interesting new mechanisms on the Internet for conveniently addressing Internet-based disputes. Networks of human mediators, dispute resolution software, and an Internet version of *The People's Court* are among the online methods of settling problems outside of court. Online businesses recognize that trust is a key to their growth, so providing a quick, inexpensive, fair way for consumers to settle e-commerce grievances is an important industry goal. The leader in these developments is probably a San Francisco firm, SquareTrade, which works with eBay, realtors, and others and, as of early 2002, claimed to have handled over $50 million in disputes and resolved over 100,000 of those disputes. [See **www.squaretrade.com/**]

Cybersettle is an online system for settling insurance disputes, often of the fender-bender or slip-and-fall variety. The parties log onto Cybersettle and type in a sum they are willing to settle for. The computer compares the bids, round by round, and automatically settles the case if the bids fall within $5,000 or 30 percent of each other. Cybersettle has patented its Computerized Dispute Resolution System and says it has settled over $80,000,000 in claims with "half of all disputes submitted . . . resolved online or within 60 days of use of the system!" [See **www.cybersettle.com/**]

What Is ADR?

Of course, any form of *negotiation and settlement* would constitute an alternative to litigation, but *mediation* and *arbitration* are the most prominent of the alternatives to formal, full-blown litigation. Given the expense, frustration, and exploding numbers of lawsuits, we are seeing increasing imagination in building other ADR options including *private trials* and *minitrials*. [For many ADR links, see **www.hg.org/adr.html**]

Mediation

Mediation introduces a neutral third party into the resolution process. Ideally, the parties devise their own solution, with the mediator as a facilitator, not a decision maker. Even if the mediator does propose a solution, it will be in the nature of a compromise, not a determination of right and wrong. The bottom line is that only the disputing parties can adopt any particular outcome. The mediator may aid the parties in a number of ways, such as opening up communication between them.

Arbitration

Arbitration is a process in which a neutral third party is given the power to determine a binding resolution of the dispute. Depending on the situation, the resolution may be either a compromise solution or a determination of the rights of the parties and a win–lose solution. Even in the latter case, however, it may be quicker and less costly than a trial, and the arbitrator may be an expert in the subject area of the dispute instead of a generalist, as a judge would be. It is procedurally more formal than mediation, with the presentation of proofs and arguments by the parties, but less formal than court adjudication.

The arbitrator's decision is legally binding, although in some cases, such as labor disputes, it may be appealed to a court.

Private Trials

"rent-a-judge"

A number of states now permit private trials, sometimes labeled "rent-a-judge," where the litigants agree on that approach. Normally a third party such as a mediation firm makes the necessary arrangements, including hiring a retired judge as well as jurors to hear the case. The proceedings are conducted much as in a courtroom. Because the parties are paying, however, the dispute comes to trial more quickly, the process normally moves along more rapidly, and the proceeding may be conducted in private. Normally, the parties agree in advance that the decision will be binding. Appeals to the formal judicial system are provided for in some states. Critics question the fairness of the private system and wonder if it will further erode faith in public trials, but the time and money saved can be quite substantial.

Minitrials

In recent years, some corporations have agreed to settle their disputes by holding informal hearings that clarify the facts and the issues that would emerge if the dispute were litigated. In the minitrial, each organization presents its version of the case to a panel of senior executives from each organization. The trial is presided over by a neutral third party who may be called on for an opinion as to what would happen were the case to be litigated. That opinion has no binding force. The executives then meet to attempt to negotiate a settlement. The neutral third party sometimes facilitates that discussion. Minitrials are voluntary and nonbinding, but if an agreement is reached, the parties can formalize it by entering a settlement contract.

ADR Assessed

ADR mechanisms are employed in a variety of roles across many industries and businesses. Almost all union contracts have some arbitration procedure. Many auto companies use ADR to resolve warranty claims as well as disputes with dealers. Consumer complaints are sometimes settled by arbitration sponsored by the Better Business Bureau. Brokerage firms as well as some banks and insurance companies require customers to arbitrate disputes over their accounts. Approximately 100 nations are parties to the New York Convention agreeing to uphold international arbitration awards.

Ordinarily, ADR costs less and is resolved more quickly than litigation. ADR is less formal and less adversarial than the judicial process. Further, the parties have more control over the proceedings in that they can choose the facilitator, they can choose when and where the dispute will be heard, and they can keep the dispute private if they wish.

Despite those strengths, alternative dispute resolution is not without its own problems. In situations involving new or complex problems, litigation may be preferable. In situations where the arbitration or other ADR method is paid for by one of the parties (ordinarily, a company), can we feel confident the process will be fair to all? ADR does not provide precedent for future disputes. Further, lawyers are troubled that ADR, when mandatory, deprives plaintiffs of their Seventh Amendment right to a jury trial.

Critics consider ADR to be particularly threatening in those now-common situations where employment contracts mandate arbitration in job discrimination disputes. Nonetheless, court decisions to date have been strongly supportive of the legality of arbitration in resolving employment claims.[31] The case that follows illustrates the commonplace use of arbitration in labor law cases (see Chapter 14) and examines the limits of an arbitrator's decision-making authority.

Boise Cascade Corporation v. Paper, Allied-Industrial, Chemical, and Energy Workers (PACE), Local 7-0159

LEGAL BRIEFCASE   309 F.3d 1075 (8th Cir. 2001)

JUDGE GOLDBERG

I. BACKGROUND

Appellee Boise Cascade Corporation ("Boise") employed Nancy Burmeister ("Burmeister"), a member of the union, for nearly 11 years as a process operator in the mill department of its pulp and paper mill in International Falls, Minnesota. The terms and conditions of employment of union members such as Burmeister are protected by a collective bargaining agreement ("CBA") between Boise and the union. This action arises out of Boise's decision to terminate Burmeister's employment, effective February 11, 2000.

Problems in Burmeister's employment began to arise long before Boise fired her. On October 26, 1996, Burmeister received a written warning from her supervisor for failing to report to work and failing to call in. Less than a month later, she received another written warning for reporting to work one hour and 15 minutes late, having unsuccessfully requested the day off after her shift was scheduled to begin. On January 28, 1997, Burmeister called her supervisor after the start of her shift to inform him that she would be late due to "truck trouble"; she never reported to work and never called back that day. Two days later, she was placed on a Last Chance Agreement ("LCA") for excessive tardiness and absences; including the foregoing occasions, she had missed a total of 45 days in the preceding 13 months.

Burmeister did not grieve either the LCA or the written warnings that preceded it. She satisfied the conditions that the LCA imposed upon her during a six-month probationary period, without incident.

On May 2, 1998, when Burmeister reported to work Boise production manager Jim Larson ("Larson") noticed that her breath smelled of alcohol, her speech was slurred, and her mannerisms were different. Burmeister admitted to having recently consumed several beers, but a urine test showed that her blood alcohol content was actually 0.28 or nearly three times the legal limit for operating a motor vehicle in Minnesota. Although Burmeister was subject to immediate termination for the violation of Boise's Drug and Alcohol Policy, Boise agreed to place her on another LCA. This LCA required Burmeister to enroll in and complete a counseling program through Boise's Employee Assistance Program ("EAP"), and subjected Burmeister to two years of random drug and alcohol testing. Using language taken verbatim from her previous LCA, the LCA also provided,

> You must understand that it is your responsibility and obligation to follow all published policies and procedures. Further violation of any mill rules and/or failure to comply with the terms and conditions of this letter could result in your immediate termination. . . . Nancy, the company's expectations are clear . . . your future with Boise Cascade is in your hands.

Burmeister and her union representative had an opportunity to read the one-and-one-half-page LCA and to confer about it privately. As the arbitrator found, Burmeister had no questions about the LCA, fully understood what was required of her under it, and told Boise that she was "fine" with it. Burmeister, Larson, and her union representative all signed the LCA.

Gradually after the 1998 LCA was implemented, Larson and Burmeister's supervisor began to notice a pattern whereby Burmeister would call shortly before the start of her shift and request immediate vacation. On October 22, 1999, Burmeister failed to report to work, without warning. Well after her shift began, she called and requested immediate vacation, which Larson and her supervisor granted after conferring. Upon Burmeister's return to work, they met with her and the union president and informed her that she was placing her job at grave risk by returning to her prior pattern of attendance problems, and specifically warned her not to miss any more shifts or make any more belated vacation requests. Burmeister admitted that she had violated Boise's unwritten rule requiring employees to notify the company of absences at least two hours prior to the start of a shift, and that her supervisors had showed leniency by not enforcing the LCA and terminating her for this violation of an unwritten attendance rule.

On Friday, February 11, 2000, Burmeister failed to report to work for her 6:00 AM shift. She had not phoned her supervisor in advance, and never did call in that day. Instead, around 8:40 AM, Burmeister's supervisor received a call from Larry Matthews ("Matthews"), an EAP counselor. Matthews told the supervisor that Burmeister "could not keep the cap on the bottle" and that he was referring her for in-patient alcohol dependency treatment. Later that day, Matthews informed Boise's human resources manager that Burmeister had been unable to report to work because she had been drinking, and asked whether Burmeister could save her job if she entered an in-patient treatment facility that weekend. Burmeister ultimately did enter such a facility on Sunday, February 13, 2000.

The following Monday, Larson and the human resources director met with union representatives to discuss Burmeister's situation. At the meeting, Larson explained that Burmeister had failed to report for work or call in beforehand; that according to Matthews, Burmeister's use of alcohol had prevented her from reporting to work; that Burmeister's absence was not due to her attendance at an in-patient treatment facility; and that after the October 22, 1999, incident, he had reminded Burmeister of her obligation not to have any more attendance problems. The union conceded each of these facts, but claimed that Burmeister should not be terminated

because she had begun in-patient treatment the previous day. Nevertheless, after further consideration, Larson and Burmeister's supervisor terminated her employment, effective February 11, 2000. On February 15, 2000, the union grieved Burmeister's termination, on the grounds that "because [Burmeister] is at this time taking part in an in-patient treatment facility, she should not be terminated." The grievance was denied, and the union appealed the matter to binding arbitration as provided by the CBA.

Arbitration was had on August 9, 2000, before Richard John Miller ("Arbitrator Miller"), who issued his written decision on September 14, 2000. Arbitrator Miller rejected the union's assertion that he was entitled to decide whether there existed just cause for Burmeister's termination, observing that the LCA, rather than the CBA, governed the dispute. Thus, he found, the sole issue was whether Burmeister had violated the LCA. Without discussing the actual language of the LCA, the arbitrator construed it to prohibit violations only of written rules, and consequently determined that Burmeister's violation of Boise's unwritten attendance rules did not constitute a violation of the LCA. Arbitrator Miller further explained,

> The reason for the grievant's failure to personally call in or be presence [sic] at work on February 11, 2000, cannot be construed as being frivolous. It is clear that the grievant needed immediate assistance through the EAP on that day to get herself into an in-patient alcohol treatment program as soon as possible, since this disease was controlling both her personal and working relationships. There is nothing in the LCA which prevented the grievant from seeking assistance through the EAP for her alcohol problem. The fact that she was not admitted to in-patient treatment until February 13, 2000, is a function of the availability of a suitable treatment center.

In sustaining the grievance, the arbitrator ordered Boise to reinstate Burmeister to her former position with full seniority and to pay her back wages from March 8, 2000, the date of her discharge from the in-patient treatment facility.

Boise brought suit in federal district court, seeking to have the arbitral award vacated. It filed a motion for summary judgment, and the union filed a cross-motion requesting confirmation of the award. The district court granted Boise's motion and vacated the arbitral award, holding that the award failed to draw its essence from the parties' agreement. The court found that the plain language of the LCA did not support the arbitrator's decision; that the arbitrator failed to discuss the operative terms of the LCA; and that the arbitrator ignored the parties' intent when they entered into the LCA.

The union appealed the district court's order.

II. DISCUSSION

* * * * *

[A]n arbitrator's decision is not totally free from judicial review, for "although the arbitrator's authority is broad, it is not unlimited" *Missouri River Servs., Inc., v. Omaha Tribe of Nebraska,* 267 F. 3d 848, 855 (8th Cir. 2001). . . . In addition to those grounds for vacation of an award set forth in the Federal Arbitration Act, 9 U.S.C. § 10 (2000) (listing such reasons as the arbitrator's corruption, fraud, evident partiality, misconduct, or ultra vires acts), courts have vacated arbitral awards that are "completely irrational" or that "evidence a manifest disregard for the law" *Hoffman v. Cargill Inc.,* 236 F. 3d 458, 461 (8th Cir. 2001). . . .

In this case, the district court found that the plain language of the LCA was unambiguous and was not susceptible of the arbitrator's interpretation that it prohibited violations of only published mill rules. The court found that while the first sentence of the relevant paragraph did instruct Burmeister to "follow all published policies and procedures," the second sentence enjoining her from "further violation of any mill rules" stood alone, and could not be read as referring only to published mill rules. The court further held that because the arbitrator failed to quote the relevant language and failed to discuss how he arrived at his interpretation, and because his interpretation contravened the parties' intent, the award did not draw its essence from the LCA.

If we owed aught but maximum deference to the arbitrator's ruling, we would likely affirm the district court's order vacating the arbitral award based on the plain text of the LCA alone. As the district court reasoned, the first sentence in question sets forth Burmeister's obligations under the LCA, and the second sentence explains the sanction attached to failure to adhere to those conditions or to any other violation of any mill rule.

However, it is not our construction of the LCA for which the parties bargained, but Arbitrator Miller's. We may not vacate the award simply because we disagree with his interpretation, unless that interpretation so directly contradicts the plain meaning of the parties' agreement that it effectively rewrites it. . . .

An arbitrator's paramount obligation is to apply the parties' agreement in a way that gives effect to their intent. . . . In *Int'l Woodworkers v. Weyerhaeuser Co.,* 7 F.3d 133 (8th Cir. 1993), we explained,

> When the arbitrator construed [an] ambiguous provision without seeking the parties' guidance as to its intent and without evidence of their relevant past practices, he acted without considering the entire agreement. In these

circumstances we do not simply disagree with his interpretation of the agreement; we conclude that he dispensed his own brand of industrial justice, and his award cannot be said to draw its essence from the collective bargaining agreement.

* * * * *

[W]e have simply followed the longstanding principle that the arbitrator is not free to alter or amend the parties' agreement, unless expressly authorized to do so. Thus, where the plain text of the agreement is unmistakably clear, it is presumed to evince the parties' intent, and the arbitrator normally need look no further, but must give effect to the parties' agreement as written.

On the other hand, where the plain language of the parties' agreement is silent or ambiguous with respect to a disputed issue, an arbitrator is obliged to consider other relevant sources of the parties' intent.

* * * * *

Thus, contrary to the union's suggestion, federal courts routinely confirm arbitral awards where the arbitrator has looked to outside sources for guidance in giving meaning to ambiguous language. . . . Conversely we have vacated awards where the arbitrator failed to consider such sources when to do so was vital to determine the parties' intent. . . .

Of course, the arbitrator must restrict his inquiry to evidence that will aid him in divining the parties' intent; he may not rely on outside sources not within the parties' contemplation at the time they drafted their agreement.

* * * * *

In this case, Arbitrator Miller did not discuss the language concerning "any mill rules," did not recognize its ambiguity, and consequently did not consider other evidence of the parties' intent. Had he done so, yet still reached the same result, his decision would have rested on a legitimate interpretation of the parties' agreement. In the absence of other strong evidence that he was merely dispensing his own brand of industrial justice, we would be obliged to confirm the award, even if we disagreed with his reasoning and conclusion. Instead, given the decision's silence on this crucial issue, we cannot know whether Arbitrator Miller simply overlooked the obvious ambiguity or whether he obliquely construed it in a hypertechnical fashion, although his admission that the result "may be unfair" to Boise suggests the latter. In either event, "we believe that where an arbitrator fails to discuss a probative contract term, and at the same time offers no clear basis for how he construed the contract to reach his decision without such consideration, there arises a strong possibility that the award was not based on the contract." *George A. Hormel & Co. v. United Food & Commercial Workers,* Local 9, 879 F.2d 347, 351 (8th Cir. 1989).

While Arbitrator Miller may have mistakenly believed that he was required to give a strict interpretation of the LCA, however unfair the result to Boise, other language in his decision suggests that he was motivated to dispense his own brand of industrial justice. Although the arbitrator stated that the sole issue before him was whether Burmeister had violated the LCA, he effectively undertook a "just cause" analysis, finding that Burmeister's absence was not "frivolous" because her absence was caused by a desire to enter an in-patient counseling program.

* * * * *

Had Arbitrator Miller considered the parties' intent in drafting the 1998 LCA, as informed by their past practice, we do not believe he would have reached the same result, for there is abundant evidence that the parties did not intend or understand the LCA to mean that Burmeister's violations of the unwritten attendance rules could not lead to her termination. . . .

Any possible doubt as to the parties' understanding of Burmeister's obligations under the 1998 LCA is vitiated by her acknowledgment that her violation of attendance rules on October 22, 1999, warranted her termination under the terms of the LCA. The union argues that Burmeister's understanding is irrelevant, as it made no such concession. However, Burmeister is an independent signatory of the 1998 LCA, so her understanding of its requirements is clearly relevant. We also note that the union's own stated ground for grieving her termination was not that the LCA did not prohibit violations of Boise's unwritten attendance rules, but that she should not be terminated because she had begun in-patient treatment. Nor did either Burmeister or her union representatives demur when she was reminded, shortly after October 22, 1999, that further violations of Boise's attendance rules would be grounds for termination. [I]t is clear that in adopting the 1998 LCA, Boise, Burmeister, and the union all understood that Burmeister could be terminated for violations of Boise's unwritten attendance rules.

In this case, there is abundant evidence that the arbitrator's decision did not consider the parties' intent, that it contra-

venes that intent, and that "additional facts exist that strongly indicate that the arbitrator did not premise his award on the contract, notwithstanding his words to the contrary" *Hormel,* 879 F.2d at 350. In these circumstances, we do not merely disagree with the arbitrator's decision; rather, we find that his award fails to draw its essence from the parties' agreement. Accordingly, we affirm the order of the district court vacating the arbitral award.

Questions

1. Why did the court vacate the arbitrator's decision?

2. Make the argument that the arbitrator's award should be sustained.

3. Kalliope and David Valchine entered court-ordered mediation to try to resolve the problems that had led them to seek a divorce. Lawyers represented both Kalliope and David at mediation. The mediation led to a marital settlement agreement between Kalliope and David. One month later, Kalliope sought to set aside the agreement, arguing that she had been coerced by her husband, her husband's attorney, and the mediator. Kalliope testified that the mediator threatened to report her to the judge for being uncooperative in refusing to sign a reasonable settlement offer. She claimed that the mediator also told her that she could sign the agreement and then object to its provisions at the final hearing.

   Should the settlement be set aside? Explain.

4. Is an arbitration clause as a condition of employment a fair method of alternate dispute resolution, if entered knowingly and voluntarily? Explain.

5. In an effort to reduce legal expenses, some major banks and other businesses follow policies providing that all customer complaints will be subject to arbitration. Is mandatory arbitration fair to consumers? Explain.

6. Economist Stephen Magee argues that one way to strengthen the American economy would be to close the law schools:

   > Every time you turn out one law school graduate you've got a 40-year problem on your hands, he says. These guys run around and generate a lot of spurious conflict. They're like heat-seeking missiles.[32]

   Comment.

Internet Exercise

At [http://www.legalreformnow.com/] study the U.S. Chamber of Commerce attack on the influence of trial lawyers. Do you agree with the Chamber? Explain.

Chapter Questions

1. Steven Levitt and John Donohue, two highly respected American scholars, have produced a study indicating that the 1973 *Roe v. Wade* Supreme Court decision legalizing abortion had the unexpected effect of reducing crime. The decline in crime rates during the early 1990s came roughly 20 years after the *Roe* decision. Children who would have been born absent abortions would have been reaching their peak criminal years of 18 to 24. The young adults who would have been at greatest risk of criminal activity, unwanted children in difficult socioeconomic circumstances, according to the study, were aborted at disproportionately high rates. Every 10 percent increase in abortion led, according to the analysis, to about a 1 percent drop in later crime. Statistically speaking, the decline in crime exceeded that which would have been expected simply because fewer children were born. Further, the study shows that the five states that legalized abortion before the 1973 *Roe* decision all saw reduced crime rates in advance of the balance of the nation. Levitt has been careful to say, "In no sense do our results condone the wanton use of abortion as a method of birth control."[33]

   a. Do those study results "make sense" to you? Explain.

   b. Could birth control and abortion be better justified if sound scientific evidence over time were to show that reduced crime would follow? Explain.

2. Professor and criminal justice expert Morgan O. Reynolds argues that sterner punishment has led to reduced crime in the United States:

   > This reflects a broader pattern: As our crime rates have fallen, serious crime rates in England have risen substantially, as a recent study from the U.S. Bureau of Justice Statistics found. For example, victim surveys show that
   >
   > - The English robbery rate was about half the U.S. rate in 1981 but was 40 percent higher than America's in 1995.
   > - The English assault rate was slightly higher than America's in 1981 but more than double by 1995.
   > - The English burglary rate was half America's in 1981 but nearly double by 1995.
   >
   > Why these dramatic increases in English crime rates, while Americans' lives and property grew safer? The obvious explanation has been too often downplayed or ignored: The United States has instituted tougher, more predictable punishment for crime. The study's authors attribute the trends they note to the increasing conviction rates and longer sentences meted out in the United States versus the decreasing conviction rates and softer sentences in England and Wales. English conviction rates for rape, burglary, assault, and auto theft have plunged by half or more since 1981, while the likelihood of serving prison time for committing a serious violent crime or a burglary has increased sustantially in the United States.[34]

   a. Do you agree that harsher and more certain punishment will reduce criminal behavior?

   b. Do "root causes" such as being born out of wedlock affect criminal behavior? Explain.

3. Crowley, who became intoxicated at a postrace party on McRoberts's boat, was driving after the party and caused a multicar accident that resulted in serious injuries to Culver, who was driving one of the other vehicles. Culver's passenger was killed, and Crowley was later convicted of reckless homicide. Culver sued McRoberts for negligence. Crowley's drinking took place in the galley of McRoberts's 40-foot boat. McRoberts did not provide the liquor and McRoberts, who was busy with recording race results, was not aware of how much drinking Crowley had done. The Indiana Dram Shop statute provided that "it is unlawful for a person to sell, barter, deliver, or give away an alcoholic beverage to another person who is in a state of intoxication if the person knows that the other person is intoxicated." Expert testimony and a blood alcohol reading suggested that Crowley may have been visibly drunk, but several witnesses on the boat said they did not observe visible signs of intoxication. Did McRoberts violate the Indiana Dram Shop law, and was McRoberts negligent in failing to properly supervise Crowley? Explain. See *Culver v. McRoberts,* 192 F.3d 1095 (7th Cir. 1999).

4. Flanagan's, a New Jersey general contractor, ordered an irrigation pumping station from Wise, a Pennsylvania sales representative for Watertronics products. Watertronics, a Wisconsin manufacturer, completed about 15 percent of the pumping station and sent an invoice to Flanagan's seeking partial payment. When payment was not forthcoming, Watertronics asked Flanagan's to submit a credit application. Flanagan's did so and then sent a check for the agreed-upon amount. In the course of their transactions, Flanagan's had a four- to five-minute phone conversation with Watertronics. After the pump was installed problems arose, and Flanagan's made no further payments. Watertronics sued in Wisconsin to collect the balance due. Flanagan's moved to dismiss for lack of jurisdiction. Rule on that motion. See *Watertronics v. Flanagan's,* 635 N.W.2d 27 (Wis. App. 2001).

5. After drinking at the Elks Lodge, Dionne was escorted to a taxi where the driver, Grader, was told to take Dionne home because he had too much to drink. Dionne would not give Grader directions to his home and then told Grader to take him to another bar. Dionne paid his fare and went into the second bar, and later that bar summoned the same cab to take Dionne home. On this occasion, Dionne told Grader to take him to a convenience store. Dionne conducted his business there with no overt signs of intoxication. He then returned to the cab and asked to be driven back to the Elks Lodge. Grader deposited Dionne at the Elks Lodge and watched as Dionne passed by his own car in the parking lot. Grader heard other voices in the lot, assumed Dionne would be fine, and resumed his work. Later that evening Dionne died in a single-car accident. His blood-alcohol level was .25. The facts are not clear as to whether Dionne drank more after leaving Grader's cab. The taxi service was sued for negligence for not taking Dionne home. How would you rule on that negligence claim? Explain. See *Mastriano v. Blyer,* 779 A.2d 951 (Sup. Jud. Ct. Maine 2001).

6. A letter to *The Wall Street Journal:*

> The problems with our legal system go much deeper than irresponsible plaintiffs, amoral lawyers, and inept juries. The trouble is, our system of checks and balances

has been corrupted; 100 percent of the executive, 100 percent of the judicial, and 43 percent of the legislative branches have been taken over by one group—lawyers.

The Constitution charges Congress to ordain and establish the courts. It is no wonder it has created a system that maximizes the incomes of its own kind. The system is rigged to drag out cases that are billed by the hour, or to find moochers and looters willing to bring huge civil suits against productive citizens and corporations in front of dumbed-down juries.[35]

Do you agree? Explain.

7. Are the flaws in our legal system of such magnitude that respect for the law is threatened? Explain.

8. According to Warren Avis, founder of Avis Rent-a-Car,

We've reached a point in this country where, in many instances, power has become more important than justice—not a matter of who is right, but of who has the most money, time, and the largest battery of lawyers to drag a case through the courts.[36]

a. Should the rich be entitled to better legal representation, just as they have access to better food, better medical care, better education, and so on? Explain.

b. Should we employ a nationwide legal services program sufficient to guarantee competent legal aid to all? Explain.

9. Peremptory challenges may not constitutionally be used to exclude a potential juror from a trial on racial or gender grounds.

a. Must a criminal jury reflect the ethnic or racial diversity of the community? Explain. See *Powers v. Ohio,* 111 S.Ct. 1364 (1991).

b. Could potential jurors lawfully be rejected on the basis of their place of residence? Explain. See *U.S. v. Bishop,* 959 F.2d 820 (9th Cir. 1992).

10. French journalist Alain Clement offered a partial explanation for Americans' increasing reliance on lawsuits to resolve conflicts:

Diverse causes explain the growth of the contentious mood in America. One could be called the devaluing of the future. In 1911, the Russian political scientist Moise Ostrgorski wrote, "Confident of the future, Americans manifest a remarkable endurance to an unhappy present, a submissive patience that is willing to bargain about not only civic rights, but even the rights of man."[37]

a. What does Clement mean?

b. How do you explain our increased reliance on litigation?

11. Maintenance of our adversary system of justice sometimes compels lawyers to engage in practices that some consider unethical. Anne Strick relates one such situation:

Once upon a time, Williston, called by a colleague "one of the most distinguished and conscientious lawyers I or any man have ever known," was defending a client in a civil suit. In the course of the trial, Williston discovered in his client's letter file material potentially damaging to the man's case. The opposition failed to demand the file; nor did Williston offer it. His client won. But, recounts Williston in his autobiography, the judge in announcing his decision made clear that his ruling was based in part on his belief in one critical fact: a fact Williston, through a letter from the file in his possession, knew to be unfounded.

Did Williston, that "most conscientious lawyer," speak up? Did he correct the court's unfounded belief, the better to serve both truth and justice? He did not.

"Though," he wrote, "I had in front of me a letter which showed his [Honor's] error," Williston kept silent. Nor did he question the propriety of his behavior. For, said he, the lawyer "is not only not obliged to disclose unfavorable evidence, but it is a violation of his duty to his client if he does so."[38]

a. Did Williston act properly? Explain.

b. Should we turn to more cooperative, less combative, approaches to dispute resolution? Explain.

12. On July 5, 1884, four sailors were cast away from their ship in a storm 1,600 miles from the Cape of Good Hope. Their lifeboat contained neither water nor much food. On the 20th day of their ordeal, Dudley and Stevens, without the assistance or agreement of Brooks, cut the throat of the fourth sailor, a 17- or 18-year-old boy. They had not eaten since day 12. Water had been available only occasionally. At the time of the death, the men were probably about 1,000 miles from land. Prior to his death, the boy was lying helplessly in the bottom of the boat. The three surviving sailors ate the boy's remains for four days, at which point they were rescued by a passing boat. They were in a seriously weakened condition.

a. Were Dudley and Stevens guilty of murder? Explain.

b. Should Brooks have been charged with a crime for eating the boy's flesh? Explain. See *The Queen v. Dudley and Stephens,* 14 Queen's Bench Division 273 (1884).

13. Tompkins was a citizen of Pennsylvania. While walking on a railroad footpath in that state, he was struck by an object protruding from a passing freight train owned by the Erie Railroad Company, a New York corporation. Tompkins, by virtue of diversity of citizenship, filed a negligence suit against Erie in a New York federal court. Erie argued for the application of Pennsylvania common law, in which case Tompkins would have been treated as a trespasser. Tompkins argued that the absence of a Pennsylvania statute addressing the topic meant that federal common law had to be applied to the case. Should the federal court apply the relevant Pennsylvania state law, or should the court be free to exercise its independent judgment about what the common law of the state is or should be? See *Erie Railroad v. Tompkins,* 304 U.S. 64 (1938).

14. As noted in the chapter, China is rapidly training lawyers and moving toward a more Western approach to judicial systems. The following quote describes China's historic view of dispute resolution:

> Most Chinese persons engage in a large variety of economic and social activities and resolve disputes involved in those activities without coming in contact with the formal legal system. As in Japan, litigation in a court of law is not considered a normal way to resolve a dispute. Custom and extrajudicial dispute-settling mechanisms are utilized not only by private parties but by public entities. Decisions declaring someone right and someone wrong are not a desirable goal. Settlements and compromises

are preferable. Even in court, Chinese litigants generally do not obtain a clear defeat or victory.[39]

In your view, would China be better off in the contemporary world to retain its traditional means of conflict settlement or should it continue its turn toward Western-style litigation? Explain.

15. Landis was employed by FINOVA. FINOVA later concluded that Landis had misrepresented certain elements of his experience that had been important in the decision to hire him. FINOVA then dismissed Landis and declared the employment contract void. That contract contained a clause requiring all employment-related disputes to be decided by arbitration. Landis sued FINOVA claiming breach of contract and defamation. FINOVA moved to compel arbitration. Landis argued that the arbitration clause was unenforceable because FINOVA had declared the agreement void. Rule on FINOVA's motion to compel arbitration. Explain. See *Landis v. FINOVA*, 2000 U.S. Dist. LEXIS 5835 (S.D.N.Y. 2000).

16. University of Chicago law professor Richard Epstein points out how quickly Americans turn to legal remedies rather than relying on informal social customs (negotiation, neighborhood groups, simply accepting small losses and disturbances rather than fighting about them) to resolve conflicts. In your view, why are social customs increasingly ineffective in settling disputes in this country?

17. Judicial reform advocates often argue that the United States should adopt the English rule providing that the winner in a lawsuit is entitled to recover its reasonable litigation expenses from the loser.
    a. In brief, what are the strengths and weaknesses of the English rule?
    b. Would you favor it? Explain. See Herbert Kritzer, "Searching for Winners in the Loser Pays Rule," *ABA Journal,* November 1992, p. 55.

18. The Mackenhausens owned Sah Kah Tay Resort on Cass Lake, Minnesota. Several local boys, age nine and under, were playing in the Mackenhausens' van, which was parked near a shed on resort property. One of the boys crawled through a gap under the locked door of the shed and took a gas tank from a boat parked in the shed. The boy read the word *flammable* on the side of the tank and decided to take the tank back to the van. Using a lighter they brought with them, the boys ignited the gasoline, causing an explosion and fire that injured several of them and killed one. The children's parents sued the Mackenhausens, claiming that the Mackenhausens maintained an attractive nuisance and that they failed to keep dangerous material under proper lock and key. The Mackenhausens conceded that they knew that children often played in the vicinity of their shed and vehicle. How would you rule on the parents' claim? Explain. See *Croaker v. Mackenhausen,* 592 N.W.2d 857 (S. Ct. Minn. 1999).

NOTES

1. "How Accountable Is the Civil Justice System?" HALT—An Organization of Americans for Legal Reform [**http://www.halt.org/about_halt/press_room/pdf/HALT_Statistic**].

2. Ibid.

3. Richard Veilleux, University of Connecticut, "Criminal Justice Poll Shows Distrust of America's Legal System" [**http://www.news.uconn.edu/2000/may2000/rel00069.htm**].

4. Ibid.

5. Ibid.

6. Martha Neil, "Gender Affects Justice," *ABA Journal,* July 2001, p. 77.

7. Paul Sisson, "Pot-Smoking Dad Gets 27-Year Term," *Waterloo/Cedar Falls Courier,* July 6, 2001, p. B1.

8. Franz Schurmann, "Justice for All Is a Fragile Ideal," *Des Moines Register,* April 25, 1993, p. 1C.

9. The Scott Krueger story was synthesized from the following sources: Jules Crittenden, "MIT Fraternity Settles Lawsuit in Freshman's Drinking Death," *Boston Herald,* November 20, 2002, p. 28; Patrick Healy, "MIT to Pay $6 M in '97 Frat Death. School Accepts Responsibility in Drinking Fatality," *Boston Globe,* September 14, 2000, p. A1; Jay Rey, "Kruegers, MIT Reach $6 Million Settlement," *Buffalo News,* September 14, 2000, p. 1A; Margery Eagan, "Apology Goes a Long Way in Easing Anguish," *Boston Herald,* September 17, 2000, p. 2; Michael John James Kuzmich, "In Vino Mortuus: Fraternal Hazing and Alcohol-Related Deaths," 31 *McGeorge Law Review* 1087 (Summer 2000).

10. Deborah Guagliardi, "We Can't Blame Fraternity Alone for Student's Death," *Buffalo News,* September 24, 1998, Viewpoints, p. 3B.

11. Eagen, *Boston Herald,* p. 2.

12. Ibid.

13. Norihiko Shirouzu, "Japan Conviction Rate Dazzles, Deceives," *The Wall Street Journal,* December 19, 1995, p. A12.

14. Reuters, "Ex-Enron Execs Seek to Move Trial," *Los Angeles Times,* November 9, 2004, p. C3.

15. Barbara Martinez, "Preparing for Vioxx Suits, Both Sides Seek Friendly Venues," *The Wall Street Journal,* November 17, 2004, p. B1.

16. Stan Darden, "Quayle Debates with ABA Head over Legal Reform," United Press International, August 13, 1991.

17. Sam Stanton, "Lawyer-Bashing Jokes Are Jurisimprudence," *San Diego Union-Tribune,* July 8, 1999, p. E-1.

18. "How Big Can It Grow?—Wal-Mart," *The Economist,* April 17, 2004, vol. 371, issue 8371, p. 74.

19. Mike France, "On the Prowl for Victims," *BusinessWeek,* January 29, 2001, p. 122.

20. Milton Bordwin, "Your Company and the Law," *Management Review,* January 2000, p. 58.

21. Charles Fleming, "Europe Learns Litigious Ways," *The Wall Street Journal,* February 24, 2004, p. A16.

22. Ibid.

23. Ibid.

24. Ibid.

25. Ichiko Fuyuno, "Japan Grooms New Lawyers," *The Wall Street Journal,* April 13, 2004, p. A18.

26. Karby Leggett, "A Trial for Chinese Justice," *The Wall Street Journal,* May 29, 2003, p. A18.

27. *Dallas Morning News,* "Juries Use Verdicts to Make a Statement," *Waterloo/Cedar Falls Courier,* July 9, 2000, p. A1.

28. Ibid.

29. Anthony Lewis, "Rule of Law to Play Growing Role in China," *Houston Chronicle,* July 7, 1998, p. A18.

30. France, "The Litigation Machine," *BusinessWeek,* p. 115.

31. See, for example, *Circuit City Stores, Inc. v. Adams,* 532 U.S. 105 (2001).

32. "An Economist Out to Be Sued," *Los Angeles Times,* October 8, 1990, p. D1.

33. John J. Donohue III and Steven D. Levitt, *Quarterly Journal of Economics* 116, no. 2 (May 2001), p. 379.

34. Morgan O. Reynolds, "Europe Surpasses America—in Crime," *The Wall Street Jounal,* October 16, 1998, p. A14.

35. Darrell Dusina, "Lawyers, Everywhere," *The Wall Street Journal,* November 23, 1998, p. A23.

36. Warren Avis, "Court before Justice," *The New York Times,* July 21, 1978, p. 25.

37. Alain Clement, "Judges, Lawyers Are the Ruling Class in U.S. Society," *Washington Post,* August 22, 1980, p. A25.

38. Anne Strick, *Injustice for All* (New York: Penguin Books, 1978), p. 123.

39. Percy Luney, "Traditions and Foreign Influences: Systems of Law in China and Japan," *Law and Contemporary Problems* 52 (Spring 1989), pp. 129, 136.

Constitutional Law and the Bill of Rights

We the people of the United States, in order to form a more perfect union, establish justice, insure domestic tranquility, provide for the common defense, promote the general welfare, and secure the blessings of liberty to ourselves and our posterity, do ordain and establish this Constitution for the United States of America.

The Preamble to our Constitution, the words that open this chapter, summarizes the founders' lofty goals for America. The idealism embodied in the Preamble is both inspiring and touching. In reading it, we should reflect on the dream of America and the Constitution's role in molding and protecting that entirely new image of a nation. That we continue to be guided, more than 210 years later, by those rather few words is testimony to the brilliance and wisdom of its creators and to our determination to build a free, democratic, just society. Our Constitution is a remarkable document, so powerful in its ideas and images that it has reshaped the world.

Creating a Constitution—The United States

You may recall that the Constitution grew out of the Articles of Confederation as enacted by Congress in 1778. The Articles contemplated a "firm league of friendship," but each state was to maintain its "sovereignty, freedom, and independence." The Articles soon proved faulty. Seven years of war had basically bankrupted the colonies. Currency was largely worthless. The 13 new states fought over economic resources, interstate disputes were routine, and the federal union that emerged under the Articles of Confederation had little real authority. As a result of this distress, and in an effort to strengthen the Articles, the Constitutional Convention was called to order in Philadelphia on May 25, 1787.

The decision to convene the Convention may have been a first in world history in that the state leaders themselves acknowledged that the existing federal government was faulty, the citizenry calmly talked things over, violence was avoided, and the decision was made to go forward with the Convention. In the hot Philadelphia summer, with windows and curtains closed to assure secrecy (as a means of encouraging open debate), the often chubby and usually heavily clothed delegates sweated their way

All 55 delegates, our Founding
Fathers, were white males

toward a new government. All 55 delegates, our Founding Fathers, were white males, and most of them were wealthy landowners, but they were also immensely talented with a wide range of interests and experiences.

The delegates agreed that a stronger central government was needed, but they were split on just how far that notion should go. Virginia, led by the brilliance of James Madison, favored a dominant central government with greatly diminished state authority. Alexander Hamilton wanted to go further yet by, among other things, instituting the Presidency as a lifetime office. On the other hand, several states, led by New Jersey, wanted to retain strong states' rights. After weeks of debate, a middle ground began to emerge that led toward our current balance of power between big states and small states and between all of the states and the central government. In the end, the delegates reached consensus on a Constitution that guaranteed the then revolutionary notion of rule by the people.

On September 17, 1787, the great document, one of the most influential expressions in human history, was formally signed. Following bitter disputes in some states, the Constitution was ratified and the new government haltingly moved forward under the leadership of George Washington and John Adams.[1]

[For a database of many nations' constitutions, see **http://www.uni-wuerzburg.de/law**]

Structure and Purpose

The United States Constitution is reprinted in this book's appendix. Take a moment to review its structure and purposes.

The Preamble identifies certain goals for our society, such as unity (among the various states), justice, domestic tranquility (peace), defense from outsiders, increasing general welfare, and liberty. Article I sets up Congress and enumerates its powers. Article I, Section 8, Clause 3 is particularly important because it gives Congress the power to regulate commerce (the Commerce Clause). Article II sets up the executive branch, headed by the president, while Article III establishes the court system. Articles IV and VI, as well as the Fourteenth Amendment, address the relationship between the federal government and the states. Article VI provides in Clause 2 (the Supremacy Clause) for the supremacy of federal law over state law. Article V provides for amendments to the Constitution. The first 10 amendments, known as the Bill of Rights, were ratified by the states and put into effect in 1791. The remaining 16 amendments (11 through 26) were adopted at various times from 1798 through 1971.

From this review we can see that the Constitution serves a number of broad roles:

1. It establishes a national government.
2. It controls the relationship between the national government and the government of the states.
3. It defines and preserves personal liberty.
4. It contains provisions to enable the government to perpetuate itself.[2]

Recall that the Constitution was enacted to protect the citizenry from the government. The Constitution does not protect the citizenry from purely private concentrations of power, such as large corporations. In fact, corporations themselves are often entitled to the protections of the Constitution. The Constitution formally limits the authority of the Congress to pass laws by specifically listing *enumerated powers* that are properly within congressional authority (such as the power to regulate commerce) and by providing certain checks or restraints (such as the due process clauses—discussed later in this chapter) in the Constitution that limit just how far Congress can go even with an enumerated power. In practice, the impact of the enumerated powers doctrine has been sharply reduced because the federal government, especially in the New Deal era, has chosen to aggressively regulate the American economy. But as we shall see in this and subsequent chapters, the aforementioned constitutional checks or restraints continue to limit government's power, particularly in this era of increasing respect for free market reasoning.

Separation of Powers

As a further means of controlling the power of government, the Constitution sets up the three federal branches and provides mechanisms for them to act as checks and balances on each other. The president, Congress, and the courts each have specialized areas of authority, as provided for by the Constitution. Congress has the sole power to legislate at the federal level, whereas the president, among other things, executes laws, makes treaties, and commands the armed forces; the Supreme Court and the inferior courts have judicial authority at the federal level. The result is a system of separation of powers that prevents too much authority from residing in any one branch. For example, the president has the power to veto acts of Congress, those vetoes can be overridden by a two-thirds vote of each house, and the judiciary can find those acts unconstitutional. [For the National Constitution Center, see **http:// www.constitutioncenter.org/**]

Federalism

A primary role of the Constitution is to balance the central federal authority with dispersed state power. As just explained, the federal government holds only those powers explicitly designated or enumerated in the Constitution. As specified by the Tenth Amendment, the states and the people hold all powers not expressly granted to the federal government in the Constitution. The resulting division of power between the federal government and the states is a key battleground for our ongoing liberal–conservative cultural and political war. Conservatives fear big government and favor bringing power as close to the people as possible, whereas liberals fear local biases and favor a more unified national approach to many issues. Our increasingly complex and interrelated lives have led to a steady expansion in federal power; but as explained hereafter the U.S. Supreme Court continues to critically examine the constitutional balance of federal/ state power. The accompanying box details a similar constitutional struggle in the European Union.

Europe United under a New Constitution?

In 2004 leaders of the 25-nation European Union approved a new constitution to bind their rather loose alliance into something more like a grand, unified state. Full adoption of the new constitution, scheduled for 2007, requires ratification by each of the 25 nations. In 2005, however, voters in France and the Netherlands resoundingly rejected the new constitution. Then Great Britain announced that it was indefinitely postponing its national referendum on the proposed constitution. On the other hand, 10 nations had approved the constitution and others intend, at this writing, to go forward with their votes. Some kind of compromise may eventually emerge, but if not, the EU can go forward in its current form as an alliance without explicit constitutional ties.

The constitution is seen as a way, among other goals, for Europe to compete in the global economic arena with the United States, Japan, and emerging powers India and China. The EU, with its 450 million inhabitants and one-quarter of the world's GNP, believes it is ready to move more aggressively to challenge the United States as the center of global economic and political leadership. Indeed, the constitution calls for a single foreign minister to speak for the 25 EU nations.

Opponents in France and the Netherlands saw the proposed constitution as a blueprint for a giant, remote, centrally managed state accompanied by declining local authority. French voters were also particularly concerned that the proposed Constitution would impose free market reforms and reduce the generous welfare state protections that laboring French, in particular, have supported. The no votes in both countries also appear to reflect general worry about the sluggish European economy, hostility to immigration (particularly cheap labor from central Europe), and fear of Islamic radicalism.

Question
Based on the American experience, do you think the Europe of the future will be better off with a powerful central government, legally supreme in many areas over its member states? Or should those states retain maximum workable independence within a reasonably cohesive confederation?

The Constitution, the Bill of Rights, and Business

The Constitution and, in particular, the Commerce Clause (Article 1, Section 8, Clause 3) profoundly shape the practice of American business. Indeed, in some important ways, the Constitution is a commercial document reflecting the economic interests of the framers. We will defer discussion of the Commerce Clause until Chapter 8. In this chapter we will devote our attention primarily to the Bill of Rights. When we think of the Bill of Rights, corporations ordinarily do not come to mind. Extensive litigation in recent years, however, serves notice that the relationship between the corporate "person" and the fundamental freedoms is both important and unclear.

The Bill of Rights protects our personal freedoms (speech, religion, and the like) from encroachment by the federal government. Furthermore, the Supreme Court has ruled that the Due Process Clause of the Fourteenth Amendment, which is directed at the states, absorbs or incorporates those fundamental freedoms and protects them against intrusion by state governments. [For the "Guide to Law Online," prepared by the United States Law Library of Congress, see **http://www.loc.gov/law/guide/**]

The First Amendment

> Congress shall make no law respecting an establishment of religion, or prohibiting the free exercise thereof; or abridging the freedom of speech, or the press; or the right of the people peaceably to assemble, and to petition the Government for a redress of grievances.

These few words constitute one of the most powerful and noble utterances in history. The freedoms guaranteed in the First Amendment reflect the basic beliefs of American life. Much of the magnificence that we often associate with America is embodied in the protections of the First Amendment. After more than 210 years, it remains a source of wonder that our vast bureaucratic system and our more than 290 million independent citizens continue to rely on that sentence as a cornerstone of our way of life. [For the First Amendment Center, see **http://www.firstamendmentcenter.org/**]

1. Freedom of Religion

The First Amendment forbids (1) the establishment of an official state religion (the Establishment Clause) and (2) undue state interference with religious practice (the Free Exercise Clause). Government may neither encourage nor discourage the practice of religion generally, nor may it give preference to one religion over another. Broadly, the idea of the First Amendment is to maintain a separation between church and state. However, the precise boundary of that separation has become one of the more contentious social issues in contemporary life. Prayer in the schools, the words "under God" in the Pledge of Allegiance, denying state-funded scholarships to divinity students—these are some of the difficult battles in the freedom of religion debate. A highly publicized and interesting example of this conflict is the question of the constitutionality of Ten Commandments displays in government spaces. [For the Freedom Forum database on the First Amendment, see **http://www.freedomforum.org/**]

Ten Commandments

In 2001 former Alabama Supreme Court Chief Justice Roy Moore designed and commissioned a 5,000-pound Ten Commandments monument and ordered it to be prominently positioned in the rotunda of the state Supreme Court building. Two federal courts ruled that the Ten Commandments monument amounted to an unconstitutional establishment of religion. The U.S. Supreme Court declined to review those rulings, the monument was wheeled away to storage, and Judge Moore was forced from the bench because he had defied court orders to remove the monument. The story is far from over, however. Perhaps hundreds of Ten Commandments displays can be found in public buildings across the United States. Indeed, the courtroom of the U.S. Supreme Court itself includes a frieze of Moses holding two tablets; but the Supreme Court frieze shows other lawgivers, including Hammurabi and Justinian, and the letters on the tablets are Hebrew.

In an effort to clarify the continuing bitter dispute, the U.S. Supreme Court handed down two Ten Commandments decisions in 2005.[3] The two 5–4 rulings offered something to both sides by allowing Texas to retain the Commandments as part of a historic display on statehouse grounds, while Kentucky officials were barred from displaying the

Commandments on their courthouse walls. The essential distinctions in the two cases are matters of purpose, context, and history. The Commandments monument in Texas was set in a historical context along with 16 other monuments and 21 markers commemorating war veterans, boy scouts, pioneers, and so on, thus conveying, in total, a secular message about America's historical values—a permissible purpose that does not entwine the government in encouraging religion or favoring one religion over another. The Kentucky case, on the other hand, involved, in the judgment of the majority, the unconstitutional purpose of advancing religion. Among other things, county officials had ordered the Ten Commandments to be posted alone and had passed resolutions affirming the central role of the Ten Commandments in Kentucky life. Secular documents were added to the display only after the lawsuit was filed.

> Christian groups announced their intention to install Ten Commandments displays in 100 communities

Clearly the Ten Commandments conflict will persist. Immediately after the decisions, Christian groups announced their intention to install Ten Commandments displays in 100 communities within a year. Polls show a strong majority of Americans believe such displays are proper. Courts must decide each situation case by case.

2. Freedom of Speech

Hustler Magazine publisher Larry Flynt: "If the First Amendment will protect a scumbag like me, then it will protect all of you. Because I am the worst."

Freedom of speech is the primary guarantor of the American approach to life. Not only is it indispensable to democracy and personal dignity, but Americans believe that the free expression of ideas is the most likely path to the best ideas. We believe in a marketplace of ideas just as we believe in a marketplace of goods.

> We cannot freely yell "Fire" in a crowded theater

Freedom of speech is not absolute. Clearly we cannot freely make slanderous statements about others, publicly utter obscenities at will, speak "fighting words" that are likely to produce a clear and present danger of violence, or yell "Fire" in a crowded theater. At the same time, in general, the state cannot tell us what we can say; that is, the state cannot, for the most part, regulate the *content* of our speech. On the other hand, the state does have greater authority to regulate the *context* of that speech; that is, the state may be able to restrict where, when, and how we say certain things if that regulation is necessary to preserve compelling state interests. We have broad free speech rights in so-called *public forums* such as downtown business districts, parks, college campuses, and public plazas. Even in those places, however, the state may need to impose reasonable time and place regulations. Thus, although the Ku Klux Klan can express hatred for black people (the content of the message), the state may restrict where and when those expressions are made (the context of the message) if necessary for the public safety. [For freedom of speech links, see **http://samsara.law.cwru.edu/links/fsp.html**]

Of course, we have no constitutional right to freedom of speech on the private property of another, such as our place of employment. What about the enclosed shopping malls that are so much a part of our lives—are they public forums where we are substantially free to speak as we wish? Several state high courts have reached that conclusion, but in a 1999 decision the Minnesota Supreme Court ruled that the giant Mall of

America is private property for speech purposes.[4] In that case, protesters inside the mall peacefully distributed leaflets and carried signs urging shoppers to boycott Macy's because it sells fur coats. Some of the protesters were arrested for trespassing after refusing to leave the mall. The Minnesota Supreme Court ruled that easy public access to the mall did not convert it from a private to a public space.

Sometimes the question becomes one of what constitutes speech. The First Amendment clearly extends to expression in forms other than actual verbiage or writing. In a leading case in this area, the Supreme Court extended First Amendment protection to the wearing of black armbands to high school as a protest against the Vietnam War where no evidence of disruption was presented.[5] Does panhandling (begging) on a public street constitute speech? [See *Loper v. New York City Police Dept.*, 802 F. Supp. 1029 (S.D.N.Y. 1992).]

The Insider

The crucial role of free, open discussion in a democratic society was well illustrated by former Brown & Williamson tobacco company executive Jeffrey Wigand's decision to publicly report what he knew about the danger of cigarettes. Wigand told Mike Wallace and a *60 Minutes* national television audience that chemicals were added to tobacco to enhance its addictive quality. Wigand then became the subject of the 1999 Oscar-nominated movie *The Insider,* starring Russell Crowe and Al Pacino.

Wigand spoke to a group of Independence, Missouri, high school students about his experience in blowing the whistle on the tobacco industry. The *Kansas City Star* summarized Wigand's message to the students:

> He told them about the bullet in the mailbox and the middle-of-the-night death threats. He said Brown & Williamson squashed the First Amendment by using courts to bully CBS into postponing the *60 Minutes* segment. The tobacco industry was desperate to shut him up, he said, because he knew the secret of how cigarette companies hustled 3,000 teens each day into becoming habitual smokers. And he knew how they ensured future sales with addictive, lethal additives.

Source: Donald Bradley, "Students Hear from 'Insider,' " *Kansas City Star,* May 6, 2000, p. B1.

Politically Correct Speech

So with some exceptions, we are largely free of government restraints on what we can say. But should it be so? Should Vicente Fox, the president of Mexico, be expected to apologize for his 2005 remark that Mexicans in the United States take jobs that "not even blacks want to do"? (He hadn't apologized at this writing, but he did convey his "regrets" after he was criticized by American black leaders.) Should we be able to publicly condemn, for example, all Muslims? Should sports teams be allowed to label themselves Redskins or Braves or the like? Should words like *fag* and *dyke* be protected in public discourse? Universities and other branches of government have often attempted to curb this "hate speech" rooted in race, sex, disability, and so on. Free speech advocates have attached the "politically correct" label to those efforts. College campuses have been the center of the politically correct speech debate. Hundreds of campuses developed speech codes in the 1990s. For example, Stanford University amended its student code to provide that

> Speech and other expression constitutes harassment by personal vilification if it is intended to insult or stigmatize an individual or a small number of individuals on the basis of their sex, race, color, handicap, religion, sexual orientation, or national and ethnic origin; is addressed directly to the individual or individuals whom it insults or stigmatizes; and makes use of insulting or "fighting" words or nonverbal symbols.

The Stanford speech code, as well as others around the nation, have been struck down as violations of the First Amendment and other constitutional provisions. On the other hand, recent court decisions have given universities considerable latitude in dealing with some speech issues. For example, the 5th Circuit Court of Appeals upheld the right of the University of Mississippi to ban flags, including the Confederate flag, at campus events.[6] Specifically banning only the Confederate flag presumably would not have met with the Court's approval. The virtue in maintaining a campus, community, and nation that welcome all is undeniable, but the great strength of free expression is likewise self-evident. Many First Amendment scholars believe the correct antidote to hate speech is simply more speech; that is, they place their faith in the marketplace of ideas rather than in rules, however well intended. [For a vigorous critique of campus "political correctness," see **www.shadowuniv.com**]

NCAA Bans Native American Nicknames

The National Collegiate Athletic Association, in 2005, announced a ban on the use of 18 Native American nicknames and mascots during its postseason tournaments except the Bowl Championship Series. The ban applies to those nicknames and mascots considered "hostile or abusive in terms of race, ethnicity or national origin." Some of the affected schools:

- University of Utah Utes
- University of Illinois Illini
- University of North Dakota Fighting Sioux

On appeal, Florida State University was granted a waiver allowing continued use of its Seminole nickname and Chief Osceola mascot because the Seminole tribe officially sanctioned those uses. Fourteen other schools, including San Diego State University (Aztecs), have either removed all Native American references or were judged not to be making references to Native Americans as part of their athletic programs.

Source: NCAA Press Release, August 5, 2005, "NCAA Executive Committee Issues Guidelines for Use of Native American Mascots at Championship Events," [**http://www2.ncaa.org/media_and_events/**]

A Campus Dispute

The decision that follows illustrates the role of the First Amendment in campus life. In this case, a fraternity's "ugly woman contest" raised claims of racism, sexism, and general insensitivity.

IOTA XI Chapter v. George Mason University

993 F.2d 386 (4th Cir. 1993)

Senior Circuit Judge Sprouse

George Mason University appeals from a summary judgment granted by the district court to the IOTA XI Chapter of Sigma Chi Fraternity in its action for declaratory judgment and an injunction seeking to nullify sanctions imposed on it by the University because it conducted an "ugly woman contest" with racist and sexist overtones. We affirm.

I

Sigma Chi has for two years held an annual "Derby Days" event, planned and conducted both as entertainment and as a source of funds for donations to charity. The "ugly woman contest," held on April 4, 1991, was one of the "Derby Days" events. The Fraternity staged the contest in the cafeteria of the student union. As part of the contest, eighteen Fraternity members were assigned to one of six sorority teams cooperating in events. The involved Fraternity members appeared in the contest dressed as caricatures of different types of women, including one member dressed as an offensive caricature of a black woman. He was painted black and wore stringy, black hair decorated with curlers, and his outfit was stuffed with pillows to exaggerate a woman's breasts and buttocks. He spoke in slang to parody African-Americans.

There is no direct evidence in the record concerning the subjective intent of the Fraternity members who conducted the contest. The Fraternity, which later apologized to the University officials for the presentation, conceded during the litigation that the contest was sophomoric and offensive.

Following the contest, a number of students protested to the University that the skit had been objectionably sexist and racist. Two hundred forty-seven students, many of them members of the foreign or minority student body, executed a petition, which stated, "[W]e are condemning the racist and sexist implications of this event in which male members dressed as women. One man in particular wore a black face, portraying a negative stereotype of black women."

On April 10, 1991, the Dean for Student Services Kenneth Bumgarner discussed the situation with representatives of the objecting students. That same day, Dean Bumgarner met with student representatives of Sigma Chi.

The Dean met again with Fraternity representatives on April 18, and the following day advised its officers of the sanctions imposed. They included suspension from all activities for the rest of the 1991 spring semester and a two-year prohibition on all social activities except preapproved pledging events and preapproved philanthropic events with an educational purpose directly related to gender discrimination and cultural diversity. The University's sanctions also required Sigma Chi to plan and implement an educational program addressing cultural differences, diversity, and the concerns of women. A few weeks later, the University made minor modifications to the sanctions, allowing Sigma Chi to engage in selected social activities with the University's advance approval.

On June 5, 1991, Sigma Chi brought this action against the University and Dean Bumgarner. It requested declaratory judgment and injunctive relief to nullify the sanctions as violative of the First and Fourteenth Amendments. Sigma Chi moved for summary judgment on its First Amendment claims on June 28, 1991.

In addition to the affidavit of Dean Bumgarner explaining his meetings with student leaders, the University submitted the affidavits of other officials, including that of University President George W. Johnson. President Johnson, by his affidavit, presented the "mission statement" of the University:

* * * * *

(3) George Mason University is committed to promoting a culturally and racially diverse student body. . . . Education here is not limited to the classroom.

(4) We are committed to teaching the values of equal opportunity and equal treatment, respect for diversity, and individual dignity.

(5) Our mission also includes achieving the goals set forth in our affirmative action plan, a plan incorporating affirmative steps designed to attract and retain minorities to this campus.

* * * * *

(7) George Mason University is a state institution of higher education and a recipient of federal funds.

* * * * *

The district court granted summary judgment to Sigma Chi on its First Amendment claim, 773 F.Supp. 792 (E.D. Va. 1991).

II

The University urges that the district court's grant of summary judgment was premature. It stresses that there remain factual issues which the district court should have weighed in its conclusion.

* * * * *

In our view, for the reasons that follow, the district court was correct in concluding that there was no outstanding issue of material fact.

III

We initially face the task of deciding whether Sigma Chi's "ugly woman contest" is sufficiently expressive to entitle it to First Amendment protection.

*   *   *   *   *

A

First Amendment principles governing live entertainment are relatively clear: Short of obscenity, it is generally protected. As the Supreme Court announced in *Schad v. Borough of Mount Ephraim,* 452 U.S. 61 (1981), "[e]ntertainment, as well as political and ideological speech, is protected; motion pictures, programs broadcast by radio and television, and live entertainment . . . fall within the First Amendment guarantee." Expression devoid of "ideas" but with entertainment value may also be protected because "[t]he line between the informing and the entertaining is too elusive." *Winters v. New York,* 333 U.S. 507, 510 (1948).

*   *   *   *   *

Even crude street skits come within the First Amendment's reach. In . . . *Schacht v. United States,* 398 U.S. 58, 61–62 (1970), . . . Justice Black [declared] that an actor participating in even a crude performance enjoys the constitutional right to freedom of speech.

Bearing on this dichotomy between low- and high-grade entertainment are the Supreme Court's holdings relating to nude dancing. See *Barnes v. Glen Theatre, Inc.,* 111 S.Ct. 2456, 2460 (1991).

[I]n *Barnes,* the Supreme Court conceded that nude dancing is expressive conduct entitled to First Amendment protection.

*   *   *   *   *

. . . [I]t appears that the low quality of entertainment does not necessarily weigh in the First Amendment inquiry. It would seem, therefore, that the Fraternity's skit, even as low-grade entertainment, was inherently expressive and thus entitled to First Amendment protection.

B

The University nevertheless contends that discovery will demonstrate that the contest does not merit characterization as a skit but only as mindless fraternity fun, devoid of any artistic expression. It argues further that entitlement to First Amendment protection exists only if the production was intended to convey a message likely to be understood by a particular audience. From the summary judgment record, the University insists, it is impossible to discern the communicative intent necessary to imbue the Fraternity's conduct with a free speech component.

As indicated, we feel that the First Amendment protects the Fraternity's skit because it is inherently expressive entertainment. Even if this were not true, however, the skit, in our view, qualifies as expressive conduct under the test articulated in *Texas v. Johnson,* 491 U.S. 397 (1989). It is true that the *Johnson* test for determining the expressiveness of conduct requires "'[a]n intent to convey a particularized message'" and a great likelihood "'that the message would be understood by those who viewed it.'"

*   *   *   *   *

[T]he affidavits establish that the punishment was meted out to the Fraternity because its boorish *message* had interfered with the described University mission. It is manifest from these circumstances that the University officials thought the Fraternity intended to convey a message. The Fraternity members' apology and postconduct contriteness suggest that they held the same view.

*   *   *   *   *

As to the second prong of the *Johnson* test, there was a great likelihood that at least some of the audience viewing the skit would understand the Fraternity's message of satire and humor. Some students paid to attend the performance and were entertained. . . .

*   *   *   *   *

. . . [W]e are persuaded that the Fraternity's "ugly woman contest" satisfies the *Johnson* test for expressive conduct.

IV

If this were not a sufficient response to the University's argument, the principles relating to content and viewpoint discrimination recently emphasized in *R.A.V. v. City of St. Paul,* 112 S.Ct. 2538 (1992), provide a definitive answer. Although the Court in *St. Paul* reviewed the constitutional effect of a city "hate speech" ordinance, and we review the constitutionality of sanctions imposed for violating University policy, *St. Paul's* rationale applies here with equal force. Noting that St. Paul's city ordinance prohibited displays of symbols that "arouse[d] anger, alarm, or resentment in others on the basis of race, color, creed, religion, or gender," but did not prohibit displays of symbols which would advance ideas of racial or religious equality, Justice Scalia stated, "The First Amendment does not permit St. Paul to impose special prohibitions on those speakers who express views on disfavored subjects."

As evidenced by their affidavits, University officials sanctioned Sigma Chi for the message conveyed by the "ugly-woman contest" because it ran counter to the views the University sought to communicate to its students and the community. The mischief was the University's punishment of those who scoffed at its goals of racial integration and gender neutrality, while permitting, even encouraging, conduct that would further the viewpoint expressed in the University's goals and probably be embraced by a majority of society as well. "The First Amendment generally prevents government from proscribing . . . expressive conduct because of disapproval of the ideas expressed."

The University, however, urges us to weigh Sigma Chi's conduct against the substantial interests inherent in educational endeavors. We agree wholeheartedly that it is the University officials' responsibility, even their obligation, to achieve the goals they have set. On the other hand, a public university has many constitutionally permissible means to protect female and minority students. We must emphasize, as have other courts, that "the manner of [its action] cannot consist of selective limitations upon speech." The University should have accomplished its goals in some fashion other than silencing speech on the basis of its viewpoint.

Affirmed.

Questions

1. Is speech that consists merely of entertainment without benefit of meaningful ideas protected by the First Amendment? Explain.

2. Explain the Court's conclusion that the fraternity skit met the *Texas v. Johnson* test of "an intent to convey a particularized message" and a great likelihood "that the message would be understood by those who viewed it."

3. *a.* Should racist/sexist remarks be forbidden in college classrooms?

   b. As noted, the Stanford University speech code, as set out above, was ruled unconstitutional. The Superior Court judge in that case said, among other things, that the code was "overbroad." What did he mean?

   c. Do we give too much attention to freedom of speech at the expense of community civility? Explain.

4. T.W., a minor, was suspended from school for three days after he drew a picture of a Confederate flag on a piece of paper. The Kansas school, Derby Unified, suspended T.W. because it believed he had violated the district's "Racial Harassment or Intimidation" policy, which prohibits students from possessing at school "any written material, either printed or in their own handwriting, that is racially divisive or creates ill will or hatred." Confederate flags were included in a list of prohibited items. The Court found that Derby Unified had a history of racial harassment. Were T.W.'s First Amendment rights violated? Explain. See *West v. Derby Unified School District # 260,* 206 F.3d 1358 (10th Cir. 2000); cert. den. 531 U.S. 825 (2000).

5. The U.S. Supreme Court and lower federal courts have repeatedly ruled that burning the American flag is speech protected by the First Amendment. Congress often considers a flag protection amendment to the Constitution to make flag burning illegal. A 1999 Gallup Poll found 63 percent of Americans favoring that amendment. How would you vote? Explain.

6. Timothy Boomer's canoe hit a rock in Michigan's Rifle River, and he fell in. A passing mother and her young children heard Boomer cuss repeatedly (they said) or once or twice (his lawyer said). A 102-year-old Michigan law forbids swearing in front of children. Boomer was ticketed and tried.

   a. Did Boomer violate the statute?

   b. Does the First Amendment protect Boomer's outburst?

Free Speech in Cyberspace?

Do you ever wonder why the Internet is so polluted with pornography? The Supreme Court just reminded us why: It blocks every attempt by Congress to regulate the pornographers. The court props open the floodgates for smut and graphic sex. Over the past five years, it has repeatedly found new constitutional rights for vulgarity, most recently invalidating the Child Online Protection Act.

Conservative activist Phyllis Schlafly probably spoke for most Americans in condemning the Supreme Court's 2004 decision striking down the Child Online Protection Act (COPA),

Congress's most recent effort to restrict pornography on the Internet. For the third time in seven years, the Supreme Court found that a federal law aimed at online smut violated the First Amendment. Our legislators and judges clearly are struggling to create new rules for dealing with the hazards of this technological era without undermining our commitment to free expression. But should we condemn the Court as Schlafly argues? Basically, the Court was concerned about the *content-based* nature of the COPA restraint on speech, and the Court considered COPA to be *overbroad* in the sense that its goal of protecting children might have been achieved with less restrictive means that would not threaten speech of interest to adults. For example, some commentators suggest that COPA might restrict production and distribution of Web sites with high, but artistically legitimate, sexual content such as the movie *The Last Tango in Paris* or the cable television version of *Sex and the City*. The Supreme Court pointed to new filtering technology that might achieve Congress's goals without undue restraint on speech.

Sources: Phyllis Schlafly, Copley News Service, "High Court Backs Pornographers," *Chattanooga Times Free Press,* July 12, 2004, p. B7; *Ashcroft v. American Civil Liberties Union,* 124 S.Ct. 2783 (2004).

Commercial Speech

Liquor ads, the location of billboards, real estate "for sale" signs, and circulars placed on car windshields are among the many forms of commercial messages that governments may want to regulate for various reasons. Does the First Amendment protect those messages from government intervention in the same manner that it protects political speech? In 1942 the U.S. Supreme Court ruled that *commercial speech* was not entitled to First Amendment protection.[7] Subsequently the Court changed its stance and extended First Amendment rights to commercial speech, but those rights were much more limited than for political speech. In more recent years the Court has been gradually expanding protection for commercial speech, and many critics have called for full parity that would allow the government to regulate commercial speech only for compelling reasons, as has long been the case for political speech. The general rule today is that the government can regulate commercial speech where those restrictions are necessary for the public welfare. The surprising importance of the First Amendment in business practice was well illustrated by recent court fights over telemarketing and Nike ads.

Do-Not-Call In 2003 the Federal Trade Commission and the Federal Communications Commission together issued rules that created a national do-not-call registry, allowing consumers to indicate that they do not want to receive unsolicited calls from telemarketers. For those spared mealtime intrusions, the rule has been a blessing, but for commercial telemarketers the registry is a big financial setback. With no chance of legislative action to override the popular registry, the only recourse for direct marketers was the courts, and a key weapon in their assault on the registry was the First Amendment. Telemarketers went to court claiming the registry amounted to an unconstitutional restriction on their free speech rights. The 10th U.S. Circuit Court of Appeals, however, upheld the constitutionality of the registry, ruling that the "do-not-call registry is a valid commercial speech regulation because it directly advances the government's important interests in safeguarding personal privacy and reducing the danger of telemarketing abuse without burdening an excessive amount of speech."[8] The U.S. Supreme Court declined to review that decision.[9]

Nike   Various news reports in 1996 and thereafter harshly criticized working conditions in Nike factories in Southeast Asia. Thereafter Nike issued advertisements and press releases to tell its side of the story. Marc Kasky, a California resident, then sued Nike, saying those ads and other public defenses included either lies or deceptions about Nike's labor practices. Kasky sued Nike on behalf of the people of California under a state law forbidding unfair business practices. Nike won at both the trial and state court of appeals on the grounds that the First Amendment protected Nike's speech from government intervention. The U.S. Supreme Court then declined to resolve the commercial speech issue and sent the case back to California on procedural grounds. Thereafter Nike settled with Kasky by guaranteeing a $1.5 million payment to a Washington worker rights group. So the Kasky case failed to resolve the ongoing commercial speech debate. Honest mistakes or misleading statements made in public debate by a professor or journalist or your neighbor, for example, are protected by the First Amendment from government regulation. Deceptive or untrue commercial speech, on the other hand, may be regulated or even prohibited. So Nike feels the law puts it at a considerable disadvantage in that its critics' remarks would ordinarily be protected political speech while Nike's response would probably be commercial speech with a lesser degree of protection.[10] And in any case, doesn't our free market in ideas sufficiently protect the consumer—even in the face of inaccurate information? The *Bad Frog* decision examines the question of free speech protection for beer advertising.

Alcohol Ban Ads in Student Papers?

A Pennsylvania law banned paid advertisements for alcohol in newspapers affiliated with educational institutions. The *Pitt News,* a student-run newspaper at the University of Pittsburgh, raised a First Amendment challenge, but the state defended the law as a means of combating underage drinking. The 3rd Circuit U.S. Court of Appeals, however, struck down the law on First Amendment grounds, ruling that the law put an undue financial and speech burden on the *Pitt News* with little evidence that the ban would actually reduce alcohol consumption.

Source: The Pitt News v. Gerald J. Pappert, 379 F.3d 96 (3d Cir. 2004).

LEGAL   BRIEFCASE

Bad Frog Brewery v. New York State Liquor Authority   134 F.3d 87 (2d Cir. 1998)

Judge Newman

BACKGROUND

Bad Frog is a Michigan corporation that manufactures and markets several different types of alcoholic beverages under its "Bad Frog" trademark. This action concerns labels used by the company in the marketing of Bad Frog Beer, Bad Frog Lemon Lager, and Bad Frog Malt Liquor. Each label prominently features an artist's rendering of a frog holding up its four-"fingered" right "hand," with the back of the "hand" shown, the second "finger" extended, and the other three "fingers" slightly curled. Bad Frog does not dispute that the frog depicted in the label artwork is making the gesture generally known as "giving the finger" and that the gesture is widely regarded as an offensive insult, conveying a message that the company has characterized as "traditionally . . . negative and nasty." Versions of the label feature slogans such as "He just don't care," "An amphibian with an attitude," "Turning bad into good," and "The beer so good . . . it's bad." Another slogan, originally used but now abandoned, was "He's mean, green and obscene."

Reprinted by permission of the trademark holder, Bad Frog Brewery.

Bad Frog's labels have been approved for use by the Federal Bureau of Alcohol, Tobacco, and Firearms, and by authorities in at least 15 states and the District of Columbia, but have been rejected by authorities in New Jersey, Ohio, and Pennsylvania.

In May 1996, Bad Frog's authorized New York distributor, Renaissance Beer Co., made an application to the New York State Liquor Authority (NYSLA) for brand label approval and registration. . . .

In September 1996, NYSLA denied Bad Frog's application. . . . Explaining its rationale for the rejection, the Authority found that the label "encourages combative behavior" and that the gesture and the slogan, "He just don't care," placed close to and in larger type than a warning concerning potential health problems,

foster a defiance to the health warning on the label, entice underage drinkers, and invite the public not to heed conventional wisdom and to disobey standards of decorum.

In addition, the Authority said that it

considered that approval of this label means that the label could appear in grocery and convenience stores, with obvious exposure on the shelf to children of tender age

and that it

is sensitive to and has concern as to [the label's] adverse effects on such a youthful audience.

Finally, the Authority said that it

has considered that within the state of New York, the gesture of "giving the finger" to someone has the insulting meaning of "**k You," or "Up Yours," . . . a confrontational, obscene gesture, known to lead to fights, shootings, and homicides . . . concludes that the encouraged use of this gesture in licensed premises is akin to yelling "fire" in a crowded theater, . . . [and] finds that to approve this admittedly obscene, provocative confrontational gesture would not be conducive to proper regulation and control and would tend to adversely affect the health, safety, and welfare of the People of the State of New York.

Bad Frog filed the present action in October 1996 and sought a preliminary injunction barring NYSLA from taking any steps to prohibit the sale of beer by Bad Frog under the controversial labels. The District Court denied the motion [and Bad Frog now appeals the District Court decision].

*   *   *   *   *

COMMERCIAL OR NONCOMMERCIAL SPEECH?

In Bad Frog's view, the commercial speech that receives reduced First Amendment protection is expression that conveys commercial information. The frog labels, it contends, do not purport to convey such information, but instead communicate only a "joke." As such, the argument continues, the labels enjoy full First Amendment protection, rather than the somewhat reduced protection accorded commercial speech.

NYSLA agrees with the District Court that the labels enjoy some First Amendment protection, but are to be assessed by the somewhat reduced standards applicable to commercial speech.

*   *   *   *   *

Bad Frog's label attempts to function, like a trademark, to identify the source of the product. The picture on a beer bottle of a frog behaving badly is reasonably to be understood as attempting to identify to consumers a product of the Bad Frog Brewery. In addition, the label serves to propose a commercial transaction. Though the label communicates no information beyond the source of the product, we think that minimal information, conveyed in the context of a proposal of a commercial transaction, suffices to invoke the protections for commercial speech. . . .

Bad Frog contends that its labels deserve full First Amendment protection because their proposal of a commercial transaction is combined with what is claimed to be political, or at least societal, commentary.

* * * * *

We are unpersuaded by Bad Frog's attempt to separate the purported social commentary in the labels from the hawking of beer. Bad Frog's labels meet the three criteria identified in *Bolger* [463 U.S. 60 (1983)]: the labels are a form of advertising, identify a specific product, and serve the economic interest of the speaker. Moreover, the purported noncommercial message is not so "inextricably intertwined" with the commercial speech as to require a finding that the entire label must be treated as "pure" speech.

* * * * *

We thus assess the prohibition of Bad Frog's labels under the commercial speech standards outlined in *Central Hudson* [447 U.S. 557 (1980)].

THE *CENTRAL HUDSON* TEST

Central Hudson sets forth the analytical framework for assessing governmental restrictions on commercial speech:

> At the outset, we must determine whether the expression is protected by the First Amendment. For commercial speech to come within that provision, it at least must concern lawful activity and not be misleading. Next, we ask whether the asserted government interest is substantial. If both inquiries yield positive answers, we must determine whether the regulation directly advances the government interest asserted, and whether it is not more extensive than is necessary to serve that interest.

* * * * *

A. Lawful Activity and Not Deceptive

We agree with the District Court that Bad Frog's labels pass *Central Hudson*'s threshold requirement that the speech "must concern lawful activity and not be misleading." The consumption of beer (at least by adults) is legal in New York, and the labels cannot be said to be deceptive, even if they are offensive.

B. Substantial State Interests

NYSLA advances two interests to support its asserted power to ban Bad Frog's labels: (i) the State's interest in "protecting children from vulgar and profane advertising," and (ii) the State's interest "in acting consistently to promote temperance, i.e., the moderate and responsible use of alcohol among those above the legal drinking age and abstention among those below the legal drinking age."

Both of the asserted interests are "substantial" within the meaning of *Central Hudson.* States have "a compelling interest in protecting the physical and psychological well-being of minors," and "[t]his interest extends to shielding minors from the influence of literature that is not obscene by adult standards."

The Supreme Court also has recognized that states have a substantial interest in regulating alcohol consumption. We agree with the District Court that New York's asserted concern for "temperance" is also a substantial state interest.

C. Direct Advancement of the State Interest

To meet the "direct advancement" requirement, a state must demonstrate that "the harms it recites are real and that its restriction will in fact alleviate them *to a material degree*" [*Edenfield v. Fane,* 507 U.S. 761, 771 (1993)].

(1) *Advancing the interest in protecting children from vulgarity.*

* * * * *

NYSLA endeavors to advance the state interest in preventing exposure of children to vulgar displays by taking only the limited step of barring such displays from the labels of alcoholic beverages. In view of the wide currency of vulgar displays throughout contemporary society, including comic books targeted directly at children, barring such displays from labels for alcoholic beverages cannot realistically be expected to reduce children's exposure to such displays to any significant degree.

* * * * *

(2) *Advancing the state interest in temperance.* We agree with the District Court that NYSLA has not established that its rejection of Bad Frog's application directly advances the state's interest in "temperance."

NYSLA maintains that the raised finger gesture and the slogan "He just don't care" urge consumers generally to defy authority and particularly to disregard the Surgeon General's warning, which appears on the label next to the gesturing frog. NYSLA also contends that the frog appeals to youngsters and promotes underage drinking.

The truth of these propositions is not so self-evident as to relieve the state of the burden of marshalling some empirical evidence to support its assumptions. All that is clear is that the gesture of "giving the finger" is offensive. Whether viewing that gesture on a beer label will encourage disregard of health warnings or encourage underage drinking remain matters of speculation.

NYSLA has not shown that its denial of Bad Frog's application directly and materially advances either of its asserted state interests.

D. Narrow Tailoring

Central Hudson's fourth criterion, sometimes referred to as "narrow tailoring," requires consideration of whether the prohibition is more extensive than necessary to serve the asserted state interest. Since NYSLA's prohibition of Bad Frog's labels has not been shown to make even an arguable advancement of the state interest in temperance, we consider here only whether the prohibition is more extensive than necessary to serve the asserted interest in insulating children from vulgarity.

*   *   *   *   *

In this case, Bad Frog has suggested numerous less intrusive alternatives to advance the asserted state interest in protecting children from vulgarity, short of a complete statewide ban on its labels. Appellant suggests "the restriction of advertising to point-of-sale locations; limitations on billboard advertising; restrictions on over-the-air advertising; and segregation of the product in the store." Even if we were to assume that the state materially advances its asserted interest by shielding children from viewing the Bad Frog labels, it is plainly excessive to prohibit the labels from all use, including placement on bottles displayed in bars and taverns where parental supervision of children is to be expected. Moreover, to whatever extent NYSLA is concerned that children will be harmfully exposed to the Bad Frog labels when wandering without parental supervision around grocery and convenience stores where beer is sold, that concern could be less intrusively dealt with by placing restrictions on the permissible locations where the appellant's products may be displayed within such stores. Or, with the labels permitted, restrictions might be imposed on placement of the frog illustration on the outside of six-packs or cases sold in such stores.

NYSLA's complete statewide ban on the use of Bad Frog's labels lacks a "reasonable fit" with the state's asserted interest in shielding minors from vulgarity, and NYSLA gave inadequate consideration to alternatives to this blanket suppression of commercial speech.

*   *   *   *   *

[W]e conclude that NYSLA has unlawfully rejected Bad Frog's application for approval of its labels.

*   *   *   *   *

[Reversed and remanded.] [For an update on Bad Frog, see **http://badfrog.com**]

Questions

1. *a.* Why did the Court of Appeals conclude that the Bad Frog label constituted commercial speech?

   b. What is the significance of that decision?

2. Why did the Court of Appeals rule in Bad Frog's favor?

3. A letter to the *Buffalo News* objecting to the *Bad Frog* decision:

   > . . . The U.S. Court of Appeals' reasoning was that "vulgar materials enjoy wide currency in society today—including comic books for children." Therefore, while offensive it is not illegal. I guess this means the sickies of the world can show us anything they want, even if we don't want to see it. They have the right to offend us, but we have no rights not to be offended.
   >
   > We all know what the extended middle finger means. I personally get offended when this gesture is directed at me, whether by humans or cartoon animals. I would like to show the Court of Appeals my opinion of their decision by extending my middle finger in their direction. I hope they enjoy this gesture. After all, it's not illegal. But maybe it should be.[11]

   a. Do you agree with the letter writer that *Bad Frog* is an unwise decision? Explain.

   b. Should "the finger" be an illegal gesture? Explain.

4. Robert Levy, a constitutional law expert, objecting to the current First Amendment treatment of commercial speech:

   > Inexplicably, advertising remains second-class speech, with less First Amendment protection than Ku Klux Klan vitriol, flag burning, even "gangsta rap." The upshot is that Time Warner can peddle rapper Ice-T's "Cop Killer" to its teen clientele. But if R. J. Reynolds were to produce a TV commercial for an adult audience featuring Tiger Woods wearing a sport coat with a Joe Camel emblem, the boot of government would come down hard on the company's neck.[12]

   Comment.

5. Two Rhode Island statutes prohibited all price advertising on liquor in the state, except for price tags and signs within a store itself which were not visible on the street. The state sought to reduce alcohol consumption. Two licensed liquor dealers challenged the statutes' constitutionality.

   a. How would you rule on that challenge? Explain.

   b. Why would the elimination of price advertising arguably contribute to reduced alcohol consumption? See *44 Liquormart, Inc. v. Rhode Island,* 116 S.Ct. 1495 (1996).

6. Hornell Brewing Co. marketed a malt liquor labeled Crazy Horse. The name brought protests on the grounds that it amounted to targeting Native Americans and because it was considered disrespectful to the memory of the highly regarded Sioux leader. Responding to that criticism, Congress attached a rider to an appropriations bill that forbade the use of the name Crazy Horse on an alcoholic beverage label. Hornell then challenged the constitutionality of the federal law.

   a. What is the nature of that challenge?

   b. How would you rule on it? Explain. See *Hornell Brewing Co. v. Nicholas Brady,* 819 F. Supp. 1227 (E.D.N.Y. 1993), and Laura Bird, "Makers of a Brew Called 'Crazy Horse' . . . ," *The Wall Street Journal,* April 14, 1993, p. B8.

7. A U.S. statute forbade the mailing of unsolicited advertisements for contraceptives. Youngs, which sold contraceptives, mailed contraceptive ads to the public at large. The ads included information regarding the public health benefits of contraceptives (such as family planning and prevention of venereal disease).

   a. Do the ads constitute commercial speech? Explain.

   b. Does the government have a "substantial interest" in preventing the mailings where the statute shields citizens from material that they are likely to find offensive and where the statute helps parents control their children's access to birth control information? Explain. See *Bolger v. Youngs Drug Products Corp.,* 463 U.S. 60 (1983).

8. The Township of Willingboro prohibited the posting of real estate "For Sale" or "Sold" signs. The town's purposes were to promote racial integration and to retard the flight of white homeowners. Is the Willingboro action constitutionally permissible? See *Linmark Associates, Inc. v. Willingboro,* 431 U.S. 85 (1977).

The Fourth Amendment

In an increasingly complex and interdependent society, the right of the individual to be free of unjustified governmental intrusions—that is, to a reasonable degree of privacy—has taken on new significance. The Fourth Amendment provides that

> [T]he right of the people to be secure in their persons, houses, papers, and effects, against unreasonable searches and seizures, shall not be violated, and no Warrants shall issue, but upon probable cause.

Some constitutional limitations on the police powers of government officials are a necessity. However, the boundaries of freedom from unreasonable search and seizure are the subject of continuing dispute. The police are under great pressure to cope with America's crime problems, but they must do so within the confines of the Constitution, which is designed to protect us all—including criminals—from the power of an unfair, overreaching government.

Certainly, the most controversial dimension of Fourth Amendment interpretation is the *exclusionary rule,* which provides that, as a matter of due process, no evidence secured in violation of the Fourth Amendment may be admitted as evidence in a court of law. As ultimately applied to all courts by the 1961 U.S. Supreme Court decision in *Mapp v. Ohio,*[13] we can see that the exclusionary rule, while a very effective device for discouraging illegal searches, seizures, and arrests, also from time to time has the effect of freeing guilty criminals.

Of course, search and seizure rules are often at issue in the government's efforts to stop illegal drug distribution. In general, a search warrant issued by a judge is necessary to comply with the Constitution in making a narcotics search. However, a warrantless search is permissible where reasonable, as in association with an arrest or where probable cause exists to believe a drug-related crime has been committed but circumstances make securing a warrant impracticable. Incident to an arrest, a search may lawfully include the person, a car, and the immediate vicinity of the arrest. Further, a police officer may lawfully secure drugs that have been abandoned or that are in plain view even though a warrant has not been obtained. As the following situations attest, search/privacy problems can reach all corners of our lives.

1. **Traffic stops.** In 1998 an Illinois police officer stopped a speeding car from Nevada. A second officer, hearing the police radio report of the stop, decided to bring his drug-sniffing dog to join the first officer. The dog led the officers to the trunk of the stopped vehicle, where the police found marijuana valued at more the $250,000. The Nevada driver, Roy I. Caballes, was convicted of drug trafficking, sentenced to 12 years' imprisonment, and fined. Caballes appealed, claiming the search was unconstitutional because the officers had no reason to believe drugs were involved. On appeal, the Illinois Supreme Court ruled for Caballes, holding that the drug-sniffing dogs can be used at a traffic stop only when the police have "specific and articulable facts" suggesting that drugs are in the vehicle.[14]

Sniffing by a dog did not constitute a search

The U.S. Supreme Court in 2005 ruled for the government, concluding that sniffing by a dog trained only to identify illegal drugs did not constitute a search because the sniffing could only reveal evidence of illegal activity. We have no reasonable expectation of privacy in illegal activity, so the dog's efforts could not reveal any information that was private and protected. Because no search actually occurred, the standard of reasonableness required by the Fourth Amendment was not implicated.[15]

2. **Testing Students.** In 1998 the school board in rural Tecumseh, Oklahoma, instituted a mandatory random urinalysis drug-testing program for all students participating in competitive extracurricular activities. The tests checked for illegal drugs but not for alcohol. Test results were not turned over to the police. An honor student, Lindsay Earls, challenged the program as a violation of her Fourth Amendment rights. A U.S. Court of Appeals agreed with her, ruling that school officials needed to provide evidence of an "identifiable drug abuse problem."[16] The U.S. Supreme Court, however, reversed that decision and held by a 5–4 margin that the school's interest in addressing drug problems outweighed students' privacy rights.[17] The Court reasoned that those participating in extracurricular activities are subjected to many rules and restrictions that diminish their expectation of privacy, and the Court said the program is a health and safety measure rather than an assault on personal privacy.

3. **September 11 and terrorism.** Surveillance is omnipresent in our lives—public spaces, streets, stores, golf courses, ball parks, and so on are routinely scanned by government and private sector cameras. Now with legitimate national fears about terrorism and the passage only a few weeks after the September 11 attacks of the federal USA Patriot Act, the Fourth Amendment seems ever more important and ever more at risk. But is reduced privacy simply the price we must pay in a dangerous world? The Patriot Act makes it easier for the government to scan an individual's financial, medical, student, and other records on the claim that the inquiry involves terrorism. Homes or businesses, under some circumstances, may now be searched and property may be seized without contemporaneous notice to the occupants. Business practice is directly affected

by the increased security concerns: The Patriot Act requires certain industries, including securities dealers, mutual funds, credit card system operators, and others to provide enhanced scrutiny of money laundering and to file Suspicious Activity Reports whenever laundering by customers is suspected. Similarly, banks are now required to verify the identities of customers opening new accounts.

Former attorney general John Ashcroft referred to the Patriot Act as "al-Quaida's worst nightmare," and clearly the act includes provisions that are vital in combating terrorism. For example, barriers have been removed so that the FBI, CIA, and police officers may now readily share information. Prior to the Patriot Act, law enforcement agencies could often more readily obtain business and financial records for white-collar criminals than for suspected terrorists. Similarly, penalties for drug traffickers had been stiffer than those for convicted terrorists. The government claims that the Patriot Act has played a big role in dismantling domestic terrorist cells, prosecuting terrorists, and strengthening border security.[18]

At this writing, Congress is debating renewal of the Patriot Act. Critics argue that the act reduces privacy protections by weakening well-settled probable cause standards for searches. Suspected terrorists have been held for months in secret captivity. Library, hospital, and bookstore records are now much more readily investigated by law enforcement agents. And the Patriot Act, with its weakened constitutional protections, has been used to solve conventional crimes such as credit fraud, child molestation, pornography, and kidnapping. Polls show that most Americans support the general idea of the Patriot Act but are skeptical about some provisions. Seventy-one percent of those responding to a 2004 poll disapprove of searches without contemporaneous notice, and half were concerned about the reduced standards for securing records from bookstores, hospitals, libraries, and banks.[19]

4. **Voyeurism and the surveillance society.**   In Washington State Richard Sorrells and Sean Glas were found guilty of violating a state voyeurism statute for taking pictures up the skirts of some women who were working and shopping in a public mall. Both men appealed their convictions and won a 2002 decision because the voyeurism law did not apply, the Washington State Supreme Court unanimously ruled, to actions in public places.[20] The women had no "reasonable expectation of privacy" in the shopping mall, so their privacy could not have been invaded. A number of states have now passed laws expanding protection against photographic voyeurism, but those laws may not meet constitutional requirements.

Meanwhile threats to privacy are growing exponentially as new technology leads toward a surveillance society. One in four cell phones sold worldwide in 2004 was expected to be equipped with a digital camera.[21] Between August 2002 and March 2004, more than 100 million photographs were exchanged over the Sprint network.[22] Hidden cameras, camera phones, and other high-tech probing devices allow voyeurism, identity theft, industrial espionage, keystroke monitoring (to capture account numbers and passwords), personal spying, and much more. Of course, a lot of good can come from spying. An employee's surreptitious filming of unsafe working conditions, for example, can be much more convincing than the employee's word alone. But the risks are enormous. We have long feared government intrusions (Big Brother is watching), but now we have democratized privacy invasions by giving all of us the technological ability to intrude. Will the legal system be able to protect us from each other? [For an overview of privacy issues around the world, see **www.epic.org**]

Questions

1. A local citizen told police that Wilson was growing marijuana in a small, roofless shed at his residence. The police flew over the shed in a small plane at a legal altitude of 500 feet and observed what they believed to be marijuana growing in the shed. They secured a warrant, conducted a search, and seized marijuana plants. Wilson moved to suppress the evidence, claiming the search was illegal. Is he correct? Explain. See *State v. Wilson,* 988 P.2d 463 (Ct. App. Wash. 1999).

2. Police stopped and arrested McFadden for riding a bicycle on a sidewalk in violation of New York City code. A search incident to the stop revealed a firearm. McFadden was later convicted of the crime of being in possession of a firearm by a previously convicted felon. McFadden appealed, claiming the search was unconstitutional. Was he correct? Explain. See *United States v. McFadden,* 238 F.3d 198 (2001); cert. den. 122 S.Ct. 223 (2001).

3. *a.* Can the police lawfully search an individual's garbage once it has been placed at the curb for disposal? A Connecticut resident, Paul DeFusco, was convicted of drug trafficking based on evidence found in his home. The police conducted the home search with a warrant secured on the basis of an informant's information as well as evidence (some short cut straws, glassine baggies, and prescription bottles) turned up in sifting through DeFusco's garbage.

   b. Explain the central issue in this case. See *State of Connecticut v. Paul DeFusco,* 620 A.2d 746 (Conn. S.Ct. 1993).

4. An informant told the police that a man, whom the informant described, was selling narcotics from the trunk of his car at a particular location. Police drove there, saw the car, and later stopped the car and arrested the driver who matched the informant's description. An officer opened the car's trunk, saw a brown bag, opened it, and found glassine bags of heroin. The car was then driven to police quarters, where another warrantless search of the trunk produced a leather pouch containing money. At trial, may the heroin and cash lawfully be introduced as evidence? Explain. See *United States v. Ross,* 456 U.S. 798 (1982).

Business Searches

Government tries to protect us from business hazards including pollution, defective products, and unsafe workplaces and business crimes such as fraud and bribery. To do so, government agents often want to enter company buildings; observe working conditions; and examine company books. We know our homes are generally protected from searches in the absence of a warrant. But for urgent circumstances such as terrorism concerns, can the same be said for a place of business? The Supreme Court has answered that question:

> The Warrant Clause of the Fourth Amendment protects commercial buildings as well as private homes. To hold otherwise would belie the origin of that Amendment, and the American colonial experience. . . . "[T]he Fourth Amendment's commands grew in large

measure out of the colonists' experience with the writs of assistance . . . [that] granted sweeping power to customs officials and other agents of the king to search at large for smuggled goods." . . . Against this background, it is untenable that the ban on warrantless searches was not intended to shield places of business as well as of residence.[23]

The importance of search and seizure law to businesses is well illustrated by the 1999 search of Coca-Cola offices in four European nations. Officials from the European Commission appeared unannounced and asked for and received access to company files. The searches were part of an ongoing inquiry into whether Coke has abused its dominant market position. The inquiry was precipitated by a complaint from Pepsi Cola.[24]

The following case involves a challenge to the constitutionality of a warrant to search a business for evidence of fraud and other crimes.

LEGAL BRIEFCASE

U.S. v. Gawrysiak 972 F. Supp. 853 (D.N.J. 1997) Affirmed 178 F.3d 1281 (3d Cir. 1999)

Judge Simandle

This matter is before the court upon the pretrial motion of defendant Edmund Danzig to suppress evidence obtained during a search conducted on October 24, 1996, at his business premises. Defendant Danzig has been charged in an indictment with one count of wire fraud, in violation of 18 U.S.C. § 1343 . . .

FACTUAL BACKGROUND

On October 18, 1996, agents from the Federal Bureau of Investigation ("FBI") obtained a warrant to search the business premises of defendant Danzig in Sarasota, Florida. The warrant was issued by United States Magistrate Judge Mark A. Pizzo of the Middle District of Florida, in Tampa, on the basis of a 24-page affidavit filed with the court by Special Agent Lynn Billings of the FBI.

By its terms, the warrant imposed four primary limitations on what items could be seized from defendant Danzig's place of business. First, the agents were only permitted to seize evidence of violations of the following federal criminal statutes: 18 U.S.C. § 371 (conspiracy), 18 U.S.C. § 1343 (wire fraud), 18 U.S.C. § 1621 (perjury), and 18 U.S.C. § 1623 (false declarations). Second, the warrant encompassed evidence concerning crimes committed by Edmund Danzig, Patrick

Gawrysiak, Thomas Fox, and their co-conspirators only. Third, the warrant only encompassed evidence of these crimes committed by those individuals between 1992 and 1995. Fourth, the warrant explained that the evidence to be seized had to pertain to one of 16 enumerated persons or entities, such as "Edmund R. Danzig," "Terra Ceia Ventures, Inc.," or "Jonathan Bowers." . . .

The affidavit submitted to Magistrate Judge Pizzo, subscribed by Special Agent Lynn M. Billings, gave the details of pervasive fraud investigations being conducted by the FBI's Special Agent Wadsworth in New Jersey and Special Agent Lynn Williams in Virginia targeting Patrick Gawrysiak and identifying Danzig as a co-conspirator. Gawrysiak, using the alias Gray, claimed to be the principal of Great American Raceways International, Inc. ("GARI"), which issued forged GARI bonds falsely claimed to be backed by U.S. Treasury bonds. Danzig was described as President of Terra Ceia Ventures, Inc., a financially troubled company that had undertaken a real estate development project on Terra Ceia Island, Florida, for which Danzig and Gawrysiak sought interim financing ("bridge financing") . . .

The affidavit laid out the contours of four known frauds allegedly involving Danzig occurring between 1992 and January 1996, which were:

1. A scheme involving misappropriation of at least $250,000 as "loans" from Moors & Cabot brokerage accounts by Thomas Fox to Edmund Danzig in 1992 and 1993.

2. A scheme involving a $60,000 loan from Jonathan Bowers in 1993 for bridge financing for the Terra Ceia project, in which Danzig allegedly falsely represented to Bowers that a $100,000 GARI bond secured repayment of Bowers's note when in fact Danzig knew the GARI bonds to be worthless

3. A scheme to gain a $1 million loan from Citizen's Bank to be collateralized by Gawrysiak's forged GARI bonds in May and June 1993.

4. A scheme to falsely represent to victim Paul Maillis that Danzig had $40 million in financing, and that Maillis's loan to Danzig would be backed by the worthless GARI bonds.

The affidavit supporting the warrant also attached numerous exhibits as examples of the forgeries and misrepresentations mentioned in the affidavit.

* * * * *

The affidavit demonstrated that evidence of Danzig's culpability for these schemes was likely to be found at his office, as well as evidence implicating others in these crimes even if Danzig is himself innocent.

* * * * *

On October 24, 1996, FBI agents executed the search, seizing from defendant's place of work approximately five boxes of various materials as well as copies of defendant's computer files.

In moving to suppress the seized items, defendant Danzig alleges primarily that (1) the search warrant issued by Judge Pizzo was overbroad and therefore invalid and (2) the law enforcement agents conducting the search acted in bad faith and with the intent to seize items beyond the scope of the warrant.

* * * * *

[FBI agent] Wadsworth testified that before commencing the search, the other five agents participating in the search met with him to discuss how to conduct the search at the Sarasota FBI at 8:00 AM. The meeting lasted approximately 30 minutes. Agent Billings gave a presentation about the search plan and made the warrant available to the others. For part of that time, Agent Wadsworth described to the other agents the type of fraudulent schemes believed to be involved in this case.... According to Agent Wadsworth, the agents also reviewed the "Search Plan" that had been drafted by Agent Billings. The Search Plan set forth the background of the government's investigation of defendants Gawrysiak and Danzig, and described the responsibilities of each of the six agents participating in the search.

* * * * *

Agent Wadsworth further testified that the agents used substantial care during the search itself. The premises before, during, and after the search were photographed by Special Agent Blake. Also, because of concern that defendant Danzig's files might contain privileged attorney/client information, Agent Huff, who is also an attorney, was assigned the responsibility of functioning as a "Chinese Wall" during the search and seizure to ensure that the other agents would not come in contact with such potentially privileged documents....

According to Agent Wadsworth, out of approximately 200 boxes of documents in defendant Danzig's office, only five boxes of documents were ultimately seized. The parties agree, however, that the agents seized approximately half of the documents in the office that pertained to the time period of 1992 through 1995. The government explains this substantial 50 percent ratio by arguing that within that time period, defendant Danzig's business affairs were pervaded by fraud.

Danzig was allowed to be present during the search. Afterward, the FBI furnished a detailed inventory of all documents taken, along with copies of same; defendant has pointed to no document that is beyond the scope permitted by the warrant, nor has defendant indicated that any seized document is within a privilege.

* * * * *

DISCUSSION

Defendant's contentions in support of his motion to suppress may be grouped into two general areas of inquiry: (1) whether Magistrate Pizzo issued a valid warrant that was sufficiently particularized and not a "general warrant" and (2) whether the government's search team acted in good faith and properly executed the warrant.

I. The Validity of the Warrant Issued by Judge Pizzo
A. Whether the Warrant Was a "General Warrant"
One of the primary arguments made by defendant on this motion is that the warrant to search defendant's premises was so overbroad as to constitute an impermissible "general warrant."

The prohibition against general warrants stems directly from the text of the Fourth Amendment to the Constitution, which requires that all warrants describe "particularly . . . the place to be searched, and the persons or things to be seized." As interpreted by the Supreme Court, this language prohibits a "'general, exploratory rummaging in a person's belongings.'"

*   *   *   *   *

In this case, the warrant imposed four significant limitations that channeled the discretion of the searching FBI agents and provided the particularized description required by the Constitution. First, the warrant provided that the agents were only permitted to seize evidence of violations of the federal criminal statutes concerning conspiracy, wire fraud, perjury, and false declarations. . . . Second, the warrant encompassed only crimes committed by Edmund Danzig, Patrick Gawrysiak, Thomas Fox, by the entities under their control. . . .

Third, the warrant encompassed only the enumerated crimes committed by those individuals between 1992 and 1995. Fourth, the warrant provided that the evidence to be seized had to pertain to one of the 16 persons or entities listed in Attachment B to the warrant. . . .

Because of these limitations, this was not a warrant that provided the searching agents with unbridled discretion to rummage through defendant's possessions in search of any evidence of criminal activity. That conclusion is confirmed by the small percentage of documents actually seized from defendant's premises, indicating that the warrant did have limits that could be and were applied by the agents conducting the search.

The scope of this warrant was indeed relatively broad. Broad phrasing in a warrant, however, does not necessarily render the warrant invalid. The court concludes that the breadth of the warrant in this case was justified by evidence before Judge Pizzo indicating that defendant Danzig's business operations were substantially pervaded by fraud during the time period in question.

*   *   *   *   *

B. Whether Magistrate Judge Pizzo Had Probable Cause to Issue the Warrant
Defendant also contends that the affidavit offered in support of the warrant did not provide probable cause concerning certain portions of the warrant.

*   *   *   *   *

In this case, the government has easily demonstrated that Judge Pizzo had probable cause to issue the warrant authorizing the search of defendant Danzig's premises. The affidavit and appendix of documents filed in support of the warrant provide significant detail concerning how each of the 16 entities/persons listed in Attachment B materially relates to the fraudulent schemes allegedly carried out by Gawrysiak and Danzig between 1992 and 1995. There was ample reason to believe that evidence concerning these crimes would be found in these premises at this time.

*   *   *   *   *

[The Court's discussion of the conduct of the agents in carrying out the search is omitted.] [The defendant's motion to suppress is denied.]

Questions

1. What reasoning and evidence allowed the Court to conclude that the warrant in *Gawrysiak* was sufficiently particularized as to meet constitutional requirements?

2. What reasoning and evidence supported the *Gawrysiak* court's conclusion that the magistrate had probable cause to issue the warrant?

3. Joseph Burger owned and operated an automobile junkyard where, among other things, he dismantled autos and sold the parts. A New York statute permitted police to conduct warrantless inspections of auto junkyards. Without objection by Burger, police conducted a warrantless inspection of his business. The inspection revealed stolen vehicles and stolen parts. Burger was charged with possession of stolen property. In court, Burger moved to suppress the evidence arising from the search on the grounds that the New York statute under which the search was conducted was unconstitutional.

   a. Does the statute violate the Fourth Amendment's prohibition of unreasonable searches and seizures? Explain.

   b. Why do many states, including New York, explicitly permit the warrantless inspection of automobile junkyards? See *New York v. Joseph Burger,* 482 U.S. 691 (1987).

4. Occupational Safety and Health Administration (OSHA) inspectors received permission from the Army Corps of Engineers to inspect a federal construction site where an accident had occurred. The contractor declined consent, but OSHA secured a federal district court order allowing inspection. OSHA found some obvious violations, but others were apparent only after initial observations led to follow-up interviews with employees and closer looks at equipment. The contractor objected to the search on Fourth Amendment grounds.

   a. Explain the nature of that objection.

   b. Decide the case. See *National Engineering & Contracting Co. v. Occupational Safety and Health Administration,* 928 F.2d 762 (6th Cir. 1991).

The Fifth Amendment

Takings—Eminent Domain

Port Chester, New York, at this writing in 2005, is clearing a business district that includes a marina, an import operation, an antiques store, and several other businesses to make room for bigger, more successful ventures, including Costco and Bed Bath & Beyond. Economic development initiatives of this kind are routine and appear to be in the general interest. What happens, however, if the owners of the property to be developed do not want to sell? Can a group of owners or even a single property owner block redevelopment by refusing to sell?[25]

The Fifth Amendment prohibits the taking of private property for *public use without just compensation* for the owner. Thus governments ordinarily use their power of *eminent domain* to buy private property for public uses such as building highways, bike trails, parks, and so on if just compensation is provided. But what about the Port Chester situation, where the condemned property is to be used for a *private* purpose? Communities across America, hungry for an improved tax base and more jobs, have made the practice routine; but are they violating the Fifth Amendment rights of the property owners? These redevelopment fights are merely the latest manifestation of a quarter-century revival of the Takings Clause. Conservative property rights activists have sought to raise the Takings Clause to a level of influence more akin to the First Amendment. The general idea is to elevate individual power and reduce government authority.[26] The following 5–4 Supreme Court decision involves a challenge to a New London, Connecticut, plan to clear a portion of the city to make way for an office/research park along with a waterfront hotel, conference center, residences, a marina, and a riverwalk.

LEGAL BRIEFCASE

Kelo v. City of New London, Connecticut Supreme Court of the United States 2005 U.S. LEXIS 5011

Justice Stevens

In 2000 the city of New London approved a development plan that, in the words of the Supreme Court of Connecticut, was "projected to create in excess of 1,000 jobs, to increase tax and other revenues, and to revitalize an economically distressed city, including its downtown and waterfront areas" (843 A.2d 500, 507 (2004)). In assembling the land needed for this project, the city's development agent has purchased property from willing sellers and proposes to use the power of

eminent domain to acquire the remainder of the property from unwilling owners in exchange for just compensation. The question presented is whether the city's proposed disposition of this property qualifies as a "public use" within the meaning of the Takings Clause of the Fifth Amendment to the Constitution.

I

The city of New London (hereinafter City) sits at the junction of the Thames River and the Long Island Sound in southeastern

Connecticut. Decades of economic decline led a state agency in 1990 to designate the City a "distressed municipality." In 1996 the Federal Government closed the Naval Undersea Warfare Center, which had been located in the Fort Trumbull area of the City and had employed over 1,500 people. In 1998 the City's unemployment rate was nearly double that of the State, and its population of just under 24,000 residents was at its lowest since 1920.

These conditions prompted state and local officials to target New London, and particularly its Fort Trumbull area, for economic revitalization. To this end, respondent New London Development Corporation (NLDC), a private nonprofit entity established some years earlier to assist the City in planning economic development, was reactivated. In January 1998 the State authorized a $5.35 million bond issue to support the NLDC's planning activities and a $10 million bond issue toward the creation of a Fort Trumbull State Park. In February the pharmaceutical company Pfizer Inc. announced that it would build a $300 million research facility on a site immediately adjacent to Fort Trumbull; local planners hoped that Pfizer would draw new business to the area. Upon obtaining state-level approval, the NLDC finalized an integrated development plan focused on 90 acres of the Fort Trumbull area.

The Fort Trumbull area is situated on a peninsula that juts into the Thames River. The area comprises approximately 115 privately owned properties, as well as the 32 acres of land formerly occupied by the naval facility (Trumbull State Park now occupies 18 of those 32 acres). The development plan encompasses seven parcels. Parcel 1 is designated for a waterfront conference hotel at the center of a "small urban village" that will include restaurants and shopping. . . . Parcel 2 will be the site of approximately 80 new residences organized into an urban neighborhood and linked by public walkway to the remainder of the development, including the state park. This parcel also includes space reserved for a new U.S. Coast Guard Museum. Parcel 3, which is located immediately north of the Pfizer facility, will contain at least 90,000 square feet of research and development office space. Parcel 4A is a 2.4-acre site that will be used either to support the adjacent state park, by providing parking or retail services for visitors, or to support the nearby marina. Parcel 4B will include a renovated marina, as well as the final stretch of the riverwalk. Parcels 5, 6, and 7 will provide land for office and retail space, parking, and water-dependent commercial uses.

*   *   *   *   *

The city council approved the plan in January 2000 and designated the NLDC as its development agent in charge of implementation. The city council also authorized the NLDC to purchase property or to acquire property by exercising eminent domain in the City's name. The NLDC successfully negotiated the purchase of most of the real estate in the 90-acre area, but its negotiations with petitioners failed. As a consequence, in November 2000 the NLDC initiated the condemnation proceedings that gave rise to this case.

II

Petitioner Susette Kelo has lived in the Fort Trumbull area since 1997. She has made extensive improvements to her house, which she prizes for its water view. Petitioner Wilhelmina Dery was born in her Fort Trumbull house in 1918 and has lived there her entire life. Her husband Charles has lived in the house since they married some 60 years ago. In all, the nine petitioners own 15 properties in Fort Trumbull. . . . There is no allegation that any of these properties is blighted or otherwise in poor condition; rather, they were condemned only because they happen to be located in the development area.

In December 2000 petitioners brought this action in the New London Superior Court. They claimed, among other things, that the taking of their properties would violate the "public use" restriction in the Fifth Amendment. After a seven-day bench trial, the Superior Court granted a permanent restraining order prohibiting the taking of the properties located in parcel 4A (park of marina support). It, however, denied petitioners relief as to the properties located in parcel 3 (office space).

After the Superior Court ruled, both sides took appeals to the Supreme Court of Connecticut. That court held that all of the City's proposed takings were valid.

*   *   *   *   *

III

Two polar propositions are perfectly clear. On the one hand, it has long been accepted that the sovereign may not take the property of *A* for the sole purpose of transferring it to another private party *B*, even though *A* is paid just compensation. On the other hand, it is equally clear that a State may transfer property from one private party to another if future "use by the public" is the purpose of the taking; the condemnation of land for a railroad is a familiar example. Neither of these propositions, however, determines the disposition of this case.

As for the first proposition, the City would no doubt be forbidden from taking petitioners' land for the purpose of conferring a private benefit on a particular party. Nor would the City be allowed to take property under the mere pretext of a public purpose, when its actual purpose was to bestow a private benefit. The takings before us, however, would be executed pursuant to a "carefully considered" development plan. The trial judge and all the members of the Supreme Court of

Connecticut agreed that there was no evidence of an illegitimate purpose in this case.

*   *   *   *   *

On the other hand, this is not a case in which the City is planning to open the condemned land—at least not in its entirety—to use by the general public. Nor will the private lessees of the land in any sense be required to operate like common carriers, making their services available to all comers. But although such a projected use would be sufficient to satisfy the public use requirement, this "Court long ago rejected any literal requirement that condemned property be put into use for the general public." Indeed, while many state courts in the mid-19th century endorsed "use by the public" as the proper definition of public use, that narrow view steadily eroded over time. Not only was the "use by the public" test difficult to administer (e.g., what proportion of the public need have access to the property? at what price?), but it proved to be impractical given the diverse and always evolving needs of society. Accordingly, when this Court began applying the Fifth Amendment to the States at the close of the 19th century, it embraced the broader and more natural interpretation of public use as "public purpose."

*   *   *   *   *

The disposition of this case therefore turns on the question whether the City's development plan serves a "public purpose." Without exception, our cases have defined that concept broadly, reflecting our longstanding policy of deference to legislative judgments in this field.

In *Berman v. Parker,* this Court upheld a redevelopment plan targeting a blighted area of Washington, D.C., in which most of the housing for the area's 5,000 inhabitants was beyond repair. Under the plan, the area would be condemned and part of it utilized for the construction of streets, schools, and other public facilities. The remainder of the land would be leased or sold to private parties for the purpose of redevelopment, including the construction of low-cost housing.

*   *   *   *   *

In *Hawaii Housing Authority v. Midkiff* the Court considered a Hawaii statute whereby fee title was taken from lessors and transferred to lessees (for just compensation) in order to reduce the concentration of land ownership. We unanimously upheld the statute and rejected the Ninth Circuit's View that it was "a naked attempt on the part of the state of Hawaii to take the property of *A* and transfer it to *B* solely for *B*'s private use and benefit."

*   *   *   *   *

IV

Those who govern the City were not confronted with the need to remove blight in the Fort Trumbull area, but their determination that the area was sufficiently distressed to justify a program of economic rejuvenation is entitled to our deference. The City has carefully formulated an economic development plan that it believes will provide appreciable benefits to the community, including—but by no means limited to—new jobs and increased tax revenue. . . . Given the comprehensive character of the plan, the thorough deliberation that preceded its adoption, and the limited scope of our review, it is appropriate for us to resolve the challenges of the individual owners, not on a piecemeal basis, but rather in light of the entire plan. Because that plan unquestionably serves a public purpose, the takings challenged here satisfy the public use requirement of the Fifth amendment.

To avoid this result, petitioners urge us to adopt a new bright-line rule that economic development does not qualify as a public use. Putting aside the unpersuasive suggestion that the City's plan will provide only purely economic benefits, neither precedent nor logic supports petitioners' proposal. Promoting economic development is a traditional and long accepted function of government.

*   *   *   *   *

It is further argued that without a bright-line rule nothing would stop a city from transferring citizen *A*'s property to citizen *B* for the sole reason that citizen *B* will put the property to a more productive use and thus pay more taxes. Such a one-to-one transfer of property, executed outside the confines of an integrated development plan, is not presented in this case. While such an unusual exercise of government power would certainly raise a suspicion that a private purpose was afoot, the hypothetical cases posited by petitioners can be confronted if and when they arise.

*   *   *   *   *

In affirming the City's authority to take petitioners' properties, we do not minimize the hardship that condemnations may entail, notwithstanding the payment of just compensation. We emphasize that nothing in our opinion precludes any State from placing further restrictions on its exercise of the takings power. Indeed, many States already impose "public use" requirements that are stricter than the federal baseline.

*   *   *   *   *

Affirmed.

AFTERWORD—PROPERTY RIGHTS REVOLUTION?

The *Kelo* decision was an angry disappointment for property rights advocates. A big government taking of Americans' life-long homes, even for just compensation, is a powerful and frightening image. Clearly, however, governments need, and have long exercised, substantial authority to take property for economic development. Now states and localities will use their own powerful legal and political systems to achieve an appropriate and difficult balance between important property rights and important public purposes. Meanwhile, a dramatic elevation of property rights and accompanying diminution of government authority will have to wait—at least until the composition of the Supreme Court shifts further to the right.

Questions

1. What reasoning was offered by Justice Stevens to support the majority view that the New London development complied with due process requirements?

2. *a.* What was the issue, the central question, in this case and how did the majority answer that question?

   b. How would you expect the dissent to answer that question?

3. From the dissenting point of view, what harm is likely to emerge from this decision?

4. Marilyn and James Nollan applied for a permit to replace their beachfront home with a larger structure. The California Coastal Commission agreed on the condition that the Nollans grant an easement on their beach that would allow the public to cross that property and thus facilitate movement between the public beaches that lay on both sides of the Nollan beach. The Nollans sued, claiming a violation of the Takings Clause. Decide. Explain. See *Nollan v. California Coastal Commission,* 483 U.S. 825 (1987).

5. Tina Bennis sued when Wayne County (Detroit), Michigan, authorities took the car she jointly owned with her husband after police arrested him for receiving oral sex from a prostitute while parked in the car. A 1925 antinuisance law permitted the seizure, but Tina Bennis claimed it amounted to an unconstitutional taking because she was an innocent half owner of the 1977 Pontiac for which the couple had paid $600. Bennis's claim eventually reached the U.S. Supreme Court. Decide the case. Explain. See *Bennis v. Michigan,* 116 S. Ct. 994 (1996).

Takings—Regulatory

We have seen how the law treats situations where the government uses its power of eminent domain to condemn property for either public or private use and pays just compensation. What happens when the government does not take the property but rather *regulates* it in a manner that deprives that property of some or all of its economic usefulness? For example, without providing just compensation, can a state lawfully limit the amount a landlord can charge for rent in an effort to preserve low-income housing? Can the state forbid billboards to enhance roadside beauty?

These *regulatory takings,* whether temporary or permanent, normally do not require government compensation because doing so would severely impair the state's ability to govern in an orderly manner. Nonetheless, in recent years the courts have been more aggressive about requiring just compensation for some regulatory takings. Three broad classes of such takings have emerged in court decisions. [For an "introduction to the takings issue," see **http://www.envpoly.org/takings/**]

1. **Total takings.**   If a governmental body acts in a way that takes *all of the economic value* of a property or permanently physically invades the property, the taking requires just compensation unless the government is preventing a nuisance or the regulation was permissible under property law at the time of the purchase of the property. When the South Carolina Coastal Commission passed erosion rules having the effect of preventing David Lucas from building any permanent structure on his $975,000 beachfront lots, Lucas sued, claiming

The South Carolina Coastal Commission passed erosion rules having the effect of preventing David Lucas from building any permanent structure on his $975,000 beachfront lots

a Fifth Amendment violation. The U.S. Supreme Court in 1992 agreed with Lucas and held that a taking requiring just compensation had occurred because the state had deprived Lucas of *all* economically beneficial use of the property, and the property did not fall in one of the two exceptions.[27]

2. **Exaction/mitigation.** A second class of regulatory takings involves situations where the government allows land development only if the owner dedicates some property interest (called an *exaction*) or money (called a *mitigation* or *impact fee*) to the government. Thus if you are developing land for housing, the city government might require that you devote a portion of that land to parks. Or you might be required to pay a fee to help the city meet the recreational needs of the citizens your development will be housing. The Supreme Court dealt with just such a case in *Dolan v. Tigard,* a 1994 decision.[28] Florence Dolan, owner of a plumbing and electrical supply store in Tigard, Oregon, applied for a city permit to nearly double the size of her store and to pave her parking lot. Concerned with increased traffic and water runoff due to the proposed expansion, the city granted the permit, subject to a pair of conditions: (1) Dolan was to dedicate the portion of her property that lay within the 100-year floodplain to the city to improve drainage for the creek that ran along her property, and (2) she was to dedicate an additional 15-foot strip of her land adjacent to the floodplain for use as a bicycle path/walkway to relieve traffic congestion. Dolan sought a variance from the requirements, but her petition was denied. She sued, and her case eventually reached the U.S. Supreme Court. The Court set out a two-part test for these exaction cases. Government can compel a dedication of private property to public use where it can show two factors. The first is a nexus or relationship between the government's legitimate purpose (flood and traffic control in *Dolan*) and the condition imposed (the land Dolan was to dedicate to public purposes). Second, if factor 1 is established, then the government must show a "rough proportionality" between the burden imposed (the land given over to public use) and the impact of the development (increased water runoff and increased traffic).[29] The Supreme Court, in a firm defense of private property rights, ruled that Tigard had failed to meet those standards, and Dolan won the case.

3. **Partial takings.** Many, perhaps most takings problems are neither total takings nor exactions, but rather fall into a case-by-case analysis that depends greatly on the facts in each instance. The primary considerations in these cases are threefold:

1. The importance of the government interest (health, safety, or the like) that generated the regulation.
2. The economic effect on the landowner.
3. The landowner's legitimate, investment-backed expectations at the time of purchase.

Broadly here, the Court is simply asking whether the regulation goes "too far" in burdening the property owner. That is, should the property owner bear the costs of the regulation or should those costs be borne by the public by paying compensation to the property owner in exchange for the value (a public beach, a park, an unobstructed view, or whatever) derived from the regulation.[30]

Zoning in the Sixth Century

Government restraints on property development are not merely a modern imposition, as we learn from the following description of a zoning law in the Byzantine Empire:

> Next came the first zoning law for the beach. Coastal vistas were so cherished, and the competition for them so keen, that by the sixth century the Emperor Justinian the Great was compelled to pass an ordinance barring construction within 100 feet of the shore to protect sea views.

Source: Lena Lencek and Gideon Bosker, *The Beach: The History of Paradise on Earth* (New York: Penguin Group, 1998). p. 31.

The Fourteenth Amendment

Due Process

The Due Process Clauses of both the Fifth Amendment (applying to the federal government) and the Fourteenth Amendment (applying to the states) forbid the government to deprive citizens of life, liberty, or property without due process of law.

Substantive Due Process

Laws that arbitrarily and unfairly infringe on fundamental personal rights and liberties such as privacy, voting, and the various freedoms specified in the Bill of Rights may be challenged on due process grounds. Basically, the purpose of the law must be so compelling as to outweigh the intrusion on personal liberty or the law will be struck down. For example, the U.S. Supreme Court ruled that a Connecticut statute forbidding the use of contraceptives violated the constitutional right to privacy (although the word *privacy* itself does not appear in the U.S. Constitution).[31] By judicial interpretation, the Fourteenth Amendment Due Process Clause "absorbs" the fundamental liberties of the *federal* Constitution and prohibits *state* laws (in this case, the Connecticut contraceptive ban) that abridge those fundamental liberties such as privacy.

Procedural Due Process

Basically, procedural due process means that the government must provide *notice* and a *fair hearing* before taking an action affecting a citizen's life, liberty, or property. A fair hearing might require, among others, the right to present evidence, the right to a decision maker free of bias, and the right to appeal. However, the precise nature of procedural due process depends on the situation. A murder trial requires meticulous attention to procedural fairness; an administrative hearing to appeal a housing officer's decision to banish a student from a dormitory, while required to meet minimal constitutional standards, can be more forgiving in its procedural niceties.

Due Process and Punitive Damages

Gore purchased a new BMW and was not told that the car had been repainted due to some minor predelivery damage. BMW's corporate policy was to advise dealers only of

> The Alabama jury awarded Gore $4,000 in compensatory damages and $4 million in punitive damages

those predelivery repairs that exceeded 3 percent of the car's suggested retail price. Gore learned of the repainting and sued, claiming he was a victim of fraud. The Alabama jury awarded Gore $4,000 in compensatory damages and $4 million in punitive damages. The $4 million award was reduced to $2 million by the Alabama Supreme Court, but BMW took the case to the U.S. Supreme Court, which found the award "grossly excessive" in relation to the state's legitimate interest in punishing and deterring wrongful conduct. The Court employed a three-factor test to determine that the award was grossly excessive and thus violative of the Due Process Clause: (1) the reprehensibility of the defendant's conduct, (2) the ratio between the plaintiff's compensatory damages and the punitive damages, and (3) a comparison between the punitive damage award and any civil or criminal penalties the state could impose for similar misconduct. By all three standards, the award was so extreme as to violate BMW's due process rights.[32] In 1997 the Alabama Supreme Court cut Gore's award to $50,000.

Big punitive awards continued to rise despite *Gore,* and the Supreme Court in 2003 strengthened and clarified its *Gore* reasoning in *State Farm v. Campbell,*[33] where a $1 million compensatory award led to a $145 million punitive award. The Court found that the award violated the Due Process Clause and suggested that a 4–1 ratio between punitive and compensatory damages, while not "binding," should be "instructive," while ratios higher than 9–1 would be appropriate only in special circumstances. On remand, the lower court then reduced punitive damages in the *State Farm* case to $9 million.

The business community is encouraged by the Supreme Court rulings, but a recent study found plaintiffs winning punitive damages in only 3.3 percent of the personal injury cases studied.[34] So perhaps the issue is not as significant as claimed by corporate interests; and perhaps substantial punitive damages are necessary to correct harmful behavior.

Equal Protection

The Fourteenth Amendment says that no state shall "deny to any person within its jurisdiction the equal protection of the laws." The Due Process Clause of the Fifth Amendment has been interpreted to provide that same protection from the federal government. Fundamentally, these laws forbid a government from treating one person (including a corporation) differently than another without a rational basis for doing so. Most notably, the Equal Protection and Due Process Clauses have played an enormous role in attacking discrimination (see Chapter 13), but they can also significantly impact routine business practice in many ways. For example, can we lawfully impose higher taxes on a gambling casino than we impose on the sale of groceries? Or can we require the oil industry to follow more rigorous environmental standards than we expect of coal mines? In general, the answer to these questions is yes, but only if the legislation can pass the rational basis test. If not, such legislation would be unconstitutional and unenforceable.

Equal Protection for Animals?

In 2002 Germany became the first European Union nation to extend constitutional protections to animals. Germany added the phrase "and animals" to a constitutional provision requiring the state to respect and protect the dignity of human beings. In 1992 Switzerland amended its constitution to treat animals as beings rather than as things (property). New Zealand's 1999 Animal Welfare Act accords nonhuman great apes the right to life, the right not to be subjected to cruelty, and protection against most experiments.

Source: Associated Press, "Germany Enshrines Rights of Animals," *Toronto Star,* May 18, 2002, p. A28.

Gay and Lesbian Marriage?

Recently, the most interesting and visible equal protection dispute has been the "cultural war" over gay marriage and civil unions. The Vermont Supreme Court made headlines across America and around the world in late 1999 when it ruled that gay and lesbian couples in that state had been denied equal protection of the law under the Vermont constitution and were entitled to the same legal benefits and protections as heterosexual couples.[35] The Court did not legalize gay marriages, but it did instruct the state legislature to find a way to extend equal protection under the law to gay couples. The legislature did so in 2000 by approving *civil unions,* which are not marriages under Vermont law, but which allow same-sex couples to join in a legally recognized relationship that confers all of the legal benefits, protections, and duties of marriage—including, for example, joint property and inheritance rights and child support duties. Civil unions are not recognized under federal law, and the federal government and many states have passed "defense of marriage laws" that specifically define marriage as a union between a man and a woman.

Then in 2003 the Massachusetts Supreme Court, by a 4–3 vote, ruled that same-sex couples have the same marital rights as heterosexuals,[36] a decision that the U.S. Supreme Court declined to review.[37] In early 2005 Connecticut like Vermont, approved civil unions. Now a full-scale judicial and legislative war looms across America. At this writing, 18 states have passed constitutional amendments specifically forbidding gay marriage. At least a dozen more are expected to do the same in 2006 or before. Congress is considering a similar amendment to the federal constitution. Lawsuits are proliferating as courts in California and Oregon, for example, are at this writing in 2005, considering the legality of about 7,000 same-sex marriages that were performed in those states. At some point presumably the U.S. Supreme Court will address the issue, and perhaps the federal Constitution along with most state constitutions will have been amended to protect "traditional" marriage. If so, will gays and lesbians have been denied equal protection under the law? And at a more fundamental level, will the people of America have strengthened or weakened our moral and ethical lives?

PRACTICING ETHICS   Gay and Lesbian Marriage

An editorial in the *Syracuse Post-Standard* (New York) in late 2004 noted the immense change portended by the gay marriage movement:

In coming months, gay marriage ceremonies will continue in Massachusetts with the backing of that state's Supreme Court. Civil unions will proliferate in Vermont, where both sides agree the subject has become a nonissue. Time will pass as gay Americans continue to go to work, pay taxes, raise families, and participate in community and political life. And more and more Americans will get used to the idea. The times they are indeed a-changing.[38]

Morally and ethically speaking, which side is "right" about gay marriage? And how do we decide? Let's look at some questions that help us sort through this moral thicket:

1. What issues should one consider in deciding whether gay marriage is morally defensible?

2. Is a civil union arrangement like the one in Vermont an acceptable "middle ground"?

3. If the American people ultimately favor gay and lesbian marriage, could we then consider it a morally defensible practice?

4. The 2000 United States census indicates that approximately 1 million children are being raised by same-sex couples, and 47 states allow gays and lesbians to adopt children.[39] Are those children at moral risk?

5. If scholarly studies ultimately demonstrate that homosexuality and lesbianism are substantially commanded by genetic characteristics, would we be morally required to permit same-sex marriage?

Gay Marriage Abroad

In 2001, The Netherlands became the first nation to legalize gay marriage. Belgium did the same in 2002, followed by Spain and Canada in 2005. Denmark, France, Norway, Sweden, and Germany permit civil unions.

Source: Rob Gillies, "Canada 4th Nation to OK Gay Marriage," *The Seattle Times,* July 21, 2005 [**http://seattletimes.nwsource.com/**].

Afterword

About 58 percent of American college freshmen (49 percent of males and 65 percent of females) believe that same-sex couples should have "the right to legal marital status."[40]

Internet Exercise

At the First Amendment Center, read Richmond School of Law Dean Rodney Smolla's overview of the First Amendment [**http://www.firstamendmentcenter.org/Speech/overview.aspx**]. According to Smolla, how do we explain the "modern American reverence for freedom of speech"?

Chapter Questions

1. Fifty-three percent of Americans responding to a 1999 poll thought the press has too much freedom in the United States.[41] The poll further found that most Americans celebrate the First Amendment but feel uncomfortable with some of the public speech that is protected by the Amendment.

   a. List some forms of speech that are protected but are troubling to many Americans.

   b. How do you feel about First Amendment protection for those forms of speech? Explain.

2. The American Civil Liberties Union of Ohio challenged the constitutionality of Ohio's state motto, "With God, All Things Are Possible."

a. Explain the nature of that constitutional challenge.

b. Decide the case. Explain. See *American Civil Liberties Union of Ohio v. Capitol Square Review and Advisory Board,* 243 F.3d 289 (6th Cir. 2001).

3. Several city ordinances in Arkansas made it illegal for "any person to place a hand-bill or advertisement on any other person's vehicle parked on public property within city limits." Church members contested the constitutionality of the ordinances, which prevented them from lawfully placing religious handbills on parked cars. Decide. Explain. See *Krantz v. City of Fort Smith,* 160 F.3d 1214 (8th Cir. 1998).

4. The Georgia Outdoor Advertising Control Act, in essence, prohibits any off-premises outdoor advertising of commercial establishments where nudity is exhibited. Cafe Erotica lawfully provides food and adult entertainment, including nude dancing, and advertises those services on billboards. Cafe Erotica challenged the constitutionality of the Advertising Control Act. Decide. Explain. See *Georgia v. Cafe Erotica,* 507 S.E.2d 732 (Ga. S. Ct. 1998).

5. Colorado School of Law Professor Pierre Schlag, summarizing the central theme raised by Ronald K. L. Collins and David M. Skover in their book *The Death of Discourse:*

> Stated most broadly, the predicament is this: with the perfection of communications technology, the refinement of capitalist rationality, and the intensification of market-created desire, the resulting culture is one that renders its own ostensible steering mecha-nism—namely, reasoned discourse—impossible. This broad scale rendition of the predica-ment is quite bleak, for there is no exit; everyone is included. We are all living in a culture that is, quite literally, doing itself in, mindlessly devoting itself to frivolous self-amusement: the unbridled pursuit of thrills, chills, titillations, fun, and ultimately, death.[42]

Do you agree with the argument that reasoned discourse is now impossible in our culture of advanced communications and obsessive, market-induced desire for plea-sure? Explain.

6. The Labor Department conducts regular investigations of business records to ensure compliance with the wages and hours provisions (such as higher pay for overtime) of the Fair Labor Standards Act. When a compliance officer sought to inspect cer-tain financial records at the Lone Steer restaurant/motel in Steele, North Dakota, the restaurant declined his admittance until the government detailed the scope of the investigation. Not receiving a satisfactory response, the Lone Steer demanded a search warrant prior to inspection. As provided for under the FLSA, the government secured an administrative subpoena, which, unlike a search warrant, does not require judicial approval. Once again, Lone Steer denied admission. The government then filed suit. Decide. Explain. See *Donovan v. Lone Steer,* 464 U.S. 408 (1984).

7. This chapter noted a number of decisions affording protection to commercial speech. Why are corporations unlikely to begin using their vast resources to speak out on the wide range of public issues from abortion to organized prayer in schools to the death penalty? Explain.

8. An Erie, Pennsylvania, public indecency ordinance prohibited knowingly or inten-tionally appearing in public in a "state of nudity." Pap's, the owners of Kandyland, an Erie establishment featuring totally nude dancers, challenged the constitutional-ity of the ordinance.

  a. Explain the nature of that constitutional challenge.

  b. Decide the case. Explain. See *City of Erie v. Pap's A.M.,* 529 U.S. 277 (2000).

9. An individual and a group applied to the Chicago Park District for permits to hold rallies advocating the legalization of marijuana. The Park District, a municipal agency, required a permit to conduct a public assembly, parade, or other event involving more than 50 individuals. Applications for permits had to be processed within 28 days, and denials had to be clearly explained. Denials could be appealed to the general superintendent and then to the courts. The Park District denied some of the permits for pro-marijuana rallies. Those denied filed suit, claiming the Park District permit rules were unconstitutional.

  a. What constitutional challenge was raised by the plaintiffs?

  b. Decide the case. Explain. See *Thomas and Windy City Hemp Development Board v. Chicago Park District,* 534 U.S. 316 (2002).

10. Tanner and others sought to distribute handbills in the interior mall of the Lloyd Corporation shopping center. The literature concerned an anti–Vietnam War meeting. Lloyd Corporation had a strict rule forbidding handbilling. When security guards terminated distributions within the center, Tanner, et al. claimed a violation of their First Amendment rights. Both the district court and the Court of Appeals found a violation of constitutional rights. The decision was appealed to the U.S. Supreme Court. Decide. Explain. See *Lloyd Corporation v. Tanner,* 407 U.S. 551 (1972).

11. Lancaster, California, located about 45 miles from Los Angeles, was trying to build its local economy but was tripped up by the United States Constitution. Costco, a big-box retailer, wanted to expand into next-door space leased to 99 Cents Only Stores. Costco told the city it would move to Palmdale if it could not expand. Lancaster tried to buy 99 Cents' lease, but the company refused. Lancaster then used its power of eminent domain to condemn the 99 Cents property for the purpose of making it available to Costco. The city noted that blight might follow if Costco left, and the city contrasted 99 Cents' under $40,000 per year in sales taxes generated with Costco's more than $400,000. 99 Cents then sued the city seeking an order blocking the effort to take the 99 Cents property.

  a. How would you have ruled on the case when it was tried in 2001? Explain.

  b. Would the result be any different today after the Supreme Court's 2005 decision in the New London, Connecticut, case? Explain. See *99 Cents Only Stores v. Lancaster Redevelopment Agency,* 237 F. Supp. 2d 1123 (C.D. Cal. 2001). Appeal dismissed, 2003 U.S. App. LEXIS 4197.

12. Long Island, New York, resident Stephanie Fuller was secretly videotaped by her landlord, who had installed a video camera in the smoke detector above her bed. Fuller's landlord was found guilty of trespassing and was fined $1,500 and sentenced to 280 hours of community service.

  a. Why was the landlord not charged with a more serious felony offense?

  b. After Fuller's experience, New York enacted a criminal unlawful surveillance statute; the statute includes language forbidding secret surveillance in places where the victim has "a reasonable expectation of privacy." What significance attaches to that language?

13. A California sales and use tax of 6 percent on all personal property sales was applied to the distribution of religious materials by religious organizations. The Jimmy Swaggart Ministries challenged the tax on constitutional grounds.

    a. What constitutional issue was raised by the plaintiff?

    b. Decide. Explain. See *Jimmy Swaggart Ministries v. Board of Equalization of California,* 493 U.S. 378 (1990).

14. Milwaukee prostitutes, who had been arrested on multiple occasions, sued to block the city from enforcing a court-ordered injunction that permanently enjoined them from engaging in certain specified activities in certain specified areas of the city. They were prohibited from "engaging in, beckoning to stop, or engaging male or female passersby in conversation, or stopping or attempting to stop motor vehicle operators by hailing, waving of arms or any other bodily gesture, or yelling in a loud voice" and other such activities. The women challenged the order on constitutional grounds.

    a. Explain the nature of that constitutional challenge.

    b. Decide the case. Explain. See *City of Milwaukee v. Burnette,* 637 N.W.2d 447 (Wis. App. 2001); 638 N.W.2d 590 (Wis. S. Ct. 2001).

15. Milagros Irizarry lived with the same man for more than two decades, during which time they raised two children. Irizarry, an employee of the Chicago public school system, received health benefits, but her male partner did not because the couple had not married. The school system provided health benefits to domestic partners of the same sex, but not to those of the opposite sex. Irizarry raised a constitutional challenge to the denial of benefits to her male partner.

    a. Explain the nature of that constitutional challenge.

    b. Decide the case. Explain. See *Irizarry v. Board of Education of the City of Chicago,* 251 F.3d 604 (7th Cir. 2001).

16. Fifteen-year-old Natalie Young, a lesbian, was sent to her New York City principal's office for wearing to school a T-shirt that said "Barbie is a lesbian." Young was suspended, and she sued the school.

    a. Was the suspension lawful? Explain.

    b. Could Young wear a shirt saying the war in Iraq is wrong?

    c. What about a shirt praising Osama bin Laden? Explain.

17. The sons of a murder victim brought a wrongful death/negligence action against a magazine, *Soldier of Fortune,* alleging that it had published an ad creating an unreasonable risk of violent crime. A former police officer had placed the ad offering his services as a bodyguard under the heading "Gun for Hire." The ad resulted in the officer being hired to kill the plaintiffs' father. The ad included the phrases "professional mercenary," "very private," and a statement indicating that "all jobs" would be considered, but it also included a list of legitimate jobs that involved the use of a gun. The plaintiffs won the negligence action and were awarded a $4.3 million judgment. *Soldier of Fortune* appealed on First Amendment grounds. Decide. See *Braun v. Soldier of Fortune Magazine, Inc.,* 968 F.2d 1110 (11th Cir. 1992); cert. den. 113 S.Ct. 1028 (1993).

18. As you have read, "hate speech" (such as racist, sexist, or homophobic remarks) is generally protected by the First Amendment. Commercial speech, often in the form of intellectually empty, symbol- and emotion-laden advertisements, is similarly protected. The Madisonian idea of the First Amendment was to protect serious political discourse. Now the First Amendment seems often to protect hate speech and commercial babble. In a 1996 book review and commentary, lawyer Paul Reidinger raised the concern that we may have "too much" free speech. Reidinger said, "The question these days is not whether government threatens free speech, but whether free speech threatens us. . . . [T]here is a tidal wave of fetid speech washing over the American landscape." Has the marketplace of ideas failed? See Paul Reidinger, "Weighing Cost of Free Speech," *ABA Journal* 82 (January 1996), p. 88.

Notes

1. Portions of this history of the United States Constitution rely upon Gordon Lloyd, "Introduction to the Constitutional Convention," [**http://teachingamericanhistory.org/convention/intro.html**].

2. Jerre Williams, *Constitutional Analysis in a Nutshell* (St. Paul: West, 1979), p. 33.

3. *McCreary County v. ACLU,* 2005 U.S. LEXIS 5211, and *Van Orden v. Perry,* 2005 U.S. LEXIS 5215.

4. *Minnesota v. Wicklund,* 589 N.W.2d 793 (S.Ct. Minn. 1999).

5. *Tinker v. Des Moines School District,* 393 U.S. 503 (1969).

6. *Barrett v. University of Mississippi,* 232 F.3d 208 (5th Cir. 2000); cert. den. 531 U.S. 1052 (2000).

7. *Valentine v. Chrestensen,* 316 U.S. 52 (1942).

8. *Mainstream Marketing Services, Inc. v. Federal Trade Commission,* 358 F.3d 1228 (10th Cir. 2004).

9. *Mainstream Marketing Services, Inc. v. FTC,* 2004 U.S. LEXIS 5564 (2004).

10. See *Kasky v. Nike, Inc.,* 45 P. 3d 243 (2002). For a discussion of *Kasky* and commercial speech, see Ryan Long, "Big Foot, Big Mouth," *Legal Times,* June 23, 2003, p. 60.

11. Norman M. Cheektowaga, "And a Rude Gesture to You, Too, Judges," *Buffalo News,* February 5, 1998, p. 3B.

12. Robert Levy, "Equality for All Speech," *National Law Journal,* September 17, 2001, p. A21.

13. 367 U.S. 643.

14. *Illinois v. Caballes,* 802 N.E. 2d 202 (Ill. S.Ct. 2003).

15. *Illinois v. Caballes,* 125 S.Ct. 834 (2005).

16. *Board of Education of Pottawatomie County v. Earls,* 122 S.Ct. 2559 (2002).

17. *Earls v. Board of Education,* 242 F.3d 1264 (10th Cir. 2001).

18. "Note to Congress," *National Review Online,* September 23, 2004.

19. Toni Lacy, "Patriot Act Blurred in the Public Mind," *USA TODAY,* [**http://www.usatoday.com/news/washington/2004-02-25-patriot**].

20. *State of Washington v. Glas,* 2002 Wash. LEXIS 596.

21. Meena Thiruvengadam, "Privacy Issues: The Popularity of Camera Phones Raises Concerns about Voyeurism and the Right to Take Photos in Public Places," *San Antonio Express-News,* August 4, 2004, p. 1E.

22. Thiruvengadam, "Privacy Issues."

23. *Marshall v. Barlow's,* 436 U.S. 307 (1978).

24. Constance Hays, "Regulators Seize Documents from Coca-Cola in Europe," *The New York Times,* July 22, 1999, p. C3.

25. A portion of the material in this paragraph was drawn from Dean Starkman, "Cities Use Eminent Domain to Clear Lots for Big-Box Stores," *The Wall Street Journal,* December 8, 2004, p. B1.

26. Starkman, "Cities Use Eminent Domain."

27. *Lucas v. So. Carolina Coastal Commission,* 112 S.Ct. 2886 (1992).

28. *Dolan v. City of Tigard,* 114 S.Ct. 2309 (1994).

29. Frank A. Vickory and Barry A. Diskin, "Advances in Private Property Protection Rights: The States in the Vanguard," *American Business Law Journal* 34, no. 4 (Summer 1997), p. 561.

30. See Vickory and Diskin, "Advances in Private Property," p. 561, and David L. Callies, "Regulatory Takings and the Supreme Court," *Stetson Law Review* 28 (Winter 1999), p. 523.

31. *Griswold v. Connecticut,* 381 U.S. 479 (1965).

32. 517 U.S. 559 (1996).

33. *State Farm v. Campbell,* 538 U.S. 408 (2003).

34. Jess Bravin, "Surprise: Judges Hand Out Most Punitive Awards," *The Wall Street Journal,* June 12, 2000, p. B1.

35. *Baker v. State,* 744 A.2d 864 (Vt. S.Ct. 1999).

36. *Goodrich v. Department of Public Health,* 798 N.E.2d 941 (Mass. S.Ct. 2003).

37. *Largess v. Supreme Judicial Court of Massachusetts,* 2004 LEXIS 7727.

38. Editorial, "Gay Marriage; Civil Rights Movement Slowed by Votes, But Not Halted," *Syracuse Post-Standard,* November 28, 2004, p. C2.

39. Liz Bradbury, "Same-Sex Couples Want Full Federal and State Rights, Benefits," *Morning Call* (Allentown, PA), December 5, 2004, p. D1.

40. "This Year's Freshmen at 4-Year Colleges: A Statistical Profile," *Chronicle of Higher Education,* February 1, 2002, pp. A36, 37.

41. Associated Press, "Americans Say Press Is Too Free," *Waterloo/Cedar Falls Courier,* July 4, 1999, p. A2.

42. Pierre Schlag, "This Could Be Your Culture—Junk Speech in a Time of Decadence," *Harvard Law Review* 109, no. 7 (1996), p. 1801.

Contracts

Preface

For both practical and philosophical reasons, a capitalist free market system simply cannot operate effectively and fairly without a reliable foundation in contract law. At the practical level, all buyers and sellers must have confidence that the deal they are about to make will be completed as specified or that they will have a remedy available if it is not completed. Otherwise, the legal risk in making deals would act as a drag on the commercial process, reducing certainty and thus depreciating the extraordinary efficiency of the free market. At the philosophical level, the fundamental point of a contract regime is personal freedom. Contract law gives each of us a reliable mechanism for freely expressing our preferences in life. From buying a tube of toothpaste, a car, or a house, to paying tuition, to accepting an employment offer, to franchising a business, to borrowing millions of dollars, to adopting a child, and so on, the direction and value of our lives are shaped and protected to a significant degree by the contractual choices we make. To a considerable extent, we define ourselves as persons by the contractual choices we make, and contract law protects those choices.

> To a considerable extent, we define ourselves as persons by the contractual choices we make

---

Contracts and Capitalism in China

Contract law has played a vital role in China's gradual movement toward free market principles and increased global commerce. Approved in 1999, China's new nationwide contract law was designed to govern all forms of contractual relationships in a manner that would encourage order, confidence, and fairness in doing business in China while making Chinese commercial and legal practice compatible with international standards. Now with China's emergence in world markets, contract disputes are inevitable:

- In late 2004 Beijing, China's municipal government, canceled a $3.5 million Windows and Office software deal with Microsoft, apparently bowing to central government pressure to buy domestically developed software. Chinese law requires preference for local products, when available, over foreign goods. Microsoft said only that it intends to continue commercial negotiations with the Beijing municipal government.
- The importance of reliable contractual relationships was unhappily obvious to the China National Petroleum Corporation (CNPC) in late 2004 when it filed suit in Moscow against the Russian oil giant Yukos. CNPC was seeking compensation for losses sustained when Yukos allegedly failed to complete contracted oil deliveries to China. A CNPC spokesman said, "The CNPC's demands for compensation for its losses are quite justified as Yukos

breached the contract first." The contract provided for 3.86 million tons of oil in 2004, but allegedly only 2.84 were delivered.

Sources: TechWeb Team, "Beijing Dumps Microsoft for Homegrown Software," *Asia Computer Weekly,* December 13, 2004; "Chinese Oil Corporation Sues Russia's Yukos for Breach of Contract," *BBC Monitoring International Reports,* October 31, 2004.

Part One—Building a Binding Contract

Introduction

We make promises routinely in our lives. Some of those create binding contracts; some do not. Thus the central question in this chapter is the following: Under what circumstances do promises become enforceable contracts?

The Uniform Commercial Code

Historically, the individual states had passed a wide variety of laws to clarify contract law, but the result was a confusing, inefficient patchwork. Thus the National Conference of Commissioners on Uniform State Laws (NCCUSL) and the American Law Institute (ALI) developed for state approval the Uniform Commercial Code (UCC), a body of rules designed to render commercial law consistent across the 50 states. *The UCC has been adopted in 49 states,* and Louisiana has adopted portions of it. With a set of uniform, predictable rules, business can be practiced with confidence and minimal legal confusion.

The UCC is divided into a series of articles addressing the multitude of potential problems that arise in complex commercial practice. For our purposes the most important of those articles is Number 2, Sales, which governs all transactions involving the sale of goods. UCC section 2-105 defines *goods* as tangible, movable, things. Hence cars, clothing, appliances, and the like are covered. Real estate, stocks, bonds, money, and so forth are not covered. Nor are contracts for *services* governed by the UCC. Of course, many transactions involve both goods and services. Characteristically, in determining whether the UCC applies, the courts have asked whether the dominant purpose of the contract is to provide a service or to sell a good.

The first question, then, in contract disputes is whether the UCC or the common law governs the situation. Throughout this chapter, you should remember that the UCC is *always* controlling (1) if the transaction is addressed by the UCC—that is, it involves a contract for the sale of goods—and (2) if a UCC rule applies to the issue in question. On the other hand, the judge-made, common law of contracts continues to govern transactions (1) not involving the sale of goods or (2) involving the sale of goods but where no specific UCC provision applies. Increasingly, in non-UCC cases, the courts are analogizing to UCC reasoning to render their judgments; that is, the common law is borrowing or absorbing UCC principles. This chapter, while focusing primarily on the common law of contracts, will introduce the role of the sales article in the practice of business. At this writing, NCCUSL/ALI–recommended revisions to the sales article are being considered by the various state legislatures. [For a brief overview of some of the recommended amendments to the UCC Article 2, see **http://www.nccusl.org/nccusl/UCC2_Synopsis.pdf**]

Article 2A of the UCC governs *leases* of goods. In essence, Article 2A mimics the sales article except that it governs leases of goods rather than sales. Because of space constraints, Article 2A will not receive further attention in this text.

What Is a Contract?

Legally enforceable contracts must exhibit all of the following features:

1. **Agreement**—a meeting of the minds of the parties based on an offer by one and an acceptance by the other. The determination as to whether the parties have actually reached agreement is based on the *objective* evidence (the parties' acts, words, and so on) as a "reasonable person" would interpret it rather than on an effort to ascertain the subjective or personal intent of the parties.

2. **Consideration.** The bargained-for legal value that one party agrees to pay or provide to secure the promise of another.

3. **Capacity.** The parties must have the legal ability to enter the contract; that is, they must be sane, sober, and of legal age.

4. **Genuineness of assent.** The parties must knowingly agree to the same thing. Their minds must meet as evidenced by the objective evidence. If that meeting does not occur because of mistake, fraud, or the like, a contract does not exist because the parties' assent was not real.

5. **Legality of purpose.** The object of the contract must not violate the law or public policy.

Contracts embracing these five features are enforceable by law and hence are distinguishable from unenforceable promises. As explained later, some contracts must be in writing to be enforceable.

Classification of Contracts

Contracts fall into a series of sometimes overlapping categories. Understanding those categories helps reveal the rather well-ordered logic of our contract system (see Figure 6.1).

Contract Formation

1. **Bilateral and unilateral contracts.**   A *bilateral contract* emerges from a situation in which *both* parties make promises. A *unilateral contract* ordinarily involves a situation in which one party makes a promise and the other *acts* in response to that promise. For example, in beginning to establish your new restaurant you promise a college friend that if he completes his degree, you will hire him. He can accept your offer/promise by the act of completing college.

FIGURE 6.1
Classification of Contracts

Contract formation
1. Bilateral/unilateral
   a. Bilateral contract—a promise for a promise.
   b. Unilateral contract—a promise for an act.
2. Express/implied
   a. Express contract—explicitly stated in writing or orally.
   b. Implied-in-fact contract—inferred from the conduct of the parties.
   c. Quasi-contract—implied contract created by a court to prevent unjust enrichment.

Contract performance
1. Executory contract—not yet fully performed.
2. Executed contract—fully performed by all parties.

Contract enforceability
1. Valid contract—includes all of the necessary ingredients of a binding contract.
2. Unenforceable contract—contract exists, but a legal defense prevents enforcement.
3. Void contract—no contract at all.
4. Voidable contract—one party has the option of either enforcing or voiding the contract.

2. **Express and implied contracts.**   When parties overtly and explicitly manifest their intention to enter an agreement, either in writing or orally, the result (if other requirements are fulfilled) is an *express contract.* For example, in managing your department at an insurance firm, you sign a form contract with a local computer store ordering a new computer. In turn, the supplier's signature on the form creates an express, bilateral agreement.

If, on the other hand, you ask your local computer service to take a look at a machine that is down and one of the service's technicians does so, you have probably entered an *implied-in-fact contract.* A court would infer a promise by you to pay a reasonable price in return for the service's promise to make a commercially reasonable effort to repair the computer. The contract is inferred on the basis of the facts—that is, by the behavior of the parties.

Suppose in managing your insurance department you have received payment for insurance that was, in fact, issued by a rival firm. In these circumstances, it would be unfair for you to be able to keep the unearned money so the courts construct an implied-in-law or quasi-contract permitting the actual insurer to collect the money. This unusual situation in which the court infers the existence of a contract is employed only when necessary to prevent unjust enrichment (as would have been the case if you were to collect an insurance premium without having issued a policy).

Contract Performance

1. **Executory contracts.**   A contract is labeled *executory* until all parties fully perform.
2. **Executed contracts.**   When all parties have completed their performances, the contract is *executed.*

Contract Enforceability

1. **Valid contracts.**   A *valid contract* meets all of the established legal requirements and thus is enforceable in court.

2. **Unenforceable contracts.**   An *unenforceable contract* meets the basic contractual requirements but remains faulty because it fails to fulfill some other legal rule. For example, an oral contract may be unenforceable if it falls in one of those categories of contracts, such as the sale of land, that must be in writing (see the Statute of Frauds later in this chapter).

3. **Void contracts.**   A *void contract* is, in fact, no contract at all because a critical legal requirement is missing; usually it is either an agreement to accomplish an illegal purpose (such as to commit a crime) or an agreement involving an incompetent (such as an individual judged by a court to be insane). In either case what is otherwise an enforceable contract is in fact void.

4. **Voidable contracts.**   A *voidable contract* is enforceable but can be canceled by one or more of the parties. The most common voidable contracts are those entered by minors who have the option, under the law, of either disaffirming or fulfilling most contracts (explained later).

The Agreement: Offer

Characteristically, an offer consists of a promise to do something or to refrain from doing something in the future. A valid offer must include all of these elements:

1. Present *intent* to enter a contract.
2. Reasonable *definiteness* in the terms of the offer.
3. *Communication* of the offer to the offeree.

Intent

Assume that you are the purchasing manager for a trucking firm, and you need a small used van to do some local light hauling. Because time is of the essence, you decide to bypass the normal bidding process and go directly to the local dealers to make a quick purchase. At the first lot you find a suitable van. In discussing it, the sales manager says, "Well, we don't usually do this, but since you've been such a good customer, I'll tell you, we paid $6,000 for this one so I guess we are gonna need about $8,000 to deal with you." You say, "Fine. That's reasonable. I'll take it." The manager then says, "Now wait a minute, I was just talking off the top of my head. I'll have to punch up the numbers to be sure."

Do you have a deal at that point? The core question is whether the sales manager made an offer. Normally, language of that kind has been treated by the courts as preliminary negotiation lacking the necessary *intent* to constitute an offer. Of course, if no offer exists, you cannot accept, and no contract can emerge absent further negotiation.

Offer?

An at-will employee (can be fired at any time) asks you, his manager, about job security. You respond, "Good employees are taken care of. You are a good employee." Does that language amount to an offer of permanent employment?

Advertisements The question of intent sometimes arises with advertisements. In buying the van for your business, suppose you were responding to an ad that said, "2003 full-size Ford cargo van, $18,000." Is that ad language an offer such that you can accept by promising to pay $18,000? Ordinarily, ads do not constitute offers, but rather are treated by the courts as invitations to deal. Were an ad actually treated as an offer, it would put the seller in the commercially impracticable position of being required to provide the advertised product at the advertised price to everyone who sought one, regardless of available supply. Presumably, that open-ended duty was not the seller's intent when issuing the ad. It follows then that the buyer, in responding to an ad, is technically making an offer, with the seller free to accept or decline.

> Suppose you were responding to an ad that said, "2003 full-size Ford cargo van, $18,000." Is that ad language an offer such that you can accept by promising to pay $18,000?

On the other hand, courts have held that some ads do manifest a present intent to make an offer. The critical terms in those ads must be highly specific and complete, leaving nothing open for negotiation.

A Jet Fighter from Pepsi?

A 1995 Pepsico promotion offered merchandise in exchange for points earned by buying Pepsi-Cola. The television ad showed a teenager modeling some of the available merchandise. A Pepsi T-shirt was displayed for 75 points and a leather jacket for 1450 points. At the end of the ad, a U.S. Marine Corps Harrier "jump jet" landed outside a school, and the boy said, "Sure beats the bus." The ad said the jet was redeemable for 7 million points. John D.R. Leonard, at the time a 21-year-old business student in Seattle, Washington, joined five investors in writing a check to Pepsi for $700,008.50 and demanded the 7 million Pepsi points. Pepsi returned the check and said it had no intention of giving Leonard the $24 million jet. Leonard sued. Who wins? Explain. See *John D.R. Leonard v. Pepsico,* 210 F.3d 88 (2d Cir. Ct. App. 2000). [For a video of the ad, see **http://www.stcl.edu/faculty-dir/ricks/casebook/pepsi1.wmv.** Other versions of the ad can be found at **pepsi2** and **pepsi3.**]

Definiteness

Suppose you have completed a management training program for a "big box" retailer. In your first assignment as an assistant manager, your boss asks you to seek bids and make the other arrangements (subject to her approval) to resurface the store's large asphalt parking lot. You secure bids, and the lowest bidder offers to complete the work "later this summer" for $98,000. You briefly explain the offer to your boss, who tells you to take care of all the details. You are busy with other matters and you put off the parking lot project for a couple of weeks. When you get back to the contractor, he says, "Sorry, man, we hadn't heard from you, and we got another deal." Can you hold that contractor to his initial offer?

One of the requirements of a binding offer is that all of its critical terms must be sufficiently clear that a court can determine both the intentions of the parties and their duties. Clearly, in the asphalt case, many critical details—such as precisely when the work would be done, the quality of the surfacing material, its thickness, and the like—had not been established. Consequently, no offer existed. In a contract for the sale of goods, UCC 2-204 relaxes the definiteness standard by providing that "one or more terms" may be missing but the court can find a contract, nonetheless, where (1) "the parties have intended to make a contract" and (2) "there is a reasonably certain basis for giving an appropriate remedy." Under the UCC, the courts can actually fill in missing terms such as specifying a reasonable price where the contract had omitted a stipulation. The following case involving Mariah Carey, the pop music star, demonstrates some of the problems that can arise when an understanding is indefinite.

Vian v. Carey 1993 U.S. Dist.

LEGAL BRIEFCASE Lexis 5460 (U.S. Dist. Ct. S.D.N.Y. 1993)

Judge Mukasey

Defendant Mariah Carey is a famous, successful and apparently wealthy entertainer. Plaintiff Joseph Vian was her stepfather before she achieved stardom, but at the start of this litigation was in the process of becoming divorced from defendant's mother. He claims defendant agreed orally that he would have a license to market singing dolls in her likeness. . . . Plaintiff claims that he and Carey had an oral contract for him to receive a license to market "Mariah dolls." These dolls would be statuettes of the singer and would play her most popular songs. Plaintiff claims that the contract was in consideration of his financial and emotional support of defendant, including picking her up from late-night recording sessions, providing her with the use of a car, paying for dental care, allowing her to use his boat for business meetings and rehearsals, and giving her various items, including unused wedding gifts from his marriage to her mother, to help furnish her apartment.

The alleged basis of the oral contract is that on at least three occasions, twice in the family car and once on Vian's boat, Vian told Carey, "Don't forget the Mariah dolls," and "I get the Mariah dolls." According to Vian, on one occasion Carey responded "okay" and on other occasions she merely smiled and nodded. Although Carey admits Vian mentioned the dolls two or three times, she testified that she thought it was a joke. For 30 years plaintiff has been in the business of designing, producing, and marketing gift and novelty items. Although it is not clear from the evidence the parties have submitted, it will be assumed that the alleged contract was formed after defendant turned 18. Under New York law, an oral agreement can form a binding

contract. . . . In determining whether a contract exists, what matters are the parties' expressed intentions, the words and deeds that constitute objective signs in a given set of circumstances.

Therefore, the issue is whether the objective circumstances indicate that the parties intended to form a contract. Without such an intent, neither a contract nor a preliminary agreement to negotiate in good faith can exist. In making such a determination, a court may look at "whether the terms of the contract have been finally resolved." In addition, a court may consider "the context of the negotiations." Plaintiff has adduced no evidence that defendant ever intended by a nod of her head or the expression "okay" to enter into a complex commercial licensing agreement involving dolls in her likeness playing her copyrighted songs. The context in which this contract between an 18-year-old girl and her stepfather allegedly was made was an informal family setting, either in the car or on plaintiff's boat, while others were present. Vian's own version of events leads to the conclusion that there was no reason for Carey to think Vian was entirely serious, let alone that he intended to bind her to an agreement at that time. He admits he never told her he was serious. The objective circumstances do not indicate that Carey intended to form a contract with plaintiff. Although plaintiff's five-page memorandum of law fails to raise the possibility, plaintiff also has not shown that Carey intended to be bound to negotiate with plaintiff at some later date over the licensing of "Mariah dolls."

There can be no meeting of the minds, required for the formation of a contract, where essential material terms are missing. Thus, even if the parties both believe themselves to be bound, there is no contract when "the terms of the agreement are so vague and indefinite that there is no basis or standard for deciding whether the agreement had been kept or broken, or to fashion a remedy, and no means by which such terms may be made certain."

. . . The word "license" was not even used. As defendant points out, no price or royalty term was mentioned, nor was the duration or geographic scope of the license, nor was Carey's right to approve the dolls. Plaintiff admits he would not have gone ahead without defendant's approval, thus conceding the materiality of that term.

* * * * *

In sum, plaintiff has not raised a triable issue of fact as to the existence of a contract. Defendant's motion for summary judgment is granted.

Questions

1. Why did the court find for Carey?

2. As noted in the text, in UCC cases judges fill in contract terms where the parties clearly intended a deal. Should the court here fill in the missing terms to provide the necessary definiteness? Explain.

3. Pilgrim Village Company had employed Petersen as a construction manager at a specified annual salary and "a share of the profits." Petersen worked at salary for several years and then asked for a 10 percent share of the profits. The company refused, and Petersen sued seeking "some share of the profits." How should the court rule on Petersen's claim? Explain. See *Petersen v. Pilgrim Village,* 42 N.W. 2d 273 (Wis. S. Ct., 1950).

Communication

As explained, an effective offer must be the product of a present intent, it must be definite, and it must be communicated to the offeree. Communication of an offer expresses the offeror's intent to make that offer. Suppose a friend tells you that your neighbor has offered to sell his classic jukebox for $10,000. You call your neighbor and say, "I accept. I'll be right over with the $10,000." Do you have a deal? No. The owner did not communicate the offer to you. The fact that it was not communicated to you may suggest that your neighbor does not want to sell or does not want to sell to you.

Duration of an Offer   Communication of an offer affords the offeree the opportunity to create a contract by accepting that offer, but how long does that opportunity last? Here are some general rules:

1. The offeror may revoke the offer anytime prior to acceptance. (Some exceptions are explained later.) Normally, revocation is effective on receipt by the offeree. Under common law the offeror has the right to revoke at any time prior to acceptance, even if he or she expressly promised to keep the offer open for a specified period.

2. The offer may specify that it is open for an express period (such as 10 days).

3. Where a time limit is not specified in the offer it will be presumed to be open for a reasonable period.

4. An offer expires if rejected or on receipt of a counteroffer.

Irrevocable Offers

Some kinds of offers may not be revoked. We will note three of them.

1. **Option contracts.** When an offeror promises to keep an offer open for a specified period and, in return, the offeree pays consideration (usually money), the parties have created an *option contract,* which is a separate agreement and is enforceable by its

terms. For example, a friend has offered to sell to you his customized car that you have long cherished, but you want to think about it for a few days. You might enter an option contract with your friend under which you pay $50 for the seller's promise to keep the offer open for seven days. You are under no obligation to buy the car, but the seller is under a binding obligation not to withdraw the offer or sell to another during the seven days.

2. **Firm offers.** Under the UCC, if the owner of that customized car is a dealer (a merchant) and he made a written, signed offer to sell that car (a good) to you, indicating that his offer would remain open for seven days, he is bound to that promise whether you paid consideration for it or not. That situation is labeled a *firm offer* as specified in UCC 2-205, which also provides that such offers will be kept open for a reasonable period if the agreement does not mention a time, but that period cannot exceed three months.

3. **Offers for unilateral contracts.** A problem sometimes arises when the offeror attempts to revoke a unilateral offer after the offeree has begun to perform. For example, your neighbor invites you to rake her leaves for $5, and then, when you are virtually done, she yells from the doorway, "Oh, sorry, I changed my mind. You go home now." Historically, the offeror (the neighbor, in this case) was free to revoke at any time; but the modern position holds that the offeror normally cannot revoke if the offeree (you) has commenced performance. If that performance is then completed (you ignore your neighbor's admonition to go home, and you finish the raking), the offeror (your neighbor) is bound to perform fully; that is, the neighbor must pay the $5.

The Agreement: Acceptance

Suppose you are in training with a large real estate firm and your boss has authorized you to enter negotiations to buy a parcel of farmland that your company hopes to develop for housing. After preliminary discussions, you extend a written offer to the owner indicating, among other terms, that your company is willing to pay $6,000 per acre for a 10-acre parcel. Assume the owner responds by writing, "I accept your offer at $6,000 per acre, but I need to keep the two-acre homesite." The offeree has used the word *accept,* but does the response constitute a legally binding acceptance?

The general rule is that an effective acceptance must be a mirror image of the offer; that is, ordinarily its terms must be the same as those in the offer. Here the offeree has changed the terms of the offer and in so doing has issued a *counteroffer,* thus extinguishing the original offer.

Communication of Acceptance

An offer may be accepted only by the offeree—that is, the person to whom the offer was directed. Because unilateral offers are accepted by performance, no communication of acceptance beyond that performance ordinarily is necessary. In the case of a bilateral contract (a promise for a promise), acceptance is not effective until communicated.

Broadly, acceptance can be accomplished by a "yes" communicated face-to-face, by a nod of the head or some other appropriate signal, by telephone, or by other unwritten means, unless the law of the state requires writing in that particular kind of transaction.

Mailbox   Confusion sometimes arises when the parties are not dealing face-to-face. In general, acceptance is effective upon dispatch by whatever mode of communication has been explicitly or implicitly authorized by the offeror. This well-settled position is labeled the *mailbox rule* and means, among other things, that an acceptance is effective when sent even if never received. [For one professor's review of the mailbox rule and related rules, see **http://www.tomwbell.com/teaching/KMailbox.pdf**]

Authorization   The offeror controls the acceptance process and may specify an exclusive manner in which an acceptance must be communicated. If so, a contract is not created if the acceptance is communicated in anything other than the stipulated fashion. Traditionally, if the offeror did not give an *express authorization* to a means of communication, an acceptance by the same or faster means than that used by the offeror was implied. *Implied authorization* might also arise from such factors as prior dealings between the parties and custom in their industry.

Modern View   Under the UCC the rules have relaxed a bit. If no specific instructions for acceptance are included in the offer, the offeree is free to accept in any reasonable manner within a reasonable period, and acceptance is effective upon dispatch. Even when the means chosen are "unreasonable," acceptance is effective on dispatch under the UCC 1-201(38) if it is actually received in a timely manner.

Consideration

Earlier we identified the five key ingredients in an enforceable contract: agreement, consideration, capacity, genuineness of assent, and legality of purpose. Having examined the offer/acceptance process, we turn now to consideration. As noted earlier, consideration is the bargained-for legal value that one party agrees to pay or provide to secure the promise of another. It is what the promisor demands and receives in exchange for his or her promise. Consideration is used by the courts to distinguish a contract (enforceable) from a gratuitous promise (unenforceable). The *promisee* must suffer a *legal detriment;* that is, the promisee must give up something of value (an act or a promise) or must refrain from doing something that she or he has a legal right to do in order to enforce the promise offered by the *promisor.* Each party, then, must pay a "price" for a contract to be enforceable. In sum, consideration consists of a detriment to the promisee that is bargained for by the promisor.

   The classic case that follows explores the idea of consideration and demonstrates that consideration can have legal value without involving monetary loss to the promisee.

Hamer v. Sidway
27 N.E. 256 (N.Y. 1891)

FACTS

In 1869 William E. Story Sr. promised his nephew, W. E. Story II, that he would pay the nephew $5,000 upon his 21st birthday if the nephew would refrain from drinking liquor, using tobacco, swearing, and playing cards or billiards for money until he reached that 21st birthday. The nephew agreed and performed his promise, but the uncle died in 1887 without paying the money, and the administrator of the estate, Sidway, declined to pay the $5,000 plus interest. The nephew had assigned (sold) his rights to the money to Louisa Hamer, who sued W. E. Story Sr.'s estate. Hamer, the plaintiff, won at the trial level, lost on appeal, and then appealed to the New York Court of Appeals.

* * * * *

Judge Parker

When the nephew arrived at the age of 21 years and on the 31st day of January 1875, he wrote to his uncle informing him that he had performed his part of the agreement and had thereby become entitled to the sum of $5,000. The uncle received the letter and a few days later and on the sixth of February, he wrote and mailed to his nephew the following letter:

> Buffalo, February 6, 1875
> W. E. Story, Jr.
> Dear Nephew:
> Your letter of the 31st came to hand all right, saying that you had lived up to the promise made to me several years ago. I have no doubt but you have, for which you shall have five thousand dollars as I promised you. I had the money in the bank the day you was 21 years old that I intend for you, and you shall have the money certain. Now, Willie I do not intend to interfere with this money in any way till I think you are capable of taking care of it and the sooner that time comes the better it will please me. I would hate very much to have you start out in some adventure that you thought all right and lose this money in one year. The first five thousand dollars that I got together cost me a heap of hard work. You would hardly believe me when I tell you that to obtain this I shoved a jackplane many a day, butchered three or four years, then came to this city, and after three months' perseverance I obtained a situation in a grocery store. I opened this store early, closed late, slept in the fourth story of the building in a room 30 by 40 feet and not a human being in the building but myself. All this I done to live as cheap as I could to save something. I don't want you to take up with this kind of fare. I was here in the cholera season '49 and '52 and the deaths averaged 80 to 125 daily and plenty of smallpox. I wanted to go home, but Mr. Fisk, the

gentleman I was working for, told me if I left then, after it got healthy he probably would not want me. I stayed. All the money I have saved I know just how I got it. It did not come to me in any mysterious way, and the reason I speak of this is that money got in this way stops longer with a fellow that gets it with hard knocks than it does when he finds it. Willie, you are 21 and you have many a thing to learn yet. This money you have earned much easier than I did besides acquiring good habits at the same time and you are quite welcome to the money; hope you will make good use of it. I was 10 long years getting this together after I was your age. Now, hoping this will be satisfactory, I stop . . .
> Truly Yours,
> W. E. STORY
> P.S.—You can consider this money on interest.

The nephew received the letter and thereafter consented that the money should remain with his uncle in accordance with the terms and conditions of the letter. The uncle died on the 29th day of January 1887, without having paid over to his nephew any portion of the said $5,000 and interest.

* * * * *

The defendant contends that the contract was without consideration to support it, and, therefore, invalid. He asserts that the promisee by refraining from the use of liquor and tobacco was not harmed but benefited; that that which he did was best for him to do independently of his uncle's promise, and insists that it follows that unless the promisor was benefited, the contract was without consideration. A contention, which if well founded, would seem to leave open for controversy in many cases whether that which the promisee did or omitted to do was, in fact, of such benefit to him as to leave no consideration to support the enforcement of the promisor's agreement. Such a rule could not be tolerated, and is without foundation in the law.

* * * * *

"In general a waiver of any legal right at the request of another party is a sufficient consideration for a promise" (Parsons on Contracts).

Pollock, in his work on contracts, says, ". . . Consideration means not so much that one party is profiting as that the other abandons some legal right in the present or limits his legal freedom of action in the future as an inducement for the promise of the first."

Now, applying this rule to the facts before us, the promisee used tobacco, occasionally drank liquor, and had a legal right to do so. That right he abandoned for a period of years upon the strength of the promise of the testator that for such forbearance he would give him $5,000. We need not speculate on the effort which may have been required to give up the use of those stimulants. It is sufficient that he restricted his lawful freedom of action within certain prescribed limits upon the faith of his uncle's agreement, and now having fully performed the conditions imposed, it is of no moment whether such performance actually proved a benefit to the promisor, and the court will not inquire into it, but were it a proper subject of inquiry, we see nothing in this record that would permit a determination that the uncle was not benefited in a legal sense.

*   *   *   *   *

Reversed.

Questions

1. *a.* What detriment, if any, was sustained by the nephew?

   b. What benefit, if any, was secured by the uncle?

   c. As a matter of law, do we need to inquire into the uncle's benefit? Explain.

2. Lampley began work as an at-will (can be dismissed or can quit at any time) employee of Celebrity Homes in Denver, Colorado, in May 1975. On July 29, 1975, Celebrity announced a profit-sharing plan for all employees if the company reached its goals for the fiscal year, April 1,1975, to March 31, 1976. Lampley was dismissed in January 1976. Celebrity distributed its profits in May 1976. Lampley sued when she did not receive a share of the profits. Celebrity argued that its promise to share its profits was a gratuity, unsupported by consideration. Decide. Explain. See *Lampley v. Celebrity Homes*, 594 P.2d 605 (Col. Ct. App. 1979). [For a detailed analysis of *Hamer v. Sidway*, see http://www.law.smu.edu/firstday/contracts/case.htm]

Adequacy of Consideration

With certain exceptions, the courts do not, as Judge Parker indicated in the *Hamer* case, inquire into the economic value of the consideration in question. Legal sufficiency depends not on the value of the consideration but on whether the promisee suffered a detriment in some way. To hold otherwise would put the courts in the place of the market in deciding the value of transactions. We are all free to make both good and bad bargains.

On the other hand, the courts will rule that consideration is found wanting in situations of pretense or sham where the parties have clearly agreed on token or nominal consideration in an effort to present the transaction as a contract rather than a gift. Likewise, an extreme inadequacy of consideration will sometimes cause the court to question a contract on the grounds of *fraud, duress,* or *unconscionability* (all are discussed later in this chapter). In these instances, the agreements would be unenforceable because of a failure of consideration. However, remember these cases are uncommon, and the courts rarely inquire into the adequacy of consideration.

Appearance of Consideration

Some agreements appear to be accompanied by consideration, but in fact, that appearance turns out to be an illusion. Hence, if one agrees to perform a preexisting duty, consideration would be found wanting. For example, if you were to pay your neighbor $50 to keep his dog chained when outdoors and a city ordinance already requires dogs to be chained if outdoors, your promise would be unenforceable because your neighbor already had a preexisting duty under the law to keep his dog chained. So performance of a preexisting legal duty does not constitute consideration because no legal detriment or benefit has arisen.

Similarly, preexisting duties sometimes arise from contracts. Suppose you hire a contractor to resurface the parking lot at your real estate office. You agree on a price of

$12,000. With a portion of the work completed, the contractor asks you to amend the agreement to add $2,000 because the project is requiring more time than anticipated. You agree. The work is completed. Could you then legally refuse to pay the additional $2,000? The answer is yes because the contractor failed to provide consideration for the modification of your contract. He was under a preexisting duty to finish the contract; hence he did not sustain a legal detriment in the modified agreement. Note, however, that UCC section 2-209(1) provides that "an agreement modifying a contract within this Article needs no consideration to be binding."

Suppose you learn from your neighbor that your friend Ames wants to sell his house. You, as a Realtor, find a buyer for the house and make all of the necessary arrangements for the sale out of regard for your friendship with Ames. Then when the transaction is complete, Ames says, "Well, this has been great of you, but I don't feel right about it. When I get my check for the sale, I'll pay you $2,000 for your hard work. I really appreciate it." What if Ames does not then pay the $2,000? Do you have recourse? No. This is a situation of *past consideration*, where the performance—arranging the sale of your friend's house—was not bargained for and was not given in exchange for the promise and thus cannot constitute consideration. In effect, the performance was a gift. Of course, past consideration is really not consideration at all. In some states, courts enforce promises to pay for benefits already received where doing so amounts to a *moral obligation* that must be enforced to prevent injustice.

Substitutes for Consideration

When necessary to achieve justice, the courts sometimes conclude that a contract exists even though consideration is clearly lacking. Moral obligation and quasi contract (discussed earlier) are two such instances; but the most prominent of these substitutes for consideration is the doctrine of *promissory estoppel,* in which the promisor is "stopped" from denying the existence of a contract where the promisee has detrimentally relied on that promise. Promissory estoppel requires the following:

1. A promise on which the promisor should expect the promisee to rely.
2. The promisee did justifiably rely on the promise.
3. Injustice can be avoided only by enforcing the promise.

Consider the following. You have been a part-time employee of a small fast-food chain restaurant while attending college. Upon graduation, you tell the manager of the restaurant that you think you could handle your own franchise. He says you need to get more experience and advises you to take a full-time position with the company. You do so. Everything goes well, and when you next approach the manager, he says, "If you can come up with the $50,000 and a good location, we will get you in a franchise right away. But you've gotta move on this. Maybe you better quit your job with us and concentrate on this thing." You take his advice and quit your job to devote your time to making the necessary financial arrangements and finding a vacant building to rent in a good location for a franchise. You show the building to the manager, and he agrees that it looks like a favorable location and one that can easily be converted to the company's needs. He says, "Looks like you have everything in place. If you can come up with $50,000 more we will make this thing happen." You refuse and decide to bring suit against the fast-food chain for breach of contract. The chain defends by saying that you did not provide consideration for its promise. No formal financing arrangement was ever agreed to, and you had not committed yourself to any franchising obligations. Under these circumstances you would probably prevail using a promissory estoppel claim. In brief, you would argue that you had changed your position in reliance on the franchisor's promises and that relief is necessary to prevent injustice. (For a similar case see *Hoffman v. Red Owl Stores,* 133 N.W. 2d 267 (Wis. S. Ct. 1965).)

Capacity

Having examined two of the required ingredients in an enforceable contract, agreement and consideration, we turn now to a third, capacity to contract. To enter a binding agreement, one must have the legal ability to do so; that is, one's mental condition and maturity must be such that the agreement was entered with understanding and in recognition of one's own interests. The three primary areas of concern are intoxication, mental impairment, and minority (infancy/youthfulness), with minority being much the more common area of dispute.

> The three primary areas of concern are intoxication, mental impairment, and minority

Intoxication

Assume you have been drinking to celebrate your 21st birthday. You enter a contract with a friend to sell him your autographed Michael Jordan basketball card for $200. You receive the money and turn over the card. Later, when sober, you regret the deal. Will a court nullify that contract on the grounds of your intoxication? That decision depends on whether you were sufficiently intoxicated that you did not understand the nature and purpose of the contract. If the objective evidence suggests that you did not understand the transaction, the contract would be considered voidable, in which case you could probably disaffirm the contract and demand the return of the card, although courts are often not sympathetic with people who attempt to escape contracts made while intoxicated. In most states, if you recovered the card, you would be required to return the $200 to your friend.

If on recovering your sobriety, your friend argued that the contract was invalid because of your intoxication, and he demanded the return of his $200 in exchange for the card, you could then *ratify* (affirm) the contract and hold him to it. If the contract had been for one of life's *necessaries* (food, shelter, clothing, medical care, tools of one's trade, or the like), you would have been liable for the reasonable value of that necessary.

Mental Incompetence

In most cases an agreement involving a mentally incompetent person is either void or voidable. The transaction would be void—that is, no contract would exist—where the impaired party had been *adjudged* insane. If the impaired party was unable to understand the purpose and effect of the contract but had not been legally adjudged insane, the contract would be voidable (void in some states) at the option of the impaired party. The competent party cannot void the contract, and the impaired party would have to pay the reasonable value of any necessaries received under the contract.

Minority

Minors may complete their contracts if they wish, but they also have an absolute right to rescind most of those contracts. They may rescind until they reach adulthood and for a reasonable time thereafter. (Many states have enacted statutes forbidding minors from disaffirming some classes of contracts such as those for marriage, student loans, and life insurance.) The minor has a right of recovery for everything given up in meeting the terms of the contract. Similarly, the minor must return everything that remains in her or his possession that was received from the contract. In many states, if nothing of the bargained-for consideration remains or if its value has depreciated, the minor has no duty to replace it but can still recover whatever she or he put into the contract. If not disaffirmed in a reasonable time after the minor reaches the age of majority, the contract is considered to be ratified, and the minor is bound to its terms. The minor is also liable for the reasonable value (not necessarily the contract price) of necessaries purchased from an adult. That is, a minor must pay the adult the reasonable value of contracted-for items such as food, clothing, shelter, medical care, basic education, and tools of the minor's trade.

> Minors may complete their contracts if they wish, but they also have an absolute right to rescind most of those contracts.

Despite the flexibility accorded to minors entering contracts, the adults who are parties to those contracts are bound to them and do not have the power to disaffirm. Hence adults put themselves at risk when they choose to bargain with minors. As noted, in many states a minor need not make restitution if the consideration is lost, destroyed, or depreciated. On the other hand, the case that follows illustrates the growing view that minors do have some monetary obligation after disaffirming a contract. [For an overview of capacity to contract law, see **http://www.outlawslegal.com/refer/contracts3.htm**]

Dodson v. Shrader

LEGAL BRIEFCASE 824 S.W. 2d 545 (Tenn. S. Ct. 1992)

Justice O'Brien

In early April of 1987, Joseph Eugene Dodson, then 16 years of age, purchased a used 1984 pickup truck from Burns and Mary Shrader. The Shraders owned and operated Shrader's Auto Sales in Columbia, Tennessee. Dodson paid $4,900 in cash for the truck, using money he borrowed from his girlfriend's grandmother. At the time of the purchase there was no inquiry by the Shraders, and no misrepresentation by Dodson, concerning his minority. However, Shrader did testify that at the time he believed Dodson to be 18 or 19 years of age.

In December 1987, nine months after the date of purchase, the truck began to develop mechanical problems. A mechanic diagnosed the problem as a burnt valve, but could not be certain without inspecting the valves inside the engine. Dodson did not want, or did not have the money, to effect these repairs. He continued to drive the truck despite the mechanical problems. One month later, in January, the truck's engine "blew up" and the truck became inoperable.

Dodson parked the vehicle in the front yard at his parents' home, where he lived. He contacted the Shraders to rescind the purchase of the truck and requested a full refund. The

Shraders refused to accept the tender of the truck or to give Dodson the refund requested.

Dodson then [sued] to rescind the contract and recover the amount paid for the truck. Before the circuit court could hear the case, the truck, while parked in Dodson's front yard, was struck on the left front fender by a hit-and-run driver. At the time of the circuit court trial, according to Shrader, the truck was worth only $500 due to the damage to the engine and the left front fender.

The case was heard in the circuit court in November 1988. The trial judge, based on previous common-law decisions, and under the doctrine of stare decisis, reluctantly granted the rescission. The Shraders were ordered, upon tender and delivery of the truck, to reimburse the $4,900 purchase price to Dodson. The Shraders appealed.

[T]he rule in Tennessee is in accord with the majority rule on the issue among our sister states. This rule is based on the underlying purpose of the "infancy doctrine," which is to protect minors from their lack of judgment and "from squandering their wealth through improvident contracts with crafty adults who would take advantage of them in the marketplace."

There is, however, a modern trend among the states, either by judicial action or by statute, in the approach to the problem of balancing the rights of minors against those of innocent merchants. As a result, two minority rules have developed that allow the other party to a contract with a minor to refund less than the full consideration paid in the event of rescission.

The first of these minority rules is called the "Benefit Rule." The rule holds that, upon rescission, recovery of the full purchase price is subject to a deduction for the minor's use of the merchandise. This rule recognizes that the traditional rule in regard to necessaries has been extended so far as to hold an infant bound by his contracts, where he failed to restore what he has received under them to the extent of the benefit actually derived by him from what he has received from the other party to the transaction.

The other minority rule holds that the minor's recovery of the full purchase price is subject to a deduction for the minor's "use" of the consideration he or she received under the contract, or for the "depreciation" or "deterioration" of the consideration in his or her possession.

We are impressed by the statement made by the Court of Appeals of Ohio:

> At a time when we see young persons between 18 and 21 years of age demanding and assuming more responsibilities in their daily lives; when we see such persons emancipated, married, and raising families; when we see such persons charged with the responsibility for committing crimes; when we see such persons being sued in tort claims for acts of negligence; when we see such persons subject to military service; when we see such persons engaged in business and acting in almost all other respects as an adult, it seems timely to reexamine the case law pertaining to contractual rights and responsibilities of infants to see if the law as pronounced and applied by the courts should be redefined.

*   *   *   *   *

We state the rule to be followed hereafter, in reference to a contract of a minor, to be where the minor has not been overreached in any way, and there has been no undue influence, and the contract is a fair and reasonable one, and the minor has actually paid money on the purchase price, and taken and used the article purchased; that he ought not be permitted to recover the amount actually paid, without allowing the vendor of the goods reasonable compensation for the use of, depreciation, and willful or negligent damage to the article purchased, while in his hands. If there has been any fraud or imposition on the part of the seller or if the contract is unfair, or any unfair advantage has been taken of the minor inducing him to make the purchase, then the rule does not apply. Whether there has been such an overreaching on the part of the seller, and the fair market value of the property returned, would always, in any case, be a question for the trier of fact. . . .

This rule is best adapted to modern conditions under which minors are permitted to, and do in fact, transact a great deal of business for themselves, long before they have reached the age of legal majority. Many young people work and earn money and collect it and spend it oftentimes without any oversight or restriction. The law does not question their right to buy if they have the money to pay for their purchases. It seems intolerably burdensome for everyone concerned if merchants and businesspeople cannot deal with them safely, in a fair and reasonable way.

*   *   *   *   *

We note that in this case, some nine months after the date of purchase, the truck purchased by the plaintiff began to develop mechanical problems. Plaintiff was informed of the probable nature of the difficulty, which apparently involved internal problems in the engine. He continued to drive the vehicle until the engine "blew up" and the truck became inoperable. Whether or not this involved gross negligence or intentional conduct on his part is a matter for determination at the trial level. It is not possible to determine from this record whether a counterclaim for tortious damage to the vehicle was asserted. After the first tender of the vehicle was made by plaintiff, and refused by the defendant, the truck was damaged by a hit-and-run driver while parked on plaintiff's property. The amount of that damage and the liability for that amount between the purchaser and the vendor, as well as the fair market value of the vehicle at the time of tender, is also an issue for the jury.

[Reversed and remanded.]

Questions

1. What was the issue in this case?

2. Distinguish the two minority rules that are summarized in this case.

3. To achieve justice in contract cases involving a minor and an adult, what would you want to know about the adult's behavior toward the minor?

4. White, a 17-year-old high school sophomore, operated a trucking business, including hiring drivers, securing jobs, and so forth. He lived with his parents and received his food, clothing, and shelter from them. Valencia operated a garage and repaired White's equipment until they had a disagreement over replacement of a motor. White then disaffirmed his contract with Valencia and refused to pay what he owed. At trial the jury found that White had caused the damage to the motor, but the court held that White could disaffirm the contract and required Valencia to refund any money paid to White under the contract. Valencia appealed.

a. Is the fact that White was in business for himself in any way relevant to the outcome of this case? Explain.

b. Decide the case. Explain. See *Valencia v. White,* 654 P.2d 287 (Ariz. Ct. App. 1982).

Genuineness of Assent

Sometimes parties appear to have concluded a binding contract, but the courts will allow them to escape that obligation because they had not, in fact, achieved an agreement. They had achieved the appearance of agreement, but not the reality. That situation arises when the contract is the product of misrepresentation, fraud, duress, undue influence, or mistake. Ordinarily, such agreements are voidable and may be rescinded because of the absence of genuine assent, the fourth of five ingredients in a binding contract.

Misrepresentation and Fraud

An innocent untruth is a *misrepresentation.* Intentional untruths constitute *fraud.* In either case, a party to a contract who has been deceived may rescind the deal, and restitution may be secured if benefits were extended to the party issuing the untruth. The test for fraud is as follows:

1. Misrepresentation of a material fact.

2. The misrepresentation was intentional.

3. The injured party justifiably relied on the misrepresentation.

4. Injury resulted.

Note that the test requires a misrepresented fact. In general, misrepresented opinions are not grounds for action; but many courts are now recognizing exceptions to that rule, especially when the innocent party has relied on opinion coming from an expert.

Is the Guru a Fraud?

Fourteen former disciples of self-proclaimed yoga guru Amrit Desai sued their former leader for losses suffered when Desai was found (according to the followers' allegations) to be a charlatan. The plaintiffs resided and labored for many years at Kripalu Ashram, a yoga retreat in

Lenox, Massachusetts. They contributed money. They received little compensation for their extensive labor. Desai promoted and claimed to follow a celibate and ascetic lifestyle. The plaintiffs committed themselves to Desai and emulated his principles until they discovered that Desai had, in fact, routinely engaged in sexual relations and had accumulated considerable wealth. Fraud was one of the plaintiffs' claims. Defend Desai against the fraud allegation. Decide. See *Dushkin v. Desai,* 18 F. Supp. 2d 117 (U.S. Dist. Ct. Mass. 1998).

Duress

Sometimes genuine assent is not secured and a contract may be rescinded because one of the parties was forced to agree. Fear lies at the heart of a *duress* claim. The party seeking to escape the contract would have to establish that a wrongful act was threatened or had occurred, causing the party to enter the contract out of fear of harm such that free will was precluded. Increasingly, courts are also setting aside contracts on the grounds of economic duress. For example, suppose you know that one of your regular customers depends on your timely delivery of steel to his factory and that he cannot expeditiously find an alternative supply. Therefore, you tell your customer that delivery will be delayed until he agrees to pay a higher price for the steel. If he agrees, the resulting contract probably could be rescinded on the grounds of economic duress.

Undue Influence

Under some circumstances, the first party to an apparent contract can escape its terms by demonstrating that the second party so dominated her will that she (the first party) did not act independently. These claims are most common in cases involving those who are old or infirm and who lose their independence of thought and action to the *undue-influence* of a caregiver or adviser.

Mistake

Most of us, on taking a new job, operate at least for a time in fear that we will make a mistake. Assume you are new to your job and are preparing a bid that your company will submit in hopes of securing the general maintenance contract for a large office building. In preparing the bid, you inadvertently submit a final price of $50,000 rather than $500,000. What happens? Do you lose your job?

In some cases, mistakes involving critical facts can be grounds for rescinding contracts. A *mutual mistake* is one in which both parties to the contract are in error about some critical fact. With exceptions, either party can rescind those contracts because genuine assent was not achieved. Your erroneous bid, however, is a *unilateral mistake;* that is, only one party to the contract made an error. The general rule is that those contracts cannot be rescinded. However, if you are able to show that the other party to the contract knew or should have known about your mistake, many courts would allow you to rescind. Certainly you would make that argument in this instance because the $50,000 bid is presumably dramatically out of line with the other bids and at odds with reasonable business expectations about the value of the contract. In cases where an error is made in *drafting* a contract, and both parties are unaware of the error (a mutual mistake), the courts will reform the contract rather than void it. That is, the contract will be rewritten to reflect what the parties actually intended.

$1.86 Round-trip on US Air

US Airways sold about 1,000 round-trip tickets in a few hours on April 23, 2005, when it posted $1.86 round-trip fares at eight airports. Most of the flights were in and out of smaller cities such as Watertown, New York and Lebanon, New Hampshire. The price was the result of a computer glitch and was corrected as soon as executives discovered the problem. Many fliers used the tickets to build frequent flier miles. Ticket price errors throughout the industry reportedly happen a few times per year.

1. As a matter of business practice, how would you have dealt with this situation had you been in charge at US Airways?
2. As a matter of law, was US Airways obligated to honor the tickets in question?

Source: Washington Post, "US Airways' $1.86 Flights Are Too Good a Deal to Last," *Waterloo/Cedar Falls Courier,* April 24, 2005, p. E8.

Legality of Purpose

Having examined agreement, consideration, capacity, and genuineness of assent, we turn now to the final requirement for the creation of a binding contract: legality of purpose (see Figure 6.2). *Illegality* refers to bargains to commit a crime or a tort (such as a deal with a coworker to embezzle funds from one's employer); but more broadly, illegality involves bargains that are forbidden by statute or violate public policy. We can identify three general categories of illegal agreements: (1) contracts that violate statutes, (2) contracts that are unconscionable, and (3) contracts that violate public policy. In general, the effect of an illegal contract is that it cannot be enforced, and the courts will not provide a remedy if its terms are unfulfilled. With exceptions, the parties to illegal deals are left where the courts find them.

1. ***Contracts violating statutes*** As noted, a contract to commit a crime or a tort is illegal and unenforceable. The states have also specified certain other agreements that are illegal. Those provisions vary from state to state, but they commonly include antigambling laws, laws forbidding the conduct of certain kinds of business on Sundays

FIGURE 6.2
Five Requirements of a Binding Contract

1. Agreement
2. Consideration
3. Capacity
4. Genuineness of assent
5. Legality of purpose

(*blue laws*), laws forbidding *usury,* and laws forbidding the practice of certain professions (law, real estate, hair care) without a license.

Who Owns the BMW?

Ryno owned Bavarian Motors in Fort Worth, Texas. In 1981 Ryno agreed to sell a 1980 BMW M-l to Tyra for $125,000. Ryno then proposed a double-or-nothing coin flip for the car. Tyra agreed and won the coin flip. Ryno then handed Tyra the keys to the car, saying, "It's yours," while handing the "German title" to the car to Tyra. On several occasions Tyra took the BMW to Ryno for servicing. The car was routinely returned to Tyra until 1982 when Ryno kept the car and sold it. Tyra sued Ryno. Who wins? Explain. See *Ryno v. Tyra,* 752 S.W.2d 148 (Tx. Ct. App. 1988).

---

2. *Unconscionable contracts.* Certain agreements are so thoroughly one-sided that fairness precludes enforcing them. Problems of *unconscionability* often arise in situations in which the bargaining power of one of the parties is much superior to the other—where one can, in effect, "twist the arm" or otherwise take advantage of the other. Both the common law of contracts and UCC 2-302 give the courts the power to modify or refuse to enforce such deals.

> Certain agreements are so thoroughly one-sided that fairness precludes enforcing them.

3. *Public policy.* The courts may decline to enforce certain otherwise binding contracts because to do so would not be in the best interest of the public. For example, an agreement between the local convenience stores to charge $1.90 for a gallon of regular gasoline would be a restraint of trade (price fixing) and as such would be contrary to public policy and to antitrust laws (see Chapter 10) and thus would be unenforceable. Similarly, suppose as a condition of being hired for a job you must sign an agreement providing that you will not leave your employer to work for one of your employer's competitors. These *noncompete clauses* (see Chapter 12) are common and may be fully lawful depending largely on whether the time and geographic restrictions imposed are reasonable. If unreasonable, the courts will either not enforce the clause or will alter it to achieve a fair result.

> If you own or manage a potentially hazardous activity such as a water slide, bungee tower, or even a health spa, you may try to protect yourself from litigation should a customer be hurt by including a release in the customer agreement.

Another commonplace public policy concern is the *exculpatory clause* or *release.* If you own or manage a potentially hazardous activity such as a water slide, bungee tower, or even a health spa, you may try to protect yourself from litigation should a customer be hurt by including a release in the customer agreement. Theoretically, such agreements are enforceable in the manner of any other contractual provision. However, the courts tend to disfavor them. The result is that sometimes they are enforced, and sometimes they are not. Many factors can influence that decision, including how sweeping the exculpation is, whether it was knowingly entered, and the relative bargaining power of the parties. The case that follows examines exculpatory clauses in greater detail.

Seigneur v. National Fitness Institute, Inc.

752 A.2d 631 (Ct. Spec. App. Md. 2000)

Judge Salmon

On September 4, 1998, Gerilynne Seigneur and her husband James filed a complaint in the Circuit Court for Montgomery County against National Fitness Institute, Inc. ("NFI"). The Seigneurs asserted that Ms. Seigneur was injured as a result of NFI's negligence while she was undergoing an initial evaluation at a fitness club owned and operated by NFI. NFI filed a motion to dismiss the complaint based on an exculpatory clause found in its contract with Ms. Seigneur. The motion for summary judgment was granted, and the Seigneurs filed this appeal in which they presented a single issue: Does the exculpatory clause in the agreement entered into by the parties validly release NFI from all liability for injuries to Ms. Seigneur caused by NFI's negligence?

I. FACTUAL BACKGROUND

NFI is a Maryland corporation operating an exercise and fitness facility. On January 30, 1996, Seigneur, after deciding to begin a weight loss and fitness program, joined NFI on a one-month trial basis. . . .

When she signed her membership contract, Seigneur had a history of serious lower back problems, including a herniated disc. Moreover, her general physical condition was poor. These facts were disclosed to NFI prior to the accident.

As part of the application process, Seigneur was required to complete and sign a document entitled "National Fitness, Inc., Health Programs Participation Agreement" ("the Participation Agreement"). Besides informing the customer of NFI's payment and fee collection policies, this agreement contained the following clause:

> Important Information: I, the undersigned applicant, agree and understand that I must report any and all injuries immediately to NFI, Inc., staff. It is further agreed that all exercises shall be undertaken by me at my sole risk and that NFI, Inc., shall not be liable to me for any claims, demands, injuries, damages, actions, or courses of action whatsoever, to my person or property arising out of or connecting with the use of the services and facilities of NFI, Inc., by me, or to the premises of NFI, Inc. Further, I do expressly hereby forever release and discharge NFI, Inc., from all claims, demands, injuries, damages, actions, or courses of action, and from all acts of active or passive negligence on the part of NFI, Inc., its servants, agents, or employees.

Seigneur signed the Participation Agreement on January 30, 1996. Kim Josties, an NFI employee, then performed an initial evaluation of Seigneur, in which Seigneur was first directed to perform various flexibility tests. Josties next directed her to the weight machines for strength testing. Seigneur worked on the leg extension machine and then the bench press. She made no complaints after using either of these devices. Seigneur next used an upper torso weight machine. Josties placed a 90-pound weight on this machine and instructed Seigneur to lift this weight once with her arms. While attempting to lift this load, Seigneur felt a tearing or ripping sensation in her right shoulder. She instantly reported this to Josties, but the instructor did not seek immediate medical attention. Instead, Josties had Seigneur proceed to the next machine, and shortly thereafter, the initial evaluation was completed.

Seigneur claims that since this incident, she has had pain and difficulty using her shoulder. In addition, she has undergone shoulder surgery for a condition that her doctor attributed to the use of NFI's upper torso machine.

* * * * *

II. ANALYSIS

A. Validity of the Exculpatory Clause

To decide this case, we must first determine whether the exculpatory clause unambiguously excused NFI's negligence.

* * * * *

In Maryland, for an exculpatory clause to be valid, it "need not contain or use the word 'negligence' or any other 'magic words.'" An exculpatory clause "is sufficient to insulate the party from his or her own negligence 'as long as [its] language . . . clearly and specifically indicates the intent to release the defendant from liability for personal injury caused by the defendant's negligence. . . .'"

In the instant case, there is no suggestion that the agreement between NFI and Seigneur was the product of fraud, mistake, undue influence, overreaching, or the like. The exculpatory clause unambiguously provides that Seigneur "expressly hereby forever releases and discharges NFI, Inc., from all claims, demands, injuries, damages, actions, or courses of action, and from all acts of active or passive negligence on the part of NFI, Inc., its servants, agents, or employees." Under these circumstances, we hold that this contract provision expresses a clear intention by the parties to release NFI from liability for all acts of negligence.

* * * * *

B. Public Policy Exception

More than 100 years ago, it was noted that "the right of parties to contract as they please is restricted only by a few well-defined and well-settled rules, and it must be a very plain case to justify a court in holding a contract to be against public policy."

* * * * *

Three exceptions have been identified where the public interest will render an exculpatory clause unenforceable. They are (1) when the party protected by the clause intentionally causes harm or engages in acts of reckless, wanton, or gross negligence; (2) when the bargaining power of one party to the contract is so grossly unequal as to put that party at the mercy of the other's negligence; and (3) when the transaction involves the public interest.

Seigneur has not alleged that NFI's agents intentionally caused her harm, or engaged in reckless, wanton, or gross acts of negligence. She does assert, however, that the second and third exceptions are applicable.

Appellants argue that NFI "possesses a decisive advantage in bargaining strength against members of the public who seek to use its services."

* * * * *

[T]here were numerous other competitors providing the same nonessential services as NFI. The exculpatory clause was prominently displayed in the Participation Agreement, and Seigneur makes no claim that she was unaware of this provision prior to her injury.

To possess a decisive bargaining advantage over a customer, the service offered must usually be deemed essential in nature. . . .

[I]n *Shields v. Sta-Fit, Inc.,* the Court pointed out that

> Health clubs are a good idea and no doubt contribute to the health of the individual participants and the community at large. But ultimately, they are not essential to the state or its citizens. And any analogy to schools, hospitals, housing (public or private), and public utilities therefore fails. Health clubs do not provide essential services.

We agree. . . .

* * * * *

NFI does not provide an essential public service such that an exculpatory clause would be "patently offensive" to the citizens of Maryland. The services offered by a health club are not of great importance or of practical necessity to the public as a whole. Nor is a health club anywhere near as socially important as institutions or businesses such as innkeepers, public utilities, common carriers, or schools.

* * * * *

[C]ourts from other jurisdictions almost universally have held that contracts relating to recreational activities do not fall within any of the categories that implicate public interest concerns.

Judgment affirmed

* * * * *

Questions

1. According to the *Seigneur* court, under what three circumstances might an exculpatory clause be unenforceable?

2. NFI's exculpatory clause had the effect of excusing the fitness club from its own negligence. Why did the court enforce that clause?

3. *a.* Would a release like that in *Seigneur* be enforceable if it involved a school district excusing itself from liability for any injury that might befall students on a class field trip? Explain.

   b. What if the school release sought to excuse the school not from its own negligence, but merely from events beyond the school's control? Explain.

4. Ning Yan went to Gay's fitness center to use a one-week complimentary pass. On each visit he signed in on a sheet that contained a standard exculpatory clause including this language: "I also understand that Vital Power Fitness Center assumes no responsibility for any injuries and/or sicknesses incurred to me. . . ." On February 18, 1999, Yan fell from the treadmill and sustained a severe head injury. He later died from that injury. No one witnessed the fall. Yan's estate claims that he struck his head against a window ledge because the treadmill was placed too close to the window. If he did strike the window ledge, who would likely win this case? Explain. See *Xu v. Gay*, 668 N.W.2d 166 (Ct. App. Mich. 2003).

Part Two—Interpreting and Enforcing Contracts

We have examined the five ingredients in a binding contract: agreement, consideration, capacity, genuineness of assent, and legality of purpose. Having established those conditions, a contract may have been created, but the door to contract problems has not been closed. Contracts often must fulfill writing formalities to be enforceable. Third parties may have claims against some contracts. And what happens when a party to a contract does not perform as called for by the agreement?

Certainly the common belief is that agreements must be in writing to be enforceable; but in most cases, oral contracts are fully enforceable. However, the exceptions are important. Oral contracts are subject to misunderstanding or to being forgotten, and fraudulent claims can readily arise from oral understandings. Consequently, our states have drawn upon the English *Statute of Frauds* in requiring the following kinds of contracts to be in writing in order to be enforceable:

> In most cases, oral contracts are fully enforceable.

1. Answering for the obligations of another (collateral contract).
2. The sale of land.
3. Promises that cannot be performed within one year.
4. Contracts for the sale of goods at a price of $500 or more.
5. A promise made in consideration of marriage.
6. An executor/administrator of an estate promising to pay the decedent's debts from the executor/administrator's own funds.

As we have noted, the state legislatures are considering various changes in the UCC, Article 2, including the Statute of Frauds (UCC 2-201—see the appendix) as recommended by the National Conference of Commissioners on Uniform State Laws (NCCUSL). Among the proposed changes, the $500 sale of goods standard would increase to $5,000, and electronic signatures and writings would meet Statute of Frauds requirements.

Failure to Comply   A fully performed oral contract, even though not in compliance with the Statute of Frauds, will not be rescinded by the courts. However, incomplete oral contracts that fail to comply with the statute are unenforceable. If a party to an unenforceable oral contract has provided partial performance in reliance on the contract, the courts will ordinarily provide compensation under quasi-contract principles for the reasonable value of that performance. Now let's consider each of the six contract categories in some detail. [For more on the Statute of Frauds, see **http://www.expertlaw.com/library/business/statute_of_frauds.html**]

1. **Collateral contract.**   Assume you have just graduated from college and a long-time family friend, Jacobs, wants to help you get started in a small printing business. You secure a bank loan on the condition that you find a creditworthy third party as a guarantor for the loan. Jacobs agrees with the bank to pay the debt if you fail to do so. Jacobs's promise to pay the debt must be in writing to be enforceable.

2. **The sale of land.**   Broadly, *land* is interpreted to include the surface itself, that which is in the soil (minerals) or permanently attached to it (buildings), and growing crops when accompanying the transfer of land. Thus if a building was permanently attached to a lot you seek for the aforementioned printing business, that building would need to be included in the written contract; but if you contracted to have a building constructed on your lot, you would not need (at least for the purposes of the Statute of Frauds) to execute a written agreement with the building contractor because you would not be contracting for an interest in land. A long-term lease (normally more than one year) for that land and building would, in most states, need to be in writing. All of these principles simply reflect the special role of land in our view of wealth and freedom.

3. **Promises that cannot be performed within one year.**   This requirement springs from a concern about faulty memories, deaths, and other impediments to the satisfactory conclusion of long-term contracts. The courts have interpreted this provision narrowly, in effect saying that such a contract need not be in writing if it is *possible,* according to its terms, to perform it within one year from the day of its creation. It follows then that a contract for an indefinite period (such as an employment contract "for the balance of the employee's life") need not be in writing to be enforceable. (It is possible that the employee will die within one year.)

4. **Contracts for the sale of goods at a price of $500 or more.**   With exceptions, under both the English-derived Statute of Frauds and UCC 2-201, contracts for the sale of goods (having a value of $500 or more under the UCC) must be in writing to be enforceable. Under the UCC, informal writing will suffice so long as it indicates that a contract was made, it contains a quantity term, and it was signed "by the party against whom enforcement is sought." Section 2-201 provides exceptions for certain transactions of $500 or more in goods in which a contract will be enforceable even though not in writing.

5. **Contracts in consideration of marriage.**   The mutual exchange of marriage promises need not be in writing, but any contract that uses marriage as the consideration to support the contract must be in writing to be enforceable. Such contracts would include, for example, prenuptial agreements that are entered prior to marriage and serve the purpose, among others, of specifying how the couple's property will be divided in the event of a divorce. Those contracts must be in writing to be enforceable.

6. **Executor/administrator's promise.**   When an individual dies, a representative is appointed to oversee the estate. A promise by that executor/administrator to pay the estate's debts must be in writing if the payment will be made from the executor/administrator's personal funds. Thus, where the executor of an estate contracts with an auctioneer to dispose of the decedent's personal property, the executor's promise to pay the auctioneer must be in writing if the funds are to come from the executor's personal resources; the promise need not be in writing if the payment is to come from the estate.

The Parol Evidence Rule

Suppose you are the purchasing manager for a large manufacturer. You entered a written contract for 50 new personal computers. During negotiations, the seller's agent said they would "throw in" 10 new printers if they got the computer order; but you failed to include a provision for the printers in the contract. Is your boss about to have a fit?

Perhaps, because you probably will not be able to introduce evidence of that oral under-standing to alter the terms of the written contract. In general, whenever a contract has been reduced to writing with the intent that the writing represents a complete and final integration of the parties' intentions, none of the parties can introduce *parol evidence* (oral or written words outside the "four corners" of the agreement) to add to, change, or contradict that contract when that evidence was expressed/created at the time of or prior to the writing. The written agreement is presumed to be the best evidence of the parties' intentions at the time they entered the contract. (The parol evidence rule under UCC sec-tion 2-202 is essentially the same as the common-law provisions discussed here.)

Exceptions   The parol evidence rule can sometimes stand in the way of achieving the purposes of the parties and the courts. Thus certain exceptions have been identified where parol evidence is admissible:

1. To add missing terms to an incomplete written contract.
2. To explain ambiguities in a written contract.
3. To prove circumstances that would invalidate a written contract; that is, to establish one of the grounds of mistake, fraud, illegality, and so forth explained earlier in this chapter.

Third Parties

We turn now to the rights and duties of those who are not parties to a contract but hold legally recognizable interests in that contract. Those interests arise when (1) contract rights are assigned to others, (2) contract duties are delegated to others, or (3) contracts have third-party beneficiary provisions.

Assignment of Rights

Ordinarily, a party to a contract is free to transfer her or his rights under the contract to a third party. Thus, if Ames owes Jones $500 for work performed, Jones can *assign* that right to Smith, who can now assert her right to collect against Ames. That transfer of rights is labeled an *assignment* (see Figure 6.3). Jones, the party making the transfer, is the *assignor;* Smith, the one receiving the right, is the *assignee;* and Ames, the party

FIGURE 6.3
Assignment of Rights

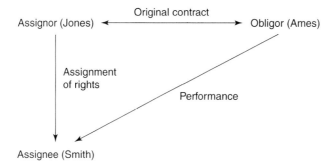

FIGURE 6.4
**Delegation of
Duties**

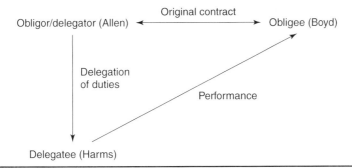

who must perform, is the *obligor*. Ames, the obligor, must now perform the contract for the benefit of the assignee; that is, Ames must pay the $500 to Smith. The completed assignment then extinguishes the assignor's rights under the contract.

Some contracts are not assignable without consent of the obligor. That would be the case where the obligor's duties are materially altered by the assignment. For example, if you have a contract to serve as a personal fitness trainer for a busy chief executive officer, your contract could not be assigned without your consent to another CEO, or movie star, or the like because the highly personal and specific obligations under the contract would necessarily be materially altered with a different client.

Delegation of Duties

The parties to a contract may also delegate their *duties* under the contract to one or more third parties. Assume Allen has secured a contract to install windows in Boyd's new office building (see Figure 6.4). Allen could delegate that duty to another contractor, Harms (although Allen would more commonly simply enter a subcontracting arrangement without actually transferring the underlying contract). A delegation of duty leaves Harms, the *delegatee,* (the one to whom the duty is delegated) primarily responsible for performance; but Allen, the *obligor/delegator,* (the one who made the delegation) remains secondarily liable in case Harms, the delegatee, fails to fulfill the duty to Boyd, the *obligee* (the one to whom the duty is owed under both the original contract and the delegation). As with the assignment of rights, some contractual duties, particularly those of a personal service nature, cannot be delegated without consent.

Third-Party Beneficiary Contracts

Normally, those not a party to a contract have no rights with respect to it. However, we have seen that third parties may be assigned rights or delegated duties under a contract. A third party may also enforce a contract where that contract was expressly intended to benefit the third party. An agreement of that nature is a third-party beneficiary contract. *Third-party beneficiaries* are of three kinds: creditor, donee, and incidental. In general, creditor and donee beneficiaries can enforce contracts made by others for their benefit; incidental beneficiaries cannot do so.

Creditor Beneficiary   Assume you decide to expand your used car business by advertising on television. Your ads appear on TV, and you owe the local station $2,000. Rather than paying the bill directly, you transfer a used car to Gleason with the understanding that he will pay off your bill with the television station. Thus the station becomes the *creditor beneficiary* of the contract between you and Gleason, and the station can sue Gleason for that money if necessary while you remain secondarily responsible for the payment.

Donee Beneficiary   When the promisee's primary purpose in entering a contract is to make a gift to another, that third party is a *donee beneficiary* of the contract. The most common of these situations involves an ordinary life insurance policy of which the owner (the promisee) pays premiums to the life insurance company (the promisor), which is obliged to pay benefits to the third party upon the death of the promisee/policy owner. If necessary, the third-party beneficiary can sue the insurance company for payment.

Incidental Beneficiary   Often a third party receives benefit from a contract although that was not the contracting parties' primary purpose or intent. For example, assume a General Motors car dealer enters into a contract to buy land adjacent to your used car lot for the purpose of opening a large dealership. You would benefit immensely from the spillover effect of the large, adjacent dealership. In such a situation, you would be an *incidental beneficiary* of the land sale contract because that contract was not intended for your benefit. If the landowner or the GM dealer failed to perform, you, as an incidental beneficiary, would have no legal rights against either of them.

   The case that follows illustrates third-party beneficiary reasoning in the colorful, factual context of a college basketball referee whose game calls incensed University of Iowa fans.

Bain v. Gillispie   357 N.W. 2d 47

LEGAL BRIEFCASE   (Ia. Ct. App. 1984)

Judge Snell

James C. Bain serves as a referee for college basketball games. During a game that took place on March 6, 1982, Bain called a foul on a University of Iowa player, which permitted free throws to a Purdue University player. That player scored the point that gave Purdue a last-minute victory. Some fans of the University of Iowa team blamed Bain for their team's loss, asserting that the foul call was clearly in error.

   John and Karen Gillispie operate a novelty store in Iowa City, specializing in University of Iowa sports memorabilia. The store is known as Hawkeye John's Trading Post. Gillispie's business is a private enterprise for profit having no association with the University of Iowa or its sports program.

   A few days after the controversial game, Gillispies began marketing T-shirts bearing a reference to Bain. It showed a man with a rope around his neck and was captioned "Jim Bain Fan Club." On learning of it, Bain sued Gillispies for injunctive relief and actual and punitive damages. Gillispies counterclaimed, alleging that Bain's conduct in officiating the game was below the standard of competence required of a professional referee. As such, it constituted malpractice, which entitles Gillispies to $175,000 plus exemplary damages.

   They claim these sums because Iowa's loss of the game to Purdue eliminated Iowa from the championship of the Big 10 Basketball Conference. This in turn destroyed a potential market for Gillispies' memorabilia touting Iowa as a Big 10 champion.

                          *   *   *   *   *

Among other claims, the Gillispies argued that they were third-party beneficiaries of the employment contract between Bain and the Big 10 Conference. The trial court granted Bain's motion for a summary judgment. The Gillispies appealed.

The trial court found that there was no issue of material fact on Gillispies' claim that they were beneficiaries under Bain's contract with the Big 10. Gillispies' argue that until the contract is produced, there exists a question of whether they are beneficiaries. There is some question of whether there is a contract between Bain and the Big 10. In his response to interrogatories, Bain stated that he had no written contract with the Big 10, but that there was a letter that defined a "working relationship." Although this letter was never produced and ordinarily we would not decide an issue without the benefit of examining the letter's contents, we nevertheless find the issue presently capable of determination. By deposition Gillispies answered that there was no contract between them and Bain, the Big 10 Athletic Conference, the University of Iowa, the players, coaches, or with anybody regarding this issue. Thus, even if the letter were considered a contract, Gillispies would be considered third-party beneficiaries. Because Gillispies would not be privy to the contract, they must be direct beneficiaries to maintain a cause of action, and not merely incidental beneficiaries.

A direct beneficiary is either a donee beneficiary or a creditor beneficiary.

*   *   *   *   *

Gillispies make no claim that they are creditor beneficiaries of Bain, the Big 10 Athletic Conference, or the University of Iowa. "The real test is said to be whether the contracting parties intended that a third person should receive a benefit that might be enforced in the courts." It is clear that the purpose of any promise that Bain might have made was not to confer a gift on Gillispies. Likewise, the Big 10 did not owe any duty to the Gillispies such that they would have been creditor beneficiaries. If a contract did exist between Bain and the Big 10, Gillispies can be considered nothing more than incidental beneficiaries and as such unable to maintain a cause of action.

Consequently, there was no genuine issue for trial that could result in Gillispies obtaining a judgment under a contract theory of recovery. The ruling of the trial court sustaining the summary judgment motion and dismissing the counterclaim is affirmed.

Questions

1. What was the issue in the third-party beneficiary portion of this case?

2. What public policy problems would have emerged if the court had held in favor of the Gillispies on their third-party beneficiary claim?

3. Jay Andreson was shopping for a diamond engagement ring at Monahan Beaches Jewelry Center. Andreson told Monahan that the ring was intended for his fiancee, Laneya Warren. Later Monahan sold a ring, which he represented to be a diamond, to Andreson for $3,974.25. Andreson gave the ring to Warren, who later discovered that the purported diamond was, in fact, cut glass or cubic zirconia. Warren sued Monahan on several counts, including breach of contract. Decide that claim. Explain. See *Warren v. Monahan Beaches Jewelry Center, Inc.,* 548 So. 2d 870 (Fla. Ct. App. 1989).

Discharge

In this section we examine some of the methods of contract discharge. Discharge can occur in many ways, but the most important of these are (1) conditions, (2) performance or breach, (3) lawful excuses, (4) agreement, and (5) operation of law.

Discharge by Conditions

Sometimes a contract is useful to one or more of the contracting parties only if some future event occurs or fails to occur. Under those circumstances, the parties may write into the contract a clause providing that performance is required only if the specified condition occurs or fails to occur. Otherwise, the duty to perform is discharged. Those conditions take three forms: conditions precedent, conditions subsequent, and conditions concurrent.

Conditions Precedent   A *conditions precedent* clause specifies that an event must occur before the parties to the contract are obliged to perform. Assume you are attempting to establish a business booking rock-and-roll acts for performances. You sign a deal with the rock group Pearl Jam, providing for a performance "contingent upon obtaining satisfactory lease arrangements for the university fieldhouse within 14 days." If you are unable to achieve an acceptable lease, both parties are discharged from performance requirements under the contract.

Conditions Subsequent   A *conditions subsequent* clause excuses performance if a future event transpires. Thus, in the Pearl Jam example, the band might include a clause providing that the agreement will be null and void if any member of the band is ill or otherwise unable to perform on the contracted evening. Hence in a contract with a condition subsequent the parties have bound themselves to perform *unless* a specified event occurs; whereas in a contract with a condition precedent the parties have no binding duties *until* the specified event occurs.

Conditions Concurrent   Here the contract simply specifies that the parties are to perform their duties at the same time. Each performance is dependent on the other. So if Pearl Jam performs as contracted, you have a simultaneous duty to pay them for their performance. Your duty to pay is conditioned on Pearl Jam's performance and vice versa.

Express or Implied Conditions   Another way of classifying the aforementioned conditions is to treat them either as express or implied. *Express conditions* are those explicitly agreed to by the parties, as in the situation where you, a concert promoter, expressly conditioned performance on your ability to secure the university fieldhouse for the concert. Express conditions are often prefaced by words such as *when, if, provided,* and so forth.

Implied-in-fact conditions are not explicitly stated in the contract but are derived by the court from the conduct of the parties and the circumstances surrounding the bargain. Suppose you contract to remove snow from your neighbor's driveway during the winter. An implied-in-fact condition of your neighbor's duty to pay would be that you would complete the work within a reasonable period.

Implied-in-law conditions (also called *constructive conditions*) are those that, although not expressly provided for in the contract or not able to be reasonably inferred from the facts, the court imposes on the contract to avoid unfairness. Hence, if you contracted to put a new roof on your neighbor's house but your written contract did not include a date for payment, the court might imply a contract clause providing that your neighbor need not pay you until the job is complete.

Whose Ring?

Barry Meyer and Robyn Mitnick became engaged on August 9, 1996, at which time Barry gave Robyn a custom-designed, $19,500 engagement ring. On November 8, 1996, Barry asked Robyn to sign a prenuptial agreement, but Robyn refused. The parties agree the engagement ended at that point, but they each blame the other for the breakup. Robyn did not return the ring, and Barry sued for its return.

1. Explain each party's argument using contract principles.
2. Does it matter who was "at fault" in the breakup? Explain.
3. Who gets the ring? Explain.

See *Meyer v. Mitnick,* 625 N.W.2d 136 (Ct. App. Mich. 2001).

Discharge by Performance or Breach of Contract

Complete performance is, of course, the normal way of discharging a contract. Failure to fully perform without a lawful excuse for that failure results in a breach of contract. The consequences of both full performance and breach of contract can be described in four parts.

Complete Performance—No Breach of Contract   Here we find the statistically normal situation in which the parties simply do precisely what the contract calls for: pay $500, provide a particular product, present the deed for a piece of land, and so on. When fully performed, a contract has been *executed.*

Substantial Performance—Nonmaterial Breach of Contract   In some cases complete performance is not achieved because of minor deviations from the agreed-upon performance. Most notably in construction contracts and in many personal or professional service contracts, the courts have recognized the doctrine of *substantial performance.* For example, assume a contractor painted a house as agreed, except that he replaced the Sears exterior paint called for in the contract with a Sherwin-Williams paint of comparable quality. Assuming the variation has not materially altered the end product and assuming that the variation was not the result of bad faith, the court will enforce the contract as written, but require a deduction for any damages sustained as a consequence of the imperfect performance.

Unacceptable Performance—Material Breach of Contract   When a party falls beneath substantial performance and does not have a lawful excuse for that failure, a *material breach* of contract has occurred. No clear line separates substantial performance (a nonmaterial breach) from unacceptable performance (a material breach). Such decisions must be made case by case. We can say that material breaches are those that fall short of what the nonbreaching party should reasonably expect—that is, full performance in some cases and substantial performance in others. A material breach discharges the nonbreaching party's duties and permits that party to sue for damages or rescind the contract and seek restitution.

Advance Refusal to Perform—Anticipatory Breach of Contract   Sometimes one of the parties, before performance is due, indicates by word or deed that she or he will not perform. Normally an *anticipatory breach* (also called *anticipatory repudiation*) is the equivalent of a material breach, discharging the nonbreaching party from any further obligations and allowing the nonbreaching party to sue for damages, if any.

An Alleged Breach and Public Policy   The brief case that follows raises many claims, including breach of contract. The case is an interesting test of the role of law. Should sports fans be able to secure a remedy through contract law when an event does not meet their expectations? The idea seems preposterous and another instance of abuse of the legal system, but consider the facts.

> **Tyson spit out his mouthpiece and bit both of Holyfield's ears**

The case deals with ex-convict and former heavyweight boxing champion Mike Tyson and his famous 1997 bout with then-champion Evander Holyfield, a fight ended by disqualification in the third round when Tyson spit out his mouthpiece and bit both of Holyfield's ears. Incensed pay-per-view customers joined in a class action seeking their money back ($50–60 each) claiming they were "ripped off" or "scammed" by Tyson. They sued Tyson, fight promoters, and fight telecasters. A lower court dismissed the complaint for failure to state a cause of action. The plaintiffs appealed.

LEGAL BRIEFCASE

Castillo v. Tyson 701 N.Y.S. 2D 423
(N.Y. S. Ct. App. Div. 2000)

Judge Ramos

Plaintiffs claim that they were entitled to view a "legitimate heavyweight title fight" fought "in accordance with the applicable rules and regulations" of the governing boxing commission—that is, a fight that was to end either in an actual or technical knockout or by decision of the judges after 12 rounds—and that they are entitled to their money back because the fight ended in a disqualification. Many legal theories are invoked in support of this claim—breach of contract, breach of implied covenant of good faith and fair dealing, unjust enrichment, breach of express and implied warranties, tortious interference with contractual relations, "wantonness," fraud, negligent representation—none of which have merit. Plaintiffs are not in contractual privity with any of the defendants, and their claim that they are third-party beneficiaries of one or more of the contracts that defendants entered into among themselves was aptly rejected by the motion court as "contrived." Nothing in these contracts can be understood as promising a fight that did not end in a disqualification. The rules of the governing commission provide for disqualification, and it is a possibility that a fight fan can reasonably expect. Plaintiffs could not reasonably rule out such a possibility by the boxer's and promoters' public statements predicting a "sensational victory" and "the biggest fight of all time,"

and assuming other representations were made promising or implying a "legitimate fight," there can be no breach of warranty claim absent privity of contract between plaintiffs and defendants and also because defendants provided only a service. Nor is a claim of fraud supported by plaintiffs' allegations that the boxer's former trainer predicted that the boxer would get himself disqualified if he failed to achieve an early knockout and that the boxer came out without his mouthpiece in the beginning of the round that he was disqualified. Plaintiffs' claim for unjust enrichment was properly dismissed by the motion court on the ground that plaintiffs received what they paid for, namely, "the right to view whatever event transpired." We have considered plaintiffs' other arguments . . . and find them unpersuasive.

Affirmed.

Questions

1. Why did the court reject the plaintiffs' breach of contract claim?

2. What is unjust enrichment, and why was that claim denied by the court?

3. The plaintiffs claim they were victims of fraud because of the suspicious behavior surrounding Tyson's disqualification. The court rejected that claim. Baseball stars Barry Bonds,

Jason Giambi, Mark McGuire (retired), and others have been accused of using steroids to enhance performance. Suppose we discover those allegations are true. Should fans be able to use contract law to sue those athletes and their teams? Explain.

4. Pelullo promoted boxers and boxing matches through his company, Banner Productions. In 1999 Echols signed an agreement with Banner giving Echols a $30,000 bonus and giving Banner "the sole and exclusive right to secure all professional boxing bouts" for Echols. Banner was to provide no fewer than three bouts per year, and Echols was to be paid not less than a specified minimum amount for each fight, but the payments could be lowered or the whole agreement canceled, at Banner's option, if Echols lost a fight. Echols lost a championship bout, and Banner said it would thereafter negotiate each purse on a bout-by-bout basis. Echols continued to fight for Banner, but various disputes over purses arose, and Echols sued. Among other claims, Echols argued that the agreement was unenforceable for indefiniteness. Decide that claim. Explain. See *Echols v. Pelullo,* 377 F.3d 272 (3d Cir. 2004).

Discharge by Lawful Excuses (for Nonperformance)

Sometimes contracts are discharged lawfully even in the event of nonperformance. This can occur when performance is either impossible or impractical.

Impossibility   After agreement is reached but performance is not yet due, circumstances may be so altered that performance is a *legal impossibility*. In such situations nonperformance is excused. *Impossibility* here refers not simply to extreme difficulty but to objective impossibility; that is, the contracted-for performance cannot be accomplished by anyone. Notable examples of such situations are a personal service contract where the promisor has died or is incapacitated by illness, a contract where the subject of the agreement was rendered illegal by a change in the law subsequent to the agreement but prior to its performance, or a contract where an ingredient essential to performance has been destroyed and no reasonable substitutes are available. [For more on impossibility of performance, see **http://www.west.net/~smith/imposbl.htm**]

Commercial Impracticability   Akin to the doctrine of impossibility is the situation in which duties are discharged because of unforeseen events that render performance exorbitantly expensive or thoroughly impractical. *Commercial impracticability* is specifically provided for in UCC 2-615, which reads, "Delay in delivery or nondelivery in whole or in part by a seller . . . is not a breach of his duty under a contract for sale if performance as agreed has been made impracticable by the occurrence of a contingency the nonoccurrence of which was a basic assumption on which the contract was made. . . ."

The UCC's commercial impracticability standard is more easily established than the impossibility doctrine of the common law, but note that only exceptional and unforeseeable events fall within the impracticability excuse for nonperformance. Mere changes in market conditions do not give rise to commercial impracticability. Historically, the commercial impracticability doctrine had been applied only to transactions involving the sale of goods, but now we see courts increasingly willing to apply it to other kinds of contracts as well.

PRACTICING ETHICS — $25,000 in Dance Lessons

In November 1959 Ryland Parker, a 37-year-old, college-educated bachelor, went to the Arthur Murray Dance Studio for three free lessons. While there, he was told that he had "exceptional potential to become an accomplished dancer." Parker signed a contract for lessons, at the bottom of which in boldface capital type were the phrases "noncancellable negotiable contract" and "I understand that no refunds will be made under the terms of this contract." Parker subsequently entered and prepaid additional contracts totaling 2,734 hours of lessons and $24,812. All of those contracts had similar language boldly displayed. Parker was severely injured in a 1961 auto accident, rendering him incapable of continuing the lessons. His repeated requests for a refund

were denied, and he sued Arthur Murray. The trial court found for Parker and ordered a refund for the unused lessons on the grounds of impossibility of performance. An appeals court affirmed that decision. See *Parker v. Arthur Murray, Inc.*, 295 N.E.2d 487 (1973).

Questions
1. In this case, did the law excuse Parker from an obligation he was ethically bound to honor? Explain.
2. If Parker did not have "exceptional potential to become an accomplished dancer," did the Arthur Murray Studio commit an ethical wrong in encouraging this 2,734-hour contract at a price of $24,812? Explain.

Discharge by Agreement

A contractual discharge is sometimes achieved by a new agreement arrived at after entering the original contract. These agreements take a variety of forms, but one—*accord and satisfaction*—will serve here to illustrate the general category. Parties reach an accord when they agree to a performance different from the one provided for in their contract. Performance of the accord is called *satisfaction,* at which point the original contract is discharged. A binding accord and satisfaction must spring from a genuine dispute between the parties, and it must include consideration as well as all of the other ingredients in a binding contract.

Discharge by Operation of Law

Under some circumstances, contractual duties are discharged by the legal system itself. Among those possibilities: (1) The contractual responsibilities of a debtor may be discharged by a bankruptcy decree. (2) Each state has a *statute of limitations* that specifies the time within which a performing party can initiate a lawsuit against a nonperforming party. For the UCC statute of limitations, see 2-725.

Remedies

> An important ingredient in successful business practice is a rudimentary understanding of your rights in the event you are the victim of a breach of contract.

An important ingredient in successful business practice is a rudimentary understanding of your rights in the event you are the victim of a breach of contract. We have looked at the elements of a binding contract and at those circumstances that discharge a party's duties under a contract. Now our concern is with what happens when one of the parties does not fulfill his or her contractual duties—that is, when the contract is breached. Remedies are provided in both law and in equity.

Remedies in Law

In general, a breach of contract allows the nonbreaching party to sue for money damages. The general goal of remedies law is to put the parties in the position they would have occupied had the contract been fulfilled. Normally, the best available substitute for actual performance is monetary damages.

Compensatory Damages   Fundamentally, the plaintiff in a breach of contract action is entitled to recover a sum equal to the actual damages suffered. The plaintiff is compensated for her losses by receiving a sum designed to "make her whole," to put her where she would have been had the contract not been breached.

Sale of Goods   A breach involving a sale of goods would be governed by the UCC. Typically the measure of *compensatory damages* would be the difference between the contract price and the market price of the goods at the time and place the goods were to be delivered (see UCC 2-708 and 2-713). Suppose you are working for a newly established computer manufacturer, and you have contracted with the Internal Revenue Service to deliver 1,000 basic laptop computers at $1,500 each, although the current market price is $1,600. If you fail to make that delivery, damages could be assessed in the amount of $100,000 ($100 × 1,000), which is the additional amount the IRS would need to pay to make the substitute purchase.

Consequential Damages   The victim of a breach may be able to recover not just the direct losses from the breach but also any indirect losses that were incurred as a consequence of that breach. Such *consequential damages* are recoverable only if they were foreseen or were reasonably foreseeable by the breaching party. For example, if you contract for a well-known local band to play for the grand opening of your new bar and dance club, you may be able to recover damages for any lost profits that you can attribute to the band's failure to appear. Those lost profits are a *consequence* of the breach. Of course, you will have some difficulty in specifying the profits lost and in proving that the loss was attributable to the band's failure to perform.

> If you contract for a well-known local band to play for the grand opening of your new bar and dance club, you may be able to recover damages for any lost profits that you can attribute to the band's failure to appear.

Incidental Damages   The costs incurred by the nonbreaching party in arranging a substitute performance or otherwise reducing the damages sustained because of the breach are recoverable as *incidental damages*. They would include such items as phone calls and transportation expenses.

Nominal Damages   In some cases of breach, the court will award only an insignificant sum, perhaps $1 (plus court costs), because the nonbreaching party has suffered no actual damages. The point of *nominal damages* is to illustrate the wrongfulness of the breach.

Punitive Damages   Sometimes when the breaching party's conduct is particularly reprehensible, the court will penalize that party by awarding *punitive damages* to the injured party. The idea is to deter such conduct in the future. Normally punitive damages cannot be awarded in breach of contract cases except when provided for by statute or when the breach is accompanied by a tort such as fraud (as where one buys a defective car having reasonably relied on the falsehoods of a salesperson).

Rescission and Restitution In some instances, including a material breach, mistake, fraud, undue influence, and duress, the wronged party may rescind (undo) the contract. The effect of a contract *rescission* is to return the parties to the positions they occupied before they entered the agreement. Generally, both parties must then make *restitution* to each other by returning whatever goods, property, and so forth were transferred under the contract or an equivalent amount of money.

Mitigation Obviously the law should penalize a breaching party, as we have discussed; but you may be surprised to learn that the law also imposes expectations on the victim (the nonbreaching party). Specifically, the nonbreaching party is required to take reasonable steps toward *mitigation*—that is, to minimize her or his damages. What happens, for example, if you are wrongfully dismissed in breach of contract from your first job after college? You are required to mitigate your damages by seeking another job. You need not take an inferior job, nor must you disturb your life by moving to another state or community; but you must take reasonable measures to minimize your claim against your former employer.

Liquidated Damages We have reviewed the legal penalties for breach and the duty to mitigate. The law also offers you the opportunity to provide some control over the penalty for breach by including in your contract a *liquidated damages* clause. Here you and the other party to the contract agree in advance about the measure of damages should either of you default on your duties. That clause is fully enforceable so long as it is not designed to be a penalty but rather a good faith effort to assess in advance an accurate measure of damages. A valid liquidated damages clause limits the nonbreaching party to recovery of the amount provided for in that clause.

Remedies in Equity

Where justice cannot be achieved via money damages alone, the courts will sometimes impose *equitable remedies*. The chief forms of equitable remedy in contract cases are specific performance, injunction, reformation, and quasi-contract.

Specific Performance In unusual circumstances the court may order the breaching party to remedy its wrong by performing its obligations precisely as provided for in the contract. Normally that *specific performance* is required only where the subject matter of the contract is unique and thus cannot be adequately compensated with money. Examples of such subject matter might include a particular piece of land, an art work, or a family heirloom. By contrast, specific performance would not be available in contracts involving conventional personal property such as a television or a car unless those items were unique (such as a one-of-a-kind Rolls Royce).

Normally the courts will not grant a specific performance remedy in personal service contracts (like an agreement by a cosmetic surgeon to perform a face-lift). If the surgeon refused to perform, specific performance probably would not be ordered. The quality of the surgery likely would not be equal to what had been bargained for; courts do not want to be in the position of supervising the completion of contracts, and as a matter of public policy, we do not want to put parties, in this case, the surgeon, in a position that amounts to involuntary servitude.

Injunction   An *injunction* is a court order that may either require or forbid a party to perform a specified act. Injunctions are granted only under exceptional circumstances. Perhaps the most common of those are the noncompetition clauses in employment contracts discussed earlier in this chapter. For example, you take a computer programming job that will afford you access to company secrets. To protect itself, the company includes a clause in your employment contract specifying that you will not take employment with a competing firm for one year after departure from your employer. If you should quit and seek to work for a competitor within one year, your former employer might be able to secure an injunction preventing you from doing so until the year has passed.

Reformation   *Reformation* is an equitable remedy that permits the court to rewrite the contract where it imperfectly expressed the parties' true intentions. Typically such situations involve mutual mistake or fraud. Thus if the parties sign a contract to sell a lot in a housing development, but the contract is written with an incorrect street address for the lot, an equity court could simply correct the error in the contract.

Quasi-Contract   What happens if one party has conferred a benefit on another, but a contract has not been created because of a failure of consideration, the application of the statute of frauds, or something of the sort? To prevent unjust enrichment, the court might then imply a contract as a matter of law. For example, assume a lawn service mistakenly trims your shrubs and you watch them do so, knowing that they are supposed to be caring for your neighbor's lawn. You have not entered a contract with the lawn service, but a court might well require you to pay the reasonable value of trimming your shrubs. To do otherwise would unjustly enrich you.

PRACTICING ETHICS) Maytag and Jobs Gone South

In 1995 the Maytag Corporation reached a $16.5 million settlement with former employees at its closed Ranson, West Virginia, vending machine plant. Eight hundred former workers had filed a class action lawsuit claiming that Maytag had lied to them before stopping operations at its Dixie–Narco vending machine plant in 1991. The Dixie–Narco employees were nonunion and were not working under written contracts; however, they claimed that Maytag had repeatedly lied to them about its plans to keep the plant open. The false promises, the lawsuit claimed, added up to an oral contract that the workers relied on to their detriment.

Maytag had spent $37 million renovating a Williston, South Carolina, factory to build soft drink vending machines. Maytag told Ranson workers that the South Carolina plant (where wages were $6 per hour lower) would supplement their work and would not result in a plant closure. Then, according to Maytag, declining business conditions forced the Ranson closing. Lawyers for the plaintiffs displayed in court an internal Maytag document that, according to published reports, showed that as early as 1989 the company had expected to phase out the Ranson operation.

Questions

1. Maytag admitted no ethical or legal violations when the settlement was reached. Do you agree that Maytag was free of wrongdoing in this episode? Explain.

2. Based on what we know of the facts prior to the settlement, do you think that Maytag breached a contract with its employees?

3. How might Maytag have been able to close the plant and yet avoid the subsequent litigation?

For a detailed account of the Ranson/Maytag story, see Barry Bearak, "Lost in America: Jobs, Trust," *Los Angeles Times*, November 26, 1995, p. Al.

Internet Exercise

Go to FindLaw's "Tips for Contracts" [**http://profs.lp.findlaw.com/contracts/contract_7 .html**]. (1) List Reed Freeman's nine suggestions for avoiding problems in building a contract. (2) Explain the meaning of a "merger clause." [For greater detail on definitions, see **http://profs.lp.findlaw.com/contracts/contract_6.html**].

Chapter Questions

1. Wardle made a standard real estate offer to buy a house owned by Kessler. The offer contained a "time is of the essence" clause specifying that the deal had to be completed on or before 11 AM on September 26, 1997. Owen then submitted a backup purchase offer for the same price as offered by Wardle. Wardle's completed contract was not delivered to Kessler until approximately 11:20 AM on September 26, so Kessler sold to Owen. Wardle then sued Kessler. Decide. Explain. See *Owen v. Kessler*, 778 N.E. 2d 953 (App. Ct. Mass. 2002).

2. A Peoples Group representative interviewed Hawley in Missouri. Hawley and Peoples completed a contract (signed by Hawley in Missouri and Peoples' president in Florida) for Hawley to recruit students in Missouri to attend a Peoples college in Florida. Hawley was to be paid a commission for the students he recruited. Hawley was to be able to participate in the Peoples health and life insurance plans, and Peoples was to provide the appropriate payroll taxes for Social Security and so forth. Hawley was to maintain certain licenses and insurance coverage, to exclusively represent Peoples' interests, and to complete Peoples' training program. Hawley was never physically present in Florida. Following training, Hawley was shot and killed while attempting to make one of his first calls in Missouri. Hawley's heirs sought Florida workers' compensation. Peoples said they could not be responsible for workers' compensation payments for Hawley's heirs because Peoples and Hawley had not entered a completed, binding contract.
   a. Explain Peoples' contract argument.
   b. Did the parties achieve a binding contract? Explain. See *Peoples Group v. Hawley*, 804 So. 2d 561 (Fla. Ct. App., 1st Dist. 2002).

3. Allen M. Campbell Co. sought a contract to build houses for the U.S. Navy. Approximately one-half hour before the housing bids were due, Virginia Metal Industries

quoted Campbell Co. a price of $193,121 to supply the necessary doors and frames. Campbell, using the Virginia Metal quote, entered a bid and won the contract. Virginia Metal refused to supply the necessary doors, and Campbell had to secure an alternative source of supply at a price $45,562 higher than Virginia Metal's quote. Campbell sued. Explain Campbell's claim. Defend Virginia Metal. Decide. See *Allen M. Campbell Co. Inc. v. Virginia Metal Industries,* 708 F.2d 930 (4th Cir. 1983).

4. The Great Minneapolis Surplus Store placed a newspaper ad saying, "Saturday 9:00 AM sharp. 3 Brand New Fur Coats. Worth $100.00. First Come. First Served. $1 each." Lefkowitz was the first customer at the store that Saturday. He demanded a coat and indicated his readiness to pay the dollar, but the store refused saying it was a "house rule" that the coats were intended for women customers only. Lefkowitz sued. Express the issue(s) in this case. Defend Great Minneapolis. Decide. Explain. See *Lefkowitz v. Great Minneapolis Surplus Store,* 86 N.W.2d 689 (Minn. S. Ct. 1957).

5. Rose Elsten and Donald Cook lived together in Tucson, Arizona, from 1969 to 1981. They were not married, but Rose used Donald's last name, and they represented themselves as husband and wife. They had two joint bank accounts. They jointly owned a house, two cars, and some shares of stock. When Rose left Donald in 1981 she received a few hundred dollars and one car, and Donald retained the balance of the property. She sued Donald on the grounds that he had breached their agreement to share their assets equally. She argued, "[E]verything we did and purchased . . . was together as husband and wife. It was just something that we agreed on." If an agreement existed, did it violate public policy? Decide Rose's lawsuit. Explain. See *Cook v. Cook,* 691 P.2d 664 (Ariz. S.Ct. 1984).

6. Sherwood agreed to purchase a cow, Rose 2d of Aberlone, from Walker at a price of 5½ cents per pound (about $80). The parties believed the cow to be barren. Sherwood came to Walker's farm to collect the cow, but at that point it was obvious that Rose was pregnant. Walker refused to give over the cow, which was then worth $750–1,000. Sherwood sued. Should he get the cow? Explain. See *Sherwood v. Walker,* 33 N.W. 919 (Mich. S. Ct. 1887).

7. Weaver leased a service station from American Oil. The lease included a clause providing that Weaver would hold American Oil harmless for any negligence by American on the premises. Weaver and an employee were burned when an American Oil employee accidentally sprayed gasoline at Weaver's station. Weaver had one and one-half years of high school education. The trial record provides no evidence that Weaver read the lease, that American's agent asked him to read it, or that Weaver's attention was drawn to the "hold harmless" clause. The clause was in fine print and contained no title heading. Is the contract enforceable against Weaver? Explain. See *Weaver v. American Oil Co.,* 276 N.E.2d 144 (Ind. S. Ct. 1971).

8. Edward Sherman wanted to sell his business, Adgraphics. He retained V.R. Brokers as an agent for the sale. On December 5, 1985, William Lyon offered $75,000 for the business. Later that day, Sherman signed a counteroffer to sell for $80,000. On December 7 at 11:35 AM Lyon signed the counteroffer, and around noon he took it to Brokers. At about 9 AM that same day, Sherman told Brokers' principal, Robert Renault, that he had decided to cancel his counteroffer. Renault told Lyon of that

decision immediately before Lyon handed the signed counteroffer to Renault. Lyon then sued for breach of contract. Decide. Explain. See *Lyon v. Adgraphics,* 540 A.2d 398 (Conn. Ct. App. 1988).

9. A building was rented "for use as a saloon" under an eight-year lease. Five years thereafter the state passed a law making the sale of liquor illegal. The renter, a brewery, argued that it no longer had any duties under the contract. Was the brewery correct? Explain. See *Heart v. East Tennessee Brewing Co.,* 113 S.W. 364 (Tenn. S. Ct. 1908).

10. The La Gasse Company contracted with the City of Fort Lauderdale to renovate one of the city's swimming pools. When the job was nearly complete, vandals severely damaged the pool and most of the work had to be redone. La Gasse sought additional compensation, which the city refused. La Gasse sued, claiming that the subject matter of the contract had been destroyed, thus discharging it from responsibility. Therefore, when it repeated the work, additional compensation was warranted. Decide. Explain. See *La Gasse Pool Construction Co. v. City of Fort Lauderdale,* 288 So. 2d 273 (Fla. Ct. App., 4th Dist. 1974).

11. After 10 PM some grocery stores in Iowa City, Iowa, refused to sell mustard, eggs, or toilet paper to younger customers. The concern was that the goods would be used by pranksters for "decorating" cars and houses rather than for more conventional consumption. Were the stores guilty of breach of contract when they declined to sell? Explain.

12. Patricia Niehaus, an employee of Delaware Valley Medical Center, requested and was granted a nine-month leave. The Medical Center employee handbook provided that any employee granted a leave could return to the same, or similar, job. The handbook also said that either party could terminate the employment relationship at any time and that the handbook did not constitute a contract. Upon completing her leave, Niehaus was denied a job of any kind with the Medical Center. Niehaus sued for breach of contract. Explain the Medical Center's defense. Decide. Explain. See *Niehaus v. Delaware Valley Medical Center,* 631 A.2d 1314 (Super. Ct. Pa. 1993), and *Delaware Valley Medical Center v. Niehaus,* 649 A.2d 433 (Pa. S.Ct. 1994).

Business Torts and Product Liability

"It was like a gust. It just came at me." (Deanine) Busche, a former University of Iowa student, told jurors. . . . "I knew my hair had caught on fire. . . . I remember smelling it. I don't know if I was blown to the ground . . . or if I threw myself on the ground."

The Facts Busche was testifying in her civil suit seeking $2.1 million from the owner of the Et Cetera Bar along with bartender Troy Kline. Busche, 23, was one of nine people burned or injured April 18, 2000, at the popular Iowa City, Iowa, bar when Kline ignited Everclear, high-proof alcohol, that he had poured into a stainless steel barwell on the bartender's side of the bar, about four feet from Busche. As the flames initially died down, Kline poured more alcohol

> Kline poured more alcohol into the barwell and a "fireball" followed

into the barwell and a "fireball" followed, according to Busche's testimony. Kline said he had previously performed the flaming trick 15 to 20 times without complaints or injuries. Kline was mimicking a stunt he had seen during a spring break trip to Acapulco. Kline had earlier been sentenced to a year of probation and 100 hours of community service for a criminal charge of reckless use of fire. The bar was fined $500 for violating city fire codes.

The Plaintiff's Case Busche claimed Kline was negligent and reckless in starting and accelerating the fire. Busche said she had seen Kline perform the stunt about a dozen times, and he had never issued a warning. Busche suffered third-degree burns over 13 percent of her body, including extensive facial burns. The broadcast journalism major said the injuries complicated her career pursuits, resulted in over $100,000 in medical bills, and left her extremely sensitive to cold and heat. She also suffered severe psychological trauma, including nightmares and fears of death.

The Defense Busche's own behavior was called into question at trial. Busche said she grabbed her purse and moved close to the bar when she saw that Kline was about to ignite the alcohol. Kline testified that Busche had earlier talked to him about spitting alcohol into fire. Defense lawyer J. Ric Gass argued that Kline's conduct was not enough to cause the flames to roar across the bar as they did. Gass asked Busche if she had caused the flash fire herself by spitting alcohol at the burning alcohol. Busche denied doing so and said she had consumed only a mixed drink, but other bar patrons indicated that the fire flared when Busche attempted to "breathe fire" by spitting alcohol on the flames. Further, Kline's hand was not burned, but Busche's mouth was blistered in a manner consistent with burning alcohol. A combustion science expert testifying for the defense said that he had been unable to re-create a fireball by pouring alcohol on fire. When the expert used a plastic tube to approximate spitting, however, the fire followed the alcohol to its source. On the other hand, after 40 interviews, police were unable to confirm that Busche contributed to her own injuries. Gass also pointed out that Busche's life since the fire had included parties, camping trips, shopping, college courses, and an internship at a Chicago television station.

The Judgment   After nearly a seven-day trial and a full day of debate, the jury found the defendants 67 percent responsible for Busche's injuries, while 33 percent of the blame was attributed to the plaintiff herself. Compensatory damages and interest were set at nearly $1.4 million. The judge reduced that sum by 33 percent. The jury also awarded Busche $275,000 in punitive damages, 75 percent of which was directed to Iowa's reparations trust fund. Et Cetera was to pay $250,000 of the punitive damages, while Kline was responsible for $25,000. In the end, Busche was expected to receive a total of over $1.1 million of the $2.1 million she had sought.

Sources: Compiled from news accounts reported by the Associated Press, *The Daily Iowan,* and *The Iowa City Press-Citizen.*

Questions

1. *a.* As nearly as you can deduce from this brief rendition of the facts, did the jury reach a correct decision? Explain.

   b. Was the decision "fair"? Explain.

2. *a.* Was Kline's stunt a moral wrong? Explain.

   b. If a racing car caught on fire and crashed into the grandstand, killing spectators, did the driver or the owner commit a moral wrong?

3. *a.* Is the sale of liquor a moral wrong?

   b. Did Kline commit a moral wrong simply by working in a bar? Explain.

Part One—Torts: An Introduction

We have looked at the Et Cetera Bar story as an ethics dilemma. Now we turn to the law that resolves claims like those raised against Et Cetera. The flaming alcohol stunt involved both *crimes* and *torts.*

At the outset we need to distinguish these two closely related wrongs. *Torts* are civil wrongs not arising from contracts. Torts involve breaches of duty to particular persons, whereas *crimes* are regarded as public wrongs breaching duties to all of society (although, of course, they are most commonly directed at a specific person or persons). Crimes are prosecuted by the state; tort actions are initiated by individuals. Criminal law punishes wrongdoers, but the point of tort law is to make whole an injured party. At the same time, many acts can be treated either as a civil wrong (a tort) or as a crime, or both. For example, a physical attack on another can, of course, lead to criminal charges, but it can also produce civil tort claims, most commonly *assault* and *battery.*

The injured party in a tort litigation can seek *compensatory damages* to make up for the harm suffered. Those damages may consist of medical expenses, lost income, and pain and suffering, among other possibilities. In some cases, *punitive damages* may be awarded to punish the wrongdoer and to discourage others from similar behavior.

Tort Categories

Fundamentally, torts are of three kinds: (1) intentional, (2) negligent, and (3) strict liability. *Intentional* torts involve voluntary acts that harm a protected interest. Intent is established by showing the defendant meant to do the act that caused the harm. The plaintiff need not show that the harm itself was intended. The defendant would be liable for all reasonably foreseeable injuries from that intentional act.

To explain, if you run an advertisement defaming a fast-food competitor by saying its food processing does not meet government standards, but you cannot prove the truth of your allegations, you will probably be guilty of the intentional tort of *injurious falsehood* (product disparagement).

Negligence involves situations in which harm is caused accidentally. Intent is absent, but because of one party's carelessness, another has suffered injury. Thus if one of your employees is making a delivery for the printing business you are managing and carelessly runs a red light, striking another car, the employee appears to be guilty of negligent conduct for which both she and your firm may be subject to civil damages. Further, you and/or your firm might bear responsibility if, for example, you hired her knowing that she had been a careless driver in the past.

Strict liability is, in essence, a no-fault concept where one is responsible for harm without proof of carelessness. Strict liability is limited to "unreasonably dangerous" products and practices about which we have decided, as a matter of social policy that responsibility for injury will automatically attach without establishing blame. Thus if a product that is (1) defective and (2) unreasonably dangerous and someone is hurt, strict (absolute) liability may attach even though fault is not established. Negligence and strict liability are explained in detail in Part II of this chapter.

Tort Law

Selected Intentional Torts against Persons

Suppose you are warehouse manager for a plumbing supply business, and a subordinate does a poor job with some work, which in turn brings your boss down on you. In your frustration, you call the subordinate into your office where you chastise him and then light up a cigar and casually but pointedly blow smoke in his face. Could he sue you for your insulting behavior? Let's look at the law in this area.

> In your frustration, you light up a cigar and casually but pointedly blow smoke in his face.

Battery

Intentionally touching another in a harmful or offensive way without legal justification or the consent of that person is a *battery*. Merely touching another's clothing or touching an occupied car may constitute a battery. Assuming no allergic response, our example of cigar smoke in the victim's face may not be physically harmful; but could it constitute a battery, nonetheless, if the touching was offensive? Few such cases have been litigated, but some decisions suggest that recipients of smoke may, under some circumstances, be able to successfully raise battery claims. On the other hand, in a crowded world, we cannot expect the law to help us erect a glass cage around ourselves such that we could sue anyone who brushes against us because we find all human contact offensive.

Assault

Intentionally causing another to reasonably believe that he or she is about to be the victim of a battery is an *assault*. The battery need not occur and the victim need not be frightened; but an assault nonetheless transpires if the victim reasonably anticipated a substantially imminent battery. Thus raising one's hand as if to strike another even though the blow never transpires constitutes the tort of assault if the victim reasonably thought herself to be in immediate danger.

False Imprisonment

If you have anticipated a career in retailing, you may have given thought to the problem of shoplifters and strategies for preserving your inventory without yourself violating customers' rights. The statutory and judge-made law of most states now protects store managers and owners from false imprisonment claims if they justifiably detain a suspected shoplifter for a reasonable period and in a reasonable manner. Broadly, *false imprisonment* occurs when someone is intentionally confined against his or her will; that is, his or her freedom of movement is restricted. That restriction might include being shut in a room, being bound, being threatened, and so on. Even a moment could conceivably constitute imprisonment, although simply sending a customer, for example, through a more distant store exit would not meet the test. The case that follows examines a common false imprisonment dilemma and provides an introduction to the torts of *wrongful discharge* and *malicious prosecution.*

Jackson v. Kmart Corp.

LEGAL BRIEFCASE

851 F. Supp. 469 (M.D. Ga. 1994)

Facts

On December 18, 1991, Rocky Malone, a loss prevention manager working at a Kmart store in Macon, Georgia, noticed two females with shopping carts full of merchandise enter a checkout lane. One of the females was Kathleen Bell. Malone . . . suspected that the two females were involved in a theft scheme. . . . Malone observed plaintiff Debbie Jackson, a cashier, scan several items from Bell's shopping cart into the computer and then void the items off the sale. [Jackson] then placed these items into a shopping cart. As Malone watched these transactions take place, he noticed Kathlene Bell staring at him. Therefore, to avoid arousing suspicion, Malone walked out of the store and . . . positioned himself . . . to observe the transactions through the windows located on the front of the building.

Subsequently, as Bell attempted to leave the store with the shopping carts, Malone stopped her and asked to see her receipt. Bell refused. Eventually, Malone recovered the receipt from one of the shopping carts. The receipt indicated that Bell had purchased only one item, which had a value of $4.99. The

carts, however, contained merchandise worth $834.86. Consequently, Bell was taken to a private security office in the rear of the store and the police were summoned.

Shortly thereafter, plaintiff [Jackson] was asked to close her register and report to an office at the rear of the store. . . . [T]he store manager questioned her about the transactions. Plaintiff, however, denied any knowledge of the attempted theft. The manager then told plaintiff that he could make a pass at [her] and that there would be nothing [she] could do about it. In addition, the manager told plaintiff that he wished she was white, because, according to the manager, shoplifting always involved blacks. The manager also refused to allow plaintiff to use the phone to call her husband and told [her] "that he was going to keep [her] there until [plaintiff told] him . . . the truth."

After being interviewed by the store manager for approximately 30 minutes, plaintiff was taken to the room where Kathleen Bell had been placed. By this time, Officer Jeffrey Lary of the Macon Police Department had arrived. Lary questioned both plaintiff and Bell about the incident. Plaintiff told Lary that although she knew Bell, she had no knowledge of the theft. Bell, however, told the officer that plaintiff was involved in the theft scheme. Subsequently, Lary was instructed by his supervisor to contact Magistrate Pam Rogers for directions. The magistrate advised Lary to make a warrantless arrest of both Bell and plaintiff.

On March 12, 1992, a grand jury indicted Kathleen Bell and plaintiff on charges of theft by deception. Kathleen Bell subsequently pleaded guilty to the charges. . . . Plaintiff was subsequently acquitted.

On October 27, 1992, plaintiff filed suit against Kmart Corporation for wrongful discharge, malicious prosecution, and false imprisonment.

*   *   *

Chief Judge Owens

I. WRONGFUL DISCHARGE

Plaintiff does not contest defendant's assertion that plaintiff was an at-will employee. Accordingly, as the law of the State of Georgia does not recognize a cause of action for wrongful discharge by an at-will employee, defendant's motion for summary judgment on this issue is **GRANTED.**

II. MALICIOUS PROSECUTION CLAIM

Official Code of Georgia Annotated . . . provides, "A criminal prosecution which is carried on maliciously and without any probable cause and which causes damage to the person prosecuted shall give him a cause of action." The elements of a malicious prosecution claim are "(1) prosecution for a criminal offense; (2) the prosecution instigated under a valid warrant, accusation, or summons; (3) termination of the prosecution in favor of the plaintiff; (4) malice; (5) want of probable cause; and (6) damage to the plaintiff."

*   *   *   *   *

The central question is whether the officials involved made an "independent decision to arrest or prosecute." Although a Kmart employee may have indicated to Officer Lary a desire to have plaintiff arrested, the record clearly indicates that this was not the "determining factor" in the decision to arrest. Prior to arresting plaintiff, Lary contacted Magistrate Pam Rogers. It was on the magistrate's recommendation that the officer arrested plaintiff; that is, the magistrate made an independent decision that an arrest should take place. Further, the record offers no support to a contention that an employee of Kmart offered the officer false information or exercised an undue influence over the decision to prosecute. Accordingly, because plaintiff has failed to put forward evidence sufficient

to establish that defendant "instigated" the prosecution of plaintiff, defendant's motion for summary judgment on the issue of malicious prosecution is **GRANTED.**

*   *   *   *   *

III. FALSE IMPRISONMENT CLAIM

"False imprisonment is the unlawful detention of the person of another, for any length of time, whereby such person is deprived of his personal liberty." O.C.G.A. § 51-7-20.

*   *   *   *   *

[Under Georgia law], a defendant is required to establish (1) that a reasonable person would have believed that plaintiff was shoplifting, *and* (2) that the manner and length of the detention were reasonable.

*   *   *   *   *

[T]he court holds that the indictment of plaintiff by the grand jury on charges of theft by deception, in that the indictment was based on the very same facts giving rise to plaintiff's detention, creates a presumption that plaintiff acted in a manner such that a reasonable person would have believed that she was shoplifting. Although the presumption may be rebutted . . . plaintiff has failed to do so. Accordingly, defendant has satisfied the first requirement of [Georgia law].

The second requirement [has two elements]. First, the manner of the detention must be reasonable. That is, "a person [should not] be subjected to gratuitous and unnecessary indignities during the course of . . . a detention." And second, the length of the detention must be reasonable.

As a general rule, "[t]he determination of whether . . . the manner and length of the detention were reasonable [are] matters for the jury, not the court, to determine." Plaintiff has put forth sufficient evidence to challenge the reasonableness of the manner in which she was detained. A jury could reasonably find that the actions of the store manager subjected plaintiff to "gratuitous and unnecessary indignities." Further, inasmuch as the reasonableness of the length of plaintiff's detention may be impacted by the manner in which she was detained, the court also finds that a genuine issue of fact exists as to the reasonableness of the length of plaintiff's detention. Accordingly, defendant's motion for summary judgment on plaintiff's claim of false imprisonment is **DENIED.**

Questions

1. Why did the plaintiff, Debbie Jackson, fail in her wrongful discharge and malicious prosecution claims?

2. If the court had found that Kmart had, in fact, instigated the prosecution of the plaintiff, Debbie Jackson, what proof

would be required for Jackson to win her malicious prosecution claim?

3. What facts arguably supported the plaintiff's false imprisonment claim?

4. Burrow selected two lamps at a Georgia Kmart. The salesman put the lamps in two cardboard boxes (not the original containers) with two end flaps up and two down. The salesman carried the boxes to the cashier and quoted the prices. Burrow paid, received a receipt, and proceeded to leave when she was stopped by the store greeter, who, according to her own testimony, said, "May I check your box, please?" According to Burrow, the greeter said she had to search the boxes and "snatched" them from Burrow's hands. Burrow said the greeter talked loudly, the episode was embarrassing, and the manager, when called, failed to help rectify the wrong. Burrow sued for false imprisonment and was awarded $25,000. Kmart appealed. Decide. Explain. See *Burrow v. Kmart Corp.*, 304 S.E.2d 460 (1983).

Fraud

Intentional misrepresentations of facts, sometimes identified by the formal title of *deceit*, can lead to tort claims. We discuss *fraud* in the contracts (Chapter 6) and consumer protection (Chapter 15) chapters. For now, simply note the general test for fraud:

1. A material fact was misrepresented.
2. The misrepresentation was intentional.
3. The injured party justifiably relied on the misrepresentation.
4. Injury resulted.

Defamation

Assume you are at a company party engaging in the networking that you understand to be essential to success. Still in the management trainee program, you are carefully watching your step. A coworker approaches and, after some casual talk, remarks, "I guess you have been warned about your boss, Smith. You know he can't be trusted. He lies when it serves his purposes." Language of that kind may constitute *slander*, the spoken form of the tort of *defamation. Libel* is defamation in print or some other tangible form such as a picture, movie, or video. Most courts also treat defamatory radio and television statements as forms of libel. The basic test for establishing defamation includes

1. A false statement.
2. Harm to the victim's reputation.
3. Publication of the statement. (The statement must reach someone other than the one being defamed.)

The law's interest here is in protecting reputations. Any living person or any organization can be the victim of defamation, although public figures such as politicians or actors face the additional burden of proving malice if they are to be successful in a defamation claim. *Malice* generally requires a showing of actual knowledge of the falsehood or reckless disregard for the truth. Libel or slander about a company's products or property would constitute the tort of *injurious falsehood,* which is discussed in the next section.

In general, a claim of slander requires a showing of actual harm, such as job loss. However, some statements are so inherently damaging that actual damage need not be shown. Those statements are labeled *slander per se* and include allegations of serious sexual misconduct, commission of a serious crime, professional incompetence, or having a loathsome disease. Similarly, libel, leaving a more permanent stain, generally does not require a showing of actual harm.

Truth acts as a complete defense to a defamation claim. Hence, if we tell the truth about others, we cannot be guilty of the tort of defamation, regardless of our evil intentions. Further, many statements are protected because of the circumstances in which they are made. We label these either *absolute* or *qualified privileges.* Absolute privileges to defame include, for example, remarks by government officials in the course of their duties or by participants in a trial. Qualified privileges to defame include statements to secure credit or a job. In those instances, the statement will not be treated as defamatory, even though false, unless it was motivated by malice. [For an overview of libel law in other countries, see **http://www.hfac.uh.edu/comm/media_libel/libel/other.html**]

Invasion of Privacy

A key ingredient in personal freedom is the right to be left alone. Our courts recognize a right of recovery in tort law when we are the victims of some kind of unconscionable exposure of our private lives. *Invasion of privacy* takes four forms:

1. **Appropriation of a person's name or likeness:**   When an individual's name or image is used without permission for commercial purposes, called an *appropriation,* that person probably has a cause of action for invasion of privacy. Typically this problem involves a company's use of a celebrity's name or picture without permission to imply that he or she has endorsed a product.

2. **Intrusion:**   An intentional invasion of a person's solitude is labeled an *intrusion* if it would be highly offensive to a reasonable person. Physical intrusions such as opening an employee's mail or more subtle strategies such as an electronic probe of an employee's bank account are examples of tortious intrusion.

3. **Public disclosure of private facts:**   This form of invasion of privacy bears a strong resemblance to defamation. Again, if the disclosure would be highly offensive to a reasonable person, the tort of *public disclosure of private facts* might be invoked. We believe that certain elements of one's life, such as debt payment practices or sexual preferences, are, with rare exceptions, no one else's business. In these cases truth does *not* constitute a good defense.

4. **False light:**   When claims are published about another that have the effect of casting the victim in a *false light* in the public mind, a tort claim may emerge. Such a claim would be much like defamation except that false light involves one's interest in being left alone, whereas defamation involves injury to reputation. Again, the claim would need to be highly offensive to the reasonable person. So if an employee's office was wrongfully searched, and he was led from the workplace by superiors in full view of other employees and in a manner that suggested that he was engaging in dishonorable conduct, a false light tort claim might be raised. Here truth would constitute a complete defense.

Intentional Infliction of Emotional Distress

Dismissals, drug tests, and sexual harassment cases have become particularly fertile grounds for *emotional distress* claims, although it should be understood that the courts have demanded compelling evidence of outrageous conduct causing severe emotional distress.

Selected Intentional Torts against Property

We will briefly examine four prominent tort claims arising from wrongs to property: trespass, conversion, nuisance, and injurious falsehood.

Trespass to *real property* (land and immovable objects attached to it) occurs with the intentional entry onto the land of another without consent. Trespass to *personal property* (movable property; all property other than real property) involves an intentional interference with a person's right to enjoy his or her personal property—for example, the manager of a parking lot refuses for a day to return a car to its owner in the mistaken belief that the owner has not paid his monthly bill.

More serious and extensive interference with personal property may be labeled a *conversion.* For example, if the parking lot company kept the car for months, and it suffered damage during the impoundment, a conversion probably occurred.

Nuisance is the situation in which enjoyment of one's land is impaired because of some tortious interference. That interference often takes the form of light, noise, smell, or vibration. Here, the owner is not deprived of the land and the land has not been physically invaded, but the full enjoyment of the land cannot be achieved because of the interference. If you opened a beer garden on the open roof of your bar, which is located near residences, you might well be sued by those neighbors on the grounds that the noise or light from the beer garden constitute a nuisance.

Injurious falsehood is a form of defamation that is directed against the property of a person. Thus falsely claiming that a competitor's product is defective or harmful would likely constitute injurious falsehood. As with defamation, the statement must be false and it must be published. Damages must result. Often malice must also be shown.

Selected Intentional Tort Defenses

Let's take a brief look at a few of the more significant defenses to the intentional torts that we have been examining.

Consent

Clearly, if you consent to the use of your picture in an advertising campaign and you subsequently feel that your public image has been harmed, you will have difficulty in pursuing a tort claim. Of course, if you gave permission under mistake, fraud, or duress, your consent was not meaningful.

Mistake

As store security manager, you are radioed by a clerk to "stop the guy in the New York Yankees cap" on suspicion of shoplifting. After stopping someone fitting that description, you later discover that someone else, also wearing a Yankees cap, was the actual suspect. If the store is sued for false imprisonment, can it successfully raise a mistake defense? Unless protected under state law, probably not. Having acted intentionally, you and, by extension, your employer probably will bear responsibility. Of course, false imprisonment does not occur unless the detention was unreasonable.

On the other hand, mistake can be a good defense, particularly in instances in which events happen rapidly. Say, for example, a store's security personnel broke up what looked like an assault and battery in the mall parking lot, only to discover that the incident was merely horsing around by the parties. A mistake defense might be appropriate here.

Necessity

In what we would broadly label emergency situations, one may intentionally commit a tort and yet be excused. A case of public necessity might involve, for example, a person's breaking into an unoccupied building late at night because he saw a fire burning inside. An example of a private necessity is when a defendant intrudes on the property of another to save himself only; he might thereafter raise a necessity defense against the tort claim of trespass.

Self-Defense

Suppose your career has taken you into retail management, and you have now decided to buy your own hardware store. You encounter the ups and downs that characterize entrepreneurial life, but you become particularly frustrated by the theft and vandalism that seem so much a part of contemporary small business practice. Finally, in an effort to stop the breaking, entering, and minor theft that has troubled your business, you build a trap in your store. You take up a few floorboards in a rear entryway where vandals have broken in, and you pound nails into those boards. Then you cover the nails with some soft felt so they are not visible; but when stepped on, the nails will pierce the felt and stab the feet of any intruder. Suppose your trap works, and an intruder is injured. Suppose the intruder then sues you for his injury. Could you cite self-defense of your property as an excuse? What if a police officer stepped on a nail responding to an alarm at your business? The *Katko* case that follows looks at the self-defense theme.

LEGAL BRIEFCASE

Katko v. Briney 183 N.W. 2d 657 (Ia. S. Ct. 1971)

FACTS

The Brineys, defendants/appellants in this case, owned an unoccupied farmhouse. During the period from 1957 to 1967, trespassers broke into the house, broke windows, and stole some items. The Brineys boarded windows and erected "no trespassing" signs on the land. On June 11, 1967, the Brineys attached a 20-gauge, loaded shotgun to a bed in the house, pointing the barrel toward the bedroom door. They attached a wire to the trigger and the bedroom doorknob so that the gun would fire if the door were opened. At first, Mr. Briney directed the gun so that it would hit an intruder in the stomach, but agreed with Mrs. Briney's suggestion to lower the barrel so that it would strike an intruder's legs. The gun could not be seen from the outside, and no warning about it was posted.

Katko, the plaintiff/appellee, worked in an Eddyville, Iowa, gas station. He and a friend, McDonough, had found antiques—old bottles and fruit jars—on their first trip to the Briney house, which Katko considered to be abandoned. On their second trip, they entered the house through a window. Katko opened the bedroom door and was shot in the right leg. Much of that leg, including part of the tibia, was blown away. Katko was hospitalized for 40 days. His leg was in a cast for approximately one year, and he was required to wear a brace for an additional year. His leg was permanently shortened by the trauma.

Katko sued the Brineys and secured a jury verdict of $30,000. The Brineys appealed to the Iowa Supreme Court.

* * * * *

Chief Justice Moore

The primary issue presented here is whether an owner may protect personal property in an unoccupied, boarded-up farmhouse against trespassers and thieves by a spring gun capable of inflicting death or serious injury.

We are not here concerned with a man's right to protect his home and members of his family. Defendant's home was several miles from the scene of the incident to which we refer.

* * * * *

Plaintiff testified he knew he had no right to break and enter the house with intent to steal bottles and fruit jars therefrom. He further testified he had entered a plea of guilty to larceny in the nighttime of property of less than $20 value from a private building. He stated he had been fined $50 and costs and paroled during good behavior from a 60-day jail sentence. Other than minor traffic charges this was plaintiff's first brush with the law. . . .

The main thrust of the defendants' defense in the trial court and on this appeal is that "the law permits use of a spring gun in a dwelling or warehouse for the purpose of preventing the unlawful entry of a burglar or thief." . . .

In the statement of issues the trial court stated plaintiff and his companion committed a felony when they broke and entered defendant's house. In instruction 2 the court referred to the early case history of the use of spring guns and stated under the law their use was prohibited except to prevent the commission of felonies of violence and where human life is in danger. The instruction included a statement that breaking and entering is not a felony of violence.

Instruction 5 stated, "You are hereby instructed that one may use reasonable force in the protection of his property, but such right is subject to the qualification that one may not use such means of force as will take human life or inflict great bodily injury. Such is the rule even though the injured party is a trespasser and is in violation of the law himself."

Instruction 6 stated, "An owner of premises is prohibited from willfully or intentionally injuring a trespasser by means of force that either takes life or inflicts great bodily injury; and therefore a person owning a premise is prohibited from setting out 'spring guns' and like dangerous devices which will likely take life or inflict great bodily injury, for the purpose of harming trespassers. The fact that the trespasser may be acting in violation of the law does not change the rule. The only time when such conduct of setting a 'spring gun' or a like dangerous device is justified would be when the trespasser was committing a felony of violence or a felony punishable by death, or where the trespasser was endangering human life by his act." . . .

The overwhelming weight of authority, both textbook and case law, supports the trial court's statement of the applicable principles of law.

Prosser on Torts, Third Edition, pages 116–18, states,

[T]he law has always placed a higher value upon human safety than upon mere rights in property; it is the accepted rule that there is no privilege to use any force calculated to cause death or serious bodily injury to repel the threat to land or chattels, unless there is also such a threat to the defendant's personal safety as to justify a self-defense . . . spring guns and other mankilling devices are not justifiable against a mere trespasser, or even a petty thief. They are privileged only against those upon whom the landowner, if he were present in person, would be free to inflict injury of the same kind.

* * * * *

In *Hooker v. Miller*, 37 Iowa 613, we held defendant vineyard owner liable for damages resulting from a spring gun shot although plaintiff was a trespasser and there to steal grapes. At pages 614, 615, this statement is made: "This court has held that a mere trespass against property other than a dwelling is not a sufficient justification to authorize the use of a deadly weapon by the owner in its defense; and that if death results in such a case it will be murder, though the killing be actually necessary to prevent the trespass. . . ."

In Wisconsin, Oregon, and England the use of spring guns and similar devices is specifically made unlawful by statute.

* * * * *

Affirmed.

Questions

1. Why did the Iowa Supreme Court rule in favor of the criminal intruder, Katko?
2. What classes of people other than intruders are of concern to the courts in cases like *Katko?*
3. Did the Iowa Supreme Court reach a just verdict? Explain.
4. A businessman in Cordele, Georgia troubled by small thefts from a cigarette machine in front of his store, allegedly booby-trapped the machine after hours with dynamite. A teenager then died when tampering with the machine. What legal action should be taken? Resolve.

[Did Katko win because he was a "hunk"? see **http://www.law .gonzaga.edu/Programs/Institute+for+Law+School+Teaching/ The+Law+Teacher+-+Newsletter/Past+Issues+of+The+Law+ Teacher/Fall+1996/default.htm**]

Introduction

We have examined intentional torts against both persons and property. Now we turn to tort and contract claims arising from products.

How does the law handle the situation where a wheel falls off a car, or a lighter explodes in a consumer's face? Product liability lawsuits deal with cases where buyers, users, and in some cases bystanders are injured or killed by defective products. Those harmed may have causes of action in torts (negligence or strict liability) or contracts (breach of warranty). If so, the manufacturers, distributors, and sellers of that product must then defend themselves against often enormously expensive claims. Part Two of this chapter explains product liability law and raises some of the public policy considerations that have caused critics to call for legal reforms to reduce the burden of product liability lawsuits.

Product Liability and Business Practice   "The business of making small airplanes is all but dead in this country, wiped out mainly by product liability lawsuits."[1] That 1991 pronouncement by *The Wall Street Journal* powerfully depicts the influence of product liability laws in the practice of American business. Today a key ingredient in a successful business is a plan for dealing with litigation costs. Product liability law addresses situations in which injuries result from defective products.

In the early 1990s, as *The Wall Street Journal* observed, the single-engine plane industry in the United States was largely dead. The major American manufacturer, Cessna Aircraft of Wichita, Kansas, stopped making small planes in 1986. Its chief rival, Piper Aircraft, struggled with bankruptcy. Single-engine aircraft production in the United States fell from a peak of 13,000 units in 1977 to 444 in 1994.[2] The problems were, in part, attributable to poor management, overproduction, high fuel costs, and recession; but the *Journal* argued that the chief cause was the legal system:

> [W]hat is happening now, according to practically every constituency except the lawyers, is a clear case of products-liability law eating a sick industry alive.[3]

Particularly troublesome for the small plane companies was the so-called liability tail that accompanied their products. Airplanes must be built to last for many years, but because product liability claims ordinarily have no time limit, a manufacturer could be sued decades after the plane had left its control. The result was that insurance fees skyrocketed, driving up airplane prices and frightening lenders and investors.[4]

Then Congress passed the General Aviation Revitalization Act, which offered protection against serious liability claims and limited claims involving planes that are more than 18 years old.[5] The result was a near-miraculous rebirth for the small plane industry. Piper, selling fewer than 50 planes per year, was left in the early 1990s with $1,000 in the bank, 45 employees, and no way to pay its electricity bill.[6] Then, as *USA TODAY* remarked, "salvation arrived" in the form of the General Aviation Act.[7] "Piper's liability risk fell from 64,000 planes to 12,000, cutting insurance costs 90 percent."[8] The results have been good for the company and good for the American economy:

> In a dramatic turnaround sparked by 1994 legislation that limited plane makers' liability from lawsuits, the new Piper Aircraft climbed out of its tailspin and now has more than 1,500 employees. Its revenue is expected to top $291 million this year (2001), up from $182 million last year.[9]

[For a general database on defective products, see **http://consumerlawpage.com/ resource/defect.shtml**]

Justice Although product liability law can sometimes be devastating to a company or industry, as was the case with small planes, it is often the only recourse for those wronged by defective products. The following story reminds us that product liability litigation compensates those who are harmed while applying important pressure to improve product quality.

READING | # Law Student Speaks to Class about Recovery from Third-Degree Burns

James Kramer

After a chemical explosion nearly took his life, University of Iowa law student Rich Webster has recovered.

The explosion, which was caused by a solvent called acetone, occurred in an Iowa City apartment managed by Webster. The accident left him with third-degree burns that covered 65 percent of his body.

Five years later, thick red scars cover Webster's cheeks and lower lip. His arms, which he said feel like they're covered in Saran Wrap, look like leather due to extensive skin grafting.

* * * * *

Webster, an Iowa City native, was removing carpet from the apartment. After reading the acetone container's warning label and applying the chemical, he opened the apartment's windows and doors and left for 15 minutes.

When he came back, the chemical's fumes ignited from the pilot light in a water heater. He jumped out a first-floor window and got help from a neighbor.

"My immediate reaction was disbelief, then panic," Webster said. "When I got to the hospital, I didn't hurt that bad because it had burned through the nerves. I thought I was going to be able to go home."

Webster spent seven weeks in the burn unit at the UI Hospitals and Clinics, where he underwent four surgical operations to graft new skin. When he first arrived there, doctors told him he had a "50–50" chance of surviving.

Several months after the incident, Webster filed a negligence lawsuit against Sunnyside, Inc., which produced the acetone; State Industries, the producer of the water heater; and Lenoch & Cilek True Value Hardware, the store from which Webster bought the product.

The case was settled out of court in 1994. Part of the settlement required Webster not to disclose monetary figures, but he said he received "a very, very substantial amount." The money covered all of his hospital bills, which amounted to over $250,000.

* * * * *

Webster's life has changed in a number of ways since his road to recovery started. Because the chemical, acetone, was in a container without an extensive warning label, he has grown more skeptical of companies.

Since the Webster case was settled, Sunnyside increased the warning on its acetone containers. In general, Webster said he feels warning labels need to be taken more seriously.

"If I read a label that has a warning on it, I automatically think it's a watered-down version," Webster said. "I think there's a problem with people not reading labels, period."

Source: *The Daily Iowan,* March 5, 1997. Reprinted by permission of the copyright holder, *The Daily Iowan.*

Negligence

The three major product liability causes of action are negligence, breach of warranty, and strict liability. In dangerously simplified terms, *negligence* is a breach of the duty of due care. A negligent act is the failure to do what a reasonable person would do or doing what a reasonable person would not do. Thus a producer or distributor has a duty to exercise reasonable care in the entire stream of events associated with the development and sale of a product. In designing, manufacturing, testing, repairing, and warning of potential dangers, those in the chain of production and distribution must meet the standard of the reasonably prudent person. Failure to do so constitutes negligence. Some decisions also extend potential liability to situations in which a product is being put to an unintended but reasonably foreseeable *misuse*.

Historically, consumers dealt face-to-face with producers and could bring breach of contract claims if injured by a defective product. However, the development in the modern era of multilayered production and distribution systems eliminated that contractual relationship between producer and consumer, making it difficult for consumers to sue producers. Then in a famous 1916 decision (*McPherson v. Buick Motor Co.*),[10] brilliant jurist Benjamin Cardozo and the New York high court ruled that a consumer could bring a negligence claim against the manufacturer of a defective automobile even though the consumer did not purchase the car directly from that manufacturer. Cardozo's view has since been broadly adopted, thus permitting victims of negligence to bring actions against all careless parties in the chain of production and distribution.

To establish a successful negligence claim, the plaintiff must meet each of the following requirements:

1. **Duty:** The plaintiff must establish that the defendant owed a duty of due care to the plaintiff. In general, the standard applied is that of the fictitious reasonable man or woman. That reasonable person acts prudently, sensibly, and responsibly. The standard of reasonableness depends, of course, on the circumstances of the situation.

2. **Breach of duty:** The plaintiff must demonstrate that the defendant breached the duty of due care by engaging in conduct that did not conform to the reasonable person standard. Breach of the duty of due care may result from either the commission of a careless act or the omission of a reasonable, prudent act. Would a reasonable man or woman discharge a firearm in a public park? Would a reasonable person foresee that failure to illuminate one's front entry steps might lead to a broken bone? More formally, we might think of reasonable behavior as that which weighs the costs and

benefits of acting or not acting. The reasonable person "takes precautions against harms when doing so costs less than the discounted value of the harms risked."[11]

3. **Causation**

   a. **Actual cause:**   Did the defendant's breach of the duty of due care in fact cause the harm in question? Commonly, the "but for" test is applied to determine cause in fact. For example, but for the defendant's failure to stop at the red light, the plaintiff pedestrian would not have been struck down in the crosswalk.

   b. **Proximate cause:**   The plaintiff must establish that the defendant's actions were the *proximate cause* of the injury. As a matter of policy, is the defendant's conduct sufficiently connected to the plaintiff's injury as to justify imposing liability? Many injuries arise from a series of events—some of them wildly improbable. Did the defendant's negligence lead directly to the plaintiff's harm, or did some intervening act break the causal link between the defendant's negligence and the harm? For example, the community's allegedly negligent maintenance resulted in a blocked road, forcing the plaintiff to detour. While on the detour route, the plaintiff's vehicle was struck by a plane that fell from the sky when attempting to land at a nearby airport. Was the community's negligence the proximate cause of the plaintiff's injury?[12]

4. **Injury:**   The plaintiff must have sustained injury, and, due to problems of proof, that injury often must be physical. [For a tort law library, see **http://www.findlaw.com/01topics/22tort/**]

The following case involves claims for emotional distress and product liability, both arising from the alleged negligence of the defendant.

Palmer v. Nan King Restaurant, Inc.   798 A.2d 583

LEGAL BRIEFCASE   (N.H.S.Ct. 2002)

Justice Nadeau

On April 25, 1997, the plaintiff purchased food for take-out from the defendant. While eating the food, the plaintiff bit into a used "band-aid." The plaintiff experienced physical and mental revulsion, as well as "extreme anxiety" that she may have contracted an infectious disease.

Several days later, the plaintiff visited her doctor and communicated her concern that she might have contracted an infectious disease. Her doctor attempted to alleviate her anxiety,

telling her that it was "highly unlikely" that she would contract an infectious disease from this incident. The plaintiff tested negative for both the human immunodeficiency virus (HIV) and hepatitis. Nevertheless, the plaintiff's doctor contemporaneously described the plaintiff as "having anxiety and being emotionally distraught." The plaintiff made no additional claim that she suffered any physical injury.

The plaintiff subsequently filed suit, alleging negligence, products liability, and breach of warranty claims. The defendant moved for summary judgment and on November 15, 2000, the trial court granted the motion, finding that there was no evidence that the plaintiff had experienced any physical injury resulting from her anxiety.

* * * * *

On appeal, the plaintiff argues that (1) freedom from emotional distress is a fundamental interest, and therefore recovery for emotional distress is available without physical manifestation; (2) because the "band-aid" in the plaintiff's mouth constituted physical impact, an emotional distress claim need not be predicated upon physical symptoms of her anxiety; (3) the plaintiff demonstrated, through the affidavit of an expert witness, the physical manifestation of her emotional distress; and (4) the trial court's ruling ignored the plaintiff's claims for products liability and breach of warranty.

The plaintiff first argues that "tranquility of mind" is a fundamental interest protected by the State Constitution. She contends that emotional distress is recognized as compensable in a variety of torts; only when a plaintiff seeks to recover for emotional distress under a traditional negligence theory must a physical manifestation of that anxiety be demonstrated. The plaintiff argues that the public policy considerations underlying this distinction, namely, the fear that allowing plaintiffs to recover for emotional distress absent some sort of physical manifestation would "open a wide door for unjust claims, which could not successfully be met," has not been realized. Therefore, allowing plaintiffs to recover for emotional distress, absent physical symptoms, would further a more pressing public policy interest.

In *Thorpe v. State,* 133 N.H. 299, 575 A.2d 351 (1990), we settled the question of recovery for mental distress under a theory of negligence by holding that "before a plaintiff can recover damages for emotional distress pursuant to a negligence cause of action, he or she must prove that physical injury resulted therefrom." [O]ur decision in *Thorpe* controls the outcome of this case.

Likewise, in *Thorpe* we disposed of the plaintiff's argument that physical impact rendered the physical manifestation requirement irrelevant. "While the plaintiff may be correct that [there was] impact, he did not charge the defendants with liability for personal injury; hence, he cannot recover. . . ." *Thorpe,* 133 N.H. at 303. Similarly in this case, the plaintiff, suffering no physical injury, did not charge the defendant with liability for personal injury and therefore cannot recover. Therefore, regardless of physical impact, in order to recover for emotional distress under a traditional negligence theory, the plaintiff must demonstrate physical symptoms of her distress.

The plaintiff next argues that summary judgment was in error because expert evidence was presented that she experienced physical symptoms related to her emotional distress. The plaintiff's doctor concluded that she was "quite concerned and distressed" and "anxious and emotionally distraught," and in his professional opinion, "her anxiety represented true emotional distress." In *Corso* we held that "the emotional harm, however, cannot be insignificant. Recovery is not to be permitted for mere upset, dismay, humiliation, grief, and anger. The emotional harm must be a painful mental experience with lasting effects." While we do not question the sincerity of the plaintiff's anxiety, recovery for mental angst, absent additional objectively verifiable physical symptoms, is inconsistent with our prior case law. In *Kenney v. Wong Len,* a case remarkably similar to this one, we allowed for the recovery of emotional distress where the plaintiff, while a customer at the defendant's restaurant, ate food containing a dead mouse. See *Kenney v. Wong Len,* 81 N.H. 427, 128 A. 343 (1925). However, in *Kenney,* "the evidence showed conclusively that the plaintiff sustained physical suffering at the time of the injury. Finding the mouse in her mouth made her sick immediately and so as to require the services of a physician."

Finally, the plaintiff made reference to products liability and breach of warranty causes of action in her pretrial statement. She contends that a physical manifestation requirement is not applicable to her products liability and breach of warranty claims and therefore the trial court's granting of summary judgment was in error. Plaintiff's negligence claim seeks recovery for the emotional distress that she suffered as a result of her encounter with the "band-aid." As the plaintiff has failed to specify otherwise, we can only assume that her products liability claim seeks recovery for the same psychic injury. For a plaintiff to successfully maintain a products liability claim, based upon the negligent actions of the defendant, the plaintiff must demonstrate all that is required to prove the underlying negligence action. As we have determined above, the plaintiff is unable to make a claim for emotional distress under a traditional negligence theory. Therefore, a products liability claim, based upon the negligence of the defendant, is equally untenable.

The plaintiff also seeks damages for breach of warranty. A review of the trial record indicates that the trial court did not specifically address the breach of warranty claim. Accordingly we remand for the limited purpose of consideration of the plaintiff's breach of warranty claim.

Affirmed in part; remanded in part.

Questions

1. Why were Palmer's negligence and product liability claims denied?

2. Why does New Hampshire law require a showing of physical injury to recover in negligence?

3. In your view, did the defendant have a duty to the plaintiff that was breached? If so, did the defendant *cause* whatever injury the plaintiff may have suffered?

4. Johnny Burnett, described by his mother, Sheila Watters, as a devoted "Dungeons & Dragons" player, killed himself. (The record did not disclose his age at the time of death.) Watters blamed the death on her son's absorption in the game. She claimed that "he lost control of his own independent will and was driven to self-destruction."

   "Dungeons & Dragons" is an adventure game set in an imaginary ancient world; the players assume the roles of various characters as suggested by illustrated booklets. The play is orchestrated by a player labeled the "Dungeon Master." The outcome of the play is determined by using dice in conjunction with tables provided with the game. The game's materials do not mention suicide or guns. More than 1 million copies of the game have been sold, many to schools where it is used as a learning tool.

   In federal district court, Watters brought a wrongful death claim against TSR, the manufacturer of "Dungeons & Dragons." The plaintiff's complaint alleged that TSR violated its duty of care in two ways: It disseminated "Dungeons & Dragons" literature to "mentally fragile persons," and it failed to warn that the "possible consequences" of playing the game might include "loss of control of the mental processes." Decide. Explain. See *Watters v. TSR, Inc.,* 904 F.2d 378 (6th Cir. 1990).

5. Plaintiff was seven months pregnant and the mother of 17-month-old James. She was standing on the sidewalk, and James was in the street. A truck being negligently driven bore down on the boy, running him over. The shock caused the mother to miscarry and suffer actual physical and emotional injury. She brought suit against the driver for harm to herself and the infant child.

   a. What is the issue in this case?

   b. Decide the case. Explain. See *Amaya v. Home Ice, Fuel & Supply Co.,* 379 P.2d 513 (Cal. S. Ct. 1963). But also see *Dillon v. Legg,* 441 P.2d 912 (Cal. S. Ct. 1968).

6. Is a fireworks manufacturer liable for harm to children who ignited an explosive that had failed to detonate in the town public display the previous day? Explain.

7. The mother of a 12-year-old boy who died in a shooting accident when a gun he was playing with accidentally discharged sued *Boys Life,* a magazine published by the Boy Scouts of America. The mother claimed that the boy was influenced to experiment with a rifle after reading a 16-page firearms advertising section in the magazine.

   a. What product liability claims would the mother raise?

   b. What constitutional defense would the Boy Scouts raise?

   c. Decide. Explain. See *Jan Way v. Boy Scouts of America,* 856 S.W.2d 230 (Tex. 1993).

Classes of Negligence Claims

Negligence claims emerging from defective products fall into three categories of analysis: (1) manufacturing defects, (2) design defects, and (3) inadequate warnings.

Manufacturing Defects

McDonald's sells a billion cups of coffee each year, in part because its coffee is extremely hot—180 to 190 degrees—which is exactly what its customers prefer and which, McDonald's believes, produces tastier coffee than the 140–145 degrees normally achieved at home. In 1992, then 79-year-old Stella Liebeck ordered coffee at an Albuquerque, New Mexico, McDonald's drive-thru. Her grandson, who was driving, pulled forward and stopped so that Liebeck could add cream and sugar to her coffee. The dashboard of the car was slanted so that the coffee could not be set on it. Liebeck, therefore, placed the coffee between her legs, and while trying to get the top off the container, she spilled the coffee on her lap, resulting in severe burns. She was hospitalized and required skin grafts. She sought a settlement with McDonald's, but according to her family,

> Liebeck sued, accusing McDonald's of gross negligence for selling coffee that was "unreasonably dangerous"

McDonald's offered only $800.[13] Liebeck sued, accusing McDonald's of gross negligence for selling coffee that was "unreasonably dangerous" and "defectively manufactured."[14]

Liebeck was awarded $200,000 in compensatory and $2.7 million in punitive damages. The jury found Liebeck 20 percent responsible for her own injury, thus reducing her compensatory award to $160,000. The judge subsequently reduced the punitive award to $480,000. The parties then settled out of court for an undisclosed amount. According to news reports, the jury awarded Liebeck $2.7 million in punitive damages because of what it perceived to be McDonald's callous attitude toward the accident and because of the more than 700 previous coffee-burn claims that had been filed against McDonald's.[15] [For the "actual facts" on the Liebeck/McDonald's episode, see **http://www.lectlaw.com/files/cur78.htm**]

A British High Court justice, however, viewed the hot coffee situation quite differently:

> By their very nature, hot drinks are hot. Otherwise, they might more properly be called warm drinks, balmy drinks, tepid drinks, cool drinks, cold drinks. . . .[16]

In that 2002 British case, 36 people were joined in an action claiming they had been scalded by McDonald's coffee, but the fast food giant won. The justice reasoned,

> Persons generally expect tea or coffee purchased to be consumed on the premises to be hot. . . . They accordingly know that care must be taken to avoid such spills.[17]

The divergent outcomes and reasoning in the American and British cases probably reflect both the poignant facts in the *Liebeck* case and the nature of the British justice system, where judges make the decisions that ordinarily reside with juries in the United States. Recent U.S. decisions have been divided. Jack in the Box quickly settled a 2002 case where a toddler knocked an uncapped container of coffee off a counter and suffered burns.[18] An Iowa jury, on the other hand, required only 75 minutes to find that McDonald's bore no responsibility for the serious burns suffered by an 18-month-old child who apparently tipped his parents' 185 degree coffee on himself.[19] [For a discussion of the impact of the *Liebeck* case on tort reform and the public's attitudes toward tort law, see "Taming Trouble Torts" at **http://www.sdcala.org/CALA%20in%20the%20News/cala_in_the_news02.htm**]

Res Ipsa   As we see with the coffee cases, improper manufacturing of products often gives rise to negligence claims. However, the extremely complex process of producing, distributing, and using a product sometimes so obscures the root of the injury in question that proof of fault is nearly impossible to establish. In those circumstances, many courts have adopted the doctrine of *res ipsa loquitur* (the thing speaks for itself), which in some cases permits the court to infer the defendant's negligence even though that negligence cannot be proven—that is, the facts suggest that the plaintiff's injury must have resulted from the defendant's negligence, but the circumstances are such that the plaintiff is unable to prove negligence. A showing of res ipsa loquitur requires that (1) the injury was caused by an instrumentality under the control of the defendant, (2) the accident ordinarily would not happen absent the defendant's negligence, and (3) there is no evidence of other causes for the accident.[20]

Design Defects

From Cessna's single-engine airplanes to five-gallon buckets (which may hold liquid sufficient to drown a child) to automobile seat belts and on across the spectrum of American products, manufacturers must think about designing products to anticipate and avoid consumer injury. Two principal lines of analysis have emerged in these cases: (1) The *risk–utility test* holds that a product is negligently designed if the benefits of a product's design are outweighed by the risks that accompany that design. (2) The *consumer expectations test* imposes on the manufacturer a duty to design its products so that they are safe not only for their intended use but also for any reasonably foreseeable use.

In 1997 members of the American Law Institute, a group of legal experts, approved the *Restatement (Third) of Torts,* which does not constitute law but represents those experts' best judgment about what the law *should* be. They have recommended a design defect standard that supports the risk–utility model and gives much less attention to consumer expectations. Further, a product would be considered defective in design only if its foreseeable risks could have been reduced or avoided by a reasonable alternative design and if failure to include that design makes the product not reasonably safe. That is, plaintiffs apparently would need to show that some better design was available and was not incorporated in the product in question. The case that follows involves, according to the California Supreme Court, a risk–benefit argument by the plaintiffs seeking civil damages after a mass murder.[21]

LEGAL BRIEFCASE

Marilyn Merrill v. Navegar, Inc. 28 P.3d 116 (Cal. S. Ct. 2001)

Justice Chin

On July 1, 1993, Gian Luigi Ferri killed eight people and wounded six—and then killed himself—during a shooting rampage at 101 California Street, a high-rise office building in San Francisco. Survivors and representatives of some of Ferri's victims (plaintiffs) sued defendant Navegar, Inc., which made two of the three weapons Ferri used.

We granted review to determine whether plaintiffs may hold Navegar liable on a common law negligence theory.

* * * * *

Navegar advertised the TEC-9/DC9 in a number of gun-related magazines and annuals. . . . A typical advertisement claimed that in light of the TEC-9/DC9's design features—including "32 rounds of firepower," a "'TEC-KOTE' finish," and "two-step disassembly for easy cleaning"—the weapon is

"ideal for self-defense or recreation," "stands out among high-capacity 9mm assault-type pistols," and "delivers more gutsy performance and reliability than ANY other gun on the market." Navegar also distributed an advertising brochure or catalog describing its guns and accessories, which it mailed to anyone interested and, on at least one occasion, printed in special issue magazines. In a page describing the TEC-KOTE finish, Navegar claimed the finish provided "natural lubicity [*sic*] to increase bullet velocities, excellent resistance to fingerprints, sweat rust, petroleum distillates of all types, gun solvents, gun cleaners, and all powder residues. Salt spray corrosion resistance, expansion and contraction of the metal will *not* result in peeling of finish" A different brochure advertising to retailers used the slogan "Intratec: Weapons that are as tough as your toughest customer."

Navegar included a manual with each TEC-9/DC9 it sold. The 1993 manual contained safety warnings, technical information, and operating instructions. It also claimed the gun was "a radically new type of semi-automatic pistol," which was "designed to deliver a high volume of firepower" and, "thanks to its dimensions and designs," could "be used in modes of fire impossible with most handguns." Regarding the latter claim, the manual described and illustrated several recommended shooting positions, including "hipfire at shortest range," a two-handed hold with the nontrigger hand placed on the upper part of the magazine well.

In early 1993 Ferri, a Southern California resident, bought a [used] TEC-9 from the Pawn & Gun Shop in Henderson, Nevada. . . . According to the salesperson, Ferri looked at a wide variety of handguns, but seemed mainly interested in a "high-capacity type" gun, "something relatively compact that holds a lot of rounds." He gave no indication he had previously heard of the TEC-9 or the Intratec brand. . . . Later that day, he returned the weapon, stating that he wanted a new gun instead.

On April 25, 1993, Ferri bought a new TEC-DC9 from Super Pawn, a gun store in Las Vegas, Nevada. . . . Ferri questioned [another] customer about the TEC-DC9. . . . The customer said that people at a shooting range would "probably laugh at" Ferri if he used a TEC-DC9 "because it wasn't really an accurate weapon" and that a .22-caliber gun was better for "plinking" than a nine-millimeter gun because ammunition for the former was much cheaper. Ferri nevertheless chose the TEC-DC9.

Ferri purchased another TEC-DC9 on May 8, 1993, at a Las Vegas gun show. . . .

To purchase the new weapons, Ferri showed an apparently valid Nevada driver's license and answered required questions about his criminal history and residency. All of the distributors and retailers were licensed by the federal Bureau of Alcohol, Tobacco, and Firearms, and [s]o far as the record shows, all of the transactions were legal . . . other than Ferri's misrepresentations as to his state of residence.

On July 1, 1993, Ferri entered 101 California Street carrying the TEC-9/DC9s and a .45-caliber Norinco Model 1911A1 pistol in a large briefcase and another bag. He had added to the TEC-DC9's Hell-Fire brand trigger systems that made the weapons fire in rapid bursts, and he was equipped with hundreds of rounds of ammunition preloaded into 40- to 50-round magazines. He went to the 34th floor, to the office of a law firm he held a grudge against, and started shooting. During his rampage, he killed eight people and wounded six on three different floors, and then killed himself.

San Francisco police investigated Ferri's crimes. . . . During a search of Ferri's apartment, the police found two TEC-DC9 manuals, one Intratec catalog (brochure), and two price lists.

The catalog and price lists had a single fold, which, according to Navegar's customer service representative, was the invariable manner of folding catalogs for inclusion with TEC-9/DC9s the company sold; in contrast, mailed catalogs were folded twice or not at all. The brochure in Ferri's apartment did not state that the TEC-KOTE finish resisted fingerprints; instead, it stated, "excellent resistance to body perspiration, rust," etc. The police also found "numerous magazines advertising weapons and paramilitary equipment," including *Soldier of Fortune* and *Guns*. However, they preserved only a few of the magazines, none of which contained a Navegar advertisement. Inspector Sanders did "not recall" finding "any TEC-DC9 magazine advertisement in Ferri's apartment," and the inspectors found "no evidence" that any advertisement caused Ferri to travel to Nevada to purchase the TEC-DC9s.

PROCEDURAL BACKGROUND

Plaintiffs' first amended complaint asserted a cause of action against Navegar for "common law negligence." In this claim, plaintiffs alleged that Navegar knew or should have known that (1) the TEC-9/DC9 is a "small, easily concealable military, assault weapon; (2) it has "no legitimate sporting . . . or self-defense purpose and is particularly well adapted to a military-style assault on large numbers of people"; (3) it is "disproportionately associated with criminal activity"; (4) it is "more attractive to criminals" because of its "firepower" and "other features"; (5) its "firepower was likely to be enhanced by the addition of products such as high-capacity magazines" and "the Hell-Fire trigger system"; and (6) it "would be used to kill or injure innocent persons in violent criminal acts such as the mass killing committed by Ferri." Plaintiffs also alleged that Navegar "acknowledges that publicity surrounding the [TEC-9/DC9s] reputation as a weapon favored by criminals increases its sales." Thus, plaintiffs alleged, Navegar "acted negligently by manufacturing, marketing, and making available for sale to the general public" the TEC-9/DC9.

* * * * *

Navegar moved for summary judgment. As to common law negligence, it argued it owed plaintiffs no duty not to advertise the TEC-9/DC9 and that plaintiffs had no evidence Ferri saw or was affected by a Navegar advertisement.

In opposing the motion, plaintiffs argued that Navegar had misconstrued the ordinary negligence claim. They explained that, contrary to Navegar's assertion, their negligence claim did "not depend on whether" Navegar had a "duty . . . not to advertise" or "whether there is a causal link between Navegar's advertising and plaintiffs' injuries. From the start, plaintiffs have made clear their ordinary negligence claim is not based on Navegar's negligent advertising but rather its decision to 'make available for sale to the general public guns . . . which [it] knew or should have known have "no legitimate sporting or self-defense purpose" and which are "particularly well-adapted to a military-style assault on large numbers of people."' Simply put, Navegar breached a duty of care by making the TEC-9 available to the general public," i.e., "by releasing the weapons for sale to the general public even though it knew or should have known that the TEC-9 was particularly attractive to criminals and particularly suited for mass killings." Plaintiffs concluded their argument regarding duty by asserting that "Navegar breached a legal duty to forebear [*sic*] distributing the TEC-9 to the general public given the likelihood that doing so would lead to the sort of violent criminal act that occurred at the 101 California Street Building."

As to causation, plaintiffs also argued that in light of their negligence theory, "whether Ferri actually saw or was influenced by any particular Navegar advertising is immaterial." They explained, "The ordinary negligence claim is directed to Navegar's conduct in making the TEC-9 available to the public. It is *that* unreasonable conduct that was a substantial factor in causing plaintiffs' injuries, not Navegar's marketing efforts." "Navegar's advertising is only material to the ordinary negligence claim in that it underscores that the criminal use of the weapon was foreseeable to Navegar. . . . *Plaintiffs are not alleging that Ferri was induced to purchase the TEC-DC9s or to commit the 101 massacre by any particular advertisements.* The significance of the advertisements is what they say about [Navegar's] knowledge of [its] market."

*   *   *   *   *

DISCUSSION

*   *   *   *   *

To prevail on their negligence claim, plaintiffs must show that Navegar owed them a legal duty, that it breached the duty, and that the breach was a proximate or legal cause of their injuries. The only elements we consider here are duty and causation.

*   *   *   *   *

[I]n the trial court, Navegar argued in effect that the Legislature, through section 1714.4, established an exception that applies in this case. Section 1714.4 provides; "(a) In a products liability action, no firearm or ammunition shall be deemed defective in design on the basis that the benefits of the product do not outweigh the risk of injury posed by its potential to cause serious injury, damage, or death when discharged.

(b) For purposes of this section: (1) The potential of a firearm or ammunition to cause serious injury, damage, or death when discharged does not make the product defective in design. (2) Injuries or damages resulting from the discharge of a firearm or ammunition are not proximately caused by its potential to cause serious injury, damage, or death, but are proximately caused by the actual discharge of the product. (c) This section shall not affect a products liability cause of action based upon the improper selection of design alternatives. (d) This section is declaratory of existing law." Navegar argues that this statute, by establishing a state policy of exempting manufacturers of legal, nondefective firearms "from liability for their criminal use," bars plaintiffs' negligence claim.

Plaintiffs respond that section 1714.4 "has no application to this case because it is not a products liability action." Plaintiffs assert that they "seek to hold Navegar liable for its negligent conduct, not for making a defective product," and that they "make no assertion that Navegar should be liable because the risks posed by the TEC-9 outweigh its benefits." More specifically, plaintiffs assert Navegar is liable because of the TEC-9/DC9's "negligent design, distribution, and marketing." . . . [W]e reject plaintiffs' argument that section 1714.4 is inapplicable because this case "is not a products liability action." . . . [I]n asserting that the TEC-9/DC9 had a "negligent design" and that Navegar "negligently designed" it, plaintiffs have in fact alleged that the TEC-9/DC9 is, in the words of section 1714.4, subdivision (a), "defective in design."

[C]ontrary to the assertion of plaintiffs, the record demonstrates that plaintiffs do, in fact, seek to hold Navegar liable precisely because, as the trial court stated, the TEC-9/DC9's "potential for harm substantially outweighs any possible benefit to be derived from [it]." In their brief, plaintiffs assert that Navegar is liable because it "designed and widely distributed a weapon uniquely suited for mass killing and lacking legitimate civilian uses." Plaintiffs further assert, "While the record contains abundant evidence of the disproportionately criminal use of the TEC-9, it is utterly 'bereft of any persuasive evidence that it is suitable or commonly employed for any other civilian use.'"

*   *   *   *   *

[T]hese allegations squarely fit within the risk–utility for defective design that applies in a products liability action. Using the words of the risk–utility test for both products liability theories, plaintiffs essentially allege, argue, and hope to prove that the TEC-9/DC9 is defective in design. Thus this is a products liability action based on negligence, which asserts that the TEC-9/DC9 was defective in design because the risks of making it available to the general public outweighed the benefits of that conduct, and that defendants knew or should have known this fact.

* * * * *

Finally, we also conclude that the evidence in the record regarding Navegar's promotional activities and the literature it distributed with the TEC-9/DC9 does not save plaintiffs' negligence claim. As we have previously explained, in opposing Navegar's summary judgment motion, plaintiffs insisted that "their ordinary negligence claim" was not "directed to" or "based on Navegar's negligent advertising but rather its decision to make [the TEC-9/DC9] available for sale to the general public. . . ." Thus, they argued, their claim depends solely on "a legal duty to forebear [sic] distributing the TEC-9 to the general public," and not on a "duty . . . not to advertise." Plaintiffs also insisted that it was Navegar's "unreasonable conduct" in "making the TEC-9 available to the public . . . that was a substantial factor in causing [their] injuries, not Navegar's marketing efforts." Thus, they maintained, "whether Ferri actually saw or was influenced by any particular Navegar advertising is immaterial." Plaintiffs further explained that under their negligence theory, "Navegar's advertising is only material to the ordinary negligence claim in that it underscores that the criminal use of the weapon was foreseeable to Navegar. . . . *Plaintiffs are not alleging that Ferri was induced to purchase the TEC-DC9s or to commit the 101 massacre by any particular advertisements.* The significance of the advertisements is what they say about [Navegar's] knowledge of [its] market."

* * * * *

In any event, the evidence in the record fails to raise a triable factual issue as to whether Navegar's advertising and literature were substantial factors in causing plaintiffs' injuries. Regarding this question, plaintiffs' counsel asserted at oral argument that "Navegar's liability does not depend on its telling the public, here's a great gun to commit a crime," but on its "communicating a message that people who want above all else in their weapons firepower, the capacity to shoot many, many rounds without the need to reload, and to use that gun in a combat fashion, this is the gun for you."

* * * * *

To the extent plaintiffs rely on allegedly more inflammatory aspects of Navegar's advertising, they fail to raise a triable factual issue regarding causation. For example, they offer no evidence, direct or circumstantial, that Ferri ever saw the promotional materials sent to dealers, which used the phrase "tough as your toughest customer," or the early version of the TEC-KOTE product brochure description, which promised "excellent resistance to fingerprints." Moreover, plaintiffs do not dispute that (1) San Francisco police inspectors did "not recall" finding "any TEC-DC9 magazine advertisement in Ferri's apartment" and found "no evidence" that any advertisement caused Ferri to travel to Nevada to purchase the TEC-DC9s; (2) "there is otherwise no Navegar magazine advertisement in the possession of the City and County of San Francisco as evidence collected in the 101 California Street shootings"; (3) the salesman at the Pawn & Gun Shop in Henderson, Nevada, where Ferri bought the used TEC-9, "never" saw Ferri in possession of any advertisement or literature for the TEC-9 or TEC-DC9, and never heard Ferri mention he had seen any advertisement for the TEC-9 or TEC-DC9; (4) when Ferri bought the first new TEC-9/DC9, he had no firearms advertisement or other type of literature in his possession and did not ask for the TEC-9/DC9 by name; and (5) when Ferri bought the second new TEC-9/DC9, he indicated he already owned another TEC-9/DC9. Plaintiffs have failed to produce, or show that they will be able to produce at trial, substantial evidence "that Navegar's marketing style was 'a factor in'" Ferri's conduct. . . .

In arguing to the contrary, plaintiffs cite evidence that Ferri went to Nevada, where the TEC-9/DC9 was available, to buy guns for his planned attack and that the two stores where he bought TEC-9/DC9s had Las Vegas Yellow Pages advertisements picturing, among other guns, assault weapons. Although this evidence does tend to show Ferri sought to purchase high-firepower guns, it does not tend to show Ferri went to Nevada or the stores in search of a TEC-9/DC9 or other assault pistol *in response to Navegar's marketing efforts.* The existence of various high-firepower rifles and pistols would have been so widely known from other sources (especially to a reader of gun magazines as, apparently, Ferri was) as to render unjustified any inference that Navegar's marketing efforts were a substantial factor in motivating Ferri's decision to seek such a gun. Thus, we agree with the trial court that "the links plaintiffs seek to establish between advertisements and carnage amount to little more than guesswork." . . .

Accordingly, we conclude the trial court properly granted Navegar summary judgment. In reaching this conclusion, we are not insensitive to the terrible tragedy that occurred on July 1, 1993, or the devastating effect of Ferri's rampage on his victims and their loved ones. But, in section 1714.4, the Legislature has set California's public policy regarding a gun manufacturer's liability under these circumstances. Given that public policy, plaintiffs may not proceed with their negligence claim.

Reversed.

DISSENTING OPINION BY JUSTICE WERDEGAR

I respectfully dissent. I cannot accept the majority's conclusion that plaintiffs are statutorily barred from suing the maker of the semiautomatic assault weapon used to massacre the victims in this case. Neither the letter of Civil Code section 1714.4 nor the legislative policy it embodies bars this action for negligence in the marketing of a firearm.

Complex though some of the issues in this case are, the statutory question addressed by the majority can be resolved simply. Civil Code section 1714.4 bars product liability actions against gunmakers based on the risk–benefit theory of product defect. The legislative policy behind the statute might, at most, be deemed also to encompass negligence claims that are substantially identical to risk–benefit product defect claims. Plaintiffs' claim is neither. Plaintiffs' claim of negligence is, at bottom, that defendant Navegar, Inc. (Navegar) acted without due care in distributing the TEC-9/DC9—a semiautomatic handgun combining portability and ease of use with an extraordinary rapidity and capacity for lethal firepower—to the general civilian public rather than restricting its sales to police and military units that might have a legitimate call for such a military-style assault pistol. Plaintiffs do *not* claim that the TEC-9/DC9 is defective; nor do they even claim that defendant acted negligently *simply by making* the TEC-9/DC9. Plaintiffs allege negligence, rather, in Navegar's *selling that firearm on the general civilian market knowing it would attract purchasers likely to misuse it,* rather than restricting sales to buyers with a lawful use for the tools of assaultive violence, such as police and military units. This theory of negligence, resting on the allegation that particular marketing choices by Navegar were imprudent, is not substantially identical to a claim of product defect and thus is within neither the letter nor the spirit of Civil Code section 1714.4.

The majority insists plaintiffs' negligent distribution claim is really one of product defect because plaintiffs' claim depends, in part, on certain of the TEC-9/DC9's features and technical characteristics. But not all claims involving a product's features are claims of defect. Here, the TEC-9/DC9's characteristics are important not to show defect but to demonstrate the foreseeability of injury from, and the consequent imprudence of, distributing this gun in a way that allows its purchase by violent criminals and the mentally deranged. Navegar's conduct was allegedly negligent not because its gun was defective but because, in light of the gun's known attractiveness to violent users and the lack of a compelling need for its availability on the civilian market, a reasonably careful distributor would have restricted sales to groups unlikely to misuse the firearm. Civil Code section 1714.4 simply does not address such a negligent distribution claim.

*　*　*　*　*

Questions

1. *a.* Why did the California Supreme Court rule in favor of Navegar in this case?

    b. Explain the plaintiffs' cause of action.

    c. Explain the dissenting opinion.

    d. Argue that the plaintiffs' claim did not involve a risk–benefit analysis of the kind forbidden by the California statute.

2. In your opinion, should gun manufacturers be liable for the criminal use of their products? Explain.

3. Some observers argued that a decision for the plaintiffs in the *Merrill/Navegar* case would have led to a product liability "slippery slope." Explain that argument. Do you agree with it? Explain.

4. Hollister was badly burned when her shirt came into contact with a burner as she leaned over her electric stove. She sued the store where she bought the shirt, claiming that it was defectively designed. What proof will Hollister need to provide to win her defective design claim? See *Hollister v. Dayton-Hudson,* 188 F.3d 414 (6th Cir. 1999).

Protect Gun Manufacturers?

At this writing, Congress is considering legislation to protect gun manufacturers from liability for the criminal and negligent wrongs of gun users. The bill would still allow causes of action in instances where gun manufacturers are linked to criminal wrongdoing and where the guns were defectively designed or produced. The legislation, if approved, likely would block the many big cases of recent years where cities and others have sued gun manufacturers to recover the public-sector cost (such as medical expenses paid from public funds) of injuries and deaths associated with handgun violence. The plaintiffs claim that guns are a public nuisance and that they are negligently marketed. Basically, the argument is that manufacturers know they are producing more guns than the lawful market can absorb and that they know about and benefit from a secondary, illegal gun market where criminals and underage users buy those "surplus" guns and put the public at risk. Most of those cases have failed thus far, but an interesting 2003 federal court of appeals case in California allowed victims' families to go to trial against gun manufacturers Glock and China North, whose weapons were used in a 1999 shooting rampage by a white supremacist. The U.S. Supreme Court declined to review that decision. On the other hand, a California Court of Appeals in early 2005 upheld the dismissal of public nuisance lawsuits filed by Los Angeles, San Francisco, and 12 other municipalities against members of the firearms industry.

Question

In your view, are manufacturers partially responsible for the vast societal damage caused by criminals' misuse of guns? Explain.

Sources: Ileto v. Glock and China North, 349 F.3d 1191 (2003); cert. den. *China N. Indus. Corp. v. Ileto,* 2005 U.S. LEXIS 452. *In Re Firearm Cases, the People v. Arcadia Machine & Tool,* 2005 Cal. App. LEXIS 211.

For the Brady Center to Prevent Gun Violence, see **www.bradycenter.org;** for the National Shooting Sports Foundation, see **http://www.nssf.org/**

Warnings

Universal Pictures issued warnings in 2001 that we might be hurt if we tried to mimic the car-racing stunts in its movie, *The Fast and the Furious.* The studio was trying to fend off lawsuits. Warnings seem to be everywhere in our lives. Some of them seem downright silly—so much so that a nonprofit group, M-LAW, sponsors a "Wacky Warning Labels" contest. Leading 2005 entries included these:

On a toilet brush: "Do not use for personal hygiene."

On a digital thermometer: "Once used rectally, the thermometer should not be used orally."[22]

Are these warnings of value in avoiding lawsuits? Some experts think so, but others are doubtful:

Rower McCarthy, a "human factors" engineer who studies the relationship between people and products, said that warnings simply [do] not work.

He said he [has] collected more than 3,500 articles about the effectiveness of warning labels and [has] found not a single reliable study that documented a reduction in accidents resulting from a warning on a product:

"Consumers who pay attention to warnings don't get hurt in the first place, and consumers who get hurt typically aren't the ones who read warnings," said McCarthy.[23]

A product may be considered defective because of inadequate warnings when reasonable warnings would have reduced or avoided the foreseeable risks and the failure to warn resulted in a product that was not reasonably safe. Courts might also consider the feasibility of an effective warning and the probable seriousness of the injury. The case that follows examines alcohol manufacturers' duty to warn. [For California's failure-to-warn law, see **http://consumerlawpage.com/article/failure.shtml**]

In 1983 Marie Brinkmeyer and a friend went to a bar to drink. Brinkmeyer was an 18-year-old, first-year college student. The legal drinking age in Texas at the time was 19. Apparently she was not asked for identification. She drank a 32-ounce pitcher of Hurricanes and an unknown number of White Russians. After leaving the bar, Brinkmeyer illegally bought a bottle of Pepe Lopez tequila, which was produced by Brown-Forman. At a party that evening, Brinkmeyer drank one-half of a glass of tequila unmixed with nonalcoholic beverages; then she began drinking straight from the tequila bottle. After drinking heavily and rapidly, Brinkmeyer lost consciousness. Friends took her to her room, placed her on her bed, and left her. The next morning she was found in her bed having died from ingesting large amounts of ethanol.

In 1983 no warning labels were required on liquor containers, but in 1988 a federal law was approved requiring warnings about the general health risks associated with drinking and specific warnings about drinking and driving and drinking while pregnant. That statute expressly precluded state warning laws.

Brinkmeyer's mother, Joyce Brune, sued Brown-Forman on grounds of negligence and strict liability (explained later in this chapter). Brune argued that alcohol is unreasonably dangerous in the absence of a warning. A jury found Brown-Forman guilty of negligence and 35 percent responsible for Brinkmeyer's death. Brune was awarded $535,000. Brown-Forman appealed.

Justice Yanez

* * * * *

It is fundamental that the existence of a legally cognizable duty is a prerequisite to all tort liability. Whether a legal duty exists under a set of facts is a question of law. Therefore, regardless of whether the theory of liability is based upon strict liability or negligence, the threshold question is whether Brown-Forman had a duty to warn of the risk of death from overconsumption of alcohol in a short period of time. We note that because there existed no federal or state legislation in 1983 regarding warnings on alcoholic beverage containers does not mean that distillers may not be found liable for a failure to warn should courts find such a duty exists. . . . [C]onsidering "the creation of new concepts of duty in tort is historically the province of the judiciary."

Therefore, we consider whether a common law duty existed in 1983 for distillers to warn that overconsumption of tequila within a short amount of time may cause death and whether there existed a duty to provide instructions about the safe use of tequila. . . . Determining whether a legal duty exists necessarily entails the interpretation and application of legal precedent as well as policy considerations. We consider social, economic, and political questions and their applicability to the facts at hand. Other factors to be considered include the extent of the risk involved, "the foreseeability and likelihood of injury weighed against the social utility of the actor's conduct, the magnitude of the burden of guarding against the injury, and the consequences of placing the burden on the defendant." We note that foreseeability alone is not a sufficient basis for creating a new duty. In a failure to warn case, we consider the extent to which the tort system is capable of devising an adequate warning.

In assessing whether a legal duty exists under the facts before us, we find Justice Kilgarlin's words distinguishing moral and legal duties particularly instructive:

> In spite of a societal dynamic to expand duty, Texas still follows a general rule that Texans do not owe others general amorphous legal duties. The rule in Texas still distinguishes between moral and legal duty. Although one may have a moral duty to prevent a blind person from crossing a busy street against a light, a person has no legal duty to do so unless additional factors exist. These other factors include the existence of familial or voluntary relationships which impose a duty, statutes or ordinances which may legally require action, or special circumstances, such as having placed the blind man in his precarious position in the first place.

The common law has long recognized that the alcoholic beverage drinker maintains the ultimate power and thus the obligation to control his own drinking behavior. We believe that the common law should remain focused on the drinker as the person primarily responsible for his behavior.

Though no Texas court has had to decide whether a distiller has a duty to warn of the risk of death from overconsuming alcohol in a short period of time, Texas courts have addressed whether alcoholic beverage manufacturers must warn of other risks and dangers associated with alcoholic beverages. All concluded that the alcoholic beverage manufacturer had no duty to warn of whatever risk or danger was asserted.

* * * * *

When choosing to enter the business of manufacturing alcoholic beverages, a manufacturer should make an effort to inform its users about risks and dangers associated with its product. That effort may include a larger public education campaign rather than simply labeling a bottle. In fact, education may be the only remedy we have in preventing binge drinking. Despite education, however, there will always be individuals who, though informed about the dangers associated with the use of alcoholic beverages, choose to misuse the product. The circumstances behind an individual's choice to misuse beverage alcohol are profoundly complex and will not be addressed by placing a few warning words on the outside of a bottle. . . . Holding an alcoholic beverage manufacturer financially responsible for the death of an individual who consumed a large quantity of alcohol in a short amount of time does not answer the more direct question about why the individual would consume a known dangerous product in such a quantity.

* * * * *

The standard for common knowledge is the overall knowledge common to the community that is a basis for determining a duty to warn, not what individual users may or may not know. Many products cannot possibly be made entirely safe for all consumption. The product sold must be dangerous to an extent beyond that which would be contemplated by the ordinary consumer who purchases it, with the ordinary knowledge common to the community as to its characteristics. . . . While morally it might appear prudent to require manufacturers of alcoholic beverages to place a warning on alcoholic beverages about the danger of death after ingesting large amounts of alcohol over a short period of time, we find no legal duty to do so.

Considering the extensive involvement of the federal and state government in regulating alcoholic beverages, we conclude that the subject of warnings on alcoholic beverages and placing instructions for use on an alcoholic beverage container should be left to the legislative process. The issues relevant to this case have for so long been political issues we conclude that courts are ill-equipped to develop effective and feasible warnings and instructions. . . .

In light of this political judgment, it would seem arbitrary for courts to hold a whiskey distiller liable for the foreseeable injurious effects to some people of whiskey which has standard ingredients and qualities. The political judgment would seem to foreclose a judicial holding that the recognized dangers of whiskey render it unreasonably dangerous. . . .

We understand that binge drinking and underage drinking are problems. However, merely because it is foreseeable that an underage drinker may gain access to alcoholic beverages and misuse them is not a reason to impose a duty to warn about death from overconsumption and impose liability for the drinker's death upon the distiller. . . .

Additionally, because of the inability to fashion effective instructions about the proper use of tequila, we conclude that no legal duty exists on the part of Brown-Forman to place instructions for proper use on its containers of tequila.

* * * * *

Even if a warning could be fashioned, there existed no evidence that Marie would have heeded the warning. The evidence was that Marie had received and disregarded warnings about the abuse of alcoholic beverages generally.

* * * * *

Finding that Brown-Forman had no legal duty to warn Marie about the dangers of consuming a large amount of tequila over a short time period and no duty to provide instructions about the proper use of tequila, we reverse the trial court's judgment, render judgment for Brown-Forman, and render that Brune take nothing.
Reversed.

Questions

1. What was the issue in this case?
2. Why did the court reverse the jury's judgment?
3. George Hacker, director of the alcohol policies project for the Center for Science in the Public Interest: "In terms of acute intoxication, I don't think it's widely known that this is a highly toxic substance when consumed too rapidly—especially among young people who are inexperienced in drinking." Comment. See Wendy Bounds, "Liquor Firm Liability Verdict Reversed," *The Wall Street Journal,* January 6, 1995, p. B2.
4. The Court in the *Brown-Forman* case favorably cites Justice Kilgarlin's view that legal and moral duties are often not one and the same. In your view, if an act (or a failure to act) is immoral, should it also be illegal? Explain.
5. Bresnahan, age 50 and 5'8" tall, was driving her Chrysler LeBaron, equipped with a driver's side air bag, at between 25 and 30 miles per hour. She was seated less than one foot from the air bag cover. Bresnahan was distracted by police lights and rear-ended a Jaguar, triggering the LeBaron air bag, which broke Bresnahan's arm and caused various abrasions. The vehicle did not include a warning about the danger of sitting too close to the air bag. Was the vehicle defective because of the absence of a warning? Explain. See *Bresnahan v. Chrysler Corp.,* 65 Cal. App. 4th 1149 (1998).
6. Laaperi installed a smoke detector in his bedroom, properly connecting it to his home's electrical system. Six months later, Laaperi's house burned and three of his children were killed. A short circuit, which caused the fire, also deprived the A.C.-powered smoke detector of electricity. Thus the detector did not sound a warning. Laaperi then claimed that Sears, Roebuck, where he purchased the detector, was guilty of negligence for failing to warn him that a fire might disable his smoke detector such that no warning would issue. How would you rule in this case? See *Laaperi v. Sears, Roebuck & Co.,* 787 F.2d 726 (1st Cir. 1986).

Negligence Defenses: Introduction

Even if the plaintiff has established all of the necessary ingredients in a negligence claim, the defendant may still prevail by asserting a good defense. The two most prominent legal defenses in these cases are (1) comparative or contributory negligence and (2) assumption of the risk.

> A trampoline at the Beta Theta Pi fraternity house at the University of Denver led to a broken neck and paralysis when a 20-year-old fraternity member, Oscar Whitlock, unsuccessfully attempted a flip at 10 PM in the dark.

A trampoline at the Beta Theta Pi fraternity house at the University of Denver led to a broken neck and paralysis when a 20-year-old fraternity member, Oscar Whitlock, unsuccessfully attempted a flip at 10 PM in the dark. Whitlock had extensive experience with trampolines. The day of the accident he had slept until 2 PM after drinking that morning until 2 AM. The trampoline was located in front of the house on university land that was leased by the fraternity. The trampoline had been used over a 10-year period by students and community members. A number of injuries had resulted. The university kept its own trampoline under lock and key because of safety concerns.

At trial the jury found the university 72 percent at fault, with the remainder of the blame lying with the plaintiff/student. He recovered 72 percent of $7,300,000 ($5,256,000). On appeal the judgment was upheld; but the dissent argued that the university had no duty to warn against obvious risks, saying that "no reasonable person could conclude that the plaintiff was not at least as negligent as the defendant." Hence the dissent was saying, in effect, that the plaintiff had *assumed the risk* and, in any case, was himself arguably more *negligent* than the university.[24]

The Colorado State Supreme Court then reviewed the appeals court decision and reversed on the grounds that the university did not maintain a "special relationship" with the plaintiff that would have justified imposing a duty of due care on the university to ensure safe use of the trampoline.[25]

Questions

Assume you own an amusement park.

1. Would the dissent's reasoning in the court of appeals decision apply to the trampoline in your amusement park business? Explain.
2. Would a warning and close supervision protect you from liability under the court of appeals decision? Explain.
3. Would you have the duty of due care for your customers that the Supreme Court said the University of Denver did not have for Whitlock? Explain.

Negligence Defenses: Rules

Let's look more closely at the central defenses in negligence cases.

Comparative Negligence

Most states have adopted *comparative negligence* as a defense. This involves weighing the relative negligence of the parties. Though the formula varies from state to state, typically the plaintiff's recovery is reduced by a percentage equal to the percentage of the plaintiff's fault in the case. Assume a plaintiff sustained $10,000 in injuries in an accident. If the plaintiff's own negligence is found to be 20 percent responsible for the injuries, then the plaintiff's recovery will be reduced to $8,000. In many states, however, when the plaintiff is more than 50 percent at fault, she or he will be barred from recovery.

Contributory Negligence

Rather than employing the comparative negligence doctrine, a few states continue to follow the historic rule that any contribution by the plaintiff to his or her own harm constitutes a complete bar to recovery. This is called *contributory negligence.* If the plaintiff is found to have contributed in any way to his or her injury, even if that contribution is minuscule, he or she is unable to recover.

Assumption of Risk

A plaintiff who willingly enters a dangerous situation and is injured, in many states, will be barred from recovery. For example, if a driver sees that the road ahead is flooded, he will not be compensated for the injuries sustained when he loses control as he attempts to drive through the water. His recovery is barred even though the road was flooded due to operator error in opening a floodgate. The requirements for use of the *assumption of risk* defense are (1) knowledge of the risk and (2) voluntary assumption of the risk. Assumption of the risk and contributory negligence are distinguishable in that the former is based on consent whereas the latter is rooted in carelessness. Increasingly, states that have adopted the comparative negligence doctrine do not treat assumption of the risk as a complete bar to recovery, but rather as a factor in negligence balancing.

Question

Muldovan and McEachern, two 17-year-old boys, were drinking and playing with a gun by handing it back and forth, pointing it at each other, and pulling the trigger. Others at the party warned them to stop, but they persisted. On one occasion, McEachern encouraged Muldovan to pull the trigger. He did so and killed McEachern, whose parents then sued Muldovan for negligence, among other causes of action.

1. What defense(s) would you offer on behalf of Muldovan? Explain.
2. Decide the case. Explain. See *Muldovan v. McEachern,* 523 S.E.2d 566 (Ga. S.Ct. 1999).

Warranties

As explained previously, negligence claims are often difficult to prove. For that reason and others, a wronged consumer may wish to raise a breach of warranty claim in addition to or in place of a negligence action. A warranty is simply a guarantee arising out of a contract. If the product does not conform to the standards of the warranty, the contract is violated (breached), and the wronged party is entitled to recovery. Note that a negligence claim arises from breach of the duty of due care, whereas a warranty claim arises from a breach of contract. [For the text of the Uniform Commercial Code, Article II, Sales, see Appendix B at the back of this text. For the UCC, in total, see **http://www .law.cornell.edu/ucc**]

Express Warranties

An express warranty exists if a seller of goods states a fact or makes a promise regarding the character or quality of the goods. (Some lease arrangements are also covered by warranty law, but we will limit our discussion to the sale of goods.) Warranties are governed primarily by the terms of the Uniform Commercial Code. The UCC is designed to codify and standardize the law of commercial practice.

UCC 2–313. Express Warranties by Affirmation, Promise, Description, Sample

1. Express warranties by the seller are created as follows:
   a. Any affirmation of fact or promise made by the seller to the buyer which relates to the goods and becomes part of the basis of the bargain creates an express warranty that the goods shall conform to the affirmation or promise.
   b. Any description of the goods which is made part of the basis of the bargain creates an express warranty that the goods shall conform to the description.
   c. Any sample or model which is made part of the basis of the bargain creates an express warranty that the whole of the goods shall conform to the sample or model.

The philosophy undergirding UCC 2–313 is straightforward. The seller who seeks to enhance the attractiveness of his or her product by offering representations as to the nature or quality of the product must fulfill those representations or fall in breach of contract and pay damages. [At this writing, the various state legislatures are considering changes to the UCC. For a summary of the changes recommended by the National Conference of Commissioners on Uniform State Laws for Article 2, Sales, including warranties, see **http://www.nccusl.org/Update/uniformact_summaries/uniformacts-s-ucc22003.asp**]

Puffing

Perhaps the area of greatest confusion in determining the existence and coverage of an express warranty is distinguishing a seller's promise from a mere expression of opinion. The latter, often referred to as sales talk or *puffing,* does not create an express warranty. The UCC requires an affirmation of fact or promise. Hence a statement of opinion is not covered by the code. For example, the sales clerk who says, "This is the best TV around," would not be guaranteeing that the television in question is the best available. The salesperson is expressing a view. We, as consumers, seem to be quite patient with sellers' exaggerations. If, on the other hand, the clerk said, "This TV has a solid walnut cabinet," when in fact it was a pine veneer stained to a walnut tone, a breach of warranty action might ultimately be in order. The test to be applied in such situations is one of reasonable expectations. An expression of opinion coming from an expert may well create an express warranty because the buyer should reasonably be able to rely on the expert's affirmations. That would particularly be the case if the buyer is not knowledgeable about the product.

Implied Warranties

A seller enters into a contract for the sale of goods and, as a consequence, an implied warranty arises by operation of law. That is, an implied warranty automatically attaches to the sale of goods unless the warranty is disclaimed (disavowed) by the seller.

Two types of implied warranties are provided for:

UCC 2–314. Implied Warranty: Merchantability; Usage of Trade

(1) Unless excluded or modified (Section 2–316), a warranty that the goods shall be merchantable is implied in a contract for their sale if the seller is a merchant with respect to goods of that kind. Under this section the serving for value of food or drink to be consumed either on the premises or elsewhere is a sale.

UCC 2–315. Implied Warranty: Fitness for Particular Purpose

Where the seller at the time of contracting has reason to know any particular purpose for which the goods are required and that the buyer is relying on the seller's skill or judgment to select or furnish suitable goods, there is unless excluded or modified under the next section an implied warranty that the goods shall be fit for such purpose.

The implied warranty of merchantability is a powerful tool for the wronged consumer in that the warranty arises automatically by operation of law. If the seller is a merchant regularly selling goods of the kind in question, the warranty of merchantability simply accompanies the sale unless the warranty is excluded via a disclaimer (explained next). The warranty arises even if the seller made no certification as to the nature or quality of the goods. UCC 2–314 enshrines the consumer's reasonable expectation that only safe goods of at least ordinary quality will appear on the market.

The implied warranty of fitness for a particular purpose likewise arises by operation of law, but only when the seller (merchant or not) knows (or has reason to know) that the goods are to be used for a specific purpose, and the seller further knows that the buyer is relying on the seller's judgment. If those conditions obtain, the warranty exists automatically unless disclaimed. For example, Chris Snapp engages an audio products clerk in a discussion regarding the proper stereo system for Chris's classic Austin Healey sports car. Chris explains the joy he expects to receive in driving his car along the winding Kentucky roads with the convertible top down and the stereo booming. Unfortunately, the stereo selected on the clerk's advice proves insufficiently powerful to be heard clearly above the rushing wind. Should Chris recover for breach of the implied warranty of fitness for a particular purpose? Merchantability?

Disclaimers

Express warranties may be disclaimed (excluded) or modified only with great difficulty. In any contract displaying both an express warranty and language disclaiming that warranty (for example, sold "as is" or "with all faults"), the warranty will remain effective unless the warranty and the disclaimer can reasonably be read as consistent.

Implied warranties may be excluded or modified by following either of the two patterns explained in UCC sections 2–316(2) and (3)(a).

2. Subject to subsection (3), to exclude or modify the implied warranty of merchantability or any part of it the language must mention merchantability and in case of a writing must be conspicuous, and to exclude or modify any implied warranty of fitness the exclusion must be by a writing and conspicuous.
3. Notwithstanding subsection (2)

a. unless the circumstances indicate otherwise, all implied warranties are excluded by expressions like as is, with all faults, or other language which in common understanding calls the buyer's attention to the exclusion of warranties and makes plain that there is no implied warranty.

Finally, when a buyer, before entering a contract, inspects the goods (or a sample thereof) or declines to inspect, no implied warranty exists with regard to defects that should have been apparent on inspection UCC 2–316(3)(b).

Magnuson–Moss Warranty Act

Although the Uniform Commercial Code embodies our primary expression of warranty rules, Congress has extended and clarified those rules by passing the Magnuson–Moss Warranty Act. Congress approved the act following a study that found widespread abuse of consumers. Warranties were often vague, deceptive, or simply incomprehensible to the average purchaser. The act, administered by the FTC, applies only to consumer products and only to written warranties. It does not require offering an express written warranty, but where such a warranty is offered and the cost of the goods is more than $10, the warranty must be labeled *full* or *limited*. A full warranty requires free repair of any defect. If repair is not achieved within a reasonable time, the buyer may elect either a refund or replacement without charge. If a limited warranty is offered, the limitation must be conspicuously displayed.

If a warranty is offered on goods costing more than $15, the warrantor must "fully and conspicuously disclose in simple and readily understandable language the terms and conditions of the warranty." The FTC has developed various rules to implement the intent of the disclosure requirement. For example, if the warrantor requires return of a completed warranty registration card to activate the warranty, that return requirement must be clearly disclosed in the warranty.

The effect of the Magnuson–Moss Act has not been entirely consistent with Congress's hopes. In practice, many sellers may have either offered limited warranties or eliminated them entirely.

The *Mitchell* case that follows summarizes warranty law as it applies to objects in food and tells us something about how the *Palmer v. Nan King* negligence case discussed earlier might have been litigated under warranty law.

Mitchell v. Fridays 748 N.E.2d 89

LEGAL BRIEFCASE (Ohio Ct. App. 2000)

Judge Waite

This timely appeal arises from the trial court's grant of summary judgment to Appellee T.G.I. Friday's and to Appellee Pro Source Distributors. For the following reasons, we affirm the judgment of the trial court.

On April 11, 1996, Appellant Sandra Mitchell was having dinner at Appellee Friday's restaurant. Appellant was eating a fried clam strip when she bit into a hard substance which she believed to be a piece of a clam shell. Appellant experienced immediate pain and later sought dental treatment. Some time later, the crown of a tooth came loose. It was determined that the crown could not be reattached and the remaining root of the tooth was extracted.

On September 2, 1997, Appellant filed a product liability action against both Friday's, who served the meal, and against Appellee Pro Source Distributing (hereinafter "Pro Source"), the supplier of the fried clams. Both Friday's and Pro Source filed motions for summary judgment which the trial court granted without explanation on June 18, 1999.

* * * * *

Appellant argues that in light of Ohio's product liability legislation, the trial court should have applied the "reasonable expectation test" to her claim. R.C. 2307.74 provides that "A product is defective [if] . . . it deviated in a material way from the design specifications, formula, or performance standards of the manufacturer." R.C. 2307.75(A) (2) provides that a product is defective in design or formulation if "it is more dangerous than an ordinary consumer would expect when used in an intended or reasonably foreseeable manner." According to Appellant, by the enactment of these statutes the "reasonable expectation" test supersedes the traditional "foreign–natural test" applied in cases where injury is caused by substances in food. Appellant asserts that there is a reasonable expectation that clams are completely cleaned of their shells and free of foreign materials.

* * * * *

In the present case, Friday's set forth in its motion for summary judgment Appellant's deposition testimony to the effect that while eating a clam strip, she bit down on "a hard, foreign substance." Appellant stated that she assumed it was a piece of a clam shell. Appellant described the size of the object as about a quarter of the size of a small fingernail or about a quarter of an inch or smaller and irregular in shape. Moreover, Friday's attached an affidavit from its manager, Eric Hicks, who immediately responded to Appellant's report of the incident. In that affidavit, Hicks confirmed that the object Appellant presented to him was indeed a piece of clam shell and that it was approximately one-quarter inch in length and irregularly shaped. . . .

There being no factual dispute here, we must decide whether Appellees are entitled to judgment as a matter of law. Both Friday's and Pro Source presented essentially the same argument, that regardless of whether the foreign–natural test or reasonable expectation test was applied, Appellant has no claim against Appellees. Appellant, however, has argued for the application only of the reasonable expectation test.

* * * * *

However, it does not appear necessary to determine which test applies to the present case. [A] similar argument was addressed in *Mathews v. Maysville Seafoods, Inc.* (1991). In *Mathews,* the plaintiff suffered a bowel injury when he swallowed a fish bone while eating a fish fillet served by the defendant. The trial court granted the defendant's motion for summary judgment. On appeal, the defendant argued for the adoption of the reasonable expectation test as opposed to the foreign–natural test.

The *Mathews* court set forth both tests. Under the foreign–natural test,

> Bones which are natural to the type of meat served cannot legitimately be called a foreign substance, and a consumer who eats meat dishes ought to anticipate and be on his guard against the presence of such bones.

The reasonable expectation test states,

> The test should be what is "reasonably expected" by the consumer in the food as served, not what might be natural to the ingredients of that food prior to preparation. . . . As applied to the action for common-law negligence, the test is related to the foreseeability of harm on the part of the defendant. The defendant is not an insurer but has the duty of ordinary care to eliminate or remove in the preparation of the food he serves such harmful substances as the consumer of the food, as served, would not ordinarily anticipate and guard against.

* * * * *

In the present case, it cannot be disputed that the piece of clam shell which caused Appellant's injury was natural to the clam strip which she consumed. Turning to the question of whether Appellant should have reasonably anticipated the presence of the clam shell, we are reminded of the Ohio Supreme Court's holding in *Allen* that, " . . . the possible presence of a piece of oyster shell in or attached to an oyster is so well known to anyone who eats oysters that we can say as a matter of law that one who eats oysters can reasonably anticipate and guard against eating such a piece of shell." The facts of the present case are virtually indistinguishable from *Allen* except for the type of injury and that, here, Appellant was eating fried clams rather than fried oysters. We therefore hold that as a matter of law, one who eats clams can reasonably anticipate and guard against eating such a piece of shell.

Affirmed.

Questions

1. *a.* Who won this case and why?

    b. Did the court adopt the foreign–natural test or the reasonable expectations test? Explain.

c. Is a walnut shell "natural" to, for example, maple nut ice cream? What about a cherry pit in a cherry pie? Explain.

2. In buying a new motor home, Leavitt told the dealer that he wanted to have plenty of power and braking capacity for driving in the mountains. He was assured by the dealer on both counts. He brought the motor home and found it unsatisfactory for mountain use. After many warranty repairs, he sued for breach of warranty.

   a. What warranty was breached, according to Leavitt?

   b. Decide the case. Explain. See *Leavitt v. Monaco Coach,* 616 N.W.2d 175 (Mich. Ct. App. 2000).

3. Priebe bought a used car without a warranty (sold as is). The seller, Autobarn, told Priebe that the car had not been in any accidents. After driving the car more than 30,000 miles, Priebe crashed the car. Priebe sued Autobarn claiming the car was dangerous to drive because of a previous, undisclosed accident. Priebe did not show that Autobarn had knowledge of the previous accident; nor did Priebe show that the value of the car was reduced by the previous accident. Priebe sued for breach of warranty. Decide. Explain. See *Priebe v. Autobarn,* 240 F.3d 584 (7th Cir. 2001).

It Could Have Been Worse

A piece of shell in food can be harmful and disturbing, as Sandra Mitchell discovered; but for Theresa VanHorn, a 29-year-old writer at MTV Networks, an apparent condom in her half-eaten muffin left her screaming and without an appetite. The piece of latex did not alarm the New York City Health Department, where an employee told her to throw the evidence away when she called to complain: "We won't get to your complaint for days, maybe weeks." Complaints of foreign objects in food are so common in New York City that the department does not have time to quickly investigate all of them. Both the city and the state did get involved, however, and VanHorn, at last report, was considering legal action.

Source: Lindsay Powers, "Eww!—Berry Muffin; Gal Finds Condom in Pastry," *New York Post,* October 24, 2004, p. 8.

Strict Liability

As it turns out, your customer has been bitten by a spider.

Sometimes things happen that businesses can neither prevent nor even explain and yet liability may attach. For example, imagine you are operating a clothing store. A customer enters and decides to try on a pair of slacks. You show her to the dressing room. Soon after, you hear a scream from the room. As it turns out, your customer has been bitten by a spider. Not surprisingly, she thinks the blame lies with your store. She sues, but her negligence and breach of warranty claims are rejected by the court. (Can you explain why she loses?) Finally, she raises a strict liability in tort argument, but the court denies that claim also. Read the overview of strict liability that follows and think about why the court denied her claim. See *Flippo v. Mode O'Day Frock Shops of Hollywood,* 449 S.W.2d 692 (Ark. S. Ct. 1970).

Strict Liability Overview

Negligence and warranty claims are helpful to the harmed consumer. However, rapid changes in the nature of commercial practice, as well as an increasing societal concern for consumer protection, led the legal community to gradually embrace yet another cause of action. *Strict liability in tort* offers the prospect of holding all of those in the chain of distribution liable for damages from a defective product, rather than imposing the entire burden on the injured consumer. Manufacturers and sellers are best positioned to prevent the distribution of defective products, and they are best able to bear the cost of injury by spreading the loss via pricing policies and insurance coverage.

Strict liability as an independent tort emerged in 1963 in the famous California case of *Greenman v. Yuba Power Products, Inc.*[26] In the ensuing 40 years, most states, have adopted strict liability in concept. The essence of the strict liability notion is expressed in Section 402A of the *Restatement (Second) of Torts.* In brief, 402A imposes liability where a product is sold in a *defective condition, unreasonably dangerous* to the user. Here is the 402A test:

1. One who sells any product in a defective condition, unreasonably dangerous to the user or consumer or to his property, is subject to liability for physical harm thereby caused to the ultimate user or consumer, or to his property, if
   a. the seller is engaged in the business of selling such a product, and,
   b. it is expected to and does reach the user or consumer without substantial change in the condition in which it is sold.
2. The rule stated in Subsection (1) applies although
   a. the seller has exercised all possible care in the preparation and sale of his product, and
   b. the user or consumer has not bought the product from or entered into any contractual relation with the seller.

Thus, we see that strict liability does not require proof of negligence on the part of the defendant. Strict liability law focuses on the condition of the *product,* rather than the conduct of the parties. Therefore, a seller who is free of actual fault may, nonetheless, be liable for injuries caused by a defective and unreasonably dangerous product, The *BIC* lighter case that follows considers the conditions under which a strict liability claim may be raised.

Price v. BIC Corporation

LEGAL BRIEFCASE · 702 A.2d 330 (N.H. S.Ct. 1997)

Justice Horton

[T]he United States District Court for the District of New Hampshire certified to us the following question of law:

Can the legal representative of a minor child injured as a result of the misuse of a product by another minor child maintain a defective design product liability claim against the product's manufacturer if the product was intended to be used only by adults and the risk that children might misuse the product was open and obvious to the product's manufacturer and its intended users?

We respond in the affirmative.

In November 1991, three-year-old Douglas Moore used a BIC model J-6 lighter to start a fire that severely burned his seventeen-month-old brother, Matthew Ryan Moore. The lighter had been purchased by the boys' mother, Mary Moore.

The packaging on BIC lighters provided the warnings "Keep out of Reach of Children" and "Keep Away from

Children." The defendant, BIC Corporation (BIC), was aware that the lighters could be used by children to ignite fires. BIC did not incorporate known and available child-resistant features into the design of the J-6 lighter even though it was possible to do so without significantly affecting the lighter's cost or effectiveness.

The plaintiff, Kathleen Price, the guardian over the estate of Matthew Ryan Moore, contends that BIC should be strictly liable because the lighter was defectively designed in that it lacked child-resistant features and adequate warnings. The plaintiff produced no evidence in response to BIC's claims that its lighters were intended to be used only by adults and that the risk that minor children might use the lighters to start fires was open and obvious to the intended users of the lighters.

BIC moved for summary judgment, asserting that New Hampshire does not permit a plaintiff to maintain a strict product liability defective design claim if the injuries complained of result from a risk that is open and obvious to the product's intended users. The federal district court asks us to clarify whether we would limit strict liability defective design claims in the manner that BIC suggests.

Nearly 30 years ago this court adopted the doctrine of strict liability of manufacturers for product defects as stated in section 402A (1) of the Restatement (Second) of Torts.

*   *   *   *   *

To maintain a defective design products liability claim, a plaintiff must first prove "that the design of the product created a defective condition unreasonably dangerous to the user. . . ." Whether a product is dangerous to an extent beyond that which would be contemplated by the ordinary consumer is determined by the jury using a risk–utility balancing test. A product's design should meet risk–utility balancing standards as seen from the point of view of the public as a whole.

Determining whether a product's design is unreasonably dangerous implicates "a multifaceted balancing process involving evaluation of many conflicting factors." These factors include the social utility and desirability of the product, as "evaluated from the point of view of the public as a whole," weighed against the risk of danger posed by its use, whether the risk of danger could have been reduced without significantly affecting either the product's effectiveness or cost, and the presence and efficacy of a warning to avoid an unreasonable risk of harm from hidden dangers or from foreseeable uses.

Manufacturer liability may still attach even if the danger is obvious to a reasonable consumer or if the user employs the product in an unintended but foreseeable manner. "The obviousness of the danger should be evaluated against the reasonableness of the steps which the manufacturer must take to reduce the danger." Further, a manufacturer's duty to warn is not limited to intended uses of its product, but also extends to all reasonably foreseeable uses to which the product may be put. "When an unreasonable danger could have been eliminated without excessive cost or loss of product efficiency, liability may attach even though the danger was obvious or there was adequate warning."

In undertaking this analysis, we caution that the term "unreasonably dangerous" should not be interpreted so broadly as to impose absolute liability on manufacturers or make them insurers of their products. In certain cases, the court may be able to keep the issue of liability from the jury if, as a matter of law, the utility of the product to the public as a whole completely outweighs the risk posed to consumers or the risk posed by use of the product is extremely remote. If the district court concludes that either of these circumstances are met, the plaintiff's defective design claims will fail.

For these reasons, we respond to the district court that barring a determination that the utility of the product completely outweighs the risk associated with its use or that the risk of harm is so remote as to be negligible, the legal representative of a minor child injured as a result of the misuse of a product by another minor child can maintain a defective design product liability claim against the product's manufacturer, even though the product was intended to be used only by adults, when the risk that children might misuse the product was open and obvious to the product's manufacturer and its intended users.

Remanded.

Questions

1. *a.* Explain the plaintiff's claim.

   b. Explain the defendant's position.

2. What evidence must a plaintiff provide to maintain a successful defective design product liability claim?

3. Is the manufacturer excused from liability if the product's danger is obvious or if the product is used in an unintended but foreseeable fashion?

4. In a similar BIC case [*Griggs v. Bic Corp.,* 981 F.2d 1429 (3rd Cir. 1992)] the court, employing a negligence analysis, found that the central question was whether the foreseeable risk was unreasonable. The court noted that residential fires started by children playing with lighters are estimated to take an average of 120 lives each year, and total damages amount to $300–$375 million or 60–75 cents per lighter sold.

   a. Is the foreseeable risk unreasonable, in your judgment?

   b. How did you reach your conclusion?

c. In your view, are the parents the responsible parties in this episode? Explain.

5. Alison Nowak, a 14-year-old girl, tried to spray her hair with Aqua Net. Because the spray valve on the recently purchased aerosol can would not work properly, she punctured the can with an opener. She was standing in her kitchen near a gas stove at the time, and the cloud of spray that gushed from the can ignited. She was severely burned.

Nowak sued Faberge, the maker of the spray, on strict liability grounds. Although the back of the can contained the warnings, "Do not puncture," and "Do not use near fire or flame," the jury determined that Faberge had not adequately warned of the fire hazard and awarded her $1.5 million. Faberge appealed. Decide. Explain. See *Nowak v. Faberge USA Inc.,* 32 F.3d 755 (3d Cir. 1994).

Coverage

All of those engaged in the preparation and distribution of a defective product may be liable for any harm caused by the defect, regardless of proof of actual fault. Furthermore, the courts have extended strict liability coverage to reach injured bystanders. Coverage generally extends to both personal injuries and property damage, but in some states the latter is excluded. Some states limit strict liability recovery to new goods, and some have limited liability to a designated period (for example, 15 years) after the manufacture or sale of the product.

Furthermore, the new *Restatement (Third) of Torts* recommends applying strict liability claims to manufacturing defects but not to design and warning defect cases. Thus, in effect, the new *Restatement* calls for the fault-based analysis explained earlier in the negligence material in *all* defective design and failure to warn cases. Of course, the courts may choose to stick with the current expansive use of the strict liability doctrine. [For a brief critique of portions of the new *Restatement,* see **http://www.cliffordlaw.com/media/articles/1272.html**]

Defenses

Assumption of risk and product misuse are both good defenses and, if factually supported, in many states can act as a complete bar to strict liability recovery. Assumption of the risk involves the plaintiff's decision to proceed to use the product despite obvious dangers associated with that use. Thus, if a pilot decided to fly knowing that the plane's wing flaps were not operating properly, she may well have assumed the risk if she subsequently crashed. When the product is used improperly, or its directions are ignored, or it is used in an unforeseeable way, the defendant would raise the misuse defense. Presumably, crop dusting with a plane not designed for that purpose would constitute misuse. Some courts, however, hold those in the chain of distribution liable for foreseeable misuses. Because strict liability is a no-fault theory, contributory negligence ordinarily is not a recognized defense.

Video Games and *The Basketball Diaries*

Michael Carneal, a 14-year-old high school freshman in Paducah, Kentucky, brought a .22-caliber pistol and five shotguns to Heath High School on December 1, 1997, where he shot and killed three students and wounded a number of others. Carneal regularly played violent video games such as "Doom and Quake" and viewed violent Internet sites. He also watched violent movies including *The Basketball Diaries,* in which a high school student dreams of killing his teacher and other students. The parents of the dead children sued several video game, movie production, and Internet content providers raising negligence and strict liability claims. Who should win that case? Explain. See *James v. Meow Media,* 300 F.3d 683 (6th Cir. 2002); cert. den. *James v. Meow Media,* 537 U.S. 1159 (2003).

Part Three—Product Liability and Public Policy

Giant tort awards involving products such as asbestos and breast implants have bank-rupted businesses and encouraged calls for tort reform. When we hear about a $28 *billion* punitive damage award in 2002 for a 64-year-old smoker suffering from lung cancer, we may wonder if the justice system has lost its bearings.[27] We may not understand that those giant awards are almost always dramatically reduced.[28] Nonetheless, the threat of tort litigation significantly affects business decision making and, in some instances, actually prevents products from reaching the market. President Bush made tort reform a center-piece of his 2005 legislative agenda. Are big tort judgments harming the American econ-omy and distorting justice, or are lawsuits Americans' only effective protection against callous corporations? Let's consider some of the evidence.

For Tort Reform Consultants Tillinghast-Towers Perrin estimated that tort suits (not lim-ited to product liability) cost the United States more than $200 billion per year, a sum equal to about 2 percent of the gross domestic product.[29] Put another way, that sum amounts to a "tort tax" of $3,236 per year for a family of four.[30] America's "tort tax" probably dou-bles that of most of western Europe, Canada, and Japan.[31] As a result, American businesses must struggle with rising costs (especially insurance), innovation is reduced, and new jobs are less plentiful. All of this comes, of course, in a fiercely competitive global market. Fur-ther, a big frustration to the critics is that much of the tort money goes to lawyers rather than to the injured plaintiffs. [For further criticism of tort claims and our legal system gen-erally, see **http://www.overlawyered.com or www.legalreformnow.com**]

Against Tort Reform Can we rely on the market and managerial ethics to protect us from dangerous products? Is the threat of litigation a powerful incentive to improve busi-ness practice? Consider, for example, the cholesterol-lowering drug Baycol, which was recently removed from the market. Its producer, Bayer, has paid more than $1 billion to settle several thousand liability cases where consumers were hospitalized, had kidney failure, or died from the drug. Bayer allegedly misled the Food and Drug Administra-tion about Baycol's dangerous propensities.[32]

More broadly, those opposing tort reform say that the tort burden simply is not of the magnitude suggested by the critics. Lawsuits, consuming less than 2 percent of spending, constitute a modest part of the cost of doing business; product liability claims are a small fraction of the total legal landscape; and studies show that insurance costs do not decline appreciably when damages are capped.[33] Furthermore, only about 3 percent of tort cases ever make it to trial; those cases that are settled before judgment often involve reasonable sums of money;[34] and punitive damages are awarded in only about 3.3 percent of tort cases won by plaintiffs.[35] Even ardent defenders of tort practice often agree, however, that the system needs to be improved so that lawyers do not gobble up so much of the money themselves and so that the system produces a more consistent form of justice.[36]

Class Actions Tort reform advocates achieved a significant victory in 2005 when Congress and President Bush approved the Class Action Fairness Act, which shifts most interstate class actions seeking more than $5 million to the federal courts. The new law was vigorously supported by corporate interests, which believe that class actions are often nuisance, "junk" cases or abusive "weapons" used by plaintiffs and lawyers to pursue defendants with deep pockets. The federal courts have generally been less receptive to class actions than the state courts, and the new law will prevent plaintiffs, in most cases, from "shopping" for the state court most favorable to their claims.

To corporate critics, on the other hand, the new class action law will simply make it harder for the "little guys" to fight corporate abuse. Individuals who are victims of discrimination, defective products, or environmental pollution, for example, often cannot afford to mount an effective claim on their own, and in any event, the individual damages involved might not be a meaningful deterrent to future wrongdoing.

Big Case: Fast Food

A helpful way to look at tort reform is to consider one of the massive claims that have emerged periodically as plaintiffs attempt to prove themselves wronged by a defective product or wrongful conduct. Tobacco smokers, Ford Explorer drivers, Vioxx users, and victims of gun violence are among those who have recently made headlines in pursuit of alleged corporate misdeeds. Some of these actions seem to make sense; others look like a quick money grab or perhaps a failure to accept personal responsibility or both. For example, what should we think of the now highly publicized lawsuits against McDonald's and other fast-food companies blaming them for plaintiffs' obesity and related health problems?

> Buoyed by the massive settlements against Big Tobacco, fast-food addicts are suing the makers of Big Macs and three other restaurant chains for the health problems they suffer. At least 10 plaintiffs—including one who downed a pound of french fries a week— accuse McDonald's, Burger King, Wendy's, and Kentucky Fried Chicken of failing to divulge nutritional information and not offering healthier menu options. . . . [T]he suit also contends that the fast-food corporations have effectively created an addiction in their consumers, especially among children and the poor.[37]

One case involves plaintiff Jazlyn Bradley, 19, of Brooklyn, New York, who measures 5'6" and 270 pounds, while the other plaintiff, Ashley Pelman, 14, of the Bronx, New York, is 4'10" and 140 pounds. They claim that eating at McDonald's three to five times per week for years caused their obesity, diabetes, coronary disease, and other health problems. Essentially they argue that they were not given sufficient notice by McDonald's of the risks of a fast-food diet and that they were misled into believing that McDonald's food was healthful. The lawsuit was twice tossed out by a lower court judge, who ruled that the plaintiffs had been unable to directly link their obesity to consumption of

McDonald's food. The judge also proclaimed that the law does not have a duty to protect us from our own excesses. Nonetheless, in early 2005 a federal court of appeals overruled the lower court and ordered the case to proceed.[38]

The appeals court decision was largely procedural; but it does open the door to similar lawsuits elsewhere, and it may allow plaintiffs to achieve access to previously secret McDonald's documents. Law professor John Banzhaf, a primary force in both the tobacco and fast-food litigations, offers at his Web site this example of the possible wrongdoing that might be revealed by fast-food company documents:

> It had been suggested, for example, that at least one fast-food company deliberately altered the temperature at which its French fries were cooked to increase their absorption of fats—and/or added unnecessary sugar.[39]

Questions

1. Are the plaintiffs (and their parents) solely responsible for their obesity? Explain.

2. Childhood obesity is an increasing problem. The *Scottish Daily Record* examined whether McDonald's unfairly targeted children as consumers of its food products:

> [I]t is worrying that one of the founding fathers of McDonald's, Ray Kroc, made an early decision that his target market was kids. He said, "A child who loves our TV commercials and brings her grandparents to a McDonald's gives us two more customers."
>
> Harry Merrick, who worked on McDonald's advertising in the sixties, said children were the easiest customers to reach. He explained, "We figured the easiest way to sell our product was to sell to children. Children aren't very quality conscious."
>
> When Burger King formed Kids Clubs in 1991, sales of children's meals increased by 300 percent. And by including a Teenie Beanie toy in the Happy Meal, McDonald's discovered it increased sales 10-fold.[40]

Journalist Eric Schlosser, author of *Fast Food America,* says, "[W]hen you are marketing to children you have an extra responsibility."[41]

   a. Do you agree with Schlosser? Explain.

   b. In your opinion, has McDonald's or Burger King breached its responsibilities to children? Explain.

   c. If advertising persuades children to favor fast foods, should they be able to sue fast-food companies if they are obese as adults? Explain.

3. Would you favor health warnings on fast-food products? Explain.

Explorer SUV Too Risky?

Internal Ford Motor Co. documents from 1993 reportedly include advice from the company's own engineers calling for stronger roof supports to prevent roof collapse in rollover accidents. Ford's engineering supervisor said the company decided against the changes because they were not required by the U.S. government. Other Ford engineers said that at least nine deaths in Explorers had been caused by suspension flaws that could have been corrected by moving the shock absorbers toward the wheels, a change Ford did not make. One of Ford's attorneys explained that Ford's decision against following the engineers' advice did not mean Ford acted in bad faith. That advice was only part of the evidence considered in assessing safety issues with the Explorer. At this writing in 2005, some 500 lawsuits claim Explorer defects.

Source: Bloomberg News, "Ford Knew of SUV Risks, Say Documents," *Des Moines Sunday Register,* February 6, 2005, p. 2D.

Too Much Law?

Perhaps, as suggested by the following analysis, the key to tort reform is simply to reduce our reliance on the law, thus providing more room for treating risk management as a matter of contractual arrangements in the free market.

READING   # Fundamental Reform of Tort Law

Paul H. Rubin

[T]he high costs of many goods and services can be traced to misguided attempts by federal regulators and courts to protect the public health and safety. The problems with the courts are especially serious, since they undermine more cost-effective means of achieving that goal.

A principal function of tort law is to deter manufacturers from causing excess harms, or, in the case of medical services, to deter malpractice. But this system has been undermined by unreasonable standards—imposed by the courts—defining parties' liability for damages.

Further, the best alternative means for securing low-cost protection has also been undermined. Before 1960, when parties agreed on an exchange of goods or services, they implicitly, if not explicitly, also agreed on the rules and limitations that would govern any liability for possible injuries. But over the past three and a half decades courts have voided such contracts, reserving for themselves the power to make determinations of liability.

* * * * *

Government intervention in the market is justified only in circumstances where the market can be expected to "fail." The most common source of market failure is the existence of some externality. An externality is said to exist when a third party, one not directly involved in a transaction, is nonetheless affected by the transaction. The classic example of a negative externality is pollution, where bystanders are harmed by the actions of polluters. Some effort at correction—by establishing or redefining property rights, by internalizing the costs of the externality, or, if all else fails, by direct government regulation—is justified by such externalities.

By this standard, much of modern tort law and much of modern government regulation purporting to protect safety and health cannot be justified, since no externalities exist that must be dealt with. Both forms of government intervention—by the courts and by regulatory agencies—stem from the fact that policymakers are unwilling to rely on private transactions to achieve efficient outcomes.

UNDERMINING CONTRACTS

Much tort law governs accidents between "strangers"—those who have no legal relationship with each other before an accident occurs. Examples include a car striking a pedestrian; two cars colliding; a passerby on the public domain being struck by a baseball flying from a stadium; a drunk punching someone for no reason in a bar. All of the above are classic tort situations, and all are cases in which there is no prior relation between the parties. In each case there is an externality, and therefore some government intervention, through regulation or through the court system, may be proper.

But many activities now governed by tort law are not of that sort. Instead, in many cases, the parties *do* have prior relations with each other, and therefore there is no externality and no need for government intervention. The major examples are product liability, where a purchaser of a product may be harmed by that product, and medical malpractice, where a patient may be harmed by some action of a physician that the patient has hired.

* * * * *

Since about 1960, as a result of a New Jersey Supreme Court case, *Henningsen v. Bloomfield Motors,* involving General Motors, courts have generally been unwilling to enforce contracts between buyers and sellers involving compensation for harms caused by accidents. No matter what terms the parties may want to govern the results of an accident, the court will decide and impose its own terms. For example, the parties may want to agree that if there is an accident, the producer of the product will pay only for lost earnings and medical costs, and will not pay anything for "pain and suffering." But if there is an injury, this voluntary agreement will have no effect. The courts will decide what level and type of damage payments from the manufacturer to the consumer are appropriate.

Source: *Regulation* 18, no. 4 (1995), p. 26. Reprinted by permission.

Questions
1. Explain Rubin's argument.
2. Why have the courts, as in the *Henningsen* case, intervened to overturn privately contracted risk and remedy arrangements?
3. Why would we want to reduce our reliance on tort law?

Part Four—Conclusion—Managing Product Liability Problems

PRACTICING ETHICS   Mitsubishi Hides Defects

How should managers react when they discover they are selling defective products? Several Mitsubishi Motors executives in Japan allegedly did not respond well to that situation. They face criminal charges of professional negligence for decades of hiding automobile and truck defects. The alleged defects, including flaws in clutches and wheel hubs, may have caused transmission parts and wheels to fall off vehicles. The problems are suspected of leading to a pair of deaths and 73 injuries. Mitsubishi has admitted covering up the defects and has apologized for them, but executives have pleaded innocent to the professional negligence charges.[42] Mitsubishi lost $1.9 billion in 2003, and its stock has lost 50 percent of its value. At this writing, Mitsubishi has created a corporate ethics committee (consisting of outsiders) to monitor senior management, and it has commissioned a thorough inquiry to reveal the full facts. [For a critical overview of Mitsubishi and its problems, see **www.mitsubishisucks.com**]

Questions
1. Mitsubishi officials have repeatedly apologized for the cover-up. Is an apology of any moral value in this situation? Explain.
2. Since the scandal broke, Mitsubishi sales have declined sharply and financial losses have been enormous. Corporate partners are putting money into Mitsubishi to help its financial recovery.
   a. Mitsubishi admits to wrongdoing. Should the company be allowed to die?
   b. Should consumers decline on moral grounds to buy Mitsubishi products?
   c. Mitsubishi is seeking government tax breaks to assist its recovery. Should the Japanese government decline that assistance because of Mitsubishi's unethical behavior? Explain.

3. In Mitsubishi's effort to redeem itself, all employees have been required to take ethics courses. Is ethics instruction likely to be of any value in improving Mitsubishi's corporate behavior? Explain.

4. Fujio Mitarai, president of Canon, Inc., commented on the Mitsubishi ethics failure:

   > Managers might often think that since they have done so much for their companies, some minor misconduct on their part should be permissible. But that would spell an end to their firms.[43]

   Mitarai went on to say that selflessness is a quality he will look for in his successor because long-term growth cannot be achieved without that quality.

   a. What do you think of Mitarai's firm stance toward "minor misconduct"?

   b. Can a successful business leader practice selflessness to a significant degree and still succeed in a highly competitive environment? Explain.

   c. Is Mitarai taking a utilitarian or formalist approach to ethical reasoning? (See Chapter 2.)

5. Successful corporate managers often possess a strong work ethic, immense know-how, energy, and other qualities. Japanese journalist Kazuo Mori, commenting on the Mitsubishi scandal, says those qualities are not at the top of his list:

   > Of all such qualities desired in managers, the most important is dedication to moral self-discipline.[44]

   a. Do you agree with Mori? Explain.

   b. Do you possess moral self-discipline? Explain.

Internet Exercise

At this writing in 2005, Congress is considering the Protection of Lawful Commerce in Arms Act. Study some of the arguments for [**http://www.nraila.org/Issues/FactSheets/Read.aspx?ID=170**] and against [**http://www.handgunfree.org/HFAMain/topics/immunity/default.htm**] the legislation. How would you vote? Explain.

Chapter Questions

1. Lydia, an adult, was intoxicated when Horton allowed Lydia to borrow his car. Lydia lost control of the car, crashed, and was rendered a quadriplegic. Lydia sued Horton for first-party negligent entrustment, claiming that Horton should have recognized that Lydia was too drunk to be entrusted with the car.
   a. Are both Lydia and Horton negligent? Explain.
   b. Who wins? Explain. See *Lydia v. Horton,* 583 S. E. 2d 750 (S. C. S. Ct. 2003).

2. Stopczynski, age 17, had used her neighbor's pool "hundreds of times." Stopczynski and her neighbor's nephew, a 34-year-old male, went to the pool. Stopczynski was noticed floating face down in the pool. She had broken her neck, apparently from diving into the four-foot deep, above-ground pool. She died a few hours later. The pool originally had stickers around the edge that said "no diving," but that edge had been replaced and the stickers were gone. Stopczynski's mother sued the property owner, Woodcox, for negligence. Decide the case. Explain. See *Stopczynski v. Woodcox,* 258 Mich. App. 226 (2003).

3. Soon after Granny's Rocker Nite Club opened in the mid-1980s, it began having a weekly "fanny" contest, which involved male and female volunteer contestants competing for cash prizes by dancing. The audience judged the contest. While attending the fanny contest on April 4, 1990, plaintiff Jeffrey Loomis, got into a fight with another patron. Loomis's right ear was bitten and torn.

Loomis's claim against Granny's Rocker had two counts, one based on the Illinois Dramshop Act and one based on negligence. The jury found for the defendant on the dramshop count, but it found that Granny's Rocker was negligent in failing to have adequate security to stop a physical altercation on the nights of the fanny contests when it knew or should have known that such contests would result in a large and rowdy group of patrons. Granny's Rocker appealed. Decide the appeal, Explain, See *Loomis v. Granny's Rocker Nite Club.* 620 N.E.2d 664 (Ill. App. 1993).

4. In 1992 Alexis Geier suffered serious injuries in an accident while driving her 1987 Honda. She was wearing a shoulder/seatbelt. She sued Honda under state product liability laws, saying the car was defective because it was not equipped with a driver's side air bag. U.S. Transportation Department standards required an air bag or automatic seatbelt by 1989 with other advances to be phased in over time. Is Geier's state product liability action blocked by the federal government's rule that did not mandate air bags until after her car was produced? Explain. See *Geier v. American Honda,* 529 U.S. 861 (2000).

5. An 11-month-old child pushed on a window screen that gave way, allowing him to fall from the second story of his aunt's house. The child's parents sued the screen maker.

   a. What product liability claims could they legitimately raise?

   b. Decide. Explain. See *Brower v. Metal Industries, Inc.,* 719 A.2d 941 (Del. S.Ct. 1998).

6. Sandage loaded a car on a transport trailer. The car door could not be fully opened because of a support bar on the trailer. He suffered a back injury when he squeezed out of the car. The trailer had been modified to add several feet to its length, and support poles, including the one in question, had been added. Sandage sued the company that modified the trailer. Sandage sued in strict liability and negligence. Decide the case. Explain. See *Sandage v. Bankhead Enterprises, Inc.,* 177 F.3d 670 (8th Cir. 1999).

7. In 1995 a young Oklahoma couple shot and paralyzed a store clerk, Patsy Byers. The young couple had repeatedly viewed Oliver Stone's 1994 movie *Natural Born Killers,* which is about a young couple who go on a killing spree. The Byers family sued Stone and Warner Brothers movie studio, the film distributor. Should a filmmaker and studio be liable for the alleged copycat behavior of those viewing a movie? Explain.

8. Embs was shopping in a self-serve grocery store. A carton of 7UP was on the floor about one foot from where she was standing. She was unaware of the carton. Several of the bottles exploded, severely injuring Embs's leg. Embs brought a strict liability action against the bottler.

   a. Raise a defense against the strict liability claim.

   b. Decide. Explain. See *Embs v. Pepsi-Cola Bottling Co. of Lexington, Kentucky, Inc.,* 528 S.W.2d 703 (Ky. Ct. App. 1975).

9. Plaintiffs Dr. Arthur Weisz and David and Irene Schwartz bought two paintings at auctions conducted by Parke-Bernet Galleries, Inc. The paintings were listed in the auction catalog as those of Raoul Dufy. It was later discovered that the paintings

were forgeries. The plaintiffs took legal action to recover their losses. Parke-Bernet defended itself by, among other arguments, asserting that the conditions of sale included a disclaimer providing that all properties were sold "as is." The conditions of sale were 15 numbered paragraphs embracing several pages in the auction catalog. The bulk of the auction catalog was devoted to descriptions of the works of art to be sold, including artists' names, dates of birth and death, and, in some instances, black-and-white reproductions of the paintings. It was established at trial that plaintiff Weisz had not previously entered bids at Parke-Bernet, and he had no awareness of the conditions of sale. Plaintiffs David and Irene Schwartz, however, were generally aware of the conditions of sale. Is the Parke-Bernet disclaimer legally binding on the plaintiffs? Explain. See *Weisz v. Parke-Bernet,* 325 N.Y.S.2d 576 (Civ. Ct. N.Y.C. 1971), but see *Schwartz v. Parke-Bernet,* 351 N.Y.S. 2d 911 (1974).

10. The plaintiff, born and raised in New England, was eating fish chowder at a restaurant when a fish bone lodged in her throat. The bone was removed, and the plaintiff sued the restaurant, claiming a breach of implied warranty under the UCC. Evidence was offered at trial to show that fish chowder recipes commonly did not provide for removal of bones. Decide. Explain. See *Webster v. Blue Ship Tea Room,* 198 N.E.2d 309 (Mass. S. Jud. Ct. 1964).

11. A passenger ran after a train as it was leaving a station. Two railroad employees boosted the passenger aboard, but as they did so a package carried by the passenger fell beneath the wheels of the train and exploded. The package, unbeknownst to the employees, contained fireworks. The force of that explosion caused a scale many feet away to topple over, injuring the plaintiff, Palsgraf. Palsgraf sued the railroad on negligence grounds.
    a. Defend the railroad.
    b. Decide. Explain. See *Palsgraf v. Long Island R.R.,* 162 N.E. 99 (N.Y. 1928).

12. Pat Stalter was injured when a bottle fell through the bottom of a soft drink carton and broke while she was shopping at Food City, a Little Rock, Arkansas, grocery store. A piece of glass went through her slacks, cutting her. A store employee said the carton was "mushy" and appeared to have been wet for some time. The bottles were in a display maintained by Coca-Cola Bottling Company. Two or three times a week the company cleaned the shelves and rotated the stock. Coca-Cola said that this process ensures that only minimal moisture is on bottles when they are placed in cartons. Most cartons are reused only once. Stalter sued Food City and Coca-Cola Bottling Company for damages.
    a. Explain the plaintiff's claims.
    b. Decide. See *Pat Stalter v. Coca-Cola Bottling Company of Arkansas and Geyer Springs Food City, Inc.,* 669 S.W.2d 460 (Ark. S. Ct. 1984).

13. Diane Elsroth was visiting her boyfriend, Michael Notarnicola, in the home of his parents. Diane complained of a headache, and Michael provided a Tylenol that his mother had bought earlier that week. Michael noted nothing unusual about the Tylenol packaging. After consuming two Tylenol capsules, Diane went to bed. She died during the night. The medical examiner concluded that the Tylenol had been contaminated with potassium cyanide. The murder was not solved. The evidence

established that the tampering with the Tylenol occurred after the product left the manufacturer's control. The packaging included a foil seal glued to the mouth of the container, a "shrink seal" around the neck and cap of the container, and a box with its ends glued shut. The manufacturer, McNeil, a wholly owned subsidiary of Johnson & Johnson, knew through its research that a determined, sophisticated tamperer could breach the packaging and reseal it in a manner that would not be visible to the average consumer. John Elsroth sued McNeil on behalf of Diane's estate. Was the Tylenol packaging defective in design? Explain. See *Elsroth v. Johnson & Johnson,* 700 F. Supp. 151 (S.D.N.Y. 1988).

14. In an attempt to commit suicide, Connie Daniell locked herself in the trunk of her 1973 Ford LTD automobile, where she remained for nine days before being freed. During the nine days, Daniell changed her mind and sought to escape, but she was unable to do so. She sued the Ford Motor Company for the injuries she sustained from her entrapment.

    a. What claims would she bring?

    b. Decide those claims. Explain. See *Daniell v. Ford Motor Company,* 581 F. Supp. 728 (N.Mex. 1984).

15. Plaintiff James L. Maguire was seriously injured when the motor vehicle in which he was a passenger was struck by another motor vehicle. Plaintiff alleges that Vikki Paulson, the driver of the other vehicle, was intoxicated at the time of the accident. Following the accident, Paulson entered guilty pleas to (1) operating a motor vehicle while under the influence of alcohol, (2) involuntary manslaughter as a consequence of the death of another passenger riding with Maguire, and (3) failure to stop at a stop sign. During the time in question in the case, Pabst Brewing Company had engaged in an advertising campaign promoting the sale of its products. Plaintiff claims the defendant Pabst was liable for his injuries because (among other claims) its advertising promoting the consumption of alcohol by those who drove to taverns constituted a danger to highway safety and because the brewer had failed to warn consumers of the dangers of alcohol consumption. Decide. Explain. See *Maguire v. Pabst Brewing Company,* 387 N.W.2d 565 (Iowa 1986).

16. Twenty-year-old Stephen Pavlik died from inhaling Zeus-brand butane while trying to "get high." His estate sued the Zeus maker, Lane. The fuel came in a small can with a printed warning reading, "DO NOT BREATHE SPRAY." The plaintiff argued that the can was defective because the warning inadequately expressed the hazard. A federal district court ruled that Pavlik was aware of the danger so the warning was adequate, and in any case, a warning would have had no effect so proximate cause could not exist. That decision was appealed. How would you rule on that appeal? Explain. See *Pavlik v. Lane Limited,* 135 F.3d 876 (3d Cir. 1998).

Notes

1. Timothy K. Smith, "Liability Costs Drive Small-Plane Business Back into Pilots, Barns," *The Wall Street Journal,* December 11, 1991, p. A1.

2. Mike Clancy, "Cessna Will Once Again Make Small Aircraft," *Des Moines Register,* March 15, 1995, p. 8S.

3. Smith, "Liability Costs," p. 8.

4. Smith, "Liability Costs."

5. Barbara Carton, "Cessna Says It Will Make More Small Airplanes," *The Wall Street Journal,* March 14, 1995, p. B1.

6. Thor Valdmanis, "6 Years after Nearly Collapsing, Piper Takes Off Again," *USA TODAY,* July 3, 2001, p. 6B.

7. Valdmanis, "6 Years after Nearly Collapsing."

8. Valdmanis, "6 Years after Nearly Collapsing."

9. Valdmanis, "6 Years after Nearly Collapsing."

10. 111 N.E. 1050 (N.Y. 1916).

11. Heidi Hurd, "The Deontology of Negligence," *Boston University Law Review* 76 (April 1996), p. 249.

12. *Doss v. Town of Big Stone Gap,* 134 S.E. 563 (Va. S. Ct. 1926).

13. Aric Press, Ginny Carrol, and Steven Waldman, "Are Lawyers Burning America?" *Newsweek,* March 20, 1995, p. 30.

14. Press, Carrol, and Waldman, "Are Lawyers Burning America?" p. 34.

15. "McDonald's Settles Lawsuit over Burn from Coffee," *The Wall Street Journal,* December 2, 1994, p. A14.

16. Editorial, "Hot Coffee? What a Litigious Idea . . ." *Santa Fe New Mexican,* March 28, 2002, p. A7.

17. Anthony Ramirez, "Hot Coffee Justice," *National Post,* April 11, 2002, p. FP15.

18. Dan Reed, "Californians Still Stirring Up Lawsuits over Hot Coffee," *San Jose Mercury News,* May 11, 2002, State and Regional News.

19. Associated Press, "Jury Sides with McDonald's in Burn Suit," *Waterloo/Cedar Falls Courier,* November 19, 1998, p. A3.

20. *Pat Stalter v. Coca-Cola Bottling Company of Arkansas and Geyer Springs Food City, Inc.,* 669 S.W.2d 460 (Ark. S. Ct. 1984).

21. For more detail on the treatment of risk–utility in the *Restatement (Third) of Torts,* see **http://library.lp.findlaw.com/articles/file/00849/002259/title/subject/topic/Products%20Liability_Risk-utility/filename/productsliability_2_916.**

22. Associated Press, "Toilet Brush, Rectal Thermometer Warnings Are Deemed Wackiest," *Waterloo/Cedar Falls Courier,* January 6, 2005, p. A2.

23. John M. Broder, "Warning Labels for Every Danger," *Des Moines Register,* March 9, 1997, p. G1.

24. *Whitlock v. University of Denver,* 712 P.2d 54 (Col. Ct. App. 1985).

25. *University of Denver v. Whitlock,* 744 P.2d 54 (Col. S. Ct. 1987).

26. 27 Cal. Rptr. 697, 377 P.2d 897 (Cal. S. Ct. 1963).

27. Associated Press, "California Jury Awards Former Smoker $28 Billion," *Waterloo/Cedar Falls Courier,* October 6, 2002, p. A10.

28. Associated Press, "Huge Awards Aside, Few Companies Forced to Write Big Checks," *Waterloo/Cedar Falls Courier,* October 12, 1997, p. C5.

29. "Stewing over Campbell," *Texas Lawyer,* September 13, 2004, p.25.

30. Editorial, "Less Litigation; Tort Reform Is a Bush Priority," *San Diego Union-Tribune,* November 15, 2004, p. B6.

31. Lou Dobbs, "Tort Reform Important to U.S. Future," *CNN,* January 6, 2005.

32. Jason Thompson, "Corporate Misconduct Helps Fuel Lawsuits," *Crain's Detroit Business,* August 30, 2004, p. 9.

33. Dan Zegart, "Tort Reform Advocates Play Fast and Loose with Facts," *The Seattle Post-Intelligencer,* November 21, 2004, p. F1.

34. Dobbs, "Tort Reform Important to U.S. Future."

35. Public Citizen, "Department of Justice Study Disproves Tort 'Reform' Myths," **http://www.citizen.org/print_article.cfm?ID=5671.**

36. Zegart, "Tort Reform Advocates Play Fast and Loose with Facts," p. F1.

37. Karen E. Crummy, "Fast-Food Junkies Sue Eateries over Fatty Food," *The Boston Herald,* July 26, 2002, Finance section, p. 1.

38. *Pelman and Bradley v. McDonald's,* 2005 U.S. App. LEXIS 1229 (U.S. Ct. App., 2d Cir.).

39. "McDonald's Obesity Law Suit Reinstated," **http://banzhaf.net/mcback.html.**

40. Annie Brown, "Operation Burger Kids," *Scottish Daily Record,* April 10, 2002, p.16.

41. Brown, "Operation Burger Kids."

42. Yuri Kageyama, "Car Launch Taken Up by Apologies at Japanese Automaker Mitsubishi Motors," *Associated Press Worldstream,* October 25, 2004.

43. Kazuo Mori, "Trust Is Most Potent Weapon," *The Nikkei Weekly (Japan),* January 11, 2005.

44. Mori, "Trust Is Most Potent Weapon."

Trade Regulation and Antitrust

Government Regulation of Business

Part One—An Introduction

PRACTICING ETHICS   Violent Video Games

Prior to Christmas 2004, the *Los Angeles Times* reported on growing concerns about violence in video games:

> This holiday season, children searching for the latest video game titles could walk into a store and buy "Grand Theft Auto: San Andreas"—which lets players kill cops, steal cars, solicit prostitutes, and then beat them to get their money back. Or kids could pick up a copy of "The Guy Game" and answer questions to get busty female characters to slip out of their clothes or engage in topless rope jumping and sack races.[1]

Should government intervene to prevent children from having access to violent or sexually explicit video games? Or will the market provide whatever protection is needed? Or perhaps we can count on the industry regulating itself as an expression of ethics and social responsibility? Indeed, the games are rated, such as, AO for adults only; but authorities have been increasingly concerned about a link between video games and violence by children. The article that follows explains recent governmental efforts to regulate some videos. [For the Entertainment Software Rating Board, see **http://www.esrb.org/index.asp**]

> Authorities have been increasingly concerned about a link between video games and violence by children.

Governor Wants to Ban Sale of Violent, Sexually Explicit Video Games to Minors

Maura Kelly Lannan

Governor Rod Blagojevich (Illinois) plans to propose a ban on the sale of violent and sexually explicit video games to minors, something other states have tried with little success.

Blagojevich's proposed legislation would prohibit the distribution, sale, rental, and availability of violent and sexually explicit video games to children younger than 18.

Current Illinois law does not prohibit selling or renting video games to children, regardless of how violent or sexually explicit the games may be. Under the governor's plan, violating the bans would be a Class A misdemeanor, punishable by up to one year in prison or a $5,000 fine.

The proposed legislation also would require retailers to label violent and sexually explicit video games. Video games now are rated with labels such as "M" for "mature."

"We already place limits on alcohol, tobacco, even adult movies. It's just logical that video games, which are so heavily marketed to young kids but many of which contain adult images, should not be available to young people or to minors," [spokeswoman Abby] Ottenhoff said.

The Illinois Retail Merchants Association blasted the governor's proposal as a way for retailers to become "the violence and sensitivity police for the state of Illinois."

"This is not just about video games. This is about the government asking their taxpaying, tax-generating, and employing companies to do what parents should be doing. It's wrong," said David Vite, president and chief executive officer of the association, which represents about 23,000 stores statewide.

Blagojevich's proposal follows calls last month by national advocacy groups for retailers to stop selling violent and sexually explicit video games to minors. The groups singled out popular and new video games that have players shoot rival gang members, watch bare-breasted women, and recreate the assassination of President Kennedy.

James Steyer, chief executive officer of Common Sense Media, a San Francisco–based advocacy group that monitors media content for children, welcomed Blagojevich's proposal, saying the video game industry does not regulate itself.

Other states, however, have tried similar bans with little success.

A federal judge in July struck down Washington State's ban on selling some violent video games to minors, calling it a violation of free speech. That state's ban sought to prevent minors from buying or renting games that portray "realistic or photographic-like depictions of aggressive conflict" in which the players kill or injure law enforcement officers.

The Judge said the Washington law was too narrow because it arbitrarily banned violence against police officers but not other depictions of violence, and too broad because it was unclear what games would fall under the ban.

Last year, a federal appeals court struck down a St. Louis County, Missouri, ordinance that required children under 17 to have parental consent before they could buy violent or sexually explicit video games or play similar arcade games. A similar ordinance in Indianapolis was struck down by a federal appeals court in Chicago.

"The courts have said that the statutes fail at all levels," said Gail Markels, senior vice president and general counsel for the Washington, D.C.–based Entertainment Software Association.

Ottenhoff said Illinois's proposal narrowly defines violent and sexually explicit video games to address concerns raised by federal courts.

In addition to proposing the legislation, Blagojevich also plans to launch a Web site where parents could read studies about the impact violent video games have on children's behavior. The site also would give parents a venue to report video games they think are inappropriate for children and to report retailers that are selling violent and sexually explicit games to minors.

Source: The Associated Press State and Local Wire, December 15, 2004. Reprinted by permission.

AFTERWORD

Governor Blagojevich's proposed video game legislation was approved by Illinois legislators and signed by the governor in July 2005. The video game industry immediately filed suit in federal court claiming the law restricts freedom of speech. Governor Blagojevich's office defended the constitutionality of the law citing the narrowly tailored nature of the new law as well as recent research linking video games and violence.

Questions

1. *a.* In your judgment, are violent and sexually explicit videos harmful to children?

    b. Would an ethical, socially responsible video store owner decline to sell violent or sexually explicit videos if evidence revealed that those videos often reach children? Explain.

2. *a.* Will the free market and industry ethics satisfactorily protect society from any harm that may emerge from video game playing or is legal intervention necessary? Explain.

    b. Does the First Amendment protect video games from government oversight?

    c. Should it? Explain.

3. A Scottish firm, Traffic Games, released in 2004 a video game that allows players to simulate the assassination of former U.S. President John F. Kennedy. The game purportedly was designed to undermine assassination conspiracy theories by showing that one person could have killed the president. The game allows slow-motion tracking of the bullets through the president's image, and blood can be viewed by pressing a blood effects button. Is the production and sale of this game an immoral act? Explain.

How Much Government?   In this chapter and all those that follow our central question will be: How much government do we need to protect us from business power? In the first three chapters we looked at the role of the free market and ethics as "regulators" of business behavior. Now we turn to the role the law plays in supplementing the market and ethics/self-regulation. The alleged link between video game violence and sexuality is one relatively small example of an enormous array of social problems springing from business practice where we have a heated debate about whether government should intervene in the market. How do we decide when a new rule is needed?

Why Regulation?

Market Failure

In theory, government intervention in a free enterprise economy would be justified only when the market is unable to serve the public interest—that is, in instances of market failure. Market failure is attributed to certain inherent imperfections in the market itself.

Imperfect Information

Can the consumer choose the best pain reliever in the absence of complete information about the virtues of the competing products? An efficient free market presumes reasoned decisions about production and consumption. Reasoned decisions require adequate information. Because we cannot have perfect information and often will not have adequate information, the government, it is argued, may impose regulations either to improve the available information or to diminish the unfavorable effect of inadequate information. Hence we have, for example, labeling mandates for consumer goods, licensure requirements for many occupations, and health standards for the processing and sale of goods.

The 2001 Nobel Prize for economics was awarded to three Americans whose research indicates that markets cannot behave as theorized—that is, rationally and efficiently—in part because buyers and sellers often do not have the information they need to make the best decisions. Put another way, their research demonstrates that we often face situations of asymmetric information where some parties to a transaction simply know more than do the other parties to that transaction, with the result that optimal efficiency cannot be achieved. Furthermore, recent research in behavioral economics suggests that we often act in ways that are contrary to our economic interests. Thus, while our free market system assumes rational decision making, we might more accurately recognize that we operate with limited or *bounded rationality*. Hence government intervention might be appropriate.

Monopoly

Of course, the government intervenes to thwart anticompetitive monopolies and oligopolies throughout the marketplace. (That process is addressed in Chapter 11.) Of immediate interest here is the so-called natural monopoly. Telephone and electrical services are classic examples of a decline in per unit production costs as the firm becomes larger.

Thus a single large firm is more efficient than several small ones, and a natural monopoly results. In such situations, the government has commonly intervened (in the form of public service commissions) to preserve the efficiencies of the large firm while preventing that firm from taking unfair advantage of the consumer. (We should note that natural monopoly theory is under increasing challenge from free market economists, and government has, of course, substantially deregulated the telephone industry and has been gradually doing the same with electric utilities.)

Externalities

When all the costs and benefits of a good or service are not fully internalized or absorbed, those costs or benefits fall elsewhere as what economists have labeled *externalities, neighborhood effects,* or *spillovers.* Pollution is a characteristic example of a negative externality. The environment is used without charge as an ingredient in the production process (commonly as a receptacle for waste). Consequently, the product is underpriced. The producer and consumer do not pay the full social cost of the product, so those remaining costs are thrust on parties external to the transaction. Government regulation is sometimes considered necessary to place the full cost on those who generated it, which in turn is expected to result in less wasteful use of resources. Positive externalities are those in which a producer confers benefits not required by the market. An example of such a positive externality is a business firm that, through no direct market compulsion, landscapes its grounds and develops a sculpture garden to contribute to the aesthetic quality of its neighborhood. Positive externalities ordinarily are not the subject of regulation.

Public Goods

Some goods and services cannot be provided through the pricing system because we have no method for excluding those who choose not to pay. For such *public goods,* the added cost of benefiting one person is zero or nearly so, and, in any case, no one can effectively be denied the benefits of the activity. National defense, insect eradication, and pollution control are examples of this phenomenon. Presumably most individuals would refuse to voluntarily pay for what others would receive free. Thus, in the absence of government regulations, public goods would not be produced in adequate quantities.

Regulatory Life Cycle?

These market failures and other forces, to be explained later, sometimes lead to government intervention (such as the Clean Air Act or the Occupational Safety and Health Act). Looking at the historical record, law school dean Joseph Tomain argues that a rather predictable pattern or life cycle typically emerges when the government decides to regulate an industry. Stage One in Tomain's life cycle is the free market itself, the period when government regulation is absent from the market in question. In Stage Two a market failure is identified, suggesting the need for government intervention. In Stage Three government regulation is imposed in the form of a rule (such as a minimum drinking age). In Stage Four regulatory failure occurs because, in brief, the benefits of the rule in question no longer exceed its costs. In Stage Five the government may respond with regulatory reform to correct the failure, or it may move to Stage Six where the regulation in question is simply eliminated. The market, thus fully deregulated, has returned to Stage One (the free market) and the regulatory life cycle is complete.[2] [To read about and submit comments on proposed rules affecting small businesses, see **http://www.sba.gov/ advo/laws/law_regalerts.html**]

Steroids

The 2004 steroid scandal in baseball allegedly involving Barry Bonds, Jason Giambi, and other major league stars led the *Des Moines Register* to argue for the value of regulation:

> Businesses forever complain about being regulated, but the truth is that reasonable regulation is good for business. It's easier to sell insurance to people who know regulators are helping keep the insurance companies solvent. It's easier to sell stocks to investors who think the SEC is on the job and easier to sell food to shoppers who trust the labels the FDA requires. Name an industry, and a case can be made that regulation helps it.
>
> Unfortunately, the barons of baseball never figured that out. The owners and players in big-league baseball resisted any regulation of performance-enhancing chemicals in their business.
>
> *   *   *   *   *
>
> Baseball had slipped in the affections of many Americans even before the scandal. Now, it's doubtful the sport can ever reclaim its good name.

In your view, should the government regulate performance-enhancing drug use in sports, or will self-regulation by the sports be sufficient?

Source: Editorial, "Baseball Barons Betrayed Game," *Des Moines Register,* December 14, 2004, p. 8A.

Philosophy and Politics

Correction of market failure arguably explains the full range of government regulation of business, but an alternative or perhaps supplemental explanation lies in the political process. Three general arguments have emerged.

1. One view is that regulation is necessary for the protection and general welfare of the public. We find the government engaging in regulatory efforts designed to achieve a more equitable distribution of income and wealth (such as, Social Security and the minimum wage). Many believe government intervention in the market is necessary to stabilize the economy, thus curbing the problems of recession, inflation, and unemployment. Affirmative action programs seek to compensate for racism and sexism. We even find the government protecting us from ourselves, both for our benefit and for the well-being of the larger society (consider seatbelt requirements).

2. Another view is that regulation is developed at the request of industry and is operated primarily for the benefit of industry. Here the various subsidies and tax advantages afforded to business might be cited. In numerous instances, government regu-

lation has been effective in reducing or entirely eliminating the entry of competitors. Government regulation has also permitted legalized price-fixing in some industries. Of course, it may be that regulation is often initiated primarily for the public welfare, but industry eventually "captures" the regulatory process and ensures its continuation for the benefit of the industry. On the other hand, some corporations seek government standards so they can do what is best for society without being undercut by their less socially responsible competitors.

3. Finally, bureaucrats who perform government regulation are themselves a powerful force in maintaining and expanding that regulation.

The Constitutional Foundation of Business Regulation

The Commerce Clause of the U.S. Constitution broadly specifies the power accorded to the federal government to regulate business activity. Article I, Section 8 of the Constitution provides that "The Congress shall have the power . . . to regulate Commerce with foreign Nations, and among the several States, and with the Indian Tribes." State authority to regulate commerce resides in the police power specified by the Constitution. *Police power* refers to the right of the state governments to promote the public health, safety, morals, and general welfare by regulating persons and property within each state's jurisdiction. The states have, in turn, delegated portions of the police power to local government units.

Supremacy Clause

Sometimes state or local law conflicts with federal law. Such situations are resolved by the Supremacy Clause of the Constitution, which provides that "This Constitution and the Laws of the United States . . . shall be the Supreme Law of the Land."

As explained in Chapter 5, ours is a *federalist* form of government wherein we divide authority among federal, state, and local units of government. Conflicts between the preferences of each level are inevitable. The Supremacy Clause, as interpreted by the Supreme Court, establishes that, in the event of an irreconcilable conflict, federal law will prevail and the state or local law will be ruled unconstitutional. Were it not so, we would have great difficulty in achieving a unified national policy on any issue.

At the same time, the Supreme Court has affirmed the states' strong role in our dual system of government by announcing that "it will read federal law to preempt state governmental functions only if Congress plainly states its intent to do so."[3]

Commerce Clause

The Commerce Clause, as interpreted by the judiciary, affords Congress exclusive jurisdiction over foreign commerce. States and localities, nevertheless, sometimes seek in various ways to regulate foreign commerce. For example, a state may seek, directly or indirectly, to impose a tax on foreign goods that compete with those locally grown or manufactured. Such efforts violate the Commerce Clause.

Federal authority over interstate commerce was designed to create a free market throughout the United States, wherein goods would move among the states, unencumbered by state and local tariffs and duties. The Constitution does not, however, expressly forbid state regulation of interstate commerce. As with foreign commerce, the states and localities pass laws to influence interstate commerce, often to favor local economic interests. The judiciary has aggressively curbed those efforts, and in the process, the reach of the federal government has been dramatically expanded. Even purely intrastate activities can be regulated by the federal government if they have a substantial effect on interstate commerce. In the 1942 case *Wickard v. Filburn,*[4] the U.S. Supreme Court, in interpreting a federal statute regulating the production and sale of wheat, found that one farmer's production of 23 acres of homegrown and largely home-consumed wheat, in combination with other similarly situated farmers growing and consuming wheat locally, could substantially affect interstate commerce and thus was subject to federal regulation. In 2005 the Supreme Court affirmed the *Wickard* reasoning in an interesting California case, *Gonzalez v. Raich,*[5] involving the federal government's constitutional authority to regulate the use of medical marijuana.

In 1996 California became the first of 10 states to decriminalize the doctor-approved medical use of marijuana. The federal Controlled Substances Act (CSA), on the other hand, forbids the use, cultivation, or possession of marijuana for any purpose. A Californian, Angel Raich, who, under a doctor's prescription, used marijuana for pain control, challenged the application of the CSA against California medical marijuana users. The heart of her claim was that the Commerce Clause does not give the federal government the authority to regulate the noncommercial cultivation and personal, medical use of marijuana that does not cross state lines. She won at the U.S. Court of Appeals for the Ninth Circuit, but the U.S. Supreme Court, by a 6–3 vote, ruled against Raich. Addressing the central question, the Court reasoned that the wholly *intrastate* use of marijuana had a substantial effect on *interstate* commerce in marijuana and thus was subject to federal regulation, as the Court had ruled decades earlier in *Wickard*. Personal consumption of marijuana, even for medical purposes, has the potential to displace demand for marijuana in the illegal interstate market, thus substantially affecting interstate commerce. To rule otherwise would hinder federal enforcement of the national drug market because authorities would not be able to determine whether marijuana in the possession of a person was grown locally or shipped across state lines.

> Angel Raich used marijuana for pain control

The immediate practical implications of the *Raich* decision are unclear. The decision does not strike down California's Compassionate Use Act or similar laws in other states; but will federal agents, for example, begin to raid the 43 cannabis clubs in San Francisco? The federal policy to date has been to pursue major cultivators and traffickers. Whether that policy will change is unknown. Medical marijuana advocates are expected to press Congress for a change in the federal law, but that campaign will be difficult.

Can States Protect American Jobs?

Americans are understandably frustrated by the market-driven loss of jobs to cheaper foreign labor markets. *The Wall Street Journal* in 2004 reported that Congress and at least 33 states were considering "Buy American" laws encouraging businesses to keep work in America. At first glance, the laws look to be shrewd efforts to regulate the market to American advantage; but as the *Journal* explains, those laws at the state level are probably unconstitutional:

> Most of the proposals would ban government contracts to companies that carry out the work overseas. In the case of state laws, this trespasses on Washington's constitutional prerogative to run foreign affairs and regulate commerce. We're all for federalism, but the Supreme Court has routinely found that Indiana isn't supposed to have an independent foreign policy. . . . This means that sooner or later state outsourcing laws are likely to be struck down by federal courts.

So although we want to keep jobs in America, the Constitution and the courts tell us that only the federal government can regulate foreign commerce. Further, global trade pacts and World Trade Organization (WTO) rules limit what Congress can do to favor America over other nations.

Source: Editorial, "The Law of Outsourcing," *The Wall Street Journal,* April 19, 2004, p. A20.

Too Much Federal Power?

For the long term, the significance of the medical marijuana decision lies in its Commerce Clause reasoning. The decision appears to reaffirm the broad reach of federal power over activities that are economic in some sense. Dissenting in *Raich,* Supreme Court Justice Thomas warned,

> If Congress can regulate this under the Commerce Clause, then it can regulate virtually anything—and the federal government is no longer one of limited and enumerated powers.[6]

Of course, we must remember that the case dealt with the sensitive subject of unlawful drug use, where the courts are more inclined to defer to federal policy. Furthermore, in recent years, the Supreme Court issued two important opinions clearly designed to demonstrate that the Commerce Clause does not accord unlimited power to the federal government. In the 1995 *United States v. Lopez* decision[7] the Supreme Court clearly spoke for states' rights.

> A 12th-grade San Antonio, Texas, student carried an unloaded, concealed gun into his high school

In 1990 the federal government approved the Gun-Free School Zones Act, which forbade "any individual knowingly to possess a firearm at a place that [he] knows . . . is a school zone."[8] A 12th-grade San Antonio, Texas, student carried an unloaded, concealed gun into his high school and was charged with violating the act. His case reached the Supreme Court, where he claimed and the Court agreed that Congress did not have the constitutional authority to regulate the matter. By a 5–4 vote the Court held that Congress exceeded its powers by defining the possession of a gun as economic activity that, through repetition elsewhere, would have a substantial effect on interstate commerce.

Strengthening its *Lopez* reasoning, the U.S. Supreme Court in the 2001 *Morrison* case[9] ruled by a 5–4 vote that Congress exceeded its Commerce Clause authority in approving some portions of the federal Violence Against Women Act (VAWA). The law allowed women who had been victims of gender-based violence to sue in federal court even though the crimes did not directly involve more than one state. In debating VAWA, Congress held hearings and developed a record on the aggregate economic impact of violence against women, including driving up medical costs and discouraging women from traveling and from holding jobs, but the Court said Congress did not have the power to regulate noneconomic violent crime simply on the basis of the total effect of that behavior on interstate commerce.

> ### Brzonkala claimed she was raped by two football players

The case involved a woman, Brzonkala, who claimed she was raped by two football players, Morrison and Crawford, when all three were students at Virginia Polytechnic Institute:

> Brzonkala alleges that soon after she met Morrison and Crawford, the two defendants pinned her down on a bed in her dormitory and forcibly raped her. Afterward, Morrison told Brzonkala, "You better not have any f* * *ing diseases." And, subsequently, Morrison announced publicly in the dormitory's dining hall, "I like to get girls drunk and f* * * the s* * * out of them."[10]

After Brzonkala complained to the university, Morrison was found guilty of abusive conduct by the VPI judicial committee and was suspended for one year, but that punishment was subsequently lifted.[11] Brzonkala then sued for civil damages in federal court, which led eventually to the Supreme Court decision. [For the federal Violence Against Women Office, see **http://www.ojp.usdoj.gov/vawo/**]

Lopez and *Morrison* denote a narrow majority sentiment in the U.S. Supreme Court to at least occasionally question the limits of federal power and thus to affirm the importance of states' rights; but *Raich* and a trio of less dramatic 2005 Supreme Court decisions suggest that the Supreme Court is not currently inclined to broadly challenge the pervasive authority of the federal government. The classic decision that follows illustrates the importance of Commerce Clause reasoning. In this case Congress used its economic authority under the Commerce Clause to open public accommodations (hotels, restaurants, and the like) to all persons, thus reshaping American social and racial practices.

LEGAL BRIEFCASE

Heart of Atlanta Motel v. United States 379 U.S. 241 (1964)

Justice Clark

This is a declaratory judgment action, attacking the constitutionality of Title II of the Civil Rights Act of 1964. [The lower court found for the United States.]

1. THE FACTUAL BACKGROUND AND CONTENTIONS OF THE PARTIES

. . . Appellant owns and operates the Heart of Atlanta Motel, which has 216 rooms available to transient guests. The motel is located on Courtland Street, two blocks from downtown Peachtree Street. It is readily accessible to interstate highways 75 and 85 and state highways 23 and 41. Appellant solicits patronage from outside the State of Georgia through various national advertising media, including magazines of national circulation; it maintains over 50 billboards and highway signs within the state, soliciting patronage for the motel; it accepts convention trade from outside Georgia, and approximately 75 percent of its registered guests are from out of state. Prior to passage of the act the motel had followed a practice of refusing to rent rooms to Negroes, and it alleged that it intended to continue to do so. In an effort to perpetuate that policy this suit was filed.

The appellant contends that Congress in passing this act exceeded its power to regulate commerce under [Article I] of the Constitution of the United States....

The appellees counter that the unavailability to Negroes of adequate accommodations interferes significantly with interstate travel, and that Congress, under the Commerce Clause, has power to remove such obstructions and restraints....

[A]ppellees proved the refusal of the motel to accept Negro transients after the passage of the act. The district court sustained the constitutionality of the sections of the act under attack and issued a permanent injunction.... It restrained the appellant from "[r]efusing to accept Negroes as guests in the motel by reason of their race or color" and from "[m]aking any distinction whatever upon the basis of race or color in the availability of the goods, services, facilities, privileges, advantages, or accommodations offered or made available to the guests of the motel, or to the general public, within or upon any of the premises of the Heart of Atlanta Motel, Inc."

2. THE HISTORY OF THE ACT

... The act as finally adopted was most comprehensive, undertaking to prevent through peaceful and voluntary settlement discrimination in voting, as well as in places of accommodation and public facilities, federally secured programs, and in employment. Since Title II is the only portion under attack here, we confine our consideration to those public accommodation provisions.

3. TITLE II OF THE ACT

This Title is divided into seven sections beginning with § 201(a), which provides,

> "All persons shall be entitled to the full and equal enjoyment of the goods, services, facilities, privileges, advantages, and accommodations of any place of public accommodation, as defined in this section, without discrimination or segregation on the ground of race, color, religion, or national origin."

4. APPLICATION OF TITLE II TO HEART OF ATLANTA MOTEL

It is admitted that the operation of the motel brings it within the provisions of § 201(a) of the act and that appellant refused to provide lodging for transient Negroes because of their race or color and that it intends to continue that policy unless restrained.

The sole question posed is, therefore, the constitutionality of the Civil Rights Act of 1964 as applied to these facts....

[Part 5 omitted.]

6. THE BASIS OF CONGRESSIONAL ACTION

While the act as adopted carried no congressional findings, the record of its passage through each house is replete with evidence of the burdens that discrimination by race or color places upon interstate commerce.... This testimony included the fact that our people have become increasingly mobile with millions of people of all races traveling from state to state; that Negroes in particular have been the subject of discrimination in transient accommodations, having to travel great distances to secure the same; that often they have been unable to obtain accommodations and have had to call upon friends to put them up overnight, and that these conditions have become so acute as to require the listing of available lodging for Negroes in a special guidebook which was itself "dramatic testimony to the difficulties" Negroes encounter in travel. These exclusionary practices were found to be nationwide, the Under Secretary of Commerce testifying that there is "no question that this discrimination in the North still exists to a large degree" and in the West and Midwest as well. This testimony indicated a qualitative as well as quantitative effect on interstate travel by Negroes. The former was the obvious impairment of the Negro traveler's pleasure and convenience that resulted when he continually was uncertain of finding lodging. As for the latter, there was evidence that this uncertainty stemming from racial discrimination had the effect of discouraging travel on the part of a substantial portion of the Negro community. This was the conclusion not only of the Under Secretary of Commerce but also of the Administrator of the Federal Aviation Agency, who wrote the Chairman of the Senate Commerce Committee that it was his "belief that air commerce is adversely affected by the denial to a substantial segment of the traveling public of adequate and desegregated public accommodations." We shall not burden this opinion with further details since the voluminous testimony presents overwhelming evidence that discrimination by hotels and motels impedes interstate travel.

7. THE POWER OF CONGRESS OVER INTERSTATE TRAVEL

The power of Congress to deal with these obstructions depends on the meaning of the Commerce Clause.

* * * * *

In short, the determinative test of the exercise of power by the Congress under the Commerce Clause is simply whether the activity sought to be regulated is "commerce which concerns more States than one" and has a real and substantial relation to the national interest. Let us now turn to this facet of the problem.

* * * * *

The same interest in protecting interstate commerce which led Congress to deal with segregation in interstate carriers and the white-slave traffic has prompted it to extend the exercise of its power to gambling, to criminal enterprises, to deceptive practices in the sale of products, to fraudulent security transactions, and to racial discrimination by owners and managers of terminal restaurants. . . .

That Congress was legislating against moral wrongs in many of these areas rendered its enactments no less valid. In framing Title II of this act Congress was also dealing with what it considered a moral problem. But that fact does not detract from the overwhelming evidence of the disruptive effect the racial discrimination has had on commercial intercourse. It was this burden which empowered Congress to enact appropriate legislation, and, given this basis for the exercise of its power, Congress was not restricted by the fact that the particular obstruction to interstate commerce with which it was dealing was also deemed a moral and social wrong.

It is said that the operation of the motel here is of a purely local character. But, assuming this to be true, "[i]f it is interstate commerce that feels the pinch, it does not matter how local the operation which applies the squeeze."

* * * * *

Thus the power of Congress to promote interstate commerce also includes the power to regulate the local incidents thereof, including local activities in both the states of origin and destination, which might have a substantial and harmful effect upon that commerce. One need only examine the evidence which we have discussed above to see that Congress may—as it has—prohibit racial discrimination by motels serving travelers, however "local" their operations may appear.

* * * * *

The only questions are (1) whether Congress had a rational basis for finding that racial discrimination by motels affected commerce, and (2) if it had such a basis, whether the means it selected to eliminate that evil are reasonable and appropriate. If they are, appellant has no "right" to select its guests as it sees fit, free from governmental regulation.

* * * * *

It is doubtful if in the long run appellant will suffer economic loss as a result of the act. Experience is to the contrary where discrimination is completely obliterated as to all public accommodations. But whether this be true or not is of no consequence since this Court has specifically held that the fact that a "member of the class which is regulated may suffer economic losses not shared by others . . . has never been a barrier" to such legislation. . . .

We, therefore, conclude that the action of the Congress in the adoption of the act as applied here to a motel which concededly serves interstate travelers is within the power granted it by the Commerce Clause of the Constitution, as interpreted by this Court for 140 years. . . .

Affirmed.

Questions

1. In your judgment, does the Commerce Clause afford the federal government the authority to regulate a local business like the Heart of Atlanta motel? Explain.

2. Should the federal government regulate local business to further the cause of racial equity? Explain.

3. What arguments were offered by the government to establish that the Heart of Atlanta racial policy affected interstate commerce? Are you persuaded by those arguments? Explain.

4. What test did the Court articulate to determine when Congress has the power to pass legislation based on the Commerce Clause?

5. Ollie's Barbecue, a neighborhood restaurant in Birmingham, Alabama, discriminated against black customers. McClung brought suit to test the application of the public accommodations section of the Civil Rights Act of 1964 to his restaurant. In the suit, the government offered no evidence to show that the restaurant ever had served interstate customers or that it was likely to do so. Decide the case. See *Katzenbach v. McClung,* 379 U.S. 294 (1964).

6. Juan Paul Robertson was charged with various narcotics offenses and with violating the federal Racketeer Influenced and Corrupt Organizations Act (RICO) by investing the proceeds from his unlawful activities in an Alaskan gold mine. He paid for some mining equipment in Los Angeles and had it shipped to Alaska. He hired seven out-of-state employees to work in the Alaskan mine. Most of the resulting gold was sold in Alaska, although Robertson transported $30,000 in gold out of the state. He was convicted on the RICO charge, but appealed claiming that the gold mine was not engaged in or affecting interstate commerce. Was Robertson's gold mine engaged in or affecting interstate commerce? Explain. See *United States v. Juan Paul Robertson,* 115 S.Ct. 1732 (1995).

7. In the San Antonio case (*Lopez*) in which a 12th-grade student brought a concealed gun to school, how would you argue that the possession of a gun in a school zone substantially affects interstate commerce?

Part Two—State and Local Regulation of Interstate Commerce

As noted, the states via their constitutional *police power* have the authority to regulate commerce within their jurisdictions for the purpose of maintaining public health, safety, and morals. We have seen, however, that the Commerce Clause accords the federal government broad authority over commerce. As explained, the federal government has exclusive authority over foreign commerce. Purely intrastate commerce, having no significant effect on interstate commerce, is within the exclusive regulatory jurisdiction of the states. Of course, purely intrastate commerce is uncommon. The confusion arises in the middle ground of interstate commerce where regulation by the federal government or state governments or both may be permissible. While federal government regulation of interstate commerce is pervasive, it is not exclusive, especially in matters involving the states' police powers.

Here we are concerned with commerce that is clearly interstate but that is subjected to state and/or local regulation. The issue is whether that regulation is unconstitutional because it (1) discriminates against interstate commerce or (2) unduly burdens interstate commerce such that the burden imposed clearly exceeds the local benefits.

In the *Granholm* case that follows, we see elements of the continuing conflict between federal and state control of interstate commerce, especially in matters of health and safety (police power). At the commercial level, the case is about another classic conflict: free trade versus protectionism. Can states lawfully protect their local wineries from out-of-state competition? The lower courts were divided on the question of whether the Commerce Clause of the federal constitution is violated when a state permits in-state wineries to ship directly to in-state customers while not permitting out-of-state wineries to do the same. Historically only a few states had allowed wineries to ship directly to customers; but gradually about half of the states allowed direct shipments, resulting in a confusing situation where some states allowed all shipments, some permitted in-state shipments only, and some forbade all shipments. In the 5–4 decision that follows, the Supreme Court narrowly resolved the split in the lower courts. The central question facing the Court was the conflict between the requirements of the Commerce Clause versus the requirements of the Twenty-First Amendment to the United States Constitution. That Amendment ended Prohibition in 1933 and gave the states broad authority to regulate the sale of alcohol.

> Can states lawfully protect their local wineries from out-of-state competition?

Granholm v. Heald   2005 U.S.

LEGAL BRIEFCASE   LEXIS 4174

Justice Kennedy

These consolidated cases present challenges to state laws regulating the sale of wine from out-of-state wineries to consumers in Michigan and New York. The details and mechanics of the two regulatory schemes differ, but the object and effect of the laws are the same: to allow in-state wineries to sell wine directly to consumers in that state but to prohibit out-of-state wineries from doing so, or, at the least, to make direct sales impractical from an economic standpoint. It is evident that the object and design of the Michigan and New York statutes is to grant in-state wineries a competitive advantage over wineries located beyond the states' borders.

* * * * *

I

Like many other states, Michigan and New York regulate the sale and importation of alcoholic beverages, including wine, through a three-tier distribution system. Separate licenses are required for producers, wholesalers, and retailers. [See FTC, Possible Anticompetitive Barriers to E-Commerce: Wine 5-7 (July 2003) hereinafter FTC Report), available at **http://www .ftc.gov/os/2003/07/winereport2.pdf**] . . . We have held previously that states can mandate a three-tier distribution scheme in the exercise of their authority under the Twenty-First Amendment. As relevant to today's cases, though, the three-tier system is, in broad terms and with refinements to be discussed, mandated by Michigan and New York only for sales from out-of-state wineries. In-state wineries, by contrast, can obtain a license for direct sales to consumers. The differential treatment between in-state and out-of-state wineries constitutes explicit discrimination against interstate commerce.

This discrimination substantially limits the direct sale of wine to consumers, an otherwise emerging and significant business. From 1994 to 1999, consumer spending on direct wine shipments doubled, reaching $500 million per year, or 3 percent of all wine sales. The expansion has been influenced by several related trends. First, the number of small wineries in the United States has significantly increased. By some estimates there are over 3,000 wineries in the country . . . more than three times the number 30 years ago. At the same time, the wholesale market has consolidated. Between 1984 and 2002, the number of licensed wholesalers dropped from 1,600 to 600. The increasing winery-to-wholesaler ratio means that many small wineries do not produce enough wine or have sufficient consumer demand for their wine to make it economical for wholesalers to carry their products. This has led many small wineries to rely on direct shipping to reach new markets. Technological improvements, in particular the ability of wineries to sell wine over the Internet, have helped make direct shipments an attractive sales channel.

Approximately 26 states allow some direct shipping of wine, with various restrictions. Thirteen of these states have reciprocity laws, which allow direct shipment from wineries outside the state, provided the state of origin affords similar nondiscriminatory treatment. In many parts of the country, however, state laws that prohibit or severely restrict direct shipments deprive consumers of access to the direct market.

The wine producers in the cases before us are small wineries that rely on direct consumer sales as an important part of their businesses. Domaine Alfred, one of the plaintiffs in the Michigan suit, is a small winery located in San Luis Obispo, California. It produces 3,000 cases of wine per year. Domaine Alfred has received requests for its wine from Michigan consumers but cannot fill the orders because of the state's direct shipment ban. Even if the winery could find a Michigan wholesaler to distribute its wine, the wholesaler's markup would render shipment through the three-tier system economically infeasible.

Similarly, Juanita Swedenburg and David Lucas, two of the plaintiffs in the New York suit, operate small wineries in Virginia (the Swedenburg Estate Vineyard) and California (the Lucas Winery). Some of their customers are tourists from other states, who purchase wine while visiting the wineries. If these customers wish to obtain Swedenburg or Lucas wines after they return home, they will be unable to do so if they reside in a state with restrictive direct shipment laws. . . .

A

We first address the background of the suit challenging the Michigan direct shipment law. Most alcoholic beverages in Michigan are distributed through the state's three-tier system. Producers or distillers of alcoholic beverages, whether located in state or out of state, generally may sell only to licensed in-state wholesalers. Wholesalers, in turn, may sell only to in-state retailers. Licensed retailers are the final link in the chain, selling alcoholic beverages to consumers at retail locations and, subject to certain restrictions, through home delivery.

Under Michigan law, wine producers, as a general matter, must distribute their wine through wholesalers. There is, however, an exception for Michigan's approximately 40 in-state wineries, which are eligible for "wine maker" licenses that allow direct shipment to in-state consumers. The cost of the license varies with the size of the winery. For a small winery, the license is $25. Out-of-state wineries can apply for a $300 "outside seller of wine" license, but this license only allows them to sell to in-state wholesalers.

* * * * *

B

New York's licensing scheme is somewhat different. It channels most wine sales through the three-tier system, but it too makes exceptions for in-state wineries. As in Michigan, the result is to allow local wineries to make direct sales to consumers in New York on terms not available to out-of-state wineries. Wineries that produce only from New York grapes can apply for a license that allows direct shipment to in-state consumers. These licensees are authorized to deliver the wines of other wineries as well, but only if the wine is made from grapes "at least seventy-five percent the volume of which were grown in New York state." An out-of-state winery may ship directly to New York consumers only if it becomes a licensed New York winery, which requires the establishment of "a branch factory, office, or storeroom within the state of New York."

* * * * *

C

We consolidated these cases and granted certiorari on the following question: "'Does a state's regulatory scheme that permits in-state wineries directly to ship alcohol to consumers but restricts the ability of out-of-state wineries to do so violate the Commerce Clause in light of § 2 of the Twenty-First Amendment?'"

II

A

Time and again this Court has held that, in all but the narrowest circumstances, state laws violate the Commerce Clause if they mandate "differential treatment of in-state and out-of-state economic interests that benefits the former and burdens the latter." This rule is essential to the foundations of the Union. The mere fact of nonresidence should not foreclose a producer in one state from access to markets in other States. States may not enact laws that burden out-of-state producers or shippers simply to give a competitive advantage to in-state businesses. This mandate "reflects a central concern of the Framers that was an immediate reason for calling the Constitutional Convention: the conviction that in order to succeed, the new Union would have to avoid the tendencies toward economic Balkanization that had plagued relations among the Colonies and later among the States under the Articles of Confederation."

* * * * *

B

The discriminatory character of the Michigan system is obvious. Michigan allows in-state wineries to ship directly to consumers, subject only to a licensing requirement. Out-of-state wineries, whether licensed or not, face a complete ban on direct shipment. The differential treatment requires all out-of-state wine, but not all in-state wine, to pass through an in-state wholesaler and retailer before reaching consumers. These two extra layers of overhead increase the cost of out-of-state wines to Michigan consumers. The cost differential, and in some cases the inability to secure a wholesaler for small shipments, can effectively bar small wineries from the Michigan market.

The New York regulatory scheme differs from Michigan's in that it does not ban direct shipments altogether. Out-of-state wineries are instead required to establish a distribution operation in New York in order to gain the privilege of direct shipment.

* * * * *

The New York scheme grants in-state wineries access to the state's consumers on preferential terms. . . . In-state producers, with the applicable licenses, can ship directly to consumers from their wineries. Out-of-state wineries must open a branch office and warehouse in New York, additional steps that drive up the cost of their wine.

* * * * *

We have no difficulty concluding that New York, like Michigan, discriminates against interstate commerce through its direct shipping laws.

III

State laws that discriminate against interstate commerce face "a virtually *per se* rule of invalidity." The Michigan and New York laws by their own terms violate this proscription. The two states, however, contend their statutes are saved by § 2 of the Twenty-First Amendment, which provides,

> The Transportation or importation into any State, Territory, or possession of the United States for delivery or use therein of intoxicating liquors, in violation of the laws thereof, is hereby prohibited.

* * * * *

"The Twenty-First Amendment grants the states virtually complete control over whether to permit importation or sale of liquor and how to structure the liquor distribution system." A state which chooses to ban the sale and consumption of alcohol altogether could bar its importation. . . . States may also assume direct control of liquor distribution through state-run outlets, or funnel sales through the three-tier system. We have previously recognized that the three-tier system itself is "unquestionably legitimate." . . . State policies are protected under the Twenty-First Amendment when they treat liquor produced out of state the same as its domestic equivalent. The instant cases, in contrast, involve straightforward attempts to discriminate in favor of local producers. The discrimination is contrary to the Commerce Clause and is not saved by the Twenty-First Amendment.

IV

Our determination that the Michigan and New York direct shipment laws are not authorized by the Twenty-First Amendment does not end the inquiry. We still must consider whether either state regime "advances a legitimate local purpose that cannot be adequately served by reasonable nondiscriminatory alternatives." The states offer two primary justifications for restricting direct shipments from out-of-state wineries: keeping alcohol out of the hands of minors and facilitating tax collection.

The states claim that allowing direct shipment from out-of-state wineries undermines their ability to police underage drinking. Minors, the states argue, have easy access to credit cards and the Internet and are likely to take advantage of direct wine shipments as a means of obtaining alcohol illegally.

The states provide little evidence that the purchase of wine over the Internet by minors is a problem. Indeed, there is some evidence to the contrary. A recent study by the staff of the FTC found that the 26 states currently allowing direct shipments report no problems with minors' increased access to wine.

* * * * *

Even were we to credit the states' largely unsupported claim that direct shipping of wine increases the risk of underage drinking, this would not justify regulations limiting only out-of-state direct shipments. As the wineries point out, minors are just as likely to order wine from in-state producers as from out-of-state ones. Michigan, for example, already allows its licensed retailers (over 7,000 of them) to deliver alcohol directly to consumers. Michigan counters that it has greater regulatory control over in-state producers than over out-of-state wineries. This does not justify Michigan's discriminatory ban on direct shipping. Out-of-state wineries face the loss of state and federal licenses if they fail to comply with state law. This provides strong incentives not to sell alcohol to minors. In addition, the states can take less restrictive steps to minimize the risk that minors will order wine by mail. For example, the Model Direct Shipping Bill developed by the National Conference of State Legislatures requires an adult signature on delivery and a label so instructing on each package.

The states' tax collection justification is also insufficient.

* * * * *

Michigan and New York benefit from provisions of federal law that supply incentives for wineries to comply with state regulations. The Tax and Trade Bureau has authority to revoke a winery's federal license if it violates state law. Without a federal license, a winery cannot operate in any state. In addition, the Twenty-First Amendment Enforcement Act gives state attorneys general the power to sue wineries in federal court to enjoin violations of state law.

These federal remedies, when combined with state licensing regimes, adequately protect states from lost tax revenue. The states have not shown that tax evasion from out-of-state wineries poses such a unique threat that it justifies their discriminatory regimes.

* * * * *

V

States have broad power to regulate liquor under § 2 of the Twenty-First Amendment. This power, however, does not allow states to ban, or severely limit, the direct shipment of out-of-state wine while simultaneously authorizing direct shipment by in-state producers. If a state chooses to allow direct shipment of wine, it must do so on evenhanded terms. Without demonstrating the need for discrimination, New York and Michigan have enacted regulations that disadvantage out-of-state wine producers. Under our Commerce Clause jurisprudence, these regulations [are unconstitutional].

* * * * *

Afterword

Dissent The dissenting opinions (not reproduced here) largely turned on the argument that the Twenty-First Amendment to the Constitution gives states broad authority to regulate liquor sales and that federal legislation (the Webb–Kenyon Act) clearly evidences congressional intent to allow state regulation of liquor, free from Commerce Clause review.

Implications *Granholm* may contribute to the broader deregulation and privatization movement (explained later in this chapter) throughout the American economy. Experts cite beer, real estate, automobiles, contact lenses, and mortgages as some of the products that may ultimately be affected by *Granholm*. For example, at this writing Costco, the giant warehouse retailer, is suing to overturn Washington State regulations that prevent Costco from buying beer directly from breweries. Rather, Costco and all retailers must buy alcoholic drinks from closely regulated wholesalers. Washington's Liquor Control Board, like those in all other states, seeks to shield the state from the hazards that can accompany liquor and beer sales; but Costco argues that the restrictive Washington rules violate the Commerce Clause by burdening interstate sales and violate the federal Sherman Antitrust Act (see Chapter 10.) If Costco succeeds, the result could be lower retail beer prices. Small, in-state wineries and microbreweries, on the other hand, argue that deregulation would drive them out of business, thus reducing consumer choice.

Questions

1. *a.* Why did the *Granholm* court strike down the New York and Michigan laws?

   b. What legal and practical justifications were presented by New York and Michigan in defense of their laws?

2. *a.* What choice now faces the states that are affected by this decision?

   b. What practical effect is this decision likely to have on the wine industry?

3. An Indiana statute prohibited the practice of backhauling municipal waste. Indiana was trying to prevent truckers from hauling trash on the homeward-bound leg of a trip after having delivered other goods on the outbound leg. On its face, the statute applied evenly to intrastate and interstate carriers. Most in-state waste was hauled in dedicated garbage trucks (those used exclusively for garbage). The Indiana statute was challenged by two companies engaged in brokering waste disposal.

   a. What constitutional challenge was raised by the plaintiffs?

   b. What defense was raised by Indiana?

   c. Decide. See *Government Suppliers Consolidating Service and Jack Castenova v. Evan Bayh and Kathy*

Prosser, 975 F.2d 1267 (7th Cir. 1992); cert. den. 113 S.Ct. 977 (1993).

4. North Dakota rules require those bringing liquor into the state to file a monthly report, and out-of-state distillers selling to federal enclaves (military bases, in this instance) must label each item indicating that it is for consumption only within the enclave. The United States challenged those rules after sellers said they would discontinue dealing with the military bases or they would raise their prices to meet the cost of dealing with the two rules.

   a. What are the constitutional foundations of the federal government's challenge?

   b. What were the state's reasons for adopting the rules?

   c. Decide. Explain. See *North Dakota v. United States,* 495 U.S. 423 (1990).

5. Premium Standard Farms, a large Missouri hog-raising operation, was pumping manure through a two-mile-long pipe into Iowa to be spread on a farm whose operator sought the manure for fertilizer. Iowa citizens objected and asked Attorney General Tom Miller to act. Can the Iowa attorney general stop the pumping? Explain.

Federalism and Free Trade

America's political structure is built on the federalist principle of a careful balance of power between the local, state, and federal governments. We prefer local control in the belief that those closest to a problem are best situated to understand and address it. At the same time, we also recognize that we cannot have a unified nation with all the benefits of that status without substantial central control. As we saw in the *Granholm* case, localities and states may pass rules to meet their needs; but the nation's needs, as expressed in the Constitution, may be undermined. If lawful, each state would be racing to erect protectionist trade barriers to benefit its citizens while burdening commerce from other states and localities. The Commerce Clause is the legal standard that prevents that kind of fracturing of the United States. Still, ample protectionism remains. Some of it, of course, may be desirable. We cannot, for example, simply move from one state to another to practice law or sell real estate. Each state sets up its own licensing rules to protect the welfare of its citizens. Of course, those rules also restrict competition.

How, for example, does a nation build an efficient, unified communications system if each local community has the power to block or increase the expense of the process of laying the necessary cables to transmit messages? Telecommunications companies are trying to spread a broadband network (the "fat" cables and equipment necessary for high-speed Internet access) across the country, but they are running into a patchwork of differing rules from community to community as they seek permission to use city streets and other rights of way for their cables. The cities, on the other hand, say the telecom companies want cheap access to valuable rights of way and that they do not fully pay for the damage they do in digging up streets.

Globalism versus Nationalism

Those protectionist tendencies that we see among our 50 states are much more pronounced around the globe. Rules are much more common in Europe, for example, than in America. We believe that tendency renders the EU nations slower and less competitive on the world scene, and we may be right. On average regulatory approval for a new gas station in Europe requires 43 months, about three times as long as the time required in the United States.[12] Put another way, estimates suggest that the cost of starting a new business in Europe is 10 times that of the United States.[13] On the other hand, EU rules cannot be ignored in the world market. As *The Wall Street Journal* expressed the new reality,

> The cost of starting a new business in Europe is 10 times that of the United States.

> Americans may not realize it, but rules governing the food they eat, the software they use and the cars they drive increasingly are set in Brussels, the unofficial capital of the EU.[14]

Pig Rights

Some European rules may seem overly intrusive or even silly to Americans, but often they are a preview of what is to come in America. The German state of North Rhine–Westphalia, concerned about mad cow disease and other food scares, decided that pigs should be raised with more of a human touch. Thus pig rights were created. *The Wall Street Journal* summarized the new standards:

> A pig should get one square meter of stall space and a straw or soft rubber mat for napping. When it's time to play, the pigs must have chains or chewy toys on hand. . . . Each pig should get at least eight hours of daylight. During the darker, shorter days of winter, farmers must compensate with lamps.
>
> But what really rankled farmers is a declaration that a farmer or farmhand must spend at least 20 seconds looking at each pig each day—and back up the loving care with paperwork showing he has enough pighands to provide quality time. Without it a farmer can't get a license to expand or start a pig-rearing business.

Should Americans be more concerned about the rights of pigs?

Source: Vanessa Fuhrmans, "I've Got You, Babe: German Farmers Told to Turn on the Charm," *The Wall Street Journal,* March 6, 2002, p. A1.

Questions

1. Journalist Max Frankel, writing in *The New York Times,* argued that the 21st century's "Great Revolution" would be the "collapse of nationhood."[15] He said that collapse would be powered largely by technology and the global financial market.
   a. Explain what Frankel meant.

    b. Do you agree? Explain.

    c. Frankel quoted finance experts George Shultz, William Simon, and Walter Wriston, who said, "The gold standard has been replaced by the information standard, an iron discipline that no government can evade." . . . "No country can hide."[16] What did they mean?

2. *a.* Can you envision a time when all of the nations of the world are able to agree on the elimination of regulatory barriers? Explain.

    b. Would you favor that development? Explain.

Summary of State and Local Regulation

The federal government receives the greater attention; but for the past decade or so, state and local government has been one of America's true growth industries. Total government jobs as a share of total employment fell in the 1990s from 17 to 16 percent.[17] The federal workforce was down about 300,000 jobs during that time, but state and local payrolls were up 18 percent to 2.7 million workers, exclusive of education-related jobs.[18]

We need to remember that this upward spiral at the state and local level, however lamentable in some ways, often springs from our demands for a better life, including improvements in education, health care, infrastructure, and so on. The states are primarily responsible for regulating the insurance industry and are heavily involved in regulating banking, securities, and liquor sales. Many businesses and professions—from funeral preparation to barbering to the practice of medicine—require a license from the state. Public utilities (gas, electricity, sewage disposal) are the subject of extensive regulation governing entry, rates, customer service, and virtually all of the companies' activities. All states have some form of public service commission charged with regulating utilities in the public interest. Many states seek to directly enhance competition via antitrust legislation. Many states have passed laws forbidding usury, false advertising, stock fraud, and other practices harmful to the consumer. Furthermore, Congress pushes federal activities such as welfare and highway safety rules back to the states, suggesting that state government growth is unlikely to abate. [For the "largest Internet compilation" of state government materials, see **http://www.hg.org/index.html**]

Licensure   Local regulation is much less economically significant than state regulation. Local government intervention in business typically involves various licensure requirements. For example, businesses like bars and theaters are often required to obtain a local permit to operate. Similarly, some 10 percent of America's jobs (practicing medicine and law, building construction, electrical work, and so on) can be occupied only by those who have successfully secured licensure from state and/or local authorities. Licensure is to protect the public from unsafe, unhealthful, and substandard goods and services, but critics contend that the presumed benefits of licensure are exceeded by its costs in increased prices, decreased services, and administrative overhead.

Rules and Community Welfare   Most of us would say, in the abstract, that we need less government in our lives; but when we are the victims of problems that the market is ill suited to resolve, those rules become much more attractive. The case that follows shows how Tampa, Florida, tried to apply its rules to the age-old problem of adult entertainment businesses but with a new twist—product distribution by the Internet rather than by face-to-face commerce.

Voyeur Dorm v. City of Tampa

265 F.3d 1232 (11th Cir. 2001); cert. den. 122 S.Ct. 1172 (2002)

LEGAL BRIEFCASE

Circuit Judge Dubina

This appeal arises from Voyeur Dorm L.C.'s alleged violation of Tampa's City Code based on the district court's characterization of Voyeur Dorm as an adult entertainment facility.

BACKGROUND

Voyeur Dorm operates an Internet-based Web site that provides a 24-hour-a-day Internet transmission portraying the lives of the residents of 2312 West Farwell Drive, Tampa, Florida. Throughout its existence, Voyeur Dorm has employed 25 to 30 different women, most of whom entered into a contract that specifies, among other things, that they are "employees," on a "stage and filming location," with "no reasonable expectation of privacy," for "entertainment purpose." Subscribers to "voyeurdorm.com" pay a subscription fee of $34.95 a month to watch the women employed at the premises and pay an added fee of $16.00 per month to "chat" with the women. From August 1998 to June 2000, Voyeur Dorm generated subscriptions and sales totaling $3,166,551.35.

In 1998 Voyeur Dorm learned that local law enforcement agencies had initiated an investigation into its business. In response, counsel for Voyeur Dorm sent a letter to Tampa's zoning coordinator requesting her interpretation of the city code as it applied to the activities occurring at 2312 West Farwell Drive. In February of 1999, Tampa's zoning coordinator, Gloria Moreda, replied to counsel's request and issued her interpretation of the city code:

* * * * *

It is my determination that the use occurring at 2312 W. Farwell Dr., is an adult use. Section 27-523 defines adult entertainment as "Any premises, except those businesses otherwise defined in this chapter, on which is offered to members of the public or any person, for a consideration, entertainment featuring or in any way including specified sexual activities, as defined in this section, or entertainment featuring the displaying or depicting of specified anatomical areas, as defined in this section; 'entertainment' as used in this definition shall include, but not be limited to, books, magazines, films, newspapers, photographs, paintings, drawings, sketches or other publications or graphic media, filmed or live plays, dances or other performances distinguished by their display or depiction of specified anatomical areas or specified anatomical activities, as defined in this section."

Please be aware that the property is zoned RS-60 Residential Single Family, and an adult use business is not permitted use. You should advise your client to cease operation at that location.

Thereafter, in April of 1999, Dan and Sharon Gold Marshlack [owners of the property located at 2312 W. Farwell] appealed the zoning coordinator's decision to Tampa's Variance Review Board. On or about July 13, 1999, the Variance Review Board conducted a hearing. At the hearing, Voyeur Dorm's counsel conceded the following: that five women live in the house; that there are cameras in the corners of all the rooms of the house; that for a fee a person can join a membership to a Web site wherein a member can view the women 24 hours a day, seven days a week; that a member, at times, can see someone disrobed; that the women receive free room and board; that the women are part of a business enterprise; and that the women are paid. At the conclusion of the hearing, the Variance Review Board unanimously upheld the zoning coordinator's determination that the use occurring at 2312 West Farwell Drive was an adult use. Subsequently, Mr. and Mrs. Marshlack filed an appeal from the decision of the Variance Review Board to the City Council. The Tampa City Council . . .

unanimously affirmed the decision of the Variance Review Board.

Voyeur Dorm filed this action in the middle district of Florida. The City of Tampa and Voyeur Dorm then filed cross-motions for summary judgment. The district court granted Tampa's motion for summary judgment, from which Voyeur Dorm now appeals.

ISSUE

1. Whether the district court properly determined that the alleged activities occurring at 2312 West Farwell Drive constitute a public offering of adult entertainment as contemplated by Tampa's zoning restrictions.

[Issues 2. and 3. are omitted.—Ed.]

DISCUSSION

The threshold inquiry is whether section 27-523 of Tampa's city code applies to the alleged activities occurring at 2312 West Farwell Drive. Because of the way we answer that inquiry, it will not be necessary for us to analyze the thorny constitutional issues presented in this case.

*   *   *   *   *

Tampa argues that Voyeur Dorm is an adult use business pursuant to the express and unambiguous language of Section 27-523 and, as such, cannot operate in a residential neighborhood. In that regard, Tampa points out that members of the public pay to watch women employed on the premises; that the employment agreement refers to the premises as "a stage and filming location;" that certain anatomical areas and sexual activities are displayed for entertainment; and that the entertainers are paid accordingly. Most importantly, Tampa asserts that nothing in the city code limits its applicability to premises where the adult entertainment is actually consumed.

In accord with Tampa's arguments, the district court specifically determined that the "plain and unambiguous language of the city code . . . does not expressly state a requirement that the members of the public paying consideration be *on* the premises viewing the adult entertainment." While the public does not congregate to a specific edifice or location in order to enjoy the entertainment provided by Voyeur Dorm, the district court found 2312 West Farwell Drive to be "a premises on which is offered to members of the public for consideration entertainment featuring specified sexual activities within the plain meaning of the city code."

Moreover, the district court relied on Supreme Court and Eleventh Circuit precedent that trumpets a city's entitlement to protect and improve the quality of residential neighborhoods. *Sammy's of Mobile, Ltd.* v. *City of Mobile* (noting that it is well established that the regulation of public health, safety, and morals is a valid and substantial state interest); *Corn v. City of Lauderdale Lakes* (noting that the "Supreme Court has held [that] restrictions may be imposed to protect 'family values, youth values, and the blessings of quiet seclusion'").

In opposition, Voyeur Dorm argues that it is not an adult use business. Specifically, Voyeur Dorm contends that section 27-523 applies to locations or premises wherein adult entertainment is actually offered to the public. Because the public does not, indeed cannot, physically attend 2312 West Farwell Drive to enjoy the adult entertainment, 2312 West Farwell Drive does not fall within the purview of Tampa's zoning ordinance.

The residence of 2312 West Farwell Drive provides no "offering [of adult entertainment] to members of the public." The offering occurs when the videotaped images are dispersed over the Internet and into the public eye for consumption. The city code cannot be applied to a location that does not, itself, offer adult entertainment to the public.

*   *   *   *   *

It does not follow, then, that a zoning ordinance designed to restrict facilities that offer adult entertainment can be applied to a particular location that does not, at that location, offer adult entertainment. Moreover, the case law relied upon by Tampa and the district court concerns adult entertainment in which customers *physically attend* the premises wherein the entertainment is performed. Here, the audience or consumers of the adult entertainment do not go to 2312 West Farwell Drive or congregate anywhere else in Tampa to enjoy the entertainment. Indeed, the public offering occurs over the Internet in "virtual space." While the district court read Section 27-523 in a literal sense, finding no requirement that the paying public be *on the premises,* we hold that section 27-523 does not apply to a residence at which there is no public offering of adult entertainment.

*   *   *   *   *

Reversed.

Questions

1. *a.* Why did the court rule against Tampa?

    b. Make the argument, as the lower court did, that the Tampa statute does apply to Voyeur Dorm.

    c. Why was Tampa concerned about Voyeur Dorm operating in a residential neighborhood?

    d. Does Tampa have any additional legal grounds for challenging Voyeur Dorm? Explain.

2. The city government in Cedar Falls, Iowa, home of the University of Northern Iowa, declined to renew the liquor

license of a local bar after 58 of 100 "bar checks" over a period of nearly two years found minors drinking illegally. One hundred and seventy four alcohol-related tickets were issued over that period.[19]

a. Could the free market satisfactorily protect the public from the various risks associated with excessive drinking by college-aged students, or are rules necessary?

b. Would you vote to renew this bar's liquor license? Explain.

3. Two Dallas, Texas, ordinances were challenged in court. One gave the police very broad authority to deny licenses to "adult" businesses such as bookstores. The other, which was directed at prostitution, barred motel owners from renting rooms for fewer than 10 hours.

a. What challenges would you raise against these ordinances?

b. How would you rule? Explain. See *FW/PBS Inc v. City of Dallas,* 493 U.S. 215 (1990).

4. The city of Los Angeles, California, enacted an ordinance that created a dress code for cab drivers and imposed fines for violations. For example, tank tops and cutoff pants are forbidden. In addition, being rude to passengers can also lead to fines.

a. By what constitutional authority does Los Angeles instruct cab drivers regarding dress and behavior?

b. Do you favor the ordinance? Explain.

5. Tattoo and body piercing statutes sometimes require liability insurance, licensing, training, and health inspections, and parents are to accompany minors. Does each of those requirements seem appropriate to you? Explain.

6. a. Can we rely on the market to protect children from excessive tanning? Explain.

b. Has the market failed? Explain.

7. Why do businesses sometimes welcome or even encourage government regulations?

Questions—Parts One and Two

1. In 1999 Matthew Hale, a law school graduate, was denied a license to practice law in Illinois because Hale is an avowed racist and the leader of a white supremacist group. A state panel assessed the character and general fitness of all those who had passed the bar exam and graduated from law school and decided that Hale's active racism disqualified him. Illinois is one of 32 states with character and fitness standards. Hale appealed on First Amendment grounds, among others. Should Hale be excluded from the practice of law, or should we let the market decide his fitness? Explain.

2. City officials in Machesney Park, Illinois, in 1999 required nine-year-old Gregory Webb to tear down his makeshift tree house on the grounds that it was a nuisance. Webb had built the structure from lawn chairs, leftover carpet, and a pet carrier, among other objects. The city was criticized for its decision.

a. Why would a city choose to exercise its police power over nuisances in this seemingly trivial case?

b. What would you do if you were the city planning and zoning director and thus responsible for the situation?

3. What is art? An Oskaloosa, Iowa, woman wanted her community to think about that question, so she began placing furniture on her lawn. She added pieces on a regular basis and arranged them in various patterns. She began to record people's responses: "A square dance." "A father with a child in his lap." She invited people to rearrange the furniture and to sit in it. She filmed the responses. Some complaints began to arrive at the city council. Neighbors found it trashy and a nuisance. After a warning, the city issued a citation saying that she needed a permit for an art exhibit or art show. She appealed to the local district court.

a. What arguments should have been included in that appeal?

b. Decide the case. Explain.

4. Notwithstanding the deregulation efforts of recent years, the larger trend in the United States over the past 50 years has been that of increased government regulation of business. How do you explain that trend?

5. As a safety measure, Arizona enacted a statute that limited the length of passenger trains to 14 cars and freight trains to 70 cars. Trains of those lengths and greater were common throughout the United States. The Southern Pacific Railroad challenged the Arizona statute.

a. What was the legal foundation of the Southern Pacific claim?

b. Decide the case. Explain. See *Southern Pacific Railroad v. Arizona,* 325 U.S. 761 (1945).

6. Taalib-Dan Abdul Uqdah owned and operated Cornrows & Co., a hair-braiding salon in Washington, D.C. The D.C. Board of Cosmetology pursued Uqdah for years because he and his 10 employees had not secured cosmetology licenses. At one point, Uqdah was fined $1,000 and ordered to close unless he and his employees went to school for nine months. The schooling would have cost about $5,000 per person and did not teach the natural African techniques that were Uqdah's practice. Uqdah's business did not use chemicals.

a. Why was the Washington, D.C., board imposing the license requirement on Uqdah?

b. Should it have done so? Explain. See Editorial, "Forgotten Civil Rights," *The Wall Street Journal,* August 14, 1992, p. A12, and Editorial, "Barring Entry," *The Wall Street Journal,* December 23, 1992, p. A8.

7. A *Journal of the American Medical Association* study indicated that a state-mandated drinking age of 21 was quite successful in reducing auto deaths among drivers aged 19 and 20. The study of Tennessee drivers found that single-vehicle nighttime crash deaths in that age group fell by 38 percent after Tennessee changed its drinking age from 19 to 21.[20]

a. What constitutional authority allows the states to regulate the age at which one may lawfully consume alcoholic beverages?

b. Were the power yours, at what age would you allow drinking? Explain.

8. Richard Moe, president of the National Trust for Historic Preservation:

> Drive down any highway leading into any town in the country, and what do you see? Fast-food outlets, office parks, and shopping malls rising out of vast barren plains of asphalt. Residential subdivisions spreading like inkblots obliterating forests and farms in their relentless march across the landscape. . . . You see the graveyard of livability. You see communities drowning in a destructive, soulless, ugly mess called sprawl.[21]

Moe's solution:

> What's needed is action by state governments to develop growth-management legislation with teeth in it, legislation that requires local government to develop rational strategies for using already developed land more efficiently [and] to make thoughtful choices about new development.[22]

  a. Do you agree with Moe's characterization of America's urban sprawl? Explain.

  b. If so, do you agree that more state and local regulation is the key to correcting the problem? Explain.

  c. If not, how do you defend the unsightliness of that sprawl?

9. Columnist George Will, in 1997, observed that the federal government is trying to shrink, that the "balance of financial, as well as intellectual, resources is tilting to the states," and that the U.S. Supreme Court has steered away from judicial activism.[23] In the late 20th century, power seemed to be leaving the federal government. Will then cited Justice Charles Fried of the Massachusetts Supreme Court, who said that the return of power to the states would not be without costs:

> Our economy of allegiance simply is not infinitely expandable. If we become more Virginian or Georgian, surely we will also feel more remote, less responsible for the poor of Kentucky or of the ghettos of Chicago. If we become more Virginian, we would be less American.[24]

  a. Make the argument that our political culture will be improved by this transfer of power.

  b. Do you approve of this transfer of power back to the states? Explain.

10. *a.* What government steps, if any, do you think would be most successful in helping Americans to stop smoking?

  b. Do you think the government should enact your proposed plan? Explain.

Part Three—Administrative Agencies and the Regulatory Process

Introduction to Administrative Agencies[25]

Suppose you start a business; a small, relatively simple business, perhaps a restaurant. If you did not realize it going into the process, you quickly come to know that the government is going to be your partner in that business. Taxes, wages, hours, sanitation, safety, advertising, zoning—at every turn a government rule shapes the conduct of your business. In many cases those rules are created and enforced by administrative agencies, a powerful subset of government little understood by the public but immensely influential in every corner of American life.

The Federal Agencies

The Federal Administrative Procedure Act defines an *agency* as any government unit other than the legislature and the courts. Thus, the *administrative law* governing those agencies technically addresses the entire executive branch of government. Our attention, however, will be directed to the prominent regulatory agencies (Federal Trade Commission, Federal Communications Commission, Securities and Exchange Commission, and the like) rather than the various executive departments (Agriculture, Defense, and so on) and nonregulatory welfare agencies (Social Security Administration and Veterans

Administration). Although our fundamental concern lies at the federal level, administrative law principles are fully applicable to the conduct of state and local governments. At the local level, planning and zoning boards and property tax assessment appeals boards are examples of administrative agencies. At the state level, one might cite public utility commissions and the various state licensure boards for law, medicine, architecture, and the like. [To search for federal government information on the World Wide Web, see **http://www. gpoaccess.gov/index.html** or **http://www.fedworld.gov/**]

History

Congress established the Interstate Commerce Commission (ICC), the first federal regulatory agency, in 1887 for the purpose of regulating railroad routes and rates. The Food and Drug Administration (FDA—1907) and the Federal Trade Commission (FTC—1914) followed, but federal regulation became pervasive only in response to the Great Depression of the 1930s. Congress created the Securities and Exchange Commission (SEC), the Federal Communications Commission (FCC), the Civil Aeronautics Board (CAB), and the National Labor Relations Board (NLRB), among others, as a response to the widely shared belief that the stock market crash and the Depression were evidence of the failure of the free market.

The next major burst of regulatory activity arrived in the 1960s and 1970s when Congress created such agencies as the Equal Employment Opportunity Commission (EEOC—1965), the Environmental Protection Agency (EPA—1970), the Occupational Safety and Health Administration (OSHA—1970), and the Consumer Product Safety Commission (CPSC—1972).

Note that the work of most of the early agencies was directed to controlling entire industries such as transportation or communications and that the primary purpose of most of those agencies was to address economic concerns. Then with the arrival of the prosperity and social turbulence of the 1960s and 1970s, Congress built a rather massive array of new agencies directed not to economic issues but to social reform in such areas as discrimination, the environment, job safety, and product safety.

As we explore later in the chapter, the free market enthusiasm of the 1980s resulted in strenuous efforts to deregulate the economy and reduce the influence of the federal agencies and the government generally. Now, at the turn of the century, we appear to be in a period of respect for the free market, tempered by concern that some government oversight remains vital to the general welfare. Federal government downsizing and further deregulation are likely, but the federal regulatory agencies will continue to be influential institutions directly affecting virtually all of American life.

Creating the Agencies

The so-called independent agencies (FTC, FCC, and SEC) were created by Congress via statutes labeled *enabling legislation.* For example, the FTC is empowered to pursue unfair trade practices by the authority of its enabling legislation.

In creating an agency, Congress delegates a portion of its authority to that body. Congress acknowledges the existence of a problem and recognizes that it is not the appropriate body to address the specific elements of that problem—hence the agency. The president, ordinarily with the advice and consent of the Senate, appoints the administrator or the several commissioners who direct each agency's affairs. Commissioners are appointed in staggered terms, typically of seven years' duration. The appointment of commissioners for most of the independent agencies must reflect an approximate political balance between the two major parties.

In effect, Congress has created a fourth branch of government. Recognizing that it possesses neither the time nor the expertise to handle problems arising from nuclear power, product safety, racial discrimination, labor unions, and much more, Congress wisely established "minigovernments" with the necessary technical resources and day-to-day authority to address those problems.

Agency Duties

The authority of the federal regulatory agencies falls broadly into three categories.

1. Control of supply. Some agencies control entry into certain economic activities. The Federal Communications Commission grants radio and television licenses. The Food and Drug Administration decides which drugs may enter the American market. The Securities and Exchange Commission (see Chapter 9) acts as a gatekeeper, preventing the entry of new securities into the marketplace until certain standards are met. The general feeling in these areas and others like them is that the market alone cannot adequately protect the public interest.

2. Control of rates. Historically, those federal agencies charged with regulating utilities and carriers (Federal Energy Regulatory Commission, ICC, and CAB) set the prices to be charged for the services offered within their jurisdictions. For example, the consumer facing an interstate change of address found little value in comparison shopping for the least expensive furniture mover because the rates, regulated by the Interstate Commerce Commission, were virtually identical. Government rate setting remains important at the state level. However, at the federal level, the deregulation movement resulted in the elimination of the CAB and the ICC and a general decline in agency rate-setting. That is, the federal government decided to reduce or eliminate its authority in decisions such as the price of airline tickets, cable TV rates, and long-distance telephone rates.

3. Control of conduct.

a. Information. A major element of government regulation is simply requiring information. Agencies commonly compel companies to disclose consumer information that would otherwise remain private. For example, warning labels may be mandated.

b. Standards. Where simply requiring information is deemed inadequate for the public need, the government may establish minimum standards that the private sector must meet. For example, a ladder might be required to safely hold at least a specified weight, or workers might lawfully be exposed to only a specified maximum level of radiation.

c. Product Banishments. In unusual instances where information alone is deemed inadequate to protect the public, products can be banned from the market. The Consumer Product Safety Commission banned the flame retardant Tris (used in children's sleepwear) because of evidence of the product's cancer-causing properties.

A Full Pint

Too much foam; too little beer. The British government announced that it may prosecute pubs that serve pints of beer with foam content greater than 5 percent. Government intervention to assure a "full" pint is so important to Britons that political debate about the issue brewed for years, and Prime Minister Tony Blair actually included the full pint among his election promises.

Source: Associated Press, "Britain Says 95% Is Close Enough to a Full Pint of Beer: Only 5% Foam Allowed, Down from Current 10%," *Ottawa Citizen,* March 19, 2002, p. A14.

Questions

1. The phrase *government regulation* embraces many functions. Define it.
2. Is the federal regulatory process limited in its goals to the correction of market failures? Should it be so limited? Explain.
3. In 1975 Scholar James Q. Wilson said, "All democratic regimes tend to shift resources from the private to the public sector and to enlarge the size of the administrative component of government."[26]
   a. Is Wilson correct? Explain.
   b. Given the striking economic and political changes around the world, would he say the same today? Explain.
4. Scholar George Stigler asked, "What benefits can a state provide to an industry?"[27] Answer Stigler's inquiry.
5. Does the real origin of government regulation of business lie in the citizens' fear? That is, do the people consider the market too risky and therefore opt for a system that affords them some protection from economic loss? Explain.
6. Have we reason for concern because the federal agencies have become a fourth branch of government not directly accountable to the public via the electoral process? Explain.

Summary of the Administrative Process

As we have noted, the administrative agencies act as minigovernments, performing quasi-executive, quasi-legislative (rule-making), and quasi-judicial (adjudicatory) roles broadly involving control of supply, rates, and conduct in large segments of American life. Let's look now at how those agencies undertake their business.

Operating the Agencies

Executive Functions

The basic executive duty of the various agencies is to implement the policy provided for in the enabling legislation and in the agencies' own rules and regulations. A large part of agency activity consists of performing mundane, repetitive tasks that are necessary for a smoothly operating society but that do not merit the day-to-day attention of Congress or the courts. Thus agencies enter into contracts, lease federal lands, register securities offerings, award grants, resolve tax disputes, settle workers' compensation claims, administer government benefits to the citizenry, and so on. Some agencies, such as the Food and Drug Administration, are charged with protecting the public by engaging in inspections and testing. Most agencies offer informal advice, both in response to requests and on their own initiative, to explain agency policy and positions. For example, each year the Federal Trade Commission receives many complaints about alleged fraud in advertising, telemarketing, identity theft, Internet commerce, and so on. Supervisory duties, including most notably the active and close attention given to the banking industry, are a further illustration of agency executive duties.

Of course, a big part of the agencies' executive duties is the protection of the public in one way or another by ensuring compliance with laws and regulations. Therefore, most agencies spend a great deal of time conducting inspections and investigations and collecting information. For example, the Occupational Safety and Health Administration regularly checks businesses for safety hazards.

Legislative Functions

The agencies create *rules* that, in effect, are laws. These rules provide the details necessary to carry out the intentions of the enabling legislation. In day-to-day business practice, the rules are likely to be much more important than the original congressional legislation. The Occupational Safety and Health Act calls for a safe and healthful workplace, but the rules necessary for interpreting and enforcing that general mandate come, not from Congress, but from OSHA.

Rules

Agencies enact three types of rules: (1) procedural rules, (2) interpretive rules, and (3) legislative rules. *Procedural rules* delineate the agency's internal operating structure and methods. *Interpretive rules* offer the agency's view of the meaning of those statutes for which the agency has administrative responsibility. Internal Revenue Service regulations are an example of interpretive rules. *Legislative rules* are policy expressions having the effect of law. The agency is exercising the law-making function delegated to it by the legislature. Federal Trade Commission rules providing for a cooling-off period of three business days within which the buyer may cancel door-to-door sales contracts are an example of agency lawmaking that significantly affects business behavior.

The Rule-Making Process

The Administrative Procedure Act (APA) provides for both *informal* (often called "notice and comment") and *formal* rule-making processes for legislative rules. Under both approaches, the process begins with the publication of a Notice of Proposed Rule Making in the *Federal Register* (a daily publication of all federal rules, regulations, and orders). Thereafter, in the case of informal rule making, the agency must permit written comments on the proposal and may hold open hearings. To enhance participation in the rule-making process, the federal government introduced an online portal where the public can comment on proposed rules [see **www.regulations.gov**]. Having received public comments, the agency either discontinues the process or prepares the final rule.

In the case of formal rule making, after providing notice, the agency must hold a public hearing conducted with most of the procedural safeguards of a trial, where all interested parties may call witnesses, challenge the agency evidence, and so on. The agency decision must be based on the formal record only.

Hybrid Rule Making.   Although not specifically provided for in the APA, agency rule making now is often achieved by a compromise (hybrid) process that combines elements of formal and informal rule making. Hybrid rule making is informal rule making with additions in the form of some trial elements (more oral testimony and hearings) that have the effect of providing a more detailed record without all of the procedural requirements of formal rule making. In routine matters, informal rule making remains the norm; but in more complex situations, hybrid procedures now are often employed.

Whether by formal, informal, or hybrid procedures, final agency rules are published in the *Federal Register* and later compiled in the *Code of Federal Regulations.*

Challenging an Agency Rule

The power and importance of the agencies and of the agency rule-making process are evident in what at this writing is an unsettled policy debate about how closely the FCC should regulate the structure of the nation's media industry. At the behest of Congress, the FCC has for some 60 years imposed various rules limiting media ownership, but in 2003 the Republican majority on the FCC loosened federal restrictions on how many local television and radio stations a company could own and on newspaper and broadcast cross-ownership. Critics objected that the relaxed rules would lead to greater media consolidation and a consequent decline in diversity of programming. A federal court of appeals struck down those new rules in 2004, and in 2005 the U.S. Supreme Court declined to review that decision.[28] Hence the FCC must once again rewrite its media ownership rules—another skirmish in the long-running battle between free market advocates and those favoring government oversight. Historically, the government has been concerned about an undue concentration of media power in too few hands and about the need to ensure as much diversity as possible in broadcast programming. More broadly, the debate is about economic policy. Will the market on its own provide for the nation's best interests? Or are restraints necessary to prevent too much concentration of power and authority in too few hands? Given the expansion of delivery systems (broadcast television, cable, Internet, satellite) and other information/entertainment sources such as newspapers, many experts believe that the government needs to take only a limited role in overseeing media ownership. Consumer advocates, on the other hand, are concerned that the media's vital free speech role will be compromised by concentrated ownership.

Little Guys Lose

The U.S. Supreme Court in 2005 ruled that cable companies are not legally required to share their high-speed lines with rival Internet service providers. ISPs such as EarthLink and Brand X (which brought the suit) do not own their networks and thus must depend on cable and phone companies for access to their customers. The smaller ISPs can still attempt to buy cable access, but they now have no guarantee that they will receive that access or that they will be able to afford it. In reaching its decision, the Court, by a 6–3 vote, deferred to the judgment of the Federal Communications Commission, which has reasoned that control over their networks will encourage the cable companies to increase investment in new products.

Following the Supreme Court decision, the Federal Communications Commission voted 4–0 to allow the big, local phone companies (Qwest, Verizon, et al.) to cut off or impose harsher terms on ISPs who had previously been guaranteed favorable access to the phone companies' broadband services (DSL–digital subscriber line). The phone companies' DSL networks were used by ISPs to provide high-speed Internet service to their customers. The FCC's deregulation decision was designed to spur competition leading to innovation and better service. Alternative forms of high-speed service, such as wireless, satellite, or broadband over power lines are anticipated. Critics, however, say that the practical effect of the deregulation decision will be to harm service and raise prices for many customers.

Sources: National Cable & Telecommunications Association v. Brand X Services, 2005 U.S. LEXIS 5018, James Granelli, "Court Lets Cable Firms Bar Rivals from Internet Lines," *Los Angeles Times,* June 28, 2005, Part C, p. 1, and Ron Orol, "Small ISPs Face Tougher Road," *Daily Deal/The Deal* [**http://www.TheDeal.com**].

Judicial Functions

Although informal procedures such as settlements are preferred, agencies commonly must turn to judicial proceedings to enforce agency rules. The National Labor Relations Board may hold a hearing to determine if an employee was wrongfully dismissed for engaging in protected union activities. The Federal Communications Commission may decide whether to remove a radio license because of a failure to serve the public interest. The Federal Trade Commission may judge whether a particular ad is misleading. Adjudicatory administrative hearings are equal in significance and much superior in numbers to all federal court trials each year.

Rule Making or Adjudication?

Many issues facing agencies could properly be resolved in either the rule-making or the adjudicatory format. The distinction between the two cannot be drawn vividly. Characteristically, however, an adjudication addresses specific parties involved in a specific present or past dispute. Rule making ordinarily involves standards to be applied to the future conduct of a class of unspecified parties. The rule-making/adjudication decision is discretionary with the agency (subject to judicial review) and is based on the nature of the issue and fairness to the parties. Regardless, the agencies are, in effect, "making law" either by setting a judicial-like precedent in the case of an adjudication or by passing a rule that has authority much like a law.

Administrative Hearing.

Typically, after an investigation, a violation of a statute and/or rule may be alleged. Affected parties are notified. An effort is made to reach a settlement via a *consent order,* in which the party being investigated agrees to steps suitable to the agency but under which the respondent makes no admission of guilt (thus retarding the likelihood of sub-sequent civil liability).

ALJ

Failing a settlement, the parties proceed much as in a civil trial. Ordinarily the case is heard by an *administrative law judge (ALJ)*. The respondent may be represented by counsel. Parties have the right to present their cases, cross-examine, file motions, raise objections, and so on. However, they do not have the right to a jury trial. The ALJ decides all questions of law and fact and then issues a decision (*order*). In general, that decision is final unless appealed to the agency/commission. After exhausting opportunities for review within the agency, appeal may be taken to the federal court system.

Controlling the Agencies

As noted, agency influence in business practice and in American life generally is enor-mous. However, none of these agencies and their thousands of employees are directly accountable to the people, and all of them operate under necessarily broad grants of power. What is to keep them from abusing their discretion? Just as with our constitu-tional system generally, certain checks and balances constrain agency conduct while allowing the latitude necessary to achieve effectiveness.

Executive Constraints

As noted, the president appoints the top administrators for the various agencies, thus sig-nificantly influencing the conservative or liberal slant of the agency. Further, the presi-dent obviously has great influence in the budget process.

The Bush administration, through the White House Office of Management and Budget (OMB), has been aggressive in applying "science-based" analysis to new rules by employ-ing such tools as "net benefits" decision making (benefits minus costs), cost-effectiveness (ratio of costs to benefits such as lives saved), and added scrutiny for rules having an economic impact exceeding $1 billion per year. This close scrutiny is designed to reduce paperwork, taxes, fines, and the other burdens that come with government intervention. But critics fear that these approaches are merely strategies for discouraging rules that the business community opposes. For example, Consumers Union claims that the Federal Communications Commission "rigged" its cost–benefit analysis in a study examining a proposed federal rule to mandate "á la carte" cable service (allow subscriptions to only those channels the consumer actually wants rather than being forced to accept packages, such as "basic" and "expanded"). Under heavy industry pressure, the FCC allegedly inflated various cost estimates to make the á la carte plan appear undesirable.[29] Clearly, agency rules and sometimes heavy-handed enforcement practices can be inefficient and costly, but the benefits are likewise undeniable. An OMB study of major federal rules estimated that their annual benefits from 1992 to 2002 ranged from $135 billion to $218 billion, while estimated annual costs ranged from only $38 billion to $44 billion.[30] [For an OMB "watchdog" see **www.ombwatch.org/**]

Congressional Constraints

Congress creates and can dissolve the agencies. Congress controls agency budgets and thus can encourage or discourage particular agency action. Broadly, Congress oversees agency action, and agencies often check with Congress before undertaking major initiatives. Congress can directly intervene by amending the enabling legislation or by passing laws that require agencies to take specific directions. The difficulty in balancing congressional and agency authority is well illustrated by an important 2001 Supreme Court decision involving the federal Clean Air Act (CAA). The case, *Whitman v. American Trucking Associations, Inc.*[31] raised the question of whether Congress had improperly delegated its authority to the Environmental Protection Agency and whether the EPA must take the cost of implementing clean air regulations into consideration when developing new rules. A unanimous Supreme Court ruled that Congress had built into the CAA constitutionally sufficient limitations on agency action, and the Court ruled that Congress clearly did not require the EPA to conduct cost–benefit analyses before establishing new rules. Thus the Court concluded that Congress can constitutionally offer agencies broad authority in carrying out Congress's general intentions.

Judicial Review

Agency rules and orders may be challenged in court. Historically, however, the courts have taken a rather narrow approach to judicial review. Two commonsense considerations support that restrained judicial stance. The first is deference to the presumed expertise of the administrative agencies. The jurists, being generalists in the field of law, have been reluctant to overrule the judgment of specialists specifically chosen to regulate within their area of expertise. Second, very crowded judicial calendars act as a natural brake on activist judicial review. For those reasons, judges have traditionally disposed of administrative law cases in an expeditious manner by readily sustaining the judgment of the agency where reasonable. Of course, the courts have overruled the agencies when appropriate, and of late we can see evidence of a firmer judicial role, including some interest in reasserting the balance of powers principle.[32]

Not surprisingly, judicial review of agency decisions raises a variety of technical issues of law. Cases turn on questions like these:

1. Does the legislature's delegation of authority meet constitutional requirements?
2. Has the agency exceeded the authority granted by the enabling legislation?
3. Are the agency's findings of fact supported by substantial evidence in the record as a whole?

These issues are close to the heart of the administrative law practitioner, but their exploration is not necessary to the layperson's understanding of the larger regulatory process. The case that follows will be our only consideration of the formalities of judicial review. This appeal from a Federal Communications Commission adjudication sheds some light on the agency regulatory process and judicial review; but, much more important, the case raises fundamental questions regarding freedom of speech in a technologically advanced society.

F.C.C. v. Pacifica Foundation

438 U.S. 726 (1978)

Justice Stevens

This case requires that we decide whether the Federal Communications Commission has any power to regulate a radio broadcast that is indecent but not obscene.

A satiric humorist named George Carlin recorded a 12-minute monologue titled "Filthy Words" before a live audience in a California theater. He began by referring to his thoughts about "the words you can't say on the public, ah, airwaves, um, the ones you definitely wouldn't say, ever." He proceeded to list those words and repeat them over and over again in a variety of colloquialisms. The transcript of the recording . . . indicates frequent laughter from the audience.

At about 2 o'clock in the afternoon on Tuesday, October 30, 1973, a New York radio station, owned by respondent Pacifica Foundation, broadcast the "Filthy Words" monologue. A few weeks later a man, who stated that he had heard the broadcast while driving with his young son, wrote a letter complaining to the commission. He stated that, although he could perhaps understand the "record's being sold for private use, I certainly cannot understand the broadcast of same over the air that, supposedly, you control."

The complaint was forwarded to the station for comment. In its response, Pacifica explained that the monologue had been played during a program about contemporary society's attitude toward language and that, immediately before its broadcast, listeners had been advised that it included "sensitive language which might be regarded as offensive to some." Pacifica characterized George Carlin as a "significant social satirist" who "like Twain and Sahl before him, examines the language of ordinary people. . . . Carlin is not mouthing obscenities; he is merely using words to satirize as harmless and essentially silly our attitudes toward those words." Pacifica stated that it was not aware of any other complaints about the broadcast.

On February 21, 1975, the commission issued a declaratory order granting the complaint and holding that Pacifica "could have been the subject of administrative sanctions." . . . The commission did not impose formal sanctions, but it did state that the order would be "associated with the station's license file, and in the event that subsequent complaints are received, the commission will then decide whether it should utilize any of the available sanctions it has been granted by Congress."

* * * * *

[T]he Commission found a power to regulate indecent broadcasting in [18 United States Code 1464] which forbids the use of "any obscene, indecent, or profane language by means of radio communications."

* * * * *

[T]he commission concluded that certain words depicted sexual and excretory activities in a patently offensive manner, noted that they "were broadcast at a time when children were undoubtedly in the audiences (in the early afternoon)" and that the prerecorded language, with these offensive words "repeated over and over," was "deliberately broadcast." . . .

In summary, the commission stated, "We therefore hold that the language as broadcast was indecent and prohibited." . . .

The United States Court of Appeals for the District of Columbia Circuit reversed, with each of the three judges on the panel writing separately. . . .

Judge Tamm concluded that the order represented censorship and was expressly prohibited by ¶ 326 of the Communications Act. Alternatively, Judge Tamm read the commission opinion as the functional equivalent of a rule and concluded that it was "overbroad." . . .

Chief Judge Bazelon's concurrence rested on the Constitution. He was persuaded that ¶ 326's prohibition against censorship is inapplicable to broadcasts forbidden by ¶ 1464. However, he concluded that ¶ 1464 must be narrowly construed to cover only language that is obscene or otherwise unprotected by the First Amendment. . . .

Judge Leventhal, in dissent, stated that the only issue was whether the commission could regulate the language "as broadcast." . . .

Emphasizing the interest in protecting children, not only from exposure to indecent language, but also from exposure to the idea that such language has official approval, . . . he concluded that the commission had correctly condemned the daytime broadcast as indecent.

Having granted the commission's petition for certiorari, . . . we must decide (1) whether the scope of judicial review encompasses more than the commission's determination that the monologue was indecent "as broadcast"; (2) whether the commission's order was a form of censorship forbidden by ¶ 326; (3) whether the broadcast was indecent within the meaning of ¶ 1464; and (4) whether the order violates the First Amendment of the United States Constitution.

(I)

The general statements in the commission's memorandum opinion do not change the character of its order. Its action was an adjudication. . . . It did not purport to engage in formal rule making or in the promulgation of any regulations. The order "was issued in a specific factual context"; questions concerning possible action in other contexts were expressly reserved for the future. The specific holding was carefully confined to the monologue "as broadcast." . . .

(II)

The relevant statutory questions are whether the commission's action is forbidden "censorship" within the meaning of ¶ 326 and whether speech that concededly is not obscene may be restricted as "indecent" under the authority of ¶ 1464.

* * * * *

The prohibition against censorship unequivocally denies the commission any power to edit proposed broadcasts in advance and to excise material considered inappropriate for the airwaves. The prohibition, however, has never been construed to deny the commission the power to review the content of completed broadcasts in the performance of its regulatory duties.

* * * * *

Entirely apart from the fact that the subsequent review of program content is not the sort of censorship at which the statute was directed, its history makes it perfectly clear that it was not intended to limit the commission's power to regulate the broadcast of obscene, indecent, or profane language. A single section of the [Radio Act of 1927] is the source of both the anticensorship provision and the commission's authority to impose sanctions for the broadcast of indecent or obscene language. Quite plainly, Congress intended to give meaning to both provisions. Respect for that intent requires that the censorship language be read as inapplicable to the prohibition on broadcasting obscene, indecent, or profane language.

We conclude, therefore, that ¶ 326 does not limit the commission's authority to impose sanctions on licensees who engage in obscene, indecent, or profane broadcasting.

(III)

The only other statutory question presented by this case is whether the afternoon broadcast of the "Filthy Words" monologue was indecent within the meaning of ¶ 1464. . . .

The commission identified several words that referred to excretory or sexual activities or organs, stated that the repetitive, deliberate use of those words in an afternoon broadcast when children are in the audience was patently offensive, and held that the broadcast was indecent. Pacifica takes issue with the commission's definition of indecency, but does not dispute the commission's preliminary determination that each of the components of its definition was present. Specifically,

Pacifica does not quarrel with the conclusion that this afternoon broadcast was patently offensive. Pacifica's claim that the broadcast was not indecent within the meaning of the statute rests entirely on the absence of prurient appeal.

The plain language of the statute does not support Pacifica's argument. The words "obscene, indecent, or profane" are written in the disjunctive, implying that each has a separate meaning. Prurient appeal is an element of the obscene, but the normal definition of "indecent" merely refers to nonconformance with accepted standards of morality.

* * * * *

Because neither our prior decisions nor the language or history of ¶ 1464 supports the conclusion that prurient appeal is an essential component of indecent language, we reject Pacifica's construction of the statute. When that construction is put to one side, there is no basis for disagreeing with the commission's conclusion that indecent language was used in this broadcast.

(IV)

Pacifica makes two constitutional attacks on the commission's order. First, it argues that the commission's construction of the statutory language broadly encompasses so much constitutionally protected speech that reversal is required even if Pacifica's broadcast of the "Filthy Words" monologue is not itself protected by the First Amendment. Second, Pacifica argues that inasmuch as the recording is not obscene, the Constitution forbids any abridgement of the right to broadcast it on the radio.

A

The first argument fails because our review is limited to the question of whether the commission has the authority to proscribe this particular broadcast. As the commission itself emphasized, its order was "issued in a specific factual context." . . .

That approach is appropriate for courts as well as the commission when regulation of indecency is at stake, for indecency is largely a function of context—it cannot be adequately judged in the abstract.

* * * * *

It is true that the commission's order may lead some broadcasters to censor themselves. At most, however, the commission's definition of indecency will deter only the broadcasting of patently offensive references to excretory and sexual organs and activities. While some of these references may be protected, they surely lie at the periphery of First Amendment concern. . . .

B

When the issue is narrowed to the facts of this case, the question is whether the First Amendment denies government any power to restrict the public broadcast of indecent language in any circumstances. For if the government has any such power, this was an appropriate occasion for its exercise.

The words of the Carlin monologue are unquestionably "speech" within the meaning of the First Amendment. It is equally clear that the commission's objections to the broadcast were based in part on its content. The order must therefore fall if, as Pacifica argues, the First Amendment prohibits all governmental regulation that depends on the content of speech. Our past cases demonstrate, however, that no such absolute rule is mandated by the Constitution.

The classic exposition of the proposition that both the content and the context of speech are critical elements of First Amendment analysis is Mr. Justice Holmes's statement . . .

> We admit that in many places and in ordinary times the defendants in saying all that was said in the circular would have been within their constitutional rights. But the character of every act depends upon the circumstances in which it was done. . . . The most stringent protection of free speech would not protect a man in falsely shouting fire in a theater and causing a panic. It does not even protect a man from an injunction against uttering words that may have all the effect of force. . . . The question in every case is whether the words used are used in such circumstances and are of such a nature as to create a clear and present danger that they will bring about the substantive evils that Congress has a right to prevent.

Other distinctions based on content have been approved. . . . The government may forbid speech calculated to provoke a fight. . . . It may pay heed to the "commonsense differences between commercial speech and other varieties.". . . It may treat libels against private citizens more severely than libels against public officials. . . . Obscenity may be wholly prohibited. . . .

The question in this case is whether a broadcast of patently offensive words dealing with sex and excretion may be regulated because of its content. Obscene materials have been denied the protection of the First Amendment because their content is so offensive to contemporary moral standards. . . . But the fact that society may find speech offensive is not a sufficient reason for suppressing it. Indeed, if it is the speaker's opinion that gives offense, that consequence is a reason for according it constitutional protection. For it is a central tenet of the First Amendment that the government must remain neutral in the marketplace of ideas. If there were any reason to believe that the commission's characterization of the

Carlin monologue as offensive could be traced to its political content—or even to the fact that it satirized contemporary attitudes about four-letter words—First Amendment protection might be required. But that is simply not this case. These words offend for the same reasons that obscenity offends.

* * * * *

In this case it is undisputed that the content of Pacifica's broadcast was "vulgar," "offensive," and "shocking." Because content of that character is not entitled to absolute constitutional protection under all circumstances, we must consider its context in order to determine whether the commission's action was constitutionally permissible.

C

We have long recognized that each medium of expression presents special First Amendment problems. . . . And of all forms of communication, it is broadcasting that has received the most limited First Amendment protection. . . . The reasons for [that distinction] are complex, but two have relevance to the present case. First, the broadcast media have established a uniquely pervasive presence in the lives of all Americans. Patently offensive, indecent material presented over the airwaves confronts the citizen, not only in public, but also in the privacy of the home, where the individual's right to be left alone plainly outweighs the First Amendment rights of an intruder. . . . Because the broadcast audience is constantly tuning in and out, prior warnings cannot completely protect the listener or viewer from unexpected program content. . . .

Second, broadcasting is uniquely accessible to children, even those too young to read. . . .

It is appropriate, in conclusion, to emphasize the narrowness of our holding. This case does not involve a two-way radio conversation between a cab driver and a dispatcher, or a telecast of an Elizabethan comedy. We have not decided that an occasional expletive in either setting would justify any sanction or, indeed, that this broadcast would justify a criminal prosecution. The commission's decision rested entirely on a nuisance rationale under which context is all-important. The concept requires consideration of a host of variables. The time of day was emphasized by the commission. The content of the program in which the language is used will also affect the composition of the audience, and differences between radio, television, and perhaps closed-circuit transmissions, may also be relevant. . . .

The judgment of the court of appeals is reversed.
[The appendix containing a transcript of the "Filthy Words" monologue is omitted.]

Questions

1. *a.* Why was the question of whether the FCC's decision constituted adjudication or rule making significant to the subsequent judicial appeals?

   b. Explain the Supreme Court's resolution of that issue.

2. Why is the two-letter word *or* critical to the outcome of this case?

3. Why was the FCC's action not considered censorship?

4. Cable television operators use signal scrambling to ensure that only paying customers have access to some programming. Congress was concerned that some sexually explicit cable programming, even though scrambled, might reach children via signal "bleeding." Section 505 of the Telecommunications Act of 1996 required cable operators to fully block sexually oriented channels or to "time channel"—that is, transmit only in hours when children are unlikely to be viewing. Most cable operators adopted the latter approach, with the result that for two-thirds of the day no viewers in the operators' service areas could receive the sexually explicit programming. Section 504 of the Telecommunications Act required cable operators to block undesired channels at individual households upon request. A supplier of sexually oriented programming challenged Section 505 on First Amendment grounds. Decide the case. Explain. See *United States v. Playboy Entertainment Group,* 529 U.S. 803 (2000).

The FCC and Indecency Today

The George Carlin case, in a sense, lives on more than 25 years after it was decided. We seem to be in the midst of a cultural war over social values, none of which is more hotly contested than the public role of sex in American life. Most famously, perhaps, Janet Jackson's "wardrobe malfunction" (when her right breast was momentarily bared during the halftime show of the 2004 Super Bowl) led to a $550,000 FCC fine levied against CBS television. Graphic depictions of sexual and excretory functions are forbidden by FCC rules on nonsatellite radio and on noncable television between 6 AM and 10 PM—hours when children are likely to be in the audience. The 10 PM to 6 AM slot, on the other hand, offers a "safe harbor" for indecent programming.

> Radio "shock jock" Howard Stern was the primary focus of recent FCC indecency complaints

Radio "shock jock" Howard Stern, fighting FCC sanctions for years, was the primary focus of recent FCC indecency complaints against the 1,200-station Clear Channel Communications empire. In 2004 Clear Channel agreed to pay $1.75 million in fines to settle the complaints. Stern has long argued that the government's oversight violates his First Amendment rights, but his explicit conversations about masturbation, intercourse, "spewing evil gunk all over everybody" and so on led Clear Channel to drop Stern, who has now moved to satellite radio.

In perhaps its most specific indecency ruling, the FCC in 2004 overruled its own staff and its own policy of many years by declaring that Bono's phrase "f---ing brilliant" at the live, 2003 Golden Globe awards show was indecent and profane. In the past, quick, nonsexual use of the "f word" had not been interpreted to violate federal law. So the FCC's ruling apparently signals a new, more socially conservative stance toward television and broadcasting. A great risk, of course, is that FCC activism will chill those ideas and expressions that have been instrumental in America's success. And at the individual level, what price in personal freedom and satisfaction do we pay when the government imposes its conception of decency on all of us? [For the complete text of the FCC indecency guidelines, see **http://www.fcc.gov/eb/Orders/2001/fcc01090.html;** for a brief overview of the history of indecency in broadcasting litigation, including links to George Carlin and Howard Stern Web sites, see **http://www.cba.uni.edu/ decencyl**]

Questions

1. The Parents Television Council filed 36 indecency complaints with the FCC alleging that popular television shows, including *Friends* and *The Simpsons,* contained indecent scenes that were either sexually explicit or used indecent or profane language. How would you vote on the following scenes?
   a. In the *Gilmore Girls*, one character says to another, "You're a dick."
   b. In *The Simpsons*, students carry picket signs with the phrases "What would Jesus glue?" and "Don't cut off my pianissimo."

2. The Parents Television Council contacted sponsors of the April 6, 2005, episode of the television program *The Shield* to complain about a "graphic" scene in which a police captain was forced to perform fellatio on a gang member at gunpoint. Kia and Castrol were among those sponsors. What would you do if you were in charge of advertising for Kia or Castrol, and you received that complaint?

3. *a.* Are you concerned about the amount of sex and violence in entertainment? Explain.
   b. Which do you think is a greater threat to American welfare, indecent entertainment materials or government rules to curb that indecency? Explain.
   c. Who is more to blame for indecency, the audience or the producers of the entertainment? Explain.

4. Employ free market reasoning to examine the FCC's indecency stance.

Chinese Censorship

In 2004 China's regulators at the State Administration for Radio, Film, and Television decided that the nation's increasingly open, frank, Westernized media market had strayed too far from its puritanical, communist past. New rules were imposed. Graphic violence and sex in prime time are now forbidden. Many Chinese welcome that development, but other rules seem unduly restrictive. As one 26-year-old math teacher put it, "We're not housewives who go to bed every night before nine." She was angry because her favorite U.S. crime show had been at least temporarily removed. Some of the new rules:

- "Pornographic portrayals . . . and base language are banned."
- Hosts of television shows must avoid vulgarity in all respects along with "overly revealing clothing" and "multicolored dyed hair".
- Broadcasters must "strictly control the exaggerated violence, murders, and horrors" in programs prior to 11 PM.

Source: Kathy Chen and Leslie Chang, "China Takes Aim at Racy, Violent TV Shows," *The Wall Street Journal,* May 24, 2004, p. B1.

Part Four—The Federal Regulatory Process Evaluated

Free market advocates seek to sharply reduce government, while others favor a constrained market where the government plays an important role in preventing and correcting market failure. The economic signature of the late 1980s and 1990s was the stunning ascendance of market economics in Eastern Europe, the former Soviet Union, Great Britain, and China. (See Chapter 1.) At the same time, the Reagan administration worked to sharply reduce the regulatory role of the federal government in American life. The Bush (senior) and Clinton administrations moved back toward the center on the question of government intervention. Philosophically, the current Bush administration clearly favors a reduced government presence in business practice, environmental protection, and some other areas, but a dramatic decline in federal rules seems unlikely. Against that historical backdrop, the argument continues—should the government be more or less involved in American business? The principal criticisms of the regulatory process follow.

Criticisms

Excessive Regulation

In brief, the argument of excessive regulation is that government rules reduce business efficiency, curb freedom, and unjustly redistribute resources. Consider some of the more specific costs.

Paper and Personnel

Government oversight remains enormous even in the conservative George W. Bush era. The *Federal Register* reached a record 75,606 pages in 2002 but did fall to 71,269 pages in 2003.[33] More ominously, the cost of administering the vast government regulatory structure grew by nearly 13 percent from 2002 to 2003 and totaled nearly $31 billion.[34] Similarly, the total number of federal government employees zoomed by more than 1 million people to a total of 12.1 million in 2003, and that growth came not only in defense and homeland security but across the board.[35] Of course, the direct costs of that growth are staggering; but as economist Robert Hahn reminds us, the direct costs are only the most visible regulatory "tax":

> The measurable costs of regulation pale against the distortions that sap the economy's dynamism. The public never sees the factories that weren't built, the new products that didn't appear, or the entrepreneurial idea that drowned in a cumbersome regulatory process.[36]

But while government has continued to grow, even during the current Republican, conservative era, President Bush has been aggressively reshaping and cutting rules in ways that advantage the business community:

> The Bush administration has cut the growth of costly business regulations by 75 percent, compared to the two previous administrations.[37]

[For more detailed criticisms of the federal regulatory process, see **http://www.heritage .org** or **http://www.cei.org** or **http://www.regulation.org**]

Around the Globe   While the cost of regulation in the United States is great, government rules are, in fact, less burdensome in America than in most nations. For example, a recent study found the United States just behind New Zealand among the world's nations in ease of starting and operating businesses.[38] Similarly, a recent World Bank study finds excess regulation stifling productivity in much of Africa, Latin America, and the former Soviet Union. On the other hand, the United States ranks along with Australia, Canada, New Zealand, and the United Kingdom, among a few others, as the least regulated and most efficient economies. In general, the World Bank study found that the least regulated economies are the strongest economies. Perhaps surprisingly, however, a critical factor in economic growth is the presence of an efficient legal system. For example, the creation of a private company in Australia requires two legal procedures and about two days, as contrasted with the system in Angola where 146 days and over $5,500 would be needed. So rules can be helpful if efficient but disastrous if excessive.[39]

No Shopping on Sunday

German federal law prevents retailers from opening on Sundays and holidays. The government considers the rules a defense of workers' rights, and in 2004 Germany's highest court upheld the constitutionality of those restrictions.

Source: "Shopping Ruling," *Des Moines Register,* June 10, 2004, p. 6C.

Insufficient Regulation

Our society is changing, complex, and in many ways troubled. Consequently, calls for new government regulations are routine. For example, aren't most Americans pleased with the FCC's do-not-call rules that keep telemarketers at a distance? Advocates of increased regulation point to the many successes of government intervention: legal equality for minorities and women; network airways substantially free of pornography and indecency; the Auto Safety Act; child labor laws; safer workplaces; cleaner air; and so on.

Would we fully trust the market to protect us from dangerous food and drugs, or would we rather maintain a vigorous Food and Drug Administration? For a number of years the government has successfully streamlined the drug approval process, thus arguably benefiting the public with quicker access to valuable medications. But recent recalls of approved drugs, such as painkillers Vioxx and Bextra, have caused the public and the government to reassess the wisdom of greater reliance on the market and the giant drug companies. Those drug withdrawals have also prompted a general reevaluation of the FDA's effectiveness:

> Adverse reactions to drugs kill more than 100,000 Americans a year. . . . Last year, a gathering of experts . . . found that the "current U.S. system for assessing the risks of therapeutics is outdated and inadequate."[40]

Few Americans are calling for a smaller, weaker FDA.

Regulation Out, Lawsuits In

Public policy problems like smoking by children, the flood of handguns, and sweatshop labor once might have been fought with new laws. But with "regulation" a bad word, the fight today has moved from Congress to the courts. That's the observation of former secretary of labor Robert Reich: "Regulating U.S. industry through lawsuits isn't the most efficient way of doing the job," he wrote, but it's "better than not regulating at all."[41]

Perhaps we need more rules in selected dimensions of American life.

> Perhaps we need more rules

Excessive Industry Influence

The industries to be regulated were often instrumental in spawning the various federal agencies. Noted economist George Stigler summarized the argument: "[R]egulation is acquired by the industry and is designed and operated primarily for its benefit."[42] Stigler further argued that, where possible, firms will encourage government regulations restricting entry (licensing), thus limiting competition: "Every industry or occupation that has enough political power to utilize the state will seek to control entry."[43]

As evidence of industry influence in agency affairs, critics argue that agency employees who leave federal service frequently turn to jobs in the industry they were formerly charged with regulating. Similarly, agency recruits are often drawn from the industry being regulated. Industry influence over the regulatory process is considerable. Industry expertise is invaluable, and the industry voice should be heard. The question is one of the "volume" of the voice.

Underrepresentation of Public Opinion

Agency critics also charge that the diffuse voice of public opinion does not receive the attention accorded the pleas of special interests. Public sentiment, being largely unorganized, often is greatly underrepresented in regulatory matters, while well-financed, skillfully organized special interests carry political weight far beyond the numbers they represent.

Bureaucratic Processes

The mechanics of agency conduct are frequently assailed. Allegations of inefficiency, incompetence, and arbitrariness are commonplace. The pace of work is said to be slow, and enforcement of policy often appears weak and ineffectual.

Deregulation

In response to the excessive regulation criticisms, both Democrats and Republicans, beginning in the late 1970s, began to reduce the quantity of federal regulatory intervention. The deregulation movement consisted primarily of shrinking the federal bureaucracy, eliminating as many government rules as possible, and expediting the process of complying with rules that could not be removed. Reduced regulation has focused on key economic sectors including transportation, banking, and telecommunications, while rule making in social arenas such as discrimination and pollution has actually increased.

In cases where a government role continued to be considered necessary, deregulation advocates argued for applying free market incentives and reasoning to achieve regulatory goals. Thus, rather than forbidding undesirable conduct (such as pollution and industrial accidents), the government might impose a tax on behaviors society wants to discourage. In effect, a business would purchase the right to engage in conduct society considers injurious or inefficient. Similarly, rather than rationing portions of the radio spectrum or the right to land at airports at peak times, the government might auction those rights to the highest bidder. Market incentives would (1) encourage companies to use cost-effective compliance means and (2) raise the price of dangerous products, thus discouraging their use. However, monitoring difficulties, particularly in the case of pollution, render the taxing or auction methods inexact at best. Some object to the idea of allowing businesses to engage in undesirable conduct or highly prized conduct merely because they have the resources to pay for those privileges.

Similarly, cost–benefit analysis would be applied to all regulations. Regulations would be imposed only if added benefits equaled or exceeded added costs. Indeed, influential scholar Cass Sunstein argues that we have moved to a "cost–benefit state" to replace the New Deal regulatory approach where big government was broadly embraced with little concern for the cost–benefit equation.[44] Sunstein, however, favors a "soft" form of cost–benefit calculation where qualitative considerations that cannot be carefully measured should nonetheless be considered, especially in health and environmental regulations.[45] [For an argument in support of deregulating marriage, see **http://www.etalkinghead .com/archives/deregulation-of-marriage-2004-03-01.html**]

Your Life? $3 Million

How much is a life worth? That question is probably the crucial cost–benefit inquiry. When imposing new environmental or car safety rules, for example, we are forced to think about how much money we should spend to save an additional life. Recently the federal Environmental Protection Agency priced a life at $6 million, while the federal Department of Transportation used a $3 million value and leading scholar Kip Viscusi's most recent study put a $7 million value on human life. Should elderly people's lives be considered less valuable than those of young people? The United States spends over $37,000 annually for medical care in the average senior citizen's final year of life, versus $7,365 on average for other years. In Europe, by contrast, expensive care is routinely denied to those facing death. In the United States, several billion dollars annually is spent to keep alive those in a persistent vegetative state (estimated at 16,000 to 35,000 people nationally). Interestingly, 80 percent of Americans surveyed say they would not want to be kept alive in a vegetative state.

How much is your life worth? Should the value of lives be a consideration in federal rules and spending decisions?

Sources: John J. Fialka, "Balancing Act: Lives vs. Regulations," *The Wall Street Journal,* May 30, 2003, p. A4; Catherine Arnst, "Getting Rational about Rationing," *BusinessWeek,* November 17, 2003, p. 140.

Further Deregulation or Reregulation?

Historian John Steele Gordon argues that capitalism needs regulation and that regulation has made the country more stable and richer:

> Capitalism without regulation and regulators is inherently unstable, Gordon claims, "as people will usually put their short-term interests ahead of the interests of the system as a whole, and either chaos or plutocracy will result. . . . The country since the New Deal has been a far richer, far more economically secure, far more just society," Gordon writes.[46]

Government regulation in America normally arises not from ideology but from actual problems.[47] America is not committed to government regulation as a matter of political policy. Rather, regulation in this country has, in many instances, resulted from an honorable effort to correct evident wrongs. Much-maligned agencies such as the EPA, OSHA, and the FDA were not born of a desire for big government and central planning. Pollution, industrial accidents, and dangerous food and drugs were clearly the impetus for the creation of those agencies. The September 11, 2001, attacks and ongoing corporate scandals have been vivid reminders of the value of government.

9/11 The fragility of civilized life was demonstrated cruelly and incontestably on September 11, 2001. The attacks brought an almost immediate plea for a strengthened government role in security. While we might not be philosophically comfortable with big government, and we certainly would like to keep more of our hard-earned money in our own pockets, 9/11 reminded us that what we think of as civilized life is permitted in good part by a big, aggressive (if sometimes misguided) government.

The Scandals Enron, WorldCom, Adelphia, and other corporate names have become infamous examples of a period of extraordinary prosperity accompanied by extraordinary managerial corruption. The result was personal financial loss for many along with declining public trust in the corporate community. As explained in Chapters 2 and 9, in particular, Congress passed the 2002 Sarbanes–Oxley (SOX) bill to strengthen criminal penalties and provide other government interventions—such as requiring executives to vouch for the accuracy of their books—to discourage future corporate misbehavior. Pressure from the electorate and the stock market effectively mandated some kind of government response. Columnist Julianne Malveaux approves:

> I say that some corporations take the capitalist message of profit maximization too seriously—and that government takes its role of containing capitalism too lightly. Capitalism is predatory. "Market forces" push wages and prices down. They encourage people to cut corners and make deals. Profit is always the bottom line. In the film *Wall Street,* Gordon Gekko took Adam Smith to the limit. "Greed is good," he said. Government's job is to regulate greed.[48]

But perhaps the solution is not in more rules. Perhaps the solution (and the blame) lies with each of us rather than with capitalism, as a student columnist from Wayne State University suggests in the following commentary.

Eric Czarnik

Is capitalism at fault for this current crisis? Despite what some Ayn Rand devotees might say, a totally unregulated capitalism isn't ideal. Although capitalism attempts to channel self-interest into safer, mutually beneficial agreements among business partners, dishonest businessmen can still satisfy their agendas while ignoring the best interests of consumers.

As we have seen, this can be successfully accomplished in many ways, such as cooking the books, insider trading, and false stock reports. These undermine the essential trust that binds suppliers and consumers together, causing capitalism to suffer immensely.

Nevertheless, acknowledging these weaknesses doesn't invalidate capitalism, which is still a far more realistic and successful economic system when compared to any other. Communism and socialism, while appealing in theory, fail to account for mankind's selfish, greedy nature. These two systems put their trust in the state while generally distrusting moral institutions like religion and the family. Amoral, self-serving, and oppressive political leaders are therefore more likely to thrive.

* * * * *

The real culprit behind these scandals isn't capitalism, per se, but shameless relativism and an arrogance that disregards the rule of law. The 1990s flourished with these two characteristics, and we're now finally reaping what we have sown.

The cultural zeitgeist of the 1990s could be summed up in one man: President Bill Clinton. During his administration, he nonchalantly sidestepped scandals, lied under oath, and debated the definition of the word "is." Meanwhile, the public collectively yawned, as it was more eager to flaunt its newfound wealth than "judge" anyone. Is it no surprise that the public's tolerance for such behavior led corporate executives to believe that they could get away with the same thing, except by manipulating numbers and figures instead of words?

We have two options for getting out of this fiasco. One option would be to have the CEOs clean up their own act—immediately. They could wisely remember the old adage, "cheaters never win." . . .

The other option would be to follow the logic of James Madison. In Federalist Paper No. 51, he proposed that "if men were angels, there would be no need for government." Because men aren't angels, Madison believed a strong central government is pertinent for our nation's stability. To executives who feel that, like Machiavelli, they're above conventional morality, tougher watchdog regulation and stiffer penalties might be necessary and fitting. Putting a few of the corrupt "suits" in orange jumpsuits would help, too.

Capitalism mostly works, and it would be a shame to abandon a system that rewards hard work and promotes social mobility. We can only hope that Wall Street listened when Bush said, "In the long run, there is no capitalism without conscience, there is no wealth without character."

Source: *The South End* via *University Wire,* July 16, 2002. Reprinted by permission.

Questions
1. Is our fundamental nature "selfish and greedy"? Explain.
2. What does Czarnik mean by "shameless relativism"?
3. *a.* Can we count on the corporate community to "clean up their own act" or must the government intervene as it did in passing the Sarbanes–Oxley Act? Explain.
   b. Do you have some other solution? Explain.

Deregulation Assessed: The Good News

A 2003 survey of about 1,400 CEOs worldwide found 18 percent of those leaders listing "overregulation" as the biggest threat to their business, exceeding all other perils including "increased competition" (17 percent), "currency fluctuations" (15 percent), and "global terrorism" (10 percent).[49] Deregulation seems to be a success in important respects although some rough spots are evident. Scholars Robert Crandall and Jerry Ellig have identified the following "patterns" in the deregulation of trucking, railroads, airlines, telecommunications, and natural gas:

- *Lower prices:* Adjusted for inflation, prices in the five industries fell between 28 and 57 percent in the decade after the deregulation.

- *More innovation:* After deregulation, airlines developed "hub-and-spoke" routing systems, enabling them to operate more efficiently. Deregulation allowed truckers and railroads to develop "intermodal" transport systems where trucks are shipped by rail for long distances. Intermodal systems are so efficient that 28 percent of America's trucks now spend some time on a railroad.

- *More business:* Falling prices ensure more demand for products. Natural gas consumption increased 21 percent in the first decade after deregulation. Falling trucking costs were a major reason United Parcel Service doubled in size between 1980 and 1995. The number of airline flights nearly doubled after a decade of deregulation.

- *Improved lives:* Airline deregulation allowed the rise of low-cost airlines such as Southwest, making airline tickets affordable for people who would otherwise have to spend hours on a bus. Telephone deregulation lowered long-distance rates, allowing more people to spend more time talking to distant friends and relatives. Natural gas deregulation dramatically reduced the cost of heating homes.[50]

As *BusinessWeek* observed,

> Deregulation dramatically increased the flexibility and responsiveness of U.S. corporations in a period of rapid technological and competitive change. Indeed, by making it easier to shift capacity where it is needed, deregulation deserves some of the credit for the current low rate of inflation.[51]

Deregulation Assessed: The Bad News

Journalist Vermont Royster argues that government is vital to civilized life:

> If I hesitate to join the hue for deregulation, even when much of the regulation is misguided, it's because I shudder at the thought of a wholly deregulated society. I prefer knowing my pharmacist has to be licensed and that somebody checks on him; so also with the butcher so that I have some assurance his scale registers a true measure.
>
> As a matter of fact, regulation to protect consumers is almost as old as civilization itself. Tourists to the ruins of Pompeii see an early version of the bureau of weights and measures, a place where the townsfolk could go to be sure they weren't cheated by the local tradesmen. Unfortunately, a little larceny is too common in the human species.
>
> So regulation in some form or other is one of the prices we pay for our complex civilization. And the more complicated society becomes, the more need for some watching over its many parts.[52]

Deregulation in practice has produced big benefits, but it has not been a painless process. Bankruptcies have been common in the airline and trucking industries. A Consumers Union study claims that deregulation has created an "increasingly Wild West marketplace" requiring some renewal of regulation in cable, phone, lending, and airline markets.[53] The current corporate scandals and the recent California electrical failure are reenergizing those with doubts about the deregulation movement. The heart of those doubts lies in fears about monopoly—that deregulated markets will allow a few firms to control vast pieces of American life. Some specific concerns:

- *Telecommunications:* The federal Telecommunications Act of 1996 substantially deregulated the phone, cable, wireless, and satellite businesses. Wireless and long-distance rates have fallen dramatically, but local phone and cable rates have been on the rise.

> ### The telecommunications merger wave has changed the nature of music radio

Furthermore, the telecommunications merger wave since 1996 has changed the nature of music radio, *Rolling Stone* claims, resulting in homogeneous, bland, unimaginative programming:

> National playlists are in the hands of corporate programmers, who are influenced by big-label money funneled into the stations by independent radio promoters. "The airwaves are a public trust, but we have given that up and let one small group of people heist all the country's programming decisions," charges Miles Copeland III, former manager of the Police.[54]

- *Transportation:* Many small communities have lost airline service or seen it decline in quality, and most of the remaining handful of big firms in the market are struggling to remain solvent.

- *Financial services:* The 1999 Financial Services Modernization Act deregulated the banking industry by removing barriers that had prevented banks and securities firms from competing in each other's markets. Congress had erected the walls in 1933 in the belief that risky securities speculation by banks had contributed to the Great Depression. The new open market has created the opportunity for "financial supermarkets" to provide loans, stock market advice, and investment banking (financing and advice for mergers, initial public offerings, and the like) all at one stop. *The Wall Street Journal* explained how the new freedom is changing banking practice:

    > Banks have made little secret since the old restrictions crumbled that they are willing to make loans in order to win investment deals. Bank of America Corp., for instance, has indicated that if a certain borrower wants a loan, then the borrower should ante up when it is time to choose a merger or deal adviser.[55]

Enhanced efficiency and strengthened global competitiveness are the expected rewards of this reduction in rules, but big problems are also likely. For example, deregulation of financial markets has increased the likelihood of conflicts of interest that may lead to fraud. Merrill Lynch, the brokerage giant, agreed in 2002 to pay a $100 million fine to settle New York State charges that it gave stock market investors favorable evaluations of companies such as bankrupt telecom giant WorldCom when it knew those companies were risky investments. Merrill Lynch did so, regulators claim, to keep or acquire the highly profitable investment banking business of WorldCom and the others whose stocks it was "pumping." These alleged conflicts of interest were facilitated by the financial markets' deregulation, which formally eliminated the aforementioned walls that Congress had put in place to separate commercial banks and investment firms.

The Winner: Open Markets, But . . .

Although Enron has raised some fears about deregulation and produced calls for new rules, the general course of the American and world economies is clearly toward open markets. In the energy area, for example, developing nations such as Brazil, the Philippines, and China, along with much of Europe, are enthusiastically introducing more competition into their closely regulated and often state-owned energy supply lines; but they are expected to do so with government rules guiding the way, according to energy expert Gerald Ducet:

> Even before Enron's collapse, he says, "the countries outside the U.S. had been more realistic about the need for strong regulation when you reform markets."[56]

Still, each new disturbance or disaster reminds us that the market needs rules. When the regional electrical power grid from Ohio to the Eastern Seaboard crashed in 2003, 50 million people received a $6 billion lesson in the limits of free markets. Even the ardently conservative *Wall Street Journal* endorsed rules under some circumstances:

> The blackout of 2003 offers a simple but powerful lesson: Markets are a great way to organize economic activity, but they need adult supervision.
>
> In the battles of communism versus capitalism and rigid regulation of economic activity versus competition, the market won. Despite persistent diatribes from the left, there is little prospect that the U.S. government is going to reinstate old regulations. . . .
>
> The spread of markets, however, is increasingly focusing attention on the need to make them work well—or risk blackouts, bankruptcies, and backlash. . . . [For example,] Congress, attempting to fix flaws in the nation's capital markets exposed by [the 2002] corporate scandals, enacted new rules to improve the information that companies provide investors and created a new institution to police the accounting industry.[57]

A Case: Get Off That Phone?

Let's close this chapter about rules by asking if we need more of them:

> At least 40 nations—from Australia to Zimbabwe—have banned talking on cell phones while driving, including nearly all of Europe. Leading the crackdown, Poland has the harshest penalties, up to $1,000, while a third offense in Ireland rings up three months in jail.
>
> Almost two of three U.S. adults have a cell phone, and 43 percent of all cell phone owners say they regularly use them while driving, according to a Harris Interactive poll. Yet 76 percent of poll respondents favor banning cell phone use while driving, except in emergencies.[58]

Connecticut, New York, New Jersey, Chicago, and Washington, D.C., all have laws requiring use of hands-free devices when talking on a cell phone and driving. Substantial evidence, however, suggests that the hands-free technology does not improve safety—probably because the distraction of talking rather than holding the phone is where the danger lies.[59] In fact, one study found that drivers wearing headsets actually drove faster than those holding their phones, and braking time slowed by 45 percent for cell phone users, a deficit that did not improve with handheld devices.[60] At the same time, drivers' minds will never be free of distractions no matter how many rules are created. In one study of random three-hour periods, 97 percent of drivers leaned or reached for something, more than 91 percent adjusted the audio, more than three-quarters talked, and more than 71 percent ate or drank.[61] A California study found that only a little more than 1 percent of the drivers involved in auto accidents were inattentive. About 11 percent of the inattentive drivers were talking on cell phones, with about two-thirds of the inattentive accidents being the result of other distractions such as daydreaming, reading street signs, or the like.[62]

Questions

1. Would you favor government rules forbidding cell phone use while driving? Explain.

2. From a *Des Moines Register* editorial:

> There's talk about airline passengers soon being allowed to use cell phones. Say it isn't so. It is hard to conceive of anything more maddening than being wedged into an airline seat next to a thoughtless cell phone addict for the duration of a three-hour flight.[63]

How would you vote on airplane cell phone use?

3. Distinguished economist Herbert Stein, now perhaps best known as father of celebrity Ben Stein, says that we are desperate for cell phone conversations to ward off our loneliness:

> It is the way of keeping contact with someone, anyone who will reassure you that you are not alone. You may think you are checking on your portfolio but deep down you are checking on your own existence.[64]

a. Are you dependent on your cell phone?

b. If so, should the government discourage that use by, for example, imposing higher taxes on cell phone purchases? Explain.

Guy Davenport: "The telephone is God's gift to the bore."

Source: Interview by John Jeremiah Sullivan, *The Paris Review*, Fall 2002.

Internet Exercise

Should the U.S. government impose new rules requiring all bicyclists to wear helmets? New Zealand has enforced a national mandatory all-age bicycle helmet law since 1994. To help with your recommendation for the United States, consider the evidence from the New Zealand experience at [**http://www.cycle-helmets.com/Zealand_helmets.html**]

Chapter Questions

1. *a.* Has deregulation affected your life? Explain.
   b. Do you *trust* the free market? The government? Both? Neither? Explain.
   c. On balance, has business deregulation been a good direction for America? Explain.

2. The *Des Moines Register* advocated a free market approach to cable television, labeling it a "nonessential activity."
   a. Should the government be involved in regulating only those products and services that we cannot do without? Explain.
   b. Do you expect deregulation of cable television to lead to lower rates? Explain.

3. A 1999 study concludes that African-American youths, especially those between 18 and 29, are 50 percent less likely to wear seat belts than whites or Hispanics. The report estimated that regular use of seat belts by all African Americans would save

1,300 lives per year, prevent 26,000 injuries, and reduce societal costs by \$2.6 billion.[65] According to the National Highway Transportation Safety Commission, if all Americans wore seat belts regularly, we would save 10,000 lives, 200,000 injuries, and \$20 billion annually.[66] Should Congress require seat belt use? Explain.

4. The Heritage Foundation and *The Wall Street Journal* jointly publish the annual global Index of Economic Freedom. In general, the nations that have been most successful in increasing their economic freedom (by reducing taxes and so forth) have enjoyed the highest rates of economic growth. When the index was first published in 1995, the United States ranked fifth in the world, and it remained near the top through the nineties. In the four years since 2001, however, the United States has fallen to 12th place on the list.[67]

   a. How would you explain that decline?

   b. What would the United States need to do differently to return to a more "economically free" culture?

   c. Should the United States take the steps you noted in part *b*?

5. Former Secretary of Labor Robert Reich: "The era of big government may be over, but the era of regulation through litigation has just begun."[68] Explain what Reich meant.

6. The Federal Communications Commission received a pair of complaints from viewers about allegedly indecent television and radio programming. In one case, a Seattle television station showed graphic scenes in a sex education class. In another, a St. Louis radio station broadcast a reading of a *Playboy* interview with Jessica Hahn, who alleged that she was raped by evangelist Jim Bakker. Sheep sounds were played in the background during the reading.

   Does either case violate the indecency standards for broadcasting as you understand them? Explain. See Daniel Pearl, "Hot Career of the Future: Indecency Screener," *The Wall Street Journal,* July 13, 1995, p. B1.

7. Transportation deregulation has resulted in an immediate loss of service to some smaller communities. Some of that loss has been compensated for with the entry of smaller, independent firms.

   a. Has deregulation endangered small-town America? Explain.

   b. Should we apply free market principles to the postal service, thus, among other consequences, compelling those in small and remote communities to pay the full cost of service rather than the "subsidized" cost now paid? Explain.

8. The expense of government regulation is not limited to the direct cost of administering the various agencies. Explain and offer examples of the other expenses produced by regulation.

9. To the extent the federal government achieves deregulation, what substitutes will citizens find for protection?

10. Pulitzer Prize–winning author and presidential adviser Arthur Schlesinger:

    The assault on the national government is represented as a disinterested movement to "return" power to the people. But the withdrawal of the national government does not transfer power to the people. It transfers power to the historical rival of the national government and the prime cause of its enlargement—the great corporate interests.[69]

a. Using 19th- and 20th-century American economic history, explain Schlesinger's claim that corporate interests are the primary cause of big government.

b. Do you agree with Schlesinger that we continue to need big government to counteract corporate interests and achieve fairness for all in American life? Explain.

11. Make the argument that increasing government rules and jobs leads to decreasing private-sector businesses and jobs.

12. *a.* How might a student such as yourself usefully employ cost–benefit reasoning to improve your academic performance?

    b. Do you do so? Explain.

13. A study by Professor Andrew Chalk of Southern Methodist University concluded, in effect, that the free market is more effective than the rules of the Federal Aviation Administration in ensuring air safety.[70] Assume the role of Professor Chalk. Explain the market mechanisms that have been influential in building our present impressive safety record in air travel.

14. Joseph Stiglitz, the chief White House economist at the time, argued in 1996 that "a huge economic literature" supports his view that "appropriately circumscribed government programs can lead to a higher-growth economy."[71] How can government programs stimulate the economy rather than act as a drag on it?

15. A major issue facing the Federal Aviation Administration is congestion in the airways caused by too many planes seeking to take off or land at peak times at high-demand airports. How might we solve that problem while maintaining reasonable service?

16. In calculating the costs and benefits of a new rule, make the argument that added regulation normally slows the economy and leads to increased deaths.

17. Eighty-three percent of teens had at least one sunburn in 1999, whereas the comparable figure in 1986 was 30 percent.[72] "'Right now, we're at the apex of the bronze goddess era,' said Atoosa Rubenstein, editor-in-chief of *CosmoGIRL* magazine.[73] More than a third of the 17-year-old girls in a recent survey reported going to a tanning salon in the previous year.[74] A 2002 study found that those using tanning devices were 1.5 to 2.5 times more likely to develop common forms of skin cancer than those not using the devices.[75] The American Academy of Dermatology Association (AADA) is urging the FDA to ban the sale and use of indoor tanning equipment for non-medical purposes and calling for state or federal laws to, among other things, forbid minors from using tanning devices.[76]

    Would you support the AADA proposals? Explain.

18. *BusinessWeek:*

    > How do you change the eating habits of several hundred million people? That's the daunting problem the World Health Organization (WHO) is trying to solve with a proposal for fighting obesity worldwide. It's a bold and necessary effort, but unfortunately, it may be undermined by the world's fattest nation: the United States. The U.N. estimates that 300 million people worldwide are obese and a further 750 million are overweight, including 22 million children under 5.

*   *   *   *   *

[The United States] is charging that the WHO's conclusions that fats and sugars cause obesity are not supported by "sufficient scientific evidence."[77]

Nonetheless, the WHO has proposed a series of nonbinding actions that governments could take to encourage citizens to curb their weight gain.

a. What strategies might the WHO endorse to help us avoid weight gain?

b. Why would the United States resist the nonbinding WHO proposals?

c. Is obesity a matter of personal responsibility? Explain.

Notes

1. P. J. Huffstutter, "Illinois Seeks to Curb Explicit Video Games," *Los Angeles Times,* December 16, 2004, p. A1.

2. Joseph P. Tomain, "American Regulatory Policy: Have We Found the 'Third Way'?" *Kansas Law Review* 48 (May 2000), p. 829.

3. "Federalism—Clear Congressional Mandate Required to Preempt State Law," *Harvard Law Review* 105, no. 1 (November 1991), p. 196.

4. 317 U.S. 111 (1942).

5. 2005 U.S. LEXIS 4656.

6. 2005 U.S. LEXIS 4656.

7. *United States v. Lopez,* 115 S.Ct. 1624 (1995).

8. 18 U.S.C. 922 (q) (1) (A).

9. *United States v. Morrison* and *Brzonkala v. Morrison,* 529 U.S. 598 (2000).

10. *Brzonkala v. Virginia Polytechnic Institute,* 169 F.3d 820, 827 (4th Cir. 1999).

11. Ibid., p. 908.

12. Bob Davis, "Why Europe Trails U.S. in High-Tech Innovation," *The Wall Street Journal,* April 1, 2002, p. A1.

13. Bob Davis, "Constitution Could Spur Europe's Economy," *The Wall Street Journal,* February 11, 2002, p. A1.

14. Brandon Mitchener, "Increasingly, Rules of Global Economy Are Set in Brussels," *The Wall Street Journal,* May 23, 2002, p. A1.

15. Max Frankel, "The Next Great Story," *The New York Times,* March 15, 1998, sec. 6, p. 30.

16. Frankel, "The Next Great Story."

17. Gene Koretz, "Uncle Sam Isn't Hiring," *BusinessWeek,* August 27, 2001, p. 38.

18. Koretz, "Uncle Sam."

19. Jennifer Jacobs, "Judge Backs City's Refusal to Renew Bar's License," *Waterloo/Cedar Falls Courier,* November 22, 1998, p. C3.

20. Associated Press, "Raising Drinking Age Does Cut Traffic Fatalities, Study Finds," *Des Moines Register,* December 23, 1988, p. 4T.

21. Richard Moe, "Mindless Madness Called Sprawl," *Des Moines Register,* January 19, 1997, p. 1C.

22. Moe, "Mindless Madness."

23. George Will, "Clinton's Terms May Leave No Footprints," *Des Moines Register,* January 19, 1997, p. 2C.

24. Will, "Clinton's Terms."

25. The organizational structure of the introductory administrative law materials owes a great deal to the suggestions of Professor Cynthia Srstka, Augustana College (South Dakota).

26. James Q. Wilson, "The Rise of the Bureaucratic State," *The Public Interest* 41 (Fall 1975), as quoted in *Perspectives on the Administrative Process,* ed. Robert L. Rabin (Boston: Little, Brown, 1979), pp. 16, 33.

27. George Stigler, "The Theory of Economic Regulation," *Bell Journal of Economics and Management Science* 2 (Spring 1971), p. 3.

28. *Prometheus Radio Project v. Federal Communications Commission,* 373 F.3d 372 (3d Cir. 2004); *FCC v. Prometheus Radio Project,* 2005 U.S. LEXIS 4811.

29. "FCC Rigs Cost–Benefit Report to Side with Industry on Cable à La Carte," [**http://www.ombwatch.org/article/articleview/2577/1/219?TopicID=1**].

30. John D. Graham, Testimony before House Government Reform Committee, "Costs, Benefits, and Impacts of Federal Regulations," Federal Document Clearing House Congressional Testimony, March 11, 2003.

31. 531 U.S. 457.

32. See *United States v. Mead Corp.,* 533 U.S.218 (2001).

33. Clyde Crews, "Federal Regulations Back to Near-Record Levels," [**http://www.heartland.org**].

34. Crews, "Federal Regulations."

35. Tom Hamburger, "Despite Bush's Credo, Government Grows," *The Wall Street Journal,* September 4, 2003, p. A4.

36. Louis Richman, "Bringing Reason to Regulation," *Fortune,* October 19, 1992, p. 94.

37. Joel Brinkley, "Out of Spotlight, Bush Overhauls U.S. Regulations," *The New York Times,* August 14, 2004 [**nytimes.com**].

38. Michael Schroeder, "Regulatory Rules Stifle Business in Poor Countries," *The Wall Street Journal,* September 8, 2004, p. A17.

39. Michael Schroeder and Terence Roth, "World Bank Faults Tight Regulation," *The Wall Street Journal,* October 7, 2003, p. A2.

40. Anna Wilde Mathews, "Vioxx Recall Raises Questions on FDA's Safety Monitoring," *The Wall Street Journal,* October 4, 2004, p. B1.

41. "Company Watch," *Business Ethics,* March–April 1999, p. 5.

42. George Stigler, "Theory of Economic Regulation," p. 3, as cited in *The Politics of Regulation,* ed. James Q. Wilson (New York: Basic Books, 1980), p. 358.

43. Stigler, "Theory of Economic Regulation," p. 5.

44. Thomas O. Garrity, "A Cost–Benefit State," *Administrative Law Review* 50, no. 1 (Winter 1998), p. 7.

45. Garrity, "A Cost–Benefit State."

46. John Steele Gordon, *An Empire of Wealth: The Epic History of American Economic Power* (New York: HarperCollins, 2004). Quoted by Wayne E. Yang, "The Wealth of America Is Wealth," [**http://www.csmonitor.com/2004/1207/p15s...**]

47. Lester Thurow, *The Zero-Sum Society* (New York: Penguin Books, 1980), p. 136.

48. Julianne Malveaux, "Corporate Scandals Prove Market Flaws," *USA TODAY,* July 19, 2002, p. 13A.

49. Marc Champion, "CEO's Worst Nightmares," *The Wall Street Journal,* January 21, 2004, p. A13.

50. Martin Wooster, "The Benefits of Deregulation," *The American Enterprise,* September–October 1997, p. 87.

51. Editorial, "Deregulation Is Great, But . . ." *BusinessWeek,* April 5, 1999, p. 130.

52. Vermont Royster, "'Regulation' Isn't a Dirty Word," *The Wall Street Journal,* September 9, 1987, p. 30.

53. Dow Jones Newswires, "Deregulation Is Likened to the 'Wild West'" *The Wall Street Journal,* June 11, 2002, p. D3.

54. Greg Kot, "What's Wrong with Radio?" *Rolling Stone,* August 16, 2001, p. 25.

55. Carrick Mollenkamp and Rick Brooks, "Collapse Raises Issue of 1999 Bank Deregulation," *The Wall Street Journal,* November 30, 2001, p. A8.

56. Anita Raghavan, Miriam Jordan, and Bhushan Bahree, "World Moves Forward on Plans for Free-Market Energy," *The Wall Street Journal,* December 6, 2001, p. A8.

57. David Wessel, "A Lesson from the Blackout: Free Markets Also Need Rules," *The Wall Street Journal,* August 28, 2003, p. A1.

58. Editorial, "Cell Phones Not the Only Driving Distraction That Needs Attention," *Waterloo/Cedar Falls Courier,* May 11, 2004, p. A6.

59. Jesse Drucker and Karen Lundegaard, "As Industry Pushes Headsets in Cars, U.S. Agency Sees Danger," *The Wall Street Journal,* July 19, 2004, p. A1.

60. Drucker and Lundegard, "As Industry Pushes Headsets."

61. Susannah Rosenblatt, "Driving While Distracted Is Common, Researchers Say," *Los Angeles Times,* August 7, 2003, p. A20.

62. Rosenblatt, "Driving While Distracted."

63. Editorial, "On a Plane, Let Cell-Phone Silence Reign," *Des Moines Register,* December 29, 2004, p. 6A.

64. James Gleick, *The Acceleration of Just about Everything* (New York: Vintage Books, 1999), p. 89.

65. R. J. King, "U.S. Seat Belt Law Is Urged: Report: Hundreds of Lives Would Be Saved, Especially among African Americans," *Detroit News,* July 20, 1999, p. B4.

66. King, "U.S. Seat Belt Law."

67. Isabel Eiras, "Four Reforms to Regain U.S. Leadership in Economic Freedom," *The Backgrounder,* no. 1815 (January 11, 2005) [**www.heritage.org/research/tradeandforeignaid/bg1815.cfm**]

68. Robert Reich, "Regulation Is Out, Litigation Is In," *USA TODAY,* February 11, 1999, p. 15A.

69. Arthur Schlesinger Jr., "In Defense of Government," *The Wall Street Journal,* June 7, 1995, p. A14.

70. Andrew Chalk, "Market Outperforms FAA as Air Safety Enforcer," *The Wall Street Journal,* September 1, 1987, p. 26.

71. Bob Davis, "In Presidential Race, the Key Question Is, 'What Causes Growth?'" *The Wall Street Journal,* September 27, 1996, p. A1.

72. Julie Sevrens Lyons, "Doctors See Growing Cancer Risk with Trendy Tans," *Milwaukee Journal,* July 29, 2002, p. 3A.

73. Lyons, "Doctors See Growing Cancer Risk."

74. Lyons, "Doctors See Growing Cancer Risk."

75. Jane E. Allen, "Young, Tan, and at Risk," *Hartford Courant,* June 25, 2002, p. D3.

76. "American Academy of Dermatology UrgesTeens to Heed Warning on Dangers of Tanning," *PR Newswire,* May 3, 2004.

77. Catherine Arnst, "Let Them Eat Cake—If They Want To," *BusinessWeek,* February 23, 2004, p. 110.

Business Organizations and Securities Regulation

Introduction

One of the fundamental decisions that must be made for a new venture is the legal form in which it will be conducted. There are three traditional forms in the United States, as well as several hybrids, some relatively recent. Each has advantages and disadvantages, and one must carefully evaluate which form is most suitable for a business or investment.

The three traditional forms, *corporations, partnerships,* and *sole proprietorships,* are discussed shortly. They can be distinguished along the following dimensions:

Nontax costs: The costs related to bringing a business form into existence and maintaining that existence.

Centralization of management: The degree to which control is centralized into a hierarchical structure.

Limited liability: The extent to which the business owners are liable for its obligations.

Free transferability of interests: Whether the business owners can transfer their interests without restriction.

Duration of existence: What events, including those impacting the business owners, end the business form's existence.

Taxes: The extent to which the business form affects the taxation of the business and the owners.

Capital structure: The debt/equity trade-off and the impact of the business form on the ability to attract capital.

Circumstances favoring a specific business form: Whether a given venture's legal characteristics mandate or favor a specific business form.

[For a table summarizing the key characteristics of each business form, see **www. bizfilings.com/learning/comparison.htm**]

Corporations

> Corporations account for 86 percent of all business revenue.

Corporations are the dominant form of business in the United States. Although only 20 percent of all businesses are corporations, they account for 86 percent of all business revenue. Indeed, 82 percent of all businesses with revenues in excess of $1 million are corporations.[1] There are good reasons for that primacy, which will become evident in the discussion to follow.

Nontax Costs

To create a corporation, a *promoter* or *incorporator* files *articles of incorporation* with the state government. A small fee is typically charged. The articles have mandatory elements, such as the corporation's name and the person designated to receive certain communications from the state (legal documents like subpoenas). Discretionary content like voting rules can be entered in the articles.

Once the articles are filed, the corporation comes into existence. The owners are called *stockholders* or *shareholders*, taken from the fact that the ownership interests are called *shares* of *stock*. An *organizational meeting* will be held, at which stock will be issued in exchange for contributions of capital or services.

Then the shareholders will elect a *board of directors*. The directors will meet to undertake the corporation's initial business. Among other things, they will appoint officers and adopt *bylaws*. Bylaws contain key policies and procedures, such as how a quorum will be determined and the percentage of shareholders that must approve a major corporate action like a merger. [For a large library of business forms, see **www.lectlaw.com/formb.htm**]

Annually the corporation will have to make modest filings with the state to keep its records up to date, usually accompanied by a small fee. [To see how Delaware computes this fee, see **www.state.de.us/corp/frtaxcalc.htm**] At least annually the board of directors and shareholders must meet.

Corporations are separate accounting entities. But the cost of their accounting systems reflects their scale of operation, not the decision to operate in the corporate form.

Centralization of Management

Large corporations have thousands of shareholders; small corporations may have only one. The vast majority of shareholders do not plan to spend their time intimately involved in the company's business. They wish to entrust their resources to the stewardship of the company's management and return to their personal affairs.

To ensure that the corporation is acting to further their interests, the shareholders elect a board of directors. Most boards have both inside and outside directors. *Inside directors* are senior executives. *Outside directors* are not employed by the company. Boards meet at regular intervals to monitor the corporation's activities, establish corporate policies, and make major decisions. It is not uncommon for some members to attend by telephone or videoconferencing.

Boards do not operate the business day-to-day. They are policy and oversight bodies. To actually run the company, boards appoint *officers,* typically a CEO or president, secretary, treasurer, and several vice presidents. Officers engage other employees to help them operate the corporation.

Corporations have centralized management. At the apex of the power pyramid is the board of directors. Immediately below is the CEO. In the next layer are the vice presidents and other top officers and executives. The pyramid further expands through layers of middle management, finally coming to the base comprised of rank-and-file employees. Great power is held by the small number of executives at the top.

> Great power is held by the small number of executives at the top.

The officers (but not the directors) are agents of the corporation. Their actions bind the corporation if undertaken within the scope of their authority, which is very broad.

Both the officers and directors have *fiduciary duties* to the corporation. A *fiduciary* is a person who acts on behalf of another (*beneficiary*) and is required to do so with great integrity. (Another fiduciary relationship is parent to minor child.) A fiduciary must act in the best interests of the beneficiary—the *duty of loyalty*. This would prohibit, for example, the directors from authorizing the corporation to lease real estate from the board chairman unless the rental terms were consistent with the market. Corporate officers and directors also owe the corporation a *duty of due care,* which requires that they act in good faith toward the corporation and in the manner a reasonably prudent person would employ under the same circumstances. [For more on board duties, see **http://boardmember.com/ network/index.pl?section=1022&article_id=11038&show=article**]

What happens if the president of a corporation makes a decision in good faith, reflecting mature judgment, but the decision turns out to be wrong and the stock declines by 30 percent? Has the president violated the duty of due care? The judicial system has developed the *business judgment rule* to help make that determination. A good statement of the rule, which is explored in the *Wrigley* case next, is this:

> The rule posits a powerful presumption . . . that a decision made by a loyal and informed board will not be overturned . . . unless it cannot be "attributed to any rational business purpose." [The] shareholder . . . challenging a board decision [must] rebut the . . . presumption [by] providing evidence that directors . . . breached any one of the triads of their fiduciary duty—good faith, loyalty, or due care. . . . If a shareholder . . . fails to meet this . . . burden, the . . . rule attaches to protect . . . officers and directors and the decisions they make, and our courts will not second-guess these business judgments.[2]

LEGAL BRIEFCASE

Shlensky v. Wrigley 237 N.E.2d 776 (Ill. App. Ct. 1968)

FACTS

Shlensky, a minority stockholder in the Chicago Cubs, sued the directors for mismanagement and negligence because of their refusal to install lights at Wrigley Field, then the only major league stadium without lights. One of the directors, Wrigley (80 percent owner), objected to lights because of his personal opinion that "baseball is a 'daytime sport' and that the installation of lights and night baseball games would have a deteriorating effect upon the surrounding neighborhood." Allegedly, the other directors deferred to Wrigley.

The Cubs were losing money. Shlensky attributed those losses to poor attendance and argued that without lights the losses would continue. His evidence was that the Chicago White Sox night games drew better than the Cubs' day games. Shlensky sought damages and an order requiring lights and night games. He lost at trial and appealed.

Justice Sullivan

[D]efendants argue that the courts will not step in and interfere with the honest business judgment of the directors unless there is a showing of fraud, illegality, or conflict of interest.

The court in *Wheeler v. The Pullman Iron & Steel Co.* said,

> It is . . . fundamental in the law of corporations that the majority of its stockholders shall control the policy of the corporation[.] Everyone purchasing [stock] impliedly agrees that he will be bound by the [lawful acts of] a majority of the shareholders, or [of their corporate agents duly chosen], and courts . . . will not undertake to control the policy or business methods of a corporation, although it may be seen that a wiser policy might be adopted and the business more successful if other methods were pursued.

Plaintiff . . . argues that the directors are acting for reasons unrelated to the . . . welfare of the Cubs. However, we are not satisfied that the motives assigned to . . . Wrigley [and] the other directors . . . are contrary to the best interests of the corporation[.] For example[,] the effect on the surrounding neighborhood might well be considered by a director who was considering the patrons who would or would not attend the games if the park were in a poor neighborhood. Furthermore, the long-run interest [in the] property value at Wrigley Field might demand all efforts to keep the neighborhood from deteriorating. [W]e do not mean to say . . . that the decision of the directors was a correct one. That is beyond our jurisdiction and ability. We are merely saying that the decision is one properly before

the directors and the motives alleged . . . showed no fraud, illegality, or conflict of interest[.]

While all . . . courts do not insist that one or more of [these] three elements must be present for a stockholder's derivative action to lie, nevertheless we feel that unless the conduct of the defendants at least borders on one of [them], the courts should not interfere. . . .

[W]e do not agree . . . that failure to follow . . . the other major league clubs in scheduling night games constituted negligence. [It] cannot be said that directors, even those of corporations that are losing money, must follow the lead of [others] in the field. Directors are elected for their business . . . judgment and the courts cannot require them to forgo their judgment because of the decisions of directors of other companies.

Affirmed.

AFTERWORD—DUTY OF CARE

Some states require proof of *intentional misconduct* or *recklessness* to establish a breach of the duty of care.

Questions

1. What was the issue in this case?
2. The Cubs added lights in 1988. How could the board be meeting its duty of due care both in the 1960s by not erecting lights and in the 1980s by doing so?
3. Charles Pritchard Sr. was CEO of a corporation. He, his wife Lillian, and his sons Charles Jr. and William were the board. The sons began running the company in the 1960s. Charles Sr. died in 1973. The sons extracted $12 million from the corporation as "loans" that were never repaid. The corporation went bankrupt. Lillian died in 1978. Corporate creditors sued Lillian's estate for $10 million, claiming that she had been negligent as a director. Lillian was never involved in corporate oversight. The defense argued that Lillian was a "simple housewife who served as a director as an accommodation to her" family. Who should win? See *Francis v. United Jersey Bank*, 432 A.2d 814 (N.J.S.Ct. 1981).

Employee, Officer, Director Liability

Wrigley involved a *shareholder derivative suit*. That action lies where the corporation is being harmed or defrauded and neither the board nor the senior executives will take action to protect it. This often involves self-dealing by these parties. The suit is brought by a minority shareholder, but any recovery inures to the corporation.

Where an employee or director commits a tort or crime while conducting corporate business, both that person and the corporation are liable for the consequences.

The doctrine that makes the employer liable for the employee's acts is *respondeat superior*.

Because officers and directors are ultimately responsible for corporate acts and because corporations are constantly being sued, these persons face a high risk of becoming involved in costly litigation. Therefore, most corporations *indemnify* them (reimburse for costs incurred). [For more, see **www.lectlaw.com/files/lws41.htm**]

Limited Liability

To a lawyer, there are two types of persons, natural and artificial. Natural persons are people. Artificial persons, like a corporation, are entities created under the law of a state (or nation) that are considered to have separate legal existence. Corporations can own property, be sued, take on debts, and otherwise act as separate entities. They even have constitutional rights. One of the great advantages of this status is that the owners of the corporation are generally not responsible for the corporation's obligations. Should the corporation find that its liabilities overwhelm its assets, its creditors cannot reach the owners' personal assets. This is the essence of limited liability, perhaps the most cherished characteristic of the corporate form. However, for smaller corporations, this feature can be severely restricted because lenders are well aware of limited liability and usually require the principal owners to *guarantee* the corporation's debts. Still, limited liability remains for obligations like breach of contract claims.

Limited liability is sometimes lost via *piercing the corporate veil*. This doctrine, explored in the *Wolfe* case that follows, usually has two elements: (1) misuse of the corporate form and (2) an unjust result if limited liability is allowed to stand.

Charles E. Wolfe v. United States   612 F. Supp. 605 (D Mon 1985)

LEGAL BRIEFCASE   Aff'd 798 F.2d 1241 (9th Cir. 1986)

Judge Battin

Charles E. Wolfe was the sole shareholder and president of [the corporation], which leased tractor-trailers. Wolfe also operated a . . . proprietorship [doing] "over-the-road" trucking[.]

[T]he corporation incurred a $114,472.91 federal tax bill. Wolfe paid the taxes . . . after the Internal Revenue Service (Service) [levied against him]. The Service contends . . . the corporation was the alter ego of Wolfe, thus justifying the piercing of the corporate veil. . . .

* * * * *

As a general rule, a corporation is treated as a legal entity, separate . . . from its shareholders[, who] enjoy limited liability.

When the corporate entity is abused, however[,] limited liability may be lost[;] courts may . . . pierce the corporate veil. . . .

The facts . . . present the classic case of a shareholder so pervasively dominating corporate affairs that the shareholder and the corporation no longer have separate identities. [He] was the sole shareholder[,] a director, and the president. [He] made all the corporate decisions without consulting the other directors. The corporation [had no] bank account[, telephone, or separate office. All expenses were paid by the proprietorship. Its] equipment was purchased on the proprietorship's credit. . . . When [it received payment,] the money was deposited into the proprietorship's bank account. . . . It is clear that the corporation and the proprietorship were operated as a single instrumentality under the sole control of Wolfe. Therefore, it was proper for the service to look to wolfe's personal assets to satisfy the taxes of his alter ego corporation.

[Held for the Internal Revenue Service]

Questions

1. Who owed the taxes?

2. How was the corporate form misused?

3. What injustice would have resulted if Wolfe had not been required to pay?

Free Transferability of Interests

The securities laws impose broad restrictions on the transfer of stock, but that topic is deferred until Part Two of this chapter.

Beyond securities regulation, the law imposes no restriction on stock transfers. It is not uncommon, however, for dispositions to be restricted by an employment contract that might, for example, require that the stock be held until the employee leaves the company.

Another common contractual restriction is a *buy–sell agreement,* which, at the minimum, forces a shareholder to offer his or her stock to the corporation or other shareholders before selling it to a third party. [For more on buy–sell agreements, see **http://smallbusiness.findlaw.com/business-structures/business-structures-quickstart/incorporate-shareholders-agreement.html**]

Duration of Existence

In general, a corporation has indefinite duration. Nothing that transpires in the lives of the stockholders automatically affects the corporation's existence.

The termination of a corporation can be voluntary or involuntary. A voluntary termination requires a vote by the shareholders. They might do so, for example, because business prospects are no longer favorable. The corporation would be *liquidated,* which involves first satisfying all creditors and then distributing the remaining assets to the shareholders. *Articles of dissolution* would then be filed, officially ending the corporation's existence.

Involuntary terminations are caused by the action of a court or the state corporate regulator. A court might end a corporation's existence if, for example, there is an irreconcilable deadlock among the shareholders. A common reason for the state to terminate a corporation is its failure to pay annual fees and make annual filings.

Taxes

Taxes are what we pay for civilized society.

As Justice Oliver Wendell Holmes said, "Taxes are what we pay for civilized society."[3] But Justice Learned Hand also said, "[T]here is nothing sinister in so arranging one's affairs as to keep taxes as low as possible."[4]

Taxation transfers an enormous percentage of the United States' economic output to the government, and still appalling deficits loom for years to come. Virtually everyone wants to minimize tax payments, preferably by legal *tax avoidance* (careful planning within the law), not by illegal *tax evasion* (committing fraud to lower taxes).

Because the corporation is a separate legal entity, it is subject to taxation in its own right. This leads to what many would say is the corporation's greatest disadvantage, *double taxation.* In the United States, a corporation pays tax on its income. When it later distributes its after-tax income to its shareholders as *dividends,* the shareholders are taxed on that amount as well—hence "double taxation." Note, however, that dividends are not mandatory. They are paid only after the board declares them, which it cannot do if the corporation's solvency (cash flow and net worth) is insufficient.

To illustrate, assume a corporation is subject to income taxes at the rate of 40 percent and its shareholders all face a rate of 35 percent (with a special rate on dividends of 15 percent). On an income of $10 million, the corporation would pay $4 million in taxes, leaving only $6 million for distribution as dividends. Upon that distribution, the shareholders would pay $900,000 in taxes. Thus, of the $10 million corporate income, only $5.1 million can actually be spent by the owners—an effective tax rate of 49 percent. Had it been possible to own the business in a form that was not subject to taxation in its own right, the total taxes would have been $3.5 million, leaving $6.5 million available for the owners to spend—27 percent more.

The 40 percent figure used for large corporations is quite close to correct. Small corporations typically face a tax rate of 15 to 25 percent, still meaningful. Thus tax considerations are important in deciding the form in which to house a business.

A growing number of large corporations are participating in "abusive *corporate tax shelters*" that generate dubious tax benefits ($1.6 billion annually[5]). The United States is vigorously attacking shelters and their promoters. [For more on abusive tax shelters, see **www.irs.gov/taxtopics/tc454.html**]

The argument that the corporate form is necessarily disadvantageous because of double taxation is misleading. In many circumstances, employing the corporate form yields clear tax advantages, especially for small- and medium-sized *closely held businesses* (corporations whose stock is not publicly held). For example, the corporation is the only form of business that comprehensively permits tax-deductible fringe benefits. [For more on fringe benefits, see **www.irs.ustreas.gov/pub/irs-pdf/p15b.pdf**]

Further, portions of a business activity can be separated into multiple business forms in a fashion that lowers the overall tax rate. For example, the real estate associated with a golf course can be owned by a partnership (whose highly favorable tax characteristics are discussed later), while the golf course operation can be housed in a corporation. The taxable income of the corporation can be kept very low by purchasing fringe benefits, establishing bonus plans, timing discretionary maintenance, and the like.

Capital Structure

A business operates by employing its assets in productive endeavors. Some assets are owned; others are leased. Still other "assets" are available on a more tenuous basis, such as key employees and favorable public sentiment toward the company (goodwill).

Businesses need access to capital to finance their activities. Capital is of two types: debt and equity—two ends of the capital spectrum with a boundary line that is very challenging to identify. *Debt capital* may be short- or long-term. Companies that provide hard disks to Dell, for example, are a source of short-term debt capital. They expect to be paid fairly quickly. A pension plan that holds Dell's 20-year bonds provides long-term debt capital. *Equity capital* (stock) has a long-term horizon. Although any given shareholder may intend to hold the stock for only a short period, the stock itself is generally expected to exist for the full life of the corporation.

The providers of both debt and equity capital hold claims against the corporation's assets. However, creditors' claims are always satisfied before equity holders' claims. Three *property rights* are associated with stock ownership: the right to participate in earnings (that is, dividends), the right to participate in assets upon liquidation, and the right to participate in control. There are two principal classes of stock: preferred and common. Where only one class exists, it is *common stock*. Common stockholders share all three property rights in proportion to their holdings.

Preferred stock was created primarily for institutional investors (which hold about 50 percent of all stock[6]) like pension funds, to fill the gap on the risk–return spectrum between long-term debt and common stock. Finance professionals find it advantageous to have many different ways to combine risk and return. Preferred stock is associated with "preferences," which relate to distributions. Preferred stockholders are paid their required annual dividend in full before any dividends are distributed to the common stockholders. In addition, preferred stockholders have a preference upon the corporation's liquidation. After the creditors are satisfied, the preferred stockholders receive the next round of distributions up to their stock's *liquidation value* (also called *redemption value*).

The cost of these two preferences is the loss of the right to participate in control. Having no vote, preferred stockholders cannot elect directors to protect their interests. To help ensure that its holders regularly receive dividends, nearly all preferred stock is *cumulative*. This means that if a preferred stock dividend is missed, then before the common stockholders get any dividends, the preferred stock *arrearage* (all dividends not paid in any prior year) must be made up. Another protection occasionally granted to preferred stockholders is a contingent right to vote if, for example, a dividend is missed twice. This voting power would continue until all arrearages have been satisfied.

Because preferred stockholders never get more than their required dividends and, upon liquidation, little more than the purchase price, all corporate growth inures to the common stockholders. If both you and Bill Gates had invested $1 million in Microsoft at the outset, you taking preferred stock and Gates taking common stock, your stock would still be worth about $1 million, whereas Gates's stock would be worth tens of billions.

Increasingly, preferred stock is being issued with both debt and equity characteristics. This poses serious classification problems for accountants and tax authorities.

Corporations carefully manage their *capital structures* (balance between debt and equity). If the debt/equity ratio is too high, it may expose a corporation to severe risk. If it is too low, opportunities for positive *financial leverage* (employing funds at a rate of return that exceeds the interest rate on the borrowed funds) may be forfeited. Executives also recognize that *interest* is tax deductible, whereas dividends are not. This places a strong emphasis on using debt capital. The capital structure must be managed to ensure that *debt covenants* are not breached. A debt covenant is a term in the lending contract that makes the otherwise long-term debt immediately payable should the condition specified not be satisfied. [For more on capital structure, see **http://pages.stern.nyu.edu/ ~adamodar/pdfiles/ovhds/capstr.pdf**]

The form of business decision must take into account the total capital needed. Large businesses need billions of dollars. Only access to the global capital markets (like the New York Stock Exchange) can fulfill this need. With few exceptions, the only form of business that has succeeded in these markets is the corporation.

Circumstances Favoring a Specific Business Form

It is not rare to find someone with a great idea but insufficient resources to take the idea to market. Some investors, like *venture capitalists,* seek out such persons. They will usually insist that the venture have limited liability, as would be true with a corporation. [For venture capitalists, see **www.vfinance.com/home.asp?Toolpage=vencaentire.asp**]

Similarly, *franchisors* normally demand that *franchisees* operate their *franchises* in a business form with limited liability. A franchise is the right to exploit the franchisor's intangible assets (trade name and business systems) and to partake of the franchisor's marketing, purchasing, and other services. The key advantages to the franchisee are a proven product or service, turnkey implementation, and access to support. The franchisor gains by earning fees and by achieving accelerated market penetration using the capital of others (franchisees). Unfortunately, franchisor fraud and oppression are common, so careful investigation is essential.

Premium franchises can be very expensive. The requirements for a Krispy Kreme franchise include a net worth of $5 million and a commitment of some $2 million.[7] [For more on franchises, see **www.ftc.gov/bcp/conline/pubs/invest/buyfran.htm;** for franchise opportunities, see **www.franchisedirect.com**]

Occasionally a valuable right (like the right to render trucking services along a particular route) is granted on the condition that it is personal to the issuee. Once the issuee ceases to use the right, it is lost—it cannot be transferred. This can pose a problem unless the right is granted to an entity with indefinite duration, like a corporation.

Partnerships

This section discusses traditional, *general partnerships*. A partnership is two or more persons (*partners*) who carry on a business as co-owners. About 8 percent of all businesses are partnerships, generating 9 percent of all revenue. Only 10 percent of businesses with revenues in excess of $1 million are partnerships.

Whereas a corporate ownership interest is called stock or share, the equity interest of a partner is called a *partnership interest.*

Partnerships have *mutual agency*. The acts of every partner within the scope of the partnership's business bind the partnership. Knowledge held by any partner is deemed held by the partnership. As agents, each partner is entitled to be reimbursed for costs personally incurred in furtherance of the partnership's business. Each partner has the right to examine all partnership records and to demand a formal determination by a court of the value of the partner's interest (an *accounting*).

Partners are in a fiduciary relationship. They owe each other the duties of loyalty, confidentiality, sharing information, and exercising due care. The *Veale* case that follows explores some of these duties.

FACTS

Veale Sr., Veale Jr., Gibson, Parker, and Rose were partners in an accounting firm. The partnership agreement permitted partners to pursue other business interests if doing so did not conflict with the partnership practice. Rose performed accounting work for Right Away Foods and Payne, receiving the compensation personally. Rose's partners claimed that he owed them a share in that he had competed with the firm in violation of the partnership agreement. The jury held for Rose. The partners appealed.

Chief Justice Nye

The partnership agreement . . . provided[:]

> Except with the expressed approval of the other partners as to each specific instance, no partner shall perform any public accounting services . . . other than . . . on behalf of this partnership.

Partners . . . occupy a fiduciary relationship . . . which requires . . . the utmost degree of good faith and honesty in dealing with one another. . . .

It is undisputed that while a partner . . . Rose rendered accounting services for Right Away Foods for which he billed and received payment personally. [The] partnership did not share in the proceeds[.] . . . There was some testimony from which the jury could have inferred that the work which Rose did for Right Away Foods . . . was of the type which did not require the services of a CPA. However, Rose . . . admitted that there was no reason why he could not have rendered [those services] as a partner in the accounting firm. . . . [In] regard to services in connection with mergers and acquisitions, [Parker testified] that he was unaware of any [such work that was not] prepared by public accounting firms. The preponderance of all the evidence clearly establishes that Rose . . . performed accounting services for Right Away Foods . . . in competition with the partnership. The [jury] was in error.

[Rose] admitted that he performed accounting services for [Payne] for which he [was paid] personally. There is no question that those services were public accounting services. His later testimony that he performed the services, in effect, after hours, or in addition to his duties to the partnership, is of no value in light of the obligations imposed by the partnership agreement and by the common understanding of the term "competition."

Reversed and remanded.

Questions

1. *a.* Why was Rose's work for Right Away Foods considered a violation of the partnership agreement?

   b. Why did Rose's "after-hours" argument fail?

2. Could Rose operate a gas station, for instance, without violating the partnership agreement?

Nontax Costs

A partnership is not a separate legal entity. No filing with the state is required to create it. Contract law governs partnership formation. If persons intend to create a partnership, a partnership is created. However, mere co-ownership of property does not create a partnership. The co-owners must intend to join in the sharing of risks and rewards.

The partnership relationship carries potentially grave risks. One would expect the contract that creates and governs the partnership, the *partnership agreement,* to specify precisely the terms of that relationship. Being a contract, it may be oral or written. The vast majority are oral, which means that if disagreements arise, the partners may find it very difficult to conclusively establish what the original agreement was. This will not be helped by the fact that when important disagreements arise, the partners often discover that their interests have become adverse and that the hopeful emotions shared at the outset have been displaced by anger and a sense of betrayal.

So if the risks are great and the problems associated with a lack of clarity can be substantial, why are partnership agreements often oral and, even if written, frequently vague?

The answer relates in part to the fact that to draft a quality partnership agreement, a host of touchy, even unpleasant, issues must be concretely addressed. The drafters must ask, "How will we change the profit-sharing arrangement if a partner becomes ill or fails to meet expectations?" "If the partnership does not work out, how will the relationship be unwound?" The soon-to-be partners usually shy away from tough questions like these, sensing that asking them will sour the high spirits in which so many partnerships are born.

Partnership agreements tend to be expensive to draft because of the opportunities for customization, because state law provides only a loose background for adequate agreements, and because the personal risks of being a partner are so significant.

The partnership form generally requires no annual recurring costs for such things as state filings (none are required) or mandatory meetings of owners.

Partnership accounting systems are the most expensive of all the business forms because of the need to keep track of extensively customized economic arrangements.

Centralization of Management

By default, management in a partnership is not centralized. Each partner has an equal right to participate in control. This can make partnerships unwieldy, particularly as the number of partners grows. Some partnerships create centralization of management by adding provisions to their partnership agreements that give management rights to a subset of partners (perhaps only one—a *managing partner*).

Limited Liability

A partnership is not a separate legal entity. Thus it does not offer limited liability. The partners are personally liable for the partnership's obligations should it default. This is clearly the greatest disadvantage of the partnership form.

The partners are *jointly liable* for contract obligations, including loans. All partners must be named in the lawsuit, and a verdict against them imposes an equal share of the total liability on each partner. Unfortunately for the more well-to-do partners, a victorious claimant can proceed against any or all of the partners to collect. If one partner is wealthy and liquid, the plaintiff may collect from that partner alone. Then the paying partner must sue the others to recoup (*right of contribution*).

The partners are *jointly and severally liable* for the torts of the partnership's employees and for the nonintentional torts of the partners. The plaintiff need sue only a subset of the partners, typically those easiest to collect from. Once again, this works to the disadvantage of the wealthier partners.

The partners may be jointly and severally liable for the crimes committed by partnership employees, but will ordinarily not be liable for crimes committed by partners (unless the other partners participate in or authorize the crime).

Free Transferability of Interests

Because partnerships have mutual agency, involve a fiduciary relationship, and do not have limited liability, the law does not allow a partner to transfer a partnership interest to a third person without the unanimous consent of the other partners.

However, a partnership interest can be assigned. The *assignment* entitles the *assignee* only to the distribution rights of the assigning partner (*assignor*). The assignee has no right to participate in control and does not have the status of partner.

Duration of Existence

Because partnerships entail mutual agency and fiduciary relationships, a partnership is automatically dissolved upon the death, incapacity, bankruptcy, expulsion, or withdrawal of any partner. Thus, events in the private lives of the partners can seriously impact the venture.

The harm from such automatic dissolution can be minimized by placing in the partnership agreement a provision to the effect that the partnership will immediately reform among the remaining partners should such a dissolution occur. The ex-partner's partnership interest will be valued and paid out.

Taxes

The greatest advantage of the partnership form is the extraordinary range of economic relationships that can be crafted. Whereas a 10 percent shareholder simply expects to get 10 percent of whatever distributions are made by the corporation, a partnership agreement can detach percentage of ownership from the stream of distributions and tax consequences. For example, assume L contributes land to a real estate development partnership, K contributes knowledge as the general contractor, and C contributes the cash necessary to undertake the venture. It would be acceptable to allocate the partnership cash flow as follows: C gets all of the net cash flow until C's initial cash contribution is recouped, then L gets all of the net cash flow until the value of L's contributed land has been distributed, then all three share the remaining net cash flow equally.

Double taxation does not apply to partnerships because they are not separate legal entities. The partnership's income is taxed only once—on the personal tax returns of the partners according to each partner's share of the partnership's income. However, partners must pay that tax whether or not the partnership actually distributes anything to them.

There are two important negative tax aspects of a partnership. First, fringe benefits provided to partners are not deductible (although fringes provided to employees are). Second, all of the partners' income is subject to self-employment tax (about 13 percent net).

Capital Structure

Because partnerships do not offer limited liability, free transferability of interests, indefinite life, or centralized management, they are (with few exceptions) not appropriate for ventures requiring large amounts of capital accessed via the financial markets.

Circumstances Favoring Specific Business Form

Whereas the partnership form is not likely to be legally required for any venture, there are two situations in which its legal characteristics are relevant to form selection. First, although partnerships are not legally separate entities, they are generally recognized as such for the purpose of property ownership. This affords opportunities for asset protection because the creditor of a partner cannot reach the partnership assets. [For a discussion of asset protection opportunities, see **www.assetprotection.com**]

Second, some experts advise that partnerships are less useful for estate planning purposes. Partnership interests can be relatively difficult to value, and they are more difficult to unitize. It is easy to transfer 10 shares of stock; it is more difficult to create easily transferable units of partnership interests. [For more on estate planning, see **www.nolo.com/lawcenter/ency/index.cfm/catID/FD1795A9-8049-422C-9087838F86A2BC2B**]

Final Comment

Under most circumstances, the disadvantages of the general partnership form are so severe that a person is generally well advised to avoid it. Instead, hybrid forms (considered shortly) like S corporations and limited liability companies are the entities of choice.

Sole Proprietorships

A sole proprietorship is nothing more than a venture undertaken by a single individual

A sole proprietorship is nothing more than a venture undertaken by a single individual, so centralization of management automatically exists. It is not a separate legal entity. Thus the owner has no limited liability. This lack of a separate legal entity also means that it terminates as soon as the proprietor ceases to engage in it—whether by incapacity, death, or any other reason. Further, a sole proprietorship is not a taxable entity. All of its revenues and expenses appear on the personal tax return of the proprietor. As in partnerships, most fringe benefits are not deductible as a business expense, and all business income is subject to self-employment tax.

A sole proprietorship comes into existence by the mere decision of the proprietor to pursue a venture. No legal filings or fees are required to establish the operation, but a business license, sales tax license, and/or other permits may be required by the state, county, and/or city where the business is located. Further, a proprietor may dispose of the proprietorship freely, but it will be deemed a transfer of the assets that underlie the business, not a transfer of the "business" in its own right. The capital structure issues for a sole proprietorship are similar to those of a partnership.

No venture is legally required to operate in proprietorship form. Doing so has several disadvantages. First, it is impossible to transfer ownership units in a proprietorship because there are none, making it a poor form for estate planning purposes. Second, the form is vulnerable to the proprietor's death or incapacity. Who will have the power to operate the business? The answer is the executor or custodian, who will be forced to continuously seek court approval to perform the activities required to operate the business. This impractical arrangement can destroy the business's value in short order. Had the venture been conducted in corporate form, the proprietor would simply have been succeeded by the next ranking executive.

Although more than two thirds of all businesses are sole proprietorships, they generate only about 5 percent of all business revenue, averaging about $50,000.

Hybrid Business Forms

Joint Ventures

Joint ventures are essentially partnerships created for a limited purpose, such as cost sharing or product development.

Limited Partnerships

The first hybrid business form in the United States was the *limited partnership*. Partnerships have advantages: great flexibility and no double taxation. Corporations have limited liability, indefinite life, freely transferable interests, and centralized management. The desire to create a business form with all of these advantages led to the limited partnership, which has two classes of partners: general and limited.

General partners are identical to the partners discussed earlier. They (often only one) make the decisions. The principal disadvantage of that status is unlimited liability. In reality, most general partners are corporations with minimal capital investment, so unlimited liability is little threat unless grounds for piercing the corporate veil exist. *Limited partners* contribute capital but do not participate in control (except to a limited extent analogous to shareholders). They do not face unlimited liability.

The law of limited partnerships provides that events that would terminate a general partnership have minimal impact on the limited partnership's existence. Limited partnerships come into existence only upon filing a *certificate of limited partnership*. Minor annual filings and fees are required. The income of the general partner is subject to self-employment tax; the income of the limited partners generally is not. Limited partnerships were extremely popular until the advent of limited liability companies, discussed later—although some continue to favor limited partnerships for estate planning.

S Corporations

Many would argue that the principal disadvantage of the corporate form is double taxation. In response, Congress created *S corporations,* essentially eliminating double taxation for corporations electing that status. An S corporation's income is taxed once—to the shareholders on their personal returns, much like partnerships. Like partnerships, S corporations may not deduct the cost of most fringe benefits provided to their owners. Unlike partnerships, to the extent the entity's income is distributed as dividends, no self-employment tax is imposed. However, the Internal Revenue Service routinely challenges attempts to distribute an excessive amount as dividends where inadequate wages have been paid to the owner.

To confine "S," the status, to smaller companies, significant restrictions on eligibility have been established. No more than 100 individuals (no nonresident aliens) and certain estates and trusts can be shareholders. Interestingly, an entire family is treated as one individual for these purposes. Only one class of stock is permitted. Despite these restrictions, one can find S corporations with multi-billion-dollar revenues. S corporations are popular. They represent about 50–60% of all corporations but tend to be much smaller, generating only 15–20% of all corporate revenue. S corporations are treated like all other corporations under state corporation law. The "S" status is relevant only for federal (and some state) tax purposes.

Limited Liability Companies (LLCs)

Wide displeasure with the lack of a business form that has the favorable characteristics both of partnerships and corporations led Wyoming to create the *limited liability company* (LLC) in 1977. The Internal Revenue Service (IRS) argued that LLCs should be taxed like corporations. Eventually, however, the IRS agreed to tax LLCs as partnerships. By 1997 LLCs were available nationally—the fastest-growing business form in the United States. Indeed, many experts say that LLCs are the form of choice for business ventures and estate plans.

To create an LLC, the owners (as few as one), called *members,* file *articles of organization*. Their equity is called *members' interests*. An *operating agreement* will be drafted to set forth the information often found in bylaws, as well as the manner in which the LLC will be managed. Minor annual filings and fees will be required. LLCs are extremely flexible, including in their management structure, which can be hierarchical (like a corporation) or horizontal (like a partnership).

Limited Liability Partnerships (LLPs)

At the same time LLCs were being conceived, the great multinational accounting firms were reeling from an episode in which the quality of their audits proved less than advertised—the savings and loan collapse of the 1980s. Over $1.6 billion in settlements (a staggering sum for that era) was paid out, and these firms feared extinction if professional liability damages could not be brought under control. Efforts to obtain tort reform that would limit such liability failed, so a new approach was sought—the *limited liability partnership* (LLP). LLPs terminate unlimited liability for malpractice. The partner committing the tort is still personally liable, but the nontortious partners are not.

To bring an LLP into existence, a document often called *application for registration* is filed. Minor annual filings and fees will be required. LLPs (and their partners) are taxed like a general partnership.

International Hybrids

Dozens of business forms exist throughout the world. For the most part, the proliferation is intended to achieve various combinations of the factors just discussed. A manager operating in a global environment must be prepared to make form of business decisions under a variety of regimes.

Uniform Acts

In the modern world, where business transactions are routinely multistate and many are multinational, differences in law among jurisdictions can present enormous difficulties. When it comes to harmonizing multistate issues, the National Conference of Commissioners on Uniform State Laws (NCCUSL) develops "uniform acts," which ideally are intended for adoption by states in their entirety. Relevant here would be the Uniform Partnership Act, the Uniform Limited Partnership Act, and the Uniform Limited Liability Company Act. Where the commissioners believe that states will not adopt the great majority of a proposed act, they develop "model acts," intended to serve as general guidelines. Relevant here would be the Model Business Corporation Act. [For more on the NCCUSL, see **www.nccusl.org/nccusl/default.asp**]

At the multinational level, the World Trade Organization will likely emerge as the vehicle for establishing international uniformity in business law.

Questions—Part One

1. Why are corporations the dominant form of business in the United States?
2. Describe the steps generally followed to bring a corporation into existence, through the election of directors.
3. Locate the form necessary to incorporate in Oregon. Does it appear difficult to incorporate there? [See **www.filinginoregon.com/forms/pdf/bizreg/111.doc**]
4. Examine the "canned" bylaws found at **www.lectlaw.com/forms/f151.htm.**
   a. For a stockholders' meeting, how many must attend to transact any business other than adjournment?
   b. Can a director participate in a board meeting by speakerphone?
   c. What does it take to remove an officer?
   d. If a board member becomes concerned about the corporation's behavior and wants to sever herself from future responsibility, can she just resign?
5. Why would it make sense to have only outside directors determine the compensation of senior executives?
6. Modell owned 80 percent of the Cleveland Stadium Corporation (Stadium) and 53 percent of the Cleveland Browns Football Company (Browns). Gries owned 43 percent of the Browns. The Browns' board consisted of Modell, the outside lawyer for both corporations, three individuals employed by both corporations, and Gries. Modell proposed that the Browns buy the Stadium for $6 million. Gries objected, saying that the Stadium appraised for only $2 million. The Browns' board approved the purchase nonetheless (all directors other than Gries voting in favor). Gries commenced a shareholders' derivative suit seeking to rescind the purchase. Who should win? See *Gries Sports Enterprises v. Cleveland Browns Football Company,* 496 N.E.2d 959 (Ohio S. Ct. 1986).
7. Is it complicated to dissolve a corporation in New York once the liabilities have been paid and the remaining assets have been distributed to the shareholders? [See **www.dos.state.ny.us/corp/pdfs/dos1337.pdf**]
8. A corporation liquidates, distributing $800,000 in cash (its only asset) to its sole shareholder. It then dissolves. A year later, the IRS seeks to impose an additional $500,000 in income taxes for the corporation's final year. Assuming the corporation actually owes this amount, how will the IRS collect?
9. A corporation is in the 40 percent tax bracket; its taxable income (before interest expense) is $1 million. The corporation borrowed, at 10 percent simple interest, $4 million to finance a new project on the first day of the year.
   a. How much in taxes must be paid?
   b. How would the taxes change if, instead of borrowing, the corporation sold 10 percent cumulative preferred stock for $4 million (par value) to finance the project?

(The preferred dividend is the product of the par value and the dividend rate [10 percent].)

10. What happens when a debt covenant is breached? What danger then exists?

11. What are the costs associated with launching a McDonald's franchise? [See **www .mcdonalds.com/content/corp/franchise/franchisinghome.html**]

12. The Patels owned the CC Motel. They formed a partnership with their son, Raj, to own and operate the motel. Title to the motel was not transferred to the partnership. The partnership agreement required Raj to approve the motel's sale. The Patels sold the motel without telling Raj and without telling the buyers of Raj's right. He learned of the pending sale and refused to agree. The buyers asked the court to compel the sale. Who should win? See *Patel v. Patel,* 260 Cal. Rptr. 255 (Cal. Ct. App. 1989).

13. Why are sole proprietorships problematic with respect to issues related to the proprietor's death or disability?

14. Assume two individuals want to be equal co-owners of a business. They will house it in either an S corporation or a general partnership. Will the total income taxes paid with respect to operating income typically be the same?
    a. What factors would favor an S corporation?
    b. What factors would favor a general partnership?

15. Why would an LLC generally be favored over a limited partnership?

16. In general, would you prefer to organize as an LLC or as an S corporation? Explain.

17. Assume you want to start a business in Norway as a partnership. What is the advantage of a "partnership with shared liability" over a general partnership? [See **www.ey.com/global/download.nsf/Norway/Establishing_a_business_in_Norway/ $file/EBIN%2φhele%2φboka.pdf**]

Part Two—Regulation of the Securities Markets

Introduction

The U.S. economy is the largest on earth, with a gross domestic product of $11.1 trillion. In considerable part this is due to its adoption of a market system intended to be restrained from exhibiting its most disagreeable side effects (such as restraints on competition) by government regulation.

The scale of modern business requires access to massive amounts of capital. The problem is that the owners of capital do not operate the businesses employing that capital and therefore reasonably fear whether their investment will be put to productive use or misappropriated by those in daily control of these businesses. In other words, to amass the capital needed to pursue global business opportunities, a large number of investors must be convinced to entrust their wealth to third parties. History shows that this trust has often been misplaced, with vast sums lost in companies with incompetent or corrupt management. As a result, the U.S. government has undertaken, principally through laws enacted since the Great Depression of 1929–1939, to promote the integrity of the capital markets. Despite some occasional major problems, the system had been heralded as the best in the world. Unfortunately, the complacent environment created by this widespread belief in the system led to disaster.

> Beginning in 2000, the United States experienced one of its greatest financial reversals.

Beginning in 2000, the United States experienced one of its greatest financial reversals. As of Monday, July 22, 2002, 100 percent of the profits earned by mutual funds in the United States since the beginning of the bull market in October 1990 had been lost. By the following Friday, losses reached $8 trillion. (The 48 percent drop is the largest since the Great Depression.[9]) About $4 trillion of this was volatile "paper" wealth, earned rather recently; but the remaining $4 trillion was "hard-earned" wealth. Although much of the decline has been recovered, for employees whose retirement funding was principally in the form of stock in employers that collapsed, such as Global Crossing, nearly all of their retirement security has been lost. These events will be discussed later, but at this juncture an understanding of how the securities markets are regulated is in order.

Initial Public Offerings

When a corporation wishes to sell a new *security* on the open market, it undertakes an *initial public offering* (IPO). If a corporation (*issuer*) and any of the persons to whom the security is offered for sale (*offerees*) are domiciled in different states (*interstate offering*), federal law governs the IPO. Should the corporation and all offerees be domiciled in the same state (*intrastate offering*), state law (considered later) applies.

The term *security* embraces both the instruments commonly understood to be such, like stocks and bonds, and a much broader class of interests called *investment contracts*. The *Howey* case that follows defines the term.

LEGAL BRIEFCASE

Securities & Exchange Commission v. W. J. Howey Co.   328 U.S. 293 (1946)

FACTS

[Howey] owns large tracts of citrus acreage in ... Florida.] Each prospective customer is offered both a land sales contract and a service contract [by which Howey maintains the groves and markets the produce]. Purchases are ... narrow strips ... arranged so that an acre consists of a row of 48 trees.... These tracts are not separately fenced[. The] purchaser has no right of entry [and] no right to specific fruit. ... All the produce is pooled[.] The purchasers [are mostly] nonresidents of Florida[,] predominantly ... professional people who lack the knowledge ... and equipment necessary for the [citrus business]. They are attracted by the expectation of substantial profits....

It is admitted that the mails and instrumentalities of interstate commerce are used in the sale of the land and service contracts and that no registration statement ... has ever been filed with the Commission[.]

Justice Murphy

[T]he Act defines . . . "security" to include the commonly known [instruments like stocks and bonds. It also includes the term] "investment contract"[.] The legal issue [is whether] the land sales contract . . . and the service contract together constitute an "investment contract"[.] An affirmative answer brings into operation the registration requirements[.]

"[I]nvestment contract" is undefined by the [Act, b]ut the term was common in many state "blue sky" laws in existence prior to the adoption of the federal statute[. An] investment contract . . . means a . . . scheme whereby a person invests his money in a common enterprise and is led to expect profits solely from the efforts of . . . a third party[.]

[These] transactions clearly involve investment contracts[.] The respondent [is] offering an opportunity to contribute money and to share in the profits of a large citrus fruit enterprise managed . . . by respondent[. It is] offering this opportunity to persons who reside in distant localities and who lack the [wherewithal to deal with] citrus products. . . .

[Respondent's] failure to [register the securities] cannot be sanctioned under the Act.

Questions

1. Would an investment in Microsoft stock satisfy the definition of *investment contract*?

2. Why do you think Congress added the term *investment contract* to the definition of *security*?

1933 Act

The federal law governing IPOs is the *Securities Act of 1933* (1933 Act), which is administered by the *Securities and Exchange Commission* (SEC). Its purpose is not to guarantee the economic merits of any investment opportunity. Rather, it seeks to ensure full disclosure of all material facts about the investment opportunity to offerees before they invest, and to eliminate fraudulent conduct in the markets. Therefore, an IPO that passes muster under the federal securities law has not been approved by the government as a good investment (although the government can find ways to discourage investments it deems poor). [For more on the SEC, see **http://www.sec.gov**]

To promote full disclosure, the 1933 act forbids any interstate offering of a new security until a *registration statement* has been filed with and approved by the SEC. The registration statement has two parts: the prospectus and the supplemental information. The *prospectus* is the major component and is delivered to offerees to satisfy the requirement for preinvestment disclosure. A prospectus has three main sections. One contains general information about the company: the industry(ies) in which it operates; the quality of its products, services, and management; its business plan, and so on. Another section contains a risk assessment dealing with problems with the business model, local operating conditions (such as political instability), and the like.

The third portion of the prospectus is the *audited financial statements*. Investors obviously invest to make money. They want to know how well the corporation under consideration has accomplished this goal in the past so, with other information, they can estimate its economic potential in the future. A corporation's ability to make a profit is shown on its *income statement,* one of the three audited financial statements.

Because the income statement seeks a measure of economic income, it employs accrual accounting, which disregards cash flows in measuring revenues and expenses. For this reason, the *statement of cash flows* is also presented in the prospectus.

The third financial statement, the *balance sheet,* is intended to show the company's assets, liabilities, and equities. Although balance sheets have numerous deficiencies (such as the use of historical cost versus current value to measure assets, and the failure to include many critical intangible assets), they attempt to describe the corporation's financial position. Liabilities pose great risks and are a major reason for sudden corporate failures.

Technically, the corporation's management prepares the financial statements. To give comfort to investors that management has prepared these statements properly and honestly, independent *certified public accountants* (CPAs) are engaged to audit them. Audits must be performed in accordance with *generally accepted auditing standards* (GAAS). GAAS are intended to ensure that the procedures used to investigate the financial statements are thorough. The objective of the investigation is to determine whether the financial statements are *not materially misleading,* in accordance with *generally accepted accounting principles* (GAAP). GAAP provide the rules for how revenues, expenses, assets, liabilities, and equity are measured and disclosed. One might paraphrase an audit: Independent experts (CPAs) are supposed to "look hard" (using GAAS) and decide whether the financial statements accurately measure the income, cash flow, and financial position of the corporation (using GAAP).

In the *supplemental information* portion of the registration statement, which is not distributed to offerees, can be found matters such as how much it is costing to "float" the IPO and what major contracts exist with unions, suppliers, or customers.

The SEC vigorously enforces the 1933 Act's prescribed relationship between solicitation or sales of a security and the registration process. This relationship has three critical stages. During the *prefiling period* (before the registration statement has been filed with the SEC), no solicitation of offerees or sales of the security are permitted. During the *waiting period* (after the registration statement has been filed, but before it has been approved by the SEC), no sales are permitted but a limited amount of solicitation is allowed. Specifically, a *tombstone ad* (name taken from its shape) may be published in forums like *The Wall Street Journal* to make the market aware of the possible future issuance. In addition, a *red herring* prospectus (the name is taken from the prominent cautionary statement in red ink required on its first page) may be distributed. This is the draft prospectus included with the filed registration statement. Once the SEC approves the registration statement, the *post-effective period* begins. Solicitations are permitted and sales may be made, but only if the offerees have first received the final prospectus.

Some companies do *shelf registrations,* which allow them to issue securities in portions over up to a two-year period under a single registration statement. This allows issuers to float the securities when market conditions are most favorable, versus having to place the entire issue shortly after the registration statement becomes effective.

Issuers typically do not want to sell the securities themselves. Instead, they employ *underwriters,* of which there are two principal kinds. A *best-efforts underwriter* acts as the issuer's sales agent, never taking title to the securities and earning its profit from sales commissions. A *firm-commitment underwriter* purchases the securities (at a discount), intending to profit by reselling them. Institutional investors and *dealers* typically purchase the securities, the former for investment, the latter for resale to retail investors.

Exemptions

Not all issuances of new securities require registration with the SEC; there are *exempt securities* and *exempt transactions*. The principal securities exempted from the registration requirement are those issued by governments, charities, educational institutions, and financial institutions such as banks and insurance companies.

A significant number of new issuances are completed using transactions that are exempted from the full registration requirement. In these cases, the SEC is notified that the transaction has occurred. In some situations, a much more modest disclosure to offerees is substituted for the prospectus. All intrastate offerings are exempt transactions, and there are others. The norm in nonliquidation corporate bankruptcy is that many creditors will exchange their debt for a new class of stock. Such issuance transactions are exempted. Corporate mergers require the exchange of securities. These issuance transactions are exempted.

Five additional exempt transactions were created as an accommodation to small issuers to lessen the financial burdens of raising capital. They are intended to be safe harbors from the general rule that all public offerings require the securities to be registered. Depending on the exemption, the presale disclosures and filings with the SEC range from none to something slightly less than a full registration statement. Most exemptions do not permit general advertising or solicitation. Note that while the exemptions apply to the registration requirement of the 1933 Act, the act's sweeping antifraud provisions, discussed later, still apply.

The Secondary Securities Markets

Once a security is issued, it can be sold repeatedly. Such sales will generally be accomplished on a *physical exchange* [such as the New York Stock Exchange (NYSE)], where agents of buyers and sellers deal directly with each other, or on an *over-the-counter market* (such as NASDAQ, the National Association of Securities Dealers Automatic Quotation system), where trades occur electronically over a computer network linking dealers across the nation.

At this writing, the NYSE is moving toward a hybrid trading model in which buy and sell orders will be processed electronically, similarly to NASDAQ. The new trading model is partly in response to demands for faster order processing and partly to address a scandal involving specialists (on-floor traders) who put themselves between buy and sell orders to appropriate a portion of the profit for themselves. In 2004 specialist firms settled criminal charges for $247 million. [For more on the secondary markets, see **www.nyse.com** and **www.nasdaq.com**]

The federal law that governs these trades is the *Securities Exchange Act of 1934* (1934 Act), which also created the SEC. Its purposes are the same as those of its 1933 counterpart: to ensure full disclosure of all material information so the market can make informed decisions and to prevent fraudulent conduct in the markets.

Even if a company's securities are not traded nationally, it is subject to the 1934 Act's registration requirements with respect to its outstanding securities if (1) it is engaged in (or its securities are traded in) interstate commerce, and (2) it has both more than $10 million in assets and more than 500 shareholders.[10]

To promote full disclosure, the SEC requires registered corporations to file a variety of reports. Annually, each must file a *Form 10-K,* which includes information similar to that found in an IPO registration statement, including audited financial statements. To increase the timeliness of information disclosures, the SEC requires additional reports. Quarterly, a *Form 10-Q* must be filed, which contains year-to-date information, including unaudited interim financial statements. Because significant events can occur between the four scheduled reporting dates, the SEC requires corporations to file a *Form 8-K* whenever a material event occurs such as change in control, major asset acquisitions and dispositions, bankruptcy, change in auditor, and resignations of directors.[11] [To retrieve filings, see **http://www.tenkwizard.com**]

Under the 1934 Act, the SEC has the power to *suspend trading* in any security "when it serves the public interest and will protect investors." Examples include when the SEC suspects price manipulation or asset misappropriation.[12] Typically the market price of a security is devastated by a suspension, which provides a strong incentive for corporations to avoid misconduct. [For more on securities law, see **http://www.findlaw.com/01topics/34securities/index.html**]

Violating Securities Laws

The consequences for noncompliance with the securities laws are potentially staggering, including damages, miscellaneous SEC remedies, and civil and criminal penalties.

Civil Damages

Perhaps the greatest deterrent to misconduct in the securities laws is the civil liability that can be imposed upon wrongdoers by harmed investors. The 1933 Act's §11 establishes this liability with respect to false or misleading registration statements related to IPOs.

Virtually anyone with a significant role in preparing the registration statement can be sued (the issuer, its directors, its underwriters, and its accountants and other experts). The liability can be vast—essentially all damages sustained by investors while the misleading registration statements were outstanding. No proof of plaintiff reliance on the content of the registration statement is required. Accounting firms and investment bankers, because of their "deep pockets," are often at the top of the list of defendants. Accounting firms have paid hundreds of millions to settle securities fraud suits.

The principal defense against a §11 claim is "due diligence." Every defendant, other than the issuer, can raise this defense. The defendant must show that, based on a reasonable investigation, he or she reasonably believed that the registration statement was not misleading. What constitutes "reasonable" is determined by reference to the conduct expected of a prudent person in the management of his or her own property.

The due diligence standard for experts (like accountants and lawyers) is much higher. Their inquiries must rise to the standards expected of professionals, not merely of prudent businesspersons. Thus, at an absolute minimum, an accounting firm that has audited the financial statements included in the registration statement must design its investigation to comport with GAAS and must evaluate the financial statement content in accordance with GAAP. Lawyers, actuaries, appraisers, and other experts whose work has a material impact on the registration statement must adhere to analogous rules established by their professional associations and regulators. The *BarChris* case explores the due diligence defense.

FACTS

Bowling as a leisure activity and sport grew rapidly in the 1950s. BarChris built alleys. By 1962 overbuilding caused construction to halt. BarChris ran into serious financial problems. It filed a registration statement (effective May 1961) for a bond IPO, and the bonds were issued. Circumstances were grave when the registration statement became effective. BarChris filed for bankruptcy in October 1962.

BarChris's financial statements dated December 31, 1960, were included in the prospectus. They were audited by Peat Marwick (predecessor to KPMG), and material errors were found. Revenues and current assets were overstated, and contingent liabilities were understated.

The prospectus overstated the demand for alley construction. It misrepresented how the IPO proceeds would be used (a large portion would actually go to pay debts recently incurred to keep the company afloat). It failed to note that because of defaults, BarChris was now operating several alleys. The bondholders sued under (Section 11 of the 1933 Act based on the prospectus being materially misleading. All defendants but BarChris raised the due diligence defense.

Judge McLean

THE "DUE DILIGENCE" DEFENSES . . .

Russo

Russo was [executive vice president and] chief executive officer[.] He was familiar with all aspects of the business. [He] knew all the relevant facts. He could not have believed that there were no untrue statements or material omissions in the prospectus. Russo has no due diligence defenses.

Vitolo and Pugliese

They were the founders[.] Despite their titles [president and vice president], their control over BarChris [was far less] than Russo's. [They are] men of limited education. It is not hard to believe that for them the prospectus was difficult reading, if indeed they read it at all. But [the] liability of a director who signs a registration statement does not depend upon whether or not he read it or, if he did, whether or not he understood what he was reading.

[I]n any case, [they] were not as naïve as they claim[.] They were members of [the] executive committee [and] must have known what was going on. [T]hey knew of the inadequacy of cash[.] They knew of their own large advances to the company[.] They knew . . . that part of the [bond] proceeds were to

be used to pay their own loans. All in all, [their situation] is not significantly different . . . from Russo's. They could not have believed that the registration statement was wholly true[.] They have not proved their due diligence defenses.

* * * * *

Trilling

[Trilling was . . . a CPA and former member of Peat Marwick. He was BarChris's controller. He signed the registration statement in that capacity, although he was not a director. [He was a] minor figure in BarChris. . . .

Trilling may well have been unaware of several of the inaccuracies in the prospectus. But he must have known of some of them. [I cannot hold] that Trilling believed the entire prospectus to be true. But even if he did, he still did not establish his due diligence defenses. [He] failed to prove, as to the [nonaudited] parts of the prospectus[,] that he made a reasonable investigation which afforded him a reasonable ground to believe that [they were true. H]e made no investigation. . . . This would have been well enough but for the fact that he signed the registration statement. As a signer, he could not avoid responsibility[. He has not proved] his due diligence defenses.

Birnbaum

Birnbaum was a young lawyer [employed as in-house counsel. He was] secretary and a director[.] He signed the [registration statement], thereby becoming responsible for the accuracy of the prospectus[.] He did not participate in the [company's] management[. H]e attended to legal matters of a routine nature. [One of his] more important duties . . . was to keep the corporate minutes[.] This necessarily informed him to a considerable extent about the company's affairs. . . .

It seems probable that Birnbaum did not know of many of the inaccuracies in the prospectus. He must, however, have appreciated some of them. In any case, he made no investigation[. He] was entitled to rely upon Peat, Marwick for the 1960 figures[.] But he was not entitled to rely upon [anyone else] for the other portions of the prospectus. As a lawyer, he should have known his obligations[.] Having failed to make [an] investigation, he did not have reasonable ground to believe that all these statements were true. Birnbaum has not established his due diligence defenses except as to the audited 1960 figures.

Auslander

Auslander [became a director shortly before the IPO. He signed] the registration statement[.]

As to the [financial statements], Auslander knew that Peat, Marwick had audited [them, so he] believed them to be correct[.] As to the [nonaudited portions of the prospectus, however, he] made no investigation[.] He relied on the assurance of Vitolo and Russo[.]

It is true that Auslander became a director on the eve of the financing. He had little opportunity to familiarize himself with the company's affairs. [But S]ection 11 imposes liability . . . upon a director, no matter how new he is. . . . He can escape liability only by using that reasonable care to investigate the facts which a prudent man would employ in the management of his own property. [A] prudent man would not act in an important matter . . . in sole reliance upon representations of persons who are comparative strangers[. Auslander] has not established his due diligence defense [except as to the financial statements.]

Grant

[Grant's] law firm was counsel to BarChris[. He] drafted the registration statement[.] As the director most directly concerned with writing [it,] more was required of him in the way of reasonable investigation[.]

I find that Grant honestly believed that the registration statement was true and [complete]. The question is whether, despite his failure to detect [the errors], Grant made a reasonable effort to that end. [BarChris's] affairs had changed for the worse[.] Grant never discovered this. He accepted the assurances of [others.]

It is claimed that a lawyer is entitled to rely on [his client's statements.] This is too broad[.] To require an audit would . . . be unreasonable. [T]o require a check of matters easily verifiable is not[.] Even honest clients can make mistakes. The statute imposes liability for untrue statements regardless of whether they are intentionally untrue.

Grant was entitled to rely on Peat, Marwick for the 1960 figures. [But as to the rest of the prospectus,] Grant was obliged to make a reasonable investigation. [H]e did not[.] Grant has not established his due diligence defenses except as to the audited 1960 figures.

The Underwriters and Coleman

The underwriters other than Drexel made no investigation of the accuracy of the prospectus. . . . They all relied upon Drexel as the "lead" underwriter. Drexel did make an investigation [through firm member] Coleman[.] Drexel's attorneys[, led by Ballard, did the work.]

[C]oleman became a director[.] He signed [the] registration statement[.] He thereby assumed a responsibility as a director and signer in addition to his responsibility as an underwriter.

[Coleman] familiarized himself with general conditions in the industry[, which appeared favorable. He read the] annual reports[.] He inquired about BarChris of certain of its banks[.]

[Early underwriting discussions] were extensive[.] Coleman and Ballard asked pertinent questions and received answers which satisfied them. [However, after] Coleman was elected a director on April 17, 1961, he made no further independent investigation[.] He assumed that Ballard was taking care of this[.]

[Ballard read some minutes.] He did not examine . . . contracts with customers. [He] examined no accounting records[.] His visit . . . lasted one day[. He] relied on the information which he got from [others. No] verification was made. [Is] it sufficient to ask questions, to obtain answers which, if true, would be thought satisfactory, and to let it go at that, without seeking to ascertain from the records whether the answers in fact are true and complete? [I hold that it] is not sufficient[.]

The purpose of Section 11 is to protect investors. To that end the underwriters are made responsible for the truth of the prospectus. [They] must make some reasonable attempt to verify the data submitted to them. . . .

Drexel is bound by [this] failure. . . . The other underwriters, who did nothing and relied solely on Drexel[,] are also bound by it. . . . The same [applies] to Coleman [as director]. . . .

Peat, Marwick . . .

The part of the registration statement . . . made upon the authority of Peat, Marwick as an expert was . . . the 1960 [audited financial statements].

The 1960 Audit

[The audit] was in general charge of [partner] Cummings[.] Most of the actual work was performed by . . . Berardi[, who was about thirty.]. He was not yet a C.P.A. He had no previous experience with the bowling industry. This was his first job as a senior accountant. . . .

Capitol Lanes

First and foremost is Berardi's failure to discover that Capitol Lanes had not been sold. . . . Berardi did become aware [of references] in BarChris's records to . . . Capitol Lanes. [He read minutes] which recited that "the Corporation [would] operate Capitol Lanes[.]" Berardi knew . . . that Capitol Lanes . . . was paying rentals [and insurance. The foregoing] should have alerted him . . . that an alley existed. . . .

The S-1 Review

The purpose of reviewing events subsequent to the date of a certified balance sheet [an S-1 review] is to ascertain whether any material change has occurred . . . which should be disclosed . . . to prevent the . . . figures from being misleading. The scope of such a review [is not] a complete audit. Peat, Marwick prepared a written program [which] conformed to generally accepted auditing standards.

Berardi made the S-1 review in May 1961. He devoted . . . 20 1/2 hours. He did not discover any of the errors or omissions[.] The question is whether, despite his failure to find out anything, his investigation was reasonable[.]

What Berardi did was [examine a] trial balance as of March 31, 1961[,] compare it with the audited December 31, 1960 figures, discuss with Trilling certain unfavorable developments[,] and read certain minutes. He did not examine any [other] "important financial records"[.] He asked questions, he got answers which he considered satisfactory, and he did nothing to verify them. . . .

There had been a material change for the worse in BarChris's financial position. That change was sufficiently serious so that the failure to disclose it made the 1960 figures misleading. Berardi did not discover it. As far as results were concerned, his S-1 review was useless.

Accountants should not be held to a standard higher than that recognized in their profession. . . . Berardi's review did not come up to that standard. He did not take some of the steps [the] written program prescribed. He did not spend an adequate amount of time on a task of this magnitude. Most important of all, he was too easily satisfied with glib answers to his inquiries. [T]here were enough danger signals in the materials which he did examine to require some further investigation on his part. [Peat, Marwick] has not established its due diligence defense.

Questions

1. *a.* Why were so many defendants not held responsible for the misleading audited financial statements?

   b. Which defendants were not successful in claiming the due diligence defense with respect to these financial statements? Why were they denied the defense?

2. Does being "new" make any difference in terms of directoral liability for a signed registration statement?

3. What would you do differently in the future if you were Peat Marwick?

Fraud

Under the 1933 Act's §17(a) and the 1934 Act's §10(b) and its related SEC Rule 10b-5, it is illegal, in connection with the sale or purchase of any security, to employ any scheme or to engage in any practice that defrauds another person participating in the financial markets. This includes making misleading statements of material facts and failing to state material facts.

The extraordinary breadth of the antifraud statutes is intentional. They cast a "broad net" and provide a potent basis for damage suits by harmed investors.

Basic Inc. v. Levinson et al.

LEGAL BRIEFCASE   485 U.S. 224 (1988)

FACTS

Beginning in . . . 1976, Combustion . . . had meetings . . . with Basic . . . concerning the possibility of a merger. During 1977 and 1978, Basic made three public statements denying . . . merger negotiations. On December 19, 1978, Basic's board endorsed [the merger].

Respondents are former Basic shareholders who sold their stock after Basic's first public [denial], and before the . . . December 1978 [announcement. They assert] that the defendants issued three false or misleading public statements . . . in violation of § 10(b) of the 1934 Act and of Rule 10b-5 [and] that they were injured by selling Basic shares at artificially depressed prices[.]

JUSTICE BLACKMUN

[Rule] 10b-5 provides, "It shall be unlawful [t]o make any untrue statement of a material fact or to omit to state a material fact necessary . . . to make the statements made . . . not misleading . . . in connection with the purchase or sale of any security."

[T]o fulfill the materiality requirement "there must be a substantial likelihood that the disclosure of the omitted fact would have been viewed by the reasonable investor as having significantly altered the 'total mix' of information made available." . . .

We turn to the question of reliance and the fraud-on-the-market theory. Succinctly put:

> The fraud on the market theory is based on the hypothesis that, in an open and developed securities market, the price of a company's stock is determined by the available material information[.] Misleading statements will . . . defraud purchasers . . . even if [they] do not directly rely on the misstatements. . . . The causal connection between the defendants' fraud and the plaintiffs' purchase . . . is no less significant than in a case of direct reliance on misrepresentations.

Requiring proof of individualized reliance from each member of the proposed plaintiff class . . . would have prevented . . . a class action, since individual issues . . . would have overwhelmed the common ones. [T]he presumption of reliance created by the fraud-on-the-market theory provided

> . . . a practical resolution to the problem of balancing the [need for] proof of reliance [against] the procedural [obstacles].

Reliance provides the requisite causal connection between a defendant's misrepresentation and a plaintiff's injury. . . .

The modern securities markets . . . differ from the face-to-face transactions contemplated by early fraud cases[. T]he market is interposed between seller and buyer and, ideally, transmits information to the investor in the processed form of a market price. Thus the market is performing a substantial part of the valuation process performed by the investor in a face-to-

face transaction. The market is acting as the unpaid agent of the investor, informing him that given all the information available to it, the value of the stock is worth the market price. . . .

Presumptions . . . assist courts [where] direct proof [is problematic.] Requiring a plaintiff to show . . . how he would have acted if omitted material information had been disclosed . . . or if the misrepresentation had not been made . . . would place an unnecessarily unrealistic evidentiary burden on the Rule 10b-5 plaintiff[.] The presumption . . . is consistent with . . . congressional policy[.] In drafting [the 1934] Act, Congress expressly relied on the premise that securities markets are affected by information, and enacted legislation to facilitate an investor's reliance on the integrity of those markets[.] Recent empirical studies . . . confirm Congress's premise that the market price . . . on well-developed markets reflects all publicly available information, [including] material misrepresentations. . . .

Any showing that severs the link between the alleged misrepresentation and [the] decision to trade [is] sufficient to rebut the presumption of reliance. For example, [petitioners] could rebut the presumption as to plaintiffs who would have divested themselves of their Basic shares without relying on the integrity of the market. For example[,] a plaintiff [might have] sold his shares because of . . . potential antitrust problems[.]

Questions

1. When is an item of undisclosed information about a company "material" for Rule 10b-5 purposes?

2. Is reliance on a misrepresentation essential in a Rule 10b-5 action?

3. *a.* Why would it be difficult for a plaintiff to demonstrate reliance in fact on a material omission?

   b. What solution did the courts create to deal with this problem?

§18 in the 1934 Act, relating to false or misleading statements in any filing required to maintain the registration of a security, is similar to the 1933 Act's §11. However, the only defense offered by §18 is that the defendant acted in good faith, without knowledge of the false or misleading nature of the statement.

Further, unlike the 1933 Act's §11 where reliance by the plaintiff on the false or misleading statements is presumed, under the 1934 Act's §18 the plaintiff must prove that he or she relied on the statements. Because bringing forward direct evidence of such reliance can be difficult, the *fraud-on-the-market* theory has evolved. It is the subject of the *Basic, Inc.* case that follows.

Insider Trading

Among the most widely known securities law violations is *insider trading*. This occurs when an "insider" buys or sells a security while in possession of material, nonpublic information. The 1934 Act forces the inside trader to pay damages to harmed third parties up to the extent that the insider profited on the transaction. The *Texas Gulf Sulphur* case that follows gives the rule for those possessing inside information.

LEGAL BRIEFCASE

SEC v. Texas Gulf Sulphur Co.   401 F.2d 833 (2d Cir. 1968)

FACTS

On November 12, 1963, TGS drilled a "discovery hole," K-55-1, in Canada that revealed possibly one of the largest ore strikes in history. Insiders (geologists at the drill site, certain company officers, and so on) began buying TGS stock at around $18. Lab testing and further test-hole drilling fully confirmed the magnitude of the strike. Rumors began to circulate. On April 12, 1964, when the stock had passed $30 and when the best estimate was 8 million recoverable tons, TGS issued a press release naysaying the rumors. On April 16, a Canadian mining journal story, based on an April 13 site visit and interview, put the tonnage at 10 million. On the same day a Canadian government official, based on information current through April 15, put the tonnage at 25 million in a public announcement. On this day the stock passed $36. By May 15, it exceeded $58. The SEC brought an insider-trading suit.

Judge Waterman

[Rule 10b-5] is based . . . on the justifiable expectation . . . that all investors trading on impersonal exchanges have relatively equal access to material information[.] The essence of the Rule is that anyone who, trading for his own account [has access] to information intended to be available only for a corporate purpose . . . may not take "advantage of such . . . knowing it is unavailable to those with whom he is dealing"—that is, the investing public. Insiders . . . are, of course[,] precluded from so unfairly dealing, but the Rule is also applicable to one possessing the information who may not be strictly termed an "insider"[. A]nyone in possession of material inside information must either disclose it to the investing public [or] abstain from trading in or recommending the securities [while it] remains undisclosed. . . .

An insider's duty to disclose [or] abstain . . . arises only in "those situations . . . which are reasonably certain to have a substantial effect on the market price [if] disclosed." . . .

[W]hether facts are material [will depend] upon a balancing of both the indicated probability that the event will occur and the anticipated magnitude of the event[. Here,] knowledge of the possibility, which surely was more than marginal, of the existence of a mine of the vast magnitude indicated by the remarkably rich drill core . . . would certainly have been an important fact to a reasonable . . . investor[. A] major factor in determining whether the K-55-1 discovery was a material fact is the importance attached to [it] by those who knew about it. [T]he timing . . . of their stock purchases . . . virtually compels the inference that the insiders were influenced by the drilling results. . . .

We hold . . . that all transactions in TGS stock . . . by individuals apprised of the drilling results of K-55-1 were made in violation of Rule 10b-5. . . .

[Coates], who placed orders . . . immediately after the official announcement[, contends that his] purchases were not proscribed . . . for the news had already been . . . disclosed. . . . The reading of [the announcement] . . . is merely the first step in the process of dissemination [intended to provide] all investors with an equal opportunity to make informed . . . judgments. [A]t the minimum Coates should have waited until the news could reasonably have been expected to appear over the media of widest circulation, the Dow Jones broad tape, rather than hastening to ensure an advantage to himself[.]

Questions

1. If you possess undisclosed inside information, what are your options for trading in the company's stock?

2. How soon after disclosure can an insider trade in the stock?

Tippees

The insider concept has been extended to include *tippees*. In some cases, the *tipper* (the insider or the "upstream" tippee) intends to improperly convey the inside information to a third party and hopes to derive personal benefit therefrom. In such a case, both the tipper and tippee are fully liable. In other cases, the tippee is deemed to "misappropriate" the inside information from the inadvertent tipper, knowing that it was confidential. This would occur, for example, if a psychiatrist learned material inside information during a session with a senior corporate executive and traded on that information. Here, the tippee, but not the tipper, would be liable. In the *O'Hagan* case, next, the U.S. Supreme Court approved the "misappropriation" theory of insider trading.

United States v. O'Hagan

LEGAL BRIEFCASE   521 U.S. 642 (1997)

FACTS

O'Hagan was a lawyer. In July 1988, Grand Metropolitan retained his law firm to represent it in a tender offer for Pillsbury common stock. O'Hagan did no work on this matter.

In August, O'Hagan began purchasing Pillsbury stock at $39. When the tender offer was announced in October, the price rose to $60. O'Hagan sold, making a profit of $4.3 million.

O'Hagan was convicted of securities fraud. The Eighth Circuit Court of Appeals reversed, rejecting §10(b) and Rule 10b-5 liability under the "misappropriation theory." The Supreme Court granted certiorari.

Justice Ginsburg

Section 10(b) . . . proscribes (1) using any deceptive device (2) in connection with the purchase or sale of securities[.] [It] does not confine its coverage to deception of a purchaser or seller [; rather, it] reaches any deceptive device used "in connection with the purchase or sale of any security." . . .

Under the . . . "classical theory" of insider trading[,] §10(b) and Rule 10b-5 are violated when [an] insider trades in the securities of his corporation on the basis of material, nonpublic information. [Such trading] qualifies as a "deceptive device" . . . because "a relationship of trust [exists] between the shareholders [and the] insiders who have obtained confidential information by reason of their position with [the] corporation." . . . That relationship . . . "gives rise to a duty to disclose [or to abstain from trading[."] The classical theory applies not only to officers, directors, and other permanent insiders[,] but also to

attorneys, accountants, consultants, and others who temporarily become fiduciaries of a corporation. . . .

The "misappropriation theory" holds that a person commits fraud "in connection with" a securities transaction . . . when he misappropriates confidential information for securities trading purposes, in breach of a duty owed to the source of the information. . . . Under this theory, a fiduciary's undisclosed, self-serving use of a principal's information to purchase or sell securities, in breach of a duty of loyalty and confidentiality, defrauds the principal of the exclusive use of that information.

* * * * *

[Rather than] premising liability on a fiduciary relationship between company insider and purchaser or seller of the company's stock, the misappropriation theory premises liability on a fiduciary-turned-trader's deception of those who entrusted him with access to confidential information.

The two theories are complementary, each addressing efforts to capitalize on nonpublic information through the purchase or sale of securities. . . .

In this case, the indictment alleged that O'Hagan, in breach of a duty of trust . . . owed to his law firm . . . and to its client[,] traded on the basis of nonpublic information [the] tender offer [.] This conduct [allegedly] constituted a fraudulent device in connection with the purchase and sale of securities. . . .

We agree[.] We observe, first, that misappropriators . . . deal in deception. A fiduciary who "[pretends] loyalty to the principal while secretly converting the principal's information for personal gain" . . . defrauds the principal. . . .

We turn next to the §10(b) requirement that the misappropriator's deceptive use of information be "in connection with the purchase or sale of [a] security." This element is satisfied because the fiduciary's fraud is consummated, not when the fiduciary gains the confidential information, but when he uses the information to purchase or sell securities. . . .

The misappropriation theory [is] well-tuned to an animating purpose of the [1934] Act: to ensure honest securities markets and thereby promote investor confidence. . . . Although informational disparity is inevitable [, an] investor's informational disadvantage vis-a-vis a misappropriator . . . stems from contrivance, not luck; it is a disadvantage that cannot be overcome with research or skill.

[Reversed and remanded.]

Questions

1. Are both insider trading theories needed to fulfill the 1934 Act's desire to keep the markets "honest?"

2. Both theories depend heavily on fiduciary relationships. Contrast the parties in the fiduciary relationships under the "classical" and "misappropriation" theories.

3. Would it have made any difference if O'Hagan had established with his broker, long before this trading, a portfolio diversification plan such that, pursuant to the plan, the identical trading would have occurred?

Short-Swing Profits

Closely related to insider trading is liability for *short-swing profits*. An insider trading case requires proof that the insider had material inside information and traded to exploit it. A short-swing profit case conclusively *presumes* that the insider had such information and did so trade any time the insider engages in any purchase and sale of an equity security issued by the insider's corporation, if both transactions occur within a six-month period. The insider's actual motive is irrelevant. All profits on any such trades must be remitted to the corporation. Here *insider* is restricted to officers, directors, and holders of more than 10 percent of any class of equity of the issuer.

Class Actions

In civil damage cases, plaintiffs typically join together in a *class-action lawsuit*. This allows plaintiffs to pool their resources and the judicial system to dispose of potentially thousands of cases within a single suit. Attorneys essentially compete to form classes.

Most securities class-action suits are based primarily on accounting irregularities. In 2004, a record $5.4 billion was paid out in 118 settlements.[13]

As noted in Part One of this chapter, major accounting firms paid over $1.6 billion in class-action damages during the savings and loan debacle of the 1980s. Responding to these payouts, accounting firms and others began intense lobbying to curtail such suits.

The lobbying paid off, and in December 1995 Congress enacted the *Private Securities Litigation Reform Act* (1995 Act). It significantly restricts fraud actions for civil damages by preventing any presumption of fraudulent conduct from the simple fact that a security's price changed significantly. Now plaintiffs must include in their pleadings concrete facts creating a strong inference that the defendant intentionally engaged in fraudulent conduct. Without that showing, the case may not proceed to the discovery phase—a sharp contrast to the way lawsuits worked before the 1995 Act.

Previously, law firms specializing in plaintiffs' securities actions groomed "professional plaintiffs" to bring damage suits. These plaintiffs would make general allegations primarily supported by a significant market price change. Then they would proceed to the discovery phase and often undertake a "fishing expedition" until sufficient facts were accumulated to motivate the defendant to settle rather than endure litigation.

Beyond pleading matters, the 1995 Act restricts joint and several liability for accountants and underwriters whose deep pockets have historically attracted plaintiffs' lawyers. Now, unless they are guilty of knowingly violating the securities laws, these defendants can be held responsible only for the damages for which they are actually responsible (plus up to a 50 percent premium if other defendants are insolvent).

Because of these significant new restraints, plaintiffs' attorneys began filing their cases in state courts based on state securities laws (rather than in federal courts under federal securities laws). To stop this end-run of the 1995 Act, Congress passed the *Securities Litigation Uniform Standards Act* in 1998 (1998 Act) to require that legal actions related to *covered securities* (those traded in the national markets) be tried in federal court under federal law, thus reimposing the 1995 Act's requirements. [For more on class-action lawsuits, see **http://securities.milberg.com**]

Additional SEC Remedies

The SEC is empowered to issue *cease-and-desist orders* if it fears dissipation of assets, harm to investors, or harm to the public interest. It can get injunctions against persons committing securities fraud. It can prohibit individuals who have violated the securities laws from serving as officers or directors of publicly traded companies. In addition, the SEC can have a defendant's ill-gotten gains disgorged. Unfortunately, the SEC's track record in collecting these amounts is poor.

Civil Penalties

The SEC may, in an insider trading case, impose a penalty of up to 300 percent of the profit gained or loss avoided by such trading.

Further, the SEC has the power to impose civil penalties generally for failures to comply with the securities laws. The penalties range up to $750,000 for individuals and $15 million for corporations.

Criminal Penalties

Both the 1933 and 1934 Acts contain criminal sanctions for *willful* (knowing and deliberate) violations of their provisions. As with criminal statutes in general, the principal problem for prosecutors is convincing the jury of guilt beyond a reasonable doubt. As a result, civil penalties are often substituted for criminal prosecutions. The SEC does not undertake criminal actions; rather the Justice Department does, generally after a referral from the SEC upon the completion of its civil investigation.

The criminal penalties are found in §24 of the 1933 Act and §32 of the 1934 Act. They impose fines of up to $25 million and imprisonment of up to 20 years.

Tender Offers

There are several ways to acquire control of a corporation. Where mergers or direct acquisitions fail, a *tender offer* (also called a *takeover*) can be attempted.

In a tender offer, the offerer announces that it wishes to acquire a specific number of shares (often the number needed to gain control). It identifies where stockholders who want to participate must tender (that is, deliver) their shares (shares are returned if the tender offer fails). It also specifies the opening bid price. If fewer than the desired number of shares are tendered, the tender offerer can either walk away or increase the offering price.

To ensure fair treatment, the 1934 Act requires that if more shares are tendered than are sought, each tendering shareholder will have a pro rata amount of stock purchased. As a further safeguard, if too few shares are tendered at the original bid price and the offerer increases the bid, all previously tendering shareholders will receive the increased price.

In dealing with a tender offer situation, the target corporation's management realizes that a change in control will likely result in its dismissal because the new controlling party will want to put its own management in place. Because of the extraordinary financial benefits attendant to being a senior corporate executive, it is understandable that the target's management will not be eager to leave. It will resist, which accounts for the term *hostile takeover*. Management has a problem, however, because it is supposed to act exclusively in the best interests of the shareholders, and the tender offer may well be in their best interests. To avoid liability, management will generally try to style its resistance as "looking out for the stockholders."

Management can resist in various ways. It could launch its own tender offer (*go private*). Or it could start using corporate cash to buy back shares in the market, driving up the price to discourage the tender offerer. In this case management has to worry that it could be sanctioned for violating §9 of the 1934 Act, which prohibits price manipulation. However, the SEC provides a safe harbor that allows management to purchase up to 25 percent of the security's average daily trading volume each day.

Another resistance tactic is *greenmail,* in which the target's management uses corporate cash to buy back the tender offerer's current stake, with a significant premium to "go away." Changes in the federal tax law discourage this technique.

Management sometimes puts takeover defenses in place by prearranging "disasters" if a tender offer is attempted. Two notorious ones are the crown jewel and poison pill defenses. The *crown jewel* tactic involves arranging a stand-by agreement with a friendly third party to purchase critical corporate assets at a reasonable price should a tender offer be launched, knowing that the third party will, by lease or otherwise, continue to make these assets available to the corporation on "friendly" terms if the tender offer fails and management maintains control. The *poison pill* tactic involves prearranging with shareholders a right to buy or to redeem a significant amount of stock at prices unfavorable to the corporation in the event of a tender offer. The former discourages the tender offerer by diluting the stock, the latter by dissipating the cash or cash-related assets (such as overfunded pension plans) that may constitute the primary reason for the takeover.

> Management will no doubt find comfort in the golden parachutes it will have negotiated.

If all else fails, the target's managers will find comfort in the *golden parachutes* (e.g., severance pay) they will have negotiated. Management serves at the pleasure of the board, but an employment contract can specify damages for early dismissal.

State Securities Regulation

Since the enactment of the Securities Act of 1933, the United States has operated under a dual regulatory environment for securities. Both the state and federal governments have been entitled to regulate IPOs and subsequent purchases and sales.

However, the lack of regulatory uniformity among the states led Congress to enact the *National Securities Markets Improvement Act* in 1996. This act preempted state registration requirements for securities traded on national markets. States continued to have concurrent jurisdiction over securities fraud until the aforementioned 1998 Act mandated that claims related to such securities be litigated in federal court under federal law. State securities regulation, known as *blue sky laws,* is thus only a shadow of its former self.

About 20 percent of the states have adopted a registration process that parallels the federal registration system; intended to ensure the full disclosure of all material information, but not to evaluate the quality of the underlying investment. About 80 percent of the states do engage in *merit reviews* of IPOs. Typically matters related to merit include the following:

1. As to debt and preferred stock issuances, ensuring that the issuer's historical cash flows demonstrate its ability to service the debt or meet the preferred stock dividend and redemption requirements.

2. As to the offering price, ensuring that such price is related to meaningful measures like book value, earnings history, or industry price/earnings ratios.

3. As to insiders, ensuring that
   a. They are not allowed to purchase stock at prices significantly discounted from the general offering price.
   b. Options held by them do not exceed 15 percent of the total stock to be issued and cannot be exercised at a price less than 85 percent of the offering price.
   c. All corporate loans to them have been repaid before the offering goes forward.
   d. All corporate transactions involving them reflect the terms one would expect in the open market.

[For more on state securities regulation, see **http://www.nasaa.org/NASAA_Newsroom/ what_s_new**]

International Securities Regulation and Corporate Governance

Referring to securities laws, a member of the International Accounting Standards Board (the body charged with establishing global financial accounting principles) said, "Apart from the U.S. there is . . . little enforcement around the world."[14] Only a little has changed since that statement was made.

> Many Asians view their securities markets as "gambling."

Many Asians view their securities markets as "gambling."[15] "[O]ne in 10 publicly traded companies [in China] has 'doctored their books.'" Further, "14 of 16 accounting firms [practicing in China] had 'severely falsified'" client financial records.[16]

Japan's Securities and Exchange Surveillance Commission has filed an average of four criminal and no civil securities complaints per year, as compared to 55 criminal and 500 civil complaints in the United States.[17] A study found that 83 percent of the Japanese have no interest in the stock market despite near-zero interest rates on bank deposits and the lowest stock prices in over a decade. Of their astonishing $14 trillion in personal savings (30 percent more than the United States' GDP), only 4 percent is invested in stocks, as opposed to 19 percent in the United States.[18] Only one-half of 1 percent of Japanese corporations have more outside than inside directors. But things may be changing as the power of foreign and domestic institutional investors (like retirement plans) increases. Companies wanting to raise capital from these sources are facing demands for more transparency, in particular more outside directors. But with more transparency has come greater legal risk. For example, in 2000, 49 Daiwa Bank directors and employees were ordered to pay $775 million to settle a class action suit related to illegal dealings in the United States.[19]

In Europe there is nothing equivalent to the U.S. SEC. The member nations of the European Union individually also have no truly analogous organizations. Almost half of Europe's securities agencies never check financial statements. In most others, only spot checks are performed and then only after a complaint has been filed. Regulators have small staffs, minimal budgets, deficient technology, and weak regulatory authority.[20] However, Germany and France are leading an effort calling for an EU-wide regulator after Citigroup engaged in August 2004 in a rapid sale/repurchase (in less than 30 minutes) in four countries of £16 billion of government bonds to make a $17 million profit.[21]

Thus far, many European countries have adopted, in response to the Sarbanes–Oxley Act, corporate governance improvements in the form of codes that specify principles of good governance. Although compliance with these principles is not required, the corporations must explain why they do not comply. Not surprisingly, two surveys of European directors and senior managers showed little enthusiasm for the codes. No more than half thought corporate governance had been improved, and only 30 percent felt corporate meltdowns were less likely to result. On the other hand, the EU has recommended such reforms as greater reliance on independent directors, disclosure of senior executive compensation and the creation of a new oversight board for auditors. [For more on international securities regulation, see **www.iosco.org/iosco.html**]

Forward-Looking Statements

In the past it was common for plaintiffs seeking damages for security law violations to use, as grounds for their suits, discrepancies between actual developments and earlier statements by management related to plans for the future and projections of financial results. The 1995 Act eliminated liability based on such *forward-looking statements* (1) if such statements contain "meaningful cautionary statements" that identify why the plans and projections may not be achieved, or (2) if the parties making the statements cannot be proven to have known that they were misleading. This safe harbor does not apply to a person who has violated the securities laws within the preceding three years. Nor does it protect statements made in audited financial reports.

RICO

In 1970 Congress enacted the *Racketeer Influenced and Corrupt Organizations Act* (RICO) to thwart organized crime. Because of its attractive treble-damages award, RICO was increasingly used in securities fraud suits. However, the aforementioned 1995 Act now forbids a securities-based RICO action unless it follows a criminal securities fraud conviction. [For more on RICO, see **http://www.lectlaw.com/files/cri18.htm**]

Selective Disclosure

The SEC, concerned that corporations were giving certain persons preferential access to material information relevant to the securities markets, promulgated Regulation Full Disclosure (FD) in October 2000. It has one principal rule: Whenever an issuer discloses material nonpublic information to "enumerated persons," it must make the same information available to the public simultaneously (if the disclosure was intentional) or "promptly" (if the disclosure was unintentional).

"Enumerated persons" are "securities market professionals [and] holders of the issuer's securities who may well trade on the basis of the information." Disclosure is made "promptly" if it occurs "'as soon as reasonably practicable' (but no later than 24 hours) after a senior official of the issuer learns of the [unintentional] disclosure[.]"

An issuer's failure to comply with Regulation FD subjects it to SEC enforcement action, but no investor may base a lawsuit for damages solely on such failure.[22]

Online Trading

One effect of widely available technology, particularly the Internet, is the disintermediation (bypassing) of full-service securities brokers by *online trading*. Whereas full-service brokers charge more and may sometimes be available only during limited hours, they typically both provide advisory services and assess the *suitability* of investments for a particular investor (that is, they take into account their needs, financial situation, investment objectives, and risk tolerance). Online brokers are less expensive and have greater availability, but they tend to leave investors mostly on their own.

> Online trading now represents about 25 percent of the total retail trades in the United States.

Online trading now represents about 25 percent of the total retail trades in the United States. But the number of complaints about online trading companies has exploded. Investors report trouble confirming trades, delays in execution, changes in a security price between submitting and completing an order,[23] and difficulties determining whether order cancellations have gone through.[24] Concern is increasing about the excessive use of margin trading and the extent to which many online traders are actually capable of evaluating investment opportunities.

Matters get worse when it comes to *day trading*. Only about 10 percent of day traders are successful.[25] They rarely hold any security more than a few hours, earning profits by exploiting volatility, not inherent value. The SEC has expressed great concern about advertising that suggests day trading is easy and certain to be profitable. It cautions that tips and analyses are frequently false.[26] And it is concerned about many day-trading companies' lax record keeping and poor compliance with other SEC requirements.[27] Nonetheless, there is an inexorable movement toward global, 24-hour-a-day electronic trading.

Broker Issues

An increasing number of complaints have been filed against brokers in recent years. These complaints have several recurring themes, including allegations that brokers have failed to execute orders or have unreasonably delayed their execution. Many instances of broker misrepresentation of investment opportunities have been reported. Worse are claims that brokers have failed to address the suitability of investments for particular investors. Additionally, brokers continue to face charges of *churning*—repeatedly and unnecessarily engaging in trades to generate commissions.

In one case, an 80-year-old woman with Alzheimer's disease entrusted $500,000 to a broker in December 1999. By February 2001, the account was worth $15,000. The broker had engaged in over 300 trades and charged the account $94,000 in fees, purchasing only high-tech stocks (versus a balanced, conservative portfolio). In addition, the broker secured a $422,000 margin loan with the account to buy more such stocks, further decimating the account when the high-tech bubble burst.[28]

READING Crisis in the Financial Markets

Kristofer Neslund

On December 2, 2001, Enron filed for bankruptcy. The collapse of the seventh largest U.S. corporation—*Fortune*'s "Most Innovative Company" for five consecutive years—cost investors $90 billion. Enron called the world's attention to extraordinary failings in corporate governance, the accounting and financial services industries, and the regulation of the markets. Its demise was not an isolated event. It was quickly followed by many scandals, at least three of which were actually larger (WorldCom, Parmalat, and Fannie Mae).

Senior managers at many corporations committed fraud and employed improper accounting methods in an effort to maximize the value of their stock options. They sought to engineer financial results, including the attainment of earnings targets, that would lead to ever-increasing stock prices. Byzantine transactions were used to hide liabilities and losses, generate phony revenues and equity, and improperly reduce taxes.

WorldCom's CEO, Bernard Ebbers, has been convicted on multiple securities-related crimes and was sentenced to 25 years in prison. Enron's CEO, Kenneth Lay, faces trial in early 2006. Matters are still evolving at Parmalat and Fannie Mae. Numerous other executives have plea bargained or are awaiting trial.

Financial services companies aided management in these scandalous events. For example, J.P. Morgan used its British Channel Islands company (Mahonia) to route $2 billion in loans to Enron under the guise of revenues, earning $100 million for its help.[29] Goldman Sachs earned a 19 percent return in 15 months on its $215 million investment in AOL–Europe. It "purchased" a 1 percent interest to enable AOL–North America to avoid consolidating AOL–Europe's $200 million loss on its financial statements, which might have jeopardized its impending $120 billion merger with Time Warner. In fact, there was no purchase because a side agreement guaranteed an immediate sale at a gain.[30] (AOL and Time Warner each recently paid $300 million to settle shareholder suits related to the merger.)[31]

Related to WorldCom, many banks have now settled investor suits alleging inadequate due diligence in underwriting the company's securities offerings, including Bank of America ($460 million), J.P. Morgan ($2 billion), and Citigroup ($2.58 billion; $6 billion for all banks).[32] Plaintiffs alleged that these banks were well aware of WorldCom's precarious financial condition when they brought the securities to market.

The big accounting firms allegedly compromised their audits as they sought to cross-sell high-profit nonaudit services, charging $3 of nonaudit services for every $1 of audit services. Many of the nonaudit services involved the sale of abusive tax shelters. The Government Accounting Office reported that 61 of the *Fortune* 500 companies had purchased shelters from their auditors, costing the U.S. government $3.4 billion (1998–2003).[33] Dozens of lawsuits now allege poor accounting, including the following new actions: (1) KPMG for $550 million based on its audits of Independent Insurance,[34] and (2) Deloitte & Touche for $2 billion with respect to its audits of Fortress Re, Inc.[35] Enron's auditor, Andersen, ceased to exist upon its conviction for criminal obstruction of justice related to the destruction of audit records.

Boards of directors are being sued for their anemic corporate oversight. In a recent WorldCom settlement, the directors will pay $20 million personally, waiving all rights to insurance and indemnification.[36] Far too frequently, boards have simply abdicated to CEOs who, in reality, controlled board membership and compensation. Many conflicts of interest have been found. At Enron, for example, some directors were personal friends of senior managers, others were academics whose institutions were receiving substantial contributions, and another was a former senior government official who had exempted Enron from regulation in its principal line of business.

Some boards even permitted their CEOs who had been convicted of felonies to continue receiving compensation while incarcerated. Martha Stewart received $500,000 during her five months of house arrest, and Andrew Wiederhorn (Fog Cutter Capital) was expected to collect millions while spending 18 months in jail.[37]

By the early 2000s, the integrity of the U.S. capital markets was in jeopardy. Senior management was engaging in widespread misconduct, unhampered by boards of directors. The "gatekeepers," especially the accounting profession and the financial services industry, were not only failing to safeguard the public interest, they were complicit in management schemes. The time was ripe for change.

Congress Responds

On July 30, 2002, the Sarbanes–Oxley Act (SOX) became law. It constitutes the most significant regulatory reform of the markets since the Great Depression.

Sarbanes–Oxley Act

Auditing/Accounting Provisions

New Public Company Accounting Oversight Board (PCAOB) to oversee audits of public companies (only 40 percent of members from accounting)—great investigatory and punitive powers.

Audit committee must consist of all independent directors (with at least one "financial expert").

Auditor now responsible directly to audit committee, which appoints auditor and sets compensation.

Most consulting forbidden for audit clients; what consulting remains requires advance written permission from audit committee.

Mandatory audit partner rotation every five years.

Enhanced scrutiny of internal control system.

One-year waiting period before auditor can join senior management of audit client.

Senior Executive/Officer/Director Provisions

CEO/CFO must certify accuracy of financial statements (penalties of up to $5 million plus 20 years in jail).

No loans from companies to senior executives/directors.

CEO/CFO performance-based compensation forfeited if accounting results revised because of misconduct.

Securities law penalties, damages, and compensation forfeiture survive bankruptcy.

Persons violating antifraud provisions barred from service as public company officer/director.

New crime for harassing whistleblowers (fines plus up to 10 years in jail).

Financial Services Provisions

Starter provisions to force analyst independence.

Other Provisions

Criminal
New destruction of evidence/obstruction of justice crime (fines plus up to 20 years in jail).
New securities fraud crime (fines plus up to 25 years in jail).
Existing securities criminal penalties increased to maximum of $25 million fine and 20 years in jail.

Miscellaneous
Faster disclosure of material events and insider transactions.
Starter provision granting SEC power to control conduct of lawyers practicing before it.

Inspections   The PCAOB completed its first inspections of the Big Four accounting firms in December 2003. Its August 2004 report uncovered "significant audit and accounting issues . . . missed by the firms and identified concerns about significant aspects of each firm's quality control systems."[38] [For more on the findings, see **www.pcaobus.com/inspections/ index.asp**]

Financial Statement Certification   The CEO/CFO financial statement certification requirement was enacted to preclude the "Claude Rains defense [which was] the typical defense of every CEO and CFO of every major company." In the famous film *Casablanca,* the wagering impresario played by Rains said he was "shocked, shocked" that gambling was going on around him. The certification requirement, which precludes this defense, is proving an extraordinary prosecution tool. Many senior executives have accepted plea bargains to avoid the potentially severe punishment, agreeing to help prosecutors pursue other senior executives.[39]

Whistleblowers   The whistleblower provisions have proven a severe disappointment thus far. Enforcement was oddly granted to the Occupational Safety and Health Administration (OSHA), which has no subpoena power, no power to place a person under oath, no budget for this enforcement, and absolutely no experience dealing with financial fraud. OSHA has ruled favorably on less than 15 percent of all claims. To illustrate, David Welch was CFO of a small bank. He refused to certify the financial statements per SOX. He expressed his concerns to the bank's auditor and was fired. He filed for whistleblower protection on December 19, 2002. His claim was denied on February 4, 2003, after a perfunctory investigation undertaken only after continuous prodding. Fourteen months later, an administrative law judge overturned the denial, but the bank plans to appeal for years through the agency-level appeals board and circuit court of appeals. In the meantime, Welch was forced to sell his family farm, owes more than $90,000 in legal fees, and has had no regular employment.[40]

Stock Analysts   Among the many corrupt practices uncovered at investment banks, the worst was likely the corruption of their "independent" stock analysts, who instead of offering objective assessments about corporations' stocks, promoted those stocks to help their banks earn hundreds of millions of dollars in underwriting fees. E-mails disclosed situations in which analysts' contempt for a corporation's securities was obvious, despite their public enthusiasm for them. On April 28, 2003, the large Wall Street firms agreed to pay $1.4 billion to settle civil actions by the SEC and the State of New York involving the improper use of stock analysts. Among the investment bankers were Citigroup, Credit Suisse First Boston, Morgan Stanley, Goldman Sachs, Lehman Bros., Bear Stearns, US Bancorp, JP Morgan, UBS Paine Webber, and Merrill Lynch. Analysts Henry Blodget (Merrill Lynch) and Jack Grubman (Citigroup) received lifetime bans from the securities industry and paid fines of $4 million and $15 million, respectively.[41]

SOX Compliance Costs   Corporations have complained loudly about the cost of complying with SOX, especially the rules related to internal control. A recent study found that corporations with revenues exceeding $5 billion will pay an average of $4.7 million to implement SOX, and $1.5 million per year to maintain compliance. It is difficult to have much sympathy given the hundreds of billions of dollars of investor losses suffered over the past few years, largely related to matters an effective internal control system would have prevented (or at least detected). As Paul Volcker (former chair of the Federal Reserve Board and current chair of the International Accounting Standards Board) and Arthur Levitt (chair of the SEC immediately prior to Enron) jointly wrote in a *Wall Street Journal* editorial,

> [W]e believe that those costs are justified in light of the benefits—the price necessary to pay for more reliability in accounting, clear accountability to shareholders, and more robust and trusted markets. [T]he investment in good corporate governance, professional integrity, and transparency will pay dividends in the form of investor confidence, more efficient markets, and more market participation in years to come.[42]

More Governance Rules

Pursuant to SOX, the NYSE and NASDAQ established special corporate governance rules for listed companies. The NYSE's requirements, adopted November 3, 2004, include the following:

- Directors: Majority independent.
  Nonmanagement directors must meet regularly.
  Nominating, corporate governance, compensation, and audit committees must be independent.
  Audit committee: Minimum of three directors.
- Must have internal audit function.
- Must adopt, and disclose on Web page, corporate governance guidelines and code of business conduct and ethics.
- Must immediately disclose waivers from business conduct and ethics code.
- Must encourage whistleblowers.
- CEO must certify annually that he/she is unaware of any violations of the above.

Source: NYSE, "Section 303A Corporate Governance Rules," November 3, 2004, at **www.nyse.com/pdfs/ section303A_final_rules.pdf.**

PRACTICING ETHICS) Shall We "Cook the Books"?

On December 15, a CEO reviews the accounting results shaping up for the fourth quarter. The $15 million projected net income is $2 million short of the target for his $750,000 bonus. He asks the CFO to lunch. She will lose a $300,000 bonus if the target isn't achieved. The CEO casually inquires whether there might be some way to "salvage the disappointing fourth-quarter performance." She ponders a moment. "What about lowering the bad debt reserve by $600,000—we can fix it next year?" She also suggests recognizing in the last week of December the income to be earned from goods actually to be shipped in the first week of January. Her "rationale" is that the contracts are already signed. That will add another $1.5 million to net income. The CEO responds, "Well, if you think that's best." The bonuses are awarded.

Question

How would you resolve the ethical issues presented here?

Questions—Part Two

1. *a.* Would the federal securities laws' registration provisions apply to a corporation if it issued stock to another corporation's stockholders as part of a merger? Explain.
   b. Would they apply later, when the combined corporation goes bankrupt and its long-term creditors all take a new class of stock in exchange for their debt securities?
2. *a.* What is contained in a registration statement under the 1933 Act?
   b. What role is played by the prospectus?
3. Describe the extent to which a corporation can sell securities (or solicit such sales) in an IPO during the following periods:
   a. Before the IPO registration statement has been filed with the SEC.

     b. After the registration statement has been filed, but before the SEC has approved it.

     c. After the SEC has approved the registration statement.

4. *a.* Is the purpose of the federal securities laws to directly cull poor investments?

   b. Is this true for state securities laws? Explain.

5. *a.* What financial statements are relevant under the 1933 and 1934 Acts?

   b. What is the role of the auditor with respect to these financial statements?

   c. What is the relevance of GAAP and GAAS to an auditor?

6. What are the three major forms a corporation uses to maintain its registration with the SEC under the 1934 Act? What do these forms contain?

7. What emergency action can the SEC take if it discovers that corporate officers are anonymously feeding the media false information that Microsoft is about to make public its intention to buy their corporation—and the stock price is "taking off"?

8. A *Fortune* 500 CFO admits to having deliberately treated $4 billion in operating expenses as assets, thereby allowing the corporation to show profits instead of losses. The auditor did not detect this fraud. The corporation's stock drops 95 percent, and bond covenants related to billions in debt are breached. At its peak price last year, the CFO sold stock (acquired through options) for $15 million, generating a $10 million gain.

   a. Why might the corporation have to file for bankruptcy protection?

   b. Why will the 1995 Act probably not stop a class-action lawsuit from proceeding to the discovery phase?

   c. What provision(s) of the securities law will probably be the basis for a class-action lawsuit by the stockholders?

   d. Why will the CFO be subject to criminal (as well as civil) securities sanctions?

   e. Will the SEC likely ever allow the CFO to be an officer or director of a publicly traded corporation in the future?

   f. Will the SEC allow the CFO to keep the $10 million gain on the stock?

   g. What kind of civil penalties could the SEC impose on the CFO?

9. Assume a midlevel manager learns that his corporation is about to go bankrupt because of soon-to-be-disclosed improprieties. He calls his lawyer to ask about his personal exposure. After advising him, the lawyer immediately sells all of her holdings in that stock. Later that day, the news breaks and the stock price tumbles 60 percent. Does anyone have insider trading liability? If so, in what amount?

10. *a.* What is the purpose of a takeover?

    b. How does a typical takeover proceed?

    c. Why (and how) might the target's management resist the takeover?

11. How well are the securities markets regulated outside the United States?

12. Can a corporation whose officers give the media occasional projections about how well they expect the corporation to perform in the future, based on factors such as new product development, the economy, the industry, and the like, be held liable when it later turns out that the actual results are materially different from those projected?

13. What is meant by an investment's *suitability*?

14. What does *churning* mean in the context of investment accounts?

15. Ivan Landreth and his sons owned all of the stock in a lumber business they operated in Tonasket,Washington. The owners offered the stock for sale. During that time a fire

severely damaged the business, but the owners made assurances of rebuilding and modernization. The stock was sold to Dennis and Bolten, and a new organization, Landreth Timber Company, was formed with the senior Landreth remaining as a consultant on the side. The new firm was unsuccessful and was sold at a loss. The Landreth Timber Company then filed suit against Ivan Landreth and his son seeking rescission of the first sale, alleging, among other arguments, that Landreth and sons had widely offered and then sold their stock without registering it as required by the Securities Act of 1933. The district court acknowledged that *stocks* fit within the definition of a *security,* and that the stock in question "possessed all of the characteristics of conventional stock." However, it held that the federal securities laws do not apply to the sale of 100 percent of the stock of a closely held corporation. Here the district court found that the purchasers had not entered into the sale with the expectation of earnings secured via the labor of others. Managerial control resided with the purchasers. Thus the sale was a commercial venture rather than a typical investment. The Court of Appeals affirmed, and the case reached the Supreme Court. Decide. See *Landreth Timber Co. v. Landreth,* 471 U.S. 681 (1985).

Internet Exercise

Using **www.securitieslaw.com** answer the following questions:

1. What duties are owed by stockbrokers and brokerage firms to customers?
2. How does a customer know when he or she has been defrauded?

Notes

1. **www.irs.ustreas.gov/taxstats/article/0,,id=120350,00.html.**
2. *Cede & Co. v. Technicolor, Inc.,* 634 A.2d 345 (Del. S. Ct. 1993).
3. *Compania General de Tabacos de Filipinas v. Collector of Internal Revenue,* 275 U.S. 87, 100 (1927) (J. Holmes dissenting).
4. *Commissioner v. Newman,* 159 F.2d 848, 850 (2d Cir 1947).
5. Mary Wisniewski, "Andersen Tax Shelters Targeted," *Australian Financial Review,* September 25, 2002.
6. **http://corpgov.net.**
7. Carlye Adler, "Would You Pay $2 Million for This Franchise?" *Fortune,* May 1, 2002, p. 36.
8. Rev. Rul. 88-76, 1988-2 C.B. 360.
9. "First the Market, Now the U.S. Economy Wobbles," *Australian Financial Review,* July 27, 2002.
10. **www.sec.gov/info/smallbus/qasbsec.htm.**
11. **www.sec.gov/about/forms/form8-k.pdf.**
12. **www.sec.gov/answers/tradingsuspension.htm.**
13. Kara Scannell, "Settlements Totaled $5.4 Billion for Securities Class Actions in '04," *The Wall Street Journal,* March 2, 2005, p. C4.
14. Daniel Schwammenthal, "Europe's Enrons May Be Lurking behind Weak Enforcement," *The Wall Street Journal,* July 31, 2002.
15. Phred Dvorak, "Japan's Securities Watchdog to Increase Its Staff by 50%," *The Wall Street Journal,* July 5, 2002.
16. "Asia Has Its Own Strains of Enronitis," *Australian Financial Review*, July 19, 2002.
17. Dvorak, "Japan's Securities Watchdog to Increase Its Staff by 50%."

18. Phred Dvorak, "Japan's Hollow 'Zombie' Firms Keep Stock Market in Doldrums," *The Wall Street Journal,* August 8, 2002.

19. Jathon Sapsford and Martin Fackler, "Directors' Roles Shift in Japan," *The Wall Street Journal,* March 10, 2005, p. A15.

20. Schwammenthal, "Europe's Enrons May Be Lurking behind Weak Enforcement."

21. "A European SEC?," *The Wall Street Journal*, March 7, 2005, p. A18; David Reilly and Edward Taylor, "German Plan Signals European SEC," *The Wall Street Journal,* March 4, 2005, p. C3.

22. SEC Final Rule: Selective Disclosure and Insider Trading, 17 CFR Parts 240, 243 and 249, October 23, 2000.

23. **www.sec.gov/news/press/pressarchive/1999/99-9.txt.**

24. **www.sec.gov/investor/pubs/onlinetips.htm.**

25. "The Return of the Day Trader," **www.cbsnews.com/stories/2002/09/30/eveningnews/main523766 .shtml.**

26. **www.sec.gov/investor/pubs/daytips.htm.**

27. **www.sec.gov/news/testimony/testarchive/1999/tsty2099.htm.**

28. "Sales-Practice Complaints to SEC Increase," *The Wall Street Journal,* April 26, 2001, p. C1.

29. Jathon Sapsford and Anita Raghavan, "Energy-Trading Venture Could Result in an Enormous Loss for J.P. Morgan," *The Wall Street Journal,* January 25, 2002.

30. Paula Dwyer, Tom Lowry, and Jack Ewing, "Goldman's 1% Solution for AOL," *BusinessWeek* online, June 17, 2004.

31. Julia Angwin, "Time Warner Agrees to Pay $300 Million in SEC Settlement," *The Wall Street Journal,* March 21, 2005.

32. Rick Brooks, "WorldCom Settlement to Cost Bank of America $460.5 Million," *The Wall Street Journal,* March 4, 2005, p. A7; Erin McClam, "JPMorgan Chase OKs $2B World-ComSettlement," Associated Press, March 16, 2005, at **www.businessweek.com/ap/ financialnews/D88SB5T81.htm?campaign_id+apn_home_up.**

33. Jonathan Weil, "Many Big Firms Buy Tax Shelters from Auditors," *The Wall Street Journal,* February 25, 2005, p. A8.

34. Alice Nixon, "PwC Sues KPMG for Over £300m," *Accountancy Magazine,* June 4, 2005.

35. "$2 Billion Claim against D&T," *WebCPA,* April 18, 2005, at **www.webcpa.com/article .cfm?articleid=10192&pg=pracacc&print=yes.**

36. "Ex-WorldCom Directors Reach Pact," NYAACPA.ORG, March 21, 2005.

37. Joann S. Lublin, "Imprisonment Doesn't Bar Pay for Select Groups of CEOs," *The Wall Street Journal,* March 2, 2005, p. B1.

38. "PCAOB Releases Big Four Findings," *SmartPros Ltd,* August 27, 2004, at **www.accountingnet .com/x44957.xml**.

39. Phyllis Plitch, "Scrushy Charges Show the Long Reach of Sarbanes-Oxley," *The Wall Street Journal,* November 4, 2003.

40. Deborah Solomon, "For Financial Whistle-Blowers, New Shield Is an Imperfect One," *The Wall Street Journal,* October 4, 2004, p. A1.

41. Colleen Debaise, "Judge Says $1.4 Billion Deal with Wall Street Firms Is 'Fair'," *The Wall Street Journal,* October 31, 2003.

42. Paul Volcker and Arthur Levitt, "In Defense of Sarbanes-Oxley, *The Wall Street Journal,* June 14, 2004, p. A16.

Antitrust Law— Restraints of Trade

Antitrust is a word that is only dimly recognizable to most of us, but antitrust law reaches all corners of our lives and significantly shapes our economic and social practices.

PRACTICING ETHICS   Antitrust Law and the Price of Beer

We recognize that college students drink astonishing amounts of beer (4 billion cans annually, according to the federal Department of Health and Human Services— enough, if stacked, to reach the moon and 70,000 miles beyond);[1] but do we understand that antitrust law can affect the consumption or at least the price of that beer? At this writing, a group of consumers in Madison, Wisconsin, home of the University of Wisconsin, is suing some local bars and the Madison–Dane County Tavern League, Inc., for price fixing, an antitrust violation.[2] The plaintiffs claim that the defendant bars agreed to fix prices by adopting a "voluntary ban on drink specials." The plaintiffs point to a September 2002 press release from the "Downtown Tavern Working Group" announcing that late-night drink specials would not be offered on Friday and Saturday nights for "at least a year."[3] The defendants said the new policy was a self-imposed effort to curb binge drinking, especially by

students, and that the policy was a response to pressure from the city and the University of Wisconsin. Further, the defendants said that the press release did not reflect an agreement of any kind and thus could not violate the law because all bar owners remained free to do as they wished.[4] A lawyer for the defendants reportedly said,

> When you combine a student with imagination with a lawyer with time on his hands, this is what you get.[5]

Questions

1. The legality of this arrangement aside, *should* bar owners be free to reach an agreement eliminating drink specials? Explain.

2. Is the Madison dispute too trivial and frivolous to justify court time? Explain.

3. Will the market satisfactorily protect youthful drinkers and society? Explain.

Part One—The Foundations of Antitrust Law

Antitrust—Early Goals

Antitrust, perhaps more than any other branch of the law, is a product of changing political and economic tides. Historically, antitrust law sought, broadly expressed, to maintain an approach to life where every American, at least in theory, had the opportunity to reach the top. More specifically, antitrust advocates were concerned about the following issues:

1. **The preservation of competition.** Antitrust law was designed to provide free, open markets permitting the virtues of capitalism to be fully expressed. The belief was (and continues to be) that competition would bring the best products and services at the lowest possible prices.

2. **The preservation of democracy.** Many businesses in competition meant that none of them could corner economic, political, or social power.

3. **The preservation of small businesses, or more generally, the preservation of the American Dream.** Antitrust was designed to preserve the opportunity for the "little people" to compete with the giants.

4. **An expression of political radicalism.** At least for a segment of society, antitrust laws were meant to be tools for reshaping America to meet the needs of all people, rather than those of big business.

During President Ronald Reagan's tenure, a free market mentality dominated, and reliance on antitrust law declined. While the federal government continued to avidly pursue collusion between competitors and certain other antitrust violations, the prevailing expectation was that the market would function most effectively in the absence of government intervention.

Antitrust Stability?

Today in the federal courts, conservative Reagan/Bush judges are powerful, and antitrust, while important in ensuring a competitive economy, is certainly not being used aggressively as a lever for social change. The political and sociological concerns noted, although not abandoned, have taken a back seat to efficiency considerations and to pragmatic, case-by-case consideration of the economic facts.

What we are seeing is a more centrist role for antitrust where, in appropriate cases, the legal system will be employed to deal with market imperfections. In both the Bush (Republican) and the Clinton (Democratic) administrations, antitrust officials seem to have held the view that consumer welfare, rather than shareholder or corporate considerations, should be the primary concern of antitrust enforcement. The result is a pragmatic, reasonably consistent, "by-the-numbers" approach to enforcement, as explained to *The Wall Street Journal* by then–Justice Department antitrust boss Charles James:

> "We don't look at a market and say, 'This is the way it should be.' We go in only when there's been a market failure." When competition fails, James says, "we will not be reluctant to intervene, and to be aggressive."
>
> Federal antitrust enforcers may be held in low regard by many businesspeople, but it is a bum rap, James maintains.
>
> "Antitrust law is an absolutely critical component of a free market economy, where market forces, not government regulation, produce the best results for consumers and businesses," he said.[6]

Antitrust Enforcement and Statutes

Federal government antitrust enforcement is divided between the Antitrust Division of the Department of Justice and the Federal Trade Commission. The government brings relatively few antitrust actions, but a government victory sends powerful messages to the business community about the risks of anticompetitive behavior. The government prefers to avoid litigation, and most cases are settled before going to court. Private parties may also sue under the antitrust laws. Those claims are, in fact, much more numerous than government litigation. [For the Justice Department Antitrust Division, see **www.usdoj.gov/atr/**]

Sherman Antitrust Act, 1890

Section 1 of the Sherman Antitrust Act forbids restraints of trade, and Section 2 forbids monopolization, attempts to monopolize, and conspiracies to monopolize. Two types of enforcement options are available to the federal government:

1. Violation of the Sherman Act opens participants to criminal penalties. The maximum corporate fine is $100 million per violation, whereas individuals may be fined $1 million and/or imprisoned for 10 years.
2. Injunctive relief is provided under civil law. The government or a private party may secure a court order preventing continuing violations of the act and affording appropriate relief (such as dissolution or divestiture).

Perhaps the most important remedy is available to private parties. An individual or organization harmed by a violation of the act may bring a civil action seeking three times the actual damages (treble damages) sustained. Only actual damages are awarded in instances where defendants "cooperate" with private plaintiffs.

Clayton Act, 1914

The Clayton Act forbids price discrimination, exclusive dealing, tying arrangements, requirements contracts, mergers restraining commerce or tending to create a monopoly, and interlocking directorates. Civil enforcement of the Clayton Act is similar to the Sherman Act in that the government may sue for injunctive relief, and private parties may seek treble damages. In general, criminal law remedies are not available under the Clayton Act. [For the texts of federal antitrust laws, along with antitrust case summaries and antitrust links, see **http://www.antitrustcases.com**]

Federal Trade Commission Act (FTC)

The Federal Trade Commission Act created a powerful, independent agency designed to devote its full attention to the elimination of anticompetitive practices in American commerce. The FTC proceeds under the Sherman Act, the Clayton Act, and Section 5 of the FTC Act itself, which declares unlawful "unfair methods of competition" and "unfair or deceptive acts or practices in or affecting commerce." The commission's primary enforcement device is the cease and desist order, but fines may be imposed. [For the FTC home page, see **http://www.ftc.gov/**]

Federal Antitrust Law and Other Regulatory Systems

State Law

Most states, through legislation and judicial decisions, have developed their own antitrust laws. Some states have recently become more aggressive in antitrust enforcement, as illustrated by their sucess in conjunction with the federal government in attacking Microsoft's alleged monopoly conduct. (See Chapter 11.)

Patents, Copyrights, and Trademarks

Each of these devices constitutes a limited, government-granted monopoly. As such, they are in direct conflict with the general thrust of antitrust law. Each device, however, serves to protect—and thus encourage—commercial creativity and development. The resulting antitrust problem is essentially that of limiting the patent, copyright, or trademark holder to the narrow terms of its privilege.

Law of Other Nations

Chapter 11 addresses the immense practical and ideological significance of international antitrust issues in this era of globalization. Journalist Steven Thomas explains:

> One challenge facing Bush's new attorney general will be how to assert U.S. interests in the world marketplace. Today half of the department's antitrust cases involve international business or cartels, up from fewer than 1 percent a decade ago.
>
> "This is a problem that is going to get much, much more serious," former U.S. antitrust chief Joel Klein said in a recent lecture. "The worst cases of antitrust abuses take place on a global basis. . . . They're stealing money from U.S. companies and consumers."[7]

[For a guide to antitrust resources on the Internet, see **http://www.antitrustinstitute. org/links.cfm**]

Part Two—Horizontal Restraints

When competitors collude, conspire, or agree among themselves, they are engaging in *horizontal restraints of trade.* Instead of competing to drive prices down and quality up, they may be fixing prices, restricting output, dividing territories, and the like. The various horizontal restraints are governed by Section 1 of the Sherman Act, which forbids contracts, combinations, or conspiracies in *restraint of trade*. What is a restraint of trade? In the *Standard Oil*[8] decision of 1911, the U.S. Supreme Court articulated what has come to be known as the *Rule of Reason.* In essence, the Court said that the Sherman Act forbids only *unreasonable* restraints of trade. The reasonableness of a restraint of trade is largely determined by balancing the pro- and anticompetitive effects of the situation in question. Thus the plaintiff must prove the existence of an anticompetitive agreement or conduct and also prove that, on balance, the agreement or conduct harms competition. [For an antitrust overview, see **http://www.law.cornell.edu/topics/antitrust.html**]

Some antitrust violations, such as horizontal price fixing, are perceived to be so injurious to competition that their mere existence constitutes unlawful conduct. Plaintiffs must prove that the violation in question occurred, but they need not prove that the violation caused, or is likely to cause, competitive harm. These *per se* violations are simply unlawful on their face.

Horizontal Price Fixing

Principal legislation—Sherman Act, Section 1:

> Every contract, combination in the form of trust or otherwise, or conspiracy, in restraint of trade or commerce, among the several States, or with foreign nations, is hereby declared to be illegal.

Competitors may not lawfully agree on prices. The principle is simple and fundamental to an efficient, fair marketplace. Establishing the presence of an unlawful price-fixing arrangement, on the other hand, ordinarily is anything but simple.

Proof

The major dilemma in price fixing and all other Sherman Act Section 1 violations is the measure of proof that satisfies the requirement of a contract, combination, or conspiracy. Evidence of collusion arises in a variety of ways. Broadly, a showing of cooperative action amounting to an agreement must be established. In general, that showing may be developed by any of the following four methods of proof:

1. **Agreement with direct evidence.** In the easiest case, the government can produce direct evidence such as writings or testimony from participants proving the existence of collusion.
2. **Agreement without direct evidence.** Here the defendants directly but covertly agree, and circumstantial evidence such as company behavior must be employed to draw an inference of collusion.
3. **Agreement based on a tacit understanding.** In this situation no direct exchange of assurances occurs, but the parties employ tactics that act as surrogates for direct assurances and thus "tell" each other that they are, in fact, in agreement.
4. **Agreement based on mutual observation.** These defendants have simply observed each others' pricing behavior over time, and they are able therefore to anticipate each other's future conduct and act accordingly without any direct collusion but with results akin to those that would have resulted from a direct agreement.[9]

Parallel Conduct

An unlawful conspiracy is to be distinguished from independent but parallel business behavior by competitors. So-called *conscious parallelism* is fully lawful because the competitors have not agreed either explicitly or by implication to follow the same course of action. Rather, their business judgment has led each to independently follow parallel paths. On the other hand, a conspiracy can sometimes be established by proof that the parallel behavior in question was not arrived at independently. (See the *Fears* case on page 392.)

Aggressive Enforcement

Both government advocates and free market champions agree that price fixing cripples the market. So government intervention, at the federal and state levels, and damage claims by wronged consumers are sometimes essential to maintaining effective competition. Antitrust law, including price-fixing prohibitions, is designed to protect the consumer from a variety of commercial arrangements—some well intentioned, some overt cheating—that nullify the favorable effects of competition. The value of free markets is undeniable. Antitrust seeks to ensure that freedom. Doubts about whether the markets, so vigorously embraced by the business community, are in fact free have grown in recent years as a series of price-fixing scandals has emerged:

> The value of free markets is undeniable. Antitrust seeks to ensure that freedom.

- At this writing in 2005, Eliot Spitzer, the attorney general of the state of New York, has insurance brokerage giant Marsh & McLennan and others reeling from charges of bid rigging. (Businesses seeking insurance often hire a broker, such as Marsh, to solicit bids for them from insurers. Marsh is accused of rigging those bids in various ways.) At this writing, three Marsh executives have pleaded guilty to criminal charges, the company has agreed to pay an $850 million settlement, and Marsh is laying off 5,500 workers because of the scandal.[10]

- Ending nine years of litigation over alleged conspiracies to fix corn syrup prices, Archer Daniels Midland, A. E. Staley, and others agreed in 2004 to pay $531 million to settle a class action against them.[11]

- In May 1999 the U.S. Justice Department secured a criminal fine of more than $750 million from three international vitamin manufacturers. Those three and three other companies later agreed to pay $1.1 billion to settle civil price-fixing claims. The companies' executives allegedly got together to divide the worldwide vitamin market and set prices for the vitamins, and then they allegedly policed themselves to see that all conspirators were adhering to the agreement.[12] [For many of the settlement documents in the vitamin civil case, see **http://www.dcd.uscourts.gov/99ms197d.pdf**]

> The companies' executives allegedly got together to divide the worldwide vitamin market and set prices for the vitamins.

These are only a few of the many examples in recent years of price-fixing conspiracies in America and around the world. The effect of these unlawful arrangements is to harm competition and raise prices. Price fixing is nothing new, but its aggressive pursuit both domestically and around the world does represent a change in policy, as explained by Phillip Warren, U.S. Department of Justice antitrust chief in San Francisco:

> "I think it's been going on [for a long time], and we have only recently been able to detect and prosecute them," Warren said. There's a long tradition of cartel activity, not in the United States but around the world. Cartels were accepted." . . .
> Prosecuting international cartels is "an important development, an exciting development, and certainly it's what keeps me coming back," Warren said. "There's no sign of it trending back at all. It's the way things are going and will continue to go."[13]

Models as Price-Fixing Victims?

The case that follows involves a $50 million class action by some 10,000 professional models alleging that at least 10 leading modeling agencies conspired for more than 20 years to fix prices on the fees the agencies charge models to represent them. A New York State law ("Article 11") imposes a cap of 10 percent on the fees that employment agencies can charge their clients, but the plaintiff models claimed the defendant modeling agencies' fees rose to 20 percent or more. The defendants claimed they were managing the models and thus were not simply employment agencies. The defendants moved for a summary judgment to dismiss the plaintiffs' claim.

LEGAL BRIEFCASE

Fears v. Wilhelmina Model Agency, et al. 2004 U.S. Dist. LEXIS 5045 (S.D. N

Judge Baer

FACTUAL BACKGROUND

Plaintiffs (the models) allege that defendants (modeling agencies), through their . . . industry's trade association, IMMA (now called MMC), had the opportunity to—and indeed did—fix prices. . . . Plaintiffs assert that defendants' price-fixing conspiracy originated with "an intention and plan collectively to evade the licensing requirements and fee restrictions imposed by New York State law ("Article 11")."

CONSPIRACY TO FIX MODELS' COMMISSIONS

In Count I of their complaint, plaintiffs assert that defendants violated [the Sherman Act] Section One by (1) initially conspiring to charge the majority of their models a commission in excess of the 10 percent statutory cap imposed by Article 11, and then (2) conspiring to increase this commission to 15 percent, and finally 20 percent.

Plaintiffs allege that defendants colluded to fix models' commissions through discussions, exchanges, and agreements at IMMA meetings and outside of IMMA's formal setting. Because the alleged conspiracy, as it involves horizontal price fixing, is illegal *per se,* this Court need only determine whether plaintiffs have established a material issue of fact as to whether defendants conspired to fix models' commissions.

* * * * *

Parallel Pricing "Plus"

While plaintiffs have not uncovered direct "smoking gun" evidence to confirm that defendants operated under an agreement to fix models' commissions, it is undisputed that there is evidence of parallel pricing, both at rates exceeding 10 percent, and at rates of 20 percent. Plaintiffs' expert, Martin A. Asher, Ph.D., concluded "from data provided by defendants" that "more than

97 percent of models who had billings within the class period, from 1998 through 2003, paid commissions in excess of 10 percent." Further, Asher reports that " approximately 91 percent of the models paid commission rates of 20 percent." Similarly, plaintiffs' second expert, John C. Beyer, Ph.D., concludes that "most models (approximately 96 percent) have been charged a commission rate of 20 percent or more." While plaintiffs' experts demonstrate parallel pricing, assuming defendants were aware of each other's pricing patterns, which the evidence suggests they were, conscious parallelism alone is insufficient to create a material issue of fact as to whether an agreement was formulated. For purposes of summary judgment, additional circumstances, referred to as "plus factors," must "provide a supplemental basis to infer a conspiracy." Among recognized plus factors, two in particular have received significant exposure in case law, both of which have a strong presence in this case—a motive to conspire and a high level of interfirm communication.

* * * * *

With regard to the first plus factor, there is no question that defendants possessed a common rational motive to conspire—the ability to raise models' commissions without suffering loss of business.

Second, it is beyond peradventure that IMMA members engaged in a concentrated degree of interfirm communication, including but hardly limited to models' commissions directly.

INTERFIRM COMMUNICATIONS

Plaintiffs assert that the conspiracy began with an agreement among defendants, collectively, to transform the structure of their businesses from employment agencies to management agencies for the express purpose of avoiding the 10 percent cap imposed upon employment agencies by Article 11.

* * * * *

Plaintiffs argue that through their conspiracy to evade Article 11, or more aptly their joint agreement to become management companies, defendants were able to raise the commission that they charged to models above Article 11's 10 percent cap, and eventually agree to uniformly charge models commissions of 20 percent—a commission rate which would have been impossible under their previous configurations. While defendants hotly contest the formation of any agreements as to models' commissions, they concede that there was significant information exchanged among IMMA members about pricing. [John Casablancas, founder of Elite Model Management] noted proudly that each company "basically knew the price practices of all the agencies . . . everybody knows what everybody else is doing." He also admitted that he "knew instantly every time an agency raised or when an agency didn't raise." Dieter Esch, then President and Chief Executive Officer of Wilhelmina, admitted that he may have announced to attendees of an IMMA meeting, in the approximate timeframe of 1996 through 1998, that he was charging a 25 percent commission to models, and Casablancas made a similar, yet even more troubling, announcement at the December 12, 1991, IMMA meeting that he too "*would be* charging 20 percent commission to all clients as a firm policy." While Casablancas's announcement does not explicitly demonstrate an agreement among IMMA members to follow course, it suggests that IMMA members were made aware of their competitors' price increases before the price increases were enacted—leaving time for others to agree to increase their fees accordingly. Further, Casablancas conceded that "the more uniformity in the prices, the more I think it was—it was something that you could then compete on the quality of your models on the service, and not just on—on rates, you know. So we were always favorable to letting everyone know as much as possible about—about our pricing policies." Casablancas also testified that "I was always hoping that as leaders, we would be followed, and that we would not be left as we were on many instances by ourselves with higher rates, and having a lot of clients segregating against us because we were too expensive." While it is possible that Elite simply took the lead in raising its commissions, with the blind hope that other members would follow, it is far more reasonable to assume that Elite sought some guarantee that the other defendants would acquiesce, to ensure that its clients would not segregate against them.

This assumption is bolstered by significant evidence of discussions and agreements concerning raising the client service fees. Elite's internal memorandum "RE: IMMA Meeting—Minutes," reports that at a January 21, 1980, IMMA meeting, trade association members acted in unison with regard to pricing decisions. The memorandum reads in part that "the suggestion of increasing client service charge from 10% which Alain Kittler suggested I [Jo Zagami] make at this meeting *was not accepted by the Association.* The general feeling was that *with the increase of model rates,* and the agencies benefiting by models' commissions, clients would not be agreeable to a higher service charge." This memorandum reveals both that one agency sought the "acceptance" of the trade association before increasing its client service fee and also strongly suggests that the "increase of model rates" was applicable to all members and not a decision made unilaterally by each company. Similarly, a memorandum recounting a November 14, 1980, IMMA meeting, makes clear that "certain members" had made "requests" "to increase the service charge from 10 to 15%." This Court can think of no other rationale for the need for such a "request," other than that members were required to act jointly with regard to price increases.

* * * * *

The evidence suggests that the management companies did approve an increase in the client service fee to 20 percent, with Elite taking the initiative in doing so. On April 14, 1987, Casablancas sent [Monique] Pillard the letter that he intended to send to his clients, announcing the increase in the service fee, and explained that "you may show [the letter] to some people at the next IMMA meeting." He explained further that "you should say that *it is our intent to send this letter* and you should be very careful that in no way can this be construed as 'price fixing'. You are merely to inform our competitors of our intention to send this letter or a similar one." The tone and tense of this letter suggests that Casablancas provided his fellow IMMA members with advance notice of Elite's intended price increase. As further evidence that Elite actually provided its competitors with notice of its intended price increase, and secured their agreement to follow suit, plaintiffs provide a May 5, 1987, memorandum from Pillard to all Elite staff, informing them of the service charge increase from 15 to 20 percent, effective June 1, and stating that "*all other agencies will go along with this increase.* Please inform your clients accordingly so that there is no misunderstanding." Only a rich fantasy life could lead one to an inference other than that Pillard was directing her staff to inform clients that the other agencies would institute similar increases so that clients would not "misunderstand" and cease utilizing Elite's services, in hopes of moving to a management company with lower fees. . . .

At a September 16, 1986, IMMA meeting, as reflected in an internal Elite memorandum, Pillard "made a point about lowering the prices of catalogs; that we are all committing suicide, if we do not stick together. Pauline's agreed with me but as usual, Bill Weinberg [of Wilhelmina] cautioned me about price fixing . . . Ha! Ha! Ha! . . . the usual bulls . . t! I warned him that by not sticking together, we would have to make 40% more volume in order to make the same figures as last year, but you know Bill, he always thinks he can get more if he acts that way." Again, it is difficult for me to escape the inference that discussions of the benefits of joint action on pricing ensued. While Wilhelmina objects to the outward discussion of price fixing, it is plausible from Pillard's reaction that Wilhelmina's objection was to the dissemination of information, not to the underlying price-fixing agreement.

* * * * *

Notably, just prior to IMMA's distribution of its standard Model Management Agreement to its members in May 1993, its counsel Edward Klagsbrun found serious antitrust problems with pertinent sections. Klagsbrun noted in an April 6, 1993, memorandum to co-IMMA counsel David Blasband ("Blasband") that "any agreement suggested by a trade association to its members who are competitors is inherently suspect and vulnerable to attack from the point of view of federal and state antitrust law."

* * * * *

Despite advice of counsel as to the antitrust problems associated with mandating any agreement, by cover letter of August 16, 1993, Hunter circulated a draft of the model contract and wrote that he felt that it was "a very good contract for IMMA Members to *endorse.*" Similarly, draft IMMA meeting minutes from September 15, 1993, reflect that "members who had received copies of the draft agreement were in agreement that the contract was ready to be adopted." . . . Shortly after IMMA adopted its standard Model Management Agreement in 1993, plaintiffs assert that four defendants, Ford, IMG, Next, and Wilhelmina, inserted substantially identical language in the section stating that models understood that managers were also "entitled to receive a service charge from clients."

* * * * *

Sufficiency of Evidence to Establish Price-Fixing Conspiracy

Despite the artful innocent explanations that defendants have offered for their parallel pricing, . . . when analyzed together, as it must be, the evidence of parallel pricing, coupled with the evidence of discussions and agreements among association members, demonstrates a material issue of disputed fact as to whether IMMA members acted independently with regard to models' commissions.

* * * * *

Plaintiffs have established that all defendants who were members of IMMA, and therefore participated in or were privy to the conversations and agreements discussed above, "had a unity of purpose or a common design and understanding, or a meeting of minds in an unlawful arrangement." (*Int'l Distribution Centers, Inc.,* 812 F. 2d at 793.) . . . Therefore, Ford's, G. Ford's, Wilhelmina's, Elite's, Next's, IMG's, Click's, Images, and MMC's motions for summary judgment on plaintiffs' claim of a conspiracy to fix models' commissions are *denied.*

* * * * *

AFTERWORD

As the *Fears* case was going to trial in June 2004, the parties agreed to an out-of-court settlement. IMG Models, one of the defendants, reportedly settled for more than $11 million.[14]

Questions

1. *a.* Explain why the Court ruled for the plaintiffs by denying the summary judgment motion.

   b. In your view, does the evidence support the judge's conclusion that the case should go to trial? Explain.

2. Does this opinion tell us that competitors cannot lawfully talk about prices? Explain.

3. Did John Casablancas of Elite Model Management appear to violate antitrust law by acting as a price leader for his industry? Explain.

4. Assume two drugstores, located across the street from each other and each involved in interstate commerce, agree to exchange a monthly list of prices charged for all nonprescription medications. Is that arrangement lawful in the absence of any further cooperation? Explain.

5. The gasoline dealers' association in a community reaches an agreement providing that (1) both major brands and independents will not give trading stamps or other premiums and (2) majors agree not to advertise their prices except on the pumps.

   a. What is the purpose of the arrangement?

   b. What violation of law might be alleged? Decide the case. Explain. See *U.S. v. Gasoline Retailers Association,* 285 F.2d 688 (7th Cir. 1961).

6. Assume that 10 real estate firms operate in the city of Gotham. Further assume that each charges a 7 percent commission on all residential sales.

   a. Does that uniformity of prices in and of itself constitute price fixing? Explain.

   b. Assume we have evidence that the firms agreed to set the 7 percent level. What defense would be raised against a price-fixing charge?

   c. Would that defense succeed? Explain. See *McLain v. Real Estate Board of New Orleans, Inc.,* 444 U.S. 232 (1980).

Refusal to Deal/Group Boycotts

In America we are free to do business with whomever we prefer, correct? Generally, yes; but antitrust problems sometimes emerge. When does a *refusal to deal* with another raise antitrust issues? The clearest problem is a *horizontal group boycott* where *competitors agree* not to deal with a supplier, customer, or another competitor. Ford and GM, for example, presumably could not jointly refuse to buy tires from Firestone. Such arrangements so thoroughly subvert the market that they normally are *per se* violations and thus do not require a detailed evaluation of competitive harm and benefits, although a showing of market power by those in the group may be required. A unilateral (individual) refusal to deal by a buyer or a seller sometimes raises antitrust concerns if the firm refusing to deal is a monopolist and harm to competition can be proven.[15]

A recent battle among the big bank card companies illustrates refusal to deal reasoning (although for technical reasons the case was not tried under the refusal to deal/boycott label). In 1996 American Express decided to open its own credit card network to compete with Visa and MasterCard. No bank, however, was willing to deal with American Express. Why would the banks turn down the potential to make more money by working with the respected American Express brand? They did so because Visa and MasterCard had rules forbidding their members from issuing American Express and Discover cards. Visa and MasterCard operate as nonprofit joint venture associations owned by the member banks that issue their credit cards. As long as those banks wanted to do business with Visa and MasterCard, the two giants, they could not deal with American Express and Discover. Were the Visa and MasterCard refusal to deal rules lawful? No, as it turns out. The antitrust division of the federal Department of Justice sued the two giants for their alleged exclusionary practices and won in the federal courts.[16] The six-year struggle turned largely on the finding that continued exclusion of Discover, American Express, and others from the market would likely harm future competition. Better products and services are to be expected from the four credit card networks (and other new entrants) when all have access to the banks that are the dominant distribution source for credit cards and future smart cards as well as the growing debit card market. A key finding was the conclusion that Visa and MasterCard, with their collective market share exceeding 70 percent, had market power.

> An athletes' advocacy group is calling on athletes to boycott colleges with low graduation rates.
>
> The International Baby Food Action Network is urging mothers to boycott Nestlé.

Consumer and Political Boycotts   Boycotts for persuasive purposes are commonplace. At this writing, for example, an athletes' advocacy group is calling on athletes to boycott colleges with low graduation rates (especially for black students); the University of Texas Student Labor Action Project is urging students to boycott Taco Bell because the taco maker buys tomatoes from a company that allegedly underpays its workers; and the International Baby Food Action Network is urging mothers to boycott Nestlé for aggressively marketing baby foods and thus allegedly undermining breastfeeding. Noncommercial, political efforts, like these, to use the power of the boycott to cause a change in behavior sometimes are subject to antitrust law. When faced with direct conflicts between antitrust principles and First Amendment freedom of expression, however, the courts have proven reluctant to find a Sherman Act violation.

Clarett Boycotted by NFL?

Antitrust shapes all dimensions of our lives, as football running back Maurice Clarett learned when he tried to enter the 2004 National Football League draft. Clarett, as a freshman, led Ohio State University to an undefeated season in 2002. Clarett was ineligible for college football in his sophomore year because of allegations that he accepted improper benefits and lied about doing so. Clarett then tried to enter the NFL draft but was barred by a league rule providing that players must have been out of high school for three seasons. Clarett sued the NFL, claiming its eligibility rules violated federal antitrust laws by, in effect, allowing competing teams to agree among themselves to boycott certain players (including Clarett, who had not yet been out of high school for three years). Clarett won at the federal district court level, but he lost on appeal when the court ruled that the eligibility rule is exempt (immune from scrutiny) from the antitrust laws. The NFL eligibility rule is the product of a collective bargaining agreement between the league and the players' union, the National Football League Players Association. Antitrust promotes competition while unions restrict it in various ways; but in balancing those competing interests, Congress and the courts have long granted unions certain exemptions from antitrust laws. At this writing, Clarett has petitioned the Supreme Court for a review of his claims.

Question

Should Clarett and future football players be free to sell their services on the open market? Or is the NFL correct to encourage players to stay in college and mature before seeking to become professionals? Explain.

Source: Clarett v. National Football League, 369 F.3d 124 (2d Cir. 2004)

Questions

1. Baptist Eye Institute, a group of nonspecialized ophthalmologists in Jacksonville, Florida, controlling approximately 15 percent of the referral market, sent nearly all of its retina cases to the Florida Retina Institute. Is BEI engaging in an unlawful group boycott against plaintiff Retina Associates, a retina care provider in competition with the Florida Retina Institute? Explain. See *Retina Associates P.A. v. Southern Baptist Hospital of Florida Inc.,* 105 F.3d 1376 (11th Cir. 1997).

2. Discon, a telephone salvage company, sold services to MECo, a subsidiary of NYNEX, a phone company for the New York/New England area. MECo switched from Discon to AT&T Technologies, a Discon competitor, and paid a higher price to AT&T than it had paid to Discon. Discon claimed that the buyer and NYNEX then received a rebate from AT&T at the end of the year. Discon argued that NYNEX was able to pass on its higher costs to its customers because NYNEX was a part of a regulated phone market. Discon claimed that NYNEX, its subsidiaries, and AT&T were engaging in a group boycott in violation of the Sherman Act in order to drive Discon out of the market. Decide. Explain. See *NYNEX Corp. v. Discon, Inc.,* 119 S.Ct. 493 (1998).

We have been studying unfair trade practices by competitors—that is, horizontal restraints of trade. Now we turn our attention to antitrust violations on the vertical axis—that is, restraints involving two or more members of a supply chain (such as a manufacturer and a retailer of that manufacturer's products).

Compact Discs

Do we need antitrust intervention by the government to bring music prices to a "fair" level? Music lovers might vote yes on that question; but of course, the government will not bring an antitrust action unless it believes the law has been broken. Consumers recently benefited from just such an intervention when 28 states sued the five largest record labels and some music retailers, claiming they had fixed compact disc prices above market levels in the 1990s. The plaintiffs claimed that the defendants established a minimum advertised pricing (MAP) system to stop discounting by retailers such as Best Buy. MAP specified the retail price beneath which compact discs were not to be sold. Retailers selling beneath that price allegedly were punished by denying them discounts and promotional payments. MAP pricing, as the states saw it, was a form of resale price maintenance or so-called "vertical price fixing." The lawsuit was settled in 2002 with the defendants agreeing to provide $143 million in cash and compact discs. All those who bought compact discs and some other forms of recordings from 1995 to 2000 were eligible for a $12.60 payment simply by filing a claim by March 3, 2003. The Federal Trade Commission estimated consumer overcharging from 1996 to 1999 at a nationwide total of $480 million.[17]

> All those who bought compact discs from 1995 to 2000 were eligible for a $12.60 payment.

Antitrust or the Market or Both?   CD prices, at this writing, are plummeting because of file sharing, Internet sales, competition from other entertainment, and deep discounts from big box retailers such as Wal-Mart. As of June 1, 2004, CD prices were down 20 percent from 18 months previously, reportedly reaching a new all-time low.[18] The CD antitrust action doubtless encouraged falling prices, and those in the music industry may indeed have been engaging in price fixing; but changing technology and the resulting fierce market appear to have provided the most powerful solution to high music prices. Still, a watchful government eye remains welcome in instances of wrongdoing and market failure.

Take Home the National Anthem?

News reports call into question the value of the CD settlement. The big record labels apparently dumped their poor sellers to meet the settlement requirements:

> . . . 48 copies of *Martha Stewart Living: Spooky Scary Sounds for Halloween,* 375 copies of *Entertainment Weekly: The Greatest Hits 1971,* 1,400 copies of Whitney Houston's CD single, *The Star-Spangled Banner,* and 206 copies of *3 Mo' Tenors.*

Source: "Labels Clean Out Warehouses in Price-Fixing Settlement," *G2 Intelligence, Inc. Online Reporter,* August 7, 2004.

Resale Price Maintenance/Vertical Territorial and Customer Restraints

Principal legislation: Sherman Act, Section 1; Federal Trade Commission Act, Section 5.

As we saw in the music business, manufacturers and distributors often seek to specify the price at which their customers may resell their products. Having sold its product, why should a manufacturer or distributor seek to influence the price at which the product is resold? The primary reasons are threefold: (1) establishing a minimum price may enhance the product's reputation for quality, (2) resale price maintenance policy seeks to prevent discount stores from undercutting regular retail outlets, and (3) to prevent *free riders.* (Why does the manufacturer or distributor prefer its products to be sold in traditional retail stores rather than in discount enterprises?) [For a summary of vertical restraints law, see **http://profs.ip.findlaw.com/antitrust/antitrust_4. html**]

Colgate Doctrine

An *agreement* between a seller and its buyer, fixing the price at which the buyer may resell the product, is a per se violation. However, under the Supreme Court's 1919 *Colgate* decision,[19] sellers may lawfully engage in resale price maintenance if they do nothing more than specify prices at which their products are to be sold and unilaterally refuse to deal with anyone who does not adhere to those prices. In some factual settings, however, some courts appear to be abandoning the *Colgate* safe harbor for sellers.[20]

Nonprice Restraints

In addition to price restraints, manufacturers commonly wish to restrict where and to whom their product may be resold. Those restrictions typically afford an exclusive sales territory to a distributor. Similarly, manufacturers may prevent distributors from selling to some classes of customers (for example, a distributor might be forbidden to sell to an unfranchised retailer). Of course, such arrangements necessarily retard or eliminate *intrabrand* competition. Because price and service competition among dealers in the same brand ordinarily benefits the consumer, the courts have frequently struck down such arrangements. Still, those territorial and customer allocations also have merits. The *GTE Sylvania* case[21] enunciated those virtues and established the position that vertical restrictions are to be judged case by case, balancing interbrand and intrabrand competitive effects while recognizing that interbrand competition is the primary concern of antitrust law. Thus the Rule of Reason is to be applied to vertical territorial and customer restraints.

At this point, a review is in order of the critical legal distinction between horizontal and vertical restraints. The former, in general, are per se unlawful. The latter are to be resolved under the Rule of Reason unless an agreement on prices is involved. As just explained, *horizontal* restrictions are those arising from an agreement among the *competitors* themselves, while *vertical* restrictions ordinarily are those imposed on *buyers* by their *suppliers.* The *Business Electronics Corporation (B.E.C.)* case that follows offers a summary of the Supreme Court's analysis of both vertical price and nonprice restraints, and it demonstrates the difficulty of proving resale price maintenance.

Business Electronics Corporation v. Sharp Electronics Corporation   485 U.S. 717(1988)

Justice Scalia

Petitioner Business Electronics Corporation seeks review of a decision of the United States Court of Appeals for the Fifth Circuit holding that a vertical restraint is per se illegal under § 1 of the Sherman Act, only if there is an express or implied agreement to set resale prices at some level. We granted certiorari to resolve a conflict in the Courts of Appeals regarding the proper dividing line between the rule that vertical price restraints are illegal per se and the rule that vertical nonprice restraints are to be judged under the Rule of Reason.

I

In 1968 petitioner became the exclusive retailer in the Houston, Texas, area of electronic calculators manufactured by respondent Sharp Electronics Corporation. In 1972 respondent appointed Gilbert Hartwell as a second retailer in the Houston area. During the relevant period, electronic calculators were primarily sold to business customers for prices up to $1,000. While much of the evidence in this case was conflicting—in particular, concerning whether petitioner was "free riding" on Hartwell's provision of presale educational and promotional services by providing inadequate services itself—a few facts are undisputed. Respondent published a list of suggested minimum retail prices, but its written dealership agreements with petitioner and Hartwell did not obligate either to observe them, or to charge any other specific price. Petitioner's retail prices were often below respondent's suggested retail prices and generally below Hartwell's retail prices, even though Hartwell too sometimes priced below respondent's suggested retail prices. Hartwell complained to respondent on a number of occasions about petitioner's prices. In June 1973 Hartwell gave respondent the ultimatum that Hartwell would terminate his dealership unless respondent ended its relationship with petitioner within 30 days. Respondent terminated petitioner's dealership in July 1973.

Petitioner brought suit in the United States District Court for the Southern District of Texas, alleging that respondent and Hartwell had conspired to terminate petitioner and that such conspiracy was illegal per se under § 1 of the Sherman Act. The case was tried to a jury. The district court submitted a liability interrogatory to the jury that asked whether "there was an agreement or understanding between Sharp Electronics Corporation and Hartwell to terminate Business Electronics as a Sharp dealer because of Business Electronics' price cut-

ting." The district court instructed the jury at length about this question:

> The Sherman Act is violated when a seller enters into an agreement or understanding with one of its dealers to terminate another dealer because of the other dealer's price cutting. Plaintiff contends that Sharp terminated Business Electronics in furtherance of Hartwell's desire to eliminate Business Electronics as a price-cutting rival.
>
> If you find that there was an agreement between Sharp and Hartwell to terminate Business Electronics because of Business Electronics' price cutting, you should answer yes to Question Number 1.

* * * * *

> A combination, agreement, or understanding to terminate a dealer because of his price cutting unreasonably restrains trade and cannot be justified for any reason. Therefore, even though the combination, agreement, or understanding may have been formed or engaged in . . . to eliminate any alleged evils of price cutting, it is still unlawful.
>
> If a dealer demands that a manufacturer terminate a price-cutting dealer, and the manufacturer agrees to do so, the agreement is illegal if the manufacturer's purpose is to eliminate the price cutting.

The jury answered Question 1 affirmatively and awarded $600,000 in damages. . . .

* * * * *

The Fifth Circuit reversed. . . .

II
A

Section 1 of the Sherman Act provides that "[e]very contract, combination in the form of trust or otherwise, or conspiracy, in restraint of trade or commerce among the several States, or with foreign nations, is declared to be illegal." Since the earliest decisions of this Court interpreting this provision, we have recognized that it was intended to prohibit only unreasonable restraints of trade. Ordinarily, whether particular concerted action violates § 1 of the Sherman Act is determined through case-by-case application of the so-called Rule of Reason. . . . Certain categories of agreements, however, have been held to be per se illegal, dispensing with the need for case-by-case evaluation. . . .

* * * * *

Although vertical agreements on resale prices have been illegal per se since *Dr. Miles Medical Co. v. John D. Park & Sons Co.,* we have recognized that the scope of per se illegality should be narrow in the context of vertical restraints. In *Continental T.V. Inc. v. GTE Sylvania Inc.* we refused to extend per se illegality to vertical nonprice restraints, specifically to a manufacturer's termination of one dealer pursuant to an exclusive territory agreement with another. We noted that especially in the vertical restraint context "departure from the Rule-of-Reason standard must be based on demonstrable economic effect rather than . . . upon formalistic line drawing." We concluded that vertical nonprice restraints had not been shown to have such a "pernicious effect on competition" and to be so "lack[ing][in] . . . redeeming value" as to justify per se illegality. Rather, we found, they had real potential to stimulate inter-brand competition, "the primary concern of antitrust law":

> [N]ew manufacturers and manufacturers entering new markets can use the restrictions in order to induce competent and aggressive retailers to make the kind of investment of capital and labor that is often required in the distribution of products unknown to the consumer. Established manufacturers can use them to induce retailers to engage in promotional activities or to provide service and repair facilities necessary to the efficient marketing of their products. Service and repair are vital for many products. . . . The availability and quality of such services affect a manufacturer's goodwill and the competitiveness of his product. Because of market imperfections such as the so-called free-rider effect, these services might not be provided by retailers in a purely competitive situation, despite the fact that each retailer's benefit would be greater if all provided the services than if none did.

Moreover we observed that a rule of per se illegality for vertical nonprice restraints was not needed or effective to protect *intra*brand competition. First, so long as interbrand competition existed, that would provide a "significant check" on any attempt to exploit intrabrand market power. In fact, in order to meet that interbrand competition, a manufacturer's dominant incentive is to lower resale prices. Second, the per se illegality of vertical restraints would create a perverse incentive for manufacturers to integrate vertically into distribution, an outcome hardly conducive to fostering the creation and maintenance of small businesses.

* * * * *

Our approach to the question presented in the present case is guided by the premises of *GTE Sylvania:* that there is a presumption in favor of a Rule-of-Reason standard; that departure from that standard must be justified by demonstrable economic effect, such as the facilitation of cartelizing, rather than formalistic distinctions; that interbrand competition is the primary concern of the antitrust laws; and that rules in this area should

be formulated with a view toward protecting the doctrine of *GTE Sylvania.* These premises lead us to conclude that the line drawn by the Fifth Circuit is the most appropriate one.

There has been no showing here that an agreement between a manufacturer and a dealer to terminate a "price cutter," without a further agreement on the price or price levels to be charged by the remaining dealer, almost always tends to restrict competition and reduce output. Any assistance to cartelizing that such an agreement might provide cannot be distinguished from the sort of minimal assistance that might be provided by vertical nonprice agreements like the exclusive territory agreement in *GTE Sylvania,* and is insufficient to justify a per se rule. Cartels are neither easy to form nor easy to maintain. . . .

The District Court's rule on the scope of per se illegality for vertical restraints would threaten to dismantle the doctrine of *GTE Sylvania.* Any agreement between a manufacturer and a dealer to terminate another dealer who happens to have charged lower prices can be alleged to have been directed against the terminated dealer's "price cutting." In the vast majority of cases, it will be extremely difficult for the manufacturer to convince a jury that its motivation was to ensure adequate services, since price cutting and some measure of service cutting usually go hand in hand. Accordingly, a manufacturer that agrees to give one dealer an exclusive territory and terminates another dealer pursuant to that agreement, or even a manufacturer that agrees with one dealer to terminate another for failure to provide contractually obligated services, exposes itself to the highly plausible claim that its real motivation was to terminate a price cutter. Moreover, even vertical restraints that do not result in dealer termination, such as the initial granting of an exclusive territory or the requirement that certain services be provided, can be attacked as designed to allow existing dealers to charge higher prices. Manufacturers would be likely to forgo legitimate and competitively useful conduct rather than risk treble damages and perhaps even criminal penalties.

We cannot avoid this difficulty by invalidating as illegal per se only those agreements imposing vertical restraints that contain the word "price," or that affect the "prices" charged by dealers. Such formalism was explicitly rejected in *GTE Sylvania.* As the above discussion indicates, all vertical restraints, including the exclusive territory agreement held not to be per se illegal in *GTE Sylvania,* have the potential to allow dealers to increase "prices" and can be characterized as intended to achieve just that. In fact, vertical nonprice restraints only accomplish the benefits identified in *GTE Sylvania* because they reduce intrabrand price competition to the point where the dealer's profit margin permits provision of the desired services. As we described it in *Monsanto,* "The manufacturer often will want to ensure that its distributors earn sufficient profit to pay for programs such as hiring and training additional salesmen or demonstrating the technical features of the product, and will want to see that 'free-riders' do not interfere."

* * * * *

. . . Petitioner has provided no support for the proposition that vertical price agreements generally underlie agreements to terminate a price cutter. That proposition is simply incompatible with the conclusion of *GTE Sylvania* and *Monsanto* that manufacturers are often motivated by a legitimate desire to have dealers provide services, combined with the reality that price cutting is frequently made possible by "free riding" on the services provided by other dealers. The district court's per se rule would therefore discourage conduct recognized by *GTE Sylvania* and *Monsanto* as beneficial to consumers.

* * * * *

Affirmed.

AFTERWORD

In 1997 the U.S. Supreme Court ruled that vertical *maximum* price fixing is to be analyzed under the Rule of Reason.[22] Thus a supplier now may lawfully specify a price beyond which the buyer may not resell the product in question so long as the arrangement does not harm competition.

Questions

1. Summarize the essence of the *B.E.C.* holding.
2. What practical effects would you expect the *B.E.C.* decision to have on the behavior of (*a*) manufacturers and (*b*) discounters?
3. *a.* What is the *Colgate* doctrine?
   b. Is the *Colgate* doctrine a practical, workable standard of conduct? Explain.
4. Assume a manufacturer communicates to its distributors a "suggested retail price" for its product. Further assume the distributors individually decide to follow that suggestion.
   a. Does that conduct violate the law? Explain.
   b. Would it matter whether the product is heavily advertised? Explain.
5. In *Continental T.V., Inc., v. GTE Sylvania Inc.,* 433 U.S. 36 (1977), the Supreme Court took the position that interbrand,

rather than intrabrand, agreements must be the primary concern of antitrust law.
   a. Why does the Court take that view?
   b. Is the Court correct? Explain.
6. The *GTE* decision distinguished vertical "nonprice" restrictions (such as location clauses) from vertical price restrictions (resale price maintenance). Make the argument that the Court's distinction was not meaningful.
7. What is the "free-rider" problem that frequently concerns the courts in cases involving vertical territorial restraints?
8. Assume a manufacturer assigns an "area of primary responsibility" to a distributor. The distributor's sales are not confined to that area, but he or she must devote his or her best efforts to that area, and failure to do so may result in termination of the distributorship. Is that arrangement lawful? Explain.
9. In 1977 Michelin failed to renew its dealership agreement with the Donald B. Rice Tire Company of Frederick, Maryland. After seven years with Michelin, approximately 80 percent of Rice's business was derived from wholesaling the tires to smaller authorized and unauthorized dealers. Other authorized dealers complained to Michelin about Rice's wholesale business. In an effort to assume primary wholesaling responsibility, Michelin chose not to renew its relationship with Rice. Rice contended that the nonrenewal was a consequence of its refusal to comply with Michelin's customer and territorial restraints, and Rice filed an antitrust action on that basis. Michelin argued that it was a new entrant into a concentrated market, and as such, restraints on intrabrand competition were necessary to induce retailers to carry Michelin tires. However, the court found frequent shortages of Michelin tires. Michelin also argued that nonrenewal was "necessary to prevent free riding by retailers on the services provided by other dealers."

Rice had not advertised in a quantity commensurate with his sales volume. He sold to unauthorized dealers who were not bound to do any advertising and could thus reap benefits of advertising by authorized dealers. Michelin wanted to encourage point-of-sales services and the offering of specialized services but feared authorized dealers would not invest the necessary expenditures because of their fear of being underpriced by unauthorized dealers. Decide the case. See *Donald B. Rice Tire Company Inc. v. Michelin Corporation,* 483 F. Supp. 750 (D. Md. 1980), 638 F.2d 15 (4th Cir. 1981), cert. den. 454 U.S. 864 (1981).

Tying Arrangements

Principal legislation: Clayton Act, Section 3; Sherman Act, Sections 1 and 2; Federal Trade Commission Act, Section 5.

> Clayton Act, Section 3. That it shall be unlawful for any person engaged in commerce, in the course of such commerce, to lease or make a sale or contract for sale of goods . . . or other commodities . . . or fix a price charged therefore, or discount from or rebate upon, such price, on the condition, agreement, or understanding that the lessee or purchaser thereof shall not use or deal in the goods . . . or other commodities of a competitor or competitors of the lessor or seller, where the effect of such lease, sale, or contract for sale or such condition, agreement, or understanding may be to substantially lessen competition or tend to create a monopoly in any line of commerce.

Giants Battle   In a clash of commercial titans, four million merchants led by Wal-Mart, Sears, and others sued Visa and MasterCard, alleging that the bank card associations engaged in unlawful *tying arrangements*. Merchants wanting to accept the very popular Visa and MasterCard charge cards were also required to accept the associations' debit cards. The result, the plaintiffs said, was billions in losses because they were forced to pay higher fees for Visa and MasterCard debit cards rather than the lower fees of competing debit cards. The parties reached a $3 billion out-of-court settlement in 2003, the largest class-action settlement in antitrust history.[23]

Yale law professor George Priest harshly criticized the class-action threat as a "bludgeon" against the two giant defendants because damages in the case could have reached $100 billion and could have been trebled under the Sherman Act. Priest argued that the Wal-Mart class needed only a 1 percent chance of victory for the $3 billion settlement to make sense to the defendants.[24] On the other hand, removing the alleged tie between charge and debit cards should significantly lower debit card fees.

The Law   The typical tying arrangement permits a customer to buy or lease a desired product (the tying product) only if she or he also buys or leases another product (the tied product). The primary antitrust concerns are twofold: (1) A party who already enjoys market power over the tying product is able to extend that power into the tied product market; and (2) competitors in the tied product market are foreclosed from equal access to that market.

In brief, proof of the following conditions constitutes a per se violation:

1. The existence of separate products. (That is, two products are present rather than one product consisting of two or more components, or two entirely separate products that happen to be elements in a single transaction.)
2. A requirement that the purchase of one of the products (the tying product) is conditioned on the purchase of another product (the tied product).
3. Market power in the tying product.
4. Substantial impact on commerce in the tied product. (Some courts require a substantial *anticompetitive* effect in the tied product market.)

Tying claims are often evaluated on a Rule of Reason basis (weighing the pro- and anticompetitive impact of the arrangement) because of increasing recognition of the gains in efficiency, and thus in consumer value, that can accompany some tie-ins. As the following case illustrates, tying arrangements often are approved by the courts in franchising situations.

Queen City Pizza, Inc. v. Domino's Pizza, Inc.

124 F.3d 430 (3d Cir. 1997) [Cert. Denied *Baughans, Inc. v. Domino's Pizza,* 523 U.S. 1059 (1998)]

LEGAL BRIEFCASE

Circuit Judge Scirica

1. FACTS AND PROCEDURAL HISTORY

A

Domino's Pizza, Inc., is a fast-food service company that sells pizza through a national network of over 4,200 stores. Domino's Pizza owns and operates approximately 700 of these stores. Independent franchisees own and operate the remaining 3,500. Domino's Pizza, Inc., is the second largest pizza company in the United States, with revenues in excess of $1.8 billion per year.

Under the franchise agreement, the franchisee receives the right to sell pizza under the "Domino's" name and format. In return, Domino's Pizza receives franchise fees and royalties.

The essence of a successful nationwide fast-food chain is product uniformity and consistency. Uniformity benefits franchisees because customers can purchase pizza from any Domino's store and be certain the pizza will taste exactly like the Domino's pizza with which they are familiar. This means that individual franchisees need not build up their own goodwill. Uniformity also benefits the franchisor. It ensures the brand name will continue to attract and hold customers, increasing franchise fees and royalties.

For these reasons, section 12.2 of the Domino's Pizza standard franchise agreement requires that all pizza ingredients, beverages, and packaging materials used by a Domino's franchisee conform to the standards set by Domino's Pizza, Inc. Section 12.2 also provides that Domino's Pizza, Inc., "may in our sole discretion require that ingredients, supplies, and materials used in the preparation, packaging, and delivery of pizza be purchased exclusively from us or from approved suppliers or distributors." Domino's Pizza reserves the right "to impose reasonable limitations on the number of approved suppliers or distributors of any product." To enforce these rights, Domino's Pizza, Inc., retains the power to inspect franchisee stores and to test materials and ingredients. Section 12.2 is subject to a reasonableness clause providing that Domino's Pizza, Inc., must "exercise reasonable judgment with respect to all determinations to be made by us under the terms of this Agreement."

Under the standard franchise agreement, Domino's Pizza, Inc., sells approximately 90 percent of the $500 million in ingredients and supplies used by Domino's franchisees. These sales, worth some $450 million per year, form a significant part of Domino's Pizza, Inc.'s, profits. Franchisees purchase only 10 percent of their ingredients and supplies from outside sources. With the exception of fresh dough, Domino's Pizza, Inc., does not manufacture the products it sells to franchisees. Instead, it purchases these products from approved suppliers and then resells them to the franchisees at a markup.

B

The plaintiffs in this case are 11 Domino's franchisees and the International Franchise Advisory Council, Inc. ("IFAC"), a Michigan corporation consisting of approximately 40 percent of the Domino's franchisees in the United States, formed to promote their common interests.

* * * * *

[The lower court dismissed the plaintiffs' antitrust complaints. We turn now to the Appeals Court's analysis of the relevant product market—Ed.]

Plaintiffs suggest the "ingredients, supplies, materials, and distribution services used by and in the operation of Domino's pizza stores" constitutes a relevant market for antitrust purposes. We disagree.

As we have noted, the outer boundaries of a relevant market are determined by reasonable interchangeability of use.

Here, the dough, tomato sauce, and paper cups that meet Domino's Pizza, Inc., standards and are used by Domino's stores are interchangeable with dough, sauce, and cups available from other suppliers and used by other pizza companies. Indeed, it is the availability of interchangeable ingredients of comparable quality from other suppliers, at lower cost, that motivates this lawsuit. Thus, the relevant market, which is defined to include all reasonably interchangeable products, cannot be restricted solely to those products currently approved by Domino's Pizza, Inc., for use by Domino's franchisees. For that reason, we must reject plaintiffs' proposed relevant market.

Of course, Domino's-approved pizza ingredients and supplies differ from other available ingredients and supplies in one crucial manner. Only Domino's-approved products may be used by Domino's franchisees without violating section 12.2 of Domino's standard franchise agreement. Plaintiffs suggest that this difference is sufficient by itself to create a relevant market in approved products. We disagree. The test for a relevant market is not commodities reasonably interchangeable by a particular plaintiff, but "commodities reasonably interchangeable by consumers for the same purposes." A court making a relevant market determination looks not to the contractual restraints assumed by a particular plaintiff when determining whether a product is interchangeable, but to the uses to which the product is put by consumers in general. Thus, the relevant inquiry here is not whether a Domino's franchisee may reasonably use both approved or nonapproved products interchangeably without triggering liability for breach of contract, but whether pizza makers in general might use such products interchangeably. Clearly, they could. Were we to adopt plaintiffs' position that contractual restraints render otherwise identical products noninterchangeable for purposes of relevant market definition, any exclusive dealing arrangement, output or requirement contract, or franchise tying agreement would support a claim for violation of antitrust laws. Perhaps for this reason, no court has defined a relevant product market with reference to the particular contractual restraints of the plaintiff.

* * * * *

[The plaintiffs alleged that Domino's unlawfully engaged in monopolization, attempted monopolization, exclusive dealing, and predatory pricing. The Court rejected those claims. We turn now to the Court's analysis of the plaintiffs' claim that Domino's imposed unlawful tying arrangements on its franchisees—Ed.]

E

Plaintiffs allege Domino's Pizza, Inc., imposed an unlawful tying arrangement by requiring franchisees to buy ingredients and supplies from them as a condition of obtaining Domino's Pizza fresh dough, in violation of § 1 of the Sherman Act. "In a tying arrangement, the seller sells one item, known as the tying product, on the condition that the buyer also purchases another item, known as the tied product." "[T]he antitrust concern over tying arrangements is limited to those situations in which the seller can exploit its power in the market for the tying product to force buyers to purchase the tied product when they otherwise would not, thereby restraining competition in the tied product market." "Even if a seller has obtained a monopoly in the tying product legitimately (as by obtaining a patent), courts have seen the expansion of that power to other product markets as illegitimate and competition suppressing." "The first inquiry in any tying case is whether the defendant has sufficient market power over the tying product, which requires a finding that two separate product markets exist and a determination precisely what the tying and tied products markets are."

Here, plaintiffs allege Domino's Pizza, Inc., used its power in the purported market for Domino's-approved dough to force plaintiffs to buy unwanted ingredients and supplies from them. This claim fails because the proposed tying market—the market in Domino's-approved dough—is not a relevant

market for antitrust purposes. Domino's dough is reasonably interchangeable with other brands of pizza dough, and does not therefore constitute a relevant market of its own. All that distinguishes this dough from other brands is that a Domino's franchisee must use it or face a suit for breach of contract. As we have noted, the particular contractual restraints assumed by a plaintiff are not sufficient by themselves to render interchangeable commodities noninterchangeable for purposes of relevant market definition. If Domino's had market power in the overall market for pizza dough and forced plaintiffs to purchase other unwanted ingredients to obtain dough, plaintiffs might possess a valid tying claim. But where the defendant's "power" to "force" plaintiffs to purchase the alleged tying product stems not from the market, but from plaintiffs' contractual agreement to purchase the tying product, no claim will lie. For that reason, plaintiffs' claim was properly dismissed.

F

Plaintiffs allege Domino's Pizza, Inc., imposed an unlawful tie-in arrangement by requiring franchisees to buy ingredients and supplies "as a condition of their continued enjoyment of rights and services under their Standard Franchise Agreement," in violation of § 1 of the Sherman Act. This claim is meritless. Though plaintiffs complain of an illegal tie-in arrangement, they have failed to point to any particular tying product or service over which Domino's Pizza, Inc., has market power. Domino's Pizza's control over plaintiffs' "continued enjoyment of rights and services under their Standard Franchise Agreement" is not a "market." Rather, it is a function of Domino's contractual powers under the franchise agreement to terminate the participation of franchisees in the franchise system if they violate the agreement. Because plaintiffs failed to plead any relevant tying market, the claim was properly dismissed.

Affirmed.

AFTERWORD

The plaintiffs in the *Queen City* case filed for a rehearing, which was denied. Circuit Judge Becker dissented from that decision:

[The majority] has endorsed the questionable theory that the kind of tying arrangements involved here "are an essential and important aspect of the franchise form of business organization." But these theories are also flawed.

I believe that the approach endorsed by the majority might have been acceptable two decades ago when franchising was in its nascent, or at least its growing, stage. But now the food franchisors are leviathans, and I am underwhelmed by the suggestion that they may be permitted with impunity to perpetuate the type of arrangements pled in the complaint. These arrangements are clearly quite onerous to the average franchisee, a relatively small businessperson whose sunk costs in the franchise represent all or most of his or her assets and who lacks the considerable resources necessary to switch or defranchise. Moreover, the amount of commerce that the franchisors are foreclosing in the tied product market—for the pizza sauce, flour, and other supplies (for which nonfranchisor–dominated suppliers, be they individual firms or a franchise cooperative, could easily meet quality control specifications) is enormous.[25] [For an explanation of tying law in *Queen City* and similar cases, see **http://www.gcwf.com/articles/interest/interest_21.html**]

Questions

1. Describe the product market as the *Queen City* court saw it.

2. Explain the potential harm of tying arrangements.

3. Explain why the majority ruled against the plaintiffs' tying claims.

4. Some recent federal court decisions differ with the analysis in *Queen City Pizza*. Do you think *Queen City* is well reasoned? Explain.

5. Judge Scirica in *Queen City* wrote, "Courts and legal commentators have long recognized that franchise tying contracts are an essential and important aspect of the franchise form of business organization because they . . . prevent franchisees from free-riding." Explain what he meant about free riding.[26]

6. When *Late Night with David Letterman* was an NBC show, the network, for some time, required those wanting to advertise on *Late Night* to also buy spots on the *Tonight Show with Johnny Carson.*

   a. Does that packaging constitute a tying arrangement?

   b. Was it lawful? Explain.

7. Chrysler included the price of a sound system in the base price of its cars. Chrysler's share of the auto market was 10 to 12 percent. Chrysler did not reveal the "subprice" for the sound systems. Independent audio dealers objected on antitrust grounds. Explain their claim. Decide. See *Town Sound and Custom Tops, Inc. v. Chrysler Motor Corp.* 959 F.2d 468 (3d Cir. 1992); cert. den., 113 S.Ct. 196 (1992).

Exclusive Dealing and Requirements Contracts

Principal legislation: Clayton Act, Section 3; Sherman Act, Section 1.

The Sharper Image catalog and retail chain specializes in upscale products sold only by the Sharper Image. In general, a retailer has every right to negotiate with its suppliers to receive those *exclusive deals*. By its nature, however, an exclusive deal cuts competitors out of a source of supply or a market for sale. Thus antitrust issues may emerge. An *exclusive dealing contract* is an agreement in which a buyer commits itself to deal only with a specific seller, thereby cutting competing sellers out of that share of the market. A *requirements contract* is one in which a seller agrees to supply all of a buyer's needs, or a buyer agrees to purchase all of a seller's output, or both. Exclusive dealing and requirements contracts, as a matter of law, are much like the refusal to deal situations previously discussed.

Pearl Jam and the Ticket Business   Exclusive dealing contracts often benefit business and consumers by ensuring a stable supply, discouraging free riders, and generally enhancing efficiency. On the other hand, those deals are sometimes anticompetitive, as the rock group Pearl Jam alleged in its famous mid-1990s collision with Ticketmaster. Pearl Jam and others pursued antitrust claims against Ticketmaster, claiming that the ticketing giant's market dominance and exclusive dealing arrangements allowed it to charge unfairly high service fees. Neither Congress nor the Justice Department nor the courts were supportive of Ticketmaster's critics because, among other things, new firms were entering the market to compete with Ticketmaster. The battle continued,

> Pearl Jam pursued antitrust claims against Ticketmaster.

however, with the jam band String Cheese Incident filing exclusive dealing and collusion claims against Ticketmaster in 2003. String Cheese said that Ticketmaster was blocking the band's right to sell tickets to its own shows through its own ticketing agency, SCI Ticketing. Ticketmaster said that SCI was simply trying to free-ride on Ticketmaster's vast infrastructure. Whatever the truth, the two settled their dispute out of court in 2004 with SCI (now Baseline Ticketing) then able to sell a satisfactory number of tickets to its own shows.

Ticketmaster is a remarkable and still growing success as it moves aggressively into the international market. Between 1990 and 2002 its sales increased from 29 to 95 million tickets, and its average revenue per ticket moved from $1.50 in 1990 to $6.11 in 2001[27]—not a bad performance for a company that began with a group of Phoenix, Arizona, college students who understood how to use technology to bring efficiency to the ticket sales business. But did that business (now a part of Barry Diller's InterActive conglomerate) abuse buyers to gain its dominance? Service fees for the $32.50 tickets to a 2003 String Cheese show at Red Rocks in Colorado, for example, were $4 through the band's SCI service but were $10.10 through Ticketmaster.[28] Some estimates put the explosion in Ticketmaster fees at more than 300 percent in a decade.[29] In its lawsuit, SCI claimed that Ticketmaster controlled 60 percent of the ticketing market. SCI further claimed that Ticketmaster controlled exclusive ticket distribution rights for 89 percent of the top 50 U.S. arenas, 88 percent of the top amphitheaters, and 70 percent of the top theaters[30]—sometimes secured, experts allege, by paybacks to the arenas. Are those exclusive deals a violation of antitrust laws?

> Ticketmaster is basically home free to this point.

As a matter of law, Ticketmaster is basically home free to this point. Ticket buyers may feel aggrieved, but they are not Ticketmaster's direct clients, and according to the court rulings to date the promoters and performance sites, rather than the public, would need to sue to pursue exclusive dealing and other antitrust complaints. They are unlikely to do so because they seem to be pleased with Ticketmaster's service. In any case, live performances are not necessary to personal survival. If fans continue to pay arguably exorbitant fees, the market has spoken. Should the law intervene when customers are willing to freely spend their money?

Price Discrimination

Principal legislation: Clayton Act, Section 2, as amended by the Robinson–Patman Act. [For the statutory language, see **http://assembler.law.cornell.edu/uscode/15/13.html**]

Price discrimination involves selling substantially identical goods (not services) at reasonably contemporaneous times to different purchasers at different prices, where the effect may substantially lessen competition or tend to create a monopoly. A seller may resist a Robinson–Patman charge by establishing one of the following defenses: (1) The price differential is attributable to cost savings. (In practice, the cost savings defense has been difficult to establish.) (2) The price differential is attributable to a good faith effort to meet the equally low price of a competitor. (3) Certain transactions are exempt from the act. Of special note is a price change made in response to a changing market. Thus prices might lawfully be altered for seasonal goods or perishables.

Discounts/Price Discrimination   Upon graduation from college, suppose you decide to open a neighborhood video rental store in your hometown. Business goes well for a time, but then Blockbuster opens a superstore nearby and rents its videos at prices significantly below yours. Blockbuster is able to secure a pricing advantage from the movie studios, so you are out of business.

> A coalition of independent video stores have sued Blockbuster.

In recent years, a coalition of independent video stores have sued Blockbuster claiming that the rental giant and the movie studios have conspired to drive the small stores out of business. Thus far, however, that litigation has failed.[31] The video cases are among a number in recent years pitting independent operators (such as neighborhood bookstores and local pharmacies) against chains (such as Barnes & Noble and big hospitals) where the independents claim that suppliers charge their giant rivals lower prices than those charged to the small stores. These complaints reflect the philosophical battle over the role of antitrust law in a rapidly changing global market. Should we use antitrust to protect small businesses, thus protecting small towns and a historic way of life in America? Or should we accept the dictates of the market, where the efficiency of giants like Wal-Mart brings low prices and high quality to all? [For a Web site devoted to "How to Stop Wal-Mart (and Other Superstores)," see **http://www.lawmall.com/wal-mart/**]

Free market advocates condemn price discrimination law as an attack on common, consumer-friendly pricing practices that often result in reduced prices. Why, the critics ask, would we assault those who engage in vigorous price competition? An American Bar Association panel recently suggested that the Federal Trade Commission should take the lead in a study to determine whether Congress should repeal Robinson–Patman.[32] In fact, the federal government seldom takes enforcement action under Robinson–Patman. Private plaintiffs, on the other hand, do make aggressive use of the act. As the following case illustrates, Robinson–Patman remains a primary legal weapon for the "little guys," relatively speaking, in their struggle against the "giants."

LEGAL BRIEFCASE

The Intimate Bookshop v. Barnes & Noble   2003 U.S.
District LEXIS 17231 (S.D. N.Y.)

District Judge Pauley

Defendants Barnes & Noble, Borders Group, and Walden move for summary judgment on plaintiff The Intimate Bookshop, Inc's, price discrimination claims. . . .

BACKGROUND

* * * * *

To summarize, Intimate was an independent bookseller that sold books through retail stores located in the mid-Atlantic

United States from 1959 until March 31, 1999. Defendants are retailers that sell books and other goods in large stores across the United States and through Internet Web sites. Defendant Borders Group is a holding company that operates bookstores through its subsidiaries, defendants Borders and Walden. Defendant Barnes & Noble operates bookstores and has an interest in defendant B&N.com, an Internet bookseller. Intimate alleges that defendants violated Sections 2(a) and 2(f) of the act through secondary-line price discrimination because they knowingly induced and/or received illegal lower, discriminatory prices on the publishers' books, and that such discriminatory prices injured competition. . . .

Price discrimination is classified into three categories under the act: (1) primary-line price discrimination, which "occurs when a seller's price discrimination harms competition with the seller's competitors;" (2) secondary-line price discrimination, which "occurs when a seller's discrimination impacts competition among the seller's customers; i.e., the favored purchasers and disfavored purchasers;" and (3) tertiary-line price discrimination, which "occurs when the seller's price discrimination harms competition between customers of the favored and disfavored purchasers, even though the favored and disfavored purchasers do not compete directly against another." *George Haug Co. v. Rolls Royce Motor Cars Inc.*, 148 F.3d 136, 141 n.2 (2d Cir. 1988)

DISCUSSION
Sections 2(a) and 2(f) of the Act

In contrast to other antitrust laws, the Robinson–Patman Act was specifically enacted to protect small businesses from discriminatory pricing by manufacturers in favor of large chain stores. . . .

Section 2(a) of the Robinson–Patman Act makes it unlawful for anyone engaged in commerce

to discriminate in price between different purchasers of commodities of like grade and quality, where . . . the effect of such discrimination may be to substantially lessen competition . . . with any person who either grants or knowingly receives the benefits of such discrimination, or with customers of either of them.

To state a claim for secondary-line price discrimination under Section 2(a), a plaintiff must show that (i) the seller conducted sales in interstate commerce; (ii) the seller discriminated in price between two buyers; (iii) the product sold to competing buyers was of the same grade and quality; and (iv) the price discrimination had an unlawful effect on competition.

Additionally, even if Intimate establishes a prima facie case of unlawful price discrimination, defendants are not liable under Sections 2(f) or 2(a) of the act if the lower, discriminatory prices they received are protected by one of the seller's affir-

mative defenses to price discrimination. Indeed, Sections 2(a) and 2(b) of the act afford sellers various defenses based on cost justifications and competitive conditions.

Robinson–Patman Act Relief

Proof of a violation itself does not create a compensable private injury under the act. A plaintiff is not entitled to "automatic damages" on a successful Section 2(a) or 2(f) price discrimination claim. Instead, a plaintiff must make some showing of "actual injury attributable to something the antitrust laws were designed to prevent." . . .

In that vein, though a plaintiff need not enumerate all possible sources of its loss, it must make some showing that the injury to its business was not caused by factors unrelated to the defendant's price discrimination. . . .

1. Survey Evidence

Intimate attempts to sustain its burden of showing actual injury and causation through a survey conducted by Dr. Bruce Kardon that purports to show that Intimate lost customers to defendants. . . . In that survey, former members of Intimate's book club were contacted and asked questions about where they purchased books and the reasons for choosing that retailer. Dr. Kardon acknowledged at his deposition, however, that his survey could not be used to show any dollar value of Intimate's lost sales to any defendant. Indeed, the survey does not even question respondents whether they stopped purchasing books from Intimate and switched to another retailer. Further, the survey did not determine the year, the geographical market, or the extent to which survey respondents shopped at a defendant's store.

Finally, the survey does not provide an adequate basis to discern whether, and the extent to which, the defendants' lawful, as opposed to unlawful, competitive conduct caused injury to Intimate.

Accordingly, this Court finds that Dr. Kardon's survey is insufficient to establish a causal link between Intimate's injuries and the defendants' allegedly unlawful conduct.

2. Expert Reports

Second, Intimate cannot meet the causation requirement through any of its other experts' reports or testimony. As noted, Intimate submitted five expert reports in addition to the Kardon Report that purportedly opine on its damages claim as well as its claim that defendants violated the act. Each of Intimate's experts admitted at their deposition, however, that (i) they could not establish any causal link between Intimate's lost sales and profits and defendants' alleged receipt of unlawful discounts; and (ii) their damages calculations and opinions are based merely on an assumption that the defendants' alleged violations of the act were the sole cause of Intimate's lost sales and profits. . . .

3. Disaggregation

Third, Intimate has provided no evidence, in any form, that defendants' alleged violation of the act, as opposed to other intervening market factors, was a material cause of its [lost] sales and profits. In fact, Wallace Kuralt, one of Intimate's owners, acknowledged at his deposition that some of Intimate's business loss may be attributable to factors other than the defendants' discriminatory activity, including (i) competition with nonparties Books-a-Million and Media Play; (ii) adverse business decisions; (iii) undercapitalization; (iv) a fire at plaintiff's flagship Chapel Hill, North Carolina, location; (v) competition with franchise bookselling chains and other independent bookstores; (vi) competition with nonparty mass merchants, such as Wal-Mart and Kmart and discount warehouses, such as Price Club, Costco, and Sam's Club; and (vii) competition with specialty book retailers such as Williams Sonoma, Office Max, Staples, and Home Depot.

*   *   *   *   *

Intimate's survey and damages models are impermissibly fraught with assumptions and speculation, which unquestionably fail to show that the alleged discriminatory prices the defendants received caused Intimate actual injury.

*   *   *   *   *

[Summary judgment dismissing the Robinson–Patman claims is granted.]

Questions

1. Why did Intimate Bookshop lose this case?
2. Explain why this case involves secondary-line price discrimination.
3. In what sense does the Robinson–Patman Act arguably reduce efficiency, thus harming consumer welfare?
4. Texaco sold gasoline at its retail tank wagon prices to Hasbrouck, an independent Texaco retailer, but granted discounts to distributors Gull and Dompier. Dompier also sold at the retail level. Gull and Dompier both delivered their gas directly to retailers and did not maintain substantial storage facilities. During the period in question, sales at the stations supplied by the two distributors grew dramatically, while Hasbrouck's sales declined. Hasbrouck filed suit against Texaco, claiming that the distributor discount constituted a Robinson–Patman violation. Texaco defended, saying the discount reflected the services the distributors performed for Texaco, and that the arrangement did not harm competition. Decide. Explain. See *Texaco v. Ricky Hasbrouck*, 496 U.S. 543 (1990).
5. Utah Pie produced frozen pies in its Salt Lake City plant. Utah's competitors, Carnation, Pet, and Continental, sometimes sold pies in Salt Lake City at prices beneath those charged in other markets. Indeed, Continental's prices in Salt Lake City were beneath its direct costs plus overhead. Pet sold to Safeway using Safeway's private label at a price lower than that at which the same pies were sold under the Pet label. Pet employed an industrial spy to infiltrate Utah Pie and gather information. Utah Pie claimed that Carnation, Pet, and Continental were in violation of Robinson–Patman. Decide. Explain. See *Utah Pie Co. v. Continental Baking Co.*, 386 U.S. 685 (1967).

Predatory Pricing

Can a giant legally reduce its prices below operating costs until a competing discounter drops out of the market and then raise those prices to supracompetitive levels? The U.S. Justice Department claimed that American Airlines did just that in attempting to monopolize air travel at the Dallas–Fort Worth Airport from 1995 to 1997. Justice argued that American Airlines engaged in what is known as *predatory pricing* by lowering its prices to drive out seven discount carriers in the expectation that it could then recover its losses by charging monopoly prices. A federal court of appeals, however, ruled for American Airlines, holding that the government was unable to prove that American had priced its flights below cost (as measured by some appropriate formulation, such as average variable cost).[33] Thus the government had failed to satisfy the standard two-part test for establishing predatory pricing:

- Pricing below cost.
- A "dangerous probability" of recouping the losses suffered from the below-cost pricing.

The *American Airlines* decision could be seen as a great victory for consumers in that it supports the right to cut prices as low as possible. But consider *BusinessWeek's* description of American's pricing practices:

> . . . Between Dallas and Kansas City, for instance, American's average one-way ticket was $108 before low-cost start-up Vanguard Airlines Inc. entered the market in early 1995. That prompted American to cut fares to $80 and almost double the number of daily flights to 14. When Vanguard gave up in December 1995, American jacked up prices to $147 and scaled back the number of flights. Justice lawyers even had memos from American execs plotting the upstart's demise.[34]

Court decisions to date have been highly skeptical of the predatory pricing theory,[35] but corporate critics remain concerned about big firms and the tactics they use in competing with their smaller rivals.

Internet Exercise

Using the Federal Trade Commission's "Frequently Asked Questions" page [**http://www.ftc.gov/bc/ compguide/question.htm**], answer these questions:

1. Shopping for a stereo loudspeaker made by Sound Corporation, I couldn't find a dealer who would sell it for less than the manufacturer's suggested retail price. Isn't that price fixing?

2. I own a retail clothing store and the Brand Company refuses to sell me any of its line of clothes. These clothes are very popular in my area, so this policy is hurting my business. Isn't it illegal for Brand to refuse to sell to me?

3. I operate two stores that sell recorded music. My business is being ruined by giant discount store chains that sell their products for less than my wholesale cost. I thought there were laws against price discrimination, but I can't afford the legal fees to fight the big corporations. Can you help?

Chapter Questions

1. After reading this chapter, what is your judgment about the antitrust system?
   a. Does it work? Explain.
   b. How might it be altered?
   c. Could we place more reliance on the market? Explain.
   d. Do the statutes and case law, as a body, seem to form a rational package? Explain.

2. Scholar and jurist Richard Posner argues,

   > T]he protection of small business whatever its intrinsic merit cannot be attained within the framework of antitrust principles and procedures. The small businessman is, in general, helped rather than hurt by monopoly, so unless the antitrust laws are stood completely on their head they are an inapt vehicle (compared, say, to tax preferences) for assisting small business.[36]

   a. Is antitrust law an inappropriate vehicle for protecting small business? Explain.
   b. Should we protect small business? Explain.

    c. How does the presence of monopolies benefit small business?

    d. If it is not the proper vehicle for protecting small business, what role should antitrust law serve? For example, should social considerations (such as the maintenance of full employment and the dispersal of political power) assume greater importance? Or should antitrust policy hew as closely as possible to economic goals? Explain.

3. Subway sandwich shops required all franchisees to employ a computerized point-of-sale (POS) system. The only approved system was provided by an unrelated company, RBS. Vendors of a competing POS system sued Subway's parent, Doctor's Associates, alleging, among other things, an unlawful tying arrangement.

    a. Describe the alleged tie.

    b. Defend Doctor's Associates (Subway).

    c. Explain what the plaintiffs would need to demonstrate in order to prevail. See *Subsolutions, Inc. v. Doctor's Associates, Inc.,* 62 F. Supp. 2d 616 (D. Conn. 1999).

4. Explain how the apparently competitive practice of guaranteeing to match the prices of any competitor may actually result in price discrimination. See Aaron S. Edlin, "Do Guaranteed-Low-Price Policies Guarantee High Prices, and Can Antitrust Rise to the Challenge?" *Harvard Law Review* 111, no. 2 (December 1997), p. 529.

5. Could Whirlpool, the appliance manufacturer, lawfully refuse to deal with any purchaser that sells the products of a competitor such as General Electric? Explain.

6. Does a businessperson create antitrust problems by joining industry trade associations, promoting common safety standards for the industry, and contributing to industry advertising campaigns such as "take the family to the movies"? Explain. See John H. Shenefield and Irwin M. Stelzer, *The Antitrust Laws—A Primer,* 2nd ed. (Washington, D.C.: The AEI Press, 1996), p. 107.

7. Tanaka played soccer at the University of Southern California, a member of the PAC 10 Conference. She became unhappy, asked if she could transfer, and was told that she could. She decided to go to another PAC 10 school, UCLA. USC, unhappy with that choice, invoked an NCAA rule limiting transfers within a conference. The rule required her to sit out one year and to lose one year of eligibility. She sued USC and the NCAA on restraint of trade grounds.

    a. Explain her claim.

    b. Decide the case. Explain your decision. See *Tanaka v. University of Southern California,* 252 F.3d 1059 (9th Cir. 2001).

8. Assume two fertilizer dealerships, Grow Quick and Fertile Fields, hold 70 percent and 30 percent, respectively, of the fertilizer business in the farm community of What Cheer, Iowa. Assume the owner of Fertile Fields learns via inquiry, hearsay, and the like of Grow Quick's price quotes. Then, each growing season the Fertile Fields owner sets her prices exactly equal to those of her competitor. Is that practice unlawful? Explain.

9. Given identical competing products, why is identical pricing virtually inevitable—at least over the long run?

10. Assume firms A, B, C, D, and E are charged with price fixing under Sherman 1 because they have a program of exchanging pricing information among themselves.

   a. What element of Robinson–Patman might be used as a defense in that Sherman 1 action?

   b. Would the court find that defense persuasive? Explain.

11. Some antitrust experts argue that a firm possessing market power should be challenged by the government with the goal of eradicating the power as quickly as possible. Others maintain that the government should be patient with short-term market power. Explain those two points of view.

12. Adidas contracts with NCAA schools and their coaches to promote its products. An NCAA rule limits the amount of advertising that may appear on uniforms and equipment. Adidas complained that those restrictions on promotional rights "artificially limit the price and quality options available to apparel manufacturers as consumers of promotional space, force manufacturers to pay additional amounts for billboard space or other advertising, decrease the selection of apparel offered to the end consumer, increase the price of the apparel for end consumers, and financially benefit the NCAA." Adidas sued the NCAA on antitrust grounds.

   a. What antitrust violations were cited by Adidas?

   b. Decide the case. Explain. See *Adidas v. NCAA,* 64 F. Supp. 2d 1097 (1999).

13. A board certified anesthesiologist was denied admission to the Jefferson Parish Hospital staff because the hospital had an exclusive services contract with a firm of anesthesiologists. The contract required all surgery patients at the hospital to use that firm for their anesthesiology work. Seventy percent of the patients in the parish were served by hospitals other than Jefferson. The anesthesiologist who was denied admission sued the hospital, claiming the contract was unlawful.

   a. What antitrust violation was raised by the plaintiff?

   b. Decide. Explain. See *Jefferson Parish Hospital District No. 2 v. Hyde,* 466 U.S. 2 (1984).

14. In 1990 the American Institute of Certified Public Accountants agreed to enforce a change in its ethics rules that allows its members to accept contingent fees and commissions from nonaudit clients. The agreement was the result of a consent order between the AICPA and the Federal Trade Commission. Likewise, in 1990 the American Institute of Architects signed a consent order with the Justice Department that forbids the institute from adopting policies that would restrain architects from bidding competitively for jobs, offering discounts, or doing work without compensation.

   a. What antitrust violation was the government seeking to stem in both of these cases?

   b. What defenses are offered by the professions for their policies?

15. Starter Sportswear had a license to manufacture and sell satin professional team jackets marketed as "authentic" because they were styled in the manner of jackets actually worn by the members of the various teams. A Starter policy statement provided that it would sell only to retailers that carry a representative amount of Starter's full

line of jackets. Starter also had a minimum order policy specifying that it wouldn't deal with retailers who sought quantities beneath that minimum order. Trans Sport, a retailer, began selling Starter jackets to other retailers who did not meet Starter's requirements. At that point, Starter declined to deal further with Trans Sport. Trans Sport then sued Starter.

a. List Trans Sport's claims against Starter.

b. Resolve those claims, raising all the relevant issues. See *Trans Sport, Inc. v. Starter Sportswear, Inc.,* 964 F. 2d 186 (2d Cir. 1992).

Notes

1. Sundeep Malladi, "U. Wisconsin Students Don't See Alcohol as a Financial Drain," *University Wire,* September 7, 2004.
2. April Barker, "Antitrust Case Targets Taverns for Cutting Drink Specials," *Wisconsin Law Journal,* September 15, 2004.
3. Barker, "Antitrust Case Targets Taverns."
4. Barker, "Antitrust Case Targets Taverns."
5. "Combustible Brew," *The Wall Street Journal,* April 9, 2004, p. W13.
6. John R. Wilke, "Microsoft Finds New Antitrust Chief Won't Blink," *The Wall Street Journal,* August 9, 2001, p. A3.
7. Steven Thomas, "First President of New Century Brings Dramatic Change," *Waterloo/Cedar Falls Courier,* January 21, 2001, p. F1.
8. *Standard Oil Co. of New Jersey v. United States,* 221 U.S. 1 (1911).
9. This analysis is drawn from William Kovacic, "The Identification and Proof of Horizontal Agreements under the Antitrust Laws," *Antitrust Bulletin* 38, no. 1 (Spring 1993), p. 5.
10. For one account of the scandal, see Monica Langley and Theo Francis, "Insurers Reel from Spitzer's Strike," *The Wall Street Journal,* October 18, 2004, p. A1.
11. Bill Myers, "$100 Million Accord in Price-Fix Lawsuit," *Chicago Daily Law Bulletin,* July 29, 2004.
12. *Washington Post,* "Vitamin Giants to Settle Antitrust Suit," *Waterloo/Cedar Falls Courier,* September 8, 1999, p. A9.
13. Jeff Chorney, "Amnesty International: S.F. Antitrust Prosecutors Are Breaking Cartels with Immunity," *The Recorder,* September 27, 2004, p. 1.
14. Warren St. John, "Behind the Catwalk, Suspicion and Suits," *The New York Times,* April 18, 2004, Sec. 9, p. 1.
15. The analysis in this paragraph relies considerably on Donald M. Falk, "Antitrust and Refusals to Deal after *Nynex v. Discon,*" *Practical Lawyer* 46, no. 3 (2000), p. 25.
16. *United States v. Visa and MasterCard,* 344 F.3d 229 (2d. Cir. 2003); cert. den. *Visa v. United States,* 2004 U.S. LEXIS 5548.
17. Martin Peers and Evan Ramstad, "Prices of CDs Likely to Drop, Thanks to FTC," *The Wall Street Journal,* May 11, 2000, p. B1.
18. "Loaded Down," *Riverside Press Enterprise,* July 11, 2004, p. E07.
19. *United States v. Colgate & Co.,* 250 U.S. 300 (1919).
20. Harold Brown, "The Direction for Antitrust Law," *New York Law Journal,* November 30, 1994, p. 3.

21. *Continental T.V., Inc. v. GTE Sylvania, Inc.,* 433 U.S. 36 (1977).

22. *State Oil Co. v. Khan,* 522 U.S. 3 (1997).

23. *Wal-Mart v. Visa and MasterCard,* 396 F.3d 96 (2005).

24. George Priest, "'Class Warfare'—A Commentary by Prof. George L. Priest" [**http://www.law.yale.edu/outside/html/Public_Affairs/375/yls._article.htm**].

25. *Queen City Pizza, Inc. v. Domino's Pizza, Inc.,* 129 F.3d 724 (3d Cir. 1997).

26. *Queen City Pizza, Inc. v. Domino's Pizza, Inc.,* 124 F.3d 430, 440 (3d Cir. 1997).

27. Steve Maich, "The Keeper of the Gate," *Financial Post,* September 26, 2003, p. FP08.

28. CBS Marketplace, "Ticketmaster Facts and Figures," March 30, 2004 [**http://www.cbc.ca/consumers/market/files/services/concertix/facts.html**].

29. Maich, "The Keeper of the Gate."

30. Steve Knopper, "Incident Fight Ticketmaster," *RollingStone.com* [**http://www.rollingstone.com/news/story/_id/5936870**].

31. *Cleveland v. Viacom,* 2003 U.S. App. LEXIS 17717 (5th Cir.); cert. den. *Cleveland v. Viacom,* 540 U.S. 1219 (2004).

32. Patricia Manson, "Antitrust Enforcement Wins Praise from ABA Panel," *Chicago Daily Law Bulletin,* February 7, 2005, p. 1.

33. *United States v. AMR Corp,* 335 F.3d 1109 (10th Cir. 2003).

34. Dan Carney, "Predatory Pricing: Cleared for Takeoff," *BusinessWeek,* May 14, 2001, p. 50.

35. See the leading decision, *Brooke Group v. Brown & Williamson,* 113 S. Ct. 2578 (1993).

36. Richard Posner, *Antitrust Law* (Chicago: University of Chicago Press, 1976), p. 4.

Antitrust Law— Monopolies and Mergers

Introduction—Microsoft and Monopoly

Is Microsoft an outsized, predatory law breaker, an amazing force for technological progress, or both? The U.S. Justice Department, 18 states, and the District of Columbia went to trial against Microsoft in 1998, claiming not that the software giant was too big, but that it had violated various antitrust laws in gaining and maintaining its market dominance. An epic legal struggle followed with major elements of the American justice system challenging the world's richest man, Bill Gates.

> An epic legal struggle followed with major elements of the American justice system challenging the world's richest man, Bill Gates.

A federal district court in 2000 and later a federal court of appeals ruled that Microsoft had violated federal antitrust laws by maintaining its 95 percent share of the Intel-compatible PC operating systems market through anticompetitive means (basically using its monopoly power to coerce customers to buy other products such as its browser, Internet Explorer).[1] The district court judge ordered Microsoft split into two companies as a remedy for its antitrust wrongs, but the court of appeals threw out that order. Thereafter, the case was settled out of court with Microsoft agreeing, among other things, to not retaliate unfairly against other software and computer makers and to disclose some software code. Judge Colleen Kollar-Kotelly reviewed the settlement and supported measures designed to stop Microsoft's exclusionary practices rather than much harsher proposed remedies that included forcing Microsoft to reveal its critical source code.

The settlement was somewhat of a victory for Microsoft, and evidence is emerging that even the settlement's comparatively gentle terms are not being scrupulously followed.[2] But the settlement also might be regarded as a victory for common sense in allowing Microsoft to go forward with its remarkable work. The decision places considerable faith in the market, as it probably should in America; but the case also represents a powerful affirmation of the government's authority to attack monopoly behavior no matter how prominent the wrongdoer.

As it turns out, the federal antitrust charges were only the beginning of Microsoft's battles. Settlements with Novell, Sun Microsystems, AOL, and others had cost Microsoft billions as of 2004. The European Union turned up the heat on Microsoft in 2004 when it found the company guilty of abusing its "near monopoly" by, among other behaviors, trying to "shut competitors out of the market."[3] The European Union Court later denied a Microsoft appeal and, among other things, ordered the company to offer versions of Windows without Windows Media Player built in. That order was designed to allow rival audio and video makers to compete more fairly with Microsoft. At this writing, Microsoft continues to appeal the various EU decisions. Other nations are contemplating further legal action against Microsoft, as are some cities and states in the United States. Four days after receiving $500 million to settle its original antitrust claims against Microsoft, Novell filed another antitrust claim arguing that Microsoft unlawfully crushed Novell's WordPerfect word processing program. This remarkable odyssey, not yet over, is a powerful testament to our hunger for fairness and justice. But it also offers a less edifying message, as CNBC journalist Alan Murray explained in *The Wall Street Journal:*

> The Microsoft saga serves as a reminder of an important truth: Capitalists, for the most part, don't care much for capitalism. Their goal is to make money. And if they can do it without messy competition, so much the better. As long as it keeps its monopoly, Microsoft can afford to share the wealth with its onetime rivals. For Microsoft, those fines and payments add up to less than a year's profit from the operating system. For the others, it's easier to take Microsoft's money than fight.[4]

Power The Microsoft battle is about whether a giant bullied its rivals, thus harming competition; but it is also about the very nature of capitalism—that is, the role of the market and government in American life. Thus the case obliges Americans to think about what we want America to be and what role the law should play in securing that ideal. Antitrust law is remote from our daily lives, but by considering the Microsoft case and other less publicized decisions, we can learn the rudiments of that law while thinking carefully about how much faith we want to place in the free market. The article that follows condemns the increasing concentration of wealth and power in the hands of a small number of corporate giants and wealthy individuals. [For links to many antitrust Web sites, see **http://www.antitrustinstitute.org/links.cfm**]

READING
Perspective on Antitrust: Keep an Eye on the Monopolists

Jeff Gates

* * * * *

It should come as no surprise in these market-myopic times that the (Microsoft) case turned on the narrow issue of competition. Yet that confuses the means with the end. The trustbusters of the 1890s had no idea how markets would be dominated a century later. That wasn't the issue. The target was not the monopoly but the monopolists—the economic royalists with their kingly prerogatives—and the keen dangers they pose to democracy. That's why they urged that monopolies be broken up and their forbidden fruits dispersed.

Jefferson and Madison were similarly insistent. They warned about monarchical tendencies in the marketplace and the impossibility of maintaining a robust democracy along side an economic oligarchy. Yet that's what today's market-obsessed perspective has wrought. The financial wealth of the top 1 percent of Americans now exceeds the combined net worth of the bottom 95 percent, according to New York University economist Edward Wolff. [Bill] Gates's wealth alone exceeds the net worth of the bottom 45 percent. The personal assets of Microsoft co-founders Paul Allen and Gates plus Berkshire Hathaway's Warren Buffet exceed the combined gross domestic products of the world's 41 poorest countries, with their 550 million citizens. So much for being a beacon of hope for democracy.

* * * * *

It's easy to pick on Gates. But he's just the most visible tip of this nation's plutocratic iceberg. The wealth of the *Forbes* 400 richest Americans grew by an average $940 million each over the past two years (topping a combined $1 trillion). That's while the modest net worth of the bottom 40 percent shrank by 80 percent between 1983 and 1995. For the well-to-do, that's an average increase in wealth of $1.3 million per day. Eighty-six percent of stock market gains between 1989 and 1997 were harvested by the top 10 percent of households, while fully 42 percent flowed to the top-most 1 percent.

Over the past three years, we've seen $3.7 trillion in mergers in the United States alone, topped by this week's $163.4 billion blending of America Online and Time Warner. Monday saw Time Warner Vice Chairman Ted Turner's net worth jump by $2.53 billion. That's more than the entire value of Turner Broadcasting System prior to its 1996 merger with Time Warner.

Why would we allow our 400 richest citizens to monopolize assets equivalent to one-eighth of the GDP? Meanwhile, as of 1997, the median household financial wealth (net worth less home equity) totaled $11,700, $1,300 less than in 1989. So now we've allowed unfettered markets to undermine not only democracy but our fiscal well-being as well, leaving 76 million baby boomers with votes yet virtually no assets, a certain formula for a politically fractious future.

* * * * *

Contrary to the misplaced focus of the current debate, antitrust isn't just about monopolizing markets. Never was. It's about redressing the antidemocratic results that accompany abuse of the market. To address only the means while leaving intact the gains mocks the very rationale for antitrust.

* * * * *

Source: *Los Angeles Times,* January 12, 2000, Metro, Part B, p. 7. Reprinted by permission. [For more on Jeff Gates and his view of free enterprise, see **www.sharedcapitalism.org**]

Questions

1. *a.* Do you see increasing concentration of wealth and power as a threat to America's long-term welfare? Explain.

   b. If that concentration is a concern, is antitrust law the best remedy?

2. Jeff Gates, in this article, says antitrust is about "redressing the antidemocratic results that accompany abuse of the market." Explain what he means.

3. Does the *Microsoft* case stand simply for the view that bigness is bad? Explain.

4. Critics have argued that technology is eliminating the imperfections of the market, making antitrust law enforcement obsolete in this high-tech era.

   a. Explain that argument.

   b. Now build the argument that high-tech industries may actually be especially susceptible to antitrust problems because of the need to maintain the compatibility of equipment (like the dominance of the VHS format in the video business).

Part One—Monopoly

Both the federal district court and the court of appeals in the *Microsoft* case concluded that the computer giant holds monopoly power in the Intel-compatible PC operating systems market. How did those courts reach that conclusion? How do we know when an organization is an unlawful monopolist? An extensive, sophisticated, yet imperfect system of analysis has emerged. [For the American Bar Association Antitrust section, see **http://www.abanet.org/antitrust**]

Principal Monopoly Legislation: Sherman Act, Section 2

> Every person who shall monopolize, or attempt to monopolize, or combine or conspire with any other person or persons, to monopolize any part of the trade or commerce among the several States, or with foreign nations, shall be deemed guilty of a felony punishable by a fine.

Section 5 of the Federal Trade Commission Act also applies to most antitrust violations.

From an economic viewpoint, a *monopoly* is a situation in which one firm holds the power to control prices and/or exclude competition in a particular market. The general legal test for monopolization is

1. The possession of monopoly power in the relevant market.
2. The willful acquisition or maintenance of that power, as distinguished from growth or development as a consequence of a superior product, business acumen, or historic accident.[5]

Thus the critical inquiries are the percentage of the market held by the alleged monopolist and the behavior that produced and maintained that market share. Antitrust law does not punish efficient companies who legitimately earn and maintain large market shares.

Indeed, high market concentration often promotes competition, whereas a fragmented market of many small firms may produce higher prices. (Imagine a retail food market of many corner grocery stores and no supermarkets.) Nonetheless, the federal government continues to rely strongly on market concentration data (*structure*) in combination with evidence of actual behavior (*conduct*) to identify anticompetitive situations. Market share alone is highly unlikely to lead to antitrust action, but a high market share acquired and/or maintained via abusive conduct (as alleged in *Microsoft*) is likely to be challenged.

Oligopoly   A few firms sharing monopoly power constitute an *oligopoly*. Scholar Thomas Piraino reminds us that oligopolistic markets are common in American life:

> The public accounting industry includes only four national firms; four automobile companies produce approximately 75 percent of the cars in the United States; seven national carriers control most domestic airline traffic; Visa and MasterCard together account for most of the transactions in the credit card market; four tobacco companies manufacture 97 percent of the cigarettes sold in the United States; and five pharmaceutical companies produce most of the nation's prescription drugs.[6]

Oligopolies may promote competition, but they also raise the threat of collusion. With a few firms controlling enormous markets, competitors may find value in unlawful cooperation. Because express collusion is illegal on its face (see Chapter 10), those rivals, as Piraino explains, may find other ways of communicating their anticompetitive messages:

> [O]ligopolists can engage in informal means of communicating and enforcing a consensus price, such as by signaling planned price increases in press releases or on the Internet.[7]

Monopolization Analysis

Although the case law is not a model of clarity, a rather straightforward framework for monopoly analysis has emerged:

1. Define the relevant *product market.*
2. Define the relevant *geographic market.*
3. Compute the defendant's *market power.*
4. Assess the defendant's *intent* (predatory or coercive conduct).
5. Raise any available *defenses.*

1. Product Market

Here the court seeks, effectively, to draw a circle that encompasses categories of goods in which the defendant's products or services compete and that excludes those not in the same competitive arena. The fundamental test is *interchangeability* as determined primarily by the price, use, and quality of the product in question.

An analysis of cross-elasticity of demand is a key ingredient in defining the product market. Assume that two products, X and Y, appear to be competitors. Assume that the price of X doubled and Y's sales volume was unchanged. What does that tell us about whether X and Y are, in fact, in the same product market?

Defining the product market is really the process we all go through in routine purchasing decisions. Let us assume that you feel a rather undefined hunger for salty snack food. You proceed to the nearby convenience store. Many options confront you, but for simplicity, let's confine them to chips, nuts, and popcorn. Of course, each of those food types is composed of variations. As you sort through the choices—corn chips, cheese curls, peanuts, potato chips, and so on—you employ the criteria of price, use, and quality in focusing your decision. In so doing, you are defining the product market for "salty junk food." Products closely matched in price, use, and quality are interchangeable, and thus are competitors in the same product market. But, for example, an imported salty cheese at $10 per quarter pound presumably is not in the same product market as salted sunflower seeds.

Expressed as a matter of elasticity, the critical question becomes something like the following: If the price of potato chips, for example, falls by 10 percent, does the sales volume of salted nuts likewise fall? If so, we have a strong indication that potato chips and salted nuts lie in the same product market and thus are competitors.

2. Geographic Market

Once the product market has been defined, we still must determine where the product can be purchased. The judicial decisions to date offer no definitive explanation of the geographic market concept. A working definition might be "any section of the country where the product is sold in commercially significant quantities." From an economic perspective, the geographic market is defined by elasticity. If prices rise or supplies are reduced within the geographic area in question (New England, for example) and demand remains steady, will products from other areas enter the market in a quantity sufficient to affect price and/or supply? If so, the geographic market must be broadened to embrace those new sources of supply. If not, the geographic market is not larger than the area in question (New England). Perhaps a better approach is to read the cases and recognize that each geographic market must simply be identified in terms of its unique economic properties.

3. Market Power

Market Share

Does the market share held by the defendant threaten competition? How large that share must be to raise monopoly concerns depends on a variety of considerations including how fragmented or concentrated the market is. The *Harvard Law Review,* however, notes some approximate boundaries:

> Market share above 70 percent typically suffices to support an inference of monopoly power. Conversely, courts have rarely found monopoly power when a firm's market share is below 50 percent, leaving some uncertainty as to market shares between 50 and 70 percent.[8]

Market share alone, however, does not establish monopoly power. Barriers to entry, economies of scale, the strength of the competition, trends in the market, and pricing patterns all help to determine whether the market remains competitive despite a single firm's large share. (Why are the courts interested in barriers to entry?)

4. Intent (Predatory or Coercive Conduct)

Assuming a threatening market share is established, the next requirement is proof of an intent to monopolize. Remember that a monopoly finding requires a showing of both market power (*structure*) and willful acquisition or maintenance of that power (*conduct*). Antitrust law is not designed to attack legitimately earned market power. Rather, the concern lies with those holding monopoly power that was earned or is maintained wrongfully. Thus a showing of deliberate, predatory, coercive, or unfair conduct (such as collusion leading to price fixing) will normally suffice to establish the requisite intent.

5. Defenses

The defendant may yet prevail if the evidence demonstrates that the monopoly was innocently acquired via "superior skill, foresight, or industry"; that is, the monopoly was earned. Sometimes a monopoly may be "thrust upon" the monopolist because the competition failed or because of "natural monopoly" conditions where the market will support only one firm or where large economies of scale exist (such as for electricity suppliers).

Attempted Monopolization

The Sherman Act forbids attempts to monopolize as well as monopoly itself. In the 1993 *Spectrum Sports* decision,[9] the Supreme Court set out a three-part test for attempted monopolization: (1) that the defendant has engaged in predatory or anticompetitive conduct with (2) a specific intent to monopolize and (3) a dangerous probability of achieving monopoly power (by which the court was insisting upon evidence of some "realistic" likelihood that monopoly would actually follow).

Monopoly Case I

The case that follows is a private antitrust action involving soft drink giant PepsiCo's claim that rival giant Coca-Cola monopolized a particular portion of the soft drink market.

LEGAL BRIEFCASE

PepsiCo v. The Coca-Cola Company 315 F.3d 101 (2d Cir. 2002; as amended 2003)

PER CURIAM

PepsiCo appeals from the judgment of the United States District Court for the Southern District of New York, granting summary judgment in favor of The Coca-Cola Company on PepsiCo's claims that Coca-Cola's enforcement of loyalty provisions in its distributorship agreements with independent food service distributors ("IFDs") that prohibit the IFDs from delivering PepsiCo products to any of their customers constitutes monopolization and attempted monopolization in violation of Section 2 of the Sherman Act....

BACKGROUND

Coca-Cola and PepsiCo, in addition to selling their famous beverages in bottles and cans, sell fountain syrup to numerous customers, including large restaurant chains, movie theater chains, and other "on-premise" accounts. PepsiCo and Coca-Cola bid for agreements to supply fountain syrup and negotiate a price directly with the customer, and then pay a fee to a distributor to deliver the product. Historically, PepsiCo delivered fountain syrup primarily through bottler distributors; Coca-Cola delivered fountain syrup through bottler distributors as well as IFDs, who can offer customers one-stop shopping for all of their restaurant supplies. In the late 1990s, PepsiCo decided it wanted to start delivering fountain syrup via IFDs, but when it sought to do so, Coca-Cola began to enforce the so-called "loyalty" or "conflict of interest" policy contained in its agreements with IFDs, which provides that distributors who supply customers with Coca-Cola may not "handle[] the soft drink products of [PepsiCo]." IFDs who breach the loyalty policy risk termination by Coca-Cola....

DISCUSSION

Section 2 of the Sherman Act

A. The Relevant Market

The parties do not dispute that the relevant geographic market is the United States. A relevant product market consists of "products that have reasonable interchangeability for the purposes for which they are produced—price, use, and qualities considered." *United States v. E.I. DuPont de Nemours & Co.* Products will be considered to be reasonably interchangeable if consumers treat them as "acceptable substitutes."

In its complaint, PepsiCo defined the relevant market as the "market for fountain-dispensed soft drinks distributed through [IFDs] throughout the United States." Pepsico sought to narrow this market definition by confining it to customers with certain characteristics, specifically "large restaurant chain accounts that are not 'heavily franchised' with low fountain 'volume per outlet.'" The district court rejected this definition....

[T]he district court held that fountain syrup delivered by bottler distributors was an "acceptable substitute" for fountain syrup delivered by IFDs—and thus had to be included in the relevant product market—because none of the numerous customers ... said that the availability of delivery via IFDs was determinative of its choice of fountain syrup.... PepsiCo's internal strategy documents, moreover, repeatedly explain that Coca-Cola has several advantages over PepsiCo in the fountain syrup business, only some of which relate to flexible delivery methods.

The district court also rejected PepsiCo's argument that the relevant market should be confined to certain customers....

The district court found that, although. . . . many customers have a preference for receiving fountain syrup through IFDs because of the advantages provided by one-stop-shopping, these customers did not constitute a discrete group, but rather were included in various groups of fountain syrup customers.

* * * * *

[T]he evidence established that there is no discrete class of customers that has such a strong preference for IFDs that it would not consider substitutes if other factors (especially price) changed; the competition between PepsiCo and Coca-Cola demonstrates that there is a high sensitivity to price change between IFD-delivered and bottler-distributor–delivered fountain syrup; and there is no industry recognition of fountain syrup delivered by IFDs as a separate market. . . . In short, as the district court observed, "the evidence shows that Coca-Cola viewed PepsiCo as a competitor, and vice versa, and that both they and fountain syrup purchasers viewed systems distribution as a competitive advantage, not a separate market."

B. Monopoly Power

* * * * *

The core element of a monopolization claim is market power, which is defined as "the ability to raise price by restricting output.". . . The pertinent inquiry in a monopolization claim, then, is whether the defendant has engaged in improper conduct that has or is likely to have the effect of controlling prices or excluding competition, thus creating or maintaining market power.

* * * * *

PepsiCo has failed to adduce direct evidence that Coca-Cola has market power (i.e., that it can control prices or exclude competition). To the contrary, the result of PepsiCo's stepped-up attack on the fountain syrup market resulted in numerous bidding wars between PepsiCo and Coca-Cola. PepsiCo was successful in obtaining several accounts, and in those cases where it lost out to Coca-Cola, it nevertheless forced Coca-Cola to drastically reduce its price and profitability to keep the account. As the district court stated, moreover, it is "most compelling, [that] no customer testified that Coca-Cola's loyalty policy prevented the customer from obtaining Pepsi."

* * * * *

In sum, we conclude, as did the district court, that PepsiCo's Section 2 antitrust claim fails because fountain syrup distributed by IFDs is not a separate submarket. Moreover, PepsiCo has not sought to argue that Coca-Cola has monopoly power in the broader fountain syrup market. Nor could it; according to PepsiCo's own figures, in 1998, the year it filed this lawsuit, IFDs accounted for only 50.2 percent of all fountain syrup deliveries by the three largest suppliers (Coca-Cola, PepsiCo, and Dr. Pepper/Seven-Up), and Coca-Cola had only a 64 percent share of the total fountain syrup sales by these three suppliers. Absent additional evidence, such as an ability to control prices or exclude competition, a 64 percent market share is insufficient to infer monopoly power. See *Tops Mkts.*, 142 F.3d at 99 (holding that "a share between 50 percent and 70 percent can occasionally show monopoly power," but only if other factors support the inference). . . .

[Affirmed.]

Questions

1. *a.* Explain PepsiCo's monopoly complaint.

   b. Define the product market from PepsiCo's point of view.

   c. How did the court respond to PepsiCo's product market definition?

2. Why did PepsiCo lose this case?

3. Why didn't PepsiCo allege that Coca-Cola was a monopolist in the total fountain syrup market?

4. The U.S. government sued DuPont, claiming monopolization of the cellophane market. DuPont produced almost 75 percent of the cellophane sold in the United States. Cellophane constituted less than 20 percent of the "flexible packaging materials" market. The lower court found "[g]reat sensitivity of customers in the flexible packaging markets to price or quality changes."

   a. What is the relevant product market?

   b. Who wins the case? Explain. See *United States v. E. I. DuPont de Nemours & Co.*, 351 U.S. 377 (1956).

Monopoly Case II

The *Syufy* case that follows reflects what is probably the dominant "ideological" view of monopoly among federal court judges. The decision embodies the free market philosophy of the Reagan and Bush administrations and their judicial appointees, and it suggests an increasing judicial acceptance of the position that dominant market shares may be earned and maintained legitimately—particularly where competition can easily enter the market. Remember, however, the *Microsoft* lesson that a dominant share gained and/or maintained by anticompetitive practices is impermissible.

The *Syufy* case is also notable because Judge Kozinski, in the spirit of the facts, managed to insert the names of nearly 200 movies in his 25-page opinion (only a small portion of which is reprinted here).

U.S. v. Syufy Enterprises

LEGAL BRIEFCASE

903 F.2d 659 (9th Cir. 1990)

Circuit Judge Kozinski

Suspect that giant film distributors like Columbia, Paramount, and Twentieth Century–Fox had fallen prey to Raymond Syufy, the canny operator of a chain of Las Vegas, Nevada, movie theaters, the U.S. Department of Justice brought this civil antitrust action to force Syufy to disgorge the theaters he had purchased in 1982–84 from his former competitors. The case is unusual in a number of respects: The Department of Justice concedes that moviegoers in Las Vegas suffered no direct injury as a result of the allegedly illegal transactions; nor does the record reflect complaints from Syufy's bought-out competitors, as the sales were made at fair prices and not precipitated by any monkey business; and the supposedly oppressed movie companies have weighed in on Syufy's side. The Justice Department nevertheless remains intent on rescuing this platoon of Goliaths from a single David.

After extensive discovery and an eight-and-a-half day trial, the learned district judge entered comprehensive findings of fact and conclusions of law, holding for Syufy. He found, *inter alia*, that Syufy's actions did not injure competition because there are no barriers to entry—others could and did enter the market—and that Syufy therefore did not have the power to control prices or exclude the competition. . . .

FACTS

Gone are the days when a movie ticket cost a dime, popcorn a nickel, and theaters had a single screen: This is the age of the multiplex. With more than 300 new films released every year—each potentially the next *Batman* or *E.T.*—many successful theaters today run a different film on each of their 6, 12, or 18 screens. . . .

Raymond Syufy understood the formula well. In 1981 he entered the Las Vegas market with a splash by opening a six-screen theater. Newly constructed and luxuriously furnished, it put existing facilities to shame. Syufy's entry into the Las Vegas market caused a stir, precipitating a titanic bidding war. Soon theaters in Las Vegas were paying some of the highest license fees in the nation, while distributors sat back and watched the easy money roll in.

It is the nature of free enterprise that fierce, no-holds-barred competition will drive out the least effective participants in the market, providing the most efficient allocation of productive resources. And so it was in the Las Vegas movie market in 1982. After a hard-fought battle among several contenders, Syufy gained the upper hand. Two of his rivals, Mann Theatres and Plitt Theatres, saw their future as rocky and decided to sell out to Syufy. While Mann and Plitt are major exhibitors nationwide, neither had a large presence in Las Vegas. Mann operated two indoor theaters with a total of three screens; Plitt operated a single theater with three screens. Things were relatively quiet until September 1984; in September Syufy entered into earnest negotiations with Cragin Industries, his largest remaining competitor. Cragin sold out to Syufy midway through October, leaving Roberts Company, a small exhibitor of mostly second-run films, as Syufy's only competitor for first-run films in Las Vegas.

It is these three transactions—Syufy's purchases of the Mann, Plitt, and Cragin theaters—that the Justice Department claims amount to antitrust violations. As government counsel explained at oral argument, the thrust of its case is that "you may not get monopoly power by buying out your competitors." . . .

DISCUSSION

* * * * *

[O]f significance is the government's concession that Syufy was only a monopsonist, not a monopolist. Thus the government argues that Syufy had market power, but that he exercised this power only against suppliers (film distributors), not against consumers (moviegoers). This is consistent with the record, which demonstrates that Syufy always treated moviegoers fairly: The movie tickets, popcorn, nuts, and the Seven-Ups cost about the same in Las Vegas as in other, comparable markets. While it is theoretically possible to have a middleman who is a monopolist upstream but not downstream, this is a somewhat counterintuitive scenario. Why, if he truly had significant market power, would Raymond Syufy have chosen to take advantage of the big movie distributors while giving a fair shake to ordinary people? And why do the distributors, the alleged victims of the monopolization scheme, think that Raymond Syufy is the best thing that ever happened to the Las Vegas movie market?

* * * * *

There is universal agreement that monopoly power is the power to exclude competition or control prices. . . .

1. Power to Exclude Competition

It is true, of course, that when Syufy acquired Mann's, Plitt's, and Cragin's theaters he temporarily diminished the number of competitors in the Las Vegas first-run film market. But this does not necessarily indicate foul play; many legitimate market arrangements diminish the number of competitors. . . . If there are no significant barriers to entry, however, eliminating competitors will not enable the survivors to reap a monopoly profit; any attempt to raise prices above the competitive level will lure into the market new competitors able and willing to offer their commercial goods or personal services for less. . . .

* * * * *

The district court. . . . found that there were no barriers to entry in the Las Vegas movie market. . . . Our review of the record discloses that the district court's finding is amply supported by the record.

* * * * *

Immediately after Syufy bought out the last of his three competitors in October 1984, he was riding high, having captured 100 percent of the first-run film market in Las Vegas. But this utopia proved to be only a mirage. That same month, a major movie distributor, Orion, stopped doing business with Syufy, sending all of its first-run films to Roberts Company, a dark-horse competitor previously relegated to the second-run market. Roberts Company took this as an invitation to step into the major league and, against all odds, began giving Syufy serious competition in the first-run market. Fighting fire with fire, Roberts opened three multiplexes within a 13-month period, each having six or more

screens. By December 1986, Roberts was operating 28 screens, trading places with Syufy, who had only 23. At the same time, Roberts was displaying a healthy portion of all first-run films. In fact, Roberts got exclusive exhibition rights to many of its films, meaning that Syufy could not show them at all.

By the end of 1987, Roberts was showing a larger percentage of first-run films than was the Redrock multiplex at the time Syufy bought it. Roberts then sold its theaters to United Artists, the largest theater chain in the country, and Syufy continued losing ground. It all boils down to this: Syufy's acquisitions did not short-circuit the operation of the natural market forces; Las Vegas's first-run film market was more competitive when this case came to trial than before Syufy bought out Mann, Plitt, and Cragin.

The Justice Department correctly points out that Syufy still has a large market share, but attributes far too much importance to this fact. In evaluating monopoly power, it is not market share that counts, but the ability to *maintain* market share. . . . Syufy seems unable to do this. In 1985 Syufy managed to lock up exclusive exhibition rights to 91 percent of all the first-run films in Las Vegas. By the first quarter of 1988, that percentage had fallen to 39 percent; United Artists had exclusive rights to another 25 percent, with the remaining 36 percent being played on both Syufy and UA screens.

Syufy's share of box office receipts also dropped off, albeit less precipitously. In 1985 Syufy raked in 93 percent of the gross box office from first-run films in Las Vegas. By the first quarter of 1988, that figure had fallen to 75 percent. The government insists that 75 percent is still a large number, and we are hard-pressed to disagree; but that's not the point.

* * * * *

The numbers reveal that Roberts/UA has steadily been eating away at Syufy's market share: In two and a half years, Syufy's percentage of exclusive exhibition rights dropped 52 percent and its percentage of box office receipts dropped 18 percent. During the same period, Roberts/UA's newly opened theaters evolved from absolute beginners, barely staying alive, into a big business.

* * * * *

2. Power to Control Prices

The crux of the Justice Department's case is that Syufy, top gun in the Las Vegas movie market, had the power to push around Hollywood's biggest players, dictating to them what prices they could charge for their movies. The district court found otherwise. This finding too has substantial support in the record.

Perhaps the most telling evidence of Syufy's inability to set prices came from movie distributors, Syufy's supposed victims. At the trial, distributors uniformly proclaimed their satisfaction with the way the Las Vegas first-run film market operates; none complained about the license fees paid by Syufy. . . . Particularly damaging to the government's case was the testimony of the former head of distribution for MGM/UA that his company "never had any difficulty. . . in acquiring the terms that we thought were reasonable,". . . explaining that the license fees Syufy paid "were comparable or better than any place in the United States. And in most cases better.". . .

The documentary evidence bears out this testimony. Syufy has at all times paid license fees far in excess of the national average, even higher than those paid by exhibitors in Los Angeles, the Mecca of Moviedom. In fact, Syufy paid a higher percentage of his gross receipts to distributors in 1987 and 1988 than he did during the intensely competitive period just before he acquired Cragin's Redrock.

While successful, Syufy is in no position to put the squeeze on distributors. . . .

*   *   *   *   *

It is a tribute to the state of competition in America that the Antitrust Division of the Department of Justice has found no worthier target than this paper tiger on which to expend limited taxpayer resources. Yet we cannot help but wonder whether bringing a lawsuit like this, and pursuing it doggedly through 27 months of pretrial proceedings, about two weeks of trial, and now the full distance on appeal, really serves the interests of free competition.

*   *   *   *   *

Affirmed.

Questions

1. At one point, Syufy held 100 percent of the first-run market. Why was Syufy not a monopolist?

2. Is this decision rooted more in structural (market share) or conduct (predatory pricing) considerations? Explain.

3. What role did the issue of Syufy's intent to monopolize play in this case? Explain.

4. Assume we have historical data showing that when the price of rolled steel has increased, the sales volume of rolled aluminum has remained constant. What, if anything, does that fact tell us about the product market for rolled steel?

5. Define the product market for championship boxing matches. See *United States v. International Boxing Club of New York, Inc.*, 358 U.S. 242 (1959).

6. Adidas provides cash, sporting goods, and the like to universities in exchange for various promotional rights, including the team's or coach's agreement to wear Adidas clothing in athletic activities. National Collegiate Athletic Association (NCAA) rules limit the amount of advertising that may appear on a uniform being used in competition. Adidas sued the NCAA claiming, among other things, that the advertising restrictions constitute an attempted monopoly by the NCAA. In pursuing its monopoly claim, Adidas defined the relevant market as "the market for the sale of NCAA Promotional Rights." The NCAA responded by saying that a market consisting solely of the sale of promotional rights by NCAA member institutions (colleges and universities) on athletic apparel used in intercollegiate activity is not a plausible relevant market.

  a. Define the relevant product market from the NCAA point of view.

  b. How would the court decide where the product market actually lies? See *Adidas America, Inc v. NCAA,* 64 F. Supp. 2d 1097 (1999).

PRACTICING ETHICS   Is Bigness Bad?

That question in decades past was a great source of debate, but today the question sounds almost naïve or quaint. In this era of consolidation and globalization, colossal corporations are a fact of life and, apparently, a competitive necessity. Nonetheless, enormous, concentrated power can be abused. *The Wall Street Journal* recently described increasing fears about *monopsony*, the monopoly variant that was the subject of the *Syufy* case:

> As more of the world's markets become dominated by a few big companies, a rare form of antitrust abuse is raising new concern: when corporations illegally drive *down* the prices of their suppliers. On the coast of

Maine, blueberry growers alleged last year that four big processors conspired to push down the price they would pay for fresh wild berries. A state court jury agreed last year and awarded millions in damages. . . . In Alabama and Pennsylvania, federal antitrust enforcers last year targeted insurance companies that imposed contracts forcing down fees charged by doctors and hospitals. The insurers abandoned the practice.[10]

Questions

1. Is bigness bad? Explain.
2. Is it wrong of Wal-Mart to drive its suppliers' prices as low as possible? Explain.
3. Under what circumstances, if any, should monopsony be unlawful? Explain.

Questions—Part One

1. *a.* The *Harvard Law Review* argues, "In the New Economy. . . there will inevitably be an increasing number of markets with only a few dominant players."[11] Why would that be so?

   b. Are we mistaken in pursuing Microsoft and other "new economy" giants with "old economy" antitrust principles? Explain.

2. The plaintiffs promote early-season, NCAA-certified basketball tournaments. The National Collegiate Athletic Association's Two in Four Rule limits college basketball teams to "not more than one certified basketball event in one academic year, and not more than two certified basketball events every four years." The promoters sued the NCAA on antitrust grounds, claiming the Two in Four rule hampers their ability to make money. The NCAA argues that the limit on games is academically motivated.

   a. Does antitrust law apply to Division I collegiate basketball? Explain.

   b. Define the product market in this case. See *Worldwide Basketball & Sports Tours, Inc. v. NCAA*, 388 F. 3d 955 (6th Cir. 2004).

3. *a.* A traditional concern about monopolies is that a lack of competition discourages efficiency and innovation. Argue that monopolies may actually *encourage* innovation.

   b. Even if monopolies do not discourage invention, we have firm economic grounds for opposing monopolies. Explain.

4. Real estate developer Ernest Coleman built an apartment complex in Stilwell, Oklahoma (population 2,700), and ordered electric service from an out-of-town utility, Ozark Electric. Stilwell officials said they would deny him city water and sewer service if he did not buy his electricity from the city-owned utility service. Because he could not buy water or sewer service elsewhere, Coleman decided to switch to Stilwell's utility.

   In 1996 the federal Justice Department sued Stilwell. Explain the federal government's complaint and decide the case. See Bryan Gruley, "Little Town Becomes First Municipality Sued by U.S. for Antitrust," *The Wall Street Journal*, June 3, 1996, p. A1.

5. Historically, perhaps the most important interpretation of the Sherman Act's proscription of monopolization was Judge Learned Hand's opinion in the *Alcoa* case. After finding that Alcoa controlled 90 percent of the aluminum ingot market, Hand had to determine whether Alcoa possessed a general intent to monopolize. Hand concluded

that Alcoa's market dominance could have resulted only from a "persistent determination" to maintain control [148 F.2d 416, 431 (2d Cir. 1945)]:

> It was not inevitable that it should always anticipate increases in the demand for ingots and be prepared to supply them. Nothing compelled it to keep doubling and redoubling its capacity before others entered the field. It insists that it never excluded competitors; but we can think of no more effective exclusion than progressively to embrace each new opportunity as it opened, and to face every newcomer with new capacity already geared into a great organization.

Comment on Judge Hand's remarks.

6. Is a monopolist who makes only a "fair" profit in violation of the law? Explain.

7. May a monopolist lawfully increase its market share, assuming it does so without recourse to predatory or exclusionary tactics? Explain. Should it be able to do so? Explain.

8. The National Football League was organized in 1920. During the 1960 season, it had 14 teams located in 13 cities—Chicago (two teams), Cleveland, New York, Philadelphia, Pittsburgh, Washington, Baltimore, Detroit, Los Angeles, San Francisco, Green Bay, Dallas, and Minneapolis. The rival American Football League commenced play in 1960 with eight teams in eight cities—Boston, Buffalo, Houston, New York, Dallas, Denver, Los Angeles, and Oakland.

   In its first season, the AFL was successful in competing for outstanding players and in acquiring a desirable television contract. "[R]epresentatives of the American League declared that the League's success was unprecedented." Nevertheless, the AFL sued the NFL, claiming monopolization. A central issue in the case was defining the geographic market. The AFL characterized the market as those 17 cities either having an NFL franchise or seriously considered for a franchise. The NFL saw the market as nationwide.

   Define the geographic market in this case. Explain. See *American Football League v. National Football League,* 323 F.2d 124 (4th Cir. 1963).

9. Several smaller airlines sued the two giants, United and American, claiming that the two violated the Sherman Act through their computerized reservation systems (CRSs). The heart of the plaintiffs' position was that United and American were monopolists who violated the law by denying other airlines reasonable access to their CRSs. American and United had the largest CRSs, but other airlines also maintained CRSs. Neither had blocked any other airline's access to its CRS, but they had charged fees (in American's case, $1.75 per booking to the airline that secured a passenger through American's CRS). United and American each controlled about 12 to 14 percent of the total air transportation market. According to the court, the plaintiffs were "unhappy" about United and American's ability to extract booking fees from them for the use of the CRSs. The U.S. Ninth Circuit Court of Appeals ruled for the defendants, and the Supreme Court declined to review this case.

   a. Explain why the plaintiffs felt wronged by American and United.

   b. Explain the defendants's argument that they could not successfully charge "excessive" prices for the use of the CRSs. See *Alaska Airlines v. United Airlines,* 948 F.2d 536 (9th Cir. 1991), cert. den. 112 S.Ct. 1603 (1992).

10. A principal fear about monopoly power is that it can lead to *predatory pricing,* where large firms price their goods below cost to drive their competition out of the market, then raise those prices to monopoly levels.

   a. As a matter of economics, explain why predatory pricing of that nature is quite unlikely.

   b. On the other hand, as a matter of economics, explain how predatory pricing might be successful where a monopolist operates in several markets and sells below cost in one or two of them.

Part Two—Mergers

Merger activity tends to occur in cycles. At this writing in 2005, market conditions are driving a renewed interest in mergers. Merger filings with the government were up 40 percent in fiscal 2004,[12] and the dollar value of 2004 mergers rose about 30 percent over 2003.[13] Recent big deals have included Kmart–Sears, Procter & Gamble–Gillette, and SBC–AT&T. The current interest in mergers follows several years of relative inactivity prompted by a worldwide economic slowdown, the chill of terrorism, corporate scandals, and the dismal results of several big mergers around the turn of the century, including the $182 billion AOL acquisition of Time Warner (stock market loss of about 75 percent) and Qwest's $56 billion takeover of US West (stock market loss of nearly 90 percent).[14] Mergers, while risky, have become a key strategy in the global commercial war.

> Big deals have included Kmart–Sears, Procter & Gamble–Gillette, and SBC–AT&T.

Why? Technological change, efficiency enhancement, and piles of available cash are often important motivators for merger activity; but the big drivers at the moment appear to be growth opportunities and cost cutting. Many companies have extracted maximum value from their own products and thus can achieve growth only by purchasing new lines, and cost savings have become essential in fierce global competition. For example, the P&G–Gillette merger will add Duracell batteries and Gillette razors to P&G's product lines while eliminating about 6,000 jobs out of a combined workforce of 140,000.[15]

Merger Virtues

Of course, mergers often have clearly beneficial effects. Some of the potential virtues of mergers include these:

1. Mergers permit the replacement of inefficient management, and the threat of replacement disciplines managers to be more productive.
2. Mergers may permit stronger competition with previously larger rivals.
3. Mergers may improve credit access.
4. Mergers may produce efficiencies and economies of scale.
5. Mergers frequently offer a pool of liquid assets for use in expansion and in innovation.
6. Very often, mergers offer tax advantages.

7. Growth by merger is often less expensive than internal growth.
8. Mergers help to satisy the personal ambitions and needs of management.

Managers

> ### Job security appears to have evaporated.

For American bosses, this deal-making fever has profound professional and personal consequences. Job security appears to have evaporated. On the other hand, rapid change means new opportunities. In this volatile managerial setting, experts now say that personal, managerial conditions have become a major factor in merger negotiations. *Across the Board* explains:

> You can't talk about the quest for bigness without discussing ego, which has played a role since the beginning of time. So what's different *today* in the land of ego that's driving today's merger mania? Big Money and Celebrity Status.
>
> According to Pearl Meyer & Partners' study of the top 200 U.S. companies, 90 percent of a CEO's pay is tied to performance, and more than half of that pay is in stock option grants. . . . Big equity stakes mean CEOs are inspired to shake things up, to acquire, to merge, to divest—anything to boost numbers and the company's stock.[16]

Scholars Mathew Hayward and Donald Hambrick measured a variation on this theme with their study of "CEO hubris" (exaggerated self-confidence). Hayward and Hambrick were interested in why acquiring firms often pay much more than market value in making acquisitions. They hypothesized that some CEOs are so convinced of their own excellence that they are sure the acquisition will pay off once they are in charge. To measure CEO hubris, Hayward and Hambrick constructed an index based on (1) recent organizational success, (2) media attention from major newspapers, and (3) self-importance as measured by high pay in comparison with the next highest subordinate. After studying acquisitions in the late 1980s and early 1990s, the authors showed that those three factors accurately predicted the size of the acquisition premium (amount by which the sale price exceeded the acquired firm's market value). They also found that acquisition premiums increased by an average of 4.8 percent for each highly favorable article about the acquiring firm's CEO. The result? On average, shareholder wealth declined for the acquiring firms.[17]

PRACTICING ETHICS   Greed?

James Kilts, chairman and CEO at Gillette, reportedly will personally earn about $153 million from his firm's acquisition by Procter & Gamble. He will also receive a $1.2 million annual pension. Much of the $153 million is attributable to value Kilts is presumed to have added to Gillette during his tenure, but $23.9 million was, according to *The Wall Street Journal*, a "one-time sweetener from P&G." That money was accompanied by a $12.6 million "change in control" payment.[18]

Question

Could we fairly apply the label "greedy" to Kilts? That is, how do we know when the market has provided an "excessive" or "unfair" reward? Explain. [For Vermont Congressman Bernie Sanders's view of corporate and CEO greed, see **http://bernie.house.gov/documents/opeds/20020711182147.asp**]

Merger Problems

Mergers often are failures.   From a shareholder's point of view, mergers often are failures. *BusinessWeek* merger investigations in 2002 and 2004 found that 61 percent of big deals hurt the acquiring firm's shareholders.[19] A study of worldwide mergers from 1997 to 1999 found 31 percent of the mergers actually reducing shareholder value, whereas 33 percent increased shareholder value. On the other hand, three-quarters of the companies involved considered the mergers successful because they were looking at results such as profitability and increasing market share.[20] In addition to the frequent financial failures with mergers, other hazards should also be noted:

1. Too much power is being concentrated in too few hands.
2. A particular merger, while not threatening in and of itself, may trigger a merger movement among industry competitors.
3. Higher market concentration may lead to higher prices.
4. Innovation may be harmed.
5. Some companies are so large that they can significantly shape political affairs.
6. Some companies may have become so large that we cannot allow them to fail.[21]

Broadly, critics argue that major elements of the American economy—communications, credit cards, energy, and so on—are becoming too concentrated for market forces to work as theorized. For example, a 2004 report from the Consumer Federation of America and the Consumers Union claims that oil industry consolidation has driven household energy costs up by an average of $1,000 annually.[22] The report blames the Federal Trade Commission for failing to block giant mergers. A General Accounting Office study in 2004 reached similar conclusions,[23] but the Federal Trade Commission's own study found that market concentration in the oil industry is "low to moderate" and is not responsible for rising gasoline prices.[24]

Should the Government Intervene?   We see that mergers can harm efficiency and consumer welfare, but in general we prefer to allow the market to work its will. The competing considerations in the free market versus government intervention debate are well illustrated by two giant 2005 mergers that, if given the expected regulatory approval, will significantly reshape the telephone industry. Verizon bought MCI and SBC took over AT&T. The result will be two nationwide giants dwarfing their phone competition. Consumers Union says the two will control 90 percent of the residential local wireline, 70 percent of long distance, and 40–50 percent of wireless.[25] Will consumers be well served by these mergers? Should the government intervene? The hope is that competition between the phone companies and the big cable providers (Comcast, Time Warner, and the like) will hold down prices and provide continuing innovation. Historical evidence suggests, however, that two big competitors often act as a cooperative *duopoly* forgoing meaningful competition.[26] New technology, such as emerging Internet phone service, might, however, prevent general consumer harm, although poorer customers and rural residents may not do well under any foreseeable scenario.[27]

Questions

1. A letter to *USA TODAY:* "A reality finally has sunk into the business world: Becoming bigger doesn't necessarily make you better. Finally, the bubble has burst about megamergers, and shareholders are seeing the fruits of making irrational decisions and destroying values."[28] How do you feel about the benefits of mergers among big corporations?

2. Mergers are often generated by the prospect of cost savings and the opportunity to simply buy a customer base. Thus bigger is often better. But the young entrepreneurs whose start-up companies have been so influential in the growth of America's high-tech economy point to two other qualities that will determine business success in the "new economy." What are those two factors, and why are they so important? See Alan W. Webber, "Mergers Get Headlines, But Young Start-Ups Keep Pace," *USA TODAY,* December 2, 1998, p. 25A.

Merger Law: Overview

Mergers are addressed by the Sherman Act, Section 1; but the Clayton Act, Section 7, offers the primary legislative oversight:

> That no person engaged in commerce shall acquire the whole or any part of the stock or the assets of another person engaged also in commerce where the effect of such acquisition may be substantially to lessen competition, or to tend to create a monopoly.

Technically, a *merger* involves the union of two or more enterprises wherein the property of all is transferred to the one remaining firm. However, antitrust law embraces all those situations in which previously independent business entities are united—whether by acquisition of stock, purchase of physical assets, creation of holding companies, consolidation, or merger.

Mergers fall, somewhat awkwardly, into three categories:

1. A *horizontal merger* involves firms that are in direct competition and occupy the same product and geographic markets. A merger of two vodka producers in the same geographic market would clearly fall in the horizontal category. Would the merger of a vodka producer and a gin producer constitute a horizontal merger?

2. A *vertical merger* involves two or more firms at different levels of the same channel of distribution, such as a furniture manufacturer and a fabric supplier.

3. A *conglomerate merger* involves firms dealing in unrelated products. Thus the conglomerate category embraces all mergers that are neither horizontal nor vertical. An example of such a merger would be the acquisition of a pet food manufacturer by a book publisher. (Conglomerate mergers currently receive little attention from the government, and we will not examine them further.)

Premerger Notification Under the Hart–Scott–Rodino Antitrust Improvements Act (HSR), mergers and acquisitions must be reported to the Federal Trade Commission and the Justice Department if those deals exceed certain dollar thresholds. The dollar thresholds change annually in accord with the gross national product; for example, in 2005 an HSR filing would have been required (depending on the size of each party involved) for an acquisition valued at more than $53.1 million. [For more HSR threshold details, see **http://www.gtlaw.com/pub/alerts/2005/0201.asp**] The parties are barred from closing the merger until 30 days after they have made the required HSR filing unless the waiting period is shortened (as it often is) or lengthened by the FTC or the Justice Department. The merging firms are required to provide documentation about the merger's impact on competition. The waiting period gives the government time and information by which to determine whether the merger should be challenged.

Remedies   After the HSR review, the government may decide that the merger is not threatening, and it will be allowed to proceed according to the parties' wishes. The government may, on the other hand, conclude that the merger is anticompetitive. The government could file suit to block the merger, but the preferred action is to work out an agreeable settlement. A settlement might involve one of the parties selling some of its assets or agreeing to forgo business in some geographic segment of the market for a while.

Critics argue that the government effectively has veto power over mergers. If merger partners do not agree to government demands, the government can sue, which results in a long, expensive process for both sides. FTC resistance was, for example, the critical consideration in Blockbuster's 2005 decision to withdraw its nearly $1 billion offer to buy video rental rival Hollywood Entertainment. From the FTC point of view, perhaps the fatal flaw with the proposed merger was that Hollywood had located about 75 percent of its stores near those of Blockbuster in an effort to "steal" some of Blockbuster's business. A merger arguably would have reduced competition and harmed consumer welfare in many of those localized markets. Further, Blockbuster already controlled 40 percent of the video rental market.[29] The Blockbuster decision, in turn, cleared the way for the nation's number three video rental company, Movie Gallery, to acquire Hollywood, a move the FTC approved. The resulting firm will control 25 percent of the market and will constitute a vigorous competitor for Blockbuster.[30]

> FTC resistance was the critical consideration in Blockbuster's 2005 decision to withdraw its nearly $1 billion offer to buy video rental rival Hollywood Entertainment.

In cases where negotiation fails and the government decides to sue, it can ask the court for a remedy, such as an order stopping the merger or an order requiring divestiture of certain assets. Government litigation is infrequent, but the resulting message to the business community is powerful. Furthermore, private parties commonly use the antitrust laws to sue for treble damages when they believe a merger has harmed them unlawfully. The threat of those private actions as well as government oversight helps to maintain a marketplace where consumers are offered the benefits of vigorous competition including lower prices, improved quality, and innovation. To the critics, the market is better equipped to make those decisions than the FTC, the Justice Department, or the courts.

Question

How would you argue that the government was mistaken in discouraging the Blockbuster acquisition of Hollywood?

Horizontal Analysis

Horizontal mergers raise anticompetitive risks because direct competitors seek to join together. Three recent lower federal court decisions have caused some experts to speculate that the courts may be demanding increased proof when challenging horizontal mergers in concentrated markets.[31] Whether proof expectations have escalated remains to be seen, but horizontal merger analysis will continue to follow the FTC/Justice Department merger guidelines, which focus on a pair of concerns:

1. **Coordinated effects/collusion:** Will the merger facilitate cooperation so that the parties might fix prices, reduce output, reduce quality, or otherwise coordinate their activities rather than competing against each other? Broadly, the government takes the position that fewer firms and thus greater market concentration increases the likelihood of collusion—a position the courts often, but not always, embrace.

2. **Unilateral effects:** Will the merger allow a firm to unilaterally raise prices, restrict output, or control innovation? Normally, unilateral effects arise with products that significantly restrain each other prior to the merger. For example, in evaluating the merger of paper products manufacturers Scott and Kimberly-Clark, the Justice Department found that Scott's facial tissue brand, Scotties, and Kimberly-Clark's facial tissue brand, Kleenex, had significantly constrained each other's prices prior to the merger and that the merger would therefore allow unilateral and profitable price increases for both Scotties and Kleenex. In response, Kimberly-Clark agreed to divest itself of Scott's facial tissue brands.[32]

Market Power

Broadly, the guidelines are designed to identify mergers that may result in *market power,* defined as the ability of a seller "profitably to maintain prices above competitive levels for a significant period of time." The guidelines set out a five-step methodology for analyzing horizontal mergers:

1. Market definition.
2. Measurement of market concentration.
3. Identification of likely anticompetitive effects.
4. Liklihood of future entrants to the market.
5. Appraisal of efficiencies and other possible defenses.

Market   The market will be defined as the smallest product and geographic market in which a hypothetical monopolist could raise prices a small but significant and nontransitory amount (usually set at 5 percent above current prices).

Market Concentration   The Herfindahl–Hirschman Index (HHI) is employed to measure market concentration. Notwithstanding the formidable title, the index is computed quite easily. The market share of each firm is squared and the results are summed. Thus if five companies each had 20 percent of a market, the index for that market would be

2,000. The HHI is useful because it measures both concentration and dispersion of market share between big and small firms. If 10 firms each have 10 percent of the market, the resulting HHI is 1,000. The larger the HHI, the more concentrated the market. The guidelines establish "safe harbors" for mergers that are considered unlikely to produce anticompetitive effects. Hence a postmerger HHI below 1,000 ordinarily would not be challenged.

On the other hand, postmerger concentration of more than 1,800 accompanied by a change in the HHI above 50 (from the premerger HHI) is potentially threatening. That threat can be overcome by showing that market harm is unlikely, which could be established by reference to such other factors in the guidelines as adverse effects, ease of entry, efficiencies, and so on. In the middle ground involving postmerger HHI figures of 1,000 to 1,800 accompanied by changes in the HHI above 100, the guidelines find that the potential for competitive concerns depends on the analysis of the other factors. To illustrate, consider again a market composed of five companies, each with 20 percent of the market. If two of them merge, the HHI would rise from 2,000 to 2,800, and the merger would be presumed threatening pending consideration of the other factors in the guidelines. Thus the government's guidelines reject the older notion of market size *alone* as a threat to the welfare of the economy.

Anticompetitive Effects Although the guidelines provide highly complex instructions about conditions likely to raise adverse competitive effects, the basic point is that the government is worried that the merger may permit cartel-like behavior in the merged firm's market.

Ease of Entry The idea here is that the newly merged firm cannot arbitrarily raise prices or otherwise abuse the market if entry by competitors is timely, likely, and sufficient, because those new competitors will force the existing firms to charge competitive prices and otherwise conform to the discipline of the market.

Defenses An otherwise unacceptable merger may be saved by certain defenses. Most prominent among them are the failing company doctrine and efficiencies. The failing company doctrine permits a merger to preserve the assets of a firm that would otherwise be lost to the market. Efficiencies include such desirable economic results as economies of scale or reduced transportation costs as a result of the merger.

Vertical Analysis

A vertical merger typically involves an alliance between a supplier and a purchaser. The primary resulting threat to competition is labeled *market foreclosure*. As illustrated in Figure 11.1, a vertical merger may deny a source of supply to a purchaser or an outlet for sale to a seller, thus potentially threatening competition in violation of the Clayton Act. The government would then look closely at that foreclosure to determine whether it actually has an anticompetitive effect. In addition to foreclosing sources of supply or outlets for sale, the government may be concerned about other anticompetitive effects such as raising rivals' costs, facilitating collusion, raising barriers to entry, increasing

FIGURE 11.1
Vertical
Merger

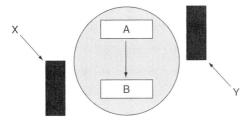

A supplies B. A and B merge. X (A's competitor) had traditionally sold
to B, and Y (B's competitor) had traditionally purchased from A. How
do we decide the legality of such a merger?

access to competitively sensitive information, encouraging discrimination in access to products and services, and reducing incentives for innovation.

The government has raised a number of vertical merger challenges in recent years, but all have been resolved through consent agreements; so we have no recent evidence about how courts treat vertical concerns. Certainly the government has not changed its generally lenient attitude toward vertical mergers, but under some conditions they will be challenged.

The Federal Trade Commission in late 2000 insisted on a consent agreement before allowing the $111 billion AOL–Time Warner vertical merger to go forward. The agreement assured that competitors would have access to AOL–Time Warner markets. The merger joined Time Warner assets CNN, HBO, *Time* magazine, the Atlanta Braves, and Bugs Bunny, among others, with AOL's online service to 26 million consumers. AOL is easily the largest Internet service provider, while Time Warner provides much of the news and entertainment content for cable and Internet service. Time Warner also owns vast cable systems that reach about 20 percent of all cable subscribers. So the general fear was that the merged company would effectively become a monopoly in telecommunications, and Time Warner customers would be forced to accept AOL's services while AOL customers would be forced to accept Time Warner's news and entertainment products.[33] That result would have foreclosed vital marketing opportunities to competitors of Time Warner and AOL. The FTC was worried that Time Warner might refuse to sell its products to competing cable television companies, or it might sell to them only at discriminatorily higher prices. Likewise, AOL–Time Warner might have refused to carry programming produced by its rivals, thus harming competition in the production of video content. The FTC had to balance those anticompetitive considerations against the efficiencies that were expected from the merger.

[For a careful analysis of the government's approach to the AOL–Time Warner merger, see **www.dbr.com/file/Cook_AOL_TimeWarner.pdf**]

Failure

At this writing five years later, the AOL–Time Warner merger has proven to be a financial failure—so much so that the company has now dropped the AOL–portion of its name, effectively conceding that the merger misfired.

Horizontal Merger Case

The Staples–Office Depot horizontal merger litigation that follows illustrates the complex factual and legal issues that must be examined in a strategically pivotal alliance like that proposed between the two office supply giants.

LEGAL BRIEFCASE

Federal Trade Commission v. Staples, Inc. and Office Depot, Inc. 970 F.Supp. 1066 (D.D.C. 1997)

Judge Hogan

BACKGROUND

* * * * *

Staples is the second largest office superstore chain in the United States with approximately 550 retail stores located in 28 states and the District of Columbia, primarily in the North east and California. In 1996 Staples' revenues from those stores were approximately $4 billion through all operations. Office Depot, the largest office superstore chain, operates over 500 retail office supply superstores that are located in 38 states and the District of Columbia, primarily in the South and Midwest. Office Depot's 1996 sales were approximately $6.1 billion. OfficeMax, Inc., is the only other office supply superstore firm in the United States.

On September 4, 1996, defendants Staples and Office Depot . . . entered into an "Agreement and Plan of Merger" whereby . . . Office Depot would become a wholly owned subsidiary of Staples. . . . The FTC filed this suit on April 9, 1997, seeking a temporary restraining order and preliminary injunction against the merger. . . .

I. Discussion

Analysis of the likely competitive effects of a merger requires determinations of (1) the "line of commerce" or product market in which to assess the transaction, (2) the "section of the country" or geographic market in which to assess the transaction, and (3) the transaction's probable effect on competition in the product and geographic markets.

II. The Geographic Market

One of the few issues about which the parties to this case do not disagree is that metropolitan areas are the appropriate geographic markets for analyzing the competitive effects of the proposed merger. In its first amended complaint, the FTC identified 42 such metropolitan areas as well as future areas which could suffer anticompetitive effects from the proposed merger. . . .

III. The Relevant Product Market

* * * * *

The Commission defines the relevant product market as "the sale of consumable office supplies through office superstores," with "consumable" meaning products that consumers buy recurrently, i.e., items which "get used up" or discarded. For example, under the Commission's definition, "consumable office supplies" would not include capital goods such as computers, fax machines, and other business machines or office furniture, but does include such products as paper, pens, file folders, self-stick notes, computer disks, and toner cartridges. The defendants characterize the FTC's product market definition as "contrived" with no basis in law or fact, and counter that the appropriate product market within which to assess the likely competitive consequences of a Staples–Office Depot combination is simply the overall sale of office products, of which a combined Staples–Office Depot accounted for 5.5 percent of total sales in North America in 1996.

* * * * *

The general rule when determining a relevant product market is that "[t]he outer boundaries of a product market are determined by the reasonable interchangeability of use [by consumers] or the cross-elasticity of demand between the product itself and substitutes for it." Interchangeability of use and cross-elasticity of demand look to the availability of substitute commodities, i.e., whether there are other products offered to consumers which are similar in character or use to the product or products in question. . . .

[T]he Commission has argued that a slight but significant increase in Staples–Office Depot's prices will not cause a considerable number of Staples–Office Depot's customers to purchase consumable office supplies from other non-superstore alternatives such as Wal-Mart, Best Buy, Quill, or Viking. On the other hand, the Commission has argued that an increase in price by Staples would result in consumers turning to another office superstore, especially Office Depot, if the consumers had that option. Therefore, the Commission concludes that the sale of consumable office supplies by office supply superstores is the appropriate relevant product market in this case, and products sold by competitors such as Wal-Mart, Best Buy, Viking, Quill, and others should be excluded. . . .

The Court acknowledges that there is, in fact, a broad market encompassing the sale of consumable office supplies by all sellers of such supplies, and that those sellers must, at some level, compete with one another. However, the mere fact that a firm may be termed a competitor in the overall marketplace does not necessarily require that it be included in the relevant product market for antitrust purposes. The Supreme Court has recognized that within a broad market, "well-defined submarkets may exist which, in themselves, constitute product markets for antitrust purposes."

* * * * *

[In defining the submarket] the FTC focused on what it termed the "pricing evidence.". . . First, the FTC presented evidence comparing Staples' prices in geographic markets where Staples is the only office superstore, to markets where Staples competes with Office Depot or OfficeMax, or both. Based on the FTC's calculations, in markets where Staples faces no office superstore competition at all, something which was termed a one-firm market during the hearing, prices are 13 percent higher than in three-firm markets where it competes with both Office Depot and OfficeMax.

* * * * *

This evidence suggests that office superstore prices are affected primarily by other office superstores and not by nonsuperstore competitors such as mass merchandisers like Wal-Mart, Kmart, or Target, wholesale clubs such as BJ's, Sam's, and Price Costco, computer or electronic stores such as Computer City and Best Buy, independent retail office supply stores, mail-order firms like Quill and Viking, and contract stationers.

* * * * *

In addition, Staples' own pricing information shows that warehouse clubs have very little effect on Staples' prices.

* * * * *

There is similar evidence with respect to the defendants' behavior when faced with entry of another competitor. The evidence shows that the defendants change their price zones when faced with entry of another superstore, but do not do so for other retailers.

* * * * *

Despite the high degree of functional interchangeability between consumable office supplies sold by the office superstores and other retailers of office supplies, the evidence presented by the Commission shows that even where Staples and Office Depot charge higher prices, certain consumers do not go elsewhere for their supplies. This further demonstrates that the sale of office supplies by nonsuperstore retailers is not responsive to the higher prices charged by Staples and Office Depot in the one-firm markets. This indicates a low cross-elasticity of demand between the consumable office supplies sold by superstores and those sold by other sellers.

* * * * *

The Court has observed that office supply superstores look far different from other sellers of office supplies. Office supply superstores are high-volume, discount office supply chain stores averaging in excess of 20,000 square feet, with over 11,000 of those square feet devoted to traditional office supplies, and carrying over 5,000 SKUs of consumable office supplies in addition to computers, office furniture, and other nonconsumables. In contrast, stores such as Kmart devote approximately 210 square feet to the sale of approximately 250 SKUs of consumable office supplies. Kinko's devotes approximately 50 square feet to the sale of 150 SKUs. Both Sam's Club and Computer City each sell approximately 200 SKUs.

In addition to the differences in SKU numbers and variety, the superstores are different from many other sellers of office supplies due to the type of customer they target and attract. The superstores' customer base overwhelmingly consists of small businesses with fewer than 20 employees and consumers with home offices. In contrast, mail-order customers are typically midsized companies with more than 20 employees. . . .

* * * * *

[T]he Court finds that the unique combination of size, selection, depth, and breadth of inventory offered by the superstores distinguishes them from other retailers.

* * * * *

While it is clear to the Court that Staples and Office Depot do not ignore sellers such as warehouse clubs, Best Buy, or Wal-Mart, the evidence clearly shows that Staples and Office Depot each consider the other superstores as the primary competition.

* * * * *

[T]he Court finds that the sale of consumable office supplies through office supply superstores is the appropriate relevant product market for purposes of considering the possible anti-competitive effects of the proposed merger between Staples and Office Depot.

* * * * *

IV. Probable Effect on Competition

[T]he Court next must consider the probable effect of a merger between Staples and Office Depot in the geographic markets previously identified. One way to do this is to examine the con-centration statistics and HHIs within the geographic markets. If the relevant product market is defined as the sale of consum-able office supplies through office supply superstores, the HHIs in many of the geographic markets are at problematic levels even before the merger. Currently, the least concentrated mar-ket is that of Grand Rapids–Muskegon–Holland, Michigan, with an HHI of 3,597, while the most concentrated is Washington, D.C., with an HHI of 6,944. In contrast, after a merger of Staples and Office Depot, the least concentrated area would be Kala-mazoo–Battle Creek, Michigan, with an HHI of 5,003, and many areas would have HHIs of 10,000. The average increase in HHI caused by the merger would be 2,715 points. The concentration statistics show that a merged Staples–Office Depot would have a dominant market share in 42 geographic markets across the country. The combined shares of Staples and Office Depot in the office superstore market would be 100 percent in 15 metro-politan areas. It is in these markets the postmerger HHI would be 10,000. In 27 other metropolitan areas, where the number of office superstore competitors would drop from three to two, the postmerger market shares would range from 45 percent to 94 percent, with postmerger HHIs ranging from 5,003 to 9,049. Even the lowest of these HHIs indicates a "highly concentrated" market.

* * * * *

The HHI calculations and market concentration evidence, however, are not the only indications that a merger between Staples and Office Depot may substantially lessen competi-tion. Much of the evidence already discussed with respect to defining the relevant product market also indicates that the merger would likely have an anticompetitive effect. The evi-dence of the defendants' own current pricing practices, for ex-ample, shows that an office superstore chain facing no com-petition from other superstores has the ability to profitably raise prices for consumable office supplies above competitive levels. The fact that Staples and Office Depot both charge higher prices where they face no superstore competition demonstrates that an office superstore can raise prices above competitive levels. The evidence also shows that defendants also change their price zones when faced with entry of an-other office superstore, but do not do so for other retailers.

* * * * *

V. Entry into the Market

"The existence and significance of barriers to entry are frequently, of course, crucial considerations in a rebuttal analysis...."

* * * * *

The Commission offered Office 1 as a specific example of the difficulty of entering the office superstore arena. Office 1 opened its first two stores in 1991. By the end of 1994, Office 1 had 17 stores, and grew to 35 stores operating in 11 Midwest-ern states as of October 11, 1996. As of that date, Office 1 was the fourth largest office supply superstore chain in the United States. Unfortunately, also as of that date, Office 1 filed for Chapter 11 bankruptcy protection. Brad Zenner, president of Office 1, testified through declaration that Office 1 failed be-cause it was severely undercapitalized in comparison with the industry leaders, Staples, Office Depot, and OfficeMax. In ad-dition, Zenner testified that when the three leaders ultimately expanded into the smaller markets where Office 1 stores were located, they seriously undercut Office 1's retail prices and profit margins. Because Office 1 lacked the capitalization of the three leaders and lacked the economies of scale enjoyed by those competitors, Office 1 could not remain profitable.

For the reasons discussed above, the Court finds it ex-tremely unlikely that a new office superstore will enter the market and thereby avert the anticompetitive effects from Sta-ples' acquisition of Office Depot.

* * * * *

VI. Efficiencies

* * * * *

First, the Court notes that the cost savings estimate of $4,947 billion over five years which was submitted to the Court ex-ceeds by almost 500 percent the figures presented to the two Boards of Directors in September 1996, when the Boards ap-proved the transaction. The cost savings claims submitted to the Court are also substantially greater than those represented in the defendants' Joint Proxy Statement/Prospectus "reflecting the best currently available estimate of management," and filed with the Securities and Exchange Commission on January 23, 1997. . . .

* * * * *

[T]he Court cannot find that the defendants have rebutted the presumption that the merger will substantially lessen competition. . .

CONCLUSION

* * * * *

[T]he Court finds that the Commission has shown a likelihood that it will succeed in proving, after a full administrative trial on the merits, that the effect of the proposed merger between Staples and Office Depot "may be substantially to lessen competition" in violation of Section 7 of the Clayton Act. . . . The FTC's motion for a preliminary injunction shall be granted.

AFTERWORD

Citing the time and money involved in battling the federal government, Staples and Office Depot officially called off their proposed merger days after Judge Hogan's decision.

Questions

1. *a.* What "general rule" did the *Staples* court employ in determining the relevant product market?

   b. What evidence supported the use of the "office supply superstore submarket" as the relevant product market?

2. *a.* What evidence supported the FTC's claim that the merger would lead to anticompetitive effects?

   b. In weighing the "public and private equities," why did the court come down on the side of the government?

3. Analysts have argued that in the *Staples* case the government was less worried about market shares than about the price impact of the merger were it to be approved. Explain what those analysts meant.

4. Three firms control the $1 billion U.S. baby food market (Gerber—65 percent, Heinz—17.4 percent, and Beech-Nut—15.4 percent). Gerber is sold in over 90 percent of American supermarkets, and it has greater brand loyalty than any other product sold in the United States. Heinz is sold in 40 percent of the supermarkets and Beech-Nut in 45 percent. The baby food HHI was 4775, which would increase by 510 HHI points if Heinz and Beech-Nut were to merge. Heinz and Beech-Nut agreed to merge. The Federal Trade Commission opposed the merger.

   a. What other facts would you want to know to decide about the legality of this proposed merger?

   b. Defend the merger.

   c. Decide. Explain. See *Federal Trade Commission v. H. J. Heinz Co.,* 246 F.3d 708 (D.C. Cir. 2001).

5. Following September 11, 2001, the federal government "bailed out" the big airlines with a multibillion-dollar aid package. Explain how that aid to the airlines, suffering from the terrorist attack and preexisting economic difficulties, probably prevented some of them from merging with each other.

6. The United States sued to block the proposed merger of two nonprofit hospitals in Rockford, Illinois, a city of 140,000 people. The two hospitals were the largest in the community with a combined market share estimated at 64 to 72 percent. If approved, the merger would have resulted in an estimated market share of 90 percent for the three largest hospitals in Rockford. The hospitals argued that the geographic market should not be limited to Rockford and parts of nearby counties as defined by the lower court judge, but should include a 10-county area of northern Illinois and southern Wisconsin centered on Rockford. That area included a number of smaller, rural hospitals. Ninety percent of hospitalized Rockford residents were hospitalized in Rockford itself. How would you rule on the legality of the merger? Explain. See *U.S. v. Rockford Memorial Corp.,* 898 F. 2d 1278 (7th Cir. 1990).

7. In 1958 Pabst Brewing Company acquired Blatz Brewing Company. Pabst was America's 10th largest brewer, while Blatz was the 18th largest. After the merger, Pabst had 4.49 percent of the nationwide beer market and was the fifth largest brewer. In the regional market of Wisconsin, Michigan, and Illinois, the merger gave Pabst 11.32 percent of the sales. After the merger, Pabst led beer sales in Wisconsin with 23.95 percent of that statewide market. The beer market was becoming increasingly concentrated, with the total number of brewers declining from 206 to 162 during the years 1957 to 1961. In *United States v. Pabst Brewing Co.,* 384 U.S. 546 (1966), the Supreme Court found the merger violated the Clayton Act, Section 7. The Court did not choose among the three geographic market configurations, saying that the crucial inquiry is whether a merger may substantially lessen competition anywhere in the United States. Thus the Court held that, under these facts, a 4.49 percent share of the market was too large.

   Respected scholar and jurist Richard Posner labeled the *Pabst* decision an "atrocity" and the product of a "fit of nonsense" on the part of the Supreme Court.[34] What economic arguments would support Posner's colorful complaint?

8. In the period 1917–19, DuPont acquired 23 percent of the stock in the then-fledgling General Motors Corporation. By 1947 DuPont supplied 68 percent of GM's automotive finish needs and 38 percent of its fabric needs. In 1955 General Motors ranked first in sales and second in assets among all U.S. industrial corporations, while accounting for approximately two-fifths of the nation's annual automobile sales. In 1949 the Justice Department challenged DuPont's 1917–19 acquisitions of GM stock.

a. Why did the government challenge DuPont's acquisition?

b. May an acquisition be properly challenged 30 years after the fact, as in DuPont? Explain.

c. Given your general understanding of finishes and fabrics, how would you defend DuPont?

d. Decide. Explain. See *United States v. E. I. DuPont de Nemours & Co.,* 353 U.S. 586 (1957).

Staples CEO Thomas Stemberg was interviewed following the *FTC v. Staples* battle:

Q: Should a company expect to be treated fairly by staff members of the antitrust regulators?

A: I do believe that the people in these agencies are well-intentioned and are trying to do the right thing for the consumer. As one who has spent the last decade or more of his business career fighting cartels and trying to induce procompetitive activity in the marketplace, their goals are very much the same as ours, which is to give the consumer the best deal possible. The antitrust regulators are some of the hardest-working people I have ever seen. They are extremely dedicated, and if you aren't prepared to go 15 rounds, you're picking a bad fight. Some of the mergers that are out there today that they are contesting, I'd be contesting if I were them, too.

Source: Del Jones, "Today's Issue: Some Lessons Learned in an Antitrust Fight," *USA TODAY,* March 30, 1998, p. 5B.

Part Three—American Antitrust Laws and the International Market

America's commercial market embraces the entire globe. Antitrust questions can become extremely complex in transactions involving multiple companies in multiple nations, where those transactions are potentially governed by U.S. and foreign antitrust laws. U.S. antitrust laws are, of course, applicable to foreign firms doing business here. The Sherman, Clayton, and FTC acts, among others, are all potentially applicable to American business abroad.

Sherman Act

The Sherman Act applies to the conduct of American business abroad when that business has a direct effect on American commerce. That the business was conducted entirely abroad or that the agreement was entered into in another nation does not excuse an American firm from the reach of the Sherman Act (assuming American courts can achieve the necessary jurisdiction).

Clayton Act

Section 7 of the Clayton Act is clearly applicable to acquisitions combining domestic and foreign firms and is potentially applicable to acquisitions not involving American firms if the effect would harm competition in the American market.

Federal Trade Commission Act

As noted earlier, the FTC shares antitrust enforcement authority with the Justice Department, and Section 5 of the act strengthens Clayton 7.

Enforcement

Under its Business Review Procedure, the Justice Department sometimes will prepare a statement of its likely response to a proposed transaction, either foreign or domestic, so that the parties will have advance notice of the government's antitrust stance.

Foreign Antitrust Laws

Compatible antitrust laws and policies around the globe have now become an important ingredient in worldwide economic efficiency. At the beginning of this chapter, we saw that the European Union took a firmer stance toward Microsoft's allegedly monopolistic conduct than did the United States. Similarly, the European Union blocked the proposed merger of General Electric and Honeywell even though the United States had earlier approved the merger—marking the first time EU regulators had stopped a deal already approved in the United States.

Historically, the United States had a much more aggressive attitude toward antitrust than the European Union, Japan, and other nations. Of course, government officials in Japan and the EU nations had been directly involved in managing their economies for the general good, and in recent years the EU has proven to be a more meticulous antitrust referee than is the U.S. government. The European Commission, the EU's executive branch, has more sweeping antitrust powers than those held by U.S. regulators. The EU regulators can, for example, block mergers and fine companies without consulting courts—power not available to their American counterparts.[35] In general, the Europeans seem to be more willing to find evidence of dominance in monopoly situations. Where U.S. regulators want not only evidence of market dominance, but also evidence of actual misconduct resulting in consumer harm, the EU regulators may be concerned about structure alone because one of their goals is simply the maintenance of multiple competitors in any particular market. For example, European regulators have been concerned that Coca-Cola's more than 50 percent market share reduces consumer choice. After six years of sparring, Coca-Cola reached a settlement with the EU in 2005 that forced Coke to turn over as much as 20 percent of its cooler and vending machine space to rivals such as Pepsi (10 percent market share). Coke is also banned from offering volume-linked rebates, exclusive dealing arrangements, and certain discounts.[36]

However, in what may signal a concession to the power of the global market, the European Union's 2004 appointees to top economic posts, including the individual who will police mergers, have strong free market preferences, are "likely to pursue a business-friendly agenda in coming years," and "are . . . instinctive pro-Americans."[37] Quick EU approval of the 2005 Procter & Gamble—Gillette merger suggests a firmer reliance on rigorous economic analysis and reduced support for the "bigness is bad" philosophy. So European Union competition law and practice may be gradually converging with the American model.[38] [For an extensive database on EU merger law, see **http://europa.eu.int/comm/competition**]

Other Nations/Globalization China, Russia, Japan, and others are either introducing new antitrust laws or adjusting existing laws and practices. For example, in 2003 China forbade price fixing and monopolies, with further laws on the way

> China forbade price fixing and monopolies.

as the Chinese have come to recognize the necessity of an orderly legal system to sustain generally open markets. Business, of course, operates in an essentially borderless world; but antitrust enforcement remains a nation-by-nation enterprise. The consequences are an often slow, expensive, unpredictable process that reduces global economic efficiency. In response, some 75 jurisdictions, including both developed and developing nations, are now working together through the International Competition Network to "formulate proposals for procedural and substantive convergence" on worldwide antitrust issues and practices. The network's proposals are not binding, but they are proving influential.[39]

Unilateral Enforcement

While American officials are encouraging worldwide antitrust cooperation, they also continue to aggressively enforce American antitrust laws as applied to international trade. U.S. antitrust enforcement is designed to encourage free and open markets around the globe. Thus, where international price fixing and other restraints of trade unlawfully interfere with American commercial interests, our antitrust laws are increasingly playing a role.

Extraterritoriality

Our most controversial expression of antitrust in trade policy was the Justice Department decision, announced in 1992, to more broadly apply American antitrust law abroad. The general idea is to sue foreign firms that violate U.S. antitrust laws even when the anticompetitive actions take place entirely overseas (extraterritorial application). In practice, the Justice Department files suit in U.S. courts against foreign companies operating in the United States if those foreign companies are taking action abroad that (1) harms competition in the United States or (2) limits American access to markets in other nations. Those lawsuits are permissible under U.S. law only where the conduct abroad has a "direct, substantial, and reasonably foreseeable" effect on the United States' domestic market. Extraterritoriality does not mean, however, that the United States will become the world's antitrust police, as illustrated by a recent Supreme Court decision involving the vitamin industry.

Several of the global vitamin giants were convicted of criminal price-fixing charges. Wronged consumers in other nations, mostly large farms feeding vitamins to cattle, sought civil damages. Attracted by treble damage possibilities that were not available in most of Europe, for example, the plaintiffs filed suit in the United States.

> "The business is outside of the U.S., the defendant is outside the U.S., and the claim is outside the U.S. How can it go to a court in the U.S.?" says Jurgen Hambrecht, chief executive of . . . one of the defendants in the vitamin suit.[40]

The U.S. Supreme Court, by an 8–0 margin in the 2004 *F. Hoffman-LaRoche* decision, agreed with Hambrecht, ruling that the parties did not have a cause of action in America.[41] Basically, the Court ruled that American intrusion in another nation's commerce is justifiable to remedy domestic harm but not to remedy foreign harm caused by foreign conduct when the foreign harm and American domestic harm are independent of each other.[42]

Internet Exercise

What evidence might suggest to the consumer that antitrust laws are being violated? For an answer, see the U.S. Department of Justice, Antitrust Division, brochure, "Antitrust Enforcement and the Consumer" [**http://www.usdoj.gov/atr/public/div_stats/9142.htm**].

Chapter Questions

1. The Chicago Skyway, a toll bridge connecting Chicago and Indiana, is owned by the City of Chicago. Chicago earned $52 million in tolls beyond the amount needed to meet bond payments and to maintain the Skyway. The excess was used to pay for other transportation expenses. Skyway tolls were higher than those of other area highways. Endsley, a bridge user, joined others in a class action against Chicago claiming that the city's control of the Skyway provided monopoly power in high-speed limited access travel between Indiana and Chicago and that the city was abusing that power by collecting excessive fees. Chicago demonstrated that at least two alternative, if less desirable, routes were in competition with the Skyway. Is Chicago a monopolist? Explain. See *Endsley v. City of Chicago,* 230 F.3d 276 (7th Cir. 2000); cert. den. 532 U.S. 972 (2001).

2. Major League Soccer (MLS) was the exclusive Division I professional soccer league in the United States, as recognized by the U.S. Soccer Federation (USSF), the national soccer governing body. MLS owned all of the league's 12 teams, set all schedules, negotiated all stadium leases, controlled all intellectual property rights, and controlled all player contracts. Partial control over some teams was transferred by MLS to certain investors. The investors did not hire their own players. Each employment contract was between the player and the league. MLS assigned the players in a manner designed to maintain competitive balance. MLS had been preceded in U.S. professional soccer by the North American Soccer League, which had failed financially. A group of players sued the MLS on antitrust grounds.

   a. What were the players' antitrust claims?

   b. Decide those claims. Explain. See *Fraser v. Major League Soccer,* 284 F.3d 47 (1st Cir. 2002).

3. Poplar Bluff is a city of 17,000 people in southeastern Missouri. Sikeston and Cape Girardeau, Missouri, both towns with populations of over 40,000, are 40 and 60 miles away from Poplar Bluff. Tenet Healthcare owns Lucy Lee Hospital in Poplar Bluff and proposed to buy Doctors' Regional Medical Center, also in Poplar Bluff. Both hospitals are profitable, but both are underutilized and have had trouble attracting specialists. The Federal Trade Commission filed suit to block the acquisition. The key question involved definition of the geographic market. The FTC proposed a relevant geographic market that essentially matched the service area: a

50-mile radius of downtown Poplar Bluff. Ninety percent of the two hospitals' patients come from that area. Four other hospitals are in that area. The merged hospital would have 84 percent of the patients in that geographic market. Tenet argues that the geographic market should encompass a 65-mile radius from downtown Poplar Bluff. That area includes 16 hospitals. How should the Court of Appeals decide where the geographic market lies? See *FTC v. Tenet Health Care Corp.*, 186 F.3d 1045 (8th Cir. 1999).

4. Staples CEO Thomas Stemberg was asked, based on his experience, "Which mergers will be contested and which ones will sail through?" How do you think the government decides which mergers to challenge? See Del Jones, "Today's Issue: Some Lessons Learned in an Antitrust Fight," *USA TODAY*, March 30, 1998, p. 5B.

5. A major concern with horizontal mergers is the increased potential for collusion. List the structural conditions that would encourage coordinated interaction between competitors.

6. Critics are concerned that increasing mergers, especially those involving media firms, threaten democracy.

   a. Explain that argument.

   b. Do you agree? Explain.

7. In 1986 distinguished economist William Shepherd argued,

   > It may not be too late to turn back from this road to serfdom by reviving the case for antitrust, but the odds aren't favorable. More probably, antitrust will continue to sink.[43]

   a. What did Shepherd mean about "this road to serfdom?"

   b. In reading this chapter, do you think antitrust has been revived? Explain.

   c. Is bigness bad, or is it necessary in today's global economy? Explain.

8. Antitrust attorney Joel Davidow says that four policy measures have been critical to the success of formerly socialist nations that are moving to a market economy: privatization, restructuring, deregulation, and adoption of competition legislation (antitrust). Now almost all of the industrial nations of the world, including former Soviet states Russia, Poland, Hungary, and Bulgaria, are taking all of these measures.

   a. Why is antitrust law important to the success of the new market economies in these formerly collectivist nations?

   b. Is antitrust important to developing nations such as India, Argentina, and Brazil? Explain. See Joel Davidow, "The Relevance of Antimonopoly Policy for Developing Countries," *Antitrust Bulletin* 37, no. 1 (Spring 1992), p. 277.

9. Is the influence of big business so persuasive that it nullifies the effective enforcement of the antitrust laws? Explain.

10. Antitrust authorities must address a critical and empirically difficult policy problem: Does seller concentration in a market ordinarily result in increased prices? That is, in a particular market, are fewer firms with larger shares likely to produce higher prices than would be the case with a more fragmented market? Free market theorists are generally untroubled by concentration. What do you think? Explain.

11. Is a monopolist required to deal with its competitors? That question was the core of a 2004 Supreme Court decision in *Verizon Communications v. Law Offices of Curtis V. Trinko.*[44] The Trinko law firm bought its local phone service from AT&T. Trinko brought a class action claiming Verizon maintained a monopoly by exclusionary practices. Trinko contended that local phone services had difficulty connecting with the giant regional Bell operating companies' (Verizon, Qwest, Bell South, and SBC) local exchange facilities, thus harming competition and consumers. The Telecommunications Act of 1996 specifically requires the regional Bell companies to provide the local phone services with fair, reasonable access. The Supreme Court, however, ruled in favor of Verizon and concluded that antitrust liability in these telephone situations would apply only where a telephone monopolist discontinues a voluntary business relationship with a competitor for the purpose of destroying that competitor. Explain why the Supreme Court decided that Verizon, a telephone monopolist, had no duty to deal with those telephone competitors with whom it had not previously dealt. See Matthew Cantor, "Is Trinko the Last Word on a Telephone Monopolist's Duty to Deal?" *New York Law Journal* 96, May 19, 2004, p. 4.

12. The Justice Department has traditionally been reluctant to accept economies of scale as a defense to an otherwise unlawful merger. Why?

13. How can a merger benefit society?

14. Which economic considerations support the view that unilateral growth is preferable to growth by merger?

15. Excel, a division of Cargill, was the second largest firm in the beef-packing market. It sought to acquire Spencer Pack, a division of Land-O-Lakes and the third largest beef packer. After the acquisition, Excel would have remained second ranked in the business, but its market share would have been only slightly smaller than that of the leader, IBP. Monfort, the nation's fifth largest beef packer, sought an injunction to block the acquisition, claiming a violation of Clayton Section 7. In effect, Monfort claimed the merger would result in a dangerous concentration of economic power in the beef-packing market, with the result that Excel would pay more for cattle and charge less for its processed beef, thus placing its competitors in a destructive and illegal price–cost squeeze. Monfort claimed Excel's initial losses in this arrangement would be covered by its wealthy parent, Cargill. Then, when the competition was driven from the market, Monfort claimed, Excel would raise its processed beef prices to supracompetitive levels. Among other defenses, Excel averred that the heavy losses Monfort claimed were merely the product of intense competition, a condition that would not constitute a violation of the antitrust laws. The district court found for Monfort, and the appeals court, considering the cost–price squeeze a form of predatory pricing, affirmed. Excel appealed to the Supreme Court. Decide. Explain. See *Cargill, Inc. v. Monfort of Colorado, Inc.,* 479 U.S. 104 (1986).

Notes

1. See *United States v. Microsoft Corporation,* 87 F. Supp. 2d 30 (D.D.C. 2000), and *Microsoft v. United States,* 253 F.3d 34 (D.C. Cir. 2001); cert. den. 122 S.Ct. 350 (2001).

2. John R. Wilke, "U.S. Criticizes Microsoft Settlement," *The Wall Street Journal,* January 19, 2004, p. B4.

3. Associated Press, "Ouch! 'Near Monopoly' Microsoft Incurs $613 Million EU Fine," *Cedar Falls/Waterloo Courier,* March 24, 2004, p. C6.

4. Alan Murray, "Microsoft Foe Quits Antitrust Crusade—with Check in Hand," *The Wall Street Journal,* December 7, 2004, p. A4.

5. *United States v. Grinnell,* 384 U.S. 563, 570-1 (1966).

6. Thomas Piraino, "Regulating Oligopoly Conduct under the Antitrust Laws," *Minnesota Law Review* 89 (November 2004), p. 9.

7. Piraino, "Regulating Oligopoly Conduct," p.11.

8. Note, "Antitrust and the Information Age: Section 2 Monopolization Analyses in the New Economy," *Harvard Law Review* 114 (March 2001), p. 1623.

9. *Spectrum Sports, Inc. v. Shirley McQuillan,* 506 U.S. 447 (1993).

10. John R. Wilke, "How Driving Prices Lower Can Violate Antitrust Statutes," *The Wall Street Journal,* January 27, 2004, p. A1.

11. Note, "Antitrust and the Information Age," pp. 1623, 1645.

12. Jaret Seiberg, "As '05 Dawns, Companies Grab Antitrust Edge . . ." *Legal Times,* December 27, 2004, p. 1.

13. Gregory Zuckerman, "Surging Economy, Stock Market Fuel Recent Revival of Big Mergers," *The Wall Street Journal,* December 14, 2004, p. A1.

14. Dennis Berman and Almar Latour, "Too Big: Learning from Mistakes," *The Wall Street Journal,* February 10, 2005, p. C1.

15. Associated Press, "P&G Pays $57 Billion for Gillette," *Waterloo/Cedar Falls Courier,* January 28, 2005, p. D6.

16. Peter Krass, "Why Do We Do It?" *Across the Board,* May/June 2001, pp. 22, 26.

17. Mathew Hayward and Donald Hambrick, "Explaining the Premiums Paid for Large Acquisitions: Evidence of CEO Hubris," *Administrative Science Quarterly* 42 (1997), p. 103.

18. Richard Cohen, "My Avaricious Hero," *Des Moines Register,* February 10, 2005, p. 9A.

19. David Henry, "Have Dealmakers Wised Up?" *BusinessWeek,* February 21, 2005, p. 36.

20. "KPMG Study Finds One-Third of Mergers, Acquisitions Boost Shareholder Returns," *AFX News Limited,* April 29, 2001 [**http://web.lexis-nexis.com/universe/doc...1&_md5=8efdeffc8d0c08b4fe812afdfa8399b9**].

21. See Michael J. Mandel, "All These Mergers Are Great, But . . .," *BusinessWeek,* October 18, 1999, p. 48; and Jeffrey Garten, "Megamergers Are a Clear and Present Danger," *BusinessWeek,* January 25, 1999, p. 28.

22. Jaret Seiberg, "Consumer Groups Slam FTC," *Daily Deal/The Deal,* September 15, 2004.

23. Dar Haddix, "Oil Mergers May Raise Prices, Alter Market," *United Press International,* May 28, 2004.

24. "Mergers Not Driving Up Gas Prices, Says FTC," *AFX.COM,* August 13, 2004.

25. Mark N. Cooper, Director of Research, Consumer Federation of America, "Technology's Impact on Communication Industry," Testimony before House Energy and Commerce Committee, *Federal Document Clearing House Congressional Testimony,* March 2, 2005.

26. Peter Grant and Anne Marie Squeo, "What about the Customers?" *The Wall Street Journal,* February 15, 2005, p. B1.

27. Grant and Squeo, "What about the Customers?"

28. Fariborz Ghadar, "Bigger Not Better," *USA TODAY,* July 6, 2001, p.11A.

29. Mike Musgrove, "Blockbuster Withdraws Hollywood Merger Bid," *The Seattle Times,* March 26, 2005 [**seattletimes.com**].

30. Rong-Gong Lin II, "Blockbuster Ends Bid for Rival Firm," *Los Angeles Times,* March 26, 2005, part C, p. 1.

31. Jon B. Dubrow, "Antitrust Defeats May Spur Concentrated-Market Deals," *Mergers and Acquisitions Journal,* January 1, 2005.

32. Note, "Analyzing Differentiated-Product Mergers: The Relevance of Structural Analysis," *Harvard Law Review* 111 (June 1998), p. 2420.

33. News Services, "FTC Gains Consumer Safeguards in AOL Deal; Time Warner Merger Has Only One More Step Left in Approval Process," *St. Louis Post-Dispatch,* December 15, 2000, p. A1.

34. Richard Posner, *Antitrust Law* (Chicago: The University of Chicago Press, 1976), p. 130.

35. James Kanter, "EU Watchdog Gets More Teeth," *The Wall Street Journal,* January 23, 2004, p. A10.

36. Corey Boles, "EU Limits Coke's Sales Tactics in Settlement of Antitrust Case," *The Wall Street Journal,* June 23, 2005, p. B6.

37. Dan Bilefsky and Marc Champion, "New EU Merger Regulator Is Business-Friendly," *The Wall Street Journal,* August 13, 2004, p. A13.

38. Wiggin & Dana LLP, "Recent Developments in Antitrust and Competition Law," *Mondaq Business Briefing,* October 15, 2004.

39. Neal R. Stoll and Shepard Goldfein, "Antitrust Trade and Practice; Competition Network: Is the Progress Living Up to the Promise?" *New York Law Journal* 114 (June 15, 2004), p. 3.

40. Robert Greenberger and Matthew Karnitschnig, "Should Foreign Antitrust Cases Be Tried in the U.S.?" *The Wall Street Journal,* June 10, 2004, p. B1.

41. *F. Hoffmann-La Roche v. Empagran S.A. et al.,* 124 S. Ct. 2359 (2004).

42. Frederick Clark, "Supreme Court Determines Extraterritorial Reach of U.S. Antitrust Laws," *The Metropolitan Corporate Counsel,* December 2004, McKenna Long section, p. 8.

43. William G. Shepherd, "Bust the Reagan Trustbusters," *Fortune,* August 4, 1986, pp. 225, 227.

44. 540 U.S. 398 (2004).

Employer–Employee Relations

Employment Law I: Employee Rights

Introduction

Jamie Pierce, a TCI of New England employee, was angry during a business meeting. He decided to leave the meeting to "cool off." But as he left the room, he shoved a half-open door, fracturing his hand. Pierce was partially disabled for about two weeks. He requested workers' compensation benefits, but his request was denied on the grounds that the injury did not grow out of his work. Pierce then sued and won—the court ruled that his injury was, in fact, job related.[1]

Managers have always had tough, demanding jobs, but in recent years the law has added complicated, frustrating new expectations. The threat of lawsuits, like Pierce's, has become an important consideration in management decision making. As union strength has declined (see Chapter 14), government rules and court decisions protecting employees have expanded. Those increased legal protections, a volatile economy, downsizing, decreased employer–employee loyalty, and other forces have led to unprecedented levels of employee litigation. [For an extensive employment law database, see **http://dir.yahoo .com/Government/Law/employment_Law/**]

Driving while Dialing

Rapidly changing technology is enhancing employee efficiency, but it too brings new litigation risks:

> Most of us have probably seen and maybe are also guilty of the daring and increasingly dangerous practice of "driving while dialing." This means cruising down the highway or zipping around city streets while chatting on a cell phone. And now, with the increasing popularity of PDAs (personal digital assistants), such as Palm Pilots and pocket PCs, some people are beginning to boldly master tapping the screens of the PDAs (as they sit in their laps) with one hand, and clutching the wheel with the other.

Solomon Smith Barney was sued by the estate of a motorcyclist who was struck and killed by an employee of the investment banking firm who was using his cell phone to speak with a client at the time. The conversation took place on a Saturday night outside of working hours. How would you rule in that lawsuit?

Source: Joseph F. Falcone III, "'Driving While Dialing' Crashes Put Employers at Risk," *The Legal Intelligencer,* February 27, 2002, p. 5.

Part One—Selection

Job Classification The nature of the selection (hiring) process and the laws governing it depend on the type of relationship the employer decides to build with the worker. The traditional, stable model of long-term direct employer–employee relationships now is often replaced with new, flexible, nontraditional staffing arrangements including outsourcing and employee leasing, along with the use of freelancers, temporary agencies, and professional employer organizations. (Firms save money and increase expertise by contracting with these PEOs to administer the firms' human resource services.) These new *contingent workers,* along with *independent contractors,* who are increasingly relied on to perform specific, shorter-term, nonrecurring jobs, permit employers to rapidly and inexpensively inflate or shrink their workforces as competitive and regulatory conditions change. The bad publicity and bad feelings associated with downsizing can be reduced with greater reliance on temps, and the cost savings can be large. Employers who choose to provide health and retirement benefits for their traditional employees need not do so for their contingent workers. Nor must they withhold income, Social Security, Medicare, and unemployment taxes. With fringe benefit costs reaching 40 percent of total compensation and averaging $15,000 (including payroll taxes) per employee, shrinking benefits has become an important consideration for many firms.[2]

Employee or Independent Contractor? The impact of many legal themes discussed in this chapter depends, initially, on whether the worker in question is considered, as a matter of law, an employee whether, long-term or contingent, or an independent contractor. That is, when an enterprise hires, for example, a trucker, programmer, or service technician, is that person an employee or an independent operator under contract to the organization but not, legally, a part of that organization?

The dominant test in settling the employee–independent contractor question is one of control. Where a worker's performance is controlled by an employer or where the employer has the right or the ability to control that work, the worker is likely to be considered an employee. A business that hires an independent contractor generally is not required to comply with a wide range of employment and labor law standards that would apply were the worker an employee. Thus a business must provide unemployment insurance, workers' compensation coverage, minimum wages, and so on to employees, but generally would not need to do so for independent contractors. [For a sample of independent contractor agreements, see **http://www.toolkit.cch.com/tools/indcon_m.asp**]

Classification Problems   Microsoft agreed in 2000 to pay $97 million to settle federal lawsuits involving independent contractors and other contingent workers who won a long court battle to establish that they were entitled to employee benefits.[3] That coverage was especially important in the *Microsoft* case because it entitled many of the workers to very valuable Microsoft stock options. Basically, the Ninth Circuit Federal Court of Appeals found that the freelancers did the same work as Microsoft employees and thus had to be treated the same for benefit purposes despite the fact that the workers had signed contracts acknowledging their temp status and agreeing that they had no right to participate in the benefit plans.[4] The U.S. Supreme Court declined to review that ruling.[5] One of Microsoft's strategies to deal with the worker classification problems was to enact a new policy providing that temporary employees could not work for more than one year before taking a hiatus of at least 100 days.[6]

Legal Problems in the Hiring Process   In conventional employer–employee relationships, contingent deals, and in some cases, independent contractor arrangements, a growing variety of potential legal problems has emerged.

- *Resume fraud:* HireRight, an Internet-based company, reviewed about 200,000 job applicants in one year and concluded that 80 percent of résumés are misleading, 20 percent list fraudulent degrees, and 40 percent have inflated salary histories.[7] Another study found that 13 percent of college students falsified their résumés even before beginning their careers.[8]

> ### 80 percent of résumés are misleading.

- *Background checks:* The 9/11/2001 attacks and the duty to provide a safe workplace have dramatically increased employers' attention to background and security checks. A recent survey found that about 80 percent of companies conducted criminal background checks in 2003, up from 51 percent in 1996, while credit checks increased to 35 percent from 19 percent in the earlier survey.[9]

- *Inappropriate questions:* About 21 percent of 1,000 workers in a national survey said they had been asked inappropriate questions in a job interview.[10] Often these questions, such as "How old are you?" and "Are you married?" raise discrimination concerns. The questions themselves are not technically unlawful, but discrimination based on the answers to those questions would be illegal. (See Chapter 13.) But what about the enormous array of awkward, intrusive, but nondiscriminatory interview questions that might leave the candidate feeling uncomfortable if not wronged? For example:

> Following a job interview this year, Megan Johnson sent a handwritten thank-you note on fine stationery. But she didn't make the impression she intended. "You aren't a Republican, are you?" asked the hiring manager during a follow-up phone call. Ms. Johnson was stumped until she remembered the small blue elephant with an upturned trunk engraved along the upper margin of her note card.[11]

The elephant was, in fact, supposed to represent good luck, but Johnson did not get the job. Furthermore, she cannot sue the company because questions about politics break no employment laws.[12]

- *Noncompete clauses:*

> In November 2002 Frank Cumbo and 10 colleagues left a New York temporary
> staffing agency to start a competing business. Two months later, their former employer
> sued all 11 for unfairly attempting to solicit business from its clients.[13]

Cumbo says he and the others built their new business from scratch and took no information with them. The lawsuit is pending at this writing. To address problems like these, employers sometimes require employees and new hires to sign agreements providing that they will neither pass trade secrets to others nor work for a competitor for a specified period. Cumbo and his colleagues had not signed such a pact, but a recent survey found that 30 percent of companies now require employees to sign noncompete agreements, and 51 percent require nondisclosure agreements.[14]

- *Arbitration:* New hires are sometimes expected to sign agreements specifying that disputes with the employer will be settled by arbitration (see Chapter 4) rather than by litigation. Employers like arbitration because they view it as less adversarial than a trial—faster, cheaper, and more consistent. Often employees see arbitration as stacked in favor of corporate interests and as a denial of the fundamental right of access to the legal system. Sherri Warner is one of those:

> When Sherri Warner claimed a former employer sexually harassed her, the California
> secretary had to abide by a legal agreement requiring any claims go to arbitration
> instead of court. Warner lost her arbitration case, but that was just the beginning of
> her problems. Warner's lawyer says she was then required to pay her former boss's
> legal fees. After three years of hearings, the total bill came to more than $200,000. . . .[15]

An important 2001 U.S. Supreme Court decision in the *Circuit City* case generally upholds the enforceability of legitimate, equitable employment arbitration agreements.[16] The federal government's antidiscrimination agency, the Equal Employment Opportunity Commission (see Chapter 13), however, retains authority to file lawsuits to secure damages for employees despite arbitration agreements that might prevent the employee herself from suing.[17]

References Historically, a job applicant's previous performance record was an important ingredient in the hiring decision, but legal difficulties have significantly reduced the usefulness of the standard reference letter. Employers fear that providing references may lead to defamation claims (*slander* when spoken; *libel* when written) by former employees. Many state courts, however, recognize what is labeled a *qualified privilege* as a defense in an employment-related defamation suit. The privilege applies where the one communicating the statement and the recipient share a legitimate, business-related interest in the information conveyed. Thus references, internal employee evaluations, and the like are protected in most states from defamation claims in the absence of malice or extreme recklessness. Similarly, a number of states have passed statutes protecting legitimate reference communications from defamation claims. Nevertheless, some recent court decisions appear to have eroded the qualified privilege a bit, leading many employers to "play it safe" by limiting their references to strictly factual details such as the date of hire, date of departure, and job title.

Broadly, a successful defamation suit requires the following conditions:

1. A false statement.
2. The statement must be "published" to a third party.
3. The employer must be responsible for the publication.
4. The plaintiff's reputation must be harmed.

Truth is a complete defense in defamation cases, and firms that avoid secondhand information, personal issues, and potential discrimination themes such as age are likely not to have problems. A mistake, however, can be expensive.

In China: Capitalism + Employer Abuse = Lawsuits

Lawsuits in China involving employers and their employees rose by more than one-third between 2001 and 2003. As China has moved from a communist economy to a more open market, legal problems have followed as employers have often abused their employees. Workers migrating from rural western provinces to the industrialized east have particularly suffered with employers simply not paying earned wages. With an estimated 100 million migrant workers being owed some $12 billion, the Chinese government in late 2004 announced new laws penalizing employers who fail to pay wages, sign contracts with workers, provide health checks, or contribute to a social security fund.

Are increased lawsuits an inevitable result of increased reliance on free markets?

Sources: "Lawmakers Blame Chinese Companies for Infringing Employees' Rights," *The Xinhua General News Service,* October 26, 2004; and "China Tackles Labor Problems with New Laws," United Press International, November 16, 2004.

Part Two—Liability

Once hired, what happens when employees make mistakes or engage in misconduct on the job that hurts others? Must the employer bear the loss in these situations? Job classification is an important first question in determining company liability for workers' job-related injuries, injuries to others, and crimes. An enterprise ordinarily will not be liable for the acts of its *independent contractors.* Employers, on the other hand, often bear legal responsibility for *employees'* accidents or wrongs. That liability often springs from the doctrine of *respondeat superior* (let the master answer), a form of *vicarious liability* (sometimes called *imputed liability*).

Scope of Employment Employer liability for employee injuries, accidents, or wrongs is largely dependent on whether the employee was on the job at the time of the incident in question. As explained later in the chapter, employers are generally liable, under workers' compensation statutes, for injuries to employees regardless of the cause of those injuries if they occurred within the *scope of employment* (on the job). Likewise, employers will be held liable under vicarious liability/respondeat superior reasoning for harm to third parties caused by the intentional or negligent acts of their employees when those acts occur within the scope of employment. A finding of employer liability, of course, does not excuse the employee from her liability, but the vicarious liability/respondeat superior reasoning does have the potential effect of opening the employer's deeper pockets to the plaintiff. The central inquiry in assigning employer liability lies in the scope of employment question; that is, broadly, did the accident happen while the employee was on the job? The following questions ordinarily determine whether the harm occurred within the scope of employment:

1. Was the employee subject to the employer's supervision?
2. Was the employee motivated, at least in part, by a desire to serve the employer's business interests?
3. Did the problem arise substantially within normal working hours and in a work location?
4. Was the act in question of the general kind the employee had been hired to perform?

> The City was held liable for a sexual assault committed by a police officer.

In a 1991 case, *Mary M. v. City of Los Angeles*,[18] the city was held liable under the doctrine of respondeat superior for a sexual assault committed by a police officer. At 2:30 AM on October 3, 1981, Sergeant Leigh Schroyer was on duty, in uniform, carrying a gun, and patrolling in his marked police car. He stopped Mary M. for erratic driving. She pleaded not to be arrested. He ordered her to enter his patrol car and took her to her home. He entered her home and said that he expected "payment" for not arresting her. He raped her and was subsequently sentenced to a term in state prison.

Mary M. sued the City of Los Angeles. The general inquiry was whether Schroyer was acting within the scope of his employment during the rape episode. The jury found for Mary M. and awarded $150,000 in damages. The Court of Appeals reversed, saying that Schroyer was not acting within the scope of his employment. The case went to the California Supreme Court. The city argued that Schroyer was acting on behalf of his own interests rather than those of the city, and that the city had not authorized his conduct. Therefore, Schroyer could not have been acting within the scope of employment. However, the court said that the correct question was not whether the rape was authorized but whether it happened in the course of a series of acts that were authorized. The court reversed, saying that a jury could find the city vicariously liable (imputed to the principal from the agent) given the unique authority of police officers in our society. [For an employment law overview, see **www.employlaw.com**]

Questions

1. Gonzalez, working for Land Transport, was driving his employer's tractor-trailer behind Nichols, who was driving his pickup. Gonzalez followed at an unsafe distance and twice attempted to pass in no-passing zones. Nichols responded with "predictable obscene gestures." While both drivers were stopped at a red light, Gonzalez left the company truck and attacked Nichols with a rubber-coated metal cable and a knife. Gonzalez was convicted of assault. Nichols sued Land Transport.
   a. What is his claim?
   b. Decide the case. Explain. See *Nichols v. Land Transport*, 233 F.3d 21 (1st Cir. 2000).

2. Williams, Hemphill, Dixon, and Osborne, while driving in Chicago, noticed some pizza boxes on top of a car parked in front of the Italian Fiesta Pizzeria. Dixon and Hemphill jumped out, discovered the boxes were empty, dropped them, and reentered their Jeep. Hall, a driver for Italian Fiesta, observed Dixon and Hemphill, yelled at them to return the pizza boxes, and then followed them in his vehicle. Dixon turned the wrong way onto a one-way street and Hall followed. Dixon then collided with another vehicle. Williams died and Hemphill was injured. Italian Fiesta was subsequently sued on negligent hiring and vicarious liability claims. The negligent hiring claim was rejected by the judge, but the vicarious liability theme was allowed to proceed to trial. The defendants provided evidence showing the pizzeria specifically informed employees that they were not to attempt to recover stolen property or punish perpetrators. Rather, the pizzeria's policy was for supervisors to contact police. Further, drivers were not penalized if property was stolen.

   a. What was the central issue in this case?

   b. Decide the case. Explain. See *Williams v. Hall,* 681 N.E.2d 1037 (Ill. App. 1997).

3. What policy justifications support the imposition of liability on an employer for the wrongs of an employee operating within the scope of employment?

Hiring/Retention/Training/Supervision

Negligence

In recent years, employers' potential liability for employee wrong has been significantly expanded by a line of cases finding employers liable for negligence in hiring an employee or retaining an employee who subsequently causes harm to a third party, or for careless training or supervision. Typically, the employer is liable on negligence grounds for hiring or retaining an employee whom the employer knew or should have known to be dangerous, incompetent, dishonest, or the like where that information was directly related to the injury suffered by the plaintiff. Note that under negligence liability an employer may be liable for acts *outside* the scope of employment. The case that follows examines the law of negligent hiring, supervision, and retention.

Yunker v. Honeywell, Inc.

LEGAL BRIEFCASE   496 N.W.2d 419 (Minn.App. 1993)

Judge Lansing

FACTS

Honeywell employed Randy Landin from 1977 to 1979 and from 1984 to 1988. From 1979 to 1984 Landin was imprisoned for the strangulation death of Nancy Miller, a Honeywell coemployee. On his release from prison, Landin reapplied at Honeywell. Honeywell rehired Landin as a custodian in Honeywell's General Offices facility in South Minneapolis in August 1984. Because of workplace confrontations Landin was twice transferred, first to the Golden Valley facility in August 1986, and then to the St. Louis Park facility in August 1987.

Kathleen Nesser was assigned to Landin's maintenance crew in April 1988. Landin and Nesser became friends and spent time together away from work. When Landin expressed a romantic interest, Nesser stopped spending time with Landin. Landin began to harass and threaten Nesser both at work and at home. At the end of June, Landin's behavior prompted Nesser to seek help from her supervisor and to request a transfer out of the St. Louis Park facility.

On July 1, 1988, Nesser found a death threat scratched on her locker door. Landin did not come to work on or after July 1, and Honeywell accepted his formal resignation on July 11, 1988. On July 19, approximately six hours after her Honeywell shift ended, Landin killed Nesser in her driveway with a close-range shotgun blast. Landin was convicted of first degree murder and sentenced to life imprisonment.

Jean Yunker, as trustee for the heirs and next-of-kin of Kathleen Nesser, brought this wrongful death action based on theories of negligent hiring, retention, and supervision of a dangerous employee. Honeywell moved for summary judgment and, for purposes of the motion, stipulated that it failed to exercise reasonable care in the hiring and supervision of Landin. The trial court concluded that Honeywell owed no legal duty to Nesser and granted summary judgment for Honeywell.

ISSUE

Did Honeywell have a duty to Kathleen Nesser to exercise reasonable care in hiring, retaining, or supervising Randy Landin?

ANALYSIS

In determining that Honeywell did not have a legal duty to Kathleen Nesser arising from its employment of Randy Landin, the district court analyzed Honeywell's duty as limited by its ability to control and protect its employees while they are involved in the employer's business or at the employer's place of business. Additionally, the court concluded that Honeywell could not have reasonably foreseen Landin's killing Nesser.

Incorporating a "scope of employment" limitation into an employer's duty borrows from the doctrine of *respondeat superior*. However, of the three theories advanced for recovery, only negligent supervision derives from the *respondeat superior* doctrine, which relies on connection to the employer's premises or chattels. We agree that negligent supervision is not a viable theory of recovery because Landin was neither on Honeywell's premises nor using Honeywell's chattels when he shot Nesser.

The remaining theories, negligent hiring and negligent retention, are based on direct, not vicarious, liability. Negligent

hiring and negligent retention do not rely on the scope of employment but address risks created by exposing members of the public to a potentially dangerous individual. These theories of recovery impose liability for an employee's intentional tort, an action almost invariably outside the scope of employment, when the employer knew or should have known that the employee was violent or aggressive and might engage in injurious conduct.

I

Minnesota first explicitly recognized a cause of action based on negligent hiring in *Ponticas* in 1983. *Ponticas* involved the employment of an apartment manager who sexually assaulted a tenant. The supreme court upheld a jury verdict finding the apartment operators negligent in failing to make a reasonable investigation into the resident manager's background before providing him with a passkey. The court defined negligent hiring as

> predicated on the negligence of an employer in placing a person with known propensities, or propensities which should have been discovered by reasonable investigation, in an employment position in which, *because of the circumstances of the employment,* it should have been foreseeable that the hired individual posed a threat of injury to others.

Honeywell argues that under *Ponticas* it is not liable for negligent hiring because, unlike providing a dangerous resident manager with a passkey, Landin's employment did not enable him to commit the act of violence against Nesser. This argument has merit, and we note that a number of jurisdictions have expressly defined the scope of an employer's duty of reasonable care in hiring as largely dependent on the type of responsibilities associated with the particular job. See *Connes,* 831 P.2d at 1321 (employer's duty in hiring is dependent on anticipated degree of contact between employee and other persons in performing employment duties).

Ponticas rejected the view that employers are required to investigate a prospective employee's criminal background in every job in which the individual has regular contact with the public. Instead, liability is determined by the totality of the circumstances surrounding the hiring and whether the employer exercised reasonable care. The court instructed that

> [t]he scope of the investigation is directly related to the severity of the risk third parties are subjected to by an incompetent employee. Although only slight care might suffice in the hiring of a yardman, a worker on a production line, or other types of employment where the employee would not constitute a high risk of injury to third persons, when the prospective employee is to be furnished a passkey permitting admittance to living quarters of tenants,

the employer has the duty to use reasonable care to investigate his competency and reliability prior to employment.

Applying these principles, we conclude that Honeywell did not owe a duty to Nesser at the time of Landin's hire. Landin was employed as a maintenance worker whose job responsibilities entailed no exposure to the general public and required only limited contact with coemployees. Unlike the caretaker in *Ponticas,* Landin's duties did not involve inherent dangers to others, and unlike the tenant in *Ponticas,* Nesser was not a reasonably foreseeable victim at the time Landin was hired.

To reverse the district court's determination on duty as it relates to hiring would extend *Ponticas* and essentially hold that ex-felons are inherently dangerous and that any harmful acts they commit against persons encountered through employment will automatically be considered foreseeable. Such a rule would deter employers from hiring workers with a criminal record and "offend our civilized concept that society must make a reasonable effort to rehabilitate those who have erred so they can be assimilated into the community."

Honeywell did not breach a legal duty to Nesser by hiring Landin because the specific nature of his employment did not create a foreseeable risk of harm, and public policy supports a limitation on this cause of action. The district court correctly determined that Honeywell is not liable to Nesser under a theory of negligent hiring.

II

In recognizing the tort of negligent hiring, *Ponticas* extended established Minnesota case law permitting recovery under theories of negligent retention.

* * * * *

The difference between negligent hiring and negligent retention focuses on when the employer was on notice that an employee posed a threat and failed to take steps to ensure the safety of third parties. The Florida appellate court has provided a useful definition:

Negligent hiring occurs when, prior to the time the employee is actually hired, the employer knew or should have known of the employee's unfitness, and the issue of liability primarily focuses upon the adequacy of the employer's pre-employment investigation into the employee's background. Negligent retention, on the other hand, occurs when, during the course of employment, the employer becomes aware or should have become aware of problems with an employee that indicated his unfitness, and the employer fails to take further action such as investigating, discharge, or reassignment.

. . . The record contains evidence of a number of episodes in Landin's postimprisonment employment at Honeywell that demonstrate a propensity for abuse and violence toward coemployees.

While at the Golden Valley facility, Landin sexually harassed female employees and challenged a male coworker to fight. After his transfer to St. Louis Park, Landin threatened to kill a coworker during an angry confrontation following a minor car accident. In another employment incident, Landin was hostile and abusive toward a female coworker after problems developed in their friendship. Landin's specific focus on Nesser was demonstrated by several workplace outbursts occurring at the end of June, and on July 1 the words "one more day and you're dead" were scratched on her locker door.

Landin's troubled work history and the escalation of abusive behavior during the summer of 1988 relate directly to the foreseeability prong of duty. The facts . . . show that it was foreseeable that Landin could act violently against a coemployee, and against Nesser in particular.

This foreseeability gives rise to a duty of care to Nesser that is not outweighed by policy considerations of employment opportunity. An ex-felon's "opportunity for gainful employment may spell the difference between recidivism and rehabilitation," but it cannot predominate over the need to maintain a safe workplace when specific actions point to future violence.

Our holding is narrow and limited only to the recognition of a legal duty owed to Nesser arising out of Honeywell's continued employment of Landin. It is important to emphasize that in reversing the summary judgment on negligent retention, we do not reach the remaining significant questions of whether Honeywell breached that duty by failing to terminate or discipline Landin, or whether such a breach was a proximate cause of Nesser's death. These are issues generally decided by a jury after a full presentation of facts . . .

DECISION

We affirm the entry of summary judgment on the theories of negligent hiring and supervision, but reverse the summary judgment on the issue of negligent retention.

AFTERWORD

Published reports indicate the *Yunker* case was settled out of court soon after this decision was handed down.

Questions

1. What did the court mean when it said that "negligent hiring and negligent retention are based on direct, not vicarious, liability"?
2. Why did the court reject the negligent supervision claim?
3. Why did the court reject the negligent hiring claim?

4. Why did the court allow the negligent retention issue to go to trial?

5. L.M. sued Iglesia Cristiana La Casa Del Senor, Inc., an Assemblies of God Church in Florida, among others, because she allegedly was sexually assaulted at age 16 by the then church pastor, Ali Pacheco. The assault occurred at a hotel where Pacheco took the victim for lunch and for a conversation about the marital problems of the victim's parents. Pacheco testified that L.M. consented to the sexual act. The local church had not investigated Pacheco's background because that duty resided exclusively in the church's district offices. Pacheco had been involved in a consensual extramarital affair, but that relationship had not been discovered during the district's background check. Pacheco was president of the church corporation and his wife was vice president. Mrs. Pacheco learned that her husband had sent gifts to the victim, but the record is unclear as to whether she knew about the gifts prior to the sexual assault.

a. What causes of action against the local church and the district church could legitimately arise from these facts?

b. Decide the case. Explain. See *Iglesia Cristiana La Casa Del Senor, Inc. v. L.M.,* 783 So.2d 360 (Fl. Ct. App. 2001).

Part Three—Fair Labor Standards Act

A note was passed to President Franklin D. Roosevelt in 1936 from a young girl:

> I wish you could do something to help us girls. We have been working in a sewing factory . . . getting our minimum pay of $11 a week. Today, the 200 of us girls have been cut down to $4 and $5 and $6 a week.[19]

Roosevelt reportedly remarked that something needed to be done about child labor. The Depression and its tragic suffering, even of those working hard, shattered many Americans' faith in the free market and led to government intervention including, in 1938, the Fair Labor Standards Act (FLSA), which is directed to these major objectives:

1. The establishment of a minimum wage that provides at least a modest standard of living for employees.
2. A flexible ceiling on hours worked weekly, the purpose of which is to increase the number of employed Americans.
3. Child labor protection.
4. Equal pay for equal work regardless of gender. (See Chapter 13.)

[For the U.S. Department of Labor home page, see **http://www.dol.gov/**]

Minimum Wage   Pat Williams of Shreveport, Louisiana, lost her home gas service in April 2001 because, according to *The Wall Street Journal,* a $477 payment was overdue. She works for $5.55 per hour in her daytime nursing assistant job and $5.15 per hour in her evening cleaning job. She is a 46-year-old mother of three. She reports having been able to live comfortably and even indulge herself occasionally while working minimum wage jobs 20 years ago. Why is she unable to have a similarly comfortable life today with her current minimum wage jobs? *The Wall Street Journal* answered:

> There's little wonder why. As a longtime low-wage worker, Ms. Williams has felt the sting of one of the most profound shifts in American economic policy during the past 20 years: a mounting disdain for the minimum wage.

This sea change began when Ronald Reagan swept into office. From 1950 through 1982, the minimum wage was allowed to fall below 45 percent of the average hourly wage in the U.S. in only four separate years. Since 1982, the minimum wage has never reached 45 percent, and it currently stands at 36 percent of that benchmark.[20]

Many politicians and economists, however, fear that a minimum wage increase from the current federal requirement of $5.15 per hour would unfairly drive up the cost of doing business and reduce the number of entry-level jobs.

Some evidence supports that view, but other studies have found that a higher minimum wage does not harm job growth. For example, in the 17 states and the District of Columbia that have minimum wages above the federal $5.15 level, job growth appears to have been at least as strong as growth in the states with the federal minimum wage.[21]

The most interesting recent development in this area is the "living wage" movement. Since 1994, more than 100 communities have passed laws aimed at pushing wages high enough to lift families above the federal poverty line. The laws typically apply only to companies contracting to provide goods and services to the cities, although some cover city employees as well. Santa Fe, New Mexico, may have the most aggressive living wage plan. All Santa Fe businesses with more than 25 employees must pay $8.50 per hour, increasing to $10.50 by 2008.[22] Critics fear that businesses will lay off staff to fall below the 25 threshold, others will decline to expand, while others will simply leave. A 2002 study found, however, that the higher minimums have been effective in reducing poverty despite some increase in unemployment.[23] [For state minimum wage laws, see **http://www.dol.gov/esa/minwage/america.htm**]

Overtime   Vickey Ramsey, a former Wal-Mart assistant manager, was working 48 hours per week, but most of that time was occupied by stocking shelves and doing other tasks normally performed by hourly workers. Ramsey was moved to an hourly role at her request, but she sued Wal-Mart for classifying her as a manager in order, she claimed, to avoid paying overtime.[24] At this writing in 2005, Wal-Mart is facing some 30 overtime lawsuits.[25] Wal-Mart is not alone. A New Jersey appeals court ruled that Pepsi improperly failed to pay overtime to delivery truck drivers and others whom the company had classified as "outside" salespeople.[26] Disneyland paid $1.7 million to settle claims that it unlawfully failed to pay workers for their time spent getting into and out of costumes and for time spent wearing costumes before reaching the work site.[27]

> Wal-Mart is facing some 30 overtime lawsuits.

In general, workers are entitled to FLSA protections, including the minimum wage and overtime (normally time and one-half for hours over 40 per week), but certain occupational classes are *exempt;* that is, those workers are not entitled to FLSA protections. In response to corporate pleas for relief from lawsuits, the Bush administration approved a 2004 revision of overtime rules. While still complicated, the new rules attempt to clarify the murky distinction between exempt and nonexempt employees.

At the simplest level, nearly all workers making less than $23,660 per year will be nonexempt (entitled to time and one-half overtime pay), whereas very few of those making $100,000 or more will be entitled to that pay. The tens of millions in between may or may not receive overtime depending on some rather vague rules. Those who fall in one of the following classes may, after close analysis of their duties, prove to be exempt from the overtime protections: executives, administrators, professional/creative workers, computer professionals, and outside salespeople. Some workers such as police officers, firefighters, and better-paid blue-collar workers are expressly granted the right to overtime pay. Others, such as insurance adjusters, dental hygienists, pharmacists, and journalists, are expressly exempt and thus not entitled to overtime. Critics say millions of workers will be ineligible for overtime pay under the new rules, but at this writing the impact is unclear. [For more details about the new overtime rules, see the federal Department of Labor guidance at **http://www.dol.gov/esa/regs/compliance/whd/fairpay/main.htm**]

Question

Answer this person's complaint: "I work at a business that offers overtime. There are two employees, myself and one other, who do the same job. The other person is always offered overtime, and I'm left working regular hours only. Is there a law that requires an employer to equally distribute overtime? Is there some place I can complain to?"[28]

Part Four—Health and Safety at Work

Jose Alatorre

An illegal Mexican immigrant, Jose Alatorre, took a job for $8.75 an hour as a welder at a dairy farm in the California Central Valley. He was 22. On his first wedding anniversary (February 22, 2001) his wife asked him to stay home, but he said he had to go to work for the morning to repair a machine. The farm's 1,700 cattle produced 200,000 gallons of waste per day. That day the waste pump clogged. Alatorre went down a 30-foot shaft, was overcome by hydrogen sulfide gas, plunged headfirst into standing manure, and drowned. Another worker died trying to rescue him.

> Alatorre was overcome by hydrogen sulfide gas.

At the time of their deaths *The New York Times* reported that the two men's lungs were packed with cow manure, and they had eight pennies and one dime in their pockets. In telling Alatorre's story, the *Times* reported on his first encounter with his wife-to-be:

> It was not a promising pickup line. "I don't own a car, I'm not legally here, and I don't earn much money," he said, flashing a smile. "It's up to you." Angelica Acevedo Hernandez followed Jose Alatorre onto the dance floor.[29]

Mexican Deaths   Perhaps we are not surprised to learn that the American workplace is particularly hazardous for Mexican workers. The Associated Press recently studied Mexican workplace deaths:

- The workplace death rate for Mexicans in a number of western and southwestern states is four times that of the average for United States–born workers in those states.
- Mexican death rates are rising while the U.S. workplace grows safer overall.
- "Though Mexicans often take the most hazardous jobs, they are more likely than others to be killed even when doing similarly risky work. . . . These accidental deaths are almost always preventable and often gruesome: Workers are impaled, shredded in machinery, buried alive. Some are as young as 15."[30] Government officials note, however, that the most recent data show, for the first time, a decline in workplace deaths among foreign-born Hispanics.[31]

Deaths, Illnesses, and Injuries

Although Mexicans working in America are significantly at risk, the total American workplace has gradually become safer because of tighter rules, improved workplace technology, and the shift to service industry jobs. Here are the data:

- Nationwide workplace deaths in 2003 totaled 5,559, up from 5,534 in 2002,[32] but the rate of fatalities remained at 4.0 per 100,000 workers, and the fatality rate fell some 11 percent from 1998 to 2003.[33]
- Injuries and illnesses continued their steady decline with a 2002 rate of 5.3 injuries and illnesses per 100 workers, down from 6.7 in 1998.[34]
- In fiscal year 2004, the federal government found nearly 87,000 workplace violations of its rules, a 9.5 percent increase over the previous five years, with serious violations up by 3 percent in one year and willful violations up by 14 percent during that year.[35] Of course, that increase might reflect more effective government oversight.

OSHA

The 1970 Occupational Safety and Health Act imposes a *general duty* on most employers to provide a workplace free of "recognized hazards causing or likely to cause death or serious physical harm to employees." Employers have an absolute duty to remove any serious and preventable workplace hazards that are generally recognized in the industry and are known to the employer or should be known to the employer. That general duty is then supplemented with numerous, detailed, and demanding *specific standards*. A federal agency, the Occupational Safety and Health Administration (OSHA), is responsible for ensuring safe workplaces. [For the OSHA home page, see **www.osha.gov**]

Standards

OSHA, through the secretary of labor, promulgates and enforces health and safety standards that identify and seek to correct specific workplace hazards and problems. These can range from exposure to cancer-causing agents (such as the chemical benzene), to the surprisingly commonplace problem of one worker restarting a machine while another is servicing it, to mundane requirements for sanitary toilet facilities in agricultural jobs. [For OSHA standards, see **http://www.osha.gov/comp-links.html**]

New Standards?

A battle is inevitable when OSHA considers new workplace safety measures. A pair of safety issues demonstrates some of the competing considerations in determining whether further government intervention is needed.

Ergonomics   Repetitive motion and overexertion injure about 1.8 million workers annually.[36] These musculoskeletal injuries, such as carpal tunnel syndrome and back strains, total one-third of all workplace injuries and cost billions of dollars.[37] Employers often try to address those problems via ergonomics, "the science of fitting the job to the worker."[38] In response to the many injuries and their high costs and after 10 years of study commencing with the George Bush Senior administration, OSHA issued new ergonomics standards at the close of the Clinton administration in 2000 that were intended to provide strict rules for adapting workplaces to employee practices (for example, changing the height of a workstation or slowing down a production line). However, with the backing of the Bush administration, Congress repealed those rules in 2001 after the business community complained about the cost of compliance. The government had estimated that the rules would cost about $4.5 billion annually[39] and save $9 billion,[40] but business groups said the costs could balloon to $125 billion.[41] A new plan was issued in 2002 to replace the mandatory rules with voluntary guidelines, but OSHA in 2003 asserted its general duty power to once again issue ergonomics citations in high-hazard workplaces such as nursing homes and grocery chains. OSHA has indicated that citations will be directed only to employers with high injury rates who do not make a good-faith effort to address those problems.

[For advice on measures to reduce repetitive stress problems for students, see **http://ergo.human.cornell.edu**]

"Going postal"

Violence "Going postal" has become, probably unfairly, a readily recognizable shorthand expression for violence in the workplace. Workplace homicides, the third leading cause of on-the-job deaths, increased to 631 in 2003 from 609 in 2002.[42] With other workplace deaths declining steadily and national overall murder rates falling precipitously in recent years, we must wonder what accounts for rather steady or, in some years, increasing workplace homicides. Stress from job insecurity, deadlines, tight work spaces, overwork, and so on seem to be ongoing problems. In a recent survey, 42 percent of office workers said yelling and verbal abuse happened frequently in their offices.[43]

But should OSHA assert its authority? Do we need new rules to curb workplace violence? Would those rules prove effective? Can management take steps to reduce workplace tensions? OSHA, at least during the Bush years, is unlikely to take an activist stance except for situations like ergonomics, where some industries clearly can improve their safety measures. Indeed, in 2004 OSHA levied a $2,500 fine and cited a Dallas janitorial firm that allegedly failed to protect employees who worked at night in Dallas Area Rapid Transit stations.[44]

Variances

Employers may seek both permanent and temporary variances (exceptions) from OSHA standards. A permanent variance may be granted only if the workplace will be as safe as if the standard were enforced. A temporary variance permits additional time to put in place the necessary compliance measures. Employees have a right to a hearing to contest variances.

Fatal Accidents: The Bright Side

Every day some new do-gooder is trying to save us from ourselves. We have so many laws and safety commissions to ensure our safety that it seems nearly impossible to have an accident. The problem is that we need accidents, and lots of them.

Danger is nature's way of eliminating stupid people. Without safety, stupid people die in accidents. Since the dead don't reproduce, our species becomes progressively more intelligent (or at least less stupid).

With safety, however well-intentioned it may be, we are devolving into half-witted mutants, because idiots, who by all rights should be dead, are spared from their rightful early graves and are free to breed even more imbeciles.

Let's do away with safety and improve our species. Take up smoking. Jaywalk. Play with blasting caps. Swim right after a big meal. Stick something small in your ear. Take your choice of dangerous activity and do it with gusto. Future generations will thank you.

Source: This letter to the editor by Lawrence A. Bullis, originally published in the *Arizona Republic,* appeared in issue number 49 of *View from the Ledge,* a 'zine published by Chuck Shepherd in St. Petersburg, Florida. Bullis lives in Phoenix.

OSHA Information Requirements

Right to Know

OSHA has adopted an employee *hazard communication standard* to protect employees from the dangers associated with chemicals and other toxins in the workplace. Chemical manufacturers and importers must develop *material safety data sheets* for all chemicals. Employers must then label all chemical containers so that employees will know about the chemical and its dangers, and employers must educate employees about chemical hazards and how to deal with them.

Records

Businesses must maintain records listing and summarizing injuries, illnesses, and deaths on the job. A summary of those records must be posted at the job. Notice of any OSHA citations of imminent dangers on the job must also be posted at the job site. OSHA reformed and simplified the record-keeping process effective in 2002. Some smaller companies, especially in nonhazardous activities, do not need to meet the record-keeping requirements.

Enforcement

OSHA's most publicized enforcement mechanism is the unannounced on-site inspection. Inspections arise at the initiative of the agency itself or at the request of employees or their representatives. The inspections must be conducted in a reasonable manner during working hours or other reasonable times, and ordinarily they must not be announced in advance. Employers can demand a warrant prior to inspection. With proper justification, warrants can easily be secured from a federal magistrate. Employer and employee representatives may accompany the inspector.

To enhance efficiency, OSHA practices a targeted, site-specific inspection plan designed to identify the workplaces most likely to have safety and health problems. The targeted sites are those that reported at least 14 injuries or illnesses for every 100 full-time workers where lost workdays or restricted activity resulted. OSHA explains its enforcement policy at its Web site:

> OSHA seeks to assist the majority of employers who want to do the right thing while focusing its enforcement resources on sites in more hazardous industries—especially those with high injury and illness rates. Less than 1 percent of inspections—about 300—came under the agency's Enhanced Enforcement Program, designed to address employers who repeatedly and willfully violate the law. . . . Outreach, education, and compliance assistance enable OSHA to play a vital role in preventing on-the-job injuries and illnesses.[45] [For an overview of "OSHA Facts," see **http://www.osha.gov/as/opa/oshafacts.html**]

Citations

Citations may be issued if violations are discovered during the inspection process. Immediate, serious threats can be restrained with a court order. Following a citation, the employer may ask to meet with an area OSHA official to discuss the problem. Often a settlement emerges from these meetings. Failing a settlement, the employer can appeal to the independent OSHA Review Commission and thereafter to the federal court of appeals. Violations may lead to fines and/or imprisonment.

Firmer Enforcement? The business community criticizes OSHA for unfairly increasing the cost of production by imposing inflexible and overzealous expectations. Labor organizations and job safety advocates, on the other hand, see OSHA as a timid, faltering safety shield. The AFL–CIO estimates that OSHA can inspect each American workplace only once each century.

> OSHA can inspect each American workplace only once each century.

Concerns about workplace deaths led *The New York Times* to conduct an eight-month investigation of OSHA enforcement policy. The *Times* concluded that OSHA officials had not fulfilled their promises to aggressively pursue the worst of workplace safety wrongs:

> Over a span of two decades, from 1982 to 2002, OSHA investigated 1,242 of these horror stories—instances in which the agency itself concluded that workers had died because of their employer's "willful" safety violations. Yet in 93 percent of those cases, OSHA declined to seek prosecution. . . . What is more, having avoided prosecution once, at least 70 employers willfully violated safety laws again, resulting in scores of additional deaths. Even these repeat violators were rarely prosecuted.[46]

PRACTICING ETHICS) Manslaughter on the Job?

When, if ever, should managerial misjudgments, carelessness, and indifference be treated as crimes with serious penalties including imprisonment? Or does the market, in most cases, provide an effective, just method of addressing workplace deaths? Consider the criminal prosecution that emerged from the aforementioned case of Jose Alatorre and a would-be rescuer who, while working, drowned in cow manure at the bottom of a 30-foot-deep sump hole. California officials decided to charge dairy manager Patrick Faria with involuntary manslaughter in the Alatorre episode. Faria was not on the site when the workplace deaths occurred, but officials reportedly had "indications that he knew the dangers of the shaft."[47] A newspaper account summarized the prosecution view:

> As a volunteer county firefighter, he aced the test on safety in confined spaces. But he hadn't relayed that information to his workers, prosecutors say, and did not supply them with proper fans to ventilate the air or a harness to extract a stricken worker. Faria could have

hired a professional crew to clean the pump for about $600, according to prosecutor Gale Filter, instead of sending down three low-wage dairyhands. "It's about money, M-O-N-E-Y," Filter told the grand jury that indicted Faria.[48]

Question

As you see it, do these facts merit a criminal conviction of involuntary manslaughter for a man who was a volunteer firefighter and a county employee of the year?

Workers' Compensation

Korey Stringer, a 27-year-old Pro Bowl tackle, died of heatstroke complications.

Korey Stringer, a 27-year-old Pro Bowl tackle, died of heatstroke complications on August 1, 2001, after going through a preseason Minnesota Vikings workout. Normally, when an employee is injured or dies on the job, the employee or the estate may not sue for damages. Rather, recovery is limited to the fixed sum provided for by the workers' compensation statute, regardless of fault. Stringer's family, however, filed a wrongful death suit trying to hold the Vikings and various individuals responsible for negligence, intentional infliction of emotional distress, and other wrongs in responding to Stringer's heatstroke. The Vikings argue that the Stringer suit is barred by the state workers' compensation law. Minnesota is one of a number of states, however, that recognize an exception to workers' compensation exclusivity provisions in cases of gross negligence by the defendants. At this writing, the Minnesota Supreme Court has agreed to review the case after two lower court defeats for the Stringer family.[49]

Early in the twentieth century, the states began enacting workers' compensation laws to provide an administrative remedy for those, like Stringer, who are injured or killed on the job. Previously, employers' superior financial resources and various technical legal defenses meant that employees often could not successfully sue to recover damages for their on-the-job injuries. Thus all states now provide some form of workers' compensation not requiring a lawsuit. Workers or their families simply apply for compensation based on illness, injury, or death. Typically, the system is governed by a state board or commission. Most decisions are routine and are accomplished by completing the necessary forms. Often a claims examiner will verify the nature and severity of the injury. In return for the ease and predictability of the system, however, workers and families are, by law, denied the right to sue, barring unusual circumstances such as gross negligence (as alleged in the Stringer case).

In most states, employers are compelled to participate in workers' compensation, depending on state law, either by purchasing insurance privately, by contributing to a state-managed fund, or by being self-insured (paying claims directly from their own funds). Firms with good safety records are rewarded with lower premium payments.

Toilet Seat

A man was taken to Covenant Medical Center [Waterloo, Iowa] to get a toilet seat removed from his backside after someone applied some sort of adhesive in a Kmart bathroom. [Fire Rescue Captain Michael Pierce:] "We had to dismantle the stall. I guess he was fairly agitated about the whole thing."

If the victim had been a Kmart employee, was he entitled to workers' compensation?

Source: Waterloo/Cedar Falls Courier, July 8, 2001, p. B5.

Benefits

A benefits schedule specifies the sum to be awarded for the injury (or death) in question. The amount of the award is normally a percentage of the worker's salary either for a specified period or indefinitely, depending on the severity of the injury. Injury benefits normally amount to one-half to two-thirds of regular wages. Death benefits ordinarily are tied to the wages of the deceased.

Coverage

Certain employment classifications such as agriculture may be excluded from workers' compensation, but about 90 percent of the labor force is covered. Most on-the-job injuries are covered, but those that are self-inflicted (including starting a fight) and others such as those springing from alcohol or drug use may not be.

Legal Requirements

In general, injuries, illnesses, and deaths are compensable where the harm (1) *arose out of the employment,* and (2) *arose in the course of employment.* (explained next in *Ciha*). Proof of employer negligence is not required, and the traditional defenses such as contributory negligence are not available to the employer. Thus workers' compensation provides a form of no-fault protection in the workplace. Workers give up the right to sue, and employers participate in an insurance system that recognizes the inevitability of workplace harm.

Although workers' compensation recovery is the exclusive remedy for workplace injury, illness, or death, some jurisdictions allow litigation in cases of intentional torts and/or gross negligence, as noted earlier. [For the Workers' Compensation Research Institute, see **http://www.wcrinet.org/**]

Litigation

Notwithstanding its no-fault character, workers' compensation has generated many lawsuits. For example, Manuel Guico had worked for two years in an Excel meat packing plant until he was fired after sustaining an injury on the job. Guico's knife slipped, cutting his thumb and a finger, and causing an 11 percent permanent partial disability. Guico had repeatedly been told to wear his steel-mesh gloves and mesh apron whenever he was using his knife, but he was not doing so when he was injured. Guico applied for and received workers' compensation benefits. Excel appealed to the courts but lost when the Nebraska Supreme Court ruled that Excel failed to show that Guico was willfully negligent.[50]

Quaker Oats Co. v. Ciha

552 N. W. 2d 143 (Iowa S. Ct. 1996)

Chief Justice McGiverin

I. BACKGROUND FACTS

In May 1991, petitioner Bradley Ciha was employed by defendant Quaker Oats Company at its Cedar Rapids plant as an area maintenance supervisor. . . . By all accounts, Ciha was considered an excellent employee. Ciha's normal workweek at Quaker Oats was Monday through Friday. On a typical weekend including Saturday and Sunday, Ciha was not on duty and was not expected to be on call to drive to the plant for emergency maintenance purposes.

For the first 48 hours on Memorial Day weekend in 1991, Ciha was assigned as "204 supervisor" for Quaker Oats. In that capacity, he was required to be on call for mechanical emergencies anywhere in the plant.

While preparing dinner at his home on Sunday, May 26, Ciha was contacted at approximately 4:15 PM through a company electronic paging device. He was informed that several large cooling fans at the plant were malfunctioning. Ciha responded to the breakdown by electing to drive his motorcycle to the plant to remedy the problem himself. To reach the plant, Ciha drove a direct route (of approximately four and a half miles) on Johnson Avenue. After reaching the plant without incident, he personally remedied the problem by cooling the fans with an air hose. At approximately 5:45 PM, Ciha telephoned his wife and informed her that she could resume dinner preparations because he was about to return home.

Ciha drove a different route from the plant to home than he drove earlier from his home to the plant. The return-home route was on Ellis Road and was admittedly not the most direct route from the plant to Ciha's home. The Ellis Road route (approximately nine miles) was scenic and subject to less traffic and traffic signals than the direct route Ciha commonly drove from home to the plant. Apparently, the Ellis Road route took approximately five to seven minutes longer to drive than the direct, Johnson Avenue route.

On his return trip from the plant to home along Ellis Road, Ciha was involved in a serious motor vehicle accident in which he suffered a broken neck and was rendered a quadriplegic. At the time of the accident, Ciha was married and resided in a home in Cedar Rapids with his wife, Kim.

Following the accident, Ciha was admitted to St. Luke's Hospital in Cedar Rapids until June 12, 1991, when he requested transfer to a specialized care facility, Craig Hospital, located in Englewood, Colorado.

In addition to the health care Ciha received while at Craig, the hospital also provided Kim specialized training in order for her to be able to care for Ciha upon his return home.

Ciha was discharged from Craig Hospital on September 14, 1991, to his home in Cedar Rapids. Since his discharge, Kim has performed necessary, extensive home nursing services. Ciha requires assistance in dressing, changing urine bags, and transferring between his wheelchair and his bed. At night, he must be repositioned in bed one to four times in order to prevent him from developing pressure sores.

Ciha first returned to work at Quaker Oats in January 1992 in a new position as materials supervisor. In this position, he works at a computer (with the aid of an adaptive device and telephone headset) in the company's purchasing department. With the aid of a modified computer, Ciha analyzes inventory and makes purchases on behalf of Quaker Oats. Quaker Oats greatly aided in Ciha's return to work by adapting the workplace and position in order for Ciha to be able to perform the job.

In his position as materials supervisor, he receives the same base salary, not including raises, as that of an area maintenance supervisor. Ciha no longer has the same opportunity, however, to earn overtime as he had as an area maintenance supervisor.

In order to return to work, Ciha relied on the county's disabled persons transportation service to and from Quaker Oats. Based on the hours of the transportation service, however, Ciha was not able to return to work full-time.

Ciha was readmitted to Craig for one week in March 1992 for a comprehensive evaluation. At the time of his readmittance, Ciha did not own a van and did not drive. While at Craig, Ciha had his driving potential assessed. A driving specialist from the hospital concluded Ciha would need to purchase a specially modified van in order to be able to drive independently. At some time thereafter, Ciha purchased the recommended van.

Many of Ciha's medical expenses from the accident were paid for through a group health and accident insurance plan available to Ciha through his employer Quaker Oats. However, there were significant limitations in coverage under the group plan. For example, in addition to a lifetime cap on medical expenses, the group plan did not provide Ciha coverage for necessary home health care services, home modifications, or motor vehicle conversions.

II. WORKERS' COMPENSATION LITIGATION

In November 1991, Ciha filed a claim for permanent partial disability benefits with the Iowa industrial commissioner's office against his employer, Quaker Oats.

Ciha's claim proceeded to an arbitration hearing.

* * * * *

[At arbitration, the deputy industrial commissioner reached several conclusions favorable to Ciha. Quaker Oats then appealed to the industrial commissioner who agreed with the deputy. Quaker Oats next took the case to the district court, which affirmed. The Iowa Supreme Court then undertook this review.]

* * * * *

IV. GOING AND COMING RULE, THE "SPECIAL ERRAND" AND "REQUIRED VEHICLE" EXCEPTIONS, AND DEVIATION

In Iowa,

> [e]very employer, not specifically excepted by the provisions of [Iowa Code chapter 85], shall provide, secure, and pay compensation according to the provisions of this chapter for any and all personal injuries sustained by an employee arising out of and in the course of the employment. . . .

To obtain such compensation, an injured employee has the burden of proving by a preponderance of the evidence that his injuries arose out of and in the course of his employment. An injury arises "out of" the employment when there is a causal relationship between the employment and the injury. "In the course of" the employment concerns the time, place, and circumstances of the injury. Stated more specifically,

> [a]n injury occurs in the course of the employment when it is within the period of employment at a place where the employee reasonably may be in performing his duties, and while he is fulfilling those duties or engaged in doing something incidental thereto. An injury in the course of employment embraces all injuries received while employed in furthering the employer's business and injuries received on the employer's premises, provided that the employee's presence must ordinarily be required at the place of the injury, or, if not so required, employee's departure from the usual place of employment must not amount to an abandonment of employment or be an act wholly foreign to his usual work. An employee does not cease to be in the course of his employment merely because he is not actually engaged in doing some specifically prescribed task, if, in the course of his employment, he does some act which he deems necessary for the benefit or interest of his employer.

First and foremost, Quaker Oats contends Ciha did not sustain his injury in the course of his employment because the injury was sustained away from the employer's premises and while Ciha was on his way home from the plant. The employer relies on the well-established "going and coming" rule, which generally provides, "[A]bsent special circumstances, injuries occurring off the employer's premises while the employee is on the way to or from work are not compensable."

Under the going and coming rule, Ciha admittedly did not sustain an injury in the course of his employment: He was injured while driving his motorcycle home from the Quaker Oats plant.

There are, however, several exceptions to the going and coming rule. . . .

The first exception to the going and coming rule relied on by the commissioner is the "special errand" exception.

Under the exception, if an employee is on a special errand or mission for his or her employer at the time of the injury, the injury is held to have arisen in the course of employment.

* * * * *

After considering all arguments raised by the parties, we believe substantial evidence supports the commissioner's conclusion that Ciha was on a special errand at the time of his injury.

[I]n answer to the question "[w]hose business was [the employee] pursuing at the time of the injury?" the answer must be Quaker Oats' business. The fact that Ciha was contacted on Sunday while he was on 204 duty was truly "special." it was unusual, sudden, and unexpected.

* * * * *

Deviation

Notwithstanding our conclusion that the special errand exception to the going and coming rule applies in the present case, Quaker Oats contends Ciha had "deviated" from his trip home from the plant to such an extent that he abandoned his employment at the time of the accident. The commissioner and district court rejected this argument, and we do the same.

* * * * *

In concluding Ciha did not deviate from his special errand, the commissioner stated,

> [Ciha] testified that he often took [the Ellis Road] route home because it was more scenic, it had less traffic, it had fewer stoplights, and the actual difference in miles between this route and the more direct route was minimal. [Ciha's] call to his wife from the plant to start the grill for their meal shows that his purpose was to return home, and that he had no other destination other than to return to his residence. The record does not show a deviation from the course of the employment.

V. CLAIMED EXPENSES UNDER IOWA CODE SECTION 85.27

Of the expenses awarded by the commissioner under Iowa Code section 85.27, Quaker Oats only challenges the award of costs for home modifications, van conversion, and home nursing services. The commissioner and district court found the home modification and van conversion expenses to be reasonable "appliances" under section 85.27. In addition, the commissioner found the claimed expenses for home nursing services and the claimed value of those services to be reasonable.

Iowa Code section 85.27 provides in pertinent part,

The employer, for all injuries compensable under this chapter or chapter 85A, shall furnish reasonable surgical, medical, dental, osteopathic, chiropractic, podiatric, physical rehabilitation, nursing, ambulance, and hospital services and supplies therefor and shall allow reasonably necessary transportation expenses incurred for such services. The employer shall also furnish reasonable and necessary crutches, artificial members, and appliances....

* * * * *

A. Home Modifications and Van Conversion

In order for Ciha to have been able to access his house in a wheelchair upon his return from Craig Hospital, various home modifications were required. The home modifications included widened doorways, a ramp into the home, a special shower, an elevator, and other items necessitated by Ciha's wheelchair-bound status. He also incurred van conversion expenses in order to be able to return to work full-time.

In his workers' compensation claim, Ciha sought and was awarded $20,788 in home modification expenses and $24,509 in van conversion expenses under Iowa Code section 85.27. The deputy concluded the home modification expenses incurred by Ciha "relate to items designed to substitute for function lost in [his] work injury." Relying on past agency decisions, the commissioner also held Quaker Oats responsible for the van conversion expenses. The commissioner further concluded,

[Ciha's] need for a ramp to enter his home, and for a special shower designed to accommodate a wheelchair, are held to be necessary and reasonable medical expenses. All of the items are related to accommodating [Ciha's] wheelchair. An appliance has been held to be a device that serves to replace a physical function lost by the injury. Just as a wheelchair seeks to replace the lost functions of standing and walking, a wheelchair ramp, a wheelchair shower, etc. also seek to replace physical functions claimant possessed before the work injury but has now lost.

Quaker Oats contends on appeal that the claimed home modification and van conversion costs are not compensable as "appliances."

* * * * *

We begin with the unusually strong medical evidence of necessity and of the record that [the claimant's] family status and past lifestyle reveal no other use for the van. That evidence refutes any contention that the van is a frill or luxury and reveals what can be described as an appliance, not greatly different from crutches or a wheelchair. The point is that a van is necessary in order to make [the claimant's] wheelchair fully useful.

* * * * *

B. Home Nursing Services

In addition to the claimed home modification and van conversion expenses, Ciha also sought $58,447 in home nursing services performed by his wife after his return home from the hospital in Colorado. At the arbitration hearing, Quaker Oats unsuccessfully contended the claimed home nursing services were not reasonable expenses under section 85.27, and also that the claimed amount of the services set forth in an affidavit prepared by Kim Ciha was unreasonable.

On appeal, Quaker Oats does not dispute that it had a duty under Iowa Code section 85.27 to provide reasonable nursing services to Ciha if his injury was compensable (which we have concluded it is). In addition, Quaker Oats agrees the services performed by Kim were "nursing" services as contemplated by section 85.27. Quaker Oats contends, however, that $58,447 in home nursing expenses claimed by Ciha is unreasonable. The commissioner and district court disagreed.

In ordering Quaker Oats to pay Ciha's home nursing services, the commissioner stated the following:

In the instant case, [Ciha's] spouse, although not a nurse or LPN, did have to receive special training to perform the services. The services themselves are clearly medical nursing services and not general care services such as dressing, bathing, feeding, etc.

We believe the affidavit and Kim's testimony establish the reasonableness of the claimed home nursing care expenses....

Industrial Disability

As a final issue, Quaker Oats contends the commissioner erred in ruling that Ciha had sustained an 80 percent permanent partial industrial disability. Quaker Oats argues Ciha's disability is only 50 to 60 percent because it, Ciha's employer, went to great lengths to accommodate claimant and also that claimant has suffered no loss of earnings.

As we have stated on many occasions, "[i]ndustrial disability measures an injured worker's lost earning capacity." Factors that should be considered include the employee's functional disability, age, education, qualifications, experience, and the ability of the employee to engage in employment for which the employee is fitted.

As a result of the accident and resulting quadriplegia, Ciha is wheelchair-bound, cannot control his bowel functions, and his lifestyle has been severely limited from that prior to the injury. He requires extensive, daily care and attention by his wife, relatives, and coworkers as he no longer has the ability to perform many basic daily living functions. Also, as a 38-year-old man, it cannot be reasonably disputed that Ciha's employability outside of the Quaker Oats workforce has been significantly and negatively affected by his injury. Although we applaud the efforts of Quaker Oats in modifying the workplace to accommodate Ciha's disability, such efforts are not determinative of Ciha's industrial disability rating. *See Thilges v. Snap-On Tools Corp.,* 528 N.W.2d 614, 617 (Iowa 1995) ("[W]e are satisfied that the commissioner was correct in viewing loss of earning capacity in terms of the injured worker's present ability to earn in the competitive job market without regard to the accommodation furnished by one's present employer.").

* * * * *

We conclude there is substantial evidence to support the commissioner's decision on this issue.

Affirmed.

Questions

1. The Iowa Supreme Court in *Quaker Oats* (and most courts in workers' compensation cases) required a two-part showing that the injury must "arise out of" and "in the course of" employment.

   a. Explain those two standards.

   b. Must an employee be engaged in a prescribed task in order to be "in the course of employment?" Explain.

   c. Why did the court conclude that Ciha was on a "special errand?"

2. Why did the court conclude that Ciha had suffered an 80 percent permanent partial industrial disability?

3. Fernandez, an exotic dancer, left her job drunk and was seriously injured in a crash while riding as a passenger in a car driven by another dancer. The crash came within one hour of leaving work. Her intoxication led to her decision to ride with her intoxicated coworker. Fernandez sought workers' compensation. She claimed that her employer, Bottoms Up Lounge in Council Bluffs, Iowa, required her to socialize with male customers when not dancing and to generate at least two drinks per hour from customers. Dancers were not required to drink, but most dancers consumed six to eight drinks per night or more. Did Fernandez's injury arise out of and in the course of employment so that she can recover workers' compensation? Explain. See *2800 Corp. v. Fernandez,* 528 N.W.2d 124 (Ia. S.Ct. 1995).

4. Joseph Smyth, a college mathematics instructor, was killed while driving his personal auto home from work. At the time, Smyth had student papers with him, which he intended to grade that evening. He often worked at home. Many faculty members took work home in the evenings. However, the college did not require that practice. Indeed, the college neither encouraged nor discouraged working at home.

   The widely adopted "going and coming rule" provides that employees injured while commuting to and from work, in general, are not covered by workers' compensation.

   a. Should Smyth (and other teachers) be exempted from the going and coming rule, thus permitting recovery by Smyth's family? Explain. See *Santa Rosa Junior College v. Workers' Compensation Appeals Board and Joann Smyth,* 708 P.2d 673 (Cal. S.Ct. 1985).

   b. Would you reach a different conclusion had a student been accompanying Smyth? Explain.

5. Casimer Gacioch worked at a Stroh Brewery. The company provided free beer at work. When he began work in 1947 he drank only three to four beers on the weekend. He was fired in 1974, by which time he was drinking 12 bottles of beer daily. After Gacioch's death, his wife sought workers' compensation benefits. The evidence indicated that Gacioch had a predisposition to alcoholism but was not an alcoholic at the time he was hired. How would you rule on the widow's workers' compensation claim? Explain. See *Gacioch v. Stroh Brewery,* 466 N.W. 2d 303 (Mich Ct. of Appeals, 1991).

Part Five—Employee Privacy

Do we have a "right to privacy" on the job? Increasingly, employers are engaging in an array of testing and monitoring procedures both before and after hiring. Drug testing, integrity tests, personality tests, spying, television and computer monitoring of work performance, and so forth are routine personnel practices in many firms. Employers have an interest in these strategies not only to hire better employees and improve productivity but to protect coworkers, reduce insurance claims, and shield consumers from poor products and service. On the other hand, job applicants and employees often feel "Big Brother" looking over their shoulders, as corporate critic Barbara Ehrenreich argues:

> Only a person of unblemished virtue can get a job at Wal-Mart—a low-level job, that is . . . A drug test eliminates the chemical miscreants; a detailed "personality test" probes the job applicant's horror of theft and willingness to turn in an erring coworker.
>
> Extreme submissiveness to authority is another desirable trait. When I applied for a job at Wal-Mart . . . I was reprimanded for getting something wrong on this test: I had agreed only "strongly" to the proposition, "All rules have to be followed to the letter at all times." The correct answer was totally agree. . . .[51]

Off the Job?   Do employers' financial goals justify policies that significantly reshape employee lives—especially their off-the-job lives? Should employers be able, for example, to require employees to lose weight or to quit smoking? One study of large employers finds 11.5 percent of the population accounting for 80 percent of health costs, with the chronically ill being particularly expensive.[52] Many employers offer wellness programs and various incentives to encourage employees to achieve more healthful lifestyles. Now some are going further by firing workers who refuse to take nicotine tests to prove they do not smoke. Others are beginning to charge higher insurance rates for those who fail to meet weight and health standards. The law offers only limited protection for employees. About half the states offer some form of "smoking discrimination" protection, and the federal Health Insurance Portability and Accountability Act (HIPAA) generally forbids discrimination based on health status or conditions.

What about "office romance"?   And what about "office romance"? Changing cultural patterns have made the workplace a primary venue for romance and marriage. A 2003 poll found 47 percent of office workers had had an office romance and 19 percent more would like to do so.[53] Managers, however, are increasingly concerned about those relationships. More than one-third of 558 companies surveyed in 2001 said employees involved in office romances could be fired, up from 27 percent taking that position in 1998.[54] Managers are concerned about productivity and fairness, but perhaps the bigger fear is the possibility of sexual harassment charges. (See Chapter 13.)

Drug Testing: Introduction

Drug testing in the corporate workplace is simply a fact of life, especially for blue-collar workers. Most *Fortune* 500 companies use some form of drug testing, although some companies, including Hewlett-Packard, have found so few job applicants testing positive that drug testing is not cost-effective for them. Regardless of the severity of the risk, many companies feel they must engage in drug testing to protect themselves against liability claims should an impaired employee cause harm and to comply with the federal Drug-Free Workplace Act. [For more details on drug testing results, see **www.questdiagnostic.com**]

Drug-Free Workplace

The Drug-Free Workplace Act of 1988 applies to employers who have contracts of $100,000 or more with the federal government or who receive aid from the government. Those employers are required to develop an antidrug policy for employees. They must provide drug-free awareness programs for employees, and they must acquaint employees with available assistance for those with drug problems, while also warning them of the penalties that accompany violation of the policy. The act requires employees to adhere to the company policy and to inform the company within five days if they are convicted of or plead no contest to a drug-related offense in the workplace. [For more drug testing information, see **http://www.courttv.com/legalcafe/work/drug_testing/**]

Drug Testing in Practice

Broadly, employment-based alcohol and drug testing occurs in six circumstances: (1) preemployment screening, (2) routine physical examinations, (3) "reasonable suspicion" testing, (4) postaccident testing, (5) random testing, and (6) follow-up testing.[55]

1. Ordinarily, private-sector, preemployment testing is lawful although some state and local laws may impose restrictions. In general, public-sector employers have less drug testing latitude because of constitutional limitations, but when challenged in court, those programs have generally been approved.
2. Drug testing as a part of periodic physical examinations is generally lawful if properly conducted. To avoid legal problems, employers should notify job applicants and current employees of drug testing in association with physicals.
3. Reasonable suspicion is something less than probable cause and means that the employer has evidence, such as lapses in performance, that would justify a drug test. Such tests, given a sound factual foundation and even-handed application, ordinarily are permissible.
4. Post accident testing involves employees who have been involved in a serious on-the-job accident. Such tests normally are permissible.
5. Selecting employees at random, without notice, for drug testing can be very effective in deterring drug use, but the practice raises significant legal questions. Some states explicitly forbid random testing, except for safety-sensitive jobs such as those in transportation. The Supreme Court has upheld such testing for public-sector employees where public safety is involved and for those having access to particularly sensitive information.[56]
6. Follow-up testing is used for employees who are returning from drug or alcohol rehabilitation. The testing acts as an incentive for recovering drug users to remain "clean." All states permit follow-up testing, but employers should create contracts with rehabilitating employees to establish testing arrangements.

Legal Challenges to Alcohol and Drug Testing

Drug use as a societal problem is undeniable, but critics are concerned that personal rights may be trampled in our zeal to attack substance abuse. Some of the doubts are that the tests (1) are often unreliable, (2) invade employee privacy, and (3) do not measure actual job impairment.

Challenges to drug testing ordinarily spring from the following claims and defenses:

1. **Federal constitution:** As explained in Chapter 5, the Fourth Amendment to the United States Constitution forbids unreasonable searches and seizures. Thus government officials ordinarily cannot conduct a search without individualized suspicion—that is, without probable cause. Certain exceptions, however, have been recognized in cases involving safety, national security, athletic participation, and other special needs. Remember that the Constitution protects us from the government, not from private-sector employers (with limited exceptions).

2. **State constitutions:** Many state constitutions offer privacy protection, but court decisions, to date, have generally not extended those protections to private-sector employers. On the other hand, certain states, such as California and Massachusetts, explicitly offer constitutional protection to private-sector employees.

3. **Federal statutes:** Drug testing could violate Title VII of the Civil Rights Act of 1964 or the Americans with Disabilities Act (see Chapter 13) if the testing fails to treat all individuals equally. The ADA protects *recovering* drug addicts and those erroneously believed to be drug users.

4. **State and local statutes:** Historically, most state and local drug testing legislation placed limits on that testing; but in recent years, fears about drug use in the workplace and often intense business community lobbying have, in some cases, relaxed those testing restraints.

5. **Common law claims:** Some of the more prominent judge-made (common law) claims that might provide a challenge to drug testing include invasion of privacy, defamation (dissemination of erroneous information about an employee), negligence (in testing or in selecting a test provider), intentional infliction of emotional distress, and wrongful discharge (discussed later in this chapter).

Monitoring

A McDonald's manager in Elmira, New York, began an affair with a McDonald's employee in another town. They exchanged "steamy" messages by voice mail. An Elmira coworker retrieved the messages and played them for the manager's wife and boss, whereupon the manager was fired. He filed suit claiming violations of a federal wiretapping law and a state eavesdropping statute.[57] The case was settled out of court.

> They exchanged "steamy" messages.

Nearly 75 percent of major U.S. companies monitor their employees on the job,[58] and misconduct can result in severe sanctions. Dow Chemical, for example, fired 50 employees and disciplined over 200 more after discovering widespread use of its computers to receive pornography.[59] Employees are, of course, concerned about privacy, while employers' worries include reduced productivity and company liability for criminal or tortious conduct (such as sexual harassment or defamation). Electronic oversight is gradually altering the workplace:

> At New York law firm Akin & Smith LLC, paralegals, receptionists, and clerks clock in by placing a finger on a sensor kept at a secretary's desk. "It keeps everyone honest," says Derek T. Smith, a managing partner at the firm.[60]

The Law

In general, employers can lawfully monitor workers' attendance, performance, e-mail, use of the Internet, and so on; but uncertainty remains. Certainly the prudent course of action is to expect employees to sign an agreement such as the following language from the Principal Financial Group employee handbook:

> The corporation's electronic mail system is business property and is to be used for business purposes. The corporation reserves the right to monitor all electronic mail messages.[61]

The primary federal legislation, the 1986 Electronic Communications Privacy Act, prohibits private individuals and organizations from intercepting wire, oral, or electronic communications. The act provides for two exceptions, however: (1) prior consent by one of the parties to the communication, and (2) employer monitoring in the "ordinary course of business" by telephone or other device furnished by a provider of wire or electronic communication service. Thus workplace monitoring of phone calls (except for purely private conversations), workplace computers, voice mail, e-mail, and Internet use are all likely to be considered lawful at this point if approached in a reasonable manner.

The case that follows is one of the few judicial examinations of privacy and monitoring. The plaintiff, Smyth, was an at-will employee (discussed later in this chapter), meaning that he did not have an employment contract for a specified period. Under the law of Pennsylvania, where the case took place, at-will employees could be fired for any reason unless the discharge violated public policy. The *Smyth* case examines whether an e-mail interception amounts to an invasion of privacy and is thus a violation of public policy. [For more information on e-mail and privacy, see **http://www.hrlawindex.com/email/email.html**]

LEGAL BRIEFCASE

Smyth v. Pillsbury Co.

914 F. Supp. 97 (E.D. Pa. 1996)

District Judge Weiner

[P]laintiff claims he was wrongfully discharged from his position as a regional operations manager by the defendant. Presently before the court is the motion of the defendant to dismiss. . . .

Defendant maintained an electronic mail communication system ("e-mail") in order to promote internal corporate communications between its employees. Defendant repeatedly assured its employees, including plaintiff, that all e-mail communications would remain confidential and privileged. Defendant further assured its employees, including plaintiff, that e-mail communications could not be intercepted and used by defendant against its employees as grounds for termination or reprimand.

In October 1994, plaintiff received certain e-mail communications from his supervisor over defendant's e-mail system on his computer at home. In reliance on defendant's assurances regarding defendant's e-mail system, plaintiff responded and exchanged e-mails with his supervisor. At some later date, contrary to the assurances of confidentiality . . . defendent, acting through its agents, servants, and employees, intercepted plaintiff's private e-mail messages made in October 1994. On January 17, 1995, defendant notified plaintiff that it was terminating his employment effective February 1, 1995, for transmitting what it deemed to be inappropriate and unprofessional comments* over defendant's e-mail system in October 1994.

* * * * *

Plaintiff claims that his termination was in violation of "public policy which precludes an employer from terminating an employee in violation of the employee's right to privacy as embodied in Pennsylvania common law." In support for this proposition, plaintiff directs our attention to a decision by our Court of Appeals in *Borse v. Piece Goods Shop, Inc.,* 963 F.2d 611 (3d Cir.1992). In *Borse,* the plaintiff sued her employer alleging wrongful discharge as a result of her refusal to submit to urinalysis screening and personal property searches at her workplace pursuant to the employer's drug and alcohol policy. After rejecting plaintiff's argument that the employer's drug and alcohol program violated public policy encompassed in the United States and Pennsylvania Constitutions, our Court of Appeals stated "our review of Pennsylvania law reveals other evidence of a public policy that may, under certain circumstances, give rise to a wrongful discharge action related to urinalysis or to personal property searches. Specifically, we refer to the Pennsylvania common law regarding tortious invasion of privacy."

* * * * *

Although the Court of Appeals in *Borse* observed that "[t]he Pennsylvania courts have not had occasion to consider whether a discharge related to an employer's tortious invasion of an employee's privacy violates public policy," the Court of

Appeals predicted that in any claim where the employee claimed that his discharge related to an invasion of his privacy "the Pennsylvania Supreme Court would examine the facts and circumstances surrounding the alleged invasion of privacy. If the court determined that the discharge was related to a substantial and highly offensive invasion of the employee's privacy, [the Court of Appeals] believe[d] that it would conclude that the discharge violated public policy." In determining whether an alleged invasion of privacy is substantial and highly offensive to a reasonable person, the Court of Appeals predicted that Pennsylvania would adopt a balancing test which balances the employee's privacy interest against the employer's interest in maintaining a drug-free workplace. [T]he Court of Appeals in *Borse* remanded the case to the district court with directions to grant Borse leave to allege how the defendant's drug and alcohol program violates her right to privacy.

* * * * *

[In the case before us] we find that plaintiff has failed to state a claim upon which relief can be granted. In the first instance, unlike urinalysis and personal property searches, we do not find a reasonable expectation of privacy in e-mail communications voluntarily made by an employee to his supervisor over the company e-mail system notwithstanding any assurances that such communications would not be intercepted by management. Once plaintiff communicated the alleged unprofessional comments to a second person (his supervisor) over an e-mail system which was apparently utilized by the entire company, any reasonable expectation of privacy was lost. Significantly, the defendant did not require plaintiff, as in the case of a urinalysis or personal property search, to disclose any personal information about himself. Rather, plaintiff voluntarily communicated the alleged unprofessional comments over the company e-mail system. We find no privacy interests in such communications.

In the second instance, even if we found that an employee had a reasonable expectation of privacy in the contents of his e-mail communications over the company e-mail system, we do not find that a reasonable person would consider the defendant's interception of these communications to be a substantial and highly offensive invasion of his privacy. Again, we note that by intercepting such communications, the company is not, as in the case of urinalysis or personal property searches, requiring the employee to disclose any personal information about himself or invading the employee's person or personal effects. Moreover, the company's interest in preventing inappropriate and unprofessional comments or even

---

*Defendant alleges in its motion to dismiss that the e-mails concerned sales management and contained threats to "kill the backstabbing bastards" and referred to the planned holiday party as the "Jim Jones Koolaid affair."

illegal activity over its e-mail system outweighs any privacy interest the employee may have in those comments.

In sum, we find that the defendant's actions did not tortiously invade the plaintiff's privacy and, therefore, did not violate public policy. As a result, the motion to dismiss is granted.

Questions

1. Why did the court reject Smyth's invasion of privacy claim?

2. Why did Pillsbury win even though it repeatedly promised employees that the e-mail system would be private and would not be used against employees?

3. In your opinion, should on-the-job e-mail messages be free from employer monitoring? Explain.

4. *a.* Does an employer have the right to search the office of an employee? Explain.

   b. What if the employer provides a locker for the employee and allows the employee to provide a lock? Explain.

Part Six—Employee Benefits and Income Maintenance

Have we reached that uncomfortable and perhaps socially destabilizing moment when the generous benefits (health insurance, life insurance, pensions) we have come to expect from our jobs are beginning a permanent decline? For decades employers used benefits to attract and retain the best employees, but the economic downturn in recent years forced employers to shift benefit burdens to employees by raising insurance deductibles and co-pays, for example. Indeed, from 2001 to 2003, nearly 9 million Americans lost their employer-provided health insurance, although most of those people subsequently moved to publicly subsidized plans such as Medicare.[62] At this writing, prosperity has returned to a considerable extent, but the benefit cuts have not been restored; and the future for improvements, especially in the prized but highly expensive health care area, does not look promising for employees. Benefits add 22 percent in value to the average employee's paycheck.[63] We prize the security of knowing that we will be shielded in the event of a health catastrophe. But can we sustain that comfort in this intense global market? A 2004 study found that a majority of surveyed companies are not raising benefits, and the small number who are increasing perks are doing so only slightly.[64] Further, *The Wall Street Journal* anticipates that any future growth in benefits will be in work/personal life balance, involving matters such as elder and child care rather than the stratospherically expensive health care costs.[65]

Even as benefits decline, American employees try harder. Almost 40 percent of us work more than 50 hours per week, and we have the stingiest vacation policies among industrialized nations with vacation allocations averaging about 10 days after three years on the job, as compared with Australia, for example, where four weeks are required by law.[66] Yet more, Expedia.com found that vacations for 2004 were expected to decline by 10 percent from 2003 as at least 20 percent of Americans report that they feel guilty about taking vacation.[67]

> We have the stingiest vacation policies among industrialized nations.

Meanwhile, the unmarried subset of the working population is increasingly aggressive in its pursuit of legal and economic benefits equal to those of families. Married employees have enhanced health care plans and unemployment benefits, for example, and differential treatment on the job allegedly is commonplace. The American Association for Single People receives complaints from singles:

> . . . In the workplace, singles are expected to put off summer vacations so married colleagues can visit Disney World while their kids are out of school. Married people get family leave and special dispensations to work at home, while singles often feel chained to their desks.[68]

Question

Are single people wronged at work and in the American economy, generally?

COBRA

Perhaps the most notable legally mandated insurance benefit is the Consolidated Budget Reconciliation Act (COBRA), which requires employers with 20 or more employees to permit departing employees to retain group health coverage at their own expense for up to 18 months as long as they are not terminated for gross misconduct.

Family Leave

The 1993 Family and Medical Leave Act (FMLA) requires up to 12 weeks of *unpaid* leave in any 12-month period for family needs such as the birth or adoption of a child, caring for a child or parent, or for the employee's own serious illness. Employees taking leave are entitled to reinstatement to the same or equivalent job. The law applies to all companies employing 50 or more workers and covers about 50 percent of the workforce. The business community has opposed the FMLA from the beginning, and experience with the law has not decreased that opposition, as *The Wall Street Journal* reported:

> While the act is helping employees, it's leaving many employers frustrated. They say the vague definition of what can trigger time off and the right of employees to take leave in increments—weeks, days, even hours—at different times make the law ripe for abuse. What's more, many human resource administrators believe employees sometimes use the law for bogus or questionable reasons. Among employers, this has earned the FMLA the nicknames "the Slacker's Protection Act" and the "Far More Leave Than Anyone Intended Act."[69]

But one FMLA advocate reminds us;

> FMLA has made an extraordinary difference in the lives of over 50 million Americans who haven't had to choose between their jobs and caring for a family member.[70]

In any case, only 16.5 percent of the workforce took leave under the FMLA in 2000,[71] and the FMLA has had no impact on males' propensity to take leave, while new mothers are taking leaves only slightly more frequently than before the FMLA.[72] Financial considerations often make FMLA leaves unattractive, but California has addressed that problem by becoming the first state to require private employers to provide *paid* time off. The program is paid for by employee payroll deductions and allows up to six weeks of leave at 55 percent of wages up to $728 per week. [For more on the FMLA, see **http://www.dol.gov/esa/whd/fmla/**]

Work Abroad?

A 2004 study found that workers in most nations around the world have greater legal rights to time off for family and medical matters than do American workers. Likewise, most of the 168 nations in the study mandate *paid* leave for pregnancy and illness.

Source: Associated Press, "Harvard Study: U.S. Policies on Time Off Rank at Bottom," *Waterloo/Cedar Falls Courier,* June 17, 2004, p. C10.

Unemployment Compensation

The tragedy of the Depression, when up to 25 percent of the workforce was unemployed, led in 1935 to the passage of the Social Security Act, one portion of which provided for an unemployment insurance program. Today all 50 states and the federal government are engaged in a cooperative system that helps protect the temporarily jobless. The system is financed through a payroll tax paid by employers.

The actual state tax rate for each employer varies, depending on the employer's *experience* ratings—the number of layoffs in its workforce. Thus employers have an incentive to retain employees.

Rules vary by state, but in general, employees qualify for unemployment benefits by reaching a specified total of annual wages. Those losing their jobs must apply to a state agency for unemployment compensation, which varies by state. Benefits may be collected up to a specified maximum period, usually 26 weeks. During that time, those collecting compensation must be ready to work and must make an effort to find suitable work. Workers who quit or who are fired for *misconduct* are ineligible for unemployment compensation. The episodes that follow illustrate the foolish and often funny cases where compensation has been denied:

- The Swiss Valley Farms dairy worker who led her coworkers in an after-hours swim in the cheese vat (filled with water at the time).[73]
- The bored production worker who removed her underwear, put the garment on the production line, and asked a supervisor if he "wanted to sniff them."[74]
- The sheriff's department dispatcher who was dismissed for refusing to remove her tongue stud. The dispatcher had initially been granted benefits, but she lost on appeal when the stud caused her to slur her words as she pleaded her case to the administrative law judge.[75]

WARN

The Worker Adjustment and Retraining Notification Act (WARN) requires firms with 100 or more employees to provide 60 days notice if they lay off one-third or more of their workers at any site employing at least 150 workers, drop 500 employees at any site, or close a plant employing at least 50 workers. A General Accounting Office study concluded, however, that the law had been ineffectual, with half of plant closings not covered by the law.

Pensions

Some employers began to adopt pension plans for their employees by the late 1800s. Comprehensive protection for pension rights did not arrive until 1974, when Congress approved the Employee Retirement Income Security Act (ERISA), under which the government regulates pension funds to help ensure their long-term financial security by reducing fraud and mismanagement. ERISA requires that fund managers keep detailed records, engage in prudent investments, and provide an annual report that has been certified by qualified, impartial third parties.

ERISA also establishes strict *vesting* rights (the point at which the employee has a nonforfeitable right to the funds) to ensure that employees actually receive the pensions to which they are entitled. Employer contributions typically vest after three years or in a six-year, graduated system.

Broadly, pensions take two forms: defined benefit plans and defined contribution plans. *Defined benefit* pensions are the traditional form of company-sponsored and company-paid plans that provide specified monthly payments upon retirement. Defined benefit plans provide security for employees who remain with a firm for many years; but for those changing jobs, benefits will likely be smaller. *Defined contribution* plans, such as the popular 401(k), specify in advance the "match" the employer will provide to go with the employee's own contributions and allow the employee a menu of investment options in which to place that retirement money; but they make no promises about the amount that will be paid upon retirement. Defined contribution plans often are attractive to employees because the money vests quickly and follows the employee who changes jobs. ERISA requires that defined benefit fund managers diversify their investments for greater safety, putting no more than 10 percent of the plan's funds in the employer's stock. Defined contribution plans, in general, have no such limit under the law. Defined benefit plans were once the norm in the business community, but defined contribution plans are now much more common. The latter are less expensive to manage, they shift the risk from employer to employee, and they are free of some ERISA requirements. [See **www.401khelpcenter .com** and **www.ebri.org** for large databases on 401(k) and other retirement topics.]

ERISA established the Pension Benefit Guaranty Corporation (PBGC), which insures defined benefit plans to protect retirees in the event that their employer's pension fund fails. The PBGC, which is funded by company contributions, guarantees that vested persons will be paid up to a specified maximum if their plan cannot meet its obligations. But even the PBGC-protected defined benefit pensions will eventually be at risk if company contributions to the PBGC fund are not significantly increased. As costs go up, however, can American companies compete successfully with lower-cost foreign competition? Can we afford the generous promises we have made to retirees? Will we see, in the decades to come, something of a generational battle between the young and the old about how big a slice of American wealth each will receive?

Unlike defined benefit plans, defined contribution arrangements are not covered by the PBGC. Thus the more relaxed and, in some ways, highly desirable 401(k) holds some big risks for employees, as we have learned in this era of corporate scandals.

Enron, WorldCom, and Pensions   Tens of thousands of employees at Enron, World-Com, and other financially devastated corporations lost most of their retirement savings in 2001–02 largely because their 401(k) plans were heavily invested in their employers' stock. Enron shares fell from a high of $90.56 in August 2000 to 36 cents in late November 2001, after the firm's alleged financial corruption became public.[76] Enron's 401(k) plan lost an estimated $850 million in two months. One employee explained his personal loss:

> "I feel like I've been betrayed," said Roy Rinard, 54, a veteran lineman at Enron subsidiary Portland General Electric in Oregon. "I have lost my savings, my plans for the future, everything." He lost the lion's share of his retirement account—once valued at more than $470,000—because he says he invested in Enron stock on the advice of plan administrators. . . . [H]is lawyer valued Rinard's 401(k) at about $40,000.[77]

That sense of betrayal, if not outrage, doubtless is exacerbated by the news that Enron executives cashed out more than $1 billion in company stock when it was near its peak value, and 600 key employees received $100 million in bonuses just before the energy giant collapsed.[78] Enron reached a $356 million settlement in 2005 with about 20,000 current and former employees, but Enron assets available after its bankruptcy suggest that claimants are likely to receive only 15–20 percent of the settlement.[79]

> 600 key employees received $100 million in bonuses just before the energy giant collapsed.

Congress and President Bush promised new laws to reduce the likelihood of future, huge employee retirement losses. At this writing, changes have been limited, but two prominent rules are in place: (1) Participants in 401(k) and similar retirement plans must receive 30 days' notice of any "blackout" periods when they cannot buy, sell, or borrow from their plans, and (2) corporate executives are forbidden from selling their company stock during blackout periods when employees are locked out of transactions involving their 401(k) holdings. Reform zeal has now cooled, but perhaps it should be so because employees doubtless must bear part of the risk, and more rules are likely to reduce efficiency and competitiveness.

Health Benefits and Retirement   In some ways, a more tragic but less spectacular retirement threat than Enron and WorldCom has been visiting hundreds of thousands of retirees across America in recent years. Many companies under tremendous financial pressure have been forced, in most cases entirely legally, to reduce or withdraw health care benefits that had once been promised to workers. Health care costs have been, for many companies, their most rapidly increasing cost of doing business. Consider GM's rather astonishing health care burdens for both its retirees and its current employees:

> Health care is one of the single biggest costs GM faces each year—representing about $1,400 per vehicle produced. The company's health plans cover 1.21 million employees, retirees, and their dependents. For 2003, the company reported that it spent $4.8 billion, or about $3,966 per person, for health care benefits.[80]

Companies feel they have no choice but to expect retirees to pay more of their own health care costs, but the retirees must endure a humiliating and frightening struggle for survival when the money they expected is no longer there. Richard Bruce, a retired Sears manager, paid $95 a month nine years ago for health care coverage for himself and his wife. As Sears' subsidy has fallen from 75 percent to less than 50 percent of his medical insurance premium, Bruce must now pay over $450 per month to maintain his coverage.[81] In a sense, only demographics and a changing economy are to blame. Many employers simply have too many retirees to support in this era of long life spans, huge medical costs, and a highly competitive world economy. Bethlehem Steel, for example, employs 13,000 people but has 74,000 retirees.[82]

Part Seven—Termination: Protection from Wrongful Discharge

Wagenseller declined to participate in a "Moon River" skit.

Catherine Wagenseller, an Arizona nurse, her boss, Kay Smith, and some co-workers joined a Colorado River rafting trip where Wagenseller declined to participate in a "Moon River" skit in which the group allegedly "mooned" the audience. Likewise, Wagenseller did not join Smith in the heavy drinking, "grouping up," public urination, and similar behaviors that allegedly marked the trip. Despite favorable job evaluations preceding the trip, Wagenseller's relationship with Smith deteriorated following the trip, and eventually she was terminated. Wagenseller, an at-will employee, sued claiming that she was wrongfully discharged. An *at-will employee,* by definition, is not under contract for a definite period of time, and as such can be fired at any time. Wagenseller, however, argued that Arizona should adopt the *public policy exception* to the at-will doctrine. She claimed that she was fired because she refused to engage in behaviors that might have violated the Arizona indecent exposure statute. The state Supreme Court agreed with Wagenseller by finding in the statute a public policy favoring privacy and decency. The case was returned to the trial level, giving Wagenseller the opportunity to prove that her refusal to violate state public policy by engaging in public indecency led to her dismissal.[83]

The *Wagenseller* decision is an exception to the long-standing American rule that at-will employees can be fired for good reasons, bad reasons, or no reason at all. Of course, the employee is likewise free to quit at any time. Furthermore, both employer and employee freely entered the bargain understanding its terms, and thus the court should, in general, enforce those terms, Critics, however, argue that the doctrine ignores the historic inequality of bargaining power between employers and employees. In recent decades the at-will rule has been softened in most states by legislative and judicially imposed limitations. Statutory exceptions to the at-will rule include our labor laws protecting union workers and the equal employment opportunity laws that forbid the dismissal of an employee for discriminatory reasons.

Fired—Guns in Their Cars

Weyerhaeuser, a large paper manufacturer in Oklahoma, learned that employees were having drug problems. Drug-sniffing dogs were used to inspect the company parking lots. The dogs detected firearms in employee vehicles. Weyerhaeuser fired those employees. Oklahoma then passed a law allowing employees to have guns in their locked vehicles on company property. At this writing, several companies are challenging the new law, citing their legal responsibility to maintain safe workplaces.

Source: Simon Romero, "An Oklahoma Version of Guns vs. Butter," *The New York Times,* November 24, 2004, p. C2.

Judicial Limitations on At-Will Principles

An increasing number of court decisions provide grounds for dismissed at-will employees to claim that they have been *wrongfully discharged.* Those judicial decisions were often provoked by transparently unjust dismissals including, for example, whistle-blowers who exposed their employers' misdeeds and employees who declined to commit perjury on behalf of their employers. Those judicial limitations to the at-will doctrine fall into three categories: (1) express or implied contracts, (2) an implied covenant of good faith and fair dealing, and (3) the tort of violating an established public policy, as in *Wagenseller.* Additional tort claims may substitute for or supplement wrongful discharge claims.

1. **Express or implied employment contracts:** A number of states have adopted a contract protection for at-will employees that arises, typically, either from the employee handbook or from employer conduct and oral representations. The notion here is that the courts will recognize a contract based either on language in the handbook or on such assurances of continued employment as routine promotions, no notice of poor performance, longevity, and oral communications.

2. **Implied covenant of good faith and fair dealing:** A few state courts have held that neither party to a contract may *act in bad faith* to deprive the other of the benefits of the contract. For example, Bruce Rubenstein gave up his job with Arbor Mortgage and took an at-will position with Huntington Mortgage with the understanding that he would be manager of a new branch office in central New Jersey. After a few weeks, however, Huntington decided on a downsizing strategy that included not opening the new branch. Rubenstein was offered a job as a loan originator, but he declined. He sued Huntington asserting, among other things, that Huntington had breached the covenant of good faith and fair dealing. Reubenstein believed that Huntington knew of the possibility of downsizing before hiring him. The court agreed that Rubenstein may have had a viable claim for breach of the implied covenant of good faith and fair dealing if the facts, at trial, proved to be as Rubenstein alleged.[84]

3. **Public policy:** Most states have now adopted some form of public policy (the general preference of the citizenry) exception providing that a dismissal is wrongful if it results from employee conduct that is consistent with the will of the people as expressed in statutes, constitutions, and the like. Those exceptions are established case by case, and they differ from state to state. In addition to the whistle-blowing and perjury situations noted, the exception often protects, for example, those fired for pursuing a lawful claim (like workers' compensation) and those fired for fulfilling a civic responsibility (like jury duty).

Additional Torts   Dismissed employees are increasingly turning to a variety of tort actions (often labeled *tag-along torts*) to enhance potential financial recovery, including punitive damages. Those tort possibilities include, among others, defamation, intentional infliction of emotional distress, interference with contract, and invasion of privacy. The following case raises public policy and false imprisonment tort claims following an employment termination.

Barrera v. ConAgra, Inc.

LEGAL BRIEFCASE   244 F.3d 663 (8th Cir. 2001)

Chief Judge Wollman

Manuel Barrera appeals from the district court's order granting summary judgment to ConAgra, Inc., and Swift & Co. (collectively, Swift), on Barrera's common law claims of retaliatory discharge in violation of public policy and false arrest and imprisonment.

On June 14, 1996, Barrera, a Mexican national who speaks very little English, was fired from his job on the cut floor of Swift's hog processing plant in Marshalltown, Iowa, after allegedly violating a company policy against eating in the employee locker room. Barrera was asked to report to human resources, where Swift alleges that he threatened the lives of several employees. The company contends that Barrera was subsequently fired and, after Swift notified local police, arrested. Although Barrera was charged with first degree harassment, the charge was eventually dismissed.

Barrera contends that he was fired in retaliation for filing a worker's compensation claim related to a slip-and-fall accident that occurred on or about March 22, 1996. He alleges that Swift staged the incident in the locker room as a pretext for his termination and that he was actually fired prior to the time he reported to human resources and before the alleged threats were made. Barrera also denies threatening to kill anyone at Swift, although he concedes that he may have threatened, depending on the translation, to "kick their asses" or "spank their buttocks."

*   *   *   *   *

In Iowa, an employer's ability to discharge an employee is limited when the discharge clearly violates the "well-recognized and defined public policy of the state." *Springer v. Weeks & Leo Co.* Discharge in retaliation for filing a worker's

compensation claim clearly violates Iowa's public policy. To prevail on a retaliatory discharge claim, Barrera must establish (1) that he engaged in a protected activity; (2) that he suffered an adverse employment action; and (3) that there existed a causal connection between the protected activity and his termination.

We agree with the district court's conclusion that Barrera failed to produce evidence sufficient to raise a genuine issue of material fact regarding causation. As the court noted, other than the timing of the discharge, Barrera produced "almost no evidence" that his termination was in any way related to his worker's compensation claim. Under Iowa law, the fact that Barrera was fired after filing a worker's compensation claim is not alone sufficient to prove causation.

Iowa law demands, rather, that Barrera produce evidence demonstrating that his worker's compensation claim was the determinative factor in Swift's decision to terminate his employment. Barrera's version of the facts, however, suggests nothing more than rude and callous behavior on Swift's part. [W]e conclude that the grant of summary judgment on Barrera's first claim was proper.

Barrera also challenges the district court's grant of summary judgment on his false arrest and imprisonment claim. In Iowa, false arrest is indistinguishable from false imprisonment, and is defined as "an unlawful restraint on freedom of movement or personal liberty." *Valadez v. City of Des Moines.* The elements of the tort are (1) detention or restraint against a person's will, and (2) unlawfulness of the detention or restraint. Barrera argues that Swift is liable for false imprisonment because the company was responsible for calling the police and requesting his arrest even though it was aware that criminal charges were unwarranted.

[A]n action for false imprisonment generally runs against the party doing the actual detention. *See* Restatement (Second) of Torts § 35 (1965) ("An actor is subject to liability to another for false imprisonment if . . . he acts intending to confine the other or a third person within boundaries *fixed by the actor.*" (emphasis added)). There is no evidence that employees of Swift detained Barrera or attempted to arrest Barrera while awaiting the arrival of the police. Barrera has cited no Iowa case that recognizes the liability of a private citizen or entity for false arrest or false imprisonment where a request for police assistance or investigation results in an arrest. Accordingly, we conclude that Barrera failed to create a genuine issue of material fact related to his claim of false imprisonment.

Affirmed.

Questions

1. Why did Barrera lose this lawsuit?
2. The criminal harassment charges against Barrera were dropped, and the court noted that Barrera (according to his account) was the victim of "rude and callous" behavior by Swift.
   a. Given this version of the facts, does it appear that Swift had legitimate grounds for dismissal?
   b. If not, should Barrera have prevailed in this appeal? Explain.
3. Schuster worked, in an at-will relationship, for Derocili for 15 months, during which time she claims he touched her inappropriately and made numerous sexual comments despite her repeated rejections of those behaviors. Schuster received bonuses and good evaluations, but in a meeting between Schuster, Derocili, and Schuster's direct supervisor, Goff, she was fired for poor performance. Schuster's sexual harassment complaint with the Delaware Department of Labor was rejected as unsubstantiated. She sued Derocili for breach of contract, but the trial court dismissed that complaint. She appealed.
   a. Does Schuster have a legitimate wrongful discharge claim? Explain.
   b. Does she have any other plausible causes of action? Explain. See *Schuster v. Derocili*, 775 A.2d 1029 (Del. S. Ct. 2000).
4. Gilmartin took a job as station manager at a Texas television station. He was hired on a year-to-year basis under an oral agreement providing that his employment would continue as long as his work was satisfactory. Gilmartin was subsequently blamed for declining profits, and he was fired. Gilmartin sued. In his pleadings, Gilmartin said that

he was informed of his annual salary, vacation time, and possible future raises, that his contract was to be renewed from year to year contingent on satisfactory performance, and that a commitment by KVTV for one to three years was "very doable." He was also told that a written agreement was not necessary. Was Gilmartin wrongfully discharged? Explain. See *Gilmartin v. KVTV-Channel 13,* 985 S.W.2d 553 (Ct. App. Tex. 1998).
5. IBP operates a large hog-processing plant in Storm Lake, Iowa. IBP prohibits possession of "look-alike drugs" on company property. An employee, Michael Huegerich, was randomly and lawfully inspected as he was entering the plant. The inspection revealed an asthma medication, Maxalert, which was identical in appearance to an illegal street drug, "speed." Maxalert contained the stimulant ephedrine. The pills actually belonged to his girlfriend and were in his possession by accident. Huegerich was terminated for possessing a look-alike drug in violation of company policy. Huegerich admitted that he was generally aware of IBP drug policies, but since he was a transfer from another IBP division, he had not gone through the company orientation program where new employees are advised of the policy against look-alike drugs. About six months after his dismissal, two IBP employees told Huegerich that they had heard he was fired for possessing speed. Huegerich then sued IBP for, among other claims, wrongful discharge and defamation.

   At trial, Huegerich provided no evidence as to how, when, and from whom the IBP employees had heard that he was terminated for possession of speed. The district court found for Huegerich in the amount of $24,000 on the wrongful discharge claim and $20,000 on the defamation claim. The court said that IBP was guilty of negligent discharge in failing to inform Huegerich about its drug policy. IBP appealed to the Iowa Supreme Court. Iowa law recognizes the doctrine of at-will employment with "narrow" exceptions for public policy violations and where a contract is created by an employer's handbook. Decide. Explain. See *Huegerich v. IBP,* 547 N.W.2d 216 (Iowa S.Ct. 1996).
6. Freeman, a television anchorperson employed by KSN, gave birth to her second child. On the day she returned from the hospital, she was notified that she had been dismissed. Six weeks later, she became unable to lactate. She sued KSN for wrongful discharge, tortious interference with contract, and negligent infliction of emotional distress. Decide. Explain. See *Freeman v. Medevac Midamerica of Kansas, Inc.,* 719 F. Supp. 995 (D Kan. 1989).

Part Eight—Immigration

Immigration is vital fuel for America's economic and cultural growth, but immigration is also a source of deep divisions in national opinion—especially since September 11, 2001. Thirteen percent of the nation's workers are immigrants, both legal and illegal.[85] About 700,000 legal immigrants enter the United States each year, and another 300,000 arrive illegally or overstay their visas.[86] In total about 30 million immigrants live in the United States, and an estimated 8.0 million of those are here illegally.[87] About one-half of the nation's farmworkers and 9 percent of restaurant employees are illegal immigrants.[88] A recent federal study found that immigrants provide a $10 billion annual boost to the American economy, and immigrants, over a lifetime, are no greater drain on public money for welfare and the like than are native-born citizens.[89] Without heavy immigration in the 1990s, unemployment probably would have been so low that wages and prices would have spiraled upward, threatening inflation.[90] A steady influx of highly skilled workers has been vital in maintaining high-tech growth.

> About one-half of the nation's farmworkers are illegal immigrants.

American Immigration Law Foreign workers seeking permanent residence in the United States on the basis of employment must have an offer of a permanent, full-time job. If so, the employer and the foreign national employee apply to the appropriate state Department of Labor for *labor certification,* which affirms that no one is available for the job and the hiring will not harm wages and working conditions in similar jobs. Some exceptions are provided for people in occupations where shortages exist and for those with exceptional abilities.

In hiring those already in the United States, federal immigration law, including the 1986 Immigration Reform and Control Act, requires employers to verify that each new hire is a U.S. citizen, a permanent resident, or a foreign national with permission to work in this country. To meet this requirement, employers must complete an employment eligibility verification form (I–9) for each new employee. New employees must present documents establishing the employee's identity and eligibility to work in the United States. The employer must examine the documents and complete the I–9 if the documents appear legitimate. Of course, employers cannot knowingly hire illegal immigrants, but neither can they discriminate against legal immigrants because of national origin and similar factors. [For an introduction to the I–9 requirements and the form itself, see **http://uscis.gov/graphics/formsfee/forms/i-9.htm**]

Internet Exercise

Using the Frequently Asked Questions portion of the Occupational Safety and Health Administration (OSHA) Web site [**http://www.osha.gov/as/opa/osha-faq.html**], answer the following:

1. What is OSHA's budget, and how many inspectors does the agency have?
2. How can I get help from OSHA to fix hazards in my workplace?
3. What cooperative programs does OSHA offer?

**Chapter
Questions**

1. In general, employers are forced to bear (or at least share) the legal burden for their employees' negligent conduct on the job.

    a. Why do we force employers to bear that responsibility?

    b. Should we do so? Explain.

2. Abplanalp, a five-year employee of Com-Co Insurance, signed an employment agreement including a restrictive covenant providing that, should he leave Com-Co, he would not use Com-Co customer lists or solicit business from Com-Co clients for three years. Abplanalp moved to Service Insurance, where he sold insurance to some friends and relatives. He did not sell to any other persons whom he came to know while working for Com-Co. Abplanalp was sued by Com-Co for violating the restrictive covenant. Decide. Explain. See *Com-Co Insurance Agency v. Service Insurance Agency,* 748 N.E.2d 298 (Ill. App. Ct. 2001).

3. Many companies refer to credit reports when investigating job applicants. The Fair Credit Reporting Act requires employers to notify applicants if they are rejected because of information in a credit report.

    a. In your judgment, does evidence of failure to pay debts constitute useful information in the job selection process? Explain.

    b. Is the use of that information an "invasion of privacy" as you understand it? Explain.

4. A group of Fargo, North Dakota, nurses were paid a subminimum wage for their "on-call" time. When on call, the nurses were required to be able to report to their hospital within 20 minutes, they were required to provide a phone number where they could be reached, and they were not to consume alcohol or drugs. After being called, nurses returned to regular pay. In three years, 36 of the 135 nurses who sued had been called in more than once. The nurses sued the hospital for violating the Fair Labor Standards Act's minimum wage provision. Decide. Explain. See *Reimer v. Champion Healthcare Corp.,* 258 F.3d 720 (8th Cir. 2001).

5. Simons, an engineer at the CIA, downloaded child pornography on his workplace computer. The computer was to be used only for work. The pornography was discovered by a search of employee computers. Simons was then convicted of receiving and possessing child pornography. Simons appealed on Fourth Amendment grounds. Decide. Explain. See *United States v. Simons,* 206 F.3d 392 (4th Cir. 2000); cert. den. 122 S.Ct. 292 (2001).

6. Guz, a longtime Bechtel employee, was dismissed during what Bechtel said was a business slump. Bechtel's personnel policy included a provision saying employees "may be terminated at the option of Bechtel." Guz sued for wrongful dismissal claiming, among other things, that Bechtel breached an implied contract to be terminated only for good cause, and that Bechtel breached the implied covenant of good faith and fair dealing. A lower court concluded that Guz's promotions, raises, favorable performance reviews, together with Bechtel's progressive discipline policy and Bechtel officials' statements of company practices supported Guz's position. Bechtel appealed. Decide. Explain. See *Guz v. Bechtel National Inc.,* 8 P.3d 1089 (S.Ct. Cal., 2000).

7. Sharon Kay Riddle sought workers' compensation claiming she had been totally and temporarily disabled by mental stress caused by the implementation of a no-smoking

ban in the electronics manufacturing plant of her employer, Ampex. Riddle had smoked one to two packs per day for 24 years. Following the plantwide ban, Riddle took leave and was diagnosed as suffering from major depression, nicotine dependence, and post-traumatic stress disorder. The administrative law judge found that Riddle had established three of the statutory requirements for her workers' compensation claim, but that she had failed to establish the fourth, which provided that work-related stress disabilities are not compensable if they are based "in whole or in part, upon facts and circumstances that are common to all fields of employment" and that the "facts and circumstances" were "not unique to [claimant's] employment." Riddle appealed the unfavorable ruling to the Colorado Court of Appeals. Is she entitled to workers' compensation? Explain. See *Riddle v. Ampex Corporation,* 839 P. 2d 489 (Colo. App. Ct. 1992).

8. As discussed in this chapter, many recent judicial decisions have afforded at-will employees much-improved protection against unfair dismissals. A special area of concern is whether at-will employees can be dismissed for off-duty conduct. The decisions are split, but the trend seems to be toward greater respect and protection for employee privacy. Nonetheless, companies still retain broad latitude to dismiss. For example, an employee convicted of selling drugs would most likely not be protected by the courts from a company dismissal.

    Virginia Rulon-Miller, an IBM salesperson, had been dating another IBM employee, Matt Blum, for several years. Her supervisors were aware of the relationship. Blum left IBM to join a competitor, QYX, and he moved from San Francisco to Philadelphia. QYX transferred him back to San Francisco, and he and Rulon-Miller resumed dating. Again, her superiors were aware of the relationship, and one mentioned that he didn't "have any problem" with her romance. Rulon-Miller did well in her sales role and was promoted to a management position, where she continued to do well, as evidenced by a $4,000 raise. Nonetheless, one week after receiving notice of the raise, Rulon-Miller was either dismissed (her version) or "transferred" (the company's version). IBM felt her romance and her concern for the success of Blum created a conflict of interest. Despite being an at-will employee, Rulon-Miller argued that she was protected by IBM's written policies that detail those circumstances under which an employee's private life can become a company issue. She filed suit, claiming wrongful discharge. Decide. Explain. See *Rulon-Miller v. IBM,* 1 BNA IER Cases 405, 162 Cal. App. 3d 241 (1984).

9. Terrell was employed by Red Giant Foods as a forklift driver. Terrell's supervisor, Rowsey, had received reports from employees that Terrell was drinking on the job. Rowsey later observed Terrell drinking in his car, parked on company property during the noon break. An hour later, Rowsey entered the unoccupied, unlocked car and found beer. Subsequently, Terrell was terminated for violating company policy against drinking on the job. Terrell filed suit.

    a. What claim(s) would Terrell raise?
    b. Decide. Explain. See *Terrell v. Rowsey and Red Giant Foods,* 647 N.E.2d 662 (Ind. App. Ct. 1995).

10. In most drug testing cases, courts have balanced the employee's privacy interests against the employer's need for information. What business justifications are

likely to be most persuasive to a court reviewing the legality of employee drug testing?

11. Millions of workers can be regarded as telecommuters. As such, they bring new legal problems to the workplace. As a manager, what legal difficulties would you want to anticipate and protect against as more and more of your employees work off-premises and often from their own homes?

12. A reader sent the following story to a newspaper question and answer forum:

    I was fired recently by my employer, an architecture firm, immediately after serving for one month on a federal grand jury. From the moment I informed my boss . . . I was harassed . . . and told I was not putting the company first. I was told to get out of my jury service, "or else." . . . I was fired exactly one week after my service ended.[91]

    Was the dismissal of this at-will employee lawful? Explain.

13. Katherine Born and Rick Gillispie were employed by a Blockbuster Video store in Iowa. Blockbuster maintained a policy that forbade dating between supervisors and their subordinates. Born and Gillispie were dismissed for violating the policy. They denied that they were romantically involved and filed suit for wrongful dismissal. Under Iowa law, an at-will employee can be discharged at any time for any reason, but Iowa law does recognize the public policy exception. To prevail in this lawsuit, what must the plaintiffs show about Iowa law? See *Katherine Born and Rick Gillispie v. Blockbuster Videos, Inc.,* 941 F.Supp. 868 (S. D. Ia. D.Ia. 1996).

14. A pregnant employee at a retail store was operating a buffing machine when propane gas that powered the machine led to a carbon monoxide buildup, causing the worker and others to be taken to a hospital. The worker's fetus sustained oxygen deprivation, resulting in injuries including abnormal motor functions, cerebral palsy, and a seizure disorder. The worker sued on negligence grounds for her child's injuries. The employer defended by arguing that workers' compensation provides the exclusive remedy in such situations. Does workers' compensation bar the child's suit? Explain. See *Snyder v. Michael's Stores, Inc.,* 945 P.2d 781 (Cal. S.Ct. 1997).

15. Lang, a white male working in a factory, called a black coworker such names as "watermelon" and "buckwheat." The coworker told Lang to stop. Lang continued the racist name-calling and his coworker then called Lang a "cracker" and a "honkey." Later, while Lang was talking with his supervisor, the coworker twice struck Lang, who then filed a workers' compensation claim.

    a. Is Lang entitled to workers' compensation?

    b. What is the key issue? Explain. See *Redman Industries v. Lang,* 326 Or. 32 (Sup. Ct. Or. 1997).

16. LaTourette worked for a California college and was attending a conference for work purposes when he suffered a heart attack. He underwent various operations including bypass surgery, subsequent to which he died in the hospital from a bacterial infection. His estate sought workers' compensation, claiming that his heart attack was a response to job stress. Is his estate entitled to workers' compensation? Explain. See *LaTourette v. Workers' Compensation Appeals Board,* 72 Cal. Rptr. 2d 217 (Sup. Ct. Cal. 1998).

Notes

1. Power, Kinder, & Sweeney, "Employee Strikes Door in Anger but Receives Workers' Comp," *Rhode Island Employment Law Letter,* May 1999.

2. Craig J. Cantoni, "The Case against Employee Benefits," *The Wall Street Journal,* August 18, 1997, p. A14.

3. "Microsoft Settles Federal Lawsuit," *Des Moines Register,* December 13, 2000, p. 8C.

4. *Donna Vizcaino v. Microsoft Corporation,* 120 F.3d 1006 (9th Cir. 1997).

5. *Microsoft Corporation v. Donna Vizcaino,* 522 U.S. 1098 (1998).

6. Staff Reporter, "Microsoft Says Temps Must Take a Hiatus after Working a Year," *The Wall Street Journal,* February 22, 2000, p. A32.

7. Sally Richards, "Résumé Fraud: Don't Lie to Get That Job!" *High Technology Careers Magazine* [**http://www.hightechcareers.com/doc699nextstep699.html**].

8. "Lying on Résumés: Why Some Can't Resist," *Dallas Morning News,* December 22, 2001, p. 8A.

9. Kris Maher, "The Jungle," *The Wall Street Journal,* January 20, 2004, p. B8.

10. Carlos Tejada, "They Asked What?" *The Wall Street Journal,* March 27, 2001, p. A1.

11. Kris Maher, "The Jungle," *The Wall Street Journal,* September 28, 2004, p. B10.

12. Maher, "The Jungle," p. B10.

13. Kris Maher, "The Jungle," *The Wall Street Journal,* June 8, 2004, p. B4.

14. Maher, "The Jungle," p. B4.

15. Stephanie Armour, "College Grads Confront Tough Job Market," *USA TODAY,* June 12, 2001, p. 1B.

16. *Circuit City Stores, Inc. v. Adams,* 532 U.S. 105 (2001).

17. See Sidney L. Gold and Hyman Lovitz, "Arbitration Agreements Don't Supersede Authority to Recover Damages," *The Legal Intelligencer,* June 6, 2002, p. 6.

18. 814 P.2d 1341 (Cal. S. Ct. 1991).

19. Jenny B. Davis, "Still Working after All These Years," *ABA Journal,* October 2001, p. 67.

20. Rick Wartzman, "As Officials Lost Faith in the Minimum Wage, Pat Williams Lived It," *The Wall Street Journal,* July 19, 2001, p. A1.

21. For a study involving 12 of the higher minimum wage states, see Gwendolyn Bounds, "Argument for Minimum-Wage Boost," *The Wall Street Journal,* July 27, 2004, p. B3.

22. Editorial, "Living in Santa Fe," *The Wall Street Journal,* July 9, 2004, p. A10.

23. Associated Press, "Study Shows 'Living Wage' Helping to Reduce Poverty," *Waterloo/Cedar Falls Courier,* March 14, 2002, p. A2.

24. Ann Zimmerman, "Big Retailers Face Overtime Suits as Bosses Do More 'Hourly' Work," *The Wall Street Journal,* May 26, 2004, p. A1.

25. Zimmerman, "Big Retailers Face Overtime Suits."

26. Michael Orey, "Lawsuits Abound from Workers Seeking Overtime Pay," *The Wall Street Journal,* May 30, 2002, p. B1.

27. Associated Press, "Disney Workers Win Pay Ruling," *Des Moines Register,* April 8, 2001, p. 2K.

28. "Call the *Courier,*" *Waterloo/Cedar Falls Courier,* February 4, 2001, p. C1.

29. David Barstow, "California Leads in Making Employer Pay for Job Deaths," *The New York Times,* December 23, 2003, p. A1.

30. Justin Pritchard, "Mexican Worker Deaths Rise in U.S. Even as Safety Improves," *Des Moines Register,* March 14, 2004, p. 1D.

31. "OSHA Enforcement Focuses on the Triple Bottom Line," *U.S. Newswire,* November 22, 2004.

32. Leigh Strope, "U.S. Workplace Deaths Up Slightly in 2003," *Des Moines Register,* September 23, 2004, p. 8C.

33. "OSHA Enforcement Focuses on the Triple Bottom Line."

34. "OSHA Enforcement Focuses on the Triple Bottom Line."

35. "OSHA Enforcement Focuses on the Triple Bottom Line."

36. Robert J. Grossman, "Making Ergonomics," *HR Magazine,* April 2000, p. 36.

37. Grossman, "Making Ergonomics."

38. Grossman, "Making Ergonomics."

39. Bloomburg News, "Poultry, Grocery Firms Face Ergonomic Rules," *Los Angeles Times,* June 12, 2002, Part 3, p. 4.

40. "U.S. Repeated Trauma Rates Decline for Third Straight Year," *CTDNEWS Workplace Solutions for Repetitive Stress Injuries* 8, no. 1 (January 1999).

41. Diane E. Lewis, "Voluntary Ergonomic Proposal Released, Business Cheers Plan; Foes Say It Lacks Teeth," *The Boston Globe,* April 6, 2002, p. C1.

42. "OSHA Prepares to Turn the Spotlight on Workplace Homicides," *Security Director's Report,* January 2005.

43. Daniel Costello, "Incidents of 'Desk Rage' Disrupt America's Offices," *The Wall Street Journal,* January 16, 2001, p. B1.

44. "OSHA Prepares to Turn the Spotlight."

45. "OSHA Facts, December 2004" [**http://www.osha.gov/as/opa/oshafacts.html**].

46. David Barstow, "U.S. Rarely Seeks Charges for Deaths in Workplace," *The New York Times,* December 22, 2003, p. Al.

47. Justin Pritchard, "Mexican Workers More Likely to Die on the Job," *Marin Independent Journal,* April 14, 2004 [**www.marinij.com**].

48. Pritchard, "Mexican Workers More Likely to Die on the Job."

49. *Stringer v. Minnesota Vikings,* 686 N. W.2d (Minn. Ct. App., 2004); *Stringer v. Minnesota Vikings,* 2004 Minn. LEXIS 752 (Minn. S. Ct.).

50. *Guico v. Excel Corp.,* 619 N.W.2d 470 (Neb. S. Ct. 2000).

51. Barbara Ehrenreich, "Two-Tiered Morality," *The New York Times,* June 30, 2002, sec. 4, p. 15.

52. Bernard Wysocki Jr., "Companies Get Tough with Smokers, Obese to Trim Costs," *The Wall Street Journal,* October 12, 2004, p. B1.

53. Sue Shellenbarger, "Getting Fired for Dating a Coworker: Office Romance Comes under Attack," *The Wall Street Journal,* February 19, 2004, p. D1.

54. Shellenbarger, "Getting Fired for Dating a Coworker."

55. Littler and Mendelson, *The 1996 Employer* (San Francisco: Littler, Mendelson, Fastiff, Tichy & Mathiason, P.C., 1996), p. 860.

56. See, e.g., *National Treasury Employees Union v. Von Raab,* 109 S.Ct. 1385 (1989).

57. Frances A. McMorris, "Is Your Office Voice Mail Private? Don't Bet on It," *The Wall Street Journal,* February 28, 1995, p. B1.

58. "Does Your Boss Watch You Work?" *Des Moines Register,* June 18, 2000, p. 3D.

59. Associated Press, "Study: Employers Monitoring Internet Use of a Third of Online U.S. Work Force," *Waterloo/Cedar Falls Courier,* July 10, 2001, p. B5.

60. Kris Maher, "Big Employer Is Watching," *The Wall Street Journal,* November 4, 2004, p. B1.

61. Mark P. Couch, "Eyes Are on Your E-Mail," *Des Moines Register,* January 26, 1997, p. 1G.

62. *Hartford Courant,* "Study Finds Millions Lost Health Insurance at Work," *Waterloo/Cedar Falls Courier,* August 3, 2004, p. D6.

63. Kathy Chu, "Good Times Return, Not Benefits," *The Wall Street Journal,* June 30, 2004, p. D2.

64. Chu, "Good Times Return, Not Benefits."

65. Chu, "Good Times Return, Not Benefits."

66. Joe Robinson, "Vacation Deficit Disorder," *Des Moines Register,* August 1, 2003, p. 9A.

67. Robinson, "Vacation Deficit Disorder."

68. Jeffrey Zaslow, "The Singles Lobby: Unmarried People Seek Economic Perks Enjoyed by Couples," *The Wall Street Journal,* June 24, 2004, p. D1.

69. Sara Munoz, "Leadership (A Special Report); A Good Idea, but . . . : Some Businesses Complain That the Family and Medical Leave Act Should Be More Aptly Named the Slackers Protection Act," *The Wall Street Journal,* January 24, 2005, p. R6.

70. Munoz, "Leadership (A Special Report)."

71. Munoz, "Leadership (A Special Report)."

72. Knight Ridder Newspapers, "Study: New Parents' Leave Is Unchanged," *Waterloo/Cedar Falls Courier,* February 21, 2003, p. A10.

73. Patt Johnson, "Getting the Boot," *Des Moines Register,* May 4, 2003, p. 1D.

74. Johnson, "Getting the Boot."

75. Clark Kauffman, "Stud-Wearing Dispatcher Gets a Tongue-Lashing," *Des Moines Register,* March 20, 2004, p. 1A.

76. Liz Pulliam Weston, "Betting It All on Company Stock Is Risky Business," *Los Angeles Times,* November 30, 2001, p. 1.

77. James T. Madore, "Enron Employees See 401(k)s Wiped Out," *Newsday,* November 30, 2001, p. A75.

78. "Enron: Deconstructing the Energy Giant's Fall," *The Scotsman,* January 11, 2002, p. 5.

79. Ellen Schultz, "Enron Settles with Employees Who Lost Retirement Money," *The Wall Street Journal,* July 12, 2005, p. A8.

80. Lee Hawkins Jr., "GM's Liabilities for Retiree Health Top $60 Billion," *The Wall Street Journal,* March 11, 2004, p. A3.

81. Sandra Guy, "Coverage Causes Pain," *Chicago Sun-Times,* June 20, 2002, p. 47.

82. Kristine Henry, "Steel Workers' Benefits in Peril," *Baltimore Sun,* July 10, 2002, p. 1A.

83. *Wagenseller v. Scottsdale Memorial Hospital,* 710 P.2d 1025 (Az. S. Ct. 1985).

84. *Rubenstein v. Huntington Mortgage Company,* N. J. Sup. Ct., App. Div., 1997. For a journalistic account of the case, see Pitney, Hardin, Kipp, and Szuch, "Employers Must Be Cautious about Failing to Disclose Business Plans That Will Affect the Jobs of New Hires," *New Jersey Employment Law Letter,* September 1997.

85. Laura Parker, "USA Just Wouldn't Work without Immigrant Labor," *USA TODAY,* July 23, 2001, p. 1A.

86. Parker, "USA Just Wouldn't Work."

87. Miriam Jordan, "Arizona Limits Illegal Immigrants' Access to Benefits," *The Wall Street Journal,* November 4, 2004, p. A4.

88. Deborah Kong, "Illegal Immigrants Abound in Some Jobs," *Des Moines Register,* March 22, 2002, p. 1A.

89. Mark Siebert, "Immigrants Aid Economy, Study Shows," *Des Moines Register,* February 18, 2001, p. 3B.

90. Adam Ninklewicz, "Keeping the Hive Humming," *BusinessWeek,* April 24, 2000, p. 50.

91. *Washington Post,* "The Boss Can't Fire You for Doing Your Civic Duty," *Waterloo/Cedar Falls Courier,* May 26, 1999, p. C8.

Employment Law II: Discrimination

Introduction

Have you shopped at Abercrombie & Fitch? Many Americans do so routinely, but as of November 2004, those customers learned that their shopping may have contributed to alleged racial and sexual discrimination. Basically, the retailer was accused of maintaining a virtually all-white image by discriminating in recruiting, hiring, and promoting women and minorities. A nationwide class action was filed claiming that Abercrombie disproportionately assigned minority employees to stockrooms and other jobs out of the public eye, while white employees were conspicuously on display as a means of projecting the company's "clean-cut, classic" image.

Abercrombie denied the charges, but it decided to settle before trial by agreeing to pay a $40 million settlement along with $10 million in attorney fees and other expenses. Some 50,000 people are expected to apply for shares in the settlement. Abercrombie agreed to manifest a more diverse image in its marketing materials, including its catalogs, shopping bags, and store posters, and the company must pursue various hiring benchmarks.[1]

Questions

1. The conservative *California Patriot* at the University of California at Berkeley:

If Abercrombie & Fitch Co. wants to promote a certain image, that is its prerogative. The goal of any business is to make a profit, and Abercrombie & Fitch may have found it profitable to use a "white image" in order to promote its clothing.

   a. The law aside, is Abercrombie simply wrong to project a "white image," if, indeed, it did so? Explain.

   b. Would it be wrong for Abercrombie to build its business plan on an ethnic or black or "hip-hop" image in its products?

2. Is discrimination based on appearance an ethical wrong? Explain.

3. Katie Hollenbeck, a junior graphic arts major, was thinking of applying for a job at Abercrombie & Fitch, but she decided that she didn't feel "appropriate" for the job after she observed all of the store's "tall, skinny white girls." Hollenbeck says that, in the long run, hiring only attractive employees will "hurt Abercrombie."[2]

   a. Would the market punish Abercrombie, even if the law had not intervened? Explain.

   b. Should the market punish Abercrombie? Explain. Put another way, should you decline to shop at Abercrombie stores? Explain.

Continuing Discrimination?   Sometimes wrongful distinctions like those alleged in the Abercrombie case can be quite subtle. For example, recent studies have found that "white-sounding" first names (Neil, Jill, and the like) on résumés generated 50 percent more responses than otherwise identical (and made-up) résumés with "black-sounding" first names (Aisha, Kareem, and so forth) when those résumés were mailed by professors in response to actual newspaper want ads.[3] The collective result of this ongoing discrimination can be crippling. For example, the already enormous wealth gap between whites and minorities continues to grow: The median net worth of white families is 11 times greater than Hispanics and 14 times that of blacks.[4] Over 88 percent of American businesses are owned by whites.[5]

At the same time, great progress is undeniable. While still trailing whites by very wide margins in most measures of welfare, more black families are now headed by married couples, more are living in homes they own, and a record 17 percent of blacks 25 and older now hold bachelor's degrees.[6] Likewise, we should note striking changes in attitudes, at least if survey responses are to be believed. According to a 2004 survey, 70 percent of whites now say they approve of marriage between blacks and whites, up from 4 percent in 1958.[7] But much remains to be done. Sixty-three percent of Americans believe that race relations will always be a problem—a finding that varies little by race.[8]

Whites in Decline?

Census projections suggest that the white share of the population will fall from its current 69 percent to 50 percent by 2050. Hispanics have passed blacks as the largest American minority group (about 13 percent to 12.7 percent), and Hispanics are expected to total more than 100 million out of an expected 420 million Americans by 2050.

Sources: Haya El Nasser, "Census Projects Growing Diversity," *USA TODAY*, March 18, 2004, p. 1A; Associated Press, "Census: Hispanics Outnumber Blacks," *MSNBC News* [**http://www.msnbc.com/news/862282.asp?0dm=N24GN**].

Part One—Employment Discrimination: The Foundation in Law

History

In 1941 A. Philip Randolph, president of the predominantly black Brotherhood of Sleeping Car Porters, organized black leaders who threatened a massive march in Washington, D.C., protesting employment discrimination. In response, President Franklin Roosevelt issued Executive Order 8802, which created a Fair Employment Practice Committee. Congress limited the committee's budget, but Roosevelt's action was a striking first step for the federal government in addressing racial discrimination.

The next big step toward racial equality was the landmark *Brown v. Board of Education*[9] decision in 1954, in which the Supreme Court forbade "separate but equal" schools. Following *Brown*, citizens engaged in sit-ins, freedom rides, boycotts, and the like to press claims for racial equality. It was a turbulent, sometimes violent, era, but those activities were critical ingredients in subsequent advances for the black population.

With the passage of the 1964 Civil Rights Act, the campaign against discrimination solidified as one of the most energetic and influential social movements in American history.[10] [For the National Civil Rights Museum, see **http://www.civilrightsmuseum.org/**]

Civil Rights Act of 1964

Title VII of the Civil Rights Act of 1964 changed American life and business practice by forbidding discrimination in employment because of race, color, religion, sex, or national origin. Relying on its authority to regulate commerce, Congress applied the act to private-sector employers with 15 or more employees, employment agencies, labor unions with 15 or more members as well as those operating a hiring hall, state and local governments, and most of the federal government. Private clubs are exempt from the act, and religious organizations may discriminate in employment on the basis of religion. Broadly, the act forbids discrimination in hiring, firing, and general conditions of employment.

Other Legislation and Orders

Title VII is the core of the federal government's authority to attack employment discrimination, but other federal laws not addressed later in this chapter should be noted:

- The Civil Rights Act of 1866 forbids all forms of racial bias arising out of contract. Employment relationships are, of course, founded in contract. Thus when a black person is discriminated against by a private employer, the act has been violated.
- The Civil Rights Act of 1991, among other things, specifies that Title VII and the Americans with Disabilities Act (ADA) are to apply to U.S. citizens working abroad for American-owned or American-controlled companies unless compliance with those American laws would require the company to violate the law of its host nation.
- EO 11246 forbids discrimination by firms doing business with the federal government and, in some instances, requires affirmative action to avoid and correct underutilization of minorities and women.

The Constitution

As explained in Chapter 5, the federal Constitution, among other purposes, protects us from wrongful government action. The Fourteenth Amendment to the Constitution provides that no state shall deny to any person life, liberty, or property without *due process of law* or deny him or her the *equal protection of the laws.* Thus citizens are protected from discrimination via state government action. Similarly, the Supreme Court has interpreted the Due Process Clause of the Fifth Amendment ("nor shall any person . . . be deprived of life, liberty, or property, without due process of law") to forbid discrimination by the federal government.

Civil Rights Enforcement

EEOC

The Equal Employment Opportunity Commission (EEOC) is the federal agency responsible for enforcing the federal laws forbidding discrimination in employment. The Commission imposes record-keeping requirements on businesses, unions, and employment agencies; issues new regulations and guidelines; investigates discrimination claims; attempts to resolve disputes via mediation and conciliation; and, if necessary, engages in litigation. Viewing litigation as a last resort, the commission simply does not have the resources to impose its will on the business community. [The EEOC home page is located at **www.eeoc.gov**]

Litigation

Normally, a victim of employment discrimination cannot immediately file a lawsuit. Rather, a complaint must be filed with the appropriate local or state fair employment practices agency, where provided for by law. After 60 days or upon termination of state or local proceedings, the grievant may turn to the EEOC for aid. Charges must be filed with the EEOC within 180 days of the discriminatory act (or 300 days if preceded by a local or state filing or 30 days after receiving notice that the state/local proceeding was terminated).

When charges reach the EEOC, most will be referred for mediation. If that process is successful, the case is over. If not, the EEOC will investigate. If no cause for the complaint is found, the EEOC will issue a *right-to-sue letter,* thus removing itself from the matter and releasing the grievant to file his or her own lawsuit because all administrative remedies have been exhausted. If grounds for complaint are found, the case will first be referred to conciliation. That failing, the commission may file a civil suit or issue a right-to-sue letter to the grievant.

Many potential employment discrimination lawsuits no longer reach the judicial system because they are resolved in arbitration. Many businesses are now including binding arbitration agreements in job offers, requiring job seekers, as a condition of employment, to waive the right to trial and turn any grievance over to arbitration. A series of U.S. Supreme Court decisions has firmly established the enforceability of those agreements when the arbitration process provided for is legitimate and fair. The Court has also ruled, however, that the EEOC retains its right to sue on behalf of an employee even if the worker has signed away his or her own rights.[11]

When job discrimination suits reach the courts, only about 30 percent of those claims are successful for plaintiffs.[12] By contrast, plaintiffs win about 43 percent of all categories of civil federal district court cases.[13] Broadly, job discrimination claims are harder to win, at least in the federal courts, than virtually all other kinds of civil suits.

Remedies

Remedies under Title VII are intended to "make the victim whole" and may include job reinstatement, back pay, and seniority relief, among other possibilities. Additionally, victims of *intentional* discrimination based on race, religion, sex, disability, or national origin can secure other compensatory damages such as pain and suffering, and they can also secure punitive damages in some instances. Combined compensatory and punitive damages, in suits involving religion, sex, disability, or national origin, are capped at $50,000 to $300,000, depending on the size of the employer's workforce. Damages are not capped for front pay (awarded for future earnings) or in cases of intentional discrimination based on race. Finally, the EEOC often negotiates consent decrees that may require new procedures to correct wrongful practices. [For the Civil Rights Division of the U.S. Justice Department, see **http://www.usdoj.gov/crt/crt-home.html**]

Title VII forbids job discrimination based on race, color, or national origin. Members of those "protected classes" cannot lawfully be denied employment opportunities merely because they are Native Americans, black, of Vietnamese ancestry, or white, for that matter.

Employment Discrimination Analysis

Title VII of the 1964 Civil Rights Act provides two primary theories of recovery for individuals—disparate treatment and disparate impact (sometimes labeled *adverse impact*). Those theories are examined below. Title VII also provides for a theory of recovery labeled *pattern or practice* discrimination where a *class* of individuals has been systematically subjected to discriminatory treatment. Normally, a pattern or practice of discrimination is identified by statistical analysis showing a significant "underutilization" in the percentage of minority employees in the employer's workforce, as compared with the percentage of qualified minority employees in the relevant labor pool.

As we turn now to a close look at disparate treatment and disparate impact analysis, keep in mind the various constitutional, statutory, and executive order protections just outlined.

Disparate Treatment

The basic elements of *disparate treatment* exist where an employer *intentionally* treats some people less favorably than others because of their race, color, religion, sex, or national origin. In a simplified form, a claim under disparate treatment analysis would proceed as follows:

1. **Plaintiff's (employee's) prima facie case** (sufficient to be presumed true unless proven otherwise): Optimally the plaintiff would present *direct evidence* of intentional disparate treatment. For example, that evidence might take the form of a letter from an employer to an employment agency indicating that "women would not be welcome as applicants for this physically taxing job." Because direct evidence is ordinarily unavailable, the plaintiff must then build the following prima facie case from which intent and hence disparate treatment may be inferred:

a. Plaintiff belongs to a protected class.

b. Plaintiff applied for a job for which the defendant was seeking applicants.

c. Plaintiff was qualified for the job.

d. Plaintiff was denied the job.

e. The position remained open, and the employer continued to seek applicants.

2. **Defendant's (employer's) case:** If the plaintiff builds a successful prima facie case, the defendant must "articulate some *legitimate, nondiscriminatory reason* for the employee's rejection" (for example, greater work experience). However, the defendant

need not prove that its decision not to hire the plaintiff was, in fact, based on that legitimate, nondiscriminatory reason. The defendant simply must raise a legitimate issue of fact disputing the plaintiff's discrimination claim.

3. **Plaintiff's response:** Assuming the defendant was successful in presenting a legitimate, nondiscriminatory reason for its action, the plaintiff must show that the reason offered by the defendant was false and thus was merely a *pretext* to hide discrimination. [For an overview of disparate treatment analysis, see **http://www.hr-guide.com/data/G701.htm**]

Question

Stalter, an African American, was fired for theft after working at a Wal-Mart loading dock for four months. Stalter ate a handful of taco chips from an open bag on the countertop in the break room. As he was eating, Ellenbecker entered the room, took the bag from Stalter, and placed it in her locker. Stalter later apologized to Ellenbecker and offered to buy a new bag. She said the incident was "no big deal" and told him to "forget about it." Management then investigated, concluded Stalter had stolen the chips, and fired him. Stalter sued, claiming his termination was race based. At court Stalter argued (a) Wal-Mart could not have reasonably believed that he committed theft, especially since the owner told him to forget about it; (b) the punishment was grossly excessive; (c) a similarly situated Caucasian employee who committed a similar offense was treated much more leniently; and (d) Wal-Mart did not investigate his claims of racial harassment. Resolve this case. Explain your reasoning. See *Stalter v. Wal-Mart Stores,* 195 F.3d 285 (7th Cir. 1999).

Disparate Impact

Disparate impact analysis involves situations in which employers use legitimate employment standards that, despite their apparent neutrality, impose a heavier burden on a protected class than on other employees. For example, a preemployment test, offered with the best of intentions and constructed to be a fair measurement device, may disproportionately exclude members of a protected class and thus be unacceptable (barring an effective defense). Alternatively, an employer surreptitiously seeking to discriminate may establish an apparently neutral, superficially valid employment test that has the effect of achieving the employer's discrimination goal. For example, a tavern might require its "bouncer" to be at least 6 feet 2 inches tall and weigh at least 200 pounds. Such a standard disproportionately excludes women, Asians, and Hispanics from consideration and probably is impermissible (barring an effective defense). Note that disparate treatment requires proof of intent, while disparate impact does not.

The Test

Disparate impact analysis requires the following:

1. The plaintiff/employee must identify the *specific employment practice or policy* (such as test score, skill, or height) that caused the alleged disparate impact on the protected class.

2. The plaintiff must prove (often with statistical evidence) that the protected class is suffering an adverse or disproportionate impact caused by the employment practice

or policy in question. The statistical analysis to establish a disparate impact (against black job applicants, for example) must be based on a comparison of the racial composition of the group of persons actually holding the jobs in question versus the racial composition of the *job-qualified* population in the relevant labor market.

3. Assuming a prima facie case is established in steps 1 and 2, the plaintiff/employee wins unless the defendant/employer demonstrates that the employment practice/policy is (a) *job related* and (b) *consistent with business necessity.*

4. If the defendant/employer succeeds in demonstrating job relatedness and business necessity, the employer wins unless the plaintiff/employee demonstrates that *an alternative, less discriminatory business practice is available and that the employer refuses to adopt it.* [For brief summaries of recent and pending Supreme Court employment discrimination cases, see **http://www.lawmemo.com/default.htm**]

The following classic case examines disparate impact analysis.

LEGAL BRIEFCASE

Griggs v. Duke Power Co.
401 U.S. 424 (1971)

Chief Justice Burger

We granted the writ in this case to resolve the question whether an employer is prohibited by the Civil Rights Act of 1964, Title VII, from requiring a high school education or passing of a standardized general intelligence test as a condition of employment in or transfer to jobs when (a) neither standard is shown to be significantly related to successful job performance, (b) both requirements operate to disqualify Negroes at a substantially higher rate than white applicants, and (c) the jobs in question formerly had been filled only by white employees as part of a longstanding practice of giving preference to whites.

Congress provided, in Title VII of the Civil Rights Act of 1964, for class actions for enforcement of provisions of the Act and this proceeding was brought by a group of incumbent Negro employees against Duke Power Company. . . .

The district court found that prior to July 2, 1965, the effective date of the Civil Rights Act of 1964, the company openly discriminated on the basis of race in the hiring and assigning of employees at its Dan River plant. The plant was organized into five operating departments: (1) Labor, (2) Coal Handling, (3) Operations, (4) Maintenance, and (5) Laboratory and Test. Negroes were employed only in the Labor Department where the highest-paying jobs paid less than the lowest-paying jobs

in the other four "operating" departments in which only whites were employed. Promotions were normally made within each department on the basis of job seniority. Transferees into a department usually began in the lowest position.

In 1955 the company instituted a policy of requiring a high school education for initial assignment to any department except Labor, and for transfer from the Coal Handling to any "inside" department (Operations, Maintenance, or Laboratory). When the company abandoned its policy of restricting Negroes to the Labor Department in 1965, completion of high school also was made a prerequisite to transfer from Labor to any other department. From the time the high school requirement was instituted to the time of trial, however, white employees hired before the time of the high school education requirement continued to perform satisfactorily and achieve promotions in the "operating" departments. Findings on this score are not challenged.

The company added a further requirement for new employees on July 2, 1965, the date on which Title VII became effective. To qualify for placement in any but the Labor Department it became necessary to register satisfactory scores on two professionally prepared aptitude tests, as well as to have a high school education. Completion of high school alone continued to render employees eligible for transfer to the four desirable departments from which Negroes had been excluded if the incumbent had been employed prior to the time of the new requirement. In September 1965 the company began to permit incumbent employees who lacked a high school education to qualify for transfer from Labor or Coal Handling to an "inside" job by passing two tests—the Wonderlic Personnel Test, which purports to measure general intelligence, and the Bennett Mechanical Comprehension Test. Neither was directed or intended to measure the ability to learn to perform a particular job or category of jobs. The requisite scores used for both initial hiring and transfer approximated the national median for high school graduates.

The District Court had found that while the company previously followed a policy of overt racial discrimination in a period prior to the Act, such conduct had ceased. The District Court also concluded that Title VII was intended to be prospective only and, consequently, the impact of prior inequities was beyond the reach of corrective action authorized by the Act.

. . . The Court of Appeals concluded there was no violation of the Act.

*   *   *   *   *

The objective of Congress in the enactment of Title VII is plain from the language of the statute. It was to achieve equality of employment opportunities and remove barriers that have operated in the past to favor an identifiable group of white employees over other employees. Under the Act, practices, procedures, or tests neutral on their face, and even neutral in terms of intent, cannot be maintained if they operate to "freeze" the status quo of prior discriminatory employment practices.

The Court of Appeals' opinion, and the partial dissent, agreed that, on the record in the present case, "whites register far better on the company's alternative requirements" than Negroes. This consequence would appear to be directly traceable to race. Basic intelligence must have the means of articulation to manifest itself fairly in a testing process. Because they are Negroes, petitioners have long received inferior education in segregated schools.

. . . Congress did not intend by Title VII, however, to guarantee a job to every person regardless of qualifications. In short, the Act does not command that any person be hired simply because he was formerly the subject of discrimination, or because he is a member of a minority group. Discriminatory preference for any group, minority or majority, is precisely and only what Congress has proscribed. . . .

. . . The Act proscribes not only overt discrimination but also practices that are fair in form, but discriminatory in operation. The touchstone is business necessity. If an employment practice which operates to exclude Negroes cannot be shown to be related to job performance, the practice is prohibited.

On the record before us, neither the high school completion requirement nor the general intelligence test is shown to bear a demonstrable relationship to successful performance of the jobs for which it was used. Both were adopted, as the Court of Appeals noted, without meaningful study of their relationship to job-performance ability. Rather, a vice president of the company testified, the requirements were instituted on the company's judgment that they generally would improve the overall quality of the workforce.

The evidence, however, shows that employees who have not completed high school or taken the tests have continued to perform satisfactorily and make progress in departments for which the high school and test criteria are not used. . . .

The Court of Appeals held that the company had adopted the diploma and test requirements without any "intention to discriminate against Negro employees." We do not suggest that either the District Court or the Court of Appeals erred in examining the employer's intent; but good intent or absence of discriminatory intent does not redeem employment procedures or testing mechanisms that operate as "built-in headwinds" for minority groups and are unrelated to measuring job capability.

*   *   *   *   *

The facts of this case demonstrate the inadequacy of broad and general testing devices as well as the infirmity of using diplomas or degrees as fixed measures of capability. . . .

The company contends that its general intelligence tests are specifically permitted by § 703(h) of the Act. That section authorizes the use of "any professionally developed ability test" that is not "designed, intended *or used* to discriminate because of race. . . ." (Emphasis added.)

The Equal Employment Opportunity Commission, having enforcement responsibility, has issued guidelines interpreting § 703(h) to permit only the use of job-related tests. The administrative interpretation of the Act by the enforcing agency is entitled to great deference. Since the Act and its legislative history support the commission's construction, this affords good reason to treat the guidelines as expressing the will of Congress.

. . . From the sum of the legislative history relevant in this case, the conclusion is inescapable that the EEOC's construction of § 703(h) to require that employment tests be job related comports with congressional intent.

Nothing in the Act precludes the use of testing or measuring procedures; obviously they are useful. What Congress has forbidden is giving these devices and mechanisms controlling force unless they are demonstrably a reasonable measure of job performance. Congress has not commanded that the less qualified be preferred over the better qualified simply because of minority origins. Far from disparaging job qualifications as such, Congress has made such qualifications the controlling factor, so that race, religion, nationality, and sex become irrelevant. What Congress has commanded is that any tests used must measure the person for the job and not the person in the abstract.

The judgment of the Court of Appeals is . . . reversed.

Questions

1. According to the Supreme Court, what was Congress's objective in enacting Title VII?

2. Had Duke Power been able to establish that its reasons for adopting the diploma and test standards were entirely without discriminatory intent, would the Supreme Court have ruled differently? Explain.

3. What is the central issue in this case?

4. Why was North Carolina's social and educational history relevant to the outcome of the case?

5. Statistical evidence showed that 35 percent of new hires in grocery and produce at Lucky Stores, a retail grocery chain, were women, while 84 percent of new hires in deli, bakery, and general merchandise were women. Statistical evidence also showed that 31 percent of those promoted into apprentice jobs in grocery and produce were women, while women comprised 75 percent of those promoted into apprentice jobs in deli, bakery, and general merchandise. Grocery and produce jobs generally were higher-paying jobs than those in deli, bakery, and general merchandise. Women received significantly fewer overtime hours than men.

    Do these facts regarding Lucky Stores suggest discrimination? Explain. See *Stender v. Lucky Stores, Inc.* 803 F. Supp. 259 (DC Cal. 1992).

6. Gregory, a black male, was offered employment by Litton Systems as a sheet metal worker. As part of a standard procedure he completed a form listing a total of 14 nontraffic arrests but no convictions. Thereupon the employment offer was withdrawn. Gregory then brought suit, claiming he was a victim of racial discrimination.

    a. Explain the foundation of his argument.

    b. Decide the case. See *Gregory v. Litton,* 412 F.2d 631 (9th Cir. 1972).

7. Eighty-one percent of the hires at Consolidated Service Systems, a small Chicago janitorial company, were of Korean origin. The EEOC brought a disparate treatment claim, saying the firm discriminated in favor of Koreans by relying primarily on word-of-mouth recruiting. Hwang, the owner, is Korean. Seventy-three percent of the job applicants were Korean. One percent of the Chicago-area workforce is Korean, and not more than 3 percent of the janitorial workforce for the area is Korean. The court found no persuasive evidence of intentional discrimination, although the government claimed that 99 applicants were denied jobs because they were not Koreans.

    a. Does restricting hiring to members of one ethnic group constitute discrimination where hiring is accomplished by word of mouth? Explain.

    b. What if a firm, using the word-of-mouth approach, hired only white applicants? Explain.

    c. In this case, the EEOC brought but dropped a disparate impact claim. Analyze the case using the disparate impact test. See *Equal Employment Opportunity Commission v. Consolidated Service Systems,* 989 F.2d 233 (7th Cir. 1993).

Statutory Defenses

In addition to the aforementioned defenses against disparate treatment and disparate impact claims, Title VII also affords specific exemptions or defenses, three of which are of particular note: (1) seniority, (2) employee testing, and (3) bona fide occupational qualification. Bona fide occupational qualifications are addressed in the next section as part of the sex discrimination discussion.

Seniority

Differences in wages and conditions of employment are permissible under the Civil Rights Act of 1964 where those differences are the result of a bona fide (good faith) seniority system, as long as the system was not intended to hide or facilitate discrimination. Seniority is important because it often determines who is laid off first and who gets promotions, vacations, and so forth. Because white people often have greater seniority than blacks, the result is that seniority may perpetuate the effects of historical discrimination. The Supreme Court has made it clear, however, that a bona fide seniority system that perpetuates past wrongs is illegal only if discriminatory intent is proven.[14]

Employee Testing

Testing is, of course, central to professional personnel practice and to maximizing employee productivity; but testing has often been, both intentionally and unintentionally, a primary vehicle in perpetuating discrimination. Only job-related tests supported by detailed, statistical evidence as to their scientific validity are lawful.

Division I College Athletics and Discrimination

In 1992 the National Collegiate Athletic Association (NCAA) Division I schools adopted Proposition 16, which determined athletic eligibility based on the student athlete's GPA and standardized test score (ACT/SAT). For example, a student athlete with a 2.0 high school GPA needed a 1010 SAT score to ensure athletic eligibility as a college freshman. Kelly Pryor, an African American, signed a National Letter of Intent (NLI) to play soccer on a scholarship at San Jose State University in the fall of 1999. Warren Spivey, an African American, signed an NLI to play football on scholarship at the University of Connecticut. Neither Pryor nor Spivey met the Proposition 16 requirements. They sued, claiming the NCAA intentionally discriminated against them because of their race. Essentially, the plaintiffs claimed that Proposition 16 achieved the NCAA goal of improving graduation rates for black athletes relative to white athletes simply by screening out greater numbers of black athletes than white athletes. The plaintiffs provided evidence indicating that the NCAA knew that Proposition 16 would disqualify black athletes in greater proportions than white athletes. In effect, the NCAA, according to the plaintiffs, had intentionally established explicit race-based goals rather than providing a racially neutral way of deciding who would qualify for scholarship eligibility. How would you rule on the case? Explain. See *Pryor v. NCAA,* 288 F.3d 548 (3d Cir. 2002).

The Four-Fifths Rule

The guidelines are rather specific regarding the meaning of *adverse impact*. An employer will generally be presumed in noncompliance with the guidelines if the selection rate (such as the percentage passing a test, being hired, or being promoted) for any protected class is less than 80 percent of the selection rate for the group with the highest rate. An employer falling below that standard must prove the job relatedness of the employment practice in question and demonstrate that a good-faith effort was made to find a selection procedure that lessened the disparate impact on protected classes. [For an extensive employment discrimination database, see **http://www.law.cornell.edu/topics/employment_discrimination.html**]

National Origin

Title VII forbids employment discrimination, including harassment, based on national origin. Marubeni America, the New York subsidiary of a big Japanese trading company, is accused at this writing in 2005 of favoring Asian employees over Americans. Yuji

A big Japanese trading company is accused of favoring Asian employees over Americans.

Takikawa, a corporate vice president, allegedly sent the following e-mail to Kevin Long, a senior human resources manager for the company, asking for help in recruiting a salesperson:

He wanted a person "who has aggressiveness [sic], high IQ. . . . We prefer male and 25–30 years [sic] old, Asian like Chinese, Japanese, of course American or others is fine. As you know, in case of American guy, once reach high income, all of a sudden stop working. . . ."[15]

Long, a white man, and another white executive have sued Marubeni claiming the company discriminates against Americans, non-Asian minorities, and women. The plaintiffs allege non-Asians are paid less and promoted less frequently than Asians.[16] The Japanese company has no African Americans or women and just one Hispanic among its top 121 officers and managers.[17] The plaintiffs claim that weekly meetings were conducted in Japanese and managers often used ethnic slurs.

The lawsuit is rare in its allegations of discrimination by "minority" Asians against Caucasians and others, but continuing globalization presumably will bring more such disputes.

English Only?   National origin claims have recently assumed greater visibility because of conflicts over "English-only" rules in workplaces. Many businesses now forbid employees to speak any language other than English on the job, and many states have designated English as their official language. The companies argue that the rules are necessary when dealing with customers, to maintain job safety, and to encourage congenial worker relations. EEOC guidelines say that employers cannot impose a blanket ban on employees speaking their primary language in the workplace, but an English-only rule at certain times is permissible if justified by business necessity and if adequately explained to the employees.

In the leading case to date, the Spun Steak Co. instituted an English-only rule for its bilingual employees to enhance safety and product quality and to address allegations that some employees were making rude comments in Spanish to English-speaking employees. The English-only rule applied to work but not to lunch, breaks, or employees' own time. The rule was upheld in court on the grounds that it was narrowly defined and did not create a discriminatory atmosphere.[18]

Question

Filipovic was born in Yugoslavia and immigrated to Illinois, where he worked as a full-time dockman for K & R Express for about 12 years. He claims to have repeatedly been called names and subjected to vulgar language by coworkers and supervisors. On four occasions over more than one year, he was subjected to comments related to his national origin, such as "dirty Commie," "Russian dick head," and "f . . . ing foreigner." Name-calling of that kind and verbal harassment generally were common on the docks, and Filipovic admits that he too engaged in name-calling. Filipovic was fired for cause. He filed suit claiming national origin discrimination and national origin harassment. Decide. Explain. See *Filipovic v. K & R Express Systems,* 176 F.3d 390 (7th Cir. 1999). Also see 391 F. 3d 859 (7th Cir. 2004).

Racial Harassment

The hangman's noose reportedly is making a symbolic comeback.

The hangman's noose, perhaps the most hurtful and disgraceful expression of American racism, reportedly is making a symbolic comeback in America's increasingly integrated workplaces. The EEOC recently responded to 25 noose cases in an 18-month period.[19] Racial epithets and notes from the "KKK" (Ku Klux Klan), along with physical and verbal threats, are alleged in some of America's biggest corporations.[20] Complaints of racial harassment doubled during the 1990s to around 10,000 annually. Some attribute the increase to blue-collar, white male anger over affirmative action and to the slide in less skilled workers' welfare due to wage increases that have lagged inflation since 1973.[21]

Recent court decisions suggest that the Supreme Court's reasoning in sexual harassment cases (explained below) will probably also apply to cases of racial or national origin harassment. In addition to overt forms of harassment such as racial slurs, some decisions suggest that the use of more subtle "code words" may constitute racial and/or national origin harassment. In *Aman v. Cort Furniture Rental Corporation,*[22] two black employees claimed that they were subjected to a racially hostile work environment in part because black employees were labeled by coworkers and managers with racist "code words" such as "all of you," "one of them," and "poor people." The court, in finding for the employees, ruled that certain phrases in the employment setting cannot be excused as mere rudeness and may, in the totality of the circumstances, add up to discrimination so severe that it creates an abusive work environment. In addition to those mentioned in *Aman,* a number of other code phrases might bring legal problems: "They're all stupid and lazy." "Your type." "All they're interested in is drugs." "You people don't understand how to save money."[23]

KKK

"Auburn University said . . . it has indefinitely suspended 15 students who wore Ku Klux Klan costumes and blackface to fraternity Halloween parties."

Source: Associated Press, "Racist Costumes Draw Suspensions," *Waterloo/Cedar Falls Courier,* November 16, 2001, p. A2.

Part Three—Sex Discrimination

Equality for Women

More than 40 years after the 1963 passage of the Equal Pay Act, American women earn, according to the Census Bureau, about 77 cents for every dollar earned by men, up dramatically from the 59 cents of the early 1960s, but still far short of equality.[24] Of course, factors beyond discrimination, including female decisions to interrupt careers for child rearing, account for some of that disparity; but allegations of sex discrimination remain common. In 2004 the securities firm Morgan Stanley agreed to pay $54 million to settle employee sex discrimination claims,[25] and Boeing settled another such suit for $72.5 million.[26] More portentously, 1.6 million current and former female employees have brought, at this writing, a class action against Wal-Mart. Basically, the suit claims that Wal-Mart pays female workers less than men for comparable work and that women are treated less favorably for promotions. Women constitute about two-thirds of Wal-Mart's employees, but only a bit more than a third of salaried managers and just 14 percent of top managers.[27] [For the AFL-CIO Web site on equal pay issues, see **www.aflcio.org/ issuespolitics/women/equalpay/**]

Glass Ceiling?   Critics say a "glass ceiling" of prejudice holds women back from roles of power. Only seven *Fortune* 500 firms have female chief executive officers following the 2005 dismissal of Carly Fiorina as Hewlett-Packard CEO, and only 7.9 percent of *Fortune* 500 bosses at the executive vice president level and above are women.[28] Fiorina's dismissal was, to some, a victory for gender equality because she was widely believed to have been assessed by her performance rather than her gender. (Fiorina had struggled in merging Compaq and HP and building the resulting business.)

The news is hardly all bad for women, however. A 2003 study shows 39 percent of women are in managerial or professional jobs, up from 36 percent in 1997 and 24 percent in 1977.[29] Lack of line experience and parenting decisions seem to be critical factors in holding women back, but desire to be the boss does not seem to be at issue. A 2004 survey of senior executives found 55 percent of women and 57 percent of men aspire to be CEOs.[30] Some experts believe that women would rise more rapidly in organizations if they manifested more of the daring, assertiveness, and self-promotion that seem to mark men rather than the conscientiousness, organization, ability to follow instructions, and the like that help women outperform males as students.[31] Similarly, a survey of executives found that successful men are primarily motivated by their own career and personal goals, while successful women give more attention to working relationships and customer satisfaction.[32]

A Double Standard?

Linda Hamburger is no wallflower, and she was working at a Florida utility company when the "F-bomb" escaped her mouth in a moment of frustration. It would not have been a big deal if it had come from a man, but Hamburger says it got her fired for insubordination.

Women in business argue that their careers can be destroyed by language that is routine when uttered by men. Further, experts argue that women may unintentionally distract men and give men ammunition for laughs at the expense of women by uttering legitimate language with a sexual subtext such as "screwed up," "stay abreast," and "get it off my chest."

Source: Del Jones, "Watch What You Say, Women Are Told," *Des Moines Register,* December 6, 2004, p. 8C.

Analysis of Sex Discrimination

Under Title VII of the Civil Rights Act of 1964, sex discrimination analysis proceeds in essentially the manner outlined earlier in the chapter: Disparate treatment (intentional discrimination) and disparate impact (discriminatory effect) are the key tests. Intentional discrimination cases are increasingly uncommon as we become better educated about both discriminatory behavior and the law. Nonetheless, these cases still emerge from time to time. For example, a federal court of appeals held that a company president's remarks could constitute direct evidence of intentional sex discrimination when he said that women were simply "not tough enough" to supervise collections and that it was "a man's job" and "I felt that a woman was not competent enough to do this job, but I think maybe you're showing me that you can do it."[33]

PRACTICING ETHICS   More Evidence in the Ongoing Gender Struggle:

- The proportion of bachelor's degrees awarded to women in the United States has reached approximately 57 percent. Among African Americans, two women earn a bachelor's degree for every man. In 1990, 57 percent of four-year college degrees went to men.
- A recent study finds that women actually learn only about two-thirds as much on the average during their college years as do men. The 2001 study of 19,000 students was published in a well-regarded academic journal, but it is the first of its kind and must be replicated before its results can be viewed with scholarly confidence.
- According to a *USA TODAY* analysis, many private colleges and universities practice what might be labeled affirmative action for boys. The newspaper says, "Private colleges routinely accept a larger percentage of male applicants than female applicants." A few admit that they "tilt the admissions scale toward boys" to maintain a gender-balanced learning environment.
- Harvard University president Lawrence Summers, in a spectacularly successful effort to be provocative, reportedly said in 2005 that women may be underrepresented in senior math and science posts because women *may* be, on average, innately inferior to men in advanced mathematics. Summers later explained that his remarks reflected the research of others rather than his personal views.

Questions

1. *a.* Should we be concerned about the declining proportion of men who are graduating from college?

   b. Have men somehow been wronged by a society that has been anxious to make up for rather obvious wrongs done to women?

2. *a.* If men actually learn more in college than women, does sexism in educational and societal practices account for that difference?

   b. Or does women's alleged innate inferiority in mathematics explain the difference?

3. *a.* Given his highly influential position in higher education, was it wrong of President Summers even to suggest that women *might* be innately inferior to men in mathematics?

   b. Is it wrong of some colleges and universities to favor men in admissions over women?

Sources: Patrick Smyth, "US Has Thrown the Gender Switch, Academics Warn," *Irish Times,* June 29, 2002, p. 13; *Washington Post,* "Women Outnumber Men on U.S. Campuses," *Waterloo/Cedar Falls Courier,* November 18, 1999, p. A10; Lamont Flowers, Steven J. Osterlind, Ernest T. Pascarella, and Christopher T. Pierson, "How Much Do Students Learn in College?" *Journal of Higher Education* 72, no. 5 (September 2001), p. 565; Editorial, "Threats to College-Diversity Programs Pose Risks for Boys," *USA TODAY,* May 23, 2003, p. 14A; Suzanne Goldenberg, "Why Women Are Poor at Science by Harvard President," *Guardian* January 18, 2005 [**http://www.guardian.co.uk/**].

Bona Fide Occupational Qualification

Often in intentional sex discrimination cases, the key inquiry involves the *bona fide occupational qualification* (*BFOQ*) defense provided by Title VII. Discrimination is lawful where sex, religion, or national origin is a BFOQ reasonably necessary to the normal operation of that business. The exclusion of race and color from the list suggests Congress thought those categories always unacceptable as bona fide occupational qualifications. The BFOQ was meant to be a very limited exception applicable to situations where specific inherent characteristics are necessary to the job (for example, wet nurse) or where authenticity (actors), privacy (nurses), or safety (guards) are required. Broadly, the BFOQ defense rests on this question: Is femaleness (maleness) necessary to perform the *essence* of the job?

Essence

An employer can lawfully insist on a woman to fill a woman's modeling role because being female goes to the essence of the job. Airlines, on the other hand, cannot hire only women as flight attendants even if customers prefer females and even if females perform the supplementary elements of the job (like charming passengers) better than most men. Those duties "are tangential to the essence of the business involved"[34] (the essence being the maintenance of safe, orderly conditions, providing service as needed, and so on). Presumably gender has little to do with the ability to perform those essential ingredients of the job.

Many employers have simply assumed that women could not perform certain tasks. Women were thought to be insufficiently aggressive for sales roles, and women were denied employment because they were assumed to have a higher turnover rate due to the desire to marry and have children. Those stereotypes are at the heart of sex discrimination litigation generally and sex as a BFOQ particularly.

The case that follows involves the application of Title VII disparate impact analysis to the physical qualifications necessary to serve as a firefighter.

LEGAL BRIEFCASE

Pietras v. Farmingville Fire District 180 F.3d 468 (2d Cir.1999); cert. den. 528 U.S. 948 (1999)

Circuit Judge Calabresi

The district court found that Farmingville's physical agility test ("PAT"), which all probationary volunteer firefighters were required to pass in order to become full-fledged volunteer firefighters, had a disparate impact on women.

* * * * *

BACKGROUND

Farmingville is the governing body of a volunteer fire department that has approximately 100 members. Pietras was a probationary (i.e., trainee) firefighter in the Farmingville Department. Even as a probationary volunteer, Pietras was entitled to numerous firefighter benefits under state law and the by-laws of the department. These included (1) a retirement pension, (2) life insurance, (3) death benefits, (4) disability insurance, and (5) some medical benefits.

Before Pietras could become a full member of the department, however, she and all other probationary volunteers were required to pass a newly instituted PAT.[1] The PAT consisted of a series of physical tasks that the applicants had to complete within a specified time limit. The most difficult of these nine labors was the "charged hose drag," which involved dragging a water-filled hose—weighing approximately 280 pounds—over a distance of 150 feet.

To determine the appropriate time limit for the PAT, Farmingville officials asked various members of the department to take the test. Forty-four firefighters participated in these trials. Of the 44 test-takers, 33 were males who served as full firefighters, 6 were male probationary members, 3 were male junior members, one was Jeanine Serpe, a female full firefighter, and one was Pietras. The average times of these subgroups were:

Sample Pool	Average Time
Full males (33)	3:12
Probationary males (6)	2:47
Junior males (3)	2:52
Full female (Serpe)	5:30
Probationary female (Pietras)	5:21

From these results, Farmingville set four minutes as the time within which the labors had to be completed. The four-minute threshold was determined by taking the average of all the (mostly male) test runs (approximately 3:30) and then adding an extra half-minute "to have some leeway." There was some concern expressed at a 1993 Farmingville Board meeting that neither Serpe nor Pietras had been able to finish the PAT in anything close to four minutes, but Farmingville nevertheless instituted the four-minute cutoff.

Following the implementation of the PAT, Pietras tried and failed the test twice. During this same period, six other female probationary firefighters took the test. Four of these women completed the PAT in under four minutes and therefore passed. One woman failed to complete the test for an unknown reason. And one woman did not complete the test despite repeated efforts to drag the water-filled hose over the required distance. All of the 24 male probationary volunteers who took the test at about this time passed.

Following her second failure to pass the PAT, Pietras was fired from her volunteer position at Farmingville.

* * * * *

[1] Pietras passed both a medical exam and a written exam that were also preconditions to becoming a full firefighter.

Pietras filed suit in district court, alleging that Farmingville had violated Title VII of the Civil Rights Act of 1964.

* * * * *

At trial . . ., Pietras presented testimony from Dr. Robert Otto, an expert exercise physiologist. Dr. Otto conducted an extensive review of the physical agility tests administered by various volunteer and paid fire departments and concluded (a) that the four-minute limit in the Farmingville test had a disparate impact on women, and (b) that it was not job related.

After reviewing the evidence, the district court ruled for Pietras.

* * * * *

[T]he court concluded that "the record is bereft of any evidence" that a four-minute time limit to finish the PAT was job related.[2]

In support of its finding of disparate impact, the court noted that the male pass rate on the PAT was 95 percent (63 out of 66) while the female pass rate was only 57 percent (4 out of 7). Relying on the "four-fifths" rule set forth in the EEOC Guidelines, the court reasoned that "a pass rate for women which is less [than] four-fifths (or 80 percent) of the pass rate for men typically signifies disparate impact sufficient to establish a *prima facie* case. . . . Therefore, the gender imbalance [in this case] more than satisfies the 80 percent standard." This statistical evidence (which was corroborated by Dr. Otto's testimony concerning the effect of the PAT on women) was deemed by the district court to be enough to establish disparate impact.

Farmingville appeals.

DISCUSSION

* * * * *

Disparate Impact

* * * * *

Farmingville asserts that, even if the statistical figures before the district court were correct, a sample of seven female test takers is simply too small to support a disparate impact finding.

* * * * *

In the case before us, however, Pietras presented more than just statistics. After conducting an exhaustive analysis of the practices of other fire departments, Dr. Otto provided expert

[2] [T]here is no evidence at all to indicate that the time chosen for the test reflected the needs of the job. In fact, the record makes clear that Farmingville selected the four-minute figure simply by taking the average of all the test scores and then arbitrarily adding some extra time.

testimony on the disparate impact of Farmingville's PAT. This expert testimony, combined with the statistics Pietras did present, comfortably tips the scales in favor of the district court's finding of disparate impact.

Affirmed.

Questions

1. *a.* Why did the court conclude that the Farmingville Fire Department had discriminated against Pietras?

   b. Did the court conclude that Farmingville intended to discriminate? Explain.

   c. What, if anything, could Farmingville have done differently to win this case?

2. *a.* Shouldn't we always choose the strongest, fastest firefighters as long as they are otherwise well qualified? Explain.

   b. Do the firefighters' rescue efforts at the World Trade Center on September 11, 2001, indicate that only men should serve as firefighters? Explain.

3. *a.* How would you argue that Women's Workout World, a health and exercise club, should be able to lawfully decline to accept men as customers and/or employees?

   b. Decide the case. Explain. See *U.S. EEOC v. Sedita*, 816 F.Supp. 1291 (N.D. Ill. 1993).

4. Dianne Rawlinson sought employment as a prison guard in Alabama. She was a 22-year-old college graduate with a degree in correctional psychology. She was denied employment because she failed to meet the 120-pound weight requirement for the job. The state also required such employees to be at least 5 feet 2 inches tall. Alabama operated four all-male, maximum security prisons. The district court characterized the Alabama prison system as one of "rampant violence." Rawlinson sued, claiming employment discrimination. Decide. Explain. See *Dothard v. Rawlinson*, 97 S.Ct. 2720 (1977).

Pietras **or** *SEPTA?*

The Southeastern Pennsylvania Transportation Authority (SEPTA) was sued on sex discrimination grounds by several female job applicants who had been rejected for employment as police officers. The women were unable to run 1.5 miles in 12 minutes, a job requirement. A disparate impact was established with evidence that 93 percent of women could not pass the test, but the Third Circuit Federal Court of Appeals ruled that the standard was consistent with business necessity and therefore did not violate Title VII. SEPTA was able to satisfy the court that running up and down subway stairs and pursuing wrongdoers required fitness like that measured by the test. Evidence also established that minimal training would allow most women to qualify.

The case against SEPTA had been pursued for a number of years by President Clinton's Justice Department, but President Bush's Justice Department decided to withdraw its support from the case, saying that officer fitness is critical to public safety.

Source: Lanning v. SEPTA, 308 F.3d 286 (3d Cir. 2002).

Hooters

Can the 40-state restaurant chain Hooters lawfully decline to hire men to be food servers? The article that follows explains the 1997 settlement of a lawsuit addressing that question.

Hooters Agrees to Hire Men in Support Roles, But It Will Still Hire Scantily Clad Women; Discrimination

CHICAGO—Hooters of America Inc. said that it will not change its policy of hiring scantily clad "Hooters girls" to serve customers despite its tentative $ 3.75 million settlement with male applicants who sued it for sex discrimination after being turned down for jobs because of their gender.

Several class-action lawsuits were filed around the country beginning in 1993 on behalf of rejected male applicants, and the suits were consolidated in Chicago.

"We've settled the entire issue," said Mike McNeil, vice president of marketing for the privately held, 204-restaurant Hooters chain. The settlement "preserves the integrity of the Hooters concept—the service of food and beverages will continue to be performed by the Hooters girls." The settlement allows Atlanta-based Hooters to continue luring customers with an exclusively female staff of Hooters Girls, but the chain agreed to create a few other support jobs, such as bartenders and hosts, that must be filled without regard to gender.

"Our business is on the female sex appeal side," McNeil said. "Over the years, there have been lots of people who have suggested [offering some male sex appeal]. Our answer is, if you think that's a good, economically viable idea, get your capital together and go ahead and do it."

In the agreement the restaurant chain agreed to set aside $2 million as compensation for men who were turned away from jobs because of their gender. Lawyers will get $.75 million. The agreement is subject to U.S. District Court approval.

The Equal Employment Opportunity Commission investigated the discrimination complaint for four years, then dropped it in 1996, saying it had more important cases to pursue. The EEOC did, however, suggest that the chain hire men.

The recommendation drew snickers and ridicule. The chain put on a mock advertising campaign featuring a burly, mustachioed man wearing a blond wig, short shorts, and stuffed shirt, with the slogan "Come on, Washington. Get a grip."

The private lawsuit settled a consolidation of legal action brought by seven men from Illinois and Maryland who argued that their failure to get jobs at Hooters was a violation of federal law.

Source: *Baltimore Sun*, October 1, 1997, p. 3C. Reprinted by permission of the copyright holder, The Associated Press.

AFTERWORD

According to published accounts, the parties agreed that a woman would continue to work behind each Hooters bar, but an assistant could be either male or female. Likewise, men or women could serve as greeters and do work such as clearing tables.

Questions

1. *a.* Explain the plaintiffs' view that Hooters' hiring policy constitutes impermissible sexual discrimination.

   b. Explain Hooters' claim that it does not violate Title VII.

2. Is Hooters' hiring policy better left to the market than to the courts? Explain.

Hooters or Jillian's?

Jillian's, a nationwide chain of family dining/entertainment facilities, agreed in 2004 to settle EEOC charges of sex discrimination involving an alleged refusal to hire men as servers and for other so-called "female" jobs. At least 100 men were expected to share a $350,000 damages payment, and Jillian's agreed to place employees without regard to gender.

Source: "Jillian's to Pay $360,000 for Sex Discrimination against Men," Equal Employment Opportunity Commission [**http://www.eeoc.gov/press/8-13-04.html**].

Parent and Manager?

Antidiscrimination law has been critical in allowing women to pursue careers and in providing some refuge from the professional disadvantages of pregnancy. The Pregnancy

Discrimination Act (PDA) amended Title VII of the Civil Rights Act of 1964 so that discrimination with regard to pregnancy is treated as a form of sex discrimination. Broadly, the PDA requires that pregnant employees be treated the same as all other employees with temporary disabilities. In general, an employer should not ask job applicants about pregnancy, and applicants have no duty to reveal that pregnancy. Nor can a pregnant employee be forced to take time off or be forced to quit due to pregnancy. Pregnancy discrimination complaints to the EEOC have been among the fastest-rising claims, with an increase of 39 percent from 1992 to 2003.[35]

In a variation on pregnancy discrimination, a federal court of appeals in 2004 recognized a particular form of gender bias that might be thought of as "maternal" or "caregiver" discrimination. In that case, the court ruled that a lower court must hear a woman's complaint that she was discriminated against merely because she is a mother. Elana Back, a school psychologist, claims that she was denied tenure, despite high performance, because her bosses doubted her ability to do her job and be a mother.[36]

Questions

1. A pregnant medical technologist was fired for taking leave because she feared being exposed to on-the-job radiation while working with equipment containing radioactive isotopes. She had sought a transfer, but no openings were available; so her employer placed her on family and sick leave. When that leave was exhausted, she was fired. Did her termination violate the PDA? Explain. See *Duncan v. Children's National Medical Center,* 702 A. 2d 207 (D.C. App. 1997); cert. den. 525 U.S. 912 (1998).

2. Ethel Roskies, a University of Montreal psychologist, reporting the results of a survey of successful professional women: "The woman who gives up marriage and children in order to further her career is making a bad bargain. We found that single childless women are significantly more depressed, report lower self-esteem and lower life satisfaction than married women with children."[37] Comment.

Equal Pay

Title VII affords broad protection from discrimination in pay because of sex. The Equal Pay Act of 1963 directly forbids discrimination on the basis of sex by paying wages to employees of one sex at a rate less than the rate paid to employees of the opposite sex for equal work on jobs requiring equal skill, effort, and responsibility and performed under similar working conditions (*equal* has been interpreted to mean "substantially equal"). The act provides for certain exceptions. Unequal wage payments are lawful if paid pursuant to (1) a seniority system, (2) a merit system, (3) a system that measures earnings by quantity or quality of production, or (4) a differential based on "any . . . factor other than sex." The employer seeking to avoid a violation of the Equal Pay Act can adjust its wage structure by raising the pay of the disfavored sex. Lowering the pay of the favored sex violates the act.

Women's Basketball Coach

Former University of Southern California head women's basketball coach Marianne Stanley sued the university for violating the Equal Pay Act because she was not as well paid as then head men's basketball coach George Raveling. Both coaches had successful won/lost records. The university defended the pay differential by pointing to Raveling's 14 years of coaching experience beyond Stanley's, his having coached the U.S. Olympic team, his marketing experience outside of coaching, and his books on basketball. Stanley could not point to similar credentials. Did the university violate the Equal Pay Act? See *Stanley v. University of Southern California*, 178 F. 3d 1069 (9th Cir. 1999); cert.den.528 U.S. 1022 (1999).

Sexual Harassment

Sexual harassment is a form of sex discrimination actionable under Title VII. As the following article clearly warns, addressing sexual harassment in the workplace has become an important component of management practice.

Settlement OKd in Smith Barney Bias Suit

READING

Times Staff and Wire Reports

A federal judge on Friday approved a unique settlement of the sex bias case against Salomon Smith Barney, allowing the investment house to close an ugly chapter in its treatment of women.

* * * * *

[T]he settlement of the class-action bias case does not constitute an admission by Smith Barney of any wrongdoing. The firm will bear all costs associated with notifying 22,000 potential claimants about the settlement.

"We believe the settlement focuses on effecting real change and progress, rather than simply delivering monetary awards," Smith Barney said in a statement.

Marianne Dalton, 37, of Westlake Village[, CA] was one of 23 women who filed the initial class-action bias complaint. A retail broker for Smith Barney's Los Angeles office in 1995, she said she repeatedly witnessed her boss changing his clothes.

"I would hear unbelievably lewd comments about his personal life" while he would strip to his underwear, Dalton said. When she reported her experiences to management, she said she was transferred to the Beverly Hills office. But she said her reputation for speaking against her boss preceded her. When she quit a year later, she could not get a similar position elsewhere.

"I was blacklisted . . . because of this case," Dalton said.

* * * * *

Dalton and the 22 other original complainants will receive a total of $1.9 million as part of the settlement, which does not include punitive damages.

Women employees alleged that they were harassed and intimidated by senior male workers who engaged in fraternity-house antics in the "boom-boom room," a basement space in a Smith Barney branch in Garden City, N.Y., on Long Island.

The suit also alleged that women were denied promotions at Smith Barney and that the firm ignored complaints of abuse and unwanted sexual advances and investigated claims in a way that subjected female workers to retaliation.

The settlement allows the women to resolve discrimination claims using an independent arbitrator instead of being forced to go to mandatory industry-sponsored arbitration.

In the proposed settlement, the firm will spend more than $15 million over four years on programs to recruit and promote women and minorities. That figure could rise under a penalty provision of the settlement.

* * * * *

Source: *Los Angeles Times*, July 25, 1998, part D, p. 2, Reprinted by permission of the copyright holder, The Associated Press.

What Is It?   Often we are not sure which behaviors constitute sexual harassment. A 1992 Roper Poll summarized 22 situations and asked the respondents which of them amounted to sexual harassment. Clear majorities found sexual harassment in only three of the situations. Those involved direct questions about sexual practices and being required to sleep with the boss in exchange for a raise. Strong majorities rejected a finding of sexual harassment in such situations as these:

- A compliment about a coworker's appearance.
- Asking a coworker for a date.
- A woman looking a man "up and down" as he walks by.
- Referring to women as "girls."

A middle ground of great confusion included such situations as these:

- A male boss calling a female "honey."
- A man looking a woman "up and down" as she walks by.
- Men in the office repeatedly discussing the appearance of female coworkers.[38]

Male Worker Harassed at Domino's

For five months, David Papa's boss at a Domino's Pizza made comments about his body, touched him, and told him she loved him. Six days after he told her to stop, she fired him.

A federal judge ordered the pizza chain to pay Papa $237,000 in damages in the first case the U.S. Equal Employment Opportunity Commission ever took to trial involving a man harassed by a woman.

Source: Associated Press, "Male Worker Harassed at Domino's, Judge Rules," *Des Moines Register,* November 23, 1995, p. 4A.

The Law of Sexual Harassment

In brief, sexual harassment, as a matter of law, consists of unwelcome sexual advances, requests for sexual favors, and other verbal or physical conduct of a sexual nature that (1) becomes a condition of employment, (2) becomes a basis for employment decisions, or (3) unreasonably interferes with work performance or creates a hostile working environment.

Sexual harassment cases have been divided into a pair of categories, *quid pro quo* (this for that, such as a sexual experience in exchange for keeping one's job) and *hostile environment* (a workplace rendered offensive and abusive by sexual comments, pictures, jokes, sexual aggression, and the like where no employment benefit is gained or lost). Note that the law of sexual harassment described hereafter appears to apply also to other forms of harassment such as race, religion, national origin, and disability.

The Test

Once we have some idea of behavior that constitutes sexual harassment, our concern turns to which remedies are available for the victims. Although the question is not settled, most courts to date have ruled that victims of sexual harassment seeking recovery under Title VII cannot sue the person who actually committed the harassment. The victim might be able to sue the wrongdoer under a state statute or by using a tort claim such as assault, but under Title VII, *personal liability* appears not to be available. This result, if the current judicial pattern continues, is not as unfair as might at first appear because well-settled principles of justice hold the employer generally responsible for workplace problems. The victim, therefore, can seek damages from the employer. A pair of 1998 U.S. Supreme Court decisions in the *Burlington Industries* and *Faragher*[39] cases considerably clarified the circumstances under which an employer is liable for sexual harassment in the workplace. The analysis proceeds as follows:

1. **Proof of sexual harassment**—The plaintiff/employee/victim must prove items *a–c*:
    a. Harassment unwelcome.
    b. Harassment because of sex.
    c. Harassment resulted in a tangible employment action, or was sufficiently severe or pervasive as to unreasonably alter the conditions of employment and create a hostile, abusive working environment.

If the plaintiff is unable to prove items *a–c*, her/his claim fails. If the plaintiff proves items *a–c*, the inquiry then turns to Part 2 and the question of whether the employer bears responsibility for the harassment.

2. **Employer liability**
    a. If the wrongdoer was a coworker, the plaintiff/employee can bring a negligence claim seeking to prove that the employer unreasonably failed to prevent or remedy the discriminatory harassment of the coworker where management knew or should have known about the harassment.
    b. If the wrongdoer was a supervisor with authority over the plaintiff/employee, and if the employee suffered a *tangible employment action* (job loss, demotion) because of the harassment, the employer is vicariously liable (*indirect* liability —see Chapter 12) for the employee's losses. That is, the employer is automatically liable for the employee's wrong and cannot offer a defense regardless of lack of knowledge, absence of negligence, or any other factor.
    c. If the wrongdoer was a supervisor with authority over the plaintiff/employee, but the employee suffered no tangible employment action, the employer can avoid liability by proving both elements of the following affirmative defense: (1) The employer exercised reasonable care to prevent and correct the harassment promptly (by instituting antiharassment training programs, for example), and (2) the employee unreasonably failed to take advantage of those opportunities. See *Pennsylvania State Police v. Suders,* 542 U.S. 129 (2005), for an analysis of the affirmative defense.

The case that follows illustrates sexual harassment analysis, and it introduces an increasingly important cause of action—*retaliation*—where a plaintiff/employee (or applicant) claims that an employer discouraged or prevented the plaintiff from enforcing his or her legal rights.

EEOC v. R&R Ventures, d/b/a Taco Bell
244 F.3d 334 (4th Cir. 2001)

Chief Judge Wilkinson

The Equal Employment Opportunity Commission (EEOC) brought this suit against R&R Ventures, owner of the Severna Park, Maryland, Taco Bell. The EEOC alleges that Edwin Wheeler, a former manager of the restaurant, sexually harassed various female employees. The district court held that Wheeler's conduct was not severe enough to create a triable issue of sexual harassment.

I.

Edwin Wheeler used to manage the Severna Park Taco Bell for R&R Ventures. Shelby Scott and Brandyn Potter worked as entry-level employees under Wheeler. R&R claims that Wheeler was a difficult manager who abused male and female employees alike. The EEOC claims, however, that Wheeler singled out his female subordinates for especially cruel treatment and that this constituted sexual harassment.

Shelby Scott was one of Wheeler's victims. She was only 15 when she started work at the Severna Park Taco Bell. Scott claims that Wheeler made sexual jokes on a daily basis and that he frequently discussed sexual positions and experiences. When Scott bent over, Wheeler told her she was giving him a "cheap thrill." He commented regularly about the size of her buttocks and breasts. He repeatedly asked Scott if she liked to be spanked. He also frequently said that women were stupid as compared to men. Wheeler made these comments every time he worked with Scott, often in front of other employees. Because of Wheeler's comments, Scott suffered an eating disorder and lost a significant amount of weight in an effort to avoid attracting attention to her body.

Although Scott repeatedly asked Wheeler to stop making sexual comments, he persisted. He did so even though Scott became visibly upset. Ultimately, Scott buckled under the pressure and resigned in June of 1996. When she resumed working at Taco Bell in August of 1996, Wheeler began harassing her again. Scott complained about Wheeler's conduct to three other managers at her store, none of whom took any action. This prompted Scott's mother to lodge several complaints with Mike Lee, then R&R's area manager. Lee did not return any of her calls. Another R&R employee, however, investigated the claims by interviewing five or six female employees who worked for Wheeler. Neither Scott nor Wheeler were interviewed as a part of this investigation and no disciplinary action resulted.

On October 27, 1996, after Scott and her mother had complained to Lee, Scott arrived early to work. Wheeler screamed at Scott, reducing her to tears, because of her early arrival. As Scott was leaving, one of the other managers told her to take the rest of the day off. When she did, Wheeler suspended her for two weeks. Scott was never returned to the work schedule.

About the same time Scott filed her charge with the EEOC, Brandyn Potter began working at the store. Potter was 20 when she started working with Wheeler. Wheeler flirted with Potter and repeatedly made sexual comments in her presence. For example, Wheeler inquired about the size of Potter's pants and complained to her about how long it had been since he had engaged in sex. Wheeler also belittled Potter in front of others, telling her she was stupid. Wheeler behaved this way every time the two worked together. Potter cried every morning at the thought of having to work with Wheeler and frequently left in tears on account of his verbal assaults.

As did Scott, Potter complained to Wheeler and asked him to stop. She also complained to another manager, Tammy Hartley, who told Potter that she was overreacting. When she decided to complain to R&R's higher management, none of the managers would give her Mike Lee's phone number. After two weeks, however, Potter obtained the number and called Lee to complain.

Lee responded by offering to move Potter to the Crofton Taco Bell while he worked out the details of transferring Wheeler. Since the Crofton assignment could not take place immediately, Lee told Potter to take a week off so she would not have to work with Wheeler. During her week off, however, Hartley called Potter and told her she would be fired if she did not come to work. When Potter arrived at the store, Wheeler confronted her. He screamed at Potter, saying that she "had no [expletive deleted] right to go to my boss and complain" and that she was a bitch. Potter left immediately and did not return until Wheeler had been transferred. When she returned, however, R&R management reduced her hours so much that she quit and found another job.

On March 30, 1999, the EEOC filed this suit. The complaint alleged that R&R was liable for a hostile working environment. The complaint also alleged that R&R retaliated against Scott and Potter for objecting to Wheeler's behavior. After discovery, the district court granted R&R's motion for summary judgment. It ruled that the alleged misconduct was not sufficiently severe or pervasive to create a hostile work environment. According to the district court, this case was "about a crude supervisor who made the life of his subordinates miserable," but whose conduct failed to rise to the level of a Title VII violation. The district court also held that there was insufficient evidence to establish a prima facie case of retaliation. The EEOC now appeals.

II.

In order to succeed on a claim of hostile workplace harassment, the EEOC must prove the following: (1) the harassment was because of sex; (2) the harassment was unwelcome; (3) the harassment was sufficiently severe or pervasive to create an abusive working environment; and (4) some basis exists for imputing liability to the employer.

A.

R&R first claims that Wheeler's harassment of his female employees was not because of sex. Rather, R&R claims that Wheeler was an "equal-opportunity" harasser who abused men and women alike. However, the allegations contained in the depositions of Scott and Potter, if proven at trial, would rebut this argument fully. While Wheeler may sometimes have been abusive toward male employees, the allegations indicate that Wheeler directed his sexually pointed comments exclusively to the young women who worked for him.

* * * * *

B.

The second element of a hostile workplace claim is whether the harassment was unwelcome. R&R does not and cannot claim that Wheeler's behavior was welcome.

C.

The third element focuses on whether the harassment was sufficiently severe or pervasive to create an abusive working environment.

* * * * *

R&R claims that Wheeler's harassment was not sufficiently severe to sustain a hostile work environment claim. In support, R&R points to the absence of any allegations of unwanted touching, overt sexual propositions, or physical threats. One of Scott's complaints, however, was that Wheeler sometimes touched her and brushed up against her. Scott's mother also claimed to have witnessed Wheeler touching an employee's breasts in an inappropriate fashion.

Even without these allegations, however, R&R's arguments are misplaced as a matter of law. In this case, Wheeler allegedly described his sex life and discussed sexual positions with Scott and Potter. He regularly asked Scott if she liked to be spanked, if she had "gotten laid," and complained about his lack of sexual prowess. On almost a daily basis he commented on Scott's buttocks and breasts, asked Potter what size pants she wore, and made inappropriate sexual remarks. He made these comments in front of other employees and customers and, in doing so, made his victims uncomfortable and visibly upset. Sometimes he even reduced them to tears. These allegations, if proven, would be more than sufficient to establish that Wheeler created an environment consumed by remarks that ridiculed and demeaned the status of women.

* * * * *

R&R next argues that Wheeler's comments were neither physically threatening nor humiliating, but merely offensive in a manner not prohibited by Title VII.

* * * * *

The facts as alleged go beyond mere offensiveness. Indeed, the incessant put-downs, innuendos, and leers directed at these young women literally caused them to become sick at the prospect of going to work.

R&R also disputes the claim that Wheeler's harassment unreasonably interfered with any employee's work performance. In support, R&R points out that although Scott quit in June of 1996, she returned in August. According to R&R, the harassment could not have been interfering with her work if she was willing to come back. As was explained in *Harris,* however, the inquiry "is not whether work has been impaired, but whether working conditions have been discriminatorily altered." We have no hesitation in concluding that Wheeler's alleged conduct was so severe, especially when considered from his victims' perspective, that it discriminatorily altered their working conditions.

D.

The fourth element of a hostile work environment claim asks if there is any basis for imputing liability to the employer.

* * * * *

In order to escape liability, R&R must prove that it exercised reasonable care in preventing and promptly correcting any sexually harassing behavior. It also must show that "the plaintiff employee unreasonably failed to take advantage of any preventive or corrective opportunities provided by the employer or to avoid harm otherwise." *Faragher,* 524 U.S. at 807.

In this case, Scott and Potter affirmatively sought to bring their complaints about Wheeler to the attention of several different managers.

* * * * *

It therefore cannot be said, as a matter of law, that Scott and Potter failed to take advantage of any corrective opportunities.

What can be said, however, is that R&R management failed to promptly correct Wheeler's harassing behavior. Hartley responded to Potter's complaints by saying that Potter was overreacting. Scott's complaints to the three other managers at the store went similarly unattended. Further, when Scott's mother complained to Mike Lee, R&R failed to interview Scott, failed to interview Wheeler, and took absolutely no corrective action. Under these circumstances, R&R cannot claim as a matter of law that it exercised reasonable care to promptly correct any sexually harassing behavior.

III.

The EEOC also appeals the grant of summary judgment on the retaliation claim. Title VII prohibits an employer from discriminating against an employee in retaliation for opposing an unlawful employment practice. To establish a prima facie case of retaliation, the EEOC must prove (1) that Scott and Potter engaged in a protected activity; (2) that R&R took an adverse action against Scott and Potter; and (3) a causal connection between the two. The district court accepted as sufficient EEOC's allegations that R&R took adverse actions against Scott and Potter. It held, however, that the EEOC could not establish that these adverse actions were a result of Scott and Potter's complaints about Wheeler.

We disagree. After complaining, Scott was suspended by Wheeler and never recalled. Potter claims that after she complained, Wheeler told her she "had no [expletive deleted] right to go to my boss" and that she was a bitch. Shortly thereafter, Potter's hours were reduced to the point that she resigned in order to find other employment. The fact that adverse actions followed so closely on the heels of Scott's and Potter's complaints supports their prima facie case of retaliation, especially since the decision to suspend Scott and to reduce Potter's hours were made by people who were well aware that they had complained.

R&R makes no attempt to provide any legitimate reason for why Scott was never recalled to work. Even the stated reason for her suspension—that she arrived for work too early—raises as many questions as it answers.

* * * * *

The above facts raise a genuine dispute on the ultimate question of R&R's retaliatory motive.

Reversed and remanded.

AFTERWORD—RETALIATION

Retaliation, as examined in the *Taco Bell* case, is forbidden by Title VII, the Americans with Disabilities Act, the Age Discrimination in Employment Act, and other federal and state laws.

Questions

1. *a.* Why did the district court issue a summary judgment in favor of the defendant?

    b. What defenses were raised by the defendant?

    c. According to this court, must a sexual harassment victim's work performance be impaired in order to win a Title VII claim? Explain.

    d. What managerial and supervisory lessons should be derived from this case?

2. Breeden, a female employee, met with two male coworkers to review the psychological evaluation reports of four job applicants. Breeden's supervisor read aloud a comment in one of the reports that said the applicant had once said to a coworker, "I hear making love to you is like making love to the Grand Canyon." The men chuckled, Breeden complained, and she eventually filed a sexual harassment complaint with the EEOC. Soon thereafter, she was transferred to another position, a move that had been contemplated for some time. Resolve the case. Explain. See *Clark County School District v. Breeden,* 121 S.Ct. 1508 (2001).

3. Truck driver Lesley Parkins claimed that she was a victim of hostile environment sexual harassment while employed by Civil Constructors beginning in 1994. Parkins alleged that coworkers subjected her to foul language, sexual stories, and touching. Parkins complained to her dispatcher, Tim Spellman, and to one of her purported harassers, Robert Strong. She saw the job superintendent and the company EEO officer almost daily, but she did not complain to either. In 1996 Parkins filed a grievance with her union—Teamsters Local 325. The union contacted the company EEO officer, who immediately launched an investigation that led to punishment for the employees. Parkins conceded that she was not harassed following the company punishment. Parkins filed suit charging Civil Constructors with sexual harassment. Parkins claimed that two of her harassers, Strong and Charles Boeke, were foremen who supervised her work. Assuming Parkins can prove that she was, in fact, sexually harassed, what must she prove in order to hold Civil Constructors liable? See *Parkins v. Civil Constructors of Illinois,* 163 F.3d 1027 (7th Cir. 1998).

4. Rena Lockard worked for a Pizza Hut franchise in Atoka, Oklahoma, in September 1993. Two male customers made sexually offensive comments to her such as, "I would like to get in your pants." Lockard told her supervisor she did not like waiting on the men, but she did not mention the sexual comments. In November 1993, the men returned to the Pizza Hut, and Lockard was instructed to wait on them. One of them asked what kind of cologne she was wearing, and Lockard replied that it was none of his business. The customer then grabbed her by the hair. Lockard told her supervisor what had happened and said that she did not want

to wait on the two men. The supervisor ordered her to do so. Lockard returned to the table where one of the men pulled her by the hair, grabbed one of her breasts, and put his mouth on her breast. Lockard then quit her job and later sued the local franchise and Pizza Hut.

a. What is the central issue(s) in this case?

b. Is the franchise and/or Pizza Hut responsible for sexual harassment by a *customer* against an employee? Explain. See *Lockard v. Pizza Hut,* 162 F.3d 1062 (10th Cir. 1998).

5. A female Internal Revenue Service agent received a number of love letters from a male coworker. The letters contained some references to sexual activity.

a. In deciding whether the conduct constituted hostile environment sexual harassment, should the court evaluate the facts from the point of view of a "reasonable person" or a "reasonable woman"? Explain.

b. Why does it matter? See *Ellison v. Brady,* 924 F. 2d 872 (9th Cir. 1991).

6. If a supervisor makes explicit sexual remarks to both sexes, has made references to sexual conduct, and has called women sexually explicit names, is the supervisor engaging in unlawful sexual harassment? Explain. See *Steiner v. Showboat Operating Co.,* 25 F.3d 1459 (9th Cir. 1994); cert.den.513 U.S. 1082 (1995); but see *Johnson v. Tower Air,* 149 F.R.D. 461 (E.D.N.Y. 1993).

Friends Writers Accused of Sexual Harassment

Amaani Lyle, hired to be a writers' assistant for the *Friends* television show, said her initial excitement gave way to feelings of degradation when the writers' conversations turned sexually explicit. At times, she felt nauseated.

> They would basically sit like teenagers in a locker room, talking about, you know . . . things they wanted to do to the cast and walking around pretending to masturbate and just ridiculous conduct.

After being told she was fired for typing too slowly, Lyle sued in 1999, claiming the writers created a hostile working environment. In sworn depositions, some of the writers admitted they told stories of oral sex, talked about anal sex, and simulated masturbation as a way of saying they were wasting time.

At this writing, the case is at the California Supreme Court.

Questions
1. *a.* What constitutional claim would you raise in defending the *Friends* writers?
   b. How would you rule on that claim?
2. *a.* Beyond that constitutional claim, how would you defend the *Friends* writers?
   b. In your opinion, who should win this case? Explain.

Source: Los Angeles Times, " . . . Sex Harassment Collide," *Waterloo/Cedar Falls Courier,* November 14, 2004, p. A3.

Same Sex? Joseph Oncale, a heterosexual who worked on an offshore oil rig, charged a supervisor and two male coworkers with sexually harassing him, including repeated taunts and several sexual assaults, one with a bar of soap while Oncale was showering. Oncale complained to superiors, but to no avail. He then quit his job and sued his employer for sexual harassment. The case went to the U.S. Supreme Court, which unanimously ruled that same-sex harassment is actionable under Title VII.[40] Oncale then settled out of court for an undisclosed amount of money. Justice Scalia, who wrote the Supreme Court opinion, explained that the harassment must be "because of sex" (that is, gender); that harassment can be motivated by hostility as well as by desire; and that common sense and social context count. Thus, smacking a football teammate on the rear end, horseplay, roughhousing, or occasional gender-related jokes, teasing, and abusive language ordinarily would not constitute harassment. [For an analysis of the significance of the *Oncale* case, see **http://www.reason.com/0301/co.cy.man.shtml**]

> ## What if the harasser bothers both genders equally?

> ## Davis, a male supervisor, grabbed the genitals of a male subordinate.

Oncale settles the big question of protection against same-sex harassment, but it raises other puzzles. For example, what if the harasser bothers both genders equally?

Thus a federal court of appeals concluded that actionable sexual harassment had not occurred where Davis, a male supervisor, had, on several occasions, grabbed the genitals of a male subordinate, Carlton. Other workers referred to Carlton as Davis's "girlfriend." Grabbing the buttocks or genitals of other workers was common in that workplace. An investigation by the company resulted in warnings, and Carlton was transferred to a different supervisor, but most workers dismissed the matter. Carlton and others sued, and the court concluded the behavior was not "because of sex." Rather, the behavior was vulgar horseplay.[41] Ordinarily, plaintiffs in same-sex harassment cases must show that the behavior was motivated by (a) sexual desire, (b) general hostility to one or other gender, or (c) the victim's failure to conform to sexual stereotypes (such as effeminate behavior by a male).

Sexual Harassment in Other Nations

American managers working abroad must deal with international differences in attitudes toward sexual behavior in the workplace, although a general shift in harassment law in the direction of the American model is evident. Italy's highest appeals court received a great deal of publicity in 2001 when it ruled that a "pat on the bottom" does not constitute sexual harassment so long as it is "isolated" and "impulsive." The same court got a bit of an international black eye in 1999 when it ruled that a woman wearing tight jeans cannot be raped, as a matter of law, because she must have helped in removing the jeans, thus providing implied consent.[42] The Italian culture manifests a more tolerant attitude toward sex in the workplace than American managers might be accustomed too. Seven of 10 Italians surveyed in 2001 said that "an erotic charge" kept within reasonable limits at work helped them through the day, boosted self-esteem, reduced friction, and established a "collegiate" work environment.[43] Now the European Union has adopted laws requiring harassment-free workplaces.[44] In Japan recent rule changes make sexual harassment law very much like the U.S. model.[45] Mexico, Taiwan, Venezuela, and other nations make sexual harassment a crime under some circumstances. Managers can go to jail.[46]

Part Four—Affirmative Action

> I do not like the sea of white faces in the audience. We have too many middle-aged white Anglo-Saxon males, and that needs to change.[47]

Former Ford Motor Co. CEO Jacques Nasser allegedly made those remarks in explaining his efforts to bring greater diversity to the Ford workforce. That evidence was provided in support of several lawsuits charging Ford with race, sex, and age discrimination as part of an effort to elevate more women and minorities to higher decision-making roles at the auto company while reducing the number of white males. Among the claims in one of the suits:

- Women and minorities are routinely promoted or hired over more qualified white males.
- Bonuses for Ford executives are tied in part to hiring and promoting more women and minorities.
- Ford Credit internal documents . . . state "diversity candidate preferred" or "female candidate preferred."[48]

Ford denied the allegations and settled with 620 claimants for $10.5 million.[49]

For more than 30 years, we have been struggling with *affirmative action* as a means of remedying past and present discriminatory wrongs. In following an affirmative action plan, employers consciously take positive steps to seek out minorities and women for hiring and promotion opportunities, and they often employ goals and timetables to measure progress toward a workforce that is representative of the qualified labor pool.

Affirmative action efforts arise in four ways: (1) Courts may order the implementation of affirmative action after a finding of wrongful discrimination, (2) employers may voluntarily adopt affirmative action plans, (3) some statutes require affirmative action, and (4) employers may adopt affirmative action to do business with government agencies. Federal contractors must meet the affirmative action standards of the Office of Federal Contract Compliance Programs. [For criticisms of affirmative action, see the Center for Equal Opportunity at **http://www.ceousa.org**]

More Black Coaches?

Fans watching Florida Atlantic play New Mexico State . . . saw a rare sight: a black Division I-A head [football] coach. The [NMS] Aggies' Tony Samuel is one of five black coaches among the 117 I-A teams. In a division where 51 percent of the players are black, having 4.27 percent of the coaches [sic] is a source of embarrassment and consternation for the NCAA.

Twenty-four percent of I-A assistant football coaches are black. Of 28 new I-A and I-AA head football coaches hired in 2003, one, Sylvester Croom at Mississippi State, was the only African American.

Questions
1. In your opinion, does the small percentage of black head football coaches reflect racist practices and values in American higher education? Explain.
2. The Black Coaches Association issued a 2004 report card for those schools conducting head football searches. Mississippi State got an "A," but so did seven schools that hired white coaches but had diverse search committees and interviewed a diverse pool of candidates. In your opinion, should a school receive an "A" if it failed to hire a black candidate? Explain.

Source: "Black Coaches Association Seeks More Diverse Searches," *Des Moines Register,* November 14, 2004, p. 5C.

The Early Law

For nearly 20 years, judicial decisions were firmly supportive of affirmative action. A massive system of relief emerged at all levels of government and in the private sector. In a 1979 case, *United Steelworkers of America v. Weber,*[50] the Court set out perhaps its most detailed "recipe" for those qualities that would allow a *voluntary affirmative action plan in the private sector* to withstand scrutiny. Weber, a white male, challenged the legality of an affirmative action plan that set aside for black employees 50 percent of the openings in a training program until the percentage of black craft workers in the plant equaled the percentage of blacks in the local labor market. The plan was the product of a collective bargaining agreement between the Steelworkers and Kaiser Aluminum and Chemical. In Kaiser's Grammercy, Louisiana, plant, only 5 of 273 skilled craft workers were black, whereas the local workforce was approximately 39 percent black. In the first year of the affirmative action plan, seven blacks and six whites were admitted to the craft training program. The most junior black employee accepted for the program had less seniority than several white employees who were not accepted. Weber was among the white males denied entry to the training program.

Weber filed suit, claiming Title VII forbade an affirmative action plan that granted a racial preference to blacks where whites dramatically exceeded blacks in skilled craft positions but where there was no proof of discrimination. The federal district court and the federal court of appeals held for Weber, but the U.S. Supreme Court reversed. Several qualities of the Steelworkers' plan were instrumental in the Court's favorable ruling:

1. The affirmative action was part of a *plan.*
2. The plan was designed to "open employment opportunities for Negroes in occupations which have been traditionally closed to them."
3. The plan was temporary.
4. The plan did not unnecessarily harm the rights of white employees. That is,
   a. The plan did not require the discharge of white employees.
   b. The plan did not create an absolute bar to the advancement of white employees.

Then, in an important 1987 public-sector decision, *Johnson v. Transportation Agency,*[51] the Supreme Court approved the extension of affirmative action to women. The political tides were turning, however. The 1980s were politically conservative years. Appointments to the Supreme Court and to the lower federal courts, by President Reagan in particular, reflected that mood. Affirmative action was under attack.

[For a wide-ranging *Washington Post* review of affirmative action, see **http://www.washingtonpost.com/wp-srv/politics/special/affirm/affirm.htm**]

Rethinking Affirmative Action

From the late 1980s to the present, a series of judicial decisions and increasing public and political skepticism have challenged the legality and the wisdom of affirmative action, at least where the government is involved. The 1989 *City of Richmond v. J. A.*

Croson Co.[52] case struck down Richmond, Virginia's, minority "set-aside" program that required prime contractors who were doing business with the city to subcontract at least 30 percent of the work to minority businesses. The Court said such race-conscious remedial plans were constitutional only if (1) the city or state could provide specific evidence of discrimination against a particular protected class in the past (rather than relying on proof of general societywide discrimination) and (2) its remedy was "narrowly tailored" to the needs of the situation.

Then in *Adarand Constructors v. Pena,* a landmark 1995 decision, the Supreme Court struck down a federal highway program that extended bidding preferences to "disadvantaged" contractors.[53] The suit was brought by Randy Pech, a white contractor whose low bid on a Colorado guardrail project was rejected in favor of the bid of a minority firm. The Supreme Court ruled that the government's preference program denied Pech his right to equal protection under the law as guaranteed by the Fifth Amendment to the federal Constitution.

The case that follows illustrates the courts' current reasoning about the constitutionality of affirmative action in a public-sector employment case involving preferences for minority and female firefighters in Chicago.

LEGAL BRIEFCASE

Reynolds v. City of Chicago
296 F.3d 524 (7th Cir. 2002)

Judge Posner

This suit by white Chicago police sergeants and lieutenants challenges, as a denial of equal protection of the laws, the promotion in 1990 and 1991 of 20 black, Hispanic, and female sergeants and lieutenants to the rank of lieutenant and captain, respectively. The challenged promotions were made pursuant to an affirmative action plan by which blacks, Hispanics, and women could be promoted "out of rank"—that is, promoted even though they had a lower score than a white male on the test for the promotion. The district judge entered judgment after a jury trial. . . . The judgment was for the city with respect to all the promotions except that of the one Hispanic in the pool, who was promoted from sergeant to lieutenant. The plaintiffs appeal the ruling that the promotions of the blacks and women ahead of them did not deny the equal protection of the laws, while the city appeals the ruling that the promotion of the Hispanic sergeant ahead of the plaintiff sergeants was a denial of equal protection.

* * * * *

The findings of fact made by the jury in this case are neither clearly erroneous nor unreasonable, and what they reveal, so far as the black and female affirmative-action promotions are concerned, is the following. Until Orlando Wilson became the City of Chicago's police commissioner in 1960, black and white police officers were segregated, with black officers being confined to the parts of Chicago that were predominantly black. However, blacks were hired roughly in proportion to their share of the Chicago population. Wilson desegregated the police force. The city presented evidence that this resulted in a *decline* in the hiring of blacks. That may seem a paradoxical consequence of desegregation, but the evidence dispels the paradox. The evidence shows that white officers didn't want to serve with blacks. There were numerous acts of racial harassment of blacks, and black applicants flunked the police medical exam at rates suspiciously higher than whites. As a result of these circumstances, applications of blacks to the police force plummeted. After reforms in the mid-1970s that are acknowledged to have eliminated or at least greatly reduced racial discrimination in the Chicago police department, the rate of black applications climbed, and black applicants no longer flunked the medical exam at rates significantly higher than whites.

The evidence that we have briefly summarized justified a finding that discrimination by members of the police force depressed the hiring of blacks during the 1960s, leading in turn to a deficit of blacks in senior positions in the 1980s. The affirmative-action promotions of blacks challenged here, promotions designed to remedy the discrimination that we have just described, involved the promotion of 11 black sergeants out of a total of 182 promotions of sergeants and 3 black lieutenants out of a total of 50 promotions of lieutenants. These affirmative-action promotions resulted in percentages of black sergeants and lieutenants that still were lower than would have been expected had there not been that decline in the entry-level hiring of blacks in the 1960s.

The evidence that the decline was the result of discrimination was not conclusive. The plaintiffs presented evidence that the decline was the result of racial tensions in the 1960s that made blacks reluctant to become police officers because it would make them unpopular with other blacks. Against this the city presented evidence that although racial tensions were not limited to Chicago during the 1960s, other cities did not experience a drop-off in black hiring for their police forces, which suggests that something other than racial tensions probably accounted for the drop-off in Chicago; that something other may have been discrimination. The conflict over this issue was one for the jury to resolve. Since remedying past discrimination is a recognized justification for affirmative action, and since the action taken was modest—the promotion out of rank of a mere handful of blacks, resulting merely in delayed promotion for some whites rather than in anyone's losing his job or failing (eventually) to get the promotion he sought and was entitled to—the conclusion that the defendant had not violated the equal protection clause followed directly from the jury's factual findings.

The case for the affirmative-action promotion of the five women was even stronger. Until the 1970s women were formally barred from being hired for most jobs in the police department, including patrol officer. As a result, few were hired and many were deterred from applying because of the truncated career opportunities.

* * * * *

The city defends the affirmative-action promotions of the blacks and the women on the further, alternative ground that they were justified by the operational needs of the police force—a ground completely different from the remedial ground that we have been discussing. One ground is enough, so we need not consider the alternative ground except with regard to the Hispanic who the district court determined had been improperly promoted. For the city's argument is not that his promotion was justifiable as a remedy against past discrimination against Hispanics—the disparity between the percentage of Hispanic policemen and the percentage of Hispanic Chicagoans in 1990 was due largely to the rapid growth of the city's Hispanic population in the 1980s—but that it was justifiable in order to make the police force more effective in performing its duties. By 1990 the population of Chicago was almost 20 percent Hispanic, but fewer than 5 percent of police lieutenants were Hispanic. Because there were only 14 Hispanic lieutenants before the affirmative-action promotion of Sergeant Denk and the police work in three shifts with the result that the number of lieutenants per shift is small, on any given shift in 1990 only two or three Hispanic lieutenants were on duty in the entire city, with its population of 2.78 million in 1990 of whom more than 500,000 were Hispanic.

The evidence presented by the city, including the testimony of a competent expert witness, established a twofold need for a larger number of Hispanic lieutenants. First, lieutenants and captains are the principal supervisors in the police department. They set the tone for the department. If there are negligible numbers of Hispanics in these ranks (and in 1990 the percentage of Hispanic captains was only half the percentage of Hispanic lieutenants), non-Hispanic police officers are less likely to be sensitized to any special problems in policing Hispanic neighborhoods. Second, the lieutenants and captains act as "ambassadors" to the various communities that make up Chicago, of which the Hispanic community is an important one. Effective police work, including the detection and apprehension of criminals, requires that the police have the trust of that community, and they are more likely to have it if they have "ambassadors" to the community of the same ethnicity.

Justifications of discrimination that are based on a public employer's operational needs are suspect because they seem to have no natural limits, unlike remedial justifications, which cease when the last traces of the discrimination that gave rise to the remedy have been eliminated. Some discrimination, whether of the old-fashioned kind or the modern "affirmative action" kind, is vicious, ignorant, political, or otherwise invidious, but much is not.

As we pointed out in *Builders Ass'n of Greater Chicago v. Cook County,* the question whether nonremedial justifications for affirmative action can ever satisfy the equal protection clause has in the absence of definitive resolution by the Supreme Court caused bitter divisions in the lower federal courts. Many courts, however, including our own, have at least left open a small window for forms of discrimination that are supported by compelling public safety concerns, such as affirmative action in the staffing of police departments and correctional institutions. Especially in a period of heightened public concern with the dangers posed by international terrorism, effective police work must be reckoned a national priority that justifies some sacrifice of competing interests. If it is indeed the case that promoting one Hispanic police sergeant out of order is important to the effectiveness of the Chicago police in protecting the people of the city from crime, the fact that this out-of-order promotion technically is "racial discrimination" does not strike us as an impressive counterweight.

The imperative need for this discrimination had, however, to be proved and not merely conjectured. [The city] had to substantiate its position with evidence. It did so. It proved that it has a compelling need to increase the number of Hispanic lieutenants; and the increase it defended—the promotion of one Hispanic sergeant—is the smallest increase it could have made.

Affirmed in part and reversed in part, and the case is remanded.

Questions

1. *a.* Why did the court uphold the constitutionality of the Chicago Police Department's affirmative action program?

b. Do you agree with the judgment of the court?

c. How did the court's analysis of the constitutionality of the Hispanic promotion differ from the analysis applied to blacks and women?

2. Frederick Claus, a white man with a degree in electrical engineering and 29 years of experience with Duquesne Light Company, was denied a promotion in favor of a black man who had not earned a bachelor's degree and did not have the required seven years of experience. Only 2 of 82 managers in that division of Duquesne Light were black. Claus sued, claiming in effect that he was a victim of "reverse discrimination." At trial, both sides conceded that the black candidate was an outstanding employee and that he was qualified to be a manager. Decide the case. Explain. See *Claus v. Duquesne Light Co.*, 46 F.3d 1115 (1994); cert. den. 115 S.Ct. 1700 (1995).

3. In 1974, Birmingham, Alabama, was accused of unlawfully excluding blacks from management roles in its fire department. After several years of litigation, Birmingham adopted an affirmative action plan that guaranteed black firefighters one of every two available promotions. The city, the Justice Department, and others applauded the arrangement, but a group of 14 white firefighters claimed they were victims of reverse discrimination. After years of wrangling, the white firefighters' claim reached the 11th Circuit Federal Court of Appeals. Was the affirmative action plan lawful? Explain. See *In re Birmingham Reverse Discrimination Employment Litig.*, 20 F.3d 1525 (11th Cir. 1994) cert. den. sub nom.; *Martin v. Wilks*, 115 S.Ct. 1695 (1995).

So Where Are We?

The Law?

Reynolds, a recent case, illustrates that affirmative action in employment remains lawful if carefully justified. On the other hand, government preference programs that push contracts toward minorities and women (as in *Croson* and *Adarand*) are reviewed with judicial skepticism. Confusion also results from differences in analysis depending on whether the cases in question are based on the Constitution or on Title VII (Title VII cases appear to allow racial preferences to a greater extent than do those analyzed under the Constitution),[54] and whether those cases address employment questions, set-asides, or other problems. The law simply is not clear; but we can be certain that the courts will now take a very close look at racial and gender preferences. We can also say that both quotas and affirmative action justified broadly by "societal discrimination" are unconstitutional. A lawful affirmative action

> Quotas are unconstitutional.

remedy in employment cases apparently will be evaluated, in most cases, by the following considerations:

- The plan addresses a compelling interest such as remedying past or present discrimination or correcting the underutilization of women and minorities.
- The plan is temporary.
- The plan is narrowly tailored to minimize layoffs and other burdens.

PRACTICING ETHICS) Diversity as a Justification for Affirmative Action?

With affirmative action under assault, many businesses, universities, government agencies, and others have focused their attention on the idea of *diversity* as a means of building both social justice and productivity. In employment, the general idea is to hire a workforce that effectively mirrors the demographic characteristics of the employer's customers and emphasizes the productive assets of all segments of society. Those characteristics are changing rapidly. Whites will shrink from 76 percent of the population in 1996 to about 50 percent in 2050.[55] Diversity advocates ask how America can hope to compete effectively against 1.3 billion Chinese, the expanding European Union, and the balance of the globe if we do not use all of our varied human resources. As business journalist Thomas Petzinger notes, "Ideas are everything in a fragmented global marketplace, and great ideas demand a diverse workforce."[56] And in any case, how can we achieve genuine social justice without complete opportunity for all?

Critics, on the other hand, view the diversity movement as merely another thinly veiled affirmative action program designed to elevate minorities and women above sometimes better-qualified white males—a more subtle form of what is often labeled "reverse discrimination." Further, those critics argue that diversity does not achieve the productivity advances claimed by its advocates. MIT management professor Thomas Kochan's five-year study of diversity's impact on industry concludes, "There are no strong positive or negative effects of gender or racial diversity on business performance."[57] Others differ, of course.

Diversity and the Law Even if useful, diversity as a justification for racial and gender preferences faces fierce legal challenges. In the name of diversity, can a business lawfully offer racial or gender preferences in hiring and promotions? We do not have an answer to that question, but the Supreme Court did address the diversity issue in its 2003 review of admission policies at the University of Michigan. In brief, the Court struck down Michigan's undergraduate admissions plan because it was not "narrowly tailored" to achieve the university's diversity goals. Using a point-based system, Michigan gave so much weight to race that it sometimes became a decisive factor in admissions decisions, and the system failed to give careful, individualized consideration to all applicants, including members of underrepresented minorities.[58] The Michigan law school's approach, however, was upheld because race was merely one factor in an array of qualities considered, and admissions decisions were reached using a case-by-case, holistic approach where race and ethnicity were relevant but not necessarily determinative.[59] So the law school decision tells us that racial diversity is a "compelling interest" that can justify consideration of race in university admissions. The Court emphasized that the preference should be temporary and that other diversity considerations (such as life circumstances, geography, and special talents) might also be important. [See the Society for Human Resource Management "Diversity Home Page" at **http://www .shrm.org/diversity/default.asp**]

Questions

1. Is diversity in employment a "compelling interest" that justifies consideration of race, ethnicity, and gender in deciding whom to hire or to reward? Explain.

2. Is affirmative action, including diversity programs, merely another form of immoral racism? Explain.

3. *a.* Do you support the use of diversity goals in university admissions decisions? Explain.

   b. Could those goals be achieved in ways other than consideration of race, ethnicity, and gender? Explain.

Religious Discrimination

Managers must bring all of their wisdom and tact to bear on increasingly common religious conflicts in the workplace. *The Wall Street Journal* points to the example of a Whirlpool factory near Nashville, Tennessee, where 200 employees, 10 percent of the workforce, are Muslims of six nationalities. To maintain their religious principles, many devout Muslim men must wear beards and skull caps, and many women must wear loose-fitting clothes and head scarves in public. Muslims pray five times daily and must first wash their hands and feet. The clothing requirements raised safety concerns. Prayers disrupted assembly line schedules. The before-prayer washing left restrooms wet and slippery. Other workers sometimes resented the rituals and worried that production would decline and the factory might not be able to remain competitive in the fierce appliance market. As the law requires, Whirlpool has made efforts to accommodate the religious needs of its workers. Substitutes are available during prayer times. Washrooms are mopped more frequently. Scarves were retained, but had to be tucked in tightly. Sometimes accommodations could not be reached, as in workers' preference for sandals where steel-toed shoes were required. And Muslim men were expected to respectfully take instructions from female managers even though their own culture and religion left the men uncomfortable in that subordinate role.[60]

The Law Title VII forbids discrimination on the basis of religion. That religious faith must be sincere and meaningful, not merely a sham to achieve advantages. Employers must take reasonable steps to prevent and remedy religious harassment. But the much more common problem is that of reasonable accommodation, as described in the Whirlpool/Muslim situation.

The leading case regarding religious discrimination is *Trans World Airlines, Inc. v. Hardison,* in which the plaintiff, who celebrated his religion on Saturdays, was unable to take that day off from his work in a parts warehouse.[61] Efforts to swap shifts or change jobs could not be worked out. The company rejected Hardison's request for a four-day week because the solution would have required the use of another employee at premium pay. The Supreme Court's ruling in the case reduced the employer's duty to a very modest standard: "To require TWA to bear more than a *de minimis cost* in order to give Hardison Saturdays off is an *undue hardship*." Saturdays off for Hardison would have imposed extra costs on TWA and would have constituted religious discrimination against other employees who would have sought Saturday off for reasons not grounded in religion. So any accommodation imposing more than a de minimis cost on the employer represents an undue hardship and is not required by Title VII. Of course, the lower courts have differed considerably on what constitutes a de minimis cost and an undue hardship. For example, an Ohio court ruled that an employee, a Seventh Day Adventist, was discriminated against when he was fired for refusing to work from sundown Friday to sundown Saturday. The employee could have been moved to an earlier shift at no cost.[62]

Question

Resolving job-related religious conflicts can be among the most emotionally demanding management dilemmas. For example, what, if anything, would you do, as a manager, if one of your subordinates wore to work an antiabortion button displaying a picture of a fetus because of her religious beliefs about abortion? See *Wilson v. U.S. West Communications,* 58 F.3d 1337 (8th Cir. 1995).

The Americans with Disabilities Act (ADA)

A Fuddruckers restaurant in St. Louis Park, Minnesota, says it fired a cook, Barbara Andresen, in 2002 because managers had received three complaints from customers about Andresen's "excessive salivation" and because coworkers allegedly saw her spitting and drooling into food. New managers had been brought in because the public perceived the restaurant to be unsanitary.

> Coworkers allegedly saw her spitting and drooling into food.

Andresen says she was fired because of her disability: excessive stuttering. The record indicated that Andresen had a great deal of trouble speaking, and she avoided situations that would require her to speak to strangers. Andresen also indicated that she heard one manager tell another that he was going to "find a way to get rid of Barb." The firing, Andresen claims, violated the Americans with Disabilities Act. Fuddruckers responded that stuttering does not constitute a disability under the ADA and that her "excessive salivation" constituted a "direct threat" to the health and safety of others (a defense provided for in the ADA). At this writing, a federal judge has denied Fuddruckers' motion for a summary judgment, thus allowing the case to go to trial. The judge noted, among other things, that Andresen's termination notice indicated that she was fired for failing to properly prepare lettuce for salad and said nothing about drooling or spitting.[63]

This situation illustrates the general purpose of the 1990 ADA, which seeks to remove barriers to a full, productive life for disabled Americans. The ADA forbids discrimination in employment, public accommodations, public services, transportation, and telecommunications. Small businesses with fewer than 15 employees are exempted from the employment portions of the ADA. The Rehabilitation Act of 1973 protects disabled workers in the public sector from employment discrimination.

Under the ADA, a disabled person (1) has a physical or mental impairment that substantially limits one or more major life activities, (2) has a record of such an impairment, or (3) is regarded as having such an impairment. The nature of major life activities (walking, seeing, hearing, performing manual tasks) is addressed in the *Williams* case that follows this discussion. One who has a history of cancer might "have a record of such an impairment." And one might be regarded by others as impaired because of a physical deformity when, in fact, that condition does not impair job performance in any material way.

Disabilities

Blindness, hearing loss, mental retardation, cosmetic disfigurement, anatomical loss, and disfiguring scars are examples of covered disabilities. Alcoholism, drug abuse, and AIDS

> The act specifically excludes job applicants and employees who *currently* use illegal drugs.

are covered. However, the act specifically excludes job applicants and employees who *currently* use illegal drugs when the employer acts on the basis of such use. Thus the act covers those who are rehabilitated and no longer using illegal drugs, those in rehabilitation and no longer using illegal drugs, and those erroneously regarded as using illegal drugs. Employers may expect the same performance and behavior from alcoholics and drug abusers as from all other employees. In sum, the act treats alcoholism and drug addiction as medical problems and protects those who are overcoming their impairments.

Specifically excluded as disabilities are homosexuality, bisexuality, exhibitionism, gambling, kleptomania, and pyromania, among others. Questions regarding which conditions constitute disabilities will continue to require litigation. For example, in interpreting the federal Rehabilitation Act and state disability laws, some courts have treated severe obesity as a disability, whereas others have not. Jennifer Portnick, a 240-pound, size 16–18, San Francisco aerobics instructor brought national publicity to job disadvantages for those who are overweight. Portnick sought to work for Jazzercise but was rejected because of her size and the company's expectation that its instructors look fit. Portnick filed a complaint under a San Francisco ordinance forbidding discrimination on the basis of weight and height, and Jazzercise agreed to change its policy. Portnick almost certainly could not have been considered disabled under the ADA, and few jurisdictions provide the protection offered in San Francisco.

Accommodation

An employer may not discriminate in hiring or employment against a *qualified person with a disability.* A qualified person is one who can perform the *essential functions* of the job. The act requires employers to make *reasonable accommodations* for disabled employees and applicants. Reasonable accommodations might include structural changes in the workplace, job reassignment, job restructuring, or new equipment.

The ADA and a Golf Cart

Casey Martin, a young golfer with a degenerative circulatory disorder in one leg, requested that the Professional Golfers Association (PGA) waive its rule requiring walking in tournaments so that Martin could ride in a cart. The request was denied, Martin sued claiming a violation of the ADA, and the case reached the U.S. Supreme Court. The primary substantive question before the Court was whether the requested accommodation (riding in a cart) would fundamentally alter the nature of the Tour tournaments. Relying on a trial court finding that Martin suffered greater fatigue even though riding than competitors who walk, the Court ruled 7–2 that Martin has a legal right to the use of the cart.

What lessons might an employer derive from the Martin decision?

Source: PGA Tour, Inc. v. Casey Martin, 532 U.S. 661(2001).

Hardship

The employer's primary defense is *undue hardship*. The employer need not make an accommodation for a disabled person if that adjustment would be unduly expensive, substantial, or disruptive. The employer can call on the hardship defense only after an appropriate accommodation has been identified. All new facilities must be accessible to disabled parties unless structurally impractical, but Congress appears to have intended that changes to existing facilities should not be required if they would involve large expense.

The ADA does not require affirmative action plans or quotas. Unqualified applicants need not be hired, and one who cannot perform the essential functions of the job after reasonable accommodations may be discharged.

Question

Davis, a Microsoft systems engineer, worked 60–80 hours per week as did others in his position. Davis was diagnosed with hepatitis C and requested a cut in his duties after his doctor told him to reduce his work to 40 hours per week. Microsoft could not identify a 40-hour position for him, and he was fired. Davis sued, claiming an ADA violation. He argued that working more than 40 hours per week was not an essential element of his job. Decide the case. Explain. See *Davis v. Microsoft Corp.,* 70 P.3d 126 (Wash. S.Ct. 2003).

The ADA in Practice

An estimated 32 million working-age Americans have disabilities. Only 30 percent of that number are working.[64] Both the economy as a whole and opportunities for minorities, single mothers, and the like climbed significantly during the 1990s, but opportunities for people with disabilities actually declined. Between 1989 and 1998, average wages for disabled workers fell by 4 percent.[65] One study found nearly an eight percentage point decline in employment of people with disabilities after approval of the ADA.[66] Some experts attribute the lack of progress to employer concerns that hiring workers with disabilities will lead to burdensome legal problems. The data, however, show quite clearly that employers win most ADA cases. In 1999 nearly 96 percent of ADA victories went to employers.[67] Some good news for those with disabilities should also be noted. Among workers aged 18–29, the employment gap between those with and without disabilities is reported at 2.5 percent and falling.[68] [For a highly regarded ADA database, see **http://www.jan.wvu.edu/links/adalinks.htm**]

> Average wages for disabled workers fell by 4 percent.

Compliance Costs

The expense of dealing with ADA expectations had been a great worry to the employment community, but the data show that those costs are quite modest:

> JAN (the President's Job Accommodation Network) reports that the median accommodation under ADA costs $500 or less. The BPA (Berkeley Planning Associates) study found that the average cost of an accommodation is very low—approximately $900—and that 51 percent of accommodations cost nothing.[69]

What Is a Disability?

The important 9–0 Supreme Court decision that follows clarifies the question of when impairments must be treated as disabilities under the ADA.

Toyota Motor Manufacturing, Kentucky v. Ella Williams

LEGAL   BRIEFCASE   534 U.S. 184 (2002)

Justice O'Conner

Under the Americans with Disabilities Act of 1990 (ADA or Act), a physical impairment that "substantially limits one or more . . . major life activities" is a "disability." Respondent (Williams), claiming to be disabled because of her carpal tunnel syndrome and other related impairments, sued petitioner (Toyota), her former employer, for failing to provide her with a reasonable accommodation as required by the ADA.

*   *   *   *   *

I

Respondent began working at petitioner's automobile manufacturing plant in Georgetown, Kentucky, in August 1990. She was soon placed on an engine fabrication assembly line, where her duties included work with pneumatic tools. Use of these tools eventually caused pain in respondent's hands, wrists, and arms. She sought treatment at petitioner's in-house medical service, where she was diagnosed with bilateral carpal tunnel syndrome and bilateral tendinitis. Respondent consulted a personal physician who placed her on permanent work restrictions that precluded her from lifting more than 20 pounds or from "frequently lifting or carrying of objects weighing up to 10 pounds," engaging in "constant repetitive . . . flexion or extension of [her] wrists or elbows," performing "overhead work," or using "vibratory or pneumatic tools."

*   *   *   *   *

[Later] petitioner placed respondent on a team in Quality Control Inspection Operations (QCIO). QCIO is responsible for four tasks: (1) "assembly paint"; (2) "paint second inspection"; (3) "shell body audit"; and (4) "ED surface repair." Respondent was initially placed on a team that performed only the first two of these tasks, and for a couple of years, she rotated on a weekly basis between them. In assembly paint, respondent visually inspected painted cars moving slowly down a conveyor. She scanned for scratches, dents, chips, or any other flaws that may have occurred during the assembly or painting process, at a rate of one car every 54 seconds. When respondent began working in assembly paint, inspection team members were required to open and shut the doors, trunk, and/or hood of each passing car. Sometime during respondent's tenure, however, the position was modified to include only visual inspection with few or no manual tasks. Paint second inspection required team members to use their hands to wipe each painted car with a glove as it moved along a conveyor. The parties agree that respondent was physically capable of performing both of these jobs and that her performance was satisfactory.

During the fall of 1996, petitioner announced that it wanted QCIO employees to be able to rotate through all four of the QCIO processes. Respondent therefore received training for the shell body audit job, in which team members apply a highlight oil to the hood, fender, doors, rear quarter panel, and trunk of passing cars at a rate of approximately one car per minute. The highlight oil has the viscosity of salad oil, and employees spread it on cars with a sponge attached to a block of wood. After they wipe each car with the oil, the employees visually inspect it for flaws. Wiping the cars required respondent to hold her hands and arms up around shoulder height for several hours at a time. [Williams experienced pain and asked to return to her original two jobs.]

*   *   *   *   *

According to respondent, petitioner refused her request and forced her to continue working in the shell body audit job, which caused her even greater physical injury. According to petitioner, respondent simply began missing work on a regular basis. Regardless, it is clear that on December 6, 1996, the last day respondent worked at petitioner's plant, she was placed under a no-work-of-any-kind restriction by her treating physicians. On January 27, 1997, respondent received a letter from petitioner that terminated her employment, citing her poor attendance record.

Respondent filed a charge of disability discrimination with the Equal Employment Opportunity Commission (EEOC).

Respondent based her claim that she was "disabled" under the ADA on the ground that her physical impairments substantially limited her in (1) manual tasks; (2) housework; (3) gardening; (4) playing with her children; (5) lifting; and (6) working, all of which, she argued, constituted major life activities under the Act. Respondent also argued, in the alternative, that she was disabled under the ADA because she had a record of a substantially limiting impairment and because she was regarded as having such an impairment.

* * * * *

The District Court held that respondent had suffered from a physical impairment, but that the impairment did not qualify as a disability because it had not "substantially limited" any "major life activity." The court rejected respondent's arguments that gardening, doing housework, and playing with children are major life activities. Although the court agreed that performing manual tasks, lifting, and working are major life activities, it found the evidence insufficient to demonstrate that respondent had been substantially limited in lifting or working.

* * * * *

The Court of Appeals for the Sixth Circuit reversed the District Court's ruling on whether respondent was disabled at the time she sought an accommodation. The Court of Appeals held that in order for respondent to demonstrate that she was disabled due to a substantial limitation in the ability to perform manual tasks at the time of her accommodation request, she had to "show that her manual disability involved a 'class' of manual activities affecting the ability to perform tasks at work." Respondent satisfied this test, according to the Court of Appeals, because her ailments "prevented her from doing the tasks associated with certain types of manual assembly line jobs, manual product handling jobs and manual building trade jobs (painting, plumbing, roofing, etc.) that require the gripping of tools and repetitive work with hands and arms extended at or above shoulder levels for extended periods of time."

* * * * *

III [II OMITTED]

The question presented by this case is whether the Sixth Circuit properly determined that respondent was disabled . . . at the time that she sought an accommodation from petitioner. The parties do not dispute that respondent's medical conditions, which include carpal tunnel syndrome, myotendinitis, and thoracic outlet compression, amount to physical impairments. The relevant question, therefore, is whether the Sixth Circuit correctly ana-

lyzed whether these impairments substantially limited respondent in the major life activity of performing manual tasks. . . .

Our consideration of this issue is guided first and foremost by the words of the disability definition itself. "Substantially" in the phrase "substantially limits" suggests "considerable" or "to a large degree."

"Major" in the phrase "major life activities" means important. "Major life activities" thus refers to those activities that are of central importance to daily life. In order for performing manual tasks to fit into this category—a category that includes such basic abilities as walking, seeing, and hearing—the manual tasks in question must be central to daily life. If each of the tasks included in the major life activity of performing manual tasks does not independently qualify as a major life activity, then together they must do so.

That these terms need to be interpreted strictly to create a demanding standard for qualifying as disabled is confirmed by the first section of the ADA. When it enacted the ADA in 1990, Congress found that "some 43,000,000 Americans have one or more physical or mental disabilities." If Congress intended everyone with a physical impairment that precluded the performance of some isolated, unimportant, or particularly difficult manual task to qualify as disabled, the number of disabled Americans would surely have been much higher.

We therefore hold that to be substantially limited in performing manual tasks, an individual must have an impairment that prevents or severely restricts the individual from doing activities that are of central importance to most people's daily lives. The impairment's impact must also be permanent or long-term.

It is insufficient for individuals attempting to prove disability status under this test to merely submit evidence of a medical diagnosis of an impairment. . . . That the Act defines "disability" "with respect to an individual" makes clear that Congress intended the existence of a disability to be determined in such a case-by-case manner.

* * * * *

An individualized assessment of the effect of an impairment is particularly necessary when the impairment is one whose symptoms vary widely from person to person. Carpal tunnel syndrome, one of respondent's impairments, is just such a condition. While cases of severe carpal tunnel syndrome are characterized by muscle atrophy and extreme sensory deficits, mild cases generally do not have either of these effects and create only intermittent symptoms of numbness and tingling. Studies have further shown that, even without surgical treatment, one-quarter of carpal tunnel cases resolve in one month, but that in 22 percent of cases, symptoms last for eight years or longer. When pregnancy is the cause of carpal tunnel syndrome, in contrast, the symptoms normally resolve within two weeks of delivery. Given these large potential differences in the severity and duration of the effects of carpal tunnel syndrome, an individual's carpal tunnel syndrome diagnosis, on its own, does not indicate whether the individual has a disability within the meaning of the ADA.

IV

The Court of Appeals' analysis of respondent's claimed disability suggested that in order to prove a substantial limitation in the major life activity of performing manual tasks, a "plaintiff must show that her manual disability involves a 'class' of manual activities," and that those activities "affect the ability to perform tasks at work." Both of these ideas lack support.

When addressing the major life activity of performing manual tasks, the central inquiry must be whether the claimant is unable to perform the variety of tasks central to most people's daily lives, not whether the claimant is unable to perform the tasks associated with her specific job.

* * * * *

[T]he manual tasks unique to any particular job are not necessarily important parts of most people's lives. As a result, occupation-specific tasks may have only limited relevance to the manual task inquiry. In this case, "repetitive work with hands and arms extended at or above shoulder levels for extended periods of time," the manual task on which the Court of Appeals relied, is not an important part of most people's daily lives. The court, therefore, should not have considered respondent's inability to do such manual work in her specialized assembly line job as sufficient proof that she was substantially limited in performing manual tasks.

At the same time, the Court of Appeals appears to have disregarded the very type of evidence that it should have focused upon. It treated as irrelevant "the fact that [respondent] can . . . tend to her personal hygiene [and] carry out personal or household chores." Yet household chores, bathing, and brushing one's teeth are among the types of manual tasks of central importance to people's daily lives, and should have been part of the assessment of whether respondent was substantially limited in performing manual tasks.

[A]t the time respondent sought an accommodation from petitioner, she admitted that she was able to do the manual

tasks required by her original two jobs in QCIO. In addition, even after her condition worsened, she could still brush her teeth, wash her face, bathe, tend her flower garden, fix breakfast, do laundry, and pick up around the house. The record also indicates that her medical conditions caused her to avoid sweeping, to quit dancing, to occasionally seek help dressing, and to reduce how often she plays with her children, gardens, and drives long distances. But these changes in her life did not amount to such severe restrictions in the activities that are of central importance to most people's daily lives that they establish a manual-task disability as a matter of law.

Reversed and remanded.

Questions
1. *a.* What is the central issue in the *Williams* case?
   b. What is the Court's holding?
   c. Does a diagnosis of carpal tunnel syndrome mean that an individual is disabled for ADA purposes?
   d. What test did the Court articulate for determining whether an individual can fulfill the major life activity of performing manual tasks?
2. Does the *Williams* decision leave workers like her unprotected in the workplace? Explain.
3. *a.* Do correctable impairments such as high blood pressure or poor vision constitute disabilities?
   b. Should they? See *Sutton and Hinton v. United Air Lines,* 119 S.Ct. 2139 (1999).
4. Chenoweth worked for Hillsborough County, Florida, reviewing files of hospital patients. She had to drive to hospitals to examine some of the records. She suffered a seizure, was diagnosed as having epilepsy, and was told not to drive at all until six months had passed without a seizure. She asked her employer to accommodate her by allowing her to work at home two days per week and by eliminating the requirement that she drive to hospitals. Her employer agreed to the former but not the latter. She sued, claiming a violation of the ADA. Decide. Explain. See *Chenoweth v. Hillsborough County,* 250 F.3d 1328 (11th Cir. 2001); cert.den. 534 U.S. 1131 (2002).

ADA Disabled?

Several recent Supreme Court decisions, in addition to *Williams*, appear to have significantly limited the impact of the ADA. For example, the Supreme Court in 2003 upheld Raytheon's refusal to rehire a recovered drug user who had been discharged for violating workplace rules. The worker argued that his addiction was a disability.[70] A leading ADA advocate has referred to the act as the "incredible shrinking law."[71]

Genetic Testing

Burlington Northern & Santa Fe Railway Co. agreed in 2002 to pay $2.2 million to 36 workers to settle an EEOC lawsuit claiming that the railroad's genetic testing program violated disability and privacy laws. The EEOC alleged that Burlington Northern engaged in DNA testing of some employees without their knowledge or permission to identify a predisposition to carpal tunnel syndrome. Among the concerns is that employers would fire employees with a predisposition to various ailments to cut future health care costs. Federal agencies are forbidden from discriminating against employees based on genetic information, and about 24 states have similar rules.

Sources: Kathy Chen, "Railroad to Settle EEOC Litigation over Genetic Test," *The Wall Street Journal,* May 9, 2002, p. D6; Kathy Chen, "U.S. Seeks to Halt Employee DNA Tests," *The Wall Street Journal,* February 12, 2001, p. B2.

Age Discrimination

Can an employee *40 years of age or older* lawfully be terminated simply and exclusively to save money? The answer to date appears to be yes,[72] but the question is one of reasonable business practice.

In addition to cost savings, age discrimination claims often arise out of management's ill-considered remarks ("We are looking for new blood") and from a desire to bring a young, fresh image to the workplace. Can a clothing store featuring styles designed for the college market lawfully prefer youthful salespersons? That question is not definitively resolved, although the EEOC certainly takes the position that age is irrelevant as long as the job's essential functions can be successfully performed. [For advice about age discrimination issues, see **http://cobrands.business.findlaw.com/employment_employee/ newcontent/workingwoman/wmnchp6_g.html**]

Downhill after 43?

Eighty-eight percent of CEOs surveyed anonymously report that they see a connection between a worker's age and productivity. In a poll of 773 chief executives in 23 countries, consultants Watson Wyatt Worldwide found that most think productivity peaks around age 43.

Source: Glenn Burkins, "Aging Workforce: Issues Companies Would Rather Not Talk About," *The Wall Street Journal,* March 24, 1998, p. A1.

The Law   Basically, an Age Discrimination in Employment Act (ADEA) plaintiff must show that she or he is 40 years of age or older, is qualified for the position in question, and either was not hired or was terminated or demoted while a younger person received more favorable treatment. Age discrimination under the ADEA is established under either disparate treatment or disparate impact analysis similar to that for race or sex. The Supreme Court endorsed the disparate impact approach in an important 2005 case[73] that increases the possibility that employment practices (such as layoffs) disproportionately impacting those 40 years of age or older may be suspect. The ADEA, however, provides some powerful defenses for employers.

Defenses   The employer may defend against an age discrimination claim by showing that the termination was based on a legitimate, nondiscriminatory reason (such as poor performance) or that age is a bona fide occupational qualification (BFOQ). To establish age as a BFOQ, an employer must demonstrate that only employees of a certain age can safely and/or efficiently complete the work in question (such as piloting airplanes). The ADEA also provides that an employer can defeat an age discrimination claim by demonstrating that a "reasonable factor other than age" (like poor attendance) was the actual reason for terminating or otherwise disfavoring an older worker. But what is reasonable? Is saving money (by dismissing higher-paid older workers) a "reasonable factor other than age?" The Supreme Court has yet to address this question, but some experts think business will be given considerable latitude in making cost-saving decisions even if older workers might be adversely affected. Nonetheless, a reduction in force that struck a disproportionate number of older workers presumably would receive close scrutiny. [For an age discrimination database, see **http://www.aarp.org/money/careers/**]

Too Young for a Job?

Being young is cool, but the job market may prefer a little gray. Jeremy Pepper, 31, became discouraged in his job search after being laid off: "I know it sounds like Generation X whining, but this discrimination is real," says Pepper of Scottsdale, Arizona. Younger workers say they have to hide their age: "During my job search, I had much more of a challenge making myself look older, since I am often mistaken for 16," says Patricia Froelich, 21, a publicist in Orlando, Florida. "I tried my hardest to look older—using everything from fake reading glasses (to) more conservative clothing and carrying a briefcase."

Federal law protects only those 40 years of age and older, but a number of state age discrimination laws do not specify an age, and others set a cutoff at 18.

Source: Stephanie Armour, "Young Workers Say Their Age Holds Them Back," *USA TODAY*, October 7, 2003 [**http://www.usatoday.com/money/workplace/2003-10-07-reverseage_x.htm**].

Questions

1. Metz alleged that he was fired in violation of the ADEA. He had been a plant manager for a company, Transit Mix, that was experiencing financial problems. His employer notified him that the plant would be closed and he would be laid off. The company then sent the assistant manager of another plant, Burzloff, to Metz's plant to inspect it and make repairs. Burzloff requested that he be allowed to manage Metz's plant;

the employer approved this request and discharged Metz. At the time of his layoff, the 54-year-old Metz had a salary of $15.75 an hour; when the 43-year-old Burzloff replaced Metz, his salary was $8.05 per hour.[74]

Metz had worked for Transit for 27 years. He had received raises each year, even though the company was not profitable during some of those years. The company decided its poor financial performance did not justify retaining Metz, whose salary was comparatively high. Metz was not asked to take a pay cut before he was dismissed. The court framed the issue in the case in this manner:

> The sole issue on appeal is whether the salary savings that can be realized by replacing a single employee in the ADEA age-protected range with a younger, lower-salaried employee constitutes a permissible, nondiscriminatory justification for the replacement.[75]

Resolve that issue. Explain. See *Metz v. Transit Mix, Inc.*, 828 F.2d 1202 (7th Cir. 1987).

2. The Insurance Company of North America (ICNA) sought to hire a "loss control representative." The ad called for a B.S. degree, two years of experience, and other qualities. The plaintiff, who had 30 years of loss control experience, applied for the job but was not interviewed. ICNA hired a 28-year-old woman with no loss control experience. The plaintiff sued claiming age discrimination. ICNA said the plaintiff was overqualified.

   a. Explain the plaintiff's argument.

   b. Decide the case. Explain. See *EEOC v. Insurance Co. of N. Am.*, 49 F.3d 1418 (9th Cir. 1995).

Sexual Orientation

A Davenport, Iowa, care center manager allegedly fired six employees because they were homosexual and, in his view, did not exhibit acceptable "moral character."[76] The manager explained,

> When I first came here, there was probably at least three—excuse my French—faggots working here and I had at least three dykes working here.[77]

Are those dismissed employees protected by our expansive network of employment antidiscrimination law? Almost certainly not. Neither federal law nor the law of most states (including Iowa) offers protection against discrimination on the basis of an employee's sexual orientation. The courts have consistently ruled that Title VII's prohibition of discrimination based on sex refers to gender only and thus does not offer protection to gays. At least 13 states and a number of cities do provide that protection, and about half of the states have laws forbidding hate crimes based on sexual orientation. Public-sector employees can call on the equal protection provisions of the federal and state constitutions for protection, although the courts have often allowed governments to discriminate against homosexuals and lesbians if officials can establish some employment necessity, such as security concerns. [For a database on the law and ethics of sexual orientation discrimination, see **http://ethics.acusd.edu/applied/ sexualorientation/**]

Gay Rights at Wal-Mart

After receiving "heartfelt" letters from employees, Wal-Mart's management decided in 2003 to include sexual orientation in its corporate antidiscrimination policy. Gays and lesbians will be protected against harassment, although domestic partners of gays and lesbians will not receive corporate benefits. With Wal-Mart's sudden shift in policy, 49 of America's 50 largest companies now provide antidiscrimination protection for gay and lesbian employees. Exxon-Mobil does not do so.

Source: Ann Zimmerman, "Wal-Mart Adds Sexual Lifestyle to Its Antidiscrimination Policy," *The Wall Street Journal*, July 3, 2003, p. B3.

Internet Exercise

Using UCLA law professor Eugene Volokh's Web site [**http://www.law.ucla.edu/faculty/volokh/harass/**], explain how sexual harassment law is regarded by some as a threat to freedom of speech.

Chapter Questions

1. Blockbuster established a grooming policy forbidding long hair for men but allowing it for women. Four men, who were fired for refusing to cut their long hair, sued Blockbuster for sex discrimination. Has Blockbuster violated title VII? Explain. See *Kenneth Harper, et al. v. Blockbuster,* 139 F.3d 1385 (11th Cir. 1998; cert. den. 525 U.S. 1000 (1998).

2. Pan American Airways, Inc., maintained a policy of excluding men from positions as flight attendants. The policy was challenged on sex discrimination grounds. Pan American defended its policy with a survey showing that 79 percent of all passengers preferred being served by females. Then Pan Am offered expert testimony to show that the passenger preference was attributable to "feminine" qualities possessed by few males. The district court ruled for Pan Am on the grounds that "all or substantially all" [the test articulated in *Weeks v. Southern Bell Telephone,* 408 F.2d 228 (5th Cir. 1969)] men were unable to successfully fulfill the duties of flight attendants. The decision was appealed. Decide. Explain. See *Diaz v. Pan American Airways, Inc.,* 311 F. Supp. 559 (S.D. Fla. 1970), 442 F.2d 385 (5th Cir. 1971), cert. den. 404 U.S. 950 (1971).

3. Can a Polynesian restaurant lawfully limit employment to "brown-skinned persons" in those jobs visible to the public? Explain.

4. Would a readily visible office wall display of nude and seminude female figures located in a common work area (for example, one poster, on display for eight years, depicted a "woman with a golf ball on her breasts and a man standing over her, golf club in hand, yelling 'fore'") in combination with obscene comments about women on a routine basis (for example, "whores," "All that bitch needs is a good lay.") give rise to an intimidating, hostile, or offensive working environment within the meaning of the sexual harassment law? Explain. See *Rabidue v. Osceola Refining Co.,* 805 F.2d 611 (6th Cir. 1986). But see *Robinson v. Jacksonville Shipyards,* 760 F. Supp. 1486 (M.D. Fla. 1991).

5. Ali Boureslan, a naturalized U.S. citizen who was born in Lebanon and was working in Saudi Arabia, was discharged by his employer, Arabian American Oil Company, a Delaware corporation. Boureslan sued ARAMCO under Title VII of the Civil Rights Act of 1964, claiming that he was discriminated against because of his race, religion, and national origin. The lower court ruled that Title VII does not reach U.S. citizens employed abroad by American firms. Boureslan appealed to the U.S. Supreme Court. Decide. Explain. See *Equal Employment Opportunity Commission v. Arabian American Oil Company,* 111 S.Ct. 1227 (1991).

6. Rodriguez managed a Wal-Mart store at Fajardo, Puerto Rico. Following an evaluation, his performance was considered unsatisfactory, and he was demoted to assistant manager at another store. Rodriguez filed suit claiming race and national origin discrimination. Rodriguez pointed to two favorable previous performance evaluations, and he argued that he was evaluated in a different manner than non–Puerto Rican managers. Rodriguez was evaluated with the use of an opinion survey given to all of his subordinates. Rodriguez claimed that non–Puerto Rican managers at other stores were not subject to opinion surveys. Assuming that claim is true, would Rodriguez be able to prevail on a disparate treatment cause of action? Explain. See *Rodriguez-Cuervos v. Wal-Mart Stores,* 181 F.3d 15 (1st Cir. 1999).

7. Define *affirmative action.*

8. Diane Piantanida went on maternity leave. While absent, her employer discovered tasks that she had not completed. Before her return, Piantanida was informed that she was being reassigned to a lesser job because of her inability to keep up in her former job. Upon objecting to the change, Piantanida claims she was told that she was being given a position "for a new mom to handle." Piantanida admits that her demotion was not based on her pregnancy or her maternity leave. Piantanida declined the offer and sued, claiming a violation of the Pregnancy Discrimination Act stemming from her status as a new mother. Decide. Explain. See *Piantanida v. Wyman Center,* 116 F.3d 340 (8th Cir. 1997).

9. Perhaps the most controversial proposed remedy for racial wrongs is the emerging movement for payments in some form to African Americans as compensation for slavery and its continuing effects. The current focus of the *reparations* movement is a proposed class-action lawsuit potentially involving as many as 35 million American descendants of slaves. The corporate defendants that allegedly profited from slavery include FleetBoston Financial Corporation, Aetna (insurance), and CSX (railroad). The lawsuit says that FleetBoston predecessor Providence Bank was founded by slave trader John Brown (who helped charter Brown University of the Ivy League). Slaves were a major source of labor for railroad building in the pre–Civil War South, and evidence allegedly links CSX forebear the Richmond, Fredericksburg & Potomac Railroad to slave labor. For example, in an 1862 contract, the railroad promised to pay $160 to Mrs. B. B. Wright to rent her two slaves, John Henry and Reuben. Aetna allegedly sold life insurance that compensated owners when slaves were lost. According to published accounts, Aetna acknowledges having records indicating at least seven such policies involving slaves.[78]

a. What issues should be considered in deciding if reparations are a necessary and appropriate remedy for slavery?

b. If links to slavery were established, would you favor requiring corporations to make reparations payments?

c. Should those corporations be expected to apologize? Explain.

10. Thornton worked as a manager at a Connecticut retail store. In accordance with his religious beliefs, Thornton notified his manager that he could no longer work on Sundays as required by company (Caldor, Inc.) policy. A Connecticut statute provided that "No person who states that a particular day of the week is observed as his Sabbath may be required by his employer to work on such day. An employee's refusal to work on his Sabbath shall not constitute grounds for his dismissal." Management offered Thornton the options of transferring to a Massachusetts store where Sunday work was not required or transferring to a lower-paying supervisory job in the Connecticut store. Thornton refused both, and he was transferred to a lower-paying clerical job in the Connecticut store. Thornton claimed a violation of the Connecticut statute. The store argued that the statute violated the Establishment Clause (see Chapter 5) of the First Amendment, which forbids establishing an official state religion and giving preference to one religion over another or over none at all. Ultimately the case reached the U.S. Supreme Court.

a. Decide. Explain.

b. Do the religious accommodation provisions of Title VII of the Civil Rights Act violate the Establishment Clause? See *Estate of Thornton v. Caldor, Inc.,* 472 U.S. 703 (1985).

11. Sanchez worked as a host and food server at a pair of Azteca restaurants. Throughout his work experience, male coworkers and a supervisor referred to him as "she" and "her." He was mocked for walking and carrying his serving tray "like a woman." He was called a "faggot" and a "female whore." This abuse occurred repeatedly.

a. Make the argument that Sanchez was *not* a victim of sexual harassment.

b. Decide the case. Explain. See *Nichols v. Azteca Restaurant Enterprises,* 256 F.3d 864 (9th Cir. 2001).

12. Must your local country club admit qualified applicants regardless of race, religion, sex, and so on? Explain.

13. A new Texas airline, flying out of Dallas's Love Field, was in a precarious financial posture. A campaign was mounted to sell itself as "the airline personification of feminine youth and vitality." In commercials, its customers, who were primarily businessmen, were promised "in-flight love," including "love potions" (cocktails), "love bites" (toasted almonds), and a ticketing process (labeled a "quickie machine") that delivered "instant gratification." A male was denied a job with the airline because of his sex. He filed a Title VII action. The airline argued that attractive females were necessary to maintain its public image under the "love campaign," a marketing approach that the company claimed had been responsible for its improved financial condition. Decide. Explain. See *Wilson v. Southwest Airlines Co.,* 517 F. Supp. 292 (ND Tex. 1981).

14. Vanderbilt is among a few American universities that acknowledge actively recruiting Jewish students for admission. About 4 percent of Vanderbilt's students are Jewish, as compared with more than 20 percent at Ivy League schools. About 2 percent of the national population is Jewish. Gordon Gee, a Mormon and the Vanderbilt chancellor, has applauded the ability and liveliness of Jewish students and the contribution they make to campus intellectual life. Assistant to the provost at Vanderbilt David Davis explained, "We want the best students to come to Vanderbilt. Jews score well on the SAT." Last year's college-bound Jewish seniors averaged 1,161 out of a possible 1,600 on the SAT, second only to Unitarians (1,209) among 35 religions while the national average was 1,020. Vanderbilt characterizes its Jewish recruitment effort as part of a broader diversity strategy. In targeting Jews for special recruitment efforts, are Vanderbilt and other universities engaging in a form of profiling or stereotyping that amounts to discrimination? Explain. See John Gerome, "Vanderbilt Recruitment Produces Unease," *Boston Globe,* May 18, 2002, p. A3.

15. On balance, have the feminist movement and accompanying legal victories improved the quality of life for American women? For American men? Explain.

16. Taylor, a black woman, worked for the Burlington County, New Jersey, sheriff's office. She heard the sheriff, in speaking to another supervisor, refer to her as a "jungle bunny." She complained to her superiors. She suffered mental distress. She discussed the matter with the media. She was shunned at work. Was Taylor a victim of a hostile working environment? Explain. See *Taylor v. Metzger,* 706 A.2d 685 (N.J. S. Ct. 1998).

17. Linda Tarr-Whelan at the Center for Policy Alternatives says, "In this economy we have a diminished sense that the work women do with people is worth the same amount as the work men do with machines and dollars."

    a. Why are "women's jobs" "worth less" than "men's"?

    b. Should we insist on pay equity by requiring equal pay for work of comparable value? Explain. See Ellen Goodman, "Gender Pay Gap Is Real: $200 Billion," *Des Moines Register,* March 17, 1999, p. 9A.

18. The author of a *Harvard Law Review* article argues for discrimination claims based on appearance:

    > The most physically unattractive members of our society face severe discrimination. . . . The unattractive ("those individuals who depart so significantly from the most commonly held notions of beauty that they incur employment discrimination") are poorly treated in such diverse contexts as employment decisions, criminal sentencing, and apartment renting. Although appearance discrimination can have a devastating economic, psychological, and social impact on individuals, its victims have not yet found a legal recourse.

    Should we treat some aspects of appearance (for example, shortness, obesity, and unattractive facial characteristics) as disabilities, thus forbidding discrimination based on those characteristics? Explain. See Note, "Facial Discrimination: Extending Handicap Law to Employment Discrimination on the Basis of Physical Appearance," *Harvard Law Review* 100, no. 8 (June 1987), p. 2035.

19. The accompanying ad for foreign exchange dealers appeared in the December 11, 1987, issue (p. 22) of *The Nation,* an English-language newspaper published in Bangkok, Thailand.

    a. Analyze the legality of the ad based on American law.

An American Bank
invites applications for
**CORPORATE FOREIGN EXCHANGE
DEALERS**
for its Bangkok branch

Qualifications:

- Thai national
- Age 23–30 years, preferably male
- University graduate in Finance, Economics, or related field
- 1–2 years' dealing experience
- Good command of both spoken and written English

Salary is negotiable and attractive benefits will be provided for the successful candidates. The bank offers excellent opportunities for career advancement.

Send application stating details of qualifications and experience, present salary, and a recent photo to

**The Nation
Class 1191
GPO Box 594
Bangkok 10501**

---

    b. Should American firms abroad adhere to American antidiscrimination policies even if those policies might put the American firms at a competitive disadvantage or offend the values and mores of the host country? Explain.

20. John D. Archbold Memorial Hospital excluded all job applicants whose weight exceeded the maximum desirable weight (based on Metropolitan Life's actuarial survey) for large-framed men and women plus 30 percent of that weight. Sandra Murray claimed she was denied a job as a respiratory therapist because her height-to-weight ratio did not meet the guidelines. Murray did not claim to be morbidly obese.

    a. Explain the plaintiff's argument.

    b. Did the hospital violate the ADA? Explain. See *Murray v. John D. Archbold Memorial Hospital,* 50 F. Supp. 2d 1368 (M.D. Ga. 1999).

Notes

1. See Jenny Strasburg, "Abercrombie to Pay $50 Million in Bias Suits," *San Francisco Chronicle,* November 10, 2004, p. C1; and Julie Tamaki, "Judge Accepts Abercrombie Plan to Settle Hiring Lawsuits," *Los Angeles Times,* November 17, 2004, p. C2.

2. Michael Lopardi, "Minority Groups Sue Abercrombie for $40 M," *University Wire,* January 27, 2005.

3. Associated Press, "Study Looks at Name Bias in Job Search," *Washington Post.com,* January 14, 2003.

4. Miriam Jordan, "Wealth Gap Widens in U.S. between Minorities, Whites," *The Wall Street Journal,* October 18, 2004, p. A2.

5. U.S. Census Bureau, "Business Owners in the U.S.," *Des Moines Register,* February 6, 2005, p. 11A.

6. Associated Press, "Census Report Shows Blacks Making Gains," *Waterloo/Cedar Falls Courier,* April 27, 2003, p. A9.

7. Adam Goodheart, "Change of Heart," *AARP The Magazine,* May/June 2004, p. 43.

8. Goodheart, "Change of Heart."

9. 347 U.S. 483 (1954).

10. A portion of this paragraph is drawn from William P. Murphy, Julius G. Getman, and James E. Jones Jr., *Discrimination in Employment,* 4th ed. (Washington: Bureau of National Affairs, 1979), pp. 1–4.

11. *EEOC v. Waffle House, Inc.,* 534 U.S. 279 (2002).

12. Jess Bravin, "U.S. Courts Are Tough on Job-Bias Suits," *The Wall Street Journal,* July 16, 2001, p. A2.

13. Bravin, "U.S. Courts Are Tough on Job-Bias Suits."

14. See *International Brotherhood of Teamsters v. United States,* 97 S.Ct. 1843 (1977); *American Tobacco v. Patterson,* 456 U.S. 63 (1982); *Firefighters Local Union No. 1784 v. Stotts,* 467 U.S. 561 (1984).

15. Kara Scannell, "Lawsuit Charges U.S. Unit of Japanese Company with Bias," *The Wall Street Journal,* January 20, 2005, p. B1.

16. Scannell, "Lawsuit Charges U.S. Unit."

17. Scannell, "Lawsuit Charges U.S. Unit."

18. *Garcia v. Spun Steak Co.,* 998 F.2d 1480, cert. den. 114 S. Ct. 2726 (1994).

19. Aaron Bernstein, "Racism in the Workplace," *BusinessWeek,* July 30, 2001, p. 64.

20. Bernstein, "Racism in the Workplace."

21. Bernstein, "Racism in the Workplace."

22. *Aman v. Cort Furniture Rental Corp.,* 85 F.3d 1074 (3d Cir. 1996).

23. *HR Focus* 74, no. 2 (February 1997), p. 11.

24. Genaro Armas, "Gender Economics: Men Still Earn More," *Des Moines Register,* June 4, 2004, p. 1A.

25. Kate Kelly and Colleen DeBaise, "Morgan Stanley Settles Bias Suit for $54 Million," The *Wall Street Journal,* July 13, 2004, p. A1.

26. J. Lynn Lunsford, "To Settle Sex-Bias Lawsuit, Boeing Agrees to Pay Up to $72.5 Million," *The Wall Street Journal,* July 19, 2004, p. B2.

27. Ann Zimmerman, "Judge Certifies Wal-Mart Suit as Class Action," *The Wall Street Journal,* June 23, 2004, p. A1.

28. Carol Hymowitz, "Carly Fiorina's Lesson in Equality," *The Wall Street Journal,* February 10, 2005, p. A9.

29. Sue Shellenbarger, "Number of Women Managers Rises," *The Wall Street Journal,* September 30, 2003, p. D2.

30. Joann S. Lublin, "Women Aspire to Be Chief as Much as Men Do," *The Wall Street Journal,* June 23, 2004, p. D2.

31. Carol Hymowitz, "Women Put Noses to the Grindstone, and Miss Opportunities," *The Wall Street Journal,* February 3, 2004, p. B1.

32. Jon Bonne, "A Gender Split in the Executive Suite," *MSNBC.com,* August 11, 2004 [**http://www.msnbc.msn.com/id/5624773/**].

33. *Haynes v. W. C. Caye & Co.,* 52 F.3d 928 (11th Cir. 1995).

34. See, generally, *Diaz v. Pan American World Airways, Inc.,* 442 F.2d 385 (5th Cir.), cert. den. 404 U.S. 950 (1971).

35. Stephanie Armour, "Pregnant Workers Report Growing Discrimination," *USA TODAY,* February 17, 2005, p. 1B.

36. *Elana Back v. Hastings on Hudson Union Free School District,* 365, F.3d 107 (2d Cir. 2004).

37. Associated Press, "Study of Career Women Finds Children Add to Satisfied Lives," *Des Moines Register,* November 22, 1992, p. 5A.

38. Allen Otten, "Uncertainty Persists on Sexual Harassment," *The Wall Street Journal,* July 29, 1992, p. B1.

39. *Burlington Industries v. Ellerth,* 524 U.S. 742 (1998); and *Faragher v. Boca Raton,* 524 U.S. 775 (1998).

40. *Oncale v. Sundowner Offshore Services,* 523 U.S. 75 (1998).

41. *EEOC v. Harbert-Yeargin,* 266 F.3d (6th Cir. 2001).

42. Associated Press, "Italian Court Clears Man over Pat on the Bottom," *Waterloo/Cedar Falls Courier,* January 25, 2001, p. A2.

43. Richard Owen, "Flirting at Work Boosts Italian Home Life: Survey," *Montreal Gazette,* September 26, 2001, p. A16.

44. Stephen Miller, "Sexual Jokes No Laughing Matter," *Glasgow Herald,* June 7, 2002, p. 4.

45. Gerald L. Maatman Jr., "A Global View of Sexual Harassment," *HRMagazine,* July 2000, p. 151.

46. Maatman, "A Global View."

47. Tom Brown, "Ford Settles Suit Alleging Bias against White Males" [**wysiwyg://38/http://www.auto.com/industry/iwirg28_20020328.htm**].

48. Mark Truby, "Lawsuits Accuse Ford of Job Bias," *Detroit News* [**wysiwyg://35/http://detnews.com/2001/autos/0106/22b01-239087.htm**].

49. Earle Eldridge, "Ford Settles 2 Lawsuits by White Male Workers," *USA TODAY,* December 19, 2001, p. 3B.

50. 443 U.S. 193 (1979).

51. 480 U.S. 616 (1987).

52. 488 U.S. 469 (1989).

53. *Adarand Constructors, Inc. v. Pena,* 115 S.Ct. 2097 (1995).

54. Charles A. Sullivan, "Circling Back to the Obvious: The Convergence of Traditional and Reverse Discrimination in Title VII Proof," *William and Mary Law Review,* 46 (December 2004), p. 1031.

55. Haya El Nasser, "Census Projects Growing Diversity," *USA TODAY,* March 18, 2004, p. 1A.

56. Thomas Petzinger, "Finding New Ways to Meet Challenges from Debt to Diversity," *The Wall Street Journal,* January 5, 1996, p. B1.

57. Fay Hansen, "Diversity's Business Case Doesn't Add Up," *Workforce,* April 2003, p. 28.

58. *Gratz v. Bollinger,* 539 U.S. 244 (2003).

59. *Grutter v. Bollinger,* 539 U.S. 306 (2003).

60. Timothy Schellhardt, "In a Factory Schedule, Where Does Religion Fit In?" *The Wall Street Journal,* March 4, 1999, p. B1.

61. 423 U.S. 63 (1977).

62. *Franks v. National Lime & Stone Co.,* 740 N.E. 2d 694 (Ohio Ct. App. 2000).

63. *Andresen v. Fuddruckers, Inc.,* No. 03-3294, 2004 WL 2931346 (D. Minn. 2004). For a journalistic account, see Donna Higgins, "Fuddruckers Loses Health Defense in 'Drooling Cook' Disability Case," *FindLaw,* January 11, 2005 [**http://news.findlaw.com**].

64. Albert Hunt, "An Army of Opposition to Disability Rights," *The Wall Street Journal,* March 15, 2001, p. A19.

65. *Los Angeles Times,* "Economic Boom Hasn't Lifted Many Disabled Workers," *Waterloo/Cedar Falls Courier,* November 23, 2000, p. A14.

66. Thomas E. DeLeire, "The Unintended Consequences of the Americans with Disabilities Act," *Regulation* 23, no. 1 (2000), p. 21.

67. Susan Stefan, "Symposium: The Americans with Disabilities Act: A Ten-Year Retrospective," *Alabama Law Review* 52 (Fall 2000), p. 271.

68. Susan J. Wells, "Is the ADA Working? *HRMagazine,* April 2001, p. 38.

69. DeLeire, "The Unintended Consequences," p. 21.

70. *Raytheon v. Hernandez,* 537 U.S. 1187 (2003).

71. Joan Biskupic, "High Court Raises Bar for ADA," *USA TODAY,* January 9, 2002, p. 3A.

72. For a general discussion of the legality of terminations of workers 40 years of age or older, see Marvin M. Goldstein and Devora L. Lindeman, "Downsizing? A Legal Roadmap," *Metropolitan Corporate Counsel,* March 1998, p. 27.

73. *Smith v. City of Jackson,* 2005 US LEXIS 2931.

74. "Age Discrimination," 56 *U.S.L.W.* 2155 (1987), summarizing *Metz v. Transit Mix, Inc.*

75. *Metz v. Transit Mix, Inc.,* 828 F.2d 1202, 1205 (7th Cir. 1987).

76. John Carlson, "Six Care Center Workers Are Fired," *Des Moines Register,* June 8, 1997, p. 1B.

77. Carlson, "Six Care Center Workers."

78. Associated Press, "Companies Sued for Allegedly Using Slaves," *Waterloo/Cedar Falls Courier,* April 1, 2002, p. B5.

Employment Law III: Labor–Management Relations

Introduction

AFL–CIO president John Sweeney remarked,

> America needs a raise, and one of the most effective solutions is a bigger and stronger labor movement, one capable of acting as a counterweight to the corporate forces now dominating our economy.[1]

Perhaps Sweeney is correct, but the American labor movement, so long a powerful voice for worker welfare, is struggling to find its way. At this writing in 2005, internal discord threatens the effectiveness of the labor movement. Already troubled by dramatic declines in membership (see below), labor is now so worried about its prospects that several large unions have split from the AFL–CIO. Although the AFL–CIO is trying to reunite the groups and the situation is certainly fluid, as the facts now stand, more than 4 million of the 13 million AFL–CIO members have left, taking with them $28 million of the $120 million AFL–CIO budget.[2] The United Food and Commercial Workers, Teamsters, the Service Employees International Union and others have decided that they are better served by working on their own. The departing unions have developed the 6-million member Change to Win coalition seeking a more effective labor voice.

This internal strife reflects the powerful economic changes that have attacked the fundamental premises of the traditional American labor movement. Outsourcing, declines in factory jobs, and increases in the service sector have reshaped the United States' economy, but the dissidents say that the AFL–CIO has been unable to respond effectively to the changed environment. More specifically, unhappy union leaders such as President James P. Hoffa of the Teamsters, say that the AFL–CIO has given too much attention to Democratic Party politics and too little to the basic task of recruiting new union workers.[3] Indeed, one of the interesting questions about the internal labor division is the effect it may have on the distribution of political power in the United States. Will the labor unions, a powerful and reliable source of money and campaign workers for the Democratic Party, be unable to provide that effort in the future? On the other hand, the split may lead to more focused union organizing that will be increasingly effective in meeting the specific needs of the various sectors of the economy. Certainly many experts expect rejuvenated and aggressive union organizing; at least in the near term.

The union news is not all bad, however. In recent years, labor leaders have been looking for new directions to rebuild their membership and their power. For example, traditionally independent physicians, frustrated by giant insurance companies and health maintenance organizations, have slowly begun to join unions. Similarly unlikely alliances are now appearing on college campuses, where graduate teaching assistants are being

> **Graduate students have gone on strike at Columbia University.**

organized. Graduate students have gone on strike at Columbia University of the Ivy League and at the University of Michigan. Undergraduate resident assistants have organized at the University of Massachusetts, and Harvard University janitors won a 16 percent raise, in part due to an alliance with students.[4] The universities claim that the graduate assistants, resident assistants, and other workers are students receiving financial aid rather than employees and thus should not be able to engage in collective bargaining under the protection of federal law. Public university graduate teaching assistants, whose work lives are governed by state law, have long been able to organize under state labor laws. In 2000 a National Labor Relations Board (NRLB) dominated by Democrats ruled that graduate student instructors at New York University, a private school, are employees under the National Labor Relations Act (NRLA).[5] Then in 2004 the Republican-dominated NLRB reversed itself and ruled that graduate student teaching assistants at private universities do not have the legal right under the NLRA to form unions because they are primarily students rather than employees. The decision reflects the often highly politicized nature of NLRB decision making and is another setback in already troubled union organizing efforts.[6]

Union Membership As recently as 1983, unions represented over 20 percent of the nonfarm labor force.[7] In 2004 that figure was 12.5 percent, down in one year from 12.9 percent.[8] Only 7.9 percent of private-sector workers belong to unions, but in the public sector, nearly 40 percent are union members.[9] Some encouraging news should be noted:

- A 2002 survey showed 50 percent of nonunion workers saying they want to join a union, the highest such number in two decades.[10]
- Following scandals at Enron, WorldCom, and others, workers' jobs and pensions often evaporated overnight. Before the scandals, workers saw themselves

> **Workers' jobs and pensions often evaporated overnight.**

as investors profiting along with management, but the recent high-tech collapse and the scandals have shaken worker faith in corporate America.[11]
- Female union membership rose by 1.4 percent in 2001.[12]
- 17.7 million immigrant workers represent a promising recruitment pool.[13]

Unions in China?

Perhaps the future of the union movement lies in communist China. Wal-Mart, with 44 stores in China, agreed in late 2004 that its workers there could form unions. The state-run All-China

Federation of Trade Unions has 134 million members and is the organization approved by the Communist Party to represent workers. All Chinese companies are required to allow unions, but Wal-Mart had resisted. Previously Wal-Mart had kept unions out of all of its stores worldwide except for one Canadian location.

Source: "Wal-Mart Agrees to Unions in China," United Press International, November 24, 2004.

[For more on union membership, see **http://www.ncpa.org/pd/unions/membership.html**]

Questions

1. *a.* Should teaching assistants be allowed to join unions? Explain.
   b. Are working people so disadvantaged in contemporary America that you feel a personal duty to support a strengthened, renewed union movement? Explain.
   c. Would such a movement benefit working-class people? Explain.
2. Do we need labor unions to counterbalance the power of big corporations? Explain.
3. Harvard economics professor Richard Freeman commented on America's "apartheid economy,"

   > From all points on the political map comes the message that something is wrong with the U.S. economy. Indeed, income inequality has jumped in the past two decades in almost every category: College graduates have gained in comparison with high school graduates, older workers in comparison with younger ones, professionals in comparison with laborers. The list goes on.

   Is the declining power of labor unions a factor in the growing income inequality in America? Explain. See Richard Freeman, "Toward an Apartheid Economy," *Harvard Business Review,* September/October 1996, p. 114. [For the federal Bureau of Labor Statistics, see **http://stats.bls.gov/**]

Part One—History

As the United States moved from an agrarian to an industrial society in the late 1880s, business competition was fierce. Costs had to be cut. By paying workers as little as possible and making them work 14- to 18-hour days, employers could prosper. Farmers began moving to the city to be near their jobs and thus left their safety net of gardens, chickens, and cows. Similarly, immigrants streamed into the big cities, and competition for jobs became heated. Wages fell, and deplorable working conditions were the norm.[14] Some of those immigrants brought with them ideas and experiences in labor conflict and class struggle that would soon contribute to dramatic changes in the American workplace.

A Grim Picture

To say that working conditions for many people at this time were unpleasant or even dismal would be a vast understatement. The term *desperate* better describes the problem. Children were impressed into service as soon as they were big enough to do a job

Children were employed in coal mines because they were small enough to fit in the confined spaces.

and then made to work 12- and 14-hour days.[15] In fact, small children were employed in coal mines for 10–12 hours each day, and at a rate of $1–3 per week, because they were small enough to fit in the confined spaces.[16] Textile companies sent men called *slavers* to New England and southern farm communities to gather young women to work in the mills.[17]

The following first-hand report from the early 20th century reveals the grim picture:

> When I moved from the North to the South in my search for work, I entered a mill village to work in a cotton mill as a spinner. There I worked 11 hours a day, five and a half days a week, for $7 a week. In a northern mill I had done the same kind of work for $22 a week, and less hours. I worked terribly hard. . . .
>
> The sanitary conditions were ghastly. When I desired a drink of water, I had to dip my cup into a pail of water that had been brought into the mill from a spring in the fields. It tasted horrible to me. Often I saw lint from the cotton in the room floating on top of the lukewarm water. All of the men chewed tobacco, and most of the women used snuff. Little imagination is needed to judge the condition of the water which I had to drink, for working in that close, hot spinning room made me thirsty. Toilet facilities were provided three stories down in the basement of the mill in a room without any ventilation. Nowhere was there any running water. . . .
>
> Everything in the village is company owned. The houses look like barns on stilts, and appear to have been thrown together. When I would go inside one of them, I could see outside through the cracks in the walls. The workers do all of their trading at the company store and bank, and use the company school and library for they have no means of leaving the village.[18]

[For a history of women in the labor movement, see **http://www.afscme.org/otherlnk/whlinks.htm**]

Compare these working-class conditions with those of John D. Rockefeller, the great tycoon of the same era. Although Rockefeller was notoriously frugal, his estate at Pocantico Hills contained

> . . . more than 75 buildings. . . . Within his estate were 75 miles of private roads on which he could take his afternoon drive; private golf links on which he could play his morning game; and anywhere from 1,000 to 1,500 employees, depending on the season.
>
> . . . Rockefeller also owned an estate at Lakewood, which he occupied in the spring; an estate at Ormond Beach in Florida for his winter use; a townhouse . . . in New York; an estate at Forest Hill, Cleveland, which he did not visit; and a house on Euclid Avenue in Cleveland, likewise unused by him.[19]

These conditions enable us to better understand the sense of injustice felt by many workers and the belief of many that a redistribution of wealth might provide the only solution to the class conflict.

Organizing Labor

The Knights of Labor, the first major labor organization in the United States, had a large following during the 1870s and 1880s.[20] The order admitted any workers to its ranks, regardless of occupation, gender, or nationality; in fact, the only people excluded from the group were gamblers, bankers, stockbrokers, and liquor dealers.[21] The Knights of Labor dedicated itself to principles of social reform, including the protection of wage and hour laws, improved health care systems, and mandatory education.[22] However, the goals of the Knights of Labor were perhaps too broad and far-reaching to bring workers any relief from their immediate problems. Great philosophical divisions within the Knights of Labor brought about its rapid decline.[23]

Skilled Workers

Samuel Gompers, who built and developed the American Federation of Labor (AFL), had more practical, attainable goals in mind for his organization. Gompers, a worker in the cigar industry, saw the need to organize workers along craft lines (such as plumbers, electricians, and machinists) so that each craft group could seek higher wages and better working conditions for its own workers, all of whom had the same type of skills and, presumably, shared the same occupational goals.[24] This approach, a national association of local unions directed to workers' pragmatic needs rather than the more politically motivated activities of the Knights of Labor, proved to be a successful formula for union organization.

Laborers

The Congress of Industrial Organizations (CIO) was organized in response to the needs of ordinary laborers not working in the skilled trades to which the AFL was devoted. The CIO was organized in 1935 and served assembly-line workers and others who often performed repetitive, physically demanding tasks. The AFL and CIO were fierce competitors, but after years of bitter conflict, the organizations agreed to stop raiding one another for members: In 1955 the two groups united forces. They function together today as the AFL–CIO. [For the AFL–CIO home page, see **http://www.aflcio.org**]

Unions and the Developing Law

Labor Protection

Responding to mounting public pressure, Congress passed the Norris–LaGuardia Act in 1932. Designed primarily to prevent antitrust problems, the act withdrew from the federal courts the right to issue injunctions against labor activities and made clear that the terminology "restraint of trade," which was the heart of the 1890 Sherman Antitrust Act, was not meant to include the organization or activities of labor.

From 1932 to 1935, labor tensions continued to mount. The nation was still caught in the Great Depression. Believing that one element essential to economic recovery was stability in the workforce, Congress addressed the labor question with the Wagner Act of 1935. This legislation gave workers for the first time the unequivocal right to organize and engage in concerted activities for their mutual aid and benefit. To protect this right, Congress identified and made illegal a number of unfair labor practices. Through the Wagner Act, Congress also established the National Labor Relations Board, an administrative agency charged with the responsibility of overseeing and ensuring fair union representation elections and investigating, prosecuting, and trying employers accused of unfair labor practices. [For the NLRB home page, see **http://www.nlrb.gov**]

Management Protection

Unions grew rapidly with the passage of the Wagner Act, and by 1947 Congress decided management might need a little help in coping with ever-growing labor organizations.[25] Congress enacted the Taft–Hartley Act, identifying as unfair labor practices certain activities unions used to exercise economic leverage over employers as part of the collective bargaining process. The Taft–Hartley Act also ensured employers' right to speak out in opposition to union organizing—in effect, protecting their First Amendment right to freedom of speech. Thus the Taft–Hartley Act signaled a move by the government away from unconditional support for labor toward a balance of rights between labor and management.[26]

Corrupt Union Leaders

In response to the growing evidence that union leaders were benefiting at the expense of the membership, Congress in 1959 enacted the Landrum–Griffin Act, requiring unions to keep records of their funds, including statements of their assets, liabilities, salaries paid, and all other expenditures. It also prohibits unions from lending money except under specified circumstances and in conformity with certain procedural rules. These financial statements and transactions must be reported annually to the government.

Members' Rights

The Landrum–Griffin Act also contains a set of provisions often referred to as the "Bill of Rights" for individual union members. These provisions are designed to protect union members by requiring that union meetings be held, that members be permitted to speak and vote at these meetings, that every employee covered by a collective bargaining agreement has the right to see a copy of that agreement, and that a union member be informed of the reasons and given a chance for a hearing if the union wishes to suspend or take disciplinary action against that member, unless he or she is being suspended for non-payment of dues.[27]

The law has also regulated the manner in which unions represent employees in the collective bargaining process. Because a union serves as employees' exclusive bargaining representative, the courts have devised a *duty of fair representation*.[28] To fulfill this duty, a union must represent employees, both in negotiating and enforcing the collective bargaining agreement, "without hostility or discrimination . . . [and] . . . with complete good faith and honesty [so as to] avoid arbitrary conduct."[29]

PRACTICING ETHICS Fairness in the Workplace?

Workplace Fairness, a nonprofit advocate for "workplace policies and practices that work for everyone," argues that America's workers are "short-changed" by "giving more and getting less":

Whether you look at job security, career opportunity, income, time spent on the job, health care, retirement security, or the right to organize, it's clear that working people are worse off today than they were several decades ago. . . . Is this because America has fallen on hard times? Hardly. Our economy is stronger than it has ever been. . . . Today's workplace has winners as well as losers. Executives and investors are winning and winning big. Workers trying to earn their livelihoods are losing.

Question

Is America now unfair to its ordinary workers? Explain.

Source: "Short-Changed, America's Workers Are Giving More and Getting Less," *Workplace Fairness* [**http://www.workplacefairness .org/sc/**].

Part Two—Labor Legislation Today

The Statutory Scheme of Labor Law and Its Goals

Today labor–management relations are governed by the National Labor Relations Act (NLRA), as enforced by the NLRB.[30] This act includes within it the Wagner Act, the Taft–Hartley Act, and portions of the Landrum–Griffin Act. The remaining provisions of the Landrum–Griffin Act make up the Labor–Management Reporting and Disclosure Act and the Bill of Rights of Members of Labor Organizations.

Right to Organize

The NLRA gives employees the right to engage in concerted activity, including strikes and collective bargaining. Section 7 of the NLRA states,

> Employees shall have the right to self-organization, to form, join, or assist labor organizations, to bargain collectively through representatives of their own choosing, and to engage in other concerted activities for the purpose of collective bargaining or other mutual aid or protection, and shall also have the right to refrain from any and all of such activities except to the extent that such right may be affected by an agreement requiring membership in a labor organization as a condition of employment.

[For a vast database of federal labor law statutes, regulations, state codes, and so on, see **http://www.law.cornell.edu/topics/labor.html**]

Nudes Organize

Complaining of low pay, cold rooms, and air laden with paint fumes and charcoal dust, models who pose nude at a Philadelphia art school voted . . . to join a union. "We were at a loss about how to get the school to pay attention to us," said Claire Hankins, 39, who led the effort to organize.

Source: "Nudes Organize," *Des Moines Register,* May 8, 2003, p. 8C.

Unfair Labor Practices by Management

The NLRA describes and outlaws certain activities by employers that would hamper or discourage employees from exercising the rights granted to them in Section 7. Thus Section 8(a) of the act makes it an unfair labor practice for an employer to

1. Interfere with, restrain, or coerce employees in the exercise of the rights given to them by Section 7.
2. Dominate, interfere, or assist with the formation of any labor organization, including contributing financial support to it.
3. Encourage or discourage membership in any labor organization by discrimination in regard to hiring, tenure of employment, promotion, salary, or any other term of employment.
4. Discharge or take any other action against an employee because he or she has filed charges or given testimony under the act.
5. Refuse to bargain collectively with a duly certified representative of the employees.

These five provisions are designed to allow employees to organize in an atmosphere free from intimidation by the employer. In addition, if employees have chosen a union as their exclusive collective bargaining representative, Section 8(a) regulates the bargaining between the employer and the union. The provisions also ensure that the employer will not be able to interfere with union activities by either seizing control of the union or rendering it impotent by refusing to bargain collectively.

Unfair Labor Practices by Unions

Section 8(b) lists activities constituting unfair labor practices by a labor organization. Some of these provisions mirror some of the activities prohibited to employers. Moreover, at least since the enactment of the Taft–Hartley Act, the law is not sympathetic to labor organizations that try to use certain coercive tactics, threats of the loss of livelihood, or any other strong-arm methods. Finally, Section 8(b) also regulates the union's collective bargaining practices, including economic action. Thus a labor organization is not permitted to

1. Restrain or coerce any employee in the exercise of his or her rights as granted by Section 7.
2. Cause or attempt to cause an employer to discriminate against an employee who has chosen not to join a particular labor organization or has been denied membership in such an organization.
3. Refuse to bargain collectively with an employer on behalf of the bargaining unit it is certified to represent.
4. Induce or attempt to induce an employer to engage in secondary boycott activities.
5. Require employees to become union members and then charge them excessive or discriminatory dues.
6. Try to make an employer compensate workers for services not performed.
7. Picket or threaten to picket an employer in an attempt to force the employer to recognize or bargain with a labor organization that is not the duly certified representative of a bargaining unit.

Representation Matters

Section 9 of the NLRA also sets forth the election procedures by which employees may choose whether to be represented by a particular union or no union at all.

Smell a Rat?

Workers at the Asbestos, Lead, and Hazardous Waste Laborers Local 78 in New York put a 30-foot inflatable rat on a flatbed truck and stuck its nose in the third-story windows of CBS Television's Manhattan office to protest against the network's use of nonunion labor on a construction project. Police deflated and confiscated the rat. CBS had no comment.

Source: Stacy Kravetz "Ratted Out," *The Wall Street Journal,* May 11, 1999, p. A1.

National Labor Relations Board (NLRB)

The NLRB is an administrative agency instrumental in regulating labor–management relations. Its primary tasks are designating appropriate bargaining units of workers (deciding which workers have a sufficient community of interest so that their needs can best be acknowledged and so that collective bargaining is efficient for the employer and the union); conducting elections for union representation within the chosen bargaining unit; certifying the results of such elections; and investigating, prosecuting, and adjudicating charges of unfair labor practices.[31]

Although the congressional mandate by which the NLRB was formed gives the agency jurisdiction theoretically to the full extent of the interstate commerce powers vested in Congress, the agency has neither the funding nor the staff to administer its duties to all of American industry. Some smaller businesses, government employees, railroad and airline workers covered by the Railway Labor Act, agricultural workers, domestic workers, independent contractors, and supervisors and other managerial employees are not protected by the board.[32]

Strippers' Rights?

Two strippers claimed they lost their jobs because of their association with the Exotic Dancers Alliance, an organization in San Francisco that tries to improve working conditions in strip clubs. The women asked the NLRB to rule on the dispute, but the board concluded, by a 2–1 vote, that it did not have jurisdiction in the case. The revenue for the strip club was about $352,200, and the jurisdictional minimum for NLRB action in retail cases is $500,000. The strippers argued that $162,000 in tips should be included in the revenue total, but the NLRB disagreed.

Source: Carlos Tejada, "No Tips: Exotic Dancers Lose a Round before the Labor Board," *The Wall Street Journal,* January 22, 2002, p. A1.

Part Three—Elections

Choosing a Bargaining Representative

Representation elections are the process by which the NLRB achieves the first of the two statutory goals under the act—employee freedom of choice. That goal, however, is sometimes in conflict with the other statutory goal—stable collective bargaining. The NLRB has devised rules to resolve such conflicts. [For the AFL–CIO view of why workers should join unions, see **http://www.aflcio.org/front/joinunions.htm**]

Election Petition

A union, employee, or employer initiates the formal organizing process by filing an election petition with the NLRB. The petition is sent to the employer, thus providing notice of union activity. Also, the employer must post notices supplied by the NLRB so that employees are aware of the petition. The NLRB then assumes its authority to closely oversee the conduct of employer and union. Of course at that point, the employer is free to simply acknowledge its employees' interest in joining a particular union and to engage in bargaining with that union. That result, normally called *voluntary recognition,* once uncommon, is becoming a favored union tactic. Some unions, feeling that elections give employers too much time and opportunity to lean on employees, have decided to apply pressure on employers to voluntarily accept the union. One of those is Unite, a union of apparel and textile workers whose tactics were summarized by *The Wall Street Journal:*

> . . . [T]he union targeted $6-an-hour workers at Up-To-Date Laundry, which washes sheets and towels for hotels and hospitals in Baltimore. In a bitter contest, the union lost a secret-ballot election by two votes. The regional NLRB office charged that firings and other labor law violations marred the election. The union geared up for a second vote, but changed course and called a strike . . . to demand recognition.
>
> In a well-orchestrated effort, the union enlisted the downtown Sheraton hotel and the University of Maryland and Johns Hopkins University medical centers to threaten to stop doing business with Up-To-Date. It took worker claims of racial and sexual harassment to state authorities and the NAACP. It persuaded the city council to summon the laundry's owner to a hearing.
>
> After a 10-week strike and a torrent of bad publicity, Up-To-Date capitulated. It recognized the union and signed a contract that provides raises of about $1.25 an hour over three years and better health and pension benefits.[33]

Failing voluntary recognition, the process proceeds according to NLRB rules. The NLRB will accept only those election petitions supported by a substantial showing of interest, which, at a minimum, must include the signatures of at least 30 percent of the employees in the bargaining unit. (In practice today, most unions will not proceed toward an election without 50 to 65 percent of the employees' signatures.) Those signatures accompany the petition, or they may appear on *authorization cards,* which unions may provide to workers to affirm their interest in an election or in union representation.

Unions Change Organizing Tactics

As noted above, unions are increasingly turning away from traditional federally supervised elections in favor of voluntary recognition strategies like Unite followed against Up-to-Date Laundry in Baltimore. *The Wall Street Journal* reports that unions often now target voluntary recognition as their goal, thus intentionally avoiding the election process. To set the foundation for voluntary recognition, the unions take the authorization card approach, which is easier and cheaper than a conventional election and which avoids a campaign battle with management. Those battles often lead to union defeats. In 2004 unions won only 56.5% of 2,299 elections. Those elections resulted in organizing only 80,000 new workers in 2004 while card check campaigns produced three times more new union members. Companies may feel forced to agree to voluntary recognition because unions have become clever in public relations campaigns designed to undermine a company's image in the community, as Unite did in its fight with Up-to-Date Laundry.

Source: Timothy Aeppel, "Not-So-Big Labor Enlists New Methods for Greater Leverage," *The Wall Street Journal,* August 29, 2005, p. A2.

Procedure

Prior to an election, the NLRB ordinarily will first attempt to settle certain issues such as whether a union contract already covers the employees or whether the election should be delayed. In determining the timing of the election, the two statutory goals of employee free choice and stable collective bargaining may conflict. For example, if the employees are already covered by a collective bargaining agreement, should they be able to choose again during the term of the agreement? Similarly, if the employees have rejected a union in an election, can they be prohibited from voting again in the name of stable collective bargaining? Alternatively, what if the employees choose to unionize in an election, but reconsider before a collective bargaining agreement is reached? Can they have another election?

To resolve these conflicts the NLRB has devised *bars* to an election. The board will prohibit an election during the term of a collective bargaining agreement, but only for a period not to exceed three years. This is known as the *contract bar rule.* An election year or certification year bar prohibits an election for 12 months following a prior election so that the employer can enjoy stable collective bargaining without negating the employees' freedom of choice.

The crucial issue to be addressed at this point, however, is normally whether the proposed bargaining unit (the designated employee group—for example, all hourly workers, all welders, or all craftspersons) is appropriate for the election.

Appropriate Bargaining Unit

The key consideration in establishing an appropriate employee bargaining unit is the community of interest among the employees. The NLRB searches for an appropriate bargaining unit because collective bargaining will not be stable and efficient if it involves employees with diverse interests. Therefore, the bargaining unit may range from a portion of a plant to multiple employers in multiple plants. Plants may have more than one appropriate bargaining unit, depending on the composition of the workforce. The NLRB makes the decision regarding the appropriate bargaining unit on the basis of such considerations as physical location of the plants; physical contact among employees; similarity of wages, benefits, and working conditions; differences in skill requirements among job categories; and common supervision.

Certain classes of employees, such as supervisors, are excluded from the bargaining unit. Obviously supervisors are excluded because they act on behalf of the employer and, through their power to direct and assign work and to discipline and discharge employees, exert control over their subordinates who are or may be in the bargaining unit. Often labor and management do not agree about the classification of workers as supervisors. In a 2001 decision, the U.S. Supreme Court emphasized the importance of three considerations in deciding which workers are supervisors: responsibility for directing other employees, the use of independent judgment, and that their authority is held on behalf of the employer.[34]

Solicitation

A 1992 Supreme Court decision in the *Lechmere* case[35] made union organizing much more difficult by ruling that employers do not have to allow on their property union organizers who are not employees. One of the results of that decision has been an increase in *salting*, the practice of union organizers applying for jobs with the intent of unionizing the other employees from the inside. The Supreme Court's 1995 *Town & Country* decision[36] held that salts are employees, thus affording them NLRA protections. Many employers saw the *Town & Country* decision as an unfair intrusion on their property rights and on their preference to remain union-free. The case that follows involves a Wal-Mart employee's efforts to interest coworkers in joining a union.

LEGAL BRIEFCASE

Wal-Mart Stores, Inc. v. National Labor Relations Board   400 F.3d 1093 (8th Cir. 2005)

Circuit Judge Melloy

Petitioner appeals the National Labor Relations Board's order finding that it violated the National Labor Relations Act by punishing employee Brian Shieldnight for union solicitation.

I.

This case arises from efforts to unionize employees at the Wal-Mart store in Tahlequah, Oklahoma. The store, like all Wal-Mart stores, maintains and enforces a policy that prohibits solicitation during employees' work time, regardless of the cause or organization.

Brian Shieldnight, an employee of the Tahlequah Wal-Mart, contacted the United Food and Commercial Workers Union, Local 1000 ("Union") about possible union representation. He obtained authorization cards from the union to organize employees at the Tahlequah store.

On January 29, 2001, Shieldnight entered the store while off-duty. He wore a T-shirt that read "Union Teamsters" on the front and "Sign a card … Ask me how!" on the back. Assistant

Store Manager John Lamont and Assistant Night Manager Tammy Flute saw Shieldnight's T-shirt and saw him speak to an associate. Flute told the associate to return to work, and Lamont ordered Shieldnight to leave associates alone. Lamont then consulted a Wal-Mart "union hotline." The hotline representative told Lamont that Shieldnight's shirt constituted solicitation and that Shieldnight should be removed from the store. Lamont and Flute sought out Shieldnight. They found him in the jewelry department talking to two friends who were not associates. Lamont informed Shieldnight that his shirt constituted a form of solicitation and that he would have to leave the store immediately. Lamont escorted Shieldnight to the front door of the store and instructed him to leave the store and Wal-Mart property.

The next incident occurred on January 30, 2001. While on duty at the store, Shieldnight invited Department Manager Debra Starr and associates Patricia Scott and James Parsons, all of whom were also on duty, to a union meeting. Shieldnight asked Starr to come to the meeting and stated that he would like her to consider signing a union authorization card. Shieldnight separately asked Scott and Parsons to attend the meeting to hear "the other side of the story."

Based on these two incidents, Co-Manager Rick Hawkins and Assistant Manager John Lamont held a written "coaching session" with Shieldnight for violating the no-solicitation rule. A "coaching session" is part of Wal-Mart's progressive discipline process. Verbal coaching and written coaching are the first two steps in a four-step process. Hawkins and Lamont explained to Shieldnight that he had violated the solicitation policy on January 29 by soliciting on the sales floor with his T-shirt and on January 30 by verbally soliciting employees while on-duty and on the sales floor. Lamont told Shieldnight that it was wrong to have sent Shieldnight off Wal-Mart property completely. Lamont clarified that while Shieldnight could not solicit on the sales floor, he could do so in the parking lot while not on duty. Hawkins, Lamont, and Shieldnight also discussed Shieldnight's questions and concerns regarding Wal-Mart employment policies, such as health insurance for associates. Lamont suggested Shieldnight should raise the matter in "grassroots" meetings that all Wal-Mart stores hold to identify the top three companywide issues. The three men arranged a time to meet in the future. That meeting never occurred.

The union subsequently filed an unfair labor practice charge against Wal-Mart. . . .

[A] divided Board panel found that Shieldnight had not engaged in solicitation when he (1) wore the T-shirt during his shift; (2) asked on-duty employees to attend a union meeting; or (3) asked a coworker to sign a union card. . . . Wal-Mart appeals. . . .

II

* * * * *

A. The T-Shirt

The union contends that Shieldnight's T-shirt did not constitute solicitation, but rather was a "union insignia." Wal-Mart argues that by encouraging people to approach him, Shieldnight's T-shirt was a form of solicitation. In *NLRB v. W. W. Grainger, Inc.,* the board held,

> "Solicitation" for a union usually means asking someone to join the union by signing his name to an authorization card in the same way that solicitation for a charity would mean asking an employee to contribute to a charitable organization . . . or in the commercial context asking an employee to buy a product or exhibiting the product for him. . . .

Ordinarily, employees may wear union insignia while on their employer's premises. . . .

The board stated that the T-shirt should be treated as union insignia because "it did not 'speak' directly to any specific individual . . . and it did not call for an immediate response, as would an oral person-to-person invitation to accept or sign an authorization card." The board found that there was "no claim or evidence that Shieldnight did anything in furtherance of the T-shirt message. . . . He merely walked around and socialized . . . about nonunion matters." Anyone, including any Wal-Mart employee who saw Shieldnight was free to ignore both Shieldnight and the message on the T-shirt. In contrast, a solicitation to sign an authorization card requires more interaction, likely a direct yes or no answer. Absent further evidence of direct inquiry by Shieldnight, the board's conclusion was supported by substantial evidence.

Wal-Mart alleges that the panel's conclusion is not reasonable because it ignores both Shieldnight's purpose and the long-held rule that an employer may implement rules against solicitation during work time to prevent interference with work productivity.

* * * * *

Wal-Mart failed to demonstrate how the T-shirt interfered in any manner with the operation of the store. Accordingly, substantial evidence supports the board's conclusion that Shieldnight's T-shirt did not constitute solicitation.

B. The Coworker Conversations

* * * * *

Shieldnight invited three coworkers to a union meeting. . . . Shieldnight's statements did not require an immediate response from the three coworkers. Instead of a solicitation that required a response, the record shows that Shieldnight's statements were more akin to a statement of fact that put his coworkers on notice that there was to be a union meeting that night and that they were welcome to attend. Nothing in the record suggests that the environment at Wal-Mart made Shieldnight's actions uniquely disruptive. Accordingly, the panel's conclusion regarding Shieldnight's conversations was supported by substantial evidence. Furthermore, the panel acted reasonably when it concluded that "simply informing another employee of an upcoming meeting or asking a brief, union-related question does not occupy enough time to be treated as a work interruption in most settings."

C. Asking Coworker to Sign a Card

The board concluded that it was not solicitation when Shieldnight asked a coworker to sign a union authorization card. . . .

In light of the totality of the circumstances, Shieldnight's actions constituted solicitation even though he did not actually offer Starr a card at the time he asked her to sign. Shieldnight had contacted the union about obtaining union representation and had obtained cards from the union for the purpose of organizing employees at the Tahlequah store. There is little doubt as to Shieldnight's intent in the words he spoke to Starr. The record indicates that Shieldnight did not have a card in his hand at the time he spoke to Starr. It is silent as to whether he had a card on his person. The fact that he did not place a card directly in front of Starr at the time of his statement makes little difference in regard to the nature of his conversation. Further, Shieldnight's actions in this instance are more analogous to a direct solicitation than when he asked his coworkers to attend the union meeting. Asking someone to sign a union card offers that individual person the choice to be represented by a union. Informing coworkers about a union meeting merely puts fellow employees on notice that a meeting is going to take place.

Accordingly, there is insufficient evidence to support the board's conclusion that Shieldnight's actions were not solicitation, and thus we reverse the board regarding the authorization card issue.

* * * * *

Questions

1. Why was the T-shirt not a form of solicitation?
2. Would statements at work such as "support the union" or "there is a meeting tonight" constitute solicitation? Explain.
3. Why was Shieldnight's invitation to three coworkers to attend a union meeting not a form of solicitation, whereas asking a coworker to sign a card was considered impermissible solicitation?

The Election for Union Representative

If the parties have agreed to conduct an election, or alternatively, the NLRB has directed that an election be conducted following a hearing, the board will require that the employer post notices and conduct the election. The union representative may be selected only by a majority of the votes cast by the employees. The NLRB oversees the election to ensure the process is carried on under "laboratory conditions."[37] In other words, elections must be held under circumstances that, to the extent possible, are free from undue or unfair influence by either the employer or by unions vying for the right to represent the bargaining unit.

The NLRB has the power to review the conduct of the employer or the union during the period between the filing of the election petition and the election itself. The board will also, if called upon, monitor the polling place itself. If the NLRB determines that objectionable conduct has taken place, it will invalidate the results of the election and another will be held.

For both employers and employees, the circulation of racist propaganda is grounds for setting aside an election. Historically, the board has set aside elections tainted by trickery such as falsehoods, allegations, misstatements, and the like. However, its current position is that misrepresentation alone will not constitute grounds for overturning an election. The burden is on the parties to correct misrepresentations and sort out the truth via the marketplace of ideas. The board will intervene only if the deceptive manner of the misrepresentation (such as a forged document) makes it impossible for the parties themselves to discern the truth. Some courts have endorsed the NLRB view; others have not.

Question

Three hours before a certification election, the union distributed a flyer listing 31 workers who were committed to the union when, in fact, some of them were not committed. The union won the election, but only 19 of 45 eligible voters actually cast ballots. The company refused to bargain with the union, claiming that it had engaged in unfair labor practices. Should the NLRB certify the union? Explain. See *NLRB v. Gormac Custom Manufacturing, Inc.*, 190 F.3d 742 (6th Cir. 1999).

Protection of Free Speech

Employers have the right to speak out against unions in the form of ads, speeches, and the like. Section 8(c) of the Taft–Hartley Act is designed to ensure employers' and labor organizations' traditional First Amendment rights as long as they do not overstep certain bounds:

> The expressing of any views, argument, or opinion, or the dissemination thereof, whether in written, printed, graphic, or visual form, shall not constitute or be evidence of an unfair labor practice . . . if such expression contains no threat of reprisal or force or promise of benefit.

Gooseplay?

During a union organizing campaign, a goose wandered from a company pond into the work area where a worker "talked" to the goose and determined that it favored the union. Workers then put a "Vote Yes" card around the goose's neck and drove the goose around the plant on a forklift. The workers were fired for disrupting work and creating a safety hazard. The union claimed the company illegally fired the workers for engaging in union organizing. An administrative law judge agreed with the union, but the NLRB reversed, saying, "Placing a 'Vote Yes' sign on a wild animal does not transform otherwise unprotected 'gooseplay' into activity protected by the National Labor Relations Act."

Source: NACCO Materials Handling Group, Inc., 331 NLRB No. 164 (Aug. 25, 2000).

Threats of Reprisal or Force

Employers cannot lawfully discriminate in employment to encourage or discourage union membership. Clearly, an employer who tells employees that, for example, they will all be discharged if they engage in union activity, has interfered with their rights. Similarly, an employer who interrogates employees about their activities or spies on them while they attend union meetings has engaged in unlawful interference. However, problems often arise in determining whether antiunion arguments by an employer are legitimate or whether they contain veiled threats. Suppose, for instance, that a company owner warns her employees that if she has to pay higher wages, she will be forced to go out of business and the employees will all lose their jobs. Such statements of economic forecast by employers are more likely to be lawful if based on objective facts not under management's control.

Promise of Benefit

Although threats of force or reprisal are clearly unlawful in union campaigns, the rationale behind the prohibition against promises of benefit is not as intuitively obvious. In the case of *NLRB v. Exchange Parts Co.,*[38] Exchange Parts sent its employees a letter shortly before a representation election that spoke of "the empty promises of the union" and "the fact that it is the company that puts things in your envelope." After mentioning a number of benefits, the letter said, "The union can't put any of those things in your envelope—only the company can do that." Further on, the letter stated, "It didn't take a union to get any of those things and . . . it won't take a union to get additional improvements in the future." Accompanying the letter was a detailed statement of the benefits granted by the company and an estimate of the monetary value of such benefits to the employees.

> The union can't put any of
> those things in your envelope.

In addition, the letter outlined further benefits, such as additional vacation days and overtime pay, that the company had recently decided to institute. In the representation election two weeks later, the union lost. The Court of Appeals did not think the employer's actions constituted an unfair labor practice. The Supreme Court disagreed, reasoning that "well-timed increases in benefits" provide a clear message that those who provide advantages are the same people who can withdraw those benefits should their wishes not be followed.

Buying Votes?

An Atlantic City, New Jersey, limousine service held a union election-day raffle for a TV/VCR. The NLRB ruled, 3–2, that the raffle was an unfair labor practice that might reasonably be interpreted to be a reward that would influence voting. A new election was ordered. The NLRB order bans election-day raffles, but minor "gifts" such as food, drinks, and buttons would be considered case by case if an objection were lodged.

Source: Carlos Tejada, "Bad Draw," *The Wall Street Journal,* September 5, 2000, p. A1.

The case that follows involves allegations that a company illegally interfered with union organizing activity.

Judge Ripple

This petition asks us to review whether Multi-Ad Services, Incorporated ("Multi-Ad") violated the National Labor Relations Act ("Act") by interfering with its employees' efforts to form a union. The National Labor Relations Board ("Board") concluded that Multi-Ad violated the Act. . . .

BACKGROUND

Multi-Ad employs 450 workers at its full-service advertising art production facility in Peoria, Illinois. Multi-Ad hired Steele in 1989 to work in the bindery department. Fifteen employees work in the department, which manufactures loose-leaf, three-ring binders. The bindery department is a small operation, accounting for a limited percentage of the company's sales and profits. Steele's performance evaluations were above average throughout his tenure at the company.

* * * * *

On July 29, 1996, Multi-Ad held a quarterly meeting for employees of the bindery, press, and finishing departments. After discussing the company's financial performance, plant production manager Jerry Ireland announced the company's plan to implement a new drug-testing policy. Following this announcement, Steele spoke up and openly criticized the policy, contending in a loud and persistent manner that such testing violated employees' right to privacy. Other employees also voiced their displeasure with the policy. Steele and Larry Clore, Multi-Ad's president, then began to argue about the policy's legality. At the end of this exchange, Steele requested a copy of Multi-Ad's laws and bylaws. Clore told Steele that he could have these materials after the meeting.

Later that day, the quarterly meeting split into separate departmental meetings. The bindery department meeting commenced around 3:00 PM, the normal quitting time for day-shift employees. At this meeting, Clore gave Steele a summary plan description of Multi-Ad's corporate structure. After Steele pointed out that he wanted the complete bylaws and not a summary, Clore responded, "Have your lawyer get them." Clore then told Steele that if he did not like the company's drug policy, "Why don't you think about leaving the company?" Steele responded that he would not give Clore the pleasure of quitting. After Clore departed, Ireland tried to continue with the meeting, but Steele announced that he was leaving because "he was on his own time now." Steele testified that Ireland said, "Okay." Ireland, however, testified that Steele's remark had shocked him and that he had said nothing

in response. Ireland also testified that he had apologized to the group for Steele's behavior. Steele, however, was not ordered to remain for the rest of the meeting, which ended shortly after his exit.

Two days later, Steele and Ireland met at Steele's request. Steele apologized for his conduct at the department meeting and then told Ireland that hourly shop workers were dissatisfied with company policies. Steele told Ireland that "management needed to just sit down with the hourly employees and work some things out." Ireland replied, "That could not be done." Steele then told Ireland that, if they could not sit down and discuss these problems, he would organize a union. Ireland asked Steele to wait until Ireland returned from his vacation to discuss the issue further. Steele agreed and made no effort to contact a union while Ireland was away.

On August 16, 1996, Steele met with Ireland and bindery department manager Marty Heathcoat in Heathcoat's office. During this meeting, the two managers asked Steele why he would want to bring a union into the company. Steele told them that it would be nice to have seniority rights, better working conditions, and raises when possible. Ireland then asked what Steele could do to improve Steele's own situation at the company and pointed out that Multi-Ad posted job openings. After Steele expressed interest in a maintenance position, Ireland told him that he would set up an interview, even though the company did not have an opening for a maintenance position. At the end of the meeting, Ireland asked Steele "what it would take to satisfy him." Steele replied that it would satisfy him if management "would sit down with the hourly employees and work something out." After Ireland responded that he could not do that, Steele informed the two managers that he was leaving the meeting and was going to attempt to organize a union. Ireland asked Steele to come back and talk some more, but Steele responded that there was nothing left to talk about. Steele left at 3:30 PM, 30 minutes after his shift had ended. No one told Steele to stay, nor was he reprimanded for having left the meeting. The next day, Steele interviewed for a maintenance position, but the interview revealed that he lacked the necessary qualifications. In any event, Steele said that he did not want the job.

Steele twice met with union officials in late August. During this time, employees began to talk about Steele's efforts at organizing a union. At a meeting of bindery department employees in late August, Heathcoat addressed rumors about a union and asked employees why they wanted a union. In response, Steele stated that everyone knew that Heathcoat was referring to Steele's desire to look into unionization. Ted DeRossett, Steele's supervisor, then warned that the bindery department would be the "first to go" if the company unionized. Steele immediately challenged the legality of closing the bindery department in such a fashion. After Steele and DeRossett began to argue heatedly, Heathcoat ended the meeting.

At another bindery department meeting in late August, management informed employees that they would be working mandatory 10-hour shifts. Steele protested that it was unfair to require employees to work overtime when in the past they had been able to decline overtime. Steele also stated that it was decisions like this that caused him to explore bringing in a union.

Shortly after the meeting, Multi-Ad announced that it was adding a second shift in the bindery department and that Steele would be the lead man. On August 29, 1996, Heathcoat and DeRossett asked Steele if he would work the second shift with a positive attitude. The two assured Steele that he could still take his scheduled vacation days from August 30 through September 3. Steele told them that he would go to the second shift, do the job, and represent the company as was expected of him.

The next day, while Steele was on vacation, Multi-Ad received a letter from Steele requesting copies of the company's policies and bylaws. When Steele returned from his vacation on September 4, Heathcoat and DeRossett were waiting for him at the plant's garage door. The two asked Steele if he still wanted to see the materials that he had requested in the letter. Steele said yes, and the two told him that he could pick up the materials in the office of Bruce Taylor, Multi-Ad's vice president of finance. Steele punched the time clock and, as he started to walk toward Taylor's office, noticed DeRossett and Heathcoat accompanying him. Steele told them that he did not need them to pick up the papers. The two replied that they were tagging along in case he had any questions. Steele told them that he could not possibly have any questions because he had not yet read the materials. Nevertheless, both managers followed Steele into Taylor's office. Ireland entered the office shortly thereafter. Steele first asked Taylor for the documents. Taylor replied that Steele already had been given the summary statement at the quarterly meeting. Steele responded that he was not asking for a summary but for complete documents. After again requesting the documents and receiving no response, Steele announced that he would no longer participate in the meeting and walked out. Heathcoat ordered him to remain or be fired. Steele ignored this command and walked back to the plant, pursued by Heathcoat and Ireland. Heathcoat repeated his order that Steele return to the office or be fired. Steele, again, refused. Ireland then told

Steele that "this is the third meeting you have walked out of, you are gone." Steele immediately demanded a termination letter.

Even though Ireland had made the decision to fire Steele, Heathcoat prepared the letter. The letter spells out the purported reasons for Steele's termination:

> He [Steele] said that he didn't come for a meeting, [sic] and then walked out of the room. I told him to get back in Bruce's [Taylor's] office to discuss this with us. He repeated himself again saying that he didn't want a meeting. Jerry Ireland then Fired [sic] him.
>
> Ted Steele has walked out of three meetings within a month because he didn't feel like hearing what was being said to him. He has said that he does not agree with corporate policies set for all the employees of Multi[-]Ad. He has interrupted the work flow of the Bindery Department by persuading it's [sic] employees that this is not a good place to work. Ted will never see eye to eye with Multi[-]Ad's policies and goals for it's [sic] employees and will not even conduct himself in a professional manner when talking to management about his concerns. Ted is terminated on 9-4-96 because of his unwillingness to abide to [sic] corporate policies.

Ireland testified that he fired Steele because he was totally disrespectful to management. Ireland also testified that Steele's exit from the meeting on September 4 was an act of insubordination, particularly after he ignored Heathcoat's order to return.

THE ADMINISTRATIVE PROCEEDINGS

On September 26, 1996, Graphic Communications Union, Local 68C, and Graphic Communications International Union, AFL–CIO, filed an unfair labor charge against Multi-Ad on behalf of its employees, including Steele. Soon thereafter, the Board's General Counsel issued a complaint and a notice of hearing. The complaint alleged that Multi-Ad violated the Act by (1) coercively interrogating Steele about his interest in forming a union during the August 16 meeting with Heathcoat and Ireland; (2) impliedly promising at the August 16 meeting to help Steele improve his employment situation without the need for representation; and (3) threatening to close the bindery department if its employees unionized. The complaint also alleges that Multi-Ad violated the Act by discharging Steele because it believed that he might contact a union to organize employees.

On May 29, 1997, the Administrative Law Judge (ALJ) conducted a hearing on the board's complaint. Based on the evidence presented at the hearing, the ALJ issued his decision on December 2, 1997, and found that Multi-Ad had committed the charged unfair labor practices. On August 25,

2000, the board issued a decision and order affirming the ALJ's conclusions.

On October 10, 2000, Multi-Ad filed this petition for review.

Substantial Evidence

Multi-Ad first challenges the Board's determination that Multi-Ad coercively interrogated Steele on August 16 in violation of the Act.

* * * * *

Substantial evidence supports the Board's conclusion that management coercively interrogated Steele on August 16. The closed-door meeting was conducted in a manager's office by Heathcoat and Ireland, two people who had authority to fire Steele. The two managers questioned Steele regarding why he would want to bring a union into the company. . . . Moreover, Ireland immediately thereafter asked Steele about his own career advancement and arranged an interview for a maintenance position, even though no such opening existed. The managers did not assure Steele that reprisals would not be taken against him for his answers, adding to the potentially coercive nature of the inquiry. Further, this meeting was conducted after company managers had expressed uneasiness over union activity. These circumstances are more than enough evidence to sustain the Board's findings.

Multi-Ad next challenges the Board's finding that it made an implied promise of benefits by asking Steele how he could help his own situation and by arranging the job interview. . . . Here, Ireland asked Steele why he wanted to form a union and then asked Steele how Steele could improve his own situation. Steele expressed an interest in a maintenance position, and Ireland arranged for an interview immediately, even though there were no such openings. The context in which this occurred is significant. Because the managers made this overture during a conversation about the need for a union, the Board reasonably could have concluded that the company was willing to confer a benefit to deter Steele from contacting a union. . . .

Next, Multi-Ad argues that substantial evidence does not support the Board's conclusion that Multi-Ad threatened to close the bindery department. Unlike an interrogation, which is coercive only if reasonable employees would perceive it as such, a threat of plant closure is per se a violation of § 8(a)(1). In this case, three employees testified unequivocally that DeRossett said that the bindery department would be the "first to go" if they brought in a union, and this evidence is more than sufficient to establish a violation.

Finally, Multi-Ad disputes the Board's conclusion that Steele's discharge violates §§ 8(a)(1) and (3). An employer violates §§ 8(a)(1) or (3) of the Act by firing employees because of their union activities. To prove a violation, the Board must prove that antiunion animus was a substantial or motivating factor in the employer's decision to make the adverse employment decision. If the Board proves such a motivation by a preponderance of the evidence, the employer can avoid a finding of an unfair labor practice by showing that it would have taken the action regardless of the employee's union activities.

[S]ubstantial evidence supports a finding that the company harbored animus, including (1) the timing of Steele's firing, which coincided with his increased efforts to organize a union; (2) the coercive interrogation of Steele regarding his interest in forming a union; (3) management's questioning of other employees about their interest in forming a union; and (4) DeRossett's warning that the bindery department would close if employees unionized. Thus, the Board met its burden of establishing antiunion animus.

Multi-Ad claims as an affirmative defense that it fired Steele for leaving three meetings without permission. The Board concluded, however, that Multi-Ad's proffered reason was pretextual and that the company fired Steele because of his efforts to unionize. That conclusion is supported by substantial evidence, including (1) Multi-Ad's written explanation of termination stating a different reason—that he was discharged because he refused to abide by corporate policies; (2) the September 4 encounter was not a "meeting"—Steele entered the office to pick up materials to which he was legally entitled and twice denied access; and (3) no manager instructed Steele to remain at the previous two meetings, both of which occurred after shift hours. . . .

Order enforced.

Questions

1. *a.* List the four unfair labor practices identified by the court.

   b. What test did the court employ in determining whether the employer coercively interrogated Steele?

   c. What evidence supported the court's conclusion that Steele's firing was motivated by antiunion animus?

   d. Why did the court conclude that the employer's stated reason for dismissing Steele was pretextual?

2. Jose Ybarra was a labor consultant for Met West. A union election was pending at the company. An employee allegedly told Ybarra that his promised raise had not been delivered. Ybarra later allegedly told the employee that management had decided that wages could not be adjusted with an election pending. The union lost the election and filed suit claiming that Ybarra's statement was an

unfair labor practice. Decide. Explain. See *Met West Agribusiness, Inc.,* 334 NLRB No. 14 (May 23, 2001).

3. During an election campaign, the general manager's office was used to interview employees in small groups of five or six. The employees had previously visited that office to discuss grievances and obtain loans. That office was the only space available for the conversations. The general manager's remarks were temperate and noncoercive. The union lost the election. Should that result be set aside for unlawful campaigning? Explain. See *NVF Company, Hartwell Division,* 210 NLRB 663 (1974).

Union Persuasion

Employers, of course, are not the only parties affected by Taft-Hartley Act Section 8(c). Unions are also restricted in the type of preelection persuasion they employ. In cases involving promises of benefits made by the union, the board has been more reluctant to set aside elections than it has when such promises have been made by management. The board's reasoning is that employees realize that union preelection promises are merely expressions of a union platform, so to speak. Employees recognize that these are benefits for which the union intends to fight. Employers, on the other hand, really do hold within their power the ability to confer or withdraw benefits. But a union promise to employees to provide "the biggest party in the history of Texas" if the union won the next day's election was an unfair labor practice.[39]

> "The biggest party in the history of Texas"

Remedies for Election Misconduct

Unfair labor practices during a representation election can result in the imposition of penalties and remedies. If the union loses the election and the employer engaged in wrongful behavior, a new election may be ordered. Under the Supreme Court's *Gissel Packing* decision,[40] the NLRB could order a company to recognize and bargain with a union even if the union had no proof of majority support, but the union could show that the employer had committed "outrageous" and "pervasive" unfair labor practices making impossible an election under "laboratory conditions." Where the employer engaged in a lesser degree of misconduct, the NLRB can also order the employer to bargain if the union can demonstrate that at some point it had enjoyed majority support (a majority of the employees had signed authorization cards) that was undermined by the employer's misconduct.

Decertification

After a union has been certified or recognized, an employee or group of employees may continue to resist the union or may lose confidence in it. After one year has passed, they can file a *decertification* petition with the NLRB. The employees must be able to demonstrate at least 30 percent support for their petition. Once a decertification petition is properly filed with the board the usual election rules are followed to determine whether the union enjoys continuing majority support. If not, the union is decertified, and at least one year must pass before a new representation election can be conducted. [For management advice about decertification, see **http://www.nrtw.org/d/decert.htm**]

Withdrawal of Recognition

An employer may unilaterally withdraw recognition of a union only where the union has, in fact, lost the support of a majority of its members. A mere suspicion or even a good-faith doubt of declining union support among workers does not meet the legal standard for withdrawal of recognition. One way of demonstrating that a union does not hold majority support is to file a petition (called an RM petition) with the NLRB for an employer-requested election. The employer may file the RM petition where the facts support a "good-faith reasonable uncertainty" about whether the union enjoys majority support. Normally, however, a union's majority status cannot be challenged during the term of a collective bargaining agreement (up to three years).

Escape the Union?

If a union clearly is about to win a representation election or already has done so, thus establishing its right to collective bargaining, management sometimes continues to resist. One strategy is to declare bankruptcy. That tactic may be lawful but only after bargaining sincerely with the union and only after convincing the bankruptcy court that fairness requires modification or rejection of the collective bargaining agreement. Similarly, a company may simply choose to shut down its business rather than engage in collective bargaining. Going out of business is fully lawful unless the reason for doing so was to discourage union efforts at plants in other locations. Likewise, companies sometimes employ the *runaway shop* strategy in which the about-to-be-unionized plant is simply shut down and replaced by another in a location less responsive to union interests. If that move was made for the purpose of thwarting union interests, it is an unfair labor practice; but if the move reflected legitimate economic goals such as reduced wages or taxes, the move is probably lawful.

Companies sometimes employ the *runaway shop* strategy.

The Union as Exclusive Bargaining Agent

Once a union has been elected and certified as the representative of a bargaining unit, it becomes the exclusive agent for all of the employees within that bargaining unit, whether they voted for the union or not. The exclusivity of the union's authority has a number of implications, but one is particularly relevant in determining whether an employer has failed to demonstrate good faith at the bargaining table. Specifically, the employer must deal with the certified representative who acts on behalf of all employees in the bargaining unit. The employer commits an unfair labor practice if she or he attempts to deal directly with the employees or recognizes someone other than the workers' chosen representative. In both instances, the issue is fairly straightforward. The employer is undermining the position of the representative by ignoring him or her.

Part Four—Collective Bargaining

Section 8(a)(5) of the NLRA requires an employer to engage in *good-faith* collective bargaining with a representative of the employees, and Section 8(b)(3) imposes the same duty on labor organizations. Failure to bargain by either an employer or representative of the employees constitutes an unfair labor practice.

What is collective bargaining? What must one do to discharge the duty imposed? According to Section 8(d) of the NRLA,

> To bargain collectively is the performance of the mutual obligation of the employer and the representatives of the employees to meet at reasonable times and confer in good faith with respect to wages, hours, and other terms and conditions of employment . . . but such obligation does not compel either party to agree to a proposal or require the making of a concession.

Note what is *not* included. The duty to bargain in good faith does not require that the parties reach agreement. The NLRB and the courts recognize that collective bargaining, like any negotiation, is consensual. Thus the act governs only the process, not the result, of collective bargaining.

Bargaining in Good Faith

Good faith is a murky area with no definitive answers. Over the years, various factors (none of which is conclusive in and of itself) have been identified by the board and the courts as being suggestive of good-faith bargaining. Some of these include the following:[41]

1. The employer must make a serious attempt to adjust differences and to reach an acceptable common ground; that is, one must bargain with an open mind and a sincere desire to reach agreement.
2. Counterproposals must be offered when another party's proposal is rejected. This must involve the give and take of an auction system.[42]
3. A position with regard to contract terms may not be constantly changed.[43]
4. The employee must be willing to incorporate oral agreements into a written contract.[44]

Mandatory Bargaining Subjects   Although employers and labor representatives are free to discuss whatever lawful subjects they mutually choose to discuss, Section 8(d) of the NLRA clearly sets out some mandatory subjects over which the parties must bargain. These are wages, hours, and "other terms and conditions of employment." Although these topics for mandatory bargaining seem simple enough, questions still arise frequently. For example, suppose the union and employer bargain over wages and agree to institute merit increases for employees. Must the employer also bargain over which employees are entitled to receive these increases or who will make the decision at the time they are to be given? What about a decision to close a plant?

Generally, the board and the courts will balance three factors. First, they look at the effect of a particular decision on the workers—how direct is it and to what extent is the effect felt? Second, they consider the degree to which bargaining would constitute an intrusion into entrepreneurial interest or, from the opposite side, an intrusion into union affairs. Third, they examine the practice historically in the industry or the company itself.[45]

Permissive and Prohibited Bargaining Subjects   Those matters not directly related to wages, hours, and terms and conditions of employment and not falling within the category of prohibited subjects are considered permissive. Either party may raise permissive subjects during the bargaining process, but neither may pursue them to the point of a bargaining impasse. Refusal to bargain over a permissive subject does not constitute an NLRA violation, and permissive subjects must simply be dropped if the parties do not reach agreement. Permissive subjects ordinarily would include such items as alteration of a defined bargaining unit, internal union affairs, and strike settlement agreements. Prohibited bargaining subjects are those that are illegal under the NLRA or other laws.

> Whether a union has a right to bargain over management's placement of hidden surveillance cameras in the workplace.

In the case that follows the NLRB had to decide whether a union has a right to bargain over management's placement of hidden surveillance cameras in the workplace. (Note that this decision has not been reviewed by the courts and will not be the "last word" in this highly contentious area.)

LEGAL BRIEFCASE

Colgate–Palmolive Co.
323 NLRB No. 82 (1997)

FACTS

Colgate–Palmolive's Jeffersonville, Indiana, plant employed approximately 750 workers. Colgate and the employees had a collective bargaining arrangement for over 20 years. In 1994 an employee discovered a surveillance camera in a restroom air vent. The union president later discussed the matter with Colgate's human resources officer, who indicated that the camera had been placed in the vent because of theft concerns and that the camera had been removed after employees objected to it. The Union filed a grievance over the matter, and the parties met for discussion where Colgate argued that it had the absolute right to install internal surveillance cameras. Later, the Union sent a letter to Colgate demanding to bargain over the subject of cameras within the plant. Colgate did not respond, and the Union filed an unfair labor practice charge. The case was heard by an administrative law judge. Evidence indicated that Colgate had installed 11 secret cameras over four years to address problems of theft and misconduct, including sleeping on the job. The cameras were placed in several offices, a fitness center, a restroom, and as a monitor for an overhead door that was not a proper exit from the building. The Union and some employees were aware of various "unhidden" cameras in the workplace and in some instances fortuitously discovered some of the hidden cameras.

The Administrative Law Judge (ALJ) concluded that the use of hidden surveillance cameras is a mandatory subject of bargaining and by failing to do so, Colgate–Palmolive violated the National Labor Relations Act. The ALJ's ruling was then appealed to the National Labor Relations Board. The NLRB decision follows.

CHAIRMAN GOULD AND MEMBERS FOX AND HIGGINS

In *Ford Motor Co. v. NLRB,* the Supreme Court described mandatory subjects of bargaining as such matters that are "plainly germane to the 'working environment'" and "not among those 'managerial decisions, which lie at the core of entrepreneurial control.'" As the judge found, the installation of surveillance cameras is both germane to the working environment, and outside the scope of managerial decisions lying at the core of entrepreneurial control.

As to the first factor—germane to the working environment—the installation of surveillance cameras is analogous to physical examinations, drug/alcohol testing requirements, and polygraph testing, all of which the Board has found to be mandatory subjects of bargaining. They are all investigatory tools or methods used by an employer to ascertain whether any of its employees has engaged in misconduct.

The Respondent [Colgate–Palmolive] acknowledges that employees caught involved in theft and/or other misconduct are subject to discipline, including discharge. Accordingly, the installation and use of surveillance cameras has the potential to affect the continued employment of employees whose actions are being monitored.

Further, as the judge finds, the use of surveillance cameras in the restroom and fitness center raises privacy concerns which add to the potential effect upon employees. We agree that these areas are part of the work environment and that the use of hidden cameras in these areas raises privacy concerns which impinged upon the employees' working conditions. The use of cameras in these or similar circumstances is unquestionably germane to the working environment.

With regard to the second criterion, we agree with the judge that the decision is not a managerial decision that lies at the core of entrepreneurial control.

* * * * *

The use of surveillance cameras is not entrepreneurial in character, is not fundamental to the basic direction of the enterprise, and impinges directly upon employment security. It is a change in the Respondent's methods used to reduce workplace theft or detect other suspected employee misconduct with serious implications for its employees' job security, which in no way touches on the discretionary "core of entrepreneurial control."

The Respondent urges that bargaining before a hidden camera is actually installed would defeat the very purpose of the camera. The very existence of secret cameras, however, is a term and condition of employment, and is thus a legitimate concern for the employees' bargaining representative. Thus, the placing of cameras, and the extent to which they will be secret or hidden, if at all, is a proper subject of negotiations between the Respondent and the union. Concededly, the Respondent also has a legitimate concern. However, bargaining about hidden cameras can embrace a host of matters other than mere location. And, even as to location, mutual accommodations can and should be negotiated. The vice in the instant case was the respondent's refusal to bargain.

* * * * *

Accordingly, we affirm the judge's finding that the union has the statutory right to engage in collective bargaining over the installation and continued use of surveillance cameras, including the circumstances under which the cameras will be activated, the general areas in which they may be placed, and how affected employees will be disciplined if improper conduct is observed.

ORDER

The National Labor Relations Board adopts the recommended Order of the administrative law judge as modified and set forth in full below and orders that the Respondent, its officers, agents, successors, and assigns, shall

1. Cease and desist from
   a. Failing and refusing to bargain with Local 15, International Chemical Workers Union, AFL–CIO with respect to the installation and use of surveillance cameras and other mandatory subjects of bargaining.
2. Take the following affirmative action necessary to effectuate the policies of the Act.
   a. On request, bargain collectively with the Union as the exclusive bargaining representative of the Respondent's employees with respect to the installation and use of surveillance cameras and other mandatory subjects of bargaining.
   b. Within 14 days after the service by the Region, post at its facility in Jeffersonville, Indiana, copies of the attached notice.

Notice to Employees
Posted by Order of the
National Labor Relations Board
An Agency of the United States Government

The National Labor Relations Board has found that we violated the National Labor Relations Act and has ordered us to post and abide by this notice. Section 7 of the Act gives employees these rights.

To organize
To form, join, or assist any union
To bargain collectively through representatives of their own choice
To act together for other mutual aid or protection

To choose not to engage in any of these protected concerted activities.

We will not fail and refuse to bargain with Local 15, International Chemical Workers Union, AFL–CIO over the installation and use of surveillance cameras within our facility and other mandatory subjects of bargaining.

We will not in any like or related manner interfere with, restrain, or coerce you in the exercise of the rights guaranteed you by Section 7 of the Act.

We will, on request, bargain collectively with the Union as the exclusive bargaining representative of our employees with respect to the installation and use of surveillance cameras within our facility and other mandatory subjects of bargaining.

Colgate–Palmolive Company.

Questions

1. What test did the ALJ and the NLRB employ to determine whether the placement of hidden surveillance cameras was a mandatory subject of bargaining?

2. Why did the union win this case?

3. If you were managing a workplace where theft, sleeping on the job, and other misconduct were at a worrisome level, would you employ hidden, secret cameras to monitor restrooms, fitness areas, and the like? Explain.

4. A mirror fell off the wall in a Consolidated Freightways bathroom. Employees discovered that management had installed cameras behind two-way bathroom mirrors in order to address "ongoing drug abuse." The employees sued, saying the cameras violated California state privacy laws.

A federal court of appeals labeled the two-way mirrors "a direct violation" of California criminal law. Consolidated argued that its collective bargaining agreement (CBA) permitted the surveillance. The CBA provided that Consolidated could not use video cameras to discipline or discharge employees for reasons other than theft or dishonesty. Consolidated also claimed that the Labor Management Relations Act preempts the employees' state claims because the claims required interpretation of the collective bargaining agreement. The lower court ruled for Consolidated. The case was appealed. How would you rule? Explain. See *Cramer v. Consolidated Freightways,* 255 F.3d 683 (2001); cert. den. 122 S.Ct. 806 (2002).

Successors and the Duty to Bargain   What bargaining duties does a firm have when it acquires or merges with another firm that has a collective bargaining agreement? Is the successor firm legally required to accept the bargained-for contractual arrangements of its predecessors? Does the successor have a duty to bargain with the union? While these questions must be settled case by case, we can safely say that a successor normally has no duty to accept the terms of the labor agreement negotiated by the previous employer, but the successor may well have to bargain with the union. The key considerations in the duty to bargain question include whether a "substantial continuity of identity" was maintained between the original firm and the successor and whether the successor retained a majority of the employees from the unionized labor force. If the general nature of the firm and a majority of its workforce are retained, the successor will be bound to recognize the union and bargain. Furthermore, if the successor deliberately avoids hiring union members from the original firm to escape bargaining duties, a bargaining order probably will be imposed. [For the Bureau of Labor Statistics and frequently asked questions about collective bargaining, see **http://www.bls.gov/cba/cbafaq.htm**]

Administering the Agreement

Union–management bargaining does not end with the negotiation of a labor agreement. Rather, bargaining continues daily as the parties work out the disputes and confusions and conflicting interpretations that are bound to arise and that cannot be entirely provided for in the labor agreement. Often this process of contract maintenance takes the form of resolving *grievances*, as in the *Colgate–Palmolive* case. Those problems are addressed through the grievance procedure that is included in collective bargaining agreements. Often the grievance procedure involves a series of steps beginning with informal discussion mechanisms. Failing there, the dissatisfied employee typically files a written complaint (the grievance). Normally, grievances are presented to management by a union representative, often with the worker also present.

Arbitration

If, after negotiation, the parties cannot resolve their dispute, the collective bargaining agreement ordinarily provides for *final and binding arbitration.* Many court decisions have vigorously supported the arbitration process as the means of settling labor–management contract maintenance disputes and tend to find disputes arbitrable unless the labor agreement explicitly and unambiguously exempts the subject at issue from the arbitration process. Further, but for rare exceptions, neither the company nor the union can turn to the courts to set aside arbitration decisions.

Fair Representation

Because grievance processing is part of a union's bargaining responsibility, the union might breach its duty if it declined to represent an employer's grievance. An employee who feels wronged when a union does not process his or her grievance has the option of appealing to the NLRB or to the courts.

Part Five—Work Stoppages

Strikes For many, the initial image of labor conflict is one of employees on strike, picketing a store or factory. Striking is, however, an extremely drastic measure under which employees must bear an immediate loss of wages and, in many instances, risk job loss. Similarly, employers bear the loss of a disruption to continued operations. As Table 14.1 shows, work stoppages have declined dramatically since World War II.

We will address two kinds of strikes:

1. *Unfair labor practice strikes* are those instituted by workers in response to the employer's commission of an unfair labor practice such as interfering with legitimate union activities or failure to bargain in good faith. These strikers can be temporarily, but not permanently, replaced.

TABLE 14.1 **U.S. Work Stoppages Involving 1,000 or More Workers**

Year	Number	Workers	Days Idle	Percentage of Estimated Working Time
		(thousands)		
1948	245	1,435	26,127	.22
1958	332	1,587	17,900	.13
1968	392	1,855	35,367	.20
1978	219	1,006	23,774	.11
1988	40	387	4,381	.02
1998	34	387	5,116	.02
2001	29	99	1,151	Less than .005
2003	14	129.2	4,091.2	.01

Source: [http://stats.bls.gov/news.release/wkstp.t01.htm].

2. *Economic Strikes* are those used purely as economic weapons to persuade an employer to provide more favorable employee benefits or better working conditions. All strikes not involving unfair labor practices fall into this category. With some exceptions, economic strikers cannot be fired, but they can be permanently replaced. In what has been labeled "the most significant change in collective bargaining to occur since the passage of the Wagner Act in 1934," employers are now increasingly willing to permanently replace economic strikers.[46] Employers had enjoyed that right where necessary "in an effort to carry on the business" since a 1938 Supreme Court decision, but for practical reasons they had rarely exercised it.[47] Later decisions imposed some limitations on that right. For example, any striker who is permanently replaced is put on a preferential hiring list and will have priority to be selected to fill subsequent vacancies. However, President Reagan's 1981 dismissal of 11,300 striking air traffic controllers effectively crushed their union (PATCO) and caused private-sector employers to reassess their long-standing reluctance to use replacements during and after strikes.[48] Thus recent years have seen some major employers like Hormel, Caterpillar, Greyhound Bus Lines, Firestone/Bridgestone, the National Football League, and Major League Baseball use, or threaten to use, strike replacements.

The following case examines when employers can legitimately decline to reinstate strikers.

LEGAL BRIEFCASE

Diamond Walnut Growers, Inc. v. NLRB 113 F.3d 1259 (D.C. Cir. 1997); cert. den. 118 S.Ct.1299 (1998)

Circuit Judge Silberman

I

Diamond Walnut processes and packages walnuts for national and international distribution. . . . Diamond's employees have for years been represented by Cannery Workers, Processors, Warehousemen, and Helpers Local 601 of the International Brotherhood of Teamsters, AFL–CIO (the union). In September of 1991, following expiration of the most recent collective bargaining agreement between Diamond and the union, nearly 500 of Diamond's permanent and seasonal employees went on strike. Diamond hired replacement workers to allow it to continue operations.

By all accounts, the strike was, and remains, a bitter affair. The strikers are alleged to have engaged in various acts of violence against the replacement workers. . . . In addition, as part of its effort to exert economic pressure on Diamond, the union undertook an international boycott of its product. The boycott included a well-publicized national bus tour during which union members distributed to the public leaflets which described Diamond's workforce as composed of "scabs" who packaged walnuts contaminated with "mold, dirt, oil, worms, and debris."

Approximately one year into the strike, the Board held a representation election. The union lost the election, but its objections prompted the Board to order a rerun to be held in October of 1993. Just over two weeks prior to the new election, a group of four striking employees, represented by a union official, approached Diamond with an unconditional offer to return to work. According to the letter presented to the company at that time by their representative, the employees were convinced that "a fair election [was] simply impossible."

Nonetheless, the employees "fe[lt] that it [was] important that the replacement workers . . . have an opportunity to hear from Union sympathizers." Thus, the group of strikers was "available and willing to return to immediate active employment." The following day, the union notified Diamond that pursuant to the above-quoted letter, two additional strikers were willing to return to work.

It is undisputed that for three of the returning strikers, neither the permanent jobs they held before the strike, nor substantially equivalent ones, were available at the time of their return. Diamond placed these three in various seasonal jobs. Prior to the strike, Willa Miller was a quality control supervisor; she was placed in a seasonal packing position even though a seasonal inspection job was available. Alfonsina Munoz had been employed as a lift truck operator and, despite the availability of a seasonal forklift job, was given a seasonal job cracking and inspecting nuts in the growers' inspection department at the front end of the production process. Mohammed Kussair, formerly an air separator machine operator, was, like Munoz, placed in a seasonal cracking and inspecting position in the growers' inspection department. . . .

The rerun election took place as scheduled, and the union lost. Following that election, the General Counsel filed a complaint alleging that Diamond had violated the National Labor Relations Act by unlawfully discriminating against Miller, Munoz, and Kussair. The General Counsel alleged that because of their protected activity, Diamond declined to put them in certain available seasonal positions for which they were qualified and that were preferable to the positions in which they were actually placed. After a hearing, an administrative law judge recommended that the charges be dismissed. He found that Diamond had "discriminated" insofar as it had placed the employees at least in part because of their protected activity, but he did not think that discrimination "unlawful."

* * * * *

[The NLRB reversed saying] "although [Diamond] was under no legal obligation . . . to reinstate the strikers . . ., once it voluntarily decided to reinstate them, it was required to act in a nondiscriminatory fashion toward the strikers." Diamond had discriminated against Miller, Munoz, and Kussair, in the Board's view, by declining "to place them in the [seasonal] positions of quality control assistant, lift truck operator, and loader, respectively, because of their union status and/or because of certain protected union activity they engaged in while on strike.". . . The Board rejected the contention that the placements were warranted by the employer's concern that the replacement workers might instigate violence against the

three and thus justified placement in well-supervised jobs, since "there [was] no evidence that Miller, Munoz, or Kussair were involved" in the strike-related violence allegedly causing Diamond's concern. The Board also dismissed the notion that the placements of Miller and Munoz were justified by their participation in the boycott and the circulation of disparaging leaflets: "[T]he strikers' conduct constituted protected . . . activity and there is no evidence indicating that such protection was lost because of threats made by Miller and Munoz to damage or sabotage [Diamond's] equipment or products." Since Diamond had failed to justify its discrimination, the Board found unfair labor practices.

* * * * *

[Diamond sought judicial review of the NLRB ruling.]

II

Diamond Walnut challenges the Board's determination that it lacked substantial business justification for refusing to place the three employees in the specific jobs they sought—quality control assistant, lift truck operator, and loader. It is undisputed that the *Fleetwood* framework governs this case. The General Counsel under *Fleetwood* must make out a *prima facie* case that the employer discriminated within the meaning of the Act, which means the employer's decision as to how to treat the three returning strikers was attributable to their protected activity. *Rose Printing* establishes that a struck employer faced with an unconditional offer to return to work is obliged to treat the returning employee like any other applicant for work (unless the employee's former job or its substantial equivalent is available, in which case the employee is preferred to any other applicant). But Miller and Munoz were not treated like any other applicant for work. Miller was qualified for a seasonal position in quality control that paid 32 cents per hour more than the packing job to which she was assigned. And Munoz was qualified to fill a forklift operating job, a position that paid between $2.75 and $5.00 per hour more than the walnut cracking and inspecting job she received. Diamond admits that it took into account Miller's and Munoz's protected activity in choosing to place them in jobs that were objectively less desirable than those for which they were qualified. Petitioner [Diamond], although it contended that the discrimination was comparatively slight, does not dispute that its action discriminated against Munoz and Miller within the meaning of the Act.

* * * * *

Under *Fleetwood,* after discrimination is shown, the burden shifts to the employer to establish that its treatment of the employees has a legitimate and substantial business justification. Petitioner declined to give Munoz the forklift driver job because of its concern that driving that piece of equipment throughout the plant would be unduly risky in two respects. First, because of the bad feeling between strikers and replacements, Munoz would be endangered if confronted by hostile replacement workers in an isolated area. Second, since Munoz had participated in the bus tour during which the union had accused the company of producing tainted walnuts, Munoz would be tempted to engage in sabotage by using the 11,000 pound vehicle to cause unspecified damage. As for Miller, who was also on the bus tour, the company declined to put her in the "sensitive position of quality control assistant" where "the final visual inspection of walnuts is made prior to leaving the plant." In that position, she would have "an easy opportunity to let defective nuts go by undetected . . . or to place a foreign object into the final product, thereby legitimizing the Union's claim of tainted walnuts."

* * * * *

A. Munoz

The Board rejected petitioner's proffered justifications for its placement of Munoz on the same ground as did the ALJ. As to Diamond's purported fear for her safety, no evidence had been produced that Munoz was thought to be responsible for any violence, so there was no reason to believe she would have been a special target. The Board said, "[T]here is no specific evidence that any replacements harbored hostility toward these three strikers, and, if such evidence did exist as [Diamond] claims, we fail to see how placing them in the positions to which they were assigned would lessen the perceived danger of retaliatory acts being committed against them." The Board discounted Diamond Walnut's contention that Munoz would be under greater protection if closely supervised, noting that petitioner had admitted that "Munoz freely roamed the plant unsupervised during her breaks."

* * * * *

As for the possibility that Munoz would engage in forklift sabotage, the Board was more terse, stating only that "the strikers' conduct [referring to the bus tour] constituted protected . . . activity," and there was no evidence indicating that such protection was lost because of threats made by Miller and Munoz. If Munoz had uttered specific threats of sabotage, however, she would have lost her protected status. . . . [T]he Board necessarily concluded that the possibility of Munoz engaging in future sabotage by misuse of her forklift was simply not a sufficient risk to constitute a substantial business justification for her treatment.

* * * * *

Similarly, the Board was reasonable in its determination that the risk of Munoz engaging in sabotage while riding around on her 11,000 pound forklift—the petitioner seems to most fear her crashing the forklift into machinery—is not a substantial business justification for her disadvantageous placement in another job. Strikes tend to be hard struggles, and although this one may have been more bitter than most, there is always a potential danger of returning strikers engaging in some form of sabotage. There is therefore undeniably some risk in employing returning strikers during a strike. But it could not be seriously argued that an employer cannot be forced to assume *any* risk of sabotage, because that would be equivalent to holding that an employer need not take back strikers during an ongoing strike at all. . . .

* * * * *

B. Miller

The Miller case is another matter. It will be recalled that petitioner declined to assign her to the post of quality control assistant, the job responsible for the final inspection of walnuts leaving the plant (she received a job paying 32 cents an hour less). The Board rejected the employer's justification, which was based on Miller's participation in the product boycott and bus tour leafleting, saying only "the strikers' conduct constituted protected . . . activity and there is no evidence indicating that such protection was lost because of threats made by Miller and Munoz to damage or sabotage . . . equipment or products." With respect to Miller, we think the Board's determination that petitioner's business justification is insubstantial is flatly unreasonable.

All strikes are a form of economic warfare, but when a union claims that a food product produced by a struck company is actually tainted it can be thought to be using the strike equivalent of a nuclear bomb; the unpleasant effects will long survive the battle. . . . The company's ability to sell the product . . . could well be destroyed.

* * * * *

The Board's counsel argues that it is unfair to assume that an employee would behave in a disloyal and improper fashion. It is unnecessary, however, for us to make that assumption to decide the Board was unreasonable. The Board accepted petitioner's contention that Miller would have been placed "in the sensitive position . . . where final visual inspection of walnuts is made prior to leaving the plant." Miller would therefore have been put in a rather acute and unusual conflict of interest in which her job for her employer could be thought to have as a function the rebutting of her union's claim. A similar conflict would be raised if she wished a bargaining unit job in the company's public relations department. This conflict makes all too likely the possibility that Miller would be *at least* inattentive to her product quality duties. . . . To make matters worse, any "mistake" by Miller on the product quality control line would not be easily attributable to her unless petitioner paid someone to stand all day looking over Miller's shoulder. . . . If Munoz ran her forklift into valuable machinery, she would run a risk of being discovered and would therefore be deterred. But Miller, as a quality control assistant, could simply avert her eye and cause the damage with apparently little risk of discovery. . . .

In short, she would have had a special motive, a unique opportunity, and little risk of detection to cause severe harm. Both the risk Diamond faced in its placement of Miller was qualitatively different than a normal risk of sabotage, and the deterrence to Miller's possible misbehavior was peculiarly inadequate.

* * * * *

[W]e are obliged to ask in the last analysis whether the Board's decision, as to whether the employer's action was substantially justified by business reasons, falls within the broad stretch of reasonableness. In this case, at least with respect to one part of the Board's decision, we conclude the Board exceeded the reasonableness limits.

So ordered.

AFTERWORD

After nearly 14 years of bitter struggle, the Diamond Walnut strike was settled in March 2005. The settlement allowed strikers to return to work with full seniority and benefits, although many of them had already returned to Diamond Walnut or had moved to other jobs. [For a time line of the Diamond Walnut strike, see **http://www.teamster.org/divisions/foodprocessing/ diamondwalnut/dwtimeline.htm**]

Questions

1. Set out the two-part test the court employed to determine whether Diamond Walnut violated the National Labor Relations Act by discriminating against its employees because of their participation in protected union activities.

2. Explain why the court found that Munoz had been wronged by Diamond but Miller had not.

3. *a.* How would you vote on federal legislation banning the practice of permanently replacing economic strikers? Explain.

   b. Is there any reason to distinguish between economic strikers and unfair labor practice strikers? Any reason not to do so? Explain.

4. A pilots' union, Airline Professionals Association, had a collective bargaining agreement with freight carrier Airborne Express (ABX). The union and ABX had a dispute about time-off provisions in the CBA. The union applied pressure to ABX by asking all pilots not to bid on open flying time not covered in the regular monthly schedule. ABX says it lost jobs due to the lack of pilots and filed a complaint saying the union was engaging in an illegal strike. A district court agreed with ABX, and the union appealed. Decide the case. Explain. See *ABX Air, Inc. v. Airline Professionals Assn.*, 266 F.3d 392 (2001); cert. den. 122 S.Ct. 1459 (2002).

Lockouts   Sometimes management takes the initiative in labor disputes by locking its doors to some or all of its employees. Both the NLRB and the courts allow lockouts as defensive acts to protect businesses against sudden strikes and to prevent sabotage or violence. Some court decisions have also expanded lawful lockouts to include those of an offensive nature designed to improve management's bargaining position. Lockouts, however, are clearly not lawful if designed to interfere with bargaining rights and other legitimate union activity.

Sports fans have learned some labor law in recent years. National Hockey League owners locked out the players and eventually cancelled the entire 2004–05 season. Since 1972 baseball has had three lockouts and five player strikes. Owners locked out National Football League game officials during the final week of the preseason 2001 schedule, then settled with them in mid-September after using college officials in the interim. National Basketball Association team owners locked out their players in 1998 and reached a settlement in 1999.

> Since 1972 baseball has had three lockouts and five player strikes.

Picketing and Boycotts

Primary Picketing   In addition to striking, unions often picket or boycott to pressure employers with which they are negotiating and to broadly publicize their concerns. Picketing is the familiar process of union members gathering and sometimes marching, placards in hand, at a place of business. Peaceful, informational picketing for a lawful purpose is protected by the NLRA. Some kinds of picketing, however, are forbidden, and all picketing can be regulated by the government to ensure public safety. Primary picketing is expressed directly to the employer with whom the picketers have a dispute. Primary picketing enjoys broad constitutional and statutory protection, but it may be unlawful if violent or coercive.

Secondary Picketing/Boycotts   Secondary picketing or boycotting is directed to a business other than the primary employer, and ordinarily it is unlawful. That is, unions are engaging in an unfair labor practice if they threaten or coerce a third party with whom they are not engaged in a dispute in order to cause that third party to put pressure on the firm that is the real target of the union's concern.

Question

George A. Hormel & Co. and the United Food and Commercial Workers Union settled a long labor dispute. Thereafter, an unhappy employee drove his car in a parade and attended a rally, both of which were designed to encourage a nationwide boycott of Hormel Products. The employee did nothing to signal his feelings beyond his presence at the two events.

Employees may lawfully be dismissed for disloyalty to their employer. Supporting a boycott of an employer's products ordinarily constitutes disloyalty except where (1) the boycott is related to an ongoing labor dispute and (2) the support does not amount to disparagement of the employer's product.

Was this Hormel employee engaged in protected activity such that his dismissal was unlawful? Explain. See *George A. Hormel and Company v. National Labor Relations Board,* 962 F.2d 1061 (D.C. Cir. 1992).

Part Six—Employees' Rights within or against the Union

The Union's Duty of Fair Representation

As you have seen in previous sections of this chapter, the union is given statutory authority to be the exclusive bargaining agent for the employees in the designated bargaining unit. This means that even if an individual employee in the bargaining unit does not agree with the union policies or is not a member of the union, he or she cannot bargain individually with the employer. Such an employee will still be bound by the terms of the collective bargaining agreement. Hence unions have a duty to fairly represent all members of the bargaining unit, whether or not they become members of the union.

The Bill of Rights of Labor Organization Members

The Bill of Rights for members of labor organizations is contained in Title 1, Section 101 of the Labor–Management Reporting and Disclosure Act (LMRDA or Landrum–Griffin Act). The Bill of Rights was designed to ensure equal voting rights, the right to sue the union, and the rights of free speech and assembly. These rights of union members are tempered by the union's right to enact and enforce "reasonable rules governing the responsibilities of its members."[49]

The NLRB and Worker Participation

Many American companies have increased worker participation in management decision making as a part of the more general effort at total quality management (TQM). The NLRA, however, provides that employer domination or interference with the formation or administration of any labor organization is an unfair labor practice. Broadly, the law is designed to prevent sham unions that, in fact, are dominated by management.

The NLRB showed, in a 2001 decision, that labor–management cooperation can be lawful, however, if employees are genuinely empowered. Crown Cork & Seal Co. set up seven employee committees at its aluminum can factory in Texas. The committees made decisions and enforced rules on production, safety, and other workplace issues. An employee complained to the NLRB, but the board said the arrangement did not violate the ban on company-sponsored unions. Here the committees were not labor organizations because they were not set up to "deal with" management about wages, grievances, and other conditions of employment. The board explained that the employer had delegated authority to employees to run the plant within certain parameters. Thus the committees were genuinely managerial in their duties and could not, therefore, be considered sham unions.[50]

Union Security Agreements and Right-to-Work Laws

To maintain their membership, unions typically seek a collective bargaining clause requiring all employees to become union members after they have been employed for some period—generally 30 days (*union shop agreements*)—or, at the least, requiring them to pay union dues and fees (*agency shop agreements*). These union security arrangements are lawful under the NLRA.

The union has a duty of fair representation for *all* members of the bargaining unit, whether those employees join the union or not. Furthermore, under the 1988 Supreme Court decision in *Communications Workers of America v. Beck*[51] nonunion employees can be compelled to pay union dues and fees only for core collective bargaining activities. Thus nonunion employees' agency shop dues and fees must be reduced by an amount equal to that applied to such noncore purposes as lobbying and political campaigning. [For the Communications Workers of America home page, see **http://www .cwa-union.org/**]

Right-to-Work   Twenty-two states, primarily in the South and West, have enacted right-to-work laws that prohibit union security arrangements in collective bargaining agreements.

In these states, nonmembers do not pay dues or fees, but as members of the bargaining unit, they must be represented by the union. Unions regard those employees as free riders, but right-to-work supporters see the matter as one of personal freedom. [For questions and answers on right-to-work laws, see **http://www.nrtw.org/a/a_prime.htm**]

Closed Shop At one time, powerful unions insisted on closed-shop arrangements wherein employers could hire only individuals who already belonged to unions, but those arrangements are now forbidden by the NLRA.

Part Seven—Other Unions

Public-Sector Unions

The public sector is a growth area for union membership. Legal regulation of public-sector labor–management relations begins with state law. Although the specific provisions of those laws vary, many of the concepts discussed earlier arising under the NLRA are applicable. Some fundamental policies and doctrines are quite different, however, Two of these doctrines that apply uniquely to the public sector are the nondelegability doctrine, which bears on the constitutionality of public-sector labor laws, and the ability of public-sector employees to strike.

The nondelegability doctrine is based on the fact that public-sector employees are, either directly or indirectly, held accountable to the electorate via the ballot box. Thus a mayor or governor, or his or her employees as representatives, have certain powers and responsibilities that cannot be given to, or delegated to, an individual or entity, such as a union or an arbitrator, that is not accountable to the voters.[52]

With regard to public employee strikes, some states prohibit them and others permit them only under restricted conditions. In either case, the rationale for treating public employees differently than private-sector employees is the role of public employees as servants of the voters. In the minds of many, public servants have a higher duty than private employees. In addition, certain public employees, including police officers and firefighters, work in positions that clearly involve public safety, and to permit them to strike might endanger the citizenry.

Internet Exercise	Using the United Auto Workers' frequently asked questions [**http://www.uaw.org/about/faqs.html**], 1. Explain "how union pay compares to nonunion pay." 2. Explain how union dues are used.
Chapter Questions	1. *a.* In your opinion, what are the average blue-collar worker's biggest sources of job dissatisfaction? Can they be eliminated through collective bargaining? Explain. *b.* In your opinion, what are the average white-collar worker's biggest sources of job dissatisfaction? What means do such workers have for eliminating those sources of dissatisfaction? Explain.

2. *a.* Imagine what the world will be like 50 years from now. In what ways do you picture the work life of the average American to have changed? Explain.

   b. Imagine the ideal work world. How close does that picture come to the one you conjured up in response to the previous question? What types, if any, of labor or other legislation would bring society closer to that ideal? Explain.

3. You are the human resources manager for a manufacturing firm that is presently the subject of an organizing campaign by a union that has filed an election petition with the NLRB just 30 days ago. Your plant manager has come to you and said that she wishes to discharge one of her employees. She further explains that the employee in question has worked for the company for three years and throughout that time has had a terrible attendance record. She adds that up to this point the employee has not received any discipline for his attendance. Upon inquiry, the plant manager tells you that the employee has been seen on the plant floor wearing a button that says "Union Yes!" In addition, the plant manager tells you that she knows that the employee is an outspoken union activist. What would you advise the plant manager to do? Why?

4. ACE/CO, a Milwaukee automobile parts manufacturer, was accused of a series of unfair labor practices springing from company conduct both before and after a disputed union representation election. Among the charges were the following:

   • ACE/CO declined to grant its usual across-the-board wage increases and told employees that the union was responsible for the failure to grant a raise.

   • ACE/CO distributed a memorandum asking employees to inform supervisors whenever they felt pressured to sign a union authorization card. One employee testified that union representatives had visited his home 13 times and that he did feel "pressured" to support the union.

   • ACE/CO included in its employee handbook a statement indicating the company's "intention to do everything possible to maintain our company's union-free status for the benefit of both our employees and [the company]."

   a. Why might ACE/CO legitimately decline to offer a wage increase during an organizing campaign?

   b. Do any of these company behaviors constitute unfair labor practices? See *NLRB v. Aluminum Casting & Engineering Co.,* 230 F.3d 286 (7th Cir. 2000).

5. When assistant manager Diane Gorrell was fired from a Bob Evans restaurant in East Peoria, Illinois, most of the employees walked off the job in protest. They stood outside the restaurant for a time and discouraged customers from entering. The restaurant was left in some disarray and problems persisted for a number of days, clearly harming business. Later all but one of the employees asked to return to their jobs, but were refused. The employees filed an unfair labor practices charge with the NLRB.

   a. Justify, as a matter of law, management's decision not to allow the employees to return to work.

   b. Explain the employees' unfair labor practices charge.

   c. Decide the case. Explain. See *Bob Evans Farms, Inc. v. NLRB,* 163 F.3d 1012 (7th Cir. 1998).

6. Seawin, an Ohio fittings manufacturer, was forced to lay off 17 employees. The company's net income had declined by 88 percent, it had lost some major customers, and it had excess inventory. At the time of the layoffs, a company vice president said that he "hoped that business . . . would turn around soon." Asked when they would be called back, employees remembered the vice president saying "probably" around two weeks to a month. Others, however, indicated that the layoffs were intended to be permanent, and the company made significant equipment and computer improvements to enhance efficiency. Soon thereafter the NLRB held a representation election at Seawin that resulted in a 31–21 vote in favor of a union. Eleven of the laid-off workers had been allowed to vote in the election. Seawin challenged the election results saying the laid-off employees should not have been allowed to vote. Was Seawin correct? Explain. See *NLRB v. Seawin, Inc.,* 248 F.3d 551 (6th Cir. 2001).

7. Midwestern Personnel Services provided truck drivers to employers in Indiana, Kentucky, and other locations. Midwestern wanted the drivers to join a union so they would be allowed to enter a unionized workplace, AK Steel, where they were to deliver cement. Midwestern management favored Teamsters Local 836 in Middletown, Ohio, for their drivers, but a majority of the drivers voted to join Teamsters Local 215 in Evansville, Indiana. Midwestern refused to recognize Local 215; management and the drivers could not reach agreement about pension rights and contract length; and the drivers went on strike. The drivers later made an unconditional offer to return to work, but Midwestern would not allow them to return because, in its view, the drivers were economic strikers. The NLRB concluded that the drivers were motivated in part by unfair labor practices, and thus should be reinstated to their jobs. Were the drivers entitled to reinstatement? Explain. See *NLRB v. Midwestern Personnel Services,* 322 F.3d 969 (7th Cir. 2003).

8. Local 582 engaged in an economic strike against Broadview Dairy of Spokane, Washington. Local 582 tried to distribute handbills at several Albertson's groceries in the Spokane area. The handbills urged customers to refrain from buying Broadview products, which Albertson's sold. Albertson's formal policy forbade all solicitations, but some groups, such as Boy Scouts and area schools, were allowed on company property to make solicitations. Albertson's ordered the union members off its property. Later, Albertson's ordered union organizers off its property where they were trying to encourage Albertson's employees to join their union. Local 582 filed an unfair labor practices charge against Albertson's. Does Albertson's have the right to exclude from its property nonemployee union representatives who engage in either nonorganizing or organizing activities? Explain. See *Albertson's Inc. v. National Labor Relations Board,* 301 F.3d 441 (6th Cir. 2002).

9. A union–management dispute led to an economic strike, at which point the employer hired replacement workers. At the end of the strike, the workforce consisted of 25 former strikers and 69 replacement workers. The agreement settling the strike provided that strikers would be recalled as vacancies arose. However, the employer did not follow the agreement when it recalled four workers (three of whom were replacements) and failed to consider any of 28 strikers who remained out of work.

Well-settled labor law provides that "economic strikers who have been permanently replaced but who have unconditionally offered to return to work are entitled to reinstatement upon the departure of the replacements." The NLRB found a violation of the National Labor Relations Act, and framed the issue as follows: "How should the layoff of the permanent replacement worker—who has a contractual right to recall—affect the reinstatement rights of unreinstated strikers?" The NLRB ruled that it would require a showing that the laid-off replacements had no "reasonable expectancy of recall." Then the burden of proof would shift to the employer to justify its failure to recall strikers when vacancies arose. The NLRB decision was appealed. Decide. Explain. See *Aqua-Chem, Inc. v. NLRB,* 910 F.2d 1487 (7th Cir., 1990); cert. den. 111 S.Ct. 2871 (1991).

10. Some employees were transferred from a unionized plant to a new location.

   a. Are the employees who were transferred to the new location still members of their original bargaining unit? Explain.

   b. What test should the National Labor Relations Board employ in deciding whether the employer must recognize and bargain with the union in the new location? See *Gitano Group, Inc.,* 308 NLRB No. 173 (1992).

11. A field organizer for the International Brotherhood of Electrical Workers sought work with a nonunion electrical firm. In applying for a job as an electrician, the organizer told the company that he would use his time during lunch and after work in an effort to organize employees. Indeed, while his application was being processed, he organized a picket line at the company to protest low wages. The foreman then told the organizer that he would not be hired because "it's kind of hard to hire you when you're out there on the other side picketing." Had he been hired, the organizer acknowledged that he would have maintained some relationship with the union, and he would likely have later returned to full-time employment with the union. Was the organizer unlawfully denied employment? Explain. See *Willmar Electric Service, Inc. v. National Labor Relations Board,* 968 F.2d 1327 (D.C. Cir. 1992); cert. den. 113 S.Ct. 1252 (1993).

12. Jerry Kirby was discharged from his job at Ford Motor Company, allegedly because of "being under the influence of alcohol, absenteeism, and threatening management." The United Auto Workers union (UAW) immediately filed a grievance on Kirby's behalf. Kirby lost through the first three steps of the grievance process, and the UAW declined to appeal to arbitration on Kirby's behalf. The UAW said that Kirby had no right to appeal because he had allowed his union membership to lapse. Kirby then filed an unfair labor practice charge against the union. Decide. Explain. See *International Union v. NLRB,* 168 F.3d 509 (D.C. Cir. 1999).

13. *a.* Can an employer lawfully discharge a group of employees who walk out in protest of working conditions?

   b. Would it matter if the collective bargaining agreement contains a no-strike clause? Explain.

14. What steps can an employer lawfully take to provide the labor necessary to keep a plant operative during a strike?

Notes

1. Associated Press, "Flow of Workers from Unions Stanched," *Des Moines Register,* February 18, 1997, p. 4A.

2. For some data on the union split and an overview of the issues dividing the parties, see Carl F. Horowitz, "Labor's Family Feud," *The American Spectator Online,* August 11, 2005 [**www.spectator.org**].

3. Peter L. Francia, "A Fruitful Division of Labor?" *The Raleigh News & Observer,* August 26, 2005, p. A17.

4. Associated Press, "Labor Issues Gain Attention of College Staff and Students," *Waterloo/Cedar Falls Courier,* March 11, 2002, p. A2.

5. Carlos Tejada, "Graduate Students at Private Universities Have Right to Unionize, Agency Rules," *The Wall Street Journal,* November 2, 2000, p. B22.

6. *Los Angeles Times,* "NLRB Rejects Students' Bid to Unionize," *Waterloo/Cedar Falls Courier,* July 18, 2004, p. A2.

7. Glenn Burkins, "Numbers of Workers in Labor Unions Grew Last Year," *The Wall Street Journal,* January 26, 1999, p. B12.

8. Editorial, "Labor of Politics," *The Wall Street Journal,* March 4, 2005, p. A14.

9. Editorial, "Labor of Politics."

10. Steven Greenhouse, "Update on Capitalism: What Do You Mean 'Us,' Boss?" *The New York Times,* September 1, 2002, Sec. 4, p. 3.

11. Greenhouse, "Update on Capitalism."

12. Carlos Tejada, "The Checkoff," *The Wall Street Journal,* January 21, 2002, p. A1.

13. Eric Brazil, "Reaching Out: Unions Widen Their World," *San Francisco Chronicle,* September 2, 2001, p. W1.

14. Isaac A. Hourwich, *Immigration and Labor* (New York: Arno Press, 1969), pp. 125–45.

15. John J. Flagler, *The Labor Movement in the United States* (Minneapolis: Lerner Publications, 1972), pp. 26–28.

16. Alan Glassman, Naomi Berger Davidson, and Thomas Cummings, *Labor Relations: Reports from the Firing Line* (New York: Business Publications, Inc., 1988), pp. 5–6.

17. Flagler, *Labor Movement,* pp. 26–28.

18. Eli Ginzberg and Hyman Berman, *The American Worker in the Twentieth Century: A History through Autobiographies* (New York: Free Press, 1963), pp. 193–95, in *I Am a Woman Worker,* ed. Andria Taylor Hourwich and Gladys L. Palmer, Affiliated Schools for Workers, 1936, pp. 17 ff.

19. Flagler, *Labor Movement,* pp. 33 and 36, quoting Frederick Lewis Allen, *The Big Change: . . . America Transforms Itself, 1900–1950* (New York: Harper, 1952).

20. Flagler, *Labor Movement,* p. 47.

21. J. David Greenstone, *Labor in American Politics* (New York: Alfred A. Knopf, 1969), p. 21.

22. Archibald Cox, with Derek Bok and Robert A. Gorman, *Cases and Materials on Labor Law,* 8th ed. (Mineola, NY: Foundation Press, 1977), pp. 7–8.

23. Greenstone, *Labor in American Politics,* p. 22.

24. Greenstone, *Labor in American Politics,* p. 23.

25. Patrick Hardin, *The Developing Labor Law* (Washington, DC: Bureau of National Affairs, 1992), pp. 31–32.

26. Hardin, *The Developing Labor Law,* p. 94.

27. Hardin, *The Developing Labor Law,* pp. 1, 108.

28. *Steele v. Louisville and Nashville Railroad,* 323 U.S. 192 (1944).

29. *Vaca v. Sipes,* 386 U.S. 171 (1967); *Miranda Fuel Co.,* 140 NLRB 181 (1962).

30. The National Labor Relations Act is found in Title 29 U.S.C. § 151 et seq.

31. Cox, *Labor Law,* pp. 113–22.

32. Cox, *Labor Law,* pp. 99–101.

33. David Wessel, "Some Workers Gain with New Union Tactics," *The Wall Street Journal,* January 31, 2002, p. A1.

34. *National Labor Relations Board v. Kentucky River Community Care, Inc.,* 121 S.Ct. 1861 (2001).

35. *Lechmere, Inc. v. NLRB,* 502 U.S. 527 (1992).

36. *NLRB v. Town & Country Electric, Inc.,* 516 U.S. 85 (1998).

37. See *Sewell Mfg. Co.,* 138 NLRB 66 (1962), which states that the board's goal is to conduct elections "in a laboratory under conditions as nearly ideal as possible to determine the uninhibited desires of employees" and "to provide an atmosphere conducive to the sober and informed exercise of the franchise free from . . . elements which prevent or impede reasonable choice."

38. 375 U.S. 409 (1964).

39. *Trencor, Inc. v. National Labor Relations Board,* 110 F.3d 268 (5th Cir. 1997).

40. *NLRB v. Gissell Packing,* 395 U.S. 575 (1969).

41. Benjamin J. Taylor and Fred Whitney, *Labor Relations Law,* 4th ed. (Englewood Cliffs, NJ: Prentice Hall, 1983), p. 406.

42. *Majure Transport Co. v. NLRB,* 198 F.2d 735 (5th Cir. 1952).

43. *NLRB v. Norfolk Shipbuilding & Drydock Corp.,* 172 F.2d 813 (4th Cir. 1949).

44. *Southern Saddlery Co.,* 90 NLRB 1205 (1950).

45. See *First National Maintenance Corporation v. NLRB,* 101 S.Ct. 2573 (1981).

46. Littler, Mendelson Fastiff and Tichy *The 1990 Employer* (San Francisco: Littler Mendelson, Fastiff and Tichy, P.C., 1990), p. V6.

47. *NLRB v. Mackay Radio & Tel. Co.,* 304 U.S. 333 (1938).

48. Littler, et al., *The 1990 Employer,* p. V6.

49. *United Steelworkers of America v. Sadlowski,* 457 U.S. 102 (1982).

50. 334 NLRB No. 92 (2001).

51. 487 U.S. 735 (1988).

52. Robert Perkovich and Mark Stein, "Challenges to Arbitration under Illinois Public Sector Labor Relations Statutes," *Hofstra Labor Law Journal* 7, no. 1 (Fall 1989), p. 197.

Selected Topics in Government–Business Relations

Consumer Protection

Introduction

Fans of Miss Cleo the "Jamaican" television "psychic" must be suffering withdrawal pains since the famous seer packed her tarot cards in the fall of 2002. Miss Cleo, who reportedly was more a California Valley Girl than the Jamaican shaman she claimed, evidently did not foresee the weight of the American legal system coming down on her. Under pressure from the U.S. Federal Trade Commission, two companies associated with Cleo, Access Resource Services and Psychic Readers Network, Inc., agreed to pay a $5 million fine and cancel $500 million in billings. Smaller settlements were subsequently reached with at least five states. Before her legal problems, Miss Cleo had been a spectacular financial success:

> Her honeyed words persuaded millions to pick up the phone and call, bringing in millions of dollars. . . . But the calls also generated 2,000 complaints across the United States from people who said they had been the victims of duplicitous marketing and outright fraud. Miss Cleo herself has not been charged, as it turns out she rarely answered the phone. Instead callers were farmed out to contract workers. . . . At $4.99 a minute, the numbers quickly added up. . . . People who had asked to be placed on a "do not call" list were contacted, while others received up to 10 calls a day, usually automated messages telling them, "Miss Cleo had a dream about them and they should call back."[1]

Doubtless the government should not always protect us from our own foolishness, but costly consumer fraud and other forms of consumer abuse (invasion of privacy, dangerous products, identity theft, false advertising, and so on) are not unusual in our consumption-driven lives. Historically we relied on the market to address those problems; but in recent decades legislatures, courts, and administrative agencies have developed laws and rulings to protect us where the market arguably has failed. This chapter surveys some of those legal interventions.

Part One—Common Law Consumer Protection

Later in this chapter we will explore government efforts to protect consumers from dangerous products, unfair lending practices, and the like. Before turning to that legislation, we need to appreciate the common law (judge-made law) that preceded and, in some respects, provided the foundation for the many federal, state, and local initiatives of recent years. In addition to the product liability protection (negligence, warranties, and strict liability) discussed in Chapter 7, injured consumers can look to several common law protections, including actions for fraud, misrepresentation, and unconscionability. [For an extensive menu of consumer law sites, see **http://www.lectlaw.com/files/cos19.htm**]

Fraud and Innocent Misrepresentation

If the market is to operate efficiently, the buyer must be able to rely on the truth of the seller's affirmations regarding a product. Regrettably, willful untruths appear to be common in American commerce. A victim of fraud is entitled to rescind the contract in question and to seek damages, including, in cases of malice, a punitive recovery. Although fraud arises in countless situations and thus is difficult to define, the legal community has generally adopted the following elements, each of which must be proven:

1. Misrepresentation of a material fact.
2. The misrepresentation was intentional.
3. The injured party justifiably relied on the misrepresentation.
4. Injury resulted.

In identifying a fraudulent expression, the law distinguishes between statements of objective, verifiable facts and simple expressions of opinion. The latter ordinarily are not fraudulent even though they are erroneous. Thus normal sales puffing ("This baby is the greatest little car you're ever gonna drive") is fully lawful, and consumers are expected to exercise good judgment in responding to such claims. However, if a misleading expression of opinion comes from an expert, and the other party does not share that expertise (such as in the sale of a diamond engagement ring), a court probably would offer a remedy.

Silence

In limited circumstances, silence may constitute fraud. Typically, that problem may emerge where party A misunderstands the facts of the situation and party B both knows the true facts and knows that A does not know those facts and cannot reasonably be expected to discover them. An example would be a cracked engine block, where the cracks were filled with a sealer and covered with a compound such that the crack is unlikely to be discovered even by capable inspection.[2] In such situations, the knowledgeable party may be under a duty to speak. Nonetheless, the general rule is that silence is fully permissible.

Of course, fraud can involve false conduct as well as false expression. A familiar example is the car seller who rolls back an odometer with the result that the buyer is misled.

A variation on the general theme of fraud is innocent misrepresentation, which differs from fraud only in that the falsehood was unintentional. The wrongdoer believed the statement or conduct in question to be true, but he or she was mistaken. In such cases, the wronged party may secure rescission of the contract, but ordinarily damages are not awarded. The following case involves a fraud claim against Harley-Davidson.

Tietsworth v. Harley-Davidson
677 N. W.2d 233 (Wis. S.Ct. 2004)

Justice Diane S. Sykes

The circuit court dismissed the entire action for failure to state a claim. [T]he court of appeals reinstated [the claims.]

* * * * *

FACTS AND PROCEDURAL HISTORY

Plaintiff Steven C. Tietsworth and the members of the proposed class own or lease 1999 or early-2000 model year Harley motorcycles equipped with Twin Cam 88 or Twin Cam 88B engines. Harley's marketing and advertising literature contained the following statement about the TC-88 engines:

> Developing [the TC-88s] was a six-year process. . . . The result is a masterpiece. We studied everything from the way oil moves through the inside, to the way a rocker cover does its job of staying oil-tight. Only 21 functional parts carry over into the new design. What does carry over is the power of a Harley-Davidson™ engine, only more so.

Harley also stated that the motorcycles were "premium" quality, and described the TC-88 engine as "eighty-eight cubic inches filled to the brim with torque and ready to take you thundering down the road."

On January 22, 2001, Harley sent a letter to Tietsworth and other owners of Harley motorcycles informing them that "the rear cam bearing in a small number of Harley-Davidson's Twin Cam 88 engines has failed. While it is unlikely that you will ever have to worry about this situation, you have our assurance that Harley-Davidson is committed to your satisfaction." The letter went on to explain that the company was extending the warranty on the cam bearing from the standard one-year/unlimited mileage warranty to a five-year/50,000 mile warranty. Separately, Harley developed a $495 "cam bearing repair kit" and made the kit available to its dealers and service departments "to expedite rear cam bearing repair."

* * * * *

The amended complaint alleges that the cam bearing mechanism in the 1999 and early-2000 model year TC-88 engines is inherently defective, causing an unreasonably dangerous propensity for premature engine failure. [T]he amended complaint alleged that Harley's failure to disclose the cam bearing defect induced the plaintiffs to purchase their motorcycles by causing them to reasonably rely upon Harley's representations regarding the "premium" quality of the motorcycles.

The amended complaint further alleges that if the plaintiffs had known of the engine defect, they either would not have purchased the product or would have paid less for it. The amended complaint does not allege that the plaintiffs' motorcycles have actually suffered engine failure, have malfunctioned in any way, or are reasonably certain to fail or malfunction. Nor does the amended complaint allege any property damage or personal injury arising out of the engine defect. Rather, the amended complaint alleges that the plaintiffs' motorcycles have diminished value, including diminished resale value, because Harley motorcycles equipped with TC-88 engines have demonstrated a "propensity" for premature engine failure and/or fail prematurely.

* * * * *

DISCUSSION
Common-Law Fraud Claim

The plaintiffs' common-law fraud claim is premised on the allegation that Harley failed to disclose or concealed the existence of the cam bearing defect prior to the plaintiffs' purchases of their motorcycles. It is well established that a nondisclosure is not actionable as a misrepresentation tort unless there is a duty to disclose. *Ollerman v. O'Rourke Co., Inc.*, 94 Wis. 2d 17, 26, 288 N.W. 2d 95 (1980). Our decision in *Ollerman* outlined the three categories of misrepresentation in Wisconsin law—intentional misrepresentation, negligent misrepresentation, and strict responsibility misrepresentation—and described the common and distinct elements of the three torts.

All misrepresentation claims share the following required elements: (1) the defendant must have made a representation of fact to the plaintiff; (2) the representation of fact must be false; and (3) the plaintiff must have believed and relied on the misrepresentation to his detriment or damage. The plaintiffs here allege intentional misrepresentation, which carries the following additional elements: (4) the defendant must have made the misrepresentation with knowledge that it was false or recklessly without caring whether it was true or false; and (5) the defendant must have made the misrepresentation with intent to deceive and to induce the plaintiff to act on it to his detriment or damage.

Ollerman reiterated the general rule that in a sales or business transaction, "silence, a failure to disclose a fact, is not an intentional misrepresentation unless the seller has a duty to disclose." The existence and scope of a duty to disclose are questions of law for the court. *Ollerman* held that "a subdivider–vendor of a residential lot has a duty to a 'noncommercial' purchaser to disclose facts which are known to the vendor, which are material to the transaction, and which are not readily discernible to the purchaser." We specified that this was a "narrow holding," premised on certain policy considerations present in noncommercial real estate transactions.

The transactions at issue here, however, are motorcycle purchases, not residential real estate purchases, and it is an open question whether the duty to disclose recognized in *Ollerman* extends more broadly to sales of consumer goods. . . .

No Legally Cognizable Injury

Ollerman also held that damages in intentional misrepresentation cases are measured according to the "benefit of the bargain" rule, "typically stated as the difference between the value of the property as represented and its actual value as purchased." . . .

[W]e have generally held that a tort claim is not capable of present enforcement (and therefore does not accrue) unless the plaintiff has suffered actual damage. . . . Actual damage is harm that has already occurred or is "reasonably certain" to occur in the future. . . . Actual damage is not the mere possibility of future harm. . . . [T]he amended complaint must adequately plead an actual injury—a loss or damage that has already occurred or is reasonably certain to occur—in order to state an actionable fraud claim. . . .

The injury complained of here is diminution in value only—the plaintiffs allege that their motorcycles are worth less than they paid for them. However, the amended complaint does not allege that the plaintiffs' motorcycles have diminished value because their engines have failed, will fail, or are reasonably certain to fail as a result of the TC-88 cam bearing defect. The amended complaint does not allege that the plaintiffs have sold their motorcycles at a loss because of the alleged engine defect. The amended complaint alleges only that the motorcycles have diminished value—primarily diminished potential resale value—because Harley motorcycles equipped with TC-88 engines have demonstrated a "propensity" for premature engine failure and/or will fail as a result of the cam bearing defect. This is insufficient to state a legally cognizable injury for purposes of a fraud claim.

Diminished value premised upon a mere possibility of future product failure is too speculative and uncertain to support a fraud claim. The plaintiffs do not specifically allege that their particular motorcycles will fail prematurely, only that the Harley product line that consists of motorcycles with TC-88 engines has demonstrated a propensity for premature engine failure. An allegation that a particular product line fails prematurely does not constitute an allegation that the plaintiffs' particular motorcycles will do so, only that there is a possibility that they will do so.

We certainly agree with the court of appeals that the damage allegations in a fraud complaint are not evaluated against a standard of "absolute certainty" for purposes of a motion to dismiss for failure to state a claim. But an allegation that a product is diminished in value because of an event or circumstance that might—or might not—occur in the future is inherently conjectural and does not allege actual benefit-of-the-bargain damages with the "reasonable certainty" required to state a fraud claim.

* * * * *

[Reversed.] [The plaintiffs' additional claims are omitted.—Ed.]

Questions

1. *a.* According to the Wisconsin Supreme Court, under what circumstances might the nondisclosure by a seller of a defect constitute misrepresentation?

   b. Did the court find that Harley-Davidson had a duty to disclose in this case? Explain.

2. *a.* What injury, if any, do the plaintiffs claim they suffered in this episode?

   b. According to the Wisconsin Supreme Court, must a plaintiff in a fraud action prove that he or she has suffered actual damages prior to bringing a claim? Explain.

   c. What is the "benefit of the bargain" rule?

3. Why did the Wisconsin Supreme Court rule for the defendant Harley-Davidson in this case?

4. Robert McGlothlin, an employee of Thomson Consumer Electronics in Bloomington, Indiana, was injured while loading televisions into a semi-trailer when the trailer's "landing gear" (retractable legs that support the front of the trailer when it is not attached to the semi-tractor) collapsed. McGlothlin sued the owner of the trailer, among others, claiming that the defendants' repair and inspection procedures for *latent* (hidden) defects were inadequate. Should the court treat latent defects differently than *patent* (observable) defects in determining when a legal duty exists? Explain. See *McGlothlin v. M & U Trucking*, 688 N.E.2d 1243 (Ind. S.Ct. 1997).

Unconscionable Contracts

The doctrine of unconscionability emerged from court decisions where jurists concluded that some contracts are so unfair or oppressive as to demand intervention. (Unconscionability is also included in state statutory laws via the Uniform Commercial Code 2–302.) The legal system intrudes on contracts only with the greatest reluctance. Mere foolishness or want of knowledge does not constitute grounds for unconscionability, nor is a contract unconscionable and hence unenforceable merely because one party is spectacularly clever and the other is not. Unconscionability takes two forms:

1. *Procedural unconscionability* is a situation where the bargaining power of the parties was so unequal that the agreement, as a practical matter, was not freely entered. Procedural unconscionability usually arises from lack of knowledge or lack of choice. A consumer may not be reasonably knowledgeable about a contract because of the use of fine print, inconspicuously displayed contract terms, or complex legalese. A consumer may not have voluntarily entered a contract because of lack of time, pressing circumstances, or market conditions.

2. *Substantive unconscionability* is a situation where the clause or contract in question was so manifestly one-sided, oppressive, or unfair as to "shock the conscience of the court." A contract price dramatically exceeding the market price, a contract that does not provide a remedy for a breach, or contract terms completely out of line with the relative risks assumed by the parties are among the conditions that might lead to a finding of substantive unconscionability.

Part Two—The Consumer and Government Regulation of Business

State Laws

Having looked at the common law foundation of consumer protection, we turn to some of the many governmental measures that provide shelter in the marketplace. Many states have enacted comprehensive consumer protection statutes, such as Pennsylvania's Unfair Practices and Consumer Protection Law. States also have specific statutes addressing such problems as door-to-door sales, debtor protection, and telemarketing fraud. We will look at only one of those, the so-called lemon laws, which address the particularly frustrating problem of a hopelessly defective vehicle.

Lemon Laws New car purchases are covered by warranty laws (see Chapter 7 for a discussion of UCC warranty provisions and the federal Magnuson–Moss Warranty Act); in addition, all 50 states have some form of law designed to provide recourse for consumers whose new vehicles turn out to be defective such that they cannot be repaired after a reasonable effort. The quarrel, of course, is about when a car is truly a lemon. Lemon laws differ significantly from state to state, but they often cover new cars for one to two years or 12,000 to 18,000 miles after purchase. Typically state

> The quarrel, of course, is about when a car is truly a lemon.

laws provide that the vehicle must have been returned to the manufacturer or dealer three or four times to repair the same defect and that defect must substantially impair the value or safety of the vehicle, *or* the vehicle must have been unavailable to the consumer for a total of at least 30 days in a 12-month period. Such a vehicle is a lemon, and the purchaser is entitled to a replacement vehicle or full refund of the purchase price. In some states, used cars may also be treated as lemons. In almost all states, the determination about whether a car is a lemon is handled by an arbitration panel. If dissatisfied with the ruling, the consumer may then file suit.

Suzuki Sucks?

Clearly one Suzuki purchaser thinks so:

> Eric Wiedemer, a 32-year-old Cincinnati auto painter, incurred corporate wrath when he created a Web gripe site to complain about a $20,000 Suziki Verona car he bought from an Alabama dealer. From the day he drove it home, he said, the engine stalled repeatedly. Unable to resolve the problem at a local Suzuki dealership, he hired a lawyer and created the Web site **www.suzukiveronasucks.com.** American Suzuki Motors Corp. bought back the car but wouldn't pay Wiedemer's legal bill and threatened possible legal action.

Suzuki said that Wiedemer's Web site contained defamatory, misleading, and inaccurate information. Several consumers have been sued because of their Web gripe sites. Consumers have often prevailed to date, but corporations do have legal rights, and false statements about verifiable facts do, in general, constitute defamation whether the victim is a person or a corporation. [For another current gripe site, see **www.myvwlemon.com**]

Source: James McNair, "Big Business Avenges Web Gripe Sites," *Des Moines Sunday Register,* February 27, 2005, p. 6D.

The case that follows examines Connecticut's lemon law requirements. [For "The Lemon Car Page," see **http://www.mindspring.com/~wf1/**]

LEGAL BRIEFCASE

General Motors Corporation v. Dohmann
722 A.2d 1205 (Conn. S.Ct. 1998)

Chief Justice Callahan

The sole issue in this appeal is whether the Connecticut "lemon law" requires the plaintiff, General Motors Corporation, to provide the defendant, Eugene Dohmann, with a replacement vehicle.

* * * * *

The arbitration panel to which the matter had been referred subsequent to the defendant having instituted an arbitration proceeding reasonably could have found the following facts. On October 26, 1996, the defendant purchased a new Chevrolet S-10 pickup truck (truck) from Maritime Motors (Maritime), a General Motors dealership located in South Norwalk. The following day, the defendant noticed defects in the paint on the truck's hood, roof, and bumpers. The defendant promptly notified Maritime of the defects and requested that the dealership provide him with a replacement vehicle. Maritime agreed to inspect the truck for defects, but refused the defendant's request for a replacement vehicle.

After inspecting the truck, Maritime agreed that the truck's paint was defective, but again refused to provide a different vehicle. Instead, the dealership offered to replace the truck's hood, the part of the truck on which the paint defects were most visible, with a hood taken from another vehicle of the same color. The defendant allowed Maritime to undertake that repair attempt. The replacement hood, however, did not fit properly and the paint was not an exact match. Dissatisfied with the repair attempt, the defendant told Maritime to reinstall the original hood, and Maritime complied.

Maritime subsequently suggested two other possible methods of curing the defects in the paint: (1) wet sanding and (2) repainting the affected areas of the truck. The defendant, however, rejected these suggestions because he believed that both wet sanding and repainting would remove the truck's original factory finish. In the defendant's view, the factory process produces a paint finish superior to that of a body shop. . . .

Thereafter, the defendant initiated an arbitration proceeding against the plaintiff. After a hearing, a three-member arbitration panel determined that (1) the truck had been subject to a reasonable number of unsuccessful repair attempts, and (2) the defective paint substantially impaired the truck's value to the defendant. Consequently, the panel concluded that the defendant was entitled to a new, comparably equipped replacement vehicle.

On appeal, the plaintiff claims that the trial court improperly affirmed the decision of the arbitration panel. Specifically, the plaintiff maintains that the record does not contain substantial evidence to support the arbitrators' findings that (1) the truck had been subject to a reasonable number of repair attempts, and (2) the defects in the paint substantially impaired the value of the truck to the defendant.

Our analysis begins with a brief overview of Connecticut's lemon law legislation. "In 1982, the Connecticut legislature enacted Public Acts 1982, No. 82–287 (Lemon Law I). For consumer buyers of new motor vehicles, the act provides supplemental remedies of repair, replacement, and refund to facilitate the enforcement of express warranties made by the manufacturers of such vehicles. These supplemental remedies come into play whenever a manufacturer or authorized dealer, after a reasonable number of repair attempts, is unable substantially to conform a new vehicle to the terms of the express warranty. . . .

"In 1984, the legislature enacted Public Acts 1984, No. 84–338 (Lemon Law II). The purpose of Lemon Law II is to provide, for consumer purchasers of new motor vehicles, an alternative to civil litigation. The key provision authorizes the department of consumer protection to establish 'an independent arbitration procedure for the settlement of disputes between consumers and manufacturers of motor vehicles which do not conform to all applicable warranties.'"

* * * * *

II

The plaintiff first claims . . . that, because the additional repairs suggested by the dealership were capable of producing a paint finish that met factory standards, the single attempt to cure the defect by replacing the truck's hood was insufficient to constitute the requisite reasonable number of repair attempts. We disagree.

Section 42–179 provides in relevant part: "(d) If the manufacturer, or its agents or authorized dealers, are unable to conform the motor vehicle to any applicable express warranty by repairing or correcting any defect or condition which substantially impairs the use, safety, or value of the motor vehicle to the consumer *after a reasonable number of [repair] attempts, the* manufacturer shall replace the motor vehicle with a new motor vehicle acceptable to the consumer . . . (e) It shall be presumed that a reasonable number of [repair] attempts have been undertaken . . . if . . . the same nonconformity has been subject to repair four or more times. . . . No claim shall be made under this section unless at least one attempt to repair a nonconformity has been made."

* * * * *

[T]he legislative program and review committee's report read in relevant part, "Generally a reasonable number of repair attempts is defined as four attempts during the first 18,000 miles or two years and the problem continues to exist. . . . In some instances, less than four repair attempts is allowed if the problem is one for which evidence exists that no repair will bring the vehicle back into conformance." The report further states, "In cases involving problems with the paint on a vehicle, a determination may be made that it is impossible for any dealer to repaint the vehicle in a manner that would match the type of finish originally achieved at the manufacturer's plant when the car was built." Consequently, if the record contains substantial evidence to support a finding that proposed additional repair attempts would not have produced a paint finish that satisfied factory paint specifications, arbitrators reasonably may find that a single repair attempt is sufficient.

The record before us reveals the following regarding the utility of additional repair attempts. The plaintiff presented affidavits of two automobile body experts who stated that body shop paint processes are capable of producing results equal to, and in some cases superior to, those produced by the original factory paint process. The state's technical expert, Gregory Carver, however, testified that the conditions under which the factory originally paints a vehicle are superior to those that exist in a body shop. Specifically Carver stated that paint bonds to the surface of a vehicle most successfully the first time it is applied, and that, therefore, it is impossible for a body shop to duplicate the bond achieved at the factory. Carver further stated that the finish of a repainted vehicle is less durable than the finish applied at the factory.

. . . [O]n the basis of Carver's testimony, the arbitration panel reasonably could have concluded that the suggested additional repair attempts would not have produced a finish that met factory paint specifications. We conclude, therefore, that the record contains substantial evidence to support the panel's conclusion that, under the circumstances, Maritime's attempt to replace the truck's hood constituted a reasonable number of repair attempts.

III

The plaintiff next claims that the arbitrators improperly concluded that the paint defects substantially impaired the value of the truck to the defendant.

*   *   *   *   *

A

Our analysis begins with the language of [the statute]. Section 42–179 (d) provides in relevant part; "If the manufacturer, or its agents or authorized dealers, are unable to conform the motor vehicle to any applicable express warranty by repairing or correcting any defect or condition which *substantially impairs the . . . value of the motor vehicle to the consumer* . . . the manufacturer shall replace the motor vehicle." The phrase "to the consumer" in § 42–179 (d) suggests that the needs and expectations of the individual consumer should be considered in a determination of whether a defect has substantially impaired the value of a vehicle. That language, therefore, suggests that the legislature intended to incorporate a subjective component into the determination of "substantial impairment" under § 42–179 (d).

Other language contained in § 42–179 (d), however, indicates that the standard for "substantial impairment" was intended to incorporate an objective component as well as a subjective component. Specifically, § 42–179 (d) provides that "*it shall be an affirmative defense to any claim under this section. . . that an alleged nonconformity does not substantially impair such . . . value . . .*" The statutory provision that permits a manufacturer to show that the value of a vehicle has not, in fact, been substantially impaired, suggests that the subjective opinion of the consumer is not dispositive. If the standard were completely subjective, the manufacturer would almost never be able to prove lack of "substantial impairment," and thus, the right to prove that the value of the vehicle had not been substantially impaired would be meaningless.

*   *   *   *   *

We conclude, therefore, that under the lemon law the standard for determining whether a defect substantially impairs the use, safety, or value of a motor vehicle to the consumer is both subjective and objective. The standard is subjective in that the fact finder first must examine the subjective desires, needs, and circumstances of the particular consumer. In light of those desires, needs, and circumstances, the fact finder then must make an objective determination as to whether the value of the motor vehicle to the consumer has, in fact, been substantially impaired. In making this determination, the fact finder must determine that the consumer's subjective desires, needs, and circumstances are reasonable.

B

Having articulated the standard for substantial impairment under the lemon law, we address the plaintiff's claim that the record does not contain substantial evidence to support a finding that the evident defects in the paint substantially impaired the truck's value to the defendant.

During the arbitration hearing, the defendant testified that he takes great pride in the appearance of the vehicles that he owns and maintains the finish of those vehicles in factory condition. Moreover, he stated that appearance was a major factor in his decision to purchase a new truck rather than a used one. On the basis of that testimony, the arbitrators reasonably could have concluded that, had the defendant known of the defects in the paint before accepting delivery, he would not have purchased the truck, and that the statutory requirement of subjective substantial impairment had been satisfied.

Carver, the state's technical expert, testified that, on a scale of 1 to 10, with 10 representing the worst amount of damage, the damage to the truck constituted a 3. Carver further stated that the paint defects could not be removed easily. Moreover, Carver corroborated the defendant's contention that wet sanding and repainting the truck would remove its finish. Finally, Carver stated that the paint defects possibly could affect the resale value of the vehicle and that if the vehicle was not maintained meticulously, the affected areas could deteriorate further. Thus, on the basis of Carver's testimony, the arbitrators reasonably could have concluded that the statutory requirement of objective substantial impairment had been satisfied.

We conclude, therefore, that the record contains substantial evidence to support a finding that the defects in the truck's paint substantially impaired its value to the defendant.

Affirmed.

Questions

1. How did the court determine when a "reasonable" number of repair attempts had been undertaken?

2. *a.* What did the court mean in saying that "the standard for determining whether a defect substantially impairs the use, safety, or value of a motor vehicle to the consumer is both subjective and objective?"

   b. What was the significance of that dual standard to the outcome of the case?

3. Dieter and Hermes agreed to buy a new 1996 Dodge Ram pickup truck from Fascona Chrysler-Plymouth-Dodge Trucks on December 12, 1995. They requested the installation of some after-market accessories—a tonneau cover, a bug shield, and rustproofing. When Dieter and Hermes returned to take delivery of the truck, they noticed it had been scratched during the installation of the accessories. The salesperson told them the scratches would be repaired. Four months later the dealership sent the truck to a body shop for repairs. After repair, Dieter and Hermes noticed swirl marks in the truck's finish. Dieter then demanded that Frascona repurchase the truck. Eight months later Dieter and Hermes sued Chrysler Corporation under Wisconsin's lemon law.

   a. Make the argument that the lemon law does not apply to the facts of this case.

   b. Decide the case. Explain. See *Dieter and Hermes v. Chrysler Corporation,* 610 N.W. 2d 832 (Wis. S.Ct. 2000).

Federal Laws and Consumer Protection Agencies

The Federal Trade Commission (FTC)

The Federal Trade Commission was created in 1914 to prevent "unfair methods of competition and unfair or deceptive acts or practices in and affecting commerce." In conducting its business, the FTC performs as a miniature government with extensive and powerful quasi-legislative and quasi-judicial roles. [For the FTC's Bureau of Consumer Protection home page, see **http://www.ftc.gov/bcp/bcp.htm**]

Rule Making

The FTC's primary legislative direction is in issuing trade regulation rules to enforce the intent of broadly drawn congressional legislation. That is, the rules specify particular acts or practices that the commission deems deceptive.

The FTC's quasi-legislative or rule-making power is extensive, as evidenced by the following examples:

- The Federal Trade Commission's Do Not Call Registry forbids telemarketers, with certain exceptions, from placing calls to the 85 million Americans who have added their phone numbers to the Federal Trade Commission's list. In February 2005 the FTC announced its first settlements in Do Not Call disputes. In this instance, two time-share sellers and a telemarketer agreed, without admitting any wrong, to pay civil penalties for the hundreds of thousands of calls placed to consumers on the Do

Not Call list. [Those wanting to be added to the list and those wanting to file complaints can visit **www.donotcall.gov**]

- The FTC announced in 2000 that the largest cigar companies had agreed to include health warning labels on packaging and in advertising. Cigar consumption grew by 70 percent from 1993 to 1998, and premium cigar sales grew by 250 percent. One 45-year-old smoker was not happy about the new rules:

It's a solution to overpopulation.

"It feels like King George is here," said Pat Godine, a Treasury Department employee. "It's a natural leaf. What if a few people die? I don't want to live 120 lives. It's a solution to overpopulation."[3]

Adjudication

On its own initiative or as a result of a citizen complaint, the FTC may investigate suspect trade practices. At that point the FTC may drop the proceeding, settle the matter, or issue a formal complaint.

Where an agreement cannot be reached, the FTC may proceed with a formal complaint, in which case the matter proceeds essentially as a trial conducted before an administrative law judge. The FTC has no authority to impose criminal sanctions.

Fraud and Deception

Unfair and deceptive trade practices, including those in advertising, are forbidden under Section 5 of the Federal Trade Commission Act. An unfair trade practice (1) must be likely to cause substantial injury to consumers, (2) must not be reasonably avoidable by consumers themselves, and (3) must not be outweighed by countervailing benefits to consumers or to competition. The FTC test for deception requires that the claim is (1) false or likely to mislead the reasonable consumer and (2) material to the consumer's decision making. Deception can take many forms, including, for example, testimonials by celebrities who do not use the endorsed product or do not have sufficient expertise to evaluate its quality. The primary areas of dispute involve quality and price.

Quality Claims

"Fewer calories," "faster acting," and "more effective" are the kinds of claims that may lead to allegations of deception unless they are factually supportable. Under the FTC's ad substantiation program, advertisers are engaging in unfair and deceptive practices if they make product claims without some reasonable foundation for those claims. For example, credible survey evidence must be in hand if an advertiser says, "Consumers prefer our brand two to one." Indeed, in recent years the FTC has settled many such claims, including a 2002 agreement with the makers of Wonder Bread regarding their claims that the bread included added calcium that could improve children's brain function and memory. The FTC said Wonder Bread had no proof that calcium helps children's brain performance. Wonder Bread has agreed not to make such claims without reliable scientific substantiation.

Pricing

Deception in price advertising sometimes takes the form of the so-called *bait and switch* practice, where a product is advertised at a very low price to attract customers although the seller actually has no intention of selling at that price. Once the customer is in the door (having taken the bait), the strategy is to switch the customer's attention to another, higher-priced product.

> **When is a sale not truly a sale?**

Sale pricing also sometimes leads to claims of deception. When is a sale not truly a sale? Do some retailers offer phony markdowns based on inflated "original" or "regular" prices? The FTC has long maintained guidelines for proving that a former price was genuine, but the problem is one that has been left largely to the states.

The Consumer Product Safety Commission (CPSC)

> **All-terrain vehicle accidents caused 357 deaths in 2002.**

All-terrain vehicle accidents caused 357 deaths in 2002, up 67 percent from 1997. That total exceeded the 2002 deaths on snowmobiles or personal watercraft, but the federal government has asserted little regulatory oversight. At this writing in 2005, the Consumer Product Safety Commission has been urged to ban the sale of adult-sized ATVs for use by children under 16; but the commission, skeptical about the wisdom of a ban, has instructed its staff to carefully review the ATV safety record to determine whether new rules are needed. The commission claims the power to ban the vehicles or order redesign if a substantial risk is established, but considerable evidence suggests that riding practices rather than design flaws are at issue.[4] The Consumer Product Safety Commission is the federal agency charged with protecting us from defects in consumer products; but with only a $62 million annual budget, the CPSC does not have the resources to routinely challenge corporations and to undertake careful investigations of thousands of products. Indeed, a 2004 *Consumer Reports* study concludes that the agency's inflation-adjusted budget has declined about 50 percent over 30 years, the staff has likewise shrunk by about 50 percent during that time, and enforcement actions were down 35 percent in 2003 from 2001.[5] In many instances, however, product recalls are undertaken voluntarily by the manufacturer. When the CPSC does decide to act, enforcement can be painfully slow. The child-safety standard for lighters, for example, required 10 years for commission approval.

On the other hand, the CPSC can be quite aggressive in encouraging industry cooperation. Graco Children's Products agreed in 2005 to pay $4 million to settle Consumer Product Safety Commission charges that Graco failed to notify the CPSC in a timely manner that some 12 million of its products could be hazardous to children. The company allegedly received reports of hundreds of injuries from its high chairs, swings, beds, and the like but failed to report the problems as the law requires.[6] [For the Consumer Product Safety Commission Web site, see **http://www.cpsc.gov/**]

Reducing Risk

The CPSC, created in 1972, is responsible for reducing the risks in using consumer products such as toys, lawn mowers, washing machines, bicycles, fireworks, pools, portable heaters, and household chemicals. The CPSC pursues product safety, initially, by *collecting data* and *issuing rules*. The commission conducts research and collects information as a foundation for regulating product safety. Via its rule-making authority, the CPSC promulgates mandatory consumer product safety, performance, and labeling standards. Public comments and suggestions are encouraged, but industry trade associations appear to have the bigger voice with the commission.

To enforce its policies and decisions, the CPSC holds both *compliance* and *enforcement* powers. In seeking compliance with safety expectations, the commission can exert a number of expectations. Manufacturers must certify before distribution that products meet federal safety standards. Manufacturing sites may be inspected, and specific product safety testing procedures can be mandated. Businesses other than retailers are required to keep product safety records. In cases of severe and imminent hazards, the CPSC may enforce its decisions by seeking a court order to remove a product from the market. In less urgent circumstances, the commission may proceed with its own administrative remedy. Preferring voluntary compliance, the commission may negotiate with the company to issue notice of its defective product or to repair or replace the product.

Where voluntary negotiations fail, the commission may proceed with an adjudicative hearing before an administrative law judge or members of the commission. That decision may be appealed to the full commission and thereafter to the federal court of appeals. Civil or criminal penalties may result. Only a few products have actually been banned from the market.

The Food and Drug Administration

The FDA is responsible for protecting the public from dangerous processed food (except meat and poultry), seafood, drugs, medical devices, radiation-emitting products, and cosmetics and for ensuring the effectiveness of drugs. [For the FDA Web site, see **http://www.fda.gov/**]

The FDA plays a broad, important role in the health and welfare of America. In recent years, the agency has, for example, banned the words *sunblock* and *waterproof* from sunscreen labels, declared nicotine-laced lollipops and lip balm illegal, and generally ensured that ad language is supported by scientific evidence. For example, Tropicana, a PepsiCo unit, settled an FTC complaint in 2005 that some of its ads saying that "heart healthy" orange juice could lower blood pressure were misleading. The settlement forbids Tropicana from making claims that "any food will have an effect on the risk of heart disease, stroke, or cancer" unless sound scientific evidence supports those claims. At this writing in 2005, the FDA is in the midst of one of its most highly publicized and interesting investigations. At FDA insistence, anti-inflammatory prescription painkillers Vioxx and Bextra have been removed from the market, and a competitor, Celebrex, is being sold only with a "black box" warning, the FDA's firmest. Scientific evidence satisfied the FDA that the enormously successful drugs dangerously raise the risk of heart attacks and strokes and may have caused, in the case of Vioxx alone, as many as 139,000 heart attacks, strokes, and deaths.[7]

Painkillers Vioxx and Bextra have been removed from the market.

Trust the Market?

Historically, the FDA was criticized for being too cautious and slow in allowing potentially helpful, new drugs on the market. The drug industry and free market advocates argued for greater faith in the market, and in 1992 the agency accelerated its drug approval process so that approval time fell from 27 to 14 months. However, at the same time the proportion of new drugs removed from the market for safety reasons jumped from 1.5 percent to 5 percent.[8] FDA officials have long complained that they do not have the financial resources to fully monitor drugs following their market entry, and some FDA scientists have said that they have felt pressure from their bosses to mute their findings and concerns about some drugs. Of course, differences of scientific opinion among experts are inevitable.

Are consumers at risk? Are consumers at risk? A 2004 survey found about two-thirds of FDA scientists are less than fully confident about the FDA's safety monitoring of prescription drugs now on the market, and one-third have some doubts about the process of approving new drugs.[9] One reason for those concerns is that drug companies may not be playing one of their crucial roles in the free market process by revealing what they know about the dangers of their own products. One Stanford University medical professor told Congress that Merck for several years had suppressed internal studies showing increased heart risks associated with Vioxx; and internal Merck e-mail suggests that Merck may have known about the increased risks as early as 1996.[10] But Merck argues that it acted responsibly in studying Vioxx carefully and removing it from the market when the evidence warranted that decision. One of the results of this regulatory battle is that thousands of lawsuits have been filed against Merck and others. The FDA, of course, is left with the very difficult job of balancing the benefits of a drug against its risks.

Consumer Privacy

Adelaide Andrews and Andrea Andrews aren't related. But for a while, a lot of people thought they were the same person. Andrea may have wanted it that way. The two met in 1993 when Adelaide visited a doctor. Andrea, the physician's receptionist, copied Adelaide's personal data, including her Social Security number and address—and then assumed her identity. Masquerading as Adelaide, Andrea racked up thousands of dollars in debt and ruined Adelaide's credit rating, which took years to put right. Such identity theft . . . has ensnared a number of prominent victims, including Tiger Woods, Ted Turner, and Oprah Winfrey.[11]

[For Federal Trade Commission advice on fighting ID theft, see **http://www.consumer.gov/idtheft/**]

Identity theft has exploded in recent years. Identity theft has exploded in recent years. In February 2005, for example, more than 145,000 personal records may have been breached at information broker Choice Point.[12] Choice Point, which collects and sells information, holds some 19 billion Social Security numbers, credit histories, job applications, vehicle registrations, lawsuits, and so on.[13] About 9.3 million U.S. adults suffered identity theft between October 2003 and September 2004.[14] Dumpster diving, stolen mail, computer hacking, a corrupt co-worker, or a credit card application improperly disposed of can lead to big financial losses and a nightmare of months or more. In most cases, consumers learn about such theft only after their Social Security numbers, credit card numbers, and other vital information have been used to make purchases, drain bank accounts, and so on. The odds of catching the bad guys in identity theft are estimated at about 1 in 700.[15]

The Choice Point scandal has critics calling for government intervention in the lightly regulated information industry. Only one state, California, requires data companies to notify consumers when their records have been compromised. California and a few other states have laws allowing consumers to completely "freeze" their credit records so that they cannot be accessed by anyone. Of course, to the credit industry, laws allowing a freeze amount to inefficient overkill. Marc Rotenberg, a privacy advocate, says the current problems "end the discussion on whether self-regulation works."[16] Nonetheless, proposed federal legislation has yet to gain traction.

Smoothly flowing information, on the other hand, is vital to efficiency in a free market economy. In some sense, we must pay for our privacy. A recent study concludes that "credit card interest rates as low as 6.9 percent are the direct result of competition in the financial services industry."[17] The authors, two university professors, argue that tighter privacy requirements could increase costs to consumers. The study examined the effects of proposed "opt-in" rules that would require express permission from consumers before their personal information could be shared. Those rules, according to the study, would "have the effect of choking off competition, raising costs, and possibly increasing the number of mailings required to achieve the same level of return."[18] So increased personal privacy may be paid for, at least in part, by reduced financial efficiency. But the potential for privacy abuse is chilling even if it might mean cheaper groceries:

> You swipe your savings card against a screen mounted on a supermarket shopping cart. As you move about the store, the screen flashes ads for products you usually buy, notes you haven't bought toothpaste in six months, and provides recipes and health information. All the while your every move—including which aisles you go down and how long you spend in each department—is tracked for marketing purposes via the savings cards, also known as loyalty cards. Such technology is in the works, and privacy advocates . . . are outraged.[19]

[For a privacy database and links, see **http://www.privacyrights.org/**]

Question

Mark Johnson of the *Tampa Tribune:*

> Comfort Inn has your number—your credit card number, that is.
>
> It only takes spending one night at a hotel or motel to put a customer and his or her credit card information into that company's database file. That dossier, however, can grow to include details such as what movies guests ordered, if they used the health club, and whether they golf.
>
> More sophisticated computer systems also can cull information from outside sources such as mailing lists, online public records, and census data to assemble a customer profile. The hotel may know the value of your house or whether you own a dog.[20]

What benefits come to customers and marketers from these intrusions on consumer privacy?

Credit Regulations

Perhaps you are operating a business selling furniture, appliances, cars, or other consumer goods, and your customers ordinarily do not pay in cash. You may have strong faith in the free market; however, Congress, the state legislatures, and most American people have decided that credit arrangements are so important, so confusing, and so potentially hurtful that they have supplemented the market's powerful messages with specific government rules. We will take an abbreviated look at several particularly important pieces of federal consumer credit legislation. [For a debtor/creditor law database, see **http://www.law.cornell.edu/topics/debtor_creditor.html**]

Truth in Lending Act (TILA)

As we increasingly turned to credit financing, consumers often did not understand the full cost of buying on credit. The TILA is part of the Consumer Credit Protection Act of 1968. Having been designed for consumer protection, it does not cover all loans. The following standards determine the TILA's applicability:

1. The debtor must be a "natural person" rather than an organization.
2. The creditor must be regularly engaged in extending credit and must be the person to whom the debt is initially payable.
3. The purpose of the credit must be "primarily for personal, family, or household purposes" not in excess of $25,000. However, "consumer real property transactions" are covered by the act. Hence home purchases fall within TILA provisions.
4. The credit must be subject to a finance charge or payable in more than four installments.

The TILA and Regulation Z interpreting the act were designed both to protect consumers from credit abuse and to assist them in becoming more informed regarding credit terms and costs so they could engage in comparison shopping. Congress presumed the increased information would stimulate competition in the finance industry. The heart of the act is the required conspicuous disclosure of the amount financed, the finance charge (the actual dollar sum to be paid for credit), the annual percentage rate (APR—the total cost of the credit expressed at an annual rate), and the number of payments. The finance charge includes not just interest but service charges, points, loan fees, carrying charges, and other costs. The TILA covers consumer loans generally, including credit cards and auto purchases, but its impact is somewhat limited by its $1,000 cap on penalties for personal property loans, as affirmed by the Supreme Court's 2004 decision in *Koons v. Nigh* (543 U.S. 50). [For consumer information on "abusive lending," see **http://www .ftc.gov/bcp/menu-lending.htm**]

The case that follows examines the application of TILA to a department store purchase.

Justice White

John E. Bell appeals from summary judgment entered against him and in favor of Respondent, the May Department Stores Company, d/b/a/ Famous Barr Company.

I. FACTUAL BACKGROUND

Bell purchased a ceiling fan on August 2, 1992, at Famous Barr and charged the purchase price of $132.16 to his Famous Barr credit card account. After installing it a few weeks later, Bell determined the fan was defective because it made an unacceptable level of noise at all speeds and he was unable to fix it. Famous Barr never inspected the fan to dispute Bell's determination.

Famous Barr billed Bell for the cost of the fan on September 1, 1992, with payment due on September 25. On or about September 23, 1992, Bell told a Famous Barr representative his fan was defective and he did not intend to pay for it. Bell also sent Famous Barr a letter memorializing this conversation, dated October 27, 1992, following the directives on the back of his Famous Barr billing statement and making a general reference to "Regulation Z." Famous Barr wrote Bell acknowledging its receipt of his letter. Famous Barr later contacted Bell in November and agreed to locate a replacement fan and reimburse Bell for the installation cost. They never discussed the details, nor did they agree when Bell should ultimately pay for the fan. Bell waited for Famous Barr to locate a replacement fan and notify him, but he was never notified.

Bell again notified Famous Barr when his November 1992 statement contained a past due notice for the unpaid fan. Famous Barr assured Bell it had simply made a mistake. From May through October 1993, however, Bell's monthly statement showed past due notices, late fees, and finance charges. Except for the disputed price of the fan, Bell *always* paid his balance in full each month. On May 4, 1993, Famous Barr informed Bell it was sending his account to three credit reporting agencies, including TRW. It made similar written threats to Bell . . . and threatened to report the most derogatory rating of "R9." Bell contacted Famous Barr to explain the dispute numerous times. He was assured no further action would be taken to collect the disputed amount and that the matter would not affect his credit rating.

* * * * *

In August 1993, the parties reached a provisional settlement agreement. Famous Barr agreed to credit Bell's account with all finance and late fee charges and reinstate his credit line. Bell agreed to pay for the fan if Famous Barr sent a letter permitting the imminent buyer of Bell's house to exchange the fan. Nevertheless, on September 1, 1993, Famous Barr assessed late fees and finance charges for nonpayment, closed Bell's account, and reported derogatory information to the credit reporting agencies.

After memorializing this settlement agreement and sending a copy to Famous Barr on September 13, 1993, Bell received written confirmation that Famous Barr would "delete all derogatory information." On October 4, 1993, Bell re-dated his September 1993 letter and mailed it with a check for the price of the fan. Later that month, however, Bell found his Famous Barr account closed due to "poor prior payment history." Bell wrote a letter to Famous Barr quoting the pertinent sections of Regulation Z and demanding the deletion of adverse or derogatory credit history from his file. Famous Barr reinstated Bell's account, faxed letters to the credit reporting agencies to that effect, and sent Bell a copy. The parties later discovered the corrective letters that Famous Barr sent to the credit reporting agencies contained the wrong account number.

In early summer 1994, Bell applied to the European American Bank ("EAB") for a TWA credit card, hoping to earn frequent flyer miles with his purchases. EAB refused to extend credit based upon derogatory Famous Barr information contained in a credit report from TRW. TRW's report did not reflect Famous Barr's request to delete all derogatory credit information. Bell also discovered Famous Barr had requested other credit reporting agencies to delete his entire 22-year credit history with Famous Barr, the large majority of which was positive. Bell sued.

II. REGULATION Z OF THE TRUTH IN LENDING ACT

Count I in Bell's petition claims Famous Barr violated [the Federal Truth in Lending Act (TILA)] by reporting him delinquent to various credit reporting agencies after receiving notice of a "billing error" and prior to resolving that error. Count I also claims Famous Barr violated [TILA] by restricting and closing his Famous Barr account after receiving notice of a "billing error" and prior to resolving that error.

* * * * *

Famous Barr argues the "billing error" alleged by Bell and essential to his claim did not occur because Bell accepted the fan.

* * * * *

Famous Barr argues Bell accepted the fan because he did not reject it. For an effective rejection, the buyer must notify the seller in accordance with the contract or within a reasonable time if the contract is silent.

* * * * *

A reasonable jury could find Bell did not accept the fan. He properly notified Famous Barr and Famous Barr duly received notice of the defective fan. Bell's rejection of the fan within three months of purchase was reasonable, especially since Bell did not install it until some weeks after he bought it and tried to fix it. Bell also notified Famous Barr of his rejection within the 60-day period prescribed by both [Regulation Z] and Famous Barr's own billing statement. In addition, Bell did not commit acts inconsistent with Famous Barr's ownership of the rejected fan. Bell neither used the fan, nor prevented Famous Barr from removing it. Famous Barr even encouraged Bell to retain it pending replacement.

Also contrary to the decision of the trial court, summary judgment is improper because a reasonable jury could find Bell attempted to resolve his dispute with Famous Barr in good faith. Bell claimed he long awaited the availability of a replacement fan. . . .

If a reasonable jury finds Bell did not accept the fan, and acted in good faith, then it can find a "billing error" existed. If a "billing error existed," Famous Barr violated the Federal Truth in Lending Act by closing Bell's account and reporting him to credit agencies. The decision of the trial court granting Famous Barr's motion for summary judgment on Count I is reversed.

* * * * *

Questions

1. *a.* In what sense did Famous Barr violate Regulation Z and the TILA?

   b. Why was the court concerned about whether Bell had accepted the fan?

2. Green Tree Financial financed Randolph's mobile home purchase. Randolph sued, claiming that Green Tree's financing document contained an arbitration clause that violates TILA because it did not provide the same level of protection as TILA accords. If the arbitration clause provides lesser protection than that provided for by TILA, as Randolph claims, should the arbitration go forward? Explain. See *Randolph v. Green Tree Financial Corp.,* 531 U.S. 79 (2000).

3. A health spa sells some memberships for cash and some on an installment basis. The price is the same whether the buyer pays cash or buys on the installment plan. The spa has an arrangement to sell the installment contracts to a financing agency at a discount (a price lower than the face value of the contract).

   a. How would you argue that the installment contract sales are in violation of TILA and Regulation Z?

   b. How would you rule on such a case? See *Joseph v. Norman's Health Club, Inc.,* 532 F.2d 86 (8th Cir. 1976).

Credit and Charge Cards

As an aggressive marketer, you may want to hand out credit cards in your student union, but the TILA provides that credit cards cannot be issued to a consumer unless requested. Cardholder liability for unauthorized use (lost or stolen card) cannot exceed $50, and the cardholder bears no liability after notifying the issuer of the missing card.

The Fair Credit and Charge Card Disclosure Act of 1988 creates extensive disclosure requirements for card issuers. The act requires notification of various cost factors when card issuers solicit applications. Details vary, depending on whether the card application was solicited by mail, telephone, or "take ones" (such as a magazine insert). In general, issuers must disclose key cost features, including APR, annual membership fees, minimum finance charges, late payment charges, and so on.

> **Credit Card Suicides**
>
> Sean Moyer, a University of Oklahoma junior, had earned the minimum wage as a part-time salesman and gift wrapper in a department store. Yet by the time he hanged himself in his bedroom closet, he had 12 credit cards and had amassed $10,000 in debt on them.

Mitzi Pool had only three cards, but they were maxed out, and $2,500 is a heavy debt load for an 18-year-old. Pool, a freshman at the University of Central Oklahoma, also hanged herself—her checkbook and credit card bills spread out on her dorm bed.

[Sixty-seven percent of college students have credit cards, and their average credit card debt exceeds $2,100.]

Sources: Associated Press, "Hooked on Credit," *Waterloo/Cedar Falls Courier,* June 9, 1999, p. C7; Associated Press, "A Different Kind of College Credit," *Waterloo/Cedar Falls Courier,* June 24, 2004, p. C10.

Consumer Credit Reports

Having a favorable credit rating is a vital feature of consumer life, and having reliable credit information is essential to efficient business practice. Thus the three national credit information giants, Equifax, Experian, and TransUnion, as well as local credit bureaus, provide retailers, employers, insurance companies, and so on with consumers' detailed credit histories. The federal Fair Credit Reporting Act (FCRA) affords consumers the following credit reporting protections, among others:

- Anyone using information from a credit reporting agency (CRA), such as Equifax, to take "adverse action" against you (denying you credit, a job, insurance) must notify you and tell you where it secured the information.
- At your request, a CRA must give you the information in your file and a list of all those who have recently sought information about you.
- If you claim that your credit file contains inaccurate information, the CRA must investigate your complaint and give you a written report. If you remain unsatisfied, you can include a brief statement in your credit file. Notice of the dispute and a summary of your statement normally must accompany future reports.
- All inaccurate information must be corrected or removed from the file, usually within 30 days.
- In most cases, negative information more than seven years old must not be reported.
- You must provide written consent before a CRA can provide information to your employer or prospective employer.
- You can sue for damages if your rights under the act have been violated.[21]

[For an extensive set of practical questions and answers about consumer rights under the Fair Credit Reporting Act, see **http://www.ftc.gov/bcp/conline/pubs/credit/fcra.htm**]

To provide consumers a ready opportunity to check the accuracy of their own credit information, the federal Fair and Accurate Credit Transactions Act of 2003 (FACT Act) guarantees consumers the right to receive free annual copies of their credit reports. One place to request a report is the Web site [**www.annualcreditreport.com**].

Question

Provide some free market reasoning supporting the credit industry position that ever more detailed government regulation of credit providers is not in the public's best interest.

Fair Credit Billing Act (FCBA)

The FCBA provides a mechanism to deal with the billing errors that accompany credit card and certain other "open-end" credit transactions. A cardholder who receives an erroneous bill must complain in writing to the creditor within 60 days of the time the bill was mailed. The creditor must acknowledge receipt of the complaint within 30 days. Then, within two billing cycles but not more than 90 days, the creditor must issue a response either by correcting the account or by forwarding a written statement to the consumer explaining why the bill is accurate. The creditor cannot threaten the consumer's credit rating or report the consumer as delinquent while the bill is in dispute, although the creditor can report that the bill is being challenged. Where a "reasonable investigation" determines the bill was correct but the consumer continues to contest it, the consumer may refuse to pay, and the creditor will then be free to commence collection procedures after giving the consumer 10 days to pay the disputed amount. If the bill is reported to a credit bureau as delinquent, that report must also indicate the consumer's belief that the money is not owed, and the consumer must be told who received the report. Penalties for a creditor in violation of the act are quite modest. The creditor forfeits the right to collect the amount in question and any accompanying finance charges, but the forfeiture cannot exceed $50 for each charge in dispute.

Electronic Fund Transfers

With ATMs, point-of-sale machines, electronic deposits, and the like we are deeply immersed in an era of "electronic money." The Electronic Fund Transfer Act provides remedies for consumers confronting electronic banking problems such as liability for lost or stolen cards and billing errors. [Space constraints preclude examining this topic, but the Federal Trade Commission has provided a detailed and readable summary of those protections at **http://www.ftc.gov/bcp/conline/pubs/credit/elbank.htm**]

Equal Credit Opportunity

The Equal Credit Opportunity Act is designed to combat bias in lending. Credit must be extended to all creditworthy applicants regardless of sex, marital status, age, race, color, religion, national origin, good-faith exercise of rights under the Consumer Credit Protection Act, and receipt of public assistance (like food stamps). ECOA was in large part a response to anger over differing treatment of women and men in the financial marketplace. Creditors often would not lend money to married women in the women's own names, and single, divorced, and widowed women were similarly disadvantaged in securing credit. [For more details about ECOA, see **http://www.ftc.gov/bcp/conline/pubs/credit/ecoa.htm**] The case that follows applies the ECOA to a "cross-dressing" male.

> ECOA was in large part a response to anger over differing treatment of women and men in the financial marketplace.

Lucas Rosa v. Park West Bank & Trust Co. 214 F.3d 213 (1st Cir. 2000)

Judge Lynch

I

[O]n July 21, 1998, [Lucas] Rosa came to the [Park West] Bank to apply for a loan. A biological male, he was dressed in traditionally feminine attire. He requested a loan application from Norma Brunelle, a bank employee. Brunelle asked Rosa for identification. Rosa produced three forms of photo identification: (1) a Massachusetts Department of Public Welfare Card; (2) a Massachusetts Identification Card; and (3) a Money Stop Check Cashing ID Card. Brunelle looked at the identification cards and told Rosa that she would not provide him with a loan application until he "went home and changed." She said that he had to be dressed like one of the identification cards in which he appeared in more traditionally male attire before she would provide him with a loan application and process his loan request.

II

Rosa sued the Bank. Rosa charged that "by requiring [him] to conform to sex stereotypes before proceeding with the credit transaction, [the Bank] unlawfully discriminated against [him] with respect to an aspect of a credit transaction on the basis of sex." He claims to have suffered emotional distress.

Without filing an answer to the complaint, the Bank moved to dismiss. . . . The district court granted the Bank's motion. The court stated,

> The issue in this case is not [Rosa's] sex, but rather how he chose to dress when applying for a loan. Because the Act does not prohibit discrimination based on the manner in which someone dresses, Park West's requirement that Rosa change his clothes does not give rise to claims of illegal discrimination. Further, even if Park West's statement or action were based upon Rosa's sexual orientation or perceived sexual orientation, the Act does not prohibit such discrimination.

PriceWaterhouse v. Hopkins, which Rosa relied on, was not to the contrary, according to the district court, because that case "neither holds, nor even suggests, that discrimination based merely on a person's attire is impermissible."

On appeal, Rosa says that the district court "fundamentally misconceived the law as applicable to the Plaintiff's claim by concluding that there may be no relationship, as a matter of law, between telling a bank customer what to wear and sex discrimination."

The Bank says that Rosa loses for two reasons. First, citing cases pertaining to gays and transsexuals, it says that the ECOA does not apply to cross-dressers. Second, the Bank says that its employee genuinely could not identify Rosa, which is why she asked him to go home and change.

III

The ECOA prohibits discrimination, "with respect to any aspect of a credit transaction[,] on the basis of race, color, religion, national origin, sex or marital status, or age." Thus to prevail, the alleged discrimination against Rosa must have been "on the basis of . . . sex."

While the district court was correct in saying that the prohibited bases of discrimination under the ECOA do not include style of dress or sexual orientation, that is not the discrimination alleged. It is alleged that the Bank's actions were taken, in whole or in part, "on the basis of . . . [the appellant's] sex." . . . Whatever facts emerge, and they may turn out to have nothing to do with sex-based discrimination, we cannot say at this point that the plaintiff has no viable theory of sex discrimination consistent with the facts alleged.

The evidence is not yet developed, and thus it is not yet clear why Brunelle told Rosa to go home and change. It may be that this case involves an instance of disparate treatment based on sex in the denial of credit. . . . It is reasonable to infer that Brunelle told Rosa to go home and change because she thought that Rosa's attire did not accord with his male gender: in other words, that Rosa did not receive the loan application because he was a man, whereas a similarly situated woman would have received the loan application. That is, the Bank may treat, for credit purposes, a woman who dresses like a man differently than a man who dresses like a woman. If so, the Bank concedes, Rosa may have a claim. Indeed, under *PriceWaterhouse,* "stereotyped remarks [including statements about dressing more 'femininely'] can certainly be evidence that gender played a part." It is also reasonable to infer, though, that Brunelle refused to give Rosa the loan application because she thought he was gay, confusing sexual orientation with cross-dressing. If so, Rosa concedes, our precedents dictate that he would have no recourse under the federal Act. It is reasonable to infer, as well, that Brunelle simply could not ascertain whether the person shown in the identification card photographs was the same person that appeared before her that day. If this were the case, Rosa again would be out of luck. It is reasonable to infer, finally, that Brunelle may have had mixed motives, some of which fall into the prohibited category.

It is too early to say what the facts will show; it is apparent, however, that, under some set of facts within the bounds of the allegations and nonconclusory facts in the complaint, Rosa may be able to prove a claim under the ECOA.

We reverse and remand.

Questions

1. *a.* Did the court of appeals find that Park West Bank had violated the ECOA? Explain.

    b. If at trial, the facts reveal that the bank employee thought Rosa was gay and demanded that he change clothes for that reason, who will win this case? Explain.

    c. According to the court of appeals, how did the lower court misunderstand this case?

2. *a.* Does federal law protect bank customers based on their style of dress? Explain.

    b. Should it offer that protection? Explain.

Debtor Protection

Personal debt is at an all-time high in America. Perhaps we live beyond our means, but Congress and the states have recognized that financial reversals are inevitable for many. Laws have been developed to protect consumers from unfair debt collection methods and to provide a way out via bankruptcy.

Do Hong Kong Debt Collectors Need Additional Legal Restraints?

Banks and other lenders [in Hong Kong] employ debt collectors who can be quite persistent, repeatedly phoning debtors to scream obscenities, waiting in front of their apartments to demand payment, or hanging the carcasses of cats and dogs outside. . . . But as long as the debt collectors don't become violent or cause any property damage, there is little legal recourse.

"Sometimes, the debt collectors may dirty the debtors' homes by throwing some grasshoppers into their residences," said Cathy Wan, the secretary of the [Law Reform Commission's] debt collection subcommittee.

Source: Margaret Wong, "Hong Kong Officials Propose Laws against Abusive Debt Collection," July 29, 2002, *The Associated Press.*

Debt Collection

The Fair Debt Collection Practices Act (FDCPA) is designed to shield debtors from unfair debt collection tactics by debt collection agencies and attorneys who routinely operate as debt collectors. The act does not extend to creditors who are themselves trying to recover money owed to them. Several thousand debt collection agencies nationwide pursue those who are delinquent in their debts. The agencies are normally paid on a commission basis and are often exceedingly aggressive and imaginative in their efforts. The FDCPA requires the collector to include a warning in the first communication with the debtor that the communication is an attempt to collect a debt, and any information obtained will be used for that purpose. In any subsequent communication except a court pleading, the collector must always disclose his or her role as a collector.

The FDCPA forbids, among others, the following practices:

- Use of obscene language.
- Contact with third parties other than for the purpose of locating the debtor. (This provision is an attempt to prevent harm to the debtor's reputation.)
- Use of or threats to use physical force.
- Contact with the debtor during "inconvenient" hours. For debtors who are employed during "normal" working hours, the period from 9 PM to 8 AM would probably be considered inconvenient.
- Repeated phone calls with the intent to harass.
- Contacting the debtor in an unfair, abusive, or deceptive manner.

The Federal Trade Commission is responsible for administering the FDCPA. A wronged debtor may also file a civil action to recover all actual damages (for example, payment for job loss occasioned by wrongful debt collection practices as well as damages for associated embarrassment and suffering). [For more details about the FDCPA, see **http://www.ftc.gov/bcp/conline/pubs/credit/fdc.htm**]

The case that follows suggests some of the problems in debt collection practices.

LEGAL BRIEFCASE

Armstrong v. Rose Law Firm

2002 U.S. Dist. LEXIS 4039 (Dist. of Minn.)

Judge Davis

BACKGROUND

Plaintiff Kathryn M. Armstrong commenced this action against Defendant The Rose Law Firm, P.A. alleging violations of the Fair Debt Collection Practices Act. In November 1999, Plaintiff wrote a check for $24.11 to Minneapolis Moto Mart for gasoline and cola. The check was returned for insufficient funds. Moto Mart turned the check over to Bonded Account Services, Inc. ("BAS"), for collection, who attempted to collect on the check without success. BAS sent Armstrong a notice of dishonor on June 17, 2000. Armstrong did not reply to that letter or otherwise make payment in response to the notice of dishonor. On August 1, 2000, Armstrong's check was referred to Defendant.

On August 10, 2000, Defendant sent a dunning letter to Armstrong. That letter indicated that Defendant had been "retained to represent the original creditor listed below as to your returned check." The letter listed the following information:

Agency: BONDED ACCOUNTS SERVICE/		
Firm File #: 204626	Amount Referred:	$44.11
Check Date: 111399	Penalties	$100.00
Original Creditor:	Settlement Offer:	$144.11
MINNEAPOLIS		
MOTO MART		

The letter then stated,

The above settlement offer includes the following: the face amount of your worthless check, a service charge of $20.00, and civil penalties pursuant to Minnesota State Law of up to $100.00 or the face value of your worthless check, whichever is greater. This is an offer of settlement and not a demand for payment. No court costs or attorneys fees are requested at this time....

* * * * *

Violation

In Count 1 of the Amended Complaint, Plaintiff alleges that Defendant's August 10, 2000, dunning letter violates the FDCPA. . . .

[T]he FDCPA prohibits debt collectors from using "any false, deceptive, or misleading representation or means in connection with the collection of any debt." The FDCPA also prohibits debt collectors from threatening to take any action that cannot legally be taken or that is not intended to be taken.

Further, the FDCPA prohibits "the collection of any amount (including any interest, fee, charge, or expense incidental to the principle obligation) unless such amount is expressly authorized by the agreement creating the debt or permitted by law." Finally, the FDCPA provides that

> within five days after the initial communication with a consumer in connection with the collection of any debt, a debt collector shall, unless the following information is contained in the initial communication or the consumer has paid the debt, send the consumer a written notice containing—(1) the amount of the debt.

Whether a debt collector has violated the FDCPA is determined from the perspective of the unsophisticated consumer. This test is designed to protect consumers of below average sophistication or intelligence, but it also contains an objective element of reasonableness that prevents liability for bizarre or idiosyncratic interpretations of collection notices. Essentially, Plaintiff here claims that Defendant violated the FDCPA by failing to state the amount of her debt in the letter, demanding an amount in the letter that was not authorized by law, and as a result, writing a misleading and deceptive letter.

1. Amount of Debt

* * * * *

[T]he Firm's dunning letter indicates that the correspondence pertains to Plaintiff's returned check. The letter lists the original creditor and check date. [T]he letter contains only one column and one set of figures. That column lists an "amount referred" of $44.11, "penalties" of $100.00, and a "settlement offer" of $144.11. The letter goes on to indicate that the settlement offer includes the face amount of Plaintiff's worthless check, a service charge of $20.00, and civil penalties pursuant to Minnesota State Law of up to $100.

The FDCPA requirement that a debt collector give a debtor written notice of the amount of debt owed is designed to avoid confusing, fraudulent, and coercive debt collection practices. In order for the notice to be meaningful, the information must

be conveyed in such a manner as to secure the understanding of the unsophisticated consumer.

* * * * *

The Court finds that the Firm's letter is not sufficient to meet the notice requirements of the FDCPA, and therefore, could mislead the unsophisticated consumer. The Firm's letter does not explicitly state the "amount of debt." Furthermore, the letter does not provide an explanation of the service charge and does not indicate that Plaintiff actually owes that amount or that the service charge is now included in the debt. Defendant confuses the matter further when on one page of its brief, it argues that Plaintiff was able to determine the amount of the debt because she remitted a money order for $44.11, and on another page of its brief, it argues that Plaintiff knew the amount of debt because she submitted a money order in the amount of $24.11. The unsophisticated consumer should not be required to subtract numbers ($44.11 "amount referred" minus $20.00 "service charge") to determine the amount of debt. Assuming that the service charge is now part of the debt (the dunning letter does not make this clear), the unsophisticated consumer should not be required to consult a dictionary to determine that "amount referred" really means the debt owed. The Firm's letter could easily be altered to remedy this defect. In its current form, the Firm's letter could be misleading.

The Firm also argues that Plaintiff's payment of $44.11 indicates that she was easily able to discern the amount of debt. The Court disagrees, not only for the reasons stated above, but also because Plaintiff paid this amount after she had the benefit of consultation with counsel.

* * * * *

Damages

. . . Plaintiff has not pled or proven a specific amount of actual damages incurred. . . . [T]herefore, the Court awards none.

With respect to statutory damages, any debt collector who fails to comply with the FDCPA may be liable for "additional damages as the court may allow, but not exceeding $1,000" and "the costs of the action, together with a reasonable attorney's fee as determined by the court." In determining the amount of statutory damages, the Court must consider the frequency and persistence of noncompliance by the debt collector, the nature of such noncompliance, and the extent to which such noncompliance was intentional.

In this case, although Defendant sent only one letter to Plaintiff, that letter was misleading with respect to the amount of debt. The nature of the noncompliance was Defendant's failure to clearly state the amount of debt in the demand letter. Based on these factors, an award of the maximum amount of statutory damages, $1,000 in this case, would be appropriate. . . .

CONCLUSION

Plaintiff's Motion for Summary Judgment is Granted.

Questions

1 *a.* Why did the federal district court conclude that the debt collector violated the FDCPA?

   b. What legal/practical standard did the court employ in assessing the adequacy of the dunning letter?

   c. Would you have understood the dunning letter had you received it? Explain.

2. Miller owed $2,501.61 to the Star Bank of Cincinnati. Payco attempted to collect the debt by sending a one-page collection form to Miller. The front side of the form included, among other words, in very large capital letters a demand for IMMEDIATE FULL PAYMENT, the words PHONE US TODAY, and the word NOW in white letters nearly two inches tall against a red background. At the bottom of the page in the smallest print on the form was the message: NOTICE: SEE REVERSE SIDE FOR IMPORTANT INFORMATION. The reverse side contained the validation notice required under the FDCPA. Does the form conform to FDCPA requirements? Explain. See *Miller v. Payco-General American Credits, Inc.,* 943 F. 2d 482 (4th Cir. 1991).

3. Why shouldn't debt collectors be able to use aggressive tactics to encourage payment of legitimate bills?

Part Four—Bankruptcy

Fresh Start?   Should we lend a hand to those who are down on their luck? Bankruptcy law was specifically designed to provide a fresh start for those whose financial problems were insurmountable. We believed that both the debtor and society benefited from the new beginning. Now, as bankruptcy filings have skyrocketed, we are downsizing the fresh start.

> In 2004, new bankruptcy filings totaled some 1.59 million.

In 2004, new bankruptcy filings totaled some 1.59 million, up from 780,000 ten years earlier.[22] Approximately 1 in 73 American households filed for bankruptcy during a 12-month period ending in March 2004.[23] Interestingly, bankruptcy patterns vary dramatically by region, with the highest rates in the southeast (such as Tennessee, with one household in every 38.7 filing for bankruptcy in that 12-month period) and the lowest rates in parts of the West and Midwest along with the Northeast (one in 156.2 households in Vermont filed for bankruptcy).[24] The credit industry sees the bankruptcy wave as more evidence of declining personal responsibility, while consumer advocates say the bankruptcies are the product of tragedies spurred by medical emergencies, job losses, and an explosion of credit cards:

> How is it that the person who wants to do right ends up so worse off?" asked Cleveland municipal judge Robert Triozzi . . . when he ruled against Discover in the company's breach-of-contract suit against another struggling credit cardholder, Ruth Owens.
>
> Owens tried for six years to pay off a $1,900 balance on her Discover card, sending the credit company a total of $3,492 in monthly payments between 1997 and 2003. Yet her balance grew to $5,564.28, even though . . . she never used the card to buy anything more. Of that total, over-limit penalty fees alone were $1,158.
>
> Triozzi denied Discover's claim, calling its attempt to collect more money from Owens "unconscionable."[25]

Students Turn to Cards

About 83 percent of college undergraduates had credit cards in 2001, up from 67 percent just three years earlier.

Source: Michael Schroeder and Suein Hwang, "Sweeping New Bankruptcy Law to Make Life Harder for Debtors," *The Wall Street Journal,* April 6, 2005, p. A1.

Reform At this writing in 2005, with President Bush in the White House and strong Republican majorities in both houses of Congress, a new bankruptcy reform law is in place after many years of political struggle. The thrust of the new legislation is to force more bankrupt parties to repay their creditors. In brief, the new legislation forces some bankruptcy filers to enter their claim under Chapter 13 of the bankruptcy code rather than the more forgiving Chapter 7. Those with income above their state's median who can pay $6,000 over five years—$100 per month—probably would be forced into Chapter 13, where the court would order a repayment plan. Those not meeting that test could file under Chapter 7, thereby achieving a fresh start by escaping most repayment responsibilities while their nonessential property would be sold to pay debtors. The new law also requires those filing for bankruptcy to pay for credit counseling. Supporters of the new law argue that it will reduce the cost of credit for all Americans, whereas opponents see the bill as a punitive assault on those already down on their luck. [For the American Bankruptcy Institute, see **http://www.abiworld.org**]

---

300 Pairs of Shoes and Bankrupt

She earned $27,000 a year but owned 300 pairs of shoes. Now the self-proclaimed "Imelda Marcos of Marina Del Rey" [California] is paying for it. This week, the 24-year-old former manager of an Ann Taylor Boutique planned to file for bankruptcy.

To support average postcollege debts and expenses, graduates would need to earn $38,000 annually. The national average wage is $34,000, and only 51 percent of students have jobs when they graduate. Scholar Elizabeth Warren says that bankruptcy filings by those 25 and under rose 51 percent during the 1990s and now represent 7 percent of the nation's total personal bankruptcy filings.

Sources: Los Angeles Times, "More Young Adults Resorting to Bankruptcy," *Waterloo/Cedar Falls Courier,* February 4, 2001, p. B7; Charles Haddad, "Congratulations, Grads—You're Bankrupt," *BusinessWeek,* May 21, 2001, p. 48.

The Law

Bankruptcy in the United States is governed exclusively by federal law; the states do not have the constitutional authority to enact bankruptcy legislation, but they do set their own rules within the limits provided by Congress. Our attention will be limited to the principal federal statute, the Bankruptcy Reform Act of 1978, as amended.

Bankruptcy is an adjudication relieving a debtor of all or part of his or her liabilities. Any person, partnership, or corporation may seek debtor relief. Three forms of bankruptcy action are important to us:

1. **Liquidation** (**Chapter 7** of the Bankruptcy Act), in which most debts are forgiven and all assets except exemptions are distributed to creditors.
2. **Reorganization** (**Chapter 11**), in which creditors are kept from the debtor's assets while the debtor, under the supervision of the court, works out a plan to continue in business while paying creditors.
3. **Adjustment of debts** of an individual with regular income (**Chapter 13**), in which individuals with limited debts are protected from creditors while paying their debts in installments. [For links to bankruptcy sites on the Internet, see **http://www.lawtrove.com/ bankruptcy/**]

Liquidation

A Chapter 7 liquidation petition can be *voluntarily* filed in federal court by the debtor (individual, partnership, or corporation), or creditors can seek an *involuntary* bankruptcy judgment. A Chapter 7 liquidation is commonly called a "straight" bankruptcy.

In a voluntary action, the debtor files a petition with the appropriate federal court. The court then has jurisdiction to proceed with the liquidation, and the petition becomes the *order for relief*. The debtor need not be insolvent to seek bankruptcy. Creditors often can compel an involuntary bankruptcy.

The debtor may challenge that bankruptcy action. The court will enter an order for relief if it finds the debtor has not been paying his or her debts when due or if most of the debtor's property is under the control of a custodian for the purpose of enforcing a lien against that property.

After the order for relief is granted, voluntary and involuntary actions proceed in a similar manner. Creditors are restrained from reaching the debtor's assets. An interim bankruptcy trustee is appointed by the court. The creditors then hold a meeting, and a permanent trustee is elected. The trustee collects the debtor's property and converts it to money, protects the interests of the debtor and creditors, may manage the debtor's business, and ultimately distributes the estate proceeds to the creditors. Debtors are allowed to keep exempt property, which varies from state to state but typically includes a car, a homestead, some household or personal items, life insurance, and other "necessities." Normally a dollar maximum is attached to each.

The debtor's nonexempt property is then divided among the creditors according to the priorities prescribed by statute. Secured creditors are paid first. If funds remain, "priority" claims, such as employees' wages and alimony/child support, are paid. Then, funds permitting, general creditors are paid. Each class must be paid in full before a class of lower priority will be compensated. Any remaining funds will return to the debtor.

When distribution is complete, the bankruptcy judge may issue an order *discharging* (relieving) the debtor of any remaining debts except for certain statutorily specified claims. Those include, for example, taxes and educational loans. The debtor might fail to receive a discharge if he or she had received one in the previous six years, if property was concealed from the court, or if good faith in the bankruptcy process was lacking in other respects.

---

910 Percent Interest

A recent survey of "payday" loans revealed annual interest rates of 182 to 910 percent. Nineteen states forbid payday loans, but lenders say that they are meeting an obvious consumer need. (Payday loans typically involve the borrower writing a check to the lender with the check dated for the borrower's payday. The borrower then receives the cash minus interest. The lender can later cash the check or "roll over" the loan.)

Source: Associated Press, "Payday Loans Charge Fees Up to 910 Percent," *Waterloo/Cedar Falls Courier,* November 14, 2001, p. C10.

Reorganization

Chapter 11 is available to individuals and most businesses. The basic thrust of this type of bankruptcy is to allow financially troubled enterprises to continue in operation while debtor adjustments are arranged. Thus both debtor and creditor may ultimately benefit more than from a straight liquidation. The debtor may voluntarily seek reorganization, or the creditors may petition for an involuntary action. When a reorganization petition is filed with the court and relief is ordered, one or more committees of creditors are appointed to participate in bankruptcy procedures. Typically the debtor continues to operate the business, although the court may appoint a trustee to replace the debtor if required because of dishonesty, fraud, or extreme mismanagement. The company, its bankers, and its suppliers will meet to work out a method for continuing operations. A plan must be developed that will satisfy the creditors that their interests are being served by the reorganization. Perhaps new capital is secured, or perhaps creditors receive some shares in the company. The plan must be approved by the creditors and confirmed by the court. The company is then required to carry out the plan.

Adjustment of Debts

Under Chapter 13, individuals (not partnerships or corporations) can seek the protection of the court to arrange a debt adjustment plan. Chapter 13 permits only voluntary bankruptcies and is restricted to those with steady incomes and somewhat limited debts. The process can begin only with a voluntary petition from the debtor. Creditors are restrained from reaching the debtor's assets. The debtor develops a repayment plan. If creditors' interests are sufficiently satisfied by the plan, the court may confirm it and appoint a trustee to oversee the plan. The debtor may then have three to five years to make the necessary payments. [For an extensive bankruptcy law database, see **http://www.law .cornell.edu/topics/bankruptcy.html**]

PRACTICING ETHICS) Bankruptcy—Who Is to Blame?

Commenting on the 2005 bankruptcy reform law, Todd Zywicki, a George Mason University law professor, said, "This is a matter of morality and personal responsibility." Consumer advocates, on the other hand, say the bankruptcy problem lies with the "enablers"—the credit card companies who encourage deeper and deeper indebtedness by bombarding consumers with billions of credit card solicitations annually.

Question
Who bears the moral blame for America's epidemic of 1.6 million bankruptcies annually? Explain.

Source: Michael Schroeder and Suein Hwang, "Sweeping New Bankruptcy Law to Make Life Harder for Debtors," *The Wall Street Journal*, April 6, 2005, p. A1.

Part Five—Consumer Protection Abroad

Aggressive consumer protection measures of the kind we have studied in this chapter are unknown to much of the world, but change is coming. European nations certainly are not new to consumer protection initiatives; but the European Union has recently recognized that a more organized, consistent, and responsive effort is necessary for economic progress and for fairness. The European Union has adopted a consumer policy strategy for the period 2002–2006. A key ingredient in this plan is to build consumer confidence in cross-border shopping, thus strengthening the European Union as a unified economic entity. That goal would be achieved with more uniform rules across EU nations, consistent enforcement, increased consumer education, and the like. [For an overview of EU consumer law and policy, see **http://europa.ev.int/comm/consumers/index_en.htm**]

The growth of formal consumer protection efforts is an acknowledgment of the market's imperfections and the need for some government intervention. As the following article suggests, China is quickly learning that lesson. Remember that China remains formally a communist state with central control. But in a burst of entrepreneurial zeal, the Chinese have adapted free market principles to fit their needs. With that growing acceptance and understanding of the market, the government and the people now see a role for legal measures to curb unscrupulous behavior.

Law Helps Chinese Consumers in Rights Protection

READING

BEIJING—Liang Zhongqiao, 64, came all the way from suburban Beijing to the downtown area to lodge a complaint about a mail-order peeler he had bought, called "Omnipotent Peeler Queen." The tool, as he demonstrated on the spot, can peel no more than one-third of an apple, let alone potatoes as advertised in a newspaper.

"I am protesting not only for myself but also for all other consumers liable to be taken in by such fake ads," he told the

China Consumers Association (CCA) and State Bureau of Quality and Technical Supervision (SBQTS), representatives of which were receiving complaints at open-air venues on Friday's International Consumer Protection Day. They received complaints about a wide variety of goods, including pork, cashmere garments, mobile phones, home decorations, and medical treatment.

The two organizations safeguard consumers' rights and interests by receiving and handling their complaints all year round. "I've organized such annual activities for four years, and I am impressed by consumers' growing awareness of rights protection," said Sun Shihua, a senior official from SBQTS. "Last year's event attracted just a few consumers, but this year people have been lining up to bring us their complaints."

He said that consumers, informed of the activities by various media organs, all came with specific questions on legal procedures, and some brought the shoddy goods they had bought to show the consumer rights activists. Bi Lian'e, a 63-year-old housewife who has been a loyal consumer of Wangzhihe fermented soy beans for many years, bought a Wangzhihe product for 3.5 yuan (about 0.42 U.S. dollars), which she found to be fake and brought Friday to the experts. She said that she would claim compensation from the supermarket at which she had bought the product. Such complaints, said Yu Shuisheng, president of the CCA, reflect the improvement of consumers' awareness of rights protection through legal channels, and will help to build a normal market system. In the past, people usually put up with fraudulent goods.

China's first law on protection of consumer rights began to take effect in 1994. Yu also attributed the improvement to China's increasingly prosperous economy, and people having "more money in their pockets and more products to choose from."

Source: Emerging Markets Datafile, Xinhua, March 15, 2002.

Internet Exercises

1. Federal law, including the Electronic Fund Transfer Act, provides significant protection for consumers who encounter electronic banking problems. To answer the following questions, go to the Internet at [**http://www.ftc.gov/bcp/conline/pubs/credit/elbank.htm**]:

   a. How can you best protect yourself in the event of an error in a bank or credit card statement or in the event of a lost credit card?

   b. If your credit card is lost or stolen, to what extent are you personally responsible for the unauthorized use of that card?

   c. Under federal law, to what extent can you stop payment on a credit card purchase when you are, for some reason, dissatisfied with the transaction?

2. Go to the Center for Auto Safety Web site [**http://www.autosafety.org/**] and find your way to your state's lemon law. Read the law of your state. Read the law for the states of Texas, Virginia, and West Virginia.

   a. Explain the differences in the laws of the states.

   b. Which of those three or four states, in your view, provides the "fairest" protection considering the viewpoints of both consumers and dealers?

Chapter Questions

1. a. An online "Ask a Lawyer" service received the following question: "Can I sue a creditor who is harassing me?" Answer that question and explain how the wronged consumer would go about that lawsuit.

   b. Answer this question that was likewise directed to "Ask a Lawyer": "What do I do if someone steals my identity?"

2. Two-thirds of American adults are either obese or overweight. The rate of overweight children ages 6 to 11 has more than doubled since 1980, and the rate for adoles-

cents has tripled. Timothy Muris, chairman of the Federal Trade Commission, objected to recent proposals to ban television commercials for "junk food" directed at kids: "Banning junk food ads on kids' programming is impractical, ineffective, and illegal." Explain what Muris meant. See Timothy J. Muris, "Don't Blame TV," *The Wall Street Journal,* June 25, 2004, p. A10.

3. DeSantis sued a debt collection agency, Computer Credit. DeSantis apparently owed $319.50 to Dr. Jeffrey A. Stahl, who assigned the debt to CC for collection. On April 27, 2000, CC sent the following collection letter to DeSantis:

> This notice will serve to inform you that your overdue balance with Dr. Jeffrey A. Stahl has been referred to Computer Credit, Inc., a debt collector. *[The] doctor insists on payment or a valid reason for your failure to make payment.* The law prohibits us from collecting any amount greater than the obligation stated above. Unless you notify us to the contrary, we will assume the amount due is correct. This communication is sent to you in an attempt to collect this debt. Any information obtained will be used for that purpose. *In the absence of a valid reason for your failure to make payment, pay the above debt or contact the doctor to settle this matter.* Payment can be sent directly to the doctor. [Italics added.]

The Fair Debt Collection Practices Act specifies that the consumer may dispute the alleged debt, in which case the debt collector must desist from collection until the debt collector obtains verification regarding the amount of the debt, if any. Given that statutory requirement, was the FDCPA violated by the italicized sentences in the collection letter? Explain. See *DeSantis v. Computer Credit, Inc.,* 269 F.3d 159 (2d Cir. 2001).

4. The Telephone Consumer Protection Act of 1991 forbids telemarketers from calling a consumer who has asked to be placed on a company's do-not-call list. Gerety, an independent contractor, called Worsham on behalf of Nationwide Insurance. Worsham asked to be placed on Nationwide's do-not-call list. Later Worsham was again solicited regarding Nationwide Insurance, although the actual source of the call was unclear. Would Nationwide be in violation of the TCPA if Gerety made the second call? Explain. See *Worsham v. Nationwide Insurance Co.,* 772 A.2d 868 (Md. Ct. App. 2001); cert. den. 778 A.2d 383 (Md. S.Ct. 2001).

5. Snow wrote a $23.12 check to a convenience store, Circle K. The check bounced, and Circle K sent the check to its attorney, Riddle, for collection. Riddle sent Snow a letter demanding payment along with a $15 service fee. Snow paid the $23.12, but refused to pay the $15. Then Snow sued Riddle for violating the Fair Debt Collection Practices Act because the collection letter did not include the required "validation notice" telling him about his legal rights under the FDCPA. Riddle responded by saying that the FDCPA does not apply to dishonored checks. Does a dishonored check constitute a debt such that the FDCPA would apply? Explain. See *Snow v. Riddle,* 143 F.3d 1350 (10th Cir. 1998).

6. Jenny Craig, Inc., reached a 1997 agreement with the Federal Trade Commission providing that the company must include the following statement in most ads: "For many dieters, weight loss is temporary." In your view, is that requirement a wise use of FTC authority? Explain.

7. Under 1998 federal rules, golf carts with a maximum speed of 25 miles per hour are exempt from most federal safety regulations and are allowed to use some public roads. The carts must be equipped with seat belts, windshields, headlights, and turn signals. The carts are widely used in retirement communities. The rules have been heavily criticized.

   a. What factors would you consider in deciding on the wisdom of this golf cart rule?

   b. How would you vote? Explain.

8. Recent studies suggest that consumer bankruptcies are much more common in some states than others. Aside from income levels, what socioeconomic factors would you expect to be closely correlated with high bankruptcy rates?

9. Playtex manufactures the market-leading spillproof cup for children, which a child uses by sucking on a spout to cause a valve to open. Gerber introduced its own version and ran ads showing an unnamed competitor's product and claiming that "Gerber's patented valve makes our cup more than 50 percent easier to drink from than the leading cup." Gerber's claims for the superiority of its cup were backed by tests from an independent laboratory. Playtex said the unnamed cup obviously was its brand and that the superiority claims were false and misleading. Playtex sought an injunction to block the Gerber ads. Would you grant that injunction? Explain. See *Playtex Products v. Gerber Products,* 981 F. Supp. 827 (S.D.N.Y. 1997).

10. Maguire, a credit card holder at Bradlees Department Store, fell behind in her payments. She received a series of dunning letters from Citicorp, which managed Bradlees' accounts, demanding that she pay the overdue amount. Later Maguire received a letter from "Debtor Assistance," which said that "your Bradlees account has recently [been] charged off." Debtor Assistance is a unit of Citicorp, but was not identified as such in the letter, beyond the phrase "a unit of CRS." The back of each Bradlees' account statement includes a notice that Citicorp Retail Services was the creditor that handled Bradlees' accounts. In general, creditors are not subject to the requirements of the Fair Debt Collections Practices Act, but Maguire sued claiming the Debtor Assistance letter violated the FDCPA. Is she correct? Explain. See *Maguire v. Citicorp Retail Services, Inc.,* 147 F.3d 232 (2d Cir. 1998).

11. A door-to-door salesman representing Your Shop at Home Services, Inc., called on Clifton and Cora Jones, who were welfare recipients. The Jones couple decided to buy a freezer from the salesman for $900. Credit charges, insurance, and so on were added to that $900 base so that the total purchase price was $1,439.69. Mr. and Mrs. Jones signed a sales agreement that accurately stipulated the price and its ingredients. The Joneses sued to reform the contract on unconscionability grounds. They had paid $619.88 toward the total purchase price. At trial, the retail value of the new freezer at the time of purchase was set at approximately $300.

    a. What is the issue in this case?

    b. Decide. Explain. See *Jones v. Star Credit Corp.,* 298 N.Y.S. 2d 264 (1969).

12. Roseman resigned from the John Hancock Insurance Company following allegations of misuse of his expense account. He reimbursed the account. Subsequently he was denied employment by another insurance firm after that firm read a Retail Credit Company credit report on him. The credit report included accurate information

regarding Roseman's resignation. Was Retail Credit in violation of the Fair Credit Reporting Act in circulating information regarding the resignation? Explain. See *Roseman v. Retail Credit Co., Inc.*, 428 F. Supp. 643 (Pa. 1977).

13. Once the government decided to intervene in the free market on behalf of consumers, two broad product safety options presented themselves: (*a*) the government could have limited its effort to generating and distributing information to consumers, or (*b*) the government could have set safety standards for all products. Assuming the government was forced to choose one or the other but not elements of both, which option should it have chosen? Explain.

14. Consumers sometimes abuse sellers. One familiar technique is shoplifting. Of course, shoplifting is a crime. However, the criminal process is cumbersome and often does not result in monetary recoveries for sellers. As a result, at least 43 states now have laws permitting store owners to impose civil fines, the collection of which is usually turned over to a lawyer or collection agency with a threat to sue in civil court, file criminal charges, or both if payment is not forthcoming. Fines may range from $50 to $5,000 or more, depending on the value of the item stolen.

    a. Defense lawyers say this civil fine system is unfair. Why?

    b. On balance, is the civil fine approach to shoplifting a good idea? Explain.

    c. Cite some examples of consumers abusing businesspeople.

15. Goswami failed to pay her $900 credit card bill. A collection agency, ACEI, mailed her a collection letter with a blue bar across the envelope saying "Priority Letter." The letter did not, in fact, constitute priority mail. The purpose of the bar was to encourage Goswami to open the envelope. Was the bar a deceptive practice in violation of the Fair Debt Collection Practices Act? Explain. See *Goswami v. American Collections Enterprise, Inc.*, 377 F.3d 488 (5th Cir. 2004); cert. den. 2005 U.S. LEXIS 5511.

Notes

1. Araminta Wordsworth, "Miss Cleo Didn't See $5M Fine in Her Future," *National Post*, November 16, 2002, p. A21.

2. *Lindberg Cadillac Co. v. Aron*, 371 S.W.3d 651 (Mo. App. 1963).

3. Knight Ridder Newspapers, "Fuming—Government Intervention Has Cigar Smokers Red Hot," *Waterloo/Cedar Falls Courier*, July 14, 2000, p. A5.

4. John J. Fialka, "As ATVs Take Off in Sales, Deaths and Injuries Mount," *The Wall Street Journal*, February 10, 2004, p. A1.

5. *Washington Post*, "Study: Dangerous Products Widely Available," *Waterloo/Cedar Falls Courier*, October 5, 2004, p. B6.

6. Christopher Conkey, "Safety Agency Takes Action on Baby Gear," *The Wall Street Journal*, March 22, 2005, p. D1.

7. Knight Ridder Newspapers, "Merck Accused of Concealing Side Effects of Vioxx during Senate Hearings," *Waterloo/Cedar Falls Courier*, November 19, 2004, p. A1.

8. Marie McCullough, "Journal Speaks Out against FDA," *Des Moines Register*, November 23, 2004, p. 3A.

9. Paul Recer, "Most FDA Scientists Critical of Drug Monitoring," *Des Moines Register*, December 17, 2004, p. 3A.

10. Knight Ridder Newspapers, "Merck Accused of Concealing."

11. Robert S. Greenberger and Glenn R. Simpson, "Identity Theft Dogs Credit Firms in the Supreme Court, Congress," *The Wall Street Journal,* April 12, 2001, p. A18.

12. Jennifer Saranow and Ron Lieber, "Freezing Out Identity Theft," *The Wall Street Journal,* March 15, 2005, p. D1.

13. Rachel Konrad, "Identity Theft Scandal Widens," *Des Moines Register,* February 19, 2005, p. 8C.

14. Saranow and Lieber, "Freezing Out Identity Theft."

15. Knight Ridder Newspapers, "Identity Thieves Get More Sophisticated," *Waterloo/Cedar Falls Courier,* October 7, 2004, p. A1.

16. Evan Perez, "Identity Theft Puts Pressure on Data Sellers," *The Wall Street Journal,* February 18, 2005, p. B1.

17. "Study Finds Privacy 'Protections' Could Increase Cost to Consumers," *Business Wire,* May 22, 2002 [**http://web.lexisnexis.com/universe/doc...V&_md5=7754ed85324cae0f83a-ac59eac3b9c50**].

18. "Study Finds Privacy 'Protections' Could Increase Costs."

19. Associated Press, "Consumers Decide: Privacy or Savings?" *Waterloo/Cedar Falls Courier,* January 18, 2002, p. C5.

20. Mark Johnson, "Credit Card Use Helps Businesses Sell Personal Data," *Tampa Tribune,* August 5, 1999, Business and Finance Section, p. 7.

21. This summary of FCRA requirements was drawn largely from the FTC document, "A Summary of Your Rights under the Fair Credit Reporting Act" [**http://www.ftc.gov/bcp/conline/edcams/fcra/summary.htm**].

22. Michael Schroeder and Suein Hwang, "Sweeping New Bankruptcy Law to Make Life Harder for Debtors," *The Wall Street Journal,* April 6, 2005, p. A1.

23. Constance Mitchell Ford, "Creditor-Friendly South Offers Preview of Bankruptcy Changes," *The Wall Street Journal,* March 10, 2005, p. A1.

24. Ford, "Creditor-Friendly South."

25. *The Washington Post,* "Punitive Charges Dog Credit Card Users," *Waterloo/Cedar Falls Courier,* March 7, 2005, p. A1.

International Ethics and Law

Introduction

The preceding chapters have addressed law and ethics in an American context. However, ours is an increasingly global economy. Evidence of our global economy is everywhere. For example, it is possible to travel the world accessing automated teller machines (ATM) for local currency. Through online banking, you can see the cash obtained, say in Japanese yen, instantaneously debited from your domestic bank account. In cities around the world, you will find such American icons as Starbucks, McDonalds, KPMG, and Citicorp adorning shops and buildings. And back in the United States, driving the local roads you can see cars from many countries. Checking the Yellow Pages, you will find sushi bars, as well as Mexican, Chinese, Thai, Greek, Indian, and many other restaurants. And on many streets you can find branches of HSBC, a British bank, and T-Mobile outlets, part of the German Corporation, Deutsche Telekom. The process of globalization is the breaking down of national boundaries and rules to allow free interchange around the world—the free interchange of people, businesses, goods, services, investments, communications, and ideas.

But what are the implications of this networked global economy? To what laws are companies subject? The laws of their "home" country? The laws of the host country? The laws where their suppliers or customers reside? What law applies if the host country and the home country are different? And what happens when a corporation changes its home country? When the German corporation, Daimler Benz, merged with Chrysler, becoming Daimler Chrysler, did the laws to which it was subject change? As firms become companies of the world, rather than of one nation, difficult issues of ethics and law arise.

The International Environment

Since Adam Smith, many have argued that it is axiomatic that a decrease in trade barriers between any number of countries will stimulate the world economy, not simply the economies of the countries involved in the specific trade agreement. This principle has been resoundingly affirmed in recent years by the 148 countries that have, as of this writing, joined the World Trade Organization (WTO) since it was created January 1, 1995. A fundamental principle set forth in the preamble to the 1994 Marrakesh Agreement establishing the WTO is that "the substantial reduction of tariffs and other barriers to trade" will contribute to the objectives of "raising standards of living, ensuring full employment and a large and steadily growing volume of real income."[1] Member countries in the WTO represent a diverse array of the world's governments: from communist to socialist to capitalist, from Buddhist to Jewish to Christian to Muslim, and from every continent. Thus the value of decreasing trade barriers is a widely shared belief in the international community.

The strength of this belief, however, is being tested as the WTO member states struggle during the current round of multilateral trade negotiations (MTN), known as the Doha Round (after the city in Qatar where the round was initiated). The Doha Round deadlocked at a September 2003 meeting in Cancun, Mexico. The primary cause was extensive domestic farm subsidy programs maintained by both the United States and the European Union (EU). Because the WTO talks are based on consensus, not on votes, even less powerful nations, particularly when they act in concert, can make their concerns felt. "Developing nations, led by Brazil and India, . . . contended that massive subsidies allow rich nations to flood global markets with farm products, depressing prices and impeding the economic development of poor countries that rely on agriculture as their primary source of exports. For example, African nations complain that American cotton subsidies contribute to the impoverishment of thousands of African growers."[2] Some commentators wondered whether the Cancun deadlock might signal an end to viable WTO multilateral trade negotiations and a return to bilateral trade talks, in which the imbalance of power between rich and poor nations is more pronounced. Fortunately, that eventuality seems to have been sidestepped, at least for the present, by an August 2004 deal brokered by Brazil, the United States, and the EU, in which wealthier nations agreed to abolish all agricultural export subsidies ultimately, but no firm deadlines were imposed. Doha Round negotiations are expected to last through 2006. [The WTO maintains an extensive online presence, including full text documents, through its Web site at **www.wto.org**]

> African nations complain that American cotton subsidies contribute to the impoverishment of thousands of African growers.

To the extent the WTO continues to be successful in reducing trade barriers to the free flow of goods and services, the global economy grows and the ethical and legal issues addressed in this chapter are magnified. However, the desire to reach some common legal ground in international business is not a recent development. For example, U.S. commercial treaties (largely bilateral), negotiated as early as 1778, have long regulated shipping and trading rights and rules between individuals of different countries. In the 20th century an unprecedented expansion of world trade was facilitated by the development of many regional trade agreements, such as the General Agreement on Tariffs and Trade (GATT—now a foundation agreement of the WTO) and the North American Free Trade Agreement (NAFTA), as well as the development of regional common markets such as the EU, the MERCOSUR Common Market (created by Argentina, Brazil, Paraguay, and Uruguay) and the East African Community (created by Kenya, Tanzania, and Uganda), among others.

It is worth taking a moment to consider recent EU developments, which make it a growing economic powerhouse. In May 2005 ten countries became new members of the EU, swelling its member states to a total of 25 and at the same time bringing its total GDP on par with that of the United States. Its population far surpasses that of the United States (457 million compared to 296 million). Eight of the new members were formerly Soviet bloc countries. Further, in December 2005 four additional countries (Bulgaria, Croatia, Romania, and Turkey) were permitted to become EU candidate countries, allowing them to pursue multiyear negotiations to resolve their eligibility for full membership. [EUROPA is the portal site of the European Union, found at **europa.eu.int**]

In the coming years it may be useful to watch the international economic roles and relationships among the United States, the EU, and China, which became a WTO member state at the end of 2001.

Countervailing Forces   While many nations are finding common ground in important respects, other forces are, in effect, limiting the globalization of world business. Interesting insights in this regard are found in *Global Trends 2015,* a U.S. government report developed under the auspices of the Central Intelligence Agency in 2000.[3] It identifies a number of regions with concerns about "the perceived adverse economic, political, and social consequences of globalization," such as east and southeast Asia, the Middle East, northern Africa, Europe, and Canada. Many of these concerns focus on protecting historical social and cultural identities from an encroaching American culture. According to the report, these concerns are likely to cause such countries to attempt to block or slow unwanted impacts of globalization through such actions as seeking greater political control over international financial and trade institutions. [For a download of the whole report, see **www.cia.gov/cia/reports/globaltrends2015**]

As evidenced in the following article, globalization to this point has not been uniformly beneficial; and it might be worth a reassessment.

Global Capitalism: Can It Be Made to Work Better?

READING

Pete Engardio

It's hard to figure how a term that once connoted so much good for the world has fallen into such disrepute. In the past decade, globalization—meaning the rise of market capitalism around the world—has undeniably contributed to America's New Economy boom. It has created millions of jobs from Malaysia to Mexico and a cornucopia of affordable goods for Western consumers. It has brought phone service to some 300 million households in developing nations and a transfer of nearly $2 trillion from rich countries to poor through equity, bond investments, and commercial loans. It has helped topple dictators by making information freely available in once sheltered societies. And now the Internet is poised to narrow the commercial and cultural gulfs separating rich nations from poor even further in the decade to come. So it's little wonder that, for many, the rage now being vented against globalization is perplexing.

*   *   *   *   *

RETHINKING

Yet it would be a grave mistake to dismiss the uproar witnessed in the past few years in Seattle, Washington, D.C., and Prague. Many of the radicals leading the protests may be on the political fringe. But they have helped to kick-start a profound rethinking about globalization among governments, mainstream economists, and corporations that, until recently, was carried on mostly in obscure think tanks.

This reassessment is badly overdue. In the late 20th century, global capitalism was pushed by leaps in technology, the failure of socialism, and East Asia's seemingly miraculous success. Now it's time to get realistic.

The plain truth is that market liberalization by itself does not lift all boats, and in some cases, it has caused severe damage. What's more, there's no point denying that multinationals have contributed to labor, environmental, and human rights abuses.

For global capitalism to move into the next stage will require a much more sophisticated look at the costs and benefits of open markets. To assess these increasingly important trade-offs, *BusinessWeek* sent more than a dozen reporters around the world, from the deserts of Chad to the factories of Guatemala, to witness firsthand the effects of global capitalism. They met workers who toil 16 hours a day for miserly pay making garments sold in the United States, as well as villagers who want oil companies off their land. But they also talked to factory laborers who have seen big gains in their standards of living as well as creative bureaucrats who have used markets to coax growth out of once moribund economies.

The overwhelming conclusion of this reporting is that there are many examples of where reckless investment has done harm—but there is no case where the hazards can't be addressed with better government and corporate policy. The real question isn't whether free markets are good or bad. It is why they are producing such wildly different results in different countries. Figuring out that answer is essential before all the benefits of global markets are realized.

The extremes of global capitalism are astonishing. While the economies of East Asia have achieved rapid growth, there has been little overall progress in much of the rest of the developing world. Income in Latin America grew by only 6 percent in the past two decades, when the continent was opening up. Average incomes in sub-Saharan Africa and the old Eastern bloc have actually contracted. The World Bank figures the number of people living on $1 a day increased, to 1.3 billion, over the past decade.

The downside of global capitalism is the disruption of whole societies. While the industrialized countries have enacted all sorts of worker and environmental safeguards since

the turn of the [twentieth] century, the global economy is pretty much still in the robber-baron age. Yet if global capitalism's flaws aren't addressed, the backlash could grow more severe.

The longer-term danger is that if the world's poor see no benefits from free trade and IMF austerity programs, political support for reform could erode. The current system is "unsustainable," says United Nations Assistant Secretary General John G. Ruggie, who, as a political economist at Columbia University, examined how previous golden ages of global capitalism, such as the one at the turn of the 19th century, unraveled.

It all adds up to a breakdown of what was known as the Washington Consensus, the world view pushed aggressively by the U.S. Treasury, the IMF, and the World Bank in the early 1990s. This dictum held that all countries should open their markets to trade, direct investment, and short-term capital as quickly as possible. The transition would be painful, but inevitably, prosperity would result.

In hindsight, it was a naïve and self-interested view. Although developing nations badly needed to import capital and foreign financial know-how, many simply could not handle the inflows. The results were huge white-elephant industrial and property projects—and foreign-currency debt bombs that started exploding in 1994.

A more realistic view is now gaining hold. It begins with a similar premise: that trade and inflows of private capital are still essential to achieving strong sustainable growth and to reducing poverty. But it acknowledges that multinationals—which account for the bulk of direct cross-border investment and one-third of trade—have social responsibilities in nations where the rule of law is weak. And this view dispenses with the erroneous notion that open markets will magically produce prosperity in all conditions. Even the IMF now warns that a high degree of openness to global capital can be dangerous for some developing nations. "The IMF push for capital market liberalization for all nations was driven by financial market ideology," says former World Bank chief economist Joseph E. Stiglitz, now a vocal IMF critic. "They have conceded defeat, but only after the damage was done."

NOT SO FAST

According to the new pragmatism, governments first must deliver political stability, sound economic management, and educated workers if they are to gain from wide-open markets. East Asia's Tigers had many of these features when they began their export drives; most of Latin America and Africa did not.

* * * * *

Source: *BusinessWeek,* November 6, 2000, pp. 72–75. Reprinted by permission.

Questions

1. This article argues that the countries that have not bene-fited from globalization are those that lack political stability, sound economic management, and educated workers. How could these factors affect the success of globalization?

2. Consider the people from the United States and elsewhere that have expressed concern about continued globalization. What do you think they are most concerned about—the free interchange of people, businesses, goods, services, invest-ments, communications, or ideas? Explain.

3. Why do you think China, one of the most communist of na-tions, wanted to join the WTO? Would it surprise you to learn that Afghanistan, Iraq, Russia, Saudi Arabia, and Uzbekistan, while not currently WTO members, are all for-mally enrolled as observer countries, which means they are (or are considering) pursuing accession negotiations to become WTO member states? Why might Iran have cho-sen not to become even an observer country?

4. Besides sushi, what manifestations of cultural globaliza-tion can you identify that have not originated in the United States?

5. On balance, do you believe globalization is a good thing or not? Explain.

The Intercultural Environment: Ethics across International Borders

The events of September 11, 2001, served to highlight the ethical and legal differences of two cultures: American and Islamic. The first step in creating an effective working relationship is to attempt to understand cultural differences. Religion often provides the fundament of a culture's ethical structure. Thus two countries with different religious heritages are likely to have divergent ethical and legal norms. For example, a basic precept in the United States is the separation of church and state. In contrast, in Islamic countries, religion is the basis for many legal, as well as ethical, standards. In reading the following article, consider what rights you believe to be "funda-mental." Keep in mind that different cultures have different concepts of those rights that should be protected.

> in Islamic countries, religion is the basis for many legal, as well as ethical, standards.

READING Islamic Law: Myths and Realities

Dennis J. Wiechman, Jerry D. Kendall, and Mohammad K. Azarian

. . . Mohammed Salam Madkoar explains the theoretical as-sumptions of Islamic Law:

> In order to protect the five important indispensables in Islam (religion, life, intellect, offspring, and property), Islamic Law has provided a worldly punishment in addition to that in the hereafter. Islam has, in fact, adopted two courses for the preservation of these five indispensables: the first is through cultivating religious consciousness in the human soul and the awakening of human awareness through moral education; the second is by inflicting deterrent punishment,

which is the basis of the Islamic criminal system. Therefore "Hudoud," Retaliation (Qesas), and Discretionary (Tazir) punishments have been prescribed according to the type of the crime committed.

Islamic Law and Jurisprudence are not always understood by the Western press. Although it is the responsibility of the mass media to bring to the world's attention violations of human rights and acts of terror, many believe that media stereotyping of all Muslims is a major problem. The recent bombing at the World Trade Center in New York City is a prime example. The media often used the term "Islamic Fundamentalists" when re-ferring to the accused in the case. They also referred to the

Egyptian connections in that case as "Islamic Fundamentalists." The media have used the label of "Islamic Fundamentalist" to imply all kinds of possible negative connotations: terrorists, kidnappers, and hostage takers. Since the media do not use the term "Fundamentalist Christian" each time a Christian does something wrong, the use of such labels is wrong for any group, Christians, Muslims, or Orthodox Jews.

A Muslim who is trying to live his religion is indeed a true believer in God. This person tries to live all of the tenets of his religion in a fundamental way. Thus, a true Muslim is a fundamentalist in the practice of that religion, but a true Muslim is not radical, because the Quran teaches tolerance and moderation in all things. When the popular media generalize from the fundamentalist believer to the "radical fundamentalist" label they do a disservice to all Muslims and others.

NO SEPARATION OF CHURCH AND STATE

To understand Islamic Law one must first understand the assumptions of Islam and the basic tenets of the religion. The meaning of the word *Islam* is "submission or surrender to Allah's (God's) will." Therefore, Muslims must first and foremost obey and submit to Allah's will. Mohammed the Prophet was called by God to translate verses from the Angel Gabriel to form the most important book in Islam, the Quran, Muslims believe.

* * * * *

The most difficult part of Islamic Law for most Westerners to grasp is that there is no separation of church and state. The religion of Islam and the government are one. Islamic Law is controlled, ruled, and regulated by the Islamic religion. The theocracy controls all public and private matters. Government, law, and religion are one. There are varying degrees of this concept in many nations, but all law, government, and civil authority rest upon it and it is a part of Islamic religion. There are civil laws in Muslim nations for Muslim and non-Muslim people. Sharia [Islamic law] is only applicable to Muslims. . . . The U.S. Constitution (Bill of Rights) prohibits the government from "establishing a religion." The U.S. Supreme Court has concluded in numerous cases that the U.S. Government can't favor one religion over another. That concept is implicit, for most U.S. legal scholars and many U.S. academicians believe that any mixture of "church and state" is inherently evil and filled with many problems.

* * * * *

CRIMES IN ISLAM

Crimes under Islamic Law can be broken down into three major categories.

1. Had crimes (most serious).

2. Tazir crimes (least serious).

3. Qesas crimes (revenge crimes restitution).

Had crimes are the most serious under Islamic Law, and Tazir crimes are the least serious. Some Western writers use the felony analogy for Had crimes and misdemeanor label for Tazir crimes. The analogy is partially accurate, but not entirely true. Common law has no comparable form of Qesas crimes. . . .

Had Crimes

Had crimes are those which are punishable by a preestablished punishment found in the Quran. These most serious of all crimes are found by an exact reference in the Quran to a specific act and a specific punishment for that act. There is no plea-bargaining or reducing the punishment for a Had crime. . . .

The Had crimes are

1. Murder.

2. Apostasy from Islam (making war upon Allah and his messengers).

3. Theft.

4. Adultery.

5. Defamation (false accusation of adultery or fornication).

6. Robbery.

7. Alcohol drinking.

* * * * *

Had crimes have fixed punishments because they are set by God and are found in the Quran. Had crimes are crimes against God's law and Tazir crimes are crimes against society. There are some safeguards for Had crimes that many in the media fail to mention. Some in the media only mention that if you steal, your hand is cut off. The Islamic judge must look at a higher level of proof and reasons why the person committed the crime. A judge can only impose the Had punishment when a person confesses to the crime or there are enough witnesses to the crime. The usual number of witnesses is two, but in the case of adultery four witnesses are required. . . .

Tazir Crimes

Tazir crimes are less serious than the Had crimes found in the Quran. Some common law writers use the analogy of misdemeanors, which is the lesser of the two categories (felony and misdemeanor) of common law crimes.

* * * * *

Tazir crimes are acts which are punished because the offender disobeys God's law and word. Tazir crimes can be punished if they harm the societal interest. [Islamic] Law places an emphasis on the societal or public interest.

* * * * *

In some Islamic nations, Tazir crimes are set by legislative parliament. Each nation is free to establish its own criminal code and there is a great disparity in punishment of some of these crimes. Some of the more common Tazir crimes are bribery, selling tainted or defective products, treason, usury, and selling obscene pictures. The consumption of alcohol in Egypt is punished much differently than in Iran or Saudi Arabia because they have far different civil laws. Islamic law has much greater flexibility than the Western media portray.

Qesas Crimes and Diya

Islamic Law has an additional category of crimes that common law nations do not have. A Qesas crime is one of retaliation. If you commit a Qesas crime, the victim has a right to seek retribution and retaliation. The exact punishment for each Qesas crime is set forth in the Quran. If you are killed, then your family has a right to seek Qesas punishment from the murderer. Punishment can come in several forms and also may include "Diya." Diya is paid to the victim's family as part of punishment. Diya is an ancient form of restitution for the victim or his family. The family also may seek to have a public execution of the offender or the family may seek to pardon the offender. Traditional Qesas crimes include

1. Murder (premeditated and nonpremeditated).
2. Premeditated offenses against human life, short of murder.
3. Murder by error.
4. Offenses by error against humanity, short of murder.

Some reporters in the mass media have criticized the thought of "blood money" as barbaric. They labeled the practice as undemocratic and inhumane. Qesas crimes are based upon the criminological assumption of retribution. The concept of retribution was found in the first statutory "Code of Hammurabi" and in the Law of Moses in the form of "an eye for an eye." Muslims add to that saying "but it is better to forgive." Contemporary common law today still is filled with the assumptions of retribution. . . . The idea of retribution is fixed in the U.S. system of justice. Qesas crime is simple retribution: if one commits a crime he knows what the punishment will be.

Diya has its roots in Islamic Law and dates to the time of the Prophet Mohammed. . . . Today, the Diya is paid by the offender to the victim if he is alive. If the victim is dead, the money is paid to the victim's family or to the victim's tribe or clan.

* * * * *

Each victim has the right to ask for retaliation and, historically, the person's family would carry out that punishment. Modern Islamic law now requires the government to carry out the Qesas punishment. . . .

CONCLUSIONS

Islamic Law is very different from English Common Law or the European Civil Law traditions. Muslims are bound to the teachings of the Prophet Mohammed whose translation of Allah or God's will is found in the Quran. Muslims are held accountable to the Sharia Law, but non-Muslims are not bound by the same standard (apostasy from Allah). Muslims and non-Muslims are both required to live by laws enacted by the various forms of government such as tax laws, traffic laws, white-collar crimes of business, and theft. These and many other crimes similar to Common Law crimes are tried in modern "Mazalim Courts." The Mazalim Courts can also hear civil law, family law, and all other cases. Islamic Law does have separate courts for Muslims for "religious crimes" and contemporary nonreligious courts for other criminal and civil matters.

Source: Office of International Criminal Justice, *Criminal Justice International Online,* 12, no. 3 (May 1996) found at **http://www.iol.ie/ ~afifi/Articles/law.htm** and reprinted by permission of *Criminal Justice International Online.*

Questions

1. If your job required that you live in a country that had laws with which you disagreed on moral grounds, would you follow the law? Explain.

2. Do the laws discussed here make logical sense to you? On what basis should you judge them?

3. Would conflicts in cultural issues such as those addressed by the laws discussed in this article impact your decision about where to conduct your business? *Should* they impact your decisions? Explain.

4. Consider the difference between fundamental rights and culturally based rights. Conduct a Web search of responses and/or criticisms of the implementation of Islamic Laws and identify those that seem culturally based and those that seem based on some concept of fundamental, universally recognized rights.

Social Responsibility to Host Country

Where a firm is involved in business abroad, does that firm have social responsibilities to the host country beyond those required by the market and the law of that country? This issue has arisen in many contexts, including the environment. For instance, are firms that engage in business that may result in a depletion of the rain forests responsible for protecting the forests, even where there are no laws that require them to do so? Chiquita, Dole, and Del Monte have all been cited as companies that have engaged in harmful environmental practices. These companies have expanded their banana plantations in Central and South America, increasing the amount of pesticides used in those areas, which has in turn led to extreme deforestation.

Another area that has received considerable press attention are the working conditions of laborers in the host country. Gap, Nike, and Wal-Mart have all received considerable negative news attention in prior years for working conditions at foreign plants used to make their apparel—from low wages to unsanitary conditions to long hours to physical and psychological abuse.

How have these companies responded? Gap made quite a stir when it released its first Social Responsibility Report in mid-2004, in which it recognized that working conditions were far from perfect in the factories of its overseas suppliers.[4] Many of the other companies just identified have responded to their critics, taken a closer look at the impacts their businesses have had worldwide, and shared their findings, often through annual social responsibility reports. [For examples of corporate social responsibility reports, see **www.chiquita.com** and select Corporate Responsibility and CR Reports; also see **http://www.gapinc.com/social_resp/social_resp.htm** and **http://www.nike.com/nikebiz/ nikebiz.jhtml?page=29&item=fy04**]

Still other companies have acted proactively: establishing social responsibility goals, implementing them, and publicizing them without requiring bad publicity as a catalyst. One example is Starbucks, which actively pursues policies to improve both environmental and labor practices of coffee producers around the globe. [For more about Starbucks' social responsibility policies and practices, see **http://www.starbucks.com/aboutus/ csrannualreport.asp**]

Substandard Working Conditions

As mentioned previously, under the moniker "sweatshops," some corporations have been chastised for allowing working conditions to prevail in their foreign operations or suppliers that Western cultures would consider substandard. Such sweatshops pose a host of commercial, economic, ethical, political, and social questions. Do businesses owe a social responsibility to the host country to improve their labor conditions?

Free market economists believe that sweatshops are necessary and beneficial; sweatshops improve global well-being; consumers in global markets pay less for the products they buy; and the economies of developing countries improve because their export sectors expand. Sweatshops have been an element of every developed country's transformation from an agrarian society to an urban-based, highly industrialized economy. If poor countries want to develop, the economists argue, a sweatshop stage is necessary. How long do you think such a stage should last, and who should act to eventually bring improvements?

[For sweatshop Web sites, see Sweatshop Watch at **www.sweatshopwatch.org;** UNITE at **www.uniteunion.org/sweatshops;** Human Rights Watch at **www.hrw.org;** Global Exchange at **www.globalexchange.org;** and the International Labour Organization at **www.ilo.org**]

Question

If you were the vice president for supply chain management for a large manufacturer or retailer, what type of labor standards would you impose on suppliers from other countries, if any?

Social Responsibility to Home Country?

Notwithstanding a potential responsibility to the countries in which a firm does business, does that firm have any special obligation to its home country? A social responsibility to a home country might necessitate imposing the values of one's home country throughout the world. The United States exports its values structure in a variety of ways, including through the extraterritorial application of its laws. When the U.S. Supreme Court declared that antidiscrimination provisions of United States statutes such as Title VII of the Civil Rights Act of 1964 did not apply extraterritorially,[5] Congress reversed the decision with its 1991 Amendments to Title VII. Accordingly, American firms that do not maintain certain Title VII standards abroad will be subject to liability in their home country.

The Foreign Corrupt Practices Act (FCPA)

Consider the problem of bribery and other forms of corruption in certain countries. Some in those countries may contend that there is nothing wrong with bribery, while other nations criticize it greatly. How would you define *bribery*? What is the main problem with it? For years, U.S. firms have tackled this problem in their own and other countries. On a governmental scale, Congress has attempted to respond harshly to corruption in other governments and to support U.S. firms that do not participate in foreign corruption.

As we saw in Chapter 2, the FCPA prohibits U.S. companies and some joint ventures from making certain payments or gifts to government officials for the purpose of influencing business decisions. Although the FCPA appears to be well motivated, some critics argue that it is inappropriate for the United States to unilaterally try to impose its sense of morality on others via foreign trade. Others argue that the FCPA unduly restricts American companies operating abroad and prevents them from effectively competing with other firms.

Social Responsibility to Humanity?

Are we in fact evolving toward the identification of common international ethical standards, standards that can be supported and implemented globally? Is this a natural progression from national standards? For example, there was a time in history when agreement was achieved only at a city level, which over time developed to state-level agreement, which then developed to agreement among federated states. Is such a progression to global standards perhaps inevitable? Does a framework that divides ethical issues between those of the "host" country and those of the "home" country remain a useful analytical tool?

> If we are moving to a concept of global social responsibility, can we do so without sacrificing the existence of wonderfully diverse and unique cultures?

If we are moving to a concept of global social responsibility, can we do so without sacrificing the existence of wonderfully diverse and unique cultures? Do we have to become the same? Or can we agree on fundamentals, but still appreciate diversity, as a garden is enriched by the presence of a wide selection of grasses, flowers, bushes, trees, and birds?

Consider the evidence. Not only are businesses interacting with stakeholders of ever more diverse nationalities (investors/owners/shareholders, customers/clients, suppliers, general citizenry impacted by business decisions), but the cultural identity of businesses themselves may be unclear. Consider the previously mentioned Daimler Chrysler—it has a rich history associated with both Germany and the United States. On the services side, consider the remaining "Big Four" accounting firms: Deloitte Touche Tohmatsu, Ernst & Young, KPMG, and PricewaterhouseCoopers. Although each of these firms started in the United States, they are each now a global network. Go to any major city in the world and you are likely to see one or more of their names emblazoned on buildings in the central business district. The previously mentioned CIA document, *Global Trends 2015,* states that MNEs (multinational enterprises) now number "more than 50,000 with nearly one-half million affiliates" and predicts a continuing growth in their numbers.[6]

There is considerable evidence of voluntary international cooperation to establish acceptable business practices. Only a few of them are listed here:

- "The International Standards Organization has become a global tool in managerial circles by creating standards such as ISO14001 for environmental auditing. Using that model, the Council on Economic Priorities Accreditation Agency (CEPAA) has developed Social Accountability 8000 (SA8000), so companies can assure an equitable and safe workplace for their employees and those of their suppliers."[7]

- The United Nations has adopted a number of documents establishing principles for worldwide adoption, many of which address issues of application to business. Perhaps the most directly related is its nonbinding "Norms on the Responsibilities of Transnational Corporations and Other Business Enterprises with Regard to Human Rights."[8]

- The Council of the Bars and Law Societies of the European Union has published a draft report for EU lawyers to use in advising clients on matters of corporate social responsibility. The report is entitled "Corporate Social Responsibility and the Role of the Legal Profession."[9]

- In 1994 a group of business leaders from Europe, Japan, and the United States developed a code of ethical conduct for global firms, known as the Caux Round Table Principles.[10]

- In 2001 the Chocolate Manufacturers Association, the World Cocoa Foundation, and executives of many major chocolate manufacturers and cocoa processors, including Hershey's, Nestlé, and Guittard Chocolates, signed an agreement accepting responsibility for labor practices on cocoa farms.[11]

Questions

1. Is it ethical for the U.S. Congress to seek to enforce federal laws on the operations of U.S. corporations abroad? Why or why not?

2. What do you think of the concept of global social responsibility? Should its development be encouraged? Is it inevitable? Does it imply the end, or at least diminishment, of the vast cultural diversity found around the world today? If so, is the cultural imperialism discussed in Chapter 1 a legitimate worry for non-Americans?

PRACTICING ETHICS   Individual Social Responsibility to Humanity?

Consider the following excerpt from a speech delivered September 28, 2001, by Jose Ramos-Horta, Nobel Peace Prize Laureate (1996) and Minister for Foreign Affairs and Cooperation for the East Timor Transition Government:

> There is no dispute that abject poverty, child labor, and prostitution are a moral indictment of all humanity.
>
> However, poverty should not only touch our conscience: It is also a matter of peace and security because it destabilizes entire countries and regions. In turn it threatens the integration of the global economy that is vital if the rich are to stay rich or if the poor are to move up, if only an inch.

> Peace will be illusory as long as the rich ignore the clamor of the poor for a better life, as long as hundreds of millions of people live below the poverty line, cannot afford a meal a day, do not have access to clean water and a roof.[12]

Questions

Must all of us, not just active international businesses, accept a social responsibility to humanity? What might answering yes to this question imply for our actions as students, employees, employers, and investors?

Laws Governing Cross-Border Business

All businesses must, of course, follow the laws of the countries in which they are physically present and operating. (Whether a business with no physical presence that solicits or performs business in a foreign country electronically must follow the laws of the foreign country will be examined in Chapter 18). Thus when Disney opened its amusement park in France, it became subject to the labor laws of France. Similarly, U.S. businesses operating abroad will be subject to the property and contract law provisions of those countries, as well as a whole compendium of other laws.

> When Disney opened its amusement park in France, it became subject to the labor laws of France.

Conversely, foreign firms often wish to establish operations in the United States, in part because Americans are more inclined to buy goods made in this country. Doing business in the United States brings with it the requirement that these foreign businesses comply with U.S. laws and regulations.

Businesses may also be required, even in their foreign operations, to continue to follow certain of the laws of their home country, as previously discussed with regard to the application of American antidiscrimination laws and the Foreign Corrupt Practices Act to U.S. corporations operating abroad. Interestingly, although there is a presumption in U.S. law against the extraterritorial application of U.S. criminal law, where Congress has clearly indicated an intent to cover actions outside of the United States, U.S. citizens can be held accountable for their actions abroad.[13]

Finally, businesses operating across national borders will also be subject to certain additional provisions, those that make up international law. The foundation and some examples of international business law will be discussed soon, but first it will be useful to explore some of the different forms of business available to companies wishing to expand their operations into foreign countries.

Forms of Global Business Expansion

Multinational Enterprise (MNE)

The term *multinational enterprise* traditionally refers to a company that conducts business in more than one country. Any of the following operations, except for a direct contract with a foreign purchaser, may qualify a company as an MNE.

Direct Contract A firm may expand its business across territorial borders using a variety of methods. The simplest, from a contractual perspective, occurs where a firm in one country enters an agreement with a firm or individual in another country. Using the example of sales, a firm might decide to sell its product to a purchaser in another country through a basic contractual agreement. This is called a *direct sale* to a foreign purchaser. In this situation, the parties agree on the terms of the sale and record them in the contract.

Where the contract is silent as to a term of the sale, the law that will apply in connection with the missing term will be the law specified in the contract; where none is specified, the applicable law will depend on the country in which the court is located. Some courts will apply the *vesting of rights doctrine,* where the applicable law is the law of the jurisdiction in which the rights in the contract vested. Other courts may apply the *most significant relationship doctrine,* where the applicable law is that of the jurisdiction that has the most significant relationship to the contract and the parties. Finally, some courts will apply the *governmental interest doctrine,* where the court will apply the law either of its own jurisdiction or of the jurisdiction that has the greatest interest in the outcome of the issue.

> One of the most complicated issues pertaining to direct sales is that of payment.

One of the most complicated issues pertaining to direct sales is that of *payment.* The seller should and usually does require an *irrevocable letter of credit,* which the buyer obtains from a bank after paying that amount to the bank (or securing that amount of credit). The bank then promises to pay the seller the amount of the contract after conforming goods have been shipped. The "irrevocable" component is that the bank may not revoke the letter of credit without the consent of both the buyer and the seller. In this way the seller is protected because the buyer already has come up with adequate funds for the purchase, confirmed by a bank. The buyer is protected because the funds are not turned over to the seller until it has been determined that the goods conform to the contract. It is important to the buyer, however, that the letter of credit be specific as to the conformance of the goods because the bank will only ensure that the goods conform to the letter of credit and not to the contract itself.

Foreign Representation A second type of foreign expansion is a sale through a representative in the foreign country, whether it is through a distributor, agent, or other type of representative. A firm may decide to sell through an *agent*—that is, it hires an individual who will remain permanently in the foreign country, negotiate contracts, and assist in the performance of the contracts. Agents are generally compensated on a commission basis. On the other hand, the firm may act through a *representative,* who may solicit and take orders but, unlike an agent, may not enter into contracts on behalf of the firm. *Distributors* purchase the goods from the seller, then negotiate sales to foreign purchasers on their own behalf. In so doing, a distributor may be more likely to invest resources to develop the foreign market for the good.

It is important to note that *exclusive dealing* agreements with distributors, where a distributor agrees to sell only the goods of one manufacturer and the manufacturer agrees to sell only to that distributor in that area, are generally not allowed abroad, although they often are legal in the United States.

Export trading companies are firms that specialize in acting as the intermediary between business and purchasers in foreign countries. The firm will take title to the goods being sold and then complete the sale in the foreign country. *Export management companies,* on the other hand, merely manage the sale but do not take title to the goods; consequently they do not share in any of the risk associated with the sale.

Joint Venture   Foreign expansion may also occur through a *joint venture* agreement between two or more parties. This type of agreement is usually for one or several specific projects and is in effect for a specified period. For instance, several Japanese automobile manufacturers have entered joint ventures with American firms to manufacture some or all of certain models in America.

Branch Office or Subsidiary   A *branch office* is a wholly owned extension of a corporate entity in a foreign country. A *subsidiary* is a separate corporation formed in a foreign country and owned in whole or in part by the parent company. For example, an Indian paper company may open a branch office in London to market and sell its products. That office would be a mere extension of the offices already established in India. On the other hand, the Indian firm may create a separate subsidiary to handle its British orders, which might then have an office in London. A subsidiary or branch office relationship may also come about through an acquisition of an existing firm in the foreign country.

The primary difference between branch offices and subsidiaries comes into play with the question of liability. In most situations where a subsidiary is sued, the parent company is not liable. For example, in *U.S. v. Philip Morris, Inc.,*[14] the district court dismissed British American Tobacco (BAT) from the government's suit against various cigarette manufacturers for recovery of health care expenses. BAT is the British parent company of the U.S. company Brown & Williamson. The subsidiary, B&W, remained a part of the suit. In contrast, the liabilities of a branch office immediately become the liabilities of the main office. In addition, the income of a branch office is considered income to the parent firm and must be reported on that firm's income tax return. Income to a subsidiary remains on the balance sheet of the subsidiary. On the other hand, there is a benefit to opening a branch office. The branch office is considered by all dealing with it as merely an arm of the parent firm. In this respect, loans and insurance may be easier to obtain for a branch, as opposed to a subsidiary.

Licensing Where a company has no interest in commencing operations in a foreign country but instead merely wants to have its product or name on the market there, the company may decide to license the rights to the name or to manufacturing the product to another company.

The benefit to this type of relationship is that the licensor (holder of the right) has the opportunity to enter the foreign market, while the licensee assumes all of the obligations of running the business.

Franchising In a franchise agreement, the franchisee pays the franchisor for a license to use trademarks, formulas, and other trade secrets. The difference between a franchising agreement and a licensing contract is that a franchise agreement may be made up of a number of licensing arrangements, as well as other obligations. For instance, in a typical fast-food franchise agreement, the franchisor will license to the franchisee the right to use its trademark, name, logo, recipes, menus, and other recognized resources.

Foundations of International Law

A firm with manufacturing plants in Argentina and Thailand, and corporate headquarters in Bangkok, enters into a contract with a French firm to distribute its products produced in the Argentinean plant. The French firm is not satisfied with the quality of the products being sent. What law would apply to this situation? Argentinean? Thai? French? Or are there, perhaps, specific provisions of international law that will govern? The answer to this question is not simple, even for seasoned lawyers; yet the firms involved will be greatly affected by the decision.

The source of law applicable to an international issue depends on the issue involved. In general, private parties are free to form agreements in whatever manner they wish. The parties to the agreement can determine, for instance, which nation's law shall govern the contract, where disagreements in connection with the contract shall be settled, and even in which language the transactions shall be made. This is considered *private law.* Whenever the parties to a transaction are from different jurisdictions and are involved in a lawsuit, the court will look to the agreement of the parties to resolve these issues. Otherwise, where the contract is silent as to the choice of law, jurisdiction, and other questions, the court must decide. Generally, the law of the jurisdiction in which the transaction occurred is applied. If the transaction is done by mail, as are many international trade negotiations, most often the law of the jurisdiction of the seller's place of business applies. Recall, however, that the parties to the contract may always reach an agreement on the law to be applied.

Public law, on the other hand, includes those rules of each nation that regulate the contractual agreement between the parties—for instance, import and export taxes, packaging requirements, and safety standards. In addition, public law regulates the relationships between nations.

Public law derives from a number of sources. The most familiar source of international public law is a *treaty* or *convention* (a contract between nations). For example, the United States, Canada, and Mexico have entered into the North American Free Trade Agreement (NAFTA), a convention regarding free trade between those countries. Some treaties and conventions are *self-executing,* which means that once the United States has signed them, a business can rely on and directly enforce their terms in court. The U.N. Convention on Contracts for the International Sale of Goods (CISG), which will be discussed soon, is an example of this. On the other hand, some treaties and conventions apply only to government signatories and not directly to private parties. Such a convention may, for example, require the United States to amend its federal statutory law to accomplish the purposes of the convention. Whether the Paris Convention (addressing international trademark issues) is self-executing or not is one of the issues the district court had to resolve in the *Piaggio* case, which appears later in this chapter.

Public law is also found in *international custom* or *generally accepted principles of law.* These terms refer to those practices that are commonly accepted as appropriate business or commercial practices between nations. For instance, sovereign immunity is an accepted principle of international law. A *custom* is derived from consistent behavior over time that is accepted as binding by the countries that engage in that behavior.

The Development of Customs

One might better understand the concept of *custom* if it is analogized to the law of sales in the United States. For years, merchants would follow certain accepted customs or principles in connection with the sale of goods. These customs or manners of dealing between merchants were later codified in the Uniform Commercial Code (UCC) that regulates the sale of goods and has certain provisions specifically related to the sale of goods between merchants. In this way, customs or practices traditionally followed by merchants have become accepted principles of law.

On the other hand, in the international legal arena, customary practices are still developing. For instance, in connection with personal privacy or information flow between countries, the custom had been that personal information moves freely between countries to encourage the free flow of information in the business world. However, the European Union in 1998 established minimum standards for the protection of personal data that must be maintained by any country receiving information from an EU country. (See Chapter 18 for more on the EU's Directive on Data Protection.)

Two factors are used to determine whether a custom exists: (1) consistency and repetition of the action or decision and (2) recognition by nations that this custom is binding. The first merely holds that the action or decision must be accepted by a number of nations for a time long enough to establish uniformity of application. The second dictates that the custom be accepted as binding by nations observing it. If the custom is accepted as merely persuasive, it does not rise to the level of a generally accepted principle of law. Through persistent objections, any nation may ensure that certain customs are not applied to cases in which it is involved.

Comity

The unique aspect of public international law is that countries are generally not subject to law in the international arena unless they consent to such jurisdiction. For instance, a country is not bound by a treaty unless that country has signed the treaty. A country is not bound by international custom unless it has traditionally participated in that custom. And prior judicial decisions are only persuasive where a country is convinced by and accepts these decisions as precedent. In fact, perhaps the most critical element in understanding international law is recognizing that it is not actually "law" in the way that we generally consider law. Countries are not bound to abide by it except through comity. *Comity* is the concept that countries *should* abide by international custom, treaties, and other sources of international direction because that is the civil way to engage in relationships. Nations must respect each other and respect some basic principles of dealing in order to have effective relationships.

The concept of comity also includes the respect one country gives to the actions another country takes in its own territory. Specifically, as stated by the Second Circuit in *Finanz AG Zurich v. Banco Economico S.A.,*[15] comity includes "the recognition which one nation allows within its territory to the legislative, executive, or judicial acts of another nation." Under this principle, U.S. courts "ordinarily refuse to review acts of foreign governments and defer to proceedings taking place in foreign countries." Thus the *Finanz* court held that a creditor could not sue in the United States to collect a debt that was subject to the jurisdiction of a bankruptcy proceeding in Brazil.

Although some believe that the origins of law are in religion and its commandments, others have argued that, instead, law derives from a natural tendency to prevent chaos. International law is that attempt to prevent chaos in the international marketplace through the application of universal principles, and comity is the means by which it is encouraged.

Regulation of International Trade

As just explained, there is no such thing as one body of international law per se that regulates international contracts and trade. Instead, a contract between firms in different countries may be subject to the laws of one country or the other, depending on (1) whether it is a sales contract subject to the U.N. CISG, discussed below, (2) whether the contract itself stipulates the applicable law and forum in which a dispute will be heard, and (3) the rules regarding conflict of laws in each jurisdiction.

Additionally, every country has domestic laws that regulate business conducted within its borders and that sometimes regulate its domestic firms outside of its borders. These laws govern the areas of employment-related activities and discrimination, product liability, intellectual property, antitrust and trade practices, and import taxes, to name a few. Consequently, a business owner may actually decide to market a good in one country over another simply because of that country's laws relating to the particular good or to commercial contracts in general. What follows is a brief look at several specific examples of the law governing international business. [For an extensive international trade law database, see **http://lexmercatoria.org**]

U.N. Convention on Contracts for the International Sale of Goods (CISG)

In 1988, 10 nations signed and became bound by the U.N. Convention on Contracts for the International Sale of Goods. By the end of 2006, the CISG will be enforceable in 65 nations. The CISG applies to contracts between parties of countries that have signed the convention and provides uniform rules for the sale of goods.

The CISG contains rules regarding the interpretation of contracts and negotiations and the form of contracts. Many obligations of the parties are enunciated by the CISG. For instance, the seller is required to deliver the goods and any documents relating to the goods, as well as to make sure that the goods conform to the contract terms. The buyer, on the other hand, is required to pay the contract price and to accept delivery of the goods. [For the Pace University CISG database, see **cisgw3.law.pace.edu**]

The CISG, however, does not answer all questions that may arise in a transaction. For instance, questions of a contract's validity are left to national law. We saw in Chapter 6, under American law, an enforceable contract requires five elements:

- *Capacity* to enter the contract.
- *Offer* and *acceptance* of the terms of the contract.
- *Consideration* for the promises in the contract.
- *Genuineness of assent.*
- *Legality of purpose* of the contract.

However, countries with civil law systems do not require consideration for a valid contract.

Generally, once a contract has been created, it is enforceable according to its terms by all parties to the contract. In the following case, read carefully to see what law the judge applies. He considers first the *private law* of the parties (that is, the express terms of the contract); then he looks to *custom;* and finally he applies the concept of *commercial impracticability.*

Transatlantic Financing Corporation v. United States

LEGAL BRIEFCASE 363 F.2d 312 (D.C. Cir. 1966)

Judge Skelly Wright

[In 1956, Transatlantic Financing, a steamship operator, contracted with the United States to ship wheat from Texas to Iran. Six days after the ship left port for Iran, the Egyptian government was at war with Israel and blocked the Suez Canal to shipping. The steamer therefore was forced to sail around the Cape of Good Hope. Transatlantic accordingly sued the United States for its added expenses as a result of this change of circumstances. Transatlantic contended that it had contracted only to travel the "usual and customary" route to Iran and that

the United States had received a greater benefit than that for which it contracted. The district court held for the United States; Transatlantic appealed.]

Transatlantic's claim is based on the following train of argument. The charter was a contract for a voyage from a Gulf port to Iran. Admiralty principles and practices, especially stemming from the doctrine of deviation, require us to [infer] into the contract the term that the voyage was to be performed by the "usual and customary" route. The usual and customary route from Texas to Iran was, at the time of contract, via Suez, so the contract was for a voyage from Texas to Iran via Suez.

When Suez was closed this contract became impossible to perform. Consequently, appellant's argument continues, when Transatlantic delivered the cargo by going around the Cape of Good Hope, in compliance with the Government's demand under claim of right, it conferred a benefit upon the United States for which it should be paid on quantum meruit.

The contract in this case does not expressly condition performance upon availability of the Suez route. Nor does it specify "via Suez" or, on the other hand, "via Suez or Cape of Good Hope." Nor are there provisions in the contract from which we may properly [infer] that the continued availability of Suez was a condition of performance. Nor is there anything in custom or trade usage, or in the surrounding circumstances generally, which would support our constructing a condition of performance. The numerous cases requiring performance around the Cape when Suez was closed indicate that the Cape route is generally regarded as an alternative means of performance. So the implied expectation that the route would be via Suez is hardly adequate proof of an allocation to the promisee of the risk of closure. In some cases, even an express expectation may not amount to a condition of performance. The doctrine of deviation supports our assumption that parties normally expect performance by the usual and customary route, but it adds nothing beyond this that is probative of an allocation of the risk.

If anything, the circumstances surrounding this contract indicate that the risk of the Canal's closure may be deemed to have been allocated to Transatlantic. We know or may safely assume that the parties were aware, as were most commercial men with interest affected by the Suez situation, that the Canal might become a dangerous area. No doubt the tension affected freight rates, and it is arguable that the risk of closure became part of the dickered terms. We do not deem the risk of closure so allocated, however. Foreseeability or even recognition of a risk does not necessarily prove its allocation. Parties to a contract are not always able to provide for all the possibilities of which they are aware, sometimes because they cannot agree, often simply because they are too busy. Moreover, that some abnormal risk was contemplated is probative but does not necessarily establish an allocation of the risk of the contingency which actually occurs. In this case, for example, nationalization by Egypt of the Canal Corporation and formation of the Suez Users Group did not necessarily indicate that the Canal would be blocked even if a confrontation resulted. The surrounding circumstances do indicate, however, a willingness by Transatlantic to assume abnormal risks, and this fact should legitimately cause us to judge the impracticability of performance by an alternative route in stricter terms than we would were the contingency unforeseen.

We turn then to the question whether occurrence of the contingency rendered performance commercially impracticable under the circumstances of this case. The goods shipped were not subject to harm from the longer, less temperate Southern route. The vessel and crew were fit to proceed around the Cape. Transatlantic was no less able than the United States to purchase insurance to cover the contingency's occurrence. If anything, it is more reasonable to expect owner–operators of vessels to insure against the hazards of war. They are in the best position to calculate the cost of performance by alternative routes (and therefore to estimate the amount of insurance required), and are undoubtedly sensitive to international troubles which uniquely affect the demand for and cost of their services. The only factor operating here in appellant's favor is the added expense, allegedly $43,972.00 above and beyond the contract price of $305,842.92, of extending a 10,000-mile voyage by approximately 3,000 miles. While it may be an overstatement to say that increased cost and difficulty of performance never constitute impracticability, to justify relief there must be more of a variation between expected cost and the cost of performing by an available alternative than is present in this case, where the promisor can legitimately be presumed to have accepted some degree of abnormal risk, and where impracticability is urged on the basis of added expense alone.

We conclude, therefore, as have most other courts considering related issues arising out of the Suez closure, that performance of this contract was not rendered legally impossible. Affirmed.

Questions

1. *a.* What did the court find with respect to the private law of the parties?

   b. What did it find with respect to the application of custom?

2. Would there be a different result in this case if the shipment had been tomatoes as opposed to wheat? Explain.

3. Would there be a different result in this case if the United States and Transatlantic agreed by contract that shipment was to arrive in Iran within a period of time that was only possible if the shipper used the canal route? Explain.

4. What do you think it would take for a court to render a contract commercially impracticable? In this case, the shipper was forced to spend almost $44,000 more than it had expected to spend in performing the $306,000 contract. What if the added cost had amounted to $100,000? Would you be persuaded that the contract was then commercially impracticable? What if the closing of the canal doubled the price of the contract? Explain.

International Trade in Services

Services, as opposed to goods, are a large component of the world's gross domestic product, currently accounting for 60 to 70 percent.[16] In the United States this percentage is even higher—services were 75 percent of gross national product (GNP) in 1998. Further, trade in services represents about 30 percent of the total dollar value of U.S. exports.[17] And the United States isn't the only country exporting services. Much furor has been seen in the popular press about the "outsourcing" and "offshoring" of U.S. service sector jobs.[18] *Outsourcing* generally refers to the contracting by U.S. companies of such services as call centers, accounting, and customer services to foreign companies located in low-wage markets. *Offshoring* refers to U.S. companies setting up their own offices in foreign low-wage markets to perform services previously done by U.S. employees. IBM, Accenture, and Google have all made plans to shift such jobs to employees in countries like India, China, and Brazil.[19] Economists are still arguing about whether the net effect on jobs in the United States is negative (through the direct loss of jobs) or positive (through corporate and consumer cost savings that permit job growth in the United States).[20]

What international agreements exist to regulate such trade in services? Although international trade in goods has been the subject of international agreement since shortly after WWII, until 1994 no similar agreement existed covering international trade in services. This was remedied with the creation of the General Agreement on Trade in Services (GATS), which is now one of the foundation agreements, with GATT, to which all member countries of the World Trade Organization (WTO) must subscribe. [The foundation agreements can be found at the WTO Web site, in the document area, at **www.wto.org**]

As might be expected, the GATS agreement is still in its infancy. It sets forth the general principles for the future of trade in services across borders, but at this time requires very little of member countries in movement toward the realization of those principles. Rather, it sets the stage for future negotiations to reduce barriers to trade in services. The services covered by GATS, and therefore by such negotiations, are broad: "any service in any sector except services supplied in the exercise of governmental authority."[21]

Two important general principles that govern international services negotiations include these:

- *Most favored nation (MFN) status:* WTO members get treatment by the host country no less favorable than that given to suppliers from any other country, whether or not the other country is a member of the WTO.

- *National treatment:* The national treatment standard calls for a comparison of the treatment accorded to suppliers from WTO member countries to the treatment accorded to domestic suppliers. As a general rule, the treatment is to be "no less favorable" than that received by domestic suppliers.

Employment-Related Regulations

When the U.S. Congress passed the Civil Rights Act of 1991, it expressly provided for *extraterritorial* application of Title VII's antidiscrimination provisions. In doing so, Congress extended American firms' liability for discrimination against their employees to situations that occur outside the United States. For instance, if a firm conducts operations in Saudi Arabia, where women are not expected to hold certain management positions, that firm is still held to Title VII's prohibition against gender discrimination. Extraterritorial application of Title VII is considered essential because over 5 million Americans work abroad. However, compliance with American civil rights laws is not required where doing so would violate the host country's laws.

One of the few internationally applied, employment-related laws is the European Works Council Directive, implemented in 1996 by 17 European nations. This directive provides that any multinational firm with at least 1,000 workers in the countries covered by the directive must comply with its regulations. The regulations include an employee voice in company deliberations, prior consultation with works councils over a wide range of employment issues, and specific rules of engagement for negotiations that are similar to the U.S. National Labor Relations Act (see Chapter 14).

The following press release summarizes a decision of the European Court of Justice in an affirmative action case. In a previous case, the court had held that an affirmative action scheme that allowed gender to serve as a tie-breaker between equal candidates was unacceptable. In the case here, a "savings clause" was put in place that would allow gender to serve as a tie-breaker unless "reasons specific to the male candidate tilt the balance in his favor." The Equal Treatment Directive of the EU generally permits no discrimination whatsoever on grounds of gender. But an exception is allowed for measures intended "to promote equal opportunity for men and women, in particular by removing existing inequalities which affect women's opportunities."

READING

Press Release No. 74/97   11 November 1997

Judgment of the Court of Justice of the ECJ in Case C-409/95

Hellmut Marschall v. *Land Nordrhein-Westfalen* (Germany)
(reference for a preliminary ruling)

[A national law which guarantees priority for women in promotions in the public sector in cases where there are male and female candidates who are equally qualified for the post in question does not conflict with community law provided that certain conditions are satisfied.]

Mr Marschall works as a tenured teacher in the service of the *Land* [of North Rhine–Westphalia, a state in Germany]. On 8 February 1994 he submitted his application for promotion to a post in the comprehensive school in Schwerte [Germany]. The competent authority informed him, however, that it planned to appoint a female candidate to the post. According to a provision of the Law governing civil servants of the *Land*, "[w]here, in the sector of the authority responsible for promotion, there are fewer women than men in the particular higher grade post

in the career bracket, women are to be given priority for promotion in the event of equal suitability, competence, and professional performance, unless reasons specific to an individual [male] candidate tilt the balance in his favour." Mr Marschall then brought an action before the Administrative Court, Gelsenkirchen, Germany, for an order directing the *Land* to promote him to the post in question.

The German court observed that the priority accorded as a matter of principle to women seemed to amount to discrimination which was not eliminated by the possibility of giving preference, exceptionally, to a male candidate. It therefore stayed proceedings and asked the Court of Justice to interpret the directive on the implementation of the principle of equal treatment for men and women as regards access to employment, vocational training and promotion, and working conditions.

That directive does not preclude measures designed in particular to remedy actual instances of inequality which affect the chances of women.

The Court of Justice considered that where a promotion is involved, men tend to be chosen in preference to women where they have equal qualifications, since they benefit from deep-rooted prejudices and from stereotypes as to the role and capacities of women.

Thus, for instance, the fear that women will interrupt their careers more frequently, that owing to household and family duties they will be less flexible in their working hours or that they will be absent from work more frequently because of pregnancy, childbirth, and breastfeeding, leads to discrimination against them.

For those reasons, the mere fact that a male and a female candidate are equally qualified does not mean that they have the same chances.

Accordingly, a provision such as that enacted by the *Land* Nordrhein–Westfalen may help to reduce actual instances

of inequality by introducing an additional criterion for promotion, namely status as a woman, and is in conformity with the directive provided that automatic priority over men is precluded.

After recalling the social prejudices mentioned above, the Court emphasized that the criteria to be used when deciding on promotions must not be such as to discriminate against women. It also approved the flexibility afforded by the German provision, which leaves a margin of discretion to the administrative authorities.

It is now for the German court to determine whether those conditions are satisfied and to decide Mr Marschall's case.

Questions

1. Are you in favor of affirmative action programs?
2. Do you believe that the suggested modification makes the affirmative action program more appropriate, or does it permit a discriminatory result to remain?
3. What do you believe will be the far-reaching impact of this decision?

Intellectual Property Regulations

Intellectual property generally refers to copyrights, patents, and trademarks. Intellectual property is one form of personal property or *personalty,* which is the legal term used to denote all forms of property, both tangible and intangible, other than real property or *realty.* Realty is comprised only of land or real estate and items permanently affixed to the land, such as buildings.

Trademarks

A *trademark* is what identifies a product, whether it is the trade name, the packaging, the logo, or other distinguishing mark. When the law protects a trademark, it grants to the holder of the mark a limited monopoly: No one else may use that mark without the holder's permission. Under section 526 of the Tariff Act of 1930, it is unlawful to import goods bearing a trademark that has been registered with the Patent Office and that is "owned by a citizen of, or by a corporation or association . . . organized within the United States" without the permission of the mark holder.

This provision regulates the importation of goods that would infringe on a trademark holder's rights in the United States. But what about an American company that wants to obtain trademark protection in other countries? Each country has distinct trademark regulations and different levels of protection offered marks registered in other countries.

Paris Convention

In 1883 several countries entered an agreement called the International Convention for the Protection of Intellectual Property, which was last revised in 1979. As of this writing,

169 countries, including the United States, are parties to the agreement, now called the *Paris Convention*. In short, according to the Paris convention, member countries ensure trademark protection to marks registered in other member countries. The convention also provides for *national treatment* requiring that any individual claiming infringement will have the same protection as would a national of that country. Thus a member country may not favor its own nationals over foreigners. The Madrid Agreement Concerning the International Registration of Marks, established after the Paris Convention, attempts to create an international trademark system. If a holder registers a trademark with the World Intellectual Property Organization (WIPO) in Switzerland, that mark is protected in all member countries requested by the holder. A Protocol relating to the agreement was concluded in 1989, with the "aim of rendering the Madrid system more flexible and more compatible with the domestic legislations of certain countries which had not been able to accede to the Agreement."[22] As of November 2, 2003, the United States became a party to the Protocol but had not acceded to the Agreement. [For extensive information on WIPO, see **www.wipo.int**]

Patents

A *patent* is a monopoly on a product, process, or device where the item or process claimed is an innovation, unique and inventive, and useful. The Paris Convention refers to patents as well as trademarks; however, it does not establish a worldwide network of protection. Instead, it requires that member countries follow simplified procedures for registration. The most important provision provides the *right of priority,* which grants the first person to obtain a patent in any member country priority over other individuals seeking to register the same patent. In addition, because a patent must be original to be registered in any country, many countries hold that patents previously awarded in other countries automatically preclude additional patent registration. The European Patent Convention was established in 1978 to create an international registration procedure for patents. Individuals who obtain patents through the European Patent Office have valid patents in each member country.

In recent years, considerable international controversy has arisen between drug companies holding patents on medicines for the treatment of HIV/AIDS and developing nations, which want to be able to manufacture, buy, and import cheap generics of these medicines to combat the AIDS epidemic. By various accounts, the cost of the generics is 80 to 90 percent less than the cost of purchases from the patent holders. At the WTO summit in Qatar in November 2001, the public health argument ultimately carried the day when WTO members agreed to recognize a public health exception to patent protection. Although the United States had previously been a strong supporter of patent recognition, its promotion of that position was significantly weakened when, in light of the anthrax scares in the fall of 2001, it threatened to break Bayer's patent for the anthrax drug Cipro if that became necessary to protect the public health. Brazil, which has permitted the manufacture of AIDS/HIV generics, by some accounts has become a model for many developing countries. Through widespread dissemination of the generics, Brazil has cut the number of AIDS-related deaths and the new infection rate by half.[23]

> WTO members agreed to recognize a public health exception to patent protection.

Copyrights

A *copyright* is a government grant giving the copyright holder exclusive control over the reproduction of a literary, musical, or artistic work. Most developed nations provide copyright protection within their borders, but many also belong to international copyright protection pacts. The Berne Convention of 1886 and the Universal Copyright Convention (UCC) of 1952 both provide a measure of international protection against the unauthorized reproduction of books, photos, drawings, movies, and the like. Copyright protection extends for a period provided by national law. For example, in the United States, a copyright currently spans the author's life plus 70 years. The United States is a party to the UCC and the Berne Convention. Thus the Second Circuit Court of Appeals upheld the application of Russian copyright law when a Russian news agency sued a Russian-language newspaper located in New York for copyright violation of an article that had originally been published in Russia.[24]

Although we should recognize that we have not yet succeeded in establishing a solid international system of protection for intellectual property, some progress was made by the WTO adoption of the Agreement on Trade-Related Aspects of Intellectual Property Rights (the TRIPS agreement) in the mid-1990s. The TRIPS agreement establishes certain minimum levels of protection for copyrights, trademarks, and patents and also requires WTO members to adopt effective enforcement measures. In furtherance of its obligations under the TRIPS agreement, the United States passed federal legislation. The validity of that legislation was upheld by the Eleventh Circuit in *U.S. v. Moghadam,*[25] when it affirmed a criminal conviction for selling bootleg CDs featuring live performances of such groups as the Beastie Boys.

The following case offers a good example of the interplay between the trademark protection offered by the Lanham Act in the United States and the global protection offered through the Paris Convention. As you read this case, also pay attention to what the judge says about the self-executing nature of the Paris Convention.

Piaggio & C.S.p.A. v. Scooterworks USA, Inc., et al.

LEGAL BRIEFCASE 1999 U.S. Dist. LEXIS 13296 (N.D. IL 1999)

Judge Marovich

Plaintiff Piaggio & C.S.p.A. ("Piaggio") has filed this action against Defendants Scooterworks USA, Inc. ("Scooterworks"), Vesparts International, L.L.C. ("Vesparts"), and Philip S. McCaleb ("McCaleb"), alleging trademark and copyright infringement. For the reasons set forth below, Scooterworks' and Vesparts' motion is granted in part and denied in part, and McCaleb's motion is denied.

BACKGROUND

Piaggio is an Italian corporation with its principal place of business in Pontedera, Italy. Scooterworks is an Illinois corporation with its principal place of business in Chicago, Illinois. Vesparts is a Nevada corporation with its principal place of business in Chicago, Illinois. McCaleb is an officer, president, and co-shareholder, together with his wife, of Scooterworks. He is also an officer, president, and shareholder of Vesparts.

Piaggio is engaged in the business of manufacturing, distributing, and selling motor scooters, motorcycles, mopeds, and light transport vehicles, as well as related parts and accessories, throughout the world, including the United States. Piaggio owns the common law rights and registration for . . . the "PIAGGIO Trademarks." Piaggio has used, for over 50 years, the PIAGGIO Trademarks on and in connection with the distribution, marketing, and sale of motorized vehicles.

In 1948, Piaggio introduced a new line of motorized scooters under trademarks using the term VESPA ("VESPA scooters"). VESPA scooters have been in continuous production since their introduction. Piaggio owns the common law rights and registration of the word mark VESPA, VESPA with Design, and other Piaggio trademarks containing the term VESPA (the "VESPA Trademarks"). Piaggio has always used its VESPA Trademarks on and in connection with the distribution, marketing, and sale of VESPA scooters, with over 16 million units produced and sold in over 150 countries, including the United States, and it has had exclusive use of the VESPA Trademarks in connection with the sale of its motor scooters.

Piaggio also owns a family of VESPA trademarks registered under Italian law. The word mark VESPA, the VESPA logo, and other Piaggio trademarks containing the term VESPA are extremely well known in Italy.

Piaggio continuously utilized VESPA trademarks on and in connection with the manufacture, distribution, and sale of VESPA scooters in the United States up through approximately 1987, at which time, for various reasons, Piaggio "temporarily suspended" sales of its VESPA scooters in the United States. Nonetheless, Piaggio has continued to aggressively market and distribute VESPA scooters all over the world and to sell parts and promote its marks in the United States. Piaggio plans to resume VESPA scooter sales in the United States within the next 12 months.

McCaleb, Scooterworks, and Vesparts are in the business of selling replacement parts and accessories for VESPA scooters, as well as other goods and services of interest to fans of VESPA scooters. Beginning in approximately 1992, McCaleb attempted, but was unsuccessful, to establish some type of business relationship between Piaggio and McCaleb's start-up business, Scooterworks.

In 1995, without Piaggio's prior approval, Scooterworks filed an application with the United States Patent and Trade Office ("PTO") to register a VESPA mark for use in connection with the sale of key chains, posters, clothes, labels, models, and related goods. The PTO refused to register Scooterworks' application because the trademark in the application was deemed identical to trademarks previously registered by Piaggio. Thereafter, Piaggio applied to register the same trademark, based upon an assignment from Scooterworks to Piaggio of Scooterworks' rights in its prior application, and was approved.

In January 1996, Piaggio and Scooterworks entered into a License Agreement dated January 4, 1996. Pursuant to the License Agreement, Piaggio gave Scooterworks the exclusive right to produce and market in the United States under the VESPA Trademark, models of VESPA scooters, for a two-year period. Throughout 1996, Scooterworks attempted to secure from Piaggio a broader agreement providing for exclusive rights to distribute the VESPA scooter and related parts under the VESPA trademark. However, no definite agreement was ever reached, and negotiations were abandoned in January 1997.

Piaggio claims that Defendants have improperly used Piaggio's PIAGGIO and VESPA Trademarks in several ways. For example, Piaggio alleges that McCaleb and Scooterworks, on their Web site and in the free catalog offered through their Web site, "repeatedly assert and imply they have an exclusive arrangement with Piaggio to import and distribute authentic VESPA replacement parts in the United States" and display the VESPA and PIAGGIO Trademarks in such a manner as "to imply that Scooterworks is sponsored, supervised, endorsed, or otherwise connected with Piaggio." However, Piaggio alleges, McCaleb and Scooterworks are not sponsored, supervised, or endorsed by Piaggio; their only connection to Piaggio is that Scooterworks markets and sells replacement parts and accessories for VESPA scooters. Piaggio also alleges that McCaleb and Scooterworks "wrongfully offer miniature VESPA motor scooters for sale" and "repeatedly misuse VESPA Trademarks by using VESPA as a generic name of a product rather than as a brand name for scooters." Piaggio asserts that although it has requested that Defendants cease their willful and wrongful acts, Defendants have refused to cooperate with Piaggio and continue in their improper and infringing activities.

On November 24, 1998, Piaggio filed its Complaint in this Court asserting 13 claims: trademark infringement, false designation, unfair competition, and antidilution under the Lanham Act, 15 U.S.C. § 1051, et seq.; trademark infringement and unfair competition under the International Convention for the Protection of Industrial Property of March 20, 1883, 21 U.S.T. 1583, as amended (the "Paris Convention"); trademark infringement, unfair competition, violation of the Uniform Deceptive Trade Practices Act, and antidilution under Illinois state law; breach of contract; copyright infringement and declaratory judgment. On January 27, 1999, Scooterworks filed a counterclaim seeking, inter alia, to cancel Piaggio's federal trademark registrations.

* * * * *

II. Paris Convention Claims—Counts IV and V

In Counts IV and V of the Complaint, Piaggio alleges claims under Articles 6 *bis* and 10 *bis,* respectively, of the Paris Convention. The Paris Convention, to which both the United States and Italy are signatories, is an international agreement which prohibits, among other things, unfair competition. Scooterworks argues that Counts IV and V should be dismissed because (1) the Paris Convention is not a self-executing treaty and there is no private right of action under the Paris Convention, and (2) even if there was a private right of action, such claims are duplicative of those asserted under the Lanham Act. This Court finds that Section 44 of the Lanham Act implements the Paris Convention but that the Paris Convention does not provide a relief distinct from that of the Lanham Act. Accordingly, Scooterworks' motion to dismiss Counts IV and V is granted.

The Lanham Act, which prohibits specific types of unfair competition, provides in section 44(b):

Any person whose country of origin is a party to any convention or treaty relating to trademarks . . . to which the United States is also a party . . . shall be entitled to the benefits of this section under the conditions expressed herein to the extent necessary to give effect to any provisions of such convention [or] treaty . . . in addition to the rights to which any owner of a mark is otherwise entitled by this chapter.

Section 44(h) of the Lanham Act extends to foreign citizens such as Piaggio "effective protections against unfair competition, and the remedies provided in this chapter for infringement of marks . . . so far as they may be appropriate in repressing acts of unfair competition."

Piaggio argues that it has pleaded acts of unfair competition over and above those acts which constitute unfair competition under the Lanham Act, and thus, its Paris Convention claims are not duplicative and should not be dismissed. However, this Court agrees with the reasoning of the courts that hold that "subsections 44(b) and 44(h) [of the Lanham Act] work together to provide foreign nationals with rights under United States law which are coextensive with the substantive provisions of the treaty involved." . . . In other words, "the Paris Convention does not provide substantive rights in the United States, [instead] Section 44 [of the Lanham Act] merely extends existing Lanham Act and state law protections to foreign nationals conducting business in the United States." . . .

Therefore, as the Court finds that the Paris Convention does not create a separate and distinct cause of action than that already available under the Lanham Act, Counts IV and V are duplicative and, accordingly, are dismissed.

Questions

1. Should it have mattered to the disposition of the case that Scooterworks filed an application with the United States PTO without Piaggio's prior approval to register a VESPA mark for use in connection with the sale of paraphernalia?

2. According to Judge Marovich, is the Paris Convention a self-executing treaty? Explain.

3. If the Lanham Act implements the Paris Convention through its section 44 but offers no new relief, why would anyone bring a claim under the Paris Convention if she or he already has a claim under the Lanham Act?

Regulation of MNEs

With globalization, the number of MNEs has vastly expanded; and precisely because their operations span the globe, regulating their activities has become quite difficult. In the absence of effective international regulatory regimes, which do not currently exist, MNEs are subject to many different overlapping, and often contradictory, national regulatory schemes. Countries that impose regulatory requirements on MNEs may, in any given circumstance, be viewed with approval or be accused of "regulatory imperialism"[26] or be charged with domestic protectionism. Consider four areas: securities regulation, imposition of financial accounting and auditing standards, anticompetitive restraints of trade, and mergers. The U.S. law covering each of these areas has previously been presented in Chapters 9 through 11, but here we want to specifically look at their international dimensions, particularly with regard to the oversight of the behavior of MNEs.

Anyone reading the business news over the past decade is quite aware of the many corporate financial scandals that have rocked the world: Enron and WorldCom in the United States; Lernout & Hauspie in Belgium; HIH Insurance in Australia; and Barings Bank in the UK. In the United States the SEC has played a major role in uncovering and pursuing financial corporate wrongdoing. But it also has a reputation outside of the United States, as one commentator put it, "as the cop on the beat for the world's securities markets."[27] For example, in the past two years the SEC has imposed a $120 million fine on the Royal Dutch/Shell Group (UK and the Netherlands); investigated and settled charges against Parmalat (Italy); and, using a provision in the recently enacted Sarbanes–Oxley Act, blocked a $25 million severance payment to the former chairman of the French corporation Vivendi Universal SA. The SEC has a broad reach because of its jurisdiction to regulate all companies that choose to list their stocks or bonds on any U.S. securities market, such as the New York Stock Exchange. It is generally conceded that, worldwide, the United States has the most stringent securities laws and enforcement. Specifically to avoid that scrutiny, and in the wake of the substantially increased regulation required by the Sarbanes–Oxley Act, some foreign corporations are delisting their securities in the United States to avoid complying with its laws and regulations.[28]

> The United States has the most stringent securities laws and enforcement.

Another aspect of the regulation of securities is the imposition of financial accounting standards. In the United States these standards also come under the regulatory authority of the SEC. However, the growth in the number of MNEs and the integration of the world's capital markets have propelled the development of internationally recognized and accepted financial accounting standards. In 2001 a set of such standards were offered for adoption under the auspices of the International Accounting Standards Board. A number of countries have already implemented these standards. For example, in the EU all publicly listed companies are required to prepare their financial statements in conformance with them not later than January 1, 2005. The SEC has initiated a harmonization project between U.S. and international standards, but no deadlines have been established for its accomplishment.[29]

Moving to international antitrust issues, Microsoft is the subject of undoubtedly the most notorious international antitrust controversy. At its heart the argument is about the identification of unacceptable trade practices by a company with monopoly market power—in this case, Microsoft's Windows operating system. In the United States alone Microsoft has faced three successive bouts of litigation brought by the U.S. Department of Justice, as well as numerous suits for damages by private plaintiffs. All of these suits apply U.S. antitrust law. However, Microsoft has also found itself being scrutinized by the European Commission for violations of the EU's Competition Law. While increasingly convergent in practice, the policies behind the U.S. and EU laws remain distinct, and Microsoft has discovered that activity not violative of one law may nevertheless be objectionable under the other.[30]

Finally, we come to antitrust laws applicable to mergers. There is as yet no multilateral agreement among the 70 or so countries with merger review systems that would seek to coordinate these processes—not even at the level of coordinating review thresholds, timetables, and required filings. Some bilateral agreements are in place, but they are simply inadequate to address the issues faced by proposed mergers among MNEs.

Imports

The General Agreement on Tariffs and Trade (GATT), now governed by the WTO, regulates import duties among signatory countries to reduce barriers to trade and to ensure fair treatment. Without GATT, it is argued, countries with stronger markets would be able to secure better deals on imports than would other countries. In addition, countries with strong market economies could use the threat of higher import taxes as a bargaining chip in other negotiations. To limit such discriminatory practices, the concepts of MFN status and national treatment are integral to GATT, just as they are to GATS, as discussed earlier in the context of international trade in services. Thus, under GATT, a reduced tariff offered to one WTO member country must be offered to all WTO members, and once a good has been imported, it must be treated just as domestic goods are treated. In addition, GATT contains several other important components that may affect where a company may want to conduct operations and to which countries that company may want to export its products.

To promote fair trade, the WTO prohibits the practice of *dumping.* Dumping occurs where a manufacturer sells its goods in a foreign country for less than their normal value. If this practice causes or threatens material injury to a domestic or established foreign manufacturer in the foreign country, the act is prohibited. The price is considered less than normal value if it is less than the price charged in the producer's home country. A firm may want to dump its goods in a foreign market for two reasons. First, its home market may be saturated and cannot support any further supply. Second, in an effort to establish itself and perhaps drive other firms out of the market, the firm may sell its goods in a foreign market at a price below other competitors and support that price with higher prices in its home country. In this way its competitors may be forced from the market; the producer may then raise prices to the normal level or above. GATT permits retaliatory duties to be imposed on countries that have dumped goods in other member countries. In theory, antidumping duties are to be imposed only to bring prices on the dumped goods back in line with what they should be. However, some commentators have argued that the computations can be manipulated and that the actual antidumping duties are just as abusive as the harm they were intended to remedy. A better approach, they argue, would be to subject imports to the same domestic predatory pricing rules that the country employs against domestic companies, as is done in Australia and New Zealand.[32]

The WTO also prohibits the payment of *unfair subsidies* by governments. This occurs where a government, in an effort to encourage growth in a certain industry, offers subsidies to producers in that industry. The producers are therefore able to sell their goods at a price lower than the prices of their worldwide competitors. Subsidies are considered unfair where governments use them to promote export trade that harms another country. Both the United States and the European Union have charged each other with providing unfair subsidies to their domestic airplane manufacturers, Boeing and Airbus, respectively. At the time of this writing, both countries have requested a suspension of the WTO dispute resolution process in order to pursue settlement negotiations.[33]

> The United States and the European Union have charged each other with providing unfair subsidies to Boeing and Airbus.

Where unfair subsidization or dumping has been found, the WTO permits the harmed country to impose *countervailing duties* on those products in an amount sufficient to counteract the effect of the subsidy. In a long-running battle between Europe and the

United States, the latter lost an appeal before the WTO that certain provisions in the U.S. corporate income tax result in unfair subsidies to U.S. exporters generally. On March 1, 2004, the EU began imposing up to $4 billion in punitive duties on U.S. imports for the violation.[34] Congress, which had twice previously amended the corporate tax laws in an attempt to address the unfair subsidy claim, passed new legislation attempting to finally settle the matter.[35]

The existence and level of import duties can have substantial impacts both on the volume of international trade itself and on the political and public relations between countries. Thus, when Congress passed the Africa Growth and Opportunity Act in June 2000, which gives 23 sub-Saharan countries the opportunity to ship certain textile products to the United States duty-free, it gave a considerable boost to foreign investment and the economy in Madagascar. In fact, exports to the United States in the first half of 2001 were up 115 percent from exports in all of 2000.[36] Conversely, when the United States increased duties on such French imports as Roquefort cheese in response to France's refusal to allow the import of American hormone-treated beef, it kicked off a reaction in France that resulted in, among other things, $100,000 of damage to a McDonald's restaurant in the town of Millau in the south of France.[37]

Questions

1. Why do developed countries like the United States impose import duties? Why would a less developed country do so?
2. If one of the premises of the WTO is that the lessening of trade barriers produces positive results, does it make sense to allow the imposition of additional import duties as a sanction against countries that practice illegal dumping or provide unfair subsidies?

Exports

Whereas imports are regulated to protect American businesses, exports by these businesses may also be regulated. Export regulation serves several purposes, articulated in the Export Administration Act of 1979, which states the following:

> It is the policy of the United States to use export controls only after full consideration of the impact on the economy of the United States and only to the extent necessary
>
> *a.* to restrict the export of goods and technology that would make a significant contribution to the military potential of any other country . . . which could prove detrimental to the national security of the United States;
>
> *b.* to restrict the export of goods and technology where necessary to further significantly the foreign policy of the United States or to fulfill its declared international obligations; and
>
> *c.* to restrict the export of goods where necessary to protect the domestic economy from the excessive drain of scarce materials and to reduce the serious inflationary impact of foreign demand.

Under the act, anyone wishing to export any type of goods or technology from the United States to a foreign country must obtain a license. Violations of the licensing requirement may bring imprisonment of up to 10 years and/or fines of up to $250,000, or five times the value of the export or $1 million, whichever is higher.

Two types of licenses are available, *general* or *validated* licenses. The shipper is responsible for determining which type is required. A commodity control list is published that specifies which goods are controlled and for which countries a validated license is required. Otherwise, a general license is available if no specific export license is required. To obtain a general license, the shipper must merely fill out a declaration form at the time of shipping. A validated license is required when a firm exports certain goods or technology to specified controlled countries. Firms must apply for the license at the Bureau of Industry and Security (formerly the Bureau of Export Administration) in the Department of Commerce prior to shipping. [For the Bureau of Industry and Security, see **www.bxa.doc.gov**]

In determining whether to award a license, the Department of Commerce will look at several factors, including the type and amount of the exported good, the importing country, the good's use or purpose, the unrestricted availability of the same or comparable item in the importing country, and the intended market in the importing country.

The CIA's report, *Global Trends 2015,* predicts that "export control regimes and sanctions will be less effective [in the future] because of the diffusion of technology, porous borders, defense industry consolidations, and reliance on foreign markets to maintain profitability."[38]

[To learn more about U.S. import and export practices, see **www.customs.ustreas.gov**]

International Dispute Resolution

As we have seen to this point, international ethical/legal relationships are highly complex. Disputes are inevitable. Resolution of these international disputes often faces several roadblocks. In the international arena, three significant international dispute resolution bodies presently exist: the International Court of Justice, the European Court of Justice, and the WTO Dispute Settlement Body. Each is discussed in turn here.

The only court that is devoted entirely to hearing cases of international public law is the International Court of Justice (ICJ) in the United Nations. The ICJ is made up of 15 judges from 15 different member countries. It may issue two types of decisions, depending on its jurisdiction. It has *advisory jurisdiction* where the United Nations asks the court for an opinion on a matter of international law. These opinions do not bind any party. It has *contentious jurisdiction* where two or more nations (not individual parties) have consented to its jurisdiction and have requested a binding opinion. Such opinions are not, however, precedent for the ICJ in later cases. [For information about the ICJ, see **www.icj-cij.org**]

The European Court of Justice (ECJ) hears cases involving European Community law. Although not required, one judge from each member nation traditionally sits on the ECJ. At first glance, the ECJ may not seem a particularly important court for American business. But in an age of MNEs, its decisions can be very important. For example, Price-WaterhouseCoopers (PWC) sought to develop consulting firms in Europe that combine under one roof the services of both accountants and lawyers, an organizational structure that has been referred to as a *multidisciplinary practice* (*MDP*). Its efforts were prohibited under the law of the Netherlands, and PWC responded that such a prohibition would violate European Community law. Unfortunately for PWC, the ECJ ruled against it and held that the Netherlands could regulate the practice of the professions to protect the public interest and that disallowing MDPs could be in the public interest.[39] [For information on the ECJ, see **http://curia.eu.int/en/transitpage.htm** and **http://europa.eu.int/institutions/court/index_en.htm**]

While the WTO Dispute Settlement Body (DSB) is not a true court, it is a significant forum for the resolution of international trade disputes between WTO members. The DSB is made up of all member governments, usually represented by ambassadors or the equivalent. The DSB establishes a panel to hear a particular dispute brought by a member state. The panel then reports back to the DSB, which can either accept or reject the panel's findings. Either side can then appeal to the WTO Appellate Body. Again, the DSB can either accept or reject the appeals report. If a WTO member fails to comply with the final decision of the DSB, the opposing party may seek compensation. If compensation is not agreed upon between the parties within 20 days, the complaining party can seek authorization for retaliation—that is, the suspension of favorable trade concessions to the noncompliant party. The reality of this power was aptly demonstrated by the DSB's 2002 authorization of $4 billion of import duties against U.S. goods by the EU based on objections to certain provisions in the U.S. corporate tax laws, as discussed previously. [For information on the WTO dispute resolution function and dispute documents, see **www.wto.org/english/tratop_e/dispu_e/dispu_e.htm**]

In addition to these three dispute resolution bodies, other treaties may also implement specific dispute resolution processes for disputes under the treaty between signatories to the agreement. For example, NAFTA provides for special tribunals before which corporations can, and have, brought complaints against governments for actions perceived to be unfair or inequitable to them as foreign investors. Under this provision, United Parcel Service (UPS) has alleged that the state-owned postal service in Canada is unfair competition.[40] Of concern to some commentators is the fact that a tribunal under NAFTA can as a practical matter operate as a further review of the decision of a domestic court. Thus, after the U.S. Supreme Court declined to review a Massachusetts case brought by a Canadian real estate company, the company took its dispute to a NAFTA tribunal (which decided that Massachusetts had not violated international law).[41] [For information on proceedings before NAFTA tribunals against the governments of Canada, Mexico, and the United States, see the U.S. State Department site at **www.state.gov/s/l/c3439.htm**, as well as a private site, **www.NaftaClaims.com**]

Of course, national courts may also rule on matters of international law and on matters involving business in international settings. In fact, because of the absence of any international courts of general jurisdiction, it is in national courts where most international business disputes are heard. When the underlying dispute seems to have little association with the forum state, and the national court agrees to rule on the substantive claim, legal commentators may lay charges of "judicial imperialism."[42] In the 2003–2004 term, the U.S. Supreme Court issued opinions in three cases where foreign plaintiffs had sought access to the U.S. judicial system. In one case, the Court prohibited foreign customers from suing international companies in the United States.[43] In another, the Court held that U.S. courts have the authority (but are not required) to order U.S. corporations to produce documents for foreign regulators (in this case the European Commission).[44]

In the third case, the Court left the door open for further human rights suits under the Alien Tort Statute,[45] such as the one discussed in the following article.

READING   U.S. Courts Handle International Law

Steven P. Garmisa

Tom Beanal—a member of an Indonesian tribe called the Amungme—filed a lawsuit in Louisiana accusing two U.S. corporations of violating international law.

A subsidiary of the American corporations operates a gigantic open-pit mine in Irian Jaya, Indonesia. According to Beanal, the American corporations are guilty of (1) human rights violations, (2) "cultural genocide" and (3) pollution.

A law that permits foreigners to sue in U.S. courts for alleged violations of international law might sound like something cooked up by stoned hippies who stumbled into law school. But Beanal relied on one of the first laws enacted by Congress—the Alien Tort Statute.

This 1789 law says that aliens can sue in federal court for wrongful conduct "committed in violation of the law of nations."

When warlord Radovan Karadzic was in Manhattan in 1993, for example, he was sued for violating international law. Muslim and Croat citizens of Bosnia–Herzegovina accused Karadzic of commanding troops that used mass rape, torture, and summary executions in a campaign of genocide. Federal appellate judges ruled the Alien Tort Statute can be used in suing Karadzic for genocide and war crimes.

With Beanal's case, U.S. District Judge Stanwood R. Duval Jr. had to decide whether the "facts" alleged in the complaint would, if true, add up to violations of international law.

Here is what Beanal alleges: The defendants (Freeport McMoRan Inc. and Freeport-McMoRan Copper & Gold Inc.) are Delaware corporations that are headquartered in New Orleans. Through a subsidiary they operate an open-pit copper, gold, and silver mine in Irian Jaya.

Security guards employed by the subsidiary allegedly arrested, detained, tortured, and murdered members of the Amungme tribe and destroyed their property. The American corporations allegedly committed "cultural genocide" on the tribe. And mining operations allegedly destroyed the rain forest and polluted the water where the Amungme live.

The McMoRan companies argued they couldn't be sued for violating international law because Beanal didn't claim they acted under authority of the Indonesian government.

Some evil acts don't violate international law unless they are performed by someone acting with government authority, Duval explained. If a home invader tortures a victim to find out where money is hidden, the crime doesn't violate international law. But when government officials arrest and torture political enemies, there's a violation of international law.

Other atrocities violate international law even if the defendants acted on their own and no government was involved. Genocide, hijacking, war crimes, and piracy violate international law even if the defendants aren't acting with official authority, Duval recounted.

One of the problems with the complaint filed by Beanal is that "cultural genocide" doesn't violate international law. The Geneva Convention on Genocide defines genocide as acts that are intended to destroy a national, ethnic, racial, or religious group.

Genocide doesn't include international destruction of a "culture," Duval decided. Yet some of the things alleged by Beanal—such as arbitrary arrest, torture, and summary execution—could add up to genocide if these acts were specifically intended to destroy the Amungme tribe.

With the other alleged human rights violations, the alleged "facts" didn't add up to a violation of international law because Beanal didn't claim the American corporations acted under the auspices of the Indonesian government. And Duval decided that the alleged "environmental torts" aren't offenses under international law. So Duval threw out the complaint. But the judge gave Beanal a chance to file an amended claim.

Source: *Chicago Sun-Times,* September 24, 1997, Section: Finance, p. 64. Reprinted by permission of Steven P. Garmisa.

Questions

1. Why might some think that a law permitting foreigners to sue in U.S. courts for international law violations is zany?

2. Do you think that "cultural genocide" such as that depicted by Beanal in this particular case should constitute a violation of international law? Does this strike you as arbitrary?

Government Defenses

As the previous article pointed out, "some evil acts don't violate international law unless they are performed by someone acting with government authority." Even where such governmental action exists, two additional doctrines, accepted as general principles of international law, may pose barriers to the judicial enforcement of a party's rights. They are the *act of state doctrine* and the *doctrine of sovereign immunity*.

Act of State Doctrine

It is generally accepted that a country has absolute rule over what occurs within its borders. Consequently, the act of state doctrine holds that a judge in one country does not have the authority to examine or challenge the acts of another country within that country's borders. For instance, an American court may not declare the acts of the British government invalid because it is presumed that the foreign country acted legally within its own territory.

One area that has caused a great deal of dispute in connection with the act of state doctrine is *expropriation*. Expropriation is the taking by a national government of property and/or rights of a foreign firm within its borders. The United States contends that international law dictates that an individual or firm be compensated for the taking by the government. Not all governments agree with this statement of law.

Doctrine of Sovereign Immunity

The doctrine of sovereign immunity is based on the concept that "the king can do no wrong." In other words, if the king makes the rules, how could the king ever be wrong? As Chief Justice Marshall explained in *The Schooner Exchange v. McFaddon*,[46] "The jurisdiction of the nation within its own territory is necessarily exclusive and absolute. It is susceptible of no limitation not imposed by itself; deriving validity from an external source would imply a diminution of its sovereignty to the extent of the restriction, and an investment of that sovereignty to the same extent in that power which could impose such restriction."

The doctrine has been codified in the United States by the Foreign Sovereign Immunities Act of 1976 (FSIA), which provides that foreign countries may not be sued in American courts, subject to several exceptions. Accordingly, it would not be possible for a U.S. citizen to sue Britain in the U.S. courts. A foreign country may be sued in American courts if the claim falls into one of the following FSIA exceptions:

1. The foreign countries have waived their immunity (they have consented to be sued in another country's courts).
2. The legal action is based on a *commercial activity* by the foreign country in the United States or outside the United States but having a direct effect in the United States.
3. The legal action is based on personal injuries "caused by an act of torture, extrajudicial killing, aircraft sabotage, hostage taking, or the provision of material support or resources" for such acts.[47]

Therefore, a country that conducts a commercial activity in a foreign country may not hide behind sovereign immunity if sued, while a country acting on its own behalf and not for a commercial purpose would be able to avail itself of the protection. This "restrictive theory of immunity" is to be contrasted with the policies of some countries, which contend that immunity is absolute—no exceptions exist. The following case examines sovereign immunity.

LEGAL BRIEFCASE

Butters v. Vance International, Inc. 225 F.3d 462 (4th Cir. 2000)

Chief Judge Wilkinson

Appellant Nyla Butters brought suit against her employer, Vance International, claiming that Vance discriminated against her on the basis of gender. The district court held that Vance was entitled to immunity from Butters' suit under the Foreign Sovereign Immunities Act, 28 U.S.C. §§ 1602–1611, because Vance's client, the Kingdom of Saudi Arabia, was responsible for Butters not being promoted.

I.

Vance International, headquartered in Oakton, Virginia, provides security services to corporations and foreign sovereigns. In October 1994, Saudi Arabia hired Vance to augment the security provided to Princess Anud, a wife of Saudi King Fhad, while the Princess was undergoing medical treatments in California. The Saudi military was responsible for protecting Princess Anud. The Princess' residence in Bel Air, California, was referred to as "Gold." Saudi Arabian Colonel Mohammed Al-Ajiji supervised all security at the site—three Saudi military officers and the Vance agents. Saudi Captain Abdullah was second in command. The Saudi government paid Vance for its services.

In August 1995, Vance hired Nyla Butters as a part-time, at-will security agent. From 1995 until April 14, 1998, . . . [on] several occasions, Butters temporarily worked in Gold's command post.

In early April 1998, Vance supervisors at Gold recommended that Butters serve a full rotation in the command post. In Colonel Mohammed's absence, Captain Abdullah rejected the recommendation. When Colonel Mohammed returned, Gregg Hall, the Vance detail leader, spoke with Mohammed. Colonel Mohammed denied Hall's request for Butters to serve a rotation in the command post. Colonel Mohammed told Hall that such an assignment was unacceptable under Islamic law,

and Saudis would consider it inappropriate for their officers to spend long periods of time in a command post with a woman present. This in turn could have political ramifications at home for the Saudi royal family. Mohammed also informed Hall that the Princess and her contingent wanted to speak only to male officers when they called the command post. In total, three Vance supervisors recommended Butters for the assignment. Saudi military officers denied every request.

* * * * *

On May 28, 1998, Butters filed a charge of gender discrimination with the California Department of Fair Employment and Housing. On October 15, 1998, Butters filed suit . . . for discriminatory constructive termination, retaliatory constructive termination, and wrongful constructive termination in violation of public policy under California's Fair Employment and Housing Act. Vance filed a motion for summary judgment with respect to these counts.

On July 30, 1999, the district court granted Vance's motion, finding Vance immune from Butters' suit under the Foreign Sovereign Immunities Act (FSIA). Under the FSIA, "a foreign state shall be immune from the jurisdiction of the courts of the United States and of the States except as provided in sections 1605 to 1607 of this chapter." 28 U.S.C. § 1604. The district court held that derivative FSIA immunity attached to Vance because it was "acting under the direct military orders of Colonel Mohammed when [it] did not allow the plaintiff to work a full rotation in the command center." Butters appeals.

II.

Butters first contends that FSIA immunity does not attach to Vance because the action here was a "commercial activity." Section 1605(a)(2) provides, "A foreign state shall not be immune from the jurisdiction of courts of the United States or of the States in any case in which the action is based upon a commercial activity carried on in the United States by the foreign state. . . ."

The FSIA defines "commercial activity" as "a regular course of commercial conduct or a particular commercial transaction or act. The commercial character of an activity shall be determined by reference to the nature of the course of conduct or particular transaction or act, rather than by reference to its purpose." 28 U.S.C. § 1603(d). In *Saudi Arabia v. Nelson,* the Supreme Court stated, "a state is immune from the jurisdiction of foreign courts as to its sovereign or public acts (jure imperii), but not as to those that are private or commercial in character (jure gestionis)." 507 U.S. 349, 359–60 (1993). The Court elaborated on the distinction: "[A] state engages in commercial activity . . . where it exercises 'only those powers that can also be exercised by private citizens,' as distinct from those 'powers peculiar to sovereigns.'" Id. At 360 (quoting *Republic of Argentina v. Weltover, Inc.,* 504 U.S. 607, 614 (1992)).

The relevant act here—a foreign sovereign's decision as to how best to secure the safety of its leaders—is quintessentially an act "peculiar to sovereigns." . . . Indeed, it is difficult to imagine an act closer to the core of a nation's sovereignty. Providing security for the royal family in this country is not a commercial act in which the state is acting "in the manner of a private player within the market." Id. at 360. . . .

One of the main concerns of the immunity framework adopted by the FSIA is to accommodate "the interests of foreign states in avoiding the embarrassment of defending the propriety of political acts before a foreign court." . . . These acts often have political, cultural, and religious components. Judicial interference with them would have serious foreign policy ramifications for the United States. We thus decline to require the Saudi government to justify to us the arrangements it believes are best suited to ensure the safety of its royal family.

III.

Butters next argues that Vance is not entitled to immunity since Vance, as opposed to the Saudi officials, was responsible for the decision not to promote Butters.

A.

If Vance was following Saudi Arabia's orders not to promote Butters, Vance would be entitled to derivative immunity under the FSIA. . . .

. . . To abrogate immunity would discourage American companies from entering lawful agreements with foreign governments and from respecting their wishes even as to sovereign acts. Under the circumstances here, imposing civil liability on the private agents of Saudi Arabia would significantly impede the Saudi government's sovereign interest in protecting its leaders while they are in the United States.

* * * * *

IV.

Any type of governmental immunity reflects a trade-off between the possibility that an official's wrongdoing will remain unpunished and the risk that government functions will be impaired. See *Harlow v. Fitzgerald,* 457 U.S. 800, 813–14 (1982) ("The resolution of immunity questions inherently requires a balance between the evils inevitable in any available alternative."). FSIA immunity presupposes a tolerance for the sovereign decisions of other countries that may reflect legal norms and cultural values quite different from our own. Here Saudi Arabia made a decision to protect a member of its royal family in a manner consistent with Islamic law and custom. The Act requires not that we approve of the diverse cultural or political motivations that may underlie another sovereign's acts, but that we respect them. We thus affirm the judgment.

Questions

1. Why did the court hold that Vance, a U.S. corporation, could avoid Butters' claim of discrimination based on a claim of sovereign immunity? Why did Butters argue that sovereign immunity would not apply?

2. How do you feel about the end result of this decision? Did Butters suffer discrimination?

Arbitration

In light of the difficulty of litigation, parties to an international contract may prefer to insert a clause that calls for international arbitration in case of a dispute. Arbitration is a nonjudicial means to settle a conflict where the parties agree to a hearing in front of a third party who will issue a binding award decision. (See Chapter 4.)

While arbitration is considered binding on the parties who consent to it, there are times when a losing party may opt not to satisfy the award to the other party. In that case, the successful party must petition a court of law to enforce the award. In that regard, the United Nations Convention on the Recognition and Enforcement of Foreign Arbitral Awards, signed by 135 countries as of 2005,[48] provides that the successful party obtain possession of the property of the losing party located in any signatory country for the purpose of satisfying the debt.

The following case illustrates the problems that may arise in collecting an award, even where an arbitration clause apparently is clear.

In the Matter of the Arbitration between Seven Seas Shipping (UK) Ltd v. Tondo Limitada, on Behalf of the Republic of Angola   1999 U.S. Dist. Lexis 9574 (S.D.N.Y. 1999)

LEGAL BRIEFCASE

District Judge Denise Cote

Seven Seas Shipping Ltd., owner of a yacht named *Mitsa,* is a British corporation with its principal place of business in Berkshire, England. The respondent, Tondo Limitada, is organized and existing under the laws of Angola, with its principal place of business in Luanda, Angola. On September 25, 1996, the two entered into a charter party agreement in which Tondo chartered the *Mitsa* to carry wheat from Houston, Texas, to Lobito, Luanda, and Namibe, Angola.

The *Mitsa* was loaded and ready to depart at Houston, Texas, on October 10, 1996, but because a letter of credit for payment that was required under the governing charter party was not in order, the vessel was not allowed to proceed to the loading berth. The problem was not remedied by Tondo until October 24, 1996. After the wheat cargo arrived and was discharged in Angola, Seven Seas presented Tondo with invoices of alleged detention damages at the loading port in Houston, and demurrage incurred in discharging at the three Angolan ports, for the total amount of $138,312.47. In response, Tondo claimed that the detention charges only amounted to $62,840.

As a result of disputes over the detention costs, pursuant to their agreement, Seven Seas sought to arbitrate. The matter was considered by the arbitrators, and on January 27, 1999, Seven Seas was awarded $95,603.28 for damages and Tondo was ordered to pay the full amount of the arbitration fees, which totaled $5,425. Seven Seas now requests an order

confirming the award as a judgment of the Court in the amount of $101,078.28 with interest at the rate of 7.75 percent until entry of judgment. Tondo has not responded to Seven Seas' motion.

DISCUSSION
1. The Standard
Whether to recognize and enforce an arbitration award is governed in the first instance in this case by the Convention on the Recognition and Enforcement of Foreign Arbitral Awards. The Convention requires contracting states such as the United States

> to recognize an agreement in writing under which the parties undertake to submit to arbitration all or any differences which have arisen or which may arise between them in respect of a defined legal relationship, whether contractual or not, concerning a subject matter capable of settlement by arbitration.

The Second Circuit has recently held that

> any commercial arbitral agreement, unless it is between two United States citizens, involves property located in the United States, and has no reasonable relationship with one or more foreign states, falls under the Convention.

Here, clause 44(a) of the [agreement] indicates that there is an agreement in writing to arbitrate all disputes that arise out of a commercial contractual relationship. According to the clause, all disputes are to be arbitrated in New York and are subject to United States law. Both parties are foreign corporations with their principal places of business outside of the United States. The agreement is, therefore, governed by the Convention.

The confirmation of an arbitration award is a summary proceeding that converts a final arbitration award into a judgment of the court. A court shall confirm an arbitration award made under the Convention "unless it finds one of the grounds for refusal or deferral of recognition or enforcement of the award specified in the said Convention." The Court may refuse recognition and enforcement of an award "at the request of the party against whom it is invoked, only if that party furnishes to the competent authority" proof of the existence of any one of five circumstances. Because Tondo has not contested Seven Seas' motion in this case, none of these grounds for refusal is relevant. Under the Convention, Article V(2), the Court may refuse to recognize an award upon its own finding that

1. the subject matter of the difference is not capable of settlement by arbitration under the law of the country where recognition is sought;

2. the recognition or enforcement of the award would be contrary to the public policy of that country.

2. Subject Matter Capable of Settlement by Arbitration

The Federal Arbitration Act governs arbitration in the United States and "reflects a legislative recognition of the 'desirability of arbitration as an alternative to the complications of litigation.'" Section 2 of the FAA provides, in relevant part,

> an agreement in writing to submit to arbitration an existing controversy . . . shall be valid, irrevocable, and enforceable, save upon such grounds as exist at law or in equity for the revocation of any contract.

This proceeding seeks confirmation of an arbitration award pursuant to the written agreement of the parties to arbitrate any controversy between them. This Court is not aware of any grounds for the revocation of this contract, and finds that the disputed subject matter is, therefore, capable of resolution by arbitration under the laws of the United States.

3. Contrary to Public Policy

The United States, as a signatory of the Convention, is in agreement with the central policy statement of the Convention, which is

> to encourage the recognition and enforcement of commercial arbitration agreements in international contracts and to unify the standards by which agreements to arbitrate are observed and arbitral awards are enforced in the signatory countries.

This statement evidences a strong public policy in support of arbitration proceedings and enforcement of arbitration awards. A court should find that enforcement is contrary to public policy only where enforcement would violate our "most basic notions of morality and justice." No understanding of the facts before this Court supports the notion that enforcement of this arbitration award would violate our basic notions of morality and justice. Instead, the confirmation of this award is quite consistent with the stated policy of the United States, and other signatories of the Convention, to encourage the resolution of commercial disputes by arbitration.

CONCLUSION

For the reasons stated above, Seven Seas' motion is granted. The arbitral award is confirmed and the Clerk of Court shall enter judgment in the amount of $101,078.28 with interest at the rate of 7.75 percent per annum from February 25, 1999 [30 days after the date of the arbitration award, during which time Tondo had an opportunity to satisfy the award without interest accruing], to the date of entry of the judgment.

Internet Exercise

Identify a multinational firm that conducts business with suppliers in developing countries. Find its code of vendor conduct on the Web and evaluate the areas of enforcement that might prove to be the most difficult.

Chapter Questions

1. Cultural values can sometimes come into conflict with outside values spread through the process of globalization. The following story originated in India.

    > A group called the Hindu Jagran Manch, or the Hindu Awakening Platform, said Valentine's Day was an affront to Indian traditional culture and warned against Feb. 14 celebrations in the city. Many conservative segments of Indian society view the day—a celebration of romantic love—as indecent.

"Valentine's Day, Mother's Day, and Father's Day . . . these are all the gimmicks of multinational companies to market their products. Valentine's Day is against the culture and ethics of Indian society," said Vinay Tewari, a Manch leader.[49]

As a result of threatened attacks by Manch, many shopkeepers in India's largest state closed for Valentine's Day. Should the shopkeepers have closed their doors? Do you understand how a celebration of "romantic love" might be offensive to some? Do you think that Valentine's Day and other U.S. holidays are promoted more for their commercial value than to further the stated purpose for the day? Consider the dates when Halloween, Thanksgiving, and Christmas decorations go up in stores.

2. America has embraced fast food. This may be part of the reason that, in the United States, obesity has risen at an epidemic rate during the past 20 years. According to the Center for Disease Control, currently more than two thirds of the adults in the United States are considered overweight or obese. Sixteen percent of those between 6 and 19 are overweight. [For more on obesity in the United States, see the Web site for the Center for Disease Control, **www.cdc.gov/nccdphp/dnpa/obesity/index.htm**] Should other countries be concerned about the influx of American fast-food chains? Why or why not? What about countries that provide universal health care? If a country is concerned about its citizens' dietary changes, what actions should it take in response? Explain.

3. What are the relative advantages and disadvantages of each form of doing business in a foreign country? Why would a firm choose one form over another?

4. Assume that you are interested in importing silk blouses from Bangkok to France. What facts might persuade you to enter into an agency agreement with a Thai blouse manufacturer rather than a distributorship and vice versa?

5. Dubai and Sharjah were Arab territories under the protection of Great Britain since 1892 but without clearly defined boundaries. The extent of territory the ruler of each controlled in each of these areas depended on which tribes offered him allegiance. Because the tribes were nomadic and moved around a great deal, the areas controlled by each ruler were indefinite. At the territories' request, Britain intervened in the 1950s, awarding certain lands to one or the other territory. However, uncertainty and dissatisfaction continued, notwithstanding the fact that the parties had requested that Britain arbitrate the boundaries. A compromise between the parties was signed in 1976 that provided for continued arbitration regarding the boundary dispute. One of the recurring issues was the choice of law to be applied because, unfortunately, no applicable law had been specified. Dubai argued that international law governed, which would dictate that equity reign; whereas Sharjah argued that the federal law of the United Arab Emirates applied, which would have given greater weight to allegiance of the tribes. What should be the result here? How would you arrive at a decision regarding the delineation of territory? What factors are important to your decision? See *Dubai–Sharjah Border Arbitration, International Court of Justice, Court of Arbitration,* October 19, 1981.

6. The WTO member nations have only just turned their consideration to the barriers between nations that impede the flow of services across boundaries. In the professions, such as medicine, law, and accounting, substantial barriers currently exist, some in the form of domestic licensure requirements, which in turn often require a particular

educational background of the applicant. Would establishing a clearinghouse for educational equivalencies around the world and requiring WTO members to honor the educational achievements received by applicants in other member countries be a good idea? Why or why not?

7. Thomas Friedman, in his 2005 book *The World Is Flat: A Brief History of the Twenty-First Century,* offers his opinion that countries with connected manufacturing supply chains won't go to war with each other. He offers an example of Dell's multicountry supply chain for the manufacture of its laptops. On balance, do you think globalization is a catalyst for bringing world peace or a tinderbox that may set international disputes on fire through the collision of differing ideals?

8. What may look to one observer like the application of objective standards may appear to another observer as improper protectionism. NAFTA, originally signed in the mid-1990s, calls for an open border for commercial truck traffic among Canada, the United States, and Mexico. But in early 2005 Mexican trucks were still not allowed into the United States, due in part to litigation brought by environmental and labor groups. Their claim was that the United States hadn't appropriately considered the environmental impact of letting Mexican trucks roll on American roads because there are no standardized emissions rules for commercial vehicles. On balance, does this argument sound to you more like a principled objection or like protection for U.S. jobs? Why? See *Dept. of Transportation v. Public Citizen,* 541 U.S. 752; (2004).

9. Original Appalachian Artworks (OAA) is the manufacturer and license holder of Cabbage Patch Kids dolls. Granada Electronics imported and distributed Cabbage Patch Kids dolls to the United States that were made in Spain by Jesmar under a license from OAA. Jesmar's license permitted manufacture and distribution of the dolls in Spain, the Canary Islands, Andorra, and Ceuta Melilla. Under the license, Jesmar agreed not to make, sell, or authorize any sale of the dolls outside its licensed territory and to sell only to those purchasers who would agree not to use or resell the licensed products outside the territory as well. Jesmar's argument that Granada's sales do not constitute "gray market" sales is that OAA's dolls sold in the United States have English-language adoption papers, birth certificates, and instructions while Granada's dolls come equipped with Spanish-language adoption papers, birth certificates, and instructions. In addition, Granada argues that the role of trademark law is to prevent an infringer from passing off its goods as being those of another. Such is not the case here. Are these sales prohibited? Explain. See *Orig. Appalachian Artworks v. Granada Electronics,* 816 F.2d 68 (2d Cir. 1987); cert. den. 484 U.S. 847 (1987).

10. Camel Manufacturing imported nylon tents to the United States. The tents held nine people and weighed over 30 pounds. The tents' floors ranged from 8 feet by 10 feet to 10 feet by 14 feet. The tents were to be used as shelter during camping. The importer categorized the goods as "sports equipment," which carried a 10 percent import duty, whereas the U.S. Customs Service considered the tents "textile articles not specifically provided for," with a duty of $.25 per pound plus 15 percent import duty. The importer appealed the decision. What should be the result? Explain. See *Camel Manufacturing Co. v. United States,* 686 F.Supp. 912 (C.I.T. 1988); aff'd 861 F.2d 1266 (Fed. Cir. 1988).

11. Should a Mexican citizen who bought a Chrysler vehicle in Mexico be allowed to sue the manufacturer in a U.S. court under U.S. product liability laws when the plaintiff's three-year-old son was killed when the passenger-side air bag deployed during an accident in Mexico? See *Gonzalez v. Chrysler Corp.*, 301 F. 3d 377 (5th Cir. 2002); cert. den. 538 U.S. 1012 (2003).

12. In 1954, Italy filed a petition with the International Court of Justice based on a 1951 war reparations declaration made by America, Britain, and France. The declaration concerned the removal of certain Albanian gold from Italy in 1943 by German authorities (who then turned over the gold to Albania). The issue that concerned Italy at this hearing was whether the gold was in fact property of Italy or Albania at the end of World War II. In fact, Italy was not asking the court to order Albania to return the gold but to order the United States, Britain, and France to make reparations to Italy under the declaration. To complicate matters, the court was also asked to decide whether, if the gold was found to be Italy's, it should still be given to Britain in settlement of a prior judgment by Britain against Albania. Britain argued that its claim for the gold from Albania had priority over Italy's claim to the gold. Notwithstanding these truly complex matters, however, the first concern of the court was whether it had jurisdiction over all of the parties. Which parties to this action must have consented to the action in order for the court to finally decide the issues presented to it and enforce a judgment? See *Monetary Gold Removed from Rome, I.C.J. Reports 1954,* p. 19.

13. Prior to 1941, Kalmich owned a business in Yugoslavia. In 1941 the Nazis confiscated his property as a result of Kalmich's Jewish heritage and faith. Bruno purchased the business from the Nazis in 1942 without knowledge of the potential unlawful conversion. Kalmich contends that because the confiscation was in violation of well-defined principles of international law prior to the German occupation, the transfer to Bruno was ineffective. Kalmich seeks to apply a 1946 Yugoslavian law called "Law Concerning the Treatment of Property Taken Away from the Owner." That law provides that where property is taken from its owners, the owner may bring an action against "responsible persons" for recovery. Does the act of state doctrine apply here? If not, what should be the result in an American court? Explain. See *Kalmich v. Bruno,* 450 F. Supp. 227 (N.D.IL 1978).

14. Zedan received a telephone call from a Saudi Arabian organization offering him an engineering position at a construction project in Saudi Arabia. The Ministry of Communications, an agency of the government, guaranteed payment to Zedan for any work he performed there, whether for the government or for a nonsovereign third party. After three years, Zedan left the country without being fully paid. After he returned to the United States, he filed an action in federal court seeking to enforce the ministry's guarantee. The ministry argued that it was protected under the Foreign Sovereign Immunities Act. Was Zedan's recruitment in the United States a commercial activity as required by the act? Did this action have a direct effect in the United States as required by the act? Explain. See *Zedan v. Kingdom of Saudi Arabia,* 849 F.2d 1511 (1988).

15. From time to time courts are called upon to determine the enforceability of an arbitration clause contained in a contract. One such case was *DiMercurio v. Sphere Drake Insurance,* 202 F.3d 71 (1st Cir. 2000). DiMercurio was injured in 1994 when

the commercial fishing vessel in which he was working sank. The vessel was owned by R&M, which was found by a court to be liable to DiMercurio for his injuries and ordered to pay $350,000 in compensation. However, because R&M had no other assets, it assigned to DiMercurio all the rights it had against Sphere Drake, the London-based insurer of the fishing vessel. When DiMercurio looked to Sphere Drake for payment, it denied the claim and invoked the arbitration clause in its insurance policy with R&M, which required the arbitration to take place in England. Should DiMercurio be required to pursue his claim through arbitration in England?

Notes

1. "Agreement Establishing the World Trade Organization," found at [**www.wto.org/english/docs_e/legal_e/legal_e.htm**].

2. Bill Sing, "Deal to Loosen Trade Reached," *Los Angeles Times,* August 1, 2004, p. A1.

3. Central Intelligence Agency, "Global Trends 2015: A Dialogue about the Future with Non-government Experts," NIC 2000–02 (December 2000), found at [**www.cia.gov.cia/publications/globaltrends2015/index.html**].

4. Amy Merrick, "Gap Offers Unusual Look at Factory Conditions," *The Wall Street Journal,* May 12, 2004, p. A1.

5. *EEOC v. Arabian American Oil Co.,* 499 U.S. 244 (1991).

6. Central Intelligence Agency, *Global Trends.*

7. [**www.westbuslaw.com/cases/topical_operational_standards.html**].

8. A copy of the draft can be found in the University of Minnesota's Human Rights Library [**www1.umn.edu/humanrts/links/NormsApril2003.html**].

9. A copy of the report can be downloaded from [**www.ccbe.org/doc/En/guidelines_csr_en.pdf**].

10. The principles can be found at [**www.cauxroundtable.org/principles.html**].

11. "Chocolate Industry Acts to End Slavery," *Waterloo/Cedar Falls Courier,* October 1, 2001, p. A2.

12. Jose Ramos-Horta, "Speech to the Northern Medical Foundation Tribute to Military Medicine and Lt-Gen. P. Cosgrove," Sydney, Australia, September 28, 2001. Copy with author's work papers.

13. See, for example, *U.S. v. Kim,* 246 F. 3d 186 (2d Cir. 2001), where a New York resident was convicted of wire fraud while working for the United Nations in Croatia.

14. 116 F. Supp. 2d 116 (D.D.C. 2000).

15. 192 F. 3d 240 (2d Cir. 1999).

16. Douglas Lavin, "Globalization Goes Upscale," *The Wall Street Journal,* February 1, 2002, p. A18.

17. See Catherine L. Mann's testimony before the Subcommittee on International Trade of the Senate Finance Committee, October 21, 1999 [**http://www.iie.com/publications/papers/mann1099.htm**].

18. Bob Davis, "Migration of Skilled Jobs Abroad Unsettles Global-Economy Fans," *The Wall Street Journal,* January 26, 2004, p. A1.

19. William M. Bulkeley, "IBM Documents Give Rare Look at Sensitive Plans on 'Offshoring,'" *The Wall Street Journal,* January 19, 2004, p. A1.

20. Michael Schroeder, "Outsourcing May Create U.S. Jobs," *The Wall Street Journal,* March 30, 2004, p. A2.

21. GATS, Art. I, para. 3(b).

22. Summary of the Madrid Agreement Concerning the International Registration of Marks (1891) and the Protocol Relating to That Agreement (1989) [**www.wipo.int/treaties/en/registration/madrid_protocol/summary_madrid.html**].

23. G. Winestock and H. Cooper, "Activists Outmaneuver Drug Makers at WTO," *The Wall Street Journal,* November 14, 2001, p. A2, A13.

24. *Itar-Tass Russian News Agency v. Russian Kurier, Inc.,* 153 F.3d 82 (2d Cir. 1998).

25. 175 F.3d 1269 (11th Cir. 1999); cert. den. 529 U.S. 1036 (2000).

26. Michael Schroeder and Silvia Ascarelli, "New Role for SEC: Policing Companies beyond U.S. Borders," *The Wall Street Journal,* July 30, 2004, p. A1.

27. Schroeder and Ascarelli, "New Role for SEC."

28. Daniel Epstein, "Goodbye, Farewell, Auf Wiedersehen, Adieu . . .," *The Wall Street Journal,* February 9, 2005, p. A10.

29. This and additional information is available from the IASB Web site generally and specifically at [**www.iasb.org/about/faq.asp?showPageContent=no&xml=18_18_24_17122003.htm**].

30. Amanda Cohen, "Surveying the Microsoft Antitrust Universe," *Berkeley Technology Law Journal* 19 (2004), p. 333.

31. For a good comparison of U.S. and EU Merger analysis and enforcement, see Cento Veljanovski, "EC Merger policy after GE/Honeywell and Airtours," *Antitrust Bulletin* 49 (Spring 2004), p. 153.

32. "Against Anti-Dumping," *The Economist* 349, no. 8093 (November 7, 1998), p. 18.

33. Peter Pae, "Aircraft Trade Issue Up in Air," *Los Angeles Times,* April 12, 2005, p. C1.

34. M. Rafiqul Islam, "Recent EU Trade Sanctions on the U.S. to Induce Compliance with the WTO Ruling in the Foreign Sales Corporations Case: Its Policy Contradiction Revisited," *Journal of World Trade* 38 (June 2004), p. 471.

35. William Chou, "The $4 Billion Question: An Analysis of Congressional Responses to the FSC/ETI Dispute under WTO Export Subsidy Standards," *Northwestern Journal of International Law & Business* 25 (Winter 2005), p. 415.

36. Helene Cooper, "Can African Nations Use Duty-Free Deal to Revamp Economy?" *The Wall Street Journal,* January 2, 2002, pp. A1, A4.

37. Keith B. Richburg, "McDonald's Attacker Convicted in France," *Washington Post,* September 14, 2000, p. A28.

38. Central Intelligence Agency, *Global Trends.*

39. *J.C.J. Wouters, J.W. Savelbergh, Price Waterhouse Belastingadviseurs BV and Algemene Raad Van de Nederlandse Orde Van Advocaten,* C-309/99, 2002 TNT 37–62 (EU Ct. 2002).

40. "NAFTA Clause May Override Labor, Environmental Laws," *Waterloo/Cedar Falls Courier,* July 12, 2001, pp. A1, A5.

41. Adam Liptak, "NAFTA Tribunals Stir U.S. Worries," *The New York Times,* April 18, 2004.

42. Klaus-Heiner Lehne, "Hands Off Our Torts," *The Wall Street Journal,* November 18, 2003, p. A20.

43. Robert S. Greenberger, "High Court Limits Antitrust Scope," *The Wall Street Journal,* June 15, 2004, p. A3.

44. Robert S. Greenberger, "Justices Deal Blow to Intel in Matter Involving EU Probe," *The Wall Street Journal,* June 22, 2004, p. A3.

45. Robert S. Greenberger and Pui-Wing Tam, "Human-Rights Suits against U.S. Firms Curbed," *The Wall Street Journal,* June 30, 2004, p. A3.

46. 11 U.S. (7 Cranch) 116 (1812).

47. *Sutherland v. Islamic Republic of Iran,* 151 F. Supp. 2d 27 (D.D.C. 2001).

48. Current information on the status of the convention can be found at [**www.uncitral.org/en-index.htm**].

49. Rupan Bhattacharya, "Valentine's Day Menace Causes Shop Closings," *Des Moines Register,* February 14, 2001, p. 2A.

Environmental Protection

Introduction

From local issues such as routing a new highway around a wetland or allowing leaf burning to colossal fears such as global warming and the loss of tropical rainforests, environmental issues mark our lives in a manner that was unimaginable a few decades ago. From the moment a firm begins to produce, service, manufacture, or create, its operations affect the environment. Imagine the small decisions made by a company: Does it pack its glassware in plastic bubbles or corrugated wrapping? Does it publish a catalog once a month or once a year? Is that catalog published on paper or only through the Internet? Does it meet with the community before choosing a disposal system? Each of these decisions will have an impact on our physical world; so it is critical to understand the law as it relates to the environment and to be aware of the ethical component of each decision.

The Global Picture

It is also important to understand the magnitude of the environmental problems we face and that their scope often extends beyond political boundaries. Environmentalists in America and around the world have a great deal to worry about. Consider the following.

- Regarding global air pollution:

    New glimpses of Earth from space show air pollution wrapping around the planet, spreading haze and hazardous gases across oceans and continents and posing new challenges for cleanup. . . . Increasingly, researchers are discovering air pollution is not a transient phenomenon. Emissions climb high into the atmosphere, borne on trade winds that circumnavigate the globe.[1]

    One study of 9,300 babies born between 1987 and 1993 in the Los Angeles basin found a strong statistical link between disruptions in fetal heart development in the second month of pregnancy and recorded levels of air pollution.[2] "Citizens in most major cities of China today wear facemasks to protect themselves from air pollutants as they walk in the streets."[3]

- Examples of pollution of and danger to the world's waterways abound. A *dead zone* (an oxygen-starved area devoid of fish) in the Gulf of Mexico, caused in part by runoff of fertilizers into the Mississippi River, in 2001 covered 8,006 square miles (that is, approaching the size of Massachusetts).[4] According to the United Nations Environment Program, there are nearly 150 such dead zones around the globe, double the number existing in 1990, covering some 27,000 square miles.[5]

- Recent studies show that the North Pole is collecting many of the world's most toxic chemicals, even chemicals such as DDT that were banned by most industrial countries in the 1970s. These chemicals accumulate in the fat of such arctic animals as the polar bear, whose survival is being threatened.[6]

- Japan has discovered it has a considerable problem with soil pollution from industrial sources. In a Tokyo suburb where Nissan Motor Corporation once had a manufacturing facility, the soil is contaminated with carcinogenic chemicals. In response to this and other such discoveries, a government-appointed panel has been charged with looking into legislation that is expected to make soil pollution a punishable offense and to force corporate Japan to clean up its act.[7]

- A report spearheaded by the U.S. Central Intelligence Agency, *Global Trends 2015*, predicts that by 2015 "nearly half the world's population—more than 3 billion people—will live in countries that are 'water-stressed'—have less than 1,700 cubic meters of water per capita per year—mostly in Africa, the Middle East, South Asia, and northern China."[8] Already by 2000, about 1.1 billion people lacked access to safe drinking water.[9] Because over 30 nations receive more than one-third of their water from outside their borders, regional tensions over water can be expected to increase.

One question raised by these illustrations is whether the process of globalization has aggravated our environmental problems. As seen in the following article, at least one observer decidedly argues yes.

READING   # Seeds of Chaos

Jeff Gersh

Like Johnny Appleseed on a huge scale, globalization is spreading the American way of making money all over the world. But at what cost to the environment?

In the winter of 1990, I spent a day and a half traveling by bus and truck from Bangkok, and another day hiking up corkscrew footpaths to reach a small Red Karen village in the northwestern hills of Thailand. Tucked into a high perch overlooking rice paddies, eight huts of reed, bamboo, and wood, elevated on stilts, were open to neighbors and friends who wished to visit. One dwelling, however, was padlocked, an odd sight in this remote place. Through its window I could see that the hut was bare—no hammock, no rice sacks or fertilizer. In one corner, as if arranged by some gifted art director to catch the light, sat a wooden soda case holding a few bottles of Coca-Cola.

This was my personal freeze-frame glimpse of globalization in progress. Those Coke bottles, icons of international marketing, represented an early wave of the sea of foreign products and capital that has since washed over Thailand and other developing countries.... Recently, Thai consumers have delighted Heinz executives by increasing their yearly spending on ketchup to nearly a dollar per person, almost half the U.S. total. Today, not only is Thailand a sought-after international market, but it is also playing the export game itself, on a grand scale: The nation is now the world's second largest producer of pickup trucks. Yet its status as an international importer–exporter is dwarfed by a country such as China, whose share of global advertising dollars, in the years from 1986 to 1996, grew 1,000 percent.

The 1990s have been a decade of frenetic economic globalization. A torrent of goods and capital has breached national boundaries that once held back the flows of international trade and financial investment.

* * * * *

Globalization is facilitated by a spate of institutional and regulatory changes, in this country and abroad, aimed at liberalizing trade and investment practices. These changes reflect the contagious U.S. enchantment with freer markets and less government intervention. Crises in Asia and Latin America have stirred great debate about how to improve the workings of global financial systems. Yet the environmental dimensions of globalization are rarely discussed—an indication that world leaders and the communities they represent have not paused to question just what it is they are globalizing.

BACKGROUND: GLOBALIZATION AND DEVELOPMENT

Buried in the hoopla over celebrated business deals and skyrocketing trade and stock markets lies another reality. As many as a billion people now live in absolute poverty. According to the United Nations, 20 percent of the populations of the world's poorest countries lack access to the most basic modern health care; 25 percent do not have adequate housing; 30 percent lack access to clean water.

Because hunger and misery cannot afford to make the distinctions of the well-fed—to choose between cutting a tree or saving it—poverty is among the greatest environmental threats in the world. For moral reasons, let alone ecological reasons, it must be vanquished.

As early as 1987, the World Commission on Environment and Development (known as the Brundtland Commission) envisioned economic development as an achievable path to sustainability—that is, to an economic system that supports citizens at a decent standard of living without degrading the environment. But the Brundtland Commission added two caveats. Sustainability through economic development, the commission said, was possible only if environmentally benign technologies were developed and shared with poorer nations, and if the ecosystems of those nations were safeguarded.

The globalization trend is not living up to the Brundtland Commission's vision. Fifty years ago, President Harry Truman introduced into the diplomatic lexicon the phrase "undeveloped areas." Today, with savvy marketing and a nod to Wall Street, the world's poor countries are labeled "emerging markets"—economic butterflies breaking from their cocoons. Less developed nations include a labor force of some 4.4 billion people who occupy three-quarters of the globe's land area. These countries have traditionally tended to be net exporters of food, fuel, minerals, and other raw materials. . . . For many of them, the rewards of participation in a global economy may seem theoretical at best. Since 1980, 100 nations have been either economically stagnant or in decline. On average, an African household today consumes one-fifth less than it did a quarter-century ago.

Other nations, such as China and Singapore, have caught fire, economically speaking. But rather than finding a new path of environmentally sustainable development, they are repeating the mistakes of the industrialized countries, and worse. In most of these nations, brisk economic development comes at great ecological expense, and environmental restoration has been postponed for some indefinite future. It has been estimated that the annual toll for environmental damage in China will reach $42 billion by the year 2000. Gold mining in the Philippines has cut large swaths of destruction in tropical forests, and many have charged that it is contaminating water sources. In Mexico, 15 U.S. wood product firms have opened for business since NAFTA was approved in 1993. Boise Cascade has a five-year plan to send 20 million board feet of tropical hardwood to the United States; the International Paper Corporation helped push for passage of Mexico's Forest Reform Law, which eases environmental restrictions and provides for privatization of industrial forests.

Still, many economists counsel patience. If these emerging markets stay on the prescribed path of development, the argument goes, they will eventually raise their per capita incomes to the threshold at which economic and political capital takes an interest in environmental reforms. Mexico City is a case in point. Since December of 1998, journalist Julia Preston reports, exposure to pollutants such as automobile exhaust has sickened half the city's 18 million people with respiratory ailments. "Mexicans have other priorities. They see pollution as a luxury problem," sociologist Jose Luis Lezama told the reporter.

The theory is that Mexico City will begin to experience relief from polluted air once per capita incomes reach about $4,000. However, economist Eban Goodstein of Lewis and Clark College projects that at the country's annual growth rate of 4 percent, citizens will need to breathe bad air for another 25 years—for another generation. . . .

Moreover, while emissions of some pollutants are expected to decrease as incomes rise, others, such as carbon dioxide, continue to grow. In 1997, General Motors made a $1 billion deal with China to build 100,000 midsized automobiles a year. In a nation of 1.2 billion people, whose cities have been particularly accommodating to bicycles and mass transit, shifting toward reliance on the automobile will degrade air quality and boost emissions of greenhouse gases. . . .

* * * * *

GLOBAL VILLAGE?

Globalization has much in common with a powerful technology. It can be harmful or beneficial, depending on how it is used and on the policies that guide its implementation. In the last five years, globalization has hastened environmental destruction and eroded community self-determination. The world is becoming not a global village, but rather a system of corporate economies. Corporations today are relatively unconstrained by national borders or by regulatory structures intended to provide them with any guiding principle beyond that of making a buck. This is not the logical outcome of a free market, but rather the result of institutional choices. . . .

Source: *Amicus Journal* 21, no. 2 (Summer 1999), p. 36. Reprinted by permission.

Questions

1. What do you think of the author's observation that "poverty is among the greatest environmental threats in the world"? Can business have any impact on this most fundamental of problems? If so, how? If not, why not?

2. If globalization is the culprit, or at least one culprit, what is the alternative? Is the poverty recited by the author caused or aggravated by globalization or would it widely exist without it?

3. Has the author provided, perhaps unwittingly, arguments in support of the development of a world government?

   a. What do you think of the idea of an across-the-board tax on international imports which could be distributed to developing countries to support environmental protection? Who would actually end up paying such a tax? Is this a further step in globalization—that is, an international taxing system (a function normally reserved to governments)?

   b. If it is true that "corporations today are relatively unconstrained by national borders or by regulatory structures intended to provide them with any guiding principle beyond that of making a buck," what can be done to address the problem? Again, is part of the solution imposing international regulatory standards on corporations?

4. Can ecobanks, ecodeposits, and ecoinvesting make a difference?

Part One—A Return to Fundamentals: The Market, Government Regulation, and Self-Regulation

The first three chapters of this text set up a framework for analyzing the substantive law topics that followed: (1) consideration of how well market forces achieve the goals we have for our society; (2) investigation of whether government intervention, through laws and regulations, can bring and has brought us closer to those societal goals; and (3) reflection on the role that self-regulation, through ethical decision making and corporate social responsibility, can and does play in realizing our goals. We will look at each of these forces in our exploration of the interplay between business and our natural environment.

Market Failure?

Without regulation, a firm may consider that dumping its garbage into a nearby canal is no big deal. In fact, perhaps the slight amount of garbage the firm dumps *is* no big deal. However, if every firm were allowed to dump that amount, the canal might become thoroughly polluted. Or consider the possibility that we may all prefer less costly cars that pollute more. Would future generations concur?

As discussed in Chapter 8, pollution in these cases would be categorized by economists as a negative "externality." Wilfred Beckerman described the economic analysis as follows:

> [T]he costs of pollution are not always borne fully, if at all, by the polluter. . . . Naturally, he has no incentive to economize in the use [of the environment] in the same way

that he has for other factors of production that carry a cost, such as labor or capital. . . . This defect of the price mechanism needs to be corrected by governmental action in order to eliminate excessive pollution.[10]

Thus environmentalists claim the market has failed to protect us from pollution and rules are necessary. The public and Congress have apparently agreed: The United States has enacted a substantial number of environmental laws since the early 1970s, addressing air pollution, pollution of our waterways, protection of rare plant and animal species, and hazardous and toxic wastes. Many of these laws will be discussed in Part Two of this chapter.

Market Incentives

As we will see, one form that our federal regulation has taken is to dictate standards with which businesses must comply. Such legislation has in fact led to steady, and at times even spectacular, strides forward in environmental protection in the United States. But this progress has not dispelled the view, particularly among economists and businesspeople, that standard-setting regulation may not be the best approach to remedy environmental problems. They believe that pollution control is not so much a matter of law as of economics. It follows that with proper incentives, the market will, in some instances, prove superior to traditional regulation in preventing and correcting environmental problems. Some examples of market incentives follow.

Pollution Credits   Perhaps the most prominent and successful example of the U.S. government employing free market tactics to address an environmental issue is the government-created market in pollution credits. In the early 1990s the United States set a cap on the number of tons of pollutants to be permitted in the air, a cap lower than the actual amount then being emitted. Pollution credits were issued to several hundred of the biggest power plants and certain factories. Credit recipients could either reduce their discharges to within their credit limit or they could buy credits from other companies who had reduced their emissions below their own credit amounts. Companies with a relatively low cost to reduce their emissions made plant improvements and then paid for some of their own improvements by selling their excess credits. Companies with a relatively high cost to reduce emissions found it more economical to help pay to reduce another company's emissions (by purchasing that plant's excess credits) than incur their own higher-cost pollution reduction.[11] Electric utilities in 1999 produced about 41 percent more electricity than in 1980 while emitting 25 percent fewer tons of sulfur dioxide.[12]

Taxes   Tax provisions can also affect behavior, either to encourage particular behavior through tax incentives or to discourage other behavior through application of additional taxes. For example, in the environmental area we have provided a tax deduction, whether or not one itemizes, for part of the cost of purchasing a new hybrid gas–electric car, such as the Toyota Prius.[13] Another example is the tax-free fringe benefit allowed to employees through a payroll deduction purchase of commuter vouchers or transit passes. The EPA in 2000 began actively seeking major employers in urban areas to enroll in the program so that the environmental benefits from the incentive would be realized.[14]

Global Examples   "When it comes to using green taxes and charges to alter the prices of goods and services to reflect their environmental effects, Europe has generally gone the furthest."[15] Thus, for example, in 1991 Sweden introduced a sulfur tax that led to a drop in the sulfur content of fuels to 50 percent below the legal requirements. "Norway's carbon tax, also levied in 1991, lowered emissions from power plants by 21 percent."[16] Australia, Greenland, Iceland, New Zealand, and the Netherlands have been quite successful using market incentives to address overfishing. "Government authorities cap the total allowable catch and then allocate quotas among fishermen, usually based on the historical catch. The quotas become a 'property right' that can be bought and sold among fishermen, helping to reduce fleet capacity. And because fishermen have access to a guaranteed share of the catch, they don't race to compete . . . prices rise and fish stocks grow."[17]

The Kyoto Protocol on global warming, which will be discussed in Part Five, also uses market incentives to achieve its goal of lower global greenhouse gas emissions.

Question

Suggested free market incentives for pollution control include government taxes or fees on pollution and government rules mandating refundable deposits on hazardous materials. Explain how those incentives would work.

Ethical Business Decision Making

On a particularly busy corner in a suburb of Auckland, New Zealand, the proprietors of a small café, Triniti of Silver, do a brisk breakfast, lunch, and coffee trade. Their menu declares their philosophy: Only organic eggs of free-range chickens are used here; only paddock-reared pigs; only certified organic beef—"we do not feel happy to encourage the inhumane treatment of animals." Just one example of grassroots, intentional, ethical business decision making.

But what can we expect in the environmental area from managers of publicly held corporations? Can we find significant examples of corporate social responsibility (discussed in Chapter 3)? The answer is a resounding yes—all one has to do is review a sampling of corporate Web sites. Why are corporate giants voluntarily doing now what they haven't done in the past? What has changed? In part, the answer may be that the market has changed and market forces are operating to reward corporate responsibility. For example, managers may believe that being "green," or being seen as being green by consumers and investors, will improve the corporate bottom line. Or a manager may believe that a proactive approach may lessen the likelihood of future regulation on an issue that is becoming increasingly visible.[18] This is one example of a pay-now-or-pay-later management analysis. Managers may take a more socially responsible approach to an environmental issue now because they think the future cost of not doing so could be enormously larger—in negative publicity, in the cost of more stringent future regulation—than the present actual cost of the action.

But does the market actually reward sound environmental practices? We cannot yet be sure, but an interesting study published in 1997 found a strong relationship between environmental high performance and high profitability.[19] Some companies simply comply with environmental laws, whereas others take affirmative steps to improve their environmental performance. The study's authors theorize that the latter companies build more skillful workers by expecting them to cope with the complexities of "clean technologies." Prevention and improvement are more complicated than mere compliance, so perhaps the environmentally active firms are actually building their performance "muscles" by their activist approach, while the compliance firms are expending their energies on the external world in an effort to fend off new rules. [For many examples of environmentally responsible actions of business, see **www.bsr.org**]

Having reviewed both market forces and ethical business decision making, we turn now in Part Two to government regulation as an approach for meeting our societal environmental goals.

Part Two—Laws and Regulations

The United States has developed a wide variety of environmental protection laws and remedies, some of which are discussed in this section. Throughout this discussion, keep in mind the following concepts:

- **Cost–benefit analysis:** Environmental protection can be expensive. How much as a society are we willing to pay? Do we want clean air at any cost? We may (or may not) be able to estimate the cost of a particular pro-environment action, but how do

  How do we value human life?

  we measure the benefit of taking the action? How do we value human life, represented by a statistical decrease in deaths or illness from exposure to environmental pollutants? Does environmental protection cause the sacrifice of short-term economic development? How can this cost be measured? These are not easy questions, and any answer will necessarily be inexact and require subjective judgments and the use of estimates. A 2003 study by the Office of Management and Budget concluded that a prior toughening of clean air regulations was well worth the cost to industry and consumers, that the "value of reductions in hospitalization and emergency room visits, premature deaths, and lost workdays resulting from improved air quality" was estimated between \$120 and \$193 billion over a 10-year period, where the cost to comply was only \$23 to \$26 billion.[20] Industry critics, however, argue that the costs of compliance were greatly understated. [For more information on cost–benefit analysis and environmental protection, see the Georgetown Environmental Law and Policy Project at **www.law.georgetown .edu/gelpi/cba/index.htm**]

- **Impact on future generations:** When performing a cost–benefit analysis, how do we deal with the cost to future generations of our not taking action? And how can we measure the value of the action to those generations? In some cases, the future generations will bear the brunt of the decision, whatever choice we make. For example, if greenhouse gases cause global warming, how do we measure that impact on future generations? This is a complex question about which there is no scientific consensus, let alone economic consensus.

- **Proving causation:** If event A occurs and event B follows, is it necessarily true that event A *caused* event B? It could simply be a coincidence that first A was observed and then B. Or there could in fact be a *correlation* between events A and B, but no actual causation. For example, event Z might cause both A and B, but no causal link may exist between A and B. In the environmental area, issues of coincidence, correlation, and causation may be extremely difficult to determine. For example, does exposure to secondhand smoke cause lung cancer in some nonsmokers? Is the observed increase in greenhouse gases a contributor to current weather patterns, such as the unusually severe hurricane season in 2004?[21] If, in the example of Z, A, and B, we spend a lot of effort trying to stop A to prevent B occurring, we will be wasting our money. On the other hand, how long can we wait to determine definitively whether a causal link exists between A and B? Our answer may depend on the severity of the harm we believe is associated with B.

- **Who pays?** Even if we decide to correct an environmental problem, who should pay for the correction? If we require corporate America to invest in pollution control devices, the cost may be shared between consumers (through increased prices) and investors (through a reduced corporate profit). If habitats of endangered species are to be preserved, current land owners may simply lose all or a portion of their investment, and workers employed on the land may lose their jobs. Who should pay?

- **The impact of politics:** Environmental protection in the United States has not been just a matter of science and cost assessment and social policy; it has also been a matter of politics. When the Bush administration came to Washington and the Clinton administration left, the country's environmental policies appeared to be poised for significant change—away from environmental protection and toward increased energy supply and consideration of the monetary costs of protection. As one commentator stated, "It's hard to imagine two presidential administrations further apart on issues of the environment and public lands."[22] An administration has considerable impact on the enforcement of our environmental laws, particularly through the regulations it chooses to pursue under the authority of the various environmental statutes. In that regard, the Bush administration has continued to be seen as more pro-business than pro-environment.[23]

The Federal Role

The federal government has long maintained a role in the protection of the environment—some would argue too great a role. As early as 1899, Congress enacted a law that required a permit to discharge refuse into navigable waters. As it became apparent that private, state, and local environmental efforts were not adequate to address the burgeoning problems, in the early 1970s Congress began to take more aggressive legislative initiatives.

National Environmental Policy Act (NEPA)

The 1970 National Environmental Policy Act (NEPA) established a strong federal presence in the promotion of a clean and healthy environment. NEPA represents a general commitment by the federal government to "use all practicable means" to conduct federal affairs in a fashion that both promotes "the general welfare" and operates in "harmony" with the environment.

NEPA established the Council on Environmental Quality (CEQ), which serves as an adviser to the president. The CEQ is a watchdog of sorts. It is required to conduct studies and collect information regarding the state of the environment. The council then develops policy and legislative proposals for the president and Congress.

> The CEQ is a watchdog of sorts.

But NEPA's primary influence results from its *environmental impact statement* (EIS) requirements. With few exceptions, "proposals for legislation and other major federal action significantly affecting the quality of the human environment" must be accompanied by an EIS explaining the impact on the environment and detailing reasonable alternatives. Completing an EIS requires undertaking a cost–benefit analysis. It also requires consideration of cause and effect links. Major federal construction projects (highways, dams, nuclear reactors) would normally require an EIS; but less visible federal programs (ongoing timber management or the abandonment of a lengthy railway) may also require EIS treatment. Although the focus here is on *federal* actions, thus exempting solely private acts from this scrutiny, a major private-sector action supported by federal funding or by one of several varieties of federal permission may also require an EIS. Hence private companies receiving federal contracts, funding, licenses, and the like may be parties to the completion of an EIS.

Environmental Protection Agency (EPA)

The private sector was not left without regulation or constraint. The Environmental Protection Agency (EPA) was created in 1970 to mount a coordinated attack on environmental problems. EPA duties include, among other things, (1) gathering information, particularly by surveying pollution problems, (2) conducting research on pollution problems, (3) assisting state and local pollution control efforts, and (4) administering many of the federal laws directed to environmental concerns. [For the EPA home page, see **www.epa.gov**]

Regulation of Air Pollution

We depend on (indeed, we emotionally embrace) the automobile. In doing so, we have opened vistas of opportunity not previously imagined. However, motor vehicles also discharge carbon monoxide, nitrogen oxide, and hydrocarbons as by-products of the combustion of fuel, which befoul our air. Industrial production and the combustion of fossil fuels in homes and industry are also significant contributors to the dilemma of dirty air.

Clean Air Act of 1990 (CAA)

Early clean air legislation in 1963 and 1965 afforded the government limited authority. The Clean Air Act amendments of 1970 and 1977 gave the EPA the power to set air quality standards and to ensure that those standards were achieved according to a timetable prescribed by the agency. Politics brought clean air to the fore in 1990, and a new Clean Air Act followed. The Clean Air Act of 1990, which phases in new standards over a period of years, generally requires tougher auto emission controls, cleaner-burning gasoline, and new equipment to capture industrial and business pollution, all of which work toward the general goal of reducing airborne pollutants by about 50 percent. Under the CAA, air quality standards are set federally, but the states are required to establish implementation plans to achieve and maintain those standards.

Particulates and Ozone

In 1997 the EPA announced new, more demanding clean air standards to reduce particulate matter and ozone coming from many sources, such as refineries, factories, and utilities. The case that follows involves a challenge by a number of industry groups to those new standards. The core of the challenge was the constitutional *nondelegation doctrine*, which provides that Congress cannot cede its power to make laws to another branch of the federal government.

LEGAL BRIEFCASE · *Whitman v. American Trucking Associations* 531 U.S. 457 (2001)

Justice Scalia

These cases present the following questions: (1) Whether § 109(b)(1) of the Clean Air Act (CAA) delegates legislative power to the Administrator of the Environmental Protection Agency (EPA). (2) Whether the Administrator may consider the costs of implementation in setting national ambient air quality standards (NAAQS) under § 109(b)(1). (3) Whether the Court of Appeals had jurisdiction to review the EPA's interpretation of Part D of Title I of the CAA, 42 U.S.C. §§ 7501–7515, with respect to implementing the revised ozone NAAQS. (4) If so, whether the EPA's interpretation of that part was permissible.

I

Section 109(a) of the CAA, 42 U.S.C. § 7409(a), requires the Administrator of the EPA to promulgate NAAQS for each air pollutant for which "air quality criteria" have been issued under § 108. Once a NAAQS has been promulgated, the Administrator must review the standard (and the criteria on which it is based) "at five-year intervals" and make "such revisions . . . as may be appropriate." These cases arose when, on July 18, 1997, the Administrator revised the NAAQS for particulate matter (PM) and ozone. American Trucking Associations, Inc., and its co-respondents . . .—which include, in addition to other private companies, the States of Michigan, Ohio, and West Virginia—challenged the new standards. . . .

The District of Columbia Circuit accepted some of the challenges and rejected others. It agreed with the . . . respondents . . . that § 109(b)(1) delegated legislative power to the Administrator in contravention of the United States Constitution, Art. I, § 1, because it found that the EPA had interpreted the statute to provide no "intelligible principle" to guide the agency's exercise of authority. *American Trucking Assns., Inc. v. EPA,* 175 F.3d 1027, 1034 (1999). The court thought, however, that the EPA could perhaps avoid the unconstitutional delegation by adopting a restrictive construction of § 109(b)(1), so instead of declaring the section unconstitutional the court remanded the NAAQS to the agency. . . . On the second issue that the Court of Appeals addressed, it unanimously rejected respondents' argument that the court should depart from the rule of *Lead Industries Assn., Inc. v. EPA,* 647 F.2d 1130, 1148 (CADC 1980), that the EPA may not consider the cost of implementing a NAAQS in setting the initial standard. . . .

The Administrator and the EPA petitioned this Court for review of the first, third, and fourth questions described in the first paragraph of this opinion. Respondents conditionally cross-petitioned for review of the second question. We granted certiorari on both petitions. . . .

II

In *Lead Industries Assn., Inc. v. EPA, supra,* at 1148, the District of Columbia Circuit held that "economic considerations [may] play no part in the promulgation of ambient air quality standards under Section 109" of the CAA. In the present cases, the court adhered to that holding, as it had done on many other occasions. Respondents argue that these decisions are incorrect. We disagree. . . .

* * * * *

III

Section 109(b)(1) of the CAA instructs the EPA to set "ambient air quality standards the attainment and maintenance of which in the judgment of the Administrator, based on [the] criteria [documents of § 108] and allowing an adequate margin of safety, are requisite to protect the public health." The Court of Appeals held that this section as interpreted by the Administrator did not provide an "intelligible principle" to guide the EPA's exercise of authority in setting NAAQS. "[The] EPA," it said, "lacked any determinate criteria for drawing lines. It has failed to state intelligibly how much is too much." The court hence found that the EPA's interpretation (but not the statute itself) violated the nondelegation doctrine. We disagree.

In a delegation challenge, the constitutional question is whether the statute has delegated legislative power to the agency. Article I, § 1, of the Constitution vests "all legislative Powers herein granted . . . in a Congress of the United States." This text permits no delegation of those powers, *Loving v. United States*, 517 U.S. 748, 771 (1996), and so we repeatedly have said that when Congress confers decisionmaking authority upon agencies *Congress* must "lay down by legislative act an intelligible principle to which the person or body authorized to [act] is directed to conform." *J. W. Hampton, Jr., & Co. v. United States*, 276 U.S. 394, 409 (1928). We have never suggested that an agency can cure an unlawful delegation of legislative power by adopting in its discretion a limiting construction of the statute. . . . Whether the statute delegates legislative power is a question for the courts, and an agency's voluntary self-denial has no bearing upon the answer.

We agree with the Solicitor General that the text of § 109(b)(1) of the CAA at a minimum requires that "for a discrete set of pollutants and based on published air quality criteria that reflect the latest scientific knowledge, [the] EPA must establish uniform national standards at a level that is requisite to protect public health from the adverse effects of the pollutant in the ambient air." Requisite, in turn, "means sufficient, but not more than necessary. . . .

The scope of discretion § 109(b)(1) allows is in fact well within the outer limits of our nondelegation precedents. In the history of the Court we have found the requisite "intelligible principle" lacking in only two statutes, one of which provided literally no guidance for the exercise of discretion, and the other of which conferred authority to regulate the entire economy on the basis of no more precise a standard than stimulating the

economy by assuring "fair competition." See *Panama Refining Co. v. Ryan,* 293 U.S. 388 (1935); *A. L. A. Schechter Poultry Corp. v. United States,* 295 U.S. 495 (1935). . . . And we have found an "intelligible principle" in various statutes authorizing regulation in the "public interest." See, e.g., *National Broadcasting Co. v. United States,* 319 U.S. 190 (1943) (FCC's power to regulate airwaves); *New York Central Securities Corp. v. United States,* 287 U.S. 12, 24–25 (1932) (ICC's power to approve railroad consolidations). In short, we have "almost never felt qualified to second-guess Congress regarding the permissible degree of policy judgment that can be left to those executing or applying the law." *Mistretta v. United States,* 488 U.S. 361, 416 (1989).

It is true enough that the degree of agency discretion that is acceptable varies according to the scope of the power congressionally conferred. While Congress need not provide any direction to the EPA regarding the manner in which it is to define "country elevators," which are to be exempt from new-stationary-source regulations governing grain elevators, see § 7411(i), it must provide substantial guidance on setting air standards that affect the entire national economy. But even in sweeping regulatory schemes we have never demanded, as the Court of Appeals did here, that statutes provide a "determinate criterion" for saying "how much [of the regulated harm] is too much." 175 F.3d at 1034. In *Touby,* for example, we did not require the statute to decree how "imminent" was too imminent, or how "necessary" was necessary enough, or even— most relevant here—how "hazardous" was too hazardous. 500 U.S. at 165-167. . . . It is therefore not conclusive for delegation purposes that, as respondents argue, ozone and particulate matter are "nonthreshold" pollutants that inflict a continuum of adverse health effects at any airborne concentration greater than zero, and hence require the EPA to make judgments of degree. "[A] certain degree of discretion, and thus of lawmaking, inheres in most executive or judicial action." *Mistretta v. United States, supra,* at 417. Section 109(b)(1) of the CAA, which to repeat we interpret as requiring the EPA to set air quality standards at the level that is "requisite"—that is, not lower or higher than is necessary—to protect the public health with an adequate margin of safety, fits comfortably within the scope of discretion permitted by our precedent.

We therefore reverse the judgment of the Court of Appeals remanding for reinterpretation that would avoid a supposed delegation of legislative power.

* * * * *

To summarize our holdings in these unusually complex cases: (1) The EPA may not consider implementation costs in setting primary and secondary NAAQS under § 109(b) of the CAA. (2) Section 109(b)(1) does not delegate legislative power to the EPA in contravention of Art. I, § 1, of the Constitution. (3) The Court of Appeals had jurisdiction to review the EPA's interpretation of Part D of Title I of the CAA, relating to the implementation of the revised ozone NAAQS. (4) The EPA's interpretation of that Part is unreasonable.

The judgment of the Court of Appeals is affirmed in part and reversed in part, and the cases are remanded for proceedings consistent with this opinion.

Questions

1. *a.* Why did the lower court find the new EPA standards unconstitutional and, therefore, strike them down?

    b. What did the Supreme Court say on the issue of unconstitutionality?

2. The Court held that it was well established that cost is not a consideration for setting clear air standards. Do you agree that should be the case? Explain.

3. The new clean-air rules were expected to save about 2,800 lives annually. Would 2,800 lives saved each year be worth the additional costs, which were expected to total at least $2.5 billion? Explain.

AFTERWORD

On remand from the Supreme Court, the D.C. Circuit Court found that the EPA had "engaged in reasoned decision-making," under the arbitrary and capricious review standard for administrative actions, and denied all of the then-pending petitions for review.[24]

Major Modification Versus Routine Maintenance and Repair

Not satisfied with air quality progress, the EPA in the late 1990s took an increasingly aggressive stance. Among other actions, in late 1999, the EPA signaled its growing frustration by taking legal action against 32 coal-fired power plants operating in 10 states (Alabama, Florida, Georgia, Illinois, Indiana, Kentucky, Mississippi, Ohio, Tennessee, and West Virginia). Some were given administrative citations and warnings, but seven utilities (for operations at 17 plants) were sued for violating EPA regulations. Most of the plants were built before the Clean Air Act of 1970 and were allowed, under "grandfather" clauses, to meet less stringent air quality requirements unless they underwent major modifications. The supposition was that the old plants would soon be phased out, but that has not happened. The EPA claimed that major renovations have been made to extend the useful lives of the plants without making the required CAA upgrades.[25]

When the Bush administration took over, there was concern that the government would drop these cases, but that did not happen. Indeed, this administration has brought similar cases against additional plants.[26] However, at the same time the Department of Justice was pursuing both the old and new cases, the Bush administration's EPA issued new regulations, which in part defined "routine maintenance" more broadly than the government's position in the previously discussed litigation.[27] Twelve states and several major cities have sued to stop the new regulations from going into force, and the D.C. Circuit Court ordered the EPA not to implement the new rules until a final determination can be made in the case.[28] While there is at this writing no final case decision, in mid-2004 the EPA reopened the public comment period on the new regulations to allow it to reconsider the controversial rules.[29]

Regulation of Water Pollution

As with the air, we often treat our water resources as free goods. Rather than paying the full cost of producing goods and services, we have simply dumped a portion of that cost into the nearest body of water. The waste from production—indeed from the totality of our life experience—has commonly been disposed of in the water at a cost beneath that required to dispose of the waste in an ecologically sound fashion. The results range from smelly to dangerous to tragic.

- *Rivers.* Around the globe, we are destroying our great river systems—sources of so much of our food, drinking water, fun, and beauty. More than half of the world's 500 major rivers are either going dry from overuse or are seriously polluted. China's giant Yellow River actually dried up for 226 days in 1997, and more than 90 percent of the Nile's natural flow either evaporates in reservoirs or is diverted for irrigation. Only four major rivers (the Amazon in South America, the Congo in Africa, the St. Lawrence in North America, and the Mekong in Southeast Asia) are considered "healthy."[30] Although we have achieved great progress, 40 percent of America's waterways remain too polluted for fishing and swimming.[31] [For more information about threatened bodies of water in the United States, see **http://www.epa.gov/owow/tmdl/atlas/index.html**]

> More than half of the world's 500 major rivers are either going dry from overuse or are seriously polluted.

- *Runoff.* Much of America's water pollution is directly attributable to our personal habits. Surface water runoff is polluted with lawn fertilizer, pet waste, grease and oil from vehicles, and all the other sludge from our modern lives. That runoff, of course, eventually debases our waterways. One of the significant problems with such runoff is that the EPA's system of tracking water pollution focuses on pollution from large facilities, which are more visible and easier to police, rather than dirty runoff from farms, storms and roads, which are known as major sources of water pollution.[32] (See the following discussion of "point source" discharges.) This is still true in spite of the new rules put in place in 1999 to reduce runoff from large hog, cattle, and poultry farms.

Federal Policy

The Clean Water Act (CWA), designed to "restore and maintain the chemical, physical, and biological integrity of the nation's waters," establishes two national goals: (1) achieving water quality sufficient for the protection and propagation of fish, shellfish, and wildlife and for recreation in and on the water; and (2) eliminating the discharge of pollutants into navigable waters. The states have primary responsibility for enforcing the CWA, but the federal government, via the Environmental Protection Agency, is empowered to assume enforcement authority if necessary.

The goals of the Clean Water Act are implemented primarily by imposing limits on the amount of pollutants that may lawfully enter the water of the United States from any "point source" (typically a pipe). The National Pollutant Discharge Elimination System (NPDES) requires all pollutant dischargers to secure an EPA permit before pouring effluent into a navigable stream. The permit specifies maximum permissible levels of effluent. Typically the permit also mandates the use of a particular pollution control process or device and requires the permit holder to monitor its own performance and report on that performance to the state or the EPA, as appropriate.

In the following case, the Supreme Court takes a look at what qualifies as "navigable waters" for purposes of regulation under the CWA. You should be aware that this decision was made by a bare majority (five) of the justices; the other four dissented.

Solid Waste Agency of Northern Cook County v. U.S. Army Corps of Engineers

531 U.S. 159 (2001)

Chief Justice Rehnquist

Section 404(a) of the Clean Water Act (CWA or Act), 33 U.S.C. § 1344(a), regulates the discharge of dredged or fill material into "navigable waters." The United States Army Corps of Engineers (Corps) has interpreted § 404(a) to confer federal authority over an abandoned sand and gravel pit in northern Illinois which provides habitat for migratory birds. We are asked to decide whether the provisions of § 404(a) may be fairly extended to these waters, and, if so, whether Congress could exercise such authority consistent with the Commerce Clause, U.S. Const., Art. I, § 8, cl. 3. We answer the first question in the negative and therefore do not reach the second.

Petitioner, the Solid Waste Agency of Northern Cook County (SWANCC), is a consortium of 23 suburban Chicago cities and villages that united in an effort to locate and develop a disposal site for baled nonhazardous solid waste. The Chicago Gravel Company informed the municipalities of the availability of a 533-acre parcel, bestriding the Illinois counties Cook and Kane, which had been the site of a sand and gravel pit mining operation for three decades up until about 1960. Long since abandoned, the old mining site eventually gave way to a successional stage forest, with its remnant excavation trenches evolving into a scattering of permanent and seasonal ponds of varying size (from under one-tenth of an acre to several acres) and depth (from several inches to several feet).

The municipalities decided to purchase the site for disposal of their baled nonhazardous solid waste. By law, SWANCC was required to file for various permits from Cook County and the State of Illinois before it could begin operation of its balefill project. In addition, because the operation called for the filling of some of the permanent and seasonal ponds, SWANCC contacted federal respondents (hereinafter respondents), including the Corps, to determine if a federal landfill permit was required under § 404(a) of the CWA.

Section 404(a) grants the Corps authority to issue permits "for the discharge of dredged or fill material into the navigable waters at specified disposal sites." *Ibid.* The term "navigable waters" is defined under the Act as "the waters of the United States, including the territorial seas." § 1362(7). The Corps has issued regulations defining the term "waters of the United States" to include

> waters such as intrastate lakes, rivers, streams (including intermittent streams), mudflats, sandflats, wetlands, sloughs, prairie potholes, wet meadows, playa lakes, or natural ponds, the use, degradation or destruction of which could affect interstate or foreign commerce. 33 CFR§ 328.3(a)(3) (1999).

In 1986, in an attempt to "clarify" the reach of its jurisdiction, the Corps stated that § 404(a) extends to intrastate waters

a. Which are or would be used as habitat by birds protected by Migratory Bird Treaties; or

b. Which are or would be used as habitat by other migratory birds which cross state lines; or

c. Which are or would be used as habitat for endangered species; or

d. Used to irrigate crops sold in interstate commerce. 51 Fed. Reg. 41217.

This last promulgation has been dubbed the "Migratory Bird Rule."

The Corps initially concluded that it had no jurisdiction over the site because it contained no "wetlands," or areas which support "vegetation typically adapted for life in saturated soil conditions[.]" However, after the Illinois Nature Preserves Commission informed the Corps that a number of migratory bird species had been observed at the site, the Corps reconsidered and ultimately asserted jurisdiction over the balefill site pursuant to subpart (b) of the "Migratory Bird Rule." The Corps found that approximately 121 bird species had been observed at the site, including several known to depend upon aquatic environments for a significant portion of their life requirements. Thus, on November 16, 1987, the Corps formally "determined that the seasonally ponded, abandoned gravel mining depressions located on the project site, while not wetlands, did qualify as 'waters of the United States' . . . based upon the following criteria: (1) the proposed site had been abandoned as a gravel mining operation; (2) the water areas and spoil piles had developed a natural character; and (3) the water areas are used as habitat by migratory bird *[sic]* which cross state lines."

* * * * *

Despite SWANCC's securing the required water quality certification from the Illinois Environmental Protection Agency, the Corps refused to issue a § 404(a) permit. The Corps found that SWANCC had not established that its proposal was the "least environmentally damaging, most practicable alternative" for disposal of nonhazardous solid waste; that SWANCC's failure to set aside sufficient funds to remediate leaks posed an "unacceptable risk to the public's drinking water supply"; and that the impact of the project upon area-sensitive species was "unmitigatable since a landfill surface cannot be redeveloped into a forested habitat."

Petitioner filed suit under the Administrative Procedure Act, 5 U.S.C. § 701 *et seq.,* in the Northern District of Illinois challenging . . . the Corps' jurisdiction over the site. . . . On appeal to the Court of Appeals for the Seventh Circuit, petitioner renewed its attack on respondents' use of the "Migratory Bird Rule" to assert jurisdiction over the site. Petitioner argued that respondents had exceeded their statutory authority in interpreting the CWA to cover nonnavigable, isolated, intrastate waters based upon the presence of migratory birds and, in the alternative, that Congress lacked the power under the Commerce Clause to grant such regulatory jurisdiction.

The Court of Appeals . . . held that the CWA reaches as many waters as the Commerce Clause allows and, given its earlier Commerce Clause ruling, it therefore followed that respondents' "Migratory Bird Rule" was a reasonable interpretation of the Act.

We granted certiorari and now reverse.

Congress passed the CWA for the stated purpose of "restoring and maintaining the chemical, physical, and biological integrity of the Nation's waters." 33 U.S.C. § 1251(a). In so doing, Congress chose to "recognize, preserve, and protect the primary responsibilities and rights of States to prevent, reduce, and eliminate pollution, to plan the development and use (including restoration, preservation, and enhancement) of land and water resources, and to consult with the Administrator in the exercise of his authority under this chapter." § 1251(b). Relevant here, § 404(a) authorizes respondents to regulate the discharge of fill material into "navigable waters," which the statute defines as "the waters of the United States, including the territorial seas," § 1362(7). Respondents have interpreted these words to cover the abandoned gravel pit at issue here because it is used as habitat for migratory birds. We conclude that the "Migratory Bird Rule" is not fairly supported by the CWA.

This is not the first time we have been called upon to evaluate the meaning of § 404(a). In *United States v. Riverside Bayview Homes, Inc.,* 474 U.S. 121 (1985), we held that the Corps had § 404(a) jurisdiction over wetlands that actually abutted on a navigable waterway. In so doing, we noted that the term "navigable" is of "limited import" and that Congress evidenced its intent to "regulate at least some waters that would not be deemed 'navigable' under the classical understanding of that term." *Id.* at 133. But our holding was based in large measure upon Congress' unequivocal acquiescence to, and approval of, the Corps' regulations interpreting the CWA to cover wetlands adjacent to navigable waters. We found that Congress' concern for the protection of water quality and aquatic ecosystems indicated its intent to regulate wetlands "inseparably bound up with the 'waters' of the United States." 474 U.S. at 134.

It was the significant nexus between the wetlands and "navigable waters" that informed our reading of the CWA in *Riverside Bayview Homes.* . . . In order to rule for respondents here, we would have to hold that the jurisdiction of the Corps extends to ponds that are *not* adjacent to open water. But we conclude that the text of the statute will not allow this.

Indeed, the Corps' *original* interpretation of the CWA, promulgated two years after its enactment, is inconsistent with that which it espouses here. Its 1974 regulations defined § 404(a)'s "navigable waters" to mean "those waters of the United States which are subject to the ebb and flow of the tide, and/or are presently, or have been in the past, or may be in the future susceptible for use for purposes of interstate or foreign commerce." 33 CFR § 209.120(d)(1). The Corps emphasized that "it is the water body's capability of use by the public for purposes of transportation or commerce which is the determinative factor." § 209.260(e)(1). Respondents put forward no persuasive evidence that the Corps mistook Congress' intent in 1974.

* * * * *

We hold that 33 CFR § 328.3(a)(3) (1999), as clarified and applied to petitioner's balefill site pursuant to the "Migratory Bird Rule," 51 Fed. Reg. 41217 (1986), exceeds the authority granted to respondents under § 404(a) of the CWA. The judgment of the Court of Appeals for the Seventh Circuit is therefore
Reversed.

QUESTIONS

1. Summarize the arguments made by the Army Corps of Engineers for finding that the government had the power to regulate this site under the CWA.

2. Explain the Supreme Court's response to each of the Army Corps of Engineers' arguments previously identified.

3. Did the Supreme Court hold that the government could not regulate this type of site or only that Congress had not in fact sought to extend its regulation to this type of site?

4. In your view, should the federal government be able to regulate bodies of water that are of significant use by migratory birds? Explain.

Regulation of Land Pollution

Pollution does not fit tidily into the three compartments (air, water, land) used for convenience in this text. Acid rain debases air and water as well as the fruits of the water and land, such as fish and trees. Similarly, the problems of land pollution addressed in this section often damage the fullness of the natural world. For most of recorded history, we felt safe and comfortable in using the Earth as a garbage dump.

Garbage

Our lifestyles result in mountains of solid waste that grow higher every year. Indeed, New York City's Fresh Kills Landfill is one of the world's largest man-made structures and one of the highest points of land on the East Coast. Each of us, on average, produces about 4.4 pounds of garbage daily, nearly 40 percent of which comes in the form of paper and paperboard.[33] Of course, we pay a great immediate price to dispose of all of the leftovers of our lives, but the long-term concern is that the waste will come back to haunt us. Even state-of-the-art landfills can leak, with the result that toxic elements can enter our groundwater. We had long assumed that much of the waste would simply decompose, but studies show that does not happen. The leading "garbologist," Professor William Rathje, explains, "The thought that after 30 or so years newspapers and food would disintegrate is off-track. Things become mummified. We found hot dogs that could be recooked and perfectly legible newspapers."[34] We do burn about 16 percent of our waste, in the process killing germs and creating steam and electricity, but the resulting fly ash, some of which escapes into the air, can be highly toxic.[35] The suggested solution, of course, is to "reduce, reuse, recycle."[36]

> We had long assumed that much of the waste would simply decompose, but studies show that does not happen.

Recycling

From the mid-1980s to the present, the EPA, environmental activists, and the garbage industry have warned about an impending trash disposal crisis. We are rapidly running out of dumping space, they have said. *The Wall Street Journal*, however, reports that both industry and EPA officials knew that we had ample waste disposal space, even as we were being warned to recycle (and, not surprisingly, as waste companies were pushing up prices):

> "I've always wondered where that crap about a landfill-capacity crisis came from," says Allen Geswein, an EPA solid-waste official. . . . The EPA, when asked, now agrees that there isn't any capacity shortage. Yet materials the agency continues to distribute warn of a shortage and cite it as one of the reasons for recycling.[37]

Of course, concern about availability of landfill sites is not the only reason to support recycling. Recycling also turns materials that would otherwise become waste into usable resources, which can reduce dependence on new materials (reducing deforestation, for example). Recycling can also reduce the amount of waste that is burned in incinerators, reducing particulate matter and other pollutants that would otherwise be released into the air. The EPA reported that the number of solid waste landfills fell to 3,581 in

1995 from 5,300 in 1992, while the national goal of recycling 25 percent of municipal garbage was reached in 1995. The agency targeted a 35 percent standard for 2005.[38]

Recycle Cars

Western European nations have generally been much more aggressive than the United States in demanding recycling. In 2000 the European Union approved new rules that require manufacturers to take back used cars for recycling with an expectation of 80 percent reuse and recycling by 2006. Studies indicate the recycling bill may reach $200 per car for collecting, transporting, dismantling, separating plastics and metals for recycling, and shredding the remainder.

Sources: "Green Light for End of Life Vehicles Directive" [**http://global.ihs.com/news/a4-2.html**] and "EU Wants Automakers to Recycle All Old Cars," *Ottawa Citizen,* July 30, 1999, p. C5.

Solid Waste Disposal Act

To attack the massive garbage problem, Congress approved the Solid Waste Disposal Act of 1965. The act, in brief, leaves solid waste problems to states and localities, but the federal government offers research and financial support.

Toxic Substances Control Act (TSCA)

In 1976 Congress approved the Toxic Substances Control Act (TSCA) to identify toxic chemicals, assess their risks, and control dangerous chemicals. Under the terms of the TSCA, the EPA requires the chemical industry to report any information it may have suggesting that a chemical poses a "substantial risk." The EPA is empowered to review and limit or stop the introduction of new chemicals.

Pollution in the Movies

Surprisingly, toxic pollution provided the central theme in two major Hollywood movies: *Erin Brockovich* and *A Civil Action.* The 2000 movie *Erin Brockovich* tells the story of a California community's battle against Pacific Gas & Electric for allegedly causing groundwater pollution. [For more information about the movie, see **www.ErinBrockovich.com;** for more on the pollutant at issue in the movie, see the National Institutes of Health site, **www.niehs.nih.gov/centers/2001news/ctrnews9.html**] In the 1998 Disney movie *A Civil Action,* John Travolta plays a plaintiff's lawyer in a true story about some middle-class families who sued two corporate giants, Beatrice Food and W. R. Grace & Co., for allegedly polluting the groundwater in East Woburn, Massachusetts, where eight children died of leukemia. [For more information about the movie from the corporate perspective, see **http://www.civil-action.com**]

Resource Conservation and Recovery Act (RCRA)

By 1976 the dangers of hazardous substances were becoming apparent to all, and Congress complemented the TSCA with the Resource Conservation and Recovery Act (RCRA). The act addresses both solid and hazardous wastes. Its solid waste provisions are more supportive than punitive in tone and approach. The federal government is authorized, among other strategies, to provide technical and financial assistance to states and localities; to prohibit future open dumping; and to establish cooperative federal, state, local, and private-enterprise programs to recover energy and valuable materials from solid waste.

Subtitle C of the RCRA is designed to ensure the safe movement and disposal of hazardous wastes. The generator of the waste must determine if that waste is hazardous under EPA guidelines and, if so, report the waste site and waste activities to the government. The waste generator must then create a manifest to be used in tracking the waste from its creation to its disposal. Along the cradle-to-grave path of the waste, all those with responsibility for it must sign the manifest and safely store and transport the waste. Once the waste reaches a licensed disposal facility, the owner or manager of that site signs the manifest and returns a copy of it to the generator.

Disposal Sites

Owners and operators of hazardous waste disposal sites must obtain government permits to begin operation. Those sites must be operated according to EPA standards, and remedial action must be taken should hazardous wastes escape from the sites. [For more information, see the EPA Web site at **www.epa.gov/ebtpages/pollutants.html**]

Superfund—Comprehensive Environmental Response, Compensation, and Liability Act of 1980 (CERCLA)

December 2005 marks the 25th anniversary of CERCLA,[39] more commonly known as the Superfund, which is designed to help clean up hazardous dumps and spills. "Under CERCLA, the EPA may take actions to clean up a site from which hazardous substances have been released or where there is the threat of such a release. CERCLA also authorizes the federal government to order private parties to undertake the cleanup activities. The government and private parties who incur response costs cleaning up a site may seek recovery of those costs from liable parties."[40] Potentially responsible parties include present owners of the site as well as past owners who operated the site when the hazardous wastes were deposited; parent firms can be liable for actions of subsidiaries; and transferors (successive owners of businesses discharging hazardous wastes) are also liable. Any parties found to be responsible are strictly liable—that is, liability attaches without proof of either intent or negligence.

Cleanup tends to be very expensive and generally requires considerable time to accomplish. The first listed Superfund site, Love Canal in Niagara Falls, New York, was finally clean enough to be delisted in 2004.[41] Originally the government began the Superfund by creating a trust fund from taxes on chemicals and petroleum; but that taxing authority lapsed in 1995, and subsequently the Superfund program has been running on annual appropriations and reserve funds. The appropriations have not kept up with the problem: Nine "mega waste sites" consume 52 percent of the budget, "leaving insufficient funds to cover the rest of the 384 long-term cleanup projects under way."[42] In 2004 industry concerns over CERCLA liability increased when a jury in Montana awarded $40.3 million to residents of Sunburst who claimed Chevron Texaco had not adequately cleaned up a site, even though state regulators had agreed that the site posed no current health risk.[43]

> Any parties found to be responsible are strictly liable

Small Business Liability Relief and Brownfields Revitalization Act

There has been considerable dissatisfaction over CERCLA for many years for a number of reasons, including the percentage of Superfund dollars that have gone to administration expenses[44] and litigation.[45] Another complaint was that so-called *brownfields* (less contaminated former industrial and commercial sites that are not on the Superfund priority list) were nevertheless covered by the successor–owner liability provisions of CERCLA, creating a disincentive for any developers to take them over and reestablish them as productive property. This complaint was largely addressed by the passage of the Small Business Liability Relief and Brownfields Revitalization Act (Brownfields Act), which President Bush signed into law on January 11, 2002.[46] This law provides liability protection for prospective purchasers and contiguous property owners and authorizes increased funding for state and local programs that assess and clean up brownfields.

Part Three—Penalties and Enforcement under Federal Law

Civil/Criminal Actions

Because of the risks associated with pollution, environmental protection agencies have been given strong enforcement authority. Often violators initially are warned and a compliance schedule is set out. If corrective action is not forthcoming, sterner measures follow, including an administrative order to comply. Where problems persist or the difficulties are more serious, the government may initiate civil or criminal actions against both firms and managers. Penalties vary with the act in question, but civil and criminal fines are provided for. Individuals may be jailed for one year or more. In some instances, an entire operation may be shut down.

Fines have long been the standard remedy in governmental pollution enforcement, but in recent years both federal and state regulators have increasingly turned to Supplemental Environmental Projects (SEPs) to settle wrongs.[47] Normally, the SEP will involve some environmental "good work" in place of a fine, such as 11 Los Angeles–area corporations, accused of polluting the drinking supply of the San Gabriel Valley, agreeing to pay $85 million for the construction of a water treatment plant to remove dangerous chemicals from the aquifer running beneath the valley floor.[48]

More and more frequently the EPA is enforcing our environmental laws with criminal suits against corporate officers. "The EPA employs more than 200 criminal investigators and works closely with 36 environmental prosecutors at the Justice Department. In 2001 alone, the EPA obtained prison sentences totaling 256 years." In one of the most publicized cases, the owner of a chemical reprocessing plant received a 17-year sentence for "disposing of hazardous waste without a permit, knowing that his actions placed others in imminent danger of death or serious bodily injury."[49] A 20-year-old employee of the facility was overcome by cyanide gas while cleaning sludge from the bottom of a 25,000-gallon tank. As a consequence of his exposure, he has been left in a Parkinson's-like condition, able to speak only with great difficulty and struggling with even the simplest physical tasks, such as brushing his teeth.[50]

> The owner of a chemical reprocessing plant received a 17-year sentence.

Question

Is the trend toward prison sentences for officers of corporate polluters a good one? Explain.

Additional Enforcement Mechanisms

Many environmental statutes require companies to monitor their own environmental performance and report that information, including violations, to the government. Government agencies generally have broad authority to conduct environmental inspections of both plants and records as necessary, although they must obtain search warrants if criminal prosecutions are anticipated. Finally, many environmental statutes allow *citizen suits,* wherein an individual is empowered to challenge government environmental decisions, such as the granting of a permit, and generally to demand both governmental and private-sector compliance with the law.

In the case that follows, a citizens' group brought suit seeking to have the Cook Inlet beluga whale listed as endangered under the Endangered Species Act.

LEGAL BRIEFCASE

Cook Inlet Beluga Whale v. Daley 156 F. Supp. 2d 16 (D.C.D.C. 2001)

Judge James Robertson

This Administrative Procedure Act (APA) case presents a challenge to the decision of the Secretary of Commerce and the National Marine Fisheries Service (NMFS) to list the Cook Inlet (CI) Beluga Whale as "depleted" under the Marine Mammal Protection Act, but not as "endangered" or "threatened" under the Endangered Species Act (ESA). The Secretary determined that the recent Beluga Whale population decrease, which everyone agrees is attributable almost exclusively to over-hunting, can be arrested using the statutory protection afforded "depleted" marine mammal species and a legislative moratorium on Native American takings. Because the plaintiffs have not sustained their burden of showing that that determination was "arbitrary, capricious, an abuse of discretion, or otherwise not in accordance with law," summary judgment will be entered in favor of the government.

FACTUAL AND PROCEDURAL BACKGROUND

The Cook Inlet Beluga Whale (Delphinapterus leucas) is a genetically distinct, geographically isolated marine mammal with a remnant population that inhabits Cook Inlet from late April or early May until October or November. NMFS estimates that in

the mid-1980s, between 1,000 and 1,300 whales inhabited the inlet. Today, the population is estimated at between 300 and 400 whales. It is not disputed that the single most significant factor in the population decline has been Native American hunting: NMFS estimates that between 1995 and 1997 the Native American subsistence harvest averaged 77 whales per year. That is why, in March 1999, the plaintiffs filed a petition to list the Cook Inlet Beluga Whale under the Endangered Species Act (ESA).[1]

The Endangered Species Act delegates to the Secretary of Commerce the authority to determine whether fish, wildlife, or plant species should be listed as endangered or threatened. A species is "endangered" when it is in "danger of extinction throughout all or a significant part of its range," and it is "threatened" when it is "likely to become an endangered species within the foreseeable future." 16 U.S.C. §§ 1532(6), (20), 1533(c). The Secretary's ESA determination is made on the basis of five statutorily prescribed factors, any one of which is sufficient to support a listing determination. 16 U.S.C. 1533(a)(1).

---

[1] The naming of the Cook Inlet Beluga Whale itself as a plaintiff is acknowledged by the Court as a beau geste, but it has no legal significance.

Within 30 days of plaintiffs' request for an ESA listing, the NMFS published formal notice that action under the ESA "may be warranted." That notice triggered a one-year status review period. On October 19, 1999, the NMFS published a proposed rule, not under the ESA, but under the Marine Mammal Protection Act (MMPA), to list the whale as "depleted." (The final rule was issued May 31, 2000.) Under the MMPA, 16 U.S.C. § 1362, the Secretary can designate a species as "depleted" if the species is listed as endangered or threatened under the ESA or if the Secretary determines that the stock is below its Optimum Sustainable Population. Once a marine mammal has been listed as "depleted," the Secretary is authorized to promulgate regulations limiting takings by Native Americans, but a listing under the MMPA does not have the regulatory, economic, and environmental fallout of a listing as "threatened" or "endangered" under the ESA.

On June 22, 2000, the NMFS determined that an ESA listing was "not warranted." It is that determination which, in plaintiffs' submission, was "arbitrary, capricious, an abuse of discretion, or otherwise not in accordance with law."

ARGUMENT

"In exercising its narrowly defined duty under the APA, the Court must consider whether the agency acted within the scope of its legal authority, adequately explained its decision, based its decision on facts in the record, and considered the relevant factors." *National Park and Conservation Ass'n v. Stanton,* 54 F. Supp. 2d 7, 11 (D.D.C. 1999). Plaintiffs argue that the agency decision in this case improperly applied the law and facts to the five-factor determination; failed to apply the best scientific and commercial data available; and improperly considered political and economic factors.

I. Statutory Factors

A decision whether or not to list a species shall be made "solely on the basis of the best scientific and commercial data available . . . after conducting a review of the status of the species and after taking into account those efforts, if any, being made by any State or foreign nation." 16 U.S.C. § 1533(b). Applying this standard, the Secretary must list a species as endangered or threatened if "any of § 1533(a)(1)'s five factors are sufficiently implicated." *Southwest Center for Biological Diversity v. Babbitt,* 215 F.3d 58, 60 (D.C. Cir. 2000). Each of the five factors is considered below.

(A) The Present or Threatened Destruction, Modification, or Curtailment of the Species' Habitat or Range The agency's conclusion that "no indication exists that the range has been, or is threatened with being modified or curtailed to an extent that appreciably diminishes the value of the habitat for both

survival and recovery of the species," was not arbitrary or capricious. There is no dispute that the Cook Inlet, the whale's habitat, has changed over time in response to the increasing demand of municipal, industrial, and recreational activities, but there is no record basis for concluding that these changes have had a deleterious effect on the whale. Plaintiffs can point only to the fact that the whales have increasingly inhabited the upper inlet in recent decades. The agency concedes that this change in whale behavior might be in response to human activities, but no data suggest that the change threatens extinction. The agency is not required to conduct further testing to determine the effect of various environmental factors, such as oil drilling, on the whale population. "The 'best available data' requirement makes it clear that the Secretary has no obligation to conduct independent studies." *Southwest Center for Biological Diversity,* 215 F.3d at 60.

(B) Overutilization All agree that Native American harvesting has been the most significant factor in the declining whale population. The agency has found "that a failure to restrict the subsistence harvest would likely cause CI beluga whales to become in danger of extinction in the foreseeable future." But the agency has also concluded that "overutilization" does not support ESA listing because it has been stopped—by designating the whale as "depleted" under the MMPA. Plaintiffs attack that conclusion as unreasonable.

If the moratorium fails to control Native American harvesting in the future, ESA listing will be warranted. That much is agreed. But plaintiffs have been unable to point to anything in the record indicating that the current whale population is unsustainable if the harvest is indeed restricted successfully. . . .

Plaintiffs argue that harvesting will still occur even after the MMPA "depleted" listing because some hunting will be permitted under co-management agreements between the agency and Native American organizations and some hunting will occur illegally. Proposed regulations governing co-management agreements, however, limit Native American hunts to two strikes annually, and there is no reason to believe that the MMPA's enforcement mechanisms, which are identical to those of the ESA, will be less effective in controlling illegal takings. Plaintiffs' concerns are reasonable, and enforcement should be carefully monitored, but the record contains support for the agency's conclusion that future takings will be minimal and that the current population is sustainable.

(C) Disease or Predation The agency concedes that both disease or predation "occur in the CI beluga population and may affect reproduction and survival," but it has concluded that these factors are not causing the stock to be threatened or

endangered. Plaintiff has not shown that conclusion to be arbitrary or capricious. . . .

(D) Inadequacy of Existing Regulatory Mechanisms We have found nothing in the record, and plaintiff has identified nothing, showing that there are inadequacies in existing regulatory mechanisms or, if there were, what the effects of such inadequacies would be. Plaintiffs argue that the MMPA is inadequate to ensure that illegal hunting does not occur and to adequately protect Cook Inlet from damaging development activities, but that argument simply asserts plaintiffs' policy preference for a remedy under the ESA and begs the question of whether ESA listing is required.

(E) Other Natural or Manmade Factors Affecting Its Continued Existence Plaintiffs argue that there are many other factors—strandings, oil spills, takings through commercial fishing, effects of pollutants, ship strikes, noise, urban runoff, etc.—that put the species at risk and that it was arbitrary and capricious for the agency to determine that "the best available information . . . indicates that these activities, alone or cumulatively, have not caused the stock to be in danger of extinction and are not likely to do so in the foreseeable future." They point to a snippet in the record indicating that "other factors could be contributing to the decline," AR-D545, at P 5, and argue that the agency failed to adequately consider the cumulative effects of all of the potential factors combined with the small population size of the Cook Inlet Beluga Whale.

It is true that the absence of "conclusive evidence" of a real threat to a species does not justify an agency's finding that ESA listing is not warranted. *Defenders of Wildlife,* 958 F. Supp. at 679. But neither is listing required simply because the agency is unable to rule out factors that could contribute to a population decline. It was not arbitrary or capricious for the agency to place its principal reliance on the cessation of Native American hunts and the Breiwick and DeMaster conclusion that the Cook Inlet Beluga Whale population could sustain itself, even accounting for stochastic events.

[Plaintiffs' remaining arguments have been omitted.]

Ordered that defendant's motion for summary judgment is granted.

Further ordered that plaintiffs' motion for summary judgment is denied.

Questions

1. Why did the plaintiffs want this beluga whale listed as endangered under the Endangered Species Act?

2. What was the standard of review that the court applied to the agency's decision?

3. What five factors are to be considered in the listing of a species as endangered under the Endangered Species Act?

Endangered Species Act
Spotted Owls or Jobs?

The *Cook Inlet* decision and the Endangered Species Act (ESA) are at the heart of one of the most interesting and poignant disputes of the long struggle between environmentalists and business. Should we save the grizzly bear, nine populations of Pacific Northwest salmon, the Delhi Sands flower-loving fly? Each is among the nearly 1,200 species officially protected by the Endangered Species Act. Most Americans don't want to lose those creatures, but as usual the question is who pays? As written, the ESA effectively forces landowners to bear the cost because the ESA forbids any practice, such as cutting trees, that results in the "taking" of any creature that is part of an endangered species. The ESA also forbids the degradation of the habitat of those species. As a result, affected communities face a dramatic decline in the economic use of property: no building, no logging, and no pesticides, for example.

The struggle was front-page news in the mid-1990s as tens of thousands of Pacific Northwest loggers struggled to retain their jobs while environmentalists fought to protect the habitat of the northern spotted owl. A compromise allowed logging on about one-third of the contested timberland under President Clinton's Northwest Forest Plan,

Should we save the grizzly bear?

but the issue reemerged in late 1999 when a federal judge halted almost all cutting in the affected areas because it was alleged that federal agents were not fulfilling their duty under the plan to conduct thorough surveys for rare plants and wildlife before logging could proceed. The issues were finally put to rest with the government's 2001 completion of a Supplemental Environmental Impact Statement (SEIS) to amend the Northwest Forest Plan, which set forth how all affected species were to be managed.[51]

Salmon or Jobs?

The remarkable spotted owl fight may pale before the struggle emerging over preserving salmon. A general scientific consensus has emerged that four lower Snake River dams have played a major role in the well-documented decline of the salmon population in the Pacific Northwest.[52] Five percent of the region's hydroelectric power comes from the dams. Farmers depend on the dams for irrigation water and for shipping their grain and fruit to market. Ralph Broetje's 4,000-acre apple and cherry orchard in eastern Washington, for example, employs 700 people full time and 600 part time.[53] Without concerted action, either to mitigate the impact of the dams or remove them, extinction of the salmon by 2017 is forecast.[54] The Clinton administration developed the 2000 Federal Salmon Plan, which enumerated 1999 actions to be taken to restore salmon populations, but also acknowledged that removing the dams would be the most effective method of restoration (although a method of last resort). A coalition led by the National Wildlife Federation, however, sued the government on the grounds that the 2000 plan was based on too many uncertainties and was therefore insufficient to protect the salmon. A federal judge agreed and ordered the plan rewritten.[55] When the Bush administration published its revision on November 30, 2004, environmentalists and conservationists protested, among other things, that instead of a plan to restore salmon populations, it was only a plan to prevent further reduction. At this writing the parties are back in court, but the clock of extinction is still ticking.[56] [To read the 2004 Federal Salmon Plan, see **www .salmonrecovery.gov/R_biop_final.shtml**]

Question

Reducing the use of lawn chemicals and retarding development near waterways would help save endangered salmon. To save those salmon, should we limit citizens' rights to live as they see fit and as they can afford to live? Explain.

State and Local Regulation

State and local governments have become increasingly aggressive in pursuing environmental concerns, but they face the same conflicts troubling federal regulators. As a result, a number of states have passed laws to protect companies from penalties and required public disclosures when managers discover environmental wrongs at their own plants. The idea is to encourage self-policing, but federal law permits state enforcement under statutes such as the Clean Water Act only if that enforcement equals federal standards. This point was reinforced by the 2004 Supreme Court ruling in *Alaska Dept. of Environmental Conservation v. EPA,*[57] in which the Court upheld an EPA order directing

Alaska to withhold permits for the expansion of a zinc mine, which the state had approved. The EPA had determined the expansion would violate the Clean Air Act because it did not require the use of best available technology to limit air pollution.

In addition to their powers and obligations under federal environmental laws, state and local governments have the right to impose various controls on citizens to protect and maintain public health, safety, and general welfare. In constitutional law, these powers are referred to as a state's *police power.* One of the areas in which states have exercised their police power is in regulating indoor air quality—that is, banning smoking in public places such as offices and restaurants.

Global Smoking Warnings

With the entry into force on February 27, 2005, of the World Health Organization (WHO) Framework Convention on Tobacco Control, smoking has become a topic of international law. As of this writing, 168 countries (including the United States and the European Union) have signed the treaty, and 64 of those have taken all actions necessary to domestically ratify it. Ratifying countries agree, among other things, that they will, within three years of ratification, ensure that all tobacco packaging contains strong health warnings and, within five years, establish advertising and promotion bans. [For the text of the framework and current information on signatory and ratifying countries, see the WHO site at **www.who.int/tobacco/en**]

PRACTICING ETHICS   Selling Tobacco Products?

According to the WHO, tobacco is the second major cause of death in the world, currently responsible for the death of 1 in 10 adults worldwide (about 5 million deaths each year). Half the people that smoke today—that is, about 650 million people—will eventually be killed by tobacco. Some companies, like Starbucks, have banned smoking in all of their establishments, even in countries that do not have a legal ban at this time.

Questions

If you were the owner/operator of a small corner market, would you sell tobacco products? What if you were the buyer for a national chain of small markets?

Part Four—Common Law Remedies

Long before the federal government became actively involved in environmental issues, courts were grappling with the problem. As early as the 1500s, city officials were ordered by a court to keep the streets clean of dung deposited by swine allowed to run loose; the air was said to be "corrupted and infected" by this practice. Legal arguments have typically revolved around the extent of a person's right to use and enjoy private property if such usage causes harm to a neighbor's property or the use of public property. More recently, tort actions of negligence and strict liability have been pursued by injured individuals. Successful plaintiffs may recover monetary damages for the harm suffered or obtain an injunction to prevent similar conduct (and therefore harm) by the defendant in the future, or both.

Nuisance   A *private nuisance* is a substantial and unreasonable invasion of the private use and enjoyment of one's land; a *public nuisance* is an unreasonable interference with a right common to the public. Harmful conduct may be both a public and private nuisance simultaneously; the case law distinctions between the two are often blurred. A classic nuisance case is a 1970 New York case, *Boomer v. Atlantic Cement Co.*[58] Neighboring landowners sued the operator of cement plant for injury to their properties from the plant's dirt, smoke, and vibration. The court recognized the wrong done and ordered the operator to pay damages. In a more recent Rhode Island case, the state sued various manufacturers of lead paint, under a public nuisance theory as well as several other theories, for injuries to itself (medical costs) and to its lead-poisoned residents. The trial resulted in a hung jury.[59]

Trespass   A *trespass* occurs and liability is imposed with any *intentional* invasion of an individual's right to the exclusive use of his or her own property. For example, in *Martin v. Reynolds Metals Co.,* 342 P.2d 790 (Or. Sup. Ct. 1959), plaintiff successfully sued in trespass for damages caused by the operation of an aluminum reduction plant, which caused certain fluoride compounds in the form of gases and particulates to become airborne, settle on the plaintiffs' land, contaminate their forage and water, and poison their cattle.

Negligence   The elements of a negligence case have been previously discussed in Chapter 7. In the environmental area, a negligence claim may be based on such occurrences as negligently fouling a neighbor's water, flooding another's land, or causing damage through the emission of excessive noise, smell, or particulate matter. A claim might also be based on the failure to correct a pollution problem where the necessary technology and resources were available to do so, where the defendant owed a duty to the harmed individual. Particularly troubling cases arise where a plaintiff claims injury from a toxic substance manufactured or otherwise supplied by defendant. Plaintiffs may have significant problems establishing *causation*. For example, does smoking cause lung cancer? Did the use of DES by pregnant women cause birth defects? Does DES cause infertility in daughters borne by mothers who took DES during their pregnancy?

Strict Liability   Certain activities, such as the use of toxic chemicals, may be seen as so abnormally dangerous as to give rise to a strict liability claim (previously discussed in Chapter 7). In an environmental law context, strict liability has been considered in circumstances in which crop dusting contaminated adjacent properties,[60] poisonous gases used for fumigation spread,[61] toxic chemicals were improperly disposed of,[62] and oil contaminated a nearby water well.[63]

Part Five—Global Warming

Without question, the most debated environmental issue has been global warming. Both the politics and the science of global warming have been controversial—a particularly potent example of the issues of coincidence, correlation, and causation discussed earlier. The phenomenon at issue is the projected overall increase in surface temperatures around the globe caused by the release of man-made carbon dioxide into the atmosphere. The primary cause of the increase is the burning of fossil fuels, especially in gasoline engines and coal-fired plants. The governments of the world, realizing that global action is required to have any significant impact on overall emissions, adopted the Kyoto Protocol on December 11, 1997. Specifically, the protocol calls for a 5 percent reduction from 1990 levels of greenhouse gas emissions, to be achieved by 2012. The protocol became binding when countries accounting for at least 55 percent of total emissions ratified, which occurred with Russia's ratification in late 2004. As of this writing, 150 countries have ratified the protocol, representing 61.6 percent of total emissions. The United States (representing 36.1 percent of total 1990 emissions)[64] is not among the ratifying countries, President Bush having announced in March 2001 that the protocol was "fatally flawed." [For current ratification status and other information about the protocol, go the official Web site for the United Nations Framework convention on Climate Change at **http://unfccc.int/essential_background/kyoto_protocol/items/2830.php**]

> President Bush announced in March 2001 that the protocol was "fatally flawed."

The Kyoto Protocol uses market incentives to achieve emission reductions. It permits industrialized countries, and the companies in them, to "generate credits toward their quotas by bankrolling projects that reduce emissions. . . . The theory is that because global warming is global, the atmosphere doesn't care whether emissions occur in, say, Germany or China. For a German company . . . financing an emissions reduction project in China is likely to be a lot cheaper than doing so at home, because in Germany, the cheap emissions improvements already have been made."[65]

Not only has the United States not ratified the Kyoto Protocol: In mid-2003 the EPA issued a decision that carbon dioxide and the other greenhouse gases are not pollutants and that any efforts on its part "to curb greenhouse-gas emissions would exceed its authority unless Congress specifically expanded its powers in new legislation."[66] Under the Clinton administration, the EPA had said that it did have the authority to regulate carbon dioxide. In response to the EPA's 2003 announcement, several state attorneys general started a lawsuit against the five largest power plant emitters of carbon dioxide under a public nuisance theory.[67]

PRACTICING ETHICS   Voluntarily Reduce Greenhouse Gas Emissions?

In spite of the nonparticipation of the United States in the Kyoto Protocol, many U.S. multinationals will come under its provisions because of their operations in ratifying countries. Many more U.S. businesses, however, are voluntarily developing emission reduction strategies. In some cases, the impetus to act may be a belief that voluntary action now may minimize the cost of required action in the future.[68] In other cases, a consensus that "humans are contributing to the warming of the planet" may cause corporate boards to more seriously evaluate potential costs and risks to their companies both from global warming itself and from their responses to it.[69]

Question

If you were a vice president of a corporation that burned significant fossil fuels in the production process but operated solely in the United States, what stance would you take on global warming?

Internet Exercise

Using the EPA's "Superfund Reforms" Web page [**www.epa.gov/oerrpage/superfund/ programs/reforms/faqs.htm**], answer the following questions:

1. How have the Superfund reforms changed the Superfund program?
2. Which reforms, if any, have not been successful, and why?

Chapter Questions

1. The United States seems to be having a love affair with sport utility vehicles (SUVs), in spite of the fact that their gas mileage is considerably poorer than most sedans. To graphically bring home the environmental irresponsibility of SUV owners, two men in the San Francisco Bay area dreamed up a scheme to address what they perceived as a market failure. Uninvited, on hundreds of SUVs they have stuck homemade bumper stickers that read, "I'm changing the environment! Ask me how!"[70]

   a. What effect do you think these self-appointed environmental police want from their actions?

   b. What effect do you think they are likely to actually have?

2. Economist B. Peter Pashigian:

   > It is widely thought that environmental controls are guided by the public-spirited ideal of correcting for "negative externalities"—the pollution costs that spill over from private operations. This view is not wrong by any means. But it is suspiciously incomplete.
   >
   > After all, there are numerous studies of regulatory programs in other fields that show how private interests have used public powers for their own enrichment.[71]

   In addition to correcting negative externalities, what forces might be influencing federal pollution control?

3. How might the government's ever-increasing environmental regulations, along with the public's call for a new environmental consciousness, favor big business interests over those of small business owners?

4. Americans' commitment to the car obviously raises serious environmental problems. The vast parking areas required to house those cars are themselves a significant environmental hazard. Explain some of the environmental problems created or encouraged by parking lots.

5. Mexico is quickly running short of water.

   > 85 percent of Mexico's economic growth and 75 percent of its 100 million people are in the north, and the water is far to the south. . . . [P]oliticians facing elections are reluctant to ask voters to spend more on any utility, let alone water. Agriculture uses 80 percent of the water and pays nothing, although it only ranks seventh in contribution to the gross national product. . . . Less than half of the capital's wastewater is treated. The rest sinks into underground lakes or flows toward the Gulf of Mexico, turning rivers into sewers. . . . Well over half of irrigation water is lost to evaporation or seepage."[72]

   Brainstorm as many possible contributions to the solution of Mexico's water problem as you can.

6. Economist Robert Crandall:

   > [O]ur best chances for regulatory reform in certain environmental areas, particularly in air pollution policy, come from the states. Probably, responsibility for

environmental regulation belongs with the states anyway, and most of it ought to be returned there.[73]

    a. What reasoning supports Crandall's notion that responsibility for environmental regulation belongs with the states?

    b. How might one reason to the contrary?

    c. If the power were yours, would environmental regulation rest primarily at the state, federal, or international level? Explain.

7. William Tucker:

> [Environmentalism is] essentially aristocratic in its roots and derives from the land and nature-based ethic that has been championed by upper classes throughout history. Large landowners and titled aristocracies . . . have usually held a set of ideals that stresses "stewardship" and the husbanding of existing resources over exploration and discovery. This view favors handicrafts over mass production and the inheritance ethic over the business ethic.[74]

Tucker went on to argue that environmentalism favors the economic and social interests of the well-off. He said people of the upper middle class see their future in universities and the government bureaucracy, with little economic stake in industrial expansion. Indeed, such expansion might threaten their suburban property values. Comment.

8. Should a state be required to prepare an environmental impact statement if it wants to use federal funds to promote statewide tourism? Does it matter which state it is? Consider Iowa and then consider Hawaii.[75]

9. A 2002 report from the EPA concludes that we have not realized the benefits from the 1990 amendments to the Clean Air Act because it is not being enforced effectively. For example, by July 2001 "only 63 percent of the 19,025 major sources of industrial pollution in the United States had obtained permits, although the law imposed a deadline of 1997." The report further noted that several states "lacked sufficient resources to run the program and . . . many states had difficulties getting EPA guidance on how the agency's regulations should be applied to a specific polluter."[76] Instead of passing additional clean air standards, should we simply vigorously enforce the standards already on the books?

10. Due to the spread of the West Nile virus in the state of New York, an insecticide spraying program was implemented to control the mosquitoes responsible for its spread. Several groups sued, arguing that the spray was a pollutant that damaged waters in violation of the Clean Water Act. What criteria should the court use to decide the outcome? See *No Spray Coalition, Inc. v. The City of New York,* 2000 U.S. Dist. LEXIS 13919, 51 ERC (BNA) 1508 (S.D.N.Y. 2000).

11. Ott Chemical Co. polluted the ground at its Michigan plant. CPC International created a wholly owned subsidiary to buy Ott, which was accomplished in 1965. CPC retained the original Ott managers. Pollution continued through 1972 when CPC sold Ott. In 1981 the U.S. EPA began a cleanup of the site. To recover some of the tens of millions in cleanup costs, the EPA sued CPC (now called Bestfoods) among other potentially responsible parties. The Superfund law places responsibility on anyone

who "owned or operated" a property when pollution was deposited. The district court held that CPC was liable because of its active participation in Ott's business and its control of Ott's decisions in that it selected the Ott board of directors and placed some CPC managers as executives at Ott.

a. Was the district court correct in holding CPC liable? Explain.

b. What test would you employ to determine whether a parent corporation should be liable for a subsidiary's pollution? See *United States v. Bestfoods,* 524 U.S. 51 (1998).

12. The Endangered Species Act provides that all federal agency actions are to be designed so that they do not jeopardize endangered or threatened species. The act had been interpreted to reach to federal agency work or funding in foreign countries, but the federal government changed that interpretation in 1986 to limit the act's reach to the United States and the high seas. A group labeled Defenders of Wildlife filed suit, seeking to reinstate the original interpretation. The case reached the U.S. Supreme Court, where Justice Scalia wrote that Defenders of Wildlife would have to submit evidence showing that at least one of its members would be "directly" affected by the interpretation. In response, one member of Defenders of Wildlife wrote that she had visited Egypt and observed the endangered Nile crocodile and hoped to return to do so again but feared that U.S. aid with the Aswan High Dam would harm the crocodiles.

a. Why did Scalia call for that evidence?

b. Decide the case. Explain. See *Lujan v. Defenders of Wildlife,* 112 S.Ct. 2130 (1992).

13. "The Aral Sea is going, gone. Once the world's fourth largest inland body of water, the Aral has shriveled to half its former area and a third of its volume. As for the region's drinking water, even the local vodka has a salty tang."[77] The Aral is the victim of the former Soviet Union's central planners, who decreed that the area would be the nation's main source of cotton. To achieve that goal, intense irrigation was required, with the result that only a trickle of fresh water was left to feed the Aral. Refilling the Aral would require tremendous dislocations in the agriculture of the vast region. If you were a member of a commission charged with developing a plan for the future of the Aral Sea, what issues would you cover?

14. Comment on the following: "The single most important and pervasive moral obligation facing mankind is to ensure survival of a healthy planet for our grandchildren and theirs."[78]

15. Professor and business ethics scholar Norman Bowie:

> Environmentalists frequently argue that business has special obligations to protect the environment. Although I agree with the environmentalists on this point, I do not agree with them as to where the obligations lie. Business does not have an obligation to protect the environment over and above what is required by law; however, business does have a moral obligation to avoid intervening in the political arena in order to defeat or weaken environmental legislation.[79]

a. Explain Professor Bowie's reasoning.

b. Do you agree with him? Explain.

Notes

1. "Satellite Findings Reveal Massive Global Pollution," *Waterloo/Cedar Falls Courier,* May 31, 2001, p. A5.

2. "Study Links Air Pollution, Birth Defects," *Waterloo/Cedar Falls Courier,* January 4, 2002, p. A8.

3. Paulette Stenzel, "Free Trade and the Environment: Recurring Issues," *Environmental and Business Forum* 6, no. 1 (May 2001), pp. 1, 6.

4. "Earth Pulse: Insatiable Appetites," *National Geographic,* March 2001.

5. "Ocean 'Dead Zones' Top Environmental Problem," *Waterloo/Cedar Falls Courier,* March 29, 2004, p. A4.

6. Marla Cone, "Toxic Arctic Threatens Lives of Polar Bears," *Des Moines Register,* June 29, 2003, p. 11A.

7. Chester Dawson, "Digging Up Trouble" *BusinessWeek Online,* January 8, 2001 [**www .businessweek.com/2001/01_02/b3714245.htm**].

8. Central Intelligence Agency, *Global Trends 2015: A Dialogue about the Future with Non-government Experts,* NIC 2000–02 (December 2000) [**www.cia.gov.cia/publications/ globaltrends2015/index.html**].

9. "Ocean 'Dead Zones' Top Environmental Problem."

10. Wilfred Beckerman, cited in Robert Solomon, *The New World of Business* (Lanham, MD: Rowman & Littlefield, 1994), p. 319.

11. Susan Lee, "How Much Is the Right to Pollute Worth?" *The Wall Street Journal,* August 1, 2001, p. A15.

12. Mark Golden, "Dirty Dealings," *The Wall Street Journal,* September 13, 1999, p. R13.

13. Tom Herman, "Tax Report," *The Wall Street Journal Online,* August 22, 2002.

14. John Fialka, "EPA Plans to Offer Incentives to Curb 'Sprawl' Pollution," *The Wall Street Journal,* October 18, 2000, p. A4.

15. "Economic Man, Cleaner Planet," *Economist,* September 29, 2001, pp. 73–75.

16. "Economic Man, Cleaner Planet."

17. "Review and Outlook: A Fish Story," *The Wall Street Journal,* November 6, 2003, p. A14.

18. Jon J. Fialka and Jeffrey Ball, "Companies Get Ready for Greenhouse-Gas Limits," *The Wall Street Journal,* October 26, 2004, p. A2.

19. Michael V. Russo and Paul A. Fouts, "A Resource-Based Perspective on Corporate Environmental Performance and Profitability," *Academy of Management Journal* 40, no. 3 (1997), p. 534.

20. Eric Pianin, "Environmental Rules Worth Their Cost, Study Says," *Des Moines Register,* September 28, 2003, p. 3A.

21. *The Baltimore Sun,* "Predicting the Global-Warming Weather: Art, Science, or Neither?," *Waterloo/Cedar Falls Courier,* November 7, 2004, p. A7.

22. Peter Coy, "Business and the Greens Share Common Ground," *BusinessWeek,* January 29, 2001, p. 45.

23. Seth Borenstein, "Bush Eases Rules, Angers Environmentalists," *Des Moines Register,* September 8, 2003, p. 4A.

24. *American Trucking v. EPA,* 283 F. 3d 355 (D.C. Cir. 2002).

25. David Stout, "7 Utilities Sued by U.S. on Charges of PollutingAir," *The New York Times,* November 4, 1999, p. A1.

26. Eric Pianin, "In Reversal, EPA to Push Cleanup of Power Plants," *Washington Post,* January 22, 2004.

27. *Los Angeles Times,* "EPA Eases Clean Air Act," *Waterloo/Cedar Falls Courier,* August 28, 2003, p. A1.

28. "Clean Air Act Changes Blocked," *Waterloo/Cedar Falls Courier,* December 25, 2003, p. A2.

29. Stephanie Ebbert, "EPA Delays Power-Plant Rules, Agrees to Reopen Comment in Case," *Boston Globe,* July 1, 2004, p. A.8

30. Jeff Nesmith, "Most Major Rivers Seriously Degraded, a Commission Finds," *Des Moines Register,* November 30, 1999, p. 4A.

31. Erin Kelly, "40% of USA's Waterways Still Not Cleaned, EPA Says," *USA TODAY,* July 31, 2000, p. 14A.

32. Traci Watson, "EPA Is Slammed on Dirty Water," *USA TODAY,* August 23, 2001, p. 3A.

33. Bernard Gavzer, "Take Out the Trash, and Put It . . . Where?" *Parade,* June 13, 1999, p. 4.

34. Gauter, "Take Out the Trash."

35. Gauter, "Take Out the Trash."

36. Gauter, "Take Out the Trash."

37. Jeff Bailey, "Curbside Recycling Comforts the Soul, but Benefits Are Scant," *The Wall Street Journal,* January 19, 1995, p. A1.

38. Scripps-Howard News Service, "White House Delays Notice of Welfare Cuts," *Waterloo/ Cedar Falls Courier,* September 15, 1996, p. F3.

39. See a Web site sponsored by the EPA [**www.clu-in.com**].

40. Rachel A. Schneider, *Federal Environmental Laws,* American Bar Association [**www.abanet .org/genpractice/lawyer/complete/98julschneid.html**].

41. Anthony DePalma, "Love Canal Declared Clean, Ending Toxic Horror," *The New York Times,* March 18, 2004, P. A1.

42. John J. Fialka, "Money Shortage Threatens Superfund," *The Wall Street Journal,* September 7, 2004, p. A2.

43. Emily Chasan, "Jury Rules against Chevron Texaco in Cleanup Suit," *The Wall Street Journal,* August 20, 2004, p. A2.

44. Tom Bliley, "Superfund Law Needs a Cleanup," *Washington Post,* August 16, 1999, p. A15.

45. Editorial, "Needed: Superfund Cleanup," *Omaha World-Herald,* November 26, 1999, p. 26.

46. [**www.epa.gov/epahome/headline_011102.htm**].

47. John Milliman and John Grosskopf, "Improving the Regulatory Enforcement Settlement Process: Applying Collaborative Solutions for Businesses and Environmental Regulatory Agencies," *Environmental Quality Management* 13 (Spring 2004), p. 25.

48. Richard Winton, "Firms to Pay $200 Million to Clean Up Water Supply," *Los Angeles Times,* September 16, 1999, p. B1.

49. "Criminal Prosecution: The Latest Threat to Help You Get Management on Board," *IOMA's Safety Director's Report* 4 (February 2004), p. 1.

50. Tom Kenworthy, "It's a New World: Polluters Go to Prison," *USA Today,* April 21, 2000, p. 3A.

51. [**www.or.blm.gov/nwfpnepa**].

52. Fredreka Schouten, "Dam-Breaking Idea Spawns Fierce Debate about Fish," *USA TODAY,* November 24, 1999, p. 22A.

53. Schouten, "Dam-Breaking Idea."

54. Paul VanDevelder, "A Political Football . . . with Fins; Clock Is Ticking as Salmon in the Pacific Northwest Face Extinction," *Los Angeles Times,* April 3, 2005, p. M6.

55. See [**http://www.wildsalmon.org/library/fed-salmon-plan.cfm**].

56. [**www.or.blm.gov/nwfpnepa**].

57. 540 U.S. 461 (2004).

58. 257 N.E. 2d 870 (N.Y. 1970).

59. *State v. Lead Indus. Ass'n, Inc.,* 2001 R.I. Super. LEXIS 37 (R.I. Super. Ct. 2001) and *Whitehouse v. Lead Indus. Ass'n,* 2003 R.I. Super. LEXIS 50 (R.I. Super. Ct. 2003).

60. *Langan v. Valicopters, Inc.,* 567 P. 2d 218 (Wash. S. Ct. 1977).

61. *Luthringer v. Moore,* 190 P. 2d 1 (Cal. S. Ct. 1948).

62. *State Dep't of Envtl. Prot. v. Ventron,* 468 A. 2d 150 (N.J. S. Ct. 1983).

63. *Branch v. W. Petroleum, Inc.,* 657 P. 2d 267 (Utah 1982).

64. Jeffrey Ball, "As Kyoto Protocol Comes Alive, So Do Pollution-Permit Markets," *The Wall Street Journal,* November 8, 2004, p. A2.

65. Ball, "As Kyoto Protocol Comes Alive."

66. Jeffrey Ball, "EPA Rejects Cap on Carbon Dioxide," *The Wall Street Journal,* August 29, 2003, p. A3.

67. "Letters to the Editor: If Feds Won't Fight Global Warming, We Will," *The Wall Street Journal,* August 18, 2004, p. A11.

68. John J. Fialka and Jeffrey Ball, "Companies Get Ready for Greenhouse-Gas Limits," *The Wall Street Journal,* October 26, 2004, p. A2.

69. Jeffrey Ball, "Conference Board Stiffens Global-Warming Stance," *The Wall Street Journal,* September 8, 2004, p. A2.

70. "'Mad Taggers' Leave Their Mark on SUV Culture," *Waterloo/Cedar Falls Courier,* December 26, 2000, p. B5.

71. B. Peter Pashigian, "How Large and Small Plants Fare under Environmental Regulation," *Regulation,* March–April 1983, p. 19.

72. "Profligate Past, Poor Planning Created Mexican Water Crisis," *Associated Press,* August 22, 2002.

73. Robert Crandall, "The Environment," in "Regulation—The First Year," *Regulation,* January–February 1982, pp. 19, 29, 31.

74. "Tucker Contra Sierra," *Regulation,* March–April 1983, pp. 48–49.

75. Ellen Goodman, "Can Tourists Love a Place to Death?" *Des Moines Register,* March 31, 2001, p. 7A.

76. John Fialka, "EPA Report Says Pollution-Control Effort Is Hurt by Bureaucracy, Lack of Funds," *The Wall Street Journal,* March 12, 2002, p. A28.

77. Hugh Pope, "Uzbeks Manage to Endure Amid Ruins of the Aral Sea," *The Wall Street Journal,* February 5, 1998, p. A18.

78. Bill Leonard, "Someday We'll Regret Damage to Our Planet," *Des Moines Register,* September 20, 2004, p. 7A.

79. Norman Bowie, with Kenneth Goodpaster, "Corporate Conscience, Money and Motorcars," in *Business Ethics Report, Highlights of Bentley College's Eighth National Conference on Business Ethics,* ed. Peter Kent, 1989, pp. 4, 6.

Internet Law and Ethics

Introduction: The Internet and Globalization

The Internet has changed our lives. The extraordinary power of nearly instantaneous communication around the globe promises remarkable new opportunities and challenges, creating and facilitating relationships (whole new "communities" of interest) among individuals, businesses, and governments that could never have occurred without it. The Internet is itself a substantial catalyst for continuing globalization, breaking down national boundaries and rules to allow free interchange of communications and ideas around the world. A government report, *Global 2015,* which seeks to envision how our world might look in 2015, states that the "IT revolution represents the most significant global transformation since the Industrial Revolution."[1]

As we enter our last chapter, we have the opportunity to consider against the backdrop of a global stage such fundamentals as what substantive law we want to govern our activities and, perhaps even more important, what process we should use to establish global standards. Now it seems more pressing for the world community to come to agreement on certain fundamental organizational principles, not just leaving the effort for consensus at a national level. The Internet has the potential for vastly expanding global relationships and, therefore, the need for international consensus.

On the other hand, the most interesting question raised by the Internet's creation and facilitation of these new relationships may be what process is going to develop to create a consensus over what the substantive law should be. What government can legitimately impose standards and sanctions? Might we in fact be evolving a world government? Is business driving the development of a medium, the expansion of which may be the catalyst for a fundamental reorganization of our global society?

Introduction: Law and the Market

Policy makers, users, and posters are all concerned about the degree to which we need to impose the force of law on Internet activities. The question is familiar: Can we count on the free market and ethics to govern Internet conduct or are government rules necessary? Put another way, which model is best for the Internet—no regulation, government regulation, self-regulation, or some combination of the three? [For links to many Internet law Web sites, see **www.willyancey.com/internet_law.htm**]

Certainly the law will play a great role in the future of the Internet. Experience confirms that a framework of law will be necessary for predictability, efficiency, and trust in the new global economy. Many of the problems law addresses in the conventional commercial world must now be revisited in the virtual world. Digital signatures, privacy, trademark infringement, freedom of speech, fraud, and taxes are among the big issues that are likely to require attention from the law. The question, of course, is how much law? Even the firmest free market advocates recognize the necessity for clear contractual principles and effective means to prevent fraud and other criminal behavior. The key regulatory question is how to maintain the vigor of the free market while establishing a limited array of binding legal standards that will bring consistency to the global Internet market.

Critical Thinking

> The Internet is a superhighway not only for information, but also for misinformation.

The Internet is a superhighway not only for information, but also for misinformation. Not only can posted information be sadly out of date, it is possible that the "information" was never accurate. Because Internet publishing is so cheap and so accessible, readers and users of the Internet must build their critical assessment skills for evaluating the worth of the information found. For example, one should always investigate who or what organization is responsible for the posted information. Information posted by an individual may not have been investigated as thoroughly as information posted by a traditional news service. In addition, the identity of the poster may indicate a particular bias or slant on the information presented. We would not expect, for example, to get a neutral evaluation of a particular lawsuit from the Web pages of the corporate defendant.

Another type of misinformation possible with the Internet is more subtle—subtle enough that Internet surfers are not likely to be aware of it. In mid-2001, a complaint was filed with the Federal Trade Commission charging that several online search engines are altering search results for businesses who pay them special fees. The allegation is that the search engines "are abandoning objective formulas to determine the order of the results they list and selling the top spots to the highest bidders—without making adequate disclosures to Internet users."[2]

Introduction: Ethics

So we see that market forces and law will blend in some uncertain, emerging formula to provide the security and confidence necessary for effective e-commerce. Now we ask what role ethics—that is, self-regulation—can play in this equation. The anonymity, the speed, the elusiveness, and the global reach of the Internet suggest very difficult new ethical problems (or old problems in a new venue). Some of those problems such as privacy, consumer fraud, and crime of all kinds will be discussed separately later in this chapter.

Selected Ethical Dilemmas

The Digital Divide

For some time there has been a concern that the Internet may worsen the income/wealth gap that splits both Americans and the globe. In many countries, including the United States, programs have been developed to address the domestic digital divide—for example, programs to provide computer access outside school hours to children without home access,[3] award programs for the development of new models to reach the unconnected population,[4] and WiFi and broadband programs to improve the public connection infrastructure.[5] But the most serious accessibility imbalance is at the global level. In recognition of this, the United Nations endorsed the holding of a World Summit on the Information Society. During the first phase in December 2003, representatives from 175 countries adopted a Declaration of Principles including a "commitment to build a people-centred, inclusive, and development-oriented Information Society, where everyone can create, access, utilize, and share information and knowledge, enabling individuals, communities, and peoples to achieve their full potential in promoting their sustainable development and improving their quality of life." The second phase, scheduled for November 2005, is to address such issues as Internet governance and financing mechanisms. [For more information, see the World Summit on the Information Society site at **www.itu.int/wsis/index.html**]

Community

We cannot know what our lives will be like as the Internet begins to assert its full technological potential, but we can be sure that much will be different. One commentator, Thomas Naylor, argues that what we really need are "more town squares and village greens where people can sit and talk, have a coffee, pass the time away, and experience real community." But what he sees is a medium, pushed by "our universities with their frantic rush to the Web," that "encourages instant gratification, superficial research, poor writing, sloppy analysis, uncritical thinking, and unrelenting conformity."[6] On the other side is the argument that "Technology has not devalued individual human life; it has elevated it, creating new opportunities, new connections, new freedoms. The human imagination has not been suppressed; it has been liberated, in ways unimaginable even a decade or two ago. . . . [T]he new technologies ensure better opportunities for a larger number. More people will have more access to more information than ever before. And that information is power."[7] [For more on the intersection of the Internet and society, see **http://cyber.law.harvard.edu**]

> More people will have more access to more information than ever before. And that information is power.

Marketing and the Internet

As anyone who has been using the Internet over several years can tell you, marketing efforts have become pervasive. Where once marketing amounted to putting up Web pages where potential customers could get product and service information, it has grown into banner ads on news sites, pop-up windows that have to be affirmatively closed to escape the advertisement, and whole Web sites designed to hook kids with interactive games that themselves promote the posters' products.[8] Even more aggressive marketing gambits are available, including "mouse-trapping" (disabling a user's ability to use the back button or to leave or close a window or page), "typo-piracy" (use of misspellings or derivations of a popular brand to divert traffic to an unintended site), mislabeling of links to send shoppers to unintended destinations, the unauthorized substitution of a new home page setting on the user's computer,[9] and spyware (software unknowingly downloaded by the user that can deliver volumes of pop-up ads, redirect browsers to undesired search engines, or steal personal information).[10] And who has not received unsolicited e-mail advertisements offering low mortgage rates, as well as many much less savory devices and services?

Questions

1. Can you think of any imaginative ways to provide widespread Internet access in developing countries? How would you deal with the reality that most Internet content is in English?

2. In your experience, has access to the Internet encouraged "superficial research, poor writing, sloppy analysis, uncritical thinking, and unrelenting conformity"? Or do you think it has given "more access to more information than ever before"? Has the issue of information reliability been raised at your college or university in the context of accessing information off the Internet?

3. What new laws can you design that would significantly reduce any of the marketing abuses described?

Part One—Jurisdiction to Adjudicate

Business in the cyberworld raises puzzling new legal problems. The Internet, after all, is borderless. We can and do communicate and conduct transactions around the world. When a dispute arises from one of those billions of communications and transactions, where will that dispute be litigated? If an American Web site provides child pornography viewed by a German on the Internet, which nation will have the authority to prosecute the offense?[11] If a Massachusetts resident posts an arguably libelous article on an Internet bulletin board sited in New York, may the Texas resident who claims harm from the libel sue the author and the bulletin board host in a Texas court?[12] These are jurisdiction questions. A party filing suit over an Internet dispute must take that claim to a court that has both *subject-matter jurisdiction* (the authority and power to address the particular kind of legal problem being raised) and *personal jurisdiction* (the power to make the defendant respond to the court). (For a general discussion of jurisdiction, see Chapter 4.)

In the United States, where the plaintiff and defendant are both residents of the forum state, personal jurisdiction ordinarily is not an issue. However, personal jurisdiction over nonresidents depends on the constitutional requirement of *due process.* In practice, the test is one of *minimum contacts:* Did the defendant have sufficient contact with the forum state that being sued there would be fair and just? Put another way, was the defendant's contact with the forum state such that he or she should expect to be subject to the state's courts? Thus, the more business a defendant does in a state, the more likely that personal jurisdiction will be found. The Internet, of course, raises special problems because the "contacts" often are electronic and fleeting.

Several cases have arisen in the United States that begin to answer this question. For example, the Fifth Circuit held that, in a case of alleged copyright violation, Texas did not have personal jurisdiction over a Vermont corporation merely because the corporation's Web site was accessible from Texas.[13] It reached this conclusion, in part, because it found that there was no specific connection between the existence of the corporation's Web site and the harm complained of by plaintiff. Thus the Vermont corporation could be sued in Texas only if it had contacts with Texas that were sufficiently "continuous and systematic" to subject the corporation generally to suit in Texas. A passive Web site could not do this. When the defendant has more contact with the forum state than mere creation of a passive Web site available to forum state computer users, the due process analysis becomes more complex and hinges on an evaluation of the defendant's specific additional contacts with the forum state. The existing decisions are often hard to reconcile and many cases have been reversed on appeal, indicating that judgments as to jurisdiction are challenging.[14]

Jurisdiction in International Suits

Jurisdictional issues like these also arise across national boundaries. In January 2001 an Italian court ruled that Italy can try to close down foreign-based Web sites that break Italian law.[15] Similarly, Germany has brought criminal actions to prevent persons from providing German residents with access to pornographic Internet sites.[16] In these international contexts, it may be useful to distinguish among three types of jurisdiction: jurisdiction to prescribe (legislate), jurisdiction to adjudicate (judicial personal jurisdiction), and jurisdiction to enforce.[17] Most countries have long had laws that prohibit or regulate expression and commerce, such as pornography, gambling, alcohol, and so on. But when they seek to apply those laws to various classes of foreigners, what is in question is their jurisdiction to adjudicate. Section 421 of the Restatement (Third) of Foreign Relations Law of the United States attempts to identify the circumstances under which countries have exercised their jurisdiction to adjudicate. It enumerates, among other circumstances, (1) when a person is present in the territory, other than transitorily; (2) when a person is domiciled, a resident, or a national of that country; (3) when a person regularly carries on business in that country; (4) when a person has carried on an activity in the country, where that activity is the subject of the dispute; and (5) when a person has done something outside the country, but it has a "substantial, direct, and foreseeable effect within" the country and that effect forms the subject of the suit.

Consider both the French court's approach and the U.S. district court's approach to the issue of jurisdiction to adjudicate in the following dispute.

YAHOO! v. La Ligue Contre Le Racisme Et L'Antisemitisme

LEGAL BRIEFCASE   169 F. Supp. 2d 1181 (N.D. Cal. 2001)

Judge Jeremy Fogel

I. PROCEDURAL HISTORY

Defendants La Ligue Contre Le Racisme Et L'Antisemitisme ("LICRA") and L'Union Des Etudiants Juifs De France, citizens of France, are nonprofit organizations dedicated to eliminating anti-Semitism. Plaintiff Yahoo!, Inc. ("Yahoo!") is a corporation organized under the laws of Delaware with its principal place of business in Santa Clara, California. Yahoo! is an Internet service provider that operates various Internet Web sites and

services that any computer user can access at the Uniform Resource Locator ("URL") **http://www.yahoo.com**. Yahoo! services ending in the suffix ".com," without an associated country code as a prefix or extension (collectively, "Yahoo!'s U.S. Services"), use the English language and target users who are residents of, utilize servers based in, and operate under the laws of the United States. Yahoo! subsidiary corporations operate regional Yahoo! sites and services in 20 other nations, including, for example, Yahoo! France, Yahoo! India, and Yahoo! Spain. Each of these regional Web sites contains the host nation's unique two-letter code as either a prefix or a suffix in its URL (Yahoo! France is found at **http://www.yahoo.fr** and Yahoo! Korea at **http://www.yahoo.kr**). Yahoo!'s regional sites use the local region's primary language, target the local citizenry, and operate under local laws.

Yahoo! provides a variety of means by which people from all over the world can communicate and interact with one another over the Internet. . . . As relevant here, Yahoo!'s auction site allows anyone to post an item for sale and solicit bids from any computer user from around the globe. Yahoo! records when a posting is made and after the requisite time period lapses sends an e-mail notification to the highest bidder and seller with their respective contact information. Yahoo! is never a party to a transaction, and the buyer and seller are responsible for arranging privately for payment and shipment of goods. Yahoo! monitors the transaction through limited regulation by prohibiting particular items from being sold (such as stolen goods, body parts, prescription and illegal drugs, weapons, and goods violating U.S. copyright laws or the Iranian and Cuban embargos). . . . Yahoo! informs auction sellers that they must comply with Yahoo!'s policies and may not offer items to buyers in jurisdictions in which the sale of such item violates the jurisdiction's applicable laws. Yahoo! does not actively regulate the content of each posting, and individuals are able to post, and have in fact posted, highly offensive matter, including Nazi-related propaganda and Third Reich memorabilia, on Yahoo!'s auction sites.

On or about April 5, 2000, LICRA sent a "cease and desist" letter to Yahoo!'s Santa Clara headquarters informing Yahoo! that the sale of Nazi and Third Reich–related goods through its auction services violates French law. LICRA threatened to take legal action unless Yahoo! took steps to prevent such sales within eight days. Defendants subsequently utilized the United States Marshal's Office to serve Yahoo! with process in California and filed a civil complaint against Yahoo! in the Tribunal de Grande Instance de Paris (the "French Court").

The French Court found that approximately 1,000 Nazi and Third Reich–related objects, including Adolf Hitler's *Mein Kampf, The Protocol of the Elders of Zion* (an infamous anti-

Semitic report produced by the Czarist secret police in the early 1900s), and purported "evidence" that the gas chambers of the Holocaust did not exist, were being offered for sale on Yahoo.com's auction site. Because any French citizen is able to access these materials on Yahoo.com directly or through a link on Yahoo.fr, the French Court concluded that the Yahoo.com auction site violates Section R645-1 of the French Criminal Code, which prohibits exhibition of Nazi propaganda and artifacts for sale. On May 20, 2000, the French Court entered an order requiring Yahoo! to (1) eliminate French citizens' access to any material on the Yahoo.com auction site that offers for sale any Nazi objects, relics, insignia, emblems, and flags; (2) eliminate French citizens' access to Web pages on Yahoo.com displaying text, extracts, or quotations from *Mein Kampf* and *Protocol of the Elders of Zion;* (3) post a warning to French citizens on Yahoo.fr that any search through Yahoo.com may lead to sites containing material prohibited by Section R645-1 of the French Criminal Code, and that such viewing of the prohibited material may result in legal action against the Internet user; (4) remove from all browser directories accessible in the French Republic index headings entitled "negationists" and from all hypertext links the equation of "negationists" under the heading "Holocaust." The order subjects Yahoo! to a penalty of 100,000 Euros for each day that it fails to comply with the order. . . .

The French Court also provided that penalties assessed against Yahoo! Inc. may not be collected from Yahoo! France. Defendants again utilized the United States Marshal's Office to serve Yahoo! in California with the French Order.

Yahoo! subsequently posted the required warning and prohibited postings in violation of Section R645-1 of the French Criminal Code from appearing on Yahoo.fr. Yahoo! also amended the auction policy of Yahoo.com to prohibit individuals from auctioning:

> Any item that promotes, glorifies, or is directly associated with groups or individuals known principally for hateful or violent positions or acts, such as Nazis or the Ku Klux Klan. Official government-issue stamps and coins are not prohibited under this policy. Expressive media, such as books and films, may be subject to more permissive standards as determined by Yahoo! in its sole discretion.

Yahoo Auction Guidelines (visited Oct. 23, 2001) [**http://user.auctions.Yahoo.com/html/guidelines.html**]. Notwithstanding these actions, the Yahoo.com auction site still offers certain items for sale (such as stamps, coins, and a copy of *Mein Kampf*) which appear to violate the French Order. . . .

Yahoo! claims that because it lacks the technology to block French citizens from accessing the Yahoo.com auction site to view materials which violate the French order or from accessing other Nazi-based content of Web sites on Yahoo.com, it cannot comply with the French order without banning Nazi-related material from Yahoo.com altogether. Yahoo! contends that such a ban would infringe impermissibly upon its rights under the First Amendment to the United States Constitution. Accordingly, Yahoo! filed a complaint in this Court seeking a declaratory judgment that the French Court's orders are neither cognizable nor enforceable under the laws of the United States.

Defendants immediately moved to dismiss on the basis that this Court lacks personal jurisdiction over them. That motion was denied. . . .

II. OVERVIEW

As this Court and others have observed, the instant case presents novel and important issues arising from the global reach of the Internet. Indeed, the specific facts of this case implicate issues of policy, politics, and culture that are beyond the purview of one nation's judiciary. Thus it is critical that the Court define at the outset what is and is not at stake in the present proceeding.

This case is *not* about the moral acceptability of promoting the symbols or propaganda of Nazism. Most would agree that such acts are profoundly offensive. By any reasonable standard of morality, the Nazis were responsible for one of the worst displays of inhumanity in recorded history. . . .

Nor is this case about the right of France or any other nation to determine its own law and social policies. A basic function of a sovereign state is to determine by law what forms of speech and conduct are acceptable within its borders. . . .

What *is* at issue here is whether it is consistent with the Constitution and laws of the United States for another nation to regulate speech by a United States resident within the United States on the basis that such speech can be accessed by Internet users in that nation. In a world in which ideas and information transcend borders and the Internet in particular renders the physical distance between speaker and audience virtually meaningless, the implications of this question go far beyond the facts of this case. The modern world is home to widely varied cultures with radically divergent value systems. There is little doubt that Internet users in the United States routinely engage in speech that violates, for example, China's laws against religious expression, the laws of various nations against advocacy of gender equality or homosexuality, or even the United Kingdom's restrictions on freedom of the press.

*   *   *   *   *

The French order prohibits the sale or display of items based on their association with a particular political organization and bans the display of Web sites based on the authors'

viewpoint with respect to the Holocaust and anti-Semitism. A United States court constitutionally could not make such an order. The First Amendment does not permit the government to engage in viewpoint-based regulation of speech absent a compelling governmental interest, such as averting a clear and present danger of imminent violence.

*   *   *   *   *

Comity

No legal judgment has any effect, of its own force, beyond the limits of the sovereignty from which its authority is derived. . . . The extent to which the United States, or any state, honors the judicial decrees of foreign nations is a matter of choice, governed by "the comity of nations." United States courts generally recognize foreign judgments and decrees unless enforcement would be prejudicial or contrary to the country's interests.

As discussed previously, the French order's content and viewpoint-based regulation of the Web pages and auction site on Yahoo.com, while entitled to great deference as an articulation of French law, clearly would be inconsistent with the First Amendment if mandated by a court in the United States. . . . The reason for limiting comity in this area is sound. "The protection to free speech and the press embodied in [the First] amendment would be seriously jeopardized by the entry of foreign judgments granted pursuant to standards deemed appropriate in [another country] but considered antithetical to the protections afforded the press by the U.S. Constitution." *Bachchan,* 585 N.Y.S.2d at 665. Absent a body of law that establishes international standards with respect to speech on the Internet and an appropriate treaty or legislation addressing enforcement of such standards to speech originating within the United States, the principle of comity is outweighed by the Court's obligation to uphold the First Amendment.

*   *   *   *   *

CONCLUSION

Yahoo! seeks a declaration from this Court that the First Amendment precludes enforcement within the United States of a French order intended to regulate the content of its speech over the Internet. . . . Accordingly, the motion for summary judgment will be granted.

AFTERWORD

This story has not yet ended. On August 23, 2004, a panel of judges from the Ninth Circuit ruled that the district court had no personal jurisdiction over LICRA and that it should have refused to hear Yahoo!'s First Amendment argument. Instead, the Ninth Circuit held that "[j]urisdiction may be obtained, and the First Amendment claim heard, once LICRA . . . ask[s] a U.S.

district court to enforce the French judgment."[18] Still not the last word: On February 10, 2005, the Ninth Circuit agreed to rehear the case *en banc* and, in the meantime, the three-judge panel decision may not be cited as precedent.[19]

Questions

1. As relayed by the district court, we do not know why the French court believed it had jurisdiction to adjudicate against Yahoo!, as opposed to Yahoo! France. Look back at the discussion of the Restatement (Third) of Foreign Relations Law of the United States immediately before this case. Why do you think the French court had jurisdiction over Yahoo! France? Yahoo!, Inc.?

2. If you were sitting on the court of appeals for the rehearing, how would you decide the jurisdiction question? Consider both the U.S. rule of minimum contacts and the restatement provision.

Part Two—Constitutional Law: Speech and Privacy

Speech

The district court opinion in *Yahoo! v. La Ligue Contre Le Racisme Et L'antisemitisme* illustrates some of the free speech issues the Internet raises. In addition to international disputes, Internet content has also raised free speech issues here at home. The Internet's anonymity, ease of use, relatively low costs, and global reach make it a natural vehicle for transporting speech messages. As we saw in Chapter 5, the First Amendment protects us from government restraints on the *content* of speech, although reasonable restraints on the context (time, place, and manner) of that speech are sometimes constitutionally permissible. Thus a court will not restrain free speech by enjoining someone from posting defamatory or copyrighted material, but the damaged parties may, of course, sue for defamation or copyright infringement after the fact.[20] [For many articles on cyberlaw free speech, search for "free speech" at **www.jcil.org/journal/search**]

Obviously, the Internet is a vast, largely unorganized, largely unpoliced competition of messages. Sometimes those messages step across legal bounds. In 2002 the Ninth Circuit Federal Court of Appeals upheld a jury verdict that an antiabortion Web site labeled "The Nuremberg Files" was devoted to unlawful threats of violence, including murder.[21] The site published detailed information on "Wanted Posters" about doctors who provide abortions, including their photos, their addresses, and names of their children. Then a doctor's name was chillingly crossed off when he was killed.

> An antiabortion Web site labeled "The Nuremberg Files" was devoted to unlawful threats of violence, including murder.

One of the most troublesome issues for free speech and the Internet is how or whether children can be protected from content that is inappropriate, while that content is nevertheless protected by the First Amendment with regard to access by adults. According to one study, nearly 20 percent of children who regularly use the Internet have received unwanted sexual solicitations online.[22] A sixth-grader, experiencing such tactics, "was worried about stumbling onto inappropriate sites on the Net when she uses it for schoolwork. 'Maybe instead of having dot-com, they should put a dot-x or something, so we wouldn't accidentally get there,' she suggested."[23]

The Supreme Court has now had the opportunity to rule on this issue in a number of contexts, the first of which was decided in 1997.[24] In this case the Court held that certain provisions of the Communications Decency Act of 1996 (CDA) were overbroad and therefore violated the First Amendment. Specifically, the Court found that "in order to deny minors access to potentially harmful speech, the CDA effectively suppresses a large amount of speech that adults have a constitutional right to receive."[25] In response, Congress passed the Child Online Protection Act (COPA), seeking to criminalize online content that is "harmful to minors" based on "contemporary community standards." In early 1999, in a lawsuit begun by the American Civil Liberties Union (ACLU), the district court imposed a temporary injunction barring the government from enforcing COPA until its constitutionality could be resolved.[26] On an appeal contesting the granting of the injunction, the Supreme Court in 2002 held in an 8–1 decision that reference to "contemporary community standards" did not make the standard unconstitutional and remanded the case to the Third Circuit.[27] Once again the Third Circuit upheld the granting of the injunction, this time finding that COPA was not narrowly tailored to serve a compelling government interest, nor was it the least restrictive means available to achieve its objective.[28] Then in 2004 the Supreme Court, in a 5–4 decision, approved the continuation of the temporary injunction and remanded the case for a trial on the merits.[29] Presumably, evidence at trial will focus on whether Congress could have chosen an alternative path that would both protect children from unsuitable content online and, at the same time, impose less on the right of free speech. [For a look at Federal Trade Commission regulations under COPA, see **www.ftc.gov/coppa/intro.htm**]

In yet another decision, the Court found the 1996 Child Pornography Prevention Act (CPPA) unconstitutional.[30] The CPPA prohibited not just actual child pornography, but also material that depicts persons who "appear to be minors" (although in fact they may just be computer-generated images) or that is advertised so it "conveys the impression" that the person depicted is a minor. In finding the statute unconstitutional, the Court reasoned in part that the government had failed to show a causal link between computer-generated images of child porn and harm to actual children.[31]

Commercial Speech

You will remember from Chapter 5 that commercial speech has been accorded reduced First Amendment protection. Thus online advertising is subject to the same kinds of government oversight as that in print and on television. One form of online commercial message receiving special attention is so-called spam (mass e-mailings). This electronic form of junk mail may be a legitimate form of commercial message at times, but it may also be an annoyance, a threat to the efficiency of the Internet because of its volume, or deceptive; or it may contain objectionable content (obscenity, viruses).

The federal CAN-SPAM Act of 2003 became effective on January 1, 2004. By the time of its passage, at least 37 states had passed antispam statutes to address some of the abuses just mentioned. The passage of the federal act has most likely preempted these state statutes,[32] although prior to the CAN-SPAM Act, at least two of the state acts had been found constitutional.[33] The federal act establishes both civil and criminal penalties for violations of its provisions, which (among other things) prohibit false or misleading header and subject line information on e-mail, require that recipients be given a method to opt out of receipt of future e-mail, mandate that commercial e-mail be clearly labeled as advertisements, and specify that a valid "snail mail" address for the sender be identified. The Federal Trade Commission (FTC) is charged with enforcing the act and brought its first criminal actions under the act in April 2004.[34] [For more information on the CAN-SPAM Act and the FTC's enforcement, see **www.ftc.gov/spam**. To report spam to the FTC, either forward it by email to spam@uce.gov or fill in an online complaint form by clicking on the "File a Complaint Online" navigator bar found at **www.ftc.gov**]

Privacy

Americans cherish the right to privacy, but the Internet opens up previously uncontemplated possibilities for intrusion. Some of the information now available online has in fact been public for decades, but most people were not aware that it was public, did not know how to obtain it, or simply never bothered. For example, local governments keep property, tax, and court records on file, all of which are open to the public, generally through visits to the local courthouse. Now, however, local governments are making this data available online, so that anyone who is simply curious can explore it.[35] Similarly, licensing bodies now often have online membership lists and sometimes also information on complaints filed and disciplinary actions taken.

But other information that may now be collected on individuals is unique to the phenomenon of the Internet. For example, one Web company, Predictive Networks, has developed software "that can track every site a Web surfer visits and build a 'digital silhouette'" of the surfer.[36] The company believes that individuals will agree to this tracking in exchange for free or reduced costs from their Internet service provider. Others, however, are concerned that less affluent citizens will be particularly vulnerable to this privacy invasion because the reduced price of the services will be a more substantial factor for them.[37]

> Software "that can track every site a Web surfer visits and build a 'digital silhouette'" of the surfer

---

Privacy in Europe

The European Union has taken quite a different tack from America's market-driven approach to online privacy. The EU's 1998 Data Protection Directive basically allows individuals to decide how their collected data can be used. Thus, if a European consumer provides personal information such as an address when buying from an online store, that store cannot legally send an ad to the purchaser without first seeking permission.[38] The directive also prohibits the transfer of data to countries outside the European Union that do not have "adequate" privacy rules.[39] The United States was one of the nations deemed inadequate, but by mid-2000 European and U.S. negotiators had reached an agreement providing U.S. companies with three voluntary safe-harbor options to choose among that, if implemented, will shield them from prosecution by EU governments under the Data Protection Directive.[40]

Privacy concerns have also been raised in the context of the Patriot Act, which was passed in the wake of the events of September 11, 2001, to strengthen the government's ability to deal with terrorism threats.[41] Many of the act's provisions actually modified preexisting laws to strengthen the government's investigatory powers. Although objections have been voiced with respect to the act, keep in mind that many parts of the law are generally viewed as reasonable law enforcement provisions.[42] Some of the provisions impacting the Internet and electronic communications include (1) extending the government's power to intercept electronic communications to include investigations of computer fraud, (2) increasing the government's "roving wiretap" powers (which may make it easier to "impact the privacy rights" of innocent users who access the Internet through public facilities), and (3) facilitating the capture of information about the sender and recipient of e-mail or other electronic communication.[43] The act also modified a provision of the Electronic Communications Privacy Act of 1986 to provide a much broader reach of the government's power to issue National Security Letters (NSLs). In essence, an NSL is an administrative subpoena issuable without any review by a court as to its reasonableness or probable cause. The ACLU brought suit on behalf of an unidentified Internet service provider (ISP), which had been presented with such a letter by the FBI ordering it to turn over certain of its subscribers' records. The law provides, and the letter stated, that neither the ISP "[n]or officer, employee, or agent thereof, shall disclose to any person" that the FBI "sought or obtained access to information or records under this section." On September 28, 2004, a federal district court found the provision unconstitutional as applied because it authorizes searches "effectively immune from any judicial process, in violation of the Fourth Amendment." It further found that this lack of judicial process, and the perpetual nature of the nondisclosure provision, could operate to violate First Amendment rights of subscribers and ISPs.[44] The government is expected to appeal.

Sixteen provisions of the Patriot Act are set to automatically expire as of December 31, 2005, unless Congress acts to extend them.[45] In that context, as of this writing, Congress is reviewing these and other Patriot Act provisions to evaluate their effectiveness and determine in each case whether expiration, amendment, or continuation is most appropriate.[46]

Another area of particular concern is the privacy of our children online. In 1998 Congress passed the Children's Online Privacy Protection Act (COPPA), which prohibits Web sites from collecting personal information from children under 13 without parental permission and requires that parents be allowed to review and correct any information collected about their children. The FTC is charged with primary enforcement responsibility for COPPA. [To take a look at the complaints, and other information, in the cases brought by the FTC under COPPA, go to **www.ftc.gov/privacy/privacyinitiatives/childrens_enf.html**]

> COPPA prohibits Web sites from collecting personal information from children under 13 without parental permission.

Yet another area drawing the interest of the public is how much employers may be allowed to access e-mail sent from or received on office computers and files stored on those computers. "In a recent survey of 840 U.S. companies by the American Management Association, 60 percent said they now use some type of software to monitor their employees' incoming and outgoing e-mail, up from 47 percent in 2001."[47] Today's software can be customized to look for such things as company officers' and competitors' names, as well as inappropriate language. Software is also available that can "track every keystroke, file download, and Internet page that appears on an employee's computer screen."[48] In part, companies may adopt some of these strategies to protect themselves from lawsuits. For example, Continental Airlines was sued for defamation and workplace harassment based on derogatory and insulting remarks posted about one employee by other coworkers on Continental's electronic bulletin board.[49] Employers wishing to implement such monitoring programs should, however, advise their employees of that fact and have all employees sign an acknowledgment so there is no question about whether an employee has any expectation of privacy on company systems.

Question

Explain why employers might want to monitor their employees' computer activities.

Freedom of Speech and the Right to Anonymity

One unique characteristic of the Internet and electronic communication through the Internet is the sender's or poster's ability to be and remain anonymous. Anonymity, of course, makes it more likely that individuals will feel free to say things about which they would otherwise keep silent. This may be a positive aspect, where the anonymous speech is truthful. But anonymity may also make individuals bolder about asserting untruths—misleading, fraudulent, or otherwise unprotected speech. So we find ever more numerous situations where one side argues to preserve its anonymity, while the other side argues that abuse of anonymity gives the right to remove the speaker's anonymity. A user's Internet service provider (ISP) has the ability to reveal the identity of the sender or poster, based on information provided by the user when contracting for service from the ISP.

In the case that follows, a Yahoo! poster asserts the First Amendment to prevent Yahoo! from responding to a subpoena from Immunomedics, a corporation claiming the anonymous poster is or was an employee who violated the company's confidentiality agreement by posting company information on a Yahoo! message board.

LEGAL BRIEFCASE

Immunomedics v. Jean Doe
775 A. 2d 773 (N.J. Super. 2001)

Judge Fall

Defendant Jean Doe, a/k/a "moonshine_fr," appeals from an order entered on December 20, 2000, denying her motion to quash a subpoena issued to Yahoo! by plaintiff, Immunomedics, Inc., seeking all personally identifiable information relating to the person or identity who posted messages on the Yahoo! Finance Message Board under the identifier "moonshine_fr" which may identify or lead to the identification of that person or entity.

Immunomedics is a publicly held biopharmaceutical Delaware corporation, with its principal place of business located at 300 American Road in Morris Plains, New Jersey. Immunomedics is focused on the development, manufacture, and commercialization of diagnostic imaging and therapeutic products for the detection and treatment of cancer and infectious diseases.

Yahoo! is an Internet Service Provider (ISP) that maintains a Web site that includes a section called Yahoo! Finance. Yahoo! Finance maintains a message board for every publicly trated company, including Immunomedics. Visitors to the Immunomedics site can obtain up-to-date information on the company, and can post and exchange messages about issues related to the operation or performance of the company.

On October 12, 2000, Immunomedics filed a complaint against Jean Doe, also known by the computer screen name "moonshine_fr" ("Moonshine"). The complaint alleged that Moonshine had "posted a message on Yahoo! Finance." Immunomedics claimed that message contained information confidential and proprietary to Immunomedics. As a result, Immunomedics asserted it had sustained injury and that Moonshine should be held liable under theories of breach of contract, breach of duty of loyalty, and negligently revealing confidential and proprietary information.

* * * * *

Of the two messages in question, the first, with Moonshine describing herself as "[a] worried employee," stated that Immunomedics was "out of stock for diagnostic products in Europe" and claimed that there would be "no more sales if [the] situation [did] not change." The second message, allegedly posted by Moonshine after the initial complaint was filed, reported that Chairman of the Company Dr. Goldenberg was going to fire the Immunomedics "european manager." In her certification to the trial court, Immunomedics' Executive Vice President and Chief Operations Officer Cynthia L. Sullivan admitted that the statements were true, but that, as an employee, Moonshine had violated the company's confidentiality agreement and "several provisions" of the company's Employee Handbook.

On or about October 20, 2000, Immunomedics served a subpoena on Yahoo!, seeking discovery of Moonshine's true identity. Yahoo!, in turn, contacted Moonshine. In response, Moonshine filed a motion to quash the subpoena on or about November 15, 2000.

The motion to quash was argued before Judge Zucker-Zarett on December 15, 2000. After considering the arguments, the judge denied Moonshine's motion, stating, in pertinent part,

> We have two issues here. We have an issue, she's an employee, she signed a confidential document saying that she was not going to speak freely about information she learned at the company. So she contracted away her right of free speech if she's an employee. Number two, free speech, anonymous, but if it harms another individual, that is another way that we have a little bit of a dent in our rights for free speech.

* * * * *

Moonshine contends the motion judge erred in denying her motion to quash the subpoena, as anonymous speech is constitutionally protected and Immunomedics' complaint is insufficient to warrant a breach of that anonymity. Immunomedics argues that, while anonymous speech is constitutionally protected, that protection can be overcome if a defendant uses that freedom in an unlawful manner. . . .

In *Dendrite International, Inc. v. John Doe No. 3* (2001), another case involving an application for expedited discovery to disclose the identity of an anonymous user of an ISP message board, we concluded that courts must decide such applications by striking a balance between the First Amendment right of an individual to speak anonymously and the right of a company to protect its proprietary interest in the pursuit of claims based on actionable conduct by the ISP message board user.

* * * * *

We hold that when such an application is made, the trial court should first require the plaintiff to undertake efforts to notify the anonymous posters that they are the subject of a subpoena or application for an order of disclosure, and withhold action to afford the fictitiously named defendants a reasonable opportunity to file and serve opposition to the application. These notification efforts should include posting a message of notification of the identity discovery request to the anonymous user on the ISP's pertinent message board.

The court shall also require the plaintiff to identify and set forth the exact statements purportedly made by each anonymous poster that plaintiff alleges constitute actionable speech.

The complaint and all information provided to the court should be carefully reviewed to determine whether plaintiff has set forth a prima facie cause of action against the fictitiously named anonymous defendants. In addition to establishing that its action can withstand a motion to dismiss for failure to state a claim upon which relief can be granted, the plaintiff must produce sufficient evidence supporting each element of its cause of action, on a prima facie basis, prior to a court ordering the disclosure of the identity of the unnamed defendant.

Finally, assuming the court concludes that the plaintiff has presented a prima facie cause of action, the court must balance the defendant's First Amendment right of anonymous free speech against the strength of the prima facie case presented and the necessity for the disclosure of the anonymous defendant's identity to allow the plaintiff to properly proceed.

The application of these procedures and standards must be undertaken and analyzed on a case-by-case basis. The guiding principle is a result based on a meaningful analysis and a proper balancing of the equities and rights at issue.

. . . Here, Immunomedics' cause of action is based on Moonshine's status as an employee and her alleged violation of a confidentiality agreement, and Moonshine's alleged breach of her common law duty of loyalty. . . .

Applying the procedure and test outlined in *Dendrite,* we conclude Judge Zucker-Zarett properly analyzed the disclosure issue, and we affirm substantially for the reasons articulated by the judge in her oral opinion delivered on December 15, 2000. We add the following. Immunomedics presented sufficient evidence that Moonshine is, or was, an employee of Immunomedics. Ms. Sullivan indicated in her certification that "all employees are bound by several Company policies and a confidentiality agreement." Within its "Confidentiality and Assignment Agreement," Immunomedics includes the following language:

> This Agreement and any disputes arising under or in connection with it shall be governed by the laws of the State of New Jersey and each of the parties hereto hereby submits to the jurisdiction of any Federal or state court sitting in the State of New Jersey over any such dispute.

Accordingly, Immunomedics clearly established a prima facie cause of action for breach of the confidentiality agreement founded on the content of Moonshine's posted messages.

In balancing Moonshine's right of anonymous free speech against the strength of the prima facie case presented and the necessity for disclosure, it is clear that the motion judge struck the proper balance in favor of identity disclosure. With evidence demonstrating Moonshine is an employee of Immunomedics, that employees execute confidentiality agreements, and the content of Moonshine's posted messages providing evidence of the breach thereof, the disclosure of Moonshine's identity, which can be reasonably calculated to be achieved by information obtained from the subpoena, was fully warranted. Although anonymous speech on the Internet is protected, there must be an avenue for redress for those who are wronged. Individuals choosing to harm another or violate an agreement through speech on the Internet cannot hope to shield their identity and avoid punishment through invocation of the First Amendment.

* * * * *

Affirmed.

Questions

1. In your opinion, should employers, police, and others who have been damaged by anonymous postings be able to obtain the identity of the poster from the hosting site or the poster's ISP? Explain.

2. An FBI agent monitored an AOL chat room suspected of being a site for exchanging child pornography. The agent did not participate in the chat room conversations. Charbonneau allegedly distributed child pornography to the chat room participants, including the FBI agent. Charbonneau was arrested.

   a. Did Charbonneau have a First Amendment free speech right to transmit child pornography online?

   b. Does the Fourth Amendment's prohibition on unreasonable searches and seizures protect the statements made in the AOL chat room? Explain. See *United States of America v. Kenneth Charbonneau,* 979 F.Supp. 1177 (S.D.Ohio, 1997).

Part Three—Crime

Crimes facilitated by the Internet include both truly new types and some old, familiar crimes in somewhat new clothing. Some of the laws already discussed in this chapter provide criminal penalties for violations of their provisions, most notably the CAN-SPAM Act, the Child Online Protection Act, and the Child Pornography Prevention Act. (But recall that enforcement of the Child Online Protection Act has been stayed pending final outcome of the suit brought by the ACLU on its constitutionality.) Other laws criminalizing specific online behavior exist as well, such as the Computer Pornography and Child Exploitation Prevention Act of 1999, which makes it unlawful to use a computer to solicit, lure, or entice a child or otherwise engage in sexual offenses with a child. But many of our long-standing, pre-Internet criminal laws can be applied to both online and offline behavior. A selection of crimes with an electronic twist will be discussed shortly.

On the international front, the Council of Europe has drafted the Convention on Cybercrime, which 38 member states and several nonmember states, including the United States, have signed, although only 10 countries have ratified it.[50] For those states, the convention went into force July 1, 2004, and requires "the criminalization of a long list of computer activities—everything from breaking into a computer to the 'deterioration' of computer data. . . . It also requires countries to make sure they can snoop through Internet data in real time. And it obliges nations to assist each other's investigations by monitoring Net communications."[51]

Computer Security   Cyberattacks on computer systems continue unabated. For a number of years, Carnegie Mellon's Software Engineering Institute, in conjunction with the U.S. Secret Service and *CSO Magazine,* has administered a survey of security and law enforcement executives to track the volume and cost of electronic crimes and system intrusions. The good news in the 2005 E-Crime Watch survey: Only 35 percent of respondents reported an increase in incidents, compared to 43 percent the prior year. On the other hand, only 13 percent of respondents reported a decrease in incidents. More good news: It seems the cost of responding has significantly decreased—estimated by respondents to be $666 million in the 2004 survey, but only $150 million in the 2005 survey. The top five crimes were viruses, spyware, phishing, illegal generation of spam, and unauthorized access, in that order.[52] [For the full 2005 E-Crime Watch report, see **www.csoonline.com/info/ecrimesurvey05.pdf**]

Fraud   With e-commerce thriving, we know that e-fraud cannot be far behind. According to the Internet Fraud Watch, online auctions result in the highest number of reported incidents of online fraud—51 percent in 2004. Nondelivery of general merchandise was the next highest reported category at 20 percent. In third place, with 8 percent of the total, were Nigerian money offers. The highest percentage of offending companies (26 percent) came from outside the United States and Canada; the largest numbers of victims were located in Alaska and Hawaii. The Internet Fraud Watch collects its statistics based on complaints reported to it, either online [see **www.fraud.org**] or by phone. It then forwards the complaints to federal, state, and local law enforcement agencies, including a database maintained by the FTC. [International fraud events can also be reported at **www.econsumer.gov**]

Phishing has become big business.   Phishing has become big business—estimated to have cost U.S. banks and credit card companies $1.2 billion in 2003. "In a phishing attack, scammers send e-mails that purport to be from a bank . . . directing customers to a site where they are asked to enter vital information, such as passwords, bank account numbers, or credit card details. The scams are so effective because the bogus e-mails and Web sites look so legitimate." It is also a global phenomenon, having affected banks in Australia, Germany, Malaysia, New Zealand, Spain, and the United Kingdom, as well as the United States.[53]

Online securities fraud has also been in the news, although perhaps not as much recently as in the late 1990s when the stock market was booming. One type is an online version of a classic "pump and dump" scheme—when someone holding a stock artificially drives its share price up by floating exaggerated or false reports of its value through Web sites, online postings, or e-mail. When the stock price jumps, the promoter sells shares at the inflated price. One of the most notorious examples was reported in 2000 when the SEC accused a 15-year old from New Jersey of stock manipulation, issued a cease and desist order, and required him to turn over his profit, plus interest—a tidy $285,000.[54]

Cyberstalking In a recent Illinois case, a former electronics store employee was sentenced to four years in prison for sending lewd photos and threatening e-mail and phone messages to a 22-year-old woman who had brought her computer in for repair.[55] This is

> Cyberstalking—the repeated use of electronic media (such as e-mail or chat rooms) to harass or threaten another person.

just one example of cyberstalking—the repeated use of electronic media (such as e-mail or chat rooms) to harass or threaten another person. It has been publicly recognized as a problem at least since 1999, when the U.S. Attorney General prepared a formal report on the growing problem.[56] Every state has laws criminalizing traditional physical stalking, although the first such law was passed only in 1990. Most of these laws require that the perpetrator make a credible threat of violence for the action to be a violation; many do not expressly include cyberstalking, although under appropriate facts it might be covered.

International Crimes Apparently one country's crime is often another country's business opportunity. Every country criminalizes certain behaviors in support of its moral attitudes and historical experiences. Some proscribed behaviors such as murder, seem fairly universal. But other behaviors are acceptable in some countries while criminalized in others. Where such crimes are facilitated by the Internet, international disputes over the appropriate reach of such laws have arisen. We have already seen one example in the *Yahoo v. La Ligue Contre Le Racisme Et L'Antisemitisme* in Part One of this chapter, where France sought to enforce its ban on the sale of Nazi memorabilia to French citizens. Both the United Kingdom and Germany have criminal laws that they have enforced based on pornographic materials posted on Web sites outside their geographic boundaries. The United Kingdom convicted a U.K. citizen operating out of his home in the United Kingdom for "publication" of pornographic materials on Web sites located in the United States. Germany convicted the German head of CompuServe for allowing German citizens access to pornographic Web sites hosted outside Germany, despite the fact that he had no technological way to block access. (Blocking access required the U.S. corporation to block access to all its customers worldwide.)[57]

PRACTICING ETHICS

Internet Gambling Bans—Necessary to Protect Public Morals or Discrimination against Foreign Gambling Operations?

The U.S. government has long held the position that Internet gambling is illegal in the United States. It has pressured U.S. businesses not to open Internet gambling sites and U.S. credit card companies not to permit charges from foreign gambling operations. On the other hand, commentators have pointed out that the government "hasn't shown the will to bust individual bettors. So the United States gets no economic benefit from online gambling yet is still saddled with the potential social cost—a growing venue for problem gamblers to feed their addiction."[58] "[O]ffshore gaming companies usually cite the United States as their biggest customer. . . . [O]f almost 12 million Internet gamblers worldwide, about 4.5 million were from the United States."[59]

In 2003 the Caribbean nation of Antigua and Barbuda filed a dispute with the WTO arguing that "if bricks-and-mortar casinos can operate in the United States, it would be illegal to stop Internet casinos from providing essentially the same service."[60] Antigua is a country "with no natural resources and a population of only about 68,000, [which] built up its Internet gambling industry to supple-

ment its tourism-driven economy."[61] That industry now generates close to $68 million. The final decision of the WTO, issued in April 2005, gave something to both parties. It ruled that some U.S. laws violated WTO trade agreements, but that others were appropriate to "protect public morals or maintain public order."[62]

Questions

What ethical arguments can you identify to allow Antigua to actively market its online gambling to U.S. citizens? What ethical arguments support the position of the U.S. government against permitting its residents to participate in gambling online?

Part Four—Commercial Law

Contracts and Uniform Laws

Internet sales have grown significantly, but for the Internet to reach its commercial potential a routine, well-settled contracts structure is essential. The basic ingredients of a binding contract, as we saw in Chapter 6, also apply to Internet transactions.

- *Capacity* to enter the contract.
- *Offer and acceptance* of the terms of the contract.
- *Consideration* for the promises in the contract.
- *Genuineness* of assent.
- *Legality* of purpose of the contract.

Thus an exchange of e-mail meeting the traditional contract requirements should result in an enforceable agreement. But what about acceptance by providing an "electronic signature" (a digital code unique to an individual), downloading some information, or opening a shrink-wrap package?

E-Signature   Electronic signatures can take a variety of forms (voice prints, distinctive marks, mathematical codes), but the key is that they are electronic symbols, sounds, or processes intended to have the same effect as a signature affixed by hand. Electronic signatures obviously will be central to trust and efficiency in online contracting. On June 30, 2000, President Clinton signed into law the Electronic Signatures in Global and National Commerce Act (E-SIGN), giving electronic signatures the same legal stature as handwritten ones, at least for most commercial purposes.[63] Consumers, however, cannot be forced to accept electronic signature agreements or to receive records and documents electronically instead of in paper form [For a look at the digital signature laws of the United

Nations, European Union, and United Kingdom, see **http://law.richmond.edu/jolt/ v11i2/article6.pdf**]

UCITA   In 1999 the National Conference of Commissioners on Uniform State Laws (NCCUSL) approved a model law designed to achieve uniformity across the United States in the law governing software and Internet transactions. The proposed law reaches all deals involving computer information or goods and is designed to address the special problems of the electronic market, including software licensure (right to use). The Uniform Computer Information Transactions Act (UCITA) addresses the substance of computer information transactions, rather than procedural aspects such as electronic signatures.

To this point, UCITA has been amended twice (2000 and 2002), but has not been well received, having been adopted in only Maryland and Virginia.[64] Until it or some other such legislation is widely approved, the Uniform Commercial Code, other applicable state and federal laws, and the common law of contracts (judge-made law) will govern electronic contractual arrangements. (The UCC, having been approved in 49 of the 50 states, is designed to provide nationwide consistency, predictability, and fairness in contract law where a sale of goods is involved.)

Shrink-Wrap Agreements   Software typically arrives in a package with license terms printed on the outside, on a document inside the package, or onscreen during the installation. Those terms often say that in opening the shrink-wrap package or using the software the buyer agrees to the terms. Whether those terms are enforceable is the subject of dispute in the courts. The likelihood is that many shrink-wrap terms will be enforceable if the buyer has a reasonable opportunity to review those terms, is clearly told how to accept the terms, and does so voluntarily. The same is probably true of *click-wrap* agreements, where one agrees to contract terms by clicking a box on a Web page. The court in *Caspi v. Microsoft Network,* 732 A.2d 528 (N.J. Super. 1999), applying a traditional contract law analysis, held the choice of forum provision in an online click-wrap agreement to be enforceable.

In the article that follows, one commentator illustrates how overreaching these terms can be.

Megalomania   How Much Does Microsoft Have the Right to Control?

READING

E. J. Heresniak

* * * * *

I have a driver's license, which warrants that I have the basic knowledge and skill to maintain my right to maneuver a ton and a half of metal and plastic at high speeds in traffic while drinking coffee and talking on the phone. . . . Having a license usually indicates you have permission to do something based on demonstrated ability or under terms you find acceptable. Those licenses I understand.

When you buy a computer program—any computer program—you don't own the program in the sense that you can do whatever you want with it. You buy a paid-up license. Nobody expects you to give the program back at the end of a term, but by retaining ownership, the maker of the software is afforded a bit of legal protection from thievery. Common sense would lead you to expect limitations in the license to prevent stealing ideas or copying the programs and handing them out on the street. But Microsoft has taken it a step further.

Microsoft's End User License Agreement, or EULA, is the fine print on Microsoft products. When you install a Microsoft program on your computer, the EULA is the thing you skip over and check "I agree" before you can continue with the installation of the program you bought or downloaded from the Web. If you check "no," that you do not agree with something in the EULA, installation stops. This is not an agreement that you reach after negotiating. The EULA is a one-way deal, and it can be dangerous and overreaching.

Here's some interesting language from the EULA for Front-Page, Microsoft's easy-to-use Web-design software package: "You may not use the Software in connection with any site that disparages Microsoft, MSN, MSNBC, Expedia, or their products or services, infringe any intellectual property or other rights of these parties, violate any state, federal, or international law, or promote racism, hatred, or pornography."

What constitutes pornography and other socially obnoxious behavior is often in the eye of the beholder. Last August, the U.S. Postal Service shut down a child-pornography ring operating a Web site in Texas. Apparently the federal government ran the site for a while in a sting operation, where they collected credit card numbers and traced them to the home addresses of people whom they then arrested for possession of bad stuff.

If the offending Texas Web site were produced with the Microsoft product FrontPage, the Microsoft license police could have shut down the site—after all, it violated the terms of their software license. So if Postal Service inspectors or the FBI ever get distracted, help is on the way. Once Microsoft gets finished innovating every conceivable computer function into Windows, we will be rid of any issues of questionable content, because licensing can giveth and licensing can taketh away.

* * * * *

I do, in fact, use FrontPage to develop my Web site. Microsoft has special deals with Internet service providers so you can get cheap rates for hosting your site with easy and automatic ways to make changes. If I decided to post this column on my Web site, I could get in trouble—not because my editors claim all the rights to the column, but because Microsoft lawyers say you can't use their Web page software for anything they might find disparaging to Microsoft or, surprisingly, to the travel site Expedia, to the cable TV network, or to MSNBC. I'm not kidding. Interestingly, after four weeks of inquiries, Microsoft public relations people hadn't figured out quite what to say about their practice—and if they've had occasion to enforce it.

* * * * *

But now it seems that computer software leasing agreements go beyond protecting intellectual property and stopping thieves. They aim to control behavior a little beyond what would be common sense.

Putting a critic in the same club as lawbreakers, copyright infringers, racists, and pornographers is stupid. Apparently, whether my Web site stays or goes depends on the meaning of the word *disparage*. Well, I think the Microsoft crowd are a bunch of monopolists who want to control the world, and plan to keep stuffing everything anyone does with a computer into an operating system that only they control. Was that disparaging?

Source: *Across the Board*, Nov/Dec 2001, p. 83.

Questions

1. Do you think Microsoft should be able to tell the licensees of its software that the software cannot be used to "disparage" Microsoft? What about its attempt to prevent its products from being used to "promote racism, hatred, or pornography"?

2. If Microsoft brought a lawsuit against one of its licensees for in fact using one of its products to "disparage" Microsoft, or to "promote racism, hatred, or pornography," what do you think the outcome would be?

Intellectual Property

Continuing expansion of electronic commerce depends to a significant extent on the business community's success in protecting its technology from theft, copying, infringement, and the like. Intellectual property, broadly, is composed of creative ideas that are the products of the human mind. Songs, computer programs, new medicines, a novel, and so on are forms of intellectual property. Recalling our discussion of market failure in

Grokster's software employs what is known as FastTrack technology. . . . StreamCast distributes a very similar product except that its software, called Morpheus, relies on what is known as Gnutella technology. A user who downloads and installs either software possesses the protocol to send requests for files directly to the computers of others using software compatible with FastTrack or Gnutella.

*　　*　　*　　*　　*

Although Grokster and StreamCast do not know when particular files are copied, a few searches using their software would show what is available on the networks the software reaches. MGM commissioned a statistician to conduct a systematic search, and his study showed that nearly 90 percent of the files available for download on the FastTrack system were copyrighted works. Grokster and StreamCast dispute this figure. . . . They also argue that potential noninfringing uses of their software are significant in kind, even if infrequent in practice. Some musical performers, for example, have gained new audiences by distributing their copyrighted works for free across peer-to-peer networks, and some distributors of unprotected content have used peer-to-peer networks to disseminate files, Shakespeare being an example. . . .

But MGM's evidence gives reason to think that the vast majority of users' downloads are acts of infringement, and because well over 100 million copies of the software in question are known to have been downloaded, and billions of files are shared across the FastTrack and Gnutella networks each month, the probable scope of copyright infringement is staggering.

Grokster and StreamCast concede the infringement in most downloads, and it is uncontested that they are aware that users employ their software primarily to download copyrighted files, even if the decentralized FastTrack and Gnutella networks fail to reveal which files are being copied, and when. . . .

Grokster and StreamCast are not, however, merely passive recipients of information about infringing use. The record is replete with evidence that from the moment Grokster and StreamCast began to distribute their free software, each one clearly voiced the objective that recipients use it to download copyrighted works, and each took active steps to encourage infringement.

After the notorious file-sharing service, Napster, was sued by copyright holders for facilitation of copyright infringement, StreamCast gave away a software program of a kind known as OpenNap, designed as compatible with the Napster program and open to Napster users for downloading files from other Napster and OpenNap users' computers. Evidence indicates

that "it was always [StreamCast's] intent to use [its OpenNap network] to be able to capture e-mail addresses of [its] initial target market so that [it] could promote [its] StreamCast Morpheus interface to them." . . .

*　　*　　*　　*　　*

StreamCast developed promotional materials to market its service as the best Napster alternative. One proposed advertisement read, "Napster Inc. has announced that it will soon begin charging you a fee. That's if the courts don't order it shut down first. What will you do to get around it?" Another proposed ad touted StreamCast's software as the "#1 alternative to Napster" and asked "when the lights went off at Napster . . . where did the users go?"

*　　*　　*　　*　　*

In addition to this evidence of express promotion, marketing, and intent to promote further, the business models employed by Grokster and StreamCast confirm that their principal object was use of their software to download copyrighted works. Grokster and StreamCast receive no revenue from users, who obtain the software itself for nothing. Instead, both companies generate income by selling advertising space, and they stream the advertising to Grokster and Morpheus users while they are employing the programs. As the number of users of each program increases, advertising opportunities become worth more.

Finally, there is no evidence that either company made an effort to filter copyrighted material from users' downloads or otherwise impede the sharing of copyrighted files. . . .

B

The District Court . . . granted summary judgment in favor of Grokster and StreamCast as to any liability arising from distribution of the then current versions of their software. Distributing that software gave rise to no liability in the court's view, because its use did not provide the distributors with actual knowledge of specific acts of infringement.

The Court of Appeals affirmed. In the court's analysis, a defendant was liable as a contributory infringer when it had knowledge of direct infringement and materially contributed to the infringement. But the court read *Sony Corp. of America v. Universal City Studios, Inc.,* 464 U.S. 417, 78 L. Ed. 2d 574, 104 S. Ct. 774 (1984), as holding that distribution of a commercial product capable of substantial noninfringing uses could not give rise to contributory liability for infringement unless the distributor had actual knowledge of specific instances of infringement and failed to act on that knowledge. The fact that the software was capable of substantial noninfringing uses in the Ninth Circuit's view meant that Grokster and StreamCast were not liable, because they had no such actual knowledge, owing to the decentralized architecture of their software. The court also held that Grokster and StreamCast did not materially contribute to their users' infringement because it was the users themselves who searched for, retrieved, and stored the infringing files, with no involvement by the defendants beyond providing the software in the first place.

II
A

*   *   *   *   *

The argument for imposing indirect liability in this case is . . . a powerful one, given the number of infringing downloads that occur every day using StreamCast's and Grokster's software. When a widely shared service or product is used to commit infringement, it may be impossible to enforce rights in the protected work effectively against all direct infringers, the only practical alternative being to go against the distributor of the copying device for secondary liability on a theory of contributory or vicarious infringement.

B

*   *   *   *   *

In *Sony Corp. v. Universal City Studios* this Court addressed a claim that secondary liability for infringement can arise from the very distribution of a commercial product. There, the product, novel at the time, was what we know today as the videocassette recorder or VCR. Copyright holders sued Sony as the manufacturer, claiming it was contributorily liable for infringement that occurred when VCR owners taped copyrighted programs because it supplied the means used to infringe, and it had constructive knowledge that infringement would occur. At the trial on the merits, the evidence showed that the principal use of the VCR was for "'time-shifting,'" or taping a program for later viewing at a more convenient time, which the Court found to be a fair, not an infringing, use. There was no evidence that Sony had expressed an object of bringing about taping in violation of copyright or had taken active steps to increase its profits from unlawful taping. Although Sony's advertisements urged consumers to buy the VCR to "'record favorite shows'" or "'build a library'" of recorded programs, neither of these uses was necessarily infringing.

On those facts, with no evidence of stated or indicated intent to promote infringing uses, the only conceivable basis for imposing liability was on a theory of contributory infringement arising from its sale of VCRs to consumers with knowledge that some would use them to infringe. But because the VCR was "capable of commercially significant noninfringing uses,"

we held the manufacturer could not be faulted solely on the basis of its distribution.

*   *   *   *   *

Because the Circuit [Court of Appeals] found the StreamCast and Grokster software capable of substantial lawful use, it concluded on the basis of its reading of *Sony* that neither company could be held liable, since there was no showing that their software, being without any central server, afforded them knowledge of specific unlawful uses.

This view of *Sony,* however, was error. . . .

C

[N]othing in *Sony* requires courts to ignore evidence of intent if there is such evidence. . . . Thus, where evidence goes beyond a product's characteristics or the knowledge that it may be put to infringing uses, and shows statements or actions directed to promoting infringement, *Sony's* . . . rule will not preclude liability. The classic case of direct evidence of unlawful purpose occurs when one induces commission of infringement by another, or "entices or persuades another" to infringe, as by advertising.

*   *   *   *   *

[T]he inducement rule is a sensible one for copyright. We adopt it here, holding that one who distributes a device with the object of promoting its use to infringe copyright, as shown by clear expression or other affirmative steps taken to foster infringement, is liable for the resulting acts of infringement by third parties. We are, of course, mindful of the need to keep from trenching on regular commerce or discouraging the development of technologies with lawful and unlawful potential. Accordingly, just as *Sony* did not find intentional inducement despite the knowledge of the VCR manufacturer that its device could be used to infringe, mere knowledge of infringing potential or of actual infringing uses would not be enough here to subject a distributor to liability. Nor would ordinary acts incident to product distribution, such as offering customers technical support or product updates, support liability in themselves. The inducement rule, instead, premises liability on purposeful, culpable expression and conduct, and thus does nothing to compromise legitimate commerce or discourage innovation having a lawful promise.

III
A

The only apparent question about treating MGM's evidence as sufficient to withstand summary judgment under the theory of inducement goes to the need on MGM's part to adduce evidence that StreamCast and Grokster communicated an inducing message to their software users.

*   *   *   *   *

Here, the . . . record is replete with evidence that Grokster and StreamCast, unlike the manufacturer and distributor in *Sony,* acted with a purpose to cause copyright violations by use of software suitable for illegal use.

Three features of this evidence of intent are particularly notable. First, each company showed itself to be aiming to satisfy a known source of demand for copyright infringement, the market comprising former Napster users.

* * * * *

Second, this evidence of unlawful objective is given added significance by MGM's showing that neither company attempted to develop filtering tools or other mechanisms to diminish the infringing activity using their software.

Third, [it] is useful to recall that StreamCast and Grokster make money by selling advertising space, by directing ads to the screens of computers employing their software. . . .

B

In addition to intent to bring about infringement and distribution of a device suitable for infringing use, the inducement theory of course requires evidence of actual infringement by recipients of the device, the software in this case. As the account of the facts indicates, there is evidence of infringe-

ment on a gigantic scale, and there is no serious issue of the adequacy of MGM's showing on this point. . . . There is substantial evidence in MGM's favor on all elements of inducement, and summary judgment in favor of Grokster and StreamCast was error.

[Vacated and remanded.]

Questions

1. *a.* Explain how the Court was able to hold software distributors like Grokster liable for the misconduct of others (those who actually used the peer-to-peer networks to download copyrighted materials).

   b. What does the Court mean by "contributory" and "vicarious" copyright infringement?

   c. Why did the Supreme Court overrule the court of appeals decision?

2. Will this decision effectively stop illegal downloading of copyrighted material? Explain.

3. As a consequence of this decision, is peer-to-peer technology now unlawful? Explain.

4. In your judgment do Grokster and other peer-to-peer software distributors have a moral responsibility regarding the unlawful use of their products by third parties? Explain.

Trademarks   Words, names, symbols, devices, or combinations thereof that are used to distinguish one seller's products from those of another are called *trademarks* when associated with products (like IBM, Coke, or Pepsi Cola) and *service marks* when associated with service businesses (United Airlines).

Although states have trademark laws, our concern will be with the federal Lanham Act. Simply using a trademark in commerce can produce legal protection, but that protection is strengthened by federal registration of the mark with the U.S. Patent and Trademark Office. A trademark owner has the exclusive right to use that mark, thus preventing confusion in consumers' minds.

Trademark infringement occurs when that exclusive right is violated and consumer confusion is likely. *Trademark dilution* occurs when the distinctiveness of the mark is gradually whittled away or blurred by a nonconfusing use on an unrelated good or service. Thus the shape of the Coke bottle was protected from dilution, as was the name Polaroid, which was, for a time, being used on heating systems. If you established your own Web site and labeled it *Mercedes,* that choice would undoubtedly be challenged as a dilution of the mark, even if you were not dealing in cars.

Domain Names   The Internet address for a Web page is called its *domain name.* Ordinarily, a business entering electronic commerce will want to use the simplest form of its name as its domain name. Rights to a domain name are secured simply by being the first to request a name and paying a registration fee. Disputes about domain names can be resolved with an arbitration process set up by the Internet Corporation for Assigned Names and Numbers (ICANN), a nonprofit organization designed to promote competition in registering commercial domain names. [For more about ICANN, see **www .icannwatch.org**]

Domain Name Disputes

"The Internet grew rapidly over the last decade as a place to do business, although no international legal standards existed to resolve domain name disputes. . . . The process of negotiating a new international treaty was considered too slow, and new national laws would most likely be too diverse. What was needed were internationally uniform and mandatory procedures to deal with what are frequently cross-border disputes." Ultimately, ICANN adopted the arbitration approach to dispute resolution. A number of organizations have been approved as arbitrators of domain name disputes. Carmen Electra, Michael Crichton, Kevin Spacey, Pamela Anderson, Celine Dion, and Bruce Springsteen have all used the process to have domain name versions of their names transferred to them, all of which were previously registered by the same Canadian company.

Sources: WIPO, "Frequently Asked Questions: Internet Domain Names" [**http://arbiter.wipo.int/center/faq/ domains.html#7**]; "People: News/Gossip/Scoops," *St. Louis Post–Dispatch*, January 17, 2004, p. 41.

In 1999 Congress approved the Anticybersquatting Consumer Protection Act, which created a cause of action where a trademark has been infringed upon by the registration of a domain name. The trademark holder must show a bad-faith intention on the part of the registrant to profit from the registration, traffic in the name, or use the name. To date, many successful suits have been brought under this act, protecting such names as vw.net,[75] sportys.com,[76] and ClassicVolvo.com.[77] The Third Circuit has held that registration of deliberate misspellings of famous marks is also a violation of the act.[78] [For information on the United Nations' World Intellectual Property Organization, which provides arbitrations pursuant to ICANN's domain name arbitration policy, see **www.wipo.int**]

Taxes

We close this chapter, and the book, with one of the most interesting public policy questions raised by the remarkable confusion (and profusion) of the Internet. It is a policy issue, like many raised by the Internet and discussed in this chapter, that crosses traditional jurisdictional lines—crossing both state boundaries in the United States and national boundaries around the world. Its resolution, either at the national level or at the international level, will require substantial negotiation, compromise and, ultimately, consensus building.

What is the issue? We will start with a national example: If you buy a CD on the Internet, your neighborhood retailer will not receive your business and your state and local governments often will not receive sales taxes as they would have if you had made the purchase at that local store. To address that issue and others, the federal government undertook a study of e-commerce tax policy. To permit time for both the study and development of a workable resolution, Congress and President Clinton imposed a moratorium on Internet taxes that expired in October 2001. Resolution, however, has proven elusive. In 1992 the Supreme Court had ruled that an out-of-state vendor cannot be required to collect sales taxes for any state in which that vendor does not have some significant presence, including a physical presence.[79] The decision was based on the Commerce Clause, the Court finding that it would be an undue burden on interstate commerce for states to be able to require out-of-state vendors to comply with each unique set of sales tax rules in each jurisdiction. While the initial Internet tax moratorium was in effect, many states joined an effort to streamline, simplify, and coordinate their sales tax laws. The idea was that if state sales taxes were more uniform, the burden on interstate commerce from requiring compliance from out-of-state vendors would disappear. As of this writing, of the 42 states that have been involved in the project, 22 have conformed their state laws to at least some of the requirements of the negotiated agreement. The provisions won't actually become operational even in those states that have passed conforming legislation until states representing at least 20 percent of the U.S. population subject to sales taxes have adopted conforming legislation. This is not expected any earlier than October 2005.[80] In the meantime, Congress has once again extended the sales tax moratorium, this time through 2007.[81] [For a Web site devoted to state and local e-commerce taxation, see **www.ryanco.com/gateway/electron.html**]

The problem is just as complex, if not more so, on an international scale. Here the issue spans the whole range of taxes, paralleling both our income tax laws and our sales tax laws. In a nutshell, what nation is entitled to tax cross-border transactions? In the international arena, certain key principles were adopted under the auspices of the Organization for Economic Cooperation and Development (OECD) in 1998, including the principle that consumption taxes (like our sales taxes) should be collected by the jurisdiction where consumption takes place.[82] But finding workable arrangements to effectuate general principles has proven elusive. The European Union amended its Value-Added Tax (VAT) to require non-EU-resident vendors to apply the VAT (for each of the EU countries) when selling "digital goods" within the EU.[83]

Reprise: Who Governs Cyberspace?

We end this chapter with some of the same questions with which we started: What substantive law should govern the taxation of international transactions (or, for that matter, the protection of intellectual property internationally, or any of the other international issues brought to the fore by the rapid development and expansion of the Internet)? What process should be used to develop international consensus over those substantive laws? And what government can legitimately impose standards and sanctions for violations of those standards?

And what government can legitimately impose standards and sanctions for violations of those standards?

Question

Comment on the following portion of John Perry Barlow's "Cyberspace Declaration of Independence":

Governments of the Industrial World, you weary giants of flesh and steel, I come from Cyberspace, the new home of Mind. On behalf of the future, I ask you of the past to leave us alone. You are not welcome among us. You have no sovereignty where we gather.

We have no elected government, nor are we likely to have one, so I address you with no greater authority than that with which liberty itself always speaks. I declare the global social space we are building to be naturally independent of the tyrannies you seek to impose on us. You have no moral right to rule us nor do you possess any methods of enforcement we have true reason to fear.[84]

Internet Exercise

Using the Cyberspace Law materials at [**http://www.findlaw.com/01topics/10cyberspace/index.html**], scroll down to the section titled "Web Guide—Laws, Databases, Web Sites and More" and click on "Jurisdiction." Then click on "Internet Jurisdiction" and read the article. Summarize the author's definitions of interactive and passive use and explain his conclusions.

Chapter Questions

1. *a.* Germany, France, the Netherlands, and Austria have laws that allow publishing groups to specify the price at which new books are to be sold at retail. That is, anyone selling one of those books at retail in those countries must sell it at the price specified by publishers or they won't be supplied with the books. Why would those countries support price fixing in book sales?

   b. Germany's *Rabattgesetz* (discount law) requires that all customers pay precisely the same price for a product. Thus an Internet concept like *Priceline.com* where buyers specify a price they are willing to pay for a product is unlawful. Why would Germany insist on identical pricing for products?

   c. How would you expect the Internet to affect those laws forbidding discounts on books and other products? See Neal Boudette, "In Europe, Surfing a Web of Red Tape," *The Wall Street Journal,* October 29, 1999, p. B1.

2. Recently journalist John Snell remarked, "Not long ago you couldn't turn around in cyberspace without bumping into a tech geek. Now you're no more than a mouse click away from a lawyer. Attorneys are everywhere."[85] What factors account for the dramatic increase in lawyers addressing Internet issues?

3. The United Nations recently warned that the worldwide growth of e-commerce may constitute a threat to the well-being of the world's developing nations as well as parts of Europe. Explain the UN concerns.

4. Psychologists are worried that the Internet will make shopping too easy. Explain their concern.

5. Are online bloggers (that is, authors of topical Web logs) entitled to protection as journalists under the First Amendment with regard to the confidentiality of their sources? What if those sources have illegally revealed corporate trade secrets?[86]

6. Bensusan Restaurant Corporation owns the famous New York City jazz club "The Blue Note," and in 1985 it registered the name as a federal trademark. Since 1980,

King has operated a small club in Columbia, Missouri, also named "The Blue Note." Around 1993, Bensusan wrote to King demanding that he discontinue use of "The Blue Note" name. King's attorney responded by saying that Bensusan had no legal right to make the demand. In 1996 King created, in Missouri, a Web site for "The Blue Note," which also contained a hyperlink to the New York club's Web site. Bensusan then sued in the Southern District of New York, alleging Lanham Act and trademark violations, among other things. The New York court dismissed the case for lack of personal jurisdiction. Bensusan appealed. Decide. Explain. See *Bensusan Restaurant Corp. v. King,* 126 F.3d 25 (2d Cir. 1997).

7. McLaren was an employee of Microsoft Corporation. In December 1996, Microsoft suspended McLaren's employment pending an investigation into accusations of sexual harassment and "inventory questions." McLaren requested access to his electronic mail to disprove the allegations against him. According to McLaren, he was told he could access his e-mail only by requesting it through company officials and telling them the location of a particular message. By memorandum, McLaren requested that no one tamper with his Microsoft office workstation or his e-mail. McLaren's employment was terminated on December 11, 1996.

   Following the termination of his employment, McLaren filed suit against the company alleging as his sole cause of action a claim for invasion of privacy. In support of his claim, McLaren alleged that, on information and belief, Microsoft had invaded his privacy by "breaking into" some or all of the personal folders maintained on his office computer and releasing the contents of the folders to third parties. According to McLaren, the personal folders were part of a computer application created by Microsoft in which e-mail messages could be stored. Access to the e-mail system was obtained through a network password. Access to personal folders could be additionally restricted by a "personal store" password created by the individual user. McLaren created and used a personal store password to restrict access to his personal folders.

   McLaren concedes in his petition that it was possible for Microsoft to "decrypt" his personal store password. McLaren alleges, however, that "[b]y allowing [him] to have a personal store password for his personal folders, [McLaren] manifested and [Microsoft] recognized an expectation that the personal folders would be free from intrusion and interference." McLaren characterizes Microsoft's decrypting or otherwise "breaking in" to his personal folders as an intentional, unjustified, and unlawful invasion of privacy.

   Did Microsoft unlawfully invade McLaren's privacy? Explain. See *McLaren v. Microsoft,* 1999 Texas App. LEXIS 4103 (5th Dist., Dallas).

8. Enza and Richard Hill ordered a Gateway 2000 computer by telephone and paid by credit card. The computer was delivered in a box that also contained the terms of sale. Those terms were to be effective unless the computer was returned within 30 days. Among those terms was a clause providing for arbitration of any problems. The Hills kept the computer for more than 30 days before complaining about its performance and components. They filed suit, and Gateway argued that the arbitration clause should be enforced. The Hills conceded that they noticed the statement of

terms, but they did not read those terms closely enough to notice the arbitration provision. Should the arbitration clause be enforced? Explain. See *Hill v. Gateway 2000,* 105 F.3d 1147 (7th Cir. 1997); cert.den.522 U.S. 808 (1997).

9. In March 1992 Danish police seized the business records of BAMSE, a computer bulletin board system based in Denmark that sold child pornography over the Internet. The records included information that Mohrbacher, who lived in Paradise, California, had downloaded two graphic interface format (GIF) images from BAMSE in January 1992.

   In March 1993 police executed a search warrant at Mohrbacher's workplace and found, among other images, two files that had been downloaded from BAMSE, one of a nude girl and one of a girl engaged in a sex act with an adult; both girls were under 12. During the execution of the warrant, Mohrbacher was cooperative, confessing that he had downloaded the two images from BAMSE. Mohrbacher was charged with transporting or shipping images by computer as prohibited by 18 U.S.C. 2252(a)(1). Mohrbacher argued that downloading is properly characterized as receiving images by computer, which is proscribed by section 2252(a)(2). He was not charged under (a)(2).

   Does downloading from a computer bulletin board constitute shipping or transporting within the meaning of 18 U.S.C. section 2252(a)(1)? Explain. See *United States of America v. Mohrbacher,* 182 F.3d 1041 (9th Cir. 1999).

10. Plaintiff Marobie-FL, Inc., released software of copyrighted clip art for use in the fire service industry. Robisheaux administered the National Association of Fire Equipment Distributors (NAFED) Web page. He received the clip art from a source that he could not remember. He placed the clip art on NAFED's Web page. At that point, the clip art could be readily accessed and downloaded by any Web user. Marobie claimed copyright infringement. Among other arguments, NAFED claimed that its display of the clip art constituted a fair use, within the meaning of federal copyright law. Decide. Explain. See *Marobie-FL v. National Ass'n of Fire Equip. Dist.,* 983 F.Supp. 1167 (N.D.Ill. 1997).

11. Intel Corporation sued a former employee for his sending of several e-mail messages to "as many as 35,000 company employees" complaining about various Intel employment practices.[87] Intel argued that the e-mail amounted to trespass against its computer system. "Hamidi breached no computer security barriers in order to communicate with Intel employees. He offered to, and did, remove from his mailing list any recipient who so wished. Hamidi's communications to individual Intel employees caused neither physical damage nor functional disruption to the company's computers, nor did they at any time deprive Intel of the use of its computers. The contents of the messages, however, caused discussion among employees and managers." Trespass? See *Intel v. Hamidi,* 71 P.3d 296 (Cal. S. Ct. 2003).

12. America Online (AOL), an Internet service provider, sued TSF Marketing and Joseph Melle, who founded TSF. AOL claimed that Melle and TSF sent unauthorized bulk e-mail advertisements (spam) to AOL subscribers. The e-mail contained the letters "aol.com" in the headers. AOL claimed that the e-mail totaled some 60 million messages over a 10-month period. Melle allegedly continued the mailings after he was

King has operated a small club in Columbia, Missouri, also named "The Blue Note." Around 1993, Bensusan wrote to King demanding that he discontinue use of "The Blue Note" name. King's attorney responded by saying that Bensusan had no legal right to make the demand. In 1996 King created, in Missouri, a Web site for "The Blue Note," which also contained a hyperlink to the New York club's Web site. Bensusan then sued in the Southern District of New York, alleging Lanham Act and trademark violations, among other things. The New York court dismissed the case for lack of personal jurisdiction. Bensusan appealed. Decide. Explain. See *Bensusan Restaurant Corp. v. King,* 126 F.3d 25 (2d Cir. 1997).

7. McLaren was an employee of Microsoft Corporation. In December 1996, Microsoft suspended McLaren's employment pending an investigation into accusations of sexual harassment and "inventory questions." McLaren requested access to his electronic mail to disprove the allegations against him. According to McLaren, he was told he could access his e-mail only by requesting it through company officials and telling them the location of a particular message. By memorandum, McLaren requested that no one tamper with his Microsoft office workstation or his e-mail. McLaren's employment was terminated on December 11, 1996.

   Following the termination of his employment, McLaren filed suit against the company alleging as his sole cause of action a claim for invasion of privacy. In support of his claim, McLaren alleged that, on information and belief, Microsoft had invaded his privacy by "breaking into" some or all of the personal folders maintained on his office computer and releasing the contents of the folders to third parties. According to McLaren, the personal folders were part of a computer application created by Microsoft in which e-mail messages could be stored. Access to the e-mail system was obtained through a network password. Access to personal folders could be additionally restricted by a "personal store" password created by the individual user. McLaren created and used a personal store password to restrict access to his personal folders.

   McLaren concedes in his petition that it was possible for Microsoft to "decrypt" his personal store password. McLaren alleges, however, that "[b]y allowing [him] to have a personal store password for his personal folders, [McLaren] manifested and [Microsoft] recognized an expectation that the personal folders would be free from intrusion and interference." McLaren characterizes Microsoft's decrypting or otherwise "breaking in" to his personal folders as an intentional, unjustified, and unlawful invasion of privacy.

   Did Microsoft unlawfully invade McLaren's privacy? Explain. See *McLaren v. Microsoft,* 1999 Texas App. LEXIS 4103 (5th Dist., Dallas).

8. Enza and Richard Hill ordered a Gateway 2000 computer by telephone and paid by credit card. The computer was delivered in a box that also contained the terms of sale. Those terms were to be effective unless the computer was returned within 30 days. Among those terms was a clause providing for arbitration of any problems. The Hills kept the computer for more than 30 days before complaining about its performance and components. They filed suit, and Gateway argued that the arbitration clause should be enforced. The Hills conceded that they noticed the statement of

terms, but they did not read those terms closely enough to notice the arbitration provision. Should the arbitration clause be enforced? Explain. See *Hill v. Gateway 2000,* 105 F.3d 1147 (7th Cir. 1997); cert.den.522 U.S. 808 (1997).

9. In March 1992 Danish police seized the business records of BAMSE, a computer bulletin board system based in Denmark that sold child pornography over the Internet. The records included information that Mohrbacher, who lived in Paradise, California, had downloaded two graphic interface format (GIF) images from BAMSE in January 1992.

   In March 1993 police executed a search warrant at Mohrbacher's workplace and found, among other images, two files that had been downloaded from BAMSE, one of a nude girl and one of a girl engaged in a sex act with an adult; both girls were under 12. During the execution of the warrant, Mohrbacher was cooperative, confessing that he had downloaded the two images from BAMSE. Mohrbacher was charged with transporting or shipping images by computer as prohibited by 18 U.S.C. 2252(a)(1). Mohrbacher argued that downloading is properly characterized as receiving images by computer, which is proscribed by section 2252(a)(2). He was not charged under (a)(2).

   Does downloading from a computer bulletin board constitute shipping or transporting within the meaning of 18 U.S.C. section 2252(a)(1)? Explain. See *United States of America v. Mohrbacher,* 182 F.3d 1041 (9th Cir. 1999).

10. Plaintiff Marobie-FL, Inc., released software of copyrighted clip art for use in the fire service industry. Robisheaux administered the National Association of Fire Equipment Distributors (NAFED) Web page. He received the clip art from a source that he could not remember. He placed the clip art on NAFED's Web page. At that point, the clip art could be readily accessed and downloaded by any Web user. Marobie claimed copyright infringement. Among other arguments, NAFED claimed that its display of the clip art constituted a fair use, within the meaning of federal copyright law. Decide. Explain. See *Marobie-FL v. National Ass'n of Fire Equip. Dist.,* 983 F.Supp. 1167 (N.D.Ill. 1997).

11. Intel Corporation sued a former employee for his sending of several e-mail messages to "as many as 35,000 company employees" complaining about various Intel employment practices.[87] Intel argued that the e-mail amounted to trespass against its computer system. "Hamidi breached no computer security barriers in order to communicate with Intel employees. He offered to, and did, remove from his mailing list any recipient who so wished. Hamidi's communications to individual Intel employees caused neither physical damage nor functional disruption to the company's computers, nor did they at any time deprive Intel of the use of its computers. The contents of the messages, however, caused discussion among employees and managers." Trespass? See *Intel v. Hamidi,* 71 P.3d 296 (Cal. S. Ct. 2003).

12. America Online (AOL), an Internet service provider, sued TSF Marketing and Joseph Melle, who founded TSF. AOL claimed that Melle and TSF sent unauthorized bulk e-mail advertisements (spam) to AOL subscribers. The e-mail contained the letters "aol.com" in the headers. AOL claimed that the e-mail totaled some 60 million messages over a 10-month period. Melle allegedly continued the mailings after he was

King has operated a small club in Columbia, Missouri, also named "The Blue Note." Around 1993, Bensusan wrote to King demanding that he discontinue use of "The Blue Note" name. King's attorney responded by saying that Bensusan had no legal right to make the demand. In 1996 King created, in Missouri, a Web site for "The Blue Note," which also contained a hyperlink to the New York club's Web site. Bensusan then sued in the Southern District of New York, alleging Lanham Act and trademark violations, among other things. The New York court dismissed the case for lack of personal jurisdiction. Bensusan appealed. Decide. Explain. See *Bensusan Restaurant Corp. v. King,* 126 F.3d 25 (2d Cir. 1997).

7. McLaren was an employee of Microsoft Corporation. In December 1996, Microsoft suspended McLaren's employment pending an investigation into accusations of sexual harassment and "inventory questions." McLaren requested access to his electronic mail to disprove the allegations against him. According to McLaren, he was told he could access his e-mail only by requesting it through company officials and telling them the location of a particular message. By memorandum, McLaren requested that no one tamper with his Microsoft office workstation or his e-mail. McLaren's employment was terminated on December 11, 1996.

   Following the termination of his employment, McLaren filed suit against the company alleging as his sole cause of action a claim for invasion of privacy. In support of his claim, McLaren alleged that, on information and belief, Microsoft had invaded his privacy by "breaking into" some or all of the personal folders maintained on his office computer and releasing the contents of the folders to third parties. According to McLaren, the personal folders were part of a computer application created by Microsoft in which e-mail messages could be stored. Access to the e-mail system was obtained through a network password. Access to personal folders could be additionally restricted by a "personal store" password created by the individual user. McLaren created and used a personal store password to restrict access to his personal folders.

   McLaren concedes in his petition that it was possible for Microsoft to "decrypt" his personal store password. McLaren alleges, however, that "[b]y allowing [him] to have a personal store password for his personal folders, [McLaren] manifested and [Microsoft] recognized an expectation that the personal folders would be free from intrusion and interference." McLaren characterizes Microsoft's decrypting or otherwise "breaking in" to his personal folders as an intentional, unjustified, and unlawful invasion of privacy.

   Did Microsoft unlawfully invade McLaren's privacy? Explain. See *McLaren v. Microsoft,* 1999 Texas App. LEXIS 4103 (5th Dist., Dallas).

8. Enza and Richard Hill ordered a Gateway 2000 computer by telephone and paid by credit card. The computer was delivered in a box that also contained the terms of sale. Those terms were to be effective unless the computer was returned within 30 days. Among those terms was a clause providing for arbitration of any problems. The Hills kept the computer for more than 30 days before complaining about its performance and components. They filed suit, and Gateway argued that the arbitration clause should be enforced. The Hills conceded that they noticed the statement of

terms, but they did not read those terms closely enough to notice the arbitration provision. Should the arbitration clause be enforced? Explain. See *Hill v. Gateway 2000,* 105 F.3d 1147 (7th Cir. 1997); cert.den.522 U.S. 808 (1997).

9. In March 1992 Danish police seized the business records of BAMSE, a computer bulletin board system based in Denmark that sold child pornography over the Internet. The records included information that Mohrbacher, who lived in Paradise, California, had downloaded two graphic interface format (GIF) images from BAMSE in January 1992.

   In March 1993 police executed a search warrant at Mohrbacher's workplace and found, among other images, two files that had been downloaded from BAMSE, one of a nude girl and one of a girl engaged in a sex act with an adult; both girls were under 12. During the execution of the warrant, Mohrbacher was cooperative, confessing that he had downloaded the two images from BAMSE. Mohrbacher was charged with transporting or shipping images by computer as prohibited by 18 U.S.C. 2252(a)(1). Mohrbacher argued that downloading is properly characterized as receiving images by computer, which is proscribed by section 2252(a)(2). He was not charged under (a)(2).

   Does downloading from a computer bulletin board constitute shipping or transporting within the meaning of 18 U.S.C. section 2252(a)(1)? Explain. See *United States of America v. Mohrbacher,* 182 F.3d 1041 (9th Cir. 1999).

10. Plaintiff Marobie-FL, Inc., released software of copyrighted clip art for use in the fire service industry. Robisheaux administered the National Association of Fire Equipment Distributors (NAFED) Web page. He received the clip art from a source that he could not remember. He placed the clip art on NAFED's Web page. At that point, the clip art could be readily accessed and downloaded by any Web user. Marobie claimed copyright infringement. Among other arguments, NAFED claimed that its display of the clip art constituted a fair use, within the meaning of federal copyright law. Decide. Explain. See *Marobie-FL v. National Ass'n of Fire Equip. Dist.,* 983 F.Supp. 1167 (N.D.Ill. 1997).

11. Intel Corporation sued a former employee for his sending of several e-mail messages to "as many as 35,000 company employees" complaining about various Intel employment practices.[87] Intel argued that the e-mail amounted to trespass against its computer system. "Hamidi breached no computer security barriers in order to communicate with Intel employees. He offered to, and did, remove from his mailing list any recipient who so wished. Hamidi's communications to individual Intel employees caused neither physical damage nor functional disruption to the company's computers, nor did they at any time deprive Intel of the use of its computers. The contents of the messages, however, caused discussion among employees and managers." Trespass? See *Intel v. Hamidi,* 71 P.3d 296 (Cal. S. Ct. 2003).

12. America Online (AOL), an Internet service provider, sued TSF Marketing and Joseph Melle, who founded TSF. AOL claimed that Melle and TSF sent unauthorized bulk e-mail advertisements (spam) to AOL subscribers. The e-mail contained the letters "aol.com" in the headers. AOL claimed that the e-mail totaled some 60 million messages over a 10-month period. Melle allegedly continued the mailings after he was

85. John Snell, "Lawyers Drawn to Unsettled Internet; Lots of Legal Issues, Large and Small, Must Be Sorted Out," *Minneapolis Star Tribune,* November 29, 1999, p. 6D.

86. See documents filed in *Apple Computer v. John Does* [**www.eff.org/Censorship/Apple_v_Does**]. For a blogger's perspective, see Benny Evangelista, "Net Buzzing on Bloggers' Status; First Amendment Issues Become Hot Topic in Chat Rooms," *San Francisco Chronicle,* March 9, 2005, p. C1.

87. Don Clark, "Court Rules against Intel in Spam Suit," *The Wall Street Journal,* July 1, 2003, p. B1.

The Constitution of the United States of America

Preamble

We the People of the United States, in Order to form a more perfect Union, establish Justice, insure domestic Tranquility, provide for the common defence, promote the general Welfare, and secure the Blessings of Liberty to ourselves and our Posterity, do ordain and establish this Constitution for the United States of America.

Article I

Section 1. All legislative Powers herein granted shall be vested in a Congress of the United States, which shall consist of a Senate and House of Representatives.

Section 2. (1) The House of Representatives shall be composed of Members chosen every second Year by the People of the several States, and the Electors in each State shall have the Qualifications requisite for Electors of the most numerous Branch of the State Legislature.

(2) No Person shall be a Representative who shall not have attained to the Age of twenty-five Years, and been seven Years a Citizen of the United States, and who shall not, when elected, be an Inhabitant of that State in which he shall be chosen.

(3) Representatives and direct Taxes shall be apportioned among the several States which may be included within this Union, according to their respective Numbers, which shall be determined by adding to the whole Number of free Persons, including those bound to Service for a Term of Years, and excluding Indians not taxed, three fifths of all other Persons.[1] The actual Enumeration shall be made within three Years after the first Meeting of the Congress of the United States, and within every subsequent Term of ten Years, in such Manner as they shall by Law direct. The Number of Representatives shall not exceed one for every thirty Thousand, but each State shall have at Least one Representative; and until such enumeration shall be made, the State of New Hampshire shall be entitled to chuse three, Massachusetts eight, Rhode Island and Providence Plantations one, Connecticut five, New York six, New Jersey four, Pennsylvania eight, Delaware one, Maryland six, Virginia ten, North Carolina five, South Carolina five, and Georgia three.

[1] Refer to the Fourteenth Amendment.

(4) When vacancies happen in the Representation from any State, the Executive Authority thereof shall issue Writs of Election to fill such Vacancies.

(5) The House of Representatives shall chuse their Speaker and other Officers; and shall have the sole Power of Impeachment.

Section 3. (1) The Senate of the United States shall be composed of two Senators from each State, chosen by the Legislature thereof,[2] for six Years; and each Senator shall have one Vote.

(2) Immediately after they shall be assembled in Consequence of the first Election, they shall be divided as equally as may be into three Classes. The Seats of the Senators of the first Class shall be vacated at the Expiration of the Second Year, of the second Class at the Expiration of the fourth Year, and of the third Class at the Expiration of the sixth Year, so that one third may be chosen every second Year; and if Vacancies happen by Resignation, or otherwise, during the Recess of the Legislature of any State, the Executive thereof may make temporary Appointments until the next Meeting of the Legislature, which shall then fill such Vacancies.[3]

(3) No Person shall be a Senator who shall not have attained to the Age of thirty Years, and been nine Years a Citizen of the United States, and who shall not, when elected, be an Inhabitant of that State for which he shall be chosen.

(4) The Vice President of the United States shall be President of the Senate, but shall have no Vote, unless they be equally divided.

(5) The Senate shall chuse their other Officers, and also a President pro tempore, in the Absence of the Vice President, or when he shall exercise the Office of President of the United States.

(6) The Senate shall have the sole Power to try all Impeachments. When sitting for that Purpose, they shall be on Oath or Affirmation. When the President of the United States is tried, the Chief Justice shall preside: And no Person shall be convicted without the Concurrence of two thirds of the Members present.

(7) Judgment in Cases of Impeachment shall not extend further than to removal from Office, and disqualification to hold and enjoy any Office of honor, Trust, or Profit under the United States: but the Party convicted shall nevertheless be liable and subject to Indictment, Trial, Judgment, and Punishment, according to Law.

Section 4. (1) The Times, Places and Manner of holding Elections for Senators and Representatives, shall be prescribed in each State by the Legislature thereof; but the Congress may at any time by Law make or alter such Regulations, except as to the Places of chusing Senators.

(2) The Congress shall assemble at least once in every year, and such Meeting shall be on the first Monday in December, unless they shall by Law appoint a different Day.[4]

Section 5. (1) Each House shall be the Judge of the Elections, Returns, and Qualifications of its own Members, and a Majority of each shall constitute a Quorum to do Business; but a smaller Number may adjourn from day to day, and may be authorized to compel the Attendance of absent Members, in such Manner, and under such Penalties as each House may provide.

[2]Refer to the Seventeenth Amendment.

[3]Ibid.

[4]Refer to the Twentieth Amendment.

(2) Each House may determine the Rules of its Proceedings, punish its Members for disorderly Behavior, and, with the Concurrence of two thirds, expel a Member.

(3) Each House shall keep a Journal of its Proceedings, and from time to time publish the same, excepting such Parts as may in their Judgment require Secrecy; and the Yeas and Nays of the Members of either House on any question shall, at the Desire of one fifth of those Present, be entered on the Journal.

(4) Neither House, during the Session of Congress, shall, without the Consent of the other, adjourn for more than three days, nor to any other Place than that in which the two Houses shall be sitting.

Section 6. (1) The Senators and Representatives shall receive a Compensation for their Services, to be ascertained by Law, and paid out of the Treasury of the United States. They shall in all Cases, except Treason, Felony and Breach of the Peace, be privileged from Arrest during their Attendance at the Session of their respective Houses, and in going to and returning from the same; and for any Speech or Debate in either House, they shall not be questioned in any other Place.

(2) No Senator or Representative shall, during the Time for which he was elected, be appointed to any civil Office under the Authority of the United States, which shall have been created, or the Emoluments whereof shall have been encreased during such time; and no Person holding any Office under the United States, shall be a Member of either House during his Continuance in Office.

Section 7. (1) All Bills for raising Revenue shall originate in the House of Representatives; but the Senate may propose or concur with Amendments as on other Bills.

(2) Every Bill which shall have passed the House of Representatives and the Senate, shall, before it becomes a Law, be presented to the President of the United States; If he approve he shall sign it, but if not he shall return it, with his Objections to the House in which it shall have originated, who shall enter the Objections at large on their Journal, and proceed to reconsider it. If after such Reconsideration two thirds of that House shall agree to pass the Bill, it shall be sent together with the Objections, to the other House, by which it shall likewise be reconsidered, and if approved by two thirds of that House, it shall become a Law. But in all such Cases the Votes of both Houses shall be determined by yeas and Nays, and the Names of the Persons voting for and against the Bill shall be entered on the Journal of each House respectively. If any Bill shall not be returned by the President within ten Days (Sundays excepted) after it shall have been presented to him, the Same shall be a Law, in like Manner as if he had signed it, unless the Congress by their Adjournment prevent its Return in which Case it shall not be a Law.

(3) Every Order, Resolution, or Vote, to Which the Concurrence of the Senate and House of Representatives may be necessary (except on a question of Adjournment) shall be presented to the President of the United States; and before the same shall take Effect, shall be approved by him, or being disapproved by him, shall be repassed by two thirds of the Senate and House of Representatives, according to the Rules and Limitations prescribed in the Case of a Bill.

Section 8. (1) The Congress shall have Power To lay and collect Taxes, Duties, Imposts and Excises, to pay the Debts and provide for the common Defence and general Welfare of the United States; but all Duties, Imposts and Excises shall be uniform throughout the United States;

(2) To borrow money on the credit of the United States;

(3) To regulate Commerce with foreign Nations, and among the several States, and with the Indian Tribes;

(4) To establish a uniform Rule of Naturalization, and uniform Laws on the subject of Bankruptcies throughout the United States;

(5) To coin Money, regulate the Value thereof, and of foreign Coin, and fix the Standard of Weights and Measures;

(6) To provide for the Punishment of counterfeiting the Securities and current Coin of the United States;

(7) To Establish Post Offices and Post Roads;

(8) To promote the Progress of Science and useful Arts, by securing for limited Times to Authors and Inventors the exclusive Right to their respective Writings and Discoveries;

(9) To constitute Tribunals inferior to the Supreme Court;

(10) To define and punish Piracies and Felonies committed on the high Seas, and Offenses against the Law of Nations;

(11) To declare War, grant Letters of Marque and Reprisal, and make Rules concerning Captures on Land and Water;

(12) To raise and support Armies, but no Appropriation of Money to that Use shall be for a longer Term than two Years;

(13) To provide and maintain a Navy;

(14) To make Rules for the Government and Regulation of the land and naval Forces;

(15) To provide for calling forth the Militia to execute the Laws of the Union, suppress Insurrections and repel Invasions;

(16) To provide for organizing, arming, and disciplining, the Militia, and for governing such Part of them as may be employed in the Service of the United States, reserving to the States respectively, the Appointment of the Officers, and the Authority of training the Militia according to the discipline prescribed by Congress;

(17) To exercise exclusive Legislation in all Cases whatsoever, over such District (not exceeding ten Miles square) as may, by Cession of particular States, and the Acceptance of Congress, become the Seat of the Government of the United States, and to exercise like Authority over all Places purchased by the Consent of the Legislature of the State in which the Same shall be, for the Election of Forts, Magazines, Arsenals, dock-Yards, and other needful Buildings;—And

(18) To make all Laws which shall be necessary and proper for carrying into Execution the foregoing Powers, and all other Powers vested by this Constitution in the Government of the United States, or in any Department or Officer thereof.

Section 9. (1) The Migration or Importation of Such Persons as any of the States now existing shall think proper to admit, shall not be prohibited by the Congress prior to the Year one thousand eight hundred and eight, but a Tax or duty may be imposed on such Importation, not exceeding ten dollars for each Person.

(2) The privilege of the Writ of Habeas Corpus shall not be suspended, unless when in Cases of Rebellion or Invasion the public Safety may require it.

(3) No Bill of Attainder or ex post facto Law shall be passed.

(4) No Capitation, or other direct, Tax shall be laid, unless in proportion to the Census or Enumeration herein before directed to the taken.[5]

---

[5]Refer to the Sixteenth Amendment.

(5) No Tax or Duty shall be laid on Articles exported from any state.

(6) No Preference shall be given by any Regulation of Commerce or Revenue to the Ports of one State over those of another; nor shall Vessels bound to, or from, one State be obliged to enter, clear, or pay Duties in another.

(7) No money shall be drawn from the Treasury, but in Consequence of Appropriations made by Law; and a regular Statement and Account of the Receipts and Expenditures of all public Money shall be published from time to time.

(8) No Title of Nobility shall be granted by the United States; And no person holding any Office of Profit or Trust under them, shall, without the Consent of the Congress, accept of any present, Emolument, Office or Title, of any kind whatever, from any King, Prince, or foreign State.

Section 10. (1) No State shall enter into any Treaty, Alliance, or Confederation; grant Letters of Marque and Reprisal; coin Money; emit Bills of Credit; make any Thing but gold and silver Coin a Tender in Payment of Debts; pass any Bill of Attainder, ex post facto Law, or Law impairing the Obligation of Contracts, or grant any Title of Nobility.

(2) No State shall, without the Consent of the Congress, lay any Imposts or Duties on Imports or Exports, except what may be absolutely necessary for executing its inspection Laws: and the net Produce of all Duties and Imposts, laid by any State on Imports or Exports, shall be for the Use of the Treasury of the United States; and all such Laws shall be subject to the Revision and Controul of the Congress.

(3) No State shall, without the Consent of Congress, lay any Duty of Tonnage, keep Troops, or Ships of War in time of Peace, enter into any Agreement or Compact with another State, or with a foreign Power, or engage in War, unless actually invaded, or in such imminent Danger as will not admit of delay.

Article II

Section 1. (1) The executive Power shall be vested in a President of the United States of America. He shall hold his Office during the Term of four Years, and, together with the Vice President, chosen for the same Term, be elected as follows:

(2) Each State shall appoint, in such Manner as the Legislature thereof may direct, a Number of Electors, equal to the whole Number of Senators and Representatives to which the State may be entitled in the Congress; but no Senator or Representative, or Person holding an Office of Trust or Profit under the United States, shall be appointed an Elector.

(3) The Electors shall meet in their respective States, and vote by Ballot for two Persons, of whom one at least shall not be an Inhabitant of the same State with themselves. And they shall make a list of all the Persons voted for, and of the Number of Votes for each; which List they shall sign and certify, and transmit sealed to the Seat of the Government of the United States, directed to the President of the Senate. The President of the Senate shall, in the Presence of the Senate and House of Representatives, open all the Certificates, and the Votes shall then be counted. The Person having the greatest Number of Votes shall be the President, if such Number be a Majority of the whole Number of Electors appointed; and if there be more than one who have such Majority, and have an equal Number of Votes, then the House of Representatives shall immediately chuse by Ballot one of them for President; and if no Person have a Majority, then from the five highest on the List the said House shall in like Manner chuse the President. But in chusing the President, the Votes

shall be taken by States, the Representation from each State have one Vote; A quorum for this Purpose shall consist of a Member or Members from two thirds of the States, and a Majority of all the States shall be necessary to a Choice. In every Case, after the Choice of the President, the Person having the greater Number of Votes of the Electors shall be the Vice President. But if there should remain two or more who have equal Votes, the Senate shall chuse from them by Ballot the Vice President.[6]

(4) The Congress may determine the Time of chusing the Electors, and the Day on which they shall give their Votes; which Day shall be the same throughout the United States.

(5) No person except a natural born Citizen, or a Citizen of the United States, at the time of the Adoption of this Constitution, shall be eligible to the Office of President; neither shall any Person be eligible to that Office who shall not have attained to the Age of thirty-five Years, and been fourteen Years a Resident within the United States.

(6) In case of the removal of the President from Office, or of his Death, Resignation or Inability to discharge the Powers and Duties of the said Office, the Same shall devolve on the Vice President, and the Congress may by Law provide for the Case of Removal, Death, Resignation or Inability, both of the President and Vice President, declaring what Officer shall then act as President, and such Officer shall act accordingly, until the Disability be removed, or a President shall be elected.[7]

(7) The President shall, at stated Times, receive for his Services, a Compensation, which shall neither be encreased nor diminished during the Period for which he shall have been elected, and he shall not receive within that Period any other Emolument from the United States, or any of them.

(8) Before he enter on the Execution of his Office, he shall take the following Oath or Affirmation: "I do solemnly swear (or affirm) that I will faithfully execute the Office of President of the United States, and will to the best of my Ability, preserve, protect, and defend the Constitution of the United States."

Section 2. (1) The President shall be Commander in Chief of the Army and Navy of the United States, and of the militia of the several States, when called into the actual Service of the United States; he may require the Opinion, in writing, of the principal Officer in each of the executive Departments, upon any Subject relating to the Duties of their respective Offices, and he shall have Power to grant Reprieves and Pardons for Offenses against the United States, except in Cases of Impeachment.

(2) He shall have Power, by and with the Advice and Consent of the Senate, to make Treaties, provided two thirds of the Senators present concur; and he shall nominate, and by and with the Advice and Consent of the Senate, shall appoint Ambassadors, other public Ministers and Consuls, Judges of the supreme Court, and all other Officers of the United States, whose Appointments are not herein otherwise provided for, and which shall be established by Law; but the Congress may by Law vest the Appointment of such inferior Officers, as they think proper, in the President alone, in the Courts of Law, or in the Heads of Departments.

---

[6]Refer to the Twelfth Amendment.

[7]Refer to the Twenty-Fifth Amendment.

(3) The President shall have Power to fill up all Vacancies that may happen during the Recess of the Senate, by granting Commissions which shall expire at the End of their next Session.

Section 3. He shall from time to time give to the Congress Information of the State of the Union, and recommend to their Consideration such Measures as he shall judge necessary and expedient; he may, on extraordinary Occasions, convene both Houses, or either of them, and in Case of Disagreement between them, with Respect to the Time of Adjournment, he may adjourn them to such Time as he shall think proper; he shall receive Ambassadors and other public Ministers; he shall take Care that the Laws be faithfully executed, and shall Commission all the Officers of the United States.

Section 4. The President, Vice President and all civil Officers of the United States, shall be removed from Office on Impeachment for, and Conviction of, Treason, Bribery, or other high Crimes and Misdemeanors.

Article III

Section 1. The judicial Power of the United States, shall be vested in one supreme Court, and in such inferior Courts as the Congress may from time to time ordain and establish. The Judges, both of the supreme and inferior Courts, shall hold their Offices during good Behaviour, and shall, at stated Times, receive for their Services a Compensation, which shall not be diminished during their Continuance in Office.

Section 2. (1) The judicial Power shall extend to all Cases, in Law and Equity, arising under this Constitution, the Laws of the United States, and Treaties made, or which shall be made, under their Authority;—to all Cases affecting Ambassadors, other public Ministers and Consuls;—to all Cases of admiralty and maritime Jurisdiction;—to Controversies to which the United States shall be a Party;—to Controversies between two or more States;—between a State and Citizens of another State,[8]—between Citizens of different states;—between Citizens of the same State claiming Lands under the Grants of different States, and between a State, or the Citizens thereof, and foreign States, Citizens or Subjects.

(2) In all Cases affecting Ambassadors, other public Ministers and Consuls, and those in which a State shall be a Party, the supreme Court shall have original Jurisdiction. In all the other Cases before mentioned, the supreme Court shall have appellate Jurisdiction, both as to Law and Fact, with such Exceptions, and under such Regulations as the Congress shall make.

(3) The trial of all Crimes, except in Cases of Impeachment, shall be by Jury; and such Trial shall be held in the State where the said Crimes shall have been committed; but when not committed within any State, the Trial shall be at such Place or Places as the Congress may by Law have directed.

Section 3. (1) Treason against the United States, shall consist only in levying War against them, or, in adhering to their enemies, giving them Aid and Comfort. No Person shall be convicted of Treason unless on the Testimony of two Witnesses to the same overt Act, or on Confession in open Court.

---

[8]Refer to the Eleventh Amendment.

(2) The Congress shall have Power to declare the Punishment of Treason, but no Attainder of Treason shall work Corruption of Blood, or Forfeiture except during the Life of the Person attainted.

Article IV

Section 1. Full Faith and Credit shall be given in each State to the public Acts, Records, and judicial Proceedings of every other State. And the Congress may by general Laws prescribe the Manner in which such Acts, Records and Proceedings shall be proved, and the Effect thereof.

Section 2. (1) The Citizens of each State shall be entitled to all Privileges and Immunities of Citizens in the several States.

(2) A Person charged in any State with Treason, Felony, or other Crime, who shall flee from Justice, and be found in another State, shall on demand of the executive Authority of the State from which he fled, be delivered up, to be removed to the State having Jurisdiction of the Crime.

(3) No Person held to Service or Labour in one State, under the Laws thereof, escaping into another, shall, in Consequence of any Law or Regulation therein, be discharged from such Service or Labour, but shall be delivered up on Claim of the Party to whom such Service or Labour may be due.[9]

Section 3. (1) New States may be admitted by the Congress into this Union; but no new State shall be formed or erected within the Jurisdiction of any other State; nor any State be formed by the Junction of two or more States, or Parts of States without the Consent of the Legislatures of the States concerned as well as of the Congress.

(2) The Congress shall have Power to dispose of and make all needful Rules and Regulations respecting the Territory or other Property belonging to the United States; and nothing in this Constitution shall be so construed as to Prejudice any Claims of the United States, or of any particular State.

Section 4. The United States shall guarantee to every State in this Union a Republican Form of Government, and shall protect each of them against Invasion; and on Application of the Legislature, or of the Executive (when the Legislature cannot be convened) against domestic Violence.

Article V

The Congress, whenever two thirds of both Houses shall deem it necessary, shall propose Amendments to this Constitution, or, on the Application of the Legislatures of two thirds of the several States, shall call a Convention for proposing Amendments, which, in either Case, shall be valid to all Intents and Purposes, as part of this Constitution, when ratified by the Legislatures of three fourths of the several States, or by Conventions in three fourths thereof, as the one or the other Mode of Ratification may be proposed by the Congress; Provided that no Amendment which may be made prior to the Year One thousand eight hundred and eight shall in any Manner affect the first and fourth Clauses in the Ninth Section

[9]Refer to the Thirteenth Amendment.

of the first Article; and that no State, without its Consent, shall be deprived of its equal Suffrage in the Senate.

Article VI

(1) All Debts contracted and Engagements entered into, before the Adoption of this Constitution shall be as valid against the United States under this Constitution, as under the Confederation.

(2) This Constitution, and the Laws of the United States which shall be made in Pursuance thereof; and all Treaties made, or which shall be made, under the Authority of the United States, shall be the supreme Law of the Land; and the Judges in every State shall be bound thereby, any Thing in the Constitution or Laws of any State to the Contrary notwithstanding.

(3) The Senators and Representatives before mentioned, and the Members of the several State Legislatures, and all executive and judicial Officers, both of the United States and of the several States, shall be bound by Oath or Affirmation, to support this Constitution, but no religious Test shall ever be required as a Qualification to any Office or public Trust under the United States.

Article VII

The Ratification of the Conventions of nine States shall be sufficient for the Establishment of this Constitution between the States so ratifying the Same.
[Amendments 1–10, the Bill of Rights, were ratified in 1791.]

Amendment I

Congress shall make no law respecting an establishment of religion, or prohibiting the free exercise thereof; or abridging the freedom of speech, or of the press; or the right of the people peaceably to assemble, and to petition the Government for a redress of grievances.

Amendment II

A well regulated Militia, being necessary to the security of a free State, the right of the people to keep and bear Arms, shall not be infringed.

Amendment III

No Soldier shall, in time of peace be quartered in any house, without the consent of the Owner, nor in time of war, but in a manner to be prescribed by law.

Amendment IV

The right of the people to be secure in their persons, houses, papers, and effects, against unreasonable searches and seizures, shall not be violated, and no Warrants shall issue, but upon probable cause, supported by Oath or affirmation, and particularly describing the place to be searched, and the persons or things to be seized.

Amendment V

No person shall be held to answer for a capital, or otherwise infamous crime, unless on a presentment or indictment of a Grand Jury, except in cases arising in the land or naval forces, or in the Militia, when in actual service in time of War or public danger; nor shall any person be subject for the same offence to be twice put in jeopardy of life or limb; nor shall be compelled in any criminal case to be a witness against himself, nor be deprived of life, liberty, or property, without due process of law; nor shall private property be taken for public use, without just compensation.

Amendment VI

In all criminal prosecutions, the accused shall enjoy the right to a speedy and public trial, by an impartial jury of the State and district wherein the crime shall have been committed, which district shall have been previously ascertained by law, and to be informed of the nature and cause of the accusation; to be confronted with the witness against him; to have compulsory process for obtaining witnesses in his favor, and to have the Assistance of Counsel for his defence.

Amendment VII

In Suits at common law, where the value in controversy shall exceed twenty dollars, the right of trial by jury shall be preserved, and no fact tried by jury, shall be otherwise re-examined in any Court of the United States, than according to the rules of the common law.

Amendment VIII

Excessive bail shall not be required, nor excessive fines imposed, nor cruel and unusual punishments inflicted.

Amendment IX

The enumeration in the Constitution, of certain rights, shall not be construed to deny or disparage others retained by the people.

Amendment X

The powers not delegated to the United States by the Constitution, nor prohibited by it to the States, are reserved to the States respectively, or to the people.

Amendment XI [1798]

The Judicial power of the United States shall not be construed to extend to any suit in law or equity, commenced or prosecuted against one of the United States by Citizens of another State, or by Citizens or Subjects of any Foreign State.

Amendment XII [1804]

The Electors shall meet in their respective states and vote by ballot for President and Vice-President, one of whom, at least, shall not be an inhabitant of the same state with themselves; they shall name in their ballots the person voted for as President, and in distinct ballots the person voted for as Vice-President, and they shall make distinct lists of all persons voted for as President, and of all persons voted for as Vice-President, and of the number of votes for each, which lists they shall sign and certify, and transmit sealed to the seat of the government of the United States, directed to the President of the Senate;—The President of the Senate shall, in the presence of the Senate and House of Representatives, open all the certificates and the votes shall then be counted;—The person having the greatest number of votes for President, shall be the President, if such number be a majority of the whole number of Electors appointed; and if no person have such majority, then from the persons having the highest numbers not exceeding three on the list of those voted for as President, the House of Representatives shall choose immediately, by ballot, the President. But in choosing the President, the votes shall be taken by states, the representation from each state having one vote; a quorum for this purpose shall consist of a member or members from two-thirds of the states, and a majority of all the states shall be necessary to a choice. And if the House of Representatives shall not choose a President whenever the right of choice shall devolve upon them before the fourth day of March next following, then the Vice-President shall act as President, as in the case of the death or other constitutional disability of the President.[10]—The person having the greatest number of votes as Vice-President, shall be the Vice-President, if such number be a majority of the whole number of Electors appointed, and if no person have a majority, then from the two highest numbers on the list, the Senate shall choose the Vice-President; a quorum for the purpose shall consist of two-thirds of the whole number of Senators, and a majority of the whole number shall be necessary to a choice. But no person constitutionally ineligible to the office of President shall be eligible to that of Vice-President of the United States.

Amendment XIII [1865]

Section 1. Neither slavery nor involuntary servitude, except as a punishment for crime whereof the party shall have been duly convicted, shall exist within the United States, or any place subject to their jurisdiction.

Section 2. Congress shall have power to enforce this article by appropriate legislation.

[10]Refer to the Twentieth Amendment.

Amendment XIV [1868]

Section 1. All persons born or naturalized in the United States, and subject to the jurisdiction thereof, are citizens of the United States and of the State wherein they reside. No State shall make or enforce any law which shall abridge the privileges or immunities of citizens of the United States; nor shall any State deprive any person of life, liberty, or property, without due process of law; nor deny to any person within its jurisdiction the equal protection of the laws.

Section 2. Representatives shall be apportioned among the several States according to their respective numbers, counting the whole number of persons in each State, excluding Indians not taxed. But when the right to vote at any election for the choice of electors for President and Vice President of the United States, Representatives in Congress, the Executive and Judicial officers of a State, or the members of the Legislature thereof, is denied to any of the male inhabitants of such State, being twenty-one years of age,[11] and citizens of the United States, or in any way abridged, except for participation in rebellion, or other crime, the basis of representation therein shall be reduced in the proportion which the number of such male citizens shall bear to the whole number of male citizens twenty-one years of age in such State.

Section 3. No person shall be a Senator or Representative in Congress, or elector of President and Vice President, or hold any office, civil or military, under the United States, or under any State, who having previously taken an oath, as a member of Congress, or as an officer of the United States, or as a member of any State legislature, or as an executive or judicial officer of any State, to support the Constitution of the United States, shall have engaged in insurrection or rebellion against the same, or given aid or comfort to the enemies thereof. But Congress may by a vote of two thirds of each House, remove such disability.

Section 4. The validity of the public debt of the United States, authorized by law, including debts incurred for payment of pensions and bounties for services in suppressing insurrection or rebellion, shall not be questioned. But neither the United States nor any State shall assume or pay any debt or obligation incurred in aid of insurrection or rebellion against the United States, or any claim for the loss or emancipation of any slave; but all such debts, obligations and claims shall be held illegal and void.

Section 5. The Congress shall have power to enforce, by appropriate legislation, the provisions of this article.

Amendment XV [1870]

Section 1. The right of citizens of the United States to vote shall not be denied or abridged by the United States or by any State on account of race, color, or previous condition of servitude.

Section 2. The Congress shall have power to enforce this article by appropriate legislation.

---

[11]Refer to the Twenty-Sixth Amendment.

Amendment XVI [1913]

The Congress shall have power to lay and collect taxes on incomes, from whatever source derived, without apportionment among the several States, and without regard to any census or enumeration.

Amendment XVII [1913]

(1) The Senate of the United States shall be composed of two Senators from each State, elected by the people thereof, for six years; and each Senator shall have one vote. The electors in each State shall have the qualifications requisite for electors of the most numerous branch of the State legislatures.

(2) When vacancies happen in the representation of any State in the Senate, the executive authority of such State shall issue writs of election to fill such vacancies: *Provided,* That the legislature of any State may empower the executive thereof to make temporary appointments until the people fill the vacancies by election as the legislature may direct.

(3) This amendment shall not be so construed as to affect the election or term of any Senator chosen before it becomes valid as part of the Constitution.

Amendment XVIII [1919]

Section 1. After one year from the ratification of this article the manufacture, sale, or transportation of intoxicating liquors within, the importation thereof into, or the exportation thereof from the United States and all territory subject to the jurisdiction thereof for beverage purposes is hereby prohibited.

Section 2. The Congress and the several States shall have concurrent power to enforce this article by appropriate legislation.

Section 3. This article shall be inoperative unless it shall have been ratified as an amendment to the Constitution by the legislatures of the several States, as provided in the Constitution, within seven years from the date of the submission hereof to the States by the Congress.[12]

Amendment XIX [1920]

(1) The right of citizens of the United States to vote shall not be denied or abridged by the United States or by any State on account of sex.

(2) Congress shall have power to enforce this article by appropriate legislation.

Amendment XX [1933]

Section 1. The terms of the President and Vice President shall end at noon on the 20th day of January, and the terms of Senators and Representatives at noon on the 3rd day of

[12]Refer to the Twenty-First Amendment.

January, of the years in which such terms would have ended if this article had not been ratified; and the terms of their successors shall then begin.

Section 2. The Congress shall assemble at least once in every year, and such meeting shall begin at noon on the 3rd day of January, unless they shall by law appoint a different day.

Section 3. If, at the time fixed for the beginning of the term of the President, the President elect shall have died, the Vice President elect shall become President. If the President shall not have been chosen before the time fixed for the beginning of his term or if the President elect shall have failed to qualify, then the Vice President elect shall act as President until a President shall have qualified; and the Congress may by law provide for the case wherein neither a President elect nor a Vice President elect shall have qualified, declaring who shall then act as President, or the manner in which one is to act shall be selected, and such person shall act accordingly until a President or Vice President shall have qualified.

Section 4. The Congress may by law provide for the case of the death of any of the persons from whom the House of Representatives may choose a President whenever the right of choice shall have devolved upon them, and for the case of the death of any of the persons from whom the Senate may choose a Vice President whenever the right of choice shall have devolved upon them.

Section 5. Sections 1 and 2 shall take effect on the 15th day of October following the ratification of this article.

Section 6. This article shall be inoperative unless it shall have been ratified as an amendment to the Constitution by the legislatures of three-fourths of the several States within seven years from the date of its submission.

Amendment XXI [1933]

Section 1. The eighteenth article of amendment to the Constitution of the United States is hereby repealed.

Section 2. The transportation or importation into any State, Territory, or possession of the United States for delivery or use therein of intoxicating liquors, in violation of the laws thereof, is hereby prohibited.

Section 3. This article shall be inoperative unless it shall have been ratified as an amendment to the Constitution by conventions in the several States, as provided in the Constitution, within seven years from the date of the submission hereof to the States by the Congress.

Amendment XXII [1951]

Section 1. No person shall be elected to the office of the President more than twice, and no person who has held the office of President, or acted as President, for more than two years of a term to which some other person was elected President shall be elected to the office of President more than once. But this Article shall not apply to any person holding the office of President when this Article was proposed by the Congress, and shall not prevent any person who may be holding the office of President, or acting as President, during the term within which this Article becomes operative from holding the office of President or acting as president during the remainder of such term.

Section 2. This article shall be inoperative unless it shall have been ratified as an amendment to the Constitution by the legislatures of three-fourths of the several States within seven years from the date of its submission to the States by the Congress.

Amendment XXIII [1961]

Section 1. The District constituting the seat of Government of the United States shall appoint in such manner as the Congress may direct:

> A number of electors of President and Vice President equal to the whole number of Senators and Representatives in Congress to which the District would be entitled if it were a State, but in no event more than the least populous state; they shall be in addition to those appointed by the states, but they shall be considered, for the purposes of the election of President and Vice Prisident, to be electors appointed by a state; and they shall meet in the District and perform such duties as provided by the twelfth article of amendment.

Section 2. The Congress shall have power to enforce this article by appropriate legislation.

Amendment XXIV [1964]

Section 1. The right of citizens of the United States to vote in any primary or other election for President or Vice President, for electors for President or Vice President, or for Senator or Representative in Congress, shall not be denied or abridged by the United States or any State by reason of failure to pay any poll tax or other tax.

Section 2. The Congress shall have power to enforce this article by appropriate legislation.

Amendment XXV [1967]

Section 1. In case of the removal of the President from office or of his death or resignation, the Vice President shall become President.

Section 2. Whenever there is a vacancy in the office of the Vice President, the President shall nominate a Vice President who shall take office upon confirmation by a majority vote of both Houses of Congress.

Section 3. Whenever the President transmits to the President pro tempore of the Senate and the Speaker of the House of Representatives his written declaration that he is unable to discharge the powers and duties of his office, and until he transmits to them a written declaration to the contrary, such powers and duties shall be discharged by the Vice President as Acting President.

Section 4. Whenever the Vice President and a majority of either the principal officers of the executive departments or of such other body as Congress may by law provide, transmit to the President pro tempore of the Senate and the Speaker of the House of Representatives their written declaration that the President is unable to discharge the powers and duties of his office, the Vice President shall immediately assume the powers and duties of the office as Acting President.

Thereafter, when the President transmits to the President pro tempore of the Senate and the Speaker of the House of Representatives his written declaration that no inability exists, he shall resume the powers and duties of his office unless the Vice President and a majority of either the principal officers of the executive departments or of such other body as Congress may by law provide, transmit within four days to the President pro tempore of the Senate and the Speaker of the House of Representatives their written declaration that the President is unable to discharge the powers and duties of his office. Thereupon Congress shall decide the issue, assembling within forty-eight hours for that purpose if not in session. If the Congress, within twenty-one days after receipt of the latter written declaration, or, if Congress is not in session, within twenty-one days after Congress is required to assemble, determines by two-thirds vote of both Houses that the President is unable to discharge the powers and duties of his office, the Vice President shall continue to discharge the same as Acting President; otherwise, the President shall resume the powers and duties of his office.

Amendment XXVI [1971]

Section 1. The right of citizens of the United States, who are eighteen years of age or older, to vote shall not be denied or abridged by the United States or by any State on account of age.

Section 2. The Congress shall have power to enforce this article by appropriate legislation.

Amendment XXVII [1992]

No law, varying the compensation for the services of the Senators and Representatives, shall take effect, until an election of Representatives shall have intervened.

Uniform Commercial Code 2000 Official Text, Article 2

Table of Sections

Article 2. Sales

Part 1. Short Title, General Construction, and Subject Matter

Part 2. Form, Formation, and Readjustment of Contract

Article 2. Sales

Part 1. Short Title, General Construction, and Subject Matter

§ 2–101. Short Title

This Article shall be known and may be cited as Uniform Commercial Code—Sales.

§ 2–102. Scope; Certain Security and Other Transactions Excluded from This Article

Unless the context otherwise requires, this Article applies to transactions in goods; it does not apply to any transaction which although in the form of an unconditional contract to sell or present sale is intended to operate only as a security transaction; nor does this Article impair or repeal any statute regulating sales to consumers, farmers, or other specified classes of buyers.

§ 2–103. Definitions and Index of Definitions

(1) In this Article unless the context otherwise requires

(a) "Buyer" means a person who buys or contracts to buy goods.

(b) "Good faith" in the case of a merchant means honesty in fact and the observance of reasonable commercial standards of fair dealing in the trade.

(c) "Receipt" of goods means taking physical possession of them.

(d) "Seller" means a person who sells or contracts to sell goods.

(2) Other definitions applying to this Article or to specified Parts thereof, and the sections in which they appear, are:

"Acceptance"	Section 2–606.
"Banker's credit"	Section 2–325.
"Between merchants"	Section 2–104.
"Cancellation"	Section 2–106(4).
"Commercial unit"	Section 2–105.
"Confirmed credit"	Section 2–325.
"Conforming to contract"	Section 2–106.
"Contract for sale"	Section 2–106.
"Cover"	Section 2–712.
"Entrusting"	Section 2–403.
"Financing agency"	Section 2–104.
"Future goods"	Section 2–105.
"Goods"	Section 2–105.
"Identification"	Section 2–501.
"Installment contract"	Section 2–612.
"Letter of credit"	Section 2–325.
"Lot"	Section 2–105.
"Merchant"	Section 2–104.
"Overseas"	Section 2–323.
"Person in position of seller"	Section 2–707.
"Present sale"	Section 2–106.
"Sale"	Section 2–106.
"Sale on approval"	Section 2–326.
"Sale or return"	Section 2–326.
"Termination"	Section 2–106.

(3) The following definitions in other Articles apply to this Article:

"Check"	Section 3–104.
"Consignee"	Section 7–102.
"Consignor"	Section 7–102.
"Consumer goods"	Section 9–102.
"Dishonor"	Section 3–502.
"Draft"	Section 3–104.

(4) In addition Article 1 contains general definitions and principles of construction and interpretation applicable throughout this Article.

§ 2–104. *Definitions: "Merchant"; "Between Merchants"; "Financing Agency"*

(1) "Merchant" means a person who deals in goods of the kind or otherwise by his occupation holds himself out as having knowledge or skill peculiar to the practices or

goods involved in the transaction or to whom such knowledge or skill may be attributed by his employment of an agent or broker or other intermediary who by his occupation holds himself out as having such knowledge or skill.

(2) "Financing agency" means a bank, finance company, or other person who in the ordinary course of business makes advances against goods or documents of title or who by arrangement with either the seller or the buyer intervenes in ordinary course to make or collect payment due or claimed under the contract for sale, as by purchasing or paying the seller's draft or making advances against it or by merely taking it for collection whether or not the documents of title accompany the draft. "Financing agency" includes also a bank or other person who similarly intervenes between persons who are in the position of seller and buyer in respect to the goods (Section 2–707).

(3) "Between merchants" means in any transaction with respect to which both parties are chargeable with the knowledge or skill of merchants.

§ 2–105. Definitions: Transferability; "Goods"; "Future" Goods; "Lot"; "Commercial Unit"

(1) "Goods" means all things (including specially manufactured goods) which are movable at the time of identification to the contract for sale other than the money in which the price is to be paid, investment securities (Article 8), and things in action. "Goods" also includes the unborn young of animals and growing crops and other identified things attached to realty as described in the section on goods to be severed from realty (Section 2–107).

(2) Goods must be both existing and identified before any interest in them can pass. Goods which are not both existing and identified are "future" goods. A purported present sale of future goods or of any interest therein operates as a contract to sell.

(3) There may be a sale of a part interest in existing identified goods.

(4) An undivided share in an identified bulk of fungible goods is sufficiently identified to be sold although the quantity of the bulk is not determined. Any agreed proportion of such a bulk or any quantity thereof agreed upon by number, weight, or other measure may to the extent of the seller's interest in the bulk be sold to the buyer who then becomes an owner in common.

(5) "Lot" means a parcel or a single article which is the subject matter of a separate sale or delivery, whether or not it is sufficient to perform the contract.

(6) "Commercial unit" means such a unit of goods as by commercial usage is a single whole for purposes of sale and division of which materially impairs its character or value on the market or in use. A commercial unit may be a single article (as a machine) or a set of articles (as a suite of furniture or an assortment of sizes) or a quantity (as a bale, gross, or carload) or any other unit treated in use or in the relevant market as a single whole.

§ 2–106. Definitions: "Contract"; "Agreement"; "Contract for Sale"; "Sale"; "Present Sale"; "Conforming" to Contract; "Termination"; "Cancellation"

(1) In this Article unless the context otherwise requires "contract" and "agreement" are limited to those relating to the present or future sale of goods. "Contract for sale" includes both a present sale of goods and a contract to sell goods at a future time. A

"sale" consists in the passing of title from the seller to the buyer for a price (Section 2–401). A "present sale" means a sale which is accomplished by the making of the contract.

(2) Goods or conduct including any part of a performance are "conforming" or conform to the contract when they are in accordance with the obligations under the contract.

(3) "Termination" occurs when either party pursuant to a power created by agreement or law puts an end to the contract otherwise than for its breach. On "termination" all obligations which are still executory on both sides are discharged, but any right based on prior breach or performance survives.

(4) "Cancellation" occurs when either party puts an end to the contract for breach by the other, and its effect is the same as that of "termination" except that the cancelling party also retains any remedy for breach of the whole contract or any unperformed balance.

§ 2–107. Goods to Be Severed from Realty: Recording

(1) A contract for the sale of minerals or the like (including oil and gas) or a structure or its materials to be removed from realty is a contract for the sale of goods within this Article if they are to be severed by the seller; but until severance a purported present sale thereof which is not effective as a transfer of an interest in land is effective only as a contract to sell.

(2) A contract for the sale apart from the land of growing crops or other things attached to realty and capable of severance without material harm thereto but not described in subsection (1) or of timber to be cut is a contract for the sale of goods within this Article whether the subject matter is to be severed by the buyer or by the seller even though it forms part of the realty at the time of contracting, and the parties can by identification effect a present sale before severance.

(3) The provisions of this section are subject to any third party rights provided by the law relating to realty records, and the contract for sale may be executed and recorded as a document transferring an interest in land and shall then constitute notice to third parties of the buyer's right under the contract for sale.

Part 2. Form, Formation, and Readjustment of Contract

§ 2–201. Formal Requirements; Statute of Frauds

(1) Except as otherwise provided in this section, a contract for the sale of goods for the price of $500 or more is not enforceable by way of action or defense unless there is some writing sufficient to indicate that a contract for sale has been made between the parties and signed by the party against whom enforcement is sought or by his authorized agent or broker. A writing is not insufficient because it omits or incorrectly states a term agreed upon, but the contract is not enforceable under this paragraph beyond the quantity of goods shown in such writing.

(2) Between merchants, if within a reasonable time a writing in confirmation of the contract and sufficient against the sender is received and the party receiving it has reason to know its contents, it satisfies the requirements of subsection (1) against such party unless written notice of objection to its contents is given within 10 days after it is received.

(3) A contract which does not satisfy the requirements of subsection (1) but which is valid in other respects is enforceable

    (a) if the goods are to be specially manufactured for the buyer and are not suitable for sale to others in the ordinary course of the seller's business and the seller, before notice of repudiation is received and under circumstances which reasonably indicate that the goods are for the buyer, has made either a substantial beginning of their manufacture or commitments for their procurement; or

    (b) if the party against whom enforcement is sought admits in his pleading, testimony, or otherwise in court that a contract for sale was made, but the contract is not enforceable under this provision beyond the quantity of goods admitted; or

    (c) with respect to goods for which payment has been made and accepted or which have been received and accepted (Section 2–606).

§ 2–202. Final Written Expression: Parol or Extrinsic Evidence

Terms with respect to which the confirmatory memoranda of the parties agree or which are otherwise set forth in a writing intended by the parties as a final expression of their agreement with respect to such terms as are included therein may not be contradicted by evidence of any prior agreement or of a contemporaneous oral agreement but may be explained or supplemented

    (a) by course and dealing or usage of trade (Section 1–205) or by course of performance (Section 2–208); and

    (b) by evidence of consistent additional terms unless the court finds the writing to have been intended also as a complete and exclusive statement of the terms of the agreement.

§ 2–203. Seals Inoperative

The affixing of a seal to a writing evidencing a contract for sale or an offer to buy or sell goods does not constitute the writing a sealed instrument and the law with respect to sealed instruments does not apply to such a contract or offer.

§ 2–204. Formation in General

(1) A contract for sale of goods may be made in any manner sufficient to show agreement, including conduct by both parties which recognizes the existence of such a contract.

(2) An agreement sufficient to constitute a contract for sale may be found even though the moment of its making is undetermined.

(3) Even though one or more terms are left open a contract for sale does not fail for indefiniteness if the parties have intended to make a contract and there is a reasonably certain basis for giving an appropriate remedy.

§ 2–205. Firm Offers

An offer by a merchant to buy or sell goods in a signed writing which by its terms gives assurance that it will be held open is not revocable, for lack of consideration, during the time stated or if no time is stated for a reasonable time, but in no event may such period of irrevocability exceed three months; but any such term of assurance on a form supplied by the offeree must be separately signed by the offerer.

§ 2–206. Offer and Acceptance in Formation of Contract

(1) Unless otherwise unambiguously indicated by the language or circumstances

    (a) an offer to make a contract shall be construed as inviting acceptance in any manner and by any medium reasonable in the circumstances;

    (b) an order or other offer to buy goods for prompt or current shipment shall be construed as inviting acceptance either by a prompt promise to ship or by the prompt or current shipment of conforming or nonconforming goods, but such a shipment of nonconforming goods does not constitute an acceptance if the seller seasonably notifies the buyer that the shipment is offered only as an accommodation to the buyer.

(2) Where the beginning of a requested performance is a reasonable mode of acceptance, an offerer who is not notified of acceptance within a reasonable time may treat the offer as having lapsed before acceptance.

§ 2–207. Additional Terms in Acceptance or Confirmation

(1) A definite and seasonable expression of acceptance or a written confirmation which is sent within a reasonable time operates as an acceptance even though it states terms additional to or different from those offered or agreed upon, unless acceptance is expressly made conditional on assent to the additional or different terms.

(2) The additional terms are to be construed as proposals for addition to the contract. Between merchants such terms become part of the contract unless

    (a) the offer expressly limits acceptance to the terms of the offer;

    (b) they materially alter it; or

    (c) notification of objection to them has already been given or is given within a reasonable time after notice of them is received.

(3) Conduct by both parties which recognizes the existence of a contract is sufficient to establish a contract for sale although the writings of the parties do not otherwise establish a contract. In such case the terms of the particular contract consist of those terms on which the writings of the parties agree, together with any supplementary terms incorporated under any other provisions of this Act.

§ 2–208. Course of Performance or Practical Construction

(1) Where the contract for sale involves repeated occasions for performance by either party with knowledge of the nature of the performance and opportunity for objection to it by the other, any course of performance accepted or acquiesced in without objection shall be relevant to determine the meaning of the agreement.

(2) The express terms of the agreement and any such course of performance, as well as any course of dealing and usage of trade, shall be construed whenever reasonable as consistent with each other; but when such construction is unreasonable, express terms shall control course of performance and course of performance shall control both course of dealing and usage of trade (Section 1–205).

(3) Subject to the provisions of the next section on modification and waiver, such course of performance shall be relevant to show a waiver or modification of any term inconsistent with such course of performance.

§ 2–209. *Modification, Rescission, and Waiver*

(1) An agreement modifying a contract within this Article needs no consideration to be binding.

(2) A signed agreement which excludes modification or rescission except by a signed writing cannot be otherwise modified or rescinded, but except as between merchants such a requirement on a form supplied by the merchant must be separately signed by the other party.

(3) The requirements of the statute of frauds section of this Article (Section 2–201) must be satisfied if the contract as modified is within its provisions.

(4) Although an attempt at modification or rescission does not satisfy the requirements of subsection (2) or (3) it can operate as a waiver.

(5) A party who has made a waiver affecting an executory portion of the contract may retract the waiver by reasonable notification received by the other party that strict performance will be required of any term waived, unless the retraction would be unjust in view of a material change of position in reliance on the waiver.

§ 2–210. *Delegation of Performance; Assignment of Rights*

(1) A party may perform his duty through a delegate unless otherwise agreed or unless the other party has a substantial interest in having his original promisor perform or control the acts required by the contract. No delegation of performance relieves the party delegating of any duty to perform or any liability for breach.

(2) Except as otherwise provided in Section 9–406, unless otherwise agreed all rights of either seller or buyer can be assigned except where the assignment would materially change the duty of the other party, or increase materially the burden or risk imposed on him by his contract, or impair materially his chance of obtaining return performance. A right to damages for breach of the whole contract or a right arising out of the assignor's due performance of his entire obligation can be assigned despite agreement otherwise.

(3) The creation, attachment, perfection, or enforcement of a security interest in the seller's interest under a contract is not a transfer that materially changes the duty of or increases materially the burden or risk imposed on the buyer or impairs materially the buyer's chance of obtaining return performance within the purview of subsection (2) unless, and then only to the extent that, enforcement actually results in a delegation of material performance of the seller. Even in that event, the creation, attachment, perfection, and enforcement of the security interest remain effective, but (i) the seller is liable to the buyer for damages caused by the delegation to the extent that the damages could not reasonably be prevented by the buyer, and (ii) a court having jurisdiction may grant other appropriate relief, including cancellation of the contract for sale or an injunction against enforcement of the security interest or consummation of the enforcement.

(4) Unless the circumstances indicate the contrary a prohibition of assignment of "the contract" is to be construed as barring only the delegation to the assignee of the assignor's performance.

(5) An assignment of "the contract" or of "all my rights under the contract" or an assignment in similar general terms is an assignment of rights and unless the language or the circumstances (as in an assignment for security) indicate the contrary, it is a delegation of performance of the duties of the assignor and its acceptance by the assignee constitutes a promise by him to perform those duties. This promise is enforceable by either the assignor or the other party to the original contract.

(6) The other party may treat any assignment which delegates performance as creating reasonable grounds for insecurity and may without prejudice to his rights against the assignor demand assurances from the assignee (Section 2–609).

Part 3. General Obligation and Construction of Contract

§ 2–301. General Obligations of Parties

The obligation of the seller is to transfer and deliver and that of the buyer is to accept and pay in accordance with the contract.

§ 2–302. Unconscionable Contract or Clause

(1) If the court as a matter of law finds the contract or any clause of the contract to have been unconscionable at the time it was made the court may refuse to enforce the contract, or it may enforce the remainder of the contract without the unconscionable clause, or it may so limit the application of any unconscionable clause as to avoid any unconscionable result.

(2) When it is claimed or appears to the court that the contract or any clause thereof may be unconscionable the parties shall be afforded a reasonable opportunity to present evidence as to its commercial setting, purpose, and effect to aid the court in making the determination.

§ 2–303. Allocation or Division of Risks

Where this Article allocates a risk or a burden as between the parties "unless otherwise agreed," the agreement may not only shift the allocation but may also divide the risk or burden.

§ 2–304. Price Payable in Money, Goods, Realty, or Otherwise

(1) The price can be made payable in money or otherwise. If it is payable in whole or in part in goods each party is a seller of the goods which he is to transfer.

(2) Even though all or part of the price is payable in an interest in realty the transfer of the goods and the seller's obligations with reference to them are subject to this Article, but not the transfer of the interest in realty or the transferor's obligations in connection therewith.

§ 2–305. Open Price Term

(1) The parties if they so intend can conclude a contract for sale even though the price is not settled. In such a case the price is a reasonable price at the time for delivery if

    (a) nothing is said as to price; or

    (b) the price is left to be agreed by the parties and they fail to agree; or

(c) the price is to be fixed in terms of some agreed market or other standard as set or recorded by a third person or agency and it is not so set or recorded.

(2) A price to be fixed by the seller or by the buyer means a price for him to fix in good faith.

(3) When a price left to be fixed otherwise than by agreement of the parties fails to be fixed through fault of one party the other may at his option treat the contract as cancelled or himself fix a reasonable price.

(4) Where, however, the parties intend not to be bound unless the price be fixed or agreed and it is not fixed or agreed there is no contract. In such a case the buyer must return any goods already received or if unable so to do must pay their reasonable value at the time of delivery and the seller must return any portion of the price paid on account.

§ 2–306. Output, Requirements, and Exclusive Dealings

(1) A term which measures the quantity by the output of the seller or the requirements of the buyer means such actual output or requirements as may occur in good faith, except that no quantity unreasonably disproportionate to any stated estimate or in the absence of a stated estimate to any normal or otherwise comparable prior output or requirements may be tendered or demanded.

(2) A lawful agreement by either the seller or the buyer for exclusive dealing in the kind of goods concerned imposes unless otherwise agreed an obligation by the seller to use best efforts to supply the goods any by the buyer to use best efforts to promote their sale.

§ 2–307. Delivery in Single Lot or Several Lots

Unless otherwise agreed all goods called for by a contract for sale must be tendered in a single delivery and payment is due only on such tender; but where the circumstances give either party the right to make or demand delivery in lots the price if it can be apportioned may be demanded for each lot.

§ 2–308. Absence of Specified Place for Delivery

Unless otherwise agreed

(a) the place for delivery of goods is the seller's place of business or if he has none his residence; but

(b) in a contract for sale of identified goods which to the knowledge of the parties at the time of contracting are in some other place, that place is the place for their delivery; and

(c) documents of title may be delivered through customary banking channels.

§ 2–309. Absence of Specific Time Provisions; Notice of Termination

(1) The time for shipment or delivery or any other action under a contract if not provided in this Article or agreed upon shall be a reasonable time.

(2) Where the contract provides for successive performance but is indefinite in duration it is valid for a reasonable time but unless otherwise agreed may be terminated at any time by either party.

(3) Termination of a contract by one party except on the happening of an agreed event requires that reasonable notification be received by the other party and an agreement dispensing with notification is invalid if its operation would be unconscionable.

§ 2–310. Open Time for Payment or Running of Credit; Authority to Ship under Reservation

Unless otherwise agreed

(a) payment is due at the time and place at which the buyer is to receive the goods even though the place of shipment is the place of delivery; and

(b) if the seller is authorized to send the goods he may ship them under reservation, and may tender the documents of title, but the buyer may inspect the goods after their arrival before payment is due unless such inspection is inconsistent with the terms of the contract (Section 2–513); and

(c) if delivery is authorized and made by way of documents of title otherwise than by subsection (b) then payment is due at the time and place at which the buyer is to receive the documents regardless of where the goods are to be received; and

(d) where the seller is required or authorized to ship the goods on credit the credit period runs from the time of shipment, but postdating the invoice or delaying its dispatch will correspondingly delay the starting of the credit period.

§ 2–311. Options and Cooperation Respecting Performance

(1) An agreement for sale which is otherwise sufficiently definite (subsection (3) of Section 2–204) to be a contract is not made invalid by the fact that it leaves particulars of performance to be specified by one of the parties. Any such specification must be made in good faith and within limits set by commercial reasonableness.

(2) Unless otherwise agreed specifications relating to assortment of the goods are at the buyer's option and except as otherwise provided in subsections (1) (c) and (3) of Section 2–319 specifications or arrangements relating to shipment are at the seller's option.

(3) Where such specification would materially affect the other party's performance but is not seasonably made or where one party's cooperation is necessary to the agreed performance of the other but is not seasonably forthcoming, the other party in addition to all other remedies

(a) is excused for any resulting delay in his own performance; and

(b) may also either proceed to perform in any reasonable manner or after the time for a material part of his own performance treat the failure to specify or to cooperate as a breach by failure to deliver or accept the goods.

§ 2–312. Warranty of Title and against Infringement; Buyer's Obligation against Infringement

(1) Subject to subsection (2) there is in a contract for sale a warranty by the seller that

(a) the title conveyed shall be good, and its transfer rightful; and

(b) the goods shall be delivered free from any security interest or other lien or encumbrance of which the buyer at the time of contracting has no knowledge.

(2) A warranty under subsection (1) will be excluded or modified only by specific language or by circumstances which give the buyer reason to know that the person selling does not claim title in himself or that he is purporting to sell only such right or title as he or a third person may have.

(3) Unless otherwise agreed a seller who is a merchant regularly dealing in goods of the kind warrants that the goods shall be delivered free of the rightful claim of any third person by way of infringement or the like; but a buyer who furnishes specifications to the seller must hold the seller harmless against any such claim which arises out of compliance with the specifications.

§ 2–313. Express Warranties by Affirmation, Promise, Description, Sample

(1) Express warranties by the seller are created as follows:

(a) Any affirmation of fact or promise made by the seller to the buyer which relates to the goods and becomes part of the basis of the bargain creates an express warranty that the goods shall conform to the affirmation or promise.

(b) Any description of the goods which is made part of the basis of the bargain creates an express warranty that the goods shall conform to the description.

(c) Any sample or model which is made part of the basis of the bargain creates an express warranty that the whole of the goods shall conform to the sample or model.

(2) It is not necessary to the creation of an express warranty that the seller use formal words such as "warrant" or "guarantee" or that he have a specific intention to make a warranty, but an affirmation merely of the value of the goods or a statement purporting to be merely the seller's opinion or commendation of the goods does not create a warranty.

§ 2–314. Implied Warranty: Merchantability; Usage of Trade

(1) Unless excluded or modified (Section 2–316), a warranty that the goods shall be merchantable is implied in a contract for their sale if the seller is a merchant with respect to goods of that kind. Under this section the serving for value of food or drink to be consumed either on the premises or elsewhere is a sale.

(2) Goods to be merchantable must be at least such as

(a) pass without objection in the trade under the contract description; and

(b) in the case of fungible goods, are of fair average quality within the description; and

(c) are fit for the ordinary purposes for which such goods are used; and

(d) run, within the variations permitted by the agreement, of even kind, quality, and quantity within each unit and among all units involved; and

(e) are adequately contained, packaged, and labeled as the agreement may require; and

(f) conform to the promises or affirmations of fact made on the container or label if any.

(3) Unless excluded or modified (Section 2–316) other implied warranties may arise from course of dealing or usage of trade.

§ 2–315. Implied Warranty: Fitness for Particular Purpose

Where the seller at the time of contracting has reason to know any particular purpose for which the goods are required and that the buyer is relying on the seller's skill or judgment to select or furnish suitable goods, there is unless excluded or modified under the next section an implied warranty that the goods shall be fit for such purpose.

§ 2–316. Exclusion or Modification of Warranties

(1) Words or conduct relevant to the creation of an express warranty and words or conduct tending to negate or limit warranty shall be construed wherever reasonable as consistent with each other, but subject to the provisions of this Article on parol or extrinsic evidence (Section 2–202) negation or limitation is inoperative to the extent that such construction is unreasonable.

(2) Subject to subsection (3), to exclude or modify the implied warranty of merchantability or any part of it the language must mention merchantability and in case of a writing must be conspicuous, and to exclude or modify any implied warranty of fitness the exclusion must be by a writing and conspicuous. Language to exclude all implied warranties of fitness is sufficient if it states, for example, that "There are no warranties which extend beyond the description on the face hereof."

(3) Notwithstanding subsection (2)

    (a) unless the circumstances indicate otherwise, all implied warranties are excluded by expressions like "as is," "with all faults," or other language which in common understanding calls the buyer's attention to the exclusion of warranties and makes plain that there is no implied warranty; and

    (b) when the buyer before entering into the contract has examined the goods or the sample or model as fully as he desired or has refused to examine the goods there is no implied warranty with regard to defects which an examination ought in the circumstances to have revealed to him; and

    (c) an implied warranty can also be excluded or modified by course of dealing or course of performance or usage of trade.

(4) Remedies for breach of warranty can be limited in accordance with the provisions of this Article on liquidation or limitation of damages and on contractual modification of remedy (Sections 2–718 and 2–719).

§ 2–317. Cumulation and Conflict of Warranties Express or Implied

Warranties whether express or implied shall be construed as consistent with each other and as cumulative, but if such construction is unreasonable the intention of the parties shall determine which warranty is dominant. In ascertaining that intention the following rules apply:

    (a) Exact or technical specifications displace an inconsistent sample or model or general language of description.

    (b) A sample from an existing bulk displaces inconsistent general language of description.

(c) Express warranties displace inconsistent implied warranties other than an implied warranty of fitness for a particular purpose.

§ 2–318. Third Party Beneficiaries of Warranties Express or Implied

Note: *If this Act is introduced in the Congress of the United States this section should be omitted. (States to select one alternative.)*

Alternative A A seller's warranty whether express or implied extends to any natural person who is in the family or household of his buyer or who is a guest in his home if it is reasonable to expect that such person may use, consume, or be affected by the goods and who is injured in person by breach of the warranty. A seller may not exclude or limit the operation of this section.

Alternative B A seller's warranty whether express or implied extends to any natural person who may reasonably be expected to use, consume, or be affected by the goods and who is injured in person by breach of the warranty. A seller may not exclude or limit the operation of this section.

Alternative C A seller's warranty whether express or implied extends to any person who may reasonably be expected to use, consume, or be affected by the goods and who is injured by breach of the warranty. A seller may not exclude or limit the operation of this section with respect to injury to the person of an individual to whom the warranty extends.

§ 2–319. F.O.B. and F.A.S. Terms

(1) Unless otherwise agreed the term F.O.B. (which means "free on board") at a named place, even though used only in connection with the stated price, is a delivery term under which

(a) when the term is F.O.B. the place of shipment, the seller must at that place ship the goods in the manner provided in this Article (Section 2–504) and bear the expense and risk of putting them into the possession of the carrier; or

(b) when the term is F.O.B. the place of destination, the seller must at his own expense and risk transport the goods to that place and there tender delivery of them in the manner provided in this Article (Section 2–503);

(c) when under either (a) or (b) the term is also F.O.B. vessel, car, or other vehicle, the seller must in addition at his own expense and risk load the goods on board. If the term is F.O.B. vessel the buyer must name the vessel and in an appropriate case the seller must comply with the provisions of this Article on the form of bill of lading (Section 2–323).

(2) Unless otherwise agreed the term F.A.S. vessel (which means "free alongside") at a named port, even though used only in connection with the stated price, is a delivery term under which the seller must

(a) at his own expense and risk deliver the goods alongside the vessel in the manner usual in that port or on a dock designated and provided by the buyer; and

(b) obtain and tender a receipt for the goods in exchange for which the carrier is under a duty to issue a bill of lading.

(3) Unless otherwise agreed in any case falling within subsection (1)(a) or (c) or subsection (2) the buyer must seasonably give any needed instructions for making delivery, including when the term is F.A.S. or F.O.B. the loading berth of the vessel and in an appropriate case its name and sailing date. The seller may treat the failure of needed instructions as a failure of cooperation under this Article (Section 2–311). He may also at his option move the goods in any reasonable manner preparatory to delivery or shipment.

(4) Under the term F.O.B. vessel or F.A.S. unless otherwise agreed the buyer must make payment against tender of the required documents and the seller may not tender nor the buyer demand delivery of the goods in substitution for the documents.

§ 2–320. C.I.F. and C. & F. Terms

(1) The term C.I.F. means that the price includes in a lump sum the cost of the goods and the insurance and freight to the named destination. The term C. & F. or C.F. means that the price so includes cost and freight to the named destination.

(2) Unless otherwise agreed and even though used only in connection with the stated price and destination, the term C.I.F. destination or its equivalent requires the seller at his own expense and risk to

(a) put the goods into the possession of a carrier at the port for shipment and obtain a negotiable bill or bills of lading covering the entire transportation to the named destination; and

(b) load the goods and obtain a receipt from the carrier (which may be contained in the bill of lading) showing that the freight has been paid or provided for; and

(c) obtain a policy or certificate of insurance, including any war risk insurance, of a kind and on terms then current at the port of shipment in the usual amount, in the currency of the contract, shown to cover the same goods covered by the bill of lading and providing for payment of loss to the order of the buyer or for the account of whom it may concern; but the seller may add to the price the amount of the premium for any such war risk insurance; and

(d) prepare an invoice of the goods and procure any other documents required to effect shipment or to comply with the contract; and

(e) forward and tender with commercial promptness all the documents in due form and with any endorsement necessary to perfect the buyer's rights.

(3) Unless otherwise agreed the term C. & F. or its equivalent has the same effect and imposes upon the seller the same obligations and risks as a C.I.F. term except the obligation as to insurance.

(4) Under the term C.I.F. or C. & F. unless otherwise agreed the buyer must make payment against tender of the required documents and the seller may not tender nor the buyer demand delivery of the goods in substitution for the documents.

§ 2–321. C.I.F. or C. & F.: "Net Landed Weights"; "Payment on Arrival"; Warranty of Condition on Arrival

Under a contract containing a term C.I.F. or C. & F.

(1) Where the price is based on or is to be adjusted according to "net landed weights," "delivered weights," "out turn" quantity or quality, or the like, unless otherwise agreed the seller must reasonably estimate the price. The payment due on tender of the documents called for by the contract is the amount so estimated, but after final adjustment of the price a settlement must be made with commercial promptness.

(2) An agreement described in subsection (1) or any warranty of quality or condition of the goods on arrival places upon the seller the risk of ordinary deterioration, shrinkage, and the like in transportation but has no effect on the place or time of identification to the contract for sale or delivery or on the passing of the risk of loss.

(3) Unless otherwise agreed where the contract provides for payment on or after arrival of the goods the seller must before payment allow such preliminary inspection as is feasible; but if the goods are lost delivery of the documents and payment are due when the goods should have arrived.

§ 2–322. Delivery "Ex-Ship"

(1) Unless otherwise agreed a term for delivery of goods "ex-ship" (which means from the carrying vessel) or in equivalent language is not restricted to a particular ship and requires delivery from a ship which has reached a place at the named port of destination where goods of the kind are usually discharged.

(2) Under such a term unless otherwise agreed

    (a) the seller must discharge all liens arising out of the carriage and furnish the buyer with a direction which puts the carrier under a duty to deliver the goods; and

    (b) the risk of loss does not pass to the buyer until the goods leave the ship's tackle or are otherwise properly unloaded.

§ 2–323. Form of Bill of Lading Required in Overseas Shipment; "Overseas"

(1) Where the contract contemplates overseas shipment and contains a term C.I.F. or C. & F. or F.O.B. vessel, the seller unless otherwise agreed must obtain a negotiable bill of lading stating that the goods have been loaded on board or, in the case of a term C.I.F. or C. & F., received for shipment.

(2) Where in a case within subsection (1) a bill of lading has been issued in a set of parts, unless otherwise agreed if the documents are not to be sent from abroad the buyer may demand tender of the full set; otherwise only one part of the bill of lading need be tendered. Even if the agreement expressly requires a full set

    (a) due tender of a single part is acceptable within the provisions of this Article on cure of improper delivery (subsection (1) of Section 2–508); and

    (b) even though the full set is demanded, if the documents are sent from abroad the person tendering an incomplete set may nevertheless require payment upon furnishing an indemnity which the buyer in good faith deems adequate.

(3) A shipment by water or by air or a contract contemplating such shipment is "overseas" insofar as by usage of trade or agreement it is subject to the commercial, financing, or shipping practices characteristic of international deep water commerce.

§ 2–324. "No Arrival, No Sale" Term

Under a term "no arrival, no sale" or terms of like meaning, unless otherwise agreed,

    (a) the seller must properly ship conforming goods and if they arrive by any means he must tender them on arrival but he assumes no obligation that the goods will arrive unless he has caused the nonarrival; and

    (b) where without fault of the seller the goods are in part lost or have so deteriorated as no longer to conform to the contract or arrive after the contract time, the buyer may proceed as if there had been casualty to identified goods (Section 2–613).

§ 2–325. "Letter of Credit" Term; "Confirmed Credit"

(1) Failure of the buyer seasonably to furnish an agreed letter of credit is a breach of the contract for sale.

(2) The delivery to seller of a proper letter of credit suspends the buyer's obligation to pay. If the letter of credit is dishonored, the seller may on seasonable notification to the buyer require payment directly from him.

(3) Unless otherwise agreed the term "letter of credit" or "banker's credit" in a contract for sale means an irrevocable credit issued by a financing agency of good repute and, where the shipment is overseas, of good international repute. The term "confirmed credit" means that the credit must also carry the direct obligation of such an agency which does business in the seller's financial market.

§ 2–326. Sale on Approval and Sale or Return; Rights of Creditors

(1) Unless otherwise agreed, if delivered goods may be returned by the buyer even though they conform to the contract, the transaction is

    (a) a "sale on approval" if the goods are delivered primarily for use, and

    (b) a "sale or return" if the goods are delivered primarily for resale.

(2) Goods held on approval are not subject to the claims of the buyer's creditors until acceptance; goods held on sale or return are subject to such claims while in the buyer's possession.

(3) Any "or return" term of a contract for sale is to be treated as a separate contract for sale within the statute of frauds section of this Article (Section 2–201) and as contradicting the sale aspect of the contract within the provisions of this Article on parol or extrinsic evidence (Section 2–202).

§ 2–327. Special Incidents of Sale on Approval and Sale or Return

(1) Under a sale on approval unless otherwise agreed

    (a) although the goods are identified to the contract the risk of loss and the title do not pass to the buyer until acceptance; and

    (b) use of the goods consistent with the purpose of trial is not acceptance but failure seasonably to notify the seller of election to return the goods is acceptance, and if the goods conform to the contract acceptance of any part is acceptance of the whole; and

(c) after due notification of election to return, the return is at the seller's risk and expense but a merchant buyer must follow any reasonable instructions.

(2) Under a sale or return unless otherwise agreed

(a) the option to return extends to the whole or any commercial unit of the goods while in substantially their original conditions, but must be exercised seasonably; and

(b) the return is at the buyer's risk and expense.

§ 2–328. Sale by Auction

(1) In a sale by auction if goods are put up in lots each lot is the subject of a separate sale.

(2) A sale by auction is complete when the auctioneer so announces by the fall of the hammer or in other customary manner. Where a bid is made while the hammer is falling in acceptance of a prior bid the auctioneer may in his discretion reopen the bidding or declare the goods sold under the bid on which the hammer was falling.

(3) Such a sale is with reserve unless the goods are in explicit terms put up without reserve. In an auction with reserve the auctioneer may withdraw the goods at any time until he announces completion of the sale. In an auction without reserve, after the auctioneer calls for bids on an article or lot, that article or lot cannot be withdrawn unless no bid is made within a reasonable time. In either case a bidder may retract his bid until the auctioneer's announcement of completion of the sale, but a bidder's retraction does not revive any previous bid.

(4) If the auctioneer knowingly receives a bid on the seller's behalf or the seller makes or procures such a bid, and notice has not been given that liberty for such bidding is reserved, the buyer may at his option avoid the sale or take the goods at the price of the last good faith bid prior to the completion of the sale. This subsection shall not apply to any bid at a forced sale.

Part 4. Title, Creditors, and Good-Faith Purchasers

§ 2–401. Passing of Title; Reservation for Security; Limited Application of This Section

Each provision of this Article with regard to the rights, obligations, and remedies of the seller, the buyer, purchasers, or other third parties applies irrespective of title to the goods except where the provision refers to such title. Insofar as situations are not covered by the other provisions of this Article and matters concerning title become material the following rules apply:

(1) Title to goods cannot pass under a contract for sale prior to their identification to the contract (Section 2–501), and unless otherwise explicitly agreed the buyer acquires by their identification a special property as limited by this Act. Any retention or reservation by the seller of the title (property) in goods shipped or delivered to the buyer is limited in effect to a reservation of a security interest. Subject to these provisions and to the provisions of the Article on Secured Transactions (Article 9), title to goods passes from the seller to the buyer in any manner and on any conditions explicitly agreed on by the parties.

(2) Unless otherwise explicitly agreed title passes to the buyer at the time and place at which the seller completes his performance with reference to the physical delivery of the goods, despite any reservation of a security interest and even though a document of title is to be delivered at a different time or place; and in particular and despite any reservation of a security interest by the bill of lading

    (a) if the contract requires or authorizes the seller to send the goods to the buyer but does not require him to deliver them at destination, title passes to the buyer at the time and place of shipment; but

    (b) if the contract requires delivery at destination, title passes on tender there.

(3) Unless otherwise explicitly agreed, where delivery is to be made without moving the goods.

    (a) if the seller is to deliver a document of title, title passes at the time when and the place where he delivers such documents; or

    (b) if the goods are at the time of contracting already identified and no documents are to be delivered, title passes at the time and place of contracting.

(4) A rejection or other refusal by the buyer to receive or retain the goods, whether or not justified, or a justified revocation of acceptance revests title to the goods in the seller. Such revesting occurs by operation of law and is not a "sale."

§ 2–402. Rights of Seller's Creditors against Sold Goods

(1) Except as provided in subsections (2) and (3), rights of unsecured creditors of the seller with respect to goods which have been identified to a contract for sale are subject to the buyer's rights to recover the goods under this Article (Sections 2–502 and 2–716).

(2) A creditor of the seller may treat a sale or an identification of goods to a contract for sale as void if as against him a retention of possession by the seller is fraudulent under any rule of law of the state where the goods are situated, except that retention of possession in good faith and current course of trade by a merchant–seller for a commercially reasonable time after a sale or identification is not fraudulent.

(3) Nothing in this Article shall be deemed to impair the rights of creditors of the seller

    (a) under the provisions of the Article on Secured Transactions (Article 9); or

    (b) where identification to the contract or delivery is made not in current course of trade but in satisfaction of or as security for a preexisting claim for money, security, or the like and is made under circumstances which under any rule of law of the state where the goods are situated would apart from this Article constitute the transaction a fraudulent transfer or voidable preference.

§ 2–403. Power to Transfer; Good-Faith Purchase of Goods; "Entrusting"

(1) A purchaser of goods acquires all title which his transferor had or had power to transfer except that a purchaser of a limited interest acquires rights only to the extent of the interest purchased. A person with voidable title has power to transfer a good title to a good-faith purchaser for value. When goods have been delivered under a transaction of purchase the purchaser has such power even though

    (a) the transferor was deceived as to the identity of the purchaser, or

(b) the delivery was in exchange for a check which is later dishonored, or

(c) it was agreed that the transaction was to be a "cash sale," or

(d) the delivery was procured through fraud punishable as larcenous under the criminal law.

(2) Any entrusting of possession of goods to a merchant who deals in goods of that kind gives him power to transfer all rights of the entruster to a buyer in ordinary course of business.

(3) "Entrusting" includes any delivery and any acquiescence in retention of possession regardless of any condition expressed between the parties to the delivery or acquiescence and regardless of whether the procurement of the entrusting or the possessor's disposition of the goods have been such as to be larcenous under the criminal law.

(4) The rights of other purchasers of goods and of lien creditors are governed by the Articles on Secured Transactions (Article 9). [Bulk Transfers/Sales (Article 6)* and Documents of Title (Article 7)].

Part 5. Performance

§ 2–501. Insurable Interest in Goods; Manner of Identification of Goods

(1) The buyer obtains a special property and an insurable interest in goods by identification of existing goods as goods to which the contract refers even though the goods so identified are nonconforming and he has an option to return or reject them. Such identification can be made at any time and in any manner explicitly agreed to by the parties. In the absence of explicit agreement identification occurs

(a) when the contract is made if it is for the sale of goods already existing and identified;

(b) if the contract is for the sale of future goods other than those described in paragraph (c), when goods are shipped, marked, or otherwise designated by the seller as goods to which the contract refers;

(c) when the crops are planted or otherwise become growing crops or the young are conceived if the contract is for the sale of unborn young to be born within 12 months after contracting or for the sale of crops to be harvested within 12 months or the next normal harvest season after contracting, whichever is longer.

(2) The seller retains an insurable interest in goods so long as title to or any security interest in the goods remains in him; and where the identification is by the seller alone he may until default or insolvency or notification to the buyer that the identification is final substitute other goods for those identified.

(3) Nothing in this section impairs any insurable interest recognized under any other statute or rule of law.

§ 2–502. Buyer's Right to Goods on Seller's Insolvency

(1) Subject to subsections (2) and (3) and even though the goods have not been shipped, a buyer who has paid a part or all of the price of goods in which he has a special property under the provisions of the immediately preceding section may on making

and keeping good a tender of any unpaid portion of their price recover them from the seller if

    (a) in the case of goods bought for personal, family, or household purposes, the seller repudiates or fails to deliver as required by the contract; or

    (b) in all cases, the seller becomes insolvent within 10 days after receipt of the first installment on their price.

(2) The buyer's right to recover the goods under subsection (1)(a) vests upon acquisition of a special property, even if the seller had not then repudiated or failed to deliver.

(3) If the identification creating his special property has been made by the buyer he acquires the right to recover the goods only if they conform to the contract for sale.

§ 2–503. *Manner of Seller's Tender of Delivery*

(1) Tender of delivery requires that the seller put and hold conforming goods at the buyer's disposition and give the buyer any notification reasonably necessary to enable him to take delivery. The manner, time, and place for tender are determined by the agreement and this Article, and in particular

    (a) tender must be at a reasonable hour, and if it is of goods they must be kept available for the period reasonably necessary to enable the buyer to take possession; but

    (b) unless otherwise agreed the buyer must furnish facilities reasonably suited to the receipt of the goods.

(2) Where the case is within the next section respecting shipment tender requires that the seller comply with its provisions.

(3) Where the seller is required to deliver at a particular destination tender requires that he comply with subsection (1) and also in any appropriate case tender documents as described in subsections (4) and (5) of this section.

(4) Where goods are in the possession of a bailee and are to be delivered without being moved

    (a) tender requires that the seller either tender a negotiable document of title covering such goods or procure acknowlcdgmcnt by the bailee of the buyer's right to possession of the goods; but

    (b) tender to the buyer of a nonnegotiable document of title or of a written direction to the bailee to deliver is sufficient tender unless the buyer seasonably objects, and receipt by the bailee of notification of the buyer's rights fixes those rights as against the bailee and all third persons; but risk of loss of the goods and of any failure by the bailee to honor the nonnegotiable document of title or to obey the direction remains on the seller untill the buyer has had a reasonable time to present the document or direction, and a refusal by the bailee to honor the document or to obey the direction defeats the tender.

(5) Where the contract requires the seller to deliver documents

    (a) he must tender all such documents in correct form, except as provided in this Article with respect to bills of lading in a set (subsection (2) of Section 2–323); and

(b) tender through customary banking channels is sufficient and dishonor of a draft accompanying the documents constitutes nonacceptance or rejection.

§ 2–504. Shipment by Seller

Where the seller is required or authorized to send the goods to the buyer and the contract does not require him to deliver them at a particular destination, then unless otherwise agreed he must

(a) put the goods in the possession of such a carrier and make such a contract for their transportation as may be reasonable having regard to the nature of the goods and other circumstances of the case; and

(b) obtain and promptly deliver or tender in due form any document necessary to enable the buyer to obtain possession of the goods or otherwise required by the agreement or by usage of trade; and

(c) promptly notify the buyer of the shipment.

Failure to notify the buyer under paragraph (c) or to make a proper contract under paragraph (a) is a ground for rejection only if material delay or loss ensues.

§ 2–505. Seller's Shipment under Reservation

(1) Where the seller has identified goods to the contract by or before shipment,

(a) his procurement of a negotiable bill of lading to his own order or otherwise reserves in him a security interest in the goods. His procurement of the bill to the order of a financing agency or of the buyer indicates in addition only the seller's expectation of transferring that interest to the person named.

(b) a nonnegotiable bill of lading to himself or his nominee reserves possession of the goods as security but except in a case of conditional delivery (subsection (2) of Section 2–507) a nonnegotiable bill of lading naming the buyer as consignee reserves no security interest even though the seller retains possession of the bill of lading.

(2) When shipment by the seller with reservation of a security interest is in violation of the contract for sale it constitutes an improper contract for transportation within the preceding section but impairs neither the rights given to the buyer by shipment and identification of the goods to the contract nor the seller's powers as a holder of a negotiable document.

§ 2–506. Rights of Financing Agency

(1) A financing agency by paying or purchasing for value a draft which relates to a shipment of goods acquires to the extent of the payment or purchase and in addition to its own rights under the draft and any document of title securing it any rights of the shipper in the goods including the right to stop delivery and the shipper's right to have the draft honored by the buyer.

(2) The right to reimbursement of a financing agency which has in good faith honored or purchased the draft under commitment to or authority from the buyer is not impaired by subsequent discovery of defects with reference to any relevant document which was apparently regular on its face.

§ 2–507. *Effect of Seller's Tender; Delivery on Condition*

(1) Tender of delivery is a condition to the buyer's duty to accept the goods and, unless otherwise agreed, to his duty to pay for them. Tender entitles the seller to acceptance of the goods and to payment according to the contract.

(2) Where payment is due and demanded on the delivery to the buyer of goods or documents of title, his right as against the seller to retain or dispose of them is conditional upon his making the payment due.

§ 2–508. *Cure by Seller of Improper Tender or Delivery; Replacement*

(1) Where any tender or delivery by the seller is rejected because nonconforming and the time for performance has not yet expired, the seller may seasonably notify the buyer of his intention to cure and may then within the contract time make a conforming delivery.

(2) Where the buyer rejects a nonconforming tender which the seller had reasonable grounds to believe would be acceptable with or without money allowance the seller may if he seasonably notifies the buyer have a further reasonable time to substitute a conforming tender.

§ 2–509. *Risk of Loss in the Absence of Breach*

(1) Where the contract requires or authorizes the seller to ship the goods by carrier

    (a) if it does not require him to deliver them at a particular destination, the risk of loss passes to the buyer when the goods are duly delivered to the carrier even though the shipment is under reservation (Section 2–505); but

    (b) if it does require him to deliver them at a particular destination and the goods are there duly tendered while in the possession of the carrier, the risk of loss passes to the buyer when the goods are there duly so tendered as to enable the buyer to take delivery.

(2) Where the goods are held by a bailee to be delivered without being moved, the risk of loss passes to the buyer

    (a) on his receipt of a negotiable document of title covering the goods; or

    (b) on acknowledgment by the bailee of the buyer's right to possession of the goods; or

    (c) after his receipt of a nonnegotiable document of title or other written direction to deliver, as provided in subsection (4)(b) of Section 2–503.

(3) In any case not within subsection (1) or (2), the risk of loss passes to the buyer on his receipt of the goods if the seller is a merchant; otherwise the risk passes to the buyer on tender of delivery.

(4) The provisions of this section are subject to contrary agreement of the parties and to the provisions of this Article on sale on approval (Section 2–327) and on effect of breach on risk of loss (Section 2–510).

§ 2–510. *Effect of Breach on Risk of Loss*

(1) Where a tender or delivery of goods so fails to conform to the contract as to give a right of rejection the risk of their loss remains on the seller until cure or acceptance.

(2) Where the buyer rightfully revokes acceptance he may to the extent of any deficiency in his effective insurance coverage treat the risk of loss as having rested on the seller from the beginning.

(3) Where the buyer as to conforming goods already identified to the contract for sale repudiates or is otherwise in breach before risk of their loss has passed to him, the seller may to the extent of any deficiency in his effective insurance coverage treat the risk of loss as resting on the buyer for a commercially reasonable time.

§ 2–511. Tender of Payment by Buyer; Payment by Check

(1) Unless otherwise agreed tender of payment is a condition to the seller's duty to tender and complete any delivery.

(2) Tender of payment is sufficient when made by any means or in any manner current in the ordinary course of business unless the seller demands payment in legal tender and gives any extension of time reasonably necessary to procure it.

(3) Subject to the provisions of this Act on the effect of an instrument on an obligation (Section 3–310), payment by check is conditional and is defeated as between the parties by dishonor of the check on due presentment.

§ 2–512. Payment by Buyer before Inspection

(1) Where the contract requires payment before inspection nonconformity of the goods does not excuse the buyer from so making payment unless

    (a) the nonconformity appears without inspection; or

    (b) despite tender of the required documents the circumstances would justify injunction against honor under this Act (Section 5–109(b)).

(2) Payment pursuant to subsection (1) does not constitute an acceptance of goods or impair the buyer's right to inspect or any of his remedies.

§ 2–513. Buyer's Right to Inspection of Goods

(1) Unless otherwise agreed and subject to subsection (3), where goods are tendered or delivered or identified to the contract for sale, the buyer has a right before payment or acceptance to inspect them at any reasonable place and time and in any reasonable manner. When the seller is required or authorized to send the goods to the buyer, the inspection may be after their arrival.

(2) Expenses of inspection must be borne by the buyer but may be recovered from the seller if the goods do not conform and are rejected.

(3) Unless otherwise agreed and subject to the provisions of this Article on C.I.F. contracts (subsection (3) of Section 2–321), the buyer is not entitled to inspect the goods before payment of the price when the contract provides

    (a) for delivery "C.O.D." or on other like terms; or

    (b) for payment against documents of title, except where such payment is due only after the goods are to become available for inspection.

(4) A place or method of inspection fixed by the parties is presumed to be exclusive but unless otherwise expressly agreed it does not postpone identification or shift the place for delivery or for passing the risk of loss. If compliance becomes impossible, inspection

shall be as provided in this section unless the place or method fixed was clearly intended as an indispensable condition, failure of which avoids the contract.

§ 2–514. *When Documents Deliverable on Acceptance; When on Payment*

Unless otherwise agreed documents against which a draft is drawn are to be delivered to the drawee on acceptance of the draft if it is payable more than three days after presentment; otherwise, only on payment.

§ 2–515. *Preserving Evidence of Goods in Dispute*

In furtherance of the adjustment of any claim or dispute

(a) either party on reasonable notification to the other and for the purpose of ascertaining the facts and preserving evidence has the right to inspect, test, and sample the goods including such of them as may be in the possession or control of the other; and

(b) the parties may agree to a third-party inspection or survey to determine the conformity or condition of the goods and may agree that the findings shall be binding upon them in any subsequent litigation or adjustment.

Part 6. Breach, Repudiation, and Excuse

§ 2–601. *Buyer's Rights on Improper Delivery*

Subject to the provisions of this Article on breach in installment contracts (Section 2–612) and unless otherwise agreed under the sections on contractual limitations of remedy (Sections 2–718 and 2–719), if the goods or the tender of delivery fail in any respect to conform to the contract, the buyer may

(a) reject the whole; or

(b) accept the whole; or

(c) accept any commercial unit or units and reject the rest.

§ 2–602. *Manner and Effect of Rightful Rejection*

(1) Rejection of goods must be within a reasonable time after their delivery or tender. It is ineffective unless the buyer seasonably notifies the seller.

(2) Subject to the provisions of the two following sections on rejected goods (Sections 2–603 and 2–604),

(a) after rejection any exercise of ownership by the buyer with respect to any commercial unit is wrongful as against the seller; and

(b) if the buyer has before rejection taken physical possession of goods in which he does not have a security interest under the provisions of this Article (subsection (3) of Section 2–711), he is under a duty after rejection to hold them with reasonable care at the seller's disposition for a time sufficient to permit the seller to remove them; but

(c) the buyer has no further obligations with regard to goods rightfully rejected.

(3) The seller's rights with respect to goods wrongfully rejected are governed by the provisions of this Article on Seller's remedies in general (Section 2–703).

§ 2–603. Merchant Buyer's Duties as to Rightfully Rejected Goods

(1) Subject to any security interest in the buyer (subsection (3) of Section 2–711), when the seller has no agent or place of business at the market of rejection a merchant buyer is under a duty after rejection of goods in his possession or control to follow any reasonable instructions received from the seller with respect to the goods and in the absence of such instructions to make reasonable efforts to sell them for the seller's account if they are perishable or threaten to decline in value speedily. Instructions are not reasonable if on demand indemnity for expenses is not forthcoming.

(2) When the buyer sells goods under subsection (1), he is entitled to reimbursement from the seller or out of the proceeds for reasonable expenses of caring for and selling them, and if the expenses include no selling commission then to such commission as is usual in the trade or if there is none to a reasonable sum not exceeding 10 percent on the gross proceeds.

(3) In complying with this section the buyer is held only to good faith and good-faith conduct hereunder is neither acceptance nor conversion nor the basis of an action for damages.

§ 2–604. Buyer's Options as to Salvage of Rightfully Rejected Goods

Subject to the provisions of the immediately preceding section on perishables if the seller gives no instructions within a reasonable time after notification of rejection the buyer may store the rejected goods for the seller's account or reship them to him or resell them for the seller's account with reimbursement as provided in the preceding section. Such action is not acceptance or conversion.

§ 2–605. Waiver of Buyer's Objections by Failure to Particularize

(1) The buyer's failure to state in connection with rejection a particular defect which is ascertainable by reasonable inspection precludes him from relying on the unstated defect to justify rejection or to establish breach

   (a) where the seller could have cured it if stated seasonably; or
   (b) between merchants when the seller has after rejection made a request in writing for a full and final written statement of all defects on which the buyer proposes to rely.

(2) Payment against documents made without reservation of rights precludes recovery of the payment for defects apparent on the face of the documents.

§ 2–606. What Constitutes Acceptance of Goods

(1) Acceptance of goods occurs when the buyer

   (a) after a reasonable opportunity to inspect the goods signifies to the seller that the goods are conforming or that he will take or retain them in spite of their nonconformity; or
   (b) fails to make an effective rejection (subsection (1) of Section 2–602), but such acceptance does not occur until the buyer has had a reasonable opportunity to inspect them; or

    (c) does any act inconsistent with the seller's ownership; but if such act is wrongful as against the seller it is an acceptance only if ratified by him.

(2) Acceptance of a part of any commercial unit is acceptance of that entire unit.

§ 2–607. *Effect of Acceptance; Notice of Breach; Burden of Establishing Breach after Acceptance; Notice of Claim or Litigation to Person Answerable Over*

(1) The buyer must pay at the contract rate for any goods accepted.

(2) Acceptance of goods by the buyer precludes rejection of the goods accepted and if made with knowledge of a nonconformity cannot be revoked because of it unless the acceptance was on the reasonable assumption that the nonconformity would be seasonably cured; but acceptance does not of itself impair any other remedy provided by this Article for nonconformity.

(3) Where a tender has been accepted

    (a) the buyer must within a reasonable time after he discovers or should have discovered any breach notify the seller of breach or be barred from any remedy; and

    (b) if the claim is one for infringement or the like (subsection (3) of Section 2–312) and the buyer is sued as a result of such a breach he must so notify the seller within a reasonable time after he receives notice of the litigation or be barred from any remedy over for liability established by the litigation.

(4) The burden is on the buyer to establish any breach with respect to the goods accepted.

(5) Where the buyer is sued for breach of a warranty or other obligation for which his seller is answerable over

    (a) he may give his seller written notice of the litigation. If the notice states that the seller may come in and defend and that if the seller does not do so he will be bound in any action against him by his buyer by any determination of fact common to the two litigations, then unless the seller after seasonable receipt of the notice does come in and defend he is so bound.

    (b) if the claim is one for infringement or the like (subsection (3) of Section 2–312) the original seller may demand in writing that his buyer turn over to him control of the litigation including settlement or else be barred from any remedy over and if he also agrees to bear all expense and to satisfy any adverse judgment, then unless the buyer after seasonable receipt of the demand does turn over control the buyer is so barred.

(6) The provisions of subsection (3), (4), and (5) apply to any obligation of a buyer to hold the seller harmless against infringement or the like (subsection (3) of Section 2–312).

§ 2–608. *Revocation of Acceptance in Whole or in Part*

(1) The buyer may revoke his acceptance of a lot or commercial unit whose nonconformity substantially impairs its value to him if he has accepted it

    (a) on the reasonable assumption that its nonconformity would be cured and it has not been seasonably cured; or

(b) without discovery of such nonconformity if his acceptance was reasonably induced either by the difficulty of discovery before acceptance or by the seller's assurances.

(2) Revocation of acceptance must occur within a reasonable time after the buyer discovers or should have discovered the ground for it and before any substantial change in condition of the goods which is not caused by their own defects. It is not effective until the buyer notifies the seller of it.

(3) A buyer who so revokes has the same rights and duties with regard to the goods involved as if he had rejected them.

§ 2–609. Right to Adequate Assurance of Performance

(1) A contract for sale imposes an obligation on each party that the other's expectation of receiving due performance will not be impaired. When reasonable grounds for insecurity arise with respect to the performance of either party the other may in writing demand adequate assurance of due performance and until he receives such assurance may if commercially reasonable suspend any performance for which he has not already received the agreed return.

(2) Between merchants the reasonableness of grounds for insecurity and the adequacy of any assurance offered shall be determined according to commercial standards.

(3) Acceptance of any improper delivery or payment does not prejudice the aggrieved party's right to demand adequate assurance of future performance.

(4) After receipt of a justified demand failure to provide within a reasonable time not exceeding 30 days such assurance of due performance as is adequate under the circumstances of the particular case is a repudiation of the contract.

§ 2–610. Anticipatory Repudiation

When either party repudiates the contract with respect to a performance not yet due the loss of which will substantially impair the value of the contract to the other, the aggrieved party may

(a) for a commercially reasonable time await performance by the repudiating party; or

(b) resort to any remedy for breach (Section 2–703 or Section 2–711), even though he has notified the repudiating party that he would await the latter's performance and has urged retraction; and

(c) in either case suspend his own performance or proceed in accordance with the provisions of this Article on the seller's right to identify goods to the contract notwithstanding breach or to salvage unfinished goods (Section 2–704).

§ 2–611. Retraction of Anticipatory Repudiation

(1) Until the repudiating party's next performance is due he can retract his repudiation unless the aggrieved party has since the repudiation cancelled or materially changed his position or otherwise indicated that he considers the repudiation final.

(2) Retraction may be by any method which clearly indicates to the aggrieved party that the repudiating party intends to perform, but must include any assurance justifiably demanded under the provisions of this Article (Section 2–609).

(3) Retraction reinstates the repudiating party's rights under the contract with due excuse and allowance to the aggrieved party for any delay occasioned by the repudiation.

§ 2–612. "Installment Contract"; Breach

(1) An "installment contract" is one which requires or authorizes the delivery of goods in separate lots to be separately accepted, even though the contract contains a clause "each delivery is a separate contract" or its equivalent.

(2) The buyer may reject any installment which is nonconforming if the nonconformity substantially impairs the value of that installment and cannot be cured or if the nonconformity is a defect in the required documents; but if the nonconformity does not fall within subsection (3) and the seller gives adequate assurance of its cure the buyer must accept that installment.

(3) Whenever nonconformity or default with respect to one or more installments substantially impairs the value of the whole contract there is a breach of the whole. But the aggrieved party reinstates the contract if he accepts a nonconforming installment without seasonably notifying of cancellation or if he brings an action with respect only to past installments or demands performance as to future installments.

§ 2–613. Casualty to Identified Goods

Where the contract requires for its performance goods identified when the contract is made, and the goods suffer casualty without fault of either party before the risk of loss passes to the buyer, or in a proper case under a "no arrival, no sale" term (Section 2–324) then

    (a) if the loss is total the contract is avoided; and

    (b) if the loss is partial or the goods have so deteriorated as no longer to conform to the contract the buyer may nevertheless demand inspection and at his option either treat the contract as voided or accept the goods with due allowance from the contract price for the deterioration or the deficiency in quantity but without further right against the seller.

§ 2–614. Substituted Performance

(1) Where without fault of either party the agreed berthing, loading, or unloading facilities fail or an agreed type of carrier becomes unavailable or the agreed manner of delivery otherwise becomes commercially impracticable but a commercially reasonable substitute is available, such substitute performance must be tendered and accepted.

(2) If the agreed means or manner of payment fails because of domestic or foreign governmental regulation, the seller may withhold or stop delivery unless the buyer provides a means or manner of payment which is commercially a substantial equivalent. If delivery has already been taken, payment by the means or in the manner provided by the regulation discharges the buyer's obligation unless the regulation is discriminatory, oppressive, or predatory.

§ 2–615. Excuse by Failure of Presupposed Conditions

Except so far as a seller may have assumed a greater obligation and subject to the preceding section on substituted performance,

(a) delay in delivery or nondelivery in whole or in part by a seller who complies with paragraphs (b) and (c) is not a breach of his duty under a contract for sale if performance as agreed has been made impracticable by the occurrence of a contingency the nonoccurrence of which was a basic assumption on which the contract was made or by compliance in good faith with any applicable foreign or domestic governmental regulation or order whether or not it later proves to be invalid.

(b) where the causes mentioned in paragraph (a) affect only a part of the seller's capacity to perform, he must allocate production and deliveries among his customers but may at his option include regular customers not then under contract as well as his own requirements for further manufacture. He may so allocate in any manner which is fair and reasonable.

(c) the seller must notify the buyer seasonably that there will be delay or nondelivery and, when allocation is required under paragraph (b), of the estimated quota thus made available for the buyer.

§ 2–616. *Procedure on Notice Claiming Excuse*

(1) Where the buyer receives notification of a material or indefinite delay or an allocation justified under the preceding section he may by written notification to the seller as to any delivery concerned, and where the prospective deficiency substantially impairs the value of the whole contract under the provisions of this Article relating to breach of installment contracts (Section 2–612), then also as to the whole,

(a) terminate and thereby discharge any unexecuted portion of the contract; or

(b) modify the contract by agreeing to take his available quota in substitution.

(2) If after receipt of such notification from the seller the buyer fails so to modify the contract within a reasonable time not exceeding 30 days the contract lapses with respect to any deliveries affected.

(3) The provisions of this section may not be negated by agreement except in so far as the seller has assumed a greater obligation under the preceding section.

Part 7. Remedies

§ 2–701. *Remedies for Breach of Collateral Contracts Not Impaired*

Remedies for breach of any obligation or promise collateral or ancillary to a contract for sale or not impaired by the provisions of this Article.

§ 2–702. *Seller's Remedies on Discovery of Buyer's Insolvency*

(1) Where the seller discovers the buyer to be insolvent he may refuse delivery except for cash including payment for all goods therefore delivered under the contract, and stop delivery under this Article (Section 2–705).

(2) Where the seller discovers that the buyer has received goods on credit while insolvent he may reclaim the goods upon demand made within 10 days after the receipt, but if misrepresentation of solvency has been made to the particular seller in writing within three months before delivery the 10-day limitation does not apply. Except as provided in this subsection the seller may not base a right to reclaim goods on the buyer's fraudulent or innocent misrepresentation of solvency or of intent to pay.

(3) The seller's right to reclaim under subsection (2) is subject to the rights of a buyer in ordinary course or other good-faith purchaser under this Article (Section 2–403). Successful reclamation of goods excludes all other remedies with respect to them.

§ 2–703. Seller's Remedies in General

Where the buyer wrongfully rejects or revokes acceptance of goods or fails to make a payment due on or before delivery or repudiates with respect to a part or the whole, then with respect to any goods directly affected and, if the breach is of the whole contract (Section 2–612), then also with respect to the whole undelivered balance, the aggrieved seller may

    (a) withhold delivery of such goods;

    (b) stop delivery by any bailee as hereafter provided (Section 2–705);

    (c) proceed under the next section respecting goods still unidentified to the contract;

    (d) resell and recover damages as hereafter provided (Section 2–706);

    (e) recover damages for nonacceptance (Section 2–708) or in a proper case the price (Section 2–709);

    (f) cancel.

§ 2–704. Seller's Right to Identify Goods to the Contract Notwithstanding Breach or to Salvage Unfinished Goods

(1) An aggrieved seller under the preceding section may

    (a) identify to the contract conforming goods not already identified if at the time he learned of the breach they are in his possession or control;

    (b) treat as the subject of resale goods which have demonstrably been intended for the particular contract even though those goods are unfinished.

(2) Where the goods are unfinished an aggrieved seller may in the exercise of reasonable commercial judgment for the purposes of avoiding loss and of effective realization either complete the manufacture and wholly identify the goods to the contract or cease manufacture and resell for scrap or salvage value or proceed in any other reasonable manner.

§ 2–705. Seller's Stoppage of Delivery in Transit or Otherwise

(1) The seller may stop delivery of goods in the possession of a carrier or other bailee when he discovers the buyer to be insolvent (Section 2–702) and may stop delivery of carload, truckload, planeload, or larger shipments of express or freight when the buyer repudiates or fails to make a payment due before delivery or if for any other reason the seller has a right to withhold or reclaim the goods.

(2) As against such buyer the seller may stop delivery until

    (a) receipt of the goods by the buyer; or

    (b) acknowledgment to the buyer by any bailee of the goods except a carrier that the bailee holds the goods for the buyer; or

    (c) such acknowledgment to the buyer by a carrier by reshipment or as warehouseman; or

    (d) negotiation to the buyer of any negotiable document of title covering the goods.

(3) (a) To stop delivery the seller must so notify as to enable the bailee by reasonable diligence to prevent delivery of the goods.

(b) After such notification the bailee must hold and deliver the goods according to the directions of the seller, but the seller is liable to the bailee for any ensuing charges or damages.

(c) If a negotiable document of title has been issued for goods, the bailee is not obliged to obey a notification to stop until surrender of the document.

(d) A carrier who has issued a nonnegotiable bill of lading is not obliged to obey a notification to stop received from a person other than the consignor.

§ 2–706. Seller's Resale Including Contract for Resale

(1) Under the conditions stated in Section 2–703 on seller's remedies, the seller may resell the goods concerned or the undelivered balance thereof. Where the resale is made in good faith and in a commercially reasonable manner the seller may recover the difference between the resale price and the contract price together with any incidental damages allowed under the provisions of this Article (Section 2–710), but less expenses saved in consequence of the buyer's breach.

(2) Except as otherwise provided in subsection (3) or unless otherwise agreed resale may be at public or private sale including sale by way of one or more contracts to sell or of identification to an existing contract of the seller. Sale may be as a unit or in parcels and at any time and place and on any terms but every aspect of the sale including the method, manner, time, place, and terms must be commercially reasonable. The resale must be reasonably identified as referring to the broken contract, but it is not necessary that the goods be in existence or that any or all of them have been identified to the contract before the breach.

(3) Where the resale is at private sale the seller must give the buyer reasonable notification of his intention to resell.

(4) Where the resale is at public sale

(a) only identified goods can be sold except where there is a recognized market for a public sale of futures in goods of the kind; and

(b) it must be made at a usual place or market for public sale if one is reasonably available and except in the case of goods which are perishable or threaten to decline in value speedily the seller must give the buyer reasonable notice of the time and place of the resale; and

(c) if the goods are not to be within the view of those attending the sale the notification of sale must state the place where the goods are located and provide for their reasonable inspection by prospective bidders; and

(d) the seller may buy.

(5) A purchaser who buys in good faith at a resale takes the goods free of any rights of the original buyer even though the seller fails to comply with one or more of the requirements of this section.

(6) The seller is not accountable to the buyer for any profit made on any resale. A person in the position of a seller (Section 2–707) or a buyer who has rightfully rejected or justifiably revoked acceptance must account for any excess over the amount of his security interest, as hereinafter defined (subsection (3) of Section 2–711).

§ 2–707. "Person in the Position of a Seller"

(1) A "person in the position of a seller" includes as against a principal an agent who has paid or become responsible for the price of goods on behalf of his principal or anyone who otherwise holds a security interest or other right in goods similar to that of a seller.

(2) A person in the position of a seller may as provided in this Article withhold or stop delivery (Section 2–705) and resell (Section 2–706) and recover incidental damages (Section 2–710).

§ 2–708. Seller's Damages for Nonacceptance or Repudiation

(1) Subject to subsection (2) and to the provisions of this Article with respect to proof of market price (Section 2–723), the measure of damages for nonacceptance or repudiation by the buyer is the difference between the market price at the time and place for tender and the unpaid contract price together with any incidental damages provided in this Article (Section 2–710), but less expenses saved in consequence of the buyer's breach.

(2) if the measure of damages provided in subsection (1) is inadequate to put the seller in as good a position as performance would have done then the measure of damages is the profit (including reasonable overhead) which the seller would have made from full performance by the buyer, together with any incidental damages provided in this Article (Section 2–710), due allowance for costs reasonably incurred and due credit for payments or proceeds of resale.

§ 2–709. Action for the Price

(1) When the buyer fails to pay the price as it becomes due the seller may recover, together with any incidental damages under the next section, the price

    (a) of goods accepted or of conforming goods lost or damaged within a commercially reasonable time after risk of their loss has passed to the buyer; and

    (b) of goods identified to the contract if the seller is unable after reasonable effort to resell them at a reasonable price or the circumstances reasonably indicate that such effort will be unavailing.

(2) Where the seller sues for the price he must hold for the buyer any goods which have been identified to the contract and are still in his control except that if resale becomes possible he may resell them at any time prior to the collection of the judgment. The net proceeds of any such resale must be credited to the buyer, and payment of the judgment entitles him to any goods not resold.

(3) After the buyer has wrongfully rejected or revoked acceptance of the goods or has failed to make a payment due or has repudiated (Section 2–610), a seller who is held not entitled to the price under this section shall nevertheless be awarded damages for nonacceptance under the preceeding section.

§ 2–710. Seller's Incidental Damages

Incidental damages to an aggrieved seller include any commercially reasonable charges, expenses, or commissions incurred in stopping delivery, in the transportation, care, and custody of goods after the buyer's breach in connection with return or resale of the goods, or otherwise resulting from the breach.

§ 2–711. *Buyer's Remedies in General; Buyer's Security Interest in Rejected Goods*

(1) Where the seller fails to make delivery or repudiates or the buyer rightfully rejects or justifiably revokes acceptance then with respect to any goods involved, and with respect to the whole if the breach goes to the whole contract (Section 2–612), the buyer may cancel and whether or not he has done so may in addition to recovering so much of the price as has been paid

  (a) "cover" and have damages under the next section as to all the goods affected whether or not they have been identified to the contract; or

  (b) recover damages for nondelivery as provided in this Article (Section 2–713).

(2) Where the seller fails to deliver or repudiates the buyer may also

  (a) if the goods have been identified recover them as provided in this Article (Section 2–502); or

  (b) in a proper case obtain specific performance or replevy the goods as provided in this Article (Section 2–716).

(3) On rightful rejection of justifiable revocation of acceptance a buyer has a security interest in goods in his possession or control for any payments made on their price and any expenses reasonably incurred in their inspection, receipt, transportation, care, and custody and may hold such goods and resell them in like manner as an aggrieved seller (Section 2–706).

§ 2–712. *"Cover"; Buyer's Procurement of Substitute Goods*

(1) After a breach within the preceding section the buyer may "cover" by making in good faith and without unreasonable delay any reasonable purchase of or contract to purchase goods in substitution for those due from the seller.

(2) The buyer may recover from the seller as damages the difference between the cost of cover and the contract price together with any incidental or consequential damages as hereinafter defined (Section 2–715), but less expenses saved in consequence of the seller's breach.

(3) Failure of the buyer to effect cover within this section does not bar him from any other remedy.

§ 2–713. *Buyer's Damages for Nondelivery or Repudiation*

(1) Subject to the provisions of this Article with respect to proof of market price (Section 2–723), the measure of damages for nondelivery or repudiation by the seller is the difference between the market price at the time when the buyer learned of the breach and the contract price together with any incidental and consequential damages provided in this Article (Section 2–715), but less expenses saved in consequence of the seller's breach.

(2) Market price is to be determined as of the place for tender or, in cases of rejection after arrival or revocation of acceptance, as of the place of arrival.

§ 2–714. *Buyer's Damages for Breach in Regard to Accepted Goods*

(1) Where the buyer has accepted goods and given notification (subsection (3) of Section 2–607) he may recover as damages for any nonconformity of tender the loss resulting

in the ordinary course of events from the seller's breach as determined in any manner which is reasonable.

(2) The measure of damages for breach of warranty is the difference at the time and place of acceptance between the value of the goods accepted and the value they would have had if they had been as warranted, unless special circumstances show proximate damages of a different amount.

(3) In a proper case any incidental and consequential damages under the next section may also be recovered.

§ 2–715. *Buyer's Incidental and Consequential Damages*

(1) Incidental damages resulting from the seller's breach include expenses reasonably incurred in inspection, receipt, transportation, and care and custody of goods rightfully rejected, any commercially reasonable charges, expenses, or commissions in connection with effecting cover, and any other reasonable expense incident to the delay or other breach.

(2) Consequential damages resulting from the seller's breach include

(a) any loss resulting from general or particular requirements and needs of which the seller at the time of contracting had reason to know and which could not reasonably be prevented by cover or otherwise; and

(b) injury to person or property proximately resulting from any breach of warranty.

§ 2–716. *Buyer's Right to Specific Performance or Replevin*

(1) Specific performance may be decreed where the goods are unique or in other proper circumstances.

(2) The decree for specific performance may include such terms and conditions as to payment of the price, damages, or other relief as the court may deem just.

(3) The buyer has a right of replevin for goods identified to the contract if after reasonable effort he is unable to effect cover for such goods or the circumstances reasonably indicate that such effort will be unvailing or if the goods have been shipped under reservation and satisfaction of the security interest in them has been made or tendered. In the case of goods bought for personal, family, or household purposes, the buyer's right of replevin vests upon acquisition of a special property, even if the seller had not then repudiated or failed to deliver.

§ 2–717. *Deduction of Damages from the Price*

The buyer on notifying the seller of his intention to do so may deduct all or any part of the damages resulting from any breach of the contract from any part of the price still due under the same contract.

§ 2–718. *Liquidation or Limitation of Damages; Deposits*

(1) Damages for breach by either party may be liquidated in the agreement but only at an amount which is reasonable in the light of the anticipated or actual harm caused by the breach, the difficulties of proof of loss, and the inconvenience of nonfeasibility of otherwise obtaining an adequate remedy. A team fixing unreasonably large liquidated damages is void as a penalty.

(2) Where the seller justifiably withholds delivery of goods because of the buyer's breach, the buyer is entitled to restitution of any amount by which the sum of his payments exceeds

  (a) the amount to which the seller is entitled by virtue of terms liquidating the seller's damages in accordance with subsection (1), or

  (b) in the absence of such terms, 20 percent of the value of the total performance for which the buyer is obligated under the contract or $500, whichever is smaller.

(3) The buyer's right to restitution under subsection (2) is subject to offset to the extent that the seller establishes

  (a) a right to recover damages under the provisions of this Article other than subsection (1), and

  (b) the amount or value of any benefits received by the buyer directly or indirectly by reason of the contract.

(4) Where a seller has received payment in goods their reasonable value or the proceeds of their resale shall be treated as payments for the purposes of subsection (2); but if the seller has notice of the buyer's breach before reselling goods received in part performance, his resale is subject to the conditions laid down in this Article on resale by an aggrieved seller (Section 2–706).

§ 2–719. Contractual Modification or Limitation of Remedy

(1) Subject to the provisions of subsections (2) and (3) of this section and of the preceding section on liquidation and limitation of damages,

  (a) the agreement may provide for remedies in addition to or in substitution for those provided in this Article and may limit or alter the measure of damages recoverable under this Article, as by limiting the buyer's remedies to return of the goods and repayment of the price or to repair and replacement of nonconforming goods or parts; and

  (b) resort to a remedy as provided is optional unless the remedy is expressly agreed to be exclusive, in which case it is the sole remedy.

(2) Where circumstances cause an exclusive or limited remedy to fail of its essential purpose, remedy may be had as provided in this Act.

(3) Consequential damages may be limited or excluded unless the limitation or exclusion is unconscionable. Limitation of consequential damages for injury to the person in the case of consumer goods is prima facie unconscionable but limitation of damages where the loss is commercial is not.

§ 2–720. Effect of "Cancellation" or "Rescission" on Claims for Antecedent Breach

Unless the contrary intention clearly appears, expressions of "cancellation" or "rescission" of the contract or the like shall not be construed as renunciation or discharge of any claim in damages for an antecedent breach.

§ 2–721. Remedies for Fraud

Remedies for material misrepresentation or fraud include all remedies available under this Article for non-fraudulent breach. Neither rescission or a claim for rescission of the contract for sale nor rejection or return of the goods shall bar or be deemed inconsistent with a claim for damages or other remedy.

§ 2–722. *Who Can Sue Third Parties for Injury to Goods*

Where a third party so deals with goods which have been identified to a contract for sale as to cause actionable injury to a party to that contract

(a) a right of action against the third party is in either party to the contract for sale who has title to or a security interest or a special property or an insurable interest in the goods; and if the goods have been destroyed or converted a right of action is also in the party who either bore the risk of loss under the contract for sale or has since the injury assumed that risk as against the other;

(b) if at the time of the injury the party plaintiff did not bear the risk of loss as against the other party to the contract for sale and there is no arrangement between them for disposition of the recovery, his suit or settlement is, subject to his own interest, as a fiduciary for the other party to the contract;

(c) either party may with the consent of the other sue for the benefit of whom it may concern.

§ 2–723. *Proof of Market Price: Time and Place*

(1) If an action based on anticipatory repudiation comes to trial before the time for performance with respect to some or all of the goods, any damages based on market price (Section 2–708 or Section 2–713) shall be determined according to the price of such goods prevailing at the time when the aggrieved party learned of the repudiation.

(2) If evidence of a price prevailing at the times or places described in this Article is not readily available the price prevailing within any reasonable time before or after the time described or at any other place which in commercial judgment or under usage of trade would serve as a reasonable substitute for the one described may be used, making any proper allowance for the cost of transporting the goods to or from such other place.

(3) Evidence of a relevant price prevailing at a time or place other than the one described in this Article offered by one party is not admissible unless and until he has given the other party such notice as the court finds sufficient to prevent unfair surprise.

§ 2–724. *Admissibility of Market Quotations*

Whenever the prevailing price or value of any goods regularly bought and sold in any established commodity market is in issue, reports in official publications or trade journals or in newspapers or periodicals of general circulation published as the reports of such market shall be admissible in evidence. The circumstances of the preparation of such a report may be shown to affect its weight but not its admissibility.

§ 2–725. *Statute of Limitations in Contracts for Sale*

(1) An action for breach of any contract for sale must be commenced within four years after the cause of action has accrued. By the original agreement the parties may reduce the period of limitation to not less than one year but may not extend it.

(2) A cause of action accrues when the breach occurs, regardless of the aggrieved party's lack of knowledge of the breach. A breach of warranty occurs when tender of

delivery is made, except that where a warranty explicitly extends to future performance of the goods and discovery of the breach must await the time of such performance the cause of action accrues when the breach is or should have been discovered.

(3) Where an action commenced within the time limited by subsection (1) is so terminated as to leave available a remedy by another action for the same breach such other action may be commenced after the expiration of the time limited and within six months after the termination of the first action unless the termination resulted from voluntary discontinuance or from dismissal for failure or neglect to prosecute.

(4) This section does not alter the law on tolling of the statute of limitations nor does it apply to causes of action which have accrued before this Act becomes effective.

A

absolute privilege   In libel and slander law, situations where a defendant is entirely excused from liability for defamatory statements because of the circumstances under which the statements were made.

acceptance   The actual or implied receipt and retention of that which is tendered or offered.

accord and satisfaction   A legally binding agreement to settle a disputed claim for a definite amount.

accredited investors   Financially sophisticated and/or wealthy individuals and institutions who understand and can withstand the risk associated with securities investments.

act of state doctrine   The view that a judge in the United States or another country does not have the authority to challenge the legality of acts by a foreign government within that foreign government's own borders.

actus reus   Wrongful act or omission.

ad substantiation   Under Federal Trade Commission policy, product claims for which reasonable evidentiary support does not exist. Constitute unfair and deceptive trade practices.

ad valorem   According to value. Hence an ad valorem tax would be based on the value of the item in question rather than, for example, a fixed rate for all such items.

adjudication   The formal pronouncement of a judgment in a legal proceeding.

adjustment of debts   Individuals with limited debts are protected from creditors while paying their debts in installments (Chapter 13 bankruptcy).

administrative agency   An agency of the government charged with administering particular legislation.

administrative law   That branch of public law addressing the operation of the government's various agencies and commissions. Also the rules and regulations established by those agencies and commissions.

administrative law judge   An officer who presides at the initial hearing on matters litigated before an administrative agency. He or she is independent of the agency staff.

Administrative Procedure Act   A federal statute specifying the procedural rules under which the government's agencies and commissions conduct their business.

adverse impact   An employee may make a prima facie case for adverse impact where the employer's facially neutral rule may result in a different impact on one protected group than on another.

adverse possession   Open and notorious possession of real property over a given length of time that denies ownership in any other claimant.

advisory jurisdiction   Power of the International Court of Justice (ICJ) to hear a dispute and to render an advisory opinion on the matter. The opinion is not binding on any party.

affidavit   A written statement sworn to by a person officially empowered to administer an oath.

affirmative action   A government or private-sector program, springing from the civil rights movement, designed to *actively promote* the employment or educational opportunities of protected classes rather than merely forbidding discrimination.

affirmative defense   A portion of a defendant's answer to a complaint in which defendant presents contentions that, if proved true, will relieve the defendant of liability even if the assertions in the complaint are correct.

agent   A person entrusted by a principal to act on behalf of that principal; one who is authorized to carry out the business of another.

agreement   A meeting of the minds based on an offer by one party and acceptance by another.

alternate dispute resolution   The growing practice of employing strategies other than conventional litigation to solve conflicts. Those strategies include negotiation, arbitration, and mediation with variations such as "minitrials" and "rent-a-judge" arrangements.

amicus curiae   A "friend of the court" who, though not a party to the case, files a brief because of a strong interest in the litigation.

annual percentage rate (APR)   The rate of interest charged for borrowing money as expressed in a standardized, yearly manner allowing for comparison among lenders' fees.

annual percentage yield (APY)   The rate of interest paid on a deposit as expressed in a standardized, yearly manner allowing for comparison of returns among institutions.

answer   The defendant's first pleading in a lawsuit, in which the defendant responds to the allegations raised in the plaintiff's complaint.

anticipatory breach   A contracting party's indication before the time for performance that he cannot or will not perform the contract. Same as **anticipatory repudiation.**

appeal   The judicial process by which a party petitions a higher court to review the decisions of a lower court or agency to correct errors.

appellant   The party filing an appeal.

appellee   The party against whom an appeal is filed.

appraisal   Assessment of the value of property by one with appropriate qualifications for the task.

appropriation   Making commercial use of an individual's name or likeness without permission.

arbitrary trademark   A trademark that is a new word or a common word that bears no relation to the product to which it is applied.

arbitration   An extrajudicial process in which a dispute is submitted to a mutually agreeable third party for a decision.

arraignment   A criminal law proceeding in which a defendant is brought before a judge to be informed of the charges and to file a plea.

assault   A show of force that would cause reasonable persons to believe that they are about to receive an intentional, unwanted, harmful physical touching.

assignee   A person to whom an assignment is made.

assignment   A transfer of property, or some right or interest therein, from one person to another.

assignor   The maker of an assignment.

assumption of risk   An affirmative defense in a negligence case in which the defendant seeks to bar recovery by the plaintiff by showing that the plaintiff knowingly exposed himself or herself to the danger that resulted in injury.

attachment   As to secured transactions, the process by which a security interest in the property of another becomes enforceable.

at-will employee   An individual not under contract for a specified term and therefore, under the general rule, subject to discharge by the employer at any time and for any reason.

B

bait-and-switch advertising   An unlawful sales tactic in which the seller attracts buyer interest by insincerely advertising a product at a dramatically reduced price while holding no genuine intent to sell the product at that price. The seller then disparages the "bait" and diverts the buyer's attention to a higher-priced product (the switch), which was the sales goal from the first.

barriers to entry   Economic or technological conditions in a market making entry by a new competitor very difficult.

battery   An intentional, unwanted, harmful physical touching.

beyond a reasonable doubt   The level of proof required for conviction in a criminal case.

bilateral contract   A contract formed by an offer requiring a reciprocal promise.

blacklists   Lists of union organizers or participants in labor activities circulated to companies to dissuade the companies from hiring the listed individuals.

blue laws   Laws forbidding certain kinds of business on Sundays.

blue sky laws   Statutes regulating the sale of stocks and other securities to prevent consumer fraud.

bona fide   In good faith; honestly.

bona fide occupational qualification (BFOQ)   A defense in a discrimination claim where the employer argues that a particular religion, sex, or national origin is a necessary qualification for a particular job.

boycott   A confederation or conspiracy involving a refusal to do business with another or an attempt by the confederation to stop others from doing business with the target person or organization.

breach of contract   Failure, without legal excuse, to perform any promise that forms the whole or part of a contract.

breach of warranty   Failure, without legal excuse, to fulfill the terms of the guarantee.

bribe   Anything of value given or taken with the corrupt intent to influence an official in the performance of her or his duties.

brief   A written document setting out for the court the facts, the law, and the argument of a party to the lawsuit.

burden of proof   The party with the burden of proof (normally the plaintiff in a civil suit and the state in a criminal case) is required to prove the truth of a claim or lose on that issue.

business judgment rule   A rule protecting business managers from liability for making bad decisions when they have acted prudently and in good faith.

bylaws   A document that governs the maintenance and operation of an organization.

C

capacity   The ability to incur legal obligations and acquire legal rights.

capitalism   Private ownership of the means of production with a largely unrestricted marketplace in goods and services.

cause in fact   The actual cause of an event. One of the required elements in a negligence claim.

cause of action   The legal theory on which a lawsuit is based.

caveat emptor   Let the buyer beware.

cease and desist order   An instruction from an agency instructing a party to refrain from a specified goal.

certificate of incorporation   An instrument from the state bestowing the right to do business under the corporate form of organization. Same as **charter.**

certiorari   A legal procedure affording an appellate court the opportunity to review a lower court decision. Also a writ asking the lower court for the record of the case.

choice of law rule   A rule of law in each jurisdiction that determines which jurisdiction's laws will be applied to a case. For instance, one state may have a choice of law rule that says that the law of the jurisdiction where the contract was signed shall govern any dispute, while another state may apply a different rule.

civil law   The branch of law dealing with private rights. Contrast with **criminal law.**

class action   A legal action brought by one on behalf of himself or herself and all others similarly situated.

Clean Air Act   Amended in 1990, establishes air quality standards and enforcement procedures for the standards.

Clean Water Act   Establishes standards for water quality relating to the protection of water life as well as for safe recreation, and the enforcement of those standards.

closed-end loan   Credit arrangement where a specified sum is borrowed and a repayment plan usually is established.

closing date   The date on which a transfer of property is made.

Code of Federal Regulations   A compilation of final federal agency rules.

codetermination   German corporate governance and labor law system in which board representation by labor unions is required.

Colgate doctrine   Sellers may lawfully engage in resale price maintenance if they do nothing more than specify prices at which their products are to be resold and unilaterally refuse to deal with anyone who does not adhere to those prices.

collateral   Property pledged as security for satisfaction of a debt.

comity   Courtesy. Nations often recognize the laws of other nations not because they must do so but because of the tradition of comity: that is, goodwill and mutual respect.

Commerce Clause   The portion of the U.S. Constitution that provides for federal regulation of foreign and interstate trade.

commercial impracticability   The standard used by the UCC to relieve a party of his or her contract obligations because of the occurrence of unforeseeable, external events beyond his or her control.

commercial speech   Speech directed toward a business purpose. Advertising is an example of commercial speech. Such speech is protected by the First Amendment, but not to the degree that we protect other varieties of speech.

Commodity Futures Trading Commission (CFTC) Federal regulatory agency responsible for overseeing futures trading.

common law   Judge-made law. To be distinguished from statutory law as created by legislative bodies.

common shares   Most universal type of corporate stock.

community property   Property acquired during marriage through the labor or skill of either spouse.

comparable worth   The legal theory that all employees should be paid the same wages for work requiring comparable skills, effort, and responsibility and having comparable worth to the employer.

comparative negligence   Defense in a negligence suit in which the plaintiff's recovery is reduced by an amount equivalent to her contribution to her own injury.

compensatory damages   Damages that will compensate a party for actual losses due to an injury suffered.

complaint   The first pleading filed by the plaintiff in a civil lawsuit.

comp time   Compensatory time. Giving an employee time off from work in place of cash for hours of overtime worked.

concerted activity   Organizing, forming, joining, or assisting labor organizations, bargaining collectively through representatives of the employees' choosing, or other activities taken for the purpose of collective bargaining or other mutual aid or protection.

concurrent conditions   When each party's obligation to perform under a contract is dependent on the other party's performance.

condemning   To appropriate land for public use.

conditions precedent   Conditions that operate to give rise to a contracting party's duty to perform.

conditions subsequent   Conditions that operate to discharge one from an obligation under a contract.

condominium or cooperative ownership   An interest in property where owners retain individual control and specific ownership over a precise segment of real estate, but own common areas as tenants in common.

confession of judgment clause   A clause stipulating that the lessee grants judgment in any action on the contract to the landlord without the formality of an ordinary proceeding.

conglomerate merger   A merger between firms operating in separate markets and having neither buyer–seller nor competitive relationships with each other.

conscious parallelism   Conduct by competitors that is very similar or identical but that is not the product of a conspiracy and thus is not, in and of itself, illegal.

consent decree   A settlement of a lawsuit arrived at by agreement of the parties. Effectively, an admission by the parties that the decree is a just determination of their rights.

consent order   The order administrative agencies issue when approving the settlement of an administrative action against some party.

consequential damages   Damages that do not flow directly and immediately from an act but rather flow from the results of the act.

consideration   A required element in an enforceable contract. The thing of value passing between the parties that results in a benefit to the one making the promise or a detriment to the one receiving the promise.

conspiracy   An agreement between two or more persons to commit an unlawful act.

constructive eviction   A breach of duty by the landlord that makes the property uninhabitable or otherwise deprives the tenant of the benefit of the lease and gives rise to the tenant's right to vacate the property and to terminate the lease.

consumer goods   Under the UCC, goods used or bought primarily for personal, family, or household purposes.

contentious jurisdiction   Power of the ICJ to hear a dispute and to render a binding opinion on the issue and the parties involved. All parties must give prior consent to contentious jurisdiction.

contingent fee   An arrangement wherein an attorney is compensated for his or her services by receiving a percentage of the award in a lawsuit rather than receiving an hourly wage or specified fee.

contingent workers   Workers that do not have an implicit or explicit contract for ongoing employment.

contract   An agreement that is legally enforceable by the courts.

contract bar rule   The NLRB prohibits an election during the term of a collective bargaining agreement, for a maximum of three years.

contract firm workers   Workers employed by a company that provides them or their services under contract or leases. Usually are assigned to only one customer and work at the customer's worksite.

contract of adhesion   One in which all the bargaining power (and all the contract terms) are unfairly on one side. This often occurs when buyers have no choice among sellers of a particular item, and when the seller uses a preprinted form contract.

contributory negligence   A defense in a negligence action wherein the defendant attempts to demonstrate that the plaintiff contributed to the harm on which the litigation was based. Contrast with **comparative negligence.**

conversion   Wrongfully exercising control over the personal property of another.

copyright   The creator's (artist, author, or the like) right to control the copying and distribution of his or her work for a period of time specified by statute.

corporate opportunity   A doctrine that prevents corporate officials from personally appropriating an opportunity that belongs to the corporation.

corporation   A form of business organization that is owned by *shareholders* who have no inherent right to manage the business, and is managed by a board of directors elected by the shareholders.

Council on Environmental Quality   Serves as an adviser to the president in connection with the preparation of the annual Environmental Quality Report.

counterclaim   A cause of action filed by the defendant in a lawsuit against the plaintiff in the same suit.

counteroffer   Response by the offeree that, in its legal effect, constitutes a rejection of the original offer and proposes a new offer to the offerer.

countervailing duties   Duties imposed by a government against the products of another government that has offered subsidies to its own producers.

covered disabilities   A physical or mental impairment that substantially limits one or more major life activities of an individual; a record of such impairment or being regarded as having such impairment.

creditor   A person to whom a debt is owed.

creditor beneficiary   Person who has given consideration, who is an intended beneficiary of a contract though not a party, and thus is entitled to enforce the contract.

crime   A public wrong, an act punishable by the state.

criminal law   Wrongs against society that the state has seen fit to label as crimes and that may result in penalties against the perpetrator(s). Contrast with **civil law.**

cumulative voting   A procedure for voting for directors that permits a shareholder to multiply the number of shares he or she owns by the number of directors to be elected and to cast the resulting total of votes for one or more directors.

curtesy interest   The right of a husband upon the death of his wife to receive all of the wife's real property as long as the two had a child between them.

D

d.b.a.   Doing business as.

de facto   In fact. Actually. As in *de facto* school segregation, which is caused by social and economic conditions rather than by government act.

de jure   Legitimate. Lawful. Of right. As in *de jure* school segregation, which is caused by government order and thus is legally correct even if morally wrong.

debenture   Any long-term debt instrument, such as a bond, issued by a company or institution, secured only by the general assets of the issuer.

deceit   A tort involving intentional misrepresentation to deceive or trick another.

deception   Trade claim that is either false or likely to mislead the reasonable consumer and that is material to the consumer's decision making.

deceptive advertising   Advertising practices likely to mislead the reasonable consumer where the practice in question is material in that it affected consumer choice.

decertification petition   Election petition stating that a current bargaining representative no longer has the support of a majority of the employees in the bargaining unit.

declaration   A document that defines the rights, responsibilities, and powers of property owners in a condominium.

declaratory judgment or order   A judicial or agency action expressing an opinion or articulating the rights of the parties without actually requiring that anything be done.

deed   An instrument transferring title to property.

deed of trust   A three-party instrument used to create a security interest in real property in which the legal title to the real property is placed in one or more trustees to secure the repayment of a sum of money or the performance of other conditions.

defamation   A false and intentional verbal or written expression that damages the reputation of another.

default   A party fails to pay money when due or when lawfully demanded.

defeasible fee simple   A title to property that is open to attack, that might be defeated by the performance of some act, or that is subject to conditions.

defendant   The party in a civil suit against whom the cause of action was brought and, in a criminal case, the party against whom charges have been filed.

delegatee   The one to whom a duty is delegated.

delegator   The one who delegates a duty.

deontological ethics   The rightness of an action depends on its conformance with duty, obligation, and moral requirements regardless of outcome.

deposition   A discovery procedure wherein a witness's sworn testimony is taken out of court, prior to trial, for subsequent use at trial.

deregulation   Returning authority to the free market by shrinking government bureaucracies and reducing government rules.

derivative suit   A lawsuit by a stockholder on behalf of the corporation where the corporation declines to act to protect the organization's rights against the conduct of an officer, director, or outsider.

derivatives   Specialized trading contracts tied to underlying assets such as bonds or currencies.

descriptive mark   A trademark that is merely descriptive of the product or its qualities.

dicta   Statements in a judicial opinion that are merely the views of the judge(s) and are not necessary for the resolution of the case.

directed verdict   A party to a lawsuit makes a motion asking the judge to instruct the jury to reach a particular decision because reasonable minds could not differ about the correct outcome of the case.

discharged   Released from liability.

disclaimer   As to warranties, a contract term wherein a party attempts to relieve itself of potential liability under that contract.

discovery   Legal procedures by which one party to a litigation may obtain information from the other party. Depositions and interrogatories are examples of discovery procedures.

disparate impact   Employment discrimination theory in which a facially neutral employment practice (such as requiring a high school diploma for new hires) results in an unfair and adverse impact on a protected class.

disparate treatment   Theory of employment discrimination wherein an individual or group is intentionally disfavored via actual discriminatory policies and practices.

dissolution   In partnership law, the change in the relation of the partners caused by any partner ceasing to be associated with the carrying on of the business.

diversity of citizenship   One standard by which federal courts may gain jurisdiction over a lawsuit. Plaintiffs and defendants must be from different states and more than $50,000 must be at issue.

divestiture   In antitrust law, a remedy wherein the court orders a defendant to dispose of specified assets.

dividend   A shareholder's earnings from his or her stock in a corporation.

doctrine of sovereign immunity   Principle that a foreign nation may not be sued in American courts, with certain exceptions.

dominant estate   The property accessed through an easement appurtenant or implied easement.

donee beneficiary   Person who has not given consideration, but is an intended beneficiary of a contract, though not a party, and is entitled to enforce the contract.

double jeopardy   The United States Constitution provides that the same individual may not be tried twice in the same tribunal for the same criminal offense.

dower interest   The right of a wife upon the death of her husband to receive a life estate in one-third of her husband's real property.

dramshop law   State laws imposing liability on the seller of intoxicating liquors when a third party is injured as a result of the intoxication of the buyer where the sale has caused or contributed to that intoxication.

due care and diligence   Corporate officers and directors must act in good faith and in a prudent manner.

due diligence   A defense against a securities violation claim where the defendant used ordinary prudence and still failed to find an error or omission in the registration statement.

due process   A constitutional principle requiring fairness in judicial proceedings and that government laws and conduct be free of arbitrariness and capriciousness.

dumping   The commercial practice of selling goods in a foreign market at a price substantially beneath that charged in the domestic market.

duress   Overpowering of the will of a person by force or fear.

duty of due care   Standard of conduct expected of a reasonable, prudent person under the circumstances.

E

easement   The right to use property without taking anything away from the property.

easement or profit appurtenant   The right of an owner of adjacent land to enter or to enter and take away from property next to it.

economies of scale   Expansion of a firm or industry's productive capacity resulting in a decline in long-run average costs of production.

efficiencies   A defense to an otherwise unlawful merger in which costs of production are reduced because of the merger.

election year or certification year bar   The NLRB prohibits an election for 12 months following a prior election.

elective share   Legislative mandate that a spouse receive a specific percentage interest in a deceased spouse's estate.

embargo   Government order prohibiting importation of some or all products from a particular country.

embezzlement   The fraudulent and unauthorized taking of the money of another while charged with the care of that money.

Emergency Planning and Community Right-to-Know Act of 1986   Amended Superfund requiring companies to inform the government upon release of any hazardous chemicals into the environment and to provide to the government an inventory of their hazardous chemicals. The act also requires states to establish emergency procedures for chemical discharges.

eminent domain   The state's power to take private property for public use.

employer identification number   Number issued to employer by federal and state governments for the purpose of record keeping associated with income and Social Security tax collections.

en banc   All of the judges hearing a case as a group rather than individually or in panels.

enabling legislation   Law that establishes an administrative agency and grants power to that agency.

enjoin   To require. A court issues an injunction requiring a certain act or ordering a party to refrain from a certain act.

enterprise law   Legal doctrine treating all companies in a corporate group as one giant organization rather than a collection of smaller, independent units.

entity law   Legal doctrine treating each company in a corporate group as a separate, independent unit.

environmental impact statement   Statement of the anticipated impact on the environment of legislation or other major federal action, and suggestions for reasonable alternatives.

Environmental Protection Agency   Created in 1970 to gather information relating to pollution and to assist in pollution control efforts and sanctions.

equal protection   The Fourteenth Amendment to the U.S. Constitution provides that all similarly situated individuals are entitled to the same advantages and must bear the same burdens under the law.

equitable remedies   Injunction, specific performance, restraining orders, and the like, as opposed to money damages.

equity   Fairness; a system of courts that developed in England. A chancellor presided to mete out fairness in cases that were not traditionally assigned to the law courts headed by the king.

essential functions of a position   Those tasks that are fundamental, as opposed to marginal or unnecessary, to the fulfillment of the position's objectives.

establishment clause   The First Amendment to the U.S. Constitution forbids the U.S. government from creating a government-supported church or religion.

estate   An interest in land or property owned by a decedent at the time of her or his death.

estate per *autre vie*   A life estate that is measured by the life of someone other than the possessor.

estoppel   A legal doctrine providing that one may not assert facts that are in conflict with one's own previous acts or deeds.

eviction   Depriving a tenant of the possession of leased premises.

excise taxes   Taxes imposed at both the state and federal levels on the sale of particular commodities, especially alcohol, tobacco, and gasoline.

exclusive dealing   Agreement to deal only with a particular buyer or a particular seller.

exculpatory clause   Portion of a contract that seeks to relieve one of the parties to the contract from any liability for breach of duty under that contract.

executed   In contract law, full performance of the terms of the bargain.

executed contract   Performances are complete.

executory contract   Not yet fully performed or completed.

exemplary damages   Same as **punitive damages.**

exempt property   Specified classes of property that are unavailable to the creditor upon default of the debtor.

exempt security   Certain kinds of securities and certain transactions involving securities are not required to meet federal registration requirements under the 1933 act.

existentialism   A philosophy emphasizing the individual's responsibility to make herself what she is to become. Existence precedes essence.

express authority   Corporate officers' powers as expressed in the bylaws or conferred by the board of directors.

express authorization   In contract law, offerer specifies a means of communication by which the offeree can accept.

express conditions   Conditions within contracts that are clear from the language.

express contract   Contract whose terms are clear from the language.

express warranty   A guarantee made by affirmation of fact or promise, by description of the goods, or by sample or model.

expropriation   A government's taking of a business's assets, such as a manufacturing facility, usually without just compensation.

extraterritoriality   The application of U.S. laws on persons, rights, or relations beyond the geographic limits of this country and even though the parties involved are not American citizens.

F

failing company doctrine   A defense to an otherwise unlawful merger in which the acquired firm is going out of business and no other purchaser is available.

fair use   A doctrine that permits the use of copyrighted works for purposes such as criticism, news reporting, training, or research.

false imprisonment   Tort of intentionally restricting the freedom of movement of another.

false light   Falsely and publicly attributing certain characteristics, conduct, or beliefs to another such that a reasonable person would be highly offended.

featherbedding   A labor law term describing the practice where workers were paid even though they did not perform any work. Featherbedding is a violation of federal labor law.

federal question   Litigation involving the federal constitution, statutes, and treaties. The federal courts have jurisdiction over cases involving federal questions.

Federal Register   Daily publication of federal agency regulations and other legal materials coming from the executive branch of government.

Federal Sentencing Guidelines   Standards established by the U.S. Sentencing Commission that rank the seriousness of individual and organizational federal crimes and provide sentences that, with little flexibility, must be applied to those crimes.

Federal Trade Commission   Agency of the federal government responsible for promoting fair trade practices in interstate commerce.

federalism   The division of authority between the federal government and the states to maintain workable cooperation while diffusing political power.

fee simple   A form of land ownership that gives the owner the right to possess and to use the land for an unlimited period of time, subject only to governmental or private restrictions, and unconditional power to dispose of the property during his or her lifetime or upon death.

felony   A crime of a serious nature ordinarily involving punishment by death or imprisonment in a penitentiary.

fiduciary   One who holds a relationship of trust with another and has an obligation to act in the best interests of the other—for example, one who manages property on behalf of another.

fiduciary duty   The responsibility of one in a position of trust with another to act in the best interests of the other.

financing statement   Document notifying others that the creditor claims an interest in the debtor's collateral. Must be filed as provided for by law to perfect a security interest.

firm offer   Under the Uniform Commercial Code, a signed, written offer by a merchant containing assurances that it will be held open, and which is not revocable for the time stated in the offer, or for a reasonable time if no such time is stated.

fixture   A thing that was originally personal property and that has actually or constructively affixed to the soil itself or to some structure legally a part of the land.

foreclose   To terminate the mortgagor's rights in the property covered by the mortgage.

franchise   A marketing arrangement in which the franchisor permits the franchisee to produce, distribute, or sell the franchisor's product using the franchisor's name or trademark.

franchisee   A holder of a franchise.

franchisor   A party granting a franchise.

fraud   An intentional misrepresentation of a material fact with intent to deceive where the misrepresentation is justifiably relied on by another and damages result.

fraud-on-the-market theory Misleading statements distort the market and thus defraud a securities buyer whether the buyer actually relies on the misstatement or not. Based on the assumption that the price of a stock reflects all of the available information about that stock.

Free Exercise Clause First Amendment provision guaranteeing all Americans the right to pursue their religious beliefs free of government intervention (with limited exceptions).

free riders Those who lawfully benefit from goods or services without paying a share of the cost of those goods or services.

Full Faith and Credit Clause Provision of the U.S. Constitution requiring each state to recognize the laws and judicial decisions of all other states.

futures Contracts to deliver or take delivery of specified quantities of commodities at a previously specified price.

G

G8 An association embracing eight of the world's leading industrial powers (Canada, France, Italy, Germany, Japan, Russia, the United Kingdom, and the United States) designed to improve worldwide economic and political conditions.

garnishment Action by a creditor to secure the property of a debtor where that property is held by a third party.

General Agreement on Tariffs and Trade Establishes and regulates import duties among signatory countries.

general duty An OSHA provision requiring that employers furnish to each employee a place of employment free from recognized hazards that cause or are likely to cause death or serious physical harm to the employee.

general warranty deed A deed that carries with it certain warranties or guarantees.

generic mark A trademark employing a common descriptive name for a product.

genuineness of assent In contract law, the parties knowingly agreed to the same thing.

going public Selling shares in a company on the open market.

good faith Honesty; an absence of intent to take advantage of another.

goods All things that are movable at the time of identification to the contract for sale except the money in which the price is to be paid, investment securities, and so forth.

grand jury A body of people convened by the state to determine whether the evidence is sufficient to bring a criminal indictment (formal accusation) against a party.

grant deed A deed that does not have the warranties contained in a warranty deed.

gray market Transactions conducted outside the usual supplier-approved channels of distribution. These transactions (unlike *black market* sales) are lawful but are often discouraged by suppliers. The gray market operates parallel to the "officially" authorized chain of distribution.

grease Payments to low-ranking authorities for the purpose of facilitating business in another nation. Not forbidden by the Foreign Corrupt Practices Act if legal in the host nation.

greenmail Takeover defense involving the target corporation's repurchase of a takeover raider's stock at a premium not offered to other shareholders.

group boycott An agreement among traders to refuse to deal with one or more other traders.

guarantor A person who promises to perform the same obligation as the principal if the principal should default.

H

Herfindahl–Hirschman Index (HHI) Calculation used by the Justice Department to determine the degree of economic concentration in a particular market and to determine the degree to which a proposed horizontal merger would further concentrate that market. Computed by squaring the market share of each firm in a market and summing those totals.

holdover lease The tenancy that exists where a tenant subject to a term lease is allowed to remain on the premises after the term has expired.

horizontal divisions of the market Competitors agree to share their market geographically or to allocate customers or products among themselves.

horizontal merger Acquisition by one company of another company competing in the same product and geographic markets.

hostile environment A form of sexual harassment in which sexual conduct, sexual remarks, sexual depictions, and the like render the workplace offensive and intimidating such that performance is affected even though no tangible employment action has occurred.

hostile takeover   The acquisition of a formerly independent business where the acquired business resists the union.

I

Immigration Reform and Control Act (IRCA)   Enacted by Congress, IRCA's purpose is to discourage the entry of illegal aliens to the United States.

implied authority   Corporate officers' powers to take actions that are reasonably necessary to achieve their express duties.

implied authorization   In contract law, where the offerer's behavior or previous dealings with the offeree suggest an agreeable means of communicating an acceptance.

implied easement   Also called easement by prescription or way of necessity. An interest created where someone has openly used an adjoining piece of property for access with no complaint from the owner for a statutorily determined period of time.

implied warranty of fitness for a particular purpose   A warranty that arises by operation of law and promises that the good warranted is reasonably useful for the buyer's purpose where the buyer was relying on the seller's expertise in making the purchase.

implied warranty of habitability   Implied warranty arising in lease or sale of residential real estate that the property will be fit for human habitability.

implied warranty of merchantability   A warranty that arises by operation of law and promises that the good warranted is at least of average, fair, reasonable quality.

implied-in-fact conditions   Conditions derived from the parties' conduct and the circumstances of the bargain.

implied-in-fact contract   Contract whose terms are implicitly understood based on the behavior of the parties.

implied-in-law conditions or constructive conditions Conditions imposed by the court to avoid unfairness.

in personam jurisdiction   The power of the court over a person.

incidental beneficiary   Person who is not a party to a contract, who benefits indirectly from the contract, who was not contemplated by the parties, and who may not enforce the contract.

incidental damages   Collateral damages that are incurred because of a breach; damages that compensate a person injured by a breach of contract for reasonable costs incurred in an attempt to avoid further loss.

incorporators   Those who initiate a new corporation.

indemnification   Corporate policy to compensate officers and directors for losses sustained in defending themselves against litigation associated with their professional duties where those duties were performed with reasonable business judgment.

indemnify   Reimburse one who has suffered a loss.

indenture   Agreement governing the conditions under which bonds are issued.

indenture trustee   Person or institution holding legal title to trust property and charged with carrying out the terms of the indenture.

independent contractor   A person who contracts with a principal to perform some task according to his or her own methods, and who is not under the principal's control regarding the physical details of the work.

indictment   A grand jury's formal accusation of a crime.

Industry Guides   Published advice to industry and the public providing Federal Trade Commission interpretations of the likely legality of specific marketing practices.

information   A prosecutor's formal accusation of a crime.

initial public offering (IPO)   A security offered for sale to the public for the first time.

injunction   A court order commanding a person or organization to do or not do a specified action.

injurious falsehood   Intentional tort based on a false statement made with malice that disparages the property of another.

innocent misrepresentation   An unintentional misrepresentation of material fact where the misrepresentation is justifiably relied on by another and damages result.

insider   In securities law, anyone with a fiduciary duty who has knowledge of material facts not available to the general public.

insider trading   Trading securities while in possession of material nonpublic information, in violation of a fiduciary duty.

intellectual property   Intangible personal property.

intent   A conscious and purposeful state of mind.

intentional infliction of emotional distress   Intentional tort based on outrageous conduct that causes severe emotional distress in another.

intentional tort   Voluntary civil wrong causing harm to a protected interest.

interference with contractual relations   Improperly causing a third party to breach or fail to perform its contract with another.

interference with prospective advantage   Improperly causing a third party not to enter a prospective contractual relationship.

interpretive rules   In administrative law, an agency's view of the meaning of statutes governing agency action.

interrogatories   An ingredient in the discovery process wherein one party in a lawsuit directs written questions to another party in the lawsuit.

intrastate offerings   Registration exemption for securities sold only to residents of the state in which the issuer is organized and doing business.

intrusion   Wrongfully entering upon or prying into the solitude or property of another.

invasion of privacy   Violation of the right to be left alone.

invitee   One who comes on the premises of another by invitation of the owner, in connection with the owner's business, and for the benefit of the owner or for the mutual benefit of the invitee and the owner.

J

joint and several liability   Liability of a group of persons in which the plaintiff may sue all members of the group collectively or one or more individuals for the entire amount.

joint liability   Liability of a group of persons in which, if one of these persons is sued, he can insist that the other liable parties be joined to the suit as codefendants, so that all must be sued collectively.

joint tenancy   An estate held by two or more jointly with an equal right in all to share in the enjoyment of the land during their lives.

joint venture   A form of business organization essentially identical to a partnership, except that it is engaged in a single project, not carrying on a business.

judgment notwithstanding the verdict (judgment n.o.v.)   A judge's decision overruling the finding of the jury.

judgment proof   Describes those against whom money judgments will have no effect because they are insolvent or their assets are beyond the reach of the court.

judicial review   A court's authority to review statutes and, if appropriate, declare them unconstitutional. Also refers to appeals from administrative agencies.

jurisdiction   The power of a judicial body to adjudicate a dispute. Also the geographical area within which that judicial body has authority to operate.

jurisprudence   The philosophy and science of law.

jury instructions   A judge's directions to the jury explaining the law that must be applied in the case at hand.

K

keiretsu   Japanese cartels of vertically related firms working together in a collaborative fashion.

L

land contract   Typically, an installment contract for the sale of land wherein the purchaser receives the deed from the owner on payment of the final installment.

landlord/lessor   A party to a lease contract who allows a tenant to possess and to use his or her property in return for rent payments.

latent defects   Imperfections that are not readily apparent upon reasonable inspection.

lease   A contract for the possession and use of land or other property, including goods, on one side, and a recompense of rent or other income on the other.

leasehold estate   A right to occupy and to use land pursuant to a lease or contract.

legal detriment   Any act or forbearance by a promisee.

legal impossibility   A party to a contract is relieved of his or her duty to perform when that performance has become objectively impossible because of the occurrence of an event unforeseen at the time of contracting.

legality of purpose   The object of the contract does not violate law or public policy.

legitimate nondiscriminatory reason (LNDR)   An employer's justification for taking adverse action against an employee or applicant where the basis for the action is something other than the individual's membership in a protected class (such as termination for dishonesty or theft).

lemon laws   State statutes providing remedies for those buying vehicles which turn out to be so thoroughly defective that they cannot be repaired after reasonable efforts.

letter of credit   A statement from a financial institution such as a bank guaranteeing that it will pay the financial obligations of a particular party.

libel   Tort of defaming or injuring another's reputation by a published writing.

license   A contractual right to use property in a certain manner.

licensee   A person lawfully on land in possession of another for purposes unconnected with business interests of the possessor.

licenses   Government-granted privileges to do some act or series of acts. Authorization to do what, without a license, would be unlawful. Same as **permits.**

lien   A claim against a piece of property in satisfaction of a debt; the financial interest of the lienholder in the property as a result of a debt or other obligation of the landowner.

life estate   A property interest that gives a person the right to possess and to use property for a time that is measured by her or his lifetime or that of another person.

life tenant   The possessor of a life estate interest.

limited liability   Maximum loss normally limited to the amount invested in the firm.

limited liability company (LLC)   Hybrid of limited partnership and corporation receiving partnership tax treatment with the operating advantages of a corporation.

limited liability partnership   A special partnership form providing some of the advantages of limited liability.

limited partnership   A form of business organization that has one or more general partners who manage the business and have unlimited liability for the obligations of the business and one or more limited partners who do not manage and have limited liability.

liquidated damages   Damages made certain by the prior agreement of the parties.

liquidation   "Straight" bankruptcy action in which all assets except exemptions are distributed to creditors (Chapter 7 bankruptcy).

lockout defense   Takeover defense where the target company manipulates its assets, shares, and so on, to make the company unattractive as a takeover candidate.

lockouts   Where employees are kept from the workplace by the employer. Where the landlord deprives the tenant of the possession of the premises by changing the locks on the property.

long-arm statute   A state enactment that accords the courts of that state the authority to claim jurisdiction over people and property beyond the borders of the state as long as certain "minimum contacts" exist between the state and the people or property.

M

mailbox rule   Rule holding that a mailed acceptance is effective upon dispatch when the offerer has used the mail to invite acceptance; the rule has been expanded to include the use of any reasonable manner of acceptance.

malice   A required element of proof in a libel or slander claim by a public figure. Proof of a defamatory statement expressed with actual knowledge of its falsity or with reckless disregard for the truth would establish malice.

malicious prosecution   Criminal prosecution carried on with malice and without probable cause with damages resulting.

malpractice   Improper or negligent conduct in the performance of duties by a professional such as a doctor or lawyer.

market failure   Economic theory arguing that the free market works imperfectly because of certain allegedly inherent defects such as monopoly, public goods, and so forth.

market foreclosure   In vertical mergers, the concern that the newly combined firm will close its doors to potential suppliers and purchasers such that competition will be harmed.

market share liability   Product liability action by which plaintiffs may be able to recover against manufacturers of defective products based on those manufacturers' market shares even though proof of causation cannot be established.

material breach   In contract law, performance that falls beneath substantial performance and does not have a lawful excuse.

mechanic's lien or materialman's lien   A claim created by law for the purpose of securing a priority of payment of the price or value of work performed and materials furnished in erecting or repairing a structure.

mediation   An extrajudicial proceeding in which a third party (the mediator) attempts to assist disputing parties to reach an agreeable, voluntary resolution of their differences.

mens rea   Evil intent.

merger   The union of two or more business organizations wherein all of the assets, rights, and liabilities of one are blended into the other with only one firm remaining.

misappropriation   In securities law, taking material, nonpublic information and engaging in insider trading in violation of a fiduciary duty.

misdemeanor   A criminal offense less serious than a felony normally requiring a fine or less than a year in a jail other than a penitentiary.

misrepresentation   The innocent assertion of a fact that is not in accord with the truth.

mitigation   Obligation of a person who has been injured by a breach of a contract to attempt to reduce the damages.

Model Business Corporation Act (MBCA)   Drafted by legal experts, the MBCA is designed to improve corporate law and to serve as a model for state legislatures in drafting their corporate laws.

mommy track   An employment track, whether formally or informally instituted, in some firms that allows for slower upward mobility for mothers who must divide their attention between their positions and their families.

monopoly   Market power permitting the holder to fix prices or exclude competition.

moot   An issue no longer requiring attention or resolution because it has ceased to be in dispute.

mortgage   An interest in land formalized by a written instrument providing security for the payment of a debt.

mortgagee   One who receives a mortgage to secure repayment of a debt.

mortgagor   One who pledges property for a particular purpose such as security for a debt.

most favored nation status (MFN)   Preferential status offered to certain countries under the GATT or WTO, which allows the MFN country to obtain the lowest applicable tariff on goods.

motion   A request to a court seeking an order or action in favor of the party entering the motion.

motion for a directed verdict   A request by a party to a lawsuit arguing that the other party has failed to prove facts sufficient to establish a claim and that the judge must, therefore, enter a verdict in favor of the moving party.

multinational enterprise   A company that conducts business in more than one country.

mutual mistake   Where both parties to the contract are in error about a material fact.

N

National Environmental Policy Act   Requires that the government "use all practicable means" to conduct federal affairs in harmony with the environment.

National Pollutant Discharge Elimination System   Requires that all who discharge pollutants obtain an EPA permit before adding pollutants to a navigable stream.

National Priorities List   A list of hazardous dump or spill sites scheduled to be cleaned using CERCLA funds.

national treatment   Concept that requires that, once goods have been imported into a country, they must be treated as if they were domestic goods (that is, no tariff may be imposed other than that at the border).

nationalization   A country taking over a private business often without adequate compensation to the ex-owners.

necessaries   That which is reasonably necessary for a minor's proper and suitable maintenance.

negative externality   A spillover in which all the costs of a good or service are not fully absorbed by the producer and thus fall on others.

negligence   Failure to do something that a reasonable person would do under the circumstances, or an action that a reasonable and prudent person would not take under the circumstances.

negligence per se   Action violating a public duty, particularly where that duty is specified by statute.

negligent tort   Unintentional, civil wrong causing harm to a protected interest. Injury to another resulting from carelessness.

nolo contendere   A no-contest plea in a criminal case in which the defendant does not admit guilt but does submit to such punishment as the court may accord.

nominal damages Small damages, oftentimes $1, awarded to show that there was a legal wrong even though the damages were very slight or nonexistent.

noncompetition clause Employee agrees not to go into business in competition with employer.

nonpossessory interest An interest in real property that is not sufficient to be an ownership or possessory interest.

nonprice restraints Resale limitations imposed by manufacturers on distributors or retailers in any of several forms (such as territorial or customer restraints) that do not directly affect price.

nonreversionary interest The interest held by the remainderman. It is called *nonreversionary* because it does not revert to the original grantor.

nonvoting stock Owners of nonvoting stock participate in firm profits and dividends but may not vote at shareholder meetings.

novation A mutual agreement between all parties concerned for the discharge of a valid existing obligation by the substitution of a new valid obligation on the part of the debtor or another, or a like agreement for the discharge of a lessee to a landlord by the substitution of a new lessee.

nuisance A class of wrongs that arises from the unreasonable, unwarrantable, or unlawful use by a person of his or her property that produces material annoyance, inconvenience, discomfort, or hurt.

O

obligee A person to whom another is bound by a promise or other obligation; a promisee.

obligor A person who is bound by a promise or other obligation; a promisor.

offer A proposal by one person to another that is intended to create legal relations on acceptance by the person to whom it is made.

oligopoly An economic condition in which the market for a particular good or service is controlled by a small number of producers or distributors.

on-call workers Workers who report to work only when called.

open-end loan Credit arrangement not involving a lump sum but permitting repeated borrowing where payment amounts are not specified.

option contract A separate contract in which an offerer agrees not to revoke her or his offer for a

stated period in exchange for some valuable consideration.

ordinance A law, rule, or regulation enacted by a local unit of government (such as a town or city).

output restriction An agreement to limit production, which is a per se violation of the Sherman Act and may have the effect of artificially stabilizing or raising prices.

over-the-counter securities Stocks, bonds, and like instruments sold directly from broker to customer rather than passing through a stock exchange.

P

parol evidence When the written document is intended as the parties' final expression of their contract, oral evidence of prior agreements or representations cannot be used to vary the terms of the document.

partial ownership interest An interest that may revert back to the original grantor.

partition A legal proceeding that enables joint tenants or tenants in common to put an end to the tenancy and to vest in each tenant a sole estate in specific property or an allotment of the lands and buildings. If division is impossible, the estate may have to be sold and the proceeds divided.

partnership An association of two or more persons where they agree to work together in a business designed to earn a profit.

past consideration Performance that is not bargained for and was not given in exchange for the promise.

patent A right conferred by the federal government allowing the holder to restrict the manufacture, distribution, and sale of the holder's invention or discovery.

patent defects Imperfections that are visible and obvious.

per curiam By the court. Refers to legal opinions offered by the court as a whole rather than those instances where an individual judge authors the opinion.

per se By itself; inherently.

per se doctrine Certain antitrust violations are considered so harmful to competition that they are always unlawful and no proof of actual harm is required.

peremptory challenge An attorney's authority to dismiss prospective members of the jury without offering any justification for that dismissal.

perfection Process by which a secured party obtains a priority claim over other possible claimants to certain collateral belonging to a debtor.

periodic tenancy   The tenancy that exists when the landlord and tenant agree that the rent will be paid in regular successive intervals until notice to terminate is given but do not agree on a specific duration of the lease.

personal jurisdiction   The authority of a particular court over the parties to a lawsuit.

personal property   Movable property. All property other than real estate.

piercing the corporate veil   Holding a shareholder responsible for acts of a corporation due to a shareholder's domination and improper use of the corporation.

plaintiff   One who initiates a lawsuit.

pleadings   The formal entry of written statements by which the parties to a lawsuit set out their contentions and thereby formulate the issues on which the litigation will be based.

police power   The government's inherent authority to enact rules to provide for the health, safety, and general welfare of the citizenry.

political action committee   A legally defined lobbying group that uses funds and activities to support certain political views.

possibility of reverter   An interest that is uncertain or may arise only upon the occurrence of a condition.

precedent   A previously decided lawsuit that may be looked to as an authoritative statement for resolving current lawsuits involving similar questions of law.

predatory pricing   Selling of goods below cost for the purpose of harming competition.

preemption doctrine   Constitutional doctrine providing that the federal government "preempts the field" where it passes laws in an area, thus denying the states the right to pass conflicting laws or, in some cases, denying the states the right to pass any laws in that area.

preemptive right   A shareholder's option to purchase new issuances of shares in proportion to the shareholder's current ownership of the corporation.

preexisting duty   Prior legal obligation or commitment, performance of which does not constitute consideration for a new agreement.

preferred shares   Shares having dividend and liquidation preferences over other classes of shares.

pretext   After an employee has established a prima facie case of discrimination and the employer has articulated a BFOQ or LNDR, the employee must show that the proffered defense is pretextual—that is, that the BFOQ is not actually bona fide (or not applied in all situations) or that the LNDR has been applied differently to this individual compared to another.

price discrimination   Selling goods of like grade and quality to different buyers at different prices without justification where competitive harm results.

price fixing   An agreement among competitors to charge a specified price for a particular product or service. Also any agreement that prevents a seller from independently setting a price or from independently establishing the quantity to be produced.

prima facie case   A litigating party may be presumed to have built a prima facie case when the evidence is such that it is legally sufficient unless contradicted or overcome by other evidence.

principal   In agency law, one under whose direction an agent acts and for whose benefit that agent acts.

private law   Individually determined agreement of the parties relating to choice of laws, where disagreements shall be settled, and the language of the transactions.

private placements   Securities sold without a public offering, thus excusing them from SEC registration requirements.

privatization   The many strategies for shifting public-sector activities back to private enterprise. Those strategies include contracting out government work to private parties, raising the user fees charged for public services, selling state-owned property and enterprises, and returning government services such as garbage collection to the private sector.

privity of contract   The legal connection that arises when two or more parties enter a contract.

procedural due process   Constitutional principle requiring that the government ensure fundamental fairness to all in the execution of our system of laws.

procedural rules   In administrative law, an agency's internal operating structure and methods.

product liability   Refers to legal responsibility of manufacturers and sellers to compensate buyers, users, and, in some cases, bystanders for harm from defective products.

profit à prendre   The right to enter property and to take something away from it, such as crops.

promisee   The person to whom a promise is made.

promisor   A person who makes a promise to another.

promissory estoppel   An equitable doctrine that protects those who foreseeably and reasonably rely on the promises of others by enforcing such promises when enforcement is necessary to avoid injustice.

promoter   A person who incorporates a business, organizes its initial management, and raises its initial capital.

prospectus   A communication, usually in the form of a pamphlet, offering a security for sale and summarizing the information needed for a prospective buyer to evaluate the security.

proximate cause   Occurrences that in a natural sequence, unbroken by potent intervening forces, produce an injury that would not have resulted in the absence of those occurrences.

proxy   Written permission from a shareholder to others to vote his or her share at a stockholders' meeting.

public disclosure of private facts   Public disclosure of private facts where disclosure of the matter in question would be highly offensive to a reasonable person.

public goods   Goods or services usually provided by government when underproduced by markets.

public law   Rules of national law that regulate transactions between parties, as well as the relationships between nations.

public policy   That which is good for the general public, as gleaned from a state's constitution, statutes, and case law.

puffing   An expression of opinion by a seller not made as a representation of fact.

punitive damages   Damages designed to punish flagrant wrongdoers and to deter them and others from engaging in similar conduct in the future.

purchase money security interest   A security interest that is (1) taken or retained by the seller of collateral to secure all or part of its purchase price or (2) taken by a debtor to acquire rights in or the use of the collateral if the value is so used.

Q

qualified person with a disability   An individual with a covered disability who can perform the essential functions of her or his position, with or without reasonable accommodation.

qualified privilege   In libel and slander law, situations where a defendant is excused from liability for defamatory statements except where the statements were motivated by malice.

quantum meruit   As much as he deserves. Describes a plea for recovery under a contract implied by law. Fair payment for work performed.

quasi-contract   The doctrine by which courts imply, as a matter of law, a promise to pay the reasonable value of goods or services when the party receiving such goods or services has knowingly done so under circumstances that make it unfair to retain them without paying for them.

quid pro quo   Exchanging one thing of value for another. In sexual harassment law, quid pro quo cases are those where employment benefits are conditioned on the subordinate's submission to sexual advances.

quitclaim deed   A deed conveying only the right, title, and interest of the grantor in the property described, as distinguished from a deed conveying the property itself.

R

ratified   The adoption or affirmance by a person of a prior act that did not previously bind her or him.

ratify   Adopting or affirming a prior, nonbinding act.

real property   Land, buildings, and things permanently attached to land or buildings.

real property or real estate   The earth's crust and all things firmly attached to it.

reasonable accommodation   An accommodation to an individual's disability or religion that does not place an undue burden on the employer, which may be determined by looking to the size of the employer, the cost to the employer, the type of employer, and the impact of the accommodation on the employer's operations.

reasonable expectations test   Measure of negligence holding that a product is negligently designed if it is not safe for its intended use and also for any reasonably foreseeable use.

reasonable person   Fictitious being the law constructs to determine whether a person's behavior falls short of what a "reasonable person" would do under the circumstances.

red herring   A preliminary securities prospectus that provides information but does not constitute an offer to sell.

redlining   Most commonly, the practice of refusing to make loans in economically unstable areas with the result that minorities are sometimes discriminated against in securing credit.

reformation   An equitable remedy in which a court effectively rewrites the terms of a contract.

registration statement Document filed with the SEC upon issuance of a new security detailing the information investors need to evaluate that security.

Regulation Z Rules of the Federal Reserve Board implementing provisions of the Federal Truth-in-Lending Act.

release Agreement to relinquish a right or a claim. Sometimes labeled a *waiver* or a *hold harmless* clause.

remainderman One who is entitled to the remainder of the estate after a particular estate carved out of it has expired.

remand To send back. For example, a higher court sends a case back to the lower court from which it came.

rent The consideration paid by a lessee to a lessor in exchange for the right to possess and to use property.

rent-strike statutes Legislation that allows a tenant to deduct from the rent payment the cost of property repairs that are otherwise the responsibility of the landlord.

reorganization A bankruptcy action in which creditors are kept from the debtor's assets while the debtor, under court supervision, works out a repayment plan and continues operations (Chapter 11 bankruptcy).

res A thing, object, or status.

res ipsa loquitur The thing speaks for itself. Rule of evidence establishing a presumption of negligence if the instrumentality causing the injury was in the exclusive control of the defendant, the injury would not ordinarily occur unless someone was negligent, and there is no evidence of other causes.

res judicata A thing decided. A doctrine of legal procedure preventing the retrial of issues already conclusively adjudicated.

resale price maintenance Manufacturer's effort to restrict the price at which its product is resold.

rescission Canceling a contract; its effect is to restore the parties to their original position.

Resource Conservation and Recovery Act Authorizes the federal government to provide assistance to states and localities in connection with solid waste, to prohibit open dumping, and to establish programs to recover energy and valuable materials from solid waste.

respondeat superior Let the master respond. Doctrine holding the employer liable for negligent acts committed by an employee while in the course of employment.

Restatement of Contracts A collection of the rules of contract law created by the American Law Institute to provide guidance to lawyers and judges.

restitution A remedy whereby one is able to obtain the return of that which he has given the other party, or an equivalent amount of money.

restraints of trade Contracts, combinations, or conspiracies resulting in obstructions of the marketplace, including monopoly, artificially inflated prices, artificially reduced supplies, or other impediments to the natural flow of commerce.

restrictive covenant An agreement restricting use of real property.

retaliation Various statutes, including Title VII of the Civil Rights Act of 1964, forbid employers from punishing employees who legitimately exercise their legal rights.

reverse Overturn the decision of a court.

RICO Federal organized crime law making it illegal to acquire or operate an enterprise by a pattern of racketeering behavior.

right of survivorship A feature of a joint tenancy that causes a co-owner's interest in property to be transferred on her or his death to the surviving co-owner(s).

right-of-way Where an easement appurtenant refers to the right to physically cross property.

right-to-know laws Federal and state laws and regulations requiring employers to assume the affirmative responsibility of acquainting employees with hazardous substances and conditions in the workplace.

risk–utility test Measure of negligence holding that a product is negligently designed if the benefits of that product's design are outweighed by the risks that accompany that design.

RM petition Employer-filed request to the National Labor Relations Board seeking an election to demonstrate that a union is no longer supported by a majority of the employees.

rule of reason For antitrust purposes, reviewing an agreement in its specific factual setting, considering its pro- and anticompetitive features, to determine if it is harmful to competition.

runaway shop An employer closes in one location and opens in another to avoid unionization.

S

scienter Intent to commit a legal wrong. Guilty knowledge.

scope of employment Limitation on master's liability to only those torts that a servant commits while "about the master's business."

scorched earth defense   Takeover defense where the target corporation takes on new debt, sells assets, and so on in an effort to make itself a less attractive target.

secondary boycott   Typically a union strategy that places pressure not on the employer with whom the union has a dispute but rather with a supplier or customer of that employer in the hope that the object of the boycott will persuade the employer to meet the union's expectations.

Securities and Exchange Commission (SEC)   Federal regulatory agency responsible for overseeing the securities markets.

security   A stock, bond, note, or other investment interest in an enterprise designed for profit and operated by one other than the investor.

    As to loans, refers to lien, promise, mortgage, or the like, given by a debtor to assure payment or performance of her debt.

security interest   A lien given by a debtor or his creditor to secure payment or performance of a debt or obligation.

self-employment tax   A Social Security tax on people who are self-employed.

separate property   Property held by either spouse at the time of marriage or property received by either spouse through a gift or inheritance.

separation of powers   The strategy of dividing government into separate and independent executive, legislative, and judicial branches, each of which acts as a check on the power of the others.

service mark   A word, mark, symbol, design, picture, or combination thereof that identifies a service provider.

servient estate   The property subject to an easement appurtenant or implied easement.

sexual harassment   Unwelcome sexual advances, requests for sexual favors, and other unwanted physical or verbal conduct of a sexual nature.

shareholder   One holding stock in a corporation.

shark repellant   Various kinds of corporate behaviors designed to make a company unattractive to potential acquirers.

shelf registration   IPO registration that permits the issuer to hold the securities for sale until favorable market conditions emerge or the issuer needs the proceeds.

short-swing profits   Profits made by an insider through sale of company stock within six months of acquisition.

slander   A defamatory statement orally communicated to at least one third party.

slander per se   Category of oral defamation not requiring proof of actual harm to recover.

small claims courts   Courts of limited powers designed to hear cases involving modest sums of money (typically limited to $2,000–$7,500, but some states permit recoveries of $15,000 or more) in hearings free of many of the formalities and burdens associated with the more conventional judicial process.

small issues   Registration exemption for securities issued in small amounts.

sole proprietorship   A form of business under which one person owns and controls the business.

sovereign immunity   The government's right to exclude itself from being sued for damages in all but those situations where it consents to be sued. In international law, sovereign immunity permits a nation to decline to be sued in the courts of other nations.

specific performance   A contract remedy whereby the defendant is ordered to perform precisely according to the terms of his contract.

standing   A stake in a dispute sufficient to afford a party the legal right to bring or join a litigation exploring the subject of the dispute.

stare decisis   Let the decision stand. A doctrine of judicial procedure expecting a court to follow precedent in all cases involving substantially similar issues unless extremely compelling circumstances dictate a change in judicial direction.

state action   Situation of a sufficiently close relationship between the state and the action in question that the action can reasonably be treated as that of the state itself.

statute   A legislative enactment.

statute of frauds   A statute specifying that certain contracts must be in writing to be enforceable.

statute of limitations   A statute requiring that certain classes of lawsuits must be brought within defined limits of time after the right to begin them accrued or the right is lost.

straight voting   A form of voting for directors that ordinarily permits a shareholder to cast a number of votes equal to the number of shares he or she owns for as many nominees as there are directors to be elected.

strict liability   Civil wrong springing from defective and "unreasonably dangerous" products where responsibility automatically attaches without proof of blame or fault.

sub S corporation   A close corporation whose shareholders have elected to be taxed essentially as partners are taxed under federal income tax law.

subject-matter jurisdiction   The authority of a particular court to judge a particular kind of dispute.

sublease   A transfer of some but not all of a tenant's remaining right to possess property under a lease.

subpoena   An order from a court or administrative agency commanding that an individual appear to give testimony or produce specified documents.

substantial performance   Performance with minor, unimportant, and unintentional deviation.

substantive due process   The Due Process Clause of the Constitution requires that a statute be fair and reasonably related to a legitimate government purpose so that persons are not improperly deprived of their property rights.

suggestive mark   A trademark that suggests the product or its qualities; one that is more than merely descriptive.

summary judgment   A judicial determination prior to trial finding that no factual dispute exists between the parties and that, as a matter of law, one of the parties is entitled to a favorable judgment.

summons   A document originating in a court and delivered to a party or organization indicating that a lawsuit has been commenced against him, her, or it. The summons constitutes notice that the defendant is expected to appear in court to answer the plaintiff's allegations.

sunset legislation   A statute providing that a particular government agency will automatically cease to exist as of a specified date unless the legislative body affirmatively acts to extend the life of the agency.

Superfund/CERCLA   Established to help pay for the cleanup of hazardous dumps and spills.

Supremacy Clause   An element of the U.S. Constitution providing that all constitutionally valid federal laws are the paramount law of the land and, as such, are superior to any conflicting state or local laws.

surety   A person who promises to perform the same obligation as the principal and is jointly liable with the principal for that performance.

suretyship   A third party agrees to answer for the debt of another.

T

takeover bid   A tender offer designed to assume control of a corporation.

teleological ethics   The rightness of an action depends on its contribution to an end; often the maximum good.

temporary workers   Workers paid by a temporary help or staffing company.

tenancy at sufferance   The leasehold interest that occurs when a tenant remains in possession of property after the expiration of a lease.

tenancy at will   A leasehold interest that occurs when a property is leased for an indefinite period and is terminable at the will of either party to the lease.

tenancy by the entirety   A form of co-ownership of property by a married couple that gives the owners a right of survivorship.

tenancy in partnership   The manner in which partners co-own partnership property, much like tenancy in common, except that partners have a right of survivorship.

tenant/lessee   A party to a lease contract who pays rent in return for the right to possess and to use property.

tenants in common   Co-owners of real property who have undivided interests in the property and equal rights to possess it.

tender offer   A public bid to the shareholders of a firm offering to buy shares at a specified price for a defined period of time.

term tenancy   The tenancy that exists where a landlord and tenant have agreed to the terms of the lease period and a specific termination date for the lease.

test of nonobviousness   Determines whether the development described in a patent application would have been obvious to an ordinary skilled worker in the art at the time the invention was made.

third-party beneficiaries   People who are not parties to a contract but who have the right to enforce it because the contract was made with the intent to benefit them.

thrust upon   Company holds a monopoly innocently because of superior performance, the failure of competition, or changing market conditions.

tippee   In securities law, one who receives inside information from another.

tipper   In securities law, one who conveys inside information to another.

tombstone ad   A securities advertisement that does not constitute an offer and that usually appears in the financial press set inside heavy black borders suggestive of a tombstone.

tort   A civil wrong, not arising from a contract, for which a court will provide a remedy.

totalitarianism   A rigid, undemocratic government according power to a particular political group and excluding all others from access to political influence. The Soviet Union, Nazi Germany, and Fascist Italy were totalitarian states.

Toxic Substances Control Act   Requires chemical manufacturers to report information relating to chemicals that pose a "substantial risk" and allows the EPA to review and limit, or to stop, the introduction of new chemicals.

Trade Regulation Rules   Directives from the Federal Trade Commission interpreting the will of Congress and specifying those practices that the commission considers unfair or deceptive.

trademark   A word, name, or other distinctive symbol registered with the government and used exclusively by the owner to identify its product.

trademark infringement   Unauthorized use of the trademark of another.

treaty or convention   A contract between nations.

treble damages   An award of damages totaling three times the amount of actual damages, authorized by some statutes in an effort to discourage further wrongful conduct.

trespass   Entering the property of another without any right, lawful authority, or invitation.

trespasser   A person who enters the property of another without any right, lawful authority, or invitation.

tying arrangement   Dealer agrees to sell or lease a product (the tying product) only on the condition that the buyer also purchases or leases another product (the tied product).

U

ultra vires   Corporate conduct beyond the scope of activities provided for under the terms of incorporation.

unconscionable   A contract so one-sided and oppressive as to be unfair.

underwriter   Professional who helps sell new securities or buys those securities for the purpose of resale.

undivided share   A share of the interest in property that is not subject to division into parts.

undue hardship   A burden imposed on an employer by accommodating an individual's disability or religion that would be too onerous for the employer to bear. See **reasonable accommodation.**

undue influence   Dominion that results in a right to rescind a contract.

unemployment taxes   Federal and state (most) taxes paid by employers as a percentage of the total payroll to fund benefits for those who have lost their jobs.

unenforceable contract   Meets basic requirements, but remains faulty.

unfair labor practice   Activities identified by Congress that employers might use to thwart workers' attempts to unionize and to undermine the economic power that would come from the workers' right to concerted activities and to unionize.

unfair subsidies   Subsidies offered to producers in a certain industry by a government to spur growth in that industry. These subsidies are considered unfair if they are used to promote export trade that harms another country.

Uniform Partnership Act (UPA)   Original uniform act for creation and operation of partnerships.

unilateral contract   A contract wherein the only acceptance of the offer that is necessary is the performance of the act.

unilateral mistake   Where one party to a contract is in error about a material fact.

union shop   In labor law, the situation where all employees of a company must join a union to retain employment. Forbidden in right-to-work states.

unjust enrichment   An unearned benefit knowingly accepted.

unsecured   Refers to a loan not backed by some kind of security.

use taxes   Normally, taxes imposed on the use, storage, or consumption of tangible personal property bought outside of the state imposing the taxes.

usury   Charging an interest rate exceeding the legally permissible maximum.

V

valid contract   Effective; sufficient in law.

venture capital funds   Organizations designed to invest in new and often risky business enterprises.

venue   The specific geographic location in which a court holding jurisdiction should properly hear a case, given the convenience of the parties and other relevant considerations.

verdict   The jury's decision as to who wins the litigation.

vertical merger   A union between two firms at different levels of the same channel of distribution.

vesting rights   The right of an individual to a present or future fixed benefit.

vicarious liability   Legal responsibility for the acts of another person because of some relationship with the person; for example, the liability of an employer for the acts of an employee.

void contract   Entirely null; no contract at all.

voidable contract   Capable of being made void; enforceable but can be canceled.

voir dire   The portion of a trial in which prospective jurors are questioned to determine their qualifications, including absence of bias, to sit in judgment in the case.

voting stock   Owners of voting stock have the right to vote at shareholder meetings.

W

waiver   Relinquishing a legal right—as in the situation where one agrees not to sue if injured while participating in a particular activity, such as attending a baseball game.

warranty   Any promise, expressed or implied, that the facts are true as specified. For example, in consumer law, the warranty of merchantability is a guarantee that the product is reasonably fit for the general purpose for which it was sold.

watered stock   Inadequate consideration received for stock.

white-collar crime   Law violations by corporations or by managerial and executive personnel in the course of their professional duties.

white knight   In a takeover battle, a friendly company that rescues the target company from a hostile takeover. Often the rescue is accomplished by a merger between the target and the white knight.

winding up   In partnership and corporation law, the orderly liquidation of the business's assets.

without reserve   At an auction advertised as "without reserve," the seller is not free to withdraw an item before the high bid is accepted.

workers' compensation laws   State statutes providing fixed recoveries for injuries and illnesses sustained in the course of employment. Under those statutes, workers need not establish fault on the part of the employer.

wrongful discharge   Tort of dismissing another from employment in violation of public policy or for other illegal reasons.

Y

yellow dog contract   An employment agreement by an employee not to become a member of a union.

Z

zoning   Restriction on the use of land as a result of public land use regulation.

zoning ordinances   Dividing a city or a county into geographical areas of restriction—for example, only residential housing would be permitted in an area zoned R.

CASE INDEX

A

ACLU v. Ashcroft, 721
ACLU v. Reno, 721
Adarand Constructors, Inc. v. Pena, 523, 525, 543
Adidas America, Inc. v. NCAA, 412, 425
A. L. A. Schechter Poultry Corp. v. United States, 668
Alaska Dept. of Environmental Conservation v. EPA, 680
Albertson's Inc. v. NLRB, 579
Allen case, 277
Allen M. Campbell Co., Inc. v. Virginia Metals Industries, 245
Aman v. Con Furniture Rental Corporation, 505, 542
Amaya v. Home Ice, Fuel & Supply Co., 262
American Civil Liberties Union of Ohio v. Capitol Square Review and Advisory Board, 203
American Football League v. National Football League, 427
American Tobacco v. Patterson, 542
American Trucking Associations, Inc. v. EPA, 667, 687
America Online, Inc. v. IMS, 719
A&M Records, Inc. v. Napster, Inc., 723
Andersen v. Fuddruckers, Inc., 544
Aqua-Chem, Inc. v. NLRB, 580
Armstrong v. Rose Law Firm, 605–607
Ashcroft v. ACLU, 721
Ashcroft v. Free Speech Coalition, 721

B

Bachchan case, 696
Bad Frog Brewery v. New York State Liquor Authority, 183–187
Bailey v. Mathers, 147
Bain v. Gillispie, 234–235
Baker v. State, 207
Barnes v. Glen Theatre, Inc., 180
Barrera v. ConAgra, Inc., 484–485
Basic, Inc. v. Max L. Levinson, 369–370
Bell v. May Department Stores Company, 599–600
Bensusan Restaurant Corp. v. King, 717
Bermen v. Parker, 196
Blakey v. Continental Airlines, 722
Board of Education of Pottawatomie County v. Earls, 206

Bob Evans Farms, Inc. v. NLRB, 578
Boise Cascade Corporation v. Paper Allied—Industrial, Chemical, and Energy Workers, 160–163
Bolger v. Youngs Drug Products Corp., 185
Boomer v. Atlantic Cement Co., 682
Borse v. Piece Goods Shop, Inc., 476
Branch v. W. Petroleum, Inc., 689
Braun v. Soldier of Fortune Magazine, Inc., 205
Bresnahan v. Chrysler Corp., 271
Brookfield Communications v. West Coast Entertainment, 719
Brower v. Metal Industries, Inc., 288
Brown Forman Corp. v. Brune, 270–271
Brown v. Board of Education, 495
Brzonkala v. Morrison, 342
Brzonkala v. Virginia Polytechnic Institute, 342
Builders Ass'n of Greater Chicago v. Cook County, 524
Burger King Corp. v. Rudzewicz, 139
Burlington Industries v. Ellerth, 543
Burrow v. Kmart Corp., 252
Business Electronics Corporation (B.E.C) v. Sharp Electronics Corporation, 399–401
Butters v. Vance International, Inc., 649–650

C

Camel Manufacturing Co. v. United States, 654
Cargill, Inc. v. Monfort of Colorado, Inc., 445
Caspi v. Microsoft Network, 707
Castillo v. Tyson, 238–239
Cede & Co. v. Technicolor, Inc., 384
Central Hudson, 185–186
Charles E. Wolfe v. United States, 349–350
Chenoweth v. Hillsborough County, 533
China N. Indus. Corp. v. Ileto, 269
Circuit City Stores, Inc. v. Adams, 490
City of Erie v. Pap's A.M., 204
City of Milwaukee v. Burnette, 205
City of Richmond v. J. A. Croson Co., 522–523, 525
Clarett v. National Football League, 396
Clark County School District v. Breeden, 518
Claus v. Duquesne Light Co., 525
Cleveland v. Viacom, 414
Colgate-Palmolive Co. case, 567–568
Com-Co Insurance Agency v. Service Insurance Agency, 487
Commissioner v. Newman, 384

Communications Workers of America v. Beck, 576
Compania General de Tabacos de Filipinas v. Collector of Internal Revenue, 384
Com v. City of Lauderdale Lakes, 313
Continental T.V, Inc. v. GTE Sylvania, Inc., 398, 414
Cook Inlet Beluga Whale v. Daley, 677–679
Cook v. Cook, 245
Croaker v. Mackenhausen, 168
Culver v. McRoberts, 167

D

Daniell v. Ford Motor Company, 290
Davis v. Microsoft Corp., 530
Defenders of Wildlife case, 679
Delaware Valley Medical Center v. Niehaus, 246
Dendrite International, Inc. v. John Doe No. 3, 702
Dept. of Transportation v. Public Citizen, 654
DeSantis v. Computer Credit, Inc., 613
Diamond Walnut Growers, Inc. v. NLRB, 571–574
Diaz. v. Pan American World Airways, Inc., 537, 543
Dieter and Hermes v. Chrysler Corporation, 592
Dillon v. Legg, 262
DiMercurio v. Sphere Drake Insurance, 655
Dodson v. Shrader, 222
Dolan v. City of Tigard, 207
Donna Vizcaino v. Microsoft Corporation, 490
Donovan v. Lone Steer, 203
Doss v. Town of Big Stone Gap, 291
Dothard v. Rawlinson, 510
Dr. Miles Medical Co. v. John D. Park & Sons Co., 399
Dubai-Sharjah Border Arbitration, International Court of Justice, Court of Arbitration, 653
Duncan v. Children's National Medical Center, 512
Dushkin v. Desai, 225

E

Earls v. Board of Education, 206
Echols v. Pellulo, 239
Edenfield v. Fane, 185

Emotional distress, intentional infliction of, 253–254
Employee benefits
    current trend, 477–478
    family leave, 478–479
    income maintenance and, 477–478
    pensions, 480–482
    unemployment compensation, 479
    WARN, 479–480
Employee leasing, 451
Employee liability, 350
Employee privacy
    alcohol and drug testing, 474
    monitoring, 474–475
Employee Retirement Income Security Act (ERISA), 480
Employee rights; *see also* Labor law
    Fair Labor Standards Act, 459–461
    health and safety at work, 462–465
    immigration, 486
    international law, 635–636
    job classification and employer liability, 454–456
    privacy, 472–475
    selection (hiring), 451–454
    termination and wrongful discharge, 482–485
    union's duty of fair representation, 575
Employee selection (hiring), 451–454
    arbitration, 453
    background checks, 452
    contingent workers, 451–452
    impermissible questions, 452
    inappropriate questions, 452
    independent contractors, 432–434, 451–452, 453–454
    negligence, 456
    noncompete clauses, 453
    references, 454
    résumé fraud, 452
    retention/training/supervision, 456–458
Employee testing, 503; *see also* Alcohol and drug testing
Employer liability
    job classification and, 454–456
    negligence, 456
    sexual harassment, 515
Employment discrimination
    affirmative action, 519–526
    age discrimination, 534–535
    Americans with Disabilities Act (ADA), 528–534
    Civil Rights Act of 1964, 496
    civil rights enforcement, 496–497
    class of individuals, 498
    Constitution and, 496
    defendant's (employer's) case, 498–499
    disparate impact, 499–500
    disparate treatment, 498–499
    employee testing as defense, 503

four-fifths rule, 503
    history of, 495–496
    national origin, 503–504
    pattern or practice of, 498
    plaintiff's prima facie case, 498
    plaintiff's response, 499
    race, color, or national origin, 498–505
    racial harassment, 505
    religious discrimination, 527–528
    remedies, 497
    seniority as defense, 503
    sex discrimination, 505–507
    sexual orientation, 536–537
    statutory defenses, 502–503
Enabling legislation, 316
Enactments, 129
Endangered Species Act (ESA), 679–680
Enforcement
    antitrust law, 442
    civil rights, 496–497
    coal-fired power plants, 669
    CPSC, 595
    environmental protection, 676–681
    horizontal restraints, 391
    OSHA, 464–465
Engardio, Pete, 619
Engle, Shaena, 74
English courts, 129
English-only rules, 504
Enron, 24, 30, 40, 50–51, 53–54, 58, 65, 68, 69, 81, 102, 334, 379–380, 481
    venue, 140
Enumerated persons, 378
Enumerated powers, 173
Environmental impact statement (EIS), 666
Environmental pollution
    air pollution, 658, 666–669
    free market and, 662–663
    land pollution, 673–676
    as negative externality, 661
    pollution credits, 662
    soil, 659
    water pollution, 669–672
Environmental protection
    civil/criminal actions, 676
    common law, 681–682
    cost-benefit analysis, 664
    ethical business decisionmaking, 663–664
    federal role, 665–666
    global picture, 658–661
    laws and regulations, 664–676
    market failure, 661–662
    market incentives, 662–663
    penalties and enforcement, 676–681
    politics, 665
    proof of causation, 664–665
    remedies under common law, 681–682
    responsibility for costs, 665
    state and local regulation, 680–681
    tax incentives, 662–663

Environmental Protection Agency (EPA), 317
    enforcement action against coal-fired power plants, 669
    general information, 666
Environmental responsibility, 99–100
Epstein, Alex, 39
Epstein, Daniel, 657
Epstein, Richard, 168
Equal Credit Opportunity Act, 602
Equal Employment Opportunity Commission (EEOC), 317, 453, 496–497
Equality as socialist goal, 16
Equal pay
    Equal Pay Act, 505, 512–513
    Fair Labor Standards Act, 459
    general information, 512–513
Equal protection
    animals, 200–201
    gay/lesbian marital rights, 201–202
Equal Treatment Directive (EU), 636
Equifax, 601
Equity capital (stock), 352
Ergonomics, 462–463
Erin Brockovich (movie), 674
Ernst & Young, 626
E-signature, 706–707
Essence of the job (BFOQ), 508
Establishment Clause, 175–176
Estate planning, 358
Ethics; *see also* Ethics: general theories; International ethics; Managerial ethics
    digital divide, 691–692
    ethics codes, 61–62
    Internet law and, 691–693
Ethics: general theories, 44–52
    act-utilitarianism, 47–48
    deontological systems, 47–48
    existentialism, 44
    formalism, 47–52
    libertarianism, 46
    moral responsibility, 44
    religion, 45–46
    rule-utilitarianism, 47–48
    teleological systems, 47–48
    universal truths, 45
    utilitarianism, 47–52
    virtue ethics, 46
Etzioni, Amitai, 13
Europe
    litigation practice, 153
    "third way" countries, 19–21
European Court of Justice (ECJ), 645–646
The European Dream: How Europe's Vision of the Future is Quietly Eclipsing the American Dream (Rifkind), 30
European Union (EU), 91
    affirmative action case, 636–637
    constitution of, 174
    consumer protection, 611

Partnerships (*continued*)
 duration of existence, 356
 free transferability of interests, 355–356
 limited liability, 355
 nontax costs, 354–355
 particular benefits of business form,
   356–357
 taxes, 356
Pascarella, Ernest T., 507
Pashigian, B. Peter, 684, 689
The Passion (movie), 86
Patents
 antitrust and, 389
 international law, 638
 U.S. law, 709
Patrick, Joseph, 54
Patriot Act, 188, 189, 699–700
Pattern or practice of discrimination, 498
Pauley, Judge, 407
Payment in direct sales arrangements, 628
Pearl Jam and Ticketmaster, 405–406
Peers, Martin, 413
Pei, Minxin, 123
Penalties for white-collar crime, 66–67
Pennar, Karen, 39
Pension Benefit Guaranty Corporation (PBGC),
   480–481
Pensions
 Enron, WorldCom retirement plans, 481
 general information, 480–482
PeopleSoft, Inc., 59
The People's Court, 158
PepsiCo/Pepsi-Cola, 191, 213
Peremptory challenges, 145
Perez, Evan, 616
Performance of contract, 237
Perkovich, Robert, 582
Perrin, Noel, 31–32, 39
Perry, Rick, 83
Perry, William, 84
Per se rule and refusal to deal, 395
Per se violations, 390, 395, 398
Personal jurisdiction, 136–139, 693
Personal liability, 515
Personal liberty, 46
Personal property, trespass to, 254
Personal virtues, 46
Peters, Ted, 96, 118
Peterson, Dane K., 119
Petition, labor representation, 554
Petitioner/appellant, 150
Petition for *certiorari,* 135
Petzinger, Thomas, Jr., 543
Pfeffer, Jeffrey, 107
Phishing, 704
Physical exchange, 365
Physical/mental examinations, 144
Pianin, Eric, 687, 688
Piercing the corporate veil, 349, 358
Pierson, Christopher T., 507

Piper Aircraft, 257
Pipes, Sally, 32, 39
Piraino, Thomas, 418, 446
Planned economy, 16
Plato, 46
Pleadings, 143–144
Plitch, Phyllis, 385
Poison pill tactic, 375
Poland and the free market, 15
Police powers, 299, 305, 681
Political action committees (PACs), 81–82,
   83–84
Political boycotts, 395
Politically correct speech, 177–178
Political rights (objectivism), 9
Politics
 buying votes, 83–84
 campaign finance reform, 82–83
 527 groups, 83
 lobbying, 83
 PACs, 81–82, 83–84
 soft money, 82
Pollution
 air pollution; *see* Air pollution
 credits, 662
 land pollution; *see* Land pollution
 soil, 659
 tax incentives, 662–663
 water pollution; *see* Water pollution
Pope, Hugh, 689
Popular culture, 87–88
Pornography on the Internet, 698, 703
Posner, Richard A., 33, 410, 414, 439, 447, 523
Post-effective period, 364
Post-trial motions, 149–150
Poverty, 24–25
Powers, Lindsay, 278
Predatory intent, 420
Predatory pricing, 409–410, 428
Preferred stock, 352
Prefiling period, 364
Pregnancy Discrimination Act (PDA),
   511–512
Premerger notification, 431–432
Preponderance of evidence, 131
Press, Aric, 291
Pretrial conference, 144
Price control, 418
Price discrimination
 discounts/price discrimination, 407
 predatory pricing, 409–410
Price fixing, horizontal, 390–394
PricewaterhouseCoopers, 626
Pricing, 594
Priest, George, 402, 414
Primary picketing, 575
Prisons
 privatization, 11
 women in, 28
Pritchard, Justin, 491

Privacy rights
 consumer privacy, 596–597
 employee privacy, 472–475
 Internet and, 699–701
Private enterprise system, law and, 123
Private law
 general information, 130
 international law perspective, 130
Private nuisance, 682
Private Securities Litigation Reform Act
   (1995 Act), 373, 377
Private trials, 159
Privatization
 adoption worldwide, 11–12
 effects of, 12
 golf courses, 10
 patterns of, 9–12
 Poland, 15
 prisons, 11
 schools, 11
 toll roads, 10
Privileges (defamation), 253
Procedural due process, 199
Procedural law, 129
Procedural rules, 320
Procedural unconscionability, 588
Procter & Gamble, 104
Procter & Gamble–Gillette, 428,
   429, 442
Prodi, Romani, 31
Product liability
 breach of warranty, 273–279
 business practice, 257–258
 fast food companies, 283–284
 guns, 268–269
 litigation and justice, 258
 mass tort claims, 282–283
 negligence, 259–273
 public policy and, 282–283
 strict liability, 278–285
 SUVs, 284–285
 tort reform and, 285–286
 video games, 281–282
Product market, 419
Profit maximization, 99–100
Promisee, 217
Promisor, 217
Promoter, 346
Property, torts against, 254
Property rights
 objectivism, 8
 private enterprise and, 123
 stock ownership, 352
Proposition 16, 503
Protected classes, 498
Proximate cause, 260
Public disclosure of private facts, 253
Public goods, 297
Public law
 general information, 130